I0754783

ROBERT SALA RAMOS
(EDITOR)

EUDALD CARBONELL
JOSÉ MARÍA BERMÚDEZ DE CASTRO
JUAN LUIS ARSUAGA
(COORDINATORS)

PLEISTOCENE AND HOLOCENE HUNTER-GATHERERS IN IBERIA AND THE GIBRALTAR STRAIT:

THE CURRENT ARCHAEOLOGICAL RECORD

BURGOS, 2014

Assistant Editors:

María Gema Chacón Navarro
Marcos Terradillos Bernal
Amèlia Bargalló Ferrerons
Cristina Vega Maeso

Published thanks to Junta de Castilla y León through Fundación Siglo para las Artes y el Turismo de Castilla y León.

Photos from the covert: 1. Handaxe from Galería, 2. Skull 5 from Sima de los Huesos, 3. and 4. Detail of Gran Dolina TD10-1, 5. Jaw of *ursus dolinensis* from Gran Dolina TD5, 6. Cutmarks from Gran Dolina, 7. Point from Sima del Elefante, upper levels, 8. Aerial view from Trinchera del Ferrocarril, and 9. Laboratory of microfauna, Arlanzón river (photos: IPHES)

Publisher: UNIVERSIDAD DE BURGOS
SERVICIO DE PUBLICACIONES E IMAGEN INSTITUCIONAL
Edificio de Administración y Servicios
C/ Don Juan de Austria, nº 1
09001 BURGOS – SPAIN

FUNDACIÓN ATAPUERCA
Carretera de Logroño, nº 44
09198 Ibeas de Juarros (Burgos).

ISBN: 978-84-92681-87-7 (Printed Edition)
978-84-92681-88-4 (e-book)

Legal Deposit: BU-206. – 2014

Photocomposition: Rico Adrados, S.L. (Burgos)
Print: Rico Adrados, S.L. (Burgos)

Contents

PREFACE

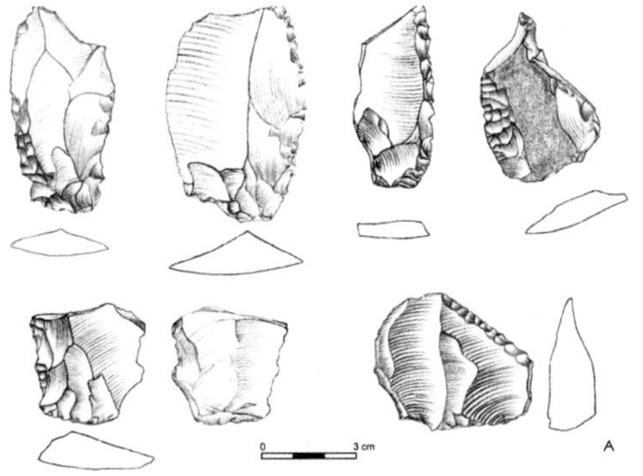

0 3 cm

A

Our group has decided to update the information available about Spanish palaeohistory for the UISPP congress. We thought that this international congress would be an ideal occasion to collate and publish two volumes on our remote history. The first volume looks at the first palaeoccupations in the prehistoric record of the Iberian Peninsula.

As you know, prehistory research is making spectacular progress thanks to fieldwork, lab work and also teamwork undertaken by archaeologists, biologists, geologists and botanists. New theoretical proposals by experts in life, earth and social sciences, as well as modern methodologies and applied technologies are all helping to shape new insights into our history, and thus build on our previous knowledge and interpretations. Yet none of this can be done without hard data.

Despite this great panoply of disciplines, it would be impossible to provide a consistent explanation of the eco-social process of human evolution without archaeological excavations. In this volume, we wish to highlight above all the empirical data that allow we archaeologists and prehistorians to advance "a posteriori" interpretations of the structures and systems of past life.

This realisation of the need to update the information widely available about fieldwork is what has led us to edit this volume about prehistory on the Iberian Peninsula, particularly in Spain. We want to present historians –and also history buffs and all other human specimens with a thirst for knowledge– with the facts that allow us to concoct the outlines needed to apply reverse engineering to reconstruct the palaeoecological evolution of our genus in a particular territorial context. We want to present information about the evolution of the *Homo* genus and its environment, which means that both the natural environment and the historic environment are the focus of this work.

An analysis of the current state of fieldwork and initiatives at prehistoric sites makes an indispensable contribution to a coherent understanding of the historic sequence of a territory. It also allows us to bring this type of scientific inquiry up to date, and places us in a better position to understand the nature of the species through the records of the past.

In recent times, the massive volume of results studied and published in specialist journals has made it necessary to draft sequential summaries in which all the data from all the research is accessible in a single monographic volume. This facilitates the necessary socialization of the work of specialists in different periods of history. Direct access to the current state of prehistoric archaeology –either in print or digital format– improves our ability to plan and discuss the past, the present and to possess a grounding to build the future.

The cascade of empirical data contained in the collective effort of this first volume is, in our opinion, of incalculable value: it is the result of the work of the majority of the Spanish teams who are working in the field and have helped to make the knowledge of this country's prehistory one of the most thorough and up to date in the world.

Bringing information about prehistoric archaeological work up to date in an orderly, concise manner in order to avoid an intractable volume has led us to the concept and structure of this book. We have arranged the sites on the basis of a regional grid, which has allowed us to organize and synthesize our discourse, and also avoid having to repeat maps and other graphic material which would make the text less palatable.

This is a reference work in which the reader can find essential information about the archaeological sites which the editors believe are the most significant for our prehistory. We apologize if this updated summary does not include every site currently in the process of investigation and publication. Our intention has been to produce a significant, up to date synthesis –necessarily abbreviated– of the current state of prehistory on the Iberian Peninsula. We do not know if this has been achieved, but whatever the case, we still think the effort was necessary and our commitment has been to coordinate this work.

The articles on the sites, all of them synthetic and systematized, open a window onto the empirical reality of our archaeological knowledge and hence the true state of our knowledge, avoiding interpretations on the basis of data and knowledge that has not been published and well checked.

This volume is thus an effort that we wish to share with all those who are interested in the study and the analysis of the past. We also hope it will serve us to update our own work and make it more visible in other areas outside the strict realm of prehistory. The transformation of the social sciences into the sciences of socialized knowledge is an evolutionary perspective of the way we understand the world.

Intervening in and influencing the state of knowledge about the history of populations is a strategic decision that has shaped the powerfully empirical nature of this proposal. When another synthesis is written, the information will probably have changed, but the underlying essence –our interest in sharing what we know with our species– will remain.

This has been our intention. The reader has the last word.

Eudald Carbonell
Vice-president of Fundación Atapuerca
Director of Institut Català de Paleoecologia Humana i Evolució Social

1

NORTH-WESTERN ATLANTIC BASINS

Site	Map numbering
As Gándaras de Budiño	1
Cova Eirós	2
Monforte de Lemos ensemble	3
Valdara	4

Arturo de Lombera-Hermida *,**,***,
Xosé Pedro Rodríguez *,**

The Paleolithic site of As Gándaras de Budiño (O Porriño, Pontevedra)

The Paleolithic site of As Gándaras de Budiño is located in O Porriño industrial park (Pontevedra) (UTMX: 531.407; UTMY: 4.661.631). It is situated in the valley of the river Louro, which runs through the southern sector of the Galician Meridiana Depression, delimited on each side by the granite heights of Faro de Budiño to the east and Serra do Galiñeiro to the west. Discovered in 1961 by Henri Nonn, in 1963 excavation and survey work began under the guidance of Dr. Emiliano Aguirre (1964). At the same time as the excavation work was being carried out, a geological and stratigraphic study of the site and of several coastal and continental deposits was conducted in order to correlate the geomorphology of Budiño with its regional context (Butzer, 1967). The archaeological excavations proved the existence of large accumulations of material, identifying workshops areas and the presence of hearths. According to D. Echaide, the lithic assemblages would correspond to the Acheulean. Due to the methodological approach used in the excavations, As Gándaras de Budiño becomes the emblematic site of Paleolithic research in Galicia.

However, the association of the Acheulean lithic assemblages with the surprising carbon dating obtained from two carbon samples, within the Upper Pleistocene and *a priori* confirmed through stratigraphic correlation of the levels of As Gándaras with the deposits from the southeast coast, would make it one of the most controversial sites (Aguirre and Butzer, 1967).

Given this problem, in 1979 Julio M. Vidal Encinas resumed excavation between 1980 and 1982, opening several trenches near the area excavated by Emiliano Aguirre and recovering many materials associated with fluvial and colluvia formations, similar to those identified previously (Vidal, 1982). Finally, in 1991 rescue archaeological excavations were carried out under the guidance of Dolores Cerqueiro Landín.

Given the problematic and controversial chronological interpretation of this site, many review papers have dealt with the stratigraphy and geomorphological context of As Gándaras de Budiño (Ramil *et al.*, 1993; Gracia *et al.*, 2004), and of its lithic assemblages (de Lombera *et al.*, 2011; Méndez, 2007; 2008).

Synthesis papers based on the stratigraphic descriptions permit the different levels to be correlated and the sequence of the depositional processes observed at the As Gándaras de Budiño site to be reconstructed (Ramil *et al.*, 1993). Initially, the Louro basin was filled by various levels of arkoses and clays during the Upper Miocene. Then, the basin was captured by the dynamic of the Miño in the Pleistocene, forming the fluvial level sequence (T+67m; T+56m; T+33m; T+24m) and small lateral channels associated with the Louro valley, level T+24m being the level related to the site (fluvial levels). Following an episode of microfracturing and dismantling of the fluvial deposits and clay baselevels, the lower colluvium deposited, formed by two units (levels 6a and 6b). The lithic industries classified as Acheulean are located in this deposit. Following a second episode of erosion, dismantling and dispersion of the lower colluvium, sedimentation of the upper colluvium occurs, now over the underlying colluvium, over the source fluvial levels, over tertiary clay mate-

* IPHES, Institut Català de Paleoecologia Humana i Evolució Social, C/ Marcel.lí Domingo s/n. Campus Sescelades, (Edifici W3), Tarragona 43007

** Area de Prehistoria, Universitat Rovira i Virgili (URV), Av. Catalunya 35, Tarragona 43002

*** Grupo de Estudos para a Prehistoria do Noroeste (GEPN). Dpto. de Historia I, Universidade de Santiago de Compostela. Praza da Universidade 1, Santiago de Compostela 15782

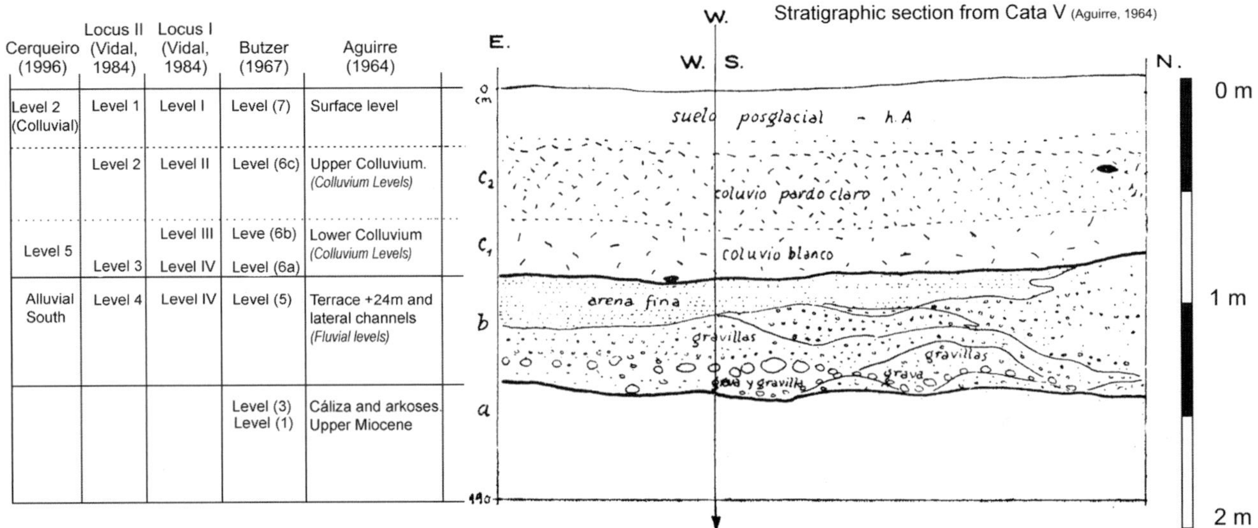

Cerqueiro (1996)	Locus II (Vidal, 1984)	Locus I (Vidal, 1984)	Butzer (1967)	Aguirre (1964)
Level 2 (Colluvial)	Level 1	Level I	Level (7)	Surface level
	Level 2	Level II	Level (6c)	Upper Colluvium. *(Colluvium Levels)*
Level 5	Level 3	Level III Level IV	Leve (6b) Level (6a)	Lower Colluvium *(Colluvium Levels)*
Alluvial South	Level 4	Level IV	Level (5)	Terrace +24m and lateral channels *(Fluvial levels)*
			Level (3) Level (1)	Cáliza and arkoses Upper Miocene

Figure 1. Stratigraphy of the As Gándaras de Budiño site and possible stratigraphic correlations between the different levels.

rials. This contains some industries as a result of disassembly of the lower levels (vg. Level 2 of Locus I). Finally different paedogenesis phenomena occur on the upper colluvium levels (Fig. 1).

The presence of lithic assemblages is constant throughout the sequence. The uniformity of the technology of the assemblages recovered from the different levels and trenches was identified from the very start. Adhering to the morphogenetic processes of the site, the origin of the lithic materials must be related to Acheulean settlements only, which are identified in the fluvial sequences associated to T+24m.

However, the materials associated to the upper colluvium showed certain volumetric and technological differences (lower incidence of Large Cutting Tools (LCT), smaller format) that, added to its stratigraphic position, led some authors to consider them as evidences of later settlements, initially linked to the Mousterian (vg. Level 2 of Locus I) (Vidal, 1982). Taphonomic reviews of colluvium levels show the existence of volumetric selection and mechanical alteration from rolling of the artefacts in the assemblages. At the same time, these assemblages show clear convergence at a technological level with those identified at the fluvial levels (de Lombera *et al.*, 2011; Méndez, 2008). For this reason, these small variations between the different sites must be understood as a consequence of the material resedimentation processes.

The lithic industry is defined by usage of local and nearby resources, the proportion of quartzite and quartz varying between the different sites (63%-26% and 73.93%-35.5%, respectively). Rock crystal appears to a lesser extent (3.2%-0.7%), related to quartz formations. Quartz is an abundant resource in the Louro basin, the source of good quality quartzite, predominant in the assemblages, is located on the terraces of the river Miño, 3 km to the south.

The assemblages are characterised by the dominance of knapping products, generally small and medium sized (30-60 mm), particularly the quartz items. Regarding the knapping strategies, the more expeditious types that performance longitudinal and bifacial reduction series (especially in quartz) predominate but with a significant presence of centripetal and discoidal cores and products, whereas Levallois products are barely represented (around 2%). The opportunistic resource of bipolar knapping on quartz is also documented, witnessed through various knapping products, as well as large blocks interpreted as anvils.

The presence of handaxes and cleavers (Fig. 2), although consistent, varies between the different sites. The majority of the handaxes are made on flake with amygdaloidal morphologies, evenly edges and silhouettes trimming, mainly using a hammerstone. There is a smaller representation of cleavers and picks. Regarding light duty tools, denticulate, scrapers and notched tools stand out.

Figure 2. Handaxes and cleavers recovered from the excavations of Emiliano Aguirre (Fotograph: Museo Municipal de Vigo. Quiñones de León).

These assemblages show a clear difference as to the management of raw materials based on their knapping quality, quartzite being used mainly for making LCT, medium and large implements, and in more complex knapping methods. Quartz, however, becomes more important for small blanks and tools. Although for the quartz tools all the phases of the *chaîne opératorie* seem to be represented, this is fragmented for the quartzite tools, basically represented by flakes, cores in an advanced stage of reduction and LCT.

Conclusions

The technical characteristics of the site of As Gándaras de Budiño place it within the peninsular Acheulean assemblages from the second half of the Middle Pleistocene. In this respect, the absolute dating obtained show the different morphogenetic processes of the Louro basin but not the age of the industries. Its location in the Meridiana Depression gives it a strategic settlement within the mobility of the Atlantic Façade, that also explain the large number of findings and their wide distribution in the area.

Arturo de Lombera-Hermida *, **, ***, Xosé Pedro Rodríguez *, **, Ramón Fábregas-Valcarce***

Cova Eirós archaeo-palaeontological site, Triacastela, Lugo

1. Cova Eirós site. Location and background

The few limestone formations in north-western Spain and the primary focus of research on river terraces and rock shelters have resulted in a small number of documented cave sites in this area, amongst which Cova Eirós (Eirós Cave) ranks amongst the most important in palaeontological and archaeological terms.

The Cova Eirós site is located in a village, Cancelo, in the Triacastela municipality (Lugo) (UTM X: 646.855; UTM Y: 4.736.428). The cave entrance is on the NNW slope of Monte Penedo in Serra do Ouribio, 780 metres asl and 25 metres above a stream, Arroyo de Bezcos. The Cova Eirós karst system is part of the Cándana limestone Series, formed during the Lower Cambrian. The cave is 104 metres long, with a mouth that currently measures 2 metres high by 3.5 metres wide. The entrance narrows after the first 7 metres into a 15 metre long neck, followed by the cave's largest space, the "Main –or Mammoth– Hall", 15 metres long, 6 metres wide at the most and up to about 5 metres high. The cave then continues inwards in a NNW direction in a series of three overlapping levels of galleries (Grandal, 1993) which are almost entirely clogged by clayey sediment interspersed with stalagmitic crusts or floors.

From the outset Cova Eirós became renowned as an outstanding palaeontological site due to the presence of bear remains. In the late 1980s, UDC conducted several digs in the middle and end sections of the cave (1988, 1989 and 1991), which recovered approx. 4,000 bones from at least 43 bears (Grandal, 1993). Based on these findings, Cova Eirós became one of the most important sites on the Iberian Peninsula for *Ursus spelaeus* remains.

AMS 14C analysis dated a bear bone at 24,090 ± 440 BP (Grandal and Vidal, 1997), consistent with the dating of a stalagmitic crust below the fertile level in the final gallery of the cave, (25,233 ± 5,027 BP) (U series) (Grandal, 1993). The most recent datings on bear bones extend the time range to a period between 24,000 and 31,000 BP (Pérez *et al.*, 2011). In addition, two datings of the stalagmite crusts in the central corridor and the final gallery have yielded 117,252 ± 75,438 BP and 97,051 ± 15,426 BP respectively, although caution is advised due to their wide standard deviation (Grandal and Vidal, 1997).

In 1993, the first archaeological dig in Cova Eirós was a 1 m^2 test pit at the cave entrance, in which five archaeological levels were identified and 550 lithic tools were recovered, all initially attributed to the Middle and Upper Palaeolithic.

Following these reports, in 2008 a new phase in the exploration of the Cova Eirós occupations was begun (Fábregas *et al.*, 2009). Initially, two test pits were dug at the mouth: Pit A at the entrance (4 m^2), which included the 1993 pit in one of its survey squares, and a second pit on the outer embankment (Cata B). The quantity and quality of the recovered material and the stratigraphic potential of the sediment led to the extension of the excavation area to nearly half the inhabitable space of the entrance sector (21 m^2) (Fig. 1).

2. The Pleistocene sequence in Cova Eirós

The 16 metre long entrance sector decreases in height to 0.8 m at the neck that leads to the interior part of the complex. A steep embankment coincides with the vertex of the mouth. The in-

* IPHES, Institut Català de Paleoecologia Humana i Evolució Social, C/ Marcel.lí Domingo s/n. Campus Sescelades, (Edifici W3), Tarragona 43007

** Area de Prehistoria, Universitat Rovira i Virgili (URV), Av. Catalunya 35, Tarragona 43002

*** Grupo de Estudos para a Prehistoria do Noroeste (GEPN). Dpto. de Historia I, Universidade de Santiago de Compostela. Praza da Universidade 1, Santiago de Compostela 15782

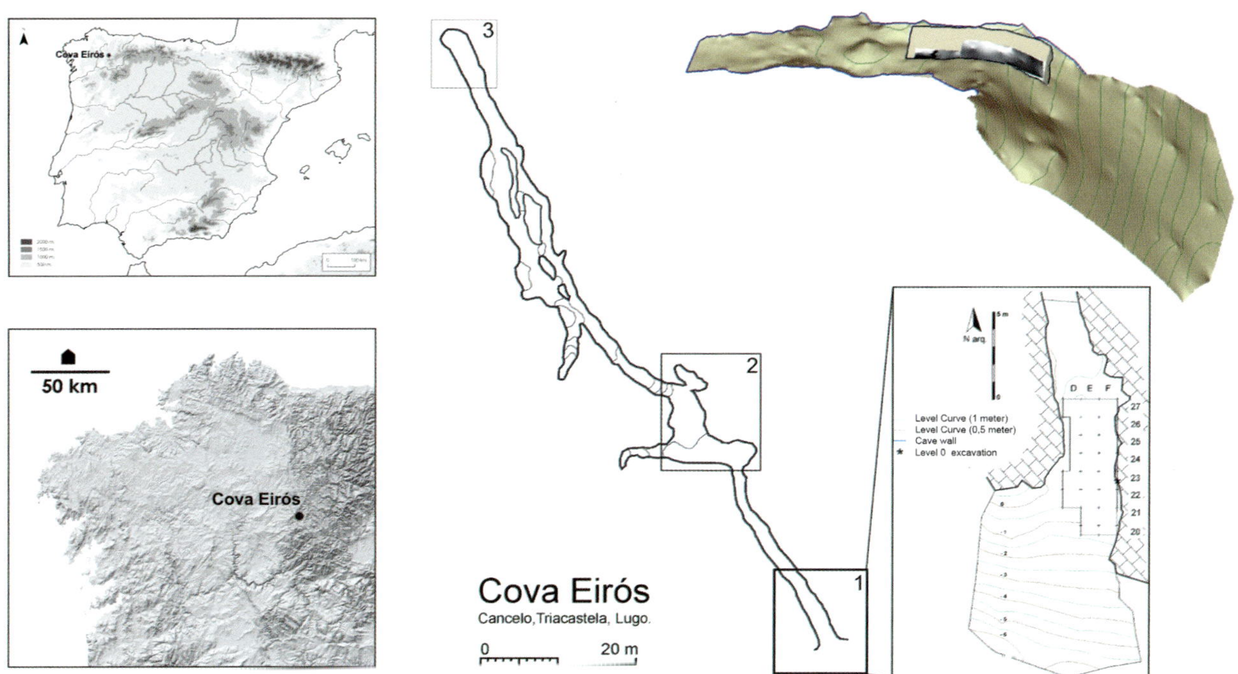

Figure 1. Location of the Cova Eirós site. Plan of the cave and the current archaeological dig with a topographic reconstruction of the entrance sector (2009). 1) Entrance sector 2) Great Hall 3) Final Gallery, Palaeontological interventions.

habitable space is thus reduced to this vertical between the ledge and the interior neck. On the west wall, however, eroded remains of a cave wall mark the former entrance area. Geophysical surveys using Georadar in this sector have detected a 3.4 m deep stratigraphic infill. Excavation has only reached the –120/140 cm level below the present floor, and occupations prior to the currently identified may thus be expected to appear in the future.

Six archaeological levels have been identified in the stratigraphic sequence, with two types of sedimentary dynamics. The lower levels are associated with *in situ* sedimentation, basically linked to gravitational input (Levels 4, 3 and 2), while the upper levels are from wind-borne matter (Levels 1A and 1B). Levels B and C levels are linked to the dynamics underway outside the cave (the slope) (Rodríguez *et al.*, 2011) (Fig. 2). The stratigraphic sequence described for the site is the following:

–Surface Level. Topsoil. Very loose and heavily bioturbated organic soil. Limestone clasts produced by rockfalls from the ceiling. First indication of disturbed archaeological material. This level also contains a perimeter stone paving which delimited two medieval silos. Potential: 10-15 cm.

–Level B: Whitish-yellow silty matrix, well compacted, containing angular limestone gravel measuring 5-13 mm along the major axis. Abrupt, irregular upper limit and gradual, diffuse lower limit. A 30 mm deep layer of very dark sediment has been identified at the bottom of this level. A considerable amount of archaeological material has been retrieved from Archaeological Level B. The upper limit of this layer, defined by limestone blocks measuring 40-140 mm on the longest axis, has a predominantly south slope. It might be related to one of the most recent processes in the reduction of the cave cornice. AMS radiocarbon dating of the archaeological level is 12,060 ± 50 BP (Beta – 308859) (Fábregas *et al.*, 2012).

–Level C: A heavily compacted clay matrix with gravel and clasts. A steep south-facing slope follows the topography of the embankment, and intersecting levels 1, 2, 3 and 4. This is interpreted as a disturbance of the levels inside the cave.

–Level 1: The upper part consists of slightly compacted fine yellow sand with a subhorizontal

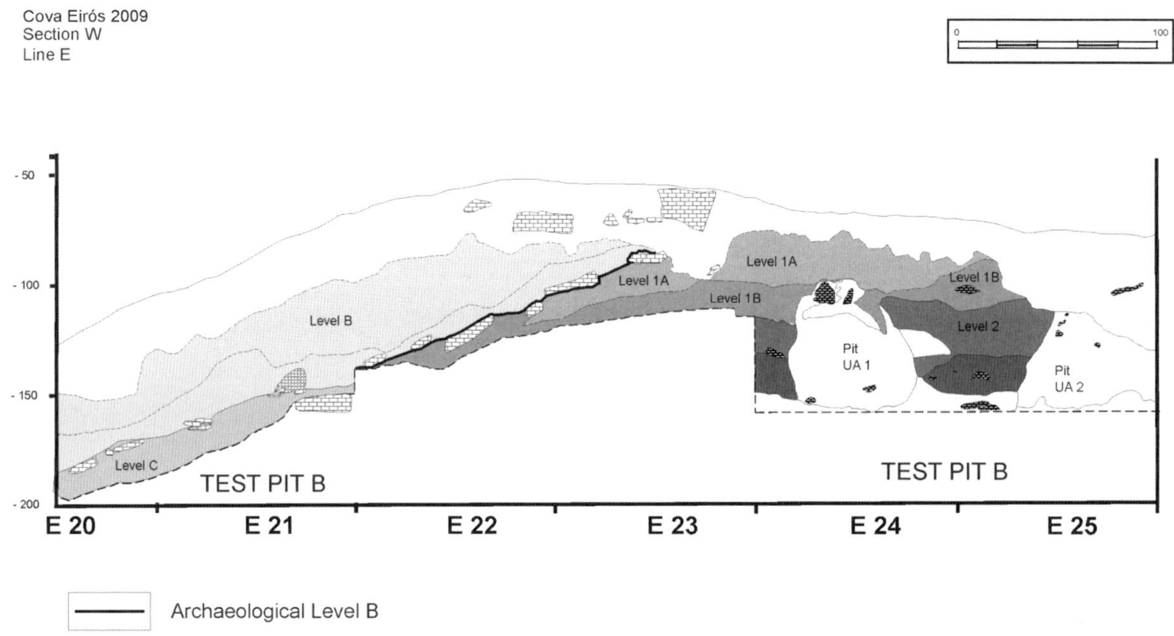

Figure 2. Stratigraphic profile West of the dig in Cova Eirós.

laminar stratification (1A). The top is archaeologically sterile. At the bottom, the sand becomes orange, more compacted and a parallel horizontal stratification (1B). The top and bottom limits of the level are net. Depth: 10 to 23 cm.

–Level 2: Orange clay-loam, more compact than the previous level. Two distinct facies: at the top (level 2a), purer sands, without concretions, while the lower limit is marked by the presence of small limestone plates. At the base (sub-level 2b) several small subangular limestone clasts (3-5 cm), heavily carbonated, with a crust in the southern sector. Net ondulating base level. Archaeological level. 34-45 cm deep. C14 AMS radiocarbon dating: 31,690 ± 240 BP (Beta – 254280)

–Level 3: Brown clay with small-sized limestone gravel. More compact and homogeneous than the overlying level. Contact with level 2 is net and undulating, indicating the existence of a gap between the two levels. Archaeological level. 20-35 cm deep. OSL dating: 84,807 ± 4919 BP (MAD-5612BIN).

–Level 4: Composed of clays and fine yellow sands, heavily carbonated with sub-rounded limestone and schist gravels. Minor lateral variations. Archaeological level: currently under excavation. Unknown depth.

3. Middle Palaeolithic occupations

Two levels attributed to the Middle Palaeolithic, the most substantial records in the study of this period in Galicia, have been identified in the lower part of the sequence.

Level 4

Level 4 has a high density of archaeological material, currently the richest of the sequence. The excavation and analysis of the data is still underway, however preliminary results point to certain aspects. As in most of the identified occupations in Cova Eirós, the lithic assemblage is dominated by quartz (90.1%), with quartzite playing a secondary role (9.7%). Knapping products are over-represented, with few cores and retouched tools on flake (sidescrapers, denticulates, etc.) which, in conjunction with the scarcity of corticality in the products, indicates that this assemblage represents the final stages of reduction. From the technological characteristics of the product, we can deduce that the predominant knapping methods are longitudinal and orthogonal strategies, although discoidal and Levallois quartz products have been identified amongst the higher quality items, particularly in the fine-grained quartzite. The technological characteristics of the lithic assemblage on this level suggest that it is Mode 3.

The faunal assemblage includes remains of bears, deer and horses. Several show evidence of human intervention (fracturing and cut marks) and thermal alteration. Several bone fragments have been attributed to *Coelodonta* sp.

The most significant discovery on this level was 5 metres from the current entrance: a combustion structure with a small (40 x 25 cm) oval focal area (Fábregas *et al.*, 2012). A large concentration of tools and skeletal remains, many of them with evidence of heat impact, was identified lying around this hearth.

Level 3

The initial excavation of this level was heavily affected by the presence of medieval silos, restricting its area to 1.5 m^2. The size of the current work area permitted excavation in the entire zone to commence, allowing us to gather more information about the Neanderthal occupations in Cova Eirós.

The detected lithic assemblage consists of 702 items. The predominant raw material is quartz (90%), followed by fine grain quartzite (8%). The identified reduction methods are Levallois, discoidal and orthogonal, with some evidence of Kombewa (Fábregas *et al.*, 2009; Rodríguez *et al.*, 2011). As in the previous level, the operational chains are fragmented, with a clear predominance of knapped products and few cores. The presence of retouched items –sidescrapers, denticulates and becs– is greater here (9.9%). This aspect is more obvious in the fine-grained quartzite, an allochthonous lithic resource, represented by Levallois flakes and points, as well as sidescrapers bearing evidence of treatment as curated tools (Fig. 3). The characteristics of the lithic assemblage on Level 3 suggest its attribution to Mode 3, with a differential management of lithic resources found in north-western Iberia in the Middle Palaeolithic, defined particularly by the relationship of Levallois techniques to fine-grained quartzite and the use of more expedient methods with quartz, although quartz Levallois products have also been found. Functional analysis of this assemblage has identified hunting-related activities (broken spear tips), butchering and hide treatment at the site (Lazuén *et al.*, 2011).

The faunal assemblage is characterized by a high percentage of fragmentation, hindering its taxonomic definition. Some of the bones show clear cut marks and fractures, pointing to the anthropic factor as the main agent in butchering-related activities, skinning and access to bone marrow. Taxonomically, *Cervus elaphus* has the highest representation, followed by *Rupicapra rupicapra* and *Capreolus capreolus*. Carnivores include numerous *Ursus spelaeus*, with many neonatal tooth remains. The presence of *Canis lupus* and *Vulpes vulpes* is also documented, indicating the alternating use of the cave by hominids and carnivores.

4. Upper Palaeolithic sequence

Level 2

The level 2 lithic assemblage contains a high percentage of small-sized quartz industry (93.3%). Although the type of raw material and the large number of knapping fragments hinder an accurate techno-typological definition, certain changes in the supply strategies –with the appearance of small amounts of rock crystal and flint– and the presence of blades in rock crystal ascribe this assemblage to be attributed to the initial Upper Palaeolithic. C14 dating places these occupations in the Aurignacian.

The faunal record includes *Cervus elaphus* and *Capreolus capreolus* and a remarkable representation of carnivores, with several remains of *Canis lupus* and *Panthera pardus*, as well as both bear species which hibernated in the cave (*Ursus arctos* and *U. spelaeus*). The faunal remains show a high level of fragmentation and some have obvious cut marks and fresh fracture. The low density of lithic tools, the identification of fragmented operational chains and the higher incidence of carnivore taxa point to occupations with little impact, perhaps related to short, repeated stays, alternated with the cave's use as a den by carnivores and ursids.

Level 1

The material is concentrated at the base of this stratum, where 729 archaeological items have been recovered (Fábregas *et al.*, 2010; Rodríguez *et al.*, 2011). The lithic assemblage is predominantly quartz (86.1%), while flint and rock crystal have a greater representation (4.8 % and 6.1 %, respectively), parallel to an increased blade and bladelet component. Two types of chaines opéra-

Figure 3. Levallois points (a) and flakes (b) in quartzite from the Middle Palaeolithic levels (Level 3 and 4).

toires have been detected at this level, depending on the type of raw material and the purpose of the reduction. In the local quartz and quartzites, more expeditious strategies (longitudinal or centripetal) were used to obtain flakes, while in the case of rock crystal and flint, production focused on blade flakes, with microblade cores and bladelets in this material as well as a few backed items (Fig. 4). While the quartz prisms are of local origin, the flint items, only found in elements from the end of the knapping sequences, are from further afar, possibly linked to the above-mentioned outcrops 12-14 km to the NE. The technical nature of the assemblage and the datings currently available ascribe this level to the end of the Gravettian.

The faunal assemblage consists of 135 items. *Rupicapra rupicapra* and *Cervus elaphus* still predominate amongst the herbivore species, but there is a significant decrease in the carnivores with respect to the previous levels, particularly ursids, a trend documented at other sites in Cantabria. One outstanding discovery on this level is a pendant made from a canine tooth of a small carnivore (Fábregas *et al.*, 2010).

The top of level 1 (1A) is a succession of small layers of fine and coarse sands of wind-borne origin. This level is sterile, indicating that the cave was probably not occupied by either humans or animals during the harshest periods of the Last Glacial Maximum, contemporary to the formation of nearby glaciers (O Queixadoiro).

Level B

Archaeological level B is linked to the final retreat of the cave ledge, defined by a line of limestone slabs and blocks, some over 30 cm in diameter. The palaeosol indicates an embankment dynamic on a steep slope towards the archaeological south. Moving inwards, this level merges with the current organic floor, and thus the preserved area is quite small (barely 3 m^2). Radiocarbon dating places this event right at the end of the Magdalenian (Fábregas *et al.*, 2010).

The lithic assemblage shows a clear specialization, with a high percentage (40.6%) of rock crystal, second only to quartz. There are two different *chaines opératoires* in the reduction strategies: the production of flake items in quartz and quartzite with longitudinal, orthogonal and, to a lesser extent, bipolar techniques; and on the other hand, specialized production centred on the exploitation of rock crystal prisms for bladelets and backed elements. Given that all parts of the sequence are represented here (cores, volumetric adjustment elements, retouched products, etc.), it follows that these items were produced *in situ*.

Faunal remains –including a deer antler– are quite scarce, possibly due to the more organic component of the sediment.

Level C

Level C is in the outer part of the embankment, with a steep south slope (lines 20-21). It contains a high density of lithic and bone material. These items show a mixture of features, evidence of the disturbance of this assemblage (Fábregas *et al.*, 2009). Taphonomicaly, the bones are in different stages of fossilization and wear. Within the lithic assemblage, Levallois flakes in quartz and quartzite akin to those recovered from levels 4 and 3 have been identified, along with rock crystal and flint blades and bladelets and flakes of the type found on levels 1 and 2. This level is therefore considered to be the result of the dismantling and disturbance of the levels inside the cave at the top of the embankment due to erosion during the retreat of the cave ledge.

5. Recent Prehistory and Early Medieval occupations

While most of the identified occupations at the site have been ascribed to various periods in the Middle and Upper Palaeolithic, there is also evidence of this cave's use in subsequent periods. In recent prehistory, it was used as a burial site, judging by the Bell-beaker ceramic material recovered at the entrance (Fábregas *et al.*, 2012), and the human remains found inside the cave (Corridor), dated at the height of the Bronze Age (Ua-38121, 3151 ±31 BP). These funerary activities can be contextualised in the late Bell-beaker horizons and the middle of the second millennium BC.

Finally, the surface level contained several storage structures (silos, UA1 and UA2), a hearth (UA06) and a perimetral pavement related to agro-pastoral activities in Cova Eirós from the late 10th to the 15th century AD (Teira *et al.*, 2012).

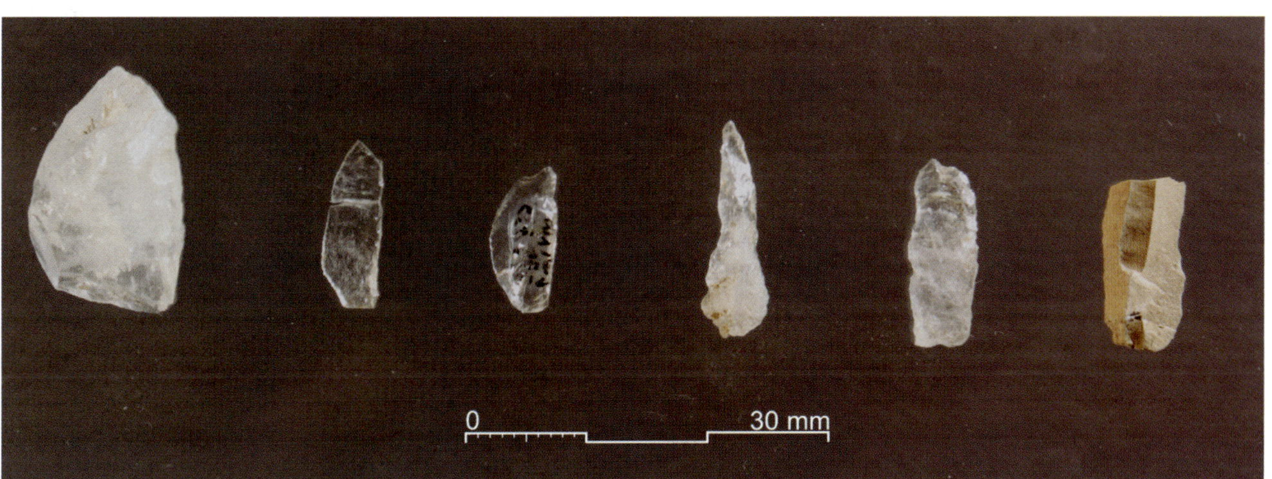

Figure 4. Core and bladelets in rock crystal, and flint bladelet from Cova Eirós, levels 1 and B.

6. Mobile and rock art

The recurrent presence of Upper Palaeolithic communities in eastern Galicia, the discovery of mobile art and, most importantly, documentation of rock art in northern Portugal indicated that rock art could probably be found in Galicia as well. In 2011, several paintings and engravings were discovered in Cova Eirós, the first Palaeolithic rock art detected in north-western Iberia (de Lombera and Fábregas, 2013). Previously, the only evidence of Palaeolithic art in this region was the Férvedes II stone pendant in Xermade (Lugo) and *Dentalium* shells found on Lower Magdalenian levels at Valdavara 1 (Becerreá, Lugo).

Mobile art

Several items of mobile art have also been found at the Cova Eirós site (Fábregas *et al.*, 2010; 2012). A small pendant in a perforated canine, probably from a fox (*Vulpes vulpes*), was found on the Gravettian level (Level 1). Several bone industry remains were also found, including a double pointed speartip from the interfaces of an Upper Palaeolithic level (1C). Both sides are decorated with a zigzag pattern composed of several parallel, discontinuous lines, whose closest equivalent would be Magdalenian items from the Altamira and El Pendo sites (Fábregas *et al.*, 2012).

Rock art

There are several parietal art forms inside Cova Eirós from the Upper Palaeolithic. The ongoing characterization, classification and dating work of these motifs will permit a precise definition of the chrono-cultural coordinates of these Palaeolithic expressions. Eleven decorated panels have been identified to date. One of the features of the series –also a constraint for their study– is the poor state of the images due to heavy washing of the paintings and also the large amount of recent graffiti which has affected many of the motifs.

The largest concentration is in the Main or Mammoth Hall, the widest space of the cave, 15 metres long and up to 5 m. high. Many painted and engraved motifs are on the walls at low or mid-height. Although figures have been identified in all sectors of this hall, the majority are on the west wall (Panels I to VI), looking inwards on the right. This sector contains the most complex themes and panels, with associations of black paintings and engravings, especially on Panel III. On the opposite wall is Panel VIII, with highly complex concepts, distribution and number of engravings, alternating signs with geometric and zoomorphic subjects. Graphic work has also been located in different recesses in the cave and the south-east gallery, an indication of the wide dispersal of these manifestations. Half of the motifs detected to date are painted elements, followed by engravings (46.4 %) and the possible use of reliefs or natural highlighting of the rock (3.6 %). However, engraved figures are most probably under-represented in the counts, as many lines have been classified together. It is also important to note that many black lines or dots may be the result of repeated visits to the interior zones of the cave during recent prehistory, early medieval and contemporary periods. The motifs are generally small and heavily influenced by the spaces and surfaces available in the cave. Quantitatively, the main themes are painted dots and lines; thin engraved lines, both individual and in sets; zoomorphs, both painted and engraved (bovids and possibly deer, equids and carnivores), many of them incomplete (partial representations of cervical-dorsal lines, hindquarters, etc.) followed by the representation of signs.

The predominant painting technique is black. FT– Raman spectrometry analysis has identified the use of charcoal as a pigment. Engravings include thin, shallow lines, in some cases striated and others associated in a dense, variegated manner. Finally, the possible use of natural enhancements of the rock surface with morphologies reminiscent of animal silhouettes, in which specific dots or lines serve to highlight certain anatomical parts of the animal, have also been documented. There is a great technique and thematic homogeneity in this art. According to technical and stylistic studies currently underway, certain techno-morphological characters permit a working hypothesis for the chrono-cultural context of this art. The presence of numerous thin linear, composite and striated engravings superimposed on other motifs, the depiction of zoomorphs with elongated bodies and members, simplified representations of limbs, bodies with filled innards (e.g. bovid Panel I, Fig. 5) and the small-sized figures all seem to suggest the end of the Magdalenian/ transition to the Mesolithic. However, the information now available prevents us from ruling out the possibility of older motifs.

7. Conclusions

The Cova Eirós site contains the most complete stratigraphic sequence now available for the study of the Middle and Upper Palaeolithic in Galicia. It allows a direct comparison of evolving technologies, subsistence strategies, adaptation to and exploitation of the territory between the Neanderthals and the *H. sapiens* of north-western Iberia. Cova Eirós is a reference point in tracing the history of the settlement of Galicia's eastern ranges (Serras Orientais) and its relationship to the open air settlements and rock-shelters elsewhere in north-western Iberia. The archaeological record and the cave art at this site point to a similarity and even convergence with historical processes identified along the Cantabrian Coast.

Acknowledgements

The archaeological work underwayat Cova Eirós is part of the research project entitled, "*Poblamiento durante el Pleistoceno medio/Holoceno en las comarcas orientales de Galicia*" (HUM2007-63662, HAR/2010-21786 financed by the Ministry of Economy and Competition.

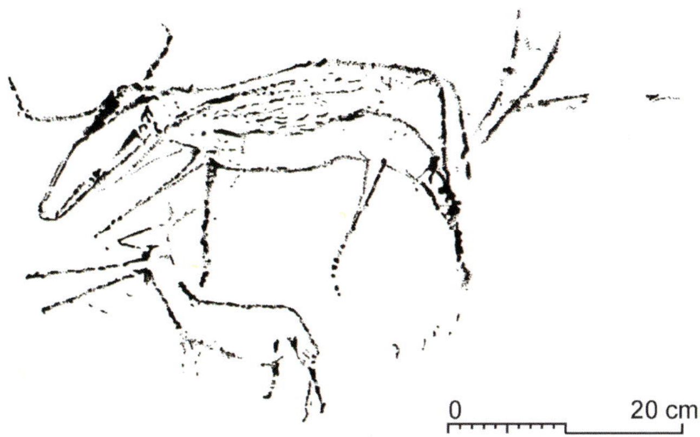

Figure 5: Photograph filtered with D-Stretch and tracing of bovid and cervid zoomorphs on Panel I.

Xosé Pedro Rodríguez*,** , Arturo de Lombera-Hermida *,**,***, Ramón Fábregas-Valcarce***

Paleolithic occupations in the Monforte de Lemos Basin (Lugo, Galicia)

Introduction

The information available about the Paleolithic in the north west of the Iberian Peninsula, particularly inland Galicia, is scarce and corresponds to accidental and sporadic finds. The only finding recorded for the Monforte de Lemos Basin (province of Lugo) was a handaxe in Vilaescura (Sober) in the mid twentieth century. Systematic research of the area started in 2006 as a consequence of accidental finding by an amateur but the findings from recent years have demonstrated the existence of a significant Paleolithic settlement in this area.

The Depresión de Monforte, irrigated by the river Cabe, is a tertiary basin surrounded by higher Paleozoic and Hercynian areas, which reach 600m high to the west (Chantada area) and 1,600m to the east (Serra do Courel). The average height of the Cabe valley is 290 metres above sea level. The origin of the Monforte basin, with a surface area of 175 Km^2, is tectonic, following the Hercynican fault lines that exist in a WNW-ESE direction. Following a neotectonic episode and subsequent fluvial rearrangement, the Pleistocene sediment linked to the paleo-channels and alluvial fans covered the banks with tertiary silts and clays of a lacustrine environment. These Quaternary deposits, arranged in a sequence of flat surfaces, are identified as river terraces, glacis and pediments (Ameijenda 2011).

Arqueological surveys

Systematic surveys, carried out between 2006 and 2010, were conditioned by the dense vegetation, which restricted the extension of the explored area. However, more than eighty open air artefact scatters were discovered, which correspond to Lower, Middle and Upper Paleolithic. These locations have different entities, from sites with dozens of artefacts per square metre to others with just one isolated finding (Fig. 1). In addition to the surveys, test pits were dug in places whose concentration of artefacts could suggest the presence of archaeological sites in a stratigraphic context (As Lamas and Valverde in the Monforte Basin, and Pedras in the granite plateau of O Saviñao) (Fábregas *et al.*, 2009; 2010). Findings were also discovered in stratigraphic context in the sites of O Regueiral and Áspera (Rodríguez *et al.*, 2008).

The geo-archaeological work has allowed us to reconstruct a relative chronological framework in accordance with the characteristics of the Quaternary surfaces and the technological interpretations of the lithic assemblages (de Lombera *et al.*, 2011). The majority of the sites located could be assigned to Mode 2 or Acheulean lithic industries. Based on the topography and morphometrics of the Quaternary deposits (considering river terraces, glacis and pediments), 7 levels of erosion were identified on the sides of the basin (Fig. 1) (Ameijenda, 2011). The majority of the archaeological findings are located in intermediary levels (N4 and N5), whereas their presence in the other levels is scarcer, except in N1. The oldest evidence, in accordance with the morphotechnic characteristics and the sedimentary contexts, are located in Chao de Fabeiro (Erosion level 7), on the north bank of the Basin (Fig. 1). At this site, 26 knapped tools were recovered, mainly in quartzite. The configuration strategies are focused in the production of pebble tools. The presence of handaxes and chopping tools and the orthogonal, longitudinal and, to a lesser extent, centripetal reduction sequences suggest their ascription to Mode 2. The majority of Mode 2 sites are located in the intermediary surfaces (erosion levels N5-N4). In N5, the most significant scatters are those of Chao Vilar

* IPHES, Institut Català de Paleoecologia Humana i Evolució Social, C/ Marcel.lí Domingo s/n. Campus Sescelades, (Edifici W3), Tarragona 43007

** Area de Prehistoria, Universitat Rovira i Virgili (URV), Av. Catalunya 35, Tarragona 43002

*** Grupo de Estudos para a Prehistoria do Noroeste (GEPN). Dpto. de Historia I, Universidade de Santiago de Compostela. Praza da Universidade 1, Santiago de Compostela 15782

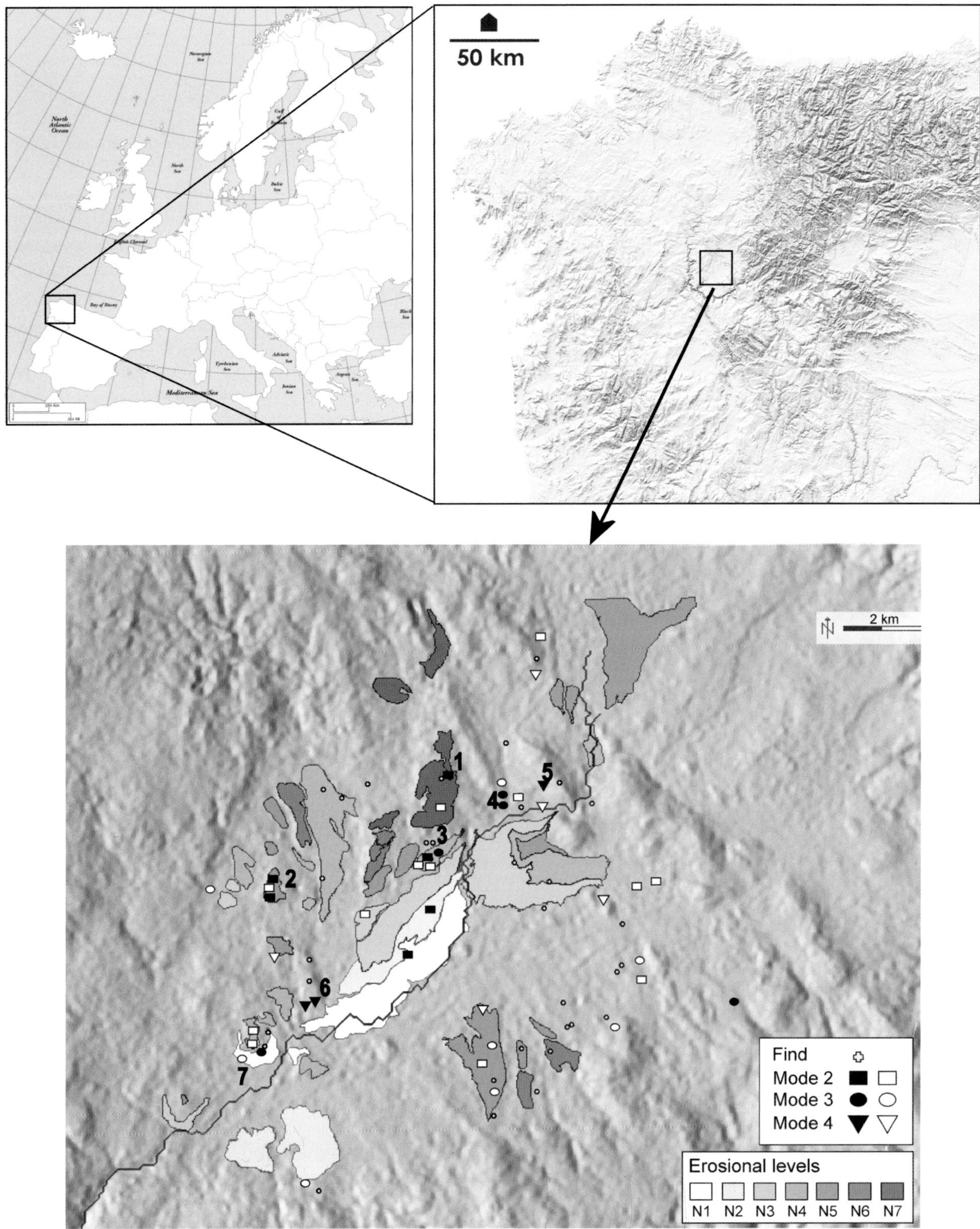

Figure 1: Location of the sites at the Monforte Basin. The squares indicate the Mode 2 findings; the circles, Mode 3 findings and the triangles, Mode 4 findings. Black indicates sites with a higher density of artefacts. The dots indicate isolated findings. The erosion levels are also specified (N1 to N7). The numbers correspond to significant sites: 1, Chao Fabeiro; 2, Chao Vilar; 3, As Lamas; 4, O Reguerial; 5, Valverde; 6, Costa Grande; 7, San Mamede.

(1-2 and 3), with 62 items (Fábregas *et al.*, 2009). As Lamas (UTM: 621.332, 4.711.619) is located in erosion level N4, where five archaeological points were discovered, which provided 241 pieces (Fig. 2.4-7). Two test pits were dug here in 2009: the test pit II revealed two archaeological levels, related to the colluviums that covered the fluvial sediments, dating by OSL in 39866 ± 3554 BP (Level 3) and 38947 ± 3150 BP (Level 2) (Fábregas *et al.*, 2010).The first level (N-II) was related to a Middle Palaeolithic occupation and the second (N-III) provided artefacts with technical characteristics and alterations (oxides), which were very similar to the pieces recovered on the surface. Its presence in a colluvium from the Upper Pleistocene should be considered the result of an episode of erosion that destroyed old sediments during the Heinrich event 4.

In these sites, the configuration strategies focus on handaxes, cleavers and trihedral picks. The majority of the handaxes are knapped on pebble and generally show a high amount of cortex on the surface. On the flake tools, the retouches create continuous and denticulate dihedral edges; sidescrapers (17.9%) and denticulate tools (13.2%) dominating over notch tools, becs and endscrapers. The most common reduction sequences are unidirectional unifacial / bifacial and centripetal, followed by the orthogonal method. The presence of the discoid method is minimum (5% of cores) and the Levallois method has only been identified in one core in Chao Vilar-II. Given the raw material used (quartzite pebbles) and its availability, the cores are knapped using natural platforms and their reduction sequences are short (60-70% of cores abandoned in initial or intermediary stages of reduction). Flakes usually show a high amount of cortex on the dorsal surface and faceted striking platforms are rare (3%).

In the Mode 2 sites, the raw material used is quartzite, followed by quartz. The presence of fluvial "neocortex" in almost all of the artefacts suggests exploitation of the secondary deposits of Quaternary age along the basin. Given that the artefact scatterings are directly on these surfaces, access to raw material was immediate and quick.

The Mode 3 sites are mainly located in erosion levels 1 and 2, particularly O Regueiral, As Gandariñas, Susao, San Mamede, Gullade and Level II of Test pit 2 of As Lamas (Fábregas *et al.*, 2007, 2009, 2010). In these site Large Cutting Tools (LCT) are almost non-existent, whereas the small lithic flake tools take on more importance. The reduction strategies are dominated by the centripetal and discoid methods. The only archaeological records in a stratigraphic context were identified in O Regueiral and As Lamas Test pit II). In the first, located in an alluvial fan, 32 artefacts were recovered (Fig. 2.8, 2.10, 2.12), some of them in a colluvium dated by the OSL in 69446 ± 5472 BP. In the site at As Lamas (Test pit 2), Level 2 is linked to the upper colluvium but the rolling and size of the lithic tools suggest a primary context of disposition (Fábregas *et al.*, 2010). In the Mode 3 sites, centripetal and discoid cores dominate (Fig. 2.9-10), while the orthogonal or longitudinal methods are less common. Some cores and tools in fine-grained quartzite could be related to the Levallois method, as they show surface hierarchisation in the reduction. However, use of the Levallois method in Monforte is quite limited, whereas discoid products are more common, particularly those related to the final stages of small quartz core reduction (Fig. 2.9). These lithic assemblages are dominated by flakes that often show centripetal disposition of the negative scars on the dorsal surface and the presence of dihedral and faceted striking platforms (Fig. 2.11-12). The configuration sequences focus on flake tools, denticulate tools (45.5%) dominating over side scrapers (27.2%) and other tools like end scrapers and points. Some large tools, like handaxes, could be present but there are very few (Fig. 2.8). In Mode 3 sites, the use of fine-grained quartzite increases in response to the most demanding reduction methods (Levallois and discoid) and the increased standardisation of flake tools.

In the sites at Valverde, Costa Grande-III, Áspera and Pedrouzos de Mourelos, Mode 4 lithic assemblages were discovered. Unlike the Upper and Middle Palaeolithic sites, these are located in high places and not on the Quaternary surfaces. Their lithic industry stands out for the presence of blade technology and a wide range of raw materials, particularly rock crystal and flint. The most significant site is Valverde, located on a hillside 350 metres above sea level (UTM: 624.434, 4.713.497). The artefacts were made of quartz, fine-grained quartzite, rock crystal and flint (Rodríguez *et al.*, 2008). Their techno-typological characteristics (cores and laminar and micro-laminar products, and leaf-shaped points), allow it to be ascribed to the Solutrean. Along with these *chaînes opératoires* from the Upper Palaeolithic, knapped in good quality raw materials (rock crystal, fine-grain quartzite and flint), bipolar knapping and the discoid method focus on the production of quartzite and quartz implements with good cutting edges (de Lombera *et al.*, 2012).

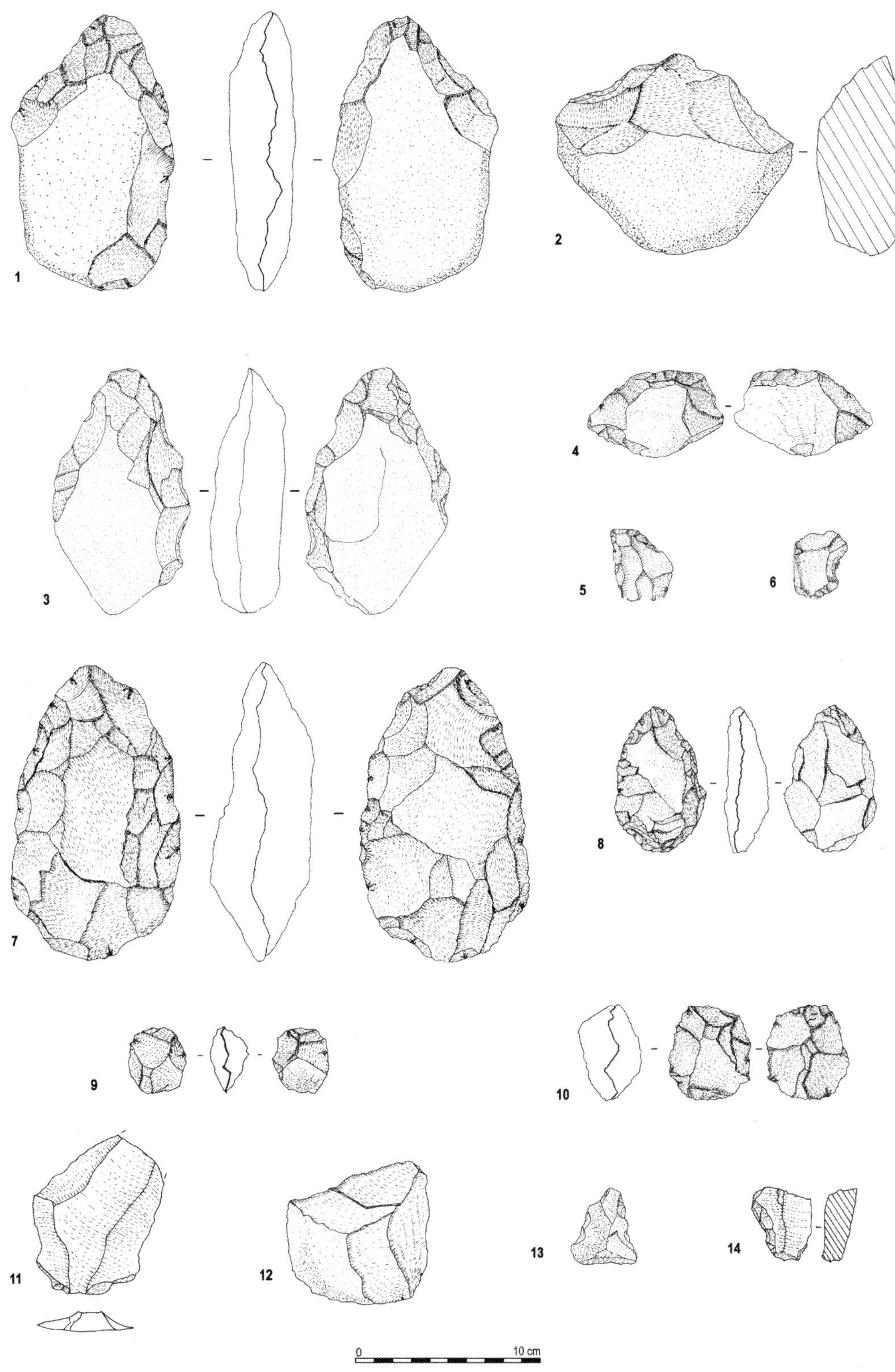

Figure 2: Lithic industry of the Monforte Basin (Mode 2 and Mode 3). 1, Quartzite handaxe (Chao Fabeiro, Mode 2); 2, Quartzite chopper Chao Fabeiro, Mode 2); 3, Quartzite handaxe (Chao Vilar, Mode 2); 4 and 5, quartzite side scrapers (As Lamas, Modo 2); 6, quartzite notch (As Lamas, Mode 2); 7, Quartzite handaxe (As Lamas, Mode 2); 8, Quartzite handaxe (O Regueiral, Mode 3); 9, quartzite discoidal core (Gullade III); 10, quartzite discoidal core (O Regueiral, Mode 3); 11 and 12, quartzite flakes (Gándara Chá and O Regueiral, Mode 3); 13 and 14, retouched quartzite flakes (Gandariñas, Mode 3).

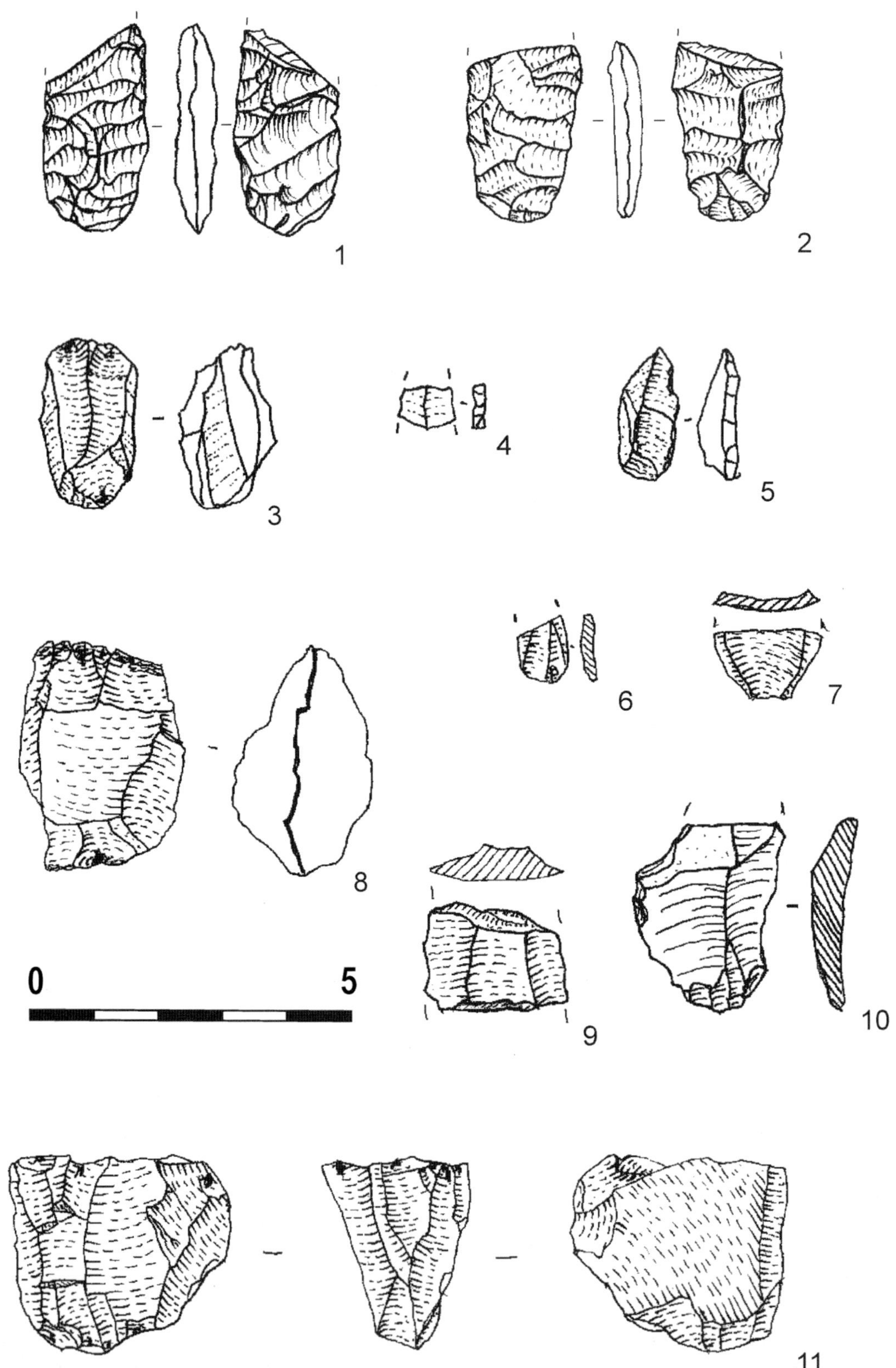

Figure 3: Lithic industry of the Monforte Basin (Mode 4). Valverde site (1-10): 1 and 2, leaf-shaped projectile fragments in flint (1) and quartzite (2); 3, micro-laminar core in rock crystal; 4 and 5, backed items in rock crystal; 6, 7 and 9: laminar and micro-laminar fragments in rock crystal (6) and quartzite (7 and 9); 8, bipolar core in quartz; 9, flint flake; 11, quartzite blade core, Áspera site.

Conclusions

The Monforte de Lemos Basin plays a strategic role due to its geographical location, as it is located in the natural route connecting inland Galicia to the western Meseta (de Lombera *et al.*, 2011). It is also framed by the two main fluvial systems of the NW of the Iberian Peninsula (the Miño and Sil) that constrain structural mobility through this territory. Secondly, due to its low altitude, the average temperatures of the valley of the Sil and the Monforte Basin during the glacial period were warmer than in the surrounding areas and comparable to those recorded on the coast. Therefore, the Monforte Basin could serve as refuge area during glacial periods, whereas the mountain and inland region, with drier and colder conditions, would be covered by icecaps and steppes. The convergence of these geological, geographical and topographical characteristics could explain the high concentration of human settlements identified during the Middle and Upper Pleistocene.

Acknowledgements

The archaeological excavations in Monforte de Lemos are part of the research project *"Poblamiento durante el Pleistoceno medio/Holoceno en las comarcas orientales de Galicia"* (HUM2007-63662, HAR/2010-21786 of the Ministry for the Economy and Competition).

Susana Alonso Fernández *, Manuel Vaquero *,**, Alicia Ameijenda Iglesias ***

La Cova and Valdavara 3 (Becerreá, Lugo)

The archaeological activity carried out since 2007 in the municipality of Becerreá (Lugo) has produced an extensive archaeological record corresponding to different chronocultural periods, including times almost unknown before in Galicia, such as the late Upper Pleistocene and the Middle Magdalenian. The work was carried out in two sites: La Cova de Valdavara, in which a well-preserved sequence was found, which includes levels from the Late Prehistory and late Upper Paleolithic, and Valdavara 3, another cave deposit with remains of the late Upper Pleistocene (Vaquero *et al.*, 2011).

La Cova de Valdavara and Valdavara 3 are situated in the karst located on the right bank of the river Naron (known in this area as Cruzul), one of the tributaries of the left bank of the river Navia, at 120m and 220m, respectively, above the current channel of the river. They are part of a cave system located in limestone formations called the Calizas de Vegadeo, from the Lower-Middle Cambrian, outcropping along a wide stretch plotted NNW-SSE between the Palaeozoic formations of the Dominio del Manto de Mondoñedo, where sandy and slate rocks predominate (Vera, 2004). Some of these caves, like Cueva de Furco or Cova da Venta (Fernández Rodríguez, 1993; Grandal, 1991), were already known for having provided some isolated archaeological or paleontological remains.

La Cova de Valdavara was discovered in the 1960s by a group of amateurs from Becerreá. The archaeological excavations were carried out between 2007 and 2013, working in three sites with different sequences and deposits: Valdavara 1, which is the original cavity found in the 1960s, Valdavara 1-2, which corresponds to the outer slope and Valdavara 2, another small cavity located barely 6 m below Valdavara 1.

In Valdavara 1 a sequence of almost one–and-a-half metres deep has been documented, consisting of two main stratigraphic units (Fig. 1). The upper unit corresponds to the Late Prehistory (Vaquero *et*

* Institut Català de Paleoecologia Humana i Evolucio Social (IPHES), Escorxador s/n, 43003 Tarragona
** Area de Prehistoria, Universitat Rovira i Virgili, Avinguda Catalunya 35, 43002 Tarragona
*** Universidade de Santiago de Compostela (USC)

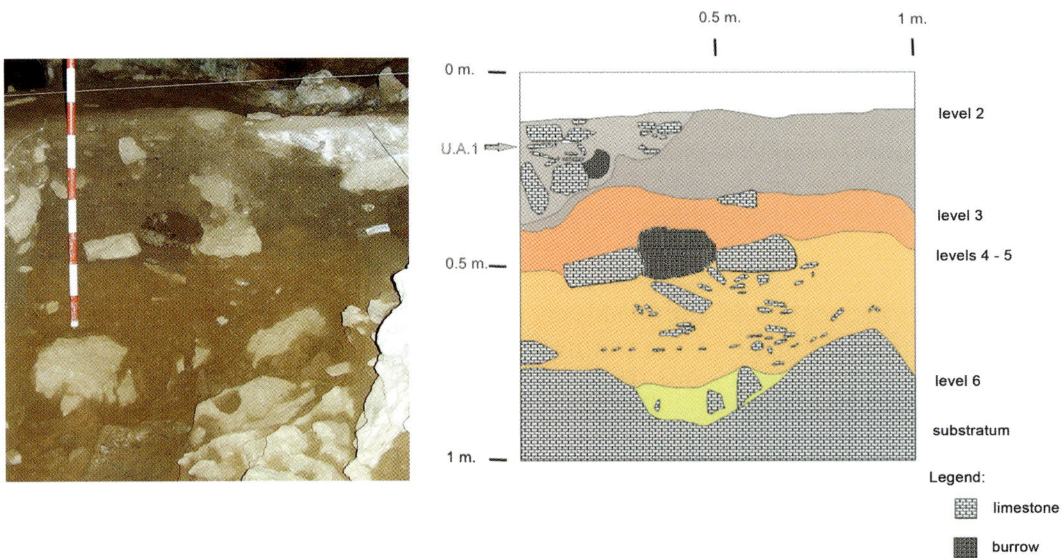

Figure 1. Stratigraphic sequence of Valdavara 1.

al., 2009). The study of the flint and quartz lithic industry, the domestic fauna and pottery recovered in this upper unit demonstrate varied use of the cavity during the Late Neolithic-Chalcolithic. The recovery of decorative seashells (*Dentalium*) infers mobility across the territory of these populations and possible contact with coastal population. Similarly, the recovery of small human remains, such as phalanges and teeth of different individuals, suggest repeated use of the cavity for burial purposes, probably as a primary burial site (Vaquero *et al.*, 2009). The variety of micro-mammals recovered is consistent with other Holocene-Chalcolithic associations from the north of the Iberian Peninsula and suggests a more Mediterranean climate (Blain *et al.*, 2009).

The lower unit corresponds to the late Upper Paleolithic, when it seems that the cavity was repeatedly occupied between 16,800 and 18,700 cal. years BP (Table 1) (Vaquero *et al.*, 2009). The evidence documented, above all in level 4, is coherent with the characteristics of the Lower and Middle Magdalenian of the Cantabrian coast: laminar flake knapping, clear dominance of burins among the retouched objects, portable art, decorative bone industry and decorative objects: including an assemblage of seashells and a pendant made from an atrophic red deer canine tooth (Fig. 2). Particularly significant is the recovery of a deciduous tooth in this level, which is the oldest human remain found in Galicia to date. A significant cultural change seems to occur at the base of this packet, characterised by the appearance of quartzite lithic objects. The wide variety of species of micro-mammals recovered has provided a large amount of environmental and paleo-environmental data for the period and suggests cooler conditions than in the upper unit (Lopez-García *et al.*, 2011).

At the site of Valdavara 1-2, under a top level that was significantly altered by post depositional processes and which contained very heterogeneous materials, a more homogeneous unit appeared (level C) with lithic artefacts in flint and quartz, indicating some technical strategies aimed at obtaining flakes. Dating of the associated remains of fauna indicates an Early Holocene chronology for this level (Fábregas *et al.*, 2010). This dating, along with the characteristics of the lithic assemblage, is coherent with attributing this level to the Macrolithic Mesolithic, which is documented for the first time in Galicia. Below this unit, we have identified another level (level D), characterised by the predominance of quartzite flakes that, if their chronology were confirmed, would correspond to the oldest occupation documented in Valdavara cave.

In Valdavara 2 a level was located at the top of the sequence containing the remains of at least three infant individuals, devoid of any associated material culture objects, but whose dating puts them in the chronological context of the Middle Bronze Age (Vaquero *et al.*, 2008, Vaquero *et al.*, 2009). Another stratigraphic unit appeared below this level with a fossil record characterised by the presence of a large number of carnivore remains but with no evidence whatsoever of human presence.

Loc.	Level	Material	Lab.ref.	Years ^{14}C	Years cal. BP	Years cal. BC
Val 1	2	Human bone	Beta-235727	4410 ± 40	5160-4840	3210-2890
Val 1	4	Bone	Beta-235728	13,770 ± 70	17,080-16,880	15,130-14,930
Val 1	4	Bone	Beta-235726	14,630 ± 70	17,890-17,730	15,940-15,780
Val 1	6	Bone	Beta-257849	15,120 ± 70	18,700-17,820	16,750-15,870
Val 1-2	C	Bone	Beta-257850	8920 ± 50	10270-9830	8320-7880
Val 1-2	C	Bone	Beta-259199	8890 ± 60	10250-9770	8300-7820
Val 2	3	Human bone	Beta-235729	3270 ± 40	3600-3400	1650-1450
Val 2	3	Human bone	Beta-235730	3250 ± 40	3600-3360	1650-1410

Table 1. Radiocarbon dating of Valdavara cave. Calibration at 2σ (p= 95%) has been performed using the cal Pal-2007-Hulu curve (Weninger and Jöris, 2004).

Between 2009 and 2011 an rescue excavation was carried out in a cavity exposed due to the consequences of the blasting of a quarry 100 metres from la Cova de Valdavara, which was named Valdavara 3. The large variety of fauna recovered from this site (lion, leopard, hyena, rhinoceros, bison, bear, fox, wolf, boar, roe deer, chamois, fallow deer), the characteristics of the micro-fauna and the first radiometric data suggest a chronology of early Upper Pleistocene, between 100,000 and 120,000 years. Although it is mainly a palaeontological assemblage, the discovery *in situ* of lithic industry stratigraphically associated to the fauna confirms human presence in the site. Although the chronology of the deposit is yet to be verified, this data places Valdavara 3 as an important reference regarding the oldest settlement in Galicia.

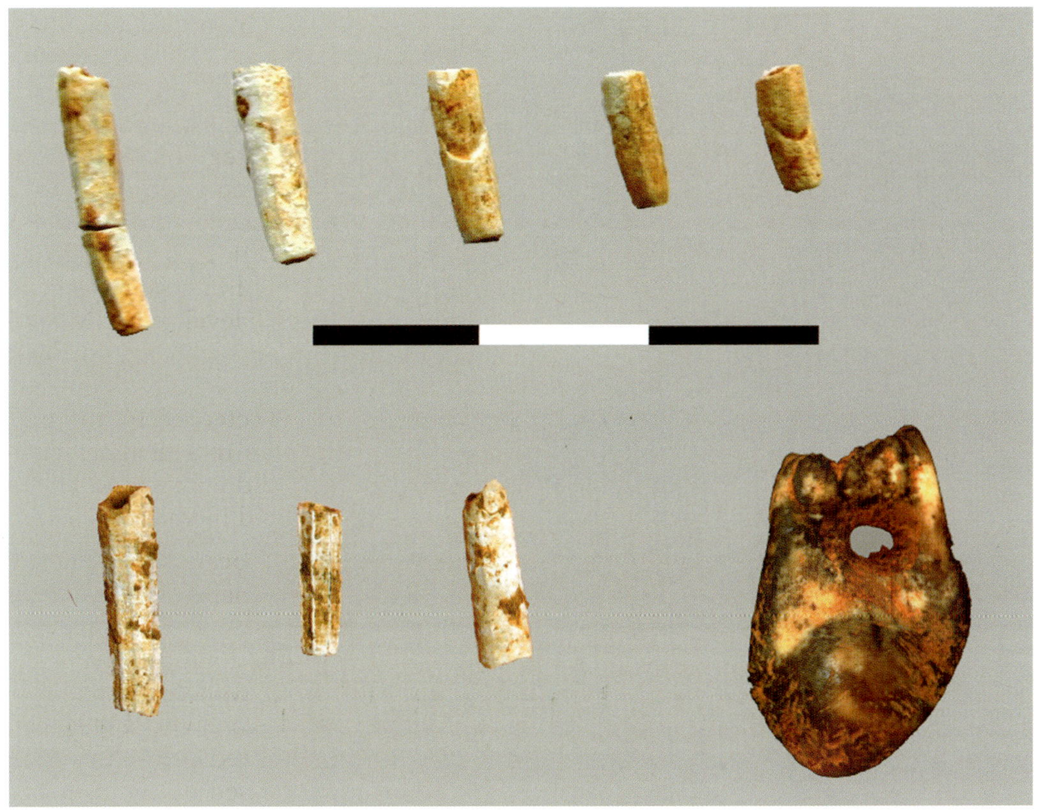

Figure 2. Personal decorative objects found in the Magdalenian levels of Valdavara 1.

2

CANTABRIAN MOUNTAINS AND COASTLINE

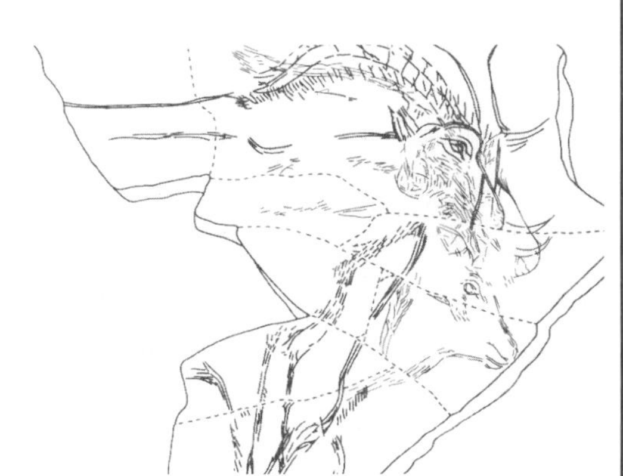

Site	Map numbering
Cueva de Aitzbitarte III and IV	5
Antoliñako Koba	6
Axlor	7
Los Azules	8
Cabo Busto	9
El Castillo	10
Cueva de la Güelga	11
Cueva de Las Caldas	12
Cueva Morín	13
Ekain	14
Cueva del Esquilleu	15
El Pendo	16
Cueva de la Riera	17
La Viña	18
Labeko Koba	19
Lezetxiki	20
Cueva del Mirón	21
Santimamiñe	22
El Sidrón	23
Sopeña	24

Jesús Altuna*, Koro Mariezkurrena*,
Joseba Ríos**

La Cueva de Aitzbitarte III and IV (Basque country)

In Aitzbitarte Hill (Rentería, Basque Country) there is a set of caves of which the two largest, III and IV, have been excavated in recent decades. The latter was worked on in the 1960's by J. M. Barandiaran (1961). E. Harlé (1908) found reindeer remains there for the first time in the Iberian Peninsula. Recently, number III has been worked on by J. Altuna (Altuna *et al.*, 2011). Both caves are located 7 km from the current coast in a straight line.

Cave III develops to the southwest. It has a large vestibule which leads to a big hall that is 60m long and averages 15m wide. Recent excavations have been conducted at the entrance of this hall and in its deep zone. Here we report the last campaigns carried out at the cave entrance. Currently, the excavations carried out in the profound area are under study.

Stratigraphy (Fig. 1) showed a Middle Paleolithic level (VI), a mixed Middle Paleolithic and Aurignacian level (Vb inferior), an Evolved Aurignacian (Vb central), three Gravettian levels (upper Vb, Va, IV), and two other levels (III and II) with Solutrean chronology but linked to the Gravettian technocomplex. Level I shows an admixed composition of reworked materials.

The level Vb central has five 14C AMS dates made in Uppsala. Four of them have provided dates to 33,605 ± 1165 to 31,000 ± 835 and an other to 28,010 ± 600 BP. The Va level has five dates the oldest one being 31,210 ± 860 and four more of 28,950 ± 655 to 26,350 ± 475. In addition the IV has six dates, five from 28,320 ± 605 to 24,240 ± 365 and an other to 22,420 ± 290. The III has seven dates, grouped from 22,580 ± 295 to 18,400 ± 215. Finally, level II also has one which dates to 19,765 ± 220 (Ua-37959).

The sedimentological study has shown that the sequence was formed under climate conditions characterized by low temperatures and humidity. Level VI is the warmest assembly. The level V, especially Vb, is gradually wetter and colder. Level IV is also damp and slightly warmer, while in level III the harshest conditions have been recorded, ameliorating gradually towards the end of the sequence.

The **pollen study** indicates a predominance of open landscapes with sparse tree representation (less than 6%).Level VI shows more arboreal presence (5.6%) with *Pinus, Juniperus* and *Betula*. The Vb central level is very cold (tree cover 1.6%) with *Pinus* and *Juniperus*. The upper Vb shows weak tree recovery (2.5%) with the same species. The Va also indicates a weak recovery in *Betula*. The IV displays an overall increase in Juniperus (3%).Due to the lack of spore pollen conservation, information was not obtained on levels III and II.

A total of 16,556 **Micromammal** remains were recovered using a 1 mm mesh sieve. The greatest part of them come from levels Vb to III. Represented species are similar in all levels, *Microtus* gr. *Agrestis-arvalis* being the most abundant, followed by *Microtus oeconomus*. *Pitymys pyrenaicus* is the most represented species of the genus *Pitymys*, and there is also evidence of *Pliomys lenki* relict species. This species representation indicates a climate characterized by cold and moist conditions, and an open landscape with scarce wood patches.

This information, obtained by sedimentological, polinical and micromammal analyses, is also confirmed by **macrommal** representation, with a good representation of open landscape animals and the presence of species usually linked with colder climates, such as *Rangifer tarandus* or *Alopex lagopus*. Bird fossil assemblages also correspond with these environmental conditions identifying the species *Lagopus mutus*, which lives today in the upper edge of coniferous forests and rocky high mountain areas in the Alps and the Pyrenees.

The lithic and bone industry reveals transformations between the Evolved Aurignacian (Vb central) and the beginning of the Gravettian (Vb superior Va

* Centro de Custodia e Investigación de los materiales Arqueológicos de Gipuzkoa. 20015 San Sebastián (GOAZ). Altuna@arkaios.com

** Centro Nacional de Investigación sobre la Evolución Humana. 09002 Burgos. joseba.rios@cenieh.es

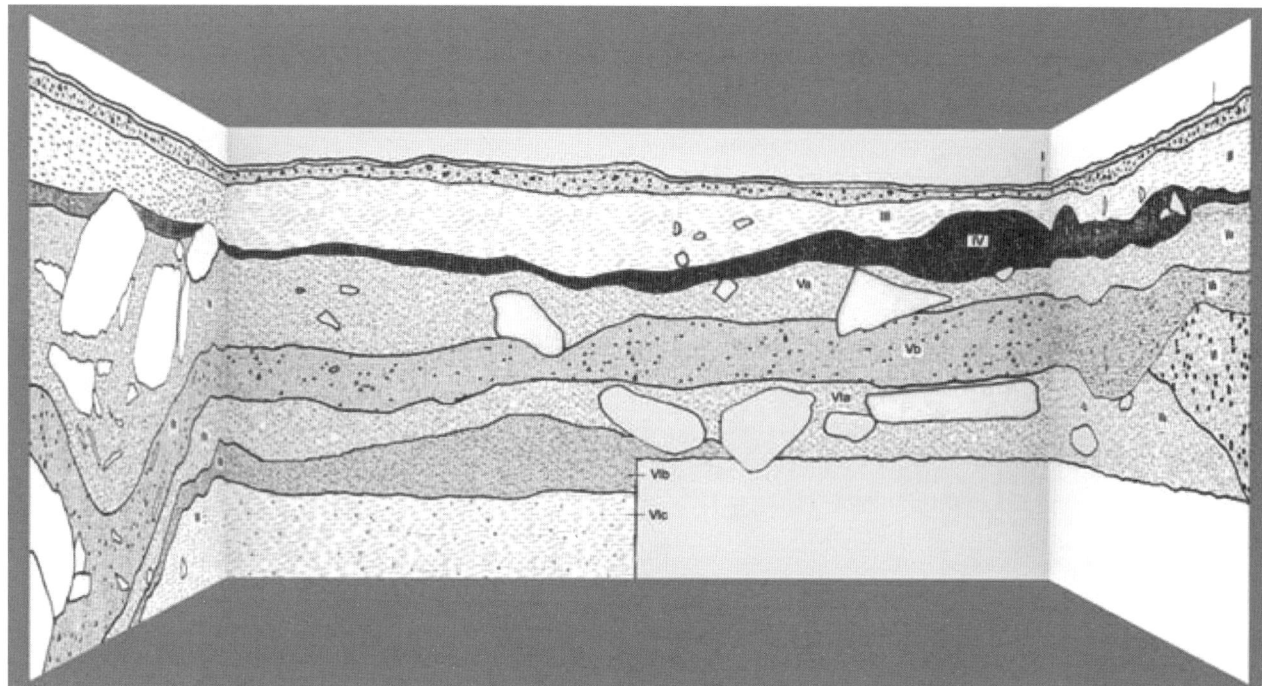

Figure 1. Stratigraphic units from Aitzbitarte cave III.

and IV) and provides data characterizing human occupations around 20,000 BP (levels III and II), which have a difficult cultural attribution in the Cantabrian regional framework.

Level VI was excavated in 1 m^2, and the scarce material recovered can only be attributed to Middle Paleolithic technocomplexes, without more precision. The upper part of this level is mixed with the lower part of Vb (Vb inferior), so the industrial complex shows an anomalous nature mixing elements from Middle Paleolithic and Evolved Aurignacian.

Level Vb central displays intense bladelet production from cores, flake edges and Vachons type cores, and also unipolar production of wide and flattened blades. The types of flint used were obtained in nearby outcrops, either the Urgonian, located in Aitzbitarte hill's limestone, or a Flysch variety from Gaitxurizketa (<10 km N).The use of flint from outcrops located between 30 and 100 km (Flysch flint from Barrika- NW- or Bidache- N) and flint coming from more distant outcrops in Chalosse (130 km, N), Salies de Bearn (100 km, N), Urbasa (90 km, S) or Treviño (125 km SW) has also been documented. The most represented formal tools are Aurignacian blades and the typical Aurignacian scrapers. Burins exhibit great variations of functions and morphologies, the most characteristic being the burin-cores (Vachons, Dihedral and Multiple) and burins on truncation. Substratum tools and splintered pieces are also very abundant, while the bladelet tools are scarce, the Dufour type retouched bladelets are the most represented type. There is also plenty of barely configured macrolithic industry. Bone industry is scarce and non-diagnostic, composed mainly by lissoirs and retouchers. Also found in this level was one engraved schist slab with nonfigurative depictions that connects with the first Cantabrian graphic traditions (Fig. 3 and 3b). The assemblage can be characterized as palimpsest of occupations with intense and varied activities, for instance the processing of fauna. The industrial characteristics along with the dates obtained on the level, allow a cultural affiliation to the Evolved Aurignacian.

The upper section (Vb superior) shows a change from level Vb central. The manufacturing of bladelet is made from unipolar prismatic cores; also laminar knapping is more regular, producing narrow blades. The retouched assemblage shows a decrease of typical Aurignacian tools and an increase of burin types, with some examples of Noailles burins (Fig. 2). From the bone industry the awls and the bone points stand out.

At the level Va the production of unipolar blades and bladelets from prismatic cores, pyramidal cores and burin-cores is remarkable. The most characteristic retouched tools are the burins, dihedral and on truncation, with some typical Noailles, and the splintered pieces. The bone technology shows a limited presence of pointed artifacts, possibly bone points, alongside other "domestic" tools.

Figure 2a. Platelet engraved from Aurignacian level

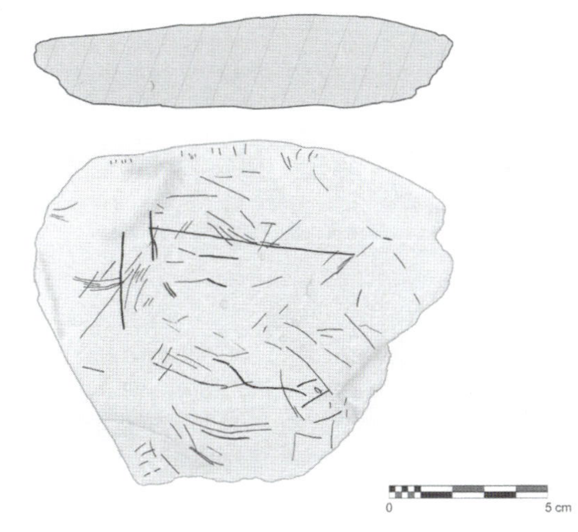

Figure 2b. Platelet engraved. Drawing..

No remarkable difference was noted in the knapping strategies between levels IV and Va. The presence of diverse tool types is notable, with some Noailles burins and splintered pieces, followed by scrapers, truncated blades and backed tools. The only evidence of bone industry is one bone point fragment. The assemblage composition also seems to be related to domestic activities.

The upper part of level Vb and levels Va and IV, are techno-typological and chronologically correlated with an early Gravettian phase. The decrease in the use of local flint (Urgonian or Gaitxurizketa) is significant in comparison with Evolved Aurignacian, as is the increase of flint coming from more distant sources, such as Chalosse or Bidache.

Level III shows a great variability in production systems identifying production of narrow and wide bladelets, both from cores or flake, and production of flakes and the importation of already produced blades. The retouched assemblage is composed of burins of various types, including Noailles and *Busqué*, backed bladelets, scrapers and two geometrics. The bone tool assemblage is the richest and most varied of the entire sequence, with two exceptional needle fragments and two bone points with flattened circular sections. In addition there is one pendant made of canine fox and one fragment of bone bead. This level corresponds to multifunctional occupations, including domestic activities and the preparation and restoration of hunting tools.

Level II is characterized by the production of different sized bladelets, especially from pyramidal cores and probably from *Busqué* type burin-cores; while flake and blade production seems to have taken place outside the cave. Regarding the retouched tools, most represented types are burins, specially Noailles and *Busqué* types. On the contrary, scrapers are scarce and there are not clear foliate types. Pieces with abrupt retouch, especially truncated and backed tools, are relatively abundant, and maybe some of them could be interpreted as fragments of shouldered points. The bone industry shows a pos-

Figure 3. Noailles burin from Gravettian levels

sible bone point fragment and bird bone tube with transverse linear engravings.

Levels III and II chronologically coincide with the beginning of regional Solutrean: nevertheless the industrial assemblage shows distinct characteristics closer to the Gravettian technocomplex. For that reason, it seems an original industry variety linked with other assemblages as Amalda (V) or Ermittia (V).

Meanwhile, level I appears extremely altered offering unreliable data.

Level III (recent Gravettian) has provided four **human teeth** belonging to three children under 13 years of age and one adult. It is, so far, the oldest known remains of our species in the Basque Country. The identified evidence is: one D_2 corresponding to newborn between 12 - 21 months, one M_1 belonging to a 5.5 - 6 year old child, one M_2 from another child aged between 11- 13 years and one P^4 from an adult.

The **macromammals** assemblage is composed of 30,261 remains, generally very fragmented, of which 2,149 have been taxonomically identified. The large number of undetermined specimens responds to the 2 mm water sieving and to the exhaustive recovery of fragments during the excavation.

The macromammals are the subsistence basis for the human groups that occupied the cave. Most represented species are the bovine (among them *Bos primigenius* and *Bison priscus*), *Cervus elaphus and Rupicapra rupicapra*. The presence of other ungulates such as *Rangifer tarandus, Capreolus capreolus* and *Capra pyrenaica*, is scarce, some of these species being absent in certain levels.

In the Vb central level (Evolved Aurignacian) *Cervus elaphus* dominates, followed by bovine and *Rupicapra rupicapra*. The *Ursus spelaeus* also has a large representation. The upper level Vb (Early Gravettian) shows a similar faunal spectrum, leading subsequently to bovine increase during Early Gravettian (Va and IV). Finally on levels III and II bovine presence decreases, and *Rupicapra rupicapra* increases. Reindeer is represented by a few remains in levels Va, IV, III and II.

There are numerous anthropogenic traces on the bones (fractures, multiple incisions, traces of fire in changing degrees). There are a few traces of Carnivore bites, probably on abandoned human faunal remains. An *Ursus spelaeus* ulna with cut-marks recovered in Vb central level is also remarkable.

On the other hand, level IV is notorious for its large hearths and for the large amount of chopped and burned small bone fragments. The elevated proportion of spongy bone fragments with high fat content, indicates that they probably served as fuel during the harshest periods with low tree cover.

The **Bird assemblage** is small, with 137 determinable remains, mostly concentrated in levels III (82) and IV (32). Identified remains correspond basically to *Lagopus mutus, Perdix perdix* and *Pyrrhocorax*. While these findings are compatible with their introduction in the cave by humans, at the moment no anthropogenic modifications have been observed in the bone fragments. Also, the appearance of rock species, especially at level III, indicates that the cavity was not permanently occupied by humans at that moment.

Fossil fish assemblage is also small, with 156 remains. The most abundant genus is *Salmon*, especially trout. The presence of *Anguilla anguilla, Trisopteros minutus* (III), *Blenius* sp. (Va and IV), *Scomber* sp. (Va) and *Platichys flesus* (Vb) is significant. This latter species occupied the seawater areas of river mouths and could be caught in the Oiartzun River.

The **mollusks** assemblage is composed by shells of marine origin, typical of the Bay of Biscay, such as: *Patella vulgate* (l. I, II and III), *Littorina littorea* (l. II, III and IV), *L. obtusata, L. fabalis* (both in l. III), *Stramonita haemastomsa, Mytilus* sp., *Pecten maximus* and *Antalis* sp. (four of them found in l. II). Three shells have been transformed into hanging ornaments.

In the **Aitzbitarte III exterior sequence** an interesting archeoestratigraphic sequence has been documented, environmental evolution and transformations in human behavior and culture, including the site function, subsistence strategies, and tool procurement, have been observed.

At this time the research focused in the interior part of the cave is very advanced, specifically in the rich Gravettian levels with Noailles burins, where subsistence strategies were based almost exclusively on bovine hunting (over 90% of the remains).

The level IV, of la Cueva de Aitzbitarte located above the III, has a poorly defined Aurignacian level, one Solutrean, two Magdalenian and another Azilian level. Also in the deepest part of the cave paleolithic paintings have recently been found (Garate *et al.*, 2013). In comparison with cave III, the absence of Gravettian occupations in cave IV is noteworthy, and likewise the late Paleolithic occupations represented in this cave (Magdalenian and Azilian) are absent from cave III.Antoliña Cave (Antoliñako koba in Basque) (DATUM ETRS 89 x: 528.685.46 Y: 4.801.186,83 Z: 285) is placed within a basin downstream of Oka or Gernika River, in area called Urdaibai (Bizkaia). It is close to the Santimamiñe classic archaeological site (Fig. 1: 1). Its mean height above sea level is 285 m; strategically orientated in the southwest direction, allowing visual control in most part of the Urdaibai basin and access to the coastal valleys of the rivers Lea and Artibai.

Mikel Aguirre*

Antoliñako Koba (Gautegiz-Arteaga, Bizkaia)

Antoliña cave (Antoliñako Koba in Basque) (DATUM ETRS 89 x: 528.685.46 Y: 4.801.186,83 Z: 285) is located in a basin downstream of the Oka or Gernika River, in an area called Urdaibai (Bizkaia). It is close to the Santimamiñe classic archaeological site (Fig. 1:1). Its average height above sea level is 285 m; it is strategically orientated toward the southwest, allowing visual control of most parts of the Urdaibai basin and access to the coastal valleys of the Lea and Artibai rivers.

The archaeological excavation was carried out between 1995 and 2008. It has allowed the identification of a major stratigraphic sequence of Aurignacian, Gravettian, Upper Solutrean, Lower advanced Magdalenian occupations, evidence of Upper Magdalenian and Azilian (Aguirre, 1996, 2001; Aguirre *et al.*, 2001). The archaeological record and paleo environmentare the most complete and richest in the Urdaibai between *c.*35, 000 BP and 14,500 BP, with some well-defined stratigraphic hiatuses in sequence with essentially anthropogenic accumulation dynamics. Are they demographic contractions in the eastern Bay of Biscay? Is this a change of strategy in territorial exploitation?

There have been some contributions to the origin of the siliceous raw materials from Antoliña (Tarriño *et al.*, 1998; Tarriño, 2006: 136-139) and the paleoenvironment from microvertebrates sequence (Zubeldia *et al.*, 2006). Currently, an interdisciplinary archaeological study is underway.

The configuration of the caves' sedimentary fill has significant lateral changes in their character and vertical development. In the west room (Fig. 1: 2), stratigraphy has little impact due to the proximity to the rock base; we call this Upper Sedimentary Set (USS) and Middle Sedimentary Set (MSS). Meanwhile, the Lower Sedimentary Set (LSS) was of considerable depth in the northern part of the gallery and lobby with archaeological levels absent. Here we will expose, from wall to roof, different documented archaeological horizons (Fig. 2).

Horizon 1 – The earliest evidence of Antoliña occupation is located in a confined level between stalagmite filtering (Fig 2) from LSS, Sbl-P (brown sandy silt with phosphates) where one marmot was identified among the poor faunal evidence, along with one scraper and a few other lithic elements. There is currently no dating for these strata, but there is some geochemical analysis (Yusta *et al.*, 2005). These levels belong to the lower half of this sedimentary base assembly. Observation has been done of forming speleothems, blocks and limit clasts, as well as different sandy layers, sometimes brecciated brown silty clay, and packages of very compact orange clays mixed with phosphates. All of this it is archaeologically sterile except for the mentioned stratum.

Horizon 2 – The top half of LSS is a thick phosphate with various clay packages and speleothems. It contains the archaeological first level of a certain entity, composed of brown sand with abundant phosphate lumps (Sb-P). This horizon displays Aurignacian industry, the most significant being the simple retouching (in denticulate and scrapers) with a few Dufour flakes.

Horizon 3 – It is covered by orange sands and phosphates (So-P) with similar archaeological lithic material and scarce fauna; poorly preserved at these levels, dating is pending. Its roof differentiates from upper zone in color, texture and small bioturbation.

Horizon 4 – Above, it is defined by one reddish brown compact sand package (Sbk), with infrequent clasts or corroded blocks and countless lateral variations (Table 1). We have data near the roof, 30,640 ± 240 BP (Beta-251304) and one on charcoal 29,990 ± 230 BP (GrA-23,898) in the lower level section. This horizon contains hue evolved Aurignacian industries, with significant percentages of substrate groups, rare Dufour bladelet and ordinary bone industry. This stratum, containing compact brown silt (L) and sand with blocks (Lbk lower / Sbk), forms the basis of the MSS.

* UNED, CA Bergara, San Martin Agirre Plaza 4, 20570 Bergara (Gipuzkoa) maguirre@bergara.uned.es

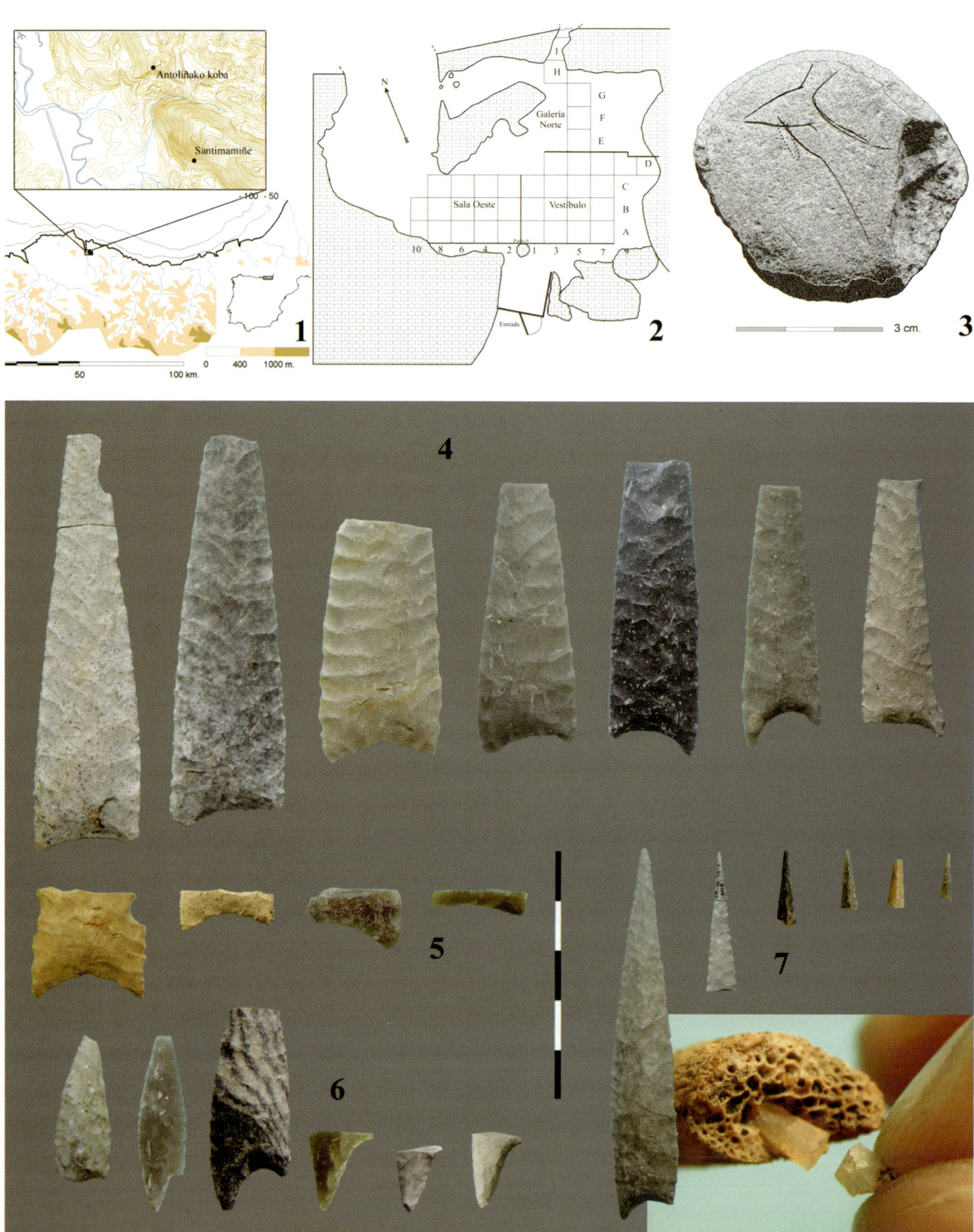

Figure 1. 1. Location of Antoliña. 2. Map of the excavation. 3. Antoliña Gravettian engraving on a pebble.4-7. Retouched falt Solutrean artifact from Antoliña. 7. Indeterminate ungulate rib with a distal tip end.

Sedimentary ensemble	Ref. Level	Cultural att.	Methhod	Material	Ref. lab.	BP Date	CalBP	68% range calBP
Upper	Lanc/ Upper Lgc	Aziliense	C14AMS	Bone	Beta-215544	10220 ± 40 BP	11932 ± 128	11804 – 12060
			C14AMS	Bone	Beta-215543	10800 ± 40 BP	12777 ± 63	12713 – 12840
	Lower Lgc	Lower Magd.	C14AMS	Bone	Beta-230281	14580 ± 70 BP	17829 ± 314	17515 – 18143
			C14AMS	Bone	Beta-230280	14630 ± 70 BP	17954 ± 379	17574 – 18333
			C14	Bone	GrN-23783	14680 ± 80 BP	18003 ± 374	17628 – 18377
			C14	Bone	GrN-23784	14680 ± 100 BP	17998 ± 378	17619 – 18376
	Lmb	Upp. Solu.	C14AMS	Bone	Beta-251301	17340 ± 100 BP	20801 ± 301	20500 – 21102
	Lmc	Upp. Solu.	C14AMS	Bone	Beta-230284	19020 ± 120 BP	22879 ± 303	22575 – 23182
			C14	Bone	GrN-23785	19280 ± 120 BP	23044 ± 283	22760 – 23327
Middle	Lab/Sab	Gravettian	C14AMS	Bone	Beta-233766	22640 ± 120 BP	27358 ± 388	26969 – 27746
	Upper Lmbk/Smbk	Gravettian	C14AMS	Bone	Beta– 215542	26080 ± 200 BP	31011 ± 356	30655 – 31367
			C14AMS	Bone	Beta– 251303	26140 ± 150 BP	31046 ± 343	30702 – 31389
			C14AMS	Bone	Beta-230282	26710 ± 180 BP	31469 ± 284	31185 – 31753
			C14AMS	Bone	Beta-251299	26720 ± 180 BP	31486 ± 273	31212 – 31759
			C14AMS	Bone	Beta-251300	27100 ± 190 BP	31822 ± 154	31667 – 31976
			C14	Bone	GrN-23786	27390 ± 320 BP	32064 ± 277	31786 – 32341
			C14AMS	Bone	Beta-230279	27520 ± 190 BP	32109 ± 222	31887 – 32331
	Lower Lmbk/Smk	Evol. Aurig.	C14AMS	Charcoal	GrA-23898	29990 ± 230 BP	34253 ± 196	34057 – 34449
			C14AMS	Bone	Beta-251304	30640 ± 240 BP	34823 ± 355	34467 – 35178

Table 1. Dating of Antoliñako koba and its calibration (2007 Calpal HULU, Weninger *et al.*, 2010).

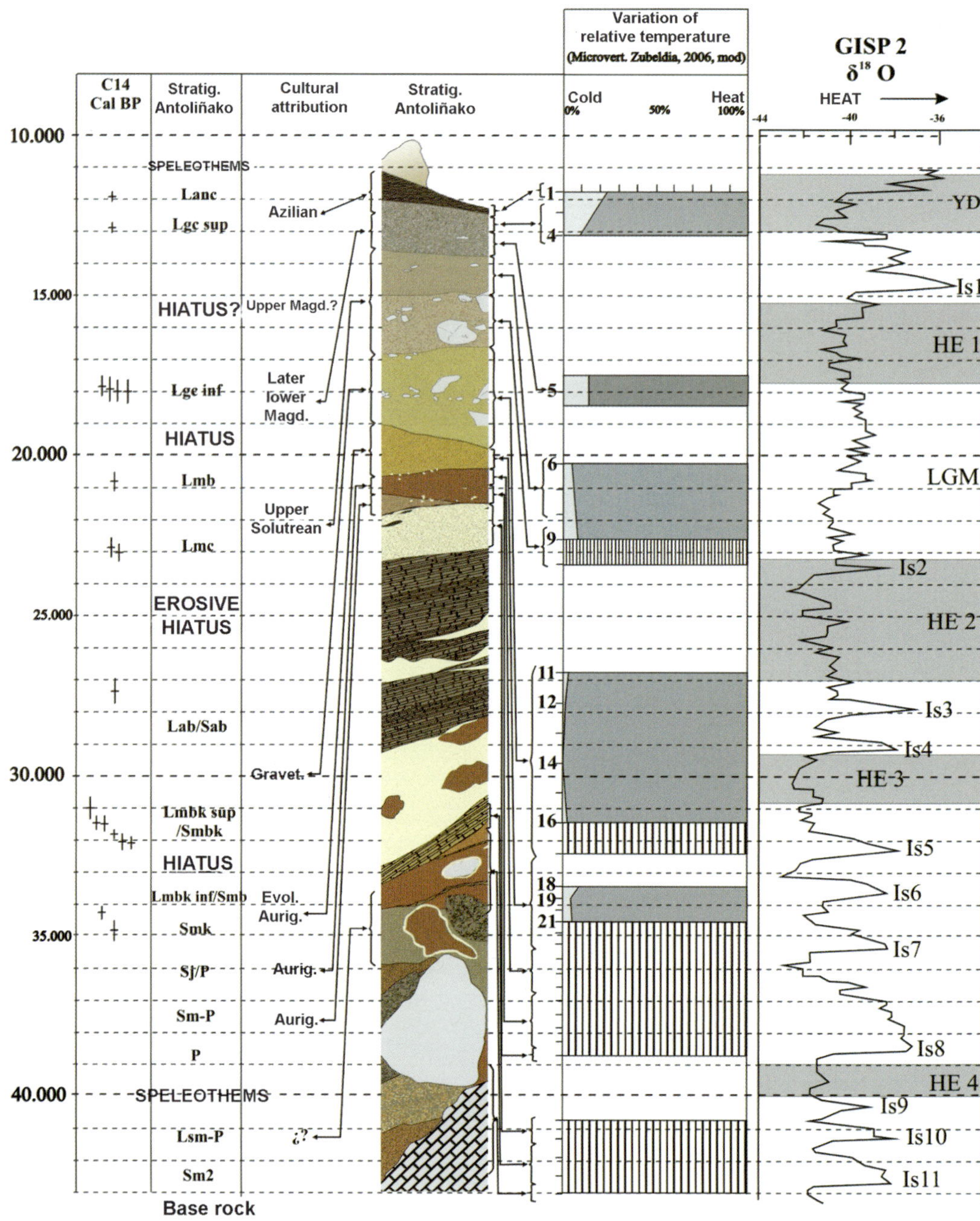

Figure 2. Test of provisional stratigraphy chrono-climatic correlation in Antoliña, such as radiocarbon and curves of temperature variation and partial processing of column sampling microvertebrates (Zubeldia *et al.*, 2006).

Horizon 5 – After a relatively short sedimentary hiatus (with no interfaces defined in the west room, but clearer in the north gallery) it develops a package with high archaeological material density at the base, compact yellowish brown silt and sand with abundant blocks (Lbk upper / Sybk) attached to Gravettian with Noailles burins (Aguirre, 2013). In the bone industry there are outstanding oval section assegais, with morphologies similar to the Isturitz. As for its implications, one small hammer-*abraseur* with deer morphology is remarkable (Fig. 1: 3) (Aguirre and Gonzalez Sainz, 2011). We have six dates found with Accelerator mass spectrometry (AMS) and ^{14}C, as one conventional, staggered consistently between *c.* 25,800 and 27,700 BP (*c.* 31,000-32,300 calBP).

The archaeological material, Gravettian type with Noailles, becomes scarcer in the upper sections, with yellow silt and sand with blocks (Lyb / Syb). Toward the roof net erosional contact occurs. It has been dated to 22,640 ± 120 BP (Beta-233766).

Horizon 6 – The USS begins over the Tardiglaciar erosive difference. It has significant Upper Solutrean occupations: the lower one of brown silt with clasts (Lbc) and the upper with brown silt blocks (Lbb). Both abundant with flat retouched pieces (Fig. 1 4 7), as well as a predominance of concave bases (about fifty) and uncommon little lateral notches. Noailles burins are present. There are three dates: 19,280 ± 120 BP (GrN-23,785) and 19,020 ± 120 BP (Beta-230284) for Bsc; and 17,340 ± 100 BP (Beta-251301) for the upper Lbb.

Horizon 7 – After another hiatus, with erosion signs on the Lbb roof, it follows grayish silt with clasts (Lgc), already in surface in one lobby section and the west room. They are greatly affected by various conditions (cattle, illegal) reaching the Solutrean levels in most of the excavated area. The bone industry evidence comprises sub-triangular and square sections and spatulate points. There are four dating between 14,510 and 14,780 BP (17,515 and 18,377 calBP), two of them completed with AMS and the others with conventional methods. The lower section of this horizon corresponds to Lower Magdalenian (Lgc lower).

Horizon 8 – Unable to establish sedimentary differentiation with upper section Lgc, (Lgc upper), in some exceptional locations it is possible to find greater density of small clasts and mollusks between the archaeological material. It is dated (Beta-215543) to 10,800 ± 40 BP. In marginal areas of the northwest room and small gallery zones of black (*negro*: n) silty-clay and silt with clasts (Lcnc), overlapping Lgc, a speleothems roof is conserved, sealed and dated in 10,220 ± 40 BP (Beta-215544), data that is very close to the previous, but not coinciding. During screening of scrambled sediment,several fragments of Magdalenian harpoons, hardly attributable to such late dates, were recovered. Logically, this fact shows occasional visits during the Magdalenian to the central section of Lgc. The composition of archaeological material of upper Lgc and Lcnc is similar (comprised of backed elements and analogous variety of mollusks) assigning it to Azilian.

González-Urquijo, Jesús*; Ibáñez, Juan José**; Lazuén, Talía***, Mozota, Millán**

Axlor

Research History

The site of Axlor (Dima, Bizcaia) is located on the northern Atlantic coast of the Iberian Peninsula. The cave mouth is located at about 320 m above sea level on an interior valley near one of the crossing points between the Atlantic and Mediterranean basins. The site was discovered by archaeologist J.M. Barandiarán in 1932 and was excavated by him between 1967 and 1974. Barandiarán described nine stratigraphic layers and defined levels III to VIII as fertile, all of them with Mousterian lithic industries (Barandiarán, 1980). The faunal remains of big mammals were studied by J. Altuna (1989). The lithic and bone industries were analyzed by A. Baldeón in his doctoral thesis

* Instituto de Prehistoria (IIIPC) / Departamento de Ciencias Históricas, Universidad de Cantabria, Avda de los Castros, s/n, 39005 Santander, gonzalje@unican.es

** Institució Milá i Fontanals, CSIC, C/Egipciaques, 15 08001 Barcelona, ibanezjj@imf.csic.es and millanm@imf.csic.es

*** PACEA (CNRS-Université de Bordeaux), Allée Geoffroy de Saint Hilaire 33615 PESSAC t.lazuen@pacea.u-bordeaux1.fr

(1985) and extensively published later (Baldeón, 1999). A. Baldeón classified all levels as Charentian Mousterian –with some variations for the two lower levels– having abundant sidescrapers.

Stratigraphic Sequence

In 2000, the excavation of the Axlor site was restarted by a team led by J. González-Urquijo and J.J. Ibáñez. The new excavation took place in contemporary levels to those of the sequence excavated by Barandiarán. Roughly, levels B to N (Fig. 1) correspond to levels III to VIII of the excavation of the 1960's and 1970's (González-Urquijo *et al.*, 2005, 2006). This sequence which chronologically corresponds to the final stages of the Middle Paleolithic. Level D is dated to 42,010 + 1,280 BP (Beta-144262) and the lower levels of sequence (M and N) date to 47,500 BP or earlier. The sequence, recognized until then, was completed, at the base, with a mass of yellow clay: level IX. The new excavations have revealed a sedimentary deposit stratigraphically located below the original sequence, with two sublevels containing archaeological material deposited around OIS 4-5. A deep drilling, down to -6.80 marks, revealed a huge sterile filling. Also, the remains of a layer of the early Upper Paleolithic were located in the upper section of the sequence (level A) corresponding to the base of level II of J.M. Barandiarán, which had been considered sterile at the time.

At the **lower levels (Axlor R),** the lithic industry is scarce (n = 414), and is knapped in flint (46.5%), quartz (27%), silicified mudstone (14%), limestone (8%), quartzite, limonite, and sandstone. In the immediate surroundings of the site, the chances to find useful rocks for knapping are limited to silicified mudstone, limestone, limonite, and sandstone. These materials are relatively easy to locate in both primary and secondary position in the nearby scree and waterways, less than 1 km (0.62 miles) from the cave. The best quality silicified mudstone is found in the formations of the Supraurgonian black Flysch a few kilometers north of Axlor. However, blocks usable for knapping can be found in Albian age outcrops, a few hundred meters from the site. Quartz can be discovered on the edges of Biscay synclinorium about 5-10 km north from the site. We do not know the origin of the quartzite found in very low amounts in fluvial deposits near Axlor. The flint basically comes from the coastal Flysch, located 35-40 km from the site.

The bulk of the set is composed of *débitage* residues (65%) and flakes (28%), whereas cores and retouched tools barely reach 1% and 5.8%, respectively. It should be noted, however, that out of the 116 flakes in the collection 48 (41%) correspond to rejuvenation flakes. The most represented utensils are the sidescrapers which are of different

Figure 1. Axlor Stratigraphy.

types: lateral, transversal, and double, four of them featuring Quina or Quina-like retouch.

A different management of flint over other raw materials can be observed in level R. Flint artifacts are smaller and much more often retouched. An important part of them are in fact rejuvenation flake from Quina sidescrapers, which sometimes have been, in turn, retouched and used (Lazuén and González Urquijo, i. p. a). The functional study of a sample of lithic tools of this layer suggests the development of

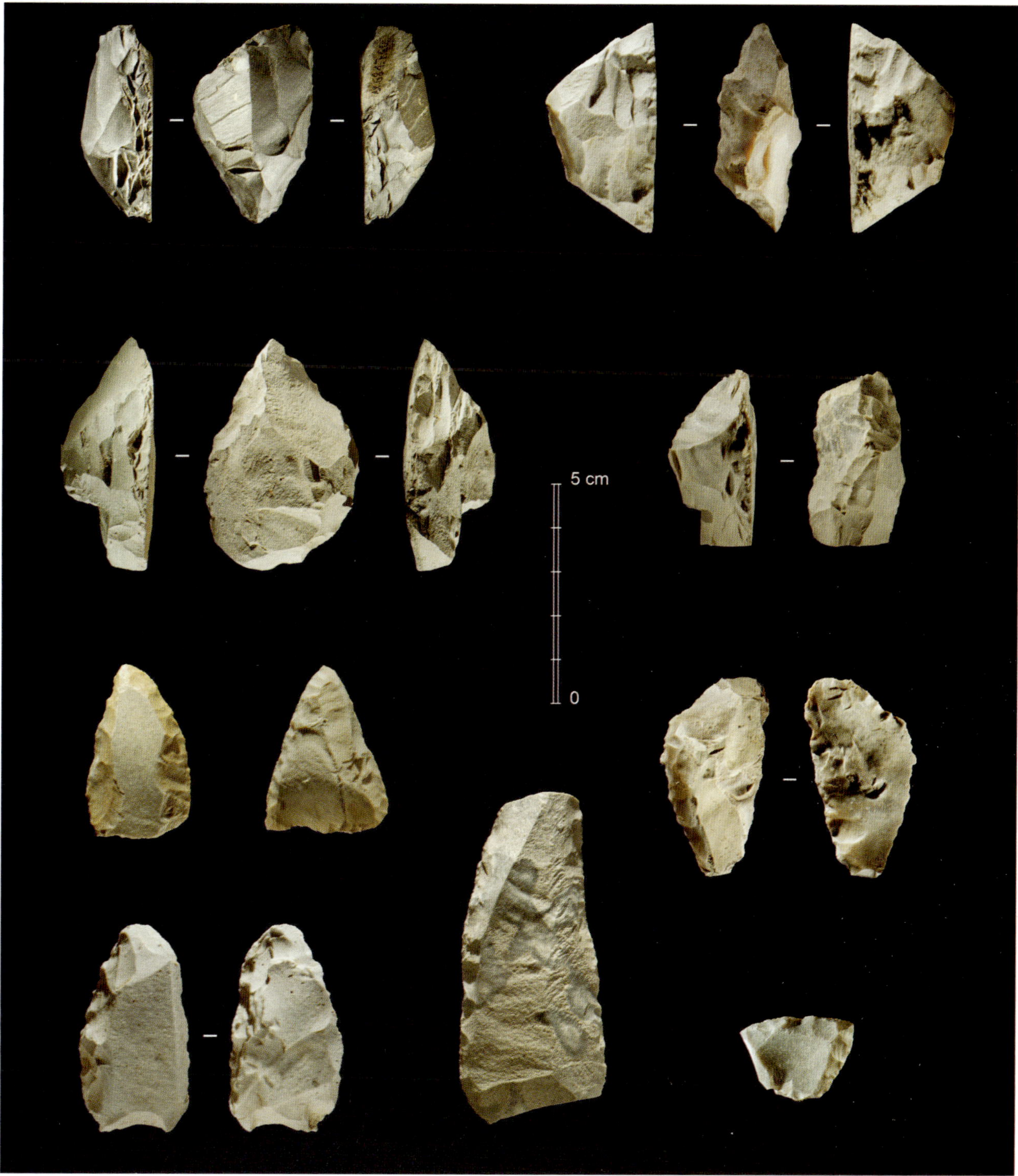

Figure 2. Quina sidescrapers.

a variety of tasks, including butchery, as well as work on non-woody plants, dry hide and wood (Lazuén and González Urquijo, in press b).

At the bottom of the modern sequence (levels M and N), the raw materials used for the lithic production are similar to those of the lower layers: flint (45%), quartz (30%), silicified mudstone (20%), quartzite, and others. Flint comes from outcrops to the north, in the coastal Flysch in the form of flakes and tools of medium or large size (> 5 cm) or small Levallois-type cores. These cores produced flakes of up to 1-1.5 cm as can be observed in the negatives of the latest extractions.

A significant portion of the tools at the site are points of Mousterian type, to be used as projectiles. The silicified mudstone is exploited often with Levallois techniques for the production of larger flakes, which are often retouched as sidescrapers. Production schemes followed with quartz are less defined.

The faunal remains of level N are composed of deer 74% (Altuna, 1989), with 20% of animals from rocky goat, chamois areas and almost no presence of large bovid and horse remains. An important behavioral feature recognized in Axlor is the intensive use of bone hammers, mainly diaphysis fragments. Nearly a thousand of them have been recovered in the campaigns conducted to date and about 500 have been technically and functionally analyzed (Mozota, 2012). Out of these, 73 are from level N and 92 from level M. These tools are obtained from faunal remains, without strict selection criteria, and without an intentional manufacture, unlike what happens in upper layers. They are mainly used for various lithic retouching techniques.

At these levels, especially in level N, the presence of abundant and well-preserved combustion structures is to be noted.

The latest part of the sequence corresponding to the final **Middle Paleolithic (levels D, C and B)** has a quite different tool management strategy. Most of the material is flint (over 60%) followed way behind by silicified mudstone and quartz (between 10% and 15% each material). At these layers the flint comes from three different sources, the coastal Flysch, the Urbasa mountain range, and the Treviño outcrops (González Urquijo *et al.*, 2005). There are hardly any cores or evidence of block knapping. Large flint artifacts are imported to the site. These are obtained through a Quina-type production of thick implements displaying a dorsal surface. These flakes are retouched as Quina sidescrapers at the site, where they are heavily used and reshaped to reach very small sizes at the time they were abandoned (Fig. 2). Some of the rejuvenation flakes, specifically the largest, appear to be the result of an intentional, or at least a preferential, selection to produce a new generation of tools.

As has been demonstrated through the analysis of a large sample of retouched artifacts from level D (n = 917, Frías, 2013), the most abundant type–about 75%– are the sidescrapers, which are very often double or multiple. The final retouched tools are very small in size. This is the result of the intensive exploitation and the use of rejuvenation which account for about 30% of the retouched implements. Unlike what was initially observed with a small sample (n = 50, Rivers, 2007), the average size of the final sidescraper reached only 2.3 x 2.2 x 0.8 mm and many of them are less than 2 cm in any their two dimensions.

The bone hammers are very abundant at these levels. According to the analyzed sample (over 200, Mozota, 2013), these are obtained after a careful selection of formats, or perhaps an intentional production of fragments during big mammals food processing. Its use is more specialized (with variations in the types of tools and predominant use of retouching tools in "Quina" tasks). In level B, these are especially massive, being adapted to the extraction of the bigger rejuvenation flakes.

The faunal remains of levels D, C and B are far more diversified, showing a progressive increase in the presence of horse and bovids to the detriment of deer. In the most recent layer of the Middle Paleolithic –level B–, deer, goat, large bovids, and horse are distributed in almost balanced shares in the spectrum of ungulate species (Altuna, 1989; Castaños, 2005).

Balance

Most of the occupations at the Axlor site occurred during the Middle Paleolithic and the most intense took place along OIS 3.The behavior that is best reflected in these occupations during OIS 3 is the variability in the technical organization of the Neanderthal societies of the period. This variability can be observed in the range of hunted animals, the formation and use of the bone industry, the management of lithic raw materials –with highly variable percentages for the different types of rocks and flint deposits in different regions–, and in the repertoire of knapping techniques or deductible territorial mobility patterns.

Manuel R. González Morales*

Los Azules cave (Cangas de Onís, Asturias)

Location and description:

Los Azules cave is located on the southern slope of Mount Llueves, today a dense forest, in Contranquil, Cangas de Onís, roughly at 30 m. above the current course of the Sella River. Its name comes from the farm property on the riverbank. It consists of a complex of small cavities on the same face of Cretaceous Albian-Lower Cenomanian limestone outcrops. The cave that has been excavated have two mouths –originally defined as Los Azules cave I (west) and II (east)– separated by a rocky pillar, which open to a single inner space. When discovered it was almost completely filled with sediment, with a thick top layer dumped by landslides from the slope, as was the case with the other adjacent cave mouths of the complex.

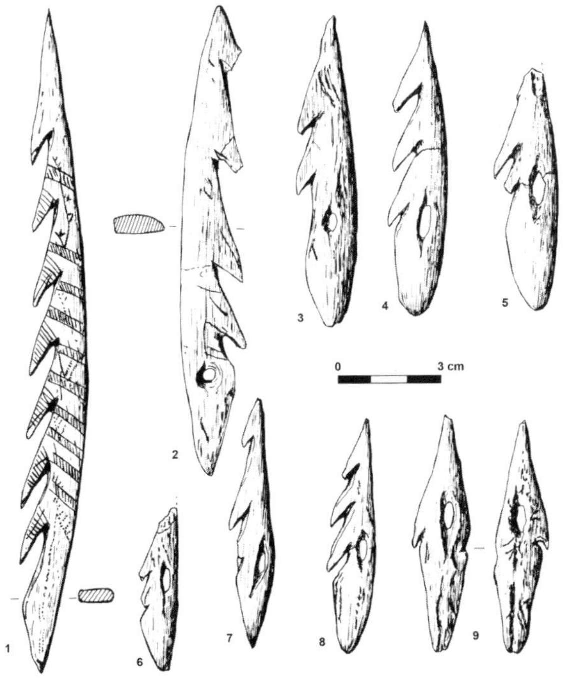

Figure 1. Azilian harpoons from Los Azules cave: 1-2: Level 5; 3-4: Level 3g; 5-9: Level 3f. (According to Fernández-Tresguerres and Junceda 1994).

Discovery and excavation:

The archaeological site was discovered accidentally in 1971 by Alberto Blanco Castaño and Francisco de la Roz Soto, who found an Azilian harpoon and some quartzite and flint flakes. Formal excavation began in 1973 under Juan Fernández-Tresguerres after finding that the site had been plundered by clandestines. In the first two campaigns became clear that the site contained a wide range of Azilian occupations and extraordinary materials, including several characteristic harpoons (Fig. 1) and rich lithic industry. At the end of the 1974 field season, the discovery of bones from a human foot on the edge of the excavated area led to a larger-scale excavation in 1975, which exhumed a burial (Fig. 2) in the Azilian level, with exceptionally well preserved remains from different skeletal parts. Subsequent excavations until the mid-90s extended the excavated area to the inner area of Los Azules cave II, and test pits were dug on the platform outside, in front of each mouth and on the bench between them.

* Instituto Internacional de Investigaciones Prehistoricas de Cantabria, 39005 Santander, Spain

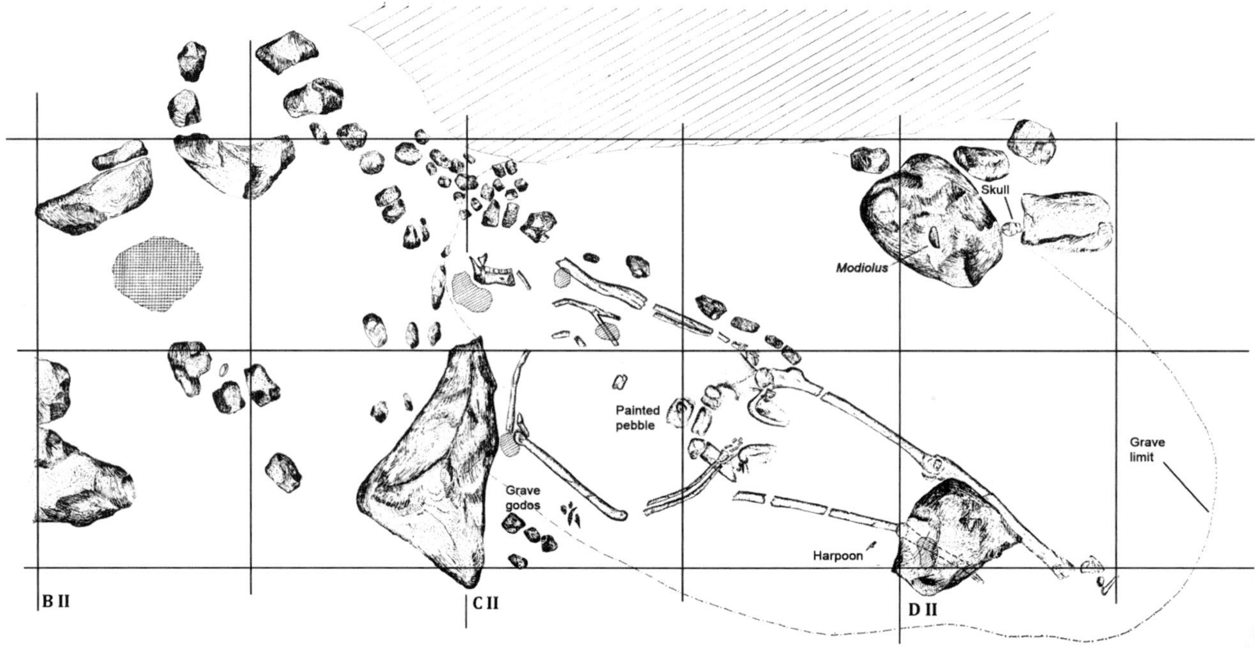

Figure 2. Plan of Los Azules cave burial (As per Fernández-Tresguerres 1976, sketch by Lorenzo Arias Páramo).

Stratigraphy:

The infill of the two cave mouths shows a relatively turbulent sedimentary history, with successive phases of water erosion and infills of clay from landslides, interstratified with clast episodes facilitated by exposure to external agents and the poor quality of the rock. The cultural sequence described by the excavators, with the exception of the aforementioned disturbances, is as follows:

Level I: Sterile.	Level 7 (layers a-c): Magdalenian.
Level 2: Late Azilian.	Level 8: Magdalenian.
Level 3 (layers a-h): Late Azilian.	Level 9: Magdalenian.
Level 4: Sterile.	Level 10: Magdalenian.
Level 5 (layers a-b): Early Azilian.	Level 11: Magdalenian.
Level 6: Late Magdalenian.	Level 12: Magdalenian.

The cave was almost completely filled up at the time of its discovery, and the surface layer formed a mound at the entrance. This is most probably due to a clay flow slopedown slope that ultimately fossilized the cave. The upper layers of level 3 (3a-d) had a limited distribution at the entrance and outside the cave, while the lower layers (especially 3d2 and 3e) extended throughout the cave and contained abundant ash, organic matter and evidence of intense human activity. From layer 3f onwards, occupations were found towards the back of the cave, also with large amounts of ashes.

Level 4, a period when the cave is not occupied, consists of yellowish clay with abundant angular limestone clasts across the entire area of the cave. Level 5, like the lower beds of Level 3, appear at the rear of the cave, filling a large erosive depression that affected Upper Magdalenian levels 6-9. These levels experienced both the erosive effect of water flowing deep into the cave and also the intense use of the space by Azilians, who dug ditches, pits and various other structures. The deepest levels (10-12) have been tentatively assigned to the Magdalenian, without further details available at present. Various structures have been found here as well, including layers of cobbles, enclosure walls, caches of ochre and others.

Lithic and bone industries:

According to Fernandez-Tresguerres, the raw material management pattern was characterized by an increased selection of materials located near the site throughout the Azilian period. Less common in the Early Azilian, this trend became more marked during the 'Azilianization' of the lithic industry. The classic Azilian progressed from careful selection to the exploitation of areas closer to the site. The Magdalenian levels showed an almost constant use of higher quality flint, a tendency that persisted into the Early Azilian. There was a massive accumulation of knapping debris in the classic Azilian, indicative of constant lithic manufacture during the occupation, including a significant presence of ultra-local quartzite collected from the banks of the Güeña and Sella Rivers, although it had limited use in the manufacture of tools, primarily limited to substrate types (denticulates, notches and retouched flakes), with a smaller number of endscrapers made from the same material, and almost no bladelets or points. Flint, on the other hand, was widely used to manufacture endscrapers, bladelets and points, with a predominance of mediocre or poor quality radiolarite. Higher quality flint is present, but in much lower proportions than in previous periods.

Fernández-Tresguerres states that the retouched tools in the Early Azilian at Los Azules cave show an industry that is well defined by "small elongated double backed points, in some cases tending to be straight and sometimes showing flat retouch on the distal dorsal face, reminiscent of the shape of late Sauveterre points". Their appearance was preceded by very short, thick points. "The rest of the industry is less distinctive from the Upper/Late Magdalenian, where small, somewhat rounded endscrapers and abundant backed bladelets are observed, often linear and in some cases double backed. Burins become less frequent. Denticulates and notches are as common as in any of the levels of this site". What is most noteworthy about Los Azules, however, is the bone industry, particularly the 105 Azilian harpoons. The sequence in this cave reflects the evolution of harpoon types from the oldest classic Azilian items (level 3 h), usually with more barbs than their more modern counterparts, in which the perforation tends to be closer to the centre of the base, later shifting towards the centre of the shaft in the central layers of level 3 (g, f and e), then returning to the centre of the base. The four harpoons from Level 5 (early Azilian) are worthy of special mention. Two are complete, one of them has a round perforation at the base –lacking in the other one–, both of them infrequent features in harpoons from this period. However, the outstanding aspect is the decoration of one of the complete harpoons –an extraordinary piece with seven barbs– and also one of the fragments, an exceptional feature for this period, specially considering the particularities of the decoration. Both items share the same decoration, based on oblique lines with short strokes connected to them, a pattern also found in decorative pendants that are chronologically midway between the late Magdalenian and the Azilian. In the case of the complete item, the initial decoration was covered by another motif based on strips of two parallel lines with the space between them filled by short oblique etched lines, a motif which also extends to the barbs. This second decorative phase almost exactly matches the decoration on a similar harpoon fragment found in La Lluera cave, more than 60 km away.

In addition to the harpoons, excavations of the upper levels of the classic Azilian unearthed an *sagaie* decorated on most of its central flank with series of short oblique lines, and a spatula made from a heavily polished deer metapodial –retaining part of the articulation– with a blunt point with one side covered with finely etched lines of dots.

Azilian burial:

During the controlled excavation of a burial in 1975, it was found to contain not only human remains but also a remarkable range of grave goods. The body had been laid on its back in a shallow depression along the west wall of the cave, dug into layers 3b-d. The base seemed to have been dusted with ochre, with several pebbles delimiting the right side. A large limestone slab was placed on the knees of the deceased, and the whole grave had been covered with a pile of stones and earth.

This adult male, more than 40 years old and 1.75 m tall, had possibly suffered bone disease from an early age, which seriously hindered his ability to walk. According to Fernandez-Tresguerres, he could made a minor contribution to the group's economy, yet he reached a relatively advanced age –evidence of a strong sense of group solidarity– and was given a unique burial, perhaps due to a specific role that he may have played in this social group. Several items recognizable as grave goods were placed around or over the corpse: stone tools, two harpoons, lithic raw material –cores and hammerstones– and deer antler fragments. Two piles of large, carefully stacked *Modiolus sp.* shells and a badger skull were placed beside the left leg. An even more striking complement was a series of pebbles painted with black points, several of them delimiting the head of the grave.

This complex burial, an exceptional discovery for the Azilian in southwestern Europe, is one of the few elements that provide a glimpse of the spiritual and social world of the last Palaeolithic hunter-gatherers.

Conclusion

Los Azules is undoubtedly the most important Azilian site on the Iberian Peninsula and a key location for the definition of the Late Magdalenian/Azilian sequence in southwestern Europe. Still pending the detailed publication of its stone and bone material and information about its sedimentology, fauna and environment, it is nevertheless clear that the series of harpoons –more than the sum of all those found at the rest of the Azilian sites in Iberia– can play a major role in determining the evolution –and extinction– of this particular technology, and act as an extraordinary basis for comparisons. The possible excavation of the Magdalenian levels or the extension of work on the Azilian layers at some point in the future would undoubtedly provide a unique source of information for research into this late Pleistocene period. The richness of materials at the site and the diversity of structures linked to the use and habitation of the cave will make a valuable contribution to our understanding of the lifestyles of the hunter-gatherers at the end of the Palaeolithic in the transit to the Mesolithic.

José Adolfo Rodríguez Asensio*

Cabo Busto: A Middle Pleistocene Site

Cabo Busto is located on the edge cliff of the Western Asturian wave-cut platform and was excavated by J.A. Rodríguez Asensio between 1993 and 1997. Two levels of human occupation have been identified in the stratigraphic sequence, level II and level V. Both belong to the Acheulean period but correspond with two different chronological spans, separated by several thousand years.

The Cantabrian wave-cut platform (locally named Rasa) is a flat coastal 5 km wide platform extending from the mountain foot hills of the ancient coastline to the actual sea cliff that is situated in this area, 60 metres above sea level. This platform descends from Cape Peñas, where it is 100 metres high, into the coast of Burela, the result of the geo-morphological process of tilting. Altogether, this sector provides one of the most relevant habitability areas at the moment of the first human population arrival to the North of the Iberian Peninsula. Several rivers in the region flow into this platform. More precisely, along their fluvial terraces, different settlements from this period have been documented. Numerous characteristics provide this area with excellent habitability conditions: it is an area where movement is easy and it offers a very rich hunting area with plenty of water. Some of the most important and well-known Lower Paleolithic sites such

* Área de Prehistoria. Dpto. de Historia. Universidad de Oviedo. Campus de El Milán. 33011 Oviedo. adolfo@uniovi.es

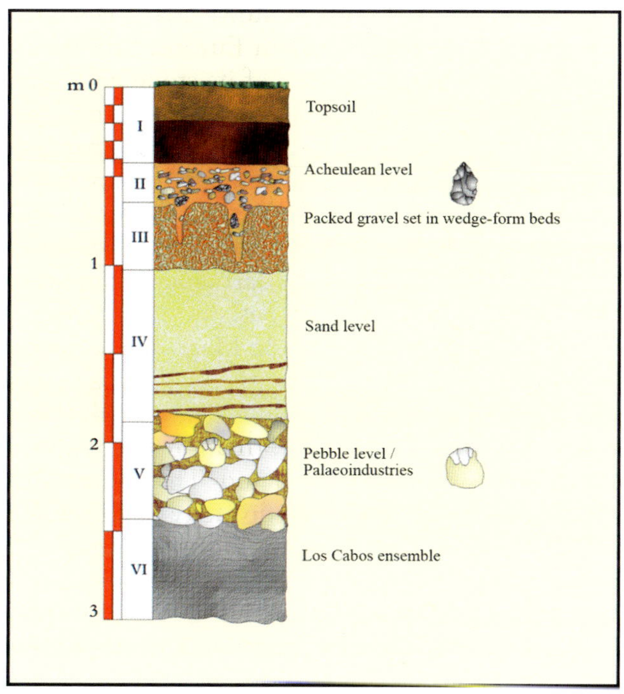

Figure 1. Stratigraphy of Cabo Busto excavation showing the two archaeological levels, II and V.

as Bañugues, Tenrero, and Louselas are located at this coastal platform.

The Esvariveror Canero river, running along the lower part of the rasa before flowing into the Cantabrian Sea, is responsible for the transportation of the geological deposits where the oldest human occupation remains have been found. Thus, it seems quite likely that this archaeological finding would not have been *in situ*, but that they have been swept along the floodplains.

The earliest level, or Busto V, has been ascribed to the Middle Pleistocene (Fig. 1). It is the oldest archaeological level documented in Asturias, and represents the first human occupation in fluvial terraces of the Cantabrian region. In the first archaeological fieldwork, the techno-typological sequence could not have been defined due to the scarce number of lithic items. However, in a recent rescue excavation carried out in 2013 due to refurbishment in a nearby pond, a large collection of lithic materials were retrieved and the old archaeological stratigraphy was also identified. The lithic assemblage, still under study, is composed primarily of massive pieces of end-products, crude bifacial tools, large retouched flakes without a clear typology, chopping tools and a minimal presence of small flakes and cores. They are primitive type materials made with elemental technology and poorly defined shape.

Based on the chronological interpretations of other similar fluvial deposits in the area dated around interglacial MIS 11, and the recent findings of lithic assemblages, a minimum relative chronology can be established for level V of Cabo Busto, corresponding with MIS 13-11, between 500 and 300 ky, during the Acheulean period.

Once these deposits settled down, ponds emerged in the landscape and, precisely at the edge of the water reservoir, remains of human occupation have been found. This evidence corresponds to level II in the archaeological sequence of Cabo Busto and techno-morphologically have been dated in the Upper Acheulean, that in Asturias region has a relative chronological span corresponding to the Riss-Würm interglacial (Fig. 1).

Level II offers different lithic assemblages made of another type of quartzite, the Ordovician quartzite, the most common variety together with the fine-grained sandstone that was used for lithic reduction in the Acheulean, both in this site and the whole settlements in Asturias. This type of raw material produces crude and primitive artefacts, in contrast to fine-grained quartzite, it is extremely tough and very difficult when knapping, but that produces very accurate tools. Typologically and technologically, the lithic collection is more elaborated and has a better shaped finish. Among the tools we can identify: a broad set of medium size subtriangular or amygdaloidal shape bifaces, also a broad and rich collection of cleavers knapped from large flakes that predetermined their morphology, very few trihedral picks, and a significant set of small size flake tools, like notched and denticulate flakes, a wide number of scrapers, Mousterian points, and, even if they are scarce, some tools obtained using llevallois techniques, like piercing tools, knives and retouched artefacts. The few core are just pebbles, although some prepared core also appear.

The paucity of any kind of pebble tools proves that it was employed in a specific *chaîne opératoire* aimed at producing bifacial artefacts and primary flake-blank. The small size of the cores and the low frequency of preparation techniques reinforce that fact.

Figure 2. *Chaîne opératoire* of Cabo Busto site.

The sourcing of raw materials would be available at the same platform where outcrops of quartzite and sandstone can be found. Also, although exceptionally, the nearby beaches can provide large pebbles and blocks for producing thick tools such as bifaces and cleavers.

The *chaîne opératoire* of Cabo Busto is simple, highly uniform, and with a low functional specialization. Its simplicity can be observed in the technical processes of production since the shape of pebbles determines the type and morphology of the tools. Concerning the high uniformity, the low technical and morphological variability indicates low diversity. Types are repeated and the unique variations are the result of the raw material characteristics more than the product of knapping intentionally. Closely related with the above mentioned uniformity comes a low functional specialization. Most of the lithic tools are polyvalent and might have been used in multiple, various, and sometimes opposed functions. These lithic assemblages can be better described as polyfunctional artifacts, although some groups such as notches and denticulates could point out certain degrees of specialization.

Therefore, the *chaîne opératoire* of Cabo Busto site is characterized by the immediacy of the strategies in the knapping process and the use of tools, and by the localism of raw material procurement and distribution strategies. Immediacy and localism can be observed in the sourcing, knapping and use of lithic artefacts. The catchment area of cobbles and pebbles can be found at the same site. Once the large blanks are transported to the campsite, flake debitage and finishing tools are used at the campsite as well. Finally, tool use would have also occurred at the campsite and we think that most of the tools were produced to obtain new tools made not of stone but of perishable materials such as wood.

In short, at the Cabo Busto platform, an archaeological sequence with two different prehistoric levels has been identified: Busto II and Busto V. The first one corresponds to the Upper Acheulean and presents similar characteristics to other known sites at the Asturian wave-cut such as Bañuges, Tenrero, and Louselas. The second level represents, so far, the only case of Middle Pleistocene human occupation at the Northern Iberian Peninsula. Also, the different raw materials employed allows discernment of both levels as unambiguously different episodes, being fine-grained quartzite used in the early occupation and Ordovician quartzite used by the Acheulean population (Rodríguez Asensio, 2001).

F. Bernaldo de Quiros *
A. Neira Campos *
J.M. Maillo Fernández **

El Castillo cave

1. Introduction

El Castillo cave is in the Puente Viesgo municipality (Cantabria), on the hill of the same name near the La Pasiega, Las Monedas and Las Chimeneas sites. This series of decorated sites makes Castillo Hill the largest known set of Palaeolithic art. The cave was discovered by H. Alcalde del Rio in 1903. Archaeological sediment covered the entire current entrance area, forcing early explorers to enter on their hands and knees (Fig 1). A H. Alcalde del Rio's first excavations unearthed the Magdalenian levels. A subsequently visit by Prince Albert I of Monaco led the recently established Institut de Paleontologie Humaine to commission H. Breuil and H. Obermaier, along with H. Alcalde del Rio, to conduct new excavations from 1910 until 1914. During this time, they discovered a long stratigraphy ranging from the Lower Palaeolithic to the Metal Ages, one of the longest known sequences in Europe. This succession of levels was largely responsible for H. Breuil's first outline of his subsequent subdivisions of the Upper Palaeolithic.

Figure 1. Plan of "El Castillo" cave.

2. Exploration of "El Castillo cave"

El Castillo cave is one of the longest known archaeological sequences, with a complete succession of Palaeolithic occupations which have been subdivided into 25 units. These include Lower and Middle Palaeolithic archaeological units (Mousterian Unit 20 to Unit 26) and all the complexes of the Upper Palaeolithic: one Transitional Aurignacian (Unit 18), Early Aurignacian (Unit 16), two Gravettian (Unit 14 and 12), one Solutrean Unit 10), one Cantabrian Lower Magdalenian (Unit 8), one Upper Magdalenian (Unit 6) and one Azilian (Unit 4). The total depth of the sequence was calculated by H. Obermaier to be 18 to 20 m (Fig. 2).

The stratigraphy included "sterile" archaeologically interlayers which isolated the series of occupations from each other. Obviously one of the problems for the initial study of the site was the system used in 1910/14. Contemporary documents show that H. Obermaier collected the material in geological strata which contained the

* Área de Prehistoria, Universidad de León, Campus de Vegazana, León. 26071 fberg@unileon.es
** Dpto. Prehistoria y Arqueología, UNED. C/ Paseo Senda del rey, 7. 28040 Madrid.
43°17'32"N, 3°57'53"W Zona 30 X 421.678 Y 4.793.734

Figure 2. Stratigraphy of "El Castillo" cave.

same type of sediment and also archaeological vestiges corresponding to a particular cultural unit (Obermaier, 1914/1925). As a result, some layers such as the Azilien and Solutrean pose no difficulties for analysis, while others evidenced a high density of occupations, which in a modern excavation would represent a process of gradual industrial transformation within certain cultural units. This is the case of Upper Magdalenian Unit 6. When H. Obermaier sketched out the stratigraphy, he clearly showed two levels of "hearths", as confirmed by Oxford AMS dating (see below).

3. New excavations

After analysing the documents and materials from the old excavation (Cabrera 1984), in 1980 we began to clear the debris and vegetation from the cave entrance. Since then, we have continued to study the stratigraphy and the site with an interdisciplinary team led by V. Cabrera and F. Bernaldo de Quirós, since 2004 by the latter. After uncovering what was left of the site, we found that the layers with the best potential for complete analysis corresponded to the sequence ranging from the first Upper Palaeolithic occupations, Obermaier's Units 16 and 18, to the base. This 5 m high series spreads out from the cave, and contains a high density of materials. Moreover, it is isolated by 40 cm of silt from the Middle Palaeolithic occupations.

Unit 16

The material culture in Unit 16 is small in number but in qualitative terms can be included without difficulty in the Archaic Aurignacian technocomplex. The lithological set is predominated by fine-grained quartzite, followed at a great distance by flint, coarse-grained quartzite or quartz. There are two sets of lithic technology systems: laminar and flakes. Laminar schemes are divided into prismatic operative schemes, and carinated scrapers and carinated burins (Cabrera Valdés *et al.*, 2002). As in other Archaic Aurignacian complexes in the region, there was a continuity in the exploitation of prismatic cores, which began with the production of blades and ended with bladelets. Both items are rectilinear with little curvature, and in the latter case, lack torsion. This feature is the same in the bladelets produced by the other above-mentioned schemes. In the case of the most common scheme, carinated scrapers, the extraction surface is broad and hence the supports are broad, straight and lack torsion. Flakes are scarce but characterized by a discoidal type of production. Typologically, Dufour bladelets (standard, with quite minor or denticulate retouch) account for 26% of the total, followed by substrate items (14%). The scrapers are Aurignacian, and one busqué type of burin stands out.

Unit 18

Stratigraphically, Unit 18 was subdivided into 18a, 18b, 18c. It lies between two sterile (17 and 19) units which are the result of two collapses of the cave cornice. Unit 19 seals Unit 20 (Middle Palaeolithic). It consists of a large fan of big blocks which form an external buttress on top of which are loam-sand clays –yellowish brown with horizontal furrows, in some cases due to runoff–marked by discontinuous layers of gravel and sand in the same clay matrix. Above this sediment are levels 18b and 18c of variable depth, depending on the zone in the cave.

Level 18c appears primarily in the longitudinal section. It consists of black sub-horizontal materials with very thin layers (<1 cm.) of charcoal but no evidence of thermal alteration or reddening. This has led us to suggest that it was formed by material cleared from hearths in other parts of the cave (Cabrera and Bernaldo de Quirós, 1984, Bernaldo de Quirós *et al.*, 2008,

2010). This interpretation is also supported by its marginal location in the cave and the high proportion of lithic microdebris in comparison with the items discovered.

Level 18b consists of a dense concentration of bones along with lithic industry, predominantly limestone, as well as quartzite and sandstone hammerstones and a smaller number of quartzite and flint flakes. The fauna largely consists of cranial elements, jawbones and remains of axial skeletons, which leads us to interpret this as a primary processing site for animal remains, with large, easy replaceable tools. Limestone is ideal raw material for this purpose.

Both levels have a brown clay matrix, characterized by a greater abundance of organic matter and less detrital calcareous elements than Unit 19. They contain medium-sized angular limestone blocks, scattered or in irregular groups, resulting from para-sedimentary rockfalls. The sterile level 18a, possibly indicative of the point prior to the rockfall, sits above these levels.

The lithic industry found in these levels is consistent with the material collected by H. Obermaier, although the difference in the occupied areas must not be overlooked. In both sub-levels, the retouching material consists of endscrapers, both simple and carinated, and few burins (primarily dihedral). Material found in the substrate such as sidescrapers and denticulates is also important. Aurignacian blades on laminar flakes (common in the Cantabria region) are also present. Raw materials include different varieties of quartzite and flint. Quantitatively, however, the predominant material is black Jurassic limestone, exogenous to the cave, found in large boulders in the surrounding valleys. This material has a high degree of alteration, particularly in excavated sector 18c. In 18b, it is almost all in the form of debris, cores and flakes amongst faunal remains. However, some of the least altered sectors of level 18c have yielded a carinated scraper and a dihedral burin, permitting the supposition that part of the abundant material made unrecognizable by subsequent alteration may have been characteristic tools.

Technologically, lithic production is predominated by discoidal operational schemes, with two well defined methods: unifacial and bifacial. Débitage began with the extraction of cortical flakes in two directions: chordal and centripetal. It is curious to note that the negatives of the thinner cores not as sharp as the thicker ones because secant exploitation is not possible in the former, and are thus produced in a sub-parallel direction to the crest separating either side of the core. This makes the final shape of the core quite similar morphologically to recurrent centripetal Levallois cores. The technique used throughout the débitage sequence is direct percussion with a hard hammerstone. A more discrete laminar operational scheme has been identified in the case of bladelets and flakelets from burin-like or unipolar pseudo-prismatic fine-grained quartzite cores. Blades were produced from limestone using prismatic and carinated burin schemes, and to a lesser extent from carinated scrapers. The technique was direct percussion with hard and also soft hammerstones.

The bone industry is scarce but significant. On level 18c we found two distal fragments of staghorn speartips, a bone fragment fishhook resembling those found on the Aurignacian levels, and an awl on a horn flake. In addition, an antler handle was discovered on 18b (Tejero *et al.*, 2005; Tejero and Bernaldo de Quirós, 2008) (Fig. 3). The discovery of this bone industry enables these levels to be linked to H. Obermaier's digs, in particular his Aurignacian D (V. Cabrera's Unit 18) where the set of ten spears and several bones with marks was found (Cabrera Valdés, 1984).

Level 18c also yielded evidence of symbolism with a distal fragment of a chisel bearing a series of short, rectilinear incisions on the left edge of the upper face, oriented transversely to the longitudinal axis of the item (Cabrera *et al.*, 2001).

Figure 3. Handle from level 18b.

We also found a mesial fragment of an ungulate metapod bearing a series of incisions on the upper face: three deep marks with an irregular contour, two of them parallel and perpendicular to the longitudinal axis of the item, while the third is in a divergent, oblique direction. More interesting is a flat bone fragment with lines painted on its upper side which form a figurative representation, interpreted as an animal head, facing the right side of the preserved fragment. SEM composition analysis detected the presence of natural graphite.

Level 18b includes several items, most notably a proximal fragment of a hyoid bone, possibly from Cervus elaphus, with lines scratched and painted in black on its upper face (Cabrera *et al.*, 2001; Tejero *et al.*, 2005; Tejero *et al.*, 2008). The theme has been interpreted as an animal foreleg. Analysis of the pigments in the painted lines indicates the presence of manganese, suggesting that it was drawn with the same manganese "pencil" used for the incision which left the marks found inside the groove. Interestingly, this is not a unique case. The use of instruments to scratch and draw at the same time has been detected in several figures at the cave in Chauvet. The same level has yielded a triangular sandstone flake with four lines etched on the flattest surface of one of the faces, while the dorsal face has a natural concavity. The incisions have a U-section and seem to have been made with the thick edge of a stone tool.

The two levels of this Unit have been attributed to a "transitional Aurignacian", an industrial complex which for us is the oldest phase of the Upper Palaeolithic, comparable to others such as Châtelperronian, Jermanovician, Bohunician, Neronian, etc., regardless of the human species which may have produced them. Many Mousterian elements are still present here, but new traits appear, possibly indicating the presence of groups of modern humans and the ensuing crisis in the Middle Palaeolithic. These complexes may therefore be considered as "transition industries" which show different local solutions to an early presence of new populations.

Unit 20

Unit 20, still under analysis, has been divided into 20 a/b, 20c, 20d and 20e. It can be provisionally characterized as Mousterian. One characteristic of its industry on almost every level is lithic production using discoidal schemes in bifacial and unifacial modes. The Levallois methods are present on some levels such as 20e, focused on the production of laminar flakelets or bladelets (Sánchez Fernández and Bernaldo de Quirós, 2008). There is also a small output of blades from Levallois cores and also from unipolar cores. Some of these cores bear evidence of alternating bifacial retouch. The lithic industry on level 20e is characterized typologically by an average index of sidescrapers, few denticulates and little Quina retouch. It can be classified as standard Mousterian. Our new excavation work has also found similar cleavers on flake to those unearthed in the old digs. These items led F. Bordes to describe the Mousterian levels of this and other Cantabrian assemblages as vasconian, although the entity of the facies was refuted for the Spanish sites.

Unit 21

Although the study of this Unit is still in a preliminary state, it has yielded one item which can be interpreted from a symbolic perspective: a 5.7 cm long quartzite pebble decorated with a line of four pitted points on its outer face and a fifth one above them in the centre of the line (Cabrera *et al.*, 2004, Bernaldo de Quirós, 2006) (Fig. 4). The nature of the pittings precludes any functional interpretation.

Figure 4. Decorated pebble from Level 21.

4. Chronology

One of the fundamental missions in our review of the cave was to define a time frame for each of the cultural assemblages in the stratigraphy. We now have datings for almost all the units in the cave, mainly from bones sampled from the same cut during the 2002 clearing process, or the material at the American Museum of Natural History, where several boxes of sediment samples (including archaeological material) were archived in the 1920's. Four us, this collection is a time capsule, since the attributions of the archaeological units were defined by Obermaier himself. In other cases, especially in Units 18 and 20, samples were taken during our excavations.

For the Upper Magdalenian, present in Unit 6, datings by I. Barandarian for art objects are 10,310 ± 120 BP for the upper sub-level and 12,390 ± 220 BP for the lower sub-level (Barandiaran, 1988). However, a rhinoceros remain from this Unit has been dated at 31,800 ± 600, showing that fossil collection is older than it might seem (Bernaldo de Quirós *et al.*, 2006). For Unit 8, attributed to the Cantabrian Lower Magdalenian with its characteristic scapula etched with deer heads and strong connections to rock art, there are two datings, both unpublished. One is a bone fragment dated at 15,540 ± 70 BP (Beta 242618) found in the stratigraphy during the 2002 clearing process, while the other is from a selected scapula fragment held at the IPH, which yielded 15,160 ± 70 BP (Beta 242620). Both dates are close to those obtained at other sites from scapulae etched with deer heads.

To learn more about the Unit 10 dates, we sent a sample from the American Museum of Natural History collection to BETA Analytic, which returned a date of 19,260 ± 90 (Beta 242619). The same process was repeated with the Gravettian units. The dates for Unit 12 ranged from 24,070 BP to 25,920 BP and for Unit 14, 29,600 BP and 29,740 BP (Bernaldo de Quirós *et al.*, 2012).

Due to complexity of Units 18 and 20 and the implications for their organization, a series of extremely important datings for the reinterpretation of the Middle-Upper Palaeolithic Transition were done. Most were in AMS C^{14} and ESR at three laboratories: Tucson, Oxford and Gif-sur-Yvette (Cabrera Valdés and Bischoff 1989, Cabrera Valdés *et al.*, 1996). The specimens were taken from different zones of the site and different excavation seasons, all independent from each other. Material from the National Archaeological Museum in Madrid and the AMNH was also dated. Despite the relatively large number of samples, the diversity of laboratories and the methods used, all results are quite consistent. We currently have over 20 datings between 40,000 and 45,000 BP for Unit 18.

We also have C^{14} datings for Unit 20, most ESR. All are staggered between 41,000 and 49,000 BP (Liberda *et al.*, 2010). For Unit 22 there is one ESR dating at 59,100 BP, and for Unit 23, a stagmitic crust which seals the base sections (Units 24, 25, and 26), there are two: 89,000 and 92,200 BP (Rink *et al.*, 1995, 1997).

5. Resource management

The management of the resources used by the populations who occupied El Castillo cave is another of the interests that have driven our work. The possibilities afforded by a site of this nature cannot be ignored. One of the research lines at the site has been the changes in resource and land use. We first did an analysis of the fauna seasonality, since the information about the season when the animals were hunted down and their age is taken from the growth marks on their teeth. For the El Castillo site, we selected 159 deer teeth (the most numerous species) from levels 18b, 18c (Transitional Aurignacian), 20a, 20b and 20c (Mousterian with cleavers). The most relevant results are that during the Mousterian, animals were captured from late autumn until spring (Pike Tay *et al.*, 1999). During the Transitional Aurignacian, they were hunted from winter and throughout spring. All ages are present in both cases, with more young adults, suggesting similar fauna resource management solutions in both cases, centred on the winter, which is consistent with an aggregation model in which the individuals in the group shared their resources at this time of year.

Several studies of the fauna are currently under way to check these results and expand our knowledge about the lifestyles of the human groups at this exciting time.

6. Conclusions

The El Castillo cave site is one of the most important records of the Middle and Upper Palaeolithic on the Iberian Peninsula and indeed in Europe. The presence of a stratigraphy representing all stages of human presence dating back more than 300,000 years enables a wide range of working hypotheses to be tested, both historically and in other disciplines (palaeontology, climatology, etc.). Our studies have focused on the transition period from the Middle to the Upper Palaeolithic. They have contributed several aspects that challenge –and indeed will continue to challenge– current views. This confirms the importance of the site and the opportunities it presents.

Mario Menéndez*, Gerd-Christian Weniger **-***, David Álvarez-Alonso1, María de Andrés-Herrero ***,Eduardo García *, Jesús F. Jordá *, Martin Kehl ****, Julio Rojo *, José M.Quesada *, Isabell Schmidh **

La Cueva de la Güelga. Cangas de Onís. Asturias

Introduction

La Cueva de la Güelga, whose name in the local language refers to wet and shady sites, opens to the heart of a limestone mountain valley, forming a *cul-de-sac*. A stream flows from the current cave aperture and has configurated a *karst* system with corresponding terrace drain caverns that were successively occupied during the Middle and Upper Paleolithic. This group of rock shelters and caves has been divided into different sectors for investigation, which has developed from 1989 to the present. *A-B* and C areas are located on the lower terrace, occupied during the Magdalenian and Solutrean. At the top is *D sector*, with occupations attributed to Châtelperronian, Aurignacian and Mousterian. This valley, closed in itself, has provided numerous lithic remains in surfaces, mostly attributable to Mode 3, surely exponents of intense and prolonged occupations. It is located 200 m above sea level, and along with Buxu and Azules caves, is a core site in the middle reaches of the Sella River, territorially linked with other coast sites, 15 km away, around the Ribadesella Bay (Menéndez, 2003).

Areas A, B and C (Upper Paleolithic): Located around the current cave entrance, they show remains of an intense Solutrean occupation swept by the river into the karst. The only evidence from the upper Solutrean, industry also present in neighboring Buxu Cave, are gap vestiges attached to the wall of the shelter and *in situ* layer (*Area* C), with notch points and concave bases. Also, A and C were excavated and assigned to Cantabrian Lower Magdalenian or Magdalenian III occupation, from the so-called *Juyofacies*. The lithic and especially the bone industry, display the existence of a group of hunters specialized in deer (55%), chamois (24%) and goats (20%), probably during the middle months of the year (spring / summer), which left at layer 3 an excellent collection of art mobilier. The hyoid hanging of deer must be highlighted, decorated assegai

* Departamento de Prehistoria y Arqueología, Universidad Nacional de Educación a Distancia. Ciudad Universitaria, Paseo Senda del Rey 7, E-28040 Madrid, Spain; mmenendez@geo.uned.es; dalvarez@gijon.uned.es; egarciasmail@gmail.com; jjorda@geo.uned.es; juliorojo@juliorojo.jazztel.es; jmquesada@geo.uned.es;

** Neanderthal Museum. Talstr. 300, 40822 Mettmann, Germany; schmidt@neanderthal.de; weniger@neanderthal.de

*** University of Cologne, Institute of Prehistoric Archaeology. Albertus-Magnus-Platz, 50923 Cologne, Germany mdeandres@neanderthal.de,

**** University of Cologne, Institute of Geography. Albertus-Magnus-Platz, 50923 Cologne, Germany; kehlm@uni-koeln.de

and bones emphasizing an adult deer tibia fragment, three heads of the same animal synchronously recorded, all done with fresh bone, but with very different styles and conventions. This occupation of the late Magdalenian is well dated, around to 14 key BP (Fig.1).

Figure 1. Engraved Magdalenian tibia.

Area D (Transition MP / UP): In the middle terrace, around11 m above the current stream bed, appears a cave entrance excavated since 2000, which was filled in by debris from a collapsed cornice that fell and formed a slope. Overall, nine archaeological layers were excavated inside the shelter, which we have called *D interior*. The result was a Châtelperronian – Aurignacian – Mousterian sequence, separated by periods of collapse and abandonment of the cavern (Quesada and Menéndez 2009). As stratigraphic variations in certain areas were observed and the Aurignacian interlayer was the utmost interest to the transition paradigm MP / UP, in 2005 a new excavation zone was determined to be opened on the outdoor terrace under the large blocks of the old collapsed shelter. This area, which has been called D exterior, provided intense Mousterian occupation. In 2012, in collaboration with the Neanderthal Museum in Mettmann and the University of Cologne (Germany), led by G-Ch.Weniger, micromorphological analysis of D zone was done on interior and exterior levels, to contrast them with the sedimentological results (Jordá *et al.*, 2013; Menéndez *et al.*, 2014). We will summarize the current geoarchaeological results and hypotheses in future work.

The geoarcheological *D sector* sequence from La Güelga comprises a series of levels generated by both anthropogenic and natural processes. These natural processes detected by the sedimentological analysis, highlight the gravitational collapse of large blocks, gelifraction and diffuse gullies of very low energy (Jordá Pardo *et al.*, 2013). The micromorphologic analysis of D interior area identifies features that indicate the nature *in situ* of both the Mousterian (L9) and Aurignacian (L5-L6) levels, whereas in the Châtelperronian levels (L1 and L2) the traits indicated were emplaced by processes of creep after a roof block fall and aren't significantly compacted by trampling. Chronological invertion seems to confirm this hypothesis.

D Interior: The sequence excavated so far consists of nine archaeological layers deposited in slope (Fig. 2), into the cave, under a strong surface layer (S1 and S2) (Quesada and Menéndez, 2009; Jordá *et al.*, 2013).

Châtelperronian (L1 and L2): Layers 1 and 2 form a sedimentological unit in slope into the cave interior. It was only useful for excavation 3.7 m^2. A flint laminar industry was found, having noted the presence of two Châtelperron points, and another assemblage of quartzite flakes, such as scrapers and denticulates. The presence of lithic manufactured the absence of bone artifacts and ^{14}C studies (Table 1) encouraged us to define this set as Châtelperronian, considering the possible underlying Aurignacian as an interstrafication. Recent dating of the lower level (L5) and sedimentological and microstratigraphic analysis carried out by the University of Cologne does not ensure that this level is *in situ*.

Under level 2 a fringe of stone blocks detached from the shelter and a layer of clay and silt appear from the outside. Levels 3 and 4 are almost sterile.

Aurignacian (L5 and L6): Under a line of stone blocks (L5) appears a clay layer (L6); shown *in situ* by the sedimentological and microstratigraphic analyses. This unit has provided a few anthropic remains, although very typical. The lithic assemblage, mostly laminar, is made on flint and quartzite. There are nosed scrapers, one Aurignacian blade and retouched flakes. Regarding bone industry, several flattened oval section awls were found, a moothed mesial fragment of assegai and one deer phalanx whistle. The chronology (pend-

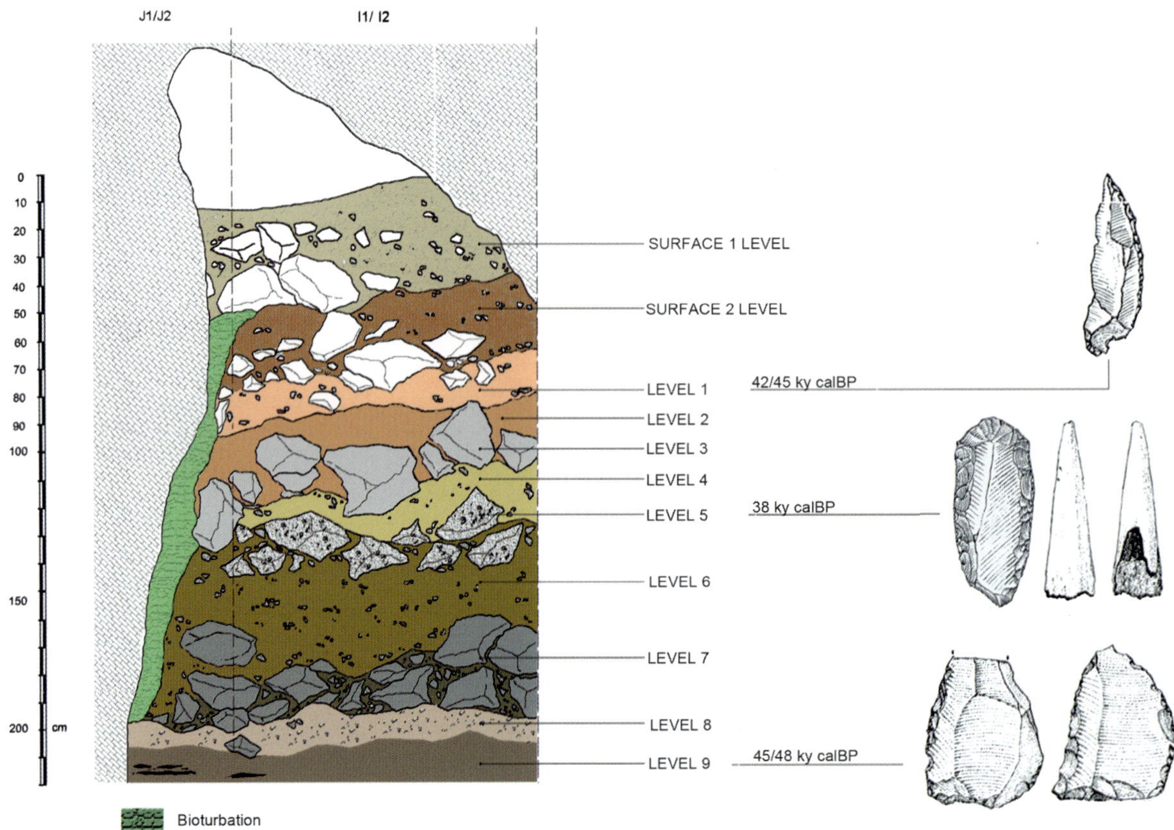

Figure 2. Overall stratigraphy of la Cueva de la Güelga.

ing new dates) places it into 38ky calBP. Despite the reduced sample, the homogeneity and conventional characters of the assemblage, the absence of contradictory elements, preliminary dating and stratigraphic position indicate an undoubted Aurignacian presence. Below this layer, a long period of cave abandonment (L7 and L8) is documented.

Mousterian: It is represented in D interior by level 9, showing intense human presence evident in combustion remains, wealth lithic industry (Mode 3), with Levallois pieces and animals bones with fleshing traces; as well as the possibility of setting spatial occupation patterns. This inside occupation matches on open air the terrace level with the 4B layer from ***D exterior.*** Both have provided a typically Mousterian lithic accumulation, consisting of local quartzite flakes retouched, denticulate and scrapers, as well as Levallois points. All phases of the operational chain are present, mostly discoid and also Levallois. Scarce flints remain, Piloña type show relationships with other sites, such as Sidrón cave in the same river basin. Premolar (15) and several human dental fragments, with Neanderthal morphology, were found. The ^{14}C dating with pretreatment by ultra filtration (OxA) places this occupation in the period 55/44 ky in OIS 3c, between H6 and H4 events (Menéndez *et al.*, 2009; Quesada and Menéndez, 2009; Jordá *et al.*, 2013). The fauna recovered, around 70,000 remains, show deer (66%) and chamois (31%) predominance, along with uncommon species and diverse ecosystems, such as mammoth (*Mammuthus primigenius*), panther *(P. pardus)*, megaloceros, rhino, wolf, boar, etc. suggesting a recurrent and prolonged use of the site by the Neanderthal populations of the River Sella basin.

Conclusions

1. The assignment Châtelperronian sediments (L1 and L2) are displaced. Their sedimento-

Zone	Level	Culture	Material	Procedure	Code	BP Date	Deviation	95% probability calibrate Date	
								CalPal 2007 Hulu	INTCAL 13
Indoor D	2	¿Châtelperronian?	Bone with marks	AMS + untrafiltration	COL2014	37429	302	42780 –41460 calBP	42320 –41400 calBP
Indoor D	2	¿Châtelperronian?	Bone with marks	AMS + untrafiltration	OxA-27958	40300	1200	45910 –42070 calBP	45890 –42090 calBP
Indoor D	5	Aurignacian	Bone with marks	AMS + untrafiltration	Beta-377233	33610	220	41730 -35570 calBP	38720 -37200 calBP
Indoor D	9	Mousterian	Bone with marks	AMS + untrafiltration	OxA-19244	43700	800	49020 –44540 calBP	48740 –45300 calBP
Indoor D	9	Mousterian	Bone with marks	AMS + untrafiltration	OxA-19245	44300	1200	50660 –44380 calBP	Out range calibration
Outdoor D	4b	Mousterian	Bone with marks	AMS + untrafiltration	OxA-20122	47400	2700	Out range calibration	Out range calibration
Outdoor D	4b	Mousterian	Bone with marks	AMS + untrafiltration	OxA-20123	>43200			
Outdoor D	4b	Mousterian	Bone with marks	AMS + untrafiltration	OxA-20124	48500	3500	Out range calibration	Out range calibration
Outdoor D	4b	Mousterian	Bone with marks	AMS + untrafiltration	OxA-20125	>43600			

Table 1. Datations of Cueva de la Güelga.

logical quality is not enough to defend such a significant hypothesis as interlayer Aurignacian. Future work should pursue an explanation for their stratigraphic position and timing (42/45 ky calBP).

2. There is an Aurignacian presence, with little information, but with a timeline around 38 ky calBP, before an intense Mousterian occupation (45/48 ky calBP).
3. There is a long period of abandonment between Aurignacian and Mousterian occupations (7/10 ky).
4. The lower Magdalenian occupation provided an excellent collection of portable art.

Mª Soledad Corchón Rodríguez*

La Cueva de las Caldas (Priorio, Northern Spain)

1. La Cueva de las Caldas in the context of the Nalón valley

The Oviedo basin, where La Cueva de las Caldas is located, forms part of the central-northern part of the Cantabrian region of Asturias and the western end of the central depression of Asturias. It is a region of Mesozoic and tertiary materials, extending towards the coast, characterized by a landscape of deep karst modelling. This territory forms the known limit of Cantabrian Upper Paleolithic deposits, as Paleozoic rocks spread westwards to the western Asturias-Leon area and no outdoor settlements are known. In terms of geomorphology, the surroundings of Las Caldas correspond to a depression whose evolution is linked to the encasement of the river Nalón. The middle section of this valley, the network of tributaries and streams that flow into the Nalón, have formed a landscape of small sheltered valleys, running laterally to the main valley, in one of which the cave is located, on the right bank of the river. It consists of a karstic complex developed in mountain limestone (Visean-Namurian, Lower Carboniferous), composed of two connected cavities –Caldas I and Caldas II–, structured in a complex network of galleries and channels over 1km long. The main entrance (Caldas I) faces SW-W, and its geographic coordinates are 5° 54´ 723´´ W, 43° 20´ 123´´ N, 160 metres above sea level. Towards the exit of Las Caldas valley, 800 m from the site, there are medicinal mineral hot springs that give the cave its name; not far from it, between 5 and 20 km away, another eighteen springs with therapeutic properties are known. At the end of the Pleistocene these circumstances, in addition to the variety of ecosystems created by the significant contrasts in altitude, generated a shelter environment with a wide range of ecosystems in the surroundings of Las Caldas: high mountains (Sierra del Aramo, 8 km ways, with peaks of 1,700 m.), low-lying hills (Peña Avis: 410 m) and sheltered valleys. This data helps to explain the large concentration of Palaeolithic sites in the middle Nalón valley: more than 20 caves and rock shelters occupied between the Aurignacian and Azilian, 13 of them with parietal art.

In the main cavity (Caldas I) the cave preserves one of the most significant stratigraphic records of the Solutrean and Magdalenianin south east Europe. The site has been open excavated to 24m^2, representing all of the occupied topographic units: *Sala I, Sala II, Pasillo I* and *Corte exterior.* The stratigraphic sequence covers a time range of *c.*10,000, from the start of the regional Solutrean (24185 ± 370 calBP, Middle Solutrean) to the Late Magdalenian (14936 ± 342 calBP). The thickest Solutrean stratigraphic units correspond to Sala I, with 17 levels that cover the entire sequence of the Cantabrian Solutrean (level 3 to base 19). Above this series are remains of eroded Magdalenian levels, one of them Late Magdalenian (level 2A). Sala II, however, only preserves one Late Solutrean level (level XIV) resting on the limestone floor, as the oldest levels were evacuated towards sala II when the hypogeum river. A thick filler of 16 Magdalenian levels was deposited on this level, with all of the stadials represented: upper, early and recent middle, upper and late Magdalenian. This deposit covers from the Lascaux interstadial to the Alleröd, and to date the levels there are 26 dating results^{14}C (Table 1).

2. The Solutrean stratigraphy of Caldas I and the outdoor engravings

The Solutrean record of Las Caldas is a reference in the Cantabrian region but its conditions of preservation are not the same in the 4 areas excavated. The outer hall, altered by the collapse of the overhang that covered the entrance, only preserves one Upper Solutrean level (level III); the same applies to Sala II, with just one level (level XIV). In the Pasillo and Sala I, although the levels do not always coincide, the record is very extensive: levels 3-18 and 3 – base 19, respectively.

* Chair in Prehistory. University of Salamanca, Department of Prehistory, c/Cervantes s/n, 37002 Salamanca, Spain. scorchon@usal.es

Lab. Ref..	^{14}C BP	CalBP_CalPal 2007-HULU (68% range calBP)	Level / Sector	Classification
Ua-15318	20250 ± 235 (AMS)	24185 ± 370 (23814 – 24555)	15 (Sala I)	Middle Solutreen
Ly-2428	19510 ± 330	23340 ± 468 (22872 – 23808)	16 (Topera)	Middle Solutreen
Ly-2426	19480 ± 260	23296 ± 413 (22882 – 23709)	12b (Pasillo)	Middle Solutreen
Ly-2425	19030 ± 320	22857 ± 404 (22452 – 23261)	12t (Pasillo)	Middle Solutreen
Ly-2429	19000 ± 280	22843 ± 379 (22464 – 23222)	18 (Topera)	Middle Solutreen
Ly-2424	19390 ± 260	23199 ± 398 (22801 – 23597)	9 (Pasillo)	Upper Solutreen
Ly-2423	18310 ± 260	21960 ± 388 (21571 – 22348)	7 (Pasillo)	Upper Solutreen
Ua-15316	18305 ± 295 (AMS)	21949 ± 412 (21537 – 22361)	11 (Sala I)	Upper Solutreen
Ua-15315	17945 ± 370 (AMS)	21541 ± 603 (20938 – 22144)	9 (Sala I)	Upper Solutreen
Ua-4302	17380 ± 215 (AMS)	20837 ± 358 (20478 – 21195)	XIVc (Sala II)	End of the Solutreen
Ly-2422	17050 ± 290	20405 ± 495 (19910 – 20900)	4 (Pasillo)	End of the Solutreen
Ly-2421	18250 ± 300	21904 ± 424 (21480 – 22328)	3 (Pasillo)	End of the Solutreen
Ua-4301	15165 ± 160 (AMS)	18324 ± 273 (18051 – 18597)	XIII (Sala II)	Lower Magdalenian
Ua-4300	14835 ± 130 (AMS)	18156 ± 282 (17874 – 18438)	XII inf (Sala II)	Lower Magdalenian
Ua-2735	14495 ± 140 (AMS)	17635 ± 282 (17353 – 17917)	XII (Sala II)	Lower Magdalenian
Ua-2734	13755 ± 120 (AMS)	16881 ± 230 (16651 – 17111)	XI (Sala II)	Lower Magdalenian
Ua-10188	13370 ± 110 (AMS)	16297 ± 436 (15860 – 16733)	IX (Sala II)	Middle Magdalenian
Ua-10189	13640 ± 150 (AMS)	16604 ± 393 (16211 – 16997)	VIII (Sala II)	Middle Magdalenian
Ly-2936	13310 ± 200	16220 ± 475 (15745 – 16695)	VIII (Sala II)	Middle Magdalenian
Ly-3318	12869 ± 160	15571 ± 512 (15059 – 16083)	VII (Sala II)	Middle Magdalenian
Ua-10190	13650 ± 140 (AMS)	16641 ± 363 (16277 – 17004)	VIc (Sala II)	Middle Magdalenian
Ly-2427	13400 ± 150	16314 ± 454 (15860 – 16768)	IV/III (Sala II)	Middle Magdalenian
Ua-10191	13185 ± 155 (AMS)	16114 ± 441 (15672 – 16555)	IIIb-IIIc (Sala II)	Middle Mag / Upper Mag
Ua-10192	12960 ± 190 (AMS)	15775 ± 529 (15245 – 16304)	II (Sala II)	Upper Magdalenian
Ua-10193	12595 ± 125 (AMSA)	14936 ± 342 (14594 – 15278)	I (Sala II)	Upper Magdalenian
Ua-10194	12590 ± 120 (AMS)	14931 ± 337 (14593 – 15268)	-II (Sala II)	Upper Magdalenian

Table 1. Cueva de Las Caldas radiocarbon dates (Weninger, B., Jöris O., Danzeglocke, U. 2007: *Calpal – Cologne University Radiocarbon Calibration Package*).

Another relevant aspect is the existence of linear and ideomorph engravings on the right wall, next to the entrance and lit by the daylight. The Solutrean engravings are deep linear grooves in a regular series. Their stratigraphic dating in the Middle Solutrean is of additional interest, as they are split by a fracture line and there are large blocks from the collapse of the right wall, which occurred during the deposit of level 15, according to the excavation carried out in Pasillo I. In the middle of the Pasillo area, the Solutrean engravings are replaced by Magdalenian engravings; the most recent, fusiform, overlapping others of fine multiple lines with claviformideomorphs and a female styling. A large quartzite plaquette engraved with a similar fusiform, from the base of the Middle Magdalenian, is a solid chronological reference for the former, overlapping the rest (Corchón *et al.*, 2009a).

2.1. Characterisation of the Solutrean levels

The excavations reveal that, based on current data, they are the oldest base levels on the Cantabrian coast. They were deposited under very wet and cold conditions in the Late Glacial Maximum (LGM: levels base 19, 19, 18). As the Middle Solutrean progressed, the environment changed to mild and very wet (GI 2), with intermittent episodes of flooding in which the cave was abandoned. These are the conditions recorded for levels 17 to 13 (Sala I) and 17 to 11 (pasillo I). This initial Cantabrian Solutrean (middle of the European sequence) is dated at 24185 ± 370 calBP (AMS, level 15, camber I), 23340 ± 468, 23296 ± 413 and 22857 ± 404 calBP (ordinary C14: levels 16, base 12 and ceiling 12, corridor).

At the beginning of the Upper Solutrean the previous very wet conditions continued (Sala I, levels 12-11); but as it progressed the climate turned very cold and wet (GS-2c), the levels near the entrance present cryoturbation (levels 9-8), and cold steppe fauna appears throughout the section (levels 9-4: mammoth and reindeer). It is dated at 23199 ± 398 and 21904 ± 424 calBP (levels 9 and 7). The Late Solutrean returns dates of 20837 ± 358 calBP for Sala II (AMS, n. XIVc), a similar date to those obtained for the Pasillo (levels 4-3, more altered due to their proximity to the entrance). During this disposition, the climate is extremely wet and cold with flooding processes and partial erosion of the deposits.

The fauna in the Solutrean levels is very abundant (84,465 remains), 14,579 of which can be identified; according to the authors of the study (Altuna and Mariezkurrena), it is the richest record of Solutrean remain in the Iberian Peninsula. There are a large number of anthropic alterations (fracture marks related to obtaining bone marrow and stripping the flesh or carving) in all levels, demonstrating that the vast majority of the ungulates were contributed by humans.

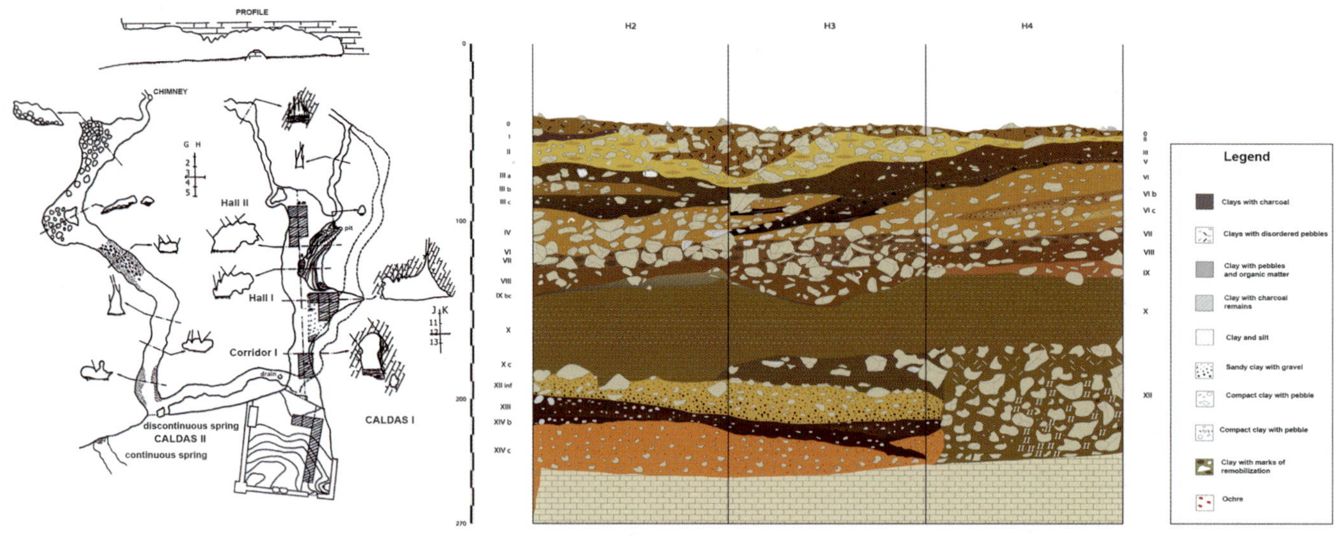

Figure 1. Karstic complex (Caldas I and II). Stratigraphy of Sala II.

The dominant species among the macro-mammals in the 17 Solutrean levels is deer (> 65%). This is followed by horse, which at the start of the Middle Solutrean exceeds 20% (level base 19), although its presence is minimum (3-4.6%) in the Upper and late Solutrean (levels 8 and 4-5). Then the mountain goat exceeds and equals the horse in some levels in the centre of the sequence; and the chamois, absent in the Middle Solutrean, increases its presence towards the end (levels 4-5: 18.9%). There are some roe remains in the Upper Solutrean. Regarding bovine species, they are represented throughout the sequence but the low number and fragmented remains do not allow us to determine whether they are aurochs or bison. Reindeer are found at the beginning of the Upper Solutrean (levels 12, 11, 10), and in a level from the middle (level 15); but do not exceed 0,2% of the remains identified. This scarcity is coherent with the general data for the Cantabrian region, where its rarity is perceived in the sites located to the west (Asturias), while the frequency is higher in the territory more to the east (Guipuzcoa). Las Caldas confirms this data, given the richness of its fauna material and the fact that the majority of the sequence corresponds to a particularly cold period (UMG).

Due to its relative rarity, 20 remains of mammoth tooth are interesting, which coincide with the most coldest phase of the Upper and Late Solutrean (levels 9, 8, 7 and 3); and fragments of the tusk of this species were used as the raw material for making a rod (level Middle Solutrean18), and portable art (engraved tusk, levels base 10-11; two pendants, levels 9 and 8, Upper Solutrean). The first tooth remains were identified by E. Aguirre and F. Poplin, and later by J. Altuna. In addition to the ungulates already mentioned, the record is completed by remains of carnivores in the Middle and Upper Solutrean (cave bear, fox, badger, marten, leopard and lynx). Even scarcer are marmot, rabbit (a distal end of humorous from this animal shows incisions from removing the flesh) and hare.

2.2. Solutrean level raw materials, technology and industries

The subsistence strategies of the Solutrean and Magdalenian groups in Las Caldas are similar in terms of extensive logistics mobility to procure exotic raw materials and exchange cultural items. The Solutrean and Magdalenian portable art used unusual local minerals, such as amber and lignite, to make necklace beads. The study of the lithic raw materials allows the traditional routes travelled and the extensive territories visited by the Palaeolithic groups in the Nalón in order to gather high quality siliceous rocks to be identified. A. Tarriño has identified fifteen local siliceous rocks in Las Caldas, including flint, lacustrine flint (Cenozoic), Jurassic flint (Mesozoic), carboniferous flint from mountain limestone (Paleozoic), Barrios quartzite and Paleozoic rock crystal. All of these are found in the vicinity of the cave, between 2 and 15km away. In addition to these, the Solutrean and Magdalenian levels show high quality allochthonous flint that constitute real lithological markers, demonstrating that these materials were transported from distant source areas (Corchón, Martínez and Tarriño, 2009). These are Flysch flint, brought to the cave from Vizcaya (Barrica) and the French Pyrenees (Bidache), 150 and 300 km away; Urbasa flint (Navarre), from 380km away and Treviño flint (Álava), 350km

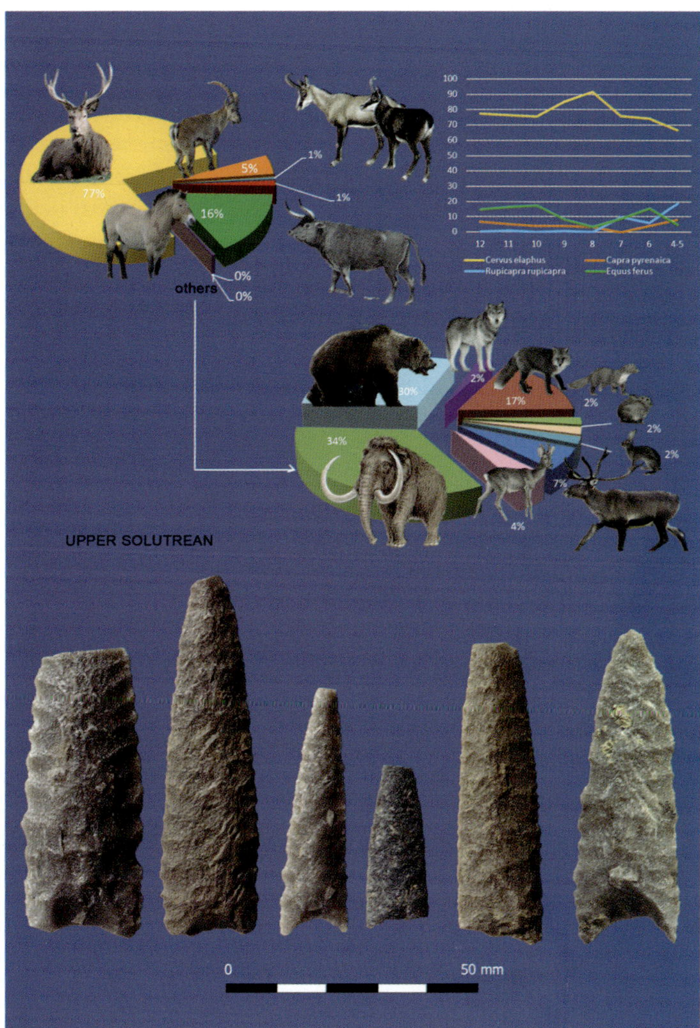

Figure 2. Upper Solutrean. Layout of the fauna and laurel-leaf blades of various sizes (Sala I).

from the cave. Finally, Chaloss flint (SW France) has been identified, the nearest source area of which is 550km away, representing the most distant Palaeolithic siliceous rock known to date. Later, new allochthonous and local varieties have been identified, one of them very suitable for laminar knapping: Piloña flint transported to Las Caldas from the eastern basin of Oviedo, 40-50 km away (Tarriño *et al.*, 2013).

The knapping technology and techniques applied to the Solutrean leaf-shaped blades are known thanks to the discovery of numerous tools in various stages of reduction, which have allowed two operational sequences to be reconstructed, one for knapping laurel-leaf blades and the other for notched points (Corchón *et al.*, 2013a). In the Middle Solutrean (levels base 19 –13, Sala I), from the oldest levels the thin bifacial laurel-leaf blades coexist, often knapped using pressure flaking and frequently in high quality foreign flint (Treviño, Urbasa, Flysch), with thick bifacial leaf-shaped blades with a rounded base and irregular percussion flaking, in many cases discarded in the preliminary knapping phases. A unique case is the use of tools that are barely operative due to their fragility: three leaf-shaped blades and a racloir delicately knapped in rock crystal (level13 and 14), as well as a bifacial laurel-leaf blade in flint associated to a necklace consisting of 7 deer canines at the base of the sequence (level base 19). However, leaf-shaped blades are only abundant in two levels (14 and 18: 18%), being scarce in the rest (3-5.5%). Other characteristic types are *points a face plane* (unifacial flat retouch points), which are often pieces in progress, and leaf-shaped racloirs for which foreign flint was also reserved. There is an abundance of retouched blades and scrapers (3%-5%), some on Solutrean blades, always prevalent over few and mediocre burins.

To summarise, even though the record is smaller than in other levels (440 tools), due to the interruptions and washing caused by flooding, in the Middle Solutrean domination of the technique is noticeable, the laminar trend of tools and the widespread use of Solutrean pressure retouch, which characterises the Upper Solutrean levels, are not fully developed. This is reflected in the many shapeless cores knapped in local quartzite and flint and the high percentages of substrate also show lower technical expertise (>25% recess, denticulate and chipped tools and scrapers) and the diverse tools (40% flake and other atypical retouched tools), in all levels.

In the Upper Solutrean (level12-7, chamberI) the record is very rich: 13,125 lithic materials recovered, 1,049 of which are tools (8%) and 96 cores (0.73%). The structure of the common tools does not show any major changes compared to the previous stadial and there are even more scrapers than burins; in all levels, the percentages are similar. Some thick leaf-shaped blades in quartzite, discarded in the knapping process have been reused as burins. Substrate still has a significant weight (14.6 – 19%), as do retouched blades (4.62 – 9.09%). The high rate of laminar flake is the most characteristic feature, consistent with the abundance of leaf-shaped blades knapped from large flakes and laminar supports. The laurel-leaf, willow-leaf, notched points and other leaf shapes in progress range between 43% and 38%, revealing the boom in flat retouch techniques across the section. Laurel-leaf blades, unifacial and bifacial, have very contrasting dimensions, with varied techniques for attaching handles-convex, straight, concave, asymmetrical base, revealing a high level of specialisation and their adaptation to different types of prey.

As regards the late Solutrean, even though there is a large sample (5,036 remains), it is considered less representative due to the erosion and flooding that occurred during and after the levels were deposited. The tools (608) reach a high percentage (12.07%), but this increase is due to the high rate of substrate. The Scrapers Index/ Burins Index ratio is inverted in favour of the latter; thick scrapers on flake appear and retouched blades are abundant, particularly towards the end (level 3). The number of leaf-shaped blades decreases to 6% (levels 3-6), in accordance with the process of gradually abandoning knapping of leaf-shaped blades in the late Solutrean in contrast with the Upper Solutrean (39% and 43%, levels 10 and 8, respectively). To sum up, the late Solutrean (levels XIV and 6-3) shows worsening of the lithic types, with few laurel-leaf blades, flakes with fine side retouches and combined tools (scraper-truncated blade, burin-truncated blade). A few racloirs, perforators, denticulate tools and some atypical raclettes complete the tools.

Bone types, which are scarce and uncharacteristic of the Middle Solutrean (assegais, rods and engraved smoothers) and of the Late Solutrean (some assegais, awls), demonstrate the creativity in the Upper Solutrean. The assegais show different formats for attaching the handle –bevelled, bi-point, with central flattening–, accompanied by rods and needles. With these, two unique pieces in the Cantabrian Solutrean have also been recovered: a large spear thrower from antler (183.3 x 17.23 x 8.78 mm), unique (level 11c), with a distal hook made by cutting and polishing and with the shaft not entirely polished and with traces of scraping and grooving and a notched point made of bone from the tibia of a deer, preserved complete (level 12 ceiling: Corchón *et al.*, 2013b). There are also many pendants, made from various materials: ivory slabs (Upper Solutrean), necklace beads in bone, antler, amber, ivory and lignite (Middle and Upper Solutrean), with perforated bones and teeth and incisors in all levels.

3. The Magdalenian sequence in Las Caldas

3.1. The Lower Magdalenian

The period between 18324 ± 273 and 16881 ± 230 calBP is occupied by the Lower Magdalenian, an extremely complex episode in the Cantabrian. In La Cueva de las Caldas the sedimentology study shows that it corresponds to the transition between the Lascaux (level XIII) to very cold and wet conditions (levels lower XII, XII, XI), with erosive and solifluction processes and in one case, with the sliding of the sediment section (level lower XII) (Fig. 1). According to Altuna and Mariezkurrena, the ungulate fauna is dominated by *Cervus elaphus* (>40%) in all levels, reaching 61 and 80% (lower XII and XIII). This is followed closely by *Equus ferus*, with a large number of remains in all levels. If we assess the meat supplied by the horse, its importance grows in the Lower Magdalenian, reaching 70% in some levels (level XII, XI). However, goat, roe and chamois have a low presence, as do bovine (aurochs-bison). These only have a significant presence in levels XIII and lower XII (4.3 and 4.6% of remains). Obviously these values increase if we look at the meat supplied, as it is a large animal that supplies an abundance of meat. As data of particular interest, level lower XII contained a *Coelodonta antiquitatis* remain. The *Rangifer tarandus*is present in levels XII and lower XII (2 and 1 remains, respectively, and one antler from level XII), in accordance with the aforementioned harshness of the environment. Roe appears in both levels (later cf.). Among the non-ungulates, wolf, fox and marmot are just as rare.

The four levels show industries with similar characteristics (*facies of the west* of Asturias), with more laminar tools and better fracturing than those in the centre of the region (eastern Cantabria-Asturias: *facies Juyo*). Of particular interest are the selection of high quality allochthonous flint for laminar knapping, the large number of burins on blades, retouched blades, back edge bladelets and scalene triangles, which exceed 40% of the total in some levels. The bone industry shows various types of assegai –single-bevelled and grooved–, rods and needles and many bone objects show line pairs, series of parallel lines, indents and other engraved symbols. The figurative subject is limited to an antler engraved with deer and a horse with a synthetic design, in level XII (Corchón, 1994).

3.2. The Middle Magdalenian

Levels IX-IV of Sala II were deposited over a thick deposit of sterile clay from flooding (>40cm, level X), which separates the section from the neighbouring Lower Magdalenian (Fig.1). The sedimentology study (Hoyos, 1995) and the material culture show that they correspond to two successive stadia. The early Middle Magdalenian (level IX-IV) is a very cold and wet episode *(GS2)* with a thick deposit (>70 cm) that offers representations of cold steppe fauna engraved on slabs: *Rangifer tarandus*, *Mammutus primigenius* and *Coelodonta antiquitatis*. Accordingly, the fauna consumed includes reindeer remains at the base (necklace of eleven serrated incisors, level IX) and in the ceiling (level VI) of the section. In the latter level, particularly cold, boar and reindeer appear together, reproducing the reindeer-roe association observed in the Lower Magdalenian. In this respect, Altuna says (Corchón, in process) that the simultaneous presence of conflicting communities of ungulates, which do not currently exist in any biotype nor among the fauna in the sites in open areas of central and western Europe during the Würm glacial stage, is not uncommon in the Cantabrian region. Its complex terrain creates a labyrinth of valleys with sunny and shady spots in the same valley, where cold steppe areas can coexist with deciduous woods.

The palaeoeconomy is based on the exploitation of deer (61%), horses (19%) and *capridae* (*Capra* and *Rupicapra*, 15%), with some bovine and carnivores. Visits to the coast provide marine mammals to the archaeological record (*Physeter macrocephalus*, *Globicefala melas*, *Halichoerus gryphus*), the majority teeth perforated to be used as pendants and a wide collection of molluscs (*Pecten maximus*, *Nucella lapillus*, *Littorina obtusata*, *Mytilus*, *Teredon-avalis*). One data of interest refers to the association of the sperm whale with *Coronula diadema* (level VIII), an ectoparasite of large cetacean that proves that the meat from these animals was transported to and consumed in the cave. In addition, the mollusc *Teredo navalis* proves that wood that had been submerged in the sea was transported to Las Caldas (Corchón *et al.*, 2008).

The advanced Middle Magdalenian (level V-IV) was deposited under harsh and very wet

Figure 3. Early Middle Magdalenian: engraved sperm whale's tooth, engraved seal and dolphin teeth, sea molluscs, remains of *Coronula Diadema*.

conditions, during the transition to the Late Glacial Maximum (GI Ie), with erosion and solifluction displacement processes. The fauna records the disappearance of steppe species and a notable reduction in large ungulates: *Equusferus* (1.5-2.3%) and *Bos/Bison* (<4%). Specialisation in deer (55%), goat (34%) and chamois (8-9.5%) is evident.

The early Middle Magdalenian ceiling is dated at 16641 ± 363 calBP (n.VIc) and its base (level IX) at 16297 ± 436 calBP, the latter probably rejuvenated by the intense humidity and carbonation of the level. The advanced Middle Magdalenian (level IV: 16314 ± 454 calBP) is also coherent with the dating of the next level, transitional to the Upper Magdalenian (level IIIb-c: 16114 ± 441 cal BP).

The early Middle Magdalenianlithic industry with more than 50,000 remains shows a high proportion of burins (20%), particularly dihedral burins (14%), doubling the number of scrapers, some knapped on blades. Retouch and Aurignacian blades account for 10% and Dufour and backed blades represent 16%. The proportion of laminar flake among the knapped remains is low, which could be explained by the use of the blades and laminar flake for knapping tools.

The advanced Middle Magdalenian, equally representative (>24,000 lithic remains), provide high levels of laminar flake, supports are second and blades/bladelets reach 40%. Similarly, 49% of cores are laminar (prismatic, pyramidal). Among the tools, burins (8%) barely exceed scrapers, some laminar, with many retouched blades (8%) and back edge bladelets with some triangles.

The bone industries and mobiliary art are particularly typical in the early Middle Magdalenian (Fig.4), offering many Pyrenean type items: relief, sculptures, trimmed contours, rims, spear throwers, pointed horses teethand engravings. With them appear protoharpoons, forked assegais, denticulate points, semi-cylindrical rods, spatulas and perforated canes, extensively engraved. The engraved lithic plaque, very numerous (*c.* 100 to 200 per level), reproduce, in addition to the typical animals horse, deer, goat, bison, aurochs, reindeer, mammoth, rhinoceros), symbolic topics: acephalous, isolated hands or legs and beast-like anthropomorphs, carrying a pack on his back or doing an activity (sitting, squatting or with extended arms).

The advanced Middle Magdalenian in terms of symbolic expression translated the palaeocological changes described. The Pyrenean volumetric models and techniques (relief, sculptures, rims, trimmed contours, etc.), the steppe fauna and the symbolic theme disappear or are very rare. In bone objects, forked assegais and protoharpoons become rarer but semi-cylindrical rods with linear decorations increase, as do needles, with a notable presence and variety (3%). The portable art shows a wide variety of complex symbols (arches, spindles, inlaid angles, eyes, rhombus, etc.), but animal symbols are limited: goat, horses, deer and salmonidae, with a synthetic design and lightly outlined limbs, appendages and manes (Fig.4).

3.3. Upper and Late Magdalenian

The Upper Magdalenian has been dated at 14936 ± 342 calBP in Sala II. Like the rest of the site in the Nalón valley, they are laminar industries that have become significantly smaller. They are characterised by the abundance of burins, the continuity of the bone point types (cylindrical and oval assegais, bevelled, round and forked based, semi-cylindrical rods with

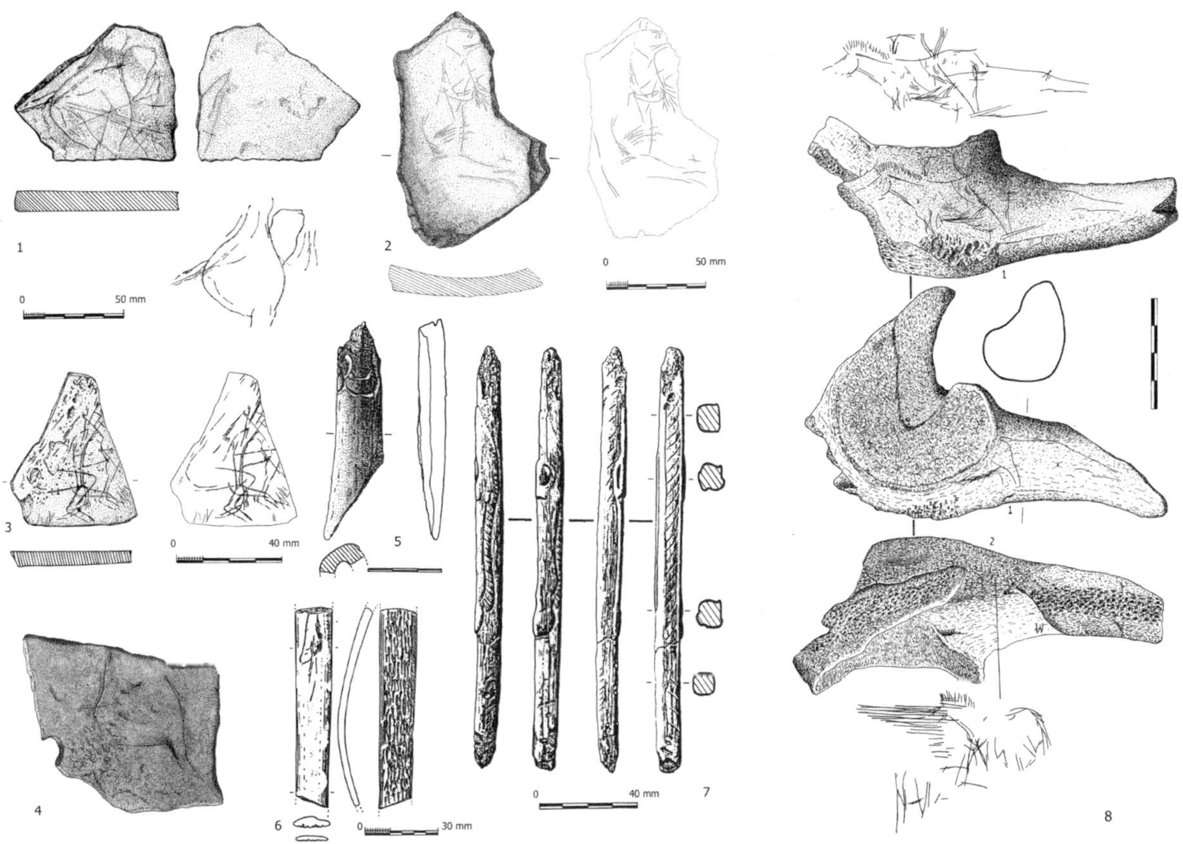

Figure 4. Early Middle Magdalenian portable art (1-7: plaquettes engraved with anthropomorphs, bone with engravings of horse legs and spear thrower with relief bison hoof) and advanced Middle Magdalenian (8: horse pelvis with engraved horses).

tuberculated decoration), with one-sided harpoons. In the most recent level, late Magdalenian (level 2A, Sala I), a harpoon with a centre perforation characteristic of the end of the sequence in the Cantabrian was collected (Corchón, 2007). In the portable art, zoomorphology symbols become rarer, and in general the highly elaborate decorations, decreasing engraved slabs. At the same time, linear decorations, usually regular series of short incisions engraved on the shaft of assegais, rods and harpoons, which combine the functional quality with simple decorative graphic schemas.

Conclusions

The data provided by research at La Cueva de las Caldas cave shows that the middle Nalón valley could have acted as a shelter during the UMG and Late Glacial Maximum. Las Caldas shows that, since the beginning of the regional Solutrean, regional organisation has arisen in the subsistence strategies. This is demonstrated by the mobility of the social groups that occupied the valley in order to collect resources and raw materials, which were sometimes transported to the cave over significant distances. In the early Middle Magdalenian this mobility implied the existence of long-distance cultural contacts, exchanges and the distribution of objects, the portable of which puts their origin in the SW French Pyrenees.

The rapid fall in the levels of occupation and cultural evidence in the Nalón valley as the Upper Magdalenian advanced is a little-known phenomenon. The break in these flows of cultural diffusion over time with the onset of milder climates are perhaps related to the glacier discharges and mass landslides documented in the High Nalón valley (Jiménez, 1997), which could have affected the middle section of the Nalón valley in warm and wet climate cycles, given that this drained the whole Macizo Central of Picos de Europa and its peak hosted significant Würm glaciers (Jiménez, 1996).

Maíllo-Fernández, José Manuel*; Arteaga, Carlos**; Iriarte-Chiapusso, María-José***; Fernández, Antonio****;, Wood, R.*****, Bernaldo de Quirós, Federico******.

Cueva Morín (Villanueva de Villaescusa, Cantabria)

Introduction

Cueva Morín is one of the key sites to understand the evolution of the Palaeolithic in Cantabrian Spain, thanks to its long stratigraphy. It contains many of the Middle and Upper Palaeolithic techno-complexes, and has provided a series of unusual finds in the region, in connection with the ways of life and funerary realm of its Palaeolithic inhabitants.

The cave is located in Villanueva de Villaescusa (Cantabria) and is also known as Mazo Moril and Cueva del Rey. It formed in a small hill of Urgonian (Aptian) limestone, in the Solia drainage basin, at 57m above sea level and 22m above the Obregón rivulet, 6 km from the modern coastline in the Bay of Santander. The cave entrance faces north-east, and leads into a short cave (González-Echegaray and Freeman, 1971). Cueva Morín is not the only cave in the hill, which in fact contains a complex series of passages, above all another cave on a lower level, called Cueva del Oso, where surveying found some lithic artefacts on the surface (Serna *et al.*, 2001).

History of research on the deposit

The cave was made known to the scientific community by H. Obermaier and P. Wernert in 1910. After several visits to the cave, two years after the discovery, in 1912, J. Carballo and P. Sierra carried out a small pit which remained unrecorded until O. Cendrero later published some of the materials the two researchers had found (Cendrero, 1915). From 1917 to 1919, J. Carballo continued working in the cave and undertook what can be considered the first serious and systematic excavation of the deposit. At this time, the Upper Palaeolithic and two Middle Palaeolithic levels were excavated (Carballo, 1923). In turn, in 1918 after he had finished his fieldwork, Carballo invited the Count of Vega del Sella to excavate the site. These new excavations, which lasted two years, were soon published by the Count (Vega del Sella, 1921), and he also informed about the Middle and Upper Palaeolithic occupations.

The site was abandoned until the mid-1960s, when from 1966 to 1969, a Spanish-American team led by the Professors J. González Echegaray and L.G. Freeman carried out further excavations. These were some of the first "modern" excavations in Palaeolithic archaeology at that time, introducing new excavation techniques and with the participation of an inter-disciplinary team to assess the totality of data obtained from the deposit (González-Echegaray and Freeman, 1971, 1973). This research, as well as the application of new excavation methods, also contributed a complete and revised sequence of the different occupations at the site, which included for the first time, a clear and well-defined Chatelperronian level.

The stratigraphic sequence comprising the deposit after this fieldwork consisted of 22 levels, attributed to the following periods: Azilian (Level 1), Magdalenian (Level 2), upper Solutrean (Level 3), Gravettian (Levels 4 and 5b), evolved Aurignacian (Levels 5a), early Aurignacian (Levels 6 and 7), archaic Aurignacian (Levels 8 and 9), Chatelperronian (Level 10), archaeologically sterile (Levels 18 to 21), and Mousterian (Level 22).

In addition to this significant cultural sequence, González Echegaray and Freeman's excavations uncovered evidence of two dwelling structures belonging respectively to the Mousterian and Au-

* Dpto. Prehistoria y Arqueología, UNED. C/ Paseo Senda del rey, 7. 28040 Madrid. jlmaillo@geo.uned.es
** Dpto. de Geografía y ordenación del territorio, Área de Geografía Física. Universidad Autónoma de Madrid.
*** IKERBASQUE /Área de Prehistoria, Universidad del País Vasco.
**** Departamento de Geografía, UNED.
***** Research School for Earth Sciences, Australian National University, Canberra, Australia
****** Área de Prehistoria, Universidad de León.

rignacian, and exhumed three pseudomorphs (one of them complete) and the badly altered grave of a fourth (Freeman, 1971a, 1973; Freeman and González-Echegaray, 1973, González-Echegaray and Freeman, 1978).

Thirty-five years later, it was necessary to update information about Cueva Morín, in relation with new methods and data introduced during that time, from both methodological and epistemological approaches to the science. For this reason, one of the authors (J. M. Maillo-Fernández), together with J. González Echegaray as co-director, carried out a research project which included a small archaeological study of a section of the deposit in 2005, in order to determine its sedimentological and geomorphologic characteristics, as well as obtain environmental (palynology) and chrono-cultural information about the deposit. The small size of the section left by the old excavations and their delicate state of conservation were deciding factors when selecting the area to excavate, in order to preserve as much of this important section as possible.

Stratigraphy, geomorphology and chronology

The most complete stratigraphic sequence in the deposit (22 levels although not all of them are archaeological) was attained by the 1966-69 excavation (Table 1).

Level	Composition	Thickness (cm)	Cultural attribution
1	Sandy-silty, 7,5 YR 3/2	2-20	Azilian
2	Silty-sand with gravel, 10 YR 2/2	5-10	Magdalenian
3	Silt, 7.5 YR 3/2	2-8	Upper Solutrean
4	Sandy silt, 5 YR 3/2	5-20	Gravettian
5	Sandy silt with gravel, 5 YR 2/1	15-30	Gravettian and final Aurignacian
6	Silty, 5 YR 3/3.5	20-30	Early Aurignacian
7	Sandy silt with clay lenses, 5 YR 2/1	10-18	Early Aurignacian
8	Silty-sand, 5 YR 3/3	10-20	Proto-Aurignacian
9	Silty-sand with fine gravel, 10 YR 3.5/3	5-8	Proto-Aurignacian
10	Clay, 10 YR 3/3	2-5	Chatelperronian
11	Sandy-silty, 2.5 YR 2/0	8-18	Mousterian
12	Silt with gravel, 7.5 YR 3/2	12-20	Mousterian
13	Clayey-silt, 7.5 YR 2/0	5-8	Mousterian
14	Silty-clay, 10YR 3.5/3	7-10	Mousterian
15	Clayey-silt, 10 YR 3.5/3	15-20	Mousterian
16	Silty-sand, 10 YR 5/6	12-15	Mousterian
17	Sandy-silt with gravel, 10 YR 4.5/5	12-22	Mousterian
18	Sandy-silt, 7.5 YR 4/4	45-70	Sterile
19	Sandy-silty, 7.5 YR 4/4	12-22	Sterile
20	n/a	2-5	Sterile
21	n/a	7-10	Sterile
22	n/a	2-5	Indeterminate Palaeolithic

Table 1. Archaeological levels in Cueva Morín.

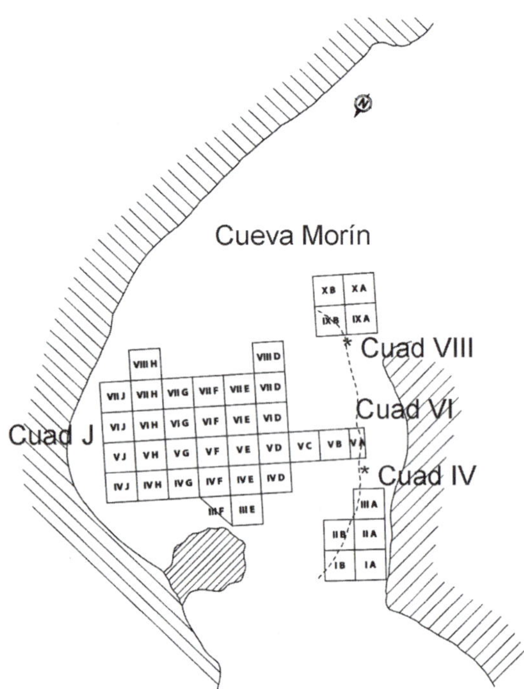

Figure 1. Plan of the cave.

The sedimentological study carried out by H. Laville and M. Hoyos (Laville and Hoyos, 1994) revealed some issues in the chrono-climatic sequence and the composition of some levels, in comparison with earlier work (Butzer, 1981). Later, J. Sanguino and collaborators, indirectly by using the other researchers' work, even cast doubts on the nature of some of the archaeological levels (Sanguino and Montes, 2005).

Therefore, an understanding of the formation of the sedimentary deposit in the cave was one of the main objectives of the fieldwork carried out in Cueva Morín in 2005. The sedimentological study performed with samples collected then has characterised sediments of two different kinds in the main section of the deposit (IB-IXB in the classic nomenclature) (Fig. 1). On the one hand, those near the cave entrance of external origin and with the classic formation process of fill in rock-shelters and caves. On the other, sediments related with water flowing from inside the cave to outside (Fig. 2). This multi-episodic flow may have alternated with the occupation in the cave, as no erosive scars are seen between the sediments of the two parts. As Count of Vega del Sella was able to observe in his excavation, it formed a meander whose channel-lag deposits may be situated around square IX, where the cave turns and the material is larger grained. The outer side of the meander, where the finer sediment is deposited, can be traced in the section of square J (Fig. 1). This current may have been active at different times in the sedimentary history of the cave, as the end of the cave is blocked by calcite and sub-angular and sub-rounded cobbles, as if it was an underground "point bar". It was abandoned, allowing later occupations, as suggested by the finds made in the central part of the cave in previous archaeological studies and as is seen in the whole main stratigraphic section.

Chronology is the Achilles heel of the deposit. Several attempts have been made to date its human occupations with very different results and leaving part of the stratigraphy unsampled (Table 2). The first attempt was during González Echegaray and Freeman's excavations (Stuckenrath, 1978). The results were partly contradictory with the stratigraphy and generally rejected by the scientific community. However, attention should be paid the determinations from Level 8, proto-Aurignacian, as they bear no relation to the stratigraphic section or the excavation in that area, where the industries have been

Figure 2. Stratigraphy of Cueva Morín.

Level	Techno-complex	Material	Context	Lab. Ref.	Date (BP)	Calibration range (cal BP, 95.4% probability range)		Reference
						from	to	
5s	Gravettian	Charcoal	Excavation	SI 953	20120 ± 340 BP	25194	23452	Stuckenrath, 1978
7	Early Aurignacian	Charcoal	Excavation	SI 954	31500 ± 880 BP	37985	33975	Stuckenrath, 1978
7	Early Aurignacian	Charcoal	Excavation	SI 955	28680 ± 840 BP	34381	31171	Stuckenrath, 1978
7	Early Aurignacian	Charcoal	Idem, soluble part in NaOH	SI 955a	27260 ± 1500 BP	35220	28610	Stuckenrath, 1978
8	Proto-Aurignacian	Charcoal	Morín III	SI 956	27710 ± 1300 BP	34925	29420	Stuckenrath, 1978
8	Proto-Aurignacian	Charcoal	Section (ABA)	GifA96263	36590 ± 770 BP	42432	39734	Maíllo-Fernández *et al.*, 2001
8	Proto-Aurignacian	Charcoal	Section	OxA19084	40060 ± 350 BP	44399	43052	Maroto *et al.*, 2012
8	Proto-Aurignacian	Charcoal	Upper part of Morín I	SI 952	27630 ± 540 BP	33022	30820	Stuckenrath, 1978
8	Proto-Aurignacian	Charcoal	Idem, soluble part in NaOH	SI 952a	27360 ± 740 BP	33445	30214	Stuckenrath, 1978
9	Proto-Aurignacian	Charcoal	Section (ABA)	GrA33891	33.430 +250 -230 BP	38470	36879	Maroto *et al.*, 2012
10	Chatelperronian	Charcoal	Section (Acid only)	GrA33823	29.380 +260 -240 BP	34033	32984	Maroto *et al.*, 2012
10	Chatelperronian	Charcoal	Section	SI951	27800 ± 560 BP	33235	30935	Stuckenrath, 1978
10	Chatelperronian	Charcoal	Idem, soluble part in NaOH	SI951a	>30340 BP	N/A		Stuckenrath, 1978
11	Mosterian	Charcoal	Section (ABA)	OxA19083*	41800 ± 450 BP	46022	44406	Maroto *et al.*, 2012
11	Mosterian	Charcoal	Scetion (ABOx-SC)	OxA19459*	43600± 600 BP	48343	45648	Maroto *et al.*, 2012
11	Mosterian	Charcoal	Section (ABA)	GifA96264	42000 ± 730 BP	46922	44120	Maíllo-Fernández *et al.*, 2001

Table 2. Radiocarbon dates from Cueva Morín. Stuckenrath's determinations (1978) were given in years BC supposing a half life of 5370 years. They have been recalculated following Stuiver and Polach (1977) using a half life of 5568 years and placing it on a time scale before 1950. These recalculated dates have been used in the calibration. The dates with an asterisk were obtained from the same sample. The determinations have been calibrated against IntCal13 (Reimer *et al.*, 2013) in OxCal v.4.2. (Ramsey, 2009).

defined. These dates correspond to the area of the "burials" which are associated with this Level 8. They are all in a span of time between 27 and 26 ky BP.

In our research project, we carried out a series of determinations with material taken from the section, and these have provided dates for the Mousterian of 40 ky BP and for Level 8 of 36.5 ky BP (Maíllo-Fernández *et al.*, 2001). Recently, Maroto and collaborators have re-analysed samples we have provided by ultrafiltration, also obtaining disconcerting results, in which the date for Level 10 (Chatelperronian) is very similar to the one obtained by Stuckenrath (Maroto *et al.*, 2012 and Table 2). Unfortunately the fragment was very poorly conserved and only the carbon prepared before the dating process could be analysed. It therefore only gives a minimum age for this level. Once again, technical improvement induced us to carry out a new attempt with material from the 1966-69 collection, with the ultrafiltration method. The low collagen content in the samples meant that results could not be obtained.

Cultural sequence

Cueva Morín is an important site for Upper and Middle Palaeolithic studies in the region owing to the long cultural sequence conserved in its deposit: 7 Mousterian levels, 1 Chatelperronian, 2 proto-Aurignacian, 2 early Aurignacian, 1 evolved Aurignacian, 2 Gravettian, 1 Solutrean, 1 Magdalenian, and 1 Azilian.

The Azilian level (Level 1) has not been dated, although *grosso modo* this techno-complex can be situated between 11,500 and 9,500 BP (Tresguerres, 2004). The layer is located near the cave entrance, and contains a dense number of objects including micro-blade tools, mostly consisting of retouched bladelets, micro-gravettes and numerous endscrapers (González Echegaray, 1971a).

Level 2 corresponds to the upper Magdalenian and is characterised by a large number of burins, truncated pieces, and carinated and nucleiform endscrapers, together with a large proportion of microlithic tools (backed bladelets, denticulates, Dufour, geometric microliths, etc.). The osseous assemblage is abundant, with fragments of sagaie points with a circular cross-section, some of them with central groove, decorated flattened rods, and pendants made from bone and red deer canine teeth (González Echegaray, 1971a).

The upper Solutrean (Level 3) is a thin layer where the lithic assemblage is not particularly rich. However, shouldered points, and to a lesser extent willow and laurel leaf points are relatively abundant. Therefore, this level can be clearly attributed to the upper Solutrean in Cantabrian Spain (González Echegaray, 1971a).

The Gravettian is represented by two layers (Levels 4 and upper 5), with a large number of backed pieces (Gravette points, micro-gravettes), truncated pieces, and some Noailles burins in the most recent level. No recent studies have examined the techno-typology in these two levels in depth, nor is any date available to situate them in the Cantabrian Gravettian, as the one obtained by Stuckenrath (1978) is clearly anomalous. Recently, the Gravettian in Cueva Morín has been identified as belonging to a late stage in which Noailles burins are scarce and backed pieces more abundant (Peña, 2011).

Similarly, the evolved Aurignacian at Cueva Morín (lower Level 5) is in need of a techno-typological reappraisal. The evolved Aurignacian is a polymorphic techno-complex in Cantabrian Spain, which hinders its characterisation (Cabrera *et al.*, 2004). Thus, in Cueva Morín, the lithic assemblage differs from the early Aurignacian in the smaller number of carinated endscrapers and a greater abundance of thick-nosed endscrapers. However, the osseous assemblage is abundant and meaningful in this level, with spindle and flat-shaped points together with the survival of split-based points.

Levels 6 and 7 in the deposit correspond to the early Aurignacian. The industry is characteristic of this techno-complex, with abundance of carinated pieces, two types of blade debitage, one for blades from prismatic cores with unipolar exploitation and another for bladelets made from carinated cores (Arrizabalaga, 1995; Cabrera *et al.*, 2004). However, the bone industry is poor and not diagnostic.

The proto-Aurignacian (Levels 8 and 9) have been reappraised recently from the technological and typological viewpoints (Arrizabalaga, 1995; Maíllo-Fernández, 2003). It is a markedly micro-blade industry, with abundant Dufour bladelets. The blade were extracted from prismatic cores with unipolar reduction, in a continuum between blades and bladelets. The relative importance of substrate tools (sidescrapers, denticulates and notches) should be stressed, as well as flake reduction schemes (Maíllo-Fernández, 2012). Level 9, because of techno-typological and sedimentological issues, may have suffered taphonomic alterations, affecting its industrial integrity.

There is no doubt that the most important level, the one that has attracted most attention to Cueva Morín, is Level 10, corresponding to the Chatelperronian. When it was identified, it was used to address the problem of the Middle-Upper Palaeolithic transition, at that time associated with the "Aurignacian-Mousterian" (González Echegaray, 1969, 1971a). The lithic assemblage has been revised on several occasions since then (Arrizabalaga, 1995, Maíllo-Fernández, 2003). However, the level and its integrity have been discussed by several scholars. K. Butzer, who carried out the first sedimentologival study of the cave, concluded that this level contained parts colluviated by later cryoturbation (Butzer, 1981: 146), probably based on the incoherence of the dates (Stuckenrath, 1978). In the review carried out by H. Laville and M. Hoyos, it was thought that it had been eroded towards the interior and scalloped towards the exterior by cryoturbation processes (Laville and Hoyos, 1994: 204). The total integrity of the level has recently been questioned following a re-interpretation of the data given by Laville and Hoyos, who thought the Cueva Morín, like nearly all the caves in Cantabrian Spain, was not apt for determining a regional palaeo-climate sequence. In this new interpretation, the scalloped part was taken as an exclusive indicator of solifluction and, taken together with the thinness of the level (2 – 5cm), it was concluded that Level 10 "is an erosive contact, altered by water currents in Levels 11 and 9" (Muñoz and Montes, 2003: 206). We carried out the first examination of the section since 1969. This allowed us to verify that Level 10 is visible in the outer part of the stratigraphic section, exactly as identified by Butzer, Laville and Hoyos, and as represented in the relevant monographs (González Echegaray, 1971b; Butzer, 1981: 143). In addition, the sedimentological curve of the Level 10 reveals that it was deposited in a low energy process and not by solifluction. The scalloping is due to a load deformation processes, which also caused scrolling, which is only found at the top of the level, although certain higher energy water action, which produced a large scroll, cannot be ruled out.

The Chatelperronian level has also been questioned from the point of view of the lithic assemblage; its existence has even been denied, arguing that it is a mixture "in equal parts" of Aurignacian and Mousterian material (Muñoz and Montes, 2003: 206). We have already reasoned at length against this hypothesis (Maíllo-Fernández, 2007a, 2008), but we might repeat that it is very hard for us to understand how the mixture of two lithic assemblages that belong to two well-defined techno-complexes (Aurignacian and Mousterian) can result in a third, completely different one (Chatelperronian).

The cultural sequence at Cueva Morín ends with a series of Mousterian levels. The most recent, Levels 11 and 12, classified as denticulate Mousterian, is characterised by discoid and partly Levallois production, with a small but significant micro-blade production (Maíllo-Fernández, 2001, 2007b). The lower section (Levels 13-17), where the predominance of cleavers is the most significant trait (Mousterian variety traditionally known as Vasconian), was attributed to the Mousterian of Acheulian tradition in the first studies (Freeman, 1971b).

Dwelling structures and burials

The 1966-69 excavation at Cueva Morín did not only reveal a chrono-stratigraphic sequence of vital importance in Cantabrian Spain, but also two dwelling structures and a series of burials.

The dwellings appeared in the central part of the cave, but belonged to different cultural periods. The oldest corresponded to Level 17 (Mousterian) and had been cut through by Vega del Sella's excavations. It is 6.6m^2 in size, and consists of a line of stones forming a curved area with sediment inside it clearly different from the rest of the level. No remains of hearths were detected inside it (Freeman, 1973).

In Level 8, proto-Aurignacian, another area was interpreted as a dwelling structure. Partially destroyed by the excavations in the early twentieth century, which do not allow its width to be determined, it was nearly three metres long and rectangular. There was no evidence that the structure had been covered, at least with posts. The sediment had been dug out to a maximum depth of 27cm, and against the innermost wall there were remains of a hearth, possibly in a pit, and on the opposite side a step 125cm long and 50cm wide, interpreted as a bench (Freeman, 1971a).

Associated with the Aurignacian, at the back of the cave, after an area interpreted by the excavators as a wall with wooden posts, were found a series of mounds that held the burials of four individuals. The most peculiar thing about these burials is that they did not contain the skeletal remains of the bodies. Instead, in the decomposition processes, they had turned into adipose and later been covered by sediment, so that the remains were turned into a positive mould that was difficult to interpret. The most complete and most recent is Morín I, found in a grave 210 x 52 cm in size. Although it is not easy to interpret, it seems that this individual was lying on its left side with flexed arms and slightly flexed legs. The excavators interpreted that its head had been amputated and deposited in the lower part of the grave. In the mount covering the body, the remains of two small hearths were found (Freeman and González Echegaray, 1973). The remains called Morín II were limited to a dark, greasy and plastic substance, similar to that in the other graves, but it could not be interpreted further. Beneath Morín I and partly destroyed by it, Morín III only consisted of two legs. Finally, Morín IV was limited to the partial remains of the grave and the mound covering it, as it had been destroyed by the other burials.

Acknowledgements

This study is dedicated to the memory of Professor Joaquín González Echegaray and Professor Leslie G. Freeman, who were truly responsible for the scientific understanding of Cueva Morín.

Jesús Altuna*
Koro Mariezkurrena*

Ekain cave (Deba, Basque Country)

Ekain cave (Deba, Basque Country), a cave famous for its rock art ensemble in its interior (Altuna, 1996), possesses an archaeological deposit at its entrance. This has been excavated in two stages; between 1969 and 1975, first directed by J. M. de Barandiarán and later by J. Altuna (Altuna and Merino, 1984) and then between 2009 and 2011, directed by J. Altuna (Altuna, 2009).

The cave is located at the confluence of two valleys, each with a small stream, in an area with biotopes of steep crags. The two streams together flow into the River Urola one and a half kilometres downstream, at a point 8 kilometres from the modern coastline. In this point, the landscape has changed to gentle hills.

The deposit in the entrance of Ekain, 5m thick, consists of 12 levels (Fig. 1).

The lowest Levels XII and XI are totally barren, both archaeologically and palaeontologically.

Level X is very rich in remains of *Ursus spelaeus*. Human influence is minimal and only a few signs of Chatelperronian remains have been identified.

Figure 1. Stratigraphy of the archaeological deposit at Ekain cave.

* Centro de Conservación e Investigación de los materiales Arqueológicos de Gipuzkoa (GOAZ). Paseo de Zarategi 84-88. 20015. San Sebastián. altuna@arkaios.com

Level IX also contains quite a large number of *Ursus spelaeus* remains, but only a little evidence of the Gravettian. Its base was dated by radiocarbon to over 30,600 BP (I-11056). These two levels contain very little knapping waste, which indicates that the artefacts found in them had been made elsewhere. The cave was therefore visited sporadically by people who did not usually live there. The site of Irikaitz, located 2km from Ekain, with Gravettian remains in its upper part, might be connected with this.

Level VIII was probably deposited in the Würm III/IV interstadial, as it no longer contains *Ursus spelaeus* remains. The lithic assemblage is scanty and not diagnostic. There are a few faunal remains, above all of *Rupicapra rupicapra*. The presence of *Sus scrofa* and *Capreolus capreolus* indicates climate amelioration in this level, which has been dated to 20,900 ± 450 BP (I-13005).

Level VII (Cantabrian lower Magdalenian) is the first level displaying intense human occupation. The sedimentological study shows that the base of the level was deposited in conditions of moderate humidity and relatively high temperatures, while these changed to cold and humid at the top of the layer. Five radiocarbon determinations have been obtained, dating to between 16,500 and 15,400 BP (all by Isotopes, Westwood, New Jersey).

The pollen analysis shows, at the base of the level, a proportion of 12% *Pinus*, 3% *Corylus* and a smaller presence of *Alnus*, *Betula* and *Quercus* t. *pedunculata*, as well as an abundance of Ericaceae and filicales triletes. This appears to correspond to the late Lascaux interstadial. The conditions worsen and the number of taxa decreases, but the climate improves again at the end of the deposition of the level, which suggests the Bölling.

The most common small mammal in the coldest phases is *Microtus oeconomus*, and *Arvicola terrestris* in the less cold phases. *Microtus* gr. *agrestis-arvalis* and *Talpa europea* also occur in significant numbers.

The lithic assemblage displays specialisation with a large number of microlithic backed bladelets used to make hunting implements. This suggests a seasonal occupation of the cave. However these occupations were prolonged as indicated by the fact that knapping was performed in the cave. Knapping waste is abundant. Equally, the readaptations of decorticating flakes and core flakes, as well as some burins and their spalls, confirm this.

The osseous assemblage clearly exhibits the particular characteristics of the Cantabrian lower Magdalenian. The most characteristic tools because of their chrono-stratigraphic position are assegai points with a square cross-section and split base, and a bi-pointed object. They belong to a single type, pointed artefacts, which seems to suggest a particular activity (hunting). The presence of antler waste rods means that certain artefacts were manufactured *in situ*.

The ungulate remains clearly support the seasonality indicated by the industry. The base of animal subsistence was red deer. The age analysis of the fawns and other young ungulates demonstrates that they were hunted in the first month of life (June) and others also in a mild season of the year. None were hunted in winter.

This raises the matter of the base site from which Ekain was used as a hunting post. Two hours away on foot is the site of Urtiaga, occupied throughout the year, with Erralla an hour and a half away (Altuna, Baldeón and Mariezkurrena, 1985). Both sites possess thick lower Magdalenian levels.

The analysis of the skeletal parts in the deposit shows that the animals were brought to the site whole, which is logical bearing in mind that many of the prey were fawns killed in their first month of life.

The osseous industry in this Level VII at Ekain displays similarities with Level F in Urtiaga.

Level VI (upper-final Magdalenian) formed in its lower part in very cold and less humid conditions than the previous level. It includes the most evidence of frost-shattering in the whole deposit. The upper part of level formed in a cold and dry climate.

The pollen studies reflect a decline in arboreal and filical species in the lower part, in which deciduous trees are practically non-existent. Carduaceae acquire their highest proportions, which Ericaceae reach a minimum level in the severest conditions (low humidity and extreme cold) in the sequence at Ekain. The level is dated by radiocarbon to 12,050 ± 190 BP (I-9240). However, the upper part of the level indicates a slight improvement, probably corresponding to the Alleröd.

The significant decrease in Ericaceae, together with the lesser tree cover, produced a decline in the *Cervus elaphus* population and consequently these animals were replaced as prey by *Capra pyrenaica*.

The faunal analysis suggests that the site was still occupied seasonally. The skeletal profiles show that the prey was brought to the cave whole less often than in Level VII. This is understandable because the preferred prey was adult ibex and the hunting sites would have been of more difficult access. The animals were butchered where they were hunted and selected parts were brought back to the cave.

The faunal assemblage also includes evidence of *Rangifer tarandus* and *Lepus timidus*, as well as salmon vertebrae. It is interesting to note that the rock art in the cave includes a painting of a salmon.

This level does not contain a single remain of marine molluscs.

The lithic assemblage further supports this seasonality. The most abundant implements are still microliths, with few medium-size tools such as burins, scrapers or denticulates. The percentage of burins increases slightly, which may be connected with the greater importance of the osseous industry in this level. The small backed tools display a change within this level, as in its lower part (Level VIb) there are no backed points, whereas the upper part (Level VIa) does contain some.

The osseous assemblage also exhibits two stages, as there are no harpoons in Level VIb, while there are in Level VIa. The harpoon assemblage in VIa is homogeneous. Their barbs are on one side, and they are somewhat flattened. The barbs are large and separated, with few of them in relation to the shaft and with deep incisions. One of them has a flat shaft, with a single row of barbs. It displays a deep longitudinal incision next to the start of the barbs on one side and profound incisions in the barbs. Another exhibits fine incisions on one of its sides, forming a decorative V-shaped motif. On the opposite side, seven short and shallow transversal incisions are similar to the so-called "hunting-marks". This specimen is similar to a harpoon found in Level D at the site of Urtiaga.

Two of the assegai points are decorated with schematic depictions of an ibex viewed from the front, like some figures in the rock art ensemble. The same level yielded an engraved sandstone plaquette representing three animals: a male ibex, a stag and a horse (Fig. 2). The ibex is the most outstanding figure as its head is depicted in great detail. Its horn displays the two typical curves of the Pyrenean species, on which the growth rings are indicated by a series of transversal lines. The red deer, drawn with finer lines, displays antlers in which the two base points, the middle points in each antler and the wider crown are indicated. The third figure, a horse, is less conspicuous and perfect than the other two.

Level V reflects more humid and less cold conditions than Level VI, although the reduction in arboreal cover and filicales persists. The lithic industry is poorer, but continues to include backed points and bladelets, scrapers, burins and denticulates. The assemblage from this level is not very characteristic but appears to represent the end of the upper Palaeolithic in the cave.

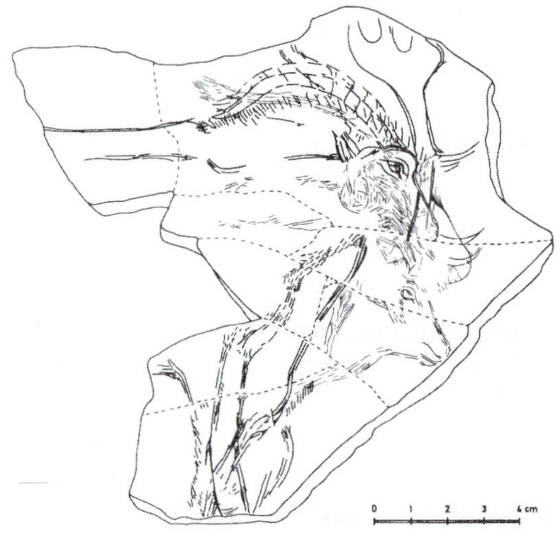

Figure 2. Plaquette from Level VI at Ekain cave.

Levels IV and III, dated in the Azilian, clearly show the climate amelioration in the Pre-Boreal, with very humid conditions and clear rise in the temperatures. Pine, which had been the main tree species, was slowly replaced by deciduous taxa such as *Corylus* and *Alnus*, with a presence of *Juglans*, *Tilia*, *Quercus*, *Betula*, *Fagus*, Cupresaceae and a large percentage of Ericaceae, which reaches its maximum values.

Microtus oeconomus disappears definitively from among the small mammals, while the bat *Myotis myotis* appears.

Red deer was the preferred prey over ibex. The representation of *Capreolus capreolus* increases and *Sus scrofa* appears in the Ekain sequence together with *Meles meles*.

Shellfish were gathered, as shown by the large number of remains of *Patella* and *Osilinus lineatus*. These resources were easily obtainable at this time, as the coastline approached the cave.

The lithic assemblage continues to indicate specialisation in hunting. The osseous industry includes a base of a typical Azilian flat harpoon with eye-shaped perforation.

Level II formed in very dry and warm conditions. It has been dated to 9540 ± 210 BP (I-11666). The lithic industry is comparable with Level III but with a more advanced Mesolithic component, including some triangles and the appearance of the micro-burin technique.

Shellfish gathering reached its greatest importance in the whole sequence at Ekain. The species represented are *Osilinus lineatus, Patella vulgata, P. depressa, P. aspera* and *Mytilus edulis*.

Remains of ungulates are scanty, with evidence of *Cervus elaphus, Capra pyrenaica* and *Sus scrofa*. The presence of 11 remains of *Bos taurus* is striking, and these were undoubtedly introduced afterwards.

A potsherd was also found in this level, and must have equally been a later intrusion. Together with the remains of *Bos taurus*, this indicates that a new excavation needed to be carried out in an intact area, in order to clarify these intrusions.

Level I is the modern surface layer.

Modern Excavations

New excavations were carried out from 2009 to 2011 and these provided some significant data (Altuna 2009, 2010 and 2011) in reference to two aspects of the deposit.

Figure 3. Contour *découpé* of a bird.

First, affecting Levels II, III and IV, a series of remains of human infants and fragments of hand-made pottery were found. One of the sherds displayed button-shaped decorations and another had finger-nail impressions. One fragment of an infant's mandible, found in Level II, refitted with another piece from Level III. This mandible has been dated to 4960 ± 60 BP (Ua-36854). The pottery and *Bos taurus* remains found in Level II in the old excavations must be ascribed to this assemblage.

When the base of Level VI was excavated, a *contour découpé* of a bird, made from a bovine rib, was found (Fig. 3) Altuna and Mariezkurrena, 2013). This displays detailed internal shaping and has been dated to 13,862 ± 129 BP (Ua-39108). Both the date and the characteristics of the find correspond to the middle Magdalenian. This occupation in this phase, which must have been very short-lived in Ekain cave, was not detected by the old excavation. Level VI begins immediately beneath it.

This representation is unique as, to date, no figures of birds have been found on this kind of object. Additionally, it was made from a bovine rib, rather than from a hyoid bone, which is also unusual in *contours découpés*.

Javier Baena Preysler *
Elena Carrion Santafé **

Cueva de El Esquilleu: a new point of reference for the Cantabrian Mousterian

As a result of collaboration between the Autonomous University of Madrid and the Consejería de Cultura of the government of Cantabria, in the context of the project HUM2004-04679/HIST "CONTEXTO CRONOLÓGICO Y CULTURAL DEL FINAL DEL PALEOLÍTICO MEDIO EN EL NORTE PENINSULAR", a series of field seasons were carried out in Cueva de El Esquilleu in Castro-Cillorigo (Cantabria) from 1997 to 2006.

The state of conservation of the sequence in Cueva de El Esquilleu, and the method used (giving priority to determining the sequence and sampling), has enabled the collection of a large amount of data from the faunal, pollen, anthracological, sedimentological, stratigraphic and, naturally, archaeological records. The research has also included a taphonomic study, technical and functional analysis, the finds of human remains, the micro-spatial reconstruction by phytolith analysis, and the study of processes of procurement of lithic resources and the functional relationship of the site with its environment. In short, this new sequence is one of the most complete Middle Palaeolithic sites in Iberia.

Figure 1. Cueva de El Esquilleu (Cantabria, Spain) and its surroundings.

El Esquilleu is a unique deposit. Although it is not at a great altitude (280m above sea level, and 68m about the River Deva), the montane environment predominates. It is a large rock-shelter, in a mostly limestone area (Valdeteja formation). It is a rugged location, different from most of the Cantabrian valleys that were occupied, and similar to only a small number of Mousterian sites in northern Spain, such as Axlor (Ríos Garaizar, 2012). The geomorphologic setting is a small basin between mountains, bounded to the south by the steep slope of the mountain valleys, which were glaciated at their heads, and very difficult connections with surrounding valleys (Fig. 1). The general nature of the Cantabrian relief, with its tendency towards dividing up the territory, is more pronounced in the Deva basin, with the connection to the coastal strip through a narrow gorge. The climate is also slightly milder than in other parts because of its particular location.

The length of the occupation (more than 50,000 years) and the stratigraphic sequence are unique in Cantabrian Spain. The excavation, formally a sounding, was carried out from 1997 to 2006, with two test excavations perpendicular to each other, one of them transversal to the rock wall. The large surface area excavated was 14m^2. In the sounding transversal to the cave wall, a depth of 4.2m was reached, and 41 stratigraphic levels were defined, 34 of them archaeologically fertile and in succession (Fig. 2). Over 100,000 lithic remains were retrieved, and about 25% of these have been described and studied from the technical viewpoint (as well as the initial typo-

* Dpto. Prehistoria y Arqueología, Universidad Autónoma de Madrid, Campus Cantoblanco, 28049 (Madrid, Spain)
** Subdirección General de Museos Estatales, Ministerio de Cultura, 28071 (Madrid, Spain)

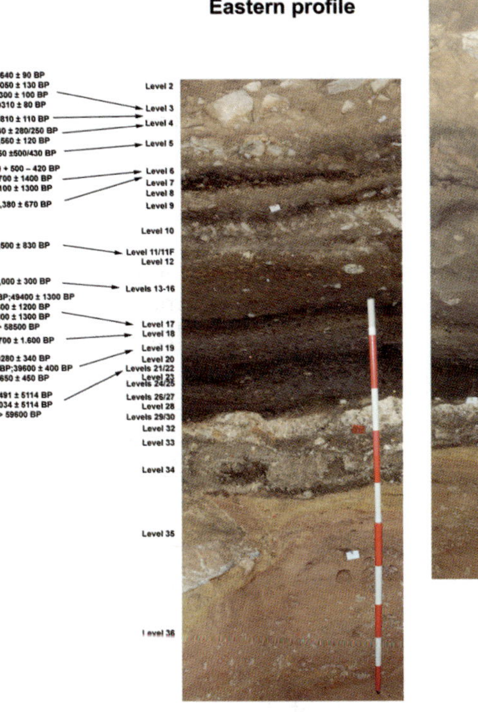

Figure 2. Stratigraphical sequence in Cueva de El Esquilleu. Eastern profile.

logical assignation and the general identification of their attribution).

The chronology at El Esquilleu covers a time from the early OIS 3, including OIS 3c and OIS 3b, the H5, H4 and H3 cold events in the middle part of OIS 3a, and probably part of OIS 2. Its levels cover a full span of time (>53 ky BP to <20 ky BP) (Jordá Pardo *et al.*, 2009; Baena *et al.*, 2012; Maroto *et al.*, 2012; Yravedra and Uzquiano, 2013). The available radiocarbon dates situate the sequence quite well between about 60 and 20 ky BP. From a conventional perspective, the El Esquilleu sequence extends beyond the natural climate limit associated with the end of the Middle Palaeolithic and enters in Würm III (H4 in terminology of Heinrich, 1988). The whole sequence is Mousterian, with a long series of determinations:

III	Charcoal	GrA-33829	3640±90 BP
III	Bone	AA-29664	12,050±130 BP
III	Bone	OxA-19967	19,300±100 BP
III	Bone	OxA-19968	19,310±80 BP
III B	Bone	OxA-19246	20,810±110 BP
IV	Charcoal	GrA-35064	22,840±280-250 BP
IV	Charcoal	GrA-35064	23,560±120 BP
V	Charcoal	GrA-35065	30,250±500-430 BP
VIF	Charcoal	AA37883	34,380±670 BP
VI	Charcoal	GrA-33816	40,110±500.420 BP
VI-1	Bone	OxA-19965	43,700±1400 BP
VI-2	Bone	OxA-19966	44,100±1300 BP
XIF	Charcoal	AA37882	36,500±830 BP
XIII	Charcoal	Beta149320	39,000±300 BP
XVII-1	Charcoal	OxA-X-2297-31	49,400±1300 BP
XVII-2	Charcoal	OxA-20320	52,600±1200 BP
XVII	Charcoal	OxA-20318	53,400±1300 BP
XVII	Charcoal	OxA-19993	>54,000 BP
XVII	Charcoal	OxA-20319	>58,500 BP
XVIII	Charcoal	OxA-19993	49,700±1600 BP
XIX-1	Charcoal	OxA-19085	39,280±340 BP
XIX-2	Charcoal	OxA-19086	>54,600 BP
XIX-3	Charcoal	OxA-V-2284-29	39,600±400 BP
XIX-4	Charcoal	OxA-V-2284-30	39,650±450 BP
XXI-I	Charcoal	OxA-20321	>59,600 BP
XXId	Burnt clay	Mad3299	(TL) 51,034±5114 BP
XXIb	Burnt clay	Mad3300	(TL) 53,491±5114 BP

Table 1. El Esquilleu dates.

The sequence is special not only because of the late age of its upper levels but also because of its early chronological start (53 ky BP for Level XXIb) in a total sequence of 41 levels. No other Middle Palaeolithic site is known in Cantabria or in the rest of Iberia, with such a continual and repeated occupation of the same place. Expressed in terms of the number of generations, if the occupation had been continual (and it was undoubtedly seasonal and possibly intermittent), these would amount to 1,600.

The dates obtained for El Esquilleu are reasonably coherent, bearing in mind the variation in types of samples, methods and laboratories. Some of the differences can be explained as laboratory errors. Thus, for example, the different dates for Level XVII (53,400 ± 1300 BP, Oxa-20318, charcoal; and >58,500 BP, OxA-20319, charcoal) and for Level XIF (36,500 ± 830 BP, AA 37882, AMS charcoal; and 34,380 ± 670 BP, AA 37883, AMS) were obtained from a single sample that was divided up.

Other cases can be regarded as inconsistent, such as (1) the three dates obtained for Level VI with results between 44 and 40 ky BP that do not match the chronological sequence of the occupation; and (2), those for Level XIX, for which the new determinations (30 ky BP) contradict the first ones obtained.

However, the date for Level III (12,050 ± 130 BP, AA29664, AMS bone) is only atypical. It fits in the archaeological sequence and the samples have passed the stress tests carried out in specific studies (Jordá Pardo *et al.*, 2009; Maroto *et al.*, 2011). Stratigraphically, it may be supposed that the sequence entered markedly colder conditions after Level VI, which may correspond to H3c (*c.* 30 ky BP). The new dates obtained for Level III (19,300 ± 100 and 19,310 ± 80 14C ky BP and 20,810 ± 110 14C BP), performed within a monographic project involving a critical reappraisal of many of the dates obtained in Iberia, support its validity. However, other clearly aberrant results, such as one recently obtained for Level III, 3640 ± 90 BP, may be explained by the intrusion of Holocene charcoal (Maroto *et al.*, 2011) or the presence of a very atypical Upper Paleolithic industries.

In this way, radiometric coherence is observed in the dates around 20 ky BP for the end of the sequence. They were obtained in different laboratories, using different pre-treatment methods (including ultrafiltration) and display C13 values that confirm the quality of the sample (Maroto *et al.*, 2011). Although many of the dates thought to be recent have been put back in time, in general terms El Esquilleu is still within an increasingly select group.

However, some unknown issues cannot be ruled out, such as a possible contamination of the samples owing to post-depositional processes or percolation problems. T aphonomical studies (Yravedra and González Castanedo, 2013) have suggested that the dates may have been obtained from bones which had not been handled by humans, and which are therefore not archaeological material. Methodologically (i.e., De la Rasilla and Santamaría, 2013), the limitations of the radiometric method itself have been pointed out, because of calibration deficiencies (Jöris *et al.*, 2011), and the divergent results caused by the specific treatment and analytical protocols (Bird *et al.*, 2010).

Technologically (Vaquero, 2013), other studies based on the nature of the lithic assemblage (whose expedient and indeterminate character has been highlighted) suggest that Level III could be a facies with an atemporal cultural attribution. In any case, a relativist position of the dates can be used, where, independently of their exact result, their relative position in the sequence can be considered (Carrión *et al.*, 2013). In addition, the internal analysis of the industries and their relationship with the environment in *chaîne opératoire* terms provides interesting information about changes in the relationship between the group and their surroundings (Carrión *et al.*, 2008).

El Esquilleu is also special because its sequence starts at an early date. There are few sites dated before 40-45 ky BP in the Cantabrian Mousterian. The classic chronologies of Castillo Level 22, Pendo XVII and Lezetxiki V have been seen to be disputable and older dates are very rare, with only El Sidrón (c. 50 ky BP; De la Rasilla *et al.*, 2013) and in a nearby region, Cueva Corazón (96.95 ky BP, by TL, Díez *et al.*, 2008). Most of the occupations that are known are concentrated in a time near the late Mousterian: Mirón, Covalejos, Arrillor, Sopeña, Morín, Amalda and Axlor (Hoyos *et al.*, 1999; Sanquino and Montes, 2005; Straus and González Morales, 2001; Maroto *et al.*, 2011, etc.). An attempt has been made to explain this circumstance by the limitation of the radiocarbon method itself (Santamaría and de La Rasilla, 2013), as the risk of rejuvenating the result increases exponentially with an increase in the age of the sample.

The litho-stratigraphic study divided the sequence into four sections according to their composition and the agents involved in their formation, by integrating taphonomic and geo-archaeological criteria, X-Ray diffraction, environmental scanning electron microscopy, and thermoluminescence (Jordá, 2008). From bottom to top, these four sections are ESQ-D (Levels XXXI to XLI), ESQ-C (Levels XII to XXX), ESQ-B (Levels I to XI) and ESQ-A (covering breccia and speleothems; the cave, which was partially filled, was initially sealed by this large formation; Jordá Pardo *et al.*, 2009).

The human occupation is located in the central Units B and C. Unit C coincided with sedimentation in the rock-shelter by diffuse run-off; the upper central Unit B consists of clasts and frost-shattered rocks with a contribution of diffuse run-off and heavier flow at the top. The characteristics of the matrix in the upper section, according to some authors, would have favoured the vertical movement of contaminating material (Santamaría and de La Rasilla, 2013).

The micro-morphological analysis (Mallol *et al.*, 2010) confirms the good state of conservation in Unit B, although it is affected in its internal structure by cryoturbation, and moderate diagenetic action in Unit C (with levels revealing intense anthropic action). In this way, in neither of these sections have any general processes been detected that might have altered the deposit in any considerable way. Below these, possibly 9m of barren sedimentation is characterised by a massive clayey matrix with highly altered limestone clasts, formed in endokarst conditions (Mallol *et al.*, 2010).

Phytolith analysis (Cabanes *et al.*, 2010) provided surprising results. The sample from the upper litho-stratigraphic section (Unit B) yielded the worst sample, but the moderate diagenesis in Unit C, and the upper levels in Unit B, favoured the conservation of a larger number of remains, which had initially been interpreted as an accumulation of ash (Jordá Pardo *et al.*, 2008). Only the detailed micro-stratigraphic study revealed a succession of hearths, with thick accumulations of ash, burnt bones and artefacts. In this way, it has been suggested that beds of grass were related to a large central area of hearth, with a possible selection of grass species, depending on their properties.

The charcoal record is irregular. Acceptable data were obtained from Level XI to Level XVII, although samples were taken as far as Level XXII. Thus, species have been identified for a span of time dated *grosso modo* between 53 and 36 ky (Uzquiano *et al.*, 2012). The study confirms the general presence of pine in the sequence, although between Levels XIV and XI, the percentage of pine decreases in favour of a greater variety of species, including *Sorbus aria*, steppe-type scrub, *Juniperus, Betula* and a large range of shrubs (possibly chosen to light the fires). This decline in pine may be explained by environmental change, which meant that fuel had to be gathered over a larger area and shrubs used in larger quantities (Uzquiano *et al.*, 2012). The data do not seem to indicate that firewood ever became scarce.

Pollen data (Ruíz Zapata and Gil García, 2005) confirm the predominance of pine throughout the sequence, and this occasionally alternates with river-bank species in optimal climate conditions, accompanied by herbaceous plants. A brief reconstruction indicates that between the old Levels XXX and XX (>50 ky BP) a possibly colder phase was represented by an open vegetation with Asteracae, Poaceae and Chenopodiaceae, and a significant presence of pine as well as some *Betula* and Cupresaceae. However, in the phase between Levels XXX and XIV, the hearths noticeably affected pollen conservation and therefore the record consists mainly of pine, birch, Cupresaceae and Asteracae. These levels are dated *grosso modo* before 39 ky BP. Between 39 and 34.5 ky BP, the palynological study reflects an optimum in humidity conditions, as pine is accompanied by a larger range of mesophile plants, especially *Betula*. This circumstance, which is found at other Cantabrian sites dated in a similar time, concords with the anthracological data obtained at El Esquilleu (Uzquiano *et al.*, 2010).

The archaeozoological record at El Esquilleu agrees with what might be expected in the area (Yravedra, 2006; Uzquiano *et al.*, 2012). Ibex and chamois (*Rupicapra rupicapra*) are the most common species, while bovids (aurochs) occasionally appear in Levels XIII and XIF, and cervids between Levels V and XIV. The presence of these animals probably denotes connections with areas on the coastal strip. In addition, in the levels in which the seasonality of the hunting could be reconstructed (basically from Level XIV to Level III, owing to lesser fragmentation of the bones), this took place mostly in the summer, with prolongations in late spring or early autumn. Only in Level XI were caprids hunted also in winter (Uzquiano *et al.*, 2012; Yravedra, 2006), which may be interpreted as a change in the seasonality pattern and a more residential use of the cave.

In general terms, therefore, it may be affirmed that the environmental data from Level XI to Level VI indicate that the site was more closely integrated in the environment, the occupation was more stable seasonally and there was a larger range of prey, occasionally including species not found in the immediate surroundings, and a wider and more varied plant catchment area. The pollen data indicates greater humidity and a certain expansion of trees in addition to pine. The provenance of raw materials also supports a changing strategy in the use of the environment in the central levels, in contrast with the lower occupations in Levels XIX to XVI. The raw materials were transported over distances of up to 30km, with connections to the coast, in lithologies involving fragmented *chaînes opératoires*, suggesting great mobility. From Level XIV onwards, the selection of raw material increased (quartzite cobbles from secondary aggregate deposits; Manzano *et al.*, 2005) and the cave acted as a central place. El Esquilleu and other sites like El Habario and El Arteu (Carrión, 2002) were then operating in a functionally combined way. However, from Level VIII, the procurement used new deposits and lithologies in the Deva valley to the south of site, and to the south-east and tributaries, and the site increasingly made use of local resources towards the end of the sequence.

In the upper levels, a detailed t phonomical study indicates an increase in carnivore activity from Level V onwards, especially in Levels IV and III, to such an extent that they may have become the main accumulating agent. The bone material in Level III displays

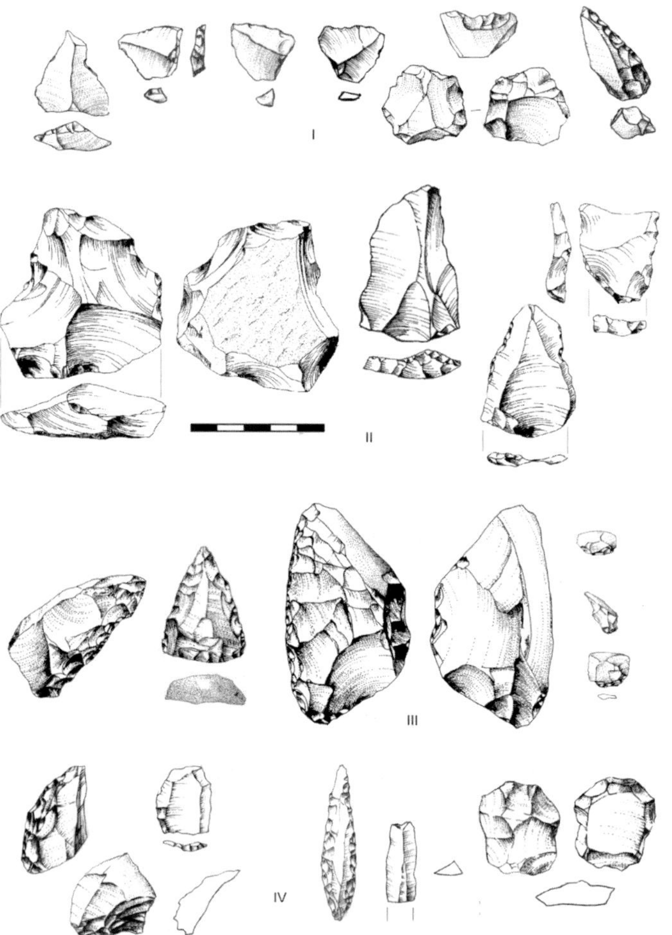

Figure 3. Lithic artefacts from El Esquilleu (I). Levels III to VI, (II) Levels VII to IX, (III) Levels XI to XV, and (IV) lower levels. (Drawn by E. Carrión).

very few anthropic marks (Yravedra and González Castanedo, 2014). The importance of carnivore action in the formation of the deposit has equally been seen at another important site in northern Spain (Level VII in Cueva de Amalda), and is defined both by distinctive marks and the differential presence of skulls and distal limb bones. This would directly explain the presence of many of the caprids in these levels (*Rupicapra rupicapra* and *Capra pyrenaica* in the case of El Esquilleu), in comparison with larger animals (such as equids and red deer) whose origin is thought to be necessarily anthropic (as in any case they would be smaller carnivores, like hyenas or foxes).

The detailed study of the material found in the hearths, which mostly appear in the litho-stratigraphic Unit C in El Esquilleu, is also significant. Hearths have been identified in Levels XXI, XXIII, XXV, XXVIII and XXIX. Charcoal from the hearth in Level XXI was dated by TL to 53,491 ± 5114 BP. This is the oldest date in the series, corresponding to the earliest occupation. The number of burnt bones and the degree of fragmentation gradually increases from Level XIV to the base of the sequence. The degree of combustion of the bones is high and quite unmistakeable evidence of intentional breakage is occasionally seen (Level XXI), indicating the bones were used as fuel in the hearths (Yravedra and Uzquiano, 2013; Uzquiano *et al.*, 2010). Although the pollen data reflects conditions of open vegetation with a predominance of grasses, the anthracological study showed that there would not have been an extreme scarcity of plant matter or of species for lighting the fires (for which Ericaceae and Fabaceae were used at El Esquilleu). Nor is the active selection of the more favourable bones for fuel seen at the site. This suggests that it was a hygienic habit, in which organic waste was thrown on to the hearths (Yravedra and Uzquiano, 2013).

Practically all the levels have yielded remains of microfauna, except the three lowest levels (XVIII to XXX) and Levels XVI, XXI and XXIII, affected by diagenesis and solution processes. Level VIII has provided the largest assemblage (Sesé in Baena *et al.*, 2005; Sesé in Uzquiano *et al.*, 2012). From the environmental viewpoint, none of the taxa in the sequence indicate extremely cold conditions. Between Levels XXVI and XIV, only indeterminate rodents are found (arvicolids). However, from Level XI onwards, a larger range of species (*Eliomys quercinus, Pliomyslenki, Microtus* cf. *lusitanicus, Microtus arvalis-agrestis,* etc.) reflects the more temperate conditions between 34.3 and 36.5 ky BP, as detected in pollen sequences at other sites in Cantabrian Spain, like Covalejos and Labeko Koba.

Finally the study of the archaeological material has provided an important sequential collection of materials, enabling a unique techno-economic study which surely corresponds to adaptive processes within the environment around the site. In this sense, a surprisingly close correlation is found between the dominant technical sequences, the investment in energy in the changing models of raw material procurement, and the climate fluctuations in the environment, especially in the last parts of the sequence (Baena *et al.*, 2012). In addition, the artefacts display great techno-typological development (Fig. 3), especially in the levels with a predominance of the Quina (Levels XX and XV-XIf), Levallois (Levels IXI and X-VIII) and discoid (Levels XXX-XXI and VI-III) techniques. Level XVII displays a clearly different nature with certain predominance of blades. In all cases, however, the dominant schemes are found together with secondary ones.

The stratigraphic sequence of the El Pendo cave (Escobedo de Camargo, Cantabria, Spain)

Ramón Montes Barquín*

1. Introduction

The El Pendo cave was discovered for science in 1878 by Marcelino Sanz de Sautuola (1880). Since then it has been the object of numerous archaeological actions, such as those performed by Juan Vilanova y Piera (at the end of the 19th century), J. Carballo and B. Larín (during the first decades of the 20th century) and Martínez Santa-Olalla (the excavations of 1953-1957), among many others. Three monographs mark the research into the cave up to the present day: that published by Carballo and Larín, in 1933, that of J. González Echegaray (1980) regarding the excavations carried out by Martínez Santaolalla, and that published by Montes and Sanguino (2001) about the actions performed between 1994 and 2000, during which the cave paintings were discovered. To these can be added numerous works on partial aspects and references in joint studies.

The international importance acquired by El Pendo is due, without doubt, to the International Field Archaeology Courses designed and delivered as a consequence of the excavations of 1953-1957 under the direction of the Spanish archaeologist Julio Martínez Santa-Olalla, courses that led to European and North American archaeologists developing an intense research activity. Leading figures from the world of prehistoric archaeology of the time, such as Cheynier and the husband and wife team of Leroi and Gourhan, personally directed the team on the excavation of the stratigraphic deposit located inside the cave, in which up to 18 different strata were documented and –in theory– covered the period from the onset of the Middle Palaeolithic to the Bronze Age. Unfortunately, these studies were not published at the time, and it was Joaquín González Echegaray who, in 1980, published a report on the excavations and a scientific interpretation of the site based on different studies, the geology section of which was written by K.W. Butzer (1980).

The interpretation, theoretically generous and at the same time very possibly frugal as far as practicality is concerned, put forward by K.W. Butzer (1980; 1981) regarding its stratigraphic column transformed El Pendo into a site of iconic proportions (on a par with the sequences of El Castillo and Cueva Morín) when it comes to establishing the general sequence of the Cantabrian (and Iberian Peninsular) Palaeolithic. However, in recent years Butzer's idyllic interpretation has been seriously questioned and doubt cast on the value of this sequence (Montes and Sanguino, dirs. 2001; Montes *et al.*, 2005). Moreover, these latest studies have redefined the series, which would,

* Unidad Técnica del Itinerario Cultural del Consejo de Europa Caminos de Arte Rupestre Prehistórico. RCDR C/San Martín del Pino, 16 – 3 bajo. 39011 Peñacastillo-Santander. rmontes@prehistour.eu.

in reality, consist of a total of 33 levels, with the base layer being subjected to a whole host of dating methods that not only show the existence of remains of up to 84 ky BP, but also the presence of severe chrono-cultural inversions that represent a clearly anomalous post-depositional accumulation when it comes to establishing a sequence of some interest (a fragment of spear –or rod– that is clearly post-Palaeolithic in appearance was found at the base of the sequence…).

2. From Classical Stratigraphic Benchmark To Inconsistent Erudite Reference.

The mouth of the El Pendo cave is situated in the village of Escobedo, which in turn forms part of the municipal district of Camargo (Cantabria, northern Spain). It lies within the karst massif of Alto del Peñajorao, one of the region's many minor coastal ranges. The landscape in the area is relatively gentle and rolling, typical, in other words, of the coastal fringe of northern Spain, being composed, as it is, of Mesozoic materials from the Lower Cretaceous and forming part of the so-called Urgonain Complex. The limestones that interest us here have been attributed to the Aptian Age. The karstification of the limestone has given rise to numerous single and compound sinkholes. As it happens, the El Pendo cave is situated in the north face of one of the many compound sinkholes to have formed in this system.

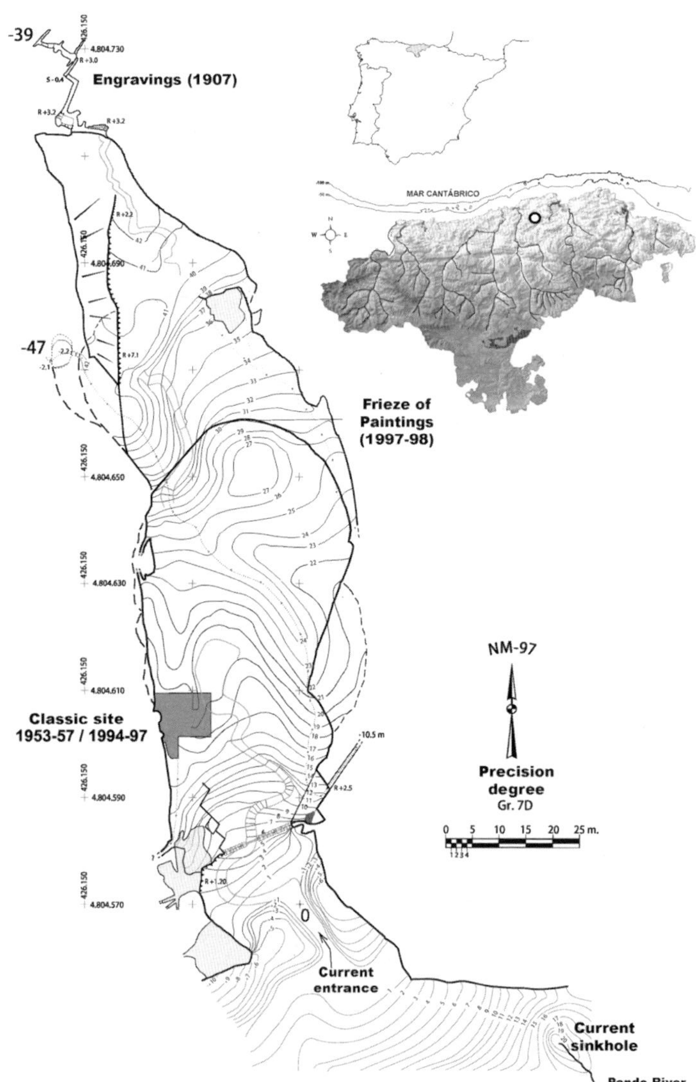

Figure 1. Location and footprint.

A precise topographic survey (carried out by Luque in 2001) places the floor of the cave's entrance at a height of 90 metres above sea level, while the height of the surface area of the place where the archaeological digs carried out between 1953 and 1957, and the more recent excavations of 1994 to 1997 were started, is 71 metres above sea level (representing a 19-metre fall over the barely 35 linear metres between the cave entrance and the dig site).

The "classical" sequence (namely the 18 levels identified by Butzer) is based on a series of cuts made in the left-hand side of the enormous rubble cone that starts a few metres in front of the fence erected at the back of the cavity's vestibule, extends over 80 metres beyond the aforementioned barrier (Fig. 1) and ends just before reaching the area in which the red paintings were discovered during the 1997 dig. González Echegaray (1980) and his collaborators interpret the sequence in accordance with the following series of human occupations: Bronze Age (level 0), Azilian (level I), the end of the Magdalenian (level II), "late Aurignacian" (levels III and IV), Gravettian (V and Va), "evolved Aurignacian" (VI), "Aurignacian I" (VII), "lower Perigordian (VIII), "archaic Aurignacian" (VIIIa and VIIIb), "denticulate Mousterian" (VIIId), Mousterian (IX and X), "denticulate Mousterian" (XI and XII), "typical Mousterian" (XIII and XIV), Mousterian (XV), "denticulate Mousterian" (XVI), "Unidentified and yet to be identified industry (XVII and XVIII)".

Regarding the characteristics and interpretation of this deposit over time, we can refer to Montes *et al* (2005). The most recent interpretation of this sedimentary deposit highlights the existence of a broad range of post-depositional processes, which are visible and may be documented in the cuts made during the excavations carried out, and concludes that, whatever the case may be, the area in which digs were undertaken in the 20th century and where the "classical sequence" was documented is nothing more

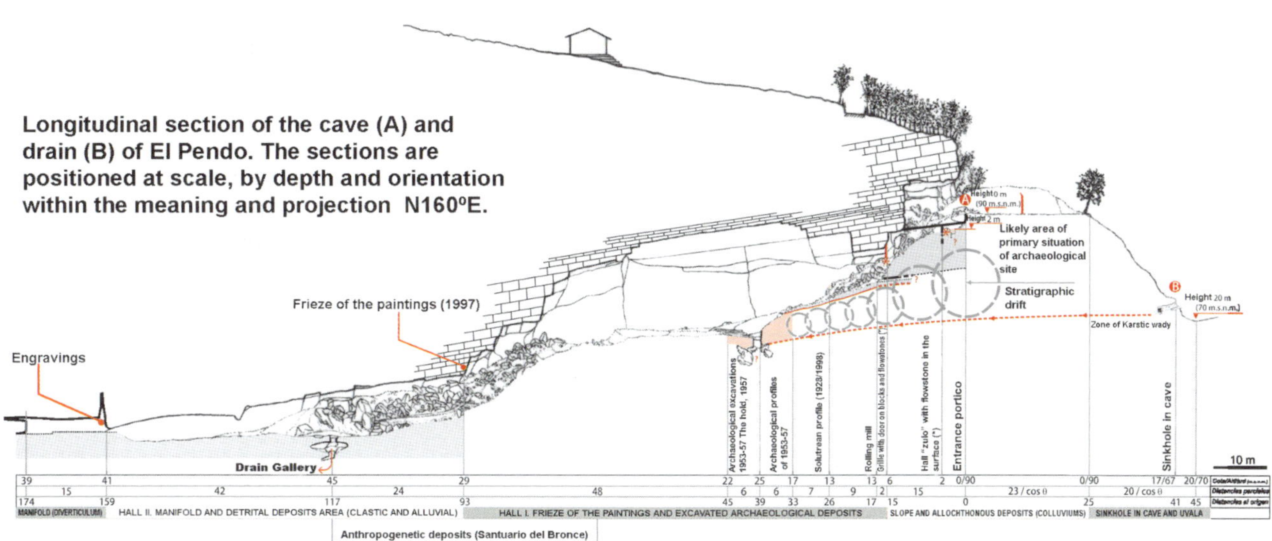

Figure 2. Cross-section of the cave.

than a monumental rubble cone brought in from an original accumulation area most likely situated in the Pleistocene vestibule of the grotto (Fig. 2). In other words, what we have here is a derived site with an infinite number of geo-archaeological problems that render it invalid as a reference for the establishment of a sequence of any chronostratigraphic value.

Few doubts currently remain regarding the fact that the general sedimentological dynamic of the site has, to a great extent, been conditioned by the action of the stream that evacuates the compound sinkhole, of which the cave system is a natural drain (currently, the grotto's active watercourse is documented as being at around 20 metres below the mouth used for accessing the site). In fact, the current floor of the sinkhole is above many of the levels that form the base section of the site.

The calcareous elements that make up the deposit would appear to have come from rock falls caused by thermoclastic processes, but these would not have occurred on the vertical plane of the sequence. The only blocks that could have fallen on this would have been those loosened from the roof of the cave by processes of chemical solution rather than cracking and fracturing. The mechanical detachment point would have to be brought back to the area close to the mouth of the cave. Finally, the alteration of the detrital elements would have been caused not only by post-sedimentary processes, but also by the length of time these elements were exposed to the weather and the climatic conditions that prevailed while they were being transported.

Three principal agents were involved in the formation of the sedimentary deposits of El Pendo cave: the slope of the accumulation cone that protrudes from the rock shelter at the mouth of the cave, the stream that drains the compound sinkhole and the topography of the cone. These three elements have acted together, with one or other of them being more influential at different times, to create the deposit we know today (Fig 2).

a) *The slope.* Starting in the vestibule of the cave is a large debris cone made up of big blocks that stretches into the cave's interior to form an accumulation cone. The distance from the point at which the slope begins in the vestibule of the cave to the area containing the main sequence column of the site is 34.6 metres, with the gradient being 44 degrees. Given the steepness of the slope, the action of gravitational flows is extremely feasible.

b) *The stream that drains the sinkhole* of El Pendo cave acts as a very effective transportation agent, capable of dislodging the detritic materials contained within it. Inside the cave it currently flows beneath the archaeo-sedimentary deposits, but its height at the point at which it disappears is a few metres above the levels of the shaft, and this was shown by the topographical survey. As was seen during the heavy rainstorm of 1983, under certain circumstances the stream is not capable of evacuating all the water that accumulates in the small basin of the sinkhole. This results in it overflowing and using the upper level of the cave, where the geoarchaeological deposit is situated, to drain off the water. The sedimentary record provides irrefutable evidence of other times when the water carried by the stream penetrated the cave.

c) Finally, *the topography of the cone* has determined the routes taken by the flows and the areas in which the materials have accumulated. The rocky escarpment of the entrance has undergone considerable chemical and mechanical alteration processes. The fallen materials have formed a rubble cone. These fallen blocks have changed the directions in which the waters flow, thereby causing lateral changes in the storm water runoff, which might explain the deposition of some materials in one area of the cave and not in others.

These three agents serve to develop the interpretation of the depositional sequence of the El Pendo cave and the sedimentary factors that have resulted in the stratigraphy that we can see today.

The study of the materials recovered during the digs carried out between 1994 and 1997 on the levels of the base of the sequence (in "the shaft"), especially of those obtained from levels 25 and 26 (which provided a significant number of finds), also provided data that showed them to be clearly inconsistent and, therefore, an unreliable chronocultural record. Apart from a few anecdotal, and at the same time tremendously symptomatic questions, such as the discovery of a fragment of spear point, or rod, in level 32, or of lithic finds that have been dubiously ascribed to the Mousterian technocomplex in many of the sequence base levels (theoretically dated as pertaining to the Middle Palaeolithic), the internal study of the lithic series, based on the operational sequence analysis methodology, supports the existence of notable anomalies. The palynological and paleontological data also revealed countless anomalies, in fact far too many to mention in detail here (Montes, Sanguino, dirs., 2001).

In addition to geological, paleoecological and archaeological studies, the most recent excavations included the use of absolute dating methods such as ESR, Thermoluminescence and Uranium/Thorium series, although Carbon 14 was not used, given the purported chronology of the lower sequence being worked on. The programme of absolute dating methods was, without doubt, essential for establishing the hypothesis that what we have here is a monumental archaeological misunderstanding. Its results clearly show the inconsistency of the El Pendo sequence that the geological data provided in such an overwhelming manner (Fig. 3).

3. The El Pendo site. A current assessment

Unfortunately, the sedimentary deposits of the El Pendo cave brought to light by the excavations of 1953-57 are the result of a major post-depositional that includes three elements: the slope of the rubble cone in question, the stream that drains the sinkhole –at the bottom of which lies the cave– and the ever-changing topography of the rubble cone in which the different cuts have been made. The entire sedimentary dynamic that has given rise to the depositional sequence can be explained by the action of these three agents.

In the geo-archaeological studies undertaken following the theory put forward by K.W. Butzer (Hoyos and Laville, 1982; Montes and Sanguino, 2001; Montes *et al.*, 2005), a great deal of evidence has been compiled and documented regarding a source of energy powerful enough to carry and transport huge quantities of materials and inflict a great deal of erosion while doing so. Episodes involving the total or partial flooding of the grotto have also been documented.

The analysis of the 33 levels which, in reality, go to make up the series, and the contacts between them, provides interesting information about the nature and origin of the sequence; this in one way can be interpreted as a geo-archaeological stratigraph that is valid as a benchmark series. Moreover, the different absolute dating methods used have confirmed the existence of significant anomalies as regards the existence of an authentic chronocultural sequence. The study of the archaeological and paleontological materials obtained from the base of the sequence have proved the limited internal cultural coherence of many of the levels.

The dynamic interpretation of the stratigraphic levels and the sedimentology shows that it is the slope movement phenomena that are mainly responsible for the formation of the deposit. The description of the processes, level by level, causes a loss of perspective, but if we examine the sequence as a whole, the El Pendo deposit is –in general terms– a macro sequence with positive grain selection. Successive infill processes have made the slope less steep, thereby reducing the potential energy, which explains the positive trend of the grain selection. The sedimentary differences are the result of the varying forces of the gravitational processes. Likewise, most of the contacts between the levels are erosive, which implies, on the one hand, an absence of the sequence's time record and, on the other, the incorporation of material, whether archaeological or not, from the underlying part of the level above. Several examples of these erosions occur.

In short, the stratigraphy of the El Pendo cave cannot be used as a reliable source of knowledge for the Upper Pleistocene in the area excavated in the 20th century. The mixtures of archaeological material from different levels means this site cannot be considered as a benchmark in the paleoclimatic and

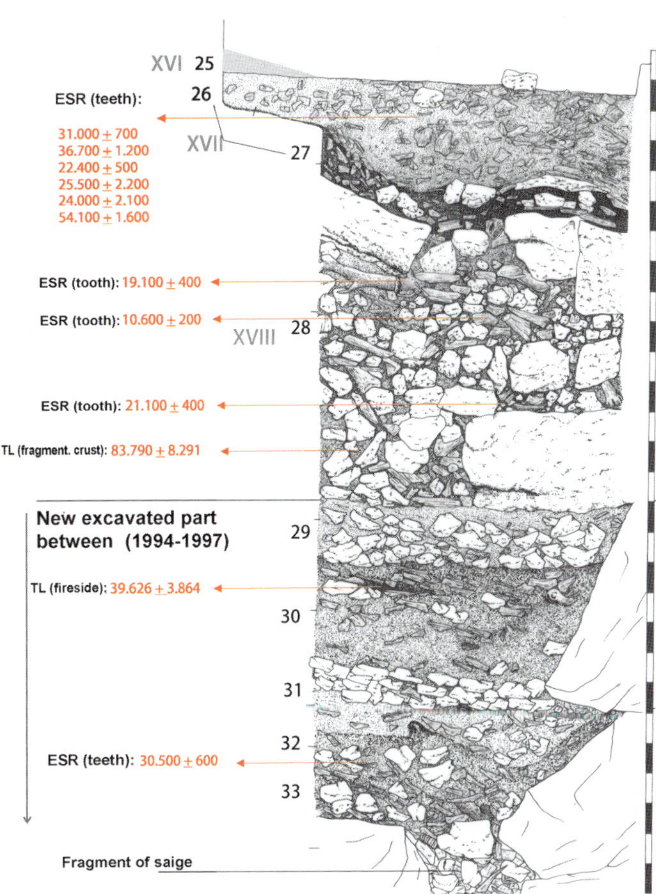

Figure 3. Stratigraphic cut and absolute dating methods.

chronocultural sequence of the Cantabrian Region despite the weight of its Historiography. Although different degrees of contamination exist in the stratigraphy, and not all the levels must be treated in the same way, the extremely large body of research to have used data from the El Pendo levels, in any section of its sequence, must be severely questioned, mainly because no guarantee exists of the synchronism of the elements contained by each level.

Despite everything, it has also been possible to document the presence of some areas in the exterior shelter (not inside the cave) that would appear not to have suffered major alterations and offer hope for future investigations (Montes and Sanguino, dir., 2001) which, under all circumstances, should be carried out away from the area we know as "the classic El Pendo site", namely, in the area that is still covered by the debris left by the collapse of the overhang of the shelter.

Lawrence Guy Straus*,** , Geoffrey A. Clark***

La Riera Cave (Posada de Llanes, Asturias)

The 1976-1979 excavation of La Riera Cave (Fig. 1), coming a decade after that of Cueva Morín in Cantabria by J. González and L.G. Freeman and done in association with M.R.González Morales, represented the continuation of a international, collaborative effort to modernize Paleolithic research in Cantabrian Spain. These Hispano-American, projects, like those that followed in El Juyo (by Freeman and González Echegaray) and Mirón (by Straus and González Morales) (both in Cantabria), were designed and conducted withexplicitly interdisciplinary,p aleoanthropological,problem-oriented foci that guided excavation methodologies, analyses and interpretations, fundamentally diverging from the solely culture-historical *raison d'être* of many traditional excavations in Spain and elsewhere.

Figure 1. La Riera in its surroundings.

The complete, monographic publication of the La Riera research (Straus and Clark 1986) has made this one of the most widely cited, extensively debated and frequently restudied excavations in the long history of Upper Paleolithic and Mesolithic research in Cantabrian Spain. A surprisingly small cave, La Riera has nonetheless played an unusually significant role in the development of scientific (and anthropological) archeology in the Iberian Peninsula, and the profession ultimately owes the importance of this site to its discovery, initial excavation and monographic publication to the Conde de la Vega del Sella, in whose footsteps the authors respectfully followed 60 years later.

La Riera Cave is located on the narrow coastal strip of eastern Asturias at 43°25'31" N x 4°52' W x 30 m above sea level. The low cave mouth faces west from the south slope of the low La Llera "*rasa*" ridge, which runs parallel to the shore west-east between the valley of the Bedón Riverand the town of Llanes. Between this ridge and the steep Sierra de Cuera range (maximum elevation: 1315 m at only 7 km from the shore), there is a depression that is drained via the Calabres stream that runs underground through a karstic system immediately adjacent to and slightly below La Riera. The Calabres resurges at the Niembro inlet 1.5 km north of La Riera and the open ocean coastline is at 1.75 km, while it would have been less than 10 km from the site during the Last Glacial Maximum. Other cave sites in this ridge include Cueto de la Mina (only 50 m from La Riera), Balmori, Tres Calabres, Bricia,etc., giving the area around the town of Posada de Llanes one of the densest concentrations of Paleolithic and Mesolithic sites (including minor cave art loci) in all of Iberia.

* Department of Anthropology, University of New Mexico, Albuquerque, NM 87131 USA
** Instituto Internacional de Investigaciones Prehistoricas de Cantabria, 39005 Santander, Spain
*** School of Human Evolution and Social Change, Arizona State University, Tempe,AZ 85287 USA

The mouth of La Riera was completely filled with archeological deposits capped by a rare intact Asturian shell midden (*"conchero"*) at the time of its discovery by Vega del Sella probably during his excavation of Cueto de la Mina in 1914-15. The Conde excavated the outer part of La Riera in 1917-18 and published a monograph on it and nearby Balmori in 1930.

He uncoverd a sequence of Solutrean, Magdalenian, Azilian and Asturian layers. His Magdalenian clearly included both Lower and Upper phase components, indicated respectively by the presence of nuecleiform endscrapers and quadrangular cross-section geometrically engraved antler points on the one hand and antler harpoons on the other. The Magdalenian horizon also included "archaic-looking" macrolithic artifacts some of which the Conde (improbably) attribued to an Acheulean deposit that had washed into the cave from the slope above the cave at this time –despite that fact that he cited the presence of other similar artifacts among the unquestioned Magdalenian assemblage. La Riera was a key site for the Conde's definition of a new Mesolithic "culture", the Asturian– also characterized by the presence of "crude" macrolithic implements (i.e., cobble picks), sometimes misinterpreted by later scholars as also being of Acheulean age (see discussion in Clark 1976, 1983). The talus slope in front of La Riera was tested and a concreted *conchero* remnant sampled by Clark in 1969 as part of his dissertation research on the Asturian (Clark 1976, 1983). This research yielded two radiocarbon dates that were among the first ever run for this techno-complex, clearly showing it to be post-Pleistocene and pre-Neolithic in age.

The 1970s excavation aimed to gather and analyze data to reconstruct the environments of the late Last Glacial and early Postglacial and to use artifactual and faunal evidence to elicit information about and to suggest explanations for variations in hunter-gatherer adaptations as their uses of the cave changed through time against the backdrop of changing conditions. Anthropological hypothesis testing was a keystone of the research and the agenda was explicitly processual, both directors having been students of L.G.Freeman at the University of Chicago and directly and indirectly influenced by the thinking of L.R.Binford and the "New Archeology" of the late 1960s-1970s. In this context, much reliance was placed on radiocarbon (as opposed to Bordesian cumulative percentage graphs of retouched stone tool frequencies) to date levels, while diagnostic artifacts such as Solutrean points, Magdalenian and Azilian harpoon types, certain Magdalenian *sagaie* forms, and Asturian picks were acknowledged generally to be temporally diagnostic. Consequently La Riera was the first Upper Paleolithic/Mesolithic site in Cantabria (and indeed in Iberia) for which a major investment was made to procure large numbers of 14C determinations–albeit with inevitable contradictions and inconsistencies, due to the number of different labs that did the dating, the use of both bone and charcoal, and the inability at the time to remove as many contaminants as can be done now, and the possibility of mixing by cryoturbation and prehistoric human activities such as hearth pit digging. Other dates on shells (corrected for marine reservoir effect) were later published by A.Craighead (1999), generally confirming the ages of the oldest Solurean, the Upper Magdalenian, the Azilian and the Asturian *conchero.*

The 7-10 m^2 excavation (of a remnant of intact deposits left by the Conde in the interior of the cave) was done by fine "dissection" of units thought to approximate more or less horizontal "living floors". This resulted in the definition of 36 levels and lenses in contrast to the Conde's 4 horizons, and in fact most of the Asturian (save small remnants) had earlier been removed, so that the new excavation mainly sampled the Solutrean, Magdalenian and (more locally) Azilian units, for a stratigraphic thickness of about 1.8 m (plus a 60 cm-deep *sondage* dug into the basal clay deposit (Levels 1-3). The resulting culture-stratigraphic sequence included a pre-Solutrean ("Aurignacian" or, more likely, undiagnostic "Gravettian") component (Levels 1-3, probably > 20 uncal. BP), several Solutrean layers with shouldered, concave base laurel and willow leaf points (Levels 4-17, 20-17 uncal. kya), Initial and Lower Magdalenian (Levels 18-19, 16.5-15.2 uncal. BP), Upper Magdalenian (Levels 20-24, 13-11.5 uncal. kya), Azilian (Levels 26-27, 11.5-10.5 uncal. kya), and Asturian (9.0-6.5 uncal. BP). Finds were piece-plotted in 3D and all sediments were screened in water through fine mesh (Fig. 2). The following analyses are published in the monograph: sedimentology (H. Laville), speleothems (R. Harmon), palynology (Arl. Leroi-Gourhan), macrobotanicals (K. Cushman), features and lithic technology (Straus and Clark), lithic raw materials (J. Ordaz, L. Suáraz and R. Esbert with Straus and Clark), osseous industry (M.González Morales), mammalian faunas (J. Altuna), fish (M. Menéndez de la Hoz with Strans and Clark), marine mollusks (J. Ortea), oxygen isotopes (M. Deith and N.J. Shackleton), human remains (M. D. Garralda). There are several background/objectives, synthesis, statistical, interpretive/conclusion chapters by Straus and Clark.

Some of the main conclusions of the research included:

There is no basis for subdividing the Solutrean into artifact-based phases and the late Solutrean intergraded with the early Magdalenian through a process of "desolultreanization", thus questioning the "reality" of these concepts as separate "cultures".

The role of the site changed notably through time (e.g, from transitory, specialized camp for hunting ibexon the nearby cliffs of the Sierra de Cuera, to major multi-functional residential hub with diversified technologies and features associated with many hunting and gathering activities, plus others such as parietal and portable art creation, to a dump for shells and other bulk garbage);

The process of subsistence intensification through both situational specialization and overall diversification, earlier thought to have begun in the Magdalenian, started here with the Solutrean and included the large-scale collection of shellfish, some fishing, and the increasingly intensive hunting of ibex and red deer, including the (ultimately

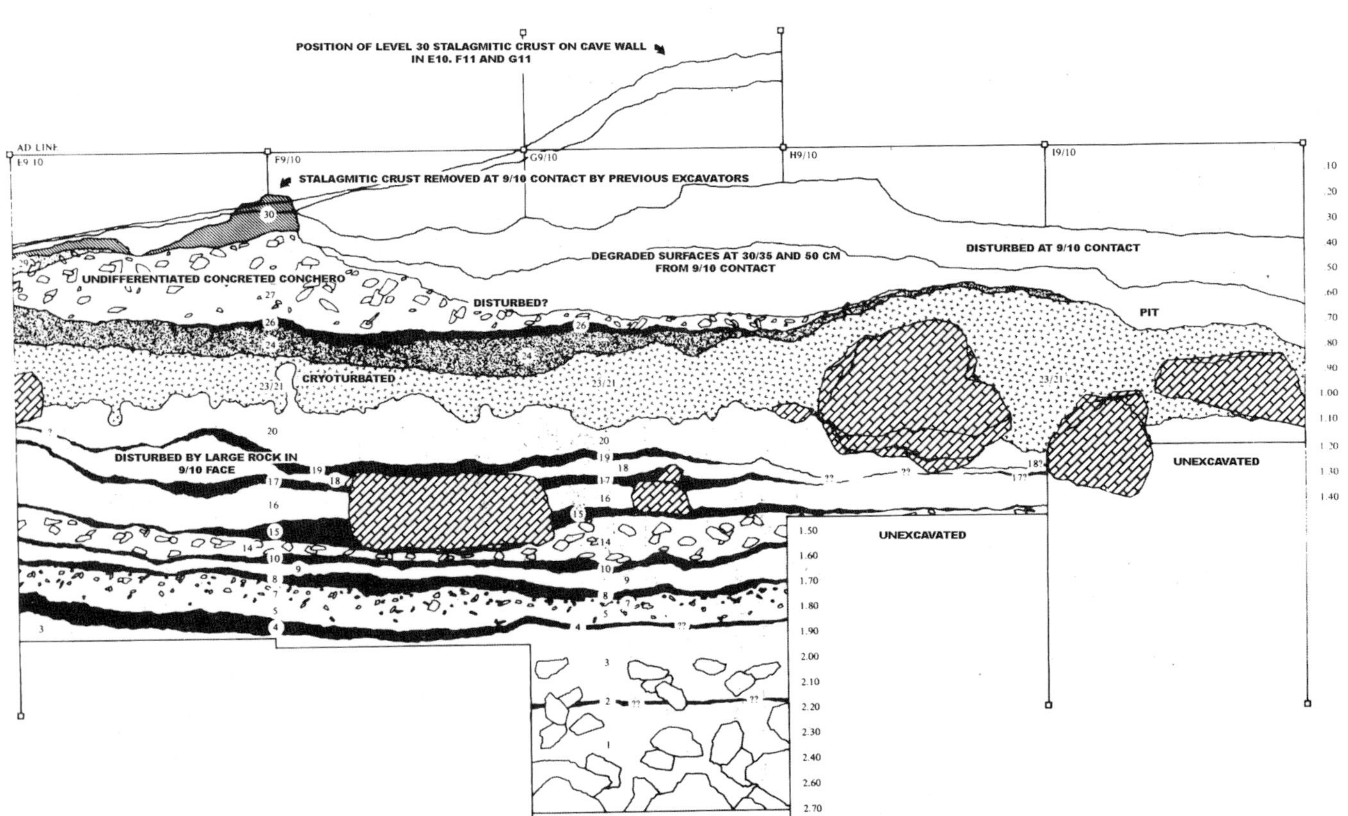

Figure 2. Stratigraphy of La Riera Cave, L.G. Strauss and G.A. Clark, (Eds.), Anthropological Research Papers, 36, Tempe, Arizona, 1986; G.A. Clark.

counter-productive) taking of ever larger numbers of young individuals, as well as the addition of woodland-adapted species (boar, roe deer) as Late Glacial and early Post-glacialconditions permitted.

There was no clear relationship between some of the changes in site use and major climatic shifts, but demographic pressure was seen as a key motor in driving subsistence change and presumably many of the main technological developments especially in the area of weaponry (e.g., Solutrean points, antler *sagaies* with backed bladelet inserts, antler harpoons, and the presumed invention of traps, nets and maybe weirs, as well as of new, more efficient hunting strategies and tactics).

In short, despite undoubted shortcomings, La Riera helped significantly to "change the nature of the conversation" about the meaning of inter-assemblage and even inter-period variability in Spain for a generation of researchers.

David Santamaría*, Elsa Duarte*, María González-Pumariega**, Lucía Martínez*, Paloma Suárez*, Javier Fernández de la Vega*, Gabriel Santos***, Tom Higham****, Rachel Wood*****, Marco de la Rasilla*

La Viña rock shelter (Asturias, Spain)

The site is located in La Manzaneda, 9 km south of Oviedo, in the middle basin of theNalón river. Facing S-SE, the rock shelter opens up inaVisean-Namurianlimestone measuring ~200m long and ~30m high and around 500m from the right bank of the river Nalón. The UTM30 ETRS89 coordinates of the site are X = 270725.79Y = 4799477.68 Z = 292 metres above sea level.

It is a large rock shelter with a surface area of approximately 225 m^2 and ~30 m long (Fig. 1), which preserves a wide stratigraphic and cultural sequence dated in the Middle and Upper Paleolithic (Fig. 2) and many parietal engravings that are partially covered by the stratigraphy (Fortea, 1994).

The shelter was discovered in 1978 by A. J. Gavelas (1981) and a little later the Prehistory Department of the University of Oviedo surveyed the rock shelter, confirming its archaeological and artistic interest. The excavations, directed by J. Fortea and integrated in the *Proyecto de Investigación Nalón medio* (Middle Nalón Research Project), started in 1980 and lasted through to 1996 (Fortea,1981, 1990, 1992, 1995, 1999 and 2001). The cultural episodes, the physical and biological environments, the rock engravings, the portable art and the mineral pigments are currently being studied.

The archaeological interventions focused on two sectors of the shelter, called central and western, coinciding with the areas where the parietal

* Área de Prehistoria. Departamento de Historia. Facultad de Filosofía y Letras. Universidad de Oviedo, c/ Teniente Alfonso Martínez s/n, 33011, Oviedo (España) santamariadavid@uniovi.es duarteelsa@uniovi.es lucia_satis@hotmail.com psuarez.ferruelo@gmail.com mrasilla@uniovi.es

** Consejería de Educación, Cultura y Deporte del Principado de Asturias, Apartado de correos nº 29, 33590 Ribadedeva. maria.glez-pumariegasolis@asturias.org

*** Departamento de Ingeniería Cartográfica y del Terreno, Facultad de Ciencias, Universidad de Salamanca, Pza. de la Merced s/n 37008 Salamanca (España) gsd@usal.es

**** Research Laboratory for Archaeology and the History of Art, University of Oxford, South Parks Road, Oxford OX1 3QY, United Kingdom thomas.higham@rlaha.ox.ac.uk

***** Research School of Earth Sciences, Australian National University, 1 Mills Road, Canberra 0200, Australia rachel.wood@anu.edu.au

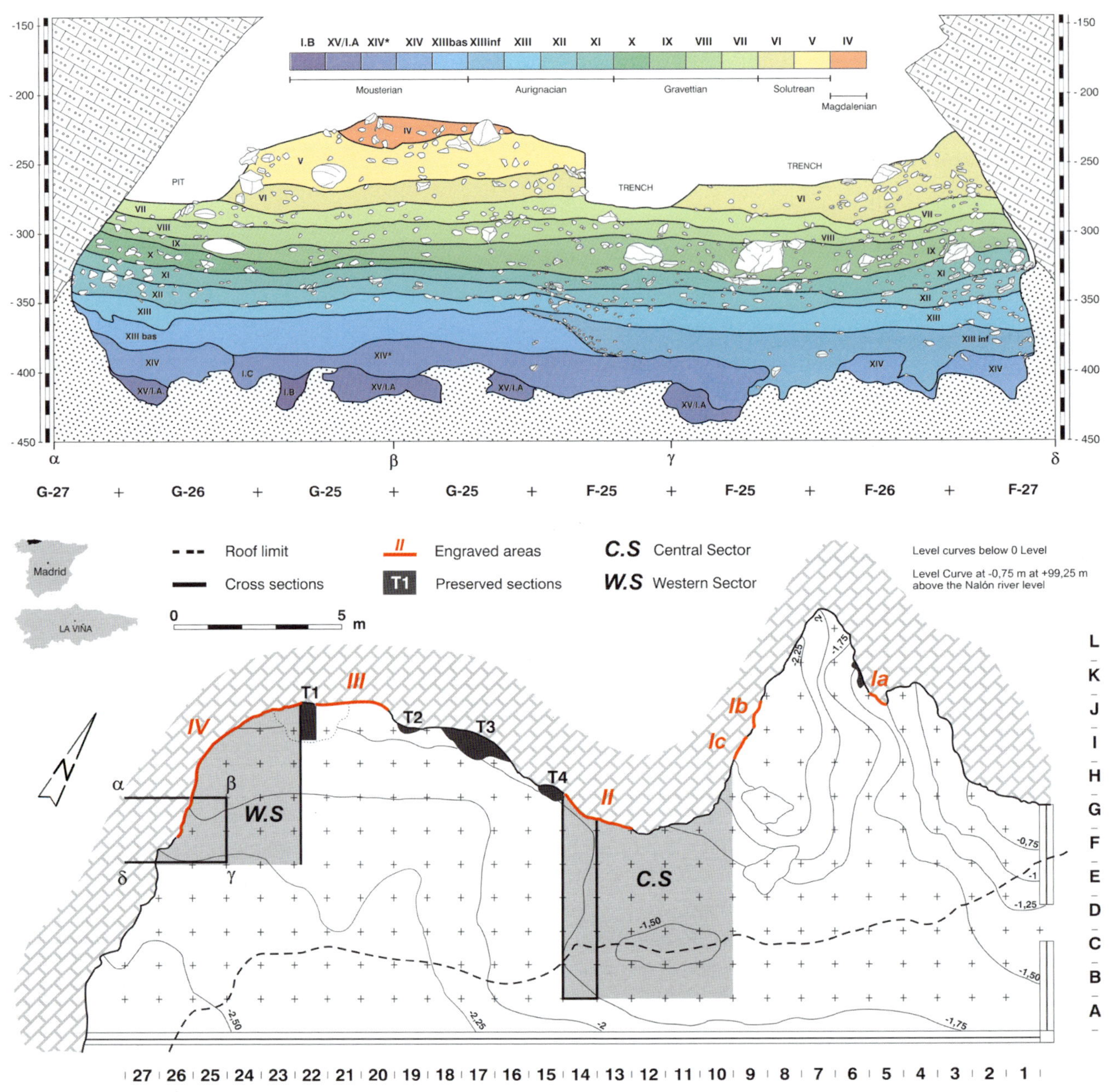

Figure 1. Floor plan and stratigraphic section of the western sector.

engravings are concentrated, and on two cores next to the wall of the shelter, which preserve remains of settlements posterior to level IV, which forms the current floor.

Central Sector. Located between lines10 and 14, its surface area is approximately 30 m². The whole area was excavated up to the topof level V and to the bedrock atline14. It presents a wide stratigraphic and cultural sequence. From top to bottom:

Strata I to III. Identified in Core 4, next to the north wall of the shelter (squareH-15).Attributed to the Tardiglacialand the Holocene (Fortea, 1990).

Stratum IV. Attributed to the Middle Magdalenian. Dated at 13,300 ± 150 (Ly-3317) and 13,360 ± 190 BP (Ly-3316) (González-Morales *et al.*, 1989; Fortea, 1990; Duarte, 2010). Contact with the underlying unit is erosional unconformity. It is very rich in lithic and bone industry and portable art.

Stratum V. Sub-divided into several levels in the area not covered by the overhang. Classified as Upper Solutrean with notched and concave base projectile points (Fortea, 1990).

Stratum VI. Sub-divided into three levels (VIa, VI band VIc). Level VI awas assigned to aphase previous to the UpperSolutrean –Middle Solutrean– and levels VI band Vic to Gravettian, the latter, VIc, with Noailles burins (Fortea, 1992).

Stratum VII. Collapse of the overhang; only outside the shelter. Sterile from an archaeological point of view.

Stratum VIII. Attributed to the Aurignacian (Fortea, 1995).

Stratum IX. The techno-typological analysis of the lithic industry puts it in the oldest Aurignacian (Suárez, 2013).

Stratum X. Classified as undetermined initial Upper Paleolithic (Suárez, 2013). Few lithic remains.

Stratum XI. Limestone bedrock. Archaeologically sterile.

Western sector. Located in lines 23 and 27, next to the western wall of the shelter. Its surface area is approximately ~17 m². It was open excavated up to the topof level V and to the bedrock at squares F-25 to F-27 and G-25 to G-27. It also presents a wide stratigraphic and cultural sequence partially dated by radiocarbon, conventional and AMS (Santamaría, 2012; Wood *et al.*, 2014, Tab. 1). From top to bottom:

Stratum I. Identified in Core 1. From the Holocene, it presents an industry with a low diagnostic typology.

Stratum II. Also identified in Core 1, without cultural assignment (Fortea, 1990).

Stratum III. Excavated in lines I and J and in Core 1. Provisionally classified as Upper Magdalenian (Fortea, 1990).

Stratum IV. Corresponds to stratum IV of the central sector. Attributed to the Middle Magdalenian (Fortea,1990, Duarte, 2010).

Stratum V. Similar to V in the central sector. Attributed to the Upper Solutrean (Fortea,1990).

Stratum VI. Middle Solutrean with *points á face plane* (unifacial flat retouch) and laurel-leaf points (Fortea,1990, Fernández de la Vega and Rasilla, 2012).

Stratum VII. End of the Gravettian with Gravette points, microgravettes points and backed bladelets (Fortea, 1992). Current research has detected a few Noailles burins, so this level best fits in to an advanced Gravettian phase.

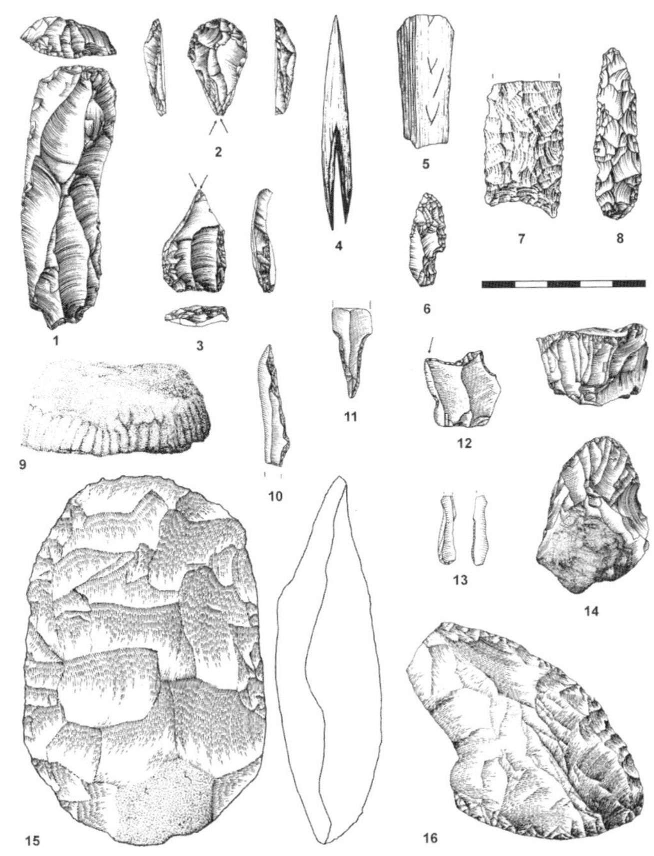

Figure 2. Selection of the archaeological materials. 1-5. Magdalenian, 6-8. Solutrean, 9-12. Gravettian, 13-14. Aurignacian, 15-16. Mousterian. Drawings: 1-9, 14 and 16 E. Duarte, 10-12 L. Martínez, 13 and 15 D. Santamaría.

Stratum VIII. Gravettian with Noailles burins, microgravette pointsand pedunculated points similar to the shape of the Font-Robert point (Fortea,1992).

Stratum IX.Gravettian with Noailles burins, microgravette points, many burins and a knapped calamite fossil deliberately modified (Fortea, 1992; Martínez and Rasilla, 2013). Dated at 24,680 ± 130 BP (OxA-21688).

Stratum X. Gravettian with Noailles burins (Fortea, 1992; Martínez and Rasilla 2013).

Stratum XI. Aurignacian with keeled and nosedendscrapers, busqué burins and Dufour subtype Roc-de-Combebladelets. This level belongs to the late Aurignacian (Martínez, 2010) and has been dated between 27,900 ± 280 (OxA-X-2290-19) and 30,600 ± 370 BP (OxA-21687).

Stratum XII. Aurignacian with keeled and nose-dendscrapers, busqué burins, Aurignacian blades and many Dufour subtype Roc-de-Combebladelets. Ascribed to the late Aurignacian (Santamaría, 2012). Two antler points of flat section were recovered from F-26. Dated at 31,500 ± 400 (OxA-21689) and 31,600 ± 400 BP (OxA-21678).

Stratum XIII.This level overlaps with level XIII basalin squaresG-25 to G-27 and XIII infin line F. Assigned to early Aurignacian (Santamaría, 2012), with many keeled endscrapers, some Aurignacian blades and Dufour subtype Dufour bladelets. A split base point ofelliptic section was recovered in square F-27.The middle and top section of this level have been dated between 30,650 ± 360 (OxA-21845) and 31,860 ± 680 BP (GifA-95463). The interfaces XIII-XIII basa land XIII-XIII infhave been dated at 35.800 ± 1000 (GifA-95550) and 36.500 ± 750 BP (Ly-6390), respectively.

Stratum XIII inf. First Aurignacian occupation of the site. This unit was partially deposited over strata XIII basal, XIV*, XIV and IA, reaching the bed rockin some areas of the sector.The contact between this unit and the underlying units (IA, XIV, XIV* and XIII basal) is erosional unconformity. Classified as polymorphic Proto-Aurignacian with microlaminarprismatic cores, keeledendscrapers, and Dufour subtype Dufour bladelets (Santamaría, 2012). Only the contact with the overlaying strata XIII (Ly-6390, *vid supra*) has been dated.

Stratum XIIIbasal. Last Mousterian level of the site. Only preserved in line G and sub-squares 3, 6 and 9 of F-25 and 1 of F-26. Towards the south the

Nº Inv	Lab Ref.	Level	Pret.	BP Date	cal BP Date	From	To
VI-1	Ly-3317	IV	C	13300±150	15986±223	16453	15515
VI-2	Ly-3316	IV	C	13360±190	16075±285	16664	15469
VI-45	OxA-21688	IX	UF	24680±130	28716±152	29016	28403
VI-35	OxAX-2290-19	XI	UF	27900±280	31800±376	32586	31190
VI-36	OxA-21686	XI	UF	**20820±130**	-	-	-
VI-39	OxA-21687	XI	UF	30600±370	34581±342	35285	33922
VI-83	OxA-19195	XI	ABA	30130±170	34180±176	34541	33848
VI-72	OxA-21678	XII	UF	31600±400	35521±415	36309	34734
VI-73	OxA-21689	XII	UF	31500±400	35431±409	36231	34671
VI-4	Ly15/OxA-4092	XIII	C	**19930±220**	-	-	-
VI-5	GifA-95463	XIII	C	31860±680	35976±828	37846	34545
VI-67	OxA-21705	XIII	UF	31160±230	35073±248	35582	34615
VI-68	OxA-21845	XIII	UF	30650±360	34621±339	35320	33967
VI-6	Ly-6390	XIII-XIII low	C	36500±750	41043±676	42341	39676
VI-7	GifA-95550	XIII-XIII bas	C	35800±1000	40412±961	42230	38560
VI-8	GifA-99230	XIII bas	C	48100±1600	50650±1820	54424	47305
VI-9	GifA-99231	XIII bas	C	**37700±590**	-	-	-
VI-10	GifA-95537	XIII bas	C	>39000	-	-	-
VI-85	OxA-19144	XIII bas	ABOx	>59300	-	-	-
VI-85	OxA-19196	XIII bas	ABA	>62000	-	-	-
VI-11	GifA-95551	XIV*	C	>39000	-	-	-

Table 1. La Viña dating. In bold, the anomalous dating values. Pre-treatment (Pret). UF: Ultrafiltration. ABA: acid/base/acid. ABOx: acid/base/oxidation. C: Conventional. The Columns age cal BP, From and Until they are calibrated with the OxCal programme based on the 2013 IntCal curve (Bronk Ramsey, 2009, Reimer *et al.*, 2013).

level forms a wedge changing to XIIIinf. The contact between these units is erosional unconformity. It is Mousterian, rich in lithic industry, with many different types of sidescrapers, some Mousterian and Tayac points, with quite a few denticulate tools, a good Chatelperron point and four bifaces with a transverse edge (Santamaría, 2012). Dated at >62,000 BP (OxA-19196).

Stratum XIV*. This unit is preserved in lines25 and 26 of the western sector. It does not overlap with XIV, but both outline a pseudo-horizontal linein section–with similar top and bottom heights. This unit is partially deposited on IB, IA and XIV in erosional unconformity. Mousterian with more sidescrapers than denticulate tools and some Mousterian points (Santamaría, 2012). Dated at >39,000 BP (GifA-95551).

Stratum XIV. This unit only appears in lines 26 and 27. Mousterian with more denticulate tools than sidescrapers (Santamaría, 2012).

Stratum XV/IA. Present in lines 25 and 27 of the western sector. Mousterian with more denticulate tools than sidescrapers (Santamaría, 2012).

Stratum IB. Preserved in sub-squares 7, 8 and 9 of G-25 and 1-2 of G-26.Mousterianwith few lithic tools and a similar proportion of sidescrapers and denticulate tools (Santamaría, 2012).

Stratum RA. Altered bedrock. Archaeologically sterile.

The erosional processes identified in the lower section of the western sector, from IB to XIII, have aided vertical and lateral displacement of archaeological materials between the Mousterian and Aurignacian levels. These contaminations have played a significant role in the techno-type configuration of the series studied, generating a local (i.e. culturally linked to the local Mousterian) and gradualtransition from Middle to Upper Palaeolithic, recognisable from at least IA but whose origin is strictly taphonomic or post-depositional. These contaminations are very evident in the Mousterian levels and less obvious or more elusive in the Aurignacian levels, clearer in XIII inf than in XIII, and undetectable in XII (Rasilla and Santamaría, 2011-12, Santamaría, 2012).

The parietal engravings are spread across five areas along the large rock wall, all of them exposed to direct sunlight (González-Pumariega,2013). Several engraving assemblages are currently unearthed e which were documented as the excavations advanced. These have been arranged into two graphic horizons that are successive over time (Fortea, 1994): the first and oldest, associated to the Aurignacian, consists of deeply engraved lines, arranged rhythmically into various groups and the second, Gravettian-Solutrean, consists of figurative (mainly deer) and non-figurative art.

Alvaro Arrizabalaga *
María-José Iriarte-Chiapuso * *

Labeko Koba (Arrasate, Gipuzkoa)

1. Introduction

The archaeological site of Labeko Koba is located on the southwestern edge of Gipuzkoa, along the upper course of the river Deba and in a highly anthropic environment (almost in the town of Arrasate). Like the whole of Gipuzkoa, it is located in a geographic area that is a mixture of Cantabrian, Pyrenean and Aquitaine environments. It was excavated between September 1987 and December 1988, under exceptional circumstances, which could be referred to as for salvage purposes rather than for emergency purposes. The work method was adapted to a certain extent to ensure complete removal of the site before the cavity was destroyed by the Arrasate ring road but

* Universidad del País Vasco (UPV-EHU). Tomás y Valiente s/n. 01006 Vitoria. alvaro.arrizabalaga@ehu.es
** Universidad del País Vasco IKERBASQUE (UPV-EHU). Tomás y Valiente s/n. 01006 Vitoria.

included the guarantees typical of this type of deposit. All of the sediment recovered while the excavation was sieved with water, allowing systematic recovery of almost one hundred percent of the assemblages at the site. In fact, the absolute dating values, the fauna spectrum identified (Fig. 1), the paleoenvironmental analyses and the lithic and bone techno-complexes allowed, in the case of Labeko Koba, the characteristics of the human settlements of the site to be defined quite well.In this respect, it could be said that Labeko Koba is one of the main sites corresponding to the initial Upper Palaeolithic excavated in the Cantabrian environment in recent decades. Sometime after the excavation, advances in the monograph (Arrizabalaga, 1989a, 1989b, 1991, 1992, 1993), a monograph with various analytical studies (Arrizabalaga and Altuna –eds.–, 2000) and a brief summary of its content (Arrizabalaga *et al.*, 2000, 2002, 2003) were published.

2. Circumstances and dating of the deposit

The post-depositional circumstances have significantly altered the archaeological remains. The majority of the surface of the site is not protected by the original overhang, so the remains deposited there have been heavily washed by the rain and exposed to the elements. This degradation particularly affects the bone (both fauna and industry) and pollen remains and significantly alters the lithic record. In fact, this circumstance imposes higher restrictions on reading and interpreting the site, much higher than those imposed by the fact that it is an excavation that has been carried out without interruption over a long period. To highlight a particularly symptomatic detail, the main stratigraphic differences of the site occur laterally (depending on whether they are located under the overhang or outside it) compared to the vertical ones, which are more attenuated (es-

Figure 1. Sample of the fauna recovered. Bone industry. Levels VII-IV (Proto aurignacian and Lower Aurignacian).

pecially in the area outside the protection of a small rock shelter).

Radiocarbon dating of the site levels has been difficult due to the taphonomic characteristics of the deposit, whose sediment has been heavily washed by rain. The dates initially available were much more recent than those estimated for the early Upper Palaeolithic of the region: Level lower IX (Châtelperronian) 34,215 + 1265 BP (Ua 3324); Level VII (Proto-Aurignacian) 31,455 + 915 BP (Ua 3321); Level V (Early Aurignacian) 30,615 + 820 BP (Ua 3322). An article was published recently (Wood et al., 2014) that presents nineteen new dates for the Labeko Koba sequence, which are much more consistent with one another and with the new regional framework for the early Upper Paleolithic after pre-treating the radiocarbon samples (in this case, ultrafiltration). In accordance with this, the dates that have not been calibrated that establish the Châtelperronianinthe site would be 38,100 ± 900 BP (OxA-22562) and 37,400 ± 800 BP (OxA-22560); the Proto-Aurignacianwould cover 35,250 ± 650 BP (OxA-21793) to 36,850 ± 800 BP (OxA-21766) and the three Early Aurignacian levels, from 35,100 ± 600 BP (OxA-21778) for level VI, from 34,750 ± 750 BP (OxA-21767) to 34,650 ± 600 BP (OxA-21779) for level V, and from 33,600 ± 500 BP (OxA-21768) to 33,550 ± 550 BP (OxA-21780) for level IV. Calibration, as demonstrated in the aforementioned article, shows additional aging of these results by between four and six millennia. Therefore, the probability curve of the oldest dating values clearly exceeds 44,000 cal BP and the most recent dating values, at least 37,000 cal BP. These dates are significantly more consistent with the new regional framework established for SW Europe (France, Italy, Germany). We must add that almost all of the new dating values have been made on bone retouch in order to minimise the risk of dating bone remains brought in by predators or scavengers that therefore do not have any direct relationship with human activity.

3. The stratigraphic sequence of Labeko Koba and its archaeological refit

We have evidence of initial visits to the cave by species that would alternate with one another throughout the occupation sequence (various carnivores and humans). Before the entrance that we excavated started to settle, at the bottom there was a pit cave that accessed the lower red karstic of Labeko Koba. In the top section of this pit cave and at the base of the debris cone that originated in it, in 1973 and 1987 three batches of material were recovered (the majority archaeozoological), named Sima (pit cave) (1973), Derrubio Superior (Upper Debris) (1987) and Derrubio Inferior (Lower Debris) (1987). The presence of a fragment of a Châtelperron points in the Sima materials, a section of a burin (in Derrubio Superior) that can be traced back to a burin in sub-level lower IX and the fauna associations in both batches indicate a precise chronological identity between these materials and the assemblage in level IX. It is therefore probable that these materials with no stratigraphy correspond to initial visits to Labeko Kobafrom hyena, cave bear and humans, using the pit cave as a den in the case of the carnivores.

Human presence, which is very occasional, is more difficult to explain but could be interpreted in relation to the procurement of biotic resources (meat, skin, antlers, bones, etc.) present in the pit cave through the activity of carnivores, the leading players in the taphocoenosis at the base of the deposit. The presence of many hyaena and bear remains in the pit cave can be explained by the difficulties of climbing back up the slope of the narrow pit cave of Labeko Koba, after throwing animals remains into it in order to eat them. Thus, some of these carnivores would die inside the lower cave. The prey includes horse and deer, species that would be relegated to more secondary positions in the levels in which humans were the principal authors of the fauna contributions.

The site sediment originated when the pit cave that fed the debris cone of the lower system became obstructed with silt. We assume that for some time the pit cave was still occasionally activated as a sink hole due to the similarity of the Palaeolithic materials of sub-level upper IX and the Derrubio Superior. However, there is not a single Dufour bladelet among the material (very overabundant in level VII), which leads us to deduce that the pit cave was definitively closed during this period, or in level VIII (sterile from an archaeological point of view). In addition, the sinkhole could have been completely obstructed before the deposition of level IX, later occasionally activating. However, what does seem to be true is that it only drags sedimentary materials included in sub-levels lower and upper IX and perhaps VIII too.

The early clogging phases of Labeko Koba, which represent almost half of the total archaeological thickness of the site, make up level IX (in some cases it reaches almost two metres thick). This level does not seem to have an anthropic origin and the majority of the material recovered from it consists of fauna remains, accumulated from hyena contributions (that have left part of their bone remains and bite marks in a large part of the series) and other carnivores (Arrizabalaga *et al.*, 2010; Villaluenga et al., 2012). As happened with the archaeological material from the lower gallery network, human presence seems to be limited to occasional visits to procure materials or meat. During these visits, they left some evidence of industry, of opportunistic character (barely knapped and the remains are crude supports or tools probably used as cutting instruments).

The arrangement of archaeological remains on the inside and some of the smaller sedimentary differences suggested, from its excavation, differentiating two sections or sub-levels in the core of level IX, separated by a horizon of fragments of a stalagmite slab. Sub-level lower IX has been attributed to a hunting base from the Châtelperronian, mainly due to the significance of three Châtelperronian points in a limited batch of lithic industry (Ríos-Garaizar 2008; Ríos-Garaizar et al., 2012). There is also a very deteriorated fragment of assegai. It is noteworthy that the scarce lithic industry from this sub-level shows typical Upper Palaeolithic characteristics, such as the high number of blades in the assemblage. Similarly the flint sources will be the same as those detected throughout the levels: Sierra de Urbasa and the Treviño syncline (to the south) and the coastal Flysch (to the north) make up the outcrops detected. These circumstances will be common to the entire series of Labeko Koba.

The environmental data on sub-level lower IX comes from several pollen and sediment samples and the ecology of the animal species taken to the site by carnivores. A certain convergence is observed in these studies, which indicate dating in the Würm-Les Cottés interstadial for this wet and relatively mild stage with the start of the stratigraphic sequence. The sedimentology study detects a high level of humidity, at the same time as an environment in which it is cold but not very cold. The pollen analyses, carried out on samples from outside the central column, showed the appearance of mesothermophile taxon (such as *Castanea*). The macro-mammals include a dominant presence (65%) of deer and a lower frequency of hyena than in the upper debris, in a spectrum that indicated a more moderate climate than the upper part of the level. Apart from a few reindeer remains, there are no indicators of a cold climate. As occurs in the rest of the stratigraphic sequence, the micro-mammals return a mild reading for the level and the avifauna does not provide any significant information in this respect.

The upper part of level IX occupies the majority of the unit and has almost no industry remains (just five flint flakes and another five possible hammer stones on Irish elk antler). From a cultural point of view, it is difficult to label this sub-level, which is sandwiched between the Châtelperronian (lower IX) and the Proto-Aurignacian (VII), separating them more clearly than the irregular level VIII. However, its environmental characteristics allow us to certify that we have entered the Pleniglacial– Würm III. The sedimentology, palynology and archaeozoology studies indicate intense cold. The sedimentology study also detects a humid environment, with little energy, which decreases at the top of the level. The steppe vegetation and the recrudescence of the climate are noticeable in the pollen record with the domination of *Poaceae* throughout the level and by the constant presence of *Ephedra*. Among the ungulates deer dominates and mammoth and woolly rhinoceros emerge strongly in the stratified sequence.

Level VIII, which is located in a dispersed fashion in different gentils throughout the cave, is characterised precisely for being archaeologically sterile. Level VII frequently rests directly on the top of level IX, without continuity. Due to this discontinuity, it has not been identified in the samples of the columns and neither do we have any paleoenvironmental information about it.

Level VII indicates a clear inflection compared to the underlying level. For the first time in the Labeko Koba sequence, the human being takes on a key role, rivalling the carnivores (mainly bears in this level), to occupy the small space available. Although we cannot identify its rhythm from the record we have, it seems to have occurred in an alternation between human occupations with certain stability over time and the use of the cave by bears as a den. In fact, the lithic industry seems to indicate that this level is the only level in Labeko Koba that presents a fairly complete and closed assemblage, which includes all of the segments of the lithic operating processes.

In particular, given the composition of the lithic industry (Fig. 2), this level clearly adheres to the Proto-Aurignacian, more specifically from the variety of the abundant retouch and semi-abrupt bladelets (often Dufour type). In general, the flint sources

Figure 2. Sample of the lithic industry.

are the same (as in the rest of the sequence) but an advance in provisioning from the outcrops to the south is noticeable in the levels of stable occupation, compared to a higher proportion of northern Flysch flint, common in more sporadic presences. However, the proximity of the outcrops and the

Figure 3. Stone with engraved lines. Level VII.

awareness of them do not seem to indicate full access, as the use of the raw material throughout the sequence is such that it allows a serious shortage of lithic resources to be detected.

Various remains have been recovered from level VII (a stone with engraved lines (Fig. 3), a small ball of amber and various decorative pieces on bone) which indicate that, at least from the Proto-Aurignacian, these groups had a symbolic universe similar to that observed throughout the Upper Palaeolithic. As a result of the irregular presence of the remains in the Cantabrian Upper Palaeolithic, we might be encountering the first evidence of this kind described for the northern Iberian Peninsula.

From an environmental point of view, the reading of level VII is not unambiguous in the light of the different analyses. The sedimentology study records significant intensification of cold. In the pollen record, the base of the level shows that the cold observed in sub-level upper IX remains stable or increases, at the same time as the level of humidity falls. However, the top section of level VII shows a significant improvement, presenting a milder and wetter landscape, from which steppe taxon disappear. Finally, the archaeozoology study detects a significant change in the proportion of ungulates, probably related to the generalisation of the human contribution. In terms of the environment, although different sections have not been distinguished, dominance of woolly rhinoceros remains have been observed at the bottom of the level, in the same way as fawn and boar are mainly located in the upper area, which could help confirm the hypothesis presented by the palynology study.

In Labeko Koba, levels VII and V are separated by level VI, which is very poor; culturally it seems to lean more towards level V than level VII due to its industrial composition. Although the lithic industry is not significant, in this level there is a bone object which has been identified as a split-based assegai, an item that delimits the occupation as an initial presence of Early Aurignacian people. A large number of stones and small blocks characterise level VI; they are often cemented by a reactivation of the cavity that dissolved and precipitated some of the carbonates contained in the stones. It is suggestive to see the result of the last phase of significant collapse of the overhang of the cave in this brecciated mass.

Sedimentology and palynology studies certify that humidity remained and increased although lower uniformity is recorded in the characterisation of the dominant temperature during the deposit of this unit. While the sedimentology study shows remission of cold in level VI, the pollen record seems to prove a worsening of the climate, with a fully stadial landscape. The archaeozoology study does not provide much information on the environment, but it does show regression in carnivore contributions (which are now small knapped objects) across the level in correlation with the higher importance of human hunting. In this respect, a large increase in the presence of bison (followed by deer and horse) sets the tone of the rest of the sequence, which stands out for several recurring characteristics. These include specialised hunting of bison, which is demonstrated by removing the carnivore remains from the assemblage, the almost non-existence of rock-dwelling animals among the species hunted or the identification of an area that was probably the preferred hunting ground on the plain of the river Aramaio, at the other end of which the Lezetxiki site is located.

The chronology of level V is also accurate, given the existence of an almost complete split-based assegai with a flattened section that could correspond to remains of this bone type. The lithic techno-complexes point in the same direction, as they present modal and group levels within the parameters observed for the Early Aurignacian in other levels in the Cantabrian (Morín cave or Polvorín cave, among others).

There is still a certain amount of paleoenvironmental information available for level V, even though pollen data comes from isolated samples. The sedimentology study records again a situation of intense cold, as do the aforementioned pollen samples, which is also relevant to the decrease in the ambient humidity. The use of bones as fuel is identified in both this record and in the upper level (level IV), after being carefully fragmented (Yravedra *et al.*, 2005). It could be concluded that, in an environment with little forest cover, this by-product would be used as fuel, after recovering the marrow that was easier to make use of. The mammoth appears again in the archaeozoological record, and this also demonstrates the climate was worsening. Regarding the economic variables, this level allows us to observe even greater specialisation in hunting bison, followed by horses, deer and other ungulates.

Level IV of Labeko Koba is more difficult to date. We have just one absolute dating. Our main argument for ascribing level IV is its close similarity to level V, in every way (environment, sediment, industry, activity). If we look at the lithic record, we can see that the majority of the tests used in the structural dynamics of the lithic industry tend to associate both levels. The lithic structure that returns the best cultural diagnosis (the modal) shows a significant similarity between the two models, even though the semi-abrupt retouch, significantly represented in level V, almost disappears from level IV. It is also possible to reference this Early Aurignacian level with others (units of Gatzarria or Morín cave). The bone industry does not provide definitive data in terms of cultural chronology, we consider level IV a more advanced phase of the Early Aurignacian. At this point, we must stress that we are not referring to an Evolved Aurignacian or évolué, in its French nomenclature, which has a series of characteristics that clearly distinguish it from the Early Aurignacian. Proximity to the model of level V seems to dominate in the assemblage of level IV.

For level IV the sedimentology study detects a progressive remission of cold. We do not have any other significant data on the climate at the time of the deposition of the level, or after, as the pollen record is highly disturbed, and the ungulate remains maintain similar conditions to those in level V, in which bison dominate, followed by horse and deer.

The last occupations of the site are detected in level III, with the cave almost clogged up. There are no dating values and almost no materials that could be dated in this level. Furthermore, the industries located in it are particularly poor. For these reasons the only object that can be used to obtain a possible dating for the level comes from the continuity between levels III and IV, both in terms of stratigraphy and other circumstances (the fauna recovered is very similar, very little coherent lithic industry and the sedimentology study indicates that tempering that started in level IV continues). Judging by this and considering that a sedimentological hiatus does not seem to occur between the start of the stratification and the clogging of the cavity, we could conclude that in terms of chronology, level III is not far from the Upper Aurignacian to which we ascribe levels V and IV.

Alvaro Arrizabalaga *

Lezetxiki (Arrasate, Gipuzkoa)

1. History of research

Although the Cave of Lezetxiki had been known since 1927, its excavation only began in 1956 after J.M. de Barandiarán's return from exile. Between 1956 and 1968, alone or in the company of several collaborators (Fernández Medrano, Boucher and Altuna, among others), Barandiarán excavated a surface area of over 100 square metres, to a depth of over nine metres in some places. The sequence included Middle and Upper Palaeolithic levels, and several fossil human remains, not precisely located, owing to the poor conservation of the sequence and the difficulties in interpreting the deposit. The excavation reports were published annually, and specialised studies of the anthropological remains (Basabe), fauna (Altuna and Chaline) and the sedimentological sequence (Kornprobst and Rat) were made known. In order to clarify certain aspects not solved by these publications, since 1996 a new team has been excavating a small sector of the deposit, under the supervision of A. Arrizabalaga and M.J. Iriarte-Chiapusso. This is in an area of about 25 square metres, next to Barandiarán's southern section, as well as a four square-metre trench on one side, called Lezetxiki II.

2. Chrono-stratigraphic sequence

Although the modern fieldwork has maintained the layout of the grid of the original excavations, the levels have been numbered differently (using letters, rather than Roman numerals) to avoid confusions. From the bottom to top, the levels dated before the Eemian are Barandiarán's Units VII and VIII, and Levels M, N, O, P and R in Arrizabalaga's sequence. Above these, Barandiarán's Mousterian levels are Units IIIb, IVa, IVc, Va and VI, which correspond to the new units F, G, I and J (Fig. 1) and L, respectively. Finally, the Aurignacian (IIIa or E), Solutrean (D) and Magdalenian (Ia or B) levels complete the sequence. The intricate topography of the cave and the enormous surface excavated explain the discrepancies between the two series, nearly all of which are concentrated in the basal part of the deposit, where Barandiarán only excavated a small side area, whereas the modern excavations have succeeded in discovering a new and older sequence.

For the same reasons, the deposit at Lezetxiki includes intensely leached outer sediments, well-protected areas inside the cave and intermediate transition or rock-shelter areas. The lateral changes in the conditions of the sedimentary fill and the state of conservation of the archaeological materials are consequently very large. This has equally caused great difficulties for the precise dating of the levels (Falguères *et al.*, 2005/2006), despite the numerous attempts with different methods (such as radiocarbon, U/Th, ESR, AAR). According to geochronological and biostratigraphic crite-

* Universidad del País Vasco (UPV-EHU). Tomás y Valiente s/n. 01006 Vitoria. alvaro.arrizabalaga@ehu.es

Figure 1: Mandible fragment of a Barbary macaque, from Level J in Lezetxiki II. Reference: Castaños *et al.*, 2011.

ria explained in several publications, the base of Lezetxiki II has been attributed to Isotope Stage 6, while Level R in Lezetxiki, the deepest level currently being excavated probably corresponds to Isotope Stage 7.

3. Interpretation of the deposit and significant aspects of the new fieldwork

The most recent fieldwork has obtained interesting information enabling a reappraisal of the deposit at Lezetxiki. Some additional research is required, and it is, therefore, likely that in the coming years a series of results of studies and dates will achieve an even better understanding of the site. Consequently, many of the observations made below should be considered provisional and pending verification in an exhaustive report.

3.1. Stratigraphic conflicts

This refers to monitoring the stratigraphic circumstances in the excavation opened on the southern side of Barandiarán's excavation. A surface area of about 20 m^2 has been opened (continuous variations in the surface area are caused by changes with depth), in the bands 18, 20, 22 and 24, by projecting the grid system of the original excavation. A square in what would be Band E has been started, which will leave a North-South section, not obtained in the classic excavation as the working strategy meant the tunnel was excavated from wall to wall.

Our experience has shown that the stratigraphy of the deposit is quite clear and continuous. It is clear in the sense that the interfaces between the levels, which are nearly always thick or very thick, are quite visible and can be identified during the fieldwork. Alternating levels with and without artefacts have been documented, and these helped Barandiarán to follow uniform criteria for the assignation of levels in most of the excavation. It is continuous from the sedimentary point of view, as the sedimentary characterisation is very homogeneous (thick layers of very compact clay, occasionally with calcareous lumps of different sizes) between the new Levels A and L (as far as Barandiarán's VI, inclusive); and no erosional contacts are seen, breaking this uniformity, except perhaps between Barandiarán's Levels IIIa and IIIb. Phenomena of stratigraphic alteration (bio– and cryoturbation) are only seen in a few places. The most common of these alterations is mechanical deformation caused by the plasticity of the clay when saturated in water.

There has been speculation about the dip of the original levels at Lezetxiki. Our observations have confirmed that they dip significantly towards the south on the north-south axis, resulting in a difference in depth of 3m over the 15m of this axis in Barandiarán's excavation. However, in our north-south section in Band E, this dip has disappeared, and the levels are nearly horizontal. It seems that this phenomenon is connected with the opening in the tunnel along a breach on its eastern side in Band 18 (the site was accessed along this breach during the excavation) on the very limit of the area currently being excavated. This breach may have caused mechanical tension on the clayey levels in Lezetxiki, causing the fall of sediment and archaeological materials towards the ravine on the east of the cave. Beyond this point, the lower parts of the tunnel would not have been affected so much by this tension and maintained an approximately horizontal position. Unfortunately, this hypothesis is difficult to verify as the sedimentary record in the affected parts of the tunnel are missing. However, the presence of particular archaeological objects in different levels in the deposit, such as objects incorrectly attributed to the osseous assemblage, and in reality the result of a post-depositional alteration known as charriage à sec, means that it should be taken seriously.

In contrast, precise information is available about the dip of the levels in the east-west axis. In the area we have been able to study, the dip has been seen to be extremely complicated, and it is impossible to describe a simple pattern for it. Some levels are sub-horizontal, whereas other dip slightly, or not so slightly, towards the east or the west. In contrast with what used to be thought, the latter dip in the most frequent. Undoubtedly, the effect of the rock-shelter that originated the rock wall makes the sediments accumulate in larger amounts against it, and then slope off towards the wall in the west, on an incline. It is very likely that this effect occurred in other parts of the tunnel (in the bands with even numbers) where the disappearance of the overhang led to the characteristic sedimentation of a rock-shelter and not of a cave. Similarly, although Lezetxiki is obviously a karst cave, its post-depositional development has been very similar to an open-air site as most of the sediment is located outside the rock overhanging the tunnel or the rock wall. For these reasons, three separate records should be considered when interpreting the fill and the evolution of the deposit: as a cave, as a rock-shelter and as an open-air site.

These circumstances have caused us to correct our previous assessment of the industrial attributions of the different levels at Lezetxiki. Apart from the central bands in the site, which were excavated first of all and in which the absence of archaeological materials in the surface layer presumably caused a shift in the numbering of the levels in comparison with the bands to the north and south, we have opted to fully respect the attributions of the archaeological materials to the levels established by the excavator during the fieldwork. Precisely because of the lack of fixed parameters in the dip of the levels, a drawing of the stratigraphic assignation of the materials may have led to an error in the definition of the industrial assemblages.

Some remarks should also be made about industrial characterisation in the sequence at Lezetxiki, particularly in the transition sub-levels between the Middle and Upper Palaeolithic. Without wishing to prejudge the chronology that will finally be assigned to sub-levels IVc, IVa and IIIa, the presence of a heterogeneous lithic assemblage, with components of ambivalent *chaînes opératoires* has always struck the attention. This duality in the appearance of the industry has variously been attributed to the archaism of EUP assemblages in northern Spain, cultural and technological mixture of models, the result of severe post-depositional alteration and careless excavation techniques, etc.

Our observations cast doubts on the latter suggestion, as we have verified the main anomalous situations detected by Barandiarán's excavation and assessed the possibility of post-depositional disturbance. Thus, as occurred in squares distant from Level IVc in Barandiarán's excavations, where blade industries were found together with Levallois points, we have located very similar tools to those that suggested the putative stratigraphic mixing. Equally, when the large number of raw materials other than flint had been stressed, we have been able to increase the proportion of these even more. This is in stratigraphic series often over a metre thick, and where it is not easy to find a simple explanation. In short, in our opinion, industrial characterisation at Lezetxiki requires cultural and technological explanations and the suspicion of mixing between levels over a metre in depth away from each other, separated by industrially barren layers, should not be raised over and over again (depending on the results when they are dated). In this respect, Levels III and IV at Lezetxiki require a new approach to their study, as clichés about the "typical" characterisation of the Mousterian and Aurignacian contribute very little at this and other sites.

3.2. *Geochronology*

The dates currently available for Lezetxiki are, for several reasons, not determinant although they mark some interesting trends in that they suggest the levels are older than was initially thought (Falguères *et al.*, 2006). One of the main objectives of the modern research at Lezetxiki is to provide the sequence with a geochronological framework allowing the levels to be interpreted in a wider regional context. During the recent fieldwork, nine charcoal and bones samples have been taken for radiocarbon dating. The four samples analysed (conventional and mass accelerator C14) have given unsatisfactory results, as the dates are much younger than would correspond to their archaeological context, and therefore they are thought to be aberrant. The paper cited above gives the principal data currently available. However, there are also some new results, involving the use of the racemisation technique and based on bio-stratigraphic criteria, described at length in the latest publications.

As described on other occasions and explained below, in the absence of sedimentary or archaeological materials to provide a context for the famous Lezetxiki humerus (Fig. 2), the true context of the human fossils found in the old excavation will hopefully be located in Lezetxiki II.

As has been pointed out, there is a certain lack of definition in the position of the three fossil human remains found in the classic excavations at Lezetxiki. Whereas the Neanderthal teeth found between Levels III and IV can easily be positioned with their coordinates among all the points in the archaeological levels, and additionally offer no difficulties in their phyletic attribution, this is not possible in the case of the humerus. We know exactly where it was found, but there still are problems in three different lines of interpretation:

1. The phyletic attribution of the humerus is confusing, as in the scientific literature it has been compared both with Neanderthal remains and pre-Neanderthal human types, such as Homo heidelbergensis (Fig. 2).
2. The humerus was found in a volume of sediment with no lithic or osseous remains. Once that sediment had been excavated, it became impossible to date any elements in that context or obtain the palaeo-environmental information. In addition, as the bone is highly mineralised, it cannot be dated directly, and this would in any case be very debatable from the methodological point of view.

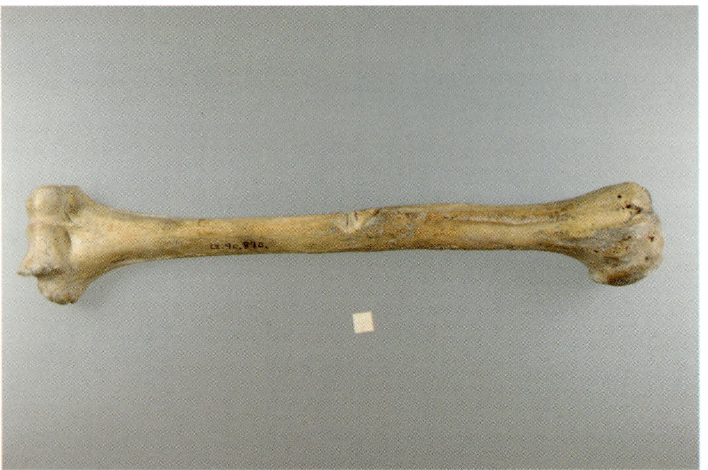

Figure 2. Human humerus from Level VIII in Cueva de Lezetxiki (J.M. Barandiarán's excavation).

3. Since 1998, a small cave we have called Lezetxiki II has been excavated and this is heading towards Cueva de Leibar. This small cave was explored during the original excavations at Lezetxiki, precisely when the human humerus was found in Cueva de Leibar, but because the position of the sieve had made access more difficult, it was not investigated further. We have always suspected that this cave might represent the actual context of the Lezetxiki humerus.

As a consequence of all this, we have slowly removed the pile of sediment sieved by the previous excavation to locate the original floor of the cave and open trench, as in some places the sediment had filled the cave to the roof. Each year we have advanced between half a metre and one metre. The 2012 fieldwork completed the excavation of Squares J15, K15, L15 and M15, in a trench one metre wide, four metres long and 320cm deep. In this, we have identified a sequence consisting of: Chalcolithic, barren, Early Upper Palaeolithic, layer of calcite, barren, possible Mousterian, and levels attributed to the MIS5 and MIS6. In 2004, a detailed survey of this cave fixed the stratigraphic relationship between Lezetxiki II and the central passage in Lezetxiki and Cueva de Leibar. As well as a small passage, now inaccessible, directly connecting the central passage in Lezetxiki with Lezetxiki II, it seems clear that there is a direct connection between Lezetxiki II and Leibar. If we continue the trench another metre (Square I15) towards the west and descend 50cm from the current floor level, we should reach the roof of Leibar Cave, in the approximate area in which the Lezetxiki humerus was found. The connection between the two caves, therefore, seems to be granted, and their stratigraphic link is very likely. It remains to be seen whether, in these circumstances, more fossil human remains have been conserved in Lezetxiki II. In any case, the new stratigraphy in Lezetxiki II, parallel to the oldest occupations in the main cave, is of the greatest interest in providing a context and geochronological background for those occupations.

3.3. *Neanderthal symbolic behaviour*

Even when it was not known whether opening a small excavation area would obtain any significant archaeological materials to modify the overall understanding of Lezetxiki, some impressive malacological remains have been recovered (Fig. 3) (Arrizabalaga *et al.*, 2011), providing an assessment of the symbolic behaviour of the last Neanderthals who occupied the cave. These are two shell fragments at the base of Level III and a further two in Sub-Level IVc. The former (one possibly from a warm-climate marine mollusc and the other a freshwater bivalve) were found precisely in the same context as the two teeth attributed to Neanderthals in Bands 16 and 18 in the excavation. Although it is very difficult to determine whether or not the shells were modified by humans, it is clear that the shells of inedible molluscs were intentionally selected and taken to the site. Both remains are polished and one of them, which is brightly coloured, was obviously selected for strictly aesthetic reasons.

The case of the two marine shells found in Level IVc is even more striking because, first, there is no doubt that Neanderthals brought them to the site (the teeth were found nearly a metre above the relative level of this find) and second, it is easier to determine that they were modified by humans, possibly complementing natural processes. These are two fragments of snail shells, probably marine species. One of them conserves the central column and a section of the outer shell wall, so that it could easily be used as a pendant by threading a cord through the gap. The other appears to be a fragment of the helical column of an even larger shell, through which a cord could be threaded, so it could also have been suspended as a pendant. Although the cord could easily have come loose through the inverse path of an open spiral, this may have been solved by blocking it with a large quartz grain (which does not come from the site) in the canal. In both cases, simple microscopic observation can identify striations over the natural polishing and other abrasions compatible with the use of these shells as pendants, following the procedure described above.

The presence of these malacological remains in levels where it can be understood that they were brought by Neanderthals suggests that it is necessary to reflect on the symbolic behaviour of this species. Although Neanderthals have traditionally been attributed extremely simple behavioural patterns, including gathering fossils and minerals that "struck their attention" and taking them to their dwellings, in recent years more sophisticated situations have been identified. It is currently believed that the last Neanderthals, at least occasionally, displayed behaviour and attitudes towards ornamental and symbolic elements similar to those recognised in modern humans in the Early Upper Palaeolithic. The debate appears to be focused on why the Neanderthals displayed this behaviour, either because it was apprehended and copied from the first modern humans in Europe, or because it represents cultural evolution intrinsic to the phyletic development of the *Homo genus*.

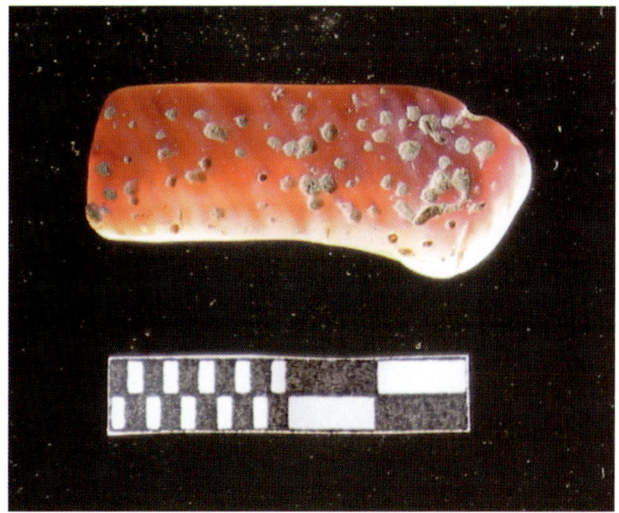

Figure 3. Fragment of a red Spondylus shell, from Level III at Lezetxiki. Reference: Arrizabalaga *et al.*, 2011.

Manuel R. González Morales*,
Lawrence Guy Straus*,**

Cueva del Mirón (Ramales de la Victoria, Cantabria)

Cueva del Mirón (Fig. 1) is a large cave situated in the second foothill chain of the Cantabrian Cordillera in eastern Cantabria, very near the border with Vizcaya. Located at 43 ° 14' 42" N and 3 ° 27' 9 " W and 260 m above sea level on the west-facing cliff of Monte Pando, about 150 m above the valley floor of the Asón River at its confluence of the Calera and Gándara, the 16 m wide x 20 m-high cave mouth dominates the broad intermontane Valle de Ruesga. It is near the crossroads of major north-south and east-west avenues of communication respectively connecting the Cantabrian coast with the Castilian *meseta* via the Asón and 920 m Los Tornos Pass and the Basque Country with the central coastal zone of Cantabria (now partly occupied by the Bay of Santander) via the Carranza and Ruesga valleys and 674 m Alisas Pass. El Mirón is surrounded by summits of ≥1000 m in elevation, yet is only 20 km from the present shore at the mouth of the Asón (about 25 km from the pleniglacial shore).

Probably more or less continuously utilized by humans for residence and (since Neolithic

Figure 1. El Mirón. Cave´s view (photo: Alejandro García Moreno).

* Instituto Internacional de Investigaciones Prehistoricas de Cantabria, 39005 Santander, España.
** Department of Anthropology, University of New Mexico, Albuquerque, NM 87131 USA.

times) for sheltering livestock, Cueva del Mirón was identified as an archeological site by H. Alcalde del Río and L. Sierra at the same time (September 1903) that they discovered Covalanas (directly above Cueva del Mirón) and La Haza (below and ca. 300 m north of it) –the second and third Paleolithic cave art sites to be recognized in Spain. Written off by archeologists as being disturbed by modern human activity, the only known (but unpublished) testing of this site –a trench dug across the middle of the inner cave gallery– was done by workers on the orders of civil engineer and amateur archeologist A. García Lorenzo during his construction of the road up the mountainside to Covalanas in the 1950s. Visited in October 1973 by LGS, the cave's potential as a major site left an indelible impression. The authors directed large-scale excavations in Cueva del Mirón between 1996-2013 (Straus and González Morales 2012).

Cueva del Mirón (Fig. 2) consists of a large, dry, sunlit vestibule measuring 30 m deep x 7-11 m wide x 12-13 m high; a dark, 7-8 m wide inner gallery that is accessible for about 80 m (after which it is filled to the ceiling with alluvial deposits and travertine); and a narrow (3-4 m-wide) connecting passage that is 20 m long and contains a ramp of colluvial-alluvial sediments-an erosional face of the inner cave's alluvial infilling. The cave has obviously undergone several cycles of deposition and erosion by running water studied by the late W.R. Farrand (2012). Indeed the inner cave trench (cleaned and deepened in 1996) revealed a sequence of Medieval, Bronze Age and Lower Magdalenian visits/occupations whose sediments fill an ancient channel that cut through the alluvium, remnant terraces of which survive along the edges of the inner cave. Above the top of the ramp in the connecting gallery breccia under a travertine remnant adhering to the cave wall yielded flakes and faunal remains dated to the Azilian period and the sedimentary infilling of a niche in the cave wall above there present erosional surface about two thirds of the way down the ramp produced artifacts and bones dating to the Initial Magdalenian. The vestibule (where geophysical prospection has shown there to be some 9 m of sedimentary deposits down to bedrock) was probably emptied of deposits by running water and progressively refilled –mainly with sediments washed down from the inner cave alluvium, but also with others washed and blown in from the exterior via the vast cave mouth, together with material deposited by humans and animals over thousands of years.

Excavations were conducted in three areas of the vestibule: the Outer Vestibule (9.5 m^2), the Vestibule Rear (maximally 17 m^2, depending on the level), and the Mid-Vestible Connecting Trench (maximally 7.5 m^2). Included within the Vestibule Rear area is a large looters' pit from which some 25 m^3 of mixed sediments were removed and dry-screened. This pit had reached the base of the culturally and organically rich Magdalenian sequence, stopping at the top of the Solutrean and thus allowing excavation of a 2-1 m *sondage* through Solutrean and Gravettian-age levels down to a horizon at the foot of the buried ramp deposit that dates to 41 uncal. kya –Final Middle Paleolithic. Sampling of the Solutrean levels was later expanded to a total of 4 m^2 after excavation of overlying Magdalenian layers in two more contiguous squares in Vestibule Rear. Also in the Vestibule Rear, excavation in a minimally connected area of 4 m^2 between the cave wall and a large engraved block yielded a secondary human burial of Lower Magdalenian age sandwiched between layers of the same period.

The site has been dated by 84 AMS and conventional radiocarbon dates (Straus and González Morales 2003, 2007, 2010; Straus et al., n.d.a) ranging from AD 1400 to 41,000 uncal. BP. The culture stratigraphic sequence revealed in the Outer Vestibule includes Lower Magdalenian (16.6-15.0 uncal. kya), possible Middle Magdalenian (ca. 15-14.6 uncal. kya), Upper Magdalenian (13-12 uncal. kya), Azilian (ca. 12-11 uncal. kya), extremely poor Mesolithic with hiati (9.5-8.4 uncal. kya), Neolithic (5.7-4.7 uncal. kya), Chalcolithic (4.1-3.8 uncal. kya) and early Bronze Age (3.7 uncal. kya) levels. The Mid-Vestible Trench cuts through possible Solutrean or Initial Magdalenian (17.4 uncal. kya), Lower Magdalenian (15.9 uncal. kya), Upper Magdalenian (12.5 uncal. kya), Azilian (11.6-10.3 uncal. kya), Neolithic (5.8-4.9 uncal. kya) and possible disturbed Chalcolithic and/or Bronze Age deposits. The Vestibule Rear includes traces of Terminal Mousterian (41.3 uncal. kya), Gravettian (27.6 uncal. kya), Solutrean (19.2-18.4 uncal. kya), Initial Magdalenian (17.6-17.0 uncal. kya), Lower Magdale-

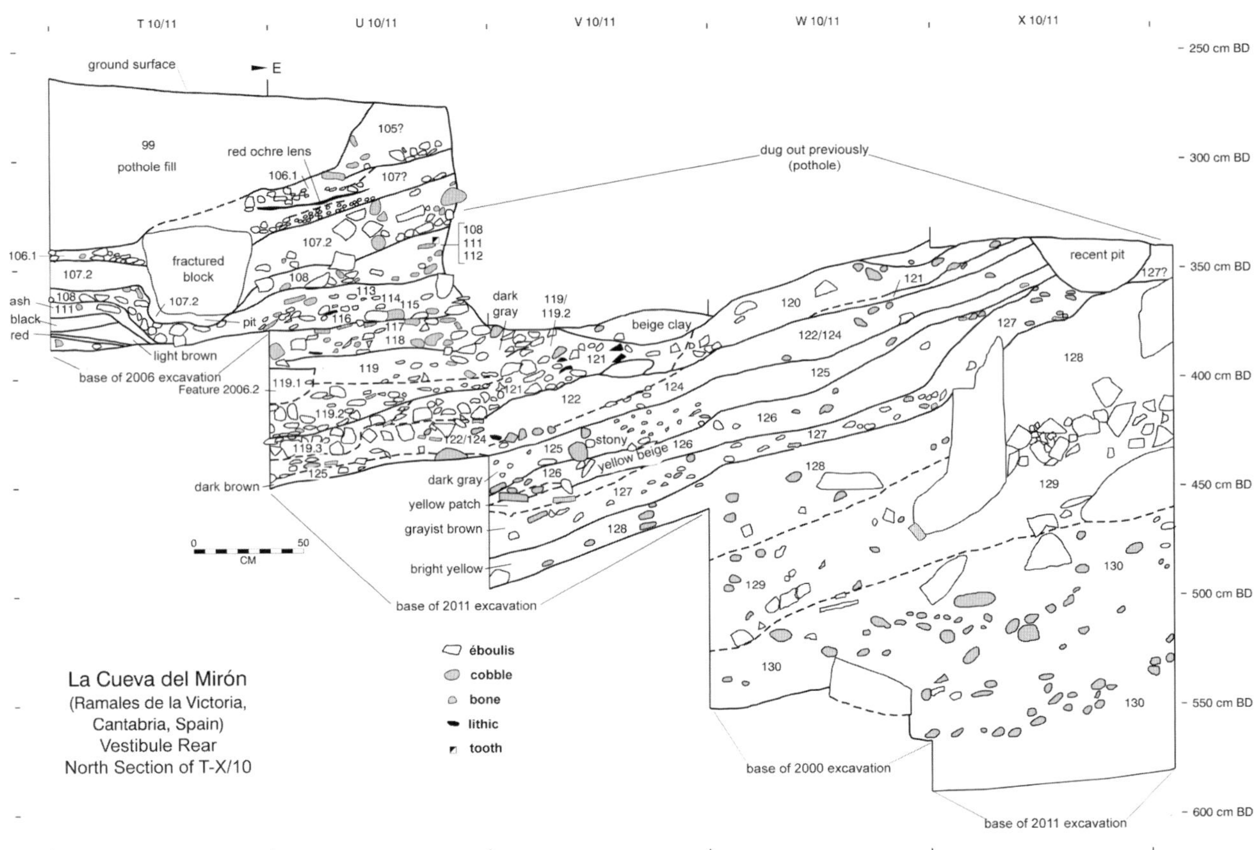

Figure 2. Stratigraphic profile of Cueva del Mirón

nian (ca. 17-14.9 uncal. kya), possible Middle Magdalenian (ca. 14.1-13.4 uncal. kya), possible Upper Magdalenian (12.5-12 uncal. kya), possible poor Azilian and Mesolithic. It is likely that sloping Neolithic, Chalcolithic and Bronze Age deposits had originally existed in the Vestibule Rear, but had been removed by shepherds to level the area for use as a corral (still in existence in 1996). The *fumiers* that characterize much of the Holocene sequence have yielded an importance series of paleomagnetic results (Carrancho *et al.*, 2013).The complete sequence of nearly 40,000 years has provided detailed micromammalian evidence of Late Pleistocene and Holocene fluctuations in climate and vegetation (Cuenca-Bescós *et al.*, 2008, 2009), as well as a less continuous palynological record (still under study by M.J. Iriarte).

While the Mousterian and Gravettian (González Morales and Straus 2013a) levels only suggest minor human visits at least to the Vestibule Rear area, the Solutrean levels seem to indicate repeated, archeologically but somewhat more visible visits, probably by parties that moved up into the mountains in summer from base camps in the coastal zone and that were heavily involved in ibex and red deer hunting, as suggested by the relatively large numbers (and relative frequencies) of foliate and shouldered points made on diverse kinds of lithics, accompanied rather enigmatically by large numbers of perforated shell, tooth, bone and stone beads (Straus and Gonzalez Morales 2009; Straus *et al.*, 2011a, 2013).

Cueva del Mirón has one of the most important sequence of Intial Magdalenian levels in the Cantabrian region, characterized by the eventual disappearance of Solutrean points and the prsence of large, thick, round-section antler points and both large flakes and "archaic" tool types on local non-flint raw materials and bladelets (unretouched, retouched and backed) on excellent quality non-local flints, but without the diagnostic tools of the somewhat older

French Badegoulian. It is with this period that the cave began to witness massive, long-term, multi-purpose human occupations, as attested by the masses of faunal remains, lithic debris and tools, hearths, fire-cracked rocks and dark brown-black, charcoal-rich sediments (Straus et al., n.d.b). A broken slate pendant with the engraving of a horse head comes from this period (González Morales and Straus 2013b). Such intensive occupations continued throughout the classic Lower Magdalenian, with thick palimpsests of living floors very similar to those of El Juyo, Altamira, Santimamiñe and El Castillo on or at the edge of the coastal zone. Remains of red deer, ibex (under study by J-M. Geiling) and salmon are extraordinarily abundant, as are stone and osseous artifacts, including large numbers of bladelets, nucleiform scrapers (on bladelet cores) (Straus *et al.*, 2008), *sagaies* of many types including iconic quadrangular-section ones with geometric or "tectiform" engraved decorations, eyed needles, and an antler spearthrower remarkably similar in form and dimensions to ones from sites in SW France (González Morales and Straus 2005, 2009). There are also "macrolithic" tools made on local nudstone, quartzite and limestone, but the flints (used especially in bladelet manufacture) mostly come from Upper Cretaceous outcrops in the coastal zone of western Vizcaya and eastern Cantabria (at distances of at least 40-50 km from the site) (Rissetto 2009). The Lower Magdalenian levels contain many, often repeatedly re-used hearths filled and surrounded by fire-cracked rocks (some previously used as anvils) and masses of heavily fragmented long bones, suggestive of processing for grease rendering via stone boiling (Nakazawa *et al.*, 2009). Notably these levels have yielded engraved fragments and one whole red deer stag scapula with the engraved and striated image of a hind head and the outline of a bovine head. The style, composition, technique and hind subject are virtually identical to engraved scapulae from several Lower Magdalenian sites in central Cantabria and eastern Asturias (notably Altamira, El Castillo and El Juyo), as well as closely resembling images on the walls of the former two and other caves, thereby defining a regional cultural marker (González Morales and Straus 2009). The DNA studies of salmon and red deer from this and the other Paleolithic horizons of Cueva del Mirón show that this region served as a refugium for these species (as it did for humans) during the Last Glacial Maximum and hence was a source area for the repopulation of more northerly regions of Europe beginning during Oldest Dryas –the time of the Initial and Lower Magdalenian (Consuegra *et al.*, 2002; Meiri *et al.*, 2013). It is to the Lower Magdalenian that belongs the secondary human burial and the fall and at least intial engraving of the 2x1x1 m limestone block behind which the mandible and some 100 other bones of the human were deposited after they had naturally lost their flesh and then been stained with red ochre (Straus *et al.*, 2011b). The sediments used to cover the bones were also stained with red ochre and glitter with hematite cystals (R. Seva, personal communication). The engraved block adjacent to the bones is also stained red and the walls of the vestibule rear are covered with masses of engravings, including the image of a horse, all possibly of Lower Magdalenian based in part on their height above the ground surface at the time (García Díez *et al.*, 2012) It is known that the block had fallen atop a layer (110) dated to 16 uncal. kya (a few centuries before the burial was done behind it) and was engraved on its sheered off flat surface during subsequent years before being covered over by dated Middle and Upper Magdalenian, Azilian and Mesolithic-age levels.

The ungulate faunal assemblages of the Middle and Upper Magdalenian and Azilian levels are dominated by red deer and ibex, all hunted during the warm season, suggesting a mobility pattern that included winter residential bases in the coastal zone (Marín 2009, 2010). Unlike the nearby cave sites of El Valle and El Horno, located on the valley floor, the Upper Magdalenian and Azilian occupations of El Mirón seem to have been of low intensity and frequency, with relatively few artifacts (though these do include an antler harpoon and an ochre-stained pebble respectively) (Gonzáez Morales and Straus 2012). The cave was only fleetingly visited during Mesolithic times when settlement was concentrated at shell middens around the newly formed Asón estuary.

Quite abruptly, locally well-made, undecorated ceramics (studied by C.Vega [2012]), domesticated sheep/goat, cattle and pig (studied by J.Altuna and K.Mariezkurrena [2012]) and wheat (studied by L. Peña-Chocarro [2012]) appeared in El Mirón as it was reoccupied intensively ca. 4650 cal. BC, making it one of the earliest known Neolithic sites in northern Atlantic Spain. Unlike most cave sites dating to the Chalcolithic and Bronze Age in Cantabrian Spain which are funerary loci, Cueva del Mirón was a major residential place for both humans and livestock (increasingly cattle), with numerous large pits (some with fire-cracked rocks), masses of ash, ceramics, a pair of arrowheads (in the Chalcolithic) and a copper pin, plus possible slag (in the Bronze Age). There are hints of later visits to the site and indeed it was inhabited by people as recently as the early post-Civil War period.

Juan Carlos López Quintana*
Amagoia Guenaga Lizasu*

Cueva de Santimamiñe (Kortezubi, Bizcaia). Stratigraphy and human occupations

1. Cueva de Santimamiñe (Kortezubi, Biscay). Geography and first excavations in its archaeological deposit

Cueva de Santimamiñe is in the Oka River basin, a coastal valley on the eastern side of the northern Spanish coast, in the Province of Biscay. Its location, on the southern slopes of Mt. Ereñozar (446.5m), is in a strategic position over the valley. The cave entrance, at an altitude of 137m, faces south/southeast, and leads into a large entrance chamber lit by daylight. The entrance and the chamber contain a stratigraphic deposit with an environmental sequence ranging from late isotope stage MIS 3 to about the middle of MIS 1.

Santimamiñe also contains a Palaeolithic art ensemble, discovered in 1916 and later studied by H. Breuil (1917), who found further engravings and defined the main graphic units in the decorated chamber. The archaeological deposit has been excavated in two stages: first, from 1918 to 1926, by T. Aranzadi, J.M. de Barandiarán and E. Eguren (Barandiarán, 1976: 11-344); and second, from 1960 to 1962, by J.M. de Barandiarán (Barandiarán, 1976: 345-419). The excavation in the cave entrance reached a depth of over 8m, with a stratigraphic sequence covering the period from the Aurignacian to the Roman age and later (Barandiarán, 1976: 421-475).

2. The 2004-2006 study of the archaeological deposit: stratigraphic sequence.

After 42 years without studying the deposit at Santimamiñe, in 2004 a new series of archaeological research began (2004-2014), with the aim of re-examining and updating the stratigraphic record at this Basque site. The research was framed within a full study and development programme initiated by the Culture Department in the Foral Deputation of Biscay. This programme includes the re-exploration, mapping and environmental monitoring of the cave, as well as a reappraisal of the archaeological deposit and the Palaeolithic art ensemble.

The archaeological work has involved 25 months of fieldwork since 2004, supervised by J.C. López Quintana and A. Guenega Lizasu. The first three years (2004-2006) were spent revising the stratigraphy of the deposit, and a first monograph-presentation of the site has already been published (López Quintana and Guenaga, 2011); from 2007 to 2014, the human occupations in the Holocene and Late Pleistocene have been the subject of a larger-scale excavation.

This reappraisal of the stratigraphy at Santimamiñe has studied a sequence 6m thick, which has been analysed and interpreted in accordance with the principles of Analytical Stratigraphy

* Asociación de Arqueología AGIRI / Círculo de Estratigrafía Analítica. Apartado de Correos nº 208, 48300 Gernika-Lumo (Bizkaia). E-mail: arkeoagiri@hotmail.com

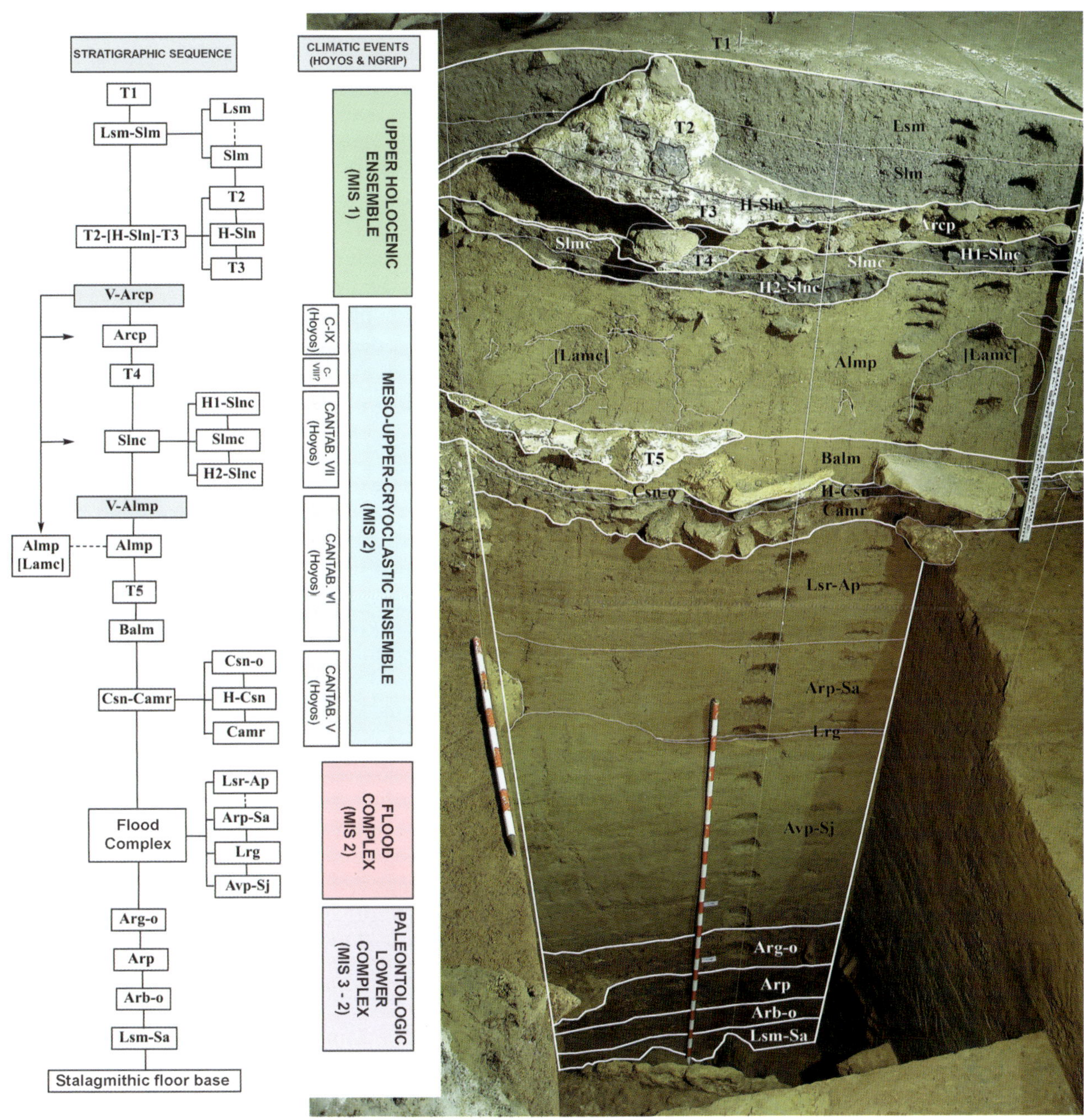

Figure 1. Frontal stratigraphic section of the deposit in Santimamiñe and an analytical matrix of the sequence.

(Laplace, 1971; Sáenz de Buruaga, 1996). This sequence consists of 27 stratigraphic units, grouped into four series according to geoclimatic and paleoethnological criteria (López Quintana and Guenaga, 2011). These four stratigraphic series will be described from the base to the top (Fig. 1).

- **Lower palaeontological series (MIS 3/MIS 2)**

The lowest part of the stratigraphic series at Santimamiñe is 1.05m thick and consists of four stratigraphic units: *Lsm-Sa*, *Arb-o*, *Arp* and *Arg-o*. The sediment is mainly fine material (clays and silts), in proportions always reaching above 95%, attesting decantation processes in a wet environment (Areso and Uriz, 2011). However, the *Arg-o* unit has yielded some indicators of a cold environment, suggesting open vegetation with the presence of reindeer. The absence of evidence of human occupation is one of the traits of this series, which contains two levels with palaeontological remains (*Arb-o* and *Arg-o*). The faunal repertoire of the former is greatly altered while the accumulation in the second evidences the site was used as a shelter by carnivores.

Radiocarbon determinations[1] (AMS) situate the series between the late isotope stage MIS 3 (*Arb-o* Unit: 26,890 ± 180 BP, Beta-259132) and the early isotope stage MIS 2 (*Arg-o* Unit: 20,530 ± 110 BP, Beta-240906).

- **Flooding Complex (MIS 2)**

The Flooding Complex is a layer of sediment 2.3 – 2.6m thick, formed by four stratigraphic units: *Avp-Sj*, *Lrg*, *Arp-Sa* and *Lsr-Ap*. They are all predominated by the fine fractions (silts and clays) and coarse components are absent. The complex is barren from archaeological and palaeontological points of view, and it formed during a mild and wet oscillation which can be dated in the GI-2 interstadial in the NGRIP climate sequence (Rasmussen *et al.*, 2008), between ca. 20,000 and 18,800 BP.

- **Cryoclastic Middle-Upper series (MIS 2)**

The Middle-Upper series, 1.8m thick, consists of 12 units with certain stratigraphic complexity: 8 levels with archaeological content, 1 barren level, 2 layers of calcite (*T4* and *T5*) and 1 erosion phase (*V-Almp*). The sedimentary trait defining this series is the evidence of cryoclastic processes, mainly in Units *Csn-Camr*, *Slnc* and *Arcp*. These three levels have provided indicators of a cold climate of differing intensity, which have been associated with the cold phases GS-2, GI-1d and GS-1 in the NGRIP sequence (Rasmussen *et al.*, 2008). This series includes the *Balm* and *Almp* levels, which almost certainly correspond to the NGRIP phase GI-1e. In M. Hoyos's regional late glacial climate sequence, this would be equivalent to his Cantabrian Phase VI (Hoyos, 1995).

This series contains the first human occupations in the cave, coinciding with the three phases of climate deterioration. The first occupation at Santimamiñe (*Csn-Camr*) took place in the late lower Magdalenian, in around 14,700 BP, according to data from the new excavation. Therefore the reappraisal of the stratigraphy at Santimamiñe has not found evidence of Early Upper Palaeolithic occupations (López Quintana and Guenaga, 2011: 56).

- **Holocene Upper series (MIS 1)**

The first stages of the Holocene are represented by the erosional hiatus *V-Arcp* and slight evidence of human activity (hearth facies *H-Sln*) included in the calcite layers *T2* and *T3* dated to 7580 ± 50 BP (Beta-240899). Above this, the stratigraphic unit *Slm-Lsm* is 0.5m thick, with a preponderance of the fine fraction. The lower part of this group (*Slm* level) contains evidence of a Neolithic occupation, between ca. 5500 and 5000 BP. After this time, human presence at Santimamiñe becomes increasingly occasional, although the cave was used for burials in the Chalcolithic-Bronze Age (*Lsm* level).

3. The sequence of occupations at Cueva de Santimamiñe: landscape and environment exploitation strategies from the lower Magdalenian to the Chalcolithic-Bronze Age.

The stratigraphic sequence at Santimamiñe hosts seven phases of human occupation, above the flooding complex and corresponding to the climate events GS-2, GI-1, GS-1 and MIS 1.

3.1. Red deer hunters in the late lower Magdalenian

The first human occupation at Santimamiñe (*Csn-Camr* Unit) took place during a cold phase, assignable to the late GS-2 stadial in the NGRIP sequence (Rasmussen *et al.*, 2008) or the early Cantabrian V (Hoyos, 1995). From its base to the top, intensification in human activity in the cave can be seen, parallel to the deterioration in environmental conditions. This took place during a short period of time, judging by the two available C14-AMS determinations: 14,670 ± 80 BP (Beta-240904) and 14,650 ± 80 BP (Beta-240905)

The *Csn-Camr* archaeozoological record is polarised towards the hunting of red deer, which make up 91.4% of the total ungulates captured (Castaños and Castaños, 2011). The percentages of chamois and ibex are surprisingly low (4.6% and 3.2%, respectively) in this landscape of crags and steep hillsides. The scanty evidence of fishing or the gathering of molluscs as food supports this idea of an extraordinarily specialised subsistence strategy.

The lithic assemblage displays the highest percentage of retouched tools in the sequence, and equally the lowest proportion of debitage prod-

[1] All the C14 dates in the text are given in uncalibrated years BP (conventional C14 age).

ucts, which means that lithic reduction tasks are scarcely represented at the site. The lithic raw materials include 23.2% of exotic flint in the total (Tarriño, 2011) with sources located between 70 and 180km away (Urbasa, Treviño, Tercis and Chalosse). This is indicative of the great territorial mobility of lower Magdalenian red deer hunters. The taphonomic study of the large mammals proposes an occupation specialised in processing the game, essentially red deer, which were taken to the cave whole to be skinned, butchered, defleshed and finally broken up to obtain the bone marrow (San Pedro and Cáceres, 2011). Antler and bone-working were other important activities at the site, which has yielded a large collection of bi-pointed assegai points with triangular-trapezoidal cross-sections.

3.2. *Evidence of human occupation during the formation of* Almp *stratigraphic unit?*

After the time of the lower Magdalenian red deer hunters, a layer of calcite (*Balm*) was dismantled, possibly by erosion related to an increase in humidity. The back of the entrance chamber again suffered ponding and displays no sign of human presence, until the humidity decreased relatively (in the middle and upper part of *Almp*) allowing occasional human occupation events. This level reflects cool wet conditions, probably in the interstadial phase GI-1e of the NGRIP sequence or, on a regional scale, in Hoyos's Cantabrian VI phase (*ca.* 13,300-12,700 BP).

In this section of the sequence, some stratigraphic alterations have been detected, as material was disturbed by the overlying *Slnc* level. This means that the archaeological record obtained should be assessed with caution (López Quintana and Guenaga, 2011: 33-36). If the faunal assemblage from *Almp* is examined as a whole, a significant change is seen from the underlying *Csn-Camr* level. The *Almp* unit has provided a diversified assemblage, in which ibex (*Capra pyrenaica*) is more abundant than red deer, in proportions of 50.3% and 40.4%. The results of the ichthyological study are in agreement with this new strategy of diversification in the consumption of resources. *Almp* reveals an increase in fishing (mainly of salmonids), as the total of the ichthyological series in the sequence goes from 2.37% in the *Csn-Camr* Unit to 28.4% in *Almp* (Roselló and Morales, 2011).

3.3. *The Upper-Final Magdalenian: diversification and full use of natural resources*

The following episode in the stratigraphic sequence at Santimamiñe is the most intense human occupation at the site, coinciding with the coldest and driest phase in the deposit (*Slnc*). Climatically, it can be included in the GI-1 interstadial of the NGRIP sequence, possibly in the GI-1d cold oscillation (Rasmussen *et al.*, 2008). In Hoyos's late glacial sequence (Hoyos, 1995), it clearly corresponds to the Cantabrian VII, dated between *ca.* 12,700 and 11,700 BP. The pollen record reveals the worst conditions in the stratigraphy, with 2% tree pollen (pine, birch and juniper), while Compositae dominate in the herbaceous-shrub layer, together with the appearance of *Artemisia* (Iriarte, 2011). A C14-AMS determination is available for the lower part of *Slnc*: 12,790 ± 70 BP (Beta-240902). Another C14-AMS determination obtained in the underlying *Almp* level, (12,250 ± 70 BP: Beta-240903), and regarded as intrusive, may have come from the disturbance of the upper part of *Slnc* (*H1-Slnc*), and closely matches the coldest and driest phase of the Cantabrian VII stage.

The archaeozoological assemblage in *Slnc* is diversified in the hunting of ungulates. Red deer (49.1%) is more common than ibex (30.7%), while some rarer species in earlier periods, such as roe deer and large bovids, become more common. Fish (almost exclusively salmonids) are indicative of the model of a diversified resource use, as this level contains the largest number of remains, with 58.58% of the whole ichthyological assemblage at the site (Roselló and Morales, 2011). As regards food processing, a sandstone slab may have been used as a refractory surface in the context of a hearth (Delgado-Raack, 2011). The most common plant species used as firewood is juniper, as well as a large number of indeterminable conifers (Euba, 2011).

The *Slnc* archaeological record reflects a subsistence model aimed towards a full use of natural resources. This diversification in subsistence strategies is associated with a relative reduction in the size of the territory being exploited and an extension in the cycles of cave occupation. Within the River Oka basin, the different ecosystems were used more exhaustively, from the valley bottom and steep crags, to the rivers and estuary, and even the shore, although less intensively because of its distance from the site. In accordance with human occupations of greater intensity and in longer cy-

Figure 2. Selection of backed points and bladelets from the *Slnc* level (Upper-Final Magdalenian).

cles during this phase, the reappraisal of the Palaeolithic rock art by C. González Sainz and R. Ruiz Idarraga is of interest. In their study, the art at Santimamiñe is interpreted as a synchronic ensemble which was probably produced during the time of the occupations in the *Slnc* level. They reject the theory that the ensemble is an accumulation of figures produced between the middle Magdalenian and the Azilian (González Sainz and Ruiz Idarraga, 2010: 150-151).

The *Slnc* level has also yielded the largest lithic assemblage in the deposit. Indeed, 62.88% of the total lithic assemblage recovered during the 2004-2006 fieldwork comes from this level, where it reflects a specialisation in backed bladelets (Fig. 2), which make up 38.36% of the retouched elements in the level (López Quintana *et al.*, 2011). In coherence with this, the most common cores are prismatic, which were used to obtain bladelet blanks. The bone assemblage consists of harpoons (with a magnificent example of a Cantabrian harpoon with a single row of barbs and a pierced base) (Fig. 3), as well as assegai points, spatulas, rods, awls, fine points or stilettos, pins and needles (González Sainz, 2011).

3.4. *The Azilian level: the last Ice Age hunter-gatherers*

The late glacial sequence at Santimamiñe concludes with the *Arcp* stratigraphic unit, assignable to the final part of the NGRIP GS-1 stadial (Rasmussen *et al.*, 2008) or Cantabrian IX phase in the regional sequence (Hoyos, 1995). Two C14-AMS determinations are available for the bottom and top of the level 10,060 ± 60 BP (Beta-240901) and 10,100 ± 60 BP (Beta-240900), respectively. The pollen re-

Figure 3. Selection of harpoons from Santimamiñe: 1924 (3 and 6), 1961 (5), 2005 (2 and 4), 2007 (7) and 2008 (1) field seasons.

cord shows an increase in tree cover, with hazel and oak appearing in the sequence for the first time (Iriarte, 2011). The climate has been defined as cold and wet, with the conditions improving in its most recent phase (Murelaga *et al.*, 2011), perhaps announcing the onset of isotope stage MIS 1.

The archaeological data suggest a more occasional occupation that in the previous levels (López Quintana and Guenaga, 2011: 439). Red deer is once more the most hunted ungulate (63.7%), while the hunting of ibex (21.9%), roe deer and large bovids (both 6.1%) decreases. The fishing of salmonids also declines significantly, with a change from the 58.58% of the total ichthyological assemblage in the underlying *Slnc* level, to 7.99% in this unit. Marine molluscs are not found in this level either; the number of sea urchin remains increases but they do not represent an important food resource since the 437 remains belong to a minimum number of only two individuals (Gutiérrez Zugasti, 2011).

The industry in the *Arcp* level has been defined as a "critical transition episode" within the Santimamiñe deposit (López Quintana *et al.*, 2011: 103). The components of the osseous assemblage disappear. In turn, the lithic assemblage is diverse, characterised by a significant number of denticulates and a decline in the backed bladelets. The percentage of exotic flint is significantly smaller than in the lower Magdalenian (*Csn-Camr* Unit), as it decreases from 23.2% to 7.8%. The Urbasa (70km away) and Chalosse (180km in a straight line) varieties are found but, in comparison with the lower Magdalenian, the Treviño and Tercis types disappear (Tarriño, 2011).

3.5. *The early Holocene: the use of estuary resources*

The area excavated in 2004-2006 yielded some Mesolithic remains (malacology, fauna and lithics), in the *H-Sln* Unit and dated to 7580 ± 50 BP (Beta-240899). In contrast, the old excavations documented a thick shell-midden layer (nearly 1m thick), whose lower section (Level IV) without pottery, was attributed to the Mesolithic and yielded a rich collection of archaeological material (Barandiarán, 1976: 429-431). With the Holocene (MIS 1), a changed is perceived at Santimamiñe in the way the cave space was used, with the human habitat now mostly in the entrance and outer area, which was excavated in last century's fieldwork (Barandiarán, 1976). This is in accordance with one of the main changes in the new climate conditions, the proliferation of open-air sites, whose clearest example is the site of Pareko Landa, but also at Goienzabal 1, Sollube Txikerra 1, Katillotxu, Garbola and Landabaso (López Quintana and Guenaga, 2009: 110 and 117).

The stratigraphic reappraisal from 2004 to 2006 found evidence of the use of malacological resources in the estuary, with a predominance of taxa gathered in rocky and muddy zones (*Ostrea edulis*, 37%, and *Scrobicularia plana*, 32%) (Gutiérrez Zugasti, 2011). The diversity of usable resources in the estuary increased significantly in the Holocene.

3.6. *The middle Holocene: Neolithic farming groups.*

The climatic conditions for the Neolithic farmers were the wettest in the sequence at Santimamiñe. The formation of the *Slm* level has been dated by C14-AMS to 5450 ± 50 BP (Beta-240898) and 5010 ± 40 BP (Beta-240897), in the late Neolithic. The pollen study shows the significant spread of tree cover (53% in the middle part of *Slm*), with a predominance of birch (37%) accompanied by hazel and oak (Iriarte, 2011).

The archaeozoological series is quite poor, although domestic species (cattle, sheep/goats and swine) predominating over wild ungulates, mainly red deer, although ibex, chamois and roe deer have also been recorded (Castaños and Castaños, 2011). It is noteworthy that, like the lithic assemblage and the pottery, two-thirds of the ungulate assemblage is found in the upper *Lsm* level, which indicates the occupation in the entrance chamber in the early Neolithic was very tenuous. At the same time, this level attests the most intense exploitation of marine molluscs (Gutiérrez Zugasti, 2011). Gathering was focused on muddy zones in the estuary, and rocky areas to a lesser extent. The peppery furrow shell *Scrobicularia plana* (86% MNI) is the most common species, followed by the grooved carpet shell *Ruditapes decussatus* (5.5%) and oysters (3%). In contrast, evidence of fishing declines drastically (the level provides 2.66% of the ichthyological assemblage at the site), with some changes in taxonomical representation, particularly a decrease in salmonids (Roselló and Morales, 2011). Evidence of charred wood increases remarkably, with a clear predominance of oak, followed by Rosaceae (*Prunus* sp.) (Euba, 2011). In the lower *Slm* level, the two main species (oak and hazel) are accompanied by testimonial evidence of strawberry tree, birch, heath, ash, Pomoideae, willow/poplar, buckthorn and pine, as well as an exceptional fragment of wild olive tree (*Olea europaea*).

The archaeological content of the *Slm* level is limited, but coherent with a Neolithic assemblage. The best represented lithic typological groups are the denticulates and endscrapers, and in second place, backed bladelets (López Quintana *et al.*, 2011). However, qualitatively, double-bevelled retouched segments, including a triangular bi-truncated piece in the style of a *Sonchamp*-point, are of particular interest. Some 95.9% of the flint is the local Cretaceous Flysch variety, available within 20km of Santimamiñe. Exotic flint is limited to 4.1%, and represented by solely the Urbasa variety, as those from further afield (Chalosse and Tercis) disappear from the record. This suggests a gradual reduction in the areas covered by the first farming groups.

One novel point is the identification of six shell fragments with signs of being used as tools (four of *Ostrea edulis*, and one each of *Mytilus galloprovincialis*, *Ruditapes decussatus* and *Patella* sp.), the first objects of this kind to be published in Cantabrian Spain (Gutiérrez Zugasti *et al.*, 2011). In general, they were used in transversal scraping actions, in some cases interspersed with longitudinal cutting tasks. Except for the *Ruditapes decussatus* fragment, possibly used to process plant matter, the other shells were used to work a soft or medium-hard animal substance.

In short, in the middle Holocene, in mild and wet climatic conditions, the cave of Santimamiñe was used, perhaps occasionally and repeatedly, by farming communities who additionally exploit the environment by hunting ungulates and gathering molluscs in the estuary. For comparison, 1.5km from Santimamiñe, in its Levels III and IV, dated between ca. 5800 and 5600 BP, the cave of Kobaederra displays a predominance of domestic fauna, which makes up 70.2% of the archaeozoological assemblage (Altuna and Mariezkurrena, 2009: 762). To date, no cultivated cereals have been found in the stratigraphic reappraisal at Santimamiñe. In the neighbouring site of Kobaederra, barley and emmer wheat have been identified in the Neolithic levels, with a date of 5375 ± 90 BP (AA-29110) obtained for a barley grain from Level IV (Zapata, 2005: 557).

3.7. Funerary use in the Chalcolithic-Bronze Age

After the Neolithic, human occupation of Santimamiñe becomes increasingly occasional, although in the middle and upper part of the *Lsm* Unit, dispersed human remains indicate a possibly very sporadic funerary use of the cave (Fig. 4). The anthropological study of the human remains (Herrasti and Etxeberria, 2011), which also included finds made by the old excavations, determined an MNI of six individuals. One of these, discovered in the 2004 field season, has been dated to 3710 ± 40 BP (Chalcolithic-Bronze Age) while its genetic study showed that it was a bearer of the T2b mitochondrial line (Cardoso *et al.*, 2011).

Figure 4. Copper chisel with an antler handle, found in Level II (Chalcolithic-Bronze Age) in 1924.

Marco de la Rasilla*, Antonio Rosas**, Juan Carlos Cañaveras***, Carles Lalueza-Fox****, David Santamaría*, Sergio SánchezMoral*****, Almudena Estalrrich**, Antonio García Tabernero**, Pablo G. Silva******, Enrique Martínez*, Gabriel Santos******, Lucía Martínez*, Elsa Duarte*, Rosa Huguet*******, Markus Bastir**, Javier Fernández de la Vega*, Paloma Suárez*, Ana Belén Díez*, Beatriz Fernández Cascón**, Soledad Cuezva*****, Ángel Fernández Cortés*****, Elena García Antón*****, Concepción Muñoz***, Javier Lario********, Pedro Carrasco******,Pedro Huerta******, Puy Ayarza******, Fernando Álvarez Lobato******, Loreto Rodríguez******, Inmaculada Picón******, Begoña Fernández******, M. Standing******, Carmen Sesé*********, Trinidad de Torres**********, José Eugenio Ortiz**********, Helène Valladas***********, Norbert Mercier***********, Nadine Tisnèrat-Laborde***********, Rainer Grün************, Stephen Eggins************, Thomas Higham*************, Rachel E. Wood*************, Ramón Julià**************, Vicente Soler***************, Ernestina Badal****************, Antonio Tarriño*****************, Domingo Carlos Salazar******************, Jesús Alonso*******************,#

El Sidrón (Piloña, Asturias)

In memory of Javier Fortea Pérez (1946-2009), Manuel Hoyos Gómez (1944-1999) and Olvido Otero González (1908-1938)

The well-known eponym El Sidrón has a very special history (Fig. 1). It started with the development of a karstic system between two types of rock (sandstone and Neogene conglomerates) as a result of the flow of a small stream. It continued with the use of the cave as a refuge and a hiding place during the Spanish Civil War and the aftermath and with the presence of some endemic species of bats and cave insects. It ended up as the

* Universidad de Oviedo. mrasilla@uniovi.es
** Grupo de Paleoantropología. Dpto. de Paleobiología. MNCN. CSIC. Madrid. arosas@mncn.csic.es
*** Universidad de Alicante. jc.canaveras@ua.es
**** Inst.de Biología Evolutiva. CSIC/UPF. Barcelona. carles.lalueza@upf.edu
***** Dpto. de Geología. MNCN. CSIC. Madrid. ssmilk@mncn.csic.es
****** Universidad de Salamanca. pgsilva@usal.es
******* Universidad Rovira i Virgili. Tarragona. rhuguet@iphes.cat
******** UNED. Madrid. javier.lario@ccia.uned.es
********* Dpto. de Paleobiología. MNCN. CSIC. Madrid. c.sese@mncn.csic.es
********** LEB. ETSIM. Universidad Politécnica de Madrid. trinidad.torres@upm.es
*********** LSCE/IPSL. CEA-CNRS-UVSQ. Francia. helene.valladas@lsce.ipsl.fr
************ Australian National University. Canberra. Rainer.Grun@anu.edu.au
************* ORAU. University of Oxford. UK. thomas.higham@rlaha.ox.ac.uk
************** ICTJA-CSIC. Barcelona. rjulia@ictja.csic.es
*************** IPNA-CSIC. Tenerife.vsoler@ipna.csic.es
**************** Universidad de Valencia.ernestina.badal@uv.es
***************** Universidad del País Vasco. antonio.tarrinno@gmail.com
****************** Max Planck Institute. EVA. Leipzig. domingo_carlos@eva.mpg.de
******************* FASE. Asturias. jesusalonso002@gmail.com

Javier Fortea Pérez fue investigador principal del proyecto hasta el año 2009.

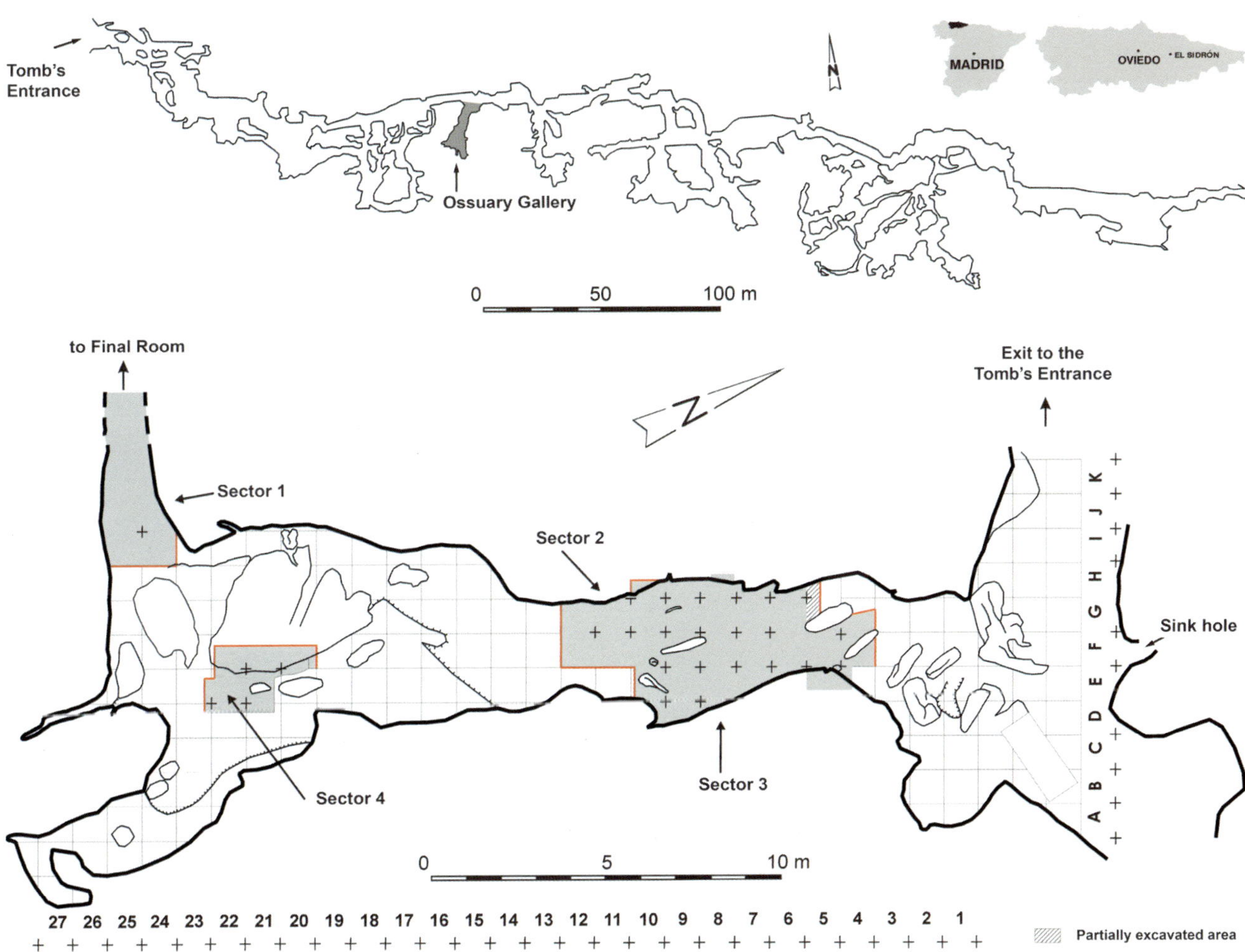

Figure 1. *Top*: Development of the karstic system and location of the entrance and the Osario Gallery. *Bottom*: Osario Gallery floorplan and excavated sectors (2013).

container of non-figurative scarce and enigmatic rock art (Pinto, 1975; Rasilla *et al.*, 2011: 189-191) and above all, a significant number of *Homo neanderthalensis* fossil remains associated to the Mousterian lithic industry.

Its incorporation into archaeological and paleoanthropological research was inevitably linked to the devastating war episode referred to above, because, for obvious reasons, the discovery of two jaws in 1994 led to legal proceedings, a police report and administrative proceedings that, after it was proved that they belonged to the Neanderthal species (Prieto *et al.*, 1998, 2001; Rosas and Aguirre, 1999), ended in 1999 with the design and immediate implementation of a research project.

The project posed a key question at the beginning: whether the material that appeared in the Osario gallery (Fig. 1) actually came from that place and whether the existing record had been removed. Both cases were proved to be true during the early stages of archaeological excavation. The project also tackled new questions: how did the remains get to this gallery? What is their chronology? What are the physical and paleobiological characteristics of the human fossils? What is the relationship between the fossils and artefacts associated with them? (Fortea, 2003, 2007b, 2007c, Rasilla *et al.*, 2011a, 2011b; Rasilla *et al.*, 2013).

Obviously, at the outset it was difficult to predict that the archaeological and anthropological record obtained would greatly exceed expectations, as this is an exceptional site due to the amount and quality of the remains and the results, inferences and interpretations obtained and obtainable.

From 2000 to the present, several parts of the karst system were excavated as the aforementioned questions were answered and according to the requirements that the study itself imposed. The intensity of activity in the Osario Gallery has been constant, GPR techniques even being used from the beginning to verify the burial theory and act accordingly, and it was confirmed that the materials were in secondary position, concentrated almost entirely in the area within sectors 2 and 3 from strip 10 to the north, with some remains in sector 4 (Fig. 1 and 2). Therefore, there was no funeral activity in this gallery.

After answering the question of how the record got there, the questions pointed in a different direction, i.e., outside the system. Its character provided clear indications that the original place of deposit was not a settlement in use. Therefore, the area where the human fossils, lithic industry and few examples of associated fauna were deposited would need to be searched in addition to the archaeological site.

To answer this question, two complementary activities were carried out. Firstly, geophysical analysis, gravimetric analysis and mechanical boreholes and archaelogical test pits were used to try to find out about the subsoil in the vertical exterior of Osario Gallery and identify shelters, galleries and channels in the karst system directly related to it and currently covered up (Fig. 2). Secondly, various boreholes were made in two shelters in the system, which had a high probability of containing the site: in La Cabañina and La Tumba. In addition, data was collected on the archaeological map made in the council and to survey the surrounding area.

The results are different. In relation to Osario Gallery and its vertical exterior, a hypothesis on the filler model has been established by implementing geological and geophysical data from both sites (Cañaveras *et al.*, 2011; Silva *et al.*, 2011), while archaeological boreholes in the shelters have not offered anything related to Mousterian / Neanderthal, although La Cabañina has delivered an interesting but modest collection of lithic material, bones, pottery and fauna –wild and domesticated according to the stage– from the late Upper Paleolithic / Mesolithic, Chalcolithic / Bronze, Iron, Roman and Medieval that support the presence of these groups and, in some cases, the use of caves for their settlement (Rasilla *et al.*, 2011c).

Similarly, the study of the lithic industry that was being carried out in El Sidrón from 2005 and a little later in La Viña rock shelter (Santamaría 2006, 2012) revealed an interesting fact related to the raw material that, in parallel, also required prospecting of this abiotic element. There is a type of flint in the area, and even in theconglomerates inside the cave, of which much of the lithic industry of El Sidrón is made but which also appears in small amounts in the Middle and Upper Paleolithic levels of La Viña.

This had an immediate corollary, as it was necessary to check whether this flint could be found in other sites and Paleolithic levels in Asturias and Cantabria and at the same time, develop a specific line of research regarding siliceous raw materials (Fortea *et al.*, 2010; Santamaría *et al.*, 2010, 2011). The information collected has allowed this raw material to be named "*Sílex de Piloña*", and from now on, studies of prehistoric lithic industry must take into account this type of siliceous rock, as its proven travelling quality makes it a region-wide lithologic trace. Although the Cantabrian region joined these studies late, we are gradually discovering the siliceous raw materials present in Asturias and that could have been used by our ancestors (Duarte *et al.*, e.p.; Tarriño *et al.*, 2013).

Inferences from different disciplines and analysis techniques

1. The arrival of the archaeological record (Sánchez-Moral *et al.*, 2007; Silva *et al.*, 2011; Cañaveras *et al.*, 2011; Santamaría *et al.*, 2010, 2011, 2012; Rasilla *et al.*, 2011a; Santos *et al.*, 2012a and b).

After the primary position had been discarded and the Osario Gallery deposit had been buried, it was necessary to explain how the accumulated material had got here, as it invariably came from an area outside this one. Initially, the contributions must have come from the southern area, following the direction of the stratification and of the water that, coming from the runoff and the drips, happens in winter and spring inside the gallery. However, the data questioned this hypothesis and transferred the vehicle to channels located in the ceiling.

This was because the vast majority of the material is concentrated between frames E-H/10 – E-H/4 and there are a few remains, with a slight increase in the number of fauna, which is always scarce, in squares D-E-F/20-23 (Fig. 1). Even if we project the archaeological evidence onto the floor

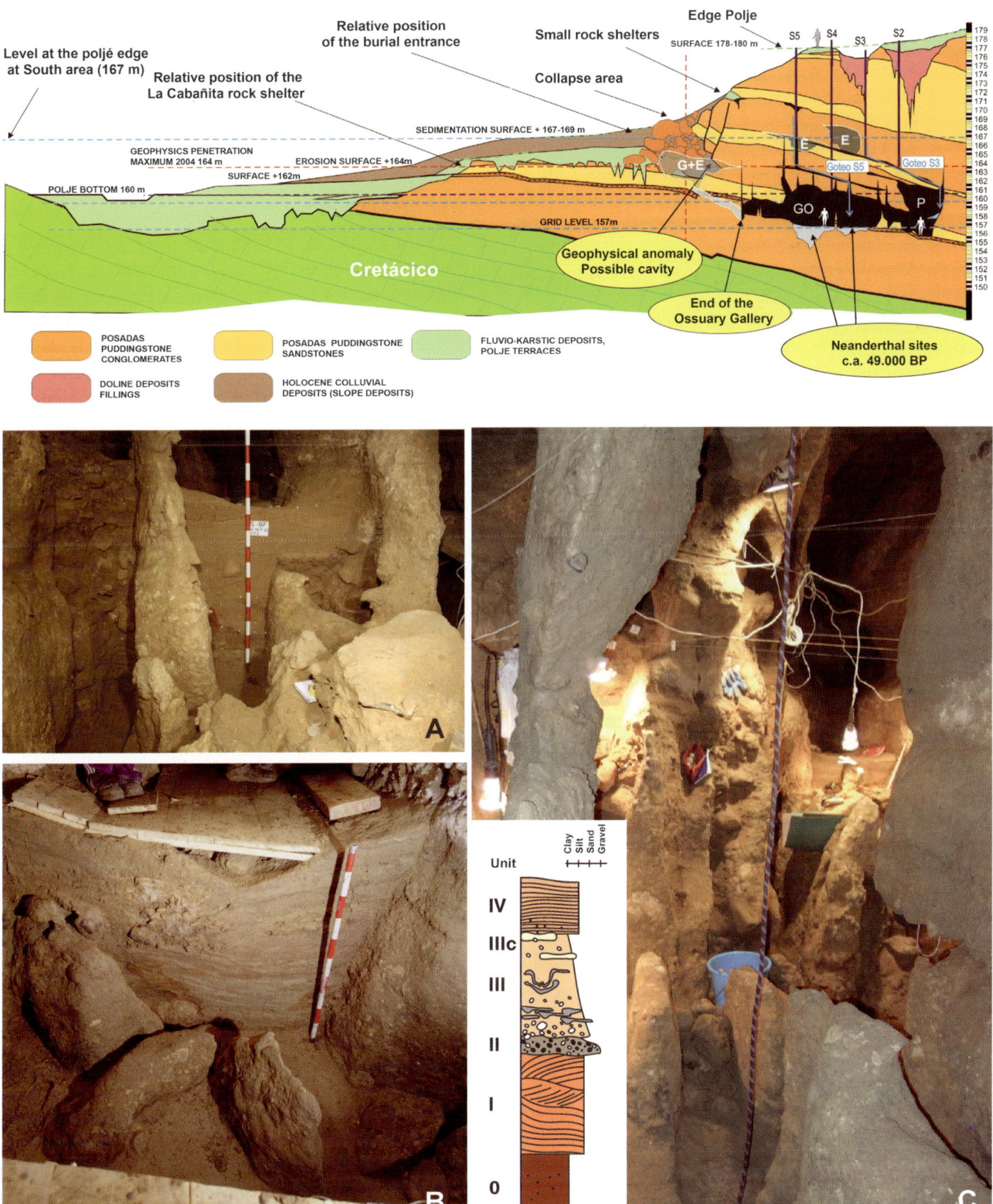

Figure 2. *Top*: Interpretive geological cut of Osario Gallery. The geological features and the most significant geomorphological levels are shown in relation to the geophysical anomalies detected, the mechanical boreholes and the profiles of Osario Gallery (GO) and Main Gallery of El Sidrón cave (P). *Bottom*: Dissolution mesomorphology in the floor of Osario Gallery. A: Details of how the partitions and shovel shapes control the texture and geometry of the deposits (area F-G / 9). B: Detail of the partitions exposed in area E-F/8-9. C: View from the north of the centre of the gallery (September 2010) and diagram of the stratigraphic series.

plan, we see a cone shape in both cases, which supports an entrance from the outside.

This phenomenon can be explained because outside, on one of the edges of a karst polje, there was a rock shelter where the archaeological record was deposited and a streamsinks a few metres down, as currently occur in La Cabañina rock shelter. For some reason, the system got blocked, coinciding with a storm or a stage of significant rainfall, the water rising up to the level of the rock shelter. When it became unblocked at a later stage, the deposit suddenly and very quickly entered the cave via channels, getting trapped in the Osario Gallery (Fig. 2). In this final position there was a post-deposition process focused mainly on the eastern wall favouring the flow of the aforementioned water and in a sinkhole that affected area E/9. Then the rock shelter broke apart and covered the quaternary sediment but its position has been located using geophysical analysis, gravimetric analysis and the corresponding topography. We are trying to access this place in order to check if there are any remains and, if there are, what the deposition process was like, as this would re-open the hypothesis that it had been a burial site.

Furthermore, we can probably deduce, based on the position of the record inside the gallery, the arrangement of the elements (fossils, tools and fauna) in the original exterior rock shelter. The majority of the material was located in a specific area that entered via a channel that took it to sectors 2 and 3 of the gallery and a little of the material –particularly the fauna– was in a different area, but nearby, and entered via another channel that took it to sector 4 of the gallery (Fig. 1).

2. Chronology of the fossils and lithic tools (Torres *et al.*, 2010, 2011; Wood *et al.*, 2013).

Both the taxa and the techno-complex to which they belong make it necessary to use different absolute dating systems, as at best, since ~55,000 BP, ^{14}C cannot be used and because depending on the result, we could be in the centre of the current debate on the Middle Paleolithic/ Upper Paleolithic – *Homo neanderthalensis/Homo sapiens*or the debate on the persistence of Neanderthal groups in the Iberian Peninsula up to chronologies around 25-24,000 BP.

It is important to point out that, firstly, for various reason, not all of the procedures chosen have returned satisfactory results (e.g. Uranium/Thorium) and secondly, problems have been brought to light that could arise according to the methods used by the laboratories and also, problems related to subsequent archaeological interpretation. To minimise this impact, several remains were dated using various procedures (AARD, ESR and ^{14}CAMS), the dates of the first two coinciding quite well and those of the third being very different and out of range (Geochron Laboratories).

As the dates could fall within the C^{14} range and in order to clear up the doubt generated, samples were sent to another laboratory (Beta Analytics). The results (between ~35,000 and ~41,000 BP) placed the El Sidrón record within the aforementioned debate. However, there was news of the dates obtained from a sample sent in 1998 to the Gif-sur-Yvette laboratory (48,500±2600 and 49,200±2500 BP) that significantly changed the vision and interpretation of the El Sidrón record.

At the same time, samples were taken to date the sediment using OSL, into which the archaeological and anthropological materials fit quite well, to the ceiling and wall, and they were correlated with those obtained using other procedures.

Finally, for the project led by Oxford University various unique European sites, including El Sidrón, were dated and the date of 48,400±3200 BP was returned.

As maybe easily inferred, there is a disagreement between the dating of Geochron/Beta and Gif/Oxford and the main reason for this is the pretreatment used to eliminate any contamination. Geochron/Beta used the conventional system whereas Gif/Oxford used more sophisticated protocols, ninhydrin and ultrafiltration, respectively.

For this reason, it is more sensible to take on the older dating values; the average value of these is 48,800±1600, and are generally more in agreement with the AAR, ESR and OSL values.

3. The nature of the anthropological collection and its paleogenomics (Rosas and Aguirre, 1999; Lalueza, 2011; Lalueza *et al.*, 2005, 2011, 2012a and b; Rosas *et al.*, 2006, 2007, 2011a, 2011c, 2012, 2013; Bastir *et al.*, 2010; Dean *et al.*, 2013; Hardy *et al.*, 2012; Engelken *et al.*, 2014, Castellano *et al.*, 2014).

What is perhaps more worthy of noteis that the existence of thirteen individuals and the practice of anthropophagy has been proved (Fig. 3). This has been possible because various specific molars and other specific bone parts have appeared and also due to the reliable presence of cut marks and deliberate fracturing of various human bones.

We have other examples from the discovery of a large number of Neanderthal individuals in the same site but in this case, it has been possible to study the mitochondrial DNA of twelve of them, which provides a new view of some of their behaviour, such as the movement of females and the higher stability of males (patrilocality) in Neanderthal groups. Various lines of research are open that will explore the interpretation of this "family" on a scale unseen before now, helped by the good general state of preservation of the fossils.

Seven adults (3♀, 3♂, 1♀ ♂?), three teenagers (2♂, 1 ¿♀ ♂?), two juniors (1♂?, 1¿♀ ♂?), one child (1♀ ♂?) and a total of ~2100 items give an illustrative source of information about laterality (right-handedness); the use of the mouth as a third hand by all adults and teenagers (grooves in the front

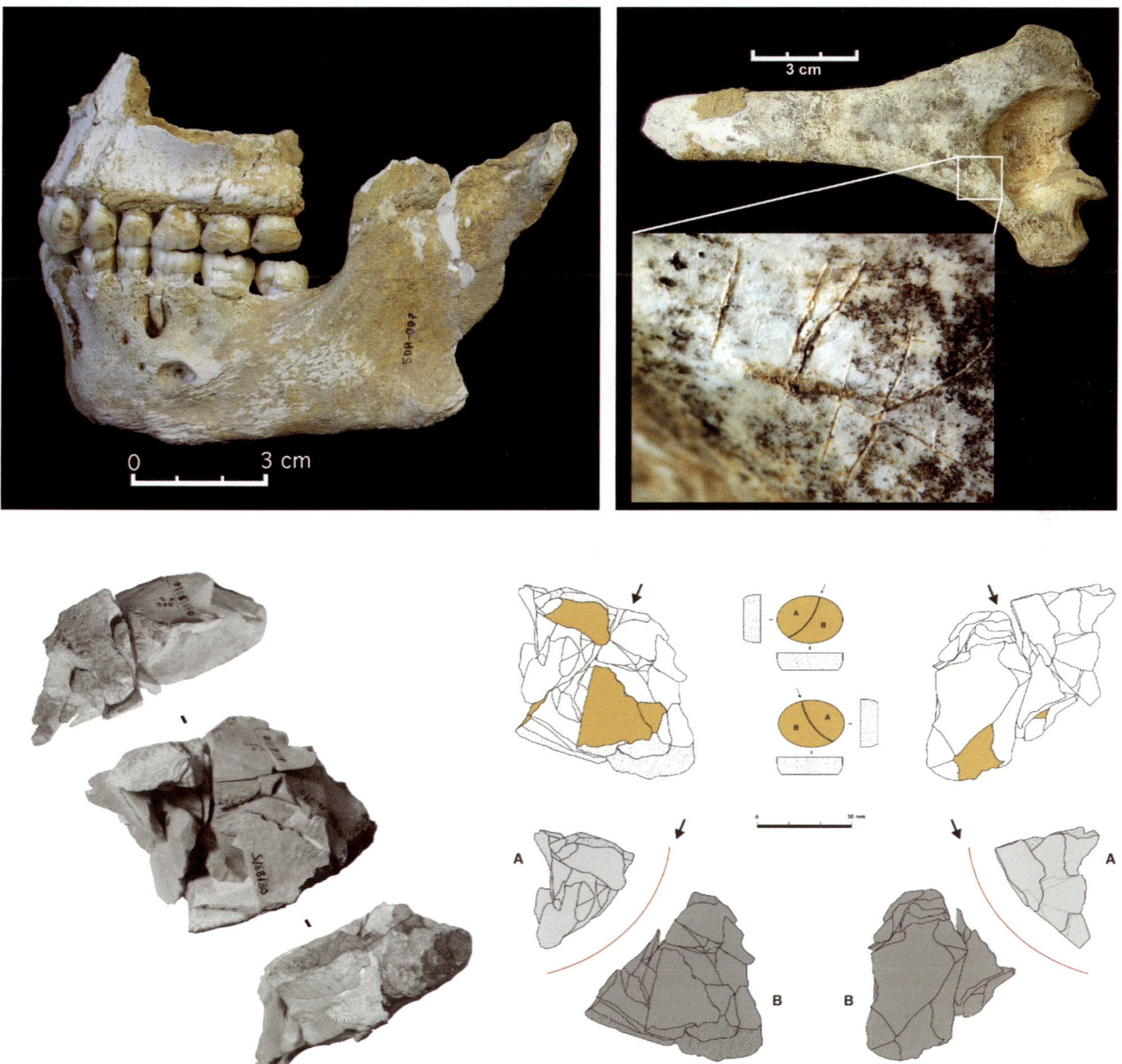

Figure 3. *Top left*: Side view of a jaw and maxilla in anatomical connection. *Top right*: Cut marks on a humorous. *Bottom*: Photo and sketch of one of the reconstructed assemblages with a total of twenty-one pieces.

teeth); episodes of physiological stress –malnutrition– (at least one hypoplasia coinciding with weaning and, in some cases, two or more); a mandibular abscess on adult 2 that must have caused chewing problems and pain; calculus present in all individuals with traces on a specimen of bitumen and consumption of medicinal plants; estimated height (between 164-171cm and between 153-161 cm: an average of 164cm); a neurocranial morphology tending towards brachycephaly; a slight anatomic variation depending on the geographic area, those from the south tending more towards a wider face and less prognathous than those from the north; and their skeletal characteristics correspond to those known as classic Neanderthal.

In addition, one adult female was red-haired and fair-skinned; one individual was blood type 0 (variant 0_{01}); Neanderthals had language, although at the moment we do not know how complex it was; one specimen could detect bitter taste but needed to eat a large quantity of the product to notice it; and the mitochondrial lineage of twelve individuals could be established. Thus, four adults (1♀, 3♂), two teenagers and one junior belong to lineage A; one adult female belongs to lineage B and one adult (♂), one teenager, one junior and one child belong to lineage C. What is significant is that each adult female has a different lineage (A, B, C) and that all adult males belong to the same lineage (A).

Therefore, at some time, a culinary practice was carried out on a group that was related to one another to some extent, which gives a very accurate snapshot of not only a biological fact but also a cultural one, their remains being left in the aforementioned rock shelter in a way that they were not affected by carnivores or rodents and could smoothly fossilise until they were discovered.

4. The qualities of the material culture and of the biotic and abiotic resources (Fortea *et al.*, 2003; 2007a, 2007b, 2007c, 2009, 2010; Rasilla *et al.*, 2011a, 2011b; Sesé, 2011; Sanchiz and Martín, 2011; Santamaría 2012; Santamaría *et al.*, 2010, 2011; Duarte *et al.*, e. p.; Tarriño *et al.*, 2013).

Associated to the human fossils, around ~400 lithic artefacts with unmistakable Mousterian type-technology conditions and a few fauna remains have been found. The type of raw material –Piloña flint– used in general stands out; the refitting of various lithic pieces that currently represents 20%, but this will increase with new yearly incorporations (Fig. 3); the arrangement of the archaeological record and the scarceness and properties of the macro-mammal fauna (deer, large bovid, chamois, horse, wolf and bear) .

The presence of Cretaceous flint in primary and secondary position in the Neogene conglomerates is of significant interest because the Neanderthals used this raw material, and some pieces of quartzite, to make their tools in direct relation to the priority activity deduced from the data exposed: tools for processing their conspecifics. This is based on the fact that this material entered Osario Gallery at the same time and the fossils and the refits also show that cores were collected from the immediate surroundings, they were knapped, different elements were used (flakes, denticulate tools, etc.) and they were left in the same place.

A key food element, such as fauna, in principle does not have any relation to the activity considered because it only has marks from carnivores and, therefore, in this case it was not directly related to humans. It reached this deposit through the activity of carnivores and when the aforementioned event occurred, allof the material that was in this part of the site entered at the same time, getting trapped in the natural traps of Osario Gallery.

Data suggests that it is a unique cultural fact and occurred quickly over time, focusing on a prominent task; therefore, it is vital to discover –and we are working on this– other Mousterian sites near El Sidrón to document this other part of human activity that is not reflected in the present one.

Ana Cristina Pinto Llona*

25.000 years of Palaeolithic occupation at Sopeña (Asturias, Spain).

Introduction

Sopeña was discovered in 2001. It has provided an ancient and intact sequence of layers that reveals an intense Middle and early Upper Palaeolithic human occupation. Due to the wealth of findings and the sophistication of recording techniques, the excavation progress is relatively slow. Much of what we know so far about Sopeña comes from the analyses of archaeological materials and features uncovered in a small 2x1 test excavation. These advances have been published in different works (Pinto Llona *et al.*, 2005, 2006, 2009, 2012). Here I will summarize published aspects of Sopeña, and the work that I see as most relevant that has been carried out thus far and is currently in.

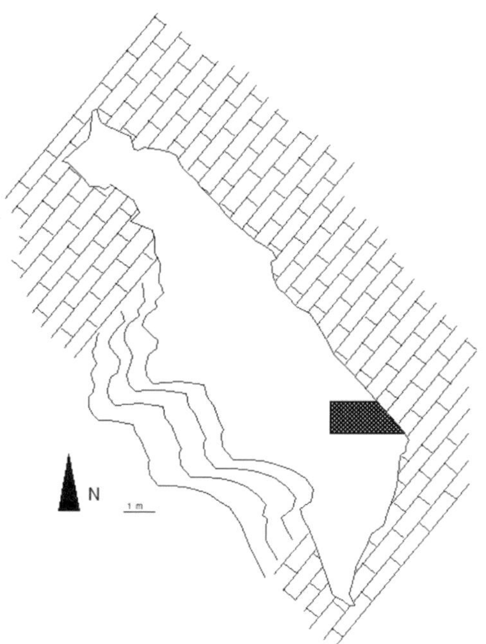

Figure. 1. Plan map of Sopeña. The shaded area indicates the test excavation.

Sopeña

Sopeña is located in the Onís county of northern Spain, bordering the Picos de Europa National Park, at 450 m. above sea level. It opens to the southwest (Fig. 1) and affords an unobstructed view of the valley of the river Güeña. It appears as a limestone shelter of modest dimensions. The entrance is protected by collapsed limestone blocks, covered by thick successive flowstone layers. Observations *in situ* and current studies (Ground Penetrating Radar) suggest that the observable floor, and the exposed stratigraphy, are the top part of much deeper sedimentary infillings, and thus that the cave is much larger than it appears to be now. All the levels are very archaeologically fertile, and lay almost horizontal. Adjacent to the flowstones, several limestone blocks of about 2 metres high, close the rockshelter to the northwest. On the upper surface of these there are deep linear engravings of the type that is sometimes assigned to the Aurignacian (Fortea Pérez, 2000-2001). On the side of one of these blocks, there is a pecked ithyphallic anthropomorph that is thought to be Neolithic in age.

Looking at the plan map of Sopeña, its sediments clearly split in two different units. An imaginary line in the middle of the site, from east to west, vertically cuts the sediment like a knife would a pudding. The stratified archaeological levels on which we are working are south of this line; they completely disappear north of it. In the northern part there is a massive flow of yellowish and unstratified sterile sediments. We are currently digging a small test excavation in this area to better understand the sedimentary history of the site. It remains to be seen if this is a natural or a prehistoric man-made feature.

The test excavation

In 2001 a 2 x 1 m test excavation was carried out (Fig. 1). The first archaeological layer (Level 0) appeared under more than one metre of cat-

* c/o J. Villarías, ILLA, CCHS-CSIC, c/ Albasanz 26-28, 28037 Madrid acpintoll@gmail.com

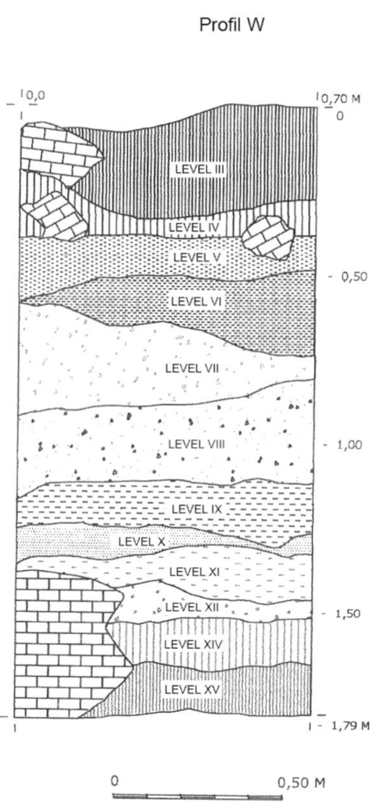

Figure 2. Stratigraphic profile of the west wall of the test excavation.

tle dung. Rockshelters in the area were used, and are still used, as cattle barns. Regularly, the dung is raked and carried to the nearby pastures as fertilizer. This practice might have scrapped away some upper deposits, although the total absence of anachronistic remains does not support this idea.

The test excavation was dug under the main fault in the limestone of the rockshelter. This excavation reached 3 metres below *Datum*, and 16 archaeological levels were exposed. Each exhibits well-defined differences in colour and texture, and in the type, size and density of other materials in it (Fig 2). We stopped the test excavation given the friability of the sediments, and also because of the presence of collapsed blocks in the lower levels that could not be removed without damaging the exposed sequence. Pale levels alternate with darker, some rich in charcoal; the sedimentation is almost horizontal, and the stratigraphic and archaeological sequence doubtlessly continues to greater depths. In view of this neat colour alternation and horizontality, and also of the micro-sedimentary analysis, I do not believe that there are inverted sequences in Sopeña. The test has been dug by the east wall, which dips further to the east as we go deeper; on the upper levels it is not possible to

LEVEL	LITHIC	% Lithic	Animal remains	% Animal remains	TOTAL	% Total
0	95	43,38	124	56,62	219	0,53
I	417	26,77	1141	73,23	1558	3,78
II	400	24,43	1237	75,57	1637	3,97
III	1153	20,62	4439	79,38	5592	13,56
IV	41	11,71	309	88,29	350	0,85
V	104	15,27	577	84,73	681	1,65
VI	115	13,79	719	86,21	834	2,02
VII	436	16,50	2206	83,50	2642	6,41
VIII	202	4,57	4220	95,43	4422	10,72
IX	662	7,91	7711	92,09	8373	20,30
X	276	7,78	3271	92,22	3547	8,60
XI	1232	48,52	1307	51,48	2539	6,16
XII	187	18,17	842	81,83	1029	2,49
XIII	130	16,09	678	83,91	808	1,96
XIV	90	7,95	1042	92,05	1132	2,74
XV	319	5,42	5567	94,58	5886	14,27

Table 1. Number of finds per level in the test excavation.

stand up, and the sediment adjacent to the wall is loose enough. Therefore, dates on materials from this area could offer aberrant results. Although we have tried to select samples from the area furthest away from the wall within test excavation, there is little doubt that dates obtained from materials recovered during the excavations now in course will give a fuller picture.

The great abundance of finds compensates for the small size of the site. In the 2 x 1 x 2 metres of the test pit more than 40,000 remains were retrieved. This fact suggests a frequent or even intense use of the site during the Mousterian, the early Upper Palaeolithic and the Gravettian. Table 1 shows the number of finds per level in the text excavation; bone fragments are more frequent in all the levels.

We did not identify any "Transitional" type tool in this sondage although they might appear elsewhere in the site. The transition Mousterian-EUP at Sopeña seems abrupt, as some dates, and also the neat qualitative difference in the lithics which are present suggest.

The lithic assemblage consists chiefly of debitage by-products and few formal artefacts, especially in the Upper Paleolithic levels. Regarding faunal remains, most bone fragments recovered are not taxonomically identifiable. Although not frequent, cut-marks on bone have been noted, and also carnivore action. We have not identified any human remains, which contrasts with the nearby site of El Sidrón (Rosas *et al.*, 2012) where the same time frame has provided many cannibalized Neanderthal remains.

Stratigraphy, archaeological attribution and absolute dates

Levels I to XI can be assigned to the Upper Palaeolithic: levels I to VII to the Gravettian and levels VIII to XI to the early Upper Paleolithic. Levels XII to XV are Mousterian. Although few in number, we have several absolute dates, listed below, that suggest a relatively rapid sedimentary accumulation for the Gravettian sequence, and a slower one for the Middle Palaeolithic (Pinto Llona *et al.*, 2012).

One AMS ^{14}C date from level XII points to this as the most recent Mousterian of the northern Iberian Peninsula (Maroto *et al.*, 2012), and this is followed almost immediately by the early Upper Palaeolithic. The dates obtained for level XII could suggest a Mousterian occupation of some 10.000 years. We consider these chronologies as a guide while more absolute dates are obtained and the current excavation progresses towards the deeper older levels.

The excavation method

The excavation of the sondage was conducted recording the depth of each level with a home-made

Level	Lithic culture	Method	Dating Lab. Ref.	Date BP ky	CalPal online CalBC
III	Gravetian	C^{14} AMS	Beta-198144	21.020 ± 100	25.168 ± 377
X	EUP	C^{14} AMS	Beta-198145	23.550 ± 180	28.496 ± 393
XI	EUP	C^{14} AMS	Beta-171157	32.870 ± 530	37.359 ± 857
XI	EUP	C^{14} AMS	GrA-39.760	34.470 + 650 – 450	39.726 ± 891
XI	EUP	ESR-LU	Williams 2005SP02	40.300 ± 4.800	
XII	Mousterian	C^{14} AMS	GrA-35.500	35.500 + 650 – 460	40.336 ± 975
XII	Mousterian	C^{14} AMS	Beta-198146	38.630 ± 800	43.052 ± 741
XII	Mousterian	ESR-LU	Williams 2005SP03	49.300 ± 5.300	
XIII	Mousterian	ESR-LU	Williams 2005SP05	57.100 ± 12.500	
XIV	Mousterian	ESR-LU	Williams 2005SP08	50.400 ± 8.700	
XV	Mousterian	ESR-LU	Williams 2005SP10	57.200 ± 12.300	

Table 2. Absolute dates of Sopeña. Level XI is the earliest Upper Paleolithic level. Level XII is Mousterian.

water level. As a rule, no vertical positions were taken of individual finds. However in the larger surface currently in excavation we have always used state-of-the-art technologies. We dig by discrete stratigraphic units within each level, using a 50 cm. grid. Using a Total Station we map in three dimensions every individual find. The position of the Total Station is rechecked and corrected several times a day, so the average error is of about 2 mm. This machine is connected to hand-held computers, equipped with GIS software (ArcView^{tm}, ArcGis^{tm}) in the cave, and also connected to a barcode scanner that transmits the correct number of the find to the database. All the archaeological finds bigger than 2 cm have been 3D mapped using this method. It allows the vertical and horizontal mapping of finds in real time, as they are dug. All the sediments are carried to the field laboratory, floated, sieved and sorted. Despite its accuracy and due to the abundance of finds, this method is slow and the excavation progresses relatively slowly. After 10 years of work we have barely started to excavate Gravettian Level IV, in a 6 x 2 metres trench.

Concluding remarks

There can be no doubt of Sopeña being a site to be taken into account in the debate about the Neanderthal to Cro-Magnon transition in northern Iberia. Whether with transitional industries or without them, continuous stratigraphic sequences *in situ* that document this time period are scarce in the north of the Iberian Peninsula. Aside from the excavation and scientific works, I have made a great effort to highlight the value of the site in the perception of the locals, doing everything possible to protect it, and to change the idea that Sopeña is only valuable as an occasional cattle –or, much worse, goat– barn. Local awareness is necessary, a consciousness of the true value of our Heritage and of the effort that we archaeologists carry out to bring it to the light. The returns will always be local, and social.

Acknowledgements

Our thanks to the Consejería de Cultura del Principado de Asturias, Concejo de Onís, National Geographic CRE, Wenner-Gren Foundation, Institute of Human Origins (ASU), Wings World Quest Foundation, Programa Ramón y Cajal del Ministerio de Ciencia e Innovación, to all the scientific collaborators of the Sopeña Project and to all excavation participants Also to Dr. Carbonell for inviting me to participate in this volume, and to the Editors for their work in coordinating it.

3

EBRO VALLEY, PYRENEES AND PRE-PYRENEES

Site	Map numbering
Abauntz	25
Arrillor	26
Atxoste	27
Cova del Parco	28
Roca dels Bous	29
Cova Gran de Santa Linya	30
Cova de l'Estret de Tragó	31
Fuente del Trucho	32
Fuentes de San Cristóbal	33
Gabasa	34
Kanpanoste Goikoa	35
Forcas	36
Nerets and Cova de les Llenes	37
Martinarri	38
Mendandia	39
Montsant valley ensemble	40

Pilar Utrilla *, Carlos Mazo *,
Rafael Domingo **

The Abauntz cave (Arraitz, Navarre, Spain)

Introduction

Close to the village of Arraitz, the cave lies at around 30 metres above the left-hand bank of the Zaldazaín River. The site has long been known about; it was mentioned by J.M. de Barandiarán as early as 1956. Hydrographically speaking, the cave is located in the Ebro Valley, but the proximity of the Cantabrian Region and the prevailing climatic conditions act as a link between the two watersheds.

The cave is strategically positioned between the flatlands to the south and the more rugged and wooded country to the north, lying, as it does, at 650 metres above sea level, close to the Velate Pass, which enables an easy crossing of the Pyrenees. It is a highland area made up of rounded rolling hills. Heavy rainfall (approximately 1,800 millimetres per year) is distributed across all four seasons.

The site has been excavated over two phases: between 1976 and 1979 under the direction of Pilar Utrilla (Utrilla, 1982), and again in 1988, 1991 and 1993 to 1996, when Carlos Mazo joined the team to co-direct the dig. Since then the team has focused on laboratory studies, some of which have been of great interest and made a considerable impact in the media.

The site's ten archaeological levels document 50,000 years of recurring visits paid by peoples with different cultural traditions and needs: the cave served as a hunting lodge during the Solutrean, as a permanent settlement during the Mousterian, Middle Magdalenian and Neolithic, was sporadically settled towards the end of the Magdalenian and during the Azilian before being used as a burial ground in the Chalcolithic and as a hideout from the invasions following the collapse of the Roman Empire, thereby providing us with one of the most complete and complex stratigraphic sequences found anywhere in the Ebro Valley (Fig. 1).

1. The Acheulean Tradition in the Mousterian. Bears and Cleavers

Signs of the oldest human presence correspond to level h, which was found in 1994 inside the cave, two metres below the preceding archaeological stratum (Solutrean); with around 8 m^2 of it being excavated. It contains no structures or hearths, although scorched bones were found. The thickness of the level is approximately 50 centimetres (Mazo *et al.*, 2013).

A number of bear teeth were dated by amino acid racemisation (T. Torres and E. Ortiz) at 47±7 ky, which would coincide with the date of AMS (GrA-16.960) >45000: both dates correspond to those of the industry, in which the relative abundance of cleavers suggests an MTA-type facies.

Some 2,000 recognisable and extremely well-preserved animal remains were found. Of these, 81.4% are of *Ursus spelaeus*, without signs of anthropic activity, which appear to be an accumulation linked with hibernation and death by natural causes. Of the rest, 10% correspond to carnivores (*Panthera pardus*, *Canis lupus*, *Vulpes vulpes*, hyenas) and only 7% to ungulates. Human consumption is documented (cut marks on the bones of *Cervus*), as is that of carnivores (gnawed bones of *Rupicapra*), which follows a pattern similar to that detected in the Moros de Gabasa Cave. Far fewer remains have been found of bovids, reindeer, ibex horses or rhinoceros. Almost 90% of the faunal remains are due to the cave being naturally used as a shelter by bears and other carnivores.

Of the 42 lithic remains the most abundant are 11 cleavers (26% of the total) (Fig. 2), which were found alongside 2 hand axes, 2 racloirs, 2 scrapers, 3 truncations and 4 retouched flakes. The cleavers are manufactured using limestone, basalt and other volcanic rocks, whereas flint was the raw material of choice for hand axes and other pieces, just as it was at Najerilla (Utrilla and Mazo, 1996d). This brings the Abauntz cave into line with other sites found in the hinterland of the Bay of Biscay coast line (Castillo, Morín, Pendo, Olha, and so forth) where cleavers were manufactured using identical technology (Mazo *et al.*, 2013), which entitles us to revive the term of *Vasconiense* (Basque) proposed by Bordes and which has today been reinstated by several authors.

2. Passing Solutreans and Gravettian Echoes

Some of the materials found in the disturbed level (Gravettian and Vachons projectile points) enable

* Área de Prehistoria. Universidad de Zaragoza. C/ Pedro Cerbuna, 12. 50009 Zaragoza
** Área de Prehistoria. Universidad de Zaragoza. Pza. Constitución, s/n. 22001 Huesca

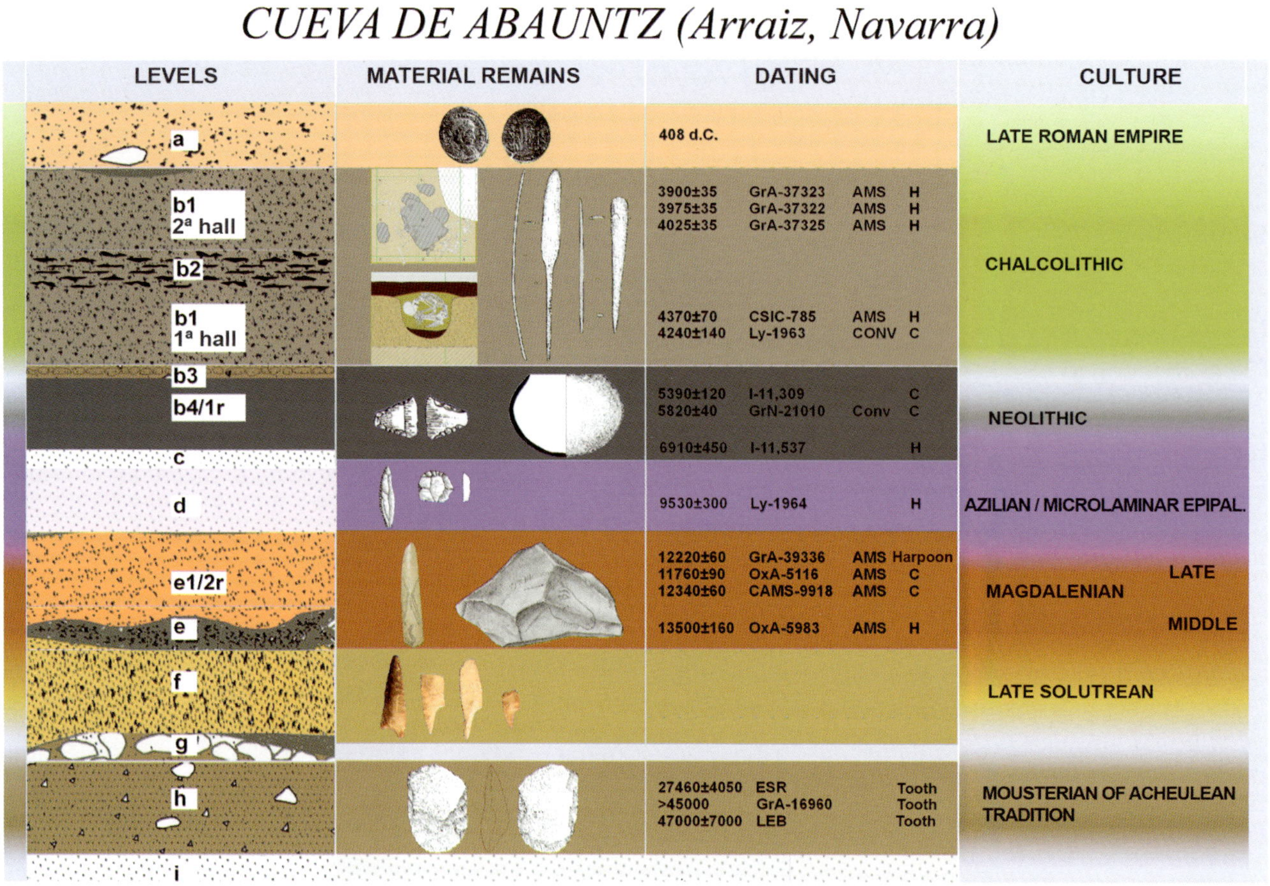

CUEVA DE ABAUNTZ (Arraiz, Navarra)

LEVELS	MATERIAL REMAINS	DATING	CULTURE
a		408 d.C.	LATE ROMAN EMPIRE
b1 2ª hall b2 b1 1ª hall		3900±35 GrA-37323 AMS H 3975±35 GrA-37322 AMS H 4025±35 GrA-37325 AMS H 4370±70 CSIC-785 AMS H 4240±140 Ly-1963 CONV C	CHALCOLITHIC
b3 b4/1r c		5390±120 I-11,309 C 5820±40 GrN-21010 Conv C 6910±450 I-11,537 H	NEOLITHIC
d		9530±300 Ly-1964 H	AZILIAN / MICROLAMINAR EPIPAL.
e1/2r		12220±60 GrA-39336 AMS Harpoon 11760±90 OxA-5116 AMS C 12340±60 CAMS-9918 AMS C	MAGDALENIAN LATE
e		13500±160 OxA-5983 AMS H	MAGDALENIAN MIDDLE
f g			LATE SOLUTREAN
h		27460±4050 ESR Tooth >45000 GrA-16960 Tooth 47000±7000 LEB Tooth	MOUSTERIAN OF ACHEULEAN TRADITION
i			

Figure 1. The stratigraphic sequence documented in the Abauntz cave indicating the archaeological levels, most significant materials, dates and cultural allocation.

one to suggest the possible presence of a Gravettian level in the cave that has since disappeared due to karst activity (Fig. 3.1).

With respect to level f, altered following the sedimentation thereof, it still contains residual elements that would appear to date back to the Upper Solutrean, though the settlement of the site is by no means intense or especially fertile. The highlights of the limited number of finds are a thick flat retouched perforator and some beautiful notched projectile points, most of which are broken, which leads one to believe that the site was used as a temporary hunting camp where broken weapons were replaced and repaired (Fig. 3).

This flat retouch is found alongside two projectile points featuring abruptly retouched notches that look like they could have come from the Cave of Salpetriere, thereby affirming the "hinge-like" nature of the site that links it with both Bay of Biscay-Atlantic and Mediterranean influences. This is the westernmost find as regards this morphotype, which is known in the foothills of the central Pyrenees (Chaves, Trucho), where the projectile points are "more like those found in the Cave of Salpetriere" than those of the coastal regions (such as those with a curved peduncle found at Ambrosio or Parpalló). This lends added further weight to the idea of a communication route with the north of the Pyrenees via the central passes (such as that of Cerdaña) as well as via the more logical coastal route (Bocaccio and Utrilla 2013, Domingo *et al.*, 2012). This technical duality found at Abauntz would reflect contacts between the peoples of the Ebro Valley with a tradition rooted in the Cave of Salpetriere and those moving along and settling the Cantabrian (Bay of Biscay) corridor running between Aquitania and what we now know as Asturias, in northern Spain.

3. Trans-Pyrenean Hunters of the Middle Magdalenian

Level e, the best known and preserved of the stratigraph, represents the only well-documented human presence during the Middle Magdalenianin the Ebro Valley, although it is clearly linked with the Cantabrian-Aquitanian world. It is dated (bone, AMS) at 13500±160 (OxA-5983; 16413±423 cal

BP). Identified during the first campaigns (Utrilla, 1982), Mazo used it to support his theory of the functionality of the Magdalenian lithic tools, which threw up a number of surprises. The burins had never been used for notching: on the truncated types the active part was the selfsame truncation, which was used for scraping skins; the blunt end of the burin was used to make the tool easier to grasp. Dihedral burins and perforators found in the same area had perforated skins; on the double burin-scraper implements the active part was the scraper blade, with the burin only being used for grasping purposes (Mazo, 1989).

Microspatial studies, palynology and functional analysis have made it possible to propose a reconstruction of the activities performed in the two main chambers of the cave (Utrilla and Mazo, 1992; Utrilla *et al.*, 2003). Significant concentrations were documented: dihedral burins and perforators in the entrance area in front of the hearth; scrapers and truncated burins in the right-hand side of Room 1, around a hearth; spears and other bone projectile points in the intermediate passageway and in Room 2. On the other hand, within the northernmost angle of the cave hardly any lithic materials were found, but there was abundant pollen from plants suitable for the preparation of rest areas: bracken and rushes.

Regarding the activities performed, we would suggest that the flint was reduced near the entrance, that is, in the best-lighted area; further in were the spaces used for working the skins (perforation and scraping), and right at the back the rest area. The interior room could have been a rest area where the weapons were stacked against the wal lor another work area used for the processing of skins, which could be sheared and/or smoked there. Several small-sized postholes were found between the passageway and Room 2, which leads one to imagine a structure for hanging skins consisting of a framework of posts that would have separated one area from the other.

Altuna and Mariezkurrena (1996) documented the only remains of *Saiga tatarica* found on the Iberian Peninsula, thereby confirming the relations between Abauntz and areas of the northern Pyrenees: 6 bones, barely 1% of one level and dominated by *Rupicapra* and, to a lesser extent, *Cervus* and *Capra*. The authors state that *Saiga tatarica* reached its maximum extension in Western Europe during the Magdalenian (especially the Middle Magdalenian, when they were to be found in places as close to Abauntz as Isturitz and Dufaure). The remains (5 phalanges and 1 central tarsal) lead one to believe that the animal was not hunted close to the site, but that these bones were attached to a skin brought in by people who came from Aquitania.

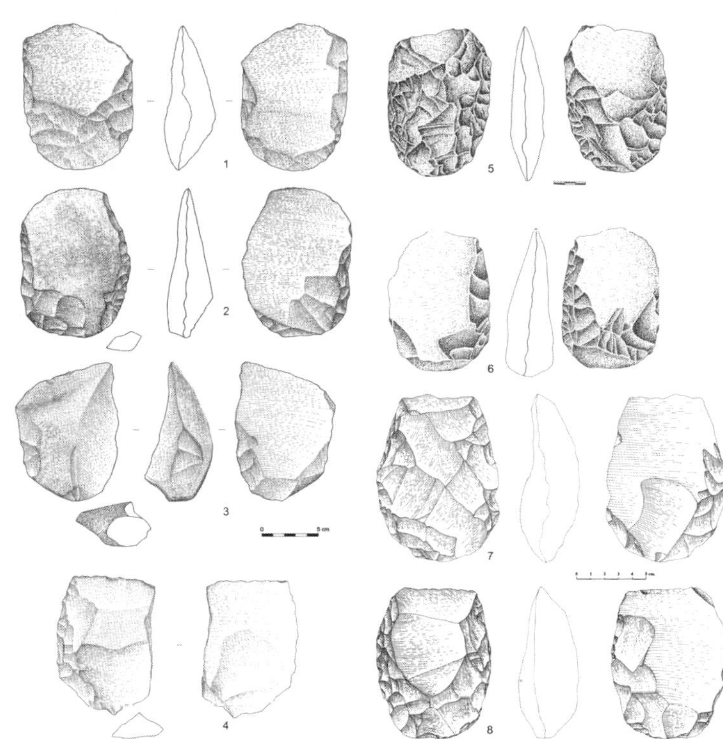

Figure 2. Cleavers found in level h of the Abauntz cave (Navarre, Spain) (1 to 4) compared with other of the Najerilla River site (La Rioja, Spain) (5 to 8).

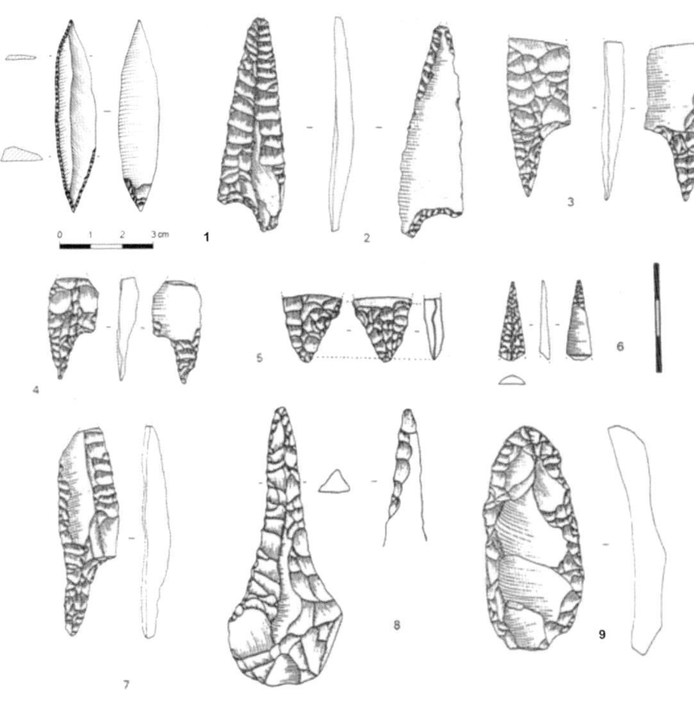

Figure 3. Vachons projectile point (No. 1) and Solutrean materials from level f

The large number of bone industry remains could be seen as confirmation that Abauntz would appear to have been dependent upon the large settlement of Isturitz, although it also presents similarities with communities of western Cantabria. The complex decorative motifs that embellish the stag horn rods of Abauntz are almost identical to those found at sites such as Caldas and La Viña in Asturias, Isturitz in Pyrénées-Atlantiques or La Madeleine in the Dordogne, which went to make up a Magdalenian koine along the entire coastline of the Bay of Biscay and in the southeast of France. Abauntz is located at a key strategic point; it is close (and with easy access) to large settlements such as Isturitz. We are able to point out three other decorative motifs found at different sites: a series of triangles framed within parallel lines (*chevrons emboités*), reversed parentheses and bison heads in profile. (Utrilla and Mazo, 1996 a and c; Utrilla *et al.*, 2013; Duarte *et al.*, 2012).

The level also provided two bones engraved with marks in multiples of seven, which evoke calendar counts referring to lunar phases that are relatively simple to follow with a minimum observation of the night sky (Utrilla, 2004; Utrilla and Martínez-Bea, 2008, Mazo *et al.*, 2008): one hyoid horse bone, perforated for suspension, and a mammoth ivory pendant. The hyoid has two series of 13 and 14 deep incised in its sides. The ivory pendant bears five series of marks with the sequence 10-14-14-14-14. This type of pendant has also been found at sites such as La Güelga and Tito Bustillo (2 at each, also in multiples of seven) or at the faraway cave of La Marche (in the French Department of Vienne), where at least three perforated hyoids bearing marks of this type have been found.

4. The Late Magdalenian of Level 2r

Dated using C14 at 11760±90 (OxA-5116; 13643±151 cal BP), this is one of the less productive levels with barely a few dozen lithic remains being found.

The most important discoveries regarding this period of settlement are three pieces of portable art, namely, three stone blocks engraved with diverse figures. After an intense period of study (Utrilla and Mazo 1996b and c; Utrilla *et al.*, 2004 and 2007-2008), in 2009 an article that was to have great media impact was published in the magazine *JHE* claiming that one of them contained Western Europe's oldest map (Utrilla *et al.*, 2009).

Included on one of the faces of block 1 is what we interpret as being the oldest representation of a map showing the immediate surroundings of a prehistoric settlement. A number of engraved lines show what would appear to be the landscape as seen from the cave: a mountain, streams and ravines running down from the hilly area to the plane... and some of the animals that inhabit these places: extremely schematic ibex (bodies in profile, head front-on indicated using two superimposed "V" shapes) places around the mountain, two young bovids on what would appear to be the plane... Then there are marks that have been interpreted as paths and fords on what would appear to be a "guide" to the immediate area for the group of humans living there or, given that the block was left abandoned there, for other hunting parties. On the same face a large stag is accompanied by a series of spiral markings which could represent the noises or odours of its bellow.

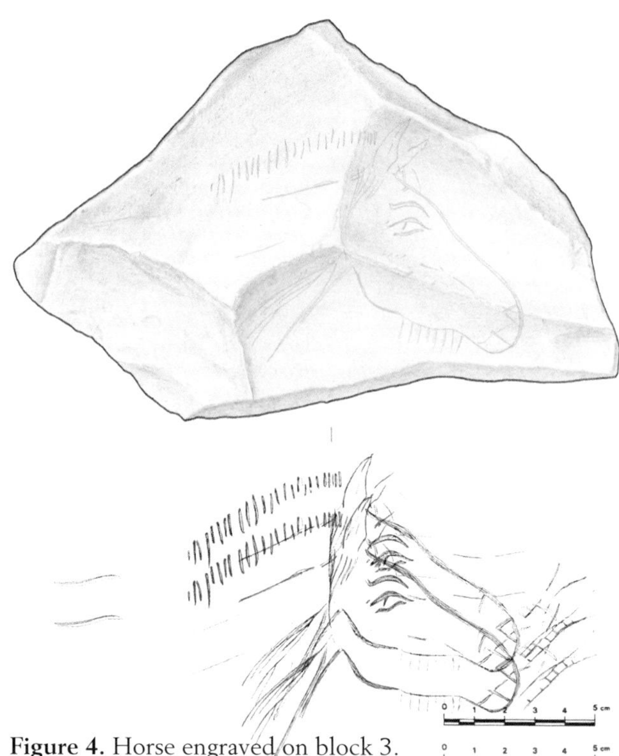

Figure 4. Horse engraved on block 3.

In contrast to the other two blocks, a natural hollow in block 2 could well have been used as a fat or bone marrow lamp. Its most eye-catching feature is the representation of a horse accompanied by several goats that repeat the schematic model found on block 1. Other marks similar to those interpreted as being symbols of the landscape can also be observed: a possible watercourse, a path...

Block 3 bears the most carefully executed representation, artistically speaking. Subtriangular in shape, it shows the engraving, with a profusion of anatomical details, of a protome of a horse, the animal that most characterises both static and portable Magdalenian art, especially in the area of the western Pyrenees (Fig. 4). Due to the frequency of its representation, is could be seen as being the "clan symbol" of a human community with strong links to Aquitanian settlements such as Isturitz, where L. Mons (1996) identifies 180 horse or figures, or Duruthy, where the symbolic value of the horse is evident (Cleyet-Merle 1996).

5. The Last Hunters: The Azilian of Level d

This level only appears in Room 1. Its formation is linked with currents of water that washed materials from the Magdalenian levels down into it. Snail shells abound in a level that is archaeologically poor, in which around 70 retouched pieces and cores were found. Small reverse blades account for almost 41% of the finds, and unguiform scrapers and Azilian projectile points are also documented for a level dated using conventional C14 at 9530±300 (Ly-1964; 10858±405 calBP). This brief human occupation of the site forms part of a complex chronocultural panorama that has yet to be fully defined (Soto *et al.*, i.p.).

6. The Neolithic of Level b4

Level b4 bears witness to a notable period of human occupation with abundant structures: a number of holes and large hearths. A sterile layer of angular stones (b3) sets this level apart from the one below it. It produced blades marked by use and featuring abrupt retouches, smooth, crudely-made pottery alongside finely-crafted vessels that are black in colour with the surface having been worked with a spatula and burnished, a small polished stone axe head and two abruptly retouched and double-bevelled geometric microliths. Five holes were identified in the central area of Room 1. One could have been used for disposing of the ashes from the adjacent hearth and another contained diverse objects and materials: a pebble-based hammer-pestle-smoothing tool, a small polished hand-axe (less than 3 centimetres in length), a retouched blade and fragments of smooth pottery that once formed part of at least two vessels, one with a rough and the other with a spatulated finish.

The level is carbon dated using the conventional C14 technique at 5390±120 (I-11309; 6158±129 cal BP), thereby placing it the Late Neolithic. The area around the cave could well have been a place of temporary residence for groups of Neolithic peoples possibly linked more with animal husbandry than with crop cultivation.

7. A Large Collective Tomb: Chalcolithic Burials.

It is impossible to ascertain the exact number of burials carried out at the site due to the fact that many of the bodies were later moved and intentionally burned; the result is a thick layer of scorched bones covering a good part of the surface area. The total would exceed one hundred. These remains have been studied by J. I. Lorenzo, D. Turbón and D. Campillo, and it was E. Fernández (2005) who carried out genetic analyses and detected the presence of Middle-Eastern and even African lineages.

It has been possible to identify four types of burial. The oldest are the shaft tombs, individual or double, which usually include bone spatulas being placed close to the femur of the deceased. One tomb, named "Alberto", contained a mature individual, curled up and accompanied by two bone spatulas, a flat retouched projectile point and two stone barrel beads. This type of shaft is more frequently found in the passageway and in Room 2. A human bone taken from one of the shafts was dated at 4370±70 (CSIC 785; 5012±124 cal BP).

The burned remains occupied a uniform surface area of around 16 m² in Room 1. It would appear that incinerating the bodies did not form part of the burial ceremony, but that it was carried out some time later, perhaps for reasons of hygiene. Around this large area of scorched bones shafts were found that look like they had been sunk to avoid it. The archaeological material found in these included leaf-shaped projectile points, many with heat cracks, and a number of necklace beads. The level was dated at 4240±140 BP (Ly-1963; 4798±205 cal BP), almost contemporary with the shaft tomb burials.

A third type of tomb consists of a stone cist structure composed of blocks sunk vertically in the ground and covered with a large slab (of non-local sandstone). It contained the remains of two adult males, two young women and two children, all with their legs folded. Remains that might have been related with the aforementioned individuals were found in nearby graves: two adult males, a woman of over 30, an infant, a child and a young woman. They were dated at 4025±35 BP.

The last type of burial is that of the deceased being deposited without any visible structure. These are the most recent interments and must have been distributed throughout the entire cave. Near the entrance of the cave the recently deceased were laid on top of the burned human remains. The materials found with them differ insofar as they include peduncle and finned projectile points alongside their leaf-shaped equivalents. An outstanding feature is that of the presence of pendants made from wild boar tusks together with diverse adornments, as well as the almost complete absence of ornamental objects in Room 2, which contrasts sharply with the profusion found in the area around the entrance. Those in the entrance were dated at 3975±35 BP and those of the second room at 3900±35 BP. (Fig. 5)

8. Romans Sheltered in the cave during the Fall of the Empire

The last human presence recorded in Abauntz cave occurred during the period of instability and social violence towards the end of Roman rule when uncon-

Figure 5. Types of Chalcolithic Burial.

trolled armed groups (bagaudae) or bands who were struggling for power sowed terror among the population, either for political or purely subsistence purposes. It was during these hard times that a series of holes were dug (a hoe was found on the site dating back to this activity) into which objects of value were put, including silver rings and more than 300 coins that enable these events to be dated at between the reigns of Constantine and Arcadian: the minimum *post quem* date is 408, the year in which the most recent coin found was minted. A hiding place used during the barbarian invasions is another viable interpretation.

9. Conclusion

The surroundings of the Abauntz cave, which is geographically located in the Ebro Basin, clearly link it with the settlements of the coastal areas of the Bay of Biscay-Aquitaine. It was used, with different functions and intensity, by numerous human groups for a period of fifty thousand years. The first of these were Neanderthals, Acheulean Tradition Mousterians, whose occupations alternated with those of bears and other carnivores that sheltered and hibernated in the cave.

The cave was sporadically used by groups of hunters during the Upper Palaeolithic: perhaps during the Gravettian and most certainly, although without dates, during the Upper Solutrean, by a human group that combined Atlantic and Mediterranean influences.

The Middle Magdalenian period of Abauntz, up until now the only contemporaneous level in the Ebro Valley, is the most intense and significant occupation. It has provided microspatial information (activity and rest areas), functional information (the "anomalous" use of truncated burins and scraper-burins used for scraping) and data about regional contacts via the decorative motifs of its bone industry that strongly bind Abauntz not only with settlements such as the super-site of Isturitz and others of the Aquitanian area, but also with sites such as La Viña and Caldas in Asturias.

At the end of the Magdalenian there was a sporadic yet extremely interesting occupation that left us with three magnificent blocks engraved with portable art: a map of the surrounds (block 1), a lamp decorated with similar subjects (block 2) and an isolated representation of a horse that could be the symbol of the Isturitz Clan (block 3).

The last hunters to visit the cave were people of the Azilian tradition: the low intensity of this particular human occupation is matched by the poor sedimentological condition of the level.

The first non-hunter gatherers present were Neolithic people who possibly used the cave for purposes of animal husbandry.

During the Chalcolithic the cave was used as a burial ground for several centuries and features three main interment methods: single shaft, cist or simply depositing the deceased on the surface, with at least one hundred people being laid to rest there. Some bodies were later intentionally burned, probably for hygienic and not ritual purposes.

The last specific use to which the cave was put dates back to the beginning of the 5th century AD, when some individuals hid objects of certain value there (silver rings and several hundred coins) against a backdrop of great insecurity and social violence, when the first groups of barbarians entered the Iberian Peninsula.

From 1976 to the present day our team has been working on the Abauntz cave, both in the field and in the laboratory. As we have seen, this is one of the most notable prehistoric sites, due to its stratigraphic strength and importance, in southwest Europe. A monograph regarding the first archaeological campaigns (Utrilla, 1982) and dozens of references made in specific or general articles bear witness to the importance of the discoveries made and the conclusions reached. A summary of all of these will appear shortly in *Quaternary International* as part of the minutes of the Conference held in Bilbao at the end of 2013.

All this research has been made possible thanks to the subsidies received from the Regional Government of Navarre and to the help received from successive research project grants awarded by the Spanish Ministry for Economic Affairs and Competitiveness (MINECO), one of which is still in force, namely, HAR 2011-27197: "Broadening New Horizons, Rethinking Ancient sites in the Ebro Valley". The signatories form part of the Consolidated Research Group "The First Settlers of the Ebro Valley", H07 of the Regional Government of Aragon.

Andoni Sáenz de Buruaga *

Arrillor cave (Araba, Basque Country): Climatic and industrial evolution during the Upper Pleistocene

1. Geographical settings

Arrillor cave is situated in the southern slope of the Basque Mountains –topographical ridge that divides the Cantabrian drainage (to the north) and the Mediterranean drainage (to the south)– in the middle of the Gorbea Massif, north of the Araba province. Administratively, Arrillor cave is located

* Círculo de Estratigrafía Analítica. Departamento de Geografía, Prehistoria y Arqueología. Facultad de Letras. Universidad del País Vasco (UPV-EHU); (andoni.buruaga@ehu.es)

Figure 1. Geographic settings of Arrillor.

in the municipality of Murua, in the Zigoitia valley (Fig. 1).

Its geographic coordinates are X=521.057, Y=4.761.540, and it is located at 710 metres a.s.l.

The entrance cave has an eastern/north-eastern orientation and lies in Urgonian limestone formation. The cave is 150 metres long, and its axis is east-west oriented. The site is situated at the southern end of a rocky spur, on the confluence of two ravines, Asunkorta (from the west), and Errkaseku (from the east); both flow together into the Zallas River, 25 metres in a straight line from Arrillor cave and 12 metres down the slope. This orographic context provides a strategic location because of the hydrographic resources available and its privileged position to monitor game movements.

2. Research on Arrillor cave

The first archaeological research was conducted in 1959 by J.M. Barandiarán and D. Fernández Medrano, who excavated a test trench, 3.5 m^2 and 1 metre deep, at the entrance of the cave (Barandiarán and Fernández Medrano 1959). The excavation provided a small collection of lithic artefacts and faunal remains of prehistoric appearance, but results at that time did not provide any precise chrono-cultural diagnosis.

Thirty years later, in 1989, A. Sáenz de Buruaga set up a systematic study project on Arrillor cave, framed in a broader research programme aimed at discovering Paleolithic sites in the territory of Araba. Since then, seven archaeological campaigns, focused on the cave entrance, have been undertaken between 1989 –1994, and in 1997.

The excavated area was divided using a 22 m^2 grid, and in some parts reached 5 metres deep. On that substantial archaeological deposit, a significant number of human occupations, particularly Mousterian evidence, occurred along different climatic episodes of the first half of the last Würm glaciation. Also, some data from Magdalenian occupation were even registered in one level (Sáenz de Buruaga, A., 1989, 1990, 1991, 1992, 1993, 1994, 1997). In 1997 regular excavation was terminated.

3. Sedimentary strata dynamics

Sedimentary stratigraphy deposited at Arrillor cave correlates with isotopic stages 3 to 1, and represents diverse events between the Würm II and the Würm IV, according to the chronostratigraphic alpine denomination

The sedimentology study is in progress, but the paleoclimatic correlations and the subsequent interpretation established during the excavation is still valid (Hoyos *et al.*, 1999). Moreover, the identification and definition of the levels at the archaeological sequence followed the theoretical basis of "Analytical Stratigraphy" (Laplace, 1971; Sáenz de Buruaga, 1996; Sáenz de Buruaga *et al.*, 1998).

The stratigraphic sequence of Arrillor has a depth of *ca.* 5 metres. It can be divided basically into three sedimentary complexes: one in the bottom part, with cryoclastic and alluvial deposits; one in the middle, of fluvial origin; and one in the upper part, also of cryoclastic formation, with severe postdepositional alterations in the middle-upper section (Fig. 2 and Tab. 1).

- The **lower sedimentary complex** encompasses a series of levels with cryoclastic origin (*Cag, Blm, Car, Clmg, Cglm* and *Clm*), coexisting with other levels of fluvial origin (*Lgj, Ln* and *Lj*). This sedimentary complex is about 50 to 115 cm thick. The presence of this type of deposits with well-differentiated sedimentary components, and its stratigraphic position in the general sequence, suggest its formation was probably during a more advanced cold temperate phase of Würm IIa, in the climatic transition from Würm IIa to Würm IIa/b.

Figure 2. Sedimentary deposits in the anterior frontal sector, of the central area of the excavation.

In these cryoclastic levels, several Mousterian lithic artefacts associated with some faunal remains were found.

- The **middle sedimentary complex** is clearly of fluvial origin. It is 245 to 305 cm thick. In general, this part formed as a result of cyclical succession of mechanical weathering, transportation and erosion, and analogous processes of deposition generated under temperate climatic conditions which, in the end, can be correlated with an interstadial phase (probably Würm IIa/b). Sand is the prevailing sedimentary component. Layers of this material, sometimes thicker and sometimes thinner, compose the deposit. At the base, silts replace sands.

On this arranged succession of yellowish sandy layers (designated *Sa*), greyish plastic clays layers (designated *Agp*), and other reddish sandy compacted layers (designated *Srk*), 10 sedimentary units (*SU*) have been identified. Though, in general, *Sa* layers and *Agp* layers are archaeologically sterile, *Srk* layers have yielded diverse archaeological evidences: basically, faunal remains and lithic artefacts that might be related with Mousterian techno-complexes. The most remarkable assemblages have been recovered at the *Amk* structural assembly (composed by layers *Amk*, *H-Amk*, and *I-Sa 8*), in the lower half of this fluvial formation, and in its upper third at level *Smk-l* (Fig. 3).

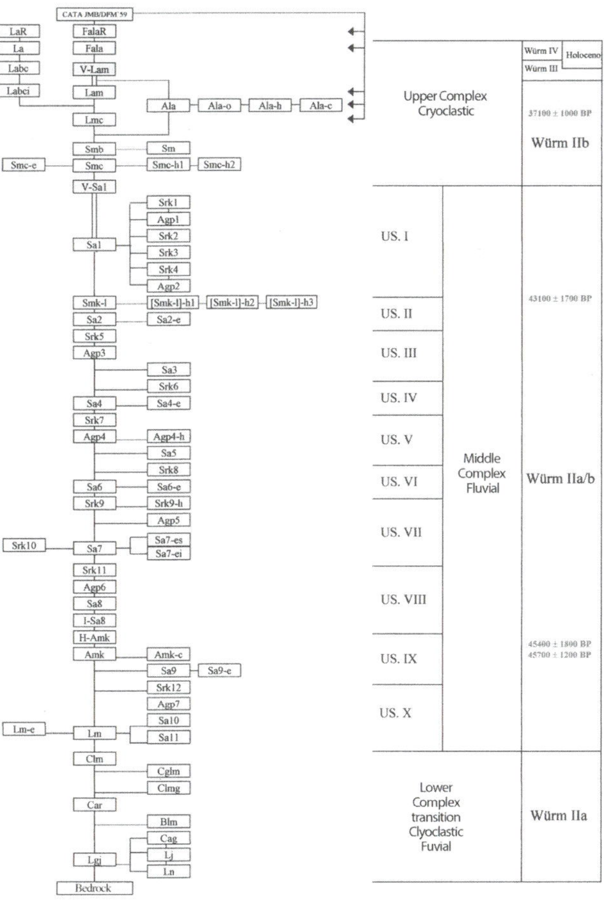

Table. 1. Analytical Matrix of the stratigraphic sequence at Arrillor cave.

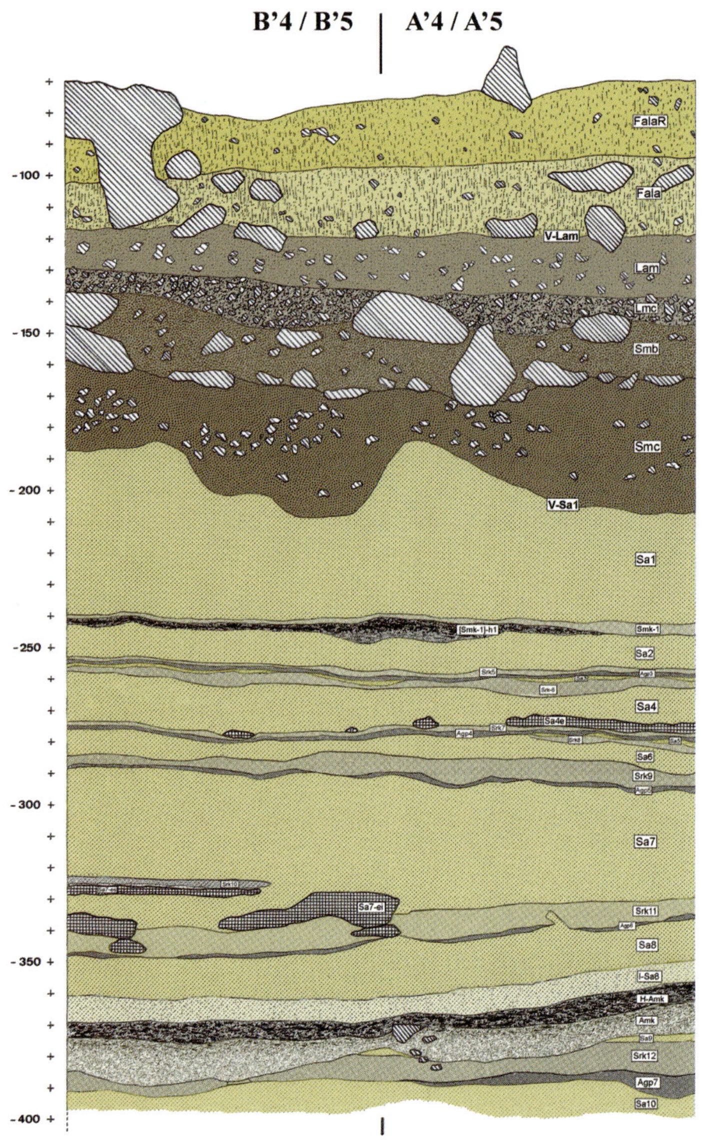

Figure 3. Stratigraphic posterior frontal profile at Arrillor: upper and middle deposits on the central area of the excavation.

- The **upper sedimentary complex** is, in general, of cryoclastic origin. It is 65 and 95 cm thick. After a net erosive contact on the base (*V-Sa 1*), an infill piles up. Two phases must be differentiated at this deposit: a) one in the lower part, which should be related to the stadial Würm IIb; and b) another one in the upper part, formed in the Würm III and IV. On top, a post Pleistocene episode is superimposed.

The Würm IIb strata initially maintains a fine brown sand composition with an increasing presence of gelifracts: first as cobbles (*Smc*), and later on as boulders (*Smb*), corresponding here with a particularly cold phase of the stadial. Afterwards, a change in the matrix is registered: sands are replaced by brown silts in a new stratigraphic episode (*Lmc*). While *Smc* and *Smb* have yielded a discrete number of faunal and lithic Mousterian evidences, *Lmc* provided a more substantial archaeological assemblage of Mousterian affiliation. This lower phase ended with stratigraphic unit (*Lam*), somewhat representative from a cultural point of view.

Furthermore, a new sedimentary hiatus (*V-Lam*), originated by a solifluxion flowstone occurred in a Holocene episode, removed, on the one hand, most of the Würm III and IV deposits from the central cave area, and on the other hand, piled up a new yellow silty-clay deposit (*Ala*). Only in a small lateral part, the stratigraphic evidences of advanced stages of Würm were preserved: first, in a level of cobbles and boulders (*Labc*), which are archaeologically sterile, and that can be related with middle and late phases of Würm III; and, later, in a yellow silt deposit (*La*), formed in the Würm IV, that contains lithic evidence of the Magdalenian period (Fig. 4).

4. Human occupations at the cave

Various archaeological references have been documented in the total 22 stratigraphic features differentiated on the sedimentary deposit of Arrillor cave. Before proceeding further, it is necessary to briefly address two issues about these particular archaeological levels: 1) with the exception of one level considered Magdalenian, the rest refer to different parts of the Mousterian period; and 2) in most of the archaeologically fertile layers, the amount of artifacts is scant and with very low diagnostic value, insufficient to provide a precise morpho-technical characterization: only layers *Amk*, *Smk-l* and *Lmc*, from bottom to top, gather the most significant and solid evidence of human occupation. In that sense, besides lithic artifacts, a very interesting collection of faunal remains has been properly identified (Castaños Ugarte, 2005). This data enhances the information regarding the environmental context of each deposit.

Figure 4. Upper deposits in a central area of the excavation. On the bottom, after a net erosive contact, the upper section of the yellow sands belonging to the middle sedimentary complex.

- The structural ensemble ***Amk***, placed on the bottom third of the middle fluvial deposit, includes the following stratigraphical units, from bottom to top: *Amk*, *H-Amk*, and *I-Sa 8*.

  In this group, a significant and varied set of lithic artefacts knapped on flint and quartzite was recovered. Among others, typical Mousterian artifacts such as sidescrapers, points, denticulates, and other pieces that are more morpho-technologically evolved such as scrapers, truncations and burins. These typological trends allow characterization as a polymorphic Mousterian, enriched with leptolithic performs of short-size pieces.

  The upper part of this sedimentary complex presents a horizon of hearths, of very dark colour, accumulated over the whole area (*H-Amk*). This horizon contains a large amount of charcoal and bones. More precisely, in this particular context the human molar (AR-1740) of a young hominid aged 9-13 years old was found (Bermúdez de Castro and Sáenz de Buruaga, 1999) (Fig. 5). Also, from this stratigraphic formation, two charcoal samples were AMS dated (45700 ±1200 B.P. (OxA-6084) and 45400 ±1800 B.P. (OxA-6251)) setting it chronologically in the middle interstadial Würm IIa/b.

Concerning the faunal remains, there is a predominance of ungulates: red deer and bison being the best represented species; on the contrary, goat and *equus* remains are scarce, and roe deer and rhinoceros are very rare.

- The ***Smk-l*** deposit, situated in the upper third of the middle fluvial complex, offers an interesting batch of lithic tools of Mousterian tradition (sidescrapers, point, etc.), and illustrative of the *levallois* debitage method, knapped almost exclusively on lidite. It could be asserted that the collection is specialized in the exploitation of this raw material (Fig. 6). Its particular techno-typological composition refers to Mousterian industries which are fairly specialized at sidescrapers and points, on large-sized and flat blanks, and using the *levallois* method.

Figure 5. Molar of a young Neanderthal retrieved at the stratigraphic deposit H-Amk and dated around 45000 years B.P. (Picture: Archaeological Museum of Araba Bibat; D.F.A.).

Figure 6. Types in lidite from level Smk-l (Picture: Archaeological Museum of Araba Bibat; D.F.A.).

The faunal spectrum still shows the predominance of ungulates, although together with bison and red deer, goat becomes more important; *Equus* on the contrary, remains very scarce.

One AMS radiocarbon date of a bone gave 43100±1700 B.P. (OxA-6250), setting the last human occupation preserved in the middle fluvial complex, at a later time in the interstadial Würm IIa/b.

- Level ***Lmc*** is situated in the bottom half of the upper cryoclastic complex. From a typological industry point of view, this level includes a more substantial lithic collection, which is well differentiated typologically from the previous repertory of the underlying levels *Smb* and *Smc*, correlated with a new cold climatic stage on Würm IIb, and associated with Mousterian industrial complex of denticulates, carenage blanks, and preferably flaking of black flint which is locally available and mediocre in quality.

Thus, in level *Lmc* there are also Mousterian industrial complex artefacts (sidescrapers, points, denticulates), together with some evolved morpho-technical types (endscrapers, burins), of acceptable quality of flint, and also of other local raw materials (quartzite, quartz). This industrial complex can be defined as Mousterian of sidescrapers and short-sized flat blanks.

The faunal assemblage is still characterized by ungulates, clearly prevailing red deer, followed by the chamois and bison, and in lesser extent rhinoceros, roe deer and *equus*.

The AMS radiocarbon date on a bone from this level provided 37100±1000 B.P. (OxA-6106), which situates the occupation on a later phase of Würm IIb, immediately previous to the moister and temperate episode of Würm II/III.

5. Concluding remarks

Systematic excavation carried out for 7 campaigns, between 1989 and 1997, on this cave, situated in the northern area of the Araba province, have provided a rich sedimentary deposit that includes significant lithic and faunal assemblage from Upper Pleistocene, as well as a Neanderthal tooth.

This deposit that is five metres thick, goes from an early phase of Würm II (or Würm IIa) to the Late Glacial of Würm IV. The most significant sedimentological and archaeological deposits concern the Mousterian period ñparticularly stratigraphic levels *Amk*, *Smk-l* and *Lmc* –, although less representative, isolated Magdalenian evidences were documented.

From bottom to top, three sedimentary complexes have been defined:

a) The lower complex, of cryoclastic and fluvial origin, includes some levels with Mousterian industries. Regarding climate conditions, this complex is related with the cold stage of the Würm IIa.

b) The middle complex: with a fluvial genesis, that preserved a considerable number of Mousterian levels and horizons. This complex developed within the moister and temperate phase of the interstadial Würm II a/b. Some sections of this complex have been dated between 46000 and 43000 B.P. (Fig. 7).

c) The upper complex: of cryoclastic formation, contains the last Mousterian industries, and preserves a small number of Late Magdalenian evidence. The sedimentary sequence seems to have been formed from different deposits associated to cold stages of Würm II (or Würm IIb), of Pleniglacial (or Würm III), and the Late Glacial (or Würm IV). One radiocarbon date from the middle-bottom deposits situates it in the late phase of Würm IIb around 37000 B.P.

Figure 7. Mousterian hearth form level Smk-l, on the upper section of the middle sedimentary complex of Arrillor.

The Arrillor Cave deposit addresses some key questions regarding the evolution process and the climatic and environmental transition from the Early Würm to the Late Würm in the inner territories of the Basque Country. Particularly worth mentioning is the preserved part around *ca.* 55000 and 35000 B.P. that offers quite remarkable sedimentological evidence.

This meaningful sequence should be contrasted with other Mousterian sites nearby, such as Axlor (Bizkaia), and Lezetxiki (Gipuzkoa), all of them in the same environmental unit of the Basque Mountains, forming a triangular arrangement where sites are separated by hardly 20 linear km (Sáenz de Buruaga, 2000: 62).

Alfonso Alday*

The site at Atxoste (Vírgala, Álava)

Atxoste is a rock shelter located by the river Berrón, south facing in the middle of an extremely varied landscape with valley and mountain resources. It gave shelter to late Upper Magdalenian communities and although its roof collapsed at the beginning of the Holocene, the conditions of the site resulted in its occupation throughout the Mesolithic (all of its phases are represented), the Neolithic, the deposition of burials being its final use in the Metal Ages.

The stratigraphic sequence is more than six metres thick and it is subdivided into several sections, where only the base layer –clay– and the surface –vegetable matter– are not of archaeological interest. We distinguish two major sedimentary units, the first from the late Pleistocene of rapid formation, and the second from the Holocene of slower constitution. The internal coherence of the sediment, the absolute dating and its cultural context guarantee the viability of the deposit that is, for the chronocultural environment in which it is encompassed, the most significant site in the Ebro basin, at least.

Excavation of the shelter was carried out, without interruption, between 1995 and 2006 under the direction of A. Alday.

Stratigraphic sequence

Level VIII sedimentary base of humid, plastic and compact clays from Maestu diapir. Its initial light brown colour turns orangey. It has no archaeological interest.

Level VII: 80 cm thick, with a dark loam clay and organic material matrix, which incorporates large blocks encrusted at different times, compressing the soil. Cold and humidity caused waterlogging and frost weathering which fractured the blocks. Thus the level will evolve internally, with different colourations, textures and higher fracturing. Culturally, it corresponds to the late Upper Magdalenian, its lithic retouching is characterised by an extensive representation of back edged arrowheads and blades and scrapers. It has no noteworthy bone industry and the fauna is very fragmented.

Level VI: dense, one–and-a-half metre thick unit whose formation was affected by the collapse of the canopy and subsequent breaking of the blocks, causing various dispositional situations. Its considerable thickness can be separated internally: from its base to –320, characterised by the significance of major fracturing and the compactness of the soil; from –320 to –270, where the soil becomes lighter and takes on a looser texture; from –270 to the top, with more compact, gritty and organic sediments. This separation is coupled with the individualisation of three cultural units: the lower from the laminar Mesolithic, where back edge tools are the most abundant retouched objects; the intermediary Sauveterrian style, where the evolution of back edge arrowheads and the introduction of geometric microliths and splintered pieces is noticeable; the top, which offers a significant industrial change as its industry rests on lithic flake and denticulate tools made from irregular materials (racloirs, perforators or other prototypes); tools that define the Mesolithic of notched and denticulate tools.

Level V with a thickness of 15-20 cm, with a loam structure, brown-red colour and constant presence of white and black (carbon) specks. There is a significant proportion of land molluscs and numerous hearths. Culturally, it adheres to the Mesolithic of notched and denticulate tools, offering a morphotechnological evolution compared to the previous episode.

Level IV: its thickness ranges from 20 to 25 cm, with clarified soil, a noticeable fall in Helix cepaea nemoralis and elements with higher fractioning. They are more compact and humid sediments. Culturally, its retouched industry adheres to geometric Mesolithic, with more trapezoids than triangles, a presence of mircoburils, back edge blades

* Área de Prehistoria Universidad del País Vasco (EHU/UPV). Tomás y Valiente s/n 01006 Vitoria-Gasteiz. a.alday@ehu.es

and a good selection of substrate elements (with a certain inheritance from lithic flake tools).

Level III: of continuous formation but where several units can be distinguished. The lower (IIIb2) of 20 cm of fine black loam, where helix colonies are represented that give a gritty feel to the soil; the intermediary (IIIb1), of 20 cm, with a horizontal disposition, with somewhat lighter loam soil and less granularity; the top, which is 20 cm thick, with finer soil and dark grey loam. This level stands out for being unctuous and greasy. Its base responds to the characteristics of geometric Mesolithic, now with a higher presence of triangles compared to trapezoids. The other two sections correspond to early Neolithic; segments in double bevel among the retouched lithic industry being very significant; Boquique style patterns, among others, on pottery; the discovery of a large windmill for grinding vegetable matter; the profile of sickles and the identification of wild and domestic fauna.

Level II: of varying thickness (between 15 and 35 cm), it presents a mixture of soils and archaeological products from the burial phase (level I) and from the last period it was occupied as shelter (level II). The soil is loose and loamy, brown in colour and with lithic elements from the Chalcolithic.

Level I: it conserves part of the organic matter from the surface level, in dry and loose brown soil, without a clear separation with respect to the

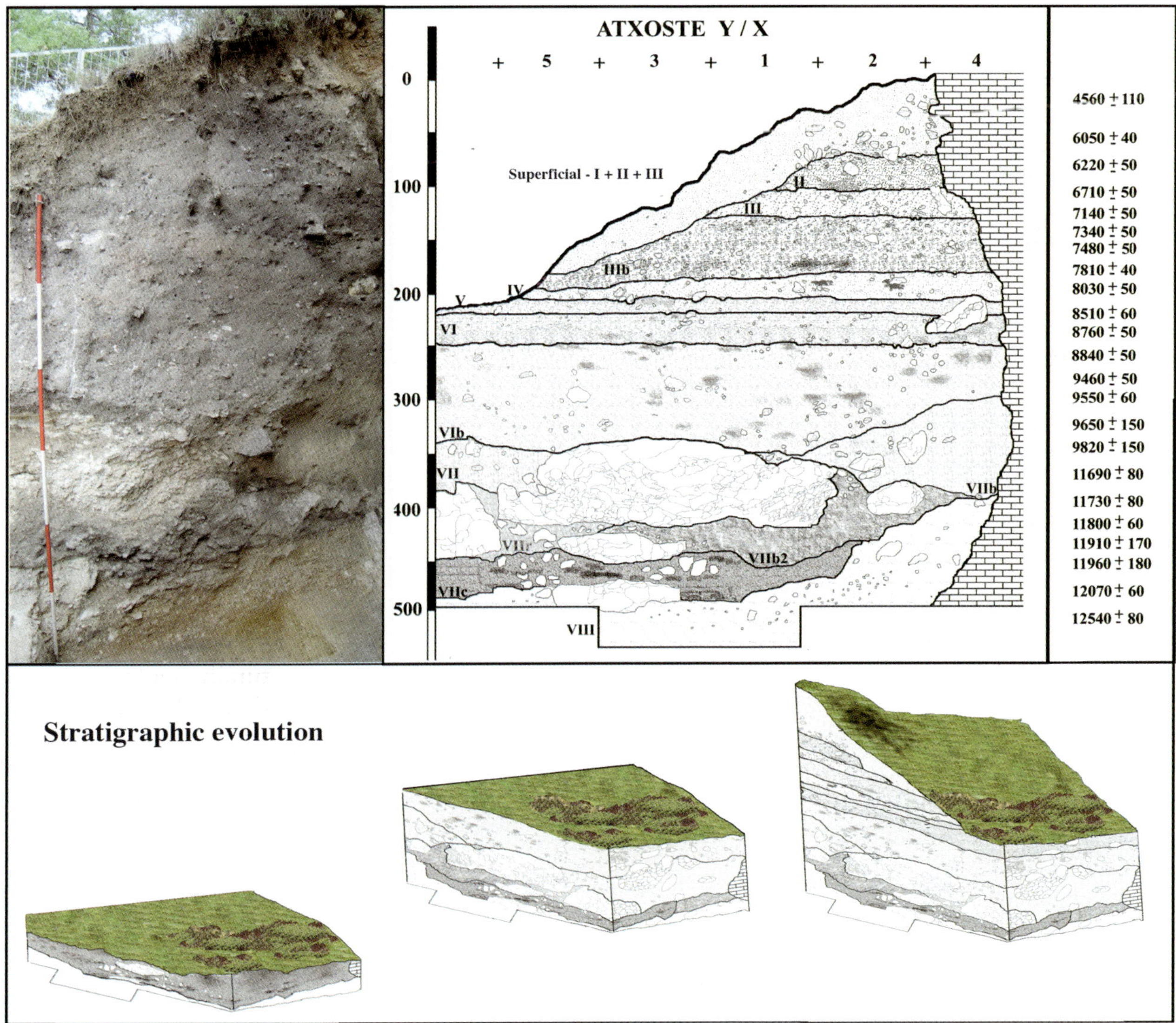

Figure 1. Stratigraphy of the site at Atxoste.

next horizon. Of the burial character ascribed to the Metal Ages, where a couple of bodies were arranged in foetal position, some in partial anatomical connection and the rest disorderly.

Surface level: organic matter with a grainy texture, dry and dusty in place, with an irregular presence of blocks. It has no archaeological interest (Fig. 1).

Level	Code	BP Date
I	GrA-9786	3360±40
	GrA-9787	3470±40
	GrA-24684	3680±50
II	GrA-24683	4980±50
III	GrA-6846	4730±50
	GrN-22739	4560±110
IIIb1	GrA-9789	6220±50
	GrA-13414	6050±40
IIIb2	GrA-13415	6940±40
	GrA-13468	7140±50
IV	GrA-13418	7340±50
	GrA-14419	6970±40
V	GrA-13447	7810±40
	GrA-13448	8030±50
VI	GrA-15700	8510±80
	GrA-15699	8760±50
VIb1	GrA-15858	9550±60
	GrA-35142	9510±50
VII	GrA-22865	11720±70
	GrA-22866	11760±70
	GrA-23107	11690±80
	GrA-22900	11800±60
D	GrA-13473	8840±50
E	GrN-26663	9650±150
	GrA-35141	9450±50
E2	GrN-26664	9510±150
	GrN-26665	9820±150
F	GrN-26666	11910±170
	GrN-26667	11960±180
F2	GrA-19554	12070±60
G	GrA-19502	12200±90
H	GrA-19870	11730±80
H2	GrA-19503	12540±80

Table 1. Carbon dating 14.

Cultural assessment

Atxoste is an archaeological deposit that contains information almost without interruption over 10000 years of prehistory; it has a rich inventory of material, flint, pottery and bone, and abundant recordings of fauna and carbon (Fig 2).

In the Late Glacial Maximum, Palaeolithic populations overflow their traditional environments of shelter to occupy more interior areas. In the Iberian Peninsula the phenomenon results in new settlements in, for example, the Ebro basin: in this context Atxoste reflects the settlement of populations in the upper reaches.

The choice of the place and repeat visits demonstrate the interest of the communities in exploiting an environment where valley and mountain ecosystems coexist. This results in the wide spectrum of fauna recovered during excavation: stag, deer, horse, boar, goat, chamois, wolf, plus smaller fauna and, anecdotally, turtle.

However, the territory does not have flint, the material used almost exclusively for making stone tools. It is collected in the outcrops of Urbasa (30km north east), Treviño and Loza (both at 30km south west), from the Cantabrian Flysch (at least 100 km) and in Neolithic times, evaporite was collected from the Ebro (around 100 km south east). The percentages vary from one variety and another according to the characteristics of each episode, reflecting, in any case, the will to exploit the region further.

The cultural stages represented refer us to various stages of the late hunter-gatherer. The Traceology define hunting practices, butchering, working hides, wood, bone... Over time, the presence of groups settling in the site stabilised; they extended their activities and in the late stage, they built a cabin next to the wall of the shelter as another sign of their geographic settling.

This model lives on in the early stages of the Neolithic, with certain innovations: renewal of lithic tools, the introduction of pottery, crop and livestock domestication (according to the identification of direct taxa or from indirect evidence associated to these practices).

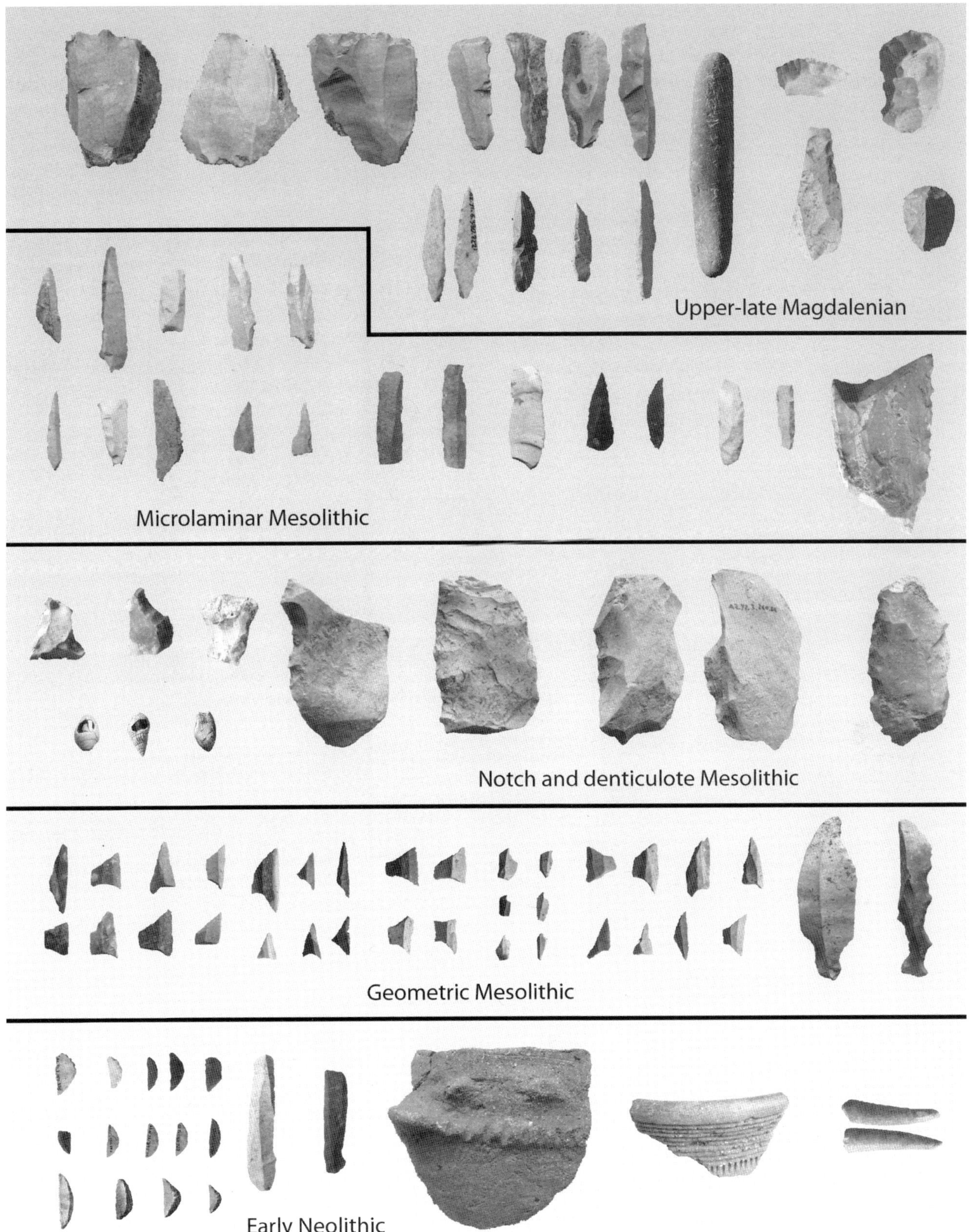

Figure 2. Archaeological materials at the site in Atxoste.

Javier Mangado*, José Miguel Tejero*, Josep Maria Fullola*, Maria Àngels Petit*, Marta Sánchez *.

Cova del Parco (Alòs de Balaguer, La Noguera, Lleida). The Magdalenian sequence

Cova del Parco is located in the pre-Pyrenees at Lleida, in the village of Alòs de Balaguer, in the Noguera region (coord. UTM 31 T – X: 329322; Y: 4642202). The archaeological site is placed 420 m above sea level and 120m above the Segre River, with a north-south orientation. A single 10.5 long by 4.5m wide gallery of triangular shape at the entrance forms the cavity, laterally communicates with a large shelter of 5.5 m by 30 m, is enclosed by a masonry wall of historic period.

The discovery of the archaeological site dates back to the middle 1970´s when the first excavations were carried out by professor Joan Maluquer de Motes in 1974, 1981 and 1984, which included almost the complete digging of the upper stratigraphic sequence containing ceramic levels. Ten years after the discovery, in 1984, a 3 m^2 trench allowed Dr. Maluquer de Motes to establish a stratigraphic sequence in six strata, finding in the deepest one a set of lithic materials of the Final Upper Palaeolithic (Maluquer de Motes, 1983-1984, 1985; Fullola *et al.*, 1988). Dr. Fullola restarted excavation activities in 1987, starting excavation campaigns which are still annually conducted and headed by several investigators from the *Seminari d'Estudis I Recerques Prehistòriques* at the University of Barcelona.

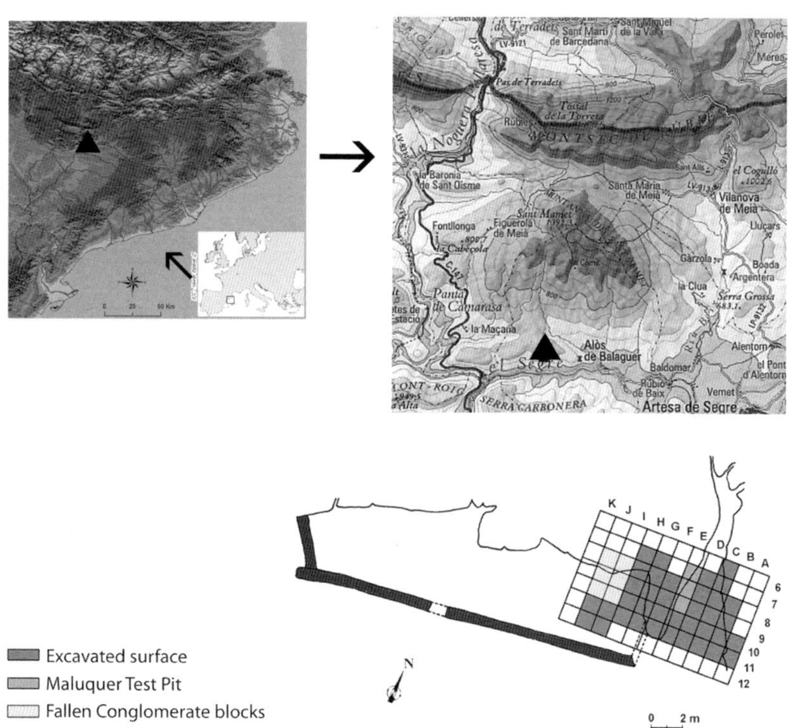

Figure 1. Location and archaeological site plan.

* SERP (Seminari d'Estudis i Recerques Prehistòriques) de la Universidad de Barcelona, área de Prehistoria, Departamento de Prehistoria, Historia Antigua y Arqueología, Facultad de Geografía e Historia, Universidad de Barcelona; calle Montalegre, 6, E-08001, Barcelona.

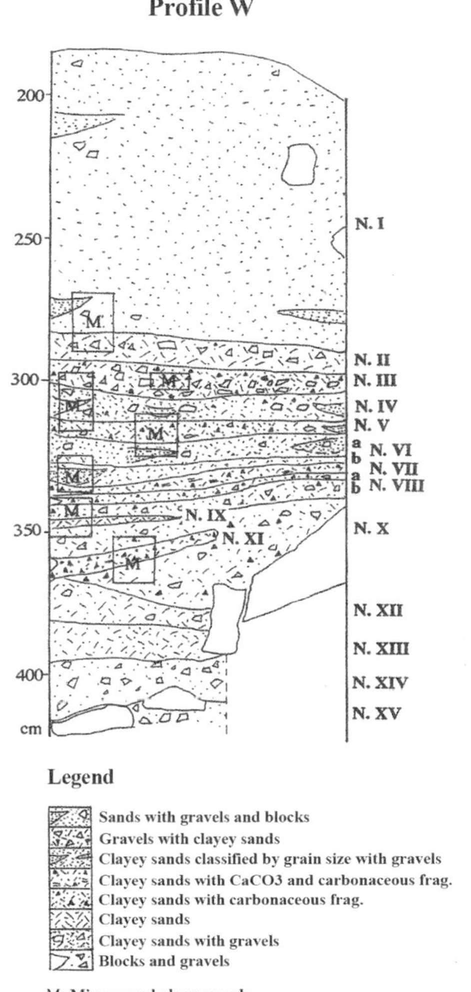

Figure 2. West sequence stratigraphy of the Dr. Maluquer-trench analysed by Bergadà (M.M. Bergadà, 1998).

1. Sedimentary Sequence and Palaeoenvironmental Evolution

The detailed analysis of the sedimentary sequence and the establishment of the palaeoenvironmental evolution from the "West stratigraphic sequence" led by Dr. Maluquer trench, were possible thanks to the studies of the PhD of M.M. Bergadà in which a sedimentary sequence in fifteen levels was established, one of the first scientific contributions from Cova del Parco to the Upper Palaeolithic in Catalonia (Bergadà, 1998:46-51, Bergadà *et al.*, 1999).

In the analysis of the sedimentary sequence two processes were observed: sedimentary as –runoffs and rock falls – and post-depositional –humidity and biological activity-. The lower levels correspond to rock falls –levels XV and XIV– being sterile from an archaeological point of view.

From level XIII to VI low intensity runoff processes, with a high human-induced activity, are produced. Climatically, the levels between XI and VII present a wet environment, except from level IX where a colder pulse is detected. From a palynological point of view, the presence of oak and fern spores in level XII demonstrate warmer and wetter conditions, as in levels VIII and VII where the presence of hazel and willow are recorded for the first time and the presence of oak remains. However, levels X and IX are cold and dry, highlighting the presence of conifers: *Pinus* and *Juniperus*, always in low percentages (Fullola *et al.*, 1997).

Sedimentation in levels VI to I presents high intensity runoffs and rock falls due to the break up processes of the wall and roof cavity. Also, from level VI to IV sedimentary crust formations can be observed pointing at arid conditions and colder pulses than the former ones. In levels III and II, especially in the first, a gravel deposit, limestone blocks, and conglomerates in cracked states were observed, related to periglacial conditions, coming up from the cavity´s wall and roof breaking up. In level II an increase in humidity was recorded. In level II contact, large limestone blocks and fallen conglomerates can be seen as a consequence of climatic process. Finally, sedimentation of notable strength in level I is due to different intensity runoff processes in the water flow. In the higher part of level I, clastic evidences are located: small rock falls and wall break up. The environmental conditions would be semi-arid with humidity pulses and cold temperatures.

In short, locates in levels XI and VII is a wet and warm environment with a cold pulse. From level VI, a semi-arid ambience is detected –storm rainfall regime– with cold pulses. Later, in level III, cold conditions still rule, however in level II humidity increases. In level I, an increase in storm rainfall eroding the slopes is produced –high sedimentation rates– in semi-arid conditions, with humidity and cold episodes (Bergadà, 1998: 79-80).

2. Cova del Parco archaeological Sequence

Archaeological materials at Cova del Parco, found during the excavations of Dr. Maluquer de Motes and housed in the Montsec Museum at Ar-

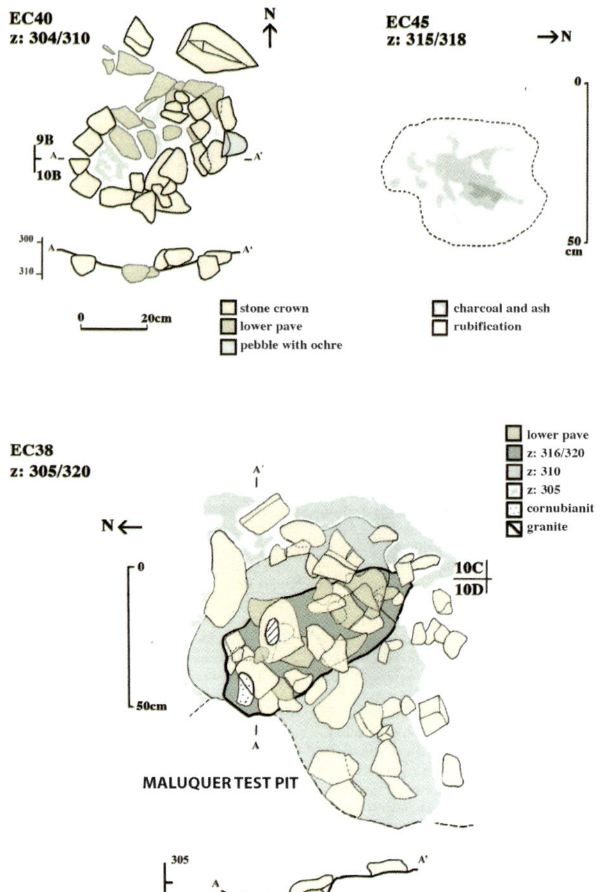

Figure 3. Some of the Magdalenian hearths at Cova del Parco.

tesa de Segre, show the different Neolithic settlements from Cardial to Recent Neolithic, as well as the III millennium Bell Beaker Culture and the Early Bronze Age (Petit, 1996).

The excavations carried out by our team from 1987 have allowed the recording of a cultural sequence presenting three stages.

Firstly, in the Neolithic levels remain, almost inexistent, the basal part of a storage structure –silo– was recorded, dated with charcoal remains in 6120±90BP (GrN-20058); the ceramic content placed the abandonment in the Epicardial Neolithic, a moment in which it was reused as a landfill with plenty of manure and ashes (Petit, 1996).

Secondly, the excavation and the register of Epipaleolithic levels in the archaeological site were developed –from 1993 to 1999-, the presence of which had formerly gone unnoticed. This was the first time that the presence of a "classic" Epipaleolithic sequence in western Catalonia defined by Fortea was recorded with some microbladelets levels to which geometrical levels with triangles and segments were overlapped, together with many microburins. The excavation allowed the establishment of its corresponding cultural and chronological sequence.

Under a very ancient Epipaleolithic geometrical horizon –level Ia2, into depths of about –175/–200 cm– dated from charcoals coming up from two combustion structures –henceforth EC, *Estructuras de Combustion* in Spanish–: EC11 and EC12 in 10930±100BP (GifA 95562) and 10770±110BP (GifA95563) respectively, and with an industry in which micro-bladelets and geometric elements of Sauveterrian type are documented –triangles and segments– (Fullola *et al.*, 1998), a micro-laminar Epipaleolithic moment had appeared –levels Ib and Ic, into depths of about –200/–230 cm.–; this was dated with charcoal from the EC15a in 11430±60BP (OxA 8656) (Fullola *et al.*, 2004).

Finally, under this microlaminar Epipaleolithic and after an abandonment period, we document a very precise stratigraphic moment –a depth between 230/-240 cm– dated in 12605±60 BP (OxA 10796), corresponding to the last Final Upper Magdalenian settlement –level II–; it was separate from the rest of the Magdalenian settlements sequence due to a huge rock fall –about –240/–260 cm.–. After this moment, the Magdalenian settlements sequence, still being excavated today, was developed.

3. Radiocarbon dating of the Magdalenian levels at Cova del Parco

The sedimentary sequence analyzed by M. M. Bergadà (1998) was dated from charcoal samples removed from the same section she described. During these years, new dating carried out from recovered charcoals during the excavation process of different EC have allowed us to establish the chronological sequence that we present, hereunder all radiocarbon dates are uncalibrated. Thus, we have distinguished a Final Upper Magdalenian, dated in 12460±60BP (OxA10797) (z-269 cm) and 12560±130BP (OxA10835) (z-271 cm) (the date 13175±60BP corresponding to OxA10798 from charcoal recovered in the inner part of the EC19 (z-273 cm), is not considered valid) from an Upper Magdalenian, placing its beginning in depths between –280/–285 cm. based on the elongated scalene triangles documentation with different dating: 12995±50BP (OxA13597) (z-285 cm), 13025±50BP (OxA13596) (z-280 cm) and 13095±55BP (OxA17730) (z-293,5 cm).

The progressive disappearance of these lithic elements, as well as, the appearance of different technological changes, for example, in the laminar support modules: typological –new spear point types– and functional –in the settlement dynamic, as well as the last radiometric dating obtained: 13255±50BP (OxA29336) (z-322 cm) and 13475±50BP (z-318 cm) establish the hypothesis of detecting the Middle Magdalenian settlements.

4. Cova del Parco Magdalenian settlements main features

We are now presenting a synoptic summary about what archaeological excavations at Cova del Parco represent in the Magdalenian. This production will be incomplete as the field work still continues.

4.1. Intrasite dynamic

We want to point out that the excavation over a $40m^2$ extension of the Magdalenian settlements at Cova del Parco is not casual. One of our main priorities in the moment of dealing with the Magdalenian study in this archaeological site has been to develop it from an socio-economic perspective and human behaviors. This is why we carried out an excavation in extension, which allowed us to observe the spatial relations between the multiple traces –artifacts and ecofacts– and the evidenced structures. The combustion structures –EC– deserve a special mention from us, as we consider that the majority of the productive, social, and cultural activities of those communities were carried out around them, this being why they have received special attention throughout these years.

However, we must not obviate that our work faces an important problem: the trench-survey carried out in 1984 by Dr. Maluquer de Motes longitudinally divided the archaeological site by its central part, affecting the whole archaeological sequence. This is why we cannot establish with absolute certainty the stratigraphic continuity among the activities developed in each area in which the site has been divided, namely: on the right side, the space properly defined as a cave, and on the left side, the outer field considered a shelter. Furthermore, the trench suffered the irremediable loss of the contextual information attached to the archaeological materials recovered during their excavation, finally forming only a material collection.

The Magdalenian settlements at Cova del Parco are characterized by great complexity, highlighted by different elements. Firstly, by the number and diversity of the discovered and excavated structures; we also have the ECs, flat and not-delimited or delimited by a stone crown, or a pave in a bucket, simple or double; and we have the "Knapping Remains Deposits" "KRD", or "DRT" in Spanish (*Depósito de Restos de Talla*)– defined as carving remains accumulation, in a very small surface coming out from a concrete technical process (Mangado *et al.*, 2009, 2010). Secondly, the complexity has been proved from several activities recorded thanks to the typological and functional lithic tool diversity (Calvo, 2004) and over hard animal materials (Tejero, 2005). Both the production and repairing of lithic tools (Langlais, 2004, 2010), osseous tools (Tejero and Fullola, 2008), and the leatherwork in different stages of the operational chain (Calvo, 2004) attest to this.

Regarding the Final Upper Magdalenian, the spatial distribution studies of the traces, as well as the analysis of the combustion structures main features –typology, micro-stratigraphy and content– show us an important and multifunctional settlement of the cave´s central area where, together with the hearths´ culinary functionality –attached to many faunal burned remains– other activities arise, mainly of the working type: lithic works/flintknapping, bone, leather... In this way, those areas closer to the walls show their functional marginality and are mainly reserved as buildup of waste areas, as faunal remains of little or void nutritional value and lithic traces which were rejected for manufacturing are recovered in them (Mangado *et al.*, 2006-2007).

The outer area, or shelter area, is also characterized for this marginal behavior in which working activities were hardly developed, such as the possible smoking of skin or food (Bergadà, 1998: 77-79).

This behavior, so different in the use of spaces regarding the activities recorded in them, will be modified as we break into the Upper Magdalenian. Thus, the EC attached to this moment increase in presence and reuse in the outer area. The shelter´s

EC shows, at the same time, a higher typological and functional variability. In this way, together with the activities of purely signaling and lighting, lithic carving work activities attached to those structures emerge, which have allowed even technological refitting among different lithic elements.

The other structures showing the settlement complexity carried out by the Magdalenian hunter-gatherers are the already mentioned –KRD– which allow us to rebuild the mobility *intrasite* (Mangado *et al.*, 2006-2007).

4.2. *Resource Management Throughout the Magdalenian at Cova del Parco*

The studies carried out throughout these years have allowed not only a certain *intrasite* perception towards the Magdalenian occupants working and life space system at Cova del Parco, but also a certain perception towards the outer area *extrasite*, beyond the archaeological site, to know the territory´s management and its resources by these communities. Accordingly, we have also observed some differences between the Final Upper Magdalenian and the Upper Magdalenian.

4.2.1. Abiotic Resources

Along the analyzed period, we have documented the presence of concrete flint types being the object of detailed petro-archaeological features which progressively reveal the way a decrease in the flint types used is variably produced as these further varieties are not represented during the Final Upper Magdalenian, the result of which we may consider a certain regionalization process of the exploitation of the resource. In this way, for the most ancient stages of the studied sequence, so far –Upper Magdalenian-, we have proved little presence of materials coming from long and/or very long distances, exceeding widely the regional state displacement; these materials were introduced in the archaeological site in both engraved bladed supports and configured cores. This discovery, which forms part of one of our ongoing PhD –MS-, and which will shortly be launched, brings to light a behavior of siliceous materials supply over the long-distance axis enclosing both the Pyrenees slopes and some neighboring territories, not strictly Pyrenean, a circumstance showing us a wide mobility of these Upper Magdalenian groups. This mobility will gradually be reduced along the Final Upper Magdalenian, during which the recorded materials are of a regional support, adopting a local resource regime during the last hunter-gatherers settlements from very Early Holocene.

The C.O.L for the tool manufacture attached to these siliceous resources, also reveals along the studied sequence a progressive adaptive behavior both to the metric features and to the raw materials knapping used in tool manufacturing. Thus, during the Upper Magdalenian the bladed module, presenting both blades and bladelets produced in the archaeological site from the core reduction sequence of high-quality raw materials, mainly pyramidal and prismatic morphologies and at the same time part of the core maintenance elements –flakes and cortical flakes– for the diverse domestic tool making –endscrapers, side-scrappers, burins, becs, etc– is recovered. Progressively, we observe minor module exploitation of raw materials and therefore a larger number of bladelets rather than blades is produced on the site, the former seeming to be produced as supports or even as finished tools –some endscrapers and burins highlight this– while at the same time, the configuration and maintenance activities of the bladelets´ cores are simplified since the volume exploitation of smaller size raw materials and from poorly modified cores are usually invoked (Langlais, 2010). Consequently, the tool technology is affected by this circumstance and the local flint of a minor knapping quality is progressively used for manufacturing different lithic tool types (Mangado, 2005).

Lithic tools of Magdalenian levels at Cova del Parco are widely dominated by the projectile elements throughout the exhumed sequence. Backed bladelets and backed points predominance reveal a wide typological variety in which the presence of truncated backed bladelets highlights, an element we used as a cultural marker to point out the transition between Final and Upper Magdalenian stage. The hunting set is supported by domestic tools showing wide diversity of working activities developed at the archaeological site, both referring to scraping, hammering, and leather work (Calvo, 2004) and to osseous tool production and maintenance (Tejero and Fullola, 2008)

4.2.2. Biotic resources

The industry in osseous raw materials at Cova del Parco includes two large subsections. The first one is referred to as domestic and hunting equipment made of bones and deer antlers. Secondly, we have a set of objects of personal ornament,

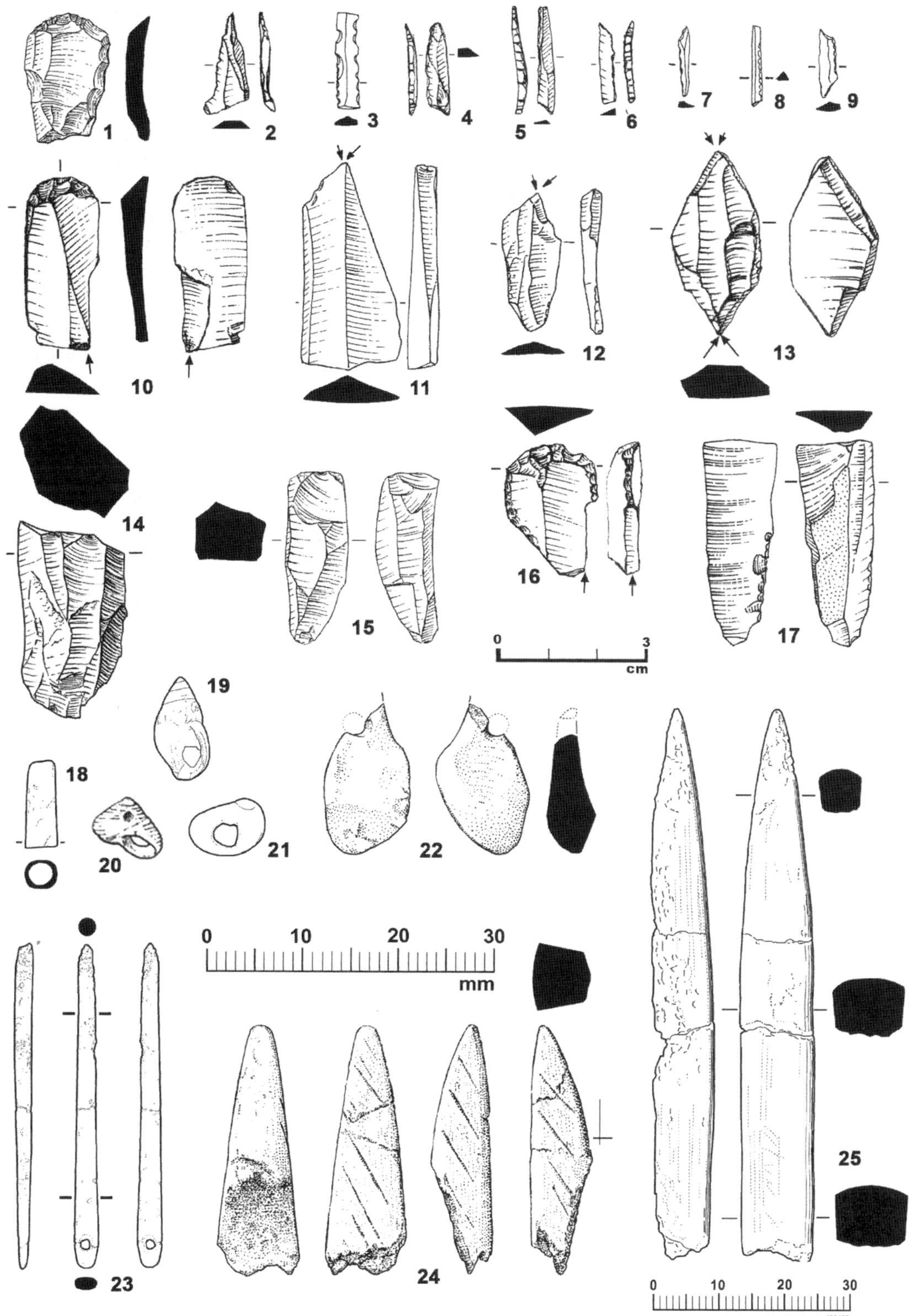

Figure 4. Upper Magdalenian settlements Lithic and bone industry at Cova del Parco (graphics R. Álvarez). 1,10,16: endscrapers. 2: bec. 3: backed bladelet. 4-9: scalene triangles. 11-13: burins. 14-15: bladelets cores. 17: retouched blade fragment. 18: *Dentalium sp*. 19: *Nasarius sp*. 20: *Homalopoma sanguineum*. 21: *Theodoxus fluviatilis*. 22: pendant of deer´s atrophied canine tooth. 23: needle. 24: spear point distal fragment. 25: spear point (*pointe de sagaie*).

which, with the exception of two pendants made of atrophied deer canine tooth, were made from different mollusks species shells. Both entities of the Cova del Parco archaeological material register form an important set from the numeric point of view and above all from a qualitative perspective, as they include not only objects but also other "technical" elements –wastes, pieces being processed, blanks–. These last ones are essential to rebuilding the technical operative sequence of the exploitation of organic material of animal origin.

This feature constitutes exactly the largest osseous industry (bone and antler) contribution in Cova del Parco to the knowledge of the site´s Magdalenian settlements and, by extension, of the Iberian Magdalenian. Although the osseous industry development is fairly recently related to the lithic technology, its huge capacity has been widely demonstrated for the better knowledge of the paleoethnographic aspects of the hunter-gatherers in the Upper Palaeolithic (Averbouh, 2000).

The analysis´ results show that the operative sequence of the bone and antler exploitation is driven to the production of the rod or *baguette* type blanks through the double longitudinal grooved procedure (Tejero 2005, Tejero and Fullola 2006, 2008, Tejero *et al.*, 2010). In the bone´s case, the blocks to be exploited are plausibly selected among the bone remains removed from the food chain without observing specific fracture patterns of technical nature. The fauna recovered in the Magdalenian levels at Cova del Parco are mainly goat´s remains (Nadal, 1998). The exploited antlers, always from deer *(Cervus elaphus)*, probably come up from shed antler collections if we abide by their modules of thick cortical tissue and the lack of deer presence among the fauna hunted at Parco. The bone and antler blanks are transformed by an overall scraping, respectively by needles and spear points (projectile elements). This correspondence between raw material and type of object, not limited to the Magdalenian, is related to the structural properties of every material, making them more efficient in transformation tasks –bone– or as projectile elements –antler– (Christensen and Tejero i.p).

With reference to the personal ornament objects, Cova del Parco has provided a set of more than one hundred pieces, with an important presence of marine gastropods (*Homalopoma sanguineum* and *Cyclopeneritea*) and fluvial gastropods (*Theodoxus fluviatilis*) (Tejero 2005, Estrada 2009, Estrada *et al.*, 2010). The shells of the different mentioned taxa –some of them keep ochre remains– were perforated probably through an indirect percussion. The use of this technique to perforate the shell of very small and relatively thin species requires very precise control of the process. This fact shows a high degree of technical expertise in the Magdalenian inhabitants of Cova del Parco. At the same time, the selection of a few varieties –difficult to work with– among the wide range of mollusks available to the Magdalenian populations at Cova del Parco shows an election guided by cultural criteria and not by a technical availability and/or efficiency.

However, most parts of faunal elements recorded during Magdalenian at Cova del Parco corresponds to hunted and consumed faunal remains. Its conservation status is usually fragile, as it appears really fragmented. Despite that, *cut marks* identification has been possible in many occasions, showing an intensive prey exploitation of mainly *Capra pyrenaica*.

5. Conclusions

The excavations during more than a decade of the Magdalenian levels at Cova del Parco by the SERP of the UB team has been the key for the understanding of the Final Upper Pleistocene settlements in the northeast of the Iberian Peninsula. Both for the large sedimentological and paleoenvironmental sequence and for the quantity and quality of the cultural traces and the exhumed human structures, this archaeological site is an essential reference point for the global study of the Magdalenian settlements in both the Pyrenees slopes.

6. Acknowledgments

In recent years, research work has been carried out as part of programme SGR2014-108 of the Generalitat de Cataluña and programme HAR2011-26193 of the MINECO.

Rafael Mora *,**, Jorge Martínez-Moreno*, Xavier Roda Gilabert *,***, Ignacio de la Torre****, Alfonso Benito-Calvo*****, Miquel Roy *,******, Sofía Samper*, Susana Vega *, Jezabel Pizarro*, Javier Plasencia*

The Mousterian site of Roca dels Bous (Lleida, Pre-pyrenees)

In a 1973 review, Emili Sunyer mentions an important Mousterian sequence in the first slopes of Pyrenees of Lleida. This short letter which brought us to Roca dels Bous (Mora, 1988), constituted the origin of our investigation of the human settlement located in the Eastern Prepyrennes (Fig. 1A). During these years, the field work carried out at Roca dels Bous, Tragó, Cova Gran de Santa Linya, and recently at Abric Pizarro, show this area to be key to analyse the human presence in the Upper Pleistocene and the Holocene in the Iberian Northeast.

Deconstructing Palimpsests

Roca dels Bous (X = 321.266, Y = 4.638.067, UTM H31 N ETRS89) is located at Cingle de la Cascalda, an Eocene limestone and Oligocene conglomerates cliff more than 40m high on the right edge of the Segre river, 275m A.S.L. (Fig. 1B). This slope´s deposit is 20m thick and has a fluvial terrace that is minted on its basis over the substrate (Fig. 1C).

The excavation is focused on the upper platform (Fig. 1C), where a first level –R3– arose, dated by ^{14}C AMS in 38.8±1.2 ky BP (AA 6481).

The excavated sequence reaches 1.5m deep. In a sedimentary level, it is a sequence of little consolidated breccia of sand and shale, plenty of angular medium-small size debris, and large autochthonous blocks coming from the weather erosion of the shelter's limestone. Up to now, 100 m^2 of levels N10 and N12 have been excavated. Other levels have been

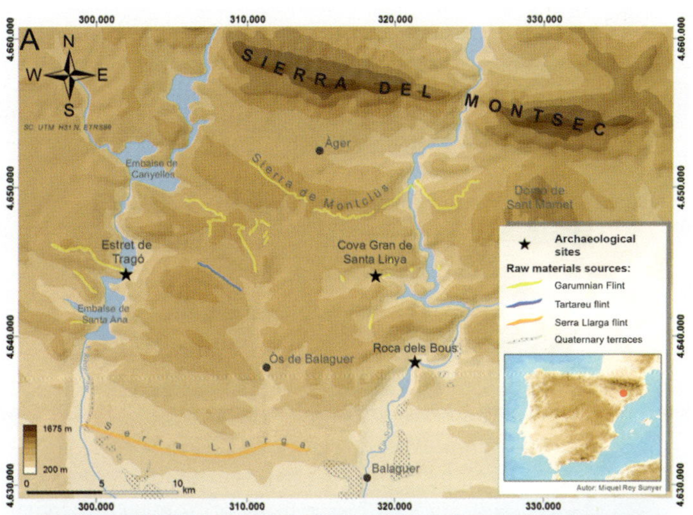

Figure 1. A) Roca dels Bous, Cova Gran de Santa Linya and Cova del'Estret de Tragó topographic location; silexand metamorphic rocks´ deposits topographic location at Noguera Prepyrenees. B) Roca dels Bous.

* Centre d'Estudis del Patrimoni Arqueològic de la Prehistòria (CEPAP). Universitat Autònoma de Barcelona. 08193 Bellaterra, Spain. cepap@uab.cat

** ICREA– Academia Program

*** Becario Programa FPI–MINECO

**** Institute of Archaeology-University College London 31-34 Gordon Square, WC1H 0PY London, United Kingdom. i.torre@ucl.ac.uk

***** Centro Nacional de Investigación sobre la Evolución Humana (CENIEH). Paseo Sierra de Atapuerca s/n. 09002 Burgos. alfonso.benito@cenieh.es

****** FI DGR– Generalitat de Catalunya Fellowship

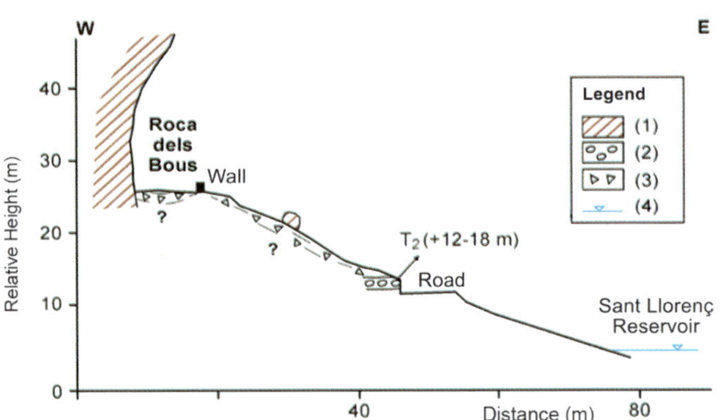

Figure 1. C) Archaeological site profile.

detected in several surveys, N14 and S9, which could be extended by similar surfaces.

The complex site formation processes of the deposit make it difficult to follow these archaeological units' dispersion. Two alluvial fans are located in the deposit´s ends, one on the E side which articulates the sediments´ income with a slope of 10º-15º to the southwest; the other, on the W side, is sub-horizontal –5º– sloping to the southeast. These riverbeds form a depression covering an important part of the excavated area.

These carbonated surfaces homogenize the sediments´ colouring. To surmount the lack of visibility, we assume that lithic and bone remains are sedimentary particles. Their systematic coordination defines accumulations with horizontal and vertical dispersion separated by sterile, delineating surfaces with inclinations and depressions derived from the sedimentary accretion of the lateral cones (Fig. 2A).

The large excavated combustion structures show the regular use of fire and confirm the archaeological geometry of these units. Similarly, they allow detection overlapping which involves the settlements´ sequence. These *fusion/fission* phenomena indicate that the sedimentary rhythms are not homogeneous (Fig. 2A). The archaeological levels are added to short-term events which were staggered during a term scale that is difficult to evaluate (Mora *et al.*, 2008; Martínez-Moreno *et al.*, 2010).

Artefacts and Behaviours

Contextualizing these processes is essential to analyze the variability observed in the Mousterian artefacts. Determining the origin of raw materials is a priority, and silex and quartzite outcrops feeding Roca dels Bous have been identified. They basically manage metamorphic rocks which abound in the fluvial deposits in this area. Silex rocks are not a local resource, although they appear in two regional outcrops: (1) the Garumnian formation which extends by Montclús and Tragómountains, (2) Serra Llarga (Oligocene) (Fig. 1A) (Roy *et al.*, 2013). There is no lack of rocks in this area to produce artefacts, so the changes in the composition of raw material and how this affects lithic assemblages describes the techno-cognitive and techno-economic environment of these Neanderthal groups. This conception can be evaluated in levels N10 and N12, resulting in remarks which affect the debate about *Mousterian variability* causes (Mora *et al.*, 2008).

In N12, excavated along 105m² and 20cm thickness, 22 hearths and the accumulation of 90 kg of rocks shaping a set of more than 23.500 artefacts are identified, of which all the segments related to the knapping process are present. The metamorphic rocks constitute 80% of the assemblage (Fig. 1C). However, retouched and small expediently knapped flint fragments are selected. These behaviors suggest the transport of finished pieces and small blanks from which little supports are obtained from 15-20 km. Retouched quartzite pieces are large with denticulate edges while the flint ones are small and instruments shaped with continuous fronts (Fig. 2B).

N10 suggests remarkable differences. This level follows along 95 m² with 10cm thickness, where 20 hearths were excavated. A radical decrease in artefacts can be seen –about 2100 pieces– which represent the transport of 11 kg of raw material. Sixty-six percent of the instruments are flint manufactured, although from the weight, the distribution between metamorphic rocks and flint is well-balanced suggesting that the flint artefacts are small, as seen in N12. There are more flint cores than quartzite cores, although they likewise point out a managing from the expedient methods as well as centripetal recurring methods which conform volumes under 5 cm (Fig. 2B). The retouched are preferably shaped of flint –80%–, the denticulate being more frequent than the continuous-edge pieces, as well as the quartzite supports (Martínez-Moreno *et al.*, 2010; Mora *et al.*, 2008).

The retouched pieces are usually fragmented and some remounts suggest that they are repaired

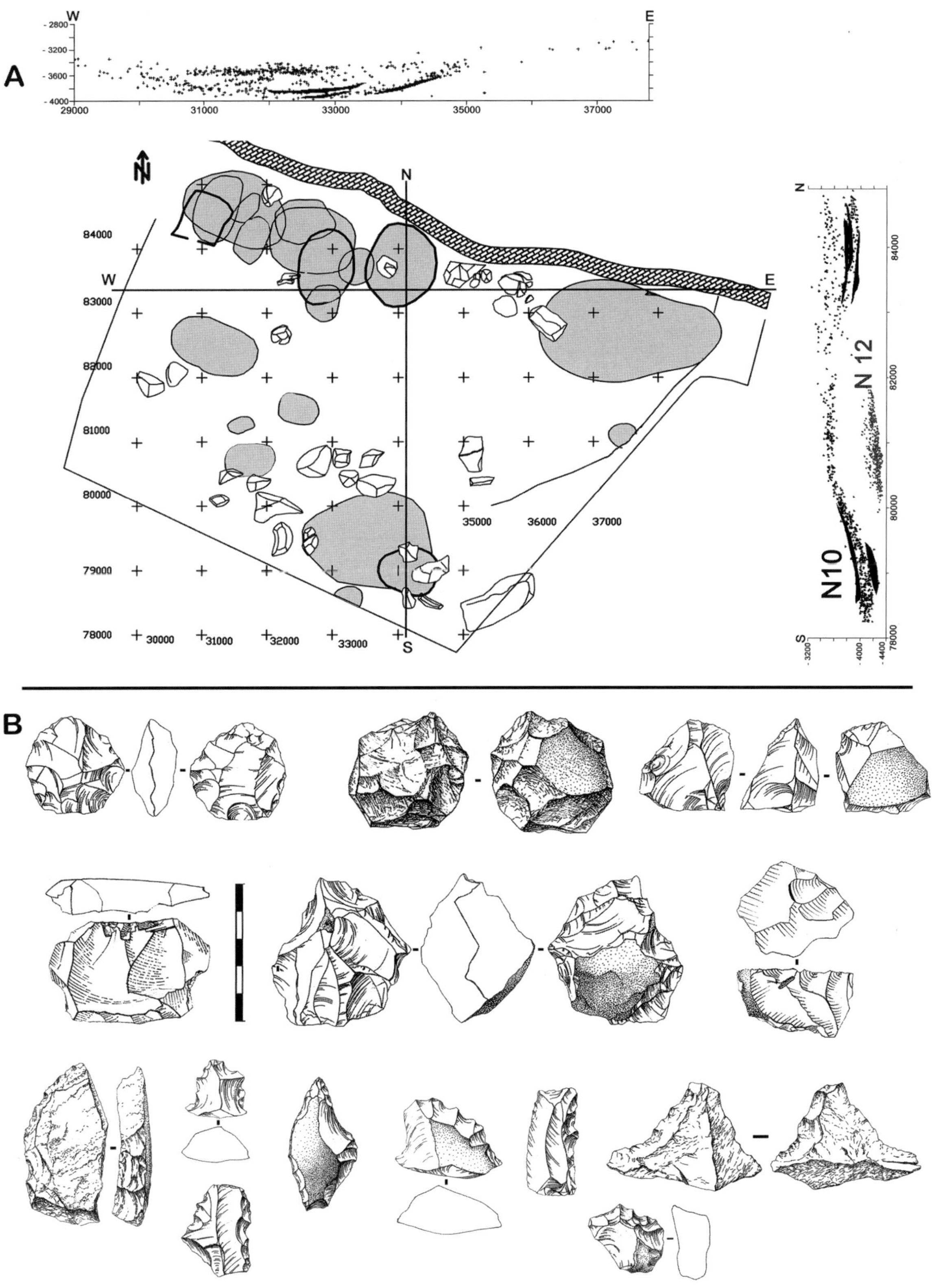

Figure 2. A) N10's excavated hearths distribution. Vertical projection, E-W –up– and N-S –right-, in which the hearths' overlapping and *fusion/fission* phenomena inside the level can be discerned. In the N-S projection, the sterile between N10 and N12 can be seen. B) Cores trends on silex and metamorphic rocks extensively exploited until configuring small volumes (up), retouched tools (down).

instruments (de la Torre *et al.*, 2012). Many retouched pieces suggest their recycling. The double patinas identified in some pieces could correspond to artefacts recovered on the site or in the surrounding landscape which are reactivated to obtain new supports (Mora *et al.*, 2008).

This intense management does not obey the lack of this material in the area, allowing us to approximate these groups techno-cognitive environment. Likewise, especially N10 suggests short-term activities; the archaeological site served as a stop in the movements between residential displacements. If so, Roca dels Bous represents a web of Neanderthal settlements inside this regional environment in the Prepyrenees of Lleida and Huesca (Mora *et al.*, 2008).

Future prospects

These arguments, discussed in other contributions (Casanova *et al.*, 2009; Martínez-Moreno *et al.*, 2010; de la Torre *et al.*, 2013), point out that these techno-typological tendencies do not respond to techno-economic factors such as the lack of raw materials in the environment. N12 notes the option of using local rocks.

These behaviours related to flint management must be attached to a fragmented *chaineo peratoire* along a wide techno-temporal scale, converting Roca dels Bous into a privileged place in the movement of Neanderthal groups (Mora *et al.*, 2008; de la Torre *et al.*, 2013).

The settlement´s strategic position allows an effective control of the seasonal animal movements, especially equids (horse and wild ass) and deer, between the Ebro Depression and the Pyrenees. This short-term settlement– pattern should be attached to annual cycle short periods in which the environment offered opportunities to obtain prey and transport them to the archaeological site.

The inferences from Roca dels Bous, and in general the pre-Pyrenees settlements at Noguera, suggest that this area will have a prominent role in the investigation of the Middle Palaeolithic in the Northeast of the Iberian Peninsula.

Rafael Mora Torcal *,**, Alfonso Benito-Calvo***, Jorge Martínez-Moreno *, Ignacio de la Torre****, Susana Vega Bolivar *, Miquel Roy *,*****, Xavier Roda Gilabert*,******, Sofia Samper Carro *

A key sequence in the Western Mediterranean Prehistory: Cova Gran de Santa Linya (Pre-Pyrenees in Lleida)

This large rock shelter was discovered in 2002 during a survey program coordinated by the Centre d'Estudis del Patrimoni Arqueològic de la Prehistòria (CEPAP). This settlement contains a large chrono-cultural sequence covering Middle Paleolithic, Early Upper Paleolithic, Magdalenian, Neolithic and Chalcolithic. The use of this site by hunter-gatherers and farmer-shepherds turned the place into a key location for analyzing human settlement of the Pyrenees during Prehistory.

Geographical situation

Cova Gran (X=318541, Y=4643877, UTM H31N ETRS89) is located in the eastern Pre-Pyrenees, in Lleida (see Fig.1A in *Roca dels Bous*

* Centre d'Estudis del Patrimoni Arqueològic de la Prehistòria (CEPAP). Universitat Autònoma de Barcelona. 08193 Bellaterra, Spain. cepap@uab.cat

** Programa ICREA- Academia.

*** Centro Nacional de Investigación sobre la Evolución Humana (CENIEH). Paseo Sierra de Atapuerca s/n. 09002 Burgos, Spain. alfonso.benito@cenieh.es

**** Institute of Archaeology-University College London 31-34 Gordon Square, WC1H 0PY London, United Kingdom. i.torre@ucl.ac.uk

***** Becario Programa FPI – MINECO

****** Becario Programa FI DGR- Generalitat de Catalunya

paper), 385m A.S.L., and in a lateral valley of the Noguera-Pallaresa river where the ravine of Sant Miquel digs into the limestone of the Upper Cretaceous creating a shelter of over 2000 m^2 (Fig. 1A). The chrono-stratigraphic sequence of the sedimentary and cultural processes of the deposit is made up from the sectors Ramp, Transition and Platform which are correlated from 40 14C AMS and T1 dates (Fig. 1B). We do not reject the appearance of new chrono-cultural segments. Cova Gran is relevant for contextualizing last 50.000 years of the human presence in the Western Mediterranean (Mora *et al.*, 2011).

The longitudinal profile of the shelter permits appreciation of the deposit shaped from two large juxtaposed platforms (Fig. 1B). The sequence of the first one –point west and external to the rock-shelter– is defined in the Ramp sector. Transition and Platform sectors record the sedimentary development under the visor.

The Ramp Sector: Archaeo-Stratigraphy of the Outer Platform

The Ramp sector –R– is a 200 m^2 platform with a 20° east gradient. The dug area extends 120 m^2 and some levels go on outwards. In this area of 2.5 m thickness, the sedimentary units S1 and 497 are differentiated, originated by different climatic processes (Fig. 1C). The basal unit S1 is a set of 2m made by medium and coarse gravels, sand-clayey matrix and limy-angular debris of a gravitational origin which indicate cold conditions. Unit 497 –0,5m– is composed of granular sediments affected by water flow indicating relatively milder environmental conditions. Relevant sin-post depositional processes are not detected (Benito Calvo *et al.*, 2011).

In sector R, 8 archaeological levels are stratified punctuated for being sterile. Unit S1 contains levels S1E, S1D, S1C, S1B1 andS1B which correspond to Mousterian, and 497D assigned to an undetermined Early Upper Paleolithic. Sedimentary unit 497, levels 497C and 497A, are attached to other stages of Early Upper Paleolithic cycle. All levels are rich in lithics, bones and hearths. Marine ornaments, especially *Nassarius incrassatus* (Martínez-Moreno *et al.*, 2011) have been recovered in 497D, 497C and 497A. These artifacts are considered markers of the irruption of *H. sapiens* in Western Europe.

The techno-typological change detected between S1B and 497D –on the roof of the unit S1– indicates several implications. In these stratigraphycally overlayed levels, recovered lithic assemblages correspond to different cultural traditions, with changes affecting raw material, knapping systems, blanks and the retouched tools (Fig. 2A). This technological change redirects to the debate about the Middle/Upper Paleolithic transition, and the possible extinction of *H. neanderthalensis* in parallel to the dispersion of *H. sapiens* in Western Europe.

S1B summarizes the general trends of the Mousterian in Cova Gran (Martínez-Moreno *et al.*, 2011; Mora *et al.*, 2012). Cores are reduced to obtain centripetal flakes similar to those observed in Tragó and Roca dels Bous (de la Torre *et al.*, 2013). The flint coming from the Garumnian formations adjacent to the site is the most used raw material in all levels. Similarly, metamorphic rocks are transported configuring large pseudo-*Levallois* blanks elaborated outside the site –Fig. 2B-. In other words, whole materials are obtained in the immediate area (see Fig. 1A article about Roca dels Bous). Regarding the retouched tools, denticulates are more common than pieces with continuous edges (Mora *et al.*, 2012).

497D shows important differences. Metamorphic rocks disappear and although the Garumnian flint is the main resource, the contribution of configured supports from Serra Llarga –20 km far away– increases. The knapping system is intended to obtain blade-elongated supports with a low morpho-technical standardization degree. This includes end-scrapers and burins on blade, backed and points on bladelet, artefacts unknown in the

Figure 1. A) Cova Gran de Santa Linya.

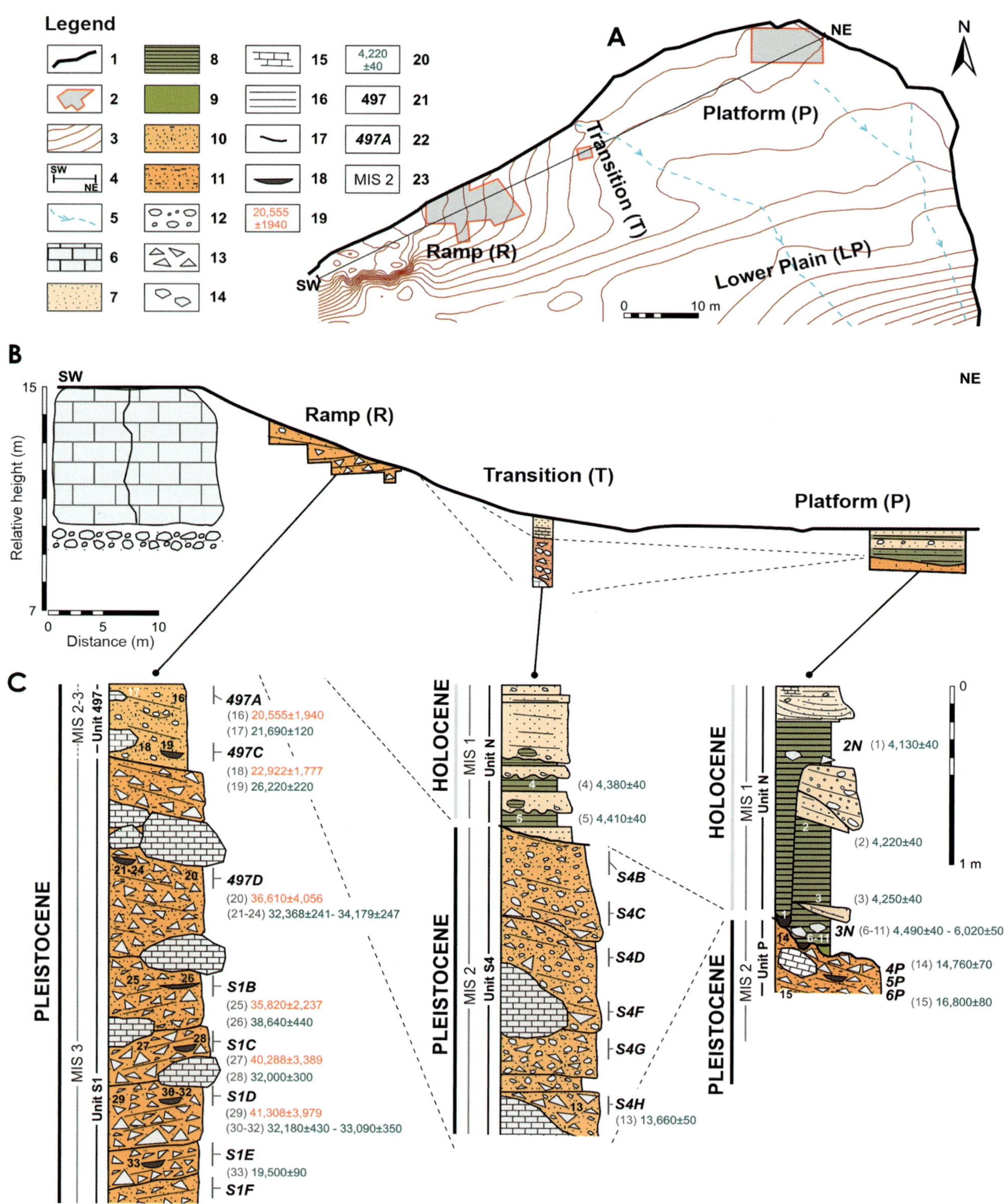

Figure 2. B) Archaeo-stratigraphic sequence: A) shelter´s floor where the dug sectors are located –Platform, Transition and Ramp– B) Longitudinal transection of the deposit. C) Sectors R, T and P chrono-stratigraphy (see Mora *et al.*, 2011).

Mousterian. Although, an important component of scrapers, denticulates and notches on flake persist –Fig. 2B–. These features do not match with the trends described in the first techno-complexes of the Upper Paleolithic in Western Europe (Martínez-Moreno *et al.*, 2010).

Some anomalies are appreciated in the dating of this sector, which can be related to the protocols used in C14 laboratories. However, the dates provided for 497D from charcoal coming from a hearth, place this level in the interval 40-38.5ka-calBP. The archaeo-stratigraphic resolution and the chronometrical intervals of these levels contribute to the debate about of Middle/Upper Paleolithic transition (Martínez-Moreno *et al.*, 2010).

Archaeo-stratigraphy of the inner platform: Transition and Platform sectors

The central platform is a surface extended under the visor of the shelter of about 2000 m^2. This delineation restricts the most ancient archaeological levels to sector R –Fig. 1B–.

This sequence is known by the Transition sector (T) –a survey of 2x2 m–, and the Platform sector (P), which embraces a dug area of 32 m^2. Two units are identified in both sectors: unit N corresponds to the Holocene, unit P is attached to the final of MIS 2 (–Fig. 1B–.)

The most ancient human presence is detected during the Last Maximum Glacial (LMG) in the sedimentary unit P of the Platform sector, made by very angular debris and falls from large blocks with limited fine sediments –Fig.1B–. Levels 4P, 5P, 6P and 8P take place in this sequence, with 1.7 m thick, dated between 20.4-18 ky calBP –stage Gs2b–. Points and backed bladelets, burin and end-scrapers on blade are associated with massive antler projectiles, needles and perforated gastropods. These artefacts can refer to the Early Magdalenian. Sector T is a survey of 3.5 m depth in which several levels with different technical features from sector P take place –Fig.1B–. A dating on the survey´s basis (17-16.8 ky calBP) allow sector T to be attributed to Middle Magdalenian and possibly Upper Magdalenian levels (Mora *et al.*, 2012).

The Holocene sequence N erodes levels P in sectors T and P, creating complex geometries over which farmer-shepherds communities settled from the Early Neolithic, just as it is identified in the Platform sector –Fig. 1B–. The most intense settlement moment occurs during the Late Neolithic –5500-5100 calBP, recording 30 domestic structures –hearths, post-holes and pits– (Mora *et al.*, 2012). Above these settlements, this area is used for stabling sheep-goat during the Late Neolithic (5000-4600 calBP), Calcolithic and Late Bronze Age (3950-3000 calBP). These accumulations, each 0.5 m thick, include several stages of intentional burning in order to condition the place for future visits. These appreciations open new perspectives to analyze the origins of pastoralism in northeast Iberia (Polo *et al.*, 2014).

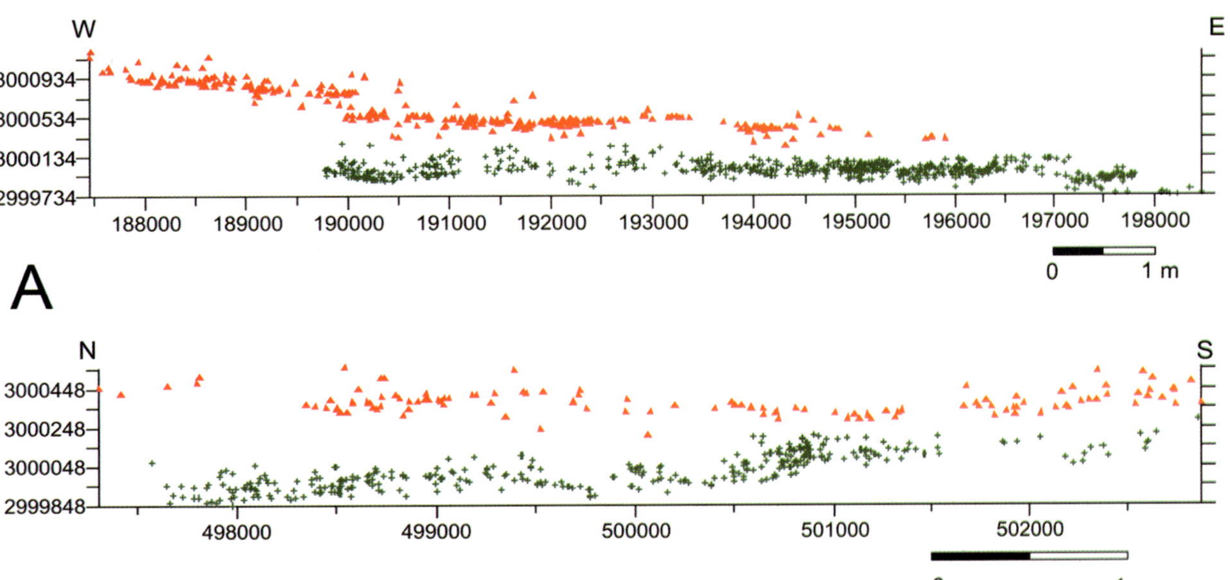

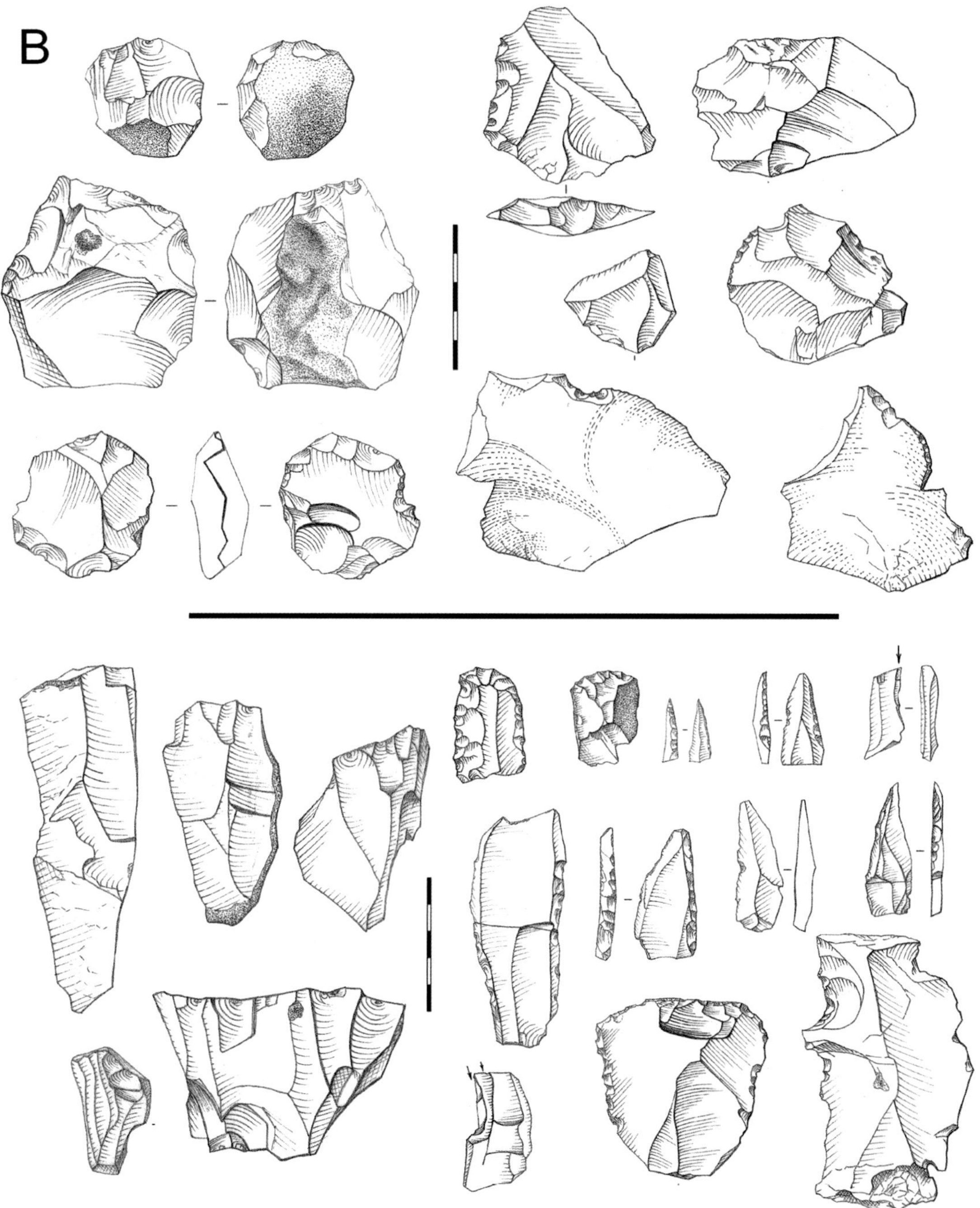

Figure 2. A) N-S and E-W projections of 497D –triangles– and S1B –points– separated by sterile. B) Lithic artifacts of S1B Middle Paleolithic –on top– and 497D initial Upper Paleolithic –below–.

Future prospects

Cova Gran de Santa Linya articulates several important research questions in the current scientific debate: the disappearance of the Neanderthals and the appearance of modern humans, hunter-gatherer adaptations during the LMG and the emergence of the first farmers. These issues are essential to analyze human presence in the southern Pyrenees, an area in which important progress is taking place. We think that this is a privileged place to analyze the course of different human groups which occupied this shelter for 50.000 years.

Joel Casanova i Martí *, Rafael Mora Torcal *,**, Xavier Roda Gilabert *,***, Jorge Martínez-Moreno *, Miquel Roy *,****, Susana Vega *

The Middle Paleolithic sequence of Cova de l'Estret de Tragó (Lleida, Pre-Pyrenees)

Cova de l'Estret de Tragó was discovered during surveys in the Noguera Ribagorçana river, conducted in 1990 by the IEI-Diputació de Lleida (see Fig. 1A in the article Roca dels Bous). This rockshelterhas a surface of 14 x 10 m and is part of karst limestone Fm. Bona (X = 301856 Y = 4644190 UTMH31N ETRS89) to 390 m (Fig. 1A). This position in the first Prepyrenees of Lleida, plays a key association between the Ebro Basin and the Pyrenees (Martínez-Moreno *et al.*, 2004; Casanova *et al.*, *2009*).

Geographical Context and Chronostratigraphic

Eight archaeological units from Middle Paleolithic are identified in Tragó. They are interbedded with sterile sediments allowing individualized analysis. The archeostratigraphy of the deposit is

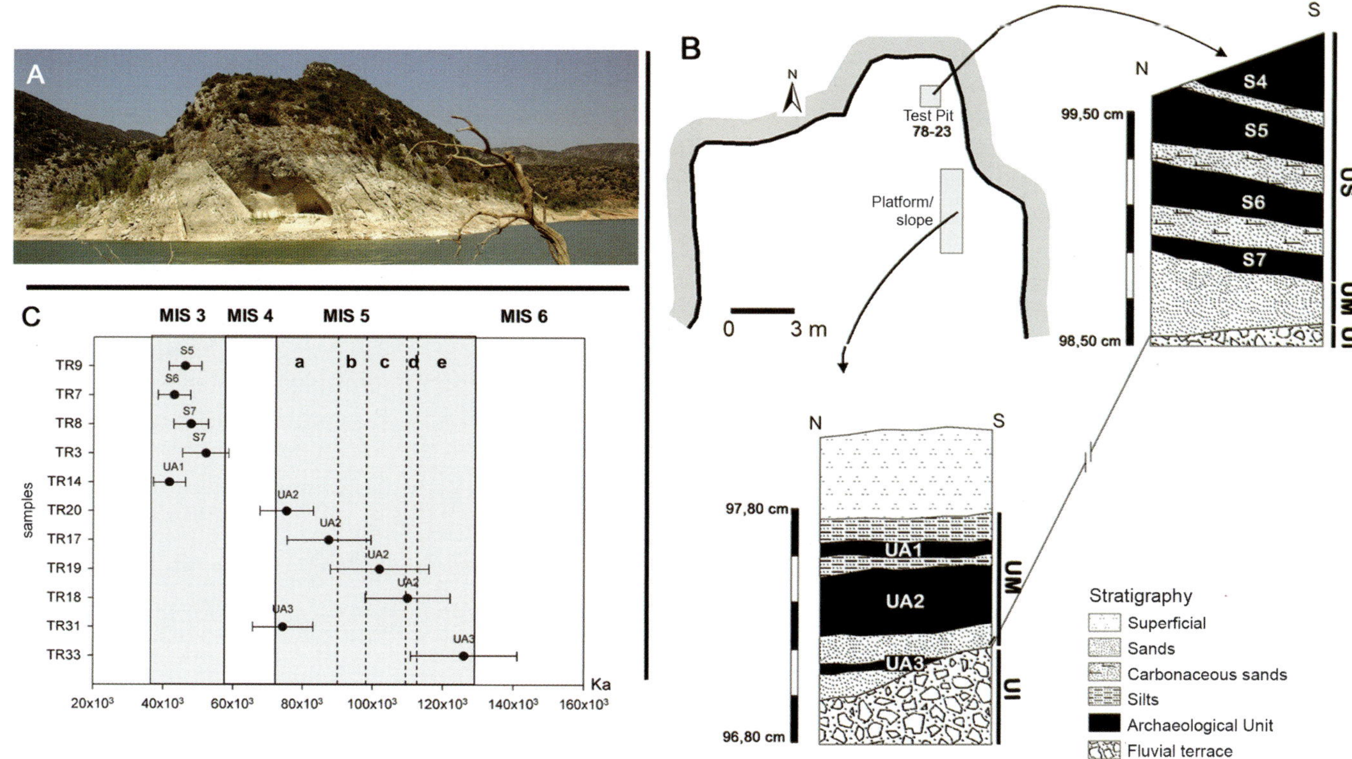

Figure 1. A) Cova del Estret de Tragó currently flooded by the Santa Anna marsh. B) Sequences of the inner rock shelter (78-23 survey) and the excavated area on the deposit platform. The *Upper Unit* (UU), *Middle Unit* (MU) and *Lower Unit* (LU) are positioned. C) Thermoluminescence series sequence.

* Centre d'Estudis del Patrimoni Arqueològic de la Prehistoria. Facultat de Lletres. Universitat Autònoma de Barcelona. 08193 Bellaterra. cepap@uab.cat

** Programa ICREA-Academia

*** Becario programa FPI-MINEC

**** Becario Programa FI-DGR. Generaltitat de Catalunya

established from the sequences obtained in the survey on the square78-23 and the excavated area (25 m²) and it can be defined in three units (Martínez-Moreno *et al., 2004;* Casanova *et al.*, 2009) (Fig. 1B):

- *Lower unit* (LU): high energy of fluvial deposit from Ribagorçana Noguerariver; containing medium and large size cobbles within a carbonated sandy matrix. This terrace constitutes the base of the site.
- *Middle unit* (MU): low to medium energy environment composed of clayey sand and silt resulting from the alternation of flooding, causing vertical migration of carbonates that precipitate on archaeological material. At this level of 1.5 m thickness, archaeological units UA3, UA1 and UA2 are excavated.
- *Upper unit* (UU): residual breccia fixed to the shelter wall dismantled in the rest of the deposit. In this survey, 1 m² and 1.10 m deep, S4, S5, S6 and S7 levels follow.

It has not been possible to correlate the archaeological levels of the *Middle unit* with the *Upper unit* (Fig. 1C). Eleven Thermoluminescence (TL) dates are available, generating chronometric ranges that frame the occupation of the settlement. The S5, S6 and S7 from the *Upper unit* levels are assigned to MIS 3 (between 43 ± 4.6 and 52.1 ± 6.7 ky). The date of UA1 (41.7 ± 4.5 ky) suggests this *Middle unit* level may be related to the *Upper unit.* The four dates obtained from UA2 are staggered in the range 75.3 ± 7.8 –110 ± 12 ky, indicating this level of 60 cm thickness is formed on the MIS 5. The UA3 has two dates and we accept the corresponding to MIS 5e stage (126 ± 15 ky). This series makes Tragó a key site to analyze the Upper Pleistocene Mousterian settlement in the northeast of the Iberian Peninsula (Casanova *et al.*, 2009).

Archaeological record

Levels excavated can be considered low resolution palimpsests with thousands of lithic and bones imbricated without apparent order (Table 1). These accumulations would be the result of repeated visits to the shelter at different time periods, interrupted by abandonment phases. There are not identified hearths, but regular fire use in the entire sequence can be recognized by the presence of abundant charcoal, and burned bone and artefacts.

Bone carbonation and difficult anatomic and/or specific bone identification are not able to calculate indices of their presence. The species identified are *Vulpes vulpes; Sus scropha, Cervus elaphus, Capreolus capreolus, Bos sp., Capra pyrenaica, Equus caballus* and *Equus* cf. *hydruntinus.* This eurythermal association describes an environment that integrates meadows with wooded areas insertedin alow/medium mountainous but sharp landscape. Abundant helical fractures on diaphysis denote intense marrow recovery (Martínez-Moreno *et al.*, 2004).

The lithic assemblage, composed by over 20,000 artifacts, is essential to characterize the

	Upper Unit				Middle Unit		
	S4	**S5**	**S6**	**S7**	**UA1**	**UA2**	**UA3**
Surface (m²)	0,5	1	1	1	23	35	13
Thickness (cm)	20	30	15	15	10	60	15
Hammers	0	4	1	1	3	75	38
Cores	1	10	14	11	15	423	229
Flakes	33	315	184	152	496	6564	2303
Flakes frag.	70	406	502	328	777	7895	2275
Chunks	15	76	185	88	73	947	452
Retouched	16	163	140	41	143	791	274

Table 1. The excavated surface and the average thickness of the archaeological levels from the *Upper* and *Middle Unit* with the number of artifacts recovered.

Mousterian in this area. Metamorphic and siliceous rocks proliferate in the environment (see Fig. 1A in the article Roca dels Bous). Flint, present in the Montes de Tragó and Serra Larga (10 km), refers to local sourcing. At diachronic levels, the metamorphic rocks are the most important in lower units UA3 and UA2. This trend is reversed in UA1 and S4, S5, S6, S7 where the flint is the majority (Casanova *et al.*, *2009;* De la Torre *et al.*, 2013).

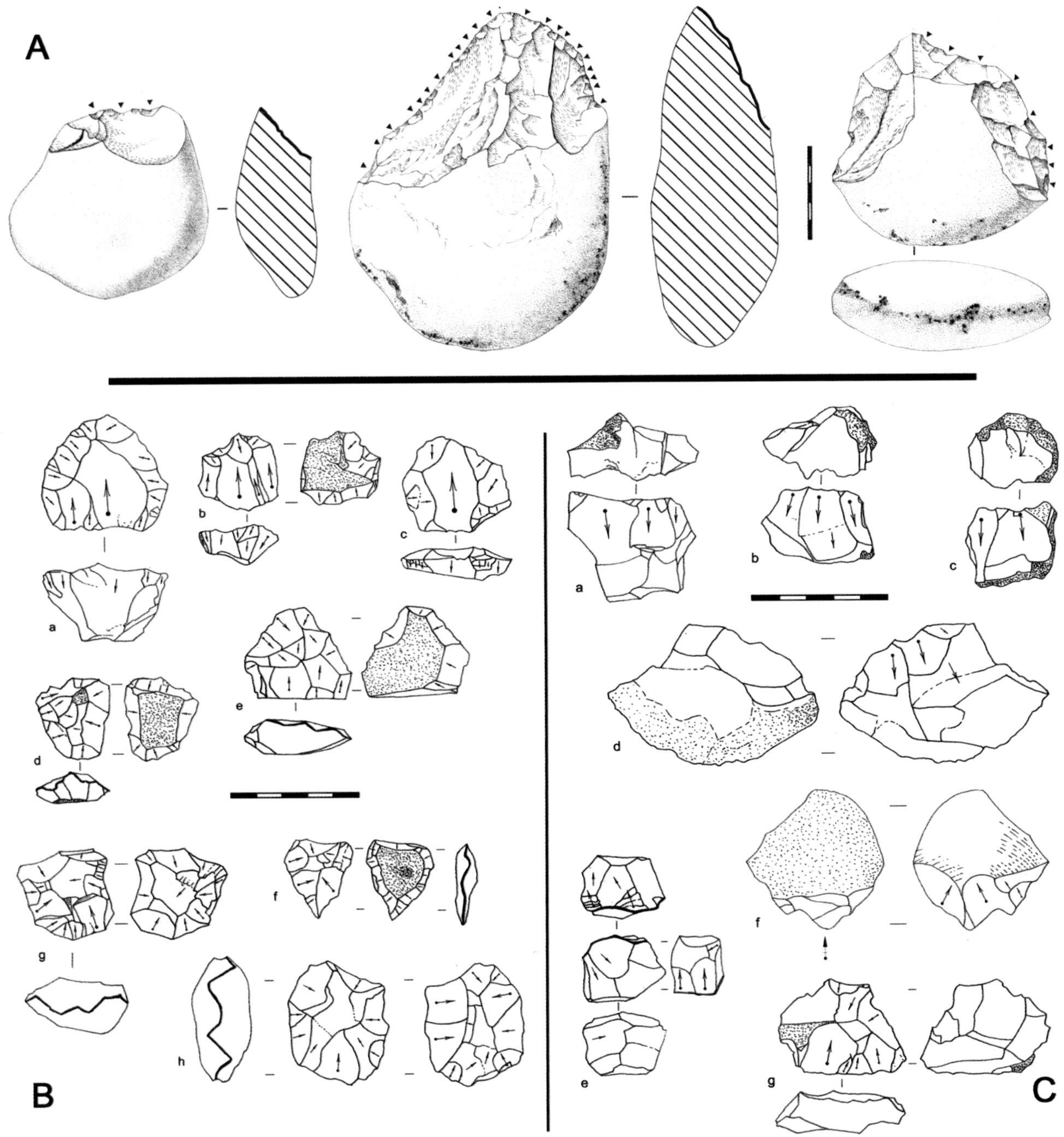

Figure. 2 A) Macrotools from UA3 related to percussion activities. B) Variability of organized knapping systems showing the configuration of small volumes. C) Expedient cores.

All categories related to knapping, including microdebitage, are represented. The *debitage* is structured from organized expedient technical systems (Fig. 2). Organized systems allow management from schemes referred to as *Levallois* and *discoid* methods. The expedient methods are applied to volumes obtaining few blanks. These strategies, present in each sequence, denote the application of complementary technical behaviors depending on specific needs (Casanova *et al.*, 2014).

The cores usually measure less than five cm and intensive management of consumption it is observed (Fig. 2).This behavior cannot be explained by the lack of raw materials in the environment, we consider it a technical choice focused on elaborating small artifacts (Casanova *et al.*, 2009).The most common blanks are flakes, points and blades are rare. Blanks were obtained with hard hammers, generating accidents like broken pieces, Siret burins and double bulbs.

This continuity in the knapping methods derived several reflections. In the *Middle Unit* levels the expedient methods are mainly against structured methods, a pattern that persisted in the *Upper Unit*. This notion of *technological stasis* denotes a cognitive arrangement in the transmission of technical knowledge that could imply that in this area a stable cultural tradition was developed (Casanova *et al.*, 2009).

In UA3 25 cobbles of metamorphic rocks and granite were knapped by *façonnage* for shaping macrotools artefacts (Fig. 2).In these pieces, modifications over the edges can be seen, relating to percussion activities (Casanova *et al., 2014).*

In the sequence, the retouched percentage is low (Table 1), selecting the flint to retouch pieces; although in UA3 and UA2 metamorphic rocks are more abundant. The most common blanks are short flakes retouched on a single edge (lateral or transverse); while double retouch edges are scarce. Denticulate and notched pieces with simple or abrupt retouch are more numerous than sidescrapers with continuous retouch. Preponderance of denticulate pieces is constant along the sequence. Although *pseudo-Levallois* retouched elements are identified, most of them are made on regular flakes or fragments.

Tragó in the Middle Paleolithic Context of Northeast Iberia

The repeated use of this area during the Upper Pleistocene between MIS 5e, MIS 5 and MIS 3 should link with the control available from the settlement on the strait of Noguera-Ribagorçana river and floodplains currently flooded by the Santa Ana reservoir. This strategic point would not be unnoticed by the Neanderthal population. The rock shelter centralizes prey acquisition and their passing through the corridor allowing ambush in the wooded areas around the river. Similarly, displacement to the rocky outcrops adjacent to the settlement can be identified.

Even though the radiometric record is inaccurate, it cannot confirm their occupation in the MIS 4. This gap could be related to climatic crisis causing the abandonment of this environment. The cyclic occupation/abandonment of the area as a result of environmental factors should be retained as a possibility.

The technical continuity from the combination of technical methods, expeditious and organized, present throughout the entire sequence is relevant. We stress the importance of *technological stasis* notion identified in other sites of the Pyrenean foothills. Likewise, we warn that these technical options articulate a cultural tradition extended into the Upper Pleistocene northeastern Iberia. A number of attributes of this entity are the panoply of knapping methods, orientation to obtain small blank, and the denticulate preferred configuration (Casanova *et al., 2009;* de la Torre *et al., 2013).*

Under this perspective, Cova Estret of Tragó is a relevant settlement to investigate the Neanderthal lifestyle in the Iberian Peninsula.

Acknowledgments

We dedicate this article to Joel Casanova i Martí. These lines are a demonstration of our respect, affection, and admiration.

Pilar Utrilla Miranda*, Vicente Baldellou Martinez**, Manuel Bea Martinez*, Lourdes Montes Ramirez*, Ramón Viñas Vallverdú***

The cave of Fuente del Trucho (Asque – Colungo, Huesca)

1. Location

The cave of Fuente del Trucho is located in the Arpan ravine on the left side of the river Vero next to the spring that gives it its name. The Paleolithic art of the mentioned cave and the Levantine and schematic art of the Arpán shelter, 870 m long –an exceptional case in the Iberian Peninsula– are located in the same ravine. The river Vero runs among canyons throughout 10 km, in this course there are only two natural entries, crossing the vertical walls, to access to the riverbed: Villacantal Bridge and Tozal de Mallata. There are Prehistoric paintings in both of them. A shallow cave, with a large 22 m wide entrance facing the southeast, gives access to a wide room, 24m deep, divided into two dissymmetrical lobes. The smallest one, at the left, has a spherical dome, blackened by organic matter and haze, and an oval window allowing sunlight to enter with zenithal lighting. The floor falls into an oblique calcite flow, several deeply drawn engravings made on it receive direct sunlight at dawn. The second lobe, in semi-gloom, presents its walls and roof covered with paintings, most of them red. The floor today presents naked rock in a great part of the room, with the exception of the right side of the cave, under the tri-lobed signs, where a messy deposit presents lithic materials which correspond to the Upper Paleolithic and the Mousterian. Towards the exterior, moving out from the painted area, the levels present a larger sequence, although in this case they seem to only be attached to the Mousterian.

2. Investigation History

The first explorers of Sierra de Guara ravines, particularly Pierre Minvielle, illustrated the archaeological deposit contained in the cave. However, the cave paintings were discovered in 1978 by a team of the Museum of Huesca and the University of Zaragoza headed by Vicente Baldellou. He entrusted the excavation of the Mousterian levels of the outside area to Anna Mir, who worked in five campaigns from 1979 –Mir, 1987– and the areas corresponding to the Upper Paleolithic were entrusted to Pilar Utrilla, who in 1980 did the first survey of the bottom of the external engravings disrupted by the presence of a very hard crust. In 2005 she restarted the excavation, in cooperation with Lourdes Montes as co-director, proceeding into the right inner area of the cave, at the bottom of the tri-lobed signs (Montes *et al.*, 2006; Utrilla *et al.*, 2010). A new campaign is expected to be started in the summer of 2014.

V. Baldellou, director of the cave art surveys in the river Vero for many years, coordinated from the begining the different procedures at Fuente del Trucho, taking care of the study of the parietal exhibitions, first in cooperation with A. Beltrán, in the progress of the *Altamira Symposium* (Beltrán and Baldellou, 1981; Beltrán, 1993) and some years later with R. Viñas, elaborating direct calques between 1989 and 1991. In the year 2000, S. Ripoll and F.J. Muñoz made photo-documentation of the roof (Ripoll *et al.*, 2001), and since the year 2011, V. Baldellou, M. Bea and P. Utrilla have carried out digital treatment and calques assembling within the project HAR 2011-27197 "*Reconsidering ancient archaeological sites. Expanding into new horizons in the Middle Valley Prehistory of river Ebro*". For this purpose, all the old photos which systematically covered every cave´s wall have been digitalized, treated with the *D Stretch* application for *Image J* and *Photoshop CS5* and collated with the original calques of Baldellou and Viñas.

In the Gravettian convention celebrated in Altamira, the two main sets of the cave were published: the roof –panel XV– and the frieze –panel VI and VII– (Utrilla *et al.*, 2013). In this convention –session A11a- the dating results made by U/Th about the cleanest crusts covering some figures –hands, points, horse and tri-lobed– were presented (Hoffman *et al.*,

* Universidad de Zaragoza utrilla@unizar.es
** Museo de Huesca
*** IPHES

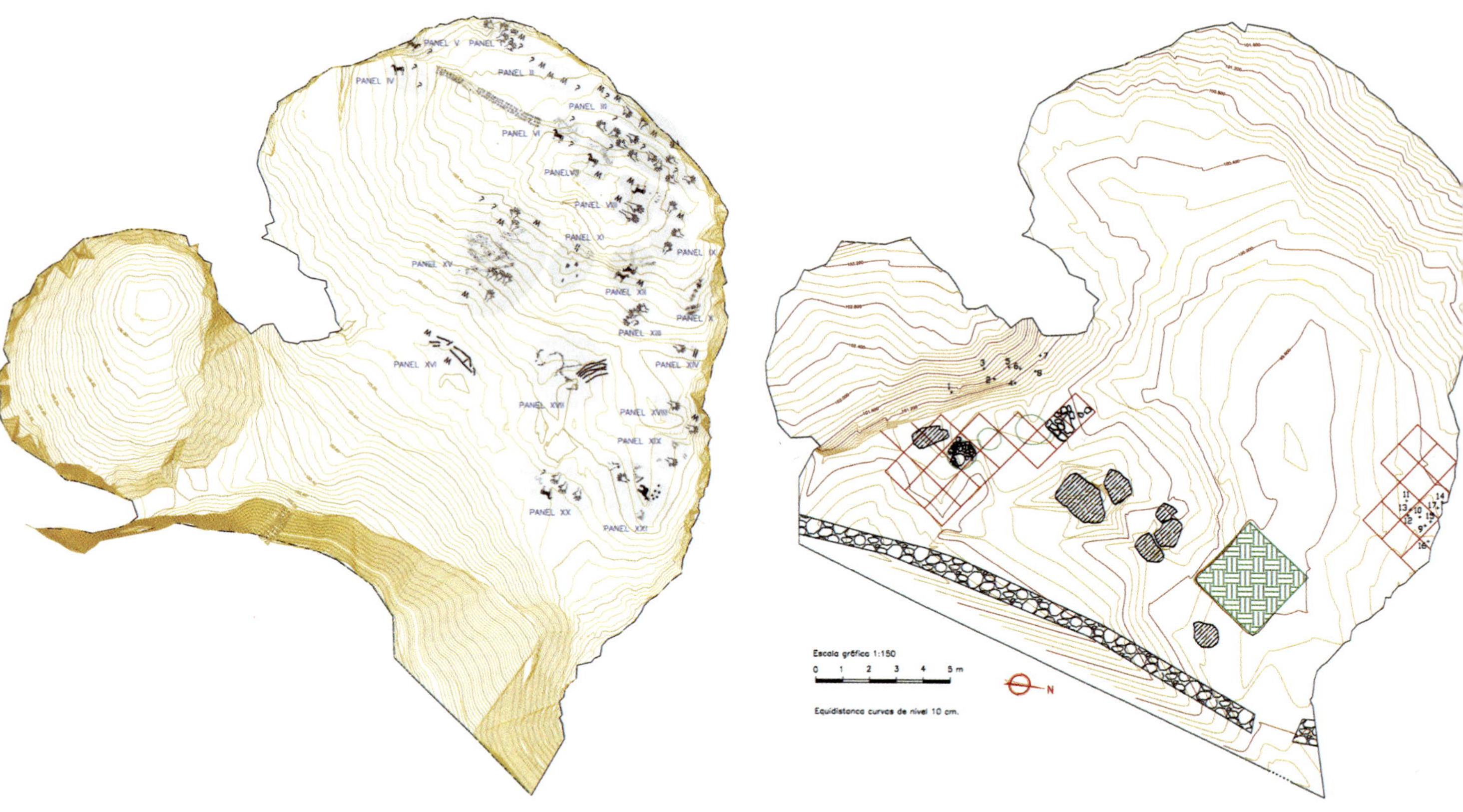

Figure 1: Roof floor –left, indicating the painted panels- and ground floor –indicating archaeological pits and the engravings´ location–. Topography J. Angás – Scanner 3D. Patrimony and Industry.

i.p.), while the Candamo convention focused on the relationship between the archaeological site and the paintings (Utrilla *et al.*, 2014).

The final study is pending on the projected haze cleaning of the dust mucking up the wall now, a splendid white support which would highlight the hundreds of paintings, most of them red, which cover the surface of the roof and the walls for decorative purposes. There are two well-defined areas in Fuente del Trucho: the paintings in a semi-gloom at the large right cave (Fig. 1.1); and the external engravings placed on the slanting floor of the small left lobe (Fig. 1.2).

3. The paintings

The provisional paintings stocklist (Ripoll *et al.*, 2001) records 22 panels with a hundred figures. Series of points, tri-lobed signs, hands and horses are the four main painted items, to which a small goat, a deer, an undefined animal –a bear, a bovid, or a horse- and several signs are added.

The points series are represented in 8 panels. They appear in horizontal lines shaping a 6 m long frieze in panel VI (Fig. 2), or forming part of more complex motifs represented in both of the walls –panel VII– and the roof –panel XV– (Fig. 3). Panel XI contains red couplet lines, also a feature of ancient Gravettian panels, usually attached to hands and fingering (González Sáinz, 2003). Regarding to the complex series of interpretations on the roof, in 1993 Beltrán proposed that they probably represent the sky dome, constellations of stars maintaining rhythms. In another vein, in 2005 Utrilla suggested that the routes of the Pyrenean ports dividing Gargas and Fuente del Trucho could have surprised the travelers, maybe losing their way or making detours, which could be represented by the complexity of some motifs.

In regards to the lineal series of the vertical frieze, in bands of 4 and 5 lines, the representation of the same motif in the Levantine art at the closer cave of Arpán draws attention. Their Paleolithic parallels are found in many caves of the Cantabrian Coast, the

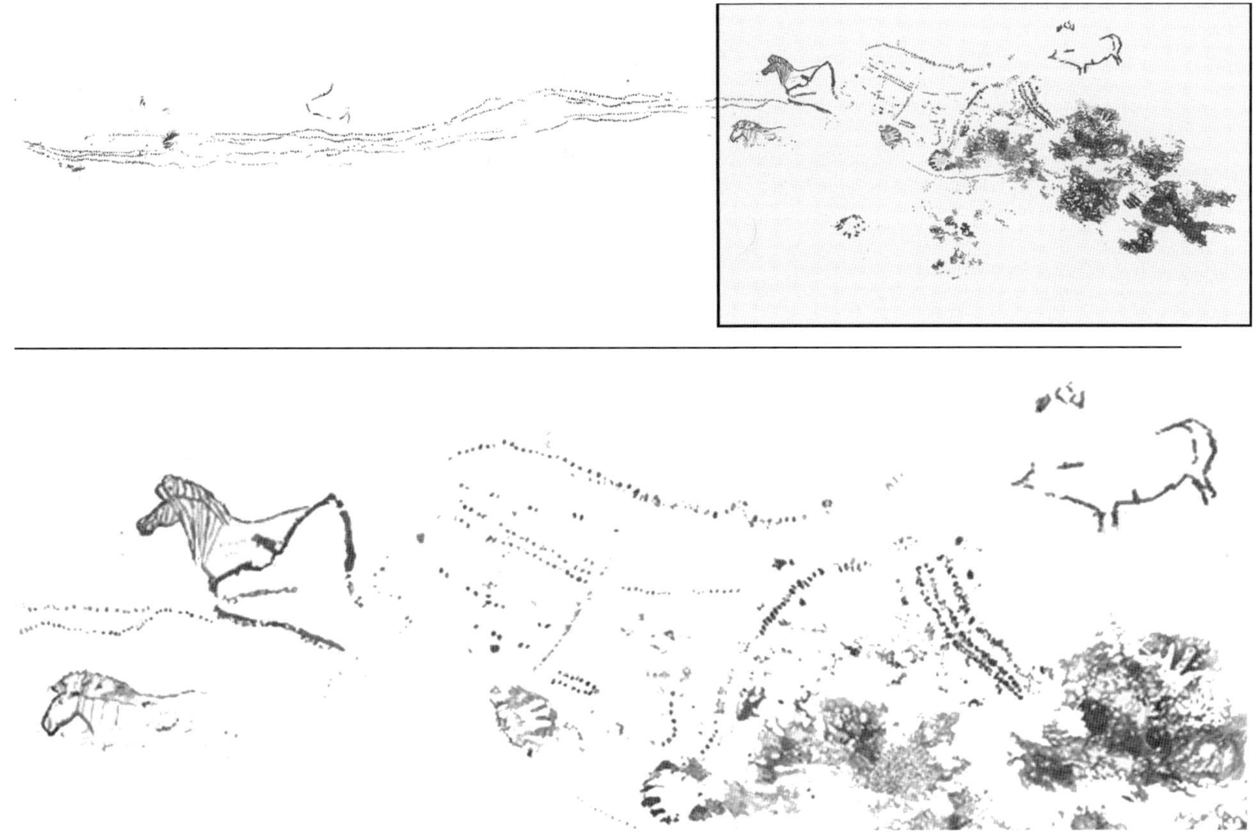

Figure 2. Frieze´s calque –panels VI and VII–. Below, detail of the listing horses, the deer, hands and points where the dating samples by U/Th were taken.

most part of them in an ancient chronology (Candamo, Llonín, Pindal, Mazaculos II, La Meaza, Chufin, Porquerizo, Castillo, la Pasiega, La Garma, Castillo or Cullalvera), the French Pyrenees (Niaux, Marsoulas, Trois Frères, Bedeilhac) or the South of the Peninsula, in this case attached to horses (Las Palomas, Atlanterra, El Moro).

The date U/Th obtained for the crust covering the series of points in panel VII, more than 31,000 years –the most ancient of the painted set– places this motif in the Aurignacian-Gravettian transition (Hoffman *et al.*, in XVII UISPP World Congress).

The hands: about forty negative hands, which could reach one hundred once the walls are cleaned, are recognized (Fig. 3). At least 13 are left hands and 6 are right hands. In some case, the forearm also appears to be painted, and in two more cases the fingers rise so short and separate that they seem to be a bear claw –panel VII (Fig. 3.2). Children´s hands are frequent. Highlighted by its size is a baby´s hand at the bottom of the cave, as is also found in Gargas (Sahly, 1975). The calcite crusts overlapping several hands can be seen (Fig. 3.4) allowing the dating of six cases by U/Th, establishing the most ancient date higher than 27,500 years and being placed in the same dating state as all the Gravettian hands (Hoffman *et al.*, i.p.). Its location presents a concentration in two areas of the vertical wall: the bottom of the cavity, with 18 samples grouped in 3 panels –I, II and III– and the right wall with 16 samples in another eight panels –VIII, IX, XIII, XIV, XVIII, XIX, XX and XXI–. However, the most interesting core is placed in the centre of the roof –panel XV–. There three black hands from children with incomplete fingers appear together with 2 red hands which could be related to the complex series of red points presenting radial motifs.

Seen as a whole, the hands at Fuente del Trucho present two peculiar features which make them different from the known hands in the Cantabrian Coast and that, on the other hand, approximate them to the French representations of the Pyrenees north side: 1) there are painted hands in black and 2) a great deal are incomplete, lacking the third finger. In fact, among

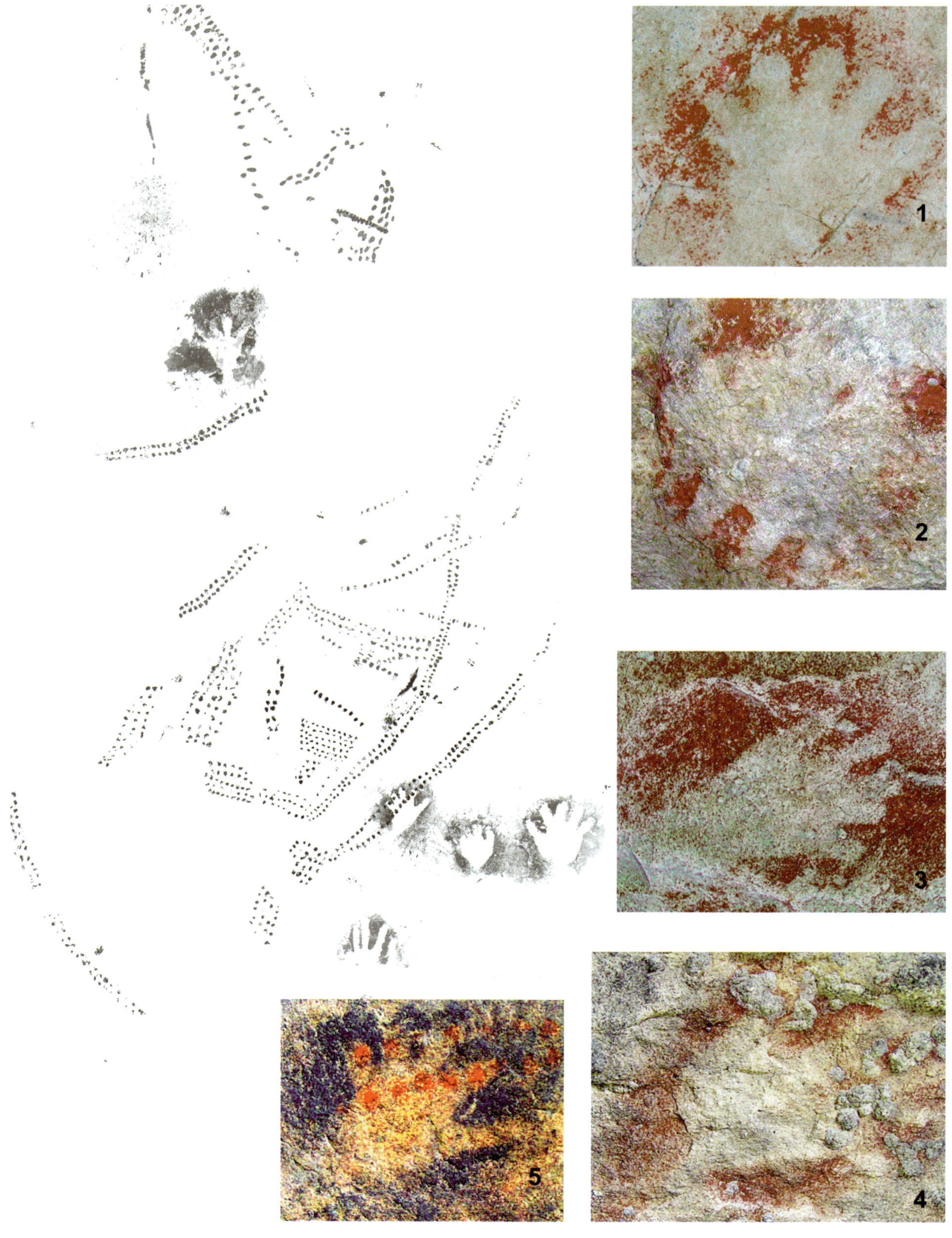

Figure 3. Calque of the points and hands series placed in the centre of the roof –panel XV- together with several hand photos. Notice the incomplete fingers in hands 1, 3 and 5, the bear claw appearance of hand number two and the chalky crusts over hand number four where the samples for U/Th were taken. Photos treated with D-Strech.

the hundreds of hands represented in the Cantabrian Coast caves –mostly at Castillo (56), the Garma (32) and Fuente del Salín (14), and in minor cases at Altamira, Tito Bustillo and Cudón– just two are painted in black; one, negative, from Gran Techo of Altamira and other, positive from Fuente del Salín and only the hand at Cudón presents incomplete fingers. Instead, in the south of the Peninsula we find two black hands with incomplete fingers at Ardales (Málaga) and with an alteration of the little finger, in red, at Maltravieso (Cáceres). However, on the French side black hands are predominant, and at the same time the majority of the incomplete hands are located in the Gargas and Tibiran caves in the same vertical as Fuente del Trucho, on the other side of the Pyrennes. This fact makes us suggest as a hypothesis that real finger loss, especially the longest middle finger, could be due to freezing when crossing the Pyrenees, with a higher incidence occuring in the weaker people, the children (Utrilla, 2005). Valuing the classic interpretation of Leroi Gourhan as a hunting code with bent fingers is not possible at Fuente del Trucho, as most of the incomplete fingers appear on children´s hands.

There are some doubts about the superposition between black hands and red points. In Ripoll´s opinion, both red hands and the black ones in panel XV are infra-placed to the red points series (Ripoll et *al.*, 2001). However, Beltrán and Baldellou observed in 1981 that "a black hand is over the red points". It is not easy to solve this issue as in the left part of the little finger some red points seem to be hidden under the black hands' halo, while in the index finger the red points appear over a colorless black (Fig. 3.5). At the moment, the U-Th dating (Hoffman *et al.*, i.p.) would lean toward a greater point antiquity, although, as it is an *ante quem* dating, both issues could be contemporary. The Gravettian crust dating recovering the hands would come after the dates, about 26,000, which have been given the cave Cosquer or the 26,860 ± 460 BP of a bone in Gragas, as the ones calibrated cal BP give dating around the 32,000, which are the ones compared to the U/Th at Fuente del Trucho. A similar dating to ours is given by the charcoal found at the foot of the panel at Fuente del Salín (calibrated about the 27, 000) (García Diez and Garrido, 2012). Regarding the hands at Castillo where the same technology has been used by the same team, the most ancient dates reach the 37,630 in the sample 0-82 (Pike *et al.*, 2012).

The horses: seven clear samples and two doubtful ones all painted in red are recognized in the inner room. Three of them –two in panel VI and one in panel VIII– are placed in the same frieze, filling an intermediate space between two bands with hand figures, and a fourth sample, in panel IV, is placed in the left of the opposite edge of the frieze in the roof. They seem to be attached to a linear series of points –panel VI– or to digitations –panel VIII– presenting on the two horses´ heads a high compositional similitude both with stiff horsehairs and listed lines on the neck (Fig. 2). This presence of this detail could date them in the Evolved Solutrean, as could be indicated in the manes on listed necks of an engraved horse on stone in the Petite Grotte de Bize which Sacchi –1986– attached to the Upper Solutrean but according to Djindjian –2013– it comes from an ancient excavation –Genson– with mixed materials, so it could belong both to Solutrean and Gravettian.

In panel VIII, associated to 5 digitalization, a fifth horse head with the long nape and nostril of a horse appears, from which a crust shaped on its back has been dated showing a possible performance before the 29,000, that is to say, in Gravettian chronology. On the other hand, the total similitude of this figure with the one represented in sector C2 of the Pasiega is surprising: the same long and fallen nape, a forward curved bow in the horsehair, and a double line on the back (Utrilla *et al.*, 2012, fig. 7). This sample is attached to two series of point curves and to a triangular sign (González Sáinz and Balbín, 2002).

In panel XII, on the roof, two opposite horses appear, one of them is a complete figure, wounded by a lance or a dart. The lack of details in the inner part, the pronounced cervical-dorsal curve and the legs in open parallel lines shaped like brackets, could classify it into the Middle Solutrean, according to the sequence of Parpalló (Villaverde, 1994). The other sample, only represented by a small elongated head and a long curved neck would fit better with the Gravettian (Utrilla *et al.*, 2012).

Deer, goat and bear: In panel VII a colorless "headless horse" was published (Ripoll *et al.*, 2001) but the digital treatment of the figure throughout the *DStrecth* application shows a small elongated head, a recognizable deer horn and a short tail (Fig. 2). This fact excludes its cataloging as a horse in spite of presenting an identical morphology to the horse in panel VI, with massive hindquarters and legs in open parallel lines (Utrilla *et al.*, 2012).

In panel XXI a little goat with an upright open nose and small parallel horns appears, framed by fissures and attached to hands and three or four tri-lobed signs (Utrilla *et al.*, 2012, fig. 9). This little goat is similar to a zoo morph at Nerja (Sanchidrián 1994, fig. 66) for which a pre-Solutrean chronology, according to the lighting traces, is proposed given the dating of 24,130±140 BP (28,532-27.832 calBP) and 20,980±100 BP (25,600-25.060 cal BP) (Medina *et al.*, 2010). This would match with the TL and U/Th dates proposed for other similar goats in panel IV/6 of the Garma about the 26.000 (González Sáinz, 2003); or the female deer with trilinear head at Antoliña in a stone of a Gravettian level dated in en 27,390±320 (31.942-30.840 calBP) (Aguirre, 2007). There is another little goat coming from the Solutrean-Gravettian II of Parpalló –number 18,100, fig. 156-, although it corresponds to the TNT type –triple naturalist trace–, more frequent in the initial Solutrean (Villaverde, 1994).

Finally, in the very centre of the line of points in panel VI, a large head is represented which could belong to both a bear and a bovine or a horse (Fig. 2).

The tri-lobed signs appear in a highlighted position in two panels: with the shape of a pointed tri-lobed in the frieze of panel VI, attached to the listed-horsehair horse (Fig. 2); and in panel XXI with the shape of three or four signs of semi-circular forehead apparently attached to the little goat, two hands and a point series (Utrilla *et al.*, 2012). The pointed tri-lobed presents several well-visible crusts on its line, over which four datings, the most ancient close to 26,000, have been obtained by the Pike and Hoffman team, confirming again the proposed Gravettian chronology.

Regarding its reading, the existence of an elongated sign crossing one of the lobes led Beltrán to identify it in 1993 as a vulvar sign, although it could also correspond to the horse´s belly. The vulvar shapes of Castillo –the scutellum– would be distantly similar motifs, or Micolón –with an inner trace in both cases–, or the triangular signs of ancient sanctuaries, as Pasiega, La Lluera II, Lloseta, Chufin o Maltravieso. However, Eric Robert has not documented on his Franco-Cantabrian Corpus of signs –2006– any sample of the same type as the ones at Trucho –personal communication-. In the opinion of Casado –1979– triangular shapes are more common in the central area of the Peninsula, with the most important core at Ojo Guareña and Maltravieso, in this case related, as in Trucho, to hands and digitations.

A last fact to report is the topographic distribution with a main and well-visible position in the panels of Fuente del Trucho, which separates again the prevailing trend of the full Cantabrian signs –quadrilateral and oval– performed "in diverticulum, lateral camarines to the communication routes or in the main composition edges, frequently noting a quest for hiding which contrasts with the wanted visibility for the animal figures" (González Sáinz, 2005).

4. The engravings panel

In a central position and in a preferential location, a large bear figure appears in a ball like hibernating position, shaped by a technique combining excision for the body and incision for the head. Also documented is an engraved head of a second bear and a claw and a foot of the same animal, both from an excision technique (Utrilla *et al.*, 2012, fig. 2, number 1 to 4). On the right of the bear, three herbivorous heads in the same vertical can be distinguished. From top to bottom, a horse and a deer looking left and a second horse with a rectangular nose looking right, maybe a feline according to Beltran´s reading –1993– , are identified. It is also difficult to identify the species of the deer: the starting of the webbed horns forward and next to the forehead excludes a deer on the interest of both a reindeer (Beltrán, 1993; Ripoll *et al.*, 2001), or a *Megaceros*, an animal fitting into the ancient chronology and of which engraved samples in the Meseta (Siega Verde, Cueva del Reno) have been documented (Alcolea and Balbín, 2003). The typical hump we saw in the Cougnac samples is not discerned, although the very small head fits with the *Megaceros*.

The set is clearly atypical, both for the performance technique –the excision on the bear and the claw– and for the subject matter of the animals represented –there are neither female deer of tri-lineal heads nor headless bison nor wild bull– although the bear finds parallels on the engraved claws in Niaux or in external sanctuaries such as Venta La Perra (Arias *et al.*, 1998).

5. The archaeological deposit

The archaeological material was obtained from two different places during the excavation carried out by Utrilla and Montes in the 2005 campaign:

1) at the bottom of the tri-lobed signs of panel XXI an altered level emerged, indicating, through the classic "*fossil director*" of the lithic industry and some absolute dating, the existence of real people from the Initial Upper Paleolithic and the Solutrean (Fig.4). Other-

wise, with some doubts, it might come from the Magdalenian with typological echoes of the former period (4 multiple borers, two of them *en étoile*) or Final-Upper (little circular endscrapers, others unguiform and two small points with a marked central peduncle, as the Teyjat type). On the other hand, a thermoluminiscent date of 13.244±945 obtained from an endscraper crackled by fire would suggest the presence of hearths in the Middle Magdalenian, but there are no significant bone materials from this period. The bone industry has only provided one sub-circular section of a spear fragment and a longitudinal section shaft fragment with a rounded and polished edge similar to a sample found in the Gravettian at Reclau Viver.

2) at the bear's bottom, in the deep trace engravings area, outside the cave. Two areas are distinguished there: one modified by the Late Middle Ages structures in shape of circular buckets and hearths paved with stone; and another adjacent one hardly explored which, in principle, could be intact, something we expect to confirm in the 2014 campaign. The first one provided some wheels and glazed pottery and a date of the hearth's coal of about 1,235±35 BP (GrA-29918), which calibrated to 68% supposing a 776 ± 63 a.C. This fact brings the settlement to the beginnings of the Muslim presence in the upper Vero, and may be related to the moment in which *Abderramán I* started a well-documented punishment campaign in this area –781–, after Charlemagne's expedition in the year 778 to Zaragoza. The second area provided altogether six backed bladelets, one of them a hump-backed piece. Recently we have dated a single bone in 31,880±220 BP (Beta 365760) (Cal BC 34,560) whose chronology is Auragnician; in any case, we cannot discard it belonging to an underneath Mousterian level that could reflect a rejuvenation produced by the roots. Together with them, there are 6 endscrapers, 2 borers and 4 scrapers. Our objective for the 2014 campaign is to check if the area is really intact, what comes up from the bone and how they fit with the next sample of Anna Mir excavation which provided two fertile levels with Mousterian materials produced.

The typological stock list of the pieces attributable to the Upper Paleolithic from the messy level of the inner survey provides 14 flat, 8 carenated and 4 nosed endscrapers. These last ones lead us to suggest, together with the existence of 15 retouched blades, some of them strangled, the presence of Aurignacian people in the archaeological site. As Gravettian elements –or Magdalenian–, 21 points and little backside leaves among Gravette, micro-Gravette, Vachons points and other short peduncles, more like the Teyjat type than the Font Robert type, could be included. Among the 12 backed bladelets, some present an oblique truncated not getting scalene. There are also 4 *écaillées* shapes which are present in Gravettian contexts. There are 7 dihedral burins and 8 truncated, one of them multiple, as the burins in Noailles, although they are really large. Four flat invasive retouched pieces and 4 notched points of the Mediterranean type should be attached to the Solutrean, one of them identical in its typometry to the ones found in the close cave of Chaves dated in 19,700 BP, a moment fitting suitably with some horse styles. A more detailed study of the lithic materials can be seen in Montes *et al.*, 2006; Montes and Utrilla, 2008; Utrilla *et al.*, 2010; and Domingo *et al.*, 2012.

6. Chronology

In short, the parietal art of Fuente del Trucho is framed within the ancient moments of Paleolithic art, at least within the Gravettian, as the U/Th dating of the crusts overlaying the points series, hands, tri-lobed and some of the horses –with elongated and fallen nose– shows. The stylistic sequence of the first Llonín horizon remains like this (Fortea *et al.*, 2004) and of the archaic panels final part of the Garma (González Sáinz, 2003). The horse with the elongated neck and small head in panel XII would be also archaic, according to the examples of Parpalló and the small goat with the upright and open nose –similar to the zoomorphals "dated" at Antoliña, Nerja, Parpalló or la Garma–. An AMS dating of 20,800±100BP (25,414-24.640 calBP), from a bone removed from aremanied level at the small goat's bottom, could place this occupation in Late Gravettian or Early Solutrean.

However, the lithic typology of some fossils heading the deposit also attests to a later Solutrean presence at the cave, highlighted by flat-retouched pieces or cutting points which would indicate a Middle and Upper Solutrean. Due to stylistic criteria fixed at Parpalló (Villaverde, 1994), the Middle period would correspond to some horses, like

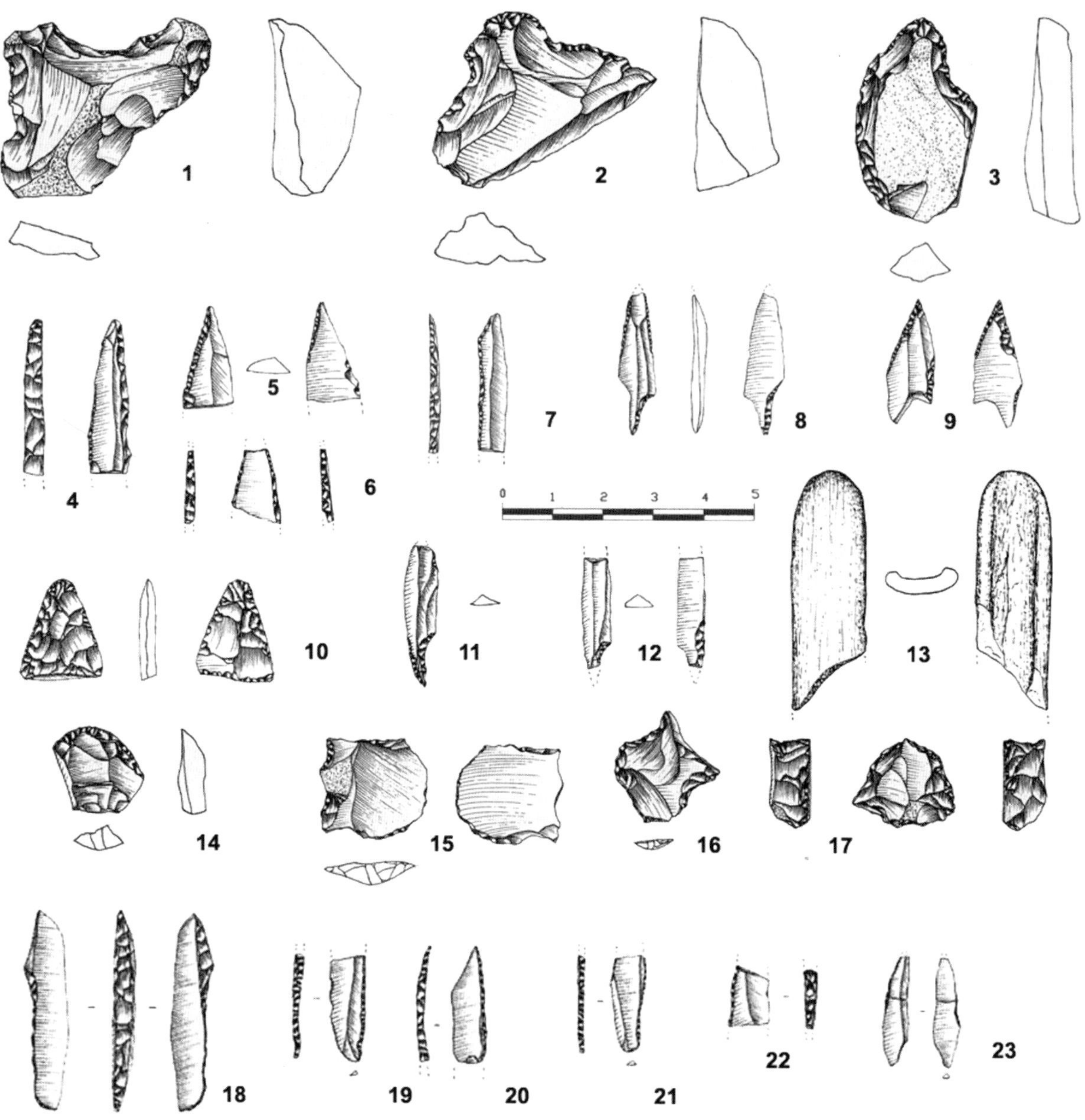

Figure 4. Lithic industry of the 2005 excavation. Numbers 1 to 17: materials found in the messy level of the inner sequence: 1 to 3 nosed endscrapers; numbers 4 to 9 backsides and peduncle points; 10 to 12 possible Solutrean pieces; 13 *lissoir* on bone; 14 to 17 Magdalenian typology pieces; numbers 18 to 23: little points and backsides from the excavation at the bottom of the engravings.

the one with legs in parallel open lines in panel XII, the one in panel IV or its twin, the deer in panel VII, and maybe the Upper Solutrean could be applied to the listed horses of the frieze, with well-marked details on the horsehair, although Bize´smoble parallel results now insecure (Djindjian, 2013). It has not been possible to determine if the horse in panel VI is overlaid on the dated tri-lobed, whose chronology was better indicated.

In conclusion, once the presence of the Gravettian and the Aurignacian at Fuente del Trucho is confirmed, we would stand before an archaeological site in an intermediate location between the forceful seat of Seriñá at Girona (La Arbreda, ReclauViver) and the Cantabrian Coast sites. Fuente del Trucho would as a result be a main point in the east-west mobility of the South Pyrenees.

Jordi Rosell Ardèvol*,**
Antoni Canals Salomó*,**

Las Fuentes de San Cristóbal (Veracruz, Huesca)

Las Fuentes de San Cristóbal was located on the left margin of the Isabéna river passing through a narrow gorge of the same name formed in the sandstones of the Areny Formation, south of the town of Veracruz (Huesca). Its coordinates were 42 ° 19'36 .6"N 0 ° 34'13 .2" E. The site was located at the base of the old A1605 road between the towns of Serraduy and Beranuy, 820 m above sea level and just 20 m above the present river bed. It was precisely the route of this road which cut the shelter section, leaving only a witness to the north of 2 m wide and 5 high (known as Profile 3 or P3); thus, a hall of 15-20 m^2 surface by 2 m high in the south direction (P1 and P2). Fills on both sides had similar characteristics: a low fluvial section and an upper dominated by the contributions of slopes. Part of P1-P2 sediments were used during the construction of the road, so the archaeological work developed between 1998 and 2002 was limited to excavating the witness P3 and the entire surface of the lower levels of P1 – P2. Following this work, the site was destroyed by the redevelopment of the existing road.

The stratigraphic section log of the site was described from the Profile 3. Later work consisted of making connections between the two sectors of the settlement. Thus, in P1-P2 5 archaeological levels were discovered, named A-G from top to bottom, and ten different levels in P3 were called consecutively M-V (Fig. 1). Subsequent correlation work revealed correspondence between the two basal levels P1-P2 (F-G) and level V from P3.

From an archaeological point of view, the higher levels of P3 included within the slope sediments, were characterized by slightly denser accumulations of artifacts (stone tools, bone fragments, and charcoal). The arrangement of these scored elements seeming paleosurfaces. They could have originally been spread over the surface of the shelter. Basal levels placed on the fluvial sediments were thicker and characterized by high density anthropogenic objects and some hearths.

The raw material used to produce most of the lithic industry was flint (73.5%), distantly followed by micritic limestone (11.3%). The other materials (porphyry, quartzite, sandstone, and quartz) were used in a testimonial way (Menéndez, 2009). The 2,199 elements studied show a representation of all categories of the operative chain, suggesting these knapping activities were performed on the site. Flakes are the most exemplified products being 95% overall. Cores (0.8%) are usually in very advanced stages of exhaustion showing discoid reduction strategies and to lesser extents the *Levallois*. Retouched elements are rare and account for only 2.2% of the recovered lithic elements. Denticulate and side scrapers are the most common elements, along with some isolated notches.

Regarding the faunal remains, the degree of fragmentation is very high, which prevents a greater degree of taxonomic identification. Ungulate remains corresponding to deer *(Cervus elaphus)* and horses *(Equus* ferus) were recognized. Evidence of rhinoceros (Rhinocerotidae indeterminate) has also been recognized. The relationship between humans and faunal remains is determined by the presence of some cut marks on bones. The appendicular elements clearly dominate different levels, with occasional dental fragments representing cranial skeletons. We have not identified remains from the axial skeleton (vertebrae and ribs). Neither was the action of carnivores recognized in the cavity. All these elements relate the presence of ungulate traces in the cavity with hunting activities of human groups, and also explain the differential carriage in favor of the limbs of prey and the consequential abandonment of other post-cranial axial parts in the catching field. The identified taxa

* Àrea de Prehistòria, Universitat Rovira i Virgili (URV), Avinguda de Catalunya 35, 43002 Tarragona, España.
** IPHES, Institut Català de Palaeoecologia Humana i Evolució Social, C/ Marcel·lí Domingo s/n (Edifici W3), 43007 Tarragona, España.

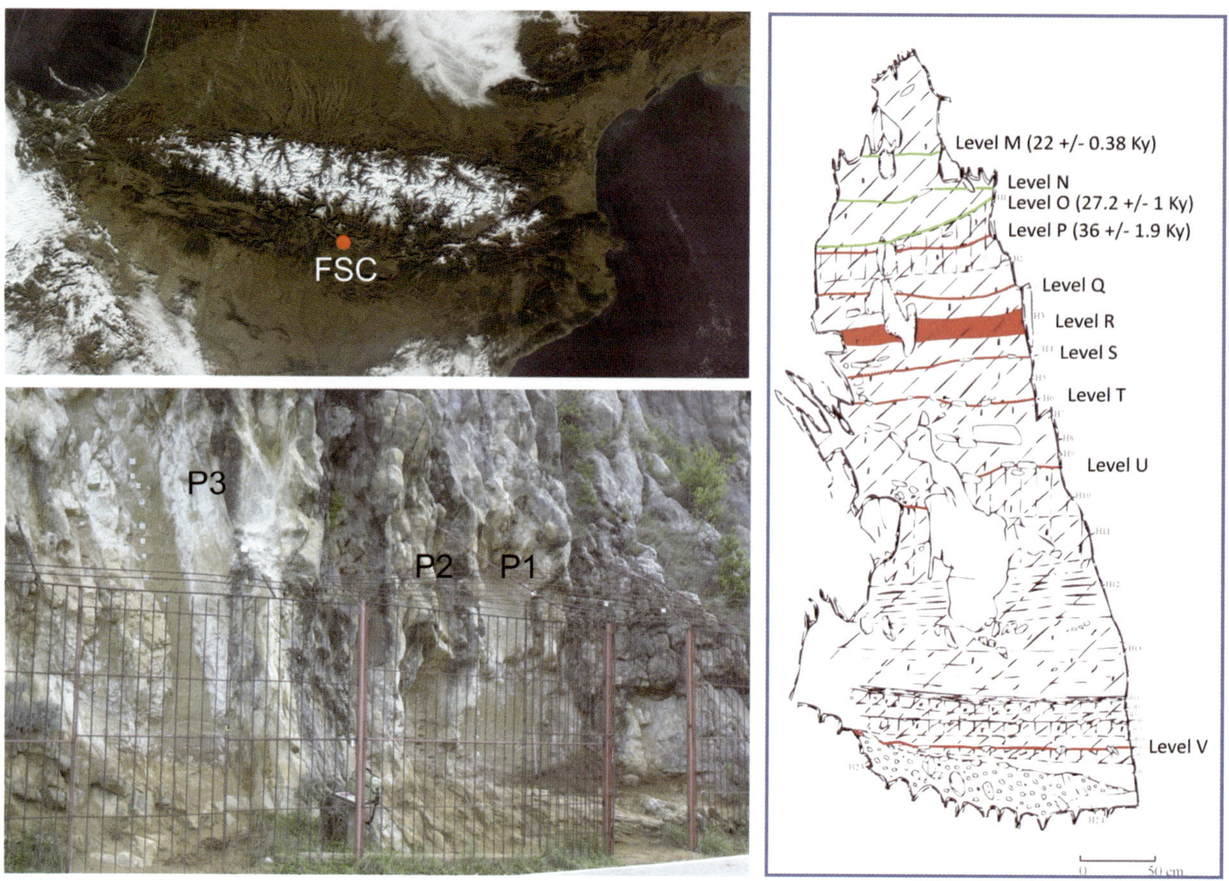

Figure 1. The geographical localization of Las Fuentes de San Cristóbal in the Pyrenees context. Overview of the site and stratigraphy of P3.

suggest hunter preferences to open environment resources, such as the plains near the bottom of the valley. Even though the steep dominates the landscape, nothing indicates its use by these human groups.

Several series made with Accelerator Mass Spectrometry (AMS) and ^{14}C datings were performed using coal from different levels (Table 1). All of them gave consistent results placing the field in a framework that covers the Middle / Up-

FSC-Level	Location	Method	Data	Lab. Ref.	Bibliography Ref.
E	P1-P2	C^{14} AMS	38.650 600	OxA-19145	Maroto *et al.*, 2012
F	P1-P2	C^{14} AMS	39.290 +490 -410	GrA-33817	Maroto *et al.*, 2012
	P1-P2		37.330 +490 -410	GrA-33904	Maroto *et al.*, 2012
G	P1-P2	C^{14} AMS	36.200 ± 350	OxA-19933	Maroto *et al.*, 2012
	P1-P2		38.550 ± 450	OxA-19934	Maroto *et al.*, 2012
M	P3	C^{14} AMS	20.220 ± 380	OxA-8591	Rosell *et al.*, 1998
O	P3	C^{14} AMS	27.200 ± 1.000	OxA-8589	Rosell *et al.*, 1998
P	P3	C^{14} AMS	36.000 ± 1.900	OxA-8591	Rosell *et al.*, 1998

Table 1. Datings obtained from different levels of Las Fuentes de San Cristóbal.

Figure 2. Point recovered in the P level dated to 36 ky.

per Paleolithic transition. Likewise the lower levels, F-G in P1-P2 and the correlation of V in P3 are placed near 39 ky. The P level from P3, where a Mousterian point was recovered, represents the last assemblage of the site associated with Middle Paleolithic technological complex (Fig. 2). Unfortunately, the O and M levels, dated to 27 and 20 ky, respectively, did not provide any diagnostic information allowing us to assign them to a specific chrono-cultural period.

Although the attachment to the Middle Paleolithic level P was initially taken with caution (Maroto *et al.*, 2005; Vaquero *et al.*, 2006), this level demonstrates the existence of human communities in inland areas of the Pre-Pyrenees with some temporal continuity between 40 and 35 ky. The discontinuity appears to have occured after the P level, as the data gap spanning a time frame of about 9,000 years displays. This lack of population could be related to the disappearance of the Middle Paleolithic human populations in the region and a late re-occupation of the territory by groups of the early Upper Paleolithic.

The cave of Los Moros 1 at Gabasa (Huesca)

Lourdes Montes*, Pilar Utrilla*

1. Presentation and history

In the 1980s, a joint project was undertaken between the University of Zaragoza and the Archaeological Museum of Huesca. Between 1981 and 1983 Pilar Utrilla and Vicente Baldellou excavated the well-known cave of Moro de Olvena with Neolithic and Bronze Age levels and in 1984 their joint interventions in two unique sites got underway: the Mousterian cave of los Moros 1 at Gabasa and the cave of Chaves, which in addition to Upper Palaeolithic levels also contained an extraordinary Neolithic deposit, which is now totally razed. The site at Gabasa, five cavities with Prehistoric and Medieval remains, was located in 1982 by M. Badía and visited by Olvena's team in the same year. In 1983, permission was requested from the Ministry of Culture to excavate all of the cavities but the excavation could not be undertaken until the summer of 1984: Utrilla directed the team that worked on the Mousterian cave and Baldellou directed the excavation of the other

* Área de Prehistoria. Universidad de Zaragoza. lmontes@unizar.es and utrilla@unizar.es.

cavities, whose deposits showed significant alterations. From 1985, the campaigns, 7 in total over 10 years, focused exclusively on the Mousterian site and in 1986, L. Montes replaced Baldellou in the joint direction until the last campaign carried out in 1994. Although it was fenced off, the cave has undergone continuous clandestine interventions, which have led to the almost complete disappearance of the control "balk" respected by excavations for further research. The cave is located on the pre-Pyrenean foothills of Huesca, at the foot of a limestone cliff, which is located to the north of the small town of Gabasa, currently the municipality of Peralta de Calasanz. The cliff is an Eocene limestone syncline that dominates one of the headwaters of the Sosa, a tributary of the left bank of the Cinca and on which the karst of the network of caves has developed, which is currently inactive. The Mousterian cave or Gabasa-1 consists of two small chambers: when it was discovered the outer chamber contained very little sedimentary deposit while the inside, a chasm partially filled with debris, housed the site (Fig. 1 and 2).

The place had been used until recently as a cattle fold and its mouth, directed eastwards, partially closed on the outside by a dry stone wall. The upper layers of soil have been repeatedly removed to be used as a fertiliser for the crop terraces that extend along the foot of the cave; in the outer chamber, which has the best living conditions, the deposit has been removed down to a thick stalagmite crust more than a metre thick. In the inner chamber, with a depth of almost three metres, the site is conserved although the fill presented a disturbed surface, particularly in the central area.In its vertical development, this chamber is a bell-type cavity, whose walls maintain carbonate stone edges of varying diameter at different heights, the footprint of water erosion. For this reason, in the site we are presenting, the excavated area greatly exceeds the contour of the walls drawn at the height "0" in the reference plan.

Over the years, there have been various publications about partial aspects of this site, but a monographic report has not yet been released:

The first presentation on the site in Bolskan extracted the first excavation campaigns (Utrilla and Montes 1986).

L. Montes's PhD thesis (1988) summarised the techno-typological study of the lithic remains, ex-

Figure 1. Location of Gabasa1cave at the foot of the cliff that dominates the town.

tending the stratigraphic context of the site to the 1987 campaign.

In the same year, the first attempt was made to reconstruct the chronostratigraphy of the cavity (Azanza *et al.*, 1988) and an initial approach to the microfauna (Gil and Lanchares 1987), which was subsequently corrected in unpublished documents (Guillén 1994; Cuenca 2002).

The first international presentation on the site was given at a conference on Neanderthals in 1986 in Lieja (Utrilla and Montes 1989).

With work more advanced, a new sediment and paleoclimate study was published (Hoyos *et al.*, 1992) whose data was used in a proposal on the end of the Middle Palaeolithic in the Ebrovalley (Utrilla and Montes 1993).

A little later, M.ª Fernanda Blasco published her thesis, a key study on the fauna of Gabasa, and an interesting summary of its taxonomic and taphonomic analyses (Blasco 1995 and 1997).

Between the two came the presentation at the meeting in Capellades in 1995 on the remains of level g, which analysed in-depth the differences between human prey and the contributions of other carnivores (Blasco *et al.*, 1996); the accumulation of remains of hyena during the last excavation campaigns led to a specific study on this animal (Blasco and Montes 1997).

In the meeting in Foz-Coa, the human remains and AMS dating were presented for the first time, with new reflections on the *Transition* (Lorenzo and Montes 2001 and Montes *et al.*, 2001).

The study of pollen preserved in hyena coprolites allowed percolation problems to be solved in the paleoclimate (González-Sampériz *et al.*, 2003 and 2005).

M.D. Garralda (2005) included the Neanderthal remains in this cavity in her review of the Iberian Peninsula for the tribute to J. Altuna; it had been previously included in M. Haber's (2003) PhD thesis on Neanderthals in the Iberian Peninsula.

A review of the *Ebro Boundary* was presented in Lieja, 2001, at the14[th]UISPP Congress (Utrilla *et al.*, 2004) and a revised and updated version was included in the volume that commemorated the centenary of the excavations of Monte Castillo (Utrilla *et al.*, 2006). In 2006, the tribute to V. Cabrera was published; this presented a review of the Middle Palaeolithic in the Ebro basin, which included a summary of the data on Gabasa (Montes *et al.*, 2006).

A detailed technology study of the levels of Gabasa based on a wide collection of the lithic remains from all of the campaigns was presented (Santamaría *et al.*, 2008),taking advantage of the meeting on technology variability organised by the UAB.

A review of the hyena remains accompanied by a new dating of level h based on racemisation in dentin was presented at the meeting on the dens of hyena and other carnivores (Utrilla *et al.*, 2010).

Other authors have used and published some specific remains from the cave in other studies: Hernández Carrasquilla (2001) published a new species of vulture identified among the bird remains and R. García González (2011) focuses in Gabasa in two separate studies on filiation of the Capra pyrenaica.

2. Stratigraphy

The archaeological levels of Gabasa, all of them of Mousterian chronology, were named during the excavation using lowercase letters, from the most recent level *a*, to the deepest, level *h* (Fig.2). The latter was presented as an open framework consisting of boulders and stone fragments, in which the fine fraction only remains *in situ* at the top, and it is accumulated loose through percolation in some points at the bottom, supported by the sub-horizontal walls of the bell-shaped chamber when closed. The colour and texture of the rest of the layers were very similar in appearance and the only significant difference was the size of the clasts.

The following proposal summarises the stratigraphic data based on a sedimentology study (Hoyos *et al.*, 1992), a basic count of the lithic remains (Montes 1988 and Santamaría *et al.*, 2008) and of the remains of fauna (Blasco, 1995), and the dates available (Montes *et al.*, 2001; Utrilla *et al.*, 2010). The sedimentology study allows the fill of the cave to be associated to the limestone lithology in which it opens, formed by sub-aerial and underground contributions, except for the fauna remains and the materials contributed by human groups. Its detritus and loose nature favoured occasional percolation of pollen and some fine fraction. The stratigraphic units were identified using Roman numerals and the archaeological levels with lowercase letters.

- Unit I (level *h*). Up to almost 2 metres thick, it is characterised by the abundance of thick elements and within these, by the dominance of great boulders over minor blocks, whereas

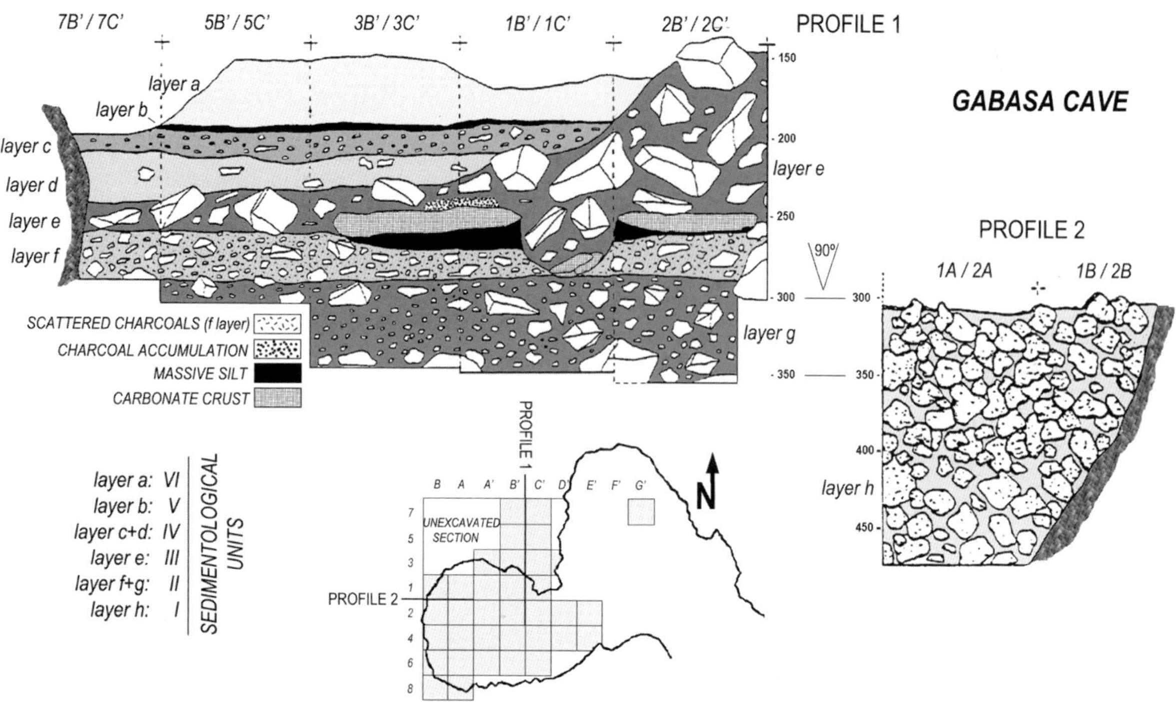

Figure 2. Stratigraphy and site at Gabasa.

the fine fraction only appears in the top area. It seems to have formed under cold and dry conditions in which freezing, significant in duration but not intensity, was responsible for the gravitational contributionand boulders and stone fragments detached from the walls. The presence of fine fraction in the top is interpreted as a change towards wetter conditions. Mixed in with this rocky framework, in level *h*, 300 lithic and 1390 fauna remains were recovered. The bones were apported both by humans and carnivores. Dating based on aminoacid racemisation in dentine of a total of 15 horse's teeth returned an average age of 140000±43000 (LEB 8538-8558). The measurement, as it is inaccurate, puts this section from the deposit in phase OIS 6, taking it out of the dates managed up until then for the entire site.

- Unit II (levels *g* + *f*). Arranged without sedimentary discontinuity with the former, the sedimentology grouping of levels *g*and *f*, an average 50 cm thick, shows a matrix of brown clays with gravel and sand that contain small stone fragments. Level *g* was distinguished from level *f* during the excavation by the disappearance from the matrix of the small calcareous concretions and scattered charcoal that appeared in it. Regarding the archaeological remains, there is a significant difference between the two layers: while more than 1200 lithic remains correspond to level *g*, level *f* yielded just 550, with an excavated area of one quarter smaller. Something similar happens with the fauna; 4194 remains in *f* compared to 8741 remains in level *g*. In the latter level, the presence of a hyena den is noteworthy, partly accounting for the large number of animal remains. For level *g* an AMS date was obtained that only specified an age earlier than 50700 BP (OxA-5675). Its immediate superposition over Unit I, without erosion traces or stratigraphic discontinuity, suggests an old chronology for this series of levels, also in the Middle Pleistocene.
- Unit III (level *e*). This level was formed in the outer chamber, from which, in a clear process of solifluction, it entered the inner cavity, resulting in partial erosion of level *f*, over which it settled. The clay matrix with gravel and calcareous sand is very similar to the previous

one but this includes large stone fragments and boulders. Its structure is responsible for the varying thickness: from 70 cm in the areas connecting the two chambers, to an average of 30 cm on the two sides of the expansion fan. The lithic remains add up to almost one thousand, whereas fauna remains amount to 4795. Although an AMS dating specifies only dates prior to 51900 BP (OxA-5674), a conventional C14 dating would put it in the late OIS-3, despite its wide deviation: 46500 +4400/-2200 BP (GrN-12809).

- Unit IV (levels *d+c*). This sedimentology unit is characterised, like the previous two, by its clay matrix, which in this case includes an abundance of stone fragments, platelets and boulders. The difference between the two archaeological levels was established by the higher compactness of level *d* and its lower clast content compared to the overlaying level *c*. The lithic remains recovered reached 531 in level *d* whereas in level *c* 253 remains were counted; besides, other 215 were attributed to *a+c*, in some areas where the lack of level *b* prevented these two layers from being distinguished *(vid. infra)*. The same happens with the fauna remains, which amount to 1862 in level *d* and 2133 in *a+c*. In this unit, the upper section, level *c*, has two AMS dates: >47800 BP (OxA-5673) and >46900 BP (CAMS-10290/Beta-68391). Perhaps, the carbon dating obtained for level *a+c* could also be related to this layer *c*, given the similarity of the result: >45900 (OxA-5672).
- Unit V (level *b*).The only archaeological level identified was sterile: a carbonate crust, with little development and discontinuous, whose absence creates the aforementioned problem to distinguish between *c* and *a*.
- Unit VI (level *a*). Another clay matrix with numerous stone fragments, platelets and boulders, whose only difference with level *c*, according to the sedimentology (the stones edges were sharpener), we were unable to identify during excavation. As we said, in some areas which did not have level *b*, the material from *a + c*are considered as a whole: 478 elements from the total of *a + c* can be singled out for definitely belonging to this level *a;* as aforementioned, 215 elements had to be attributed imprecisely to a + c. In the fauna, the total of *a + c* amounted to 2133 elements. Regarding its chronology, in addition to the generic AMS dating prior to 39900 BP (OxA-5671), we must remember the one obtained from another charcoal from *a + c*, which we have indicated in level *c*.

3. Paleoclimate characteristation of the record from Gabasa

The attempts at paleoclimate reconstruction of the Gabasa deposit were corrected in the aforementioned subsequent studies, qualifying the interpretation of the site. After the initial merely climatic estimate, made using provisional data on the fauna, pollen and sedimentology in the early campaigns (Azanza *et al.*, 1988), a revision of these was undertaken, proposing two options based on the sedimentology analysis (Hoyos *et al.*, 1992),which determined cold conditions for the bordering levels, *a* and *h*, whereas the centre of the deposit was considered warm in general, with some cooler oscillations in levels *g-f* and particularly in *e*, and with varying humidity: the first option put the development of the sequence in the Würm II (based on the dating of level *e*, the only one available at the time),whereas the second placed the central unit (levels *c-g*) in the interstadial Würm II-III, with two bordering levels, level *h* at the base, placed in Würm II, and level *a*,at ceiling level, as the start of Würm III.

The subsequent study of the fauna carried out by F. Blasco (1995) backed the majority of these observations, particularly in relation to the dryness/humidity of the conditions that affected the levels of the deposit (except *a*, dry according to the fauna assemblage). The testimonial presence of Cuon and Leopard confirmed the warm nature of the central unit of the sequence, but being aware of the low determining value of the macrofaunain identifying the oscillations in climate that could have arisen during the period in question. A brief microfauna analysis of a random sample carried out by P. Guillem ratified the determination of the macrofauna and the sedimentology as regards the warm/dryness of the deposit, coinciding with the fauna as regards level *a*, also dry (Blasco 1995: 60).

A little later, the series of AMS dates obtained by R. Hedges at the Oxford laboratory and another by Beta Analytic, although inaccurate (between >39.9 ky BP for level *a* and >50.7 ky BP for level *g*) steered us towards the first paleoclimate proposal mentioned earlier, which put the entire sequence at least in the Würm II (Montes *et al.*, 2001).

However, new results from a pollen study of hyena coprolites in this site (González-Sampériz *et al.*, 2003 and 2005), qualified this proposal, keeping the entire Gabasa deposit in Würm II with permanent conditionsof dryness and cold or cool temperatures, except at the top (level *a*). The proportion of *Quercus* t. *ilex-coccifera* in level *a*, dated at an inaccurate > 39900 BP, would suggest milder and warmer conditions, however, that could be related to the start of the interstadial Würm II-III, as documented in the apparently contemporary levels of Beneyto X, Carigüela V or in the base of Arbreda. The top of the Gabasa sequence could therefore be included in the globally warm conditions of OIS 3, distinguishing it from the rest of the site. The warm nature that the palynology study would assign to this level is not consistent with the cold nature assigned by the sedimentology based on the proliferation of frost weathering inside stone fragments (including frost weathering of platelets). As the study showed (González-Sampériz *et al.*, 2005: 593), this difference could be resolved by considering the presence of platelets as an occasional occurrence and not as something from the general environment. We currently live in a climate considered warm but on some winter days with heavy or prolonged frost, frost weathering of platelets can be generated in the cave at Gabasa. At the start of some excavation campaigns we noticed these types of platelets on the surface of the cave and the consequent scar on the roof of the cave, which proves that it is of recent origin. This could have been normal in the area, the Ebro valley, where marked continentality is one of the most significant characteristics of the climate.

Later, the earliest settlement, level *h* was dated by T. Torres and J.E. Ortiz at 140±43 ky (LEB 8538-8558) by aminoacid racemisation in the dentine of horse's teeth (Utrilla *et al.*, 2010). This dating, except for the problem posed by its very wide range, *a priori* placed the old thick deposit of level *h* in the early Middle Pleistocene. The new date offered was a surprise and led us to evaluate a more extensive chronology, with longer hiatuses in the filling process: clear discontinuity between units II *(g+f)* and III *(e)*; interruptions in the sediment in the core of IV *(d+c)*; viscous and mass transport to the inner chamber of levels III (*e*) and VI (*a*)... This meant considering a chrono-stratigraphy review of the deposit and suggested that the lower part (lithological levels I and II, or archaeological level s*h* and *g+f*) corresponded to an older chronology, from the Middle Pleistocene. The discontinuity that marked the base of level III *(e)*would represent the start of a new sedimentary phase, whose chronological distance from the previous one we cannot identify using the vague "prior to" dates that we have for the site. The upper units (III to VIII), could be immediately posterior but also more recent, if we would accept the conventional date of level *e*.

4. The lithic and bone remains and the interpretation of the site

In Gabasa 6 human bones attributed to the Neanderthal have been recovered (Utrilla 2000; Lorenzo and Montes 2001; Garralda 2005): a first upper premolar (P3) from level *f* attributed to a young person; a lower right molar (M2) also from level *f*, perhaps from a female adult and another lower right molar (M1) from the remained sediments, this one with a toothpick groove and probably from a male adult. Corresponding to level *e* are a right clavicle, without its apophysis and a first toe phalanx from a left foot and finally, the remained sediments also included a first metatarsal from a adult right foot.

The magnificent collection of fauna studied by Fernanda Blasco (1995 and 1997) presents more than 23,000 remains, over half of which can be determined. From these, 23 species of mammal have been distinguished: 9 ungulates *(Equus caballus, Equus hydruntinus, Bos* sp., *Rhinocerotidae, Cervus elaphus, Capra pyrenaica, Rupicapra rupicapra, Capreolus capreolus, Sus scropha)*; 10 carnivores *(Ursus spelaeus, Crocuta spelaea, Panthera spelaea, Panthera leo, Panthera pardus, Canis lupus, Cuon alpinus, Vulpes vulpes, Lynx spelaea, Felis sylvestris)*, 2 mustelids *(Meles meles, Mustela putorius)* and 2 lagomorphs *(Oryctolagus cunniculus, Lepus sp.)* In addition, 20 species of bird and a very significant collection of microfauna were identified. Almost half of the remains allow the species to be identified, which suggests extraordinary conservation of the collection and a low bone processing index. M.F. Blasco's PhD thesis, expressed very cautiously due to the chronological estimates available at the time of the study, suggests the possible presence of older types of horse and hyena among the remains: possible dating of the lower levels *(f, g, h)* in the Middle Pleistocene would fit into these approaches.

The taphonomic study of these fauna remains, their distribution over the site and the relationship with the human artefacts suggest alternating use of the cave between humans and carnivores. Therefore,

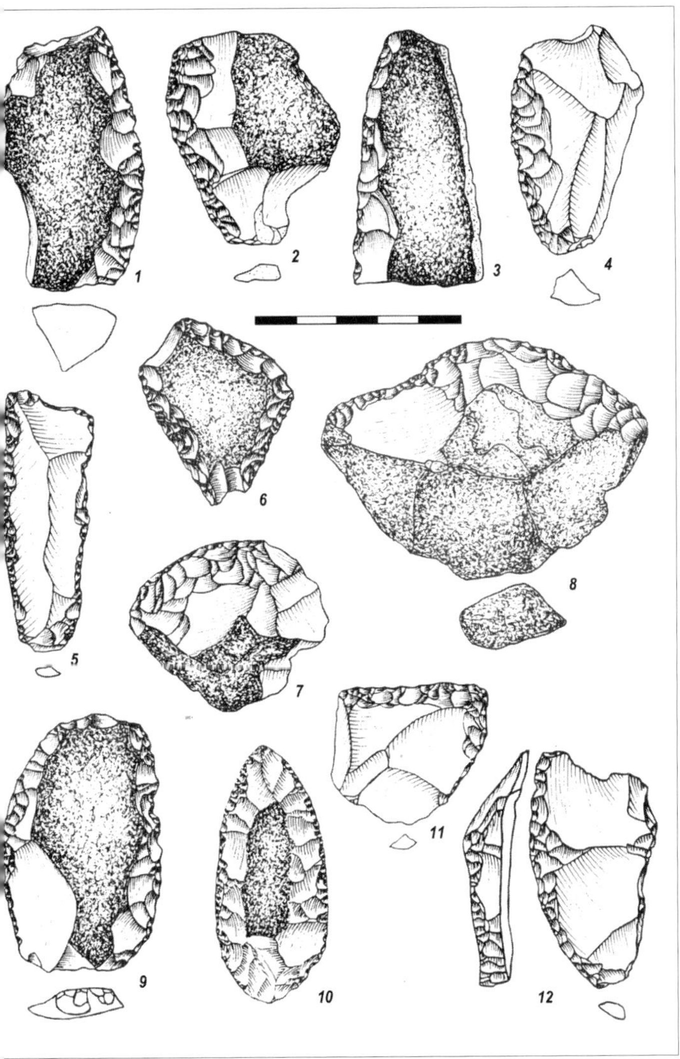

Figure 3. Gabasa: scrapersand Mousterian point (no. 10) from levels a+c (1-4), d (5-8) and e (9-12).

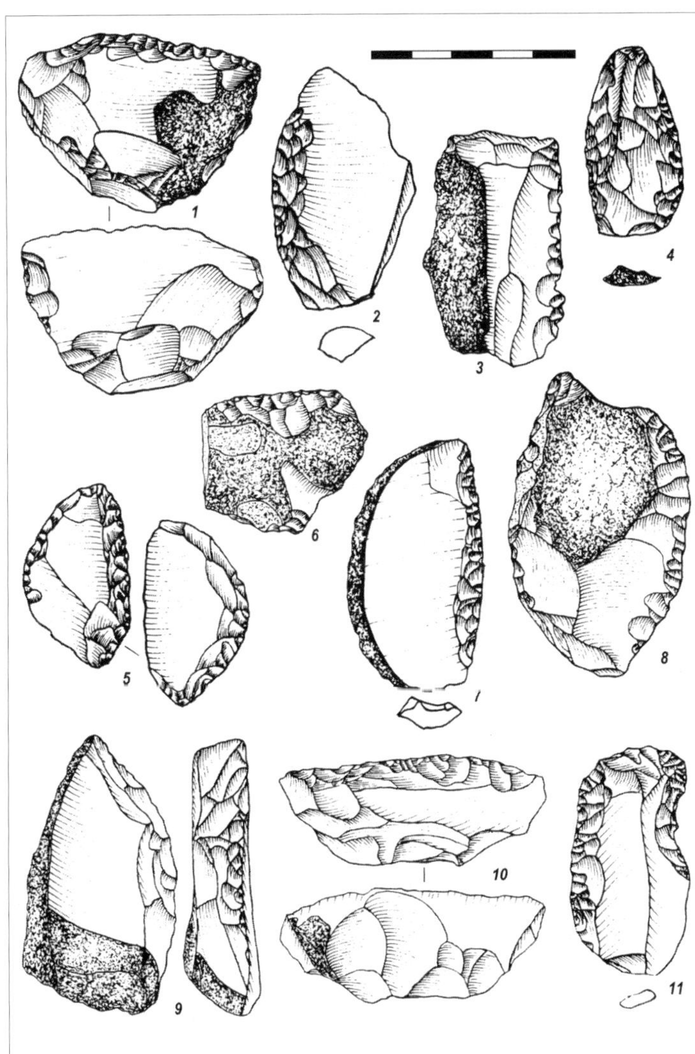

Figure 4. Gabasa: scraper and limace (no. 4) from levels f (1-4), g (5-8) and h (9-11).

the Neanderthals, who mainly hunted horses and red deers, must have occupied the cave in the summer, whereas the carnivores, whose prey marks are present on ibex's bones, always adults, would occupy the cave at other times. We know that the foals and fawns were hunted by humans from the clear marks (slits, grooves...) left by the flint instruments on the bones, while processing the prey. However, it is not currently possible to determine the pattern (in the same year or in different years) this alternate occupation followed (Blasco 1995; Blasco *et al.*, 1996).

Regarding the instruments recovered, the lithic remains currently analysed typologically relate these assemblages to the *facies* «typical, rich in scrapers» of the Mousterian: they are basically assemblages with many scrapersand untransformed lithic flakes, in addition to a few but very good points and slightly exploited cores (Fig. 3 and 4). In the two more recent levels (*a* and *c*),the technology and typology change (an increase in certain backed knives), which is reflected in an artificial increase in the group of tools from the Upper Paleolithic and which could fit into the type B Mousterian Acheulean tradition (Montes 1988; Utrilla and Montes 1993).

The lithic assemblage of Gabasa-1 show a high level of technological homogeneity throughout the sequence (Santamaría *et al.*, 2008). The main operating sequence in all levels is discoid. However, two secondary operating sequences have been identified; Levallois and Quina, whose reconstruction and individualisation require more detailed study. Raw materials would have been supplied from the surrounding area of the site; the selected nodules were tested *in situ* and then brought into the site. Production of supports was mainly done using simple albeit very economical and fast (discoid) knapping methods and techniques. The supports obtained (cortical products, flakes "à dos débordant", ordinary flakes and centripetal ones) were mainly transformed into scrapers and, to a lesser extent, denticulated and notched tools, and used, along with unretouched flakes, to process prey (fawn and foals). The low incidence of retouched flakes in the assemblage suggests that some of the tools were brought into the site. The typological differences of level *a+c* are related to changes in the transformation of supports into tools, characterised by a significant decrease in the group of scrapers and different treatment of the flakes "à dos débordant", which are not so much transformed into scrapers but are used in a raw state.

To summarise, it is a magnificent site that, considering the type of fauna found (ibex, horse and deer dominating over other herbivores and a variety of carnivores, including cave hyena) and the lithic industry recovered, is interpreted as a hunting camp specialising in fawn and foals, which contradicts the cliché of peremptory and indiscriminate hunting with a lack of specialisation of the Neanderthals. Subsequent processing of the prey (cutting, deboning and preparation of the skins) would be done using the unvaried but abundant lithic material recovered, which would explain the extraction of flakes from cores *in situ* and the minimum transformation of these supports into specific tools, points and scrapers, which would be brought along already finished. Some big tools knapped on pebbles (hammers, choppers and chopping-tools) could have been used in butchery tasks. Humans would alternate occupation of the cave with other predators, from season to season, particularly the cave hyena and wolf, which would use it as a den and whose prey would have been mainly ibex. Seasonal occupation of the site would explain the minimum preparation of the site (there are barely any stable hearths, although there is a lot of charcoal in the sediment; the failure to remove the angular clasts, some of which were very big and would have made the settlement very uncomfortable) and the conservation of the fauna, truly extraordinary, given that a minimum amount of the prey hunted was consumed in the cave.

Alfonso Alday*

Kanpanoste and Kanpanoste Goikoa sites (Vírgala, Álava, Basque Country)

Two shelters are presented together due to their geographic proximity –roughly 200m apart– and their shared stratigraphic sequences resulting from the same activities by Meso-Neolithic communities, parallel to the neighbouring Atxoste site. The shelters are in the southern foothills of Azáceta Pass. Kanpanoste faces west and Kanpanoste Goikoa west-northwest. The first, next to Berrón River, retains a visor measuring almost 12 m long and 2 m wide. The second, more difficult to reach, provides better shelter with a 13m long x 3 m wide roof, although originally it was larger.

As usual at sites from this period and zone, their features include a good strategic location, which facilitated surveillance and access to the open spaces of the Arraia Valley and the mountain landscape in the immediate hinterland.

Kanpanoste:

Archaeological work by A. Saenz de Buruaga in 1990 distinguished three sedimentary units in a 1 m deep sequence, one of which contains two distinct sections (Fig. 1).

Lanh Level: 45cm deep, dipping south-north, consisting of a fine, compact silt-clay matrix, blackish in colour, with fewer larger fraction ele-

* Área de Prehistoria Universidad del País Vasco (EHU/UPV). Tomás y Valiente s/n 01006 Vitoria-Gasteiz a.alday@ehu.es

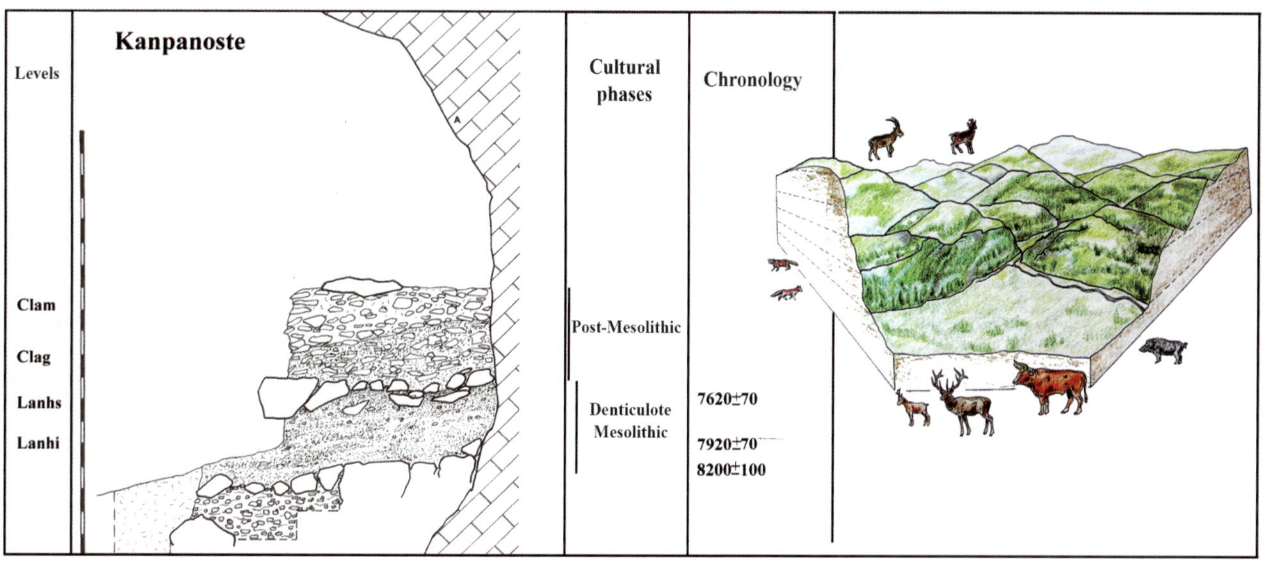

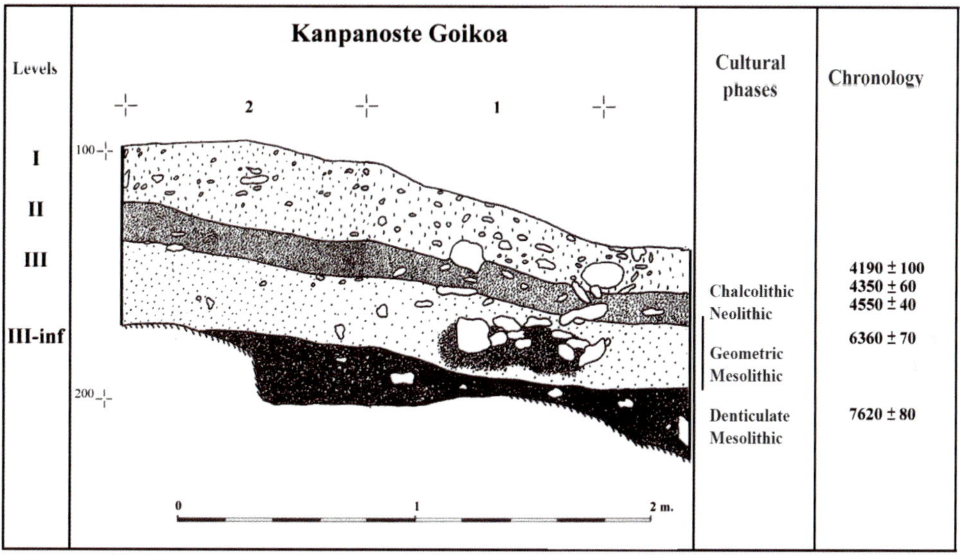

Figure 1. Top: Stratigraphic section and ecological features of Kanpanoste. Bottom: Stratigraphic section of Kanpanoste Goika.

ments and a major component of *Helix nemoralis*. It is divided into two units for sedimentological and archaeological reasons. The upper unit (Lanhs) includes blocks, while the lower level (Lanhi) does not. The lithic industry in both units is predominated by *campiñoide*-style notches and denticulates on flakes, followed by denticulates, sidescrapers denticulates, endscrapers and awls. The lack of microliths on the lower horizon and their presence on the level indicate a differential nuance in a changing industry. This unit also contains an interesting collection of perforated *nasaridas* and an atrophied deer canine which were probably part of a personal adornment. The inventory is completed with a set of stone macrotools for use as hammers/retouchers, scraping or processing plants. The scarce fauna includes wild boar, the predominant species, followed by roe deer red deer and chamois. Culturally, the material can be identified with Mesolithic notches and denticulates.

Clag Level: The defining feature of this 18 cm deep level is the considerable volume of edged clasts, associated with a greyish, ash-like silt-clay fraction with a loose structure. It is in erosive contact with the other two strata at both the wall and the ceiling. It is poor in archaeological material, with visits during the Chalcolithic, Neolithic and the late Mesolithic identified from a few denticulates, two geometrics, a speartip with flat retouch and a few flat ceramic fragments.

Clam Level: With an average depth of 20 cm, this level contains many angular clasts in a fine brown silt-clay matrix, loose but rough to touch, with a major input of present-day organic matter. This level lack archaeological interest.

Level	Code	BP Date
Lanhi	GrN-22441	8200±70
	GrN-22442	7920±100
Lanhs	GrN-22440	7620±70

Table 1. Radiocarbon references of Kanpanoste.

Three other analyses have yielded rejuvenated dates due to sample mineralization

Kanpanoste Goikoa

Archaeological work by A. Alday in 1992 and 1993 detected four sedimentary units, some of which contain several cultural episodes in a one meter thick sequence.

Level III-bottom: This level rests on the rocky base of the shelter, limestone with weathering processes which enriched the section with small-sized gravel. Average depth of 20cm, lying on a south-north dip, and also more gently east-west. Fine, silty, compact matrix with no large components except for the base. Dark brown colour. The retouched lithic industry is not large but significant. Half are notches and *campiñoide*-style denticulates on flake, accompanied by endscrapers and sidescrapers in the same style. Red deer, auroch and wild boar clearly predominated the identified game. Culturally ascribed to Mesolithic notches and denticulates.

Level III– top: A more gradual process than the previous level, with a 20cm potential, a lighter brown soil with a homogeneous silty matrix and an increased proportion of angular clasts, detached from the wall and ceiling of the shelter. Colonies of gastropods, mainly *Helix cepaea*, are mixed with the sediment, and similarly, numerous charcoal remains resulting of different fires. In fact, a hearth consisting of two rings of limestone blocks organises most of the space. The sedimentation is interrupted by one large and several small blocks which became detached from the roof. Although the notches and *campiñoide*-style denticulates are the most numerous typological group in the retouched lithic industry, by this stage these items had lost much of their role, replaced by geometric reinforcement (triangles and trapezoids, accompanied by microburins) and backs. Flakes with minimal retouch also made a major contribution. The same fauna spectrum remains, with a slight increase in deer and chamois. This level is culturally ascribed to the geometric Mesolithic.

Level II: A steep dip makes its potential (20cm average) vary from one point to another, although it is homogeneous, with very silty soils in a loose, ash coloured structure, with not an excessive amount of angular clasts and limestone slabs. Colonies of terrestrial gastropods were isolated in some sectors, and there is evidence of lit fires in the associations of charcoal and slabs. The worked stone industry has a greater influence than flakes, with a tendency to use simple flakes with marginal retouch and backs as the predominant tools, although geometric items are also present (13% of triangles, trapezoids and double bevel segments, accompanied by microburins) as are endscrapers (10%). Small pottery shards, a few pebbles and slabs, and a grinder for plant processing complete the record. Wild animals combine with ovicaprids, cattle and domestic pigs. Although the homogeneous sediment hinders an internal breakdown of this level, a detailed vertical analysis of the materials has revealed three cultural horizons: geometric Mesolithic at the base (with an industry that has evolved from the top of Level III); Early Neolithic in the middle (with some ceramics, double bevelled segments, a sickle for cutting vegetable and mill); and initial Chalcolithic at the top (indicated by small tips with flat retouch).

Level I: The current floor level, 20 cm deep, has a wedge layout, with a dry, dusty silty matrix in the first few centimetres, light brown tending to yellow, and a quite uneven component of blocks and clasts in its 20 cm depth. There are few lithic items (10 retouched tools), ceramics (19 frag-

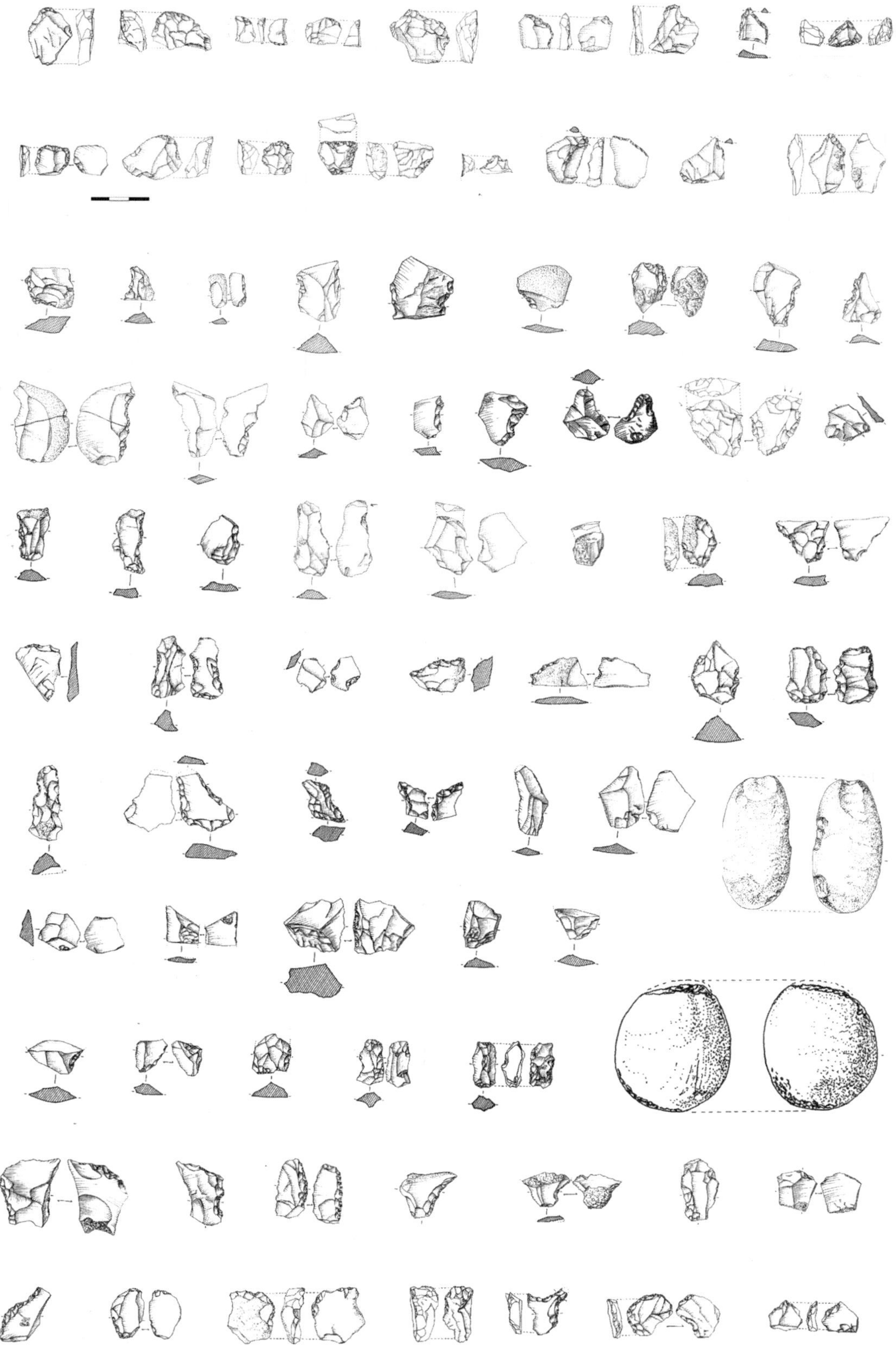

Figure 2. Selection of prehistoric materials of Kanpanoste (de A. Cava).

ments, one with Boquique decoration), or faunal remains (10 fragments).

Level	Code	BP Date
III-lower*	GrN-20215 GrN-20455	7620±80 7860±330
III-upper*	GrN-20214 GrN-20289	6360±70 6550±260
II*	GrN-20213 GrN-20267	3430±60 4350±60
II (domestic cereal)	GrA-9790	4550±40
II (domestic ovi-caprid)	GrN-202738	4190±100

Table 2. Radiocarbon references for the Kanpanoste Goika site.

* The laboratory divided the sample into two (carbonaceous and collagen). Due to the small amount of collagen available and hence the breadth of the standard deviation, the dating for the upper Level III should be accepted with some reservations, given the regional context.

Cultural material

The discrete amount of the material inventories for Kanpanoste Goikoa and Kanpanoste (Fig. 2) would rank these sites in a modest position if they were analysed individually. However, their strength lies in their complementarity. They are part of a system of territorial occupation which also involved the Atxoste, Mendandia and Fuente Hoz shelters, as well as several open air sites in Entzia, Urbasa and a few valleys in today's Alava province. In fact, the Kanpanoste assemblage was used as a basis to describe the Mesolithic notch and denticulate techno-typological unit. The roots of this territory date back to 8600 BP, and remained in place for a millennium. The presence of seashells from both the Cantabrian and the Mediterranean and the circulation of siliceous materials suggest a thoughtful articulation of the space. The features of the lithic industry, flake blanks tending to be carenated and in pieces, denticulate fronts often resulting from recycled material, loss of microlithics, apparent roughness in items which actually follow preset patterns (in which there is a notable lack of hunting equipment) are shared by many sites in the Ebro River basin and the Mediterranean fringe, which shaped a break in the evolution from the early Holocene microflake assemblages to those which characterize the geometric Mesolithic.

Carlos Mazo, Pilar Utrilla*

Forcas I and Forcas II sites

The Sierra de Castillo de Laguarres and the Sierra de Torón form a pre-Pyrenean structural unit split by the river Ésera where it passes through the Alto Aragon village of Graus. At this point rise Peña del Morrón (599 m) and Peña de las Forcas (635 m), on either side of the river and up to 300 m above the current riverbed. The latter, located on the left bank of the Ésera and of its tributary the Isábena, represents the most western point of the Sierra del Castillo de Laguarres. The place, which stands on the Aquitanian Miocene conglomerates, records the presence of two prehistoric sites, Forcas I and Forcas II, whose stratigraphic deposits show prolonged occupation, almost continuous, from the Lower Magdalenian up to the Late Neolithic, with two subsequent occupations in the Chalcolithic and early Roman Empire (Fig. 1). In both cases, occupation took place under the protection of narrow, very shallow rock-shelters, generated at the base of the conglomerate by the action of the river. The coordinates of Forcas I are X: 280.125;

* Área de Prehistoria. Universidad de Zaragoza.

Y: 4.673.241 and those of Forcas II are X: 280.242; Y: 4.673.709, and the height is 471 m and 470 m respectively. It cannot be said that they are sites with a clear archaeological sensitivity (indeed Forcas II is oriented to the north and almost on the shore of a river that flooded it at times, as shown by the levels of sand and silt in the deposit). However, the geography and topography give the site an advantageous position because the Ésera narrows there and the place becomes a checkpoint and obligatory pass between the mountain and the Barasona valley, now covered by a reservoir; because the location provides access to various biotope resources and because the Isábena acts as a transversal pass that connects the Ésera valley with Noguera Ribagorzana to the east.

Forcas I was discovered by Jean Vaquer in 1990 and excavated by Carlos Mazo and Pilar Utrilla between 1990 and 1992. It was seriously affected by aggregate mining, which restricted its extension (unknown) to just a narrow 23 linear metre strip of stratigraphic deposit that stuck to the wall of the conglomerate, which at this points runs North to South. In this deposit, 14 stratigraphic units have been recorded (from 4 to 17) with 9 fertile archaeological levels and more than 8000 lithic remains have been recovered. The assemblage represented by the bone industry is very inconspicuous and there are also very few identifiable fauna remains.

Occupation starts at level 15, corresponding to a Lower Magdalenian of the classic Cantabrian type, with a date of 14440 ± 70 BP, typologically well authenticated by the presence nucleiform endscrapers and rabots, and which would fit in well with the Lower Magdalenian of the area, particularly with the neighbouring Alonsé cave, with which it shares not only similar radiometric dates but also a similar technology in laminated cores (*débitage sur tranche transversale à encoche*), which are also present in contemporary levels on the other side of the Pyrenees. Moving up the sequence, levels 14 and 13d are classified as Upper Magdalenian while levels 13a and 11 correspond to the Late Magdalenian. The first two share the aforementioned laminar core technology, while the second two offer clear typological similarity as regards group indices and even primary types, with a variety of scrapers, the presence of burins in a similar proportion and retouched laminar flake. From level 10a, the surface conserved decreases significantly and consequently also the number of elements recovered. Despite the chronological difference between levels 10 and 9, the typological similarity between their industries is almost exact.

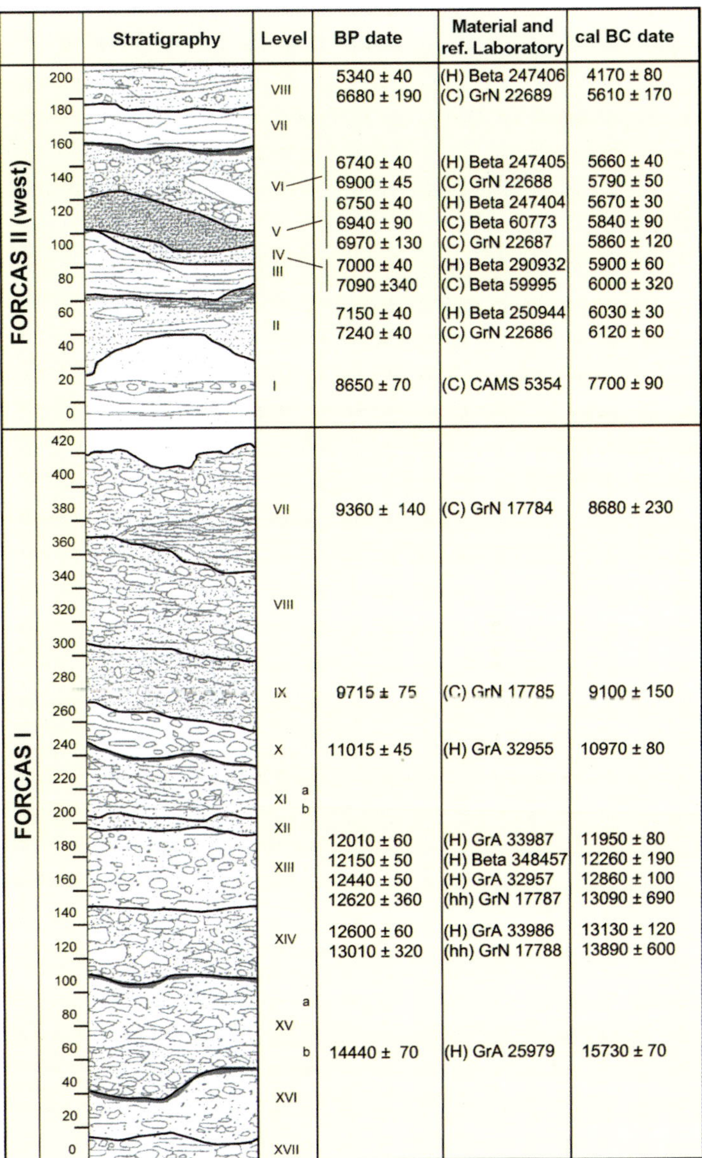

Figure 1. Stratigraphy of the two rock-shelters at Forcas.

In both levels, the lithic industry, although scarce, is based on thumbnail scrapers, consistent with a generic Epipaleolithic or Azilian.

Occupation of the site ends at level 7, which was confined to a very small space and offered very few retouched components. Its industrial characterisation is not categorical. Its stratigraphic position and chronology (9360 ± 140 BP) correspond to a microlaminar Epipaleolithic, and the laminar and microlaminar components (which account for more than one third) and a good representation of laminar cores would certainly support this but if we look at the retouched pieces, only two microgravettes would only fit in with it and a scalene triangle, which would go well in Sauveterrian industries of the Preboreal.

Forcas II is 560 m north of Forcas I, at the confluence of the river Isábena with the Ésera. It was discovered in 1991 and excavated in two phases during 1991-1992 and 1996-1997. It is also a long shelter, which offers more protection than Forcas I, but it also has a very small overhang and faces north. This orientation and its immediate proximity to the river (which flooded it several times, as shown by the flood silt levels) make the site seem like a place that is not suitable for continued occupation, but it is suitable for a temporary settlement, in the summer, as a hunting ground, which was the proposed interpretation.

The site had also undergone some destruction and clearing processes and three very different areas are distinguishable: the western area of the long shelter records a stratigraphic sequence consisting of 8 levels, 6 of which are archaeologically fertile. The base unit is I, consisting of fine sand from the river. Between levels Ia and Ic, sterile, is the first occupation of the site, level Ib, which corresponds to a macrolithic Mesolithic with notch and denticulate tools (8650 ± 70 BP) with a poor industry, as is common in old macrolithic contexts (prior to 8500 BP) like those observed in nearby sites, such as Legunova and Peña 14. An industry of crude instruments made with local raw materials such as quartzite and limestone. Levels II (7240 ± 40 and 7150 ± 40 BP) and IV (7000 ± 40 BP) correspond to a geometric Mesolithic, with rough retouched instruments and microburins and they are separated by a sterile level of sand from the river (level III). In level II, always with balanced modules, although there are some long pieces, asymmetric trapezoids and concave sided trapezoids dominate, along with scalene triangles and scalene triangles with a small concave side. In level IV, the symmetric and asymmetric trapezoids appear equally, followed by trapezoids with a small retouched base. Scalene triangles dominate among the triangles. The trapezoids include micro-trapezoids and the triangles include obtuse and both types include some with inverse retouch (Fig. 2). A few segments also appear, either as curved back edge blades or as rough retouch segments. In general, level IV differs from level II in the range of sizes, types and positions of the retouches, perhaps the result of a possible ultra-Pyrenean influence. This level also includes a plaquette engraved with precise geometric designs. In the peninsula Mesolithic similar laminates are found in Cocina II, located in the same chronological and stratigraphic time as the one in Forcas, that is, at the end of the geometric Mesolithic, at a time immediately prior to the cardium, and in a level, layer 6, in unbroken contact with level 5; now with cardium pottery. However, they differ in the support of the plaquette; that of the Alto Aragon site is smaller, flatter and tabular and the engraving is very shallow compared to the deep lines of the platelets at Cocina. However, the nearest plaquette with the most similar decoration are in southern Italy, on the plaquette of Grotta delle Veneri.

In Forcas II, the chronology of the geometric Mesolithic is later, unlike Bajo Aragon and Alto Ebro, and it is not so deeply rooted. There are only 250 years between its appearance in level II and the first pottery in level V, which appeared very early; furthermore, there is no break in the stratigraphy, and, therefore, levels IV and V are in direct contact, closely linked and with no transition.

Levels V (6940 ± 90) and VI (6900 ± 45 and 6740 ± 40) represent the moment of old Neolithic transition. As in the previous phase, in level V triangles dominate over trapezoids and, in addition, double bevel retouch appears, which would be exclusive in level VI. Both contain the oldest pottery in the Ebro valley, cardium or impressed ware (undoubtedly exchanged or borrowed from Neolithic groups, perhaps from SE France through the valleys of Tet and Aude and the valley of Segre-Cinca), but all within a hunter-gather economy.

After a moment of abandonment, which corresponds to sterile level 7, consisting of silt, level VIII, the most recent area of this rock-shelter, is clearly Neolithic with drills, sickle elements with a cereal patina and domestic fauna. In the pottery productions, the decoration is restricted to straight cords.

In the central area, the most affected by the clearance, a wall canvas consisting of 5 layers of irregular ashlar, some fragments of *terra sigillata* and a thin walled glass were recorded. The TSH materials offer a dating corresponding to I-III century and the structure might have been used to control the transport routes during the early Roman Empire, and more specifically the river crossing, which has historically been crossed at this point, where there is an old bridge today.

Finally, in the eastern area the evidence of occupation starts in level 7 and continues through 6 and 5 and the three levels could belong to the same cultural horizon, considering the high level of coincidence in the technology and forms of the pottery remains, particularly in levels 6 and 5. At the base of level 7, there

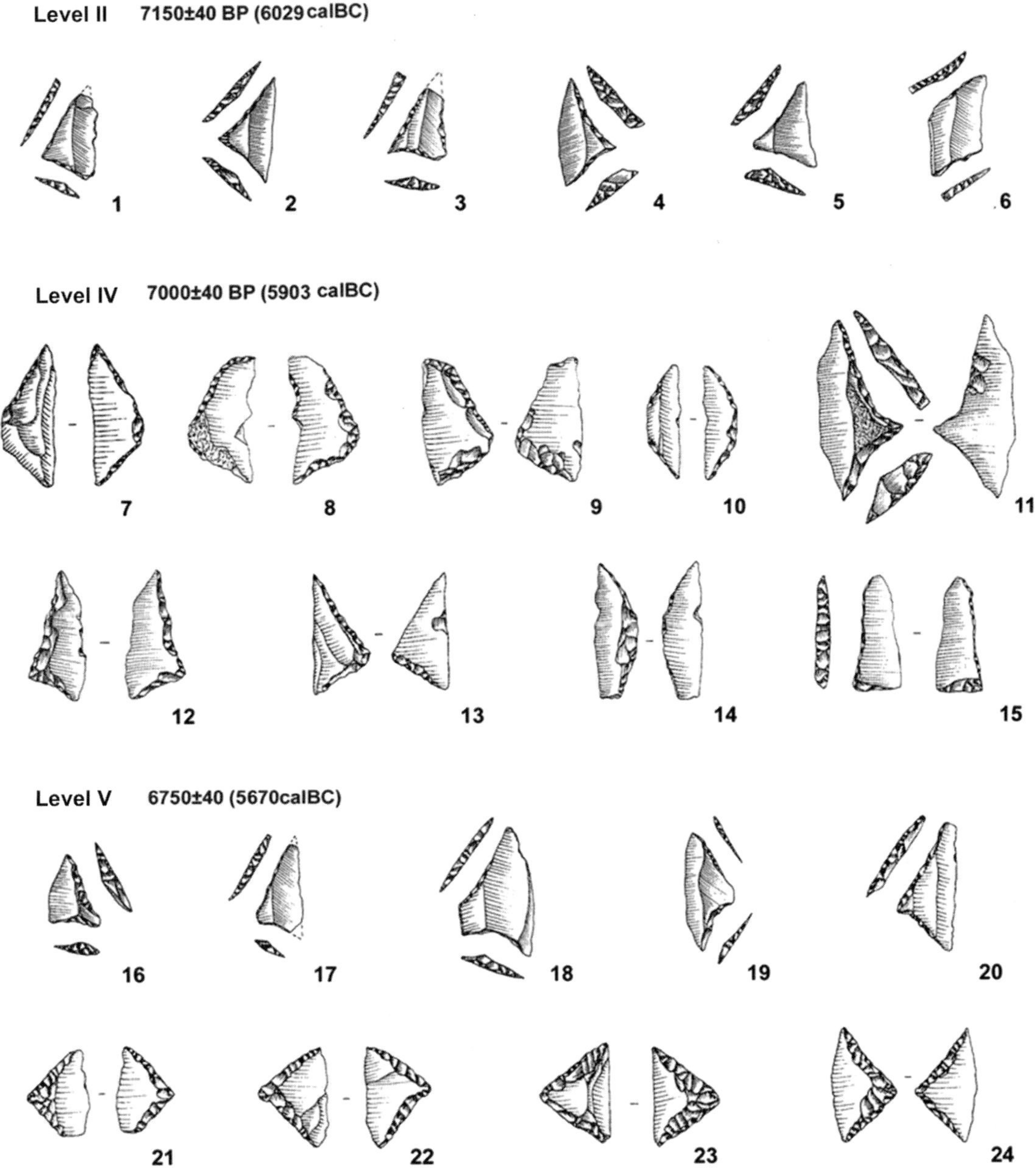

Figure 2. Evolution of the geometrics in the Mesolithic-Neolithic transition of Forcas II.

are human remains, some of which are among the ashes of a circular structure and inside a crack closed with stones, next to a wall, and which are related to a single burial time around 4430 ± 40 BP. These remains were accompanied by pottery fragments, including some examples with elongated and parallel mammae-like lumps ("Veraza" style), similar to others that appeared in the Early Bronze age levels at the nearby cave of Moro de Olvena. The limit between level 7 and the neighbouring level 6 is dated at 3920 ± 30. There are few decorations and the Beaker decorations are included in the Pyrenean group, contemporary in a large part of its development with Ciempozuelos or Salamó (phase II of Aragon), although they could also be placed in phase III, late Beaker, which would coincide with the Pyrenean *barbelé* type, contemporary to the Tarragon group of Arbolí, as is the case with the cave at Moro de Olvena.

Jordi Rosell *,**, Xose Pedro Rodríguez *,** Ruth Blasco***, Edgard Camarós *,**, Maite Arilla *,**, Andrea Picin *,**,****, Eneko Iriarte *****

Nerets and La Cova de les Llenes archaeological sites (Pallars Jussà, Lleida)

Nerets and Cova de les Llenes archaeological sites are located in the Pre-Pyrenean area of the Pallars Jussà (Lleida). The current configuration of this area rises from the Alpine Orogeny which formed an important fold of cretaceous materials resulting in two anticlines, one in the south represented by Serra del Montsec (1700 m above sea level) and another in the north, with the Serres de Sant Gervàs and Boumort (2200 m above sea level).From the geomorphologic point of view, the syncline forms a sedimentary basin known as Conca de Tremp (Conca de Baix and Conca de Dalt), where the tertiary landings show several Mesozoic outcrops. The whole area is crossed by an important hydrographic network from north to south whose two main rivers are the Noguera Pallaresa and its affluent the Flamisell. Both rivers rise from glacier valleys of the Axial Pyrenees.

The Nerets archaeological site is located in the central part of this basin, specifically in the Mesozoic sandstones of the Arén Formation located to the east of the town, Talarn. This site was discovered by chance, in 1989, by a local amateur thanks to the discovery of surface archaeological material (Rosell and Rodríguez, 1991; Rodríguez and Rosell, 1993). Nerets hill has a height of 625 meters above sea level, with good visibility over the river Noguera Pallaresa. In 1995 an archaeological intervention was carried out, directed by Jordi Rosell. The aim was to conduct a systematic recognition and survey of areas with greater concentrations of lithic materials on the surface. An excavation took place in the lower part of the hill, affecting 6 m^2 initially, later expanding to 16 m^2. During this intervention, some lithic industry was recovered but no faunal remains were located. The stratigraphic sequence described during the excavation of 1995 was formed by a pack of conglomerates of large heterometrical pebbles and very rounded polygenic with a matrix of slimes and fine sands from the base to the roof (Fig. 1). Most of the lithic industry was found in this level. A higher metric pack of fine to medium-sized sands with clays was also identified. This layer also provided lithic industry. At some points, this sequence was covered by a carbonate crust dating to U/Th en >75 ky. The current ground was placed on a higher level. The total described sequence was 60cm high.

The 1009 lithic objects recovered at Nerets come from the non-systematic survey of 1989 and mainly from the systematic survey and the excavation of 1995 (Rodriguez, 2004) (Table 1). All the material displays great consistency. In this assemblage, sequences of systematic production of flakes and of tool configuration have been identified. The shortage of debitage remains could be due to the fact that most part of the recovered material was recovered on the surface.

Among the raw materials, a clear predominance of quartzite is identified –almost 80%– (Tab. 1). Also noted is the use of hornfels, sandstone, and quartz. The rest of the raw materials do not even reach 1%. The presence of some knapping flint objects could be the result of a different dynamic from the rest, as the features of these objects are quite different from the other items. The most used raw materials appear in the present riverbed of the river Noguera Pallaresa or in some of its ancient terraces which are very close to the archaeological site. A differential management of the raw material has been observed: the quartzite is used in both processes of production and instruments-configuration; on the other hand, the hornfels is mainly used for shaping large-size instruments of pebble (Fig. 1.1). This rock is used in exploitation processes as it does not offer skills as good as the quartzite.

* Àrea de Prehistòria, Universitat Rovira i Virgili (URV), Avinguda de Catalunya 35, 43002 Tarragona, España.
** IPHES, Institut Català de Palaeoecologia Humana i Evolució Social, C/ Marcel·lí Domingo s/n (Edifici W3), 43007 Tarragona, España.
*** The Gibraltar Museum, 18–20 Bomb House Lane, Gibraltar.
**** Neanderthal Museum, Talstrasse 300, 40822 Mettmann, Alemania.
***** Departamento de Ciencias Históricas y Geografía, Universidad de Burgos, Villadiego, s/n, 09001 Burgos, España.

	Bn		BN1G						BP		BN2G				FRAGS		INDET		TOTAL	
			BN1GC		BN1GE		BN1G Ind.				BN2GC		BN2GE							
Quartzite	52	6,5%	41	5,2%	53	6,7%	3	0,4%	424	53,3%	67	8,4%	5	0,6%	146	18,4%	4	0,5%	795	78,79%
Hornfels	17	18,7%	14	15,4%	3	3,3%	2	2,2%	24	26,4%	5	5,5%	0	0%	22	24,2%	4	4,4%	91	9,02%
Sandstone	14	28,6%	9	18,4%	1	2%	1	2%	9	18,4%	2	4,1%	0	0%	12	24,5%	1	2%	49	4,86%
Quartz	6	23,1%	0	0%	2	7,7%	0	0%	8	30,8%	0	0%	0	0%	9	34,6%	1	3,8%	26	2,58%
Schist	0	0%	0	0%	0	0%	0	0%	3	42,9%	0	0%	0	0%	4	57,1%	0	0%	7	0,69%
Limestone	1	20%	1	20%	0	0%	0	0%	2	40%	0	0%	0	0%	0	0%	1	20%	5	0,50%
Slate	1	12,5%	0	0%	0	0%	0	0%	4	50%	0	0%	0	0%	3	37,5%	0	0%	8	0,79%
Porphyry	2	100%	0	0%	0	0%	0	0%	0	0%	0	0%	0	0%	0	0%	0	0%	2	0,20%
Flint	0	0%	0	0%	1	9,1%	0	0%	4	36,4%	4	36,4%	0	0%	2	18,2%	0	0%	11	1,09%
Indet	3	20%	2	13,3%	1	6,7%	0	0%	3	20%	0	0%	0	0%	4	26,7%	2	13,3%	15	1,49%
Total	96	9,5%	67	6,6%	61	6,0%	6	0,6%	481	47,7%	78	7,7%	5	0,5%	202	20,0%	13	1,3%	1009	

Table 1. Raw materials and structural categories of objects in Nerets archaeological site (Rodríguez, 2004). Nb=Natural bases (pebbles, cobbles or blocks selected in order to flake them or use them as hammers); NB1G= Negative Bases of first Generation; NB1gc= Negative Bases of first Generation of Configuration (tools on pebble); NB1GE=Negative Bases of first Generation of Exploitation (cores on pebble); PB= Positive Bases (flakes); NB2G= Negative Bases of second Generation; NB2GC= Negative Bases of second Generation of Configuration (retouched flakes); NB2GE= Negative Bases of second Generation of Exploitation (cores on flakes); Frags= Fragments; Indet.= Not determinable objects.

The most common exploitation strategy to produce flakes consisted of a bifacial-centripetal knapping prioritizing one of the sides (flaked side) over the other (the one of preparation), with the aim of pre-setting the final morphology of the products (Levallois method) (Fig. 1.3, 1.5). Bifacial-centripetal cores were also recovered without predetermination. The resulting flakes of these centripetal strategies have also been located in the archaeological record (Fig. 1.4, 1.6). Operational Themes, exploiting transverse planes of thick pebbles by using extractions based on horizontal planes, are also implemented. To carry out this kind of process, quartzite is used mainly when the method chosen requires a predetermination of the final product. The objects produced are medium-format flakes with dihedral-shaped or trihedral-shaped edges. In the most representative exploitation strategies, all the Operational Units involved in the production processes are present. The existence of cortical objects and flakes to prepare the exploitation of cores show this. On the other hand, cores which were left in different stages of exploitation, from the initial stages to almost exhausted cores, have been recovered (Fig. 1.5). All of these features suggest that the exploitation was developed in the archaeological site.

The configured items (pebbles and flakes) are 18.3% of Nerets lithic industry (except for the smaller pieces). In the pebble tools, dihedral edges in the distal-transversal area are usually configured, with an upright and/or convex delineation (choppers and chopping tools) (Fig. 1.2). The configuration of lateral-transversal dihedrals and trihedrals are also important (pick) (Fig. 1.1). Transversal dihedrals are the largest part among the retouched flakes. In these kinds of instruments, the second aim is the configuration of lateral dihedrals followed by the configuration of trihedrals and denticulate. From the typological point of view, the side scrapers are predominant among the retouched flakes, with 13 elements (Fig. 1.7), followed by denticulates (n=11) and isolated notches (n=5). There are five featureless abrupts: two denticulates and three continuous. Three end scrapers, two truncates and one burin have also been found. It does not seem to be a selection of a specific type of flake to be configured. In fact, both cortical non-faceted products (of quartzite and hornfels) and bi-faceted or multi-faceted platforms (of quartzite) with an established morphology are configured. It seems to be a type of selection related to the size of the retouched blanks: the average sizes of retouched flakes are 24 mm longer than the non-retouched ones.

If we add the effectives of instruments of pebble and of flake, we observe that in 68% of the items

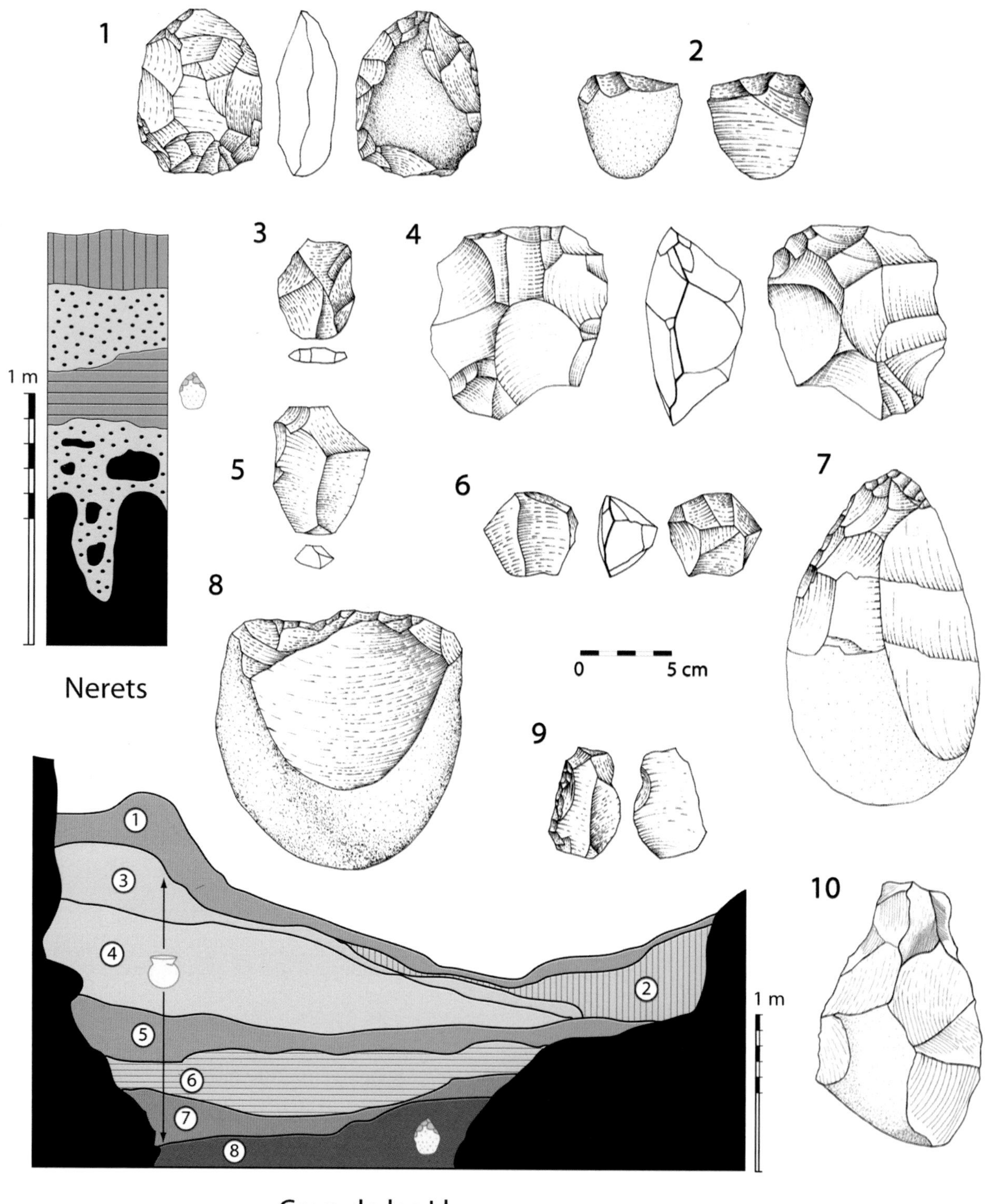

Figure 1. Nerets stratigraphic and lithics (Rodriguez, 2004) (1-9) and Cova de les Llenes. (10): 1, Quartzite handaxe (on flake):2, retouched flake with a dihedral transversal edge (cleaver); 3, Quartzite flake (Levallois); 4, Bifacial Core of quartzite (Levallois); 5, Flake of quartzite (Levallois); 6, centripetal-bifacial core of quartzite in the final exploitation stage (Levallois); 7, unifacial-angular of hornfels with distal trihedral (pick); 8, Unifacial pebble of quartzite (chopper); 9, Quartzite flake with a side scraper retouch (on the left side) and a notch (on the right side); 10, Quartzite handaxe.

dihedral edges of upright or convex delineation have been configured. Adding concave dihedrals (notches), the percentage of dihedral edges reaches 72%. The configuration of transversal dihedrals must be noted. Distal trihedrals have been configured in almost a fifth of all the items. Denticulate edges are not very large (they are present in 6.9% of the items). There are four objects classified as hand axes (3.4% of the items) (Fig. 1.8), and eight items (6.9%) fit into the cleaver morphological type (Fig. 1.9).

The absence of faunal remains makes an interpretation of the archaeological site´s role impossible. Nevertheless, with the available lithic record we can suggest that Nerets, due to its easily accessible location on a hill controlling a narrow passage of the river Noguera Pallaresa, was a place usually visited by human groups to develop processes of production and configuration of items potentially usable for processing tasks of faunal resources. Unfortunately, there are hardly criteria, except from the morphotechnical, which assign this site to a determined chronology. According to these criteria, Nerets could be placed in an advanced stage of the Middle Pleistocene, with technology including pebble tools- with some operational standards characteristics of Mode 2 – and complex production strategies (Levallois method) (Rodríguez, 2004). Accordingly, we could place Nerets in a phase of transition from Mode 2 to Mode 3.

Recently, similar deposits have been discovered in other basin locations. The industry recovered in these places presents important similarities with the industry discovered at Nerets, which shows an important flow of human groups in this area during the end of the Middle Pleistocene, which may be related to warm periods. Unfortunately, these kinds of deposits have not recovered any information about the climatic or ecological context in which human occupation was developed. This has made prospections move towards the anticlines, looking for caves that have allowed the preservation of other kind of registers beyond the lithic. But the erosion, caused by both the influence of glaciarism at the end of Pleistocene and a very active river network, has caused the previous sedimentary deposits to be conserved only in some caves with very particular features or in those placed in high points far from the rivers.

One of these cavities is La Cova de les Llenes (Conca de Dalt). This cave is a 250 m long karstic tube. The current entrance is placed on a cliff of 180 m over the river Flamisell and through the Congost d'Erinyà. The height is about 750 m above sea level. The cave was archaeologically studied for the first time at the end of the 1940´s by Professor Juan Maluquer de Motes (1951), who conducted just one excavation campaign at the entrance of the cave looking for Neolithic materials. The only existing description of the stratigraphic sequence of the cave, which discusses a basal layer made of Pleistocene materials where remains of cave bears appear, is the fruit of this campaign. This description caused the cave to be visited by the current investigation team and, after carrying out a preliminary archaeological action in February 2013, resulted in the first excavation campaign in August 2013.

This first campaign was focused on the entrance of the cave where the sample and the stratigraphy of Professor Maluquer de Motes were recovered, and an excavation of 25m² was initiated. The stratigraphy shows a higher strata of anthropic origin –levels 1 to 6- with a high content of ash and charcoal related to industrial or pre- industrial cremation activities of an unspecified date. Below, level 7 is formed by yellowish-brown shales presenting a mixture of Pleistocene materials and ceramic elements from the Neolithic and the Bronze Age. Level 8 is the first intact figuring; it is formed by green to brownish shales with some blocks of sandstones from the breakage of walls and the roof. Many faunal remains have been recovered on level 8 as well as lithic items corresponding to the beginning of the Middle Paleolithic, with very similar features to the items from Nerets.

The preservation of level 8 is related to the development of some stalagmite crusts which blocked the cave entrance. These crusts, today in dating process, were probably formed before the maximum development of the glaciers at the Pyrenees during the MIS 3. Their presence preserved the sediments until the beginning of the Holocene when they were dismantled due to the regression of the cave´s mouth, allowing the entrance of human groups during the Neolithic. Currently, remains of these crusts in the entrance walls can be seen, but at the end of the cavity they remain intact covering all the Pleistocene deposits.

The lithic industry in level 8 is mainly made of quartzite and other metamorphic rocks from the Flamisell river and from the Paleogene conglomerate formations of the area (Fig. 1. 10). The flakes are the predominant elements and, together with the few recovered cores, show both Levallois and discoidal reduction sequences. The faunal spectrum is mainly composed of bear remains (*Ursus spelaeus*), hyenas (*Crocuta* sp.), tares (*Hemitragus* sp.), horses (*Equus ferus*) and deers (*Cervus elaphus*). The relationship between the faunal remains and lithic industry is determined by the presence of some cutmarks as well as anthropogenic fractures. However, the most important activities developed in this cave seem to be related to carnivores. Pending geochronologic and paleo-ecological information, the faunal composition and the lithic industry seem to be consistent with the end of the Middle Pleistocene of the Iberian Peninsula.

In conclusion, Nerets and La Cova de les Llenes are part of a regional project with the aim of studying Neanderthal groups from the Late Middle Pleistocene in an area placed at the gateway to the Pyrenees. The study of these kinds of archaeological sites is important to understand the capacities of these human communities and their development in marginal areas far from places with great genetic flows of the same period, which the Mediterranean corridor might be.

Acknowledgements

This research is financed by the projects CGL2012-38434-C03-03, CGL2012-38358, CGL-BOS-2012-34717 and HAR2010-18952-C02-01 of the Ministry of Science and Innovation of the Spanish Government. Ruth Blasco is a post-doctoral fellow of the Beatriu de Pinós-A program of the Generalitat de Catalunya, co-financed with the Marie Curie Actions, EU-FP7. Edgard Camarós is a pre-doctoral fellow FI in the Generalitat de Catalunya, co-financed with funds of the European Social Fund. We would like to thank Jordi Fábregas for the help provided with his comments and all the members of the "Tritons" team for the logistic support during the fieldwork.

Alfonso Alday*

Martinarri rock shelter (Obécuri, Treviño)

Martinarri is a south-facing rock shelter with a roof that rises almost 3m above the current floor, and a 15m long and 3-4 m deep area, followed by a large terrace where prehistoric archaeological work has detected prehistoric activity. It lies in a large basin, now covered by dense forest on sandy, hilly terrain where sandstone outcrops containing shelters are the exception. This suggests that the prehistoric communities which settled here had detailed knowledge and control of the zone, as they chose the shelter with the best conditions in the district. The relatively monotonous catchment area consists of gentle hills and gorges, 80% lying between 700 and 900 m asl, which does not match the usual landscape patterns at Meso-neolithic sites, a possible reason for the smaller potential of the stratigraphic and cultural sequence. The flint supply points were probably the chert outcrops in Loza and Treviño (20 km away), Urbasa (30 km) and the coastal Flysch (100 km).

The site is still under excavation, with four annual digs since 2008 directed by A. Alday in a small area which has nevertheless yielded a high density of archaeological material and defined the complete stratigraphic sequence.

Stratigraphic sequence and archaeological content

Five sedimentary layers have been identified in the shelter, supplemented by several more on the adjacent platform. Each unit is practically horizontal, and basically composed of the substrate sands. Post-deposition phenomena (erosion, gullies, landslides) have not affected the strata, laid down in continuity without sterile units. Several negative structures (mainly post holes) enter each layer (Fig. 1).

Surface: A thin layer of humus and loose sands with seemingly recent carbonaceous stains and

* Área de Prehistoria Universidad del País Vasco (EHU/UPV). Tomás y Valiente s/n 01006 Vitoria-Gasteiz. a.alday@ehu.es.

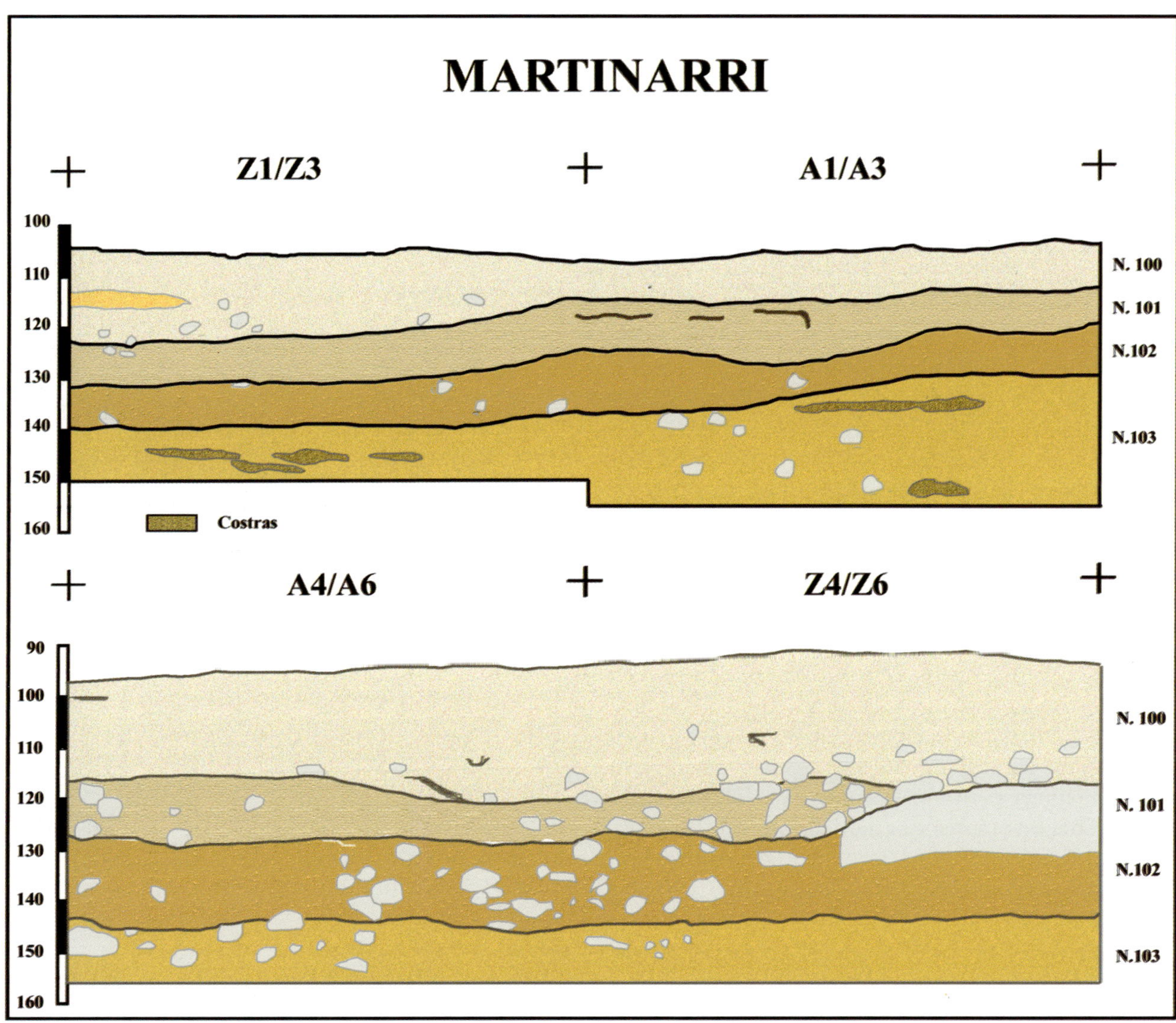

Figure 1. Martinarri stratigraphic sections (costra: crust).

a herbaceous layer covering the outer quadrats. Few archaeological materials, including faunal remains, knapping debris, the odd core, a various blade flakes, two endscrapers, retouched blades and an abrupt retouch.

Level 100: 15cm deep, with a compacted sandy texture and weathered sandy sections broken off from the shelter. Fifteen small diameter circular/oval holes have been interpreted as the product of inserted stakes, possibly related to the prehistoric level where ceramic material was found on the adjacent terrace. One thousand lithic items have been recovered from this level, the majority knapping debris and blade flakes, along with two dozen backs, a dozen scrapers, notches and denticulates and several micro-triangles and a few segmentiforms. There are over 1000 faunal fragments. Culturally this layer is attributed to the Mesolithic microindustry of Sauveterrian inspiration.

Level 101: Up to 23cm deep, with light brown soil enriched with material of increasing size with depth. Evidence of lit fires which reached high temperatures. Abundant prehistoric material: over 5,000 lithic items including 300 blade flakes and over 200 retouched items (half of them blades and backed points, four dozen endscrapers, two retouched blades and a series of abrupt retouches, burins, notches and denticulates). The assemblage also includes the presence of micro triangles and segments. There are at least 3,000 small faunal fragments. The level shows cultural similarities to the higher level, and is ascribed to the Mesolithic microindustry of Sauveterrian inspiration (Fig. 2).

Level 102: 20cm deep, characterized by compacted sand and an increasing larger fraction (many clasts and a few blocks). Its excavation revealed two large sandstone slabs which were part of a hitherto undefined anthropic structure. This is E.U 4, with an oval area of dark soil associated with blocks, interpreted as a hearth. The level has an extraordinary archaeological record consisting of over 6,000 lithic items, the majority knapping debris, many cores and approx. 200 blades without retouch. Amongst the tools (n = 250), the majority are backs (approx. 200), followed by scrapers (n = 60), retouched blades, drills, burins, endscrapers, notches and abrupt retouches. Once again microlithic triangles were collected. The presence of sandstone slabs and cobbles (usually in horizontal association) is also significant. One atrophic deer canine used as a pendant figures amongst more than 4,000 faunal items. This level is ascribed culturally to the Mesolithic microindustry of Sauveterrian inspiration, with typometric and formal variations from the other assemblages.

Level 103: This 15 cm deep layer is filled with dry, sandy sediment with no organic elements. Its grainy texture is either compact (a hard to dig breccia) or darker and lenticular, rich in archaeological material. The presence of blocks is irregular. The remarkable material record includes 3,300 lithic items including almost 100 blade flakes, 35 backed flakes, 12 endscrapers, and fewer abrupt retouches, sidescrapers and denticulates. 1,300 faunal fragments were recovered. This level is ascribed culturally to the Upper-late Magdalenian (Fig. 2).

A test pit on the open air terrace revealed an even deeper stratigraphy exceeding one metre, which can be subdivided into six units. The most notable feature here is the ceramic material including decorated fragments in Unit B, possibly from the end of Metal Age. We have associated this episode with the above-mentioned posts on level 101. The lower levels maintain the features outlined for the interior of the shelter, with minor nuances.

Level	**Code**	**BP Date**
101	Beta – 314962	340±30
102	GrA-46014	8455±45
103	GrA-45940	11890±50

Table 1. Radiochronological references for the Martinarri site.

The dating for level 101, based on a charcoal specimen collected in one of the holes, does not match the cultural material recovered, but rather the action of possibly contemporary shepherds.

Cultural overview

Although fieldwork in Martinarri is still in progress, the material recovered to date shows the quality of the site due to both the richness of its contents and the chronological-cultural periods involved. Martinarri has confirmed an integrated exploitation of today's Alava province at the end of the Pleistocene, which signalled the definitive 'colonization' of inland zones. Not far from this site are other roughly contemporary shelters: Atxoste to the north, and Montico de Charratu and Peña del Castillo to the west. Portugain, Kukuma, Socuevas, Berniollo and possibly Bardallo as well (the latter two open air sites, are a little further away in the same district).

One of the features of this series of campsites is the lack of a bone industry, along with backed flakes and endscrapers as the lynchpins of the lithic component, leaving burins to one side, and the substrate –Portugain, linked to the exploitation of the Urbasa siliceous outcrop, diverges from this pattern. The industrial content is compatible with intense hunting. In fact, it is highly likely that the vast Alava plain– whose boundary walls contain other points in this chronology, and the valleys that flank it provided shelter for a wide range of large mammals with a biomass apt for consumption. Moreover, the diversity of occupied spaces and the exploitation of a variety of flint indicate detailed knowledge of this territory

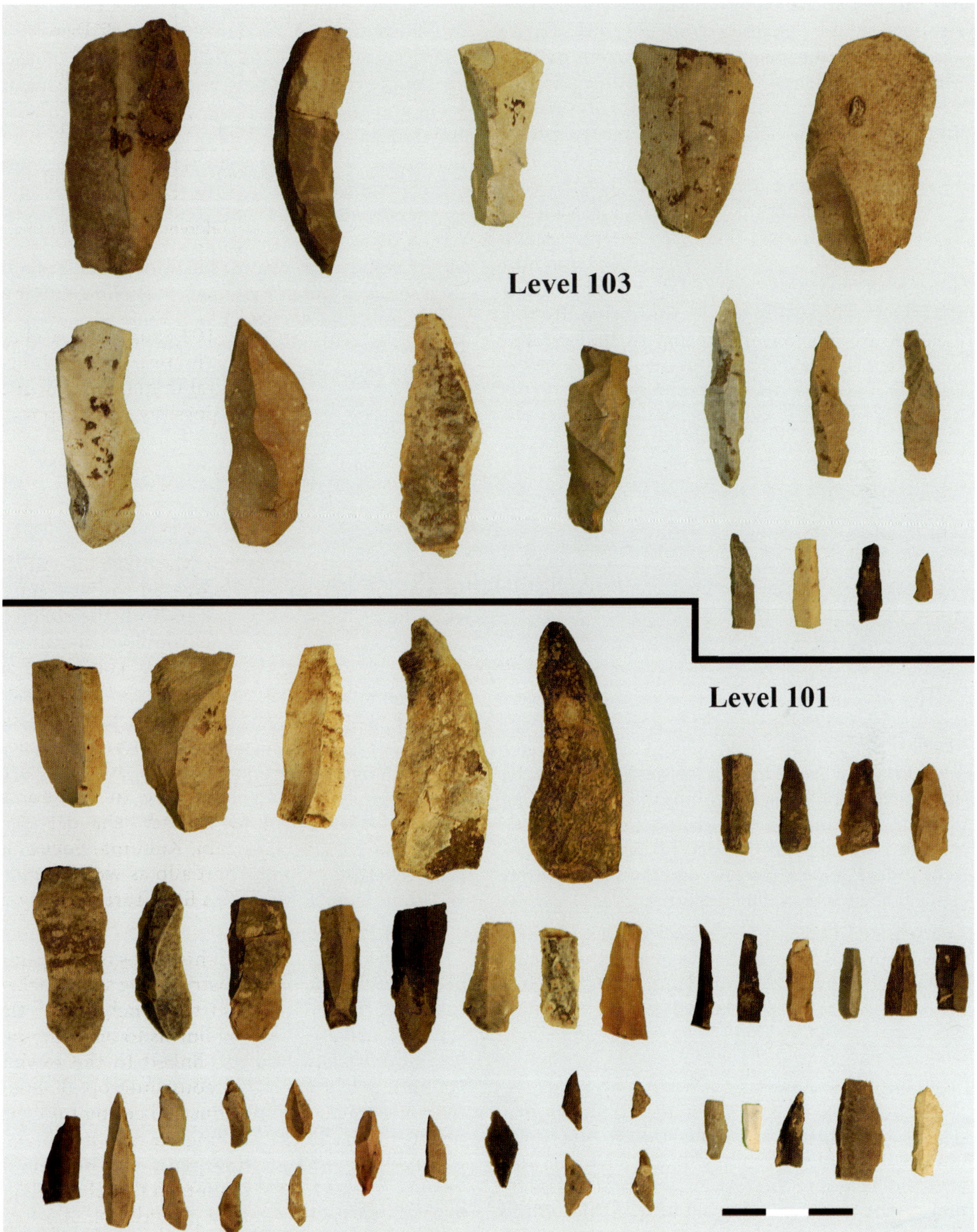

Figure 2. Selection of prehistoric materials from Martinarri.

and interest in its comprehensive exploitation. The settlement dynamics coincide with a pattern found in the neighbouring Aragon, part of a late glacial process common to other parts of Europe, characterized by settlements in new territories from a base in traditional refuge zones. The upper levels reveal a techno-industrial line which has only been identified relatively recently in this area: microblade assemblages with a Sauveterre inspiration (Fig. 2). The appearance of micro triangles and subsequently segments, along with changes in the styles and dimensions of backed tools, justify this identification. By this stage, it was no longer unusual to find double backed tools, worked bases, items which include fine apical retouches opposite the backs or even arched designs. A tendency towards microliths, more so amongst tips than blades, is another striking evolution between the Magdalenian level and those higher up. Martinarri is not an isolated case, since similar changes have been described at the Atxoste and Socuevas sites, which coexisted with other assemblages such as Mendandia and Las Orcillas with industries which seem to follow similar trends. Parco Cave, at the other extreme of the Ebro River basin, a long series of north Pyrenean sites and Cantabrian assemblages such as Ekain must all be taken into account in assessments and interpretations of this collection from Martinarri.

Alfonso Alday*

Mendandia (Sáseta, Treviño)

The roof of this east-facing rock shelter covers roughly 52 m². Alongside there is a 385 m² platform on a steep slope overlooking the Ayuda River 40/50m below, at a distance of roughly 100m. Its strategic position provides commanding views along the river gorge and also immediate access to the mid-altitude pastures, with a range of local landscapes from valleys, gorges, plateaus and grasslands to forests and abundant wildlife resources.

Excavated between 1992-1995 and in 1997 by A. Alday in a 13 m² area, the site yielded a vast range of material which was classified into five sedimentological divisions and six industrial sections.

Stratigraphic sequence

This is a continuous sequence –with no erosive or infertile phases– of eminently human origin and gradual changes in the texture, tone and composition of the sediment. It spans several Mesolithic and Neolithic periods between 8500 and 6400 BP (Fig. 1 and 2).

Level V: Surveyed in a 70cm cut, which only showed prehistoric interest at the top. The malleable clayey soil has an orange colour, gradually lightening. Small coarse fraction. The record includes 920 fauna fragments and 196 lithic items, including 6 retouched endscrapers, 1 awl, 2 denticulates, 1 abrupt retouch and 1 sidescraper. One perforated *Nassa reticulata* was also found. This level is ascribed culturally to the laminar Mesolithic technology.

Level IV: More than 40cm deep in some areas, with a slight dip from west to east. Dark brown with blackish tones, compact silty structure with little large fraction, a wet and greasy aspect, small isolated puddles and breccia. Colonies of *helix* and frequent presence of charcoal and fire are noteworthy aspects. 47,579 bone fragments were inventoried. The lithic industry includes 11,284 items, with 94 cores and 354 retouched objects (35 endscrapers, 58 awls, 9 burins, 8 abrupt flakes, 2 composite items, 3 backed bladelets, 23 short notches, 139 short denticulates, 4 notches on blades, 1 denticulate on irregular flake, 4 serrated items, 6 abrupt re-

* Área de Prehistoria Universidad del País Vasco (EHU/UPV). Tomás y Valiente s/n 01006 Vitoria-Gasteiz. a.alday@ehu.es.

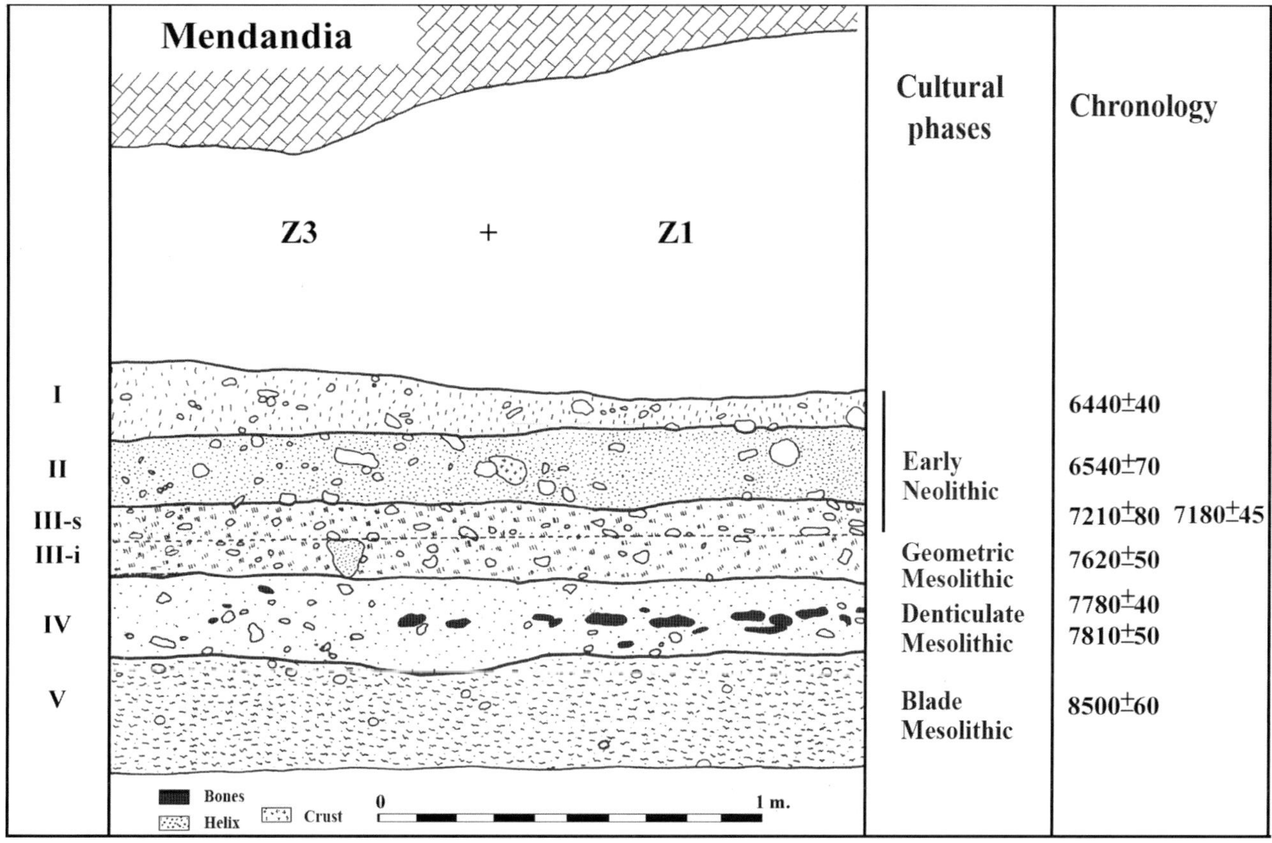

Figure 1. Mendandia stratigraphic section.

touches, 4 geometric items, 1 microburin and 57 miscellaneous items). The bone record contains few items, which includes two nasarids. This assemblage is culturally ascribed to the Mesolithic notch and denticulate industry.

Level III: A continuous 25cm deep horizon containing 2 cultural entities: dry, silty structure, fine grained, greyish colour. Colonies of terrestrial molluscs are common, and there is clear evidence of fire. 15,562 bone fragments were found in the lower part of this level (III-inf). The lithic industry consists of 3,869 items, with 50 cores and 237 retouched objects (20 endscrapers, 15 awls, 3 abrupt flakes, 11 backed bladelets, 11 short notches, 56 short denticulates, 9 notches on flake, 3 denticulates on flake, 2 abrupt retouches, 33 geometrics, 20 microburins and 54 miscellaneous items). Adornments include atrophied deer canines, *Nasa, Natica catena* and *Cypraea*. Culturally ascribed to the geometric Mesolithic.

The upper part of level III (III-sup) contained 12,518 bone fragments. The lithic industry included 1,282 items with 106 retouched objects (13 endscrapers, 6 awls, 1 abrupt on flake, 22 backed bladelets, 4 short notches, 11 short denticulates, 2 notches on flake, 1 denticulate on blade flake, 2 serrated edges with abrupt retouch, 4 abrupt retouches on blade, 18 geometrics, 6 microburins and 16 miscellaneous items). 343 ceramic fragments were counted, with lines and incisions used in decoration. Culturally ascribed to the Early Neolithic.

Level II: A 20 cm deep homogeneous level with a brown colour, silty and plastic structure, some clasts, and 4,766 bone fragments. The lithic industry includes 953 items, including 75 retouched objects (5 endscrapers, 3 awls, 10 backed bladelets, 1 notch on flake 1 denticulate on flake, 3 notches on blade, 1 denticulate on blade, 1 serrated edge, 3 abrupt retouches, 21 geometrics, 6 microburins and 19 sidescrapers). There were 794 ceramic sherds, several of them decorated with impressions below the lip, finger-drawn lines and ungulations. This level is culturally ascribed to the Early Neolithic.

Level I is the current floor, from 10 to 20cm deep. Brown-grey matrix, malleable, silty composition, initially dry and dusty, then compacted, moist and more granulous when excavated. Abundant small clasts, few cobbles and 1,044 bone fragments. The lithic industry consists of 182 items with only 8 retouched objects (two endscrapers, one awl, one denticulate on flake, 2 denticulate on blade, 1 abrupt flake and 1 segment). 33 undecorated ceramic shards were found. This level is culturally ascribed to the Early Neolithic.

Level	Code	BP Date
I	GrN-22740	6440±40
II	GrN-22741	6540±70
III-upper	GrN-22742	7180±45
	GrN-19658	7210±80
	Ua-34366	7265±60
III-lower	GrN-22743	7620±50
IV	GrN-22745	7780±40
	GrN-22744	7810±50
V	GrA-6874	8500±60

Table 1. Radiochronological references for the Mendandia site.

Lithic and ceramic industry

The density of the lithic industry and its coordination with the stratigraphic sequence have played an important role in resolving the evolution of the population at this site. The typological groups have a relatively balanced composition at each level: only level IV shows a rupture between denticulates and scrapers, and between these two elements, miscellaneous and scrapers, and the other categories (Fig. 2).

The upper horizons (I to III-inf), characterized by the geometric basis of their industries, show a sequential evolution: double bevelled segments characterize the three most recent episodes –Neolithic–, while triangles and abrupt trapezoids represent the oldest –Mesolithic– period. It is interesting to note the presence of occlusal forms, which individualize the geometrism of the upper Ebro River basin in comparison to other areas of the same basin and the Cantabrian coast, as an example of a personal stylistic development.

Level IV has yielded an extraordinary amount of lithic industry, with a proliferation of notches, denticulates and awls on flake and fragments, flake retouch used in the manufacturing process. Although this industry seems to be quite rough, in fact it was well thought out and organized to shape tools with predetermined faces, suitable for woodworking, as proven in traceological analyses. Its techno-typological and chronological concordance with other Iberian sites lends considerable content to the Mesolithic notch and denticulate industry, for which the Mendandia phase is major point of reference.

The small amount of material on level V consists of endscrapers and backed blades, indicating its affiliation to the laminar Mesolithic industry.

The inhabitants of Mendandia collected flint from outcrops in Loza and Treviño, some 15 km away, Urbasa (35 km away), Flysch (80 km) and the Ebro Evaporite (100 km).

Most of the ceramic material is from indeterminate parts of recipients (92.5%) including edges (n = 83), a few handles and lids. Originally they were simple forms such as bols, a few in a closed "S" shape. The decoration shows evidence of technical evolution: the motifs are on edges or lips, with incision used in the earliest periods and imprints in the most recent. The three C14 dates for the upper level III show the surprising antiquity of this record. Perhaps for this reason the assemblage is difficult to identify stylistically, while the ceramic material from higher levels concords well with early Neolithic imprinted ceramics (Table 1).

Lifestyles

Hunting was one of the most privileged activities in Mendandia. The strategic location of the shelter facilitated the groups' capture of a wide variety of species, 90% of which were roe deer, deer and aurochs, followed by wild boar, goat, horse and chamois, and an anecdotal presence of fox, wolf, marten, badger, bobcat, rabbit and hare.

The estimated age of the prey shows that hunting was mainly practiced in late spring and early summer. The proportion of each anatomical part, supplemented with anthracological data, suggests that certain items were smoked for their (presumed) transfer to another campsite. A genetic study has suggested that some of the old Neolithic bovids may have been domesticated. Altuna and Mariezkurrena also suggest that the age and sex spectrum of the faunal assemblage in this

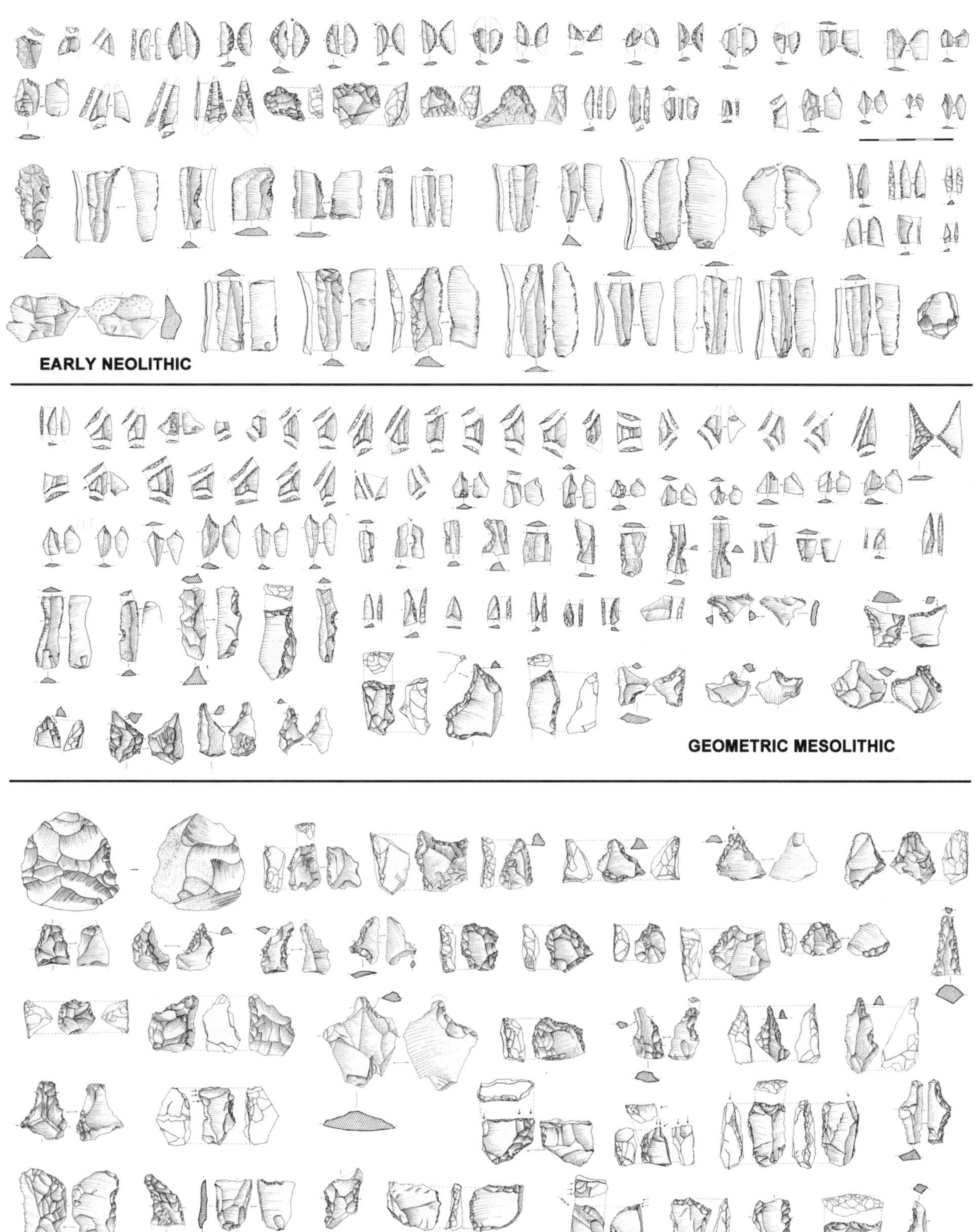

Figure 2. Selection of prehistoric materials in Mendandia.

herd may evidence quasi-domestication. Palynological data contained the excavation report show that the Neolithic landscape was compatible with agriculture, which would concur with the identification of flint blades used to cut grain.

Traceology has revealed a wide range of activities performed in this shelter, from butchering, leather and woodwork –linked to the numerous fires–, and flint knapping to the use of materials for colouring.

The Montsant Valley (Localities of Valle del Montsant Priorat, Tarragona), A key core region for Prehistory in the NE of Iberian Peninsula

Pilar García-Argüelles*
Jordi Nadal*
Josep Mª Fullola*

In recent years, research work has been carried out as part of programme SGR2014-108 of the Generalitat de Cataluña and programme HAR2011-26193 of the MINECO

1. Presentation

The middle course valley of the Montsant River, an affluent of the Siurana, the final tributary of the Ebro before its connection to the sea, contains a concentration of prehistoric sites, specifically from the Late Upper Palaeolithic and Epipalaeolithic, that makes it a benchmark area in the Iberian Peninsula when researching these two phases of prehistory. This area is located in the district of Priorato, in the province of Tarragona (Catalonia, Spain), in the NE of the Iberian Peninsula (Fig. 1).

The presence of material evidence of the prehistoric population has been known since the 1930s, when Salvador Vilaseca prospected the area and discovered different many flint artefacts from the El Filador and Els Colls shelters. His work in this area, practically all of which was in the municipality of Margalef de Montsant, continued through to the end of the 1960s, with special emphasis on the aforementioned shelter, El Filador, where he carried out different excavation campaigns until 1968. His numerous publications (Vilaseca 1936; 1949; 1953; 1960; 1968; 1973) demonstrated the vital importance of the sector studied for Epipalaeolithic times. The work by Javier Fortea in the early 1970s, re-examining the materials from El Filador for his PhD, elevated the site to a preeminent position within the cultural and material evolution of the Epipalaeolithic in the Iberian Peninsula (Fortea, 1973).

Starting in 1978, the University of Barcelona began an excavation programme in the middle course of the Montsant. The programme began with the re-excavation of El Filador (1979-1997), and the systematic prospecting in the area soon produced results. Excavation was done at three other sites, the Els Colls shelter (1982-1991), the Boix cave (1983-1984) and the L'Hort de la Boquera shelter (since 1998); other surface settlements were located, such as L'Hort d'en Marquet or El Planot (the latter with Mousterian materials, located in the highest terrace of the river), and other settlements already mentioned by Vilaseca, and with very positive potential for the future, were surveyed, such as the cova de la Jaia or Tormos d'en Celoni, among many others. In addition to this, in 1981, the only known example of cave art with an engraved Palaeolithic figure in the NE of the peninsula was discovered; this was a figure of a deer, found in the inner galleries of the cova de la Taverna (Fullola and Viñas, 1985; Fig 4.2), and while initially this appeared out of place, it is much more coherent in light of the Late Palaeolithic chronological context of the sites in the Montsant Valley that we present in this paper. In regard to a different matter, the construction of a dam required an urgent excavation in

* Adscripción de los tres autores: SERP (Seminari d'Estudis i Recerques Prehistòriques) de la Universidad de Barcelona, área de Prehistoria, Departamento de Prehistoria, Historia Antigua y Arqueología, Facultad de Geografía e Historia, Universidad de Barcelona; calle Montalegre, 6, E-08001, Barcelona. Correspondent author: garciaarguelles@ub.edu

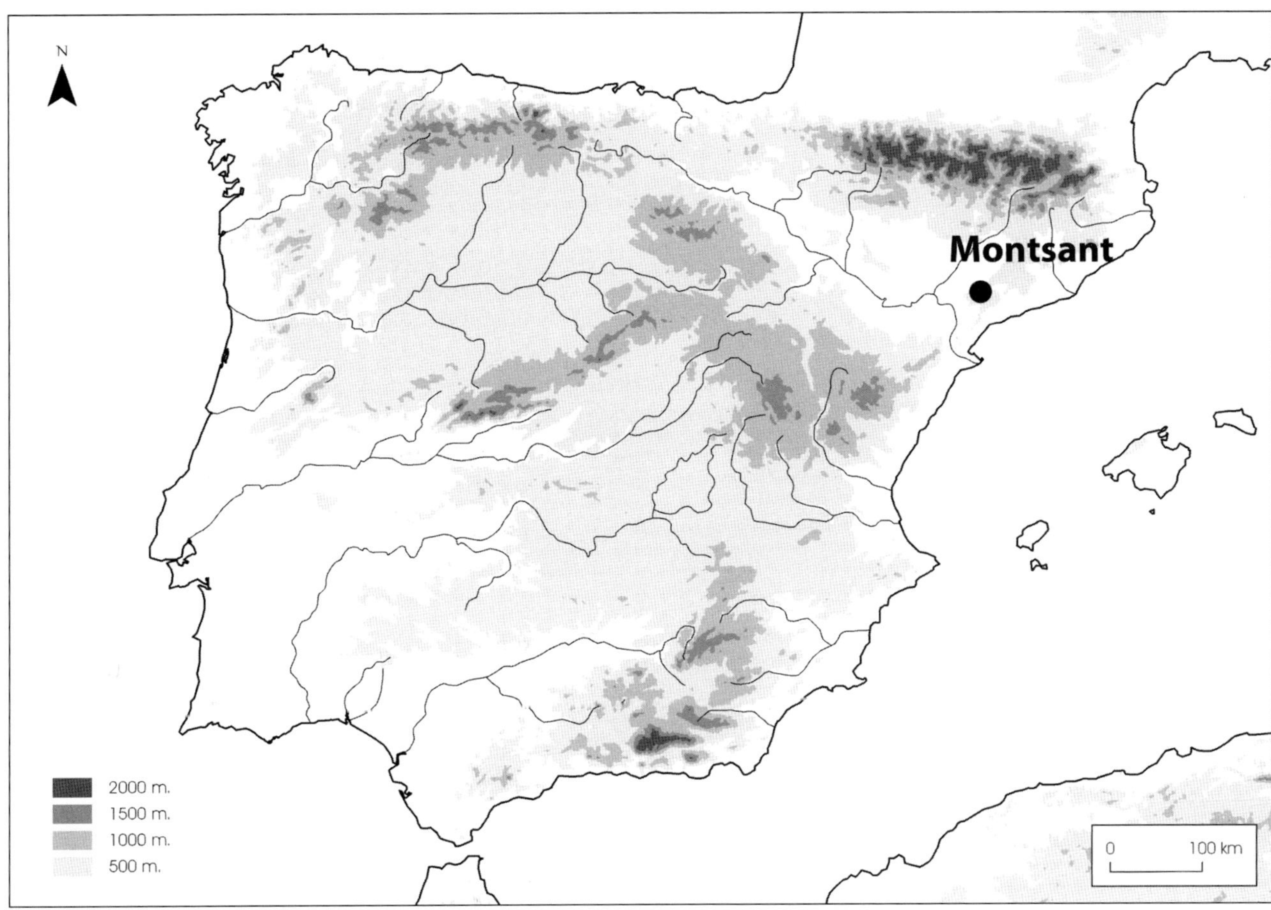

Figure 1. Location of the Montsant Valley, in the NE of the Iberian Peninsula.

the L'Auferí shelter, which was carried out by archaeologists from our group in the early 1990s.

All of these excavations clearly demonstrated the richness of the area; in consequence, since 1978, the University of Barcelona, first with research programmes directed by one of us (JMF) and later, since 1986, through the SERP (Seminari d'Estudis i Recerques Prehistòriques), and with different co-directors of the different excavations, with special dedication by the other two authors of this paper (PG-A and JN), has been working continuously in the middle sector of the Montsant, in the municipality of Margalef de Montsant.

2. Geoarchaeological information

The Montsant Valley gets its name from the Montsant Range, located to the SW of the Central Catalan Depression. Geographically, the Montsant Range is oriented NE to SW, with a total length of 19 km, and approximately 30 km from the Mediterranean coast. Geologically, Oligocene conglomerates predominate, reaching thicknesses of up to 300 m, with a sandy matrix and calcareous cement. Alternating with the conglomerates are layers of red clays, gypsum, and flint nodules, which erode much more easily and create rounded shapes, which served as shelters under which the Prehistoric peoples lived.

In the area between Margalef de Montsant and Bisbal de Falset, the river loses a significant part of its erosion capacity, which has protected the different archaeological sites in the area.

Dr. Bergadà (Bergadà, 1998) has proposed an evolutionary and chronological reconstruction of the sedimentary sequence of the middle course of the Montsant River.

Prior to 10.950BP

Phase 1: alluvial deposit with significant intensity, with several m of gravel and sand, located mainly on the concave bank of the river. Probably occurred during the Upper Pleistocene, which would correspond to terrace level T2. Level IV of L'Hort de la Boquera and level IX of the Els Colls shelter.

Phase 2: period of lower alluvial intensity, with sand deposits. Level VII of the Els Colls shelter and level II of L'Hort de la Boquera.

Phase 3: time of flooding with local additions (falling blocks), level IV and V of the Els Colls shelter.

From 10,950– 10,050 BP

Phase 4: flat flood area (bioturbated sandy silts) with local additions, falling blocks from the ledges of the Els Colls shelter (levels IV, III and II) and from L'Hort de la Boquera (level II), with local runoff contributions.

The environmental conditions were wet and cold, based on the data from the Els Colls shelter, while L'Hort de la Boquera had less moist conditions. Runoff processes began to operate, level III and IV of L'Hort de la Boquera, and the slope deposits began to form in a semi-arid environment.

From 10,050– 9,000 BP

Phase 5: the river began to carve its path (T1b) with energetic sedimentation of gravel and sand; level XII of the El Filador shelter.

Phase 6: lower intensity, levels XI, X, and VIII-IX of the El Filador shelter.

Phase 7: flat flood area (bioturbated sandy silt) of this terrace level. This would correspond to the rest of the sequence studied in the El Filador shelter. The runoff processes triggered the creation of alluvial cones.

After 9,000BP

Phase 8: the river carves its path and forms terrace T1a.

3. Archaeological sites

In this section, we will summarise the principal sites in which we have excavated in the area of the middle course of the Montsant River since 1978 and present the most significant findings.

3a. El Filador

The El Filador site is located in the municipality of Margalef de Montsant, to the north of the Priorato district, in the province of Tarragona (E(X):311907.8m-N(Y)4572589.3m UTM 31N/ ETR S89). It is a large shelter approximately 100 m long, although the archaeological site is located in the central part. It is located 15 m above the current level of the Montsant River, on the left bank, approximately 340 masl, just opposite the town of Margalef de Montsant.

The intermittent news of El Filador given by Salvador Vilaseca were based on prospecting studies prior to the Civil War and in short campaigns during the 1950s and 1960s (Vilaseca 1936; 1949; 1953; 1968; 1973). Since 1979, the University of Barcelona has been in charge of the excavations, (Fullola and García-Argüelles, 1980), directed through the SERP from 1986 to 1997.

Our stratigraphic survey (García-Argüelles *et al.*, 2005; Fig 2) shows 11 distinct levels, characterised as follows:

Level 1: Thickness of approximately 15 cm; consisting of disturbed earth, with the incorporation of modern materials. In fact, traces of the level remained in the northwest zone only.

Level 2: 25 cm thick, and also very localized in the northwest zone, where it covers 11 m^2. On the whole, ashen grey, with characteristics of intense combustion, and consequently, significant alteration of its composition. This corresponds to the first archaeological level.

Level 3: Very thin, with a thickness of approximately 15 cm, and located in the NW sector of the shelter, covering just 8 m^2.

Level T: This torrential addition overlaid level 4 and covered the entire surface area of the site. This addition came from a lateral flow. Its thickness decreases from one metre, in the SE sector, until it disappears on the opposite side. It also included materials belonging to level 4 in its matrix of pebbles and gravel.

Level 4: This level already appeared throughout the entire extension of the site, 20 m^2, and in some sectors presented interspersing of torrential additions, mainly in the SE sector. Thickness approximately 25 cm.

Level 5-6: This is one of the double levels based on the sedimentological study, but from the archaeological point of view, it was impossible to differentiate it. Thickness between 10 and 20 cm; covered 8 m² and was also concentrated in the NW sector.

Level 7: This is one of the thickest levels, 41 cm, and 27 m² excavated. In the SE zone, this level was connected directly with level 4, and since they had the same composition, it was very difficult to distinguish between them.

Level 8-9: Had the same characteristics as level 5-6 and a thickness of 76 cm, although just 28 cm correspond to the archaeological level; the rest was made up of flood sand.

Levels 10 and 11, sterile from the archaeological point of view, and that reached the underlying terrace of the Montsant River, T1.

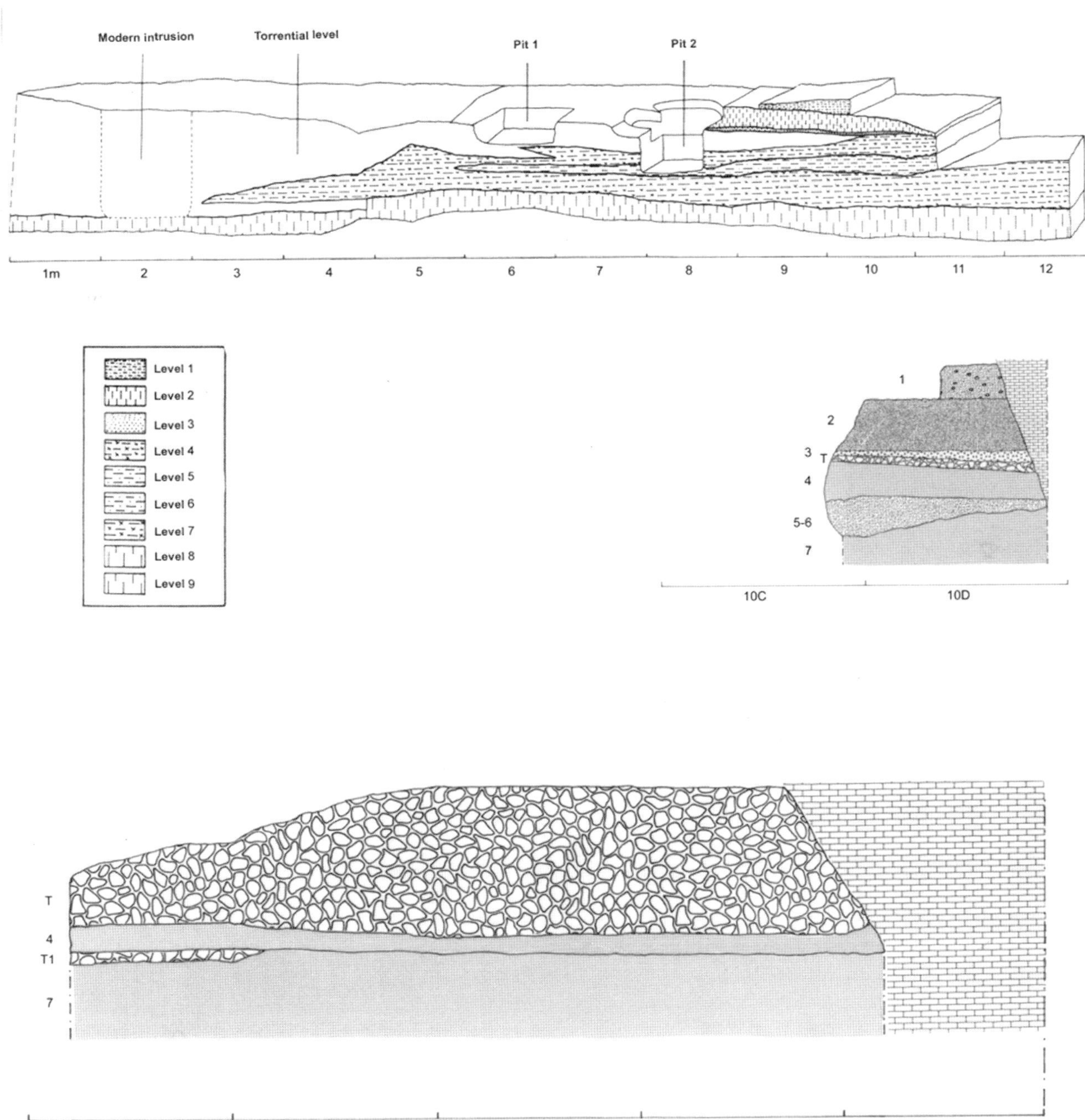

Figure 2: Stratigraphic diagram of the El Filador shelter, and cross-sections at metres 4 and 10 (from García-Argüelles *et al.*, 2005: 69).

Culturally, El Filador presents a continuous sequence from microlaminar phases, which today we tend to assimilate into a transition with the end of the Upper Palaeolithic, until the moment of Notches and Denticulates, with some ceramic remains, at the end of the occupation.

The lower levels, 8-9, are the ones that appear to correspond to the microlaminar phases, with radiocarbon dating ranging from 11,000 to 10,880 BP uncalibrated; this indicates a range between the twelfth and thirteenth millennium calBC. Backed blades (43%) and backed points (14.4%) predominate. These are followed by **burins** (16.7%), denticulates (5.2%), and **burins** (2%). There are also two large non-delineated structures of soil rubificated by fire, as well as different anthropically-contributed stone blocks and two knapping zones (Fig 3.2).

Levels 7, 4 and 3 form the largest part of the geometric Epipalaeolithic package. Abrupt retouching predominates, accounting for more than 80%, with few scrapers and even fewer burins. Micro-burins, a clear indicator of the geometric production, account for between 30 and 45% of the retouched elements. Segments of circles and triangles are the geometric forms present; the former predominates over the latter in the initial moments, with this proportion reversing in level 3 (fig 3.3). There are no trapezoids. In level 7, four sandstone polishers intended for producing arrow shafts were found. There are various pebbles with traces of red paint; in one case, in level 4, up to six red lines were clearly visible (fig 4.3); in another, from level 7, a red stripe covered the entire perimeter; and the other examples were entirely covered in ochre, as if they had been submerged in it. An anvil stone for knapping made up of two stones appeared in level 7, in relation to two combustion structures. Other structures on level 4, in addition to ashes and rubifacted earth at the base, presented a fill which included hundreds of shells from *Cepaea nemoralis*. On this same level, three slate plates were found, intentionally cut in a double bevel; two of these included a palimpsest of finely engraved lines, with traces of ochre in the grooves; the most plausible interpretation is that they were used as supports for cutting soft materials such as skins, which had been prepared with ochre. Level 4 also produced a bone punch, with an oval cross-section, made of a bovine metatarsal, an exceptional case of conservation in soil that has very negatively affected materials of animal origin. The datings obtained for this set of levels are centred on the 10th millennium BP uncalibrated.

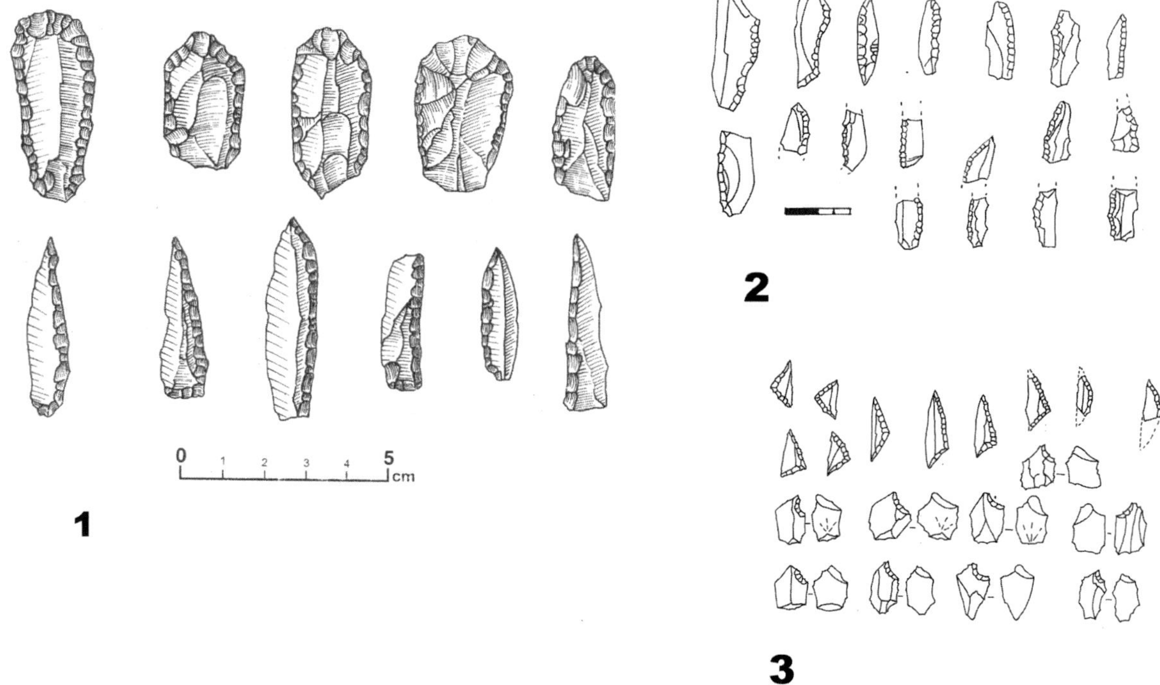

Figure 3. 1 –Materials from the Late Upper Palaeolithic of L'Hort de la Boquera, 2– Microlaminar materials from the Epipalaeolithic, levels 8-9 of El Filador, 3– Materials from the geometric Epipalaeolithic, levels 4-7 of El Filador.

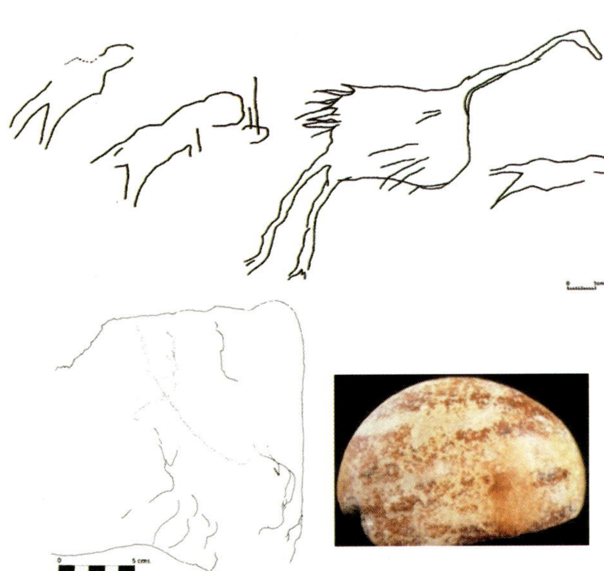

Figure 4: 1– Tracking of naturalist figures engraved in a calcareous block, from the Late Upper Palaeolithic from L'Hort de la Boquera, 2– Tracing of the Palaeolithic engraving of a deer in the Cova de la Taverna, 3– Painted pebble from level 4, geometric Epipalaeolithic, from El Filador (58 x41 x 18 mm).

Levels 5-6 are interspersed between level 7 and level 4 in one part of the site, in an area of just 10 m², in the NW sector of the shelter. Their origins indicate slow, periodic flooding, based on finer granulometry than in levels 7, 4, and 3. The occupations were, therefore much more sporadic and localized in one part of the site. Culturally, however, the representation of geometric elements continues to be significant (12.5% of segments and 7.5% of triangles), along with 42.5% micro-burins; backed bladelets and backed point accounted for 15%, and 12.5% endscrapers; burins are still virtually non-existent. Dated at 9,988±97 BP uncalibrated.

Level 2 of the El Filador shelter covered only 11 m² and was located in the NW section of the site. Unlike the rest of the sedimentary package, it was grey, as a result of intense combustion.

Industrially, the high percentage of denticulates, especially notches and *épines* (36%) and side scrapers (13.3%), along with an increase in burins (11%) and the spectacular drop in abrupt retouching (barely 3.9%), means that this level 2 of El Filador enters into the Notches and Denticulates phase recently defined in the Ebro Valley (Alday 2006).

It is also important to highlight the presence of two conical shaped basins filled with flint, twelve fragments of ceramic that is difficult to attribute, small fragments of bone, and charcoal. These basins were obviously excavated during a more recent time. Two carbon datings place this in the second half of the ninth millennium BP uncalibrated.

From the El Filador sequence, we can infer a series of general reflections, which are described below.

The end of the Upper Palaeolithic culture chronologically "merged" with the microlaminar complex and makes it difficult to distinguish the technological identity of some levels or sites through the record. Some settlements are attributed to the Late Upper Palaeolithic or the microlaminar Epipalaeolithic, depending on the subjective criteria of the researchers, due to the lack of definition of the industry recovered and the vagueness of its chronology. In theory, this does not affect the records of El Filador itself, but does affect other nearby sites, such as Els Colls, which we will see later in this paper, with chronologies that immediately precede or coincide with it.

Emphasising that it is difficult to distinguish the oldest microlaminar sites from those of the Late Upper Palaeolithic, the microlaminar technical complex probably developed fully (with possible earlier roots) in the 12th millennium BP and would reach its *floruit* in the 11th millennium BP (depending, we repeat, on the number of absolute datings) to languish throughout the 10th millennium BP, a phase in which there are few datings.

The transition from the microlaminar to geometric complex should not be understood as a break, because the appearance of geometric elements does not mean the disappearance of the microlaminar component. On the contrary, we see that the backed elements continue to be very important (24% in level 7, and 24.2% in level 4). And in fact, according to the dating table, the geometric complex began at the same time as the maximum expansion of the microlaminar complex, in the 11th millennium BP. This could lead us to think that the technological innovation represented by the appearance of Epipalaeolithic geometrism would be used initially on certain occasions, and in certain circumstances, or to carry out specific functions, while for others, the preference would be to continue with the backed elements of the microlaminar complex. Finally, the presence of the geometric component was ultimately superimposed on the microlaminar deposits with no geometric elements, at the time of the maximum expansion of the Filador facies – which technologically were Sauveterroid – in the 10th millennium BP (García-Argüelles and Nadal, 1998; García-Argüelles *et al.*, 2013). This, in turn, is presented in some sites, with a much lower frequency, until the 9th millennium BP.

We need to contradict the assertion by other authors regarding the high percentage of denticulates in all levels of El Filador. This is true only in level 2, of Notches and Denticulates / Neolithic, and we would like to reassert the data: on level 8-9 we have 10 denticulate elements; on level 7, 16; on level 5-6, 1; on level 4, 9 and on level 3, 4 (5.8%). There is not a high percentage of denticulate tools, so El Filador cannot be used to talk about a new facies of Notches and Denticulates, located between the microlaminar and geometric, which other researchers have located in the Ebro river basin and the Central Plateau, at sites such as Forcas (Utrilla and Mazo, 1997), Mendandia, Atxose, Peña 14, or El Ángel (Alday, 2002).

El Filador does not have the latest facies of the geometric Epipalaeolithic of the Fortea classification, which is characterised by the presence of trapezoids and the disappearance of the micro-burin technique. In our area, we have la Balma of la Margineda (level 4) and those of the Ebro Valley (Pontet, Botiquería, Forcas) According to the datings of Balma Margineda, its chronology would be the 9th millennium, coinciding with the most modern, and recent datings of the Filador facies – Sauveterroid.

In addition to the lack of data for trapezoidal facies in Catalonia, the presence of a series of technical complexes that had not been attributed to the typology established by Fortea has been consolidated, and have been cited as sites with "atypical" industry. With an increasingly expanding record, this group has consolidated itself as the cultural model for the 9th millennium BP, which could explain the lack of sites with trapezoids. The chronologies of these sites extend to the 8th millennium BP. In any case, for the time being, the evolution detected in the Ebro Valley does not appear to be reproduced: Microlaminar Epipalaeolithic, Mesolithic with Notches and Denticulates, and Mesolithic geometric with trapezoids (Utrilla, 2002). The Catalonian record for the 8th millennium BP is still too poor.

At El Filador, we are missing the last two facies which could clarify the transition to a Neolithic without datings and with the small quantity of ceramic of level 2. The southern zone of Catalonia still has a gap, as noted by Martí and Juan-Cabanilles (1997:237), despite the fact that there have already been significant new developments in the Pyrenees areas (Petit *et al.*, 1996; Pallarès, Bordas and Mora 1997).

The technological and economic model that we observed in El Filador was successful in the area for just over two millennia. After that, there is a chronological and cultural hiatus until the arrival of the Neolithic. Other sites in the area such as El Auferí (Adserias *et al.*, 1996) or L'Hort de la Boquera corroborate this coherent development and an occupation of the territory that leads to a rational exploitation of the biotic and abiotic resources in one of the few areas in which these spatial distribution studies have been able to be carried out in a geographically limited area.

3b. L'Hort de la Boquera

This is a small shelter, no more than 9 m long and 4 m deep, that has lost part of its ledge and that conserves an excavatable surface area of no more than 20 m^2, half of which is below the conserved section of the ledge. It is oriented S-SE, is located on the right bank of the Montsant River, approximately 25 m above the current level, and approximately 400 masl (E(X):312108.8m-N(Y)4573254.3m UTM 31N/ETR S89).

Its stratigraphy is arranged on 4 levels, level I, which contains 2 sublevels (Ia and Ib) was formed by the processes of streams and falling blocks from the ledge. This level is archaeologically sterile. Level II is made up of a sandy silt matrix. It has a thickness of 47 cm, and is the only archaeological level at the site in which different habitation moments have been detected, as we will discuss later in this paper. The stratigraphy of the site is completed with level III, which is made up of fine sand that contains some flint remains, but that do not indicate stable human occupation, and level IV, made up mainly of pebbles and gravel, and which rests on terrace T2 of the Montsant Rivers, 24 m above the current level (Fullola, 1978; Bergadà, 1993:157-165; García-Argüelles *et al.*, i.p.).

In regard to the human activity of level II, so far, more than 30,000 lithic elements have been recovered, mainly made of flint, but there is also a small number of elements made of slate and limestone.

2.15% of the elements have been retouched and endscrapers and backed elements predominate. Denticulates and truncated tools were found in smaller proportions. Burins play a smaller role, on fracture, on retouch, and dihedrals (Fig 3.1). There are also round slate plates with bevelled edges and markings that are currently being studied. In this sense, there is a large limestone block on which a figure of a bird, possibly a crane, has been engraved, surrounded by other clearer figures that can be interpreted as anthropomorphic (García-Argüelles *et al.*, i.p.; Fig 4.1). It appears that the presence of portable figurative art begins to be constant in the sites of the Late Upper Palaeolithic in southern Catalonia, as in the case of Molí del Salt and Sant Gregori (Falset).

Paleo-environmentally, the paleobotanical data is limited to the data provided by the anthracological studies conducted by Dr. Allué. There is a significant presence of *Pinus sylvestris* type and some elements of *Juniperus* sp.. In terms of fauna, despite the deficient conservation of bone, they cannot be said to be scarce. Only the presence of *Capra pyrenaica* and *Oryctolagus cuniculus* can be cited. The group is completed by different *Cepaea nemoralis*, which are abundant in El Filador. The gathering of terrestrial molluscs in the Catalonian area is very frequent in the Epipaleolithic sites, but not for Palaeolithic occupations. In this sense, L'Hort de la Boquera is one of the first indicators of the expansion of the dietary spectrum in the northeast of the Iberian Peninsula during the Pleistocene-Holocene transition.

The datings of the phases of occupations range from 12,250±60 BP to 11,850±45 BP and 11,775±45 BP, which places it, along with the cultural characteristics that we just mentioned, in a phase that corresponds to the Late Upper Palaeolithic. (Mangado *et al.*, 2010; Fullola *et al.*, 2012).

3c. *Els Colls*

This is a shelter which is more than 50 m long and between 2 and 8 m high, and up to 6 m deep in some sectors. It is oriented towards the SW and is located on the right bank of the Montsant River, 20.7 m above the current level, and approximately 400 masl (E(X):312108.8m-N(Y)4573254.3m UTM 31N/ETR S89).

Sedimentalogically, 8 levels have been identified (Bergadà, 1993:186-191); level I was formed recently. Level II is the most archaeologically rich, with more than 9,000 lithic elements. This occupation is settled on fallen blocks of conglomerate (level III). During the excavation, we observed that the blocks of conglomerate were directly above level IV, whose lithic material presented, in many cases, fracturing of the pieces (Bergadà, 1998). This level IV was excavated in a smaller sector of the shelter, and therefore offered fewer lithic elements (1,500). Below level V, to the river terrace, the levels are sterile.

Abrupt elements predominate in level II (backed bladelets and backed points). In terms of simple retouched tools, side scrapers are most prevalent, and there are also burins, which in many cases are double burins, and on truncated elements. Fauna is not very abundant and appears to be highly fragmented; most elements belong to large mammals and are splinters whose size indicates intense activity for the exploitation of hunting products (deer, wild goat, etc.). In many cases, the elements present evidence of combustion processes, connected with the appearance of a home on level II. There are traces of pollen, mainly from *Pinus* and *Quercus* t.*ilex*. Three absolute datings have been obtained, two by C14: 10,950±120 BP and 10,050±85 BP, and a third by thermoluminescence 13,000±1,000 BP. (Fullola *et al.*, 1993).

In the underlying level IV, we documented a predominance of simple retouching, endscrapers, and denticulates, followed by abrupt retouched tools such as backed bladelets and backed points. The study of the spatial distribution of the archaeological material has determined the existence of an important area of knapping and a combustion structure. There are no traces of fauna.

The archaeological levels of the Els Colls shelter present a series of industrial characteristics that are chronologically and culturally homogeneous. The large dimensions of different backed elements could lead us to think of early phases of the Upper Palaeolithic, but the rest of the sites in the valley, the aforementioned datings, and other technological details clearly place the site in the Late Upper Palaeolithic (Rodríguez Baylach, unpublished).

3d. *La Cova del Boix*

The cave is an opening in a cliff on the left bank of the Montsant River. It has a single chamber approximately 25 m wide by 15 m deep, open in the NE direction (E(X):313992.0m-N(Y)4573860.0 UTM 31/ETR S89) (García-Argüelles and Fullola, 2002).

It was excavated in 1982/83. The stratigraphy is inverted due to the disturbances caused by the use of the space by *carboneros* (charcoal makers) who used the cave as a shelter. However, the recovered materials indicated that prehistoric occupation had existed. Just over one thousand lithic elements were recovered, of which 41 are retouched pieces; backed elements clearly predominate, with some endscrapers, which outnumber the burins. There are some traces of fauna, but it is difficult to distinguish between the old elements and the modern additions. Remains from wild animals such as *Cervus elaphus* or *Capra pyrenaica* which can be attributed to prehistoric additions have been recovered.

No radiocarbon dating is available for this site, but its industrial characteristics place it closer to the cases mentioned before of Els Colls and L'Hort de la Boquera, which involves a chronological-cultural attribution to the Late Upper Palaeolithic with the characteristic of a higher proportion of endscrapers with respect to burins (García-Argüelles and Fullola, 2002).

3e. L'Abric de l'Auferí

This is the only site that was excavated as an emergency excavation due to the impact of the construction of the Margalef reservoir. It was excavated in the early 1990s under the direction of the members of our group Maria Adserias and Raül Bartolí. Once again, this is a shelter that opens in the southern direction, on the left bank of the River, approximately 22 m above the current level (E(X):315173.8m-N(Y)4574478.8m UTM 31N/ ETR S89) (Adserias and Bartrolí, 2007).

In this excavation, two sectors were opened. In one, abundant ceramics were found in the first level, which was one of the few cases of Montsant sites with occupation with Neolithic chronology. The most interesting sector is the one described in sector II, which contains 5 levels. Level I corresponds to the surface level of sandy matrix, with a large quantity of gravel from 1 to 3 cm, and a significant organic component; it incorporates archaeological materials from the lower levels as a result of agricultural disturbances. Level II is located in the parts protected by the shelter ledge. Its matrix is made up of the degraded materials of the wall of the shelter and incorporates archaeological material from the previous level in the contact zone. Level III, divided into two sublevels, presents, in its lower section, the true archaeological level, with many lithic elements but with no ceramic. Level IV, with a silty matrix, only presented a few lithic elements incorporated from the upper level; and level V corresponds to the terrace on which the site is settled, which consists mostly of river pebbles. More than 20,000 lithic elements were collected, almost all flint, of which 3.4% are retouched, with endscrapers predominating, followed by elements with abrupt retouching and finally, burins. Traces of fauna are very scarce and very poorly conserved; it can only be said that *Capra pyrenaica*, along with *Cervus elaphus* and *Oryctolagus cuniculus* predominate. There is one reliable radiocarbon dating, which also corresponds to the base of the sequence, level V, which is sterile. The date is 12,317±114 BP, and for the reasons mentioned regarding the location of the sample, it was not taken into consideration by the excavation directors (M.Adserias personal communication). Nevertheless, in our opinion, it gives a *post quem* date for the archaeological package of level III and is similar to the ones obtained at other sites in the area, with significant technotypological similarities, such as L'Hort de la Boquera and Els Colls. (Adserias *et al.*, 1996).

3f. Other sites in the middle valley of the Montsant River

Having presented the principal excavated sites, it is important to remember that, as mentioned in the introduction, that the research by S. Vilaseca and our own excavations have identified many other sites, whether caves, shelters, or outside, in the middle valley of the Montsant River. This makes this one of the areas with the highest concentration of archaeological stations in the northeast of the Iberian Peninsula.

L' Hort d'en Marquet, located in 1980, is an area with an abundance of flint on the surface and which presents, in one of the areas in which lithic material has been found, stratigraphy that is currently very degraded due to human activities during historic times. In a second level of this sequence, with a thickness of approximately 10-15 centimetres, a concentration of archaeological material was detected. This consists of retouched pieces that included scrapers, burins, and knapped dorsal elements. Without absolute dating, and with the data from the other excavated sites (Els Colls and L'Hort de la Boquera), it is very feasible that the site corresponds to the Late Upper Palaeolithic. (Fullola and García-Argüelles, 1980) .

El Planot would be another one of these sites. This is a surface site, the only one located on the upper terrace of the river, more than 30 m above the current level, on the borders of the municipalities of Margalef de Montsant and La Bisbal de Falset.

Approximately 50 pieces were recovered, with side scrapers and denticulate tools predominating. For this reason, along with its location on the upper terrace, the site is supposed to correspond to a Mousterian chronology (Fullola and García-Argüelles, 1982-83).

4. Conclusion

After describing some of the most important sites, we feel that the archaeological importance of the Montsant Valley has been clearly explained, especially in regard to the final phases of the hunter-gatherer communities of the Late Upper Palaeolithic and the Epipalaeolithic. In this sense, beyond this chronological margin, for now, we have just one site that could be attributed to the Middle Palaeolithic (El Planot) and two occupations that could be attributed to the Neolithic (on the upper levels of l'Auferí and El Filador). It is quite likely that the geographic and agricultural attractiveness of the area for hunter-gatherers was lost, at least in regard to agricultural potential.

The majority of the Montsant sites are very homogeneous in regard to a series of characteristics, which include chronology, when reliable datings are available. Most of them are occupations in shelters located on the second terrace level of the river, at heights above the current level that range from 20 to 25 metres. They are located on both sides of the Montsant, but they all coincide at a position of convergence between the river and the end of cliffs that face it, and that mark the start of the ranges between which it runs, the Montsant Range on the left, and the Llena Range on the right.

The most recurrent animal species is the *Capra pyrenaica*. The sites normally have a single phase, with a single archaeological level (Boix, L'Auferí, L'Hort de la Boquera), or several archaeological levels that correspond to the same chronological-cultural phases (Els Colls). The predominant lithic elements are backed elements or endscrapers, which are always more abundant than burins. Its datings range between the middle of the 8th and middle of the 12th millennia BP, which would make them coincide with the final phases of the Magdelenian. Despite this, though, they do present some specific aspects, such as the aforementioned scarcity of burins and the predominance of endscrapers, the lack of bone industry (although this may be due to post-depositional biases) or in some cases, the presence of figurative portable art on lithic supports (L'Hort de la Boquera), which starts to become generalised in the Tarragona sites of this time (Molí del Salt, perhaps Sant Gregori), and that brings them closer to synchronic sites in the neighbouring zone of Castellón. Based on all of this, we think that it could be attributed to the Late Upper Palaeolithic, coinciding with what we know as the Late Upper Magdalenian, with some regionally-specific characteristics. For now, according to the data on the lithic industry, fauna, and locations of the sites, we suppose that these sites from the Late Upper Palaeolithic in the Montsant Valley could present a similar pattern of occupation: sites close to the river, which would allow the gathering of flint, which was available in abundance in the river, and which were possibly exploited for food resources. They would also facilitate access from the cliffs to the higher areas of the surrounding mountain ranges for specialised hunting of mountain goats, or that took advantage of the intersection between cliffs and the river to wait for this prey when it descended from the mountains to be captured.

Finally, and although the site currently represents an exception to the model explained before, we have the El Filador shelter, which, thanks to its stratigraphic sequence and its complete dating series, as well as the reinterpretation of some of its levels, continues to serve as a reference for the systematization of the different facies of the Epipalaeolithic in the northeast area of the Iberian Peninsula, with the presence of microlaminar, geometric, notches and denticulates moments (García-Argüelles *et al.*, 2005; García-Argüelles *et al.*, 2013).

4

MEDITERRANEAN BASINS. NORTH OF THE EBRO RIVER

Site	Map numbering
Abric Romaní	41
La Cansaladeta	42
La Cativera	43
Cinglera del Capelló	44
Reclau Viver ensemble	45
St. Julià de Ramis Pleistocene ensemble La Selva and Puig d´en Roca ensemble	46
Montgrí Middle Pleistocene ensembles	47
Cova de l'Arbreda	48
Cova del Gegant	49
Cova del Rinoceront	50
Els Vinyets	51
Barranc de la Boella	52
Molí del Salt	53

Site	Map numbering
Cova de les Teixoneres and Cova del Toll	54
Vallparadís	55

Josep Vallverdú*,**, Ethel Allué*,**, Amelia Bargalló*,**, Isabel Cáceres*,**, Gerard Campeny*,**, María Gema Chacón*,**,***, Maria Joanna Gabucio*,**, Bruno Gómez*,**, Juan Manuel López-García****, Mónica Fernández*,**, Juan Marín*,**, Francesca Romagnoli*,**,*****, Palmira Saladié*,**, Alex Solé*,**, Manuel Vaquero*,**, Eudald Carbonell*,**,******.

Abric Romaní (Capellades, Anoia)

1. Location and research history

The *l'Abric Romaní* site is a large rock shelter located on the north side of the travertine cliff known as *Cinglera del Capelló* (Capellades, Barcelona). *La Cinglera* is a 60m thick escarpment made from lacustrine-spring travertine mesa formed by a multilayer groundwater springs of the Capellades region. Capellades village lies on this travertine mesa at 300-320m above sea level.

Cinglera del Capelló was thoroughly explored by Amador Romaní at the beginning of the twentieth century. A. Romaní was a businessman in the paper industry of Capellades and a naturalist associated to the *Institució Catalana d'Història Natural,* in turn associated with the *Institut d'Estudis Catalans. The Abric Romaní,* also known locally as *Balma del fossar vell* before it was discovered in 1909, is one of the first sites in the Iberian Peninsula in which Mousterian lithic industries were identified. The first excavation campaigns at *Abric Romaní* were sponsored by the *Institut d'Estudis Catalans,* first directed by Father Nobert Font i Sagué and then by mining engineer Lluís Marià Vidal.

One hundred years after it was discovered, three long periods of research activity and archaeological excavations can be identified. The first runs until the 1930s and its results are related to the argument over the age and the presence of Neanderthals in Catalonia. This phase ends with the publication of the Abric Romaní findings in the *Història de Catalunya* d'Antoni Rovira i Virgili, based on the *Atlas de Prehistòria* made by Amador Romaní, with a depth of 10m (Fig. 1). The second period was led by Dr Eduardo Ripoll and the 5th INQUA Congress held in Spain. The work of Dr Ripoll was based on reviewing the stratigraphy and extending the studies carried out by Amador Romaní. There were also specific studies dedicated to the Upper Paleolithic lithic industries, found in the layer two of the nomenclature of Amador Romaní, by Dr Georges Laplace. Professors Henry de Lumley and Eduardo Ripoll published the stratigraphy review and Mousterian lithic industry in various papers in the first half of the 1960s.

The last period of excavation work and research started in 1983 and is still going on. The early years of this project were led by a work group associated to the *Universitat Autònoma de Barcelona* and the *Centre de Recerques Paleoecosocials* (CRPES) under the direction of Dr Eudald Carbonell, Artur Cebrià and Dr Rafael Mora. The research programme of this last excavation phase adheres to an approach based on the excavation of large surface which are seemingly very well preserved. The dating of the travertine based on the Uranium series and the pollen preserved in the calcareous sediments have returned very important results on the paleoecology of the *Abric Romaní* and the region of Capellades. The *Abric Romaní* scree desposits are an singular archive in continental settings and

* IPHES, Institut Català de Paleoecologia Humana i Evolució Social, C. Marcel.lí Domingo s/n, Campus Sescelades URV (Edifici W3), 43007 Tarragona, Spain
** Àrea de Prehistòria, Universitat Rovira i Virgili (URV), Avinguda de Catalunya 35, 43002 Tarragona, Spain
*** UMR7194 – Département de Préhistoire, Muséum national d'Histoire naturelle, 1, rue René Panhard, 75013 Paris, France
**** Sezione di Scienze Preistoriche e Antropologiche, Dipartamento di Studi Umanistici, Università degli Studi di Ferrara, Ferrara, Italy
***** Cattedra di Preistoria, Dipartimento di Storia, Geografia, Archeologia, Arte e Spettacolo, Università degli Studi di Firenze, Via S. Egidio 21, 50122 Firenze, Italy
****** Visiting professor, Institute of Vertebrate Paleontology and Paleoanthropology of Beijing (IVPP), PR China

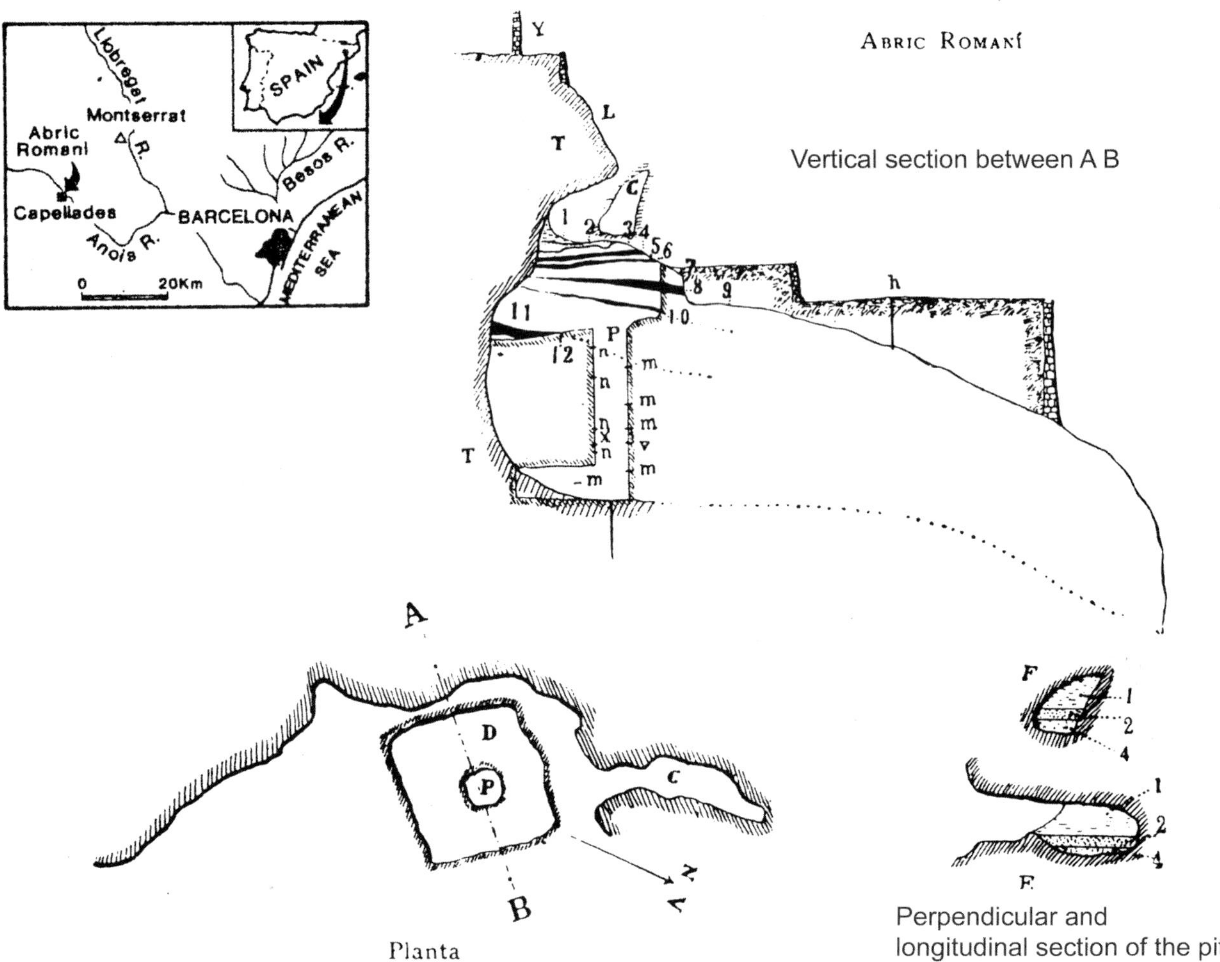

Figure 1. Location of *the Abric Romaní* in the NE of the Iberian Peninsula and sketch of the section of the site with the work carried out by Amador Romaní during the first quarter of the nineteenth century. The stratigraphic sketch of the Abric Romaní was published in the *Història de Catalunya* in 1928, in which the execution of shaft 1 is noteworthy.

complements the global paleoenvironmental archives of the Upper Pleistocene.

The excavation and research team from the *Universitat Rovira i Virgili* in Tarragona, under the direction of Dr Eudald Carbonell, started to work in Abric Romaní during the large surface excavation work in level H in 1989. This team is currently continuing with the work within the *Institut Català de Paleoecologia Humana i Evolució Social* (IPHES). The interest of the research and development of these excavations is based on the spatial documentation on the structures and the archaeological materials. The large surface excavation work has occupied 9 archaeological levels (form H to P) and three monographs dedicated to levels H, I and J have been published. From archaeological level K, the large surface excavation work is complete and it is not affected by the pits of previous phases of archaeological work. The thickness of the large surface excavation sediment is around 10m deep. In addition, Amador Romaní's shaft 1 was excavated to an additional 6m deep and its base was dated at 70,000 BP. A mechanical borehole from level P has documented another 30 m of deposits, which is located around 9 m below the last travertine of the rock-shelter. Therefore, the talus scree deposits accumulated at the foot Abric Romaní escarpment is at least 40 m thick. This thick places the base of the talus scree at the foot of the escarpment at 260 m above sea level. This elevation of 260 m is very close to the elevation of the +20-25 m terrace encaised in the valley of the river Anoia.

2. Stratigraphy and chronology

The Sedimentary Geology of the talus scree deposits at *Abric Romaní* escarpment has an evident zonation caused by the dripline of the carbonate curtains in the roof of the archaeological site. In the region of Capellades the carbonate curtains are called *Capelló*. These carbonate curtains are formed by plants being encrusted by calcite and develop along the lacustrine travertine escarpment concurrently with the alveolar weathering, or tafoni, of the cliff wall. In some archaeological levels, such as levels J and M, the distance between the back wall and the dripline of the rock-shelter can be more than 12 m. Therefore, during the fastest growth periods of the carbonate curtain in the *Abric Romaní*, there is a wide surface habitable at the foot of the wall protected from the weather by the shelter roof.

The stratigraphy of *the Abric Romaní* has repeatedly been described during various research excavation projects. Amador Romaní distinguished sand stratum and stalagmite stratum. The work of Ripoll and de Lumley recognises three types of sediments–rocks: gravel and sand deposits; reddish calcareous deposits and calcareous deposits (travertine). In the stratigraphic descriptions from the start of the third phase of research, the attention given to the different variants of travertine lithofacies is noteworthy. All of these descriptions are based on observing outcrops of the upper part of the stratigraphic sequence of the rock-shelter and they coincide in describing the three main lithofacies described by Dr Ripoll and Dr de Lumley.

The works of Amador Romaní's in the shaft 1 confirmed the volumetric significance of the travertine and calcareous sediments in the stratigraphic succession of the *Abric Romaní* rock-shelter. The travertine was widely dated and published in Nature by J.L. Bischoff. This work details the high chronological resolution of the stratigraphic succesion and the potential of the site to illustrate the latest archaeological assemblages of the material culture of the Neanderthals in the northeast of the Iberian Peninsula. The high temporal resolution of the sediment of *the Abric Romaní* was characterised by its high sedimentation rate, estimated at 0.6m per 1000 years. The dates have been established using the uranium series and situate the deposits of the *Abric Romaní* in marine isotope stage 3 (40 – 60 ky BP). Later, the same geochronologist published the calendar chronology of the travertine containing the Upper Paleolithic industries in the layer 2, or level A of the current archaeological stratigraphy, and calibrated the radiocarbon chronology of the carbon in this layer (level A). The results confirmed a consistent and reliable group of calendar dates of high temporal resolution for the travertine at the top of the shelter sediment sequence and also confirmed the old age of the Upper Paleolithic *at Abric Romaní* (42.6 ky BP) .

Sampling of shaft 1 also offered the opportunity to research the pollen biostratigraphy of the *Abric Romaní*. The pollen study was carried out by Dr F. Burjachs and Dr R. Julià from the *Institut* Jaume Almera in Barcelona. The samples were taken from shaft 1 and different profiles available in the old archaeological pits from the top portion of the stratigraphy of the *Abric*. The pollen record was divided into 5 bio-zones which register abrupt climate changes. Bio-zones 1, 2 and 3 show variations in the arboreal / non-arboreal content in a chronostratigraphy interval similar to the variation in the isotopic content of the oxygen identified in the ice core samples from Greenland. The upper bio-zones of the sediment sequence are more difficult to correlate. However, the pollen curve for the *Abric Romaní shows a singular relation between* age models of paleoclimatic change recorded in prehistoric caves and rock shelters and global stratotypes of environmental change based on in marine and glaciological settings.

From archaeological level K, large surface excavation in *the Abric Romaní* started documenting a large area without pits from the old research projects. Two stratigraphic profiles were preserved in the centre of the shelter. However, as the depth of the large surface excavation increased, it was clear that the outcrop of the *coveta Nord* section of the site was the best stratigraphic pannel to explain the Sedimentary Geology of the rock-shelter (Fig. 2). A few years later, one of the profiles reserved from the shelter wall was excavated while the volume of the other was reduced in order not to affect the spatial documentation of the archaeological levels excavated in large surface.

2.1. The coveta Nord section

The roof of the rock-shelter presents the carbonate curtain welded with the deposits of the stratigraphy of the rock-shelter after the level J. This welding determines the increase in the frequency of the endokarstic sedimentary process which forms bio-chemical sediments in the strati-

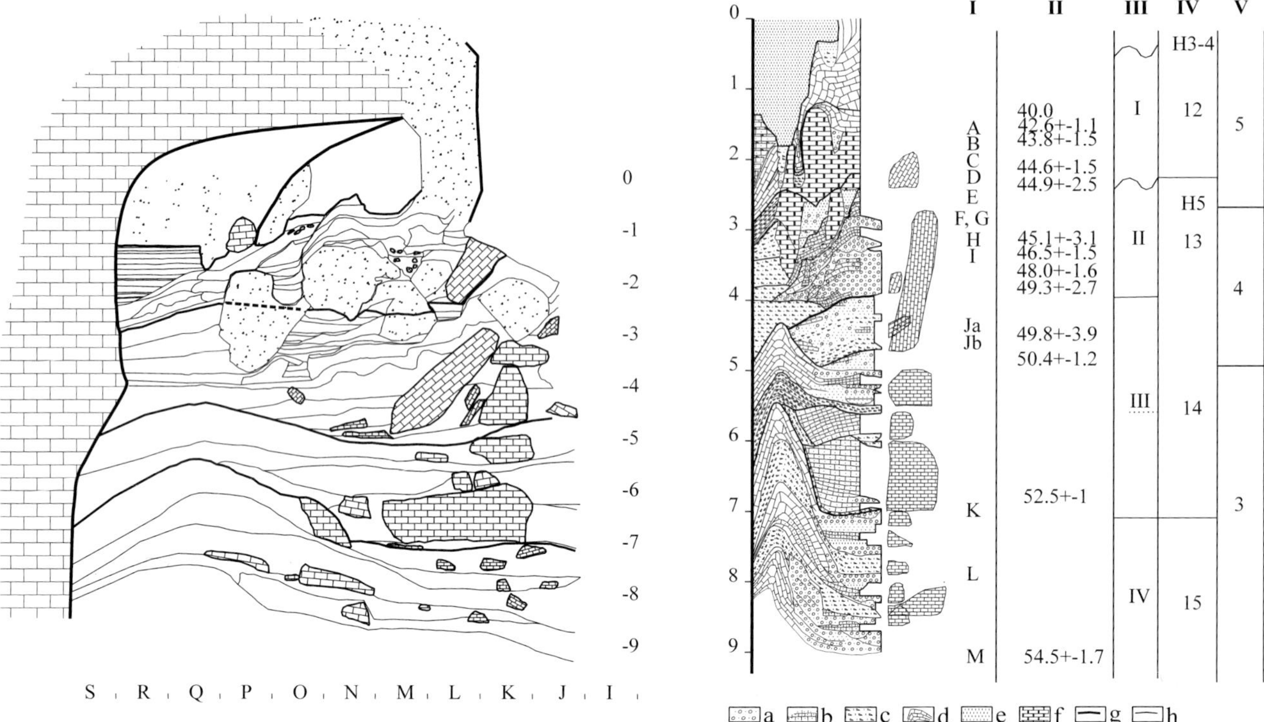

Figure 2. Sketch of the *coveta Nord* section of *Abric Romaní* and its synthetic lithostratigraphic logs
Legend: a, conglomerates and tuffaceous sands; b, bryophyte bio-constructions; c, crystalline angular gravel; d, cementation and algal laminated bio-constructions . e, calcareous sands and siliciclastic red muds; f, recrystallizated stalagmitic massif; g, boundary surfaces ; f, sequence boundaries; Comments on the column: I, archaeological levels; II, Uranium series dates; III, sequence numbering; IV, Bond cycle boundaries with the D-O Greenland event numbers and the Heinrich events of the North Atlantic with the GISP2 temporal scale ; V, pollen zones.

graphic record of the upper part of the *Abric Romaní* succesion. The rest of the sedimentary succesion could be described by the predominance of the clastic processes alternated with the biochemical processes, particularly near the wall of the shelter. In the dripline, the stratigraphy shows the importance of fragmentation of the curtain of the rock-shelter. These clastic processes were highlighted in the first stratigraphy studies of the last research period, as large blocks in the shaft 1 and used as a criterion to separate stratigraphic ensembles. The growth or shrinkage of the carbonate curtain of Abric influences the location of the dripline. The temporal drifting of the dripline results in clear zoning of the deposits accumulated at the foot of the travertine escarpment: an interior zone, between the back-wall and the dripline of the rock-shelter and an exterior zone, from the dripline to the slope of the talus scree.

The *coveta Nord* section fit as best stratigraphic outcrop for understanding the talus scree deposits (*talus d'eboulis*) in a rock shelter setting. Many of the facies described as sediments formed by precipitation (travertine) are quickly buried and recrystallization is relatively limited and allows uranium series dating. The *coveta Nord* section has allowed the stratigraphic description work to be reviewed to set out 5 allostratigraphical units or sequences. These sequences are based on hierarchisation of the discontinuities or boundary surfaces of the sedimentary bodies. The even numbered sequences contain deposits of dominant clastic facies and indicate shrinkage of the carbonate curtain of the shelter curtain. The odd numbered sequences contain dominant calcium carbonate precipitation and represent the *Capelló* accretion. It is noteworthy that the collapse of the carbonated curtain is time transgressive: it occurs regularly over all sequences.

The upper chronostratigraphic horizon of the sequence is the most recent travertine dated in the *Abric Romani* averaged at 40 ky BP. This discontinuity has a clear lithological change between the most recent travertine and red calcareous and siliciclastic sediments in the *coveta Nord* section. These deposits have been dated using OSL at 29.5 ± 1.9 ky BP. The chronostratigraphic horizon of the bottom of sequence unit I, which separates sequences I and II, has dates measured at 44.9 ± 2.5 and 44.6 ± 1.5 ky BP by Uranium series. These dates between the last travertines averaged in 40 ky and 44.9 above level E are close to the Greenland interstadial 12 time span, also known as Hengelo interstadial in the pollen biostratigraphy of Grand Pile.

The chronostratigraphic horizon separating sequence II from III are the travertine in which archaeological level Jb lies and the average date measured is 50.0 ± 1.6 ky BP. The bottom boundary of the sequence III has a calendar date of 52.5 ± 1 and their chronostratigraphic boundaries, of level K, can be correlated with Greenland interstadial 14, also known as Glinde interstadial. Dating of the base of sequence 4 has not yet been determined but it contains a date group prior to Greenland interstadial 14.

The sediment sequences of *Abric Romaní* show the climatic control in the rhythmicity of the carbonate curtain growth and shrinkage. Uranium series dating of the *Abric Romaní* sequences indicate the formation of calcium carbonate precipitation deposits and fragmentation during the abrupt environmental oscillations, with a magnitude of the time scale of the Bond cycles or long periods of cooling. These long periods of cooling end with a maximum period of cooling correlated with the Henrich events in the North Atlantic. Therefore, the red calcareous and siliciclastic sediments at the top of sequence II, which contains level E, shows the aeolian deposits during the chronology of Henrich 5. At the top of sequence I, although formed by red calcareous and siliciclastic sediments too, from the top with an OSL dating of around Henrich 3, the date determined in the most recent travertine of *Abric Romaní*, dated at 40 ky, is significant as this date is very close to the chronology of the Heinrich 4 event in the North Atlantic (39 ky BP).

To sum up, the chronostratigraphy and the sequences of *Abric Romaní* cover the oscillations described in the Oxygen isotope stratigraphy in the Greenland ice cores. Up until now we have been able to group sediment sequences and chronological intervals for stadials and interstadials 9 to 14 and we are now, in the archaeological levels P and Q, very close to reaching Greenland interstadial-stadial 16-17. The environmental change age model provided by the *Abric Romaní* sequences is independent and the dates measured are calendar dates (U-series dates). These environmental change dates, established by a group of dates and stratum delimited by discontinuities, show better correlation with the cronology of ice-core GISP2 age model than the GRIP age model.

3. Paleoenvironment

Paleoenvironmental research of the *Abric Romaní* sequence has provided a lot of valuable data for reconstructing the paleoecology of the human occupations. The paleoenvironment reconstruction data comes from several proxies that include paleobotany (palynology and anthracology) and micro-vertebrates (micro-mammals, amphibians and reptiles) that complement and allow habitat and climate aspects to be understood in order to define the landscape in which Neanderthals lived.

The palynological sequence throughout the phases shows a dominance of *Pinus* that characterises tree formations during the whole period (Fig. 3). At the base of the sequence, between 70 and 67 ky BP, the data reflects a warm climate phase with a dominance of tree pollen, including *Quercus* evergreens and *Olea / Phillyrea*. Between 66 and 59 ky BP gramineae dominate, reflecting a colder phase. Between 57 and 50 ky BP and *Pinus* and gramineae (*Artemisia* and Poaceae) dominate with a presence of meso and thermophilic taxa at times, indicating climate oscillations during this period. Between 50 and 47 ky BP the data reflects the dominance of Asteraceae, Poaceae and *Artemisia*, suggesting steppe vegetation and cold conditions. Finally, around 46 ky a warm climate trend is identified with an increase in *Quercus* and *Olea-Phillyrea* (Fig. 3). Anthracological data for levels D to O shows a dominant taxon in the anthrocological set, which is *Pinus sylvestris* and represents more than 90% of identifiable material. The dominance of this species is conditioned by the selection of this taxon for use as fuel. Level O presents other taxa in addition to *Pinus* such as as *Prunus* and *Juniperus* and in level D, mesophile species in charcoal fragments are identified such as deciduous *Acer*, *Quercus sp* and other unidentifiable angiosperms, which may reflect a change due to more favourable climate conditions that are consistent with the palynological data. Scots pine forests are the dominant tree formations throughout the sequence, which are characterised for being forest with many clearings without much taxonomic diversity.

Microvertebrates at *Abric Romani* come from the study of levels D, E, J, N and O. The species identified are insectivores: *Russula Crocidura*, *Sorex gr. coronatus* and *Talpa europaea-araneus*, Chiroptera: *Miniopterus schreibersii*, *Pipistrellus pipistrellus*, *Nyctalus lasiopterus*; and rodents: *Microtus arvalis*, *M. agrestis*, *Iberomys cabrerae*, *Terricola duodecimcostatus*, *T. cf. pyrenaicus*, *Arvicola sapidus*, *Apodemus sylvaticus* and *Eliomys quercinus*. Similarly, water environments are identified, such as *Arvicola sapidus*. The herpetofauna study represents amphibians and reptiles providing 3 anuran: *Bufo bufo*, *Bufo calamites*, *Rana temporaria*; and 3 reptiles: *Lacertidae indet.*, *Anguis fragilis* and *Vipera aspis* (Fig. 3). This data reflect domination of open forest species and species that require humidity and colder climate conditions than the current ones.

The paleoenvironmental data on *Abric Romani* reflects a mosaic landscape: forests; grasslands; riparian forests, which are larger or smaller according to the warmer or cooler climate phases. In general, the sequence data reflects colder temperatures than current ones, which is proven by the presence of certain micro-vertebrates and the distribution of *Pinus sylvestris*.

4. The lithic industry

The general characteristic of all archaeological levels of the *Abric Romani* is the fragmentation of the operative sequences, although refitting studies shows that full or almost full knapping sequences have been found in some levels. The main objective of the lithic sequences is to obtain as many knapped products as possible and these are there-

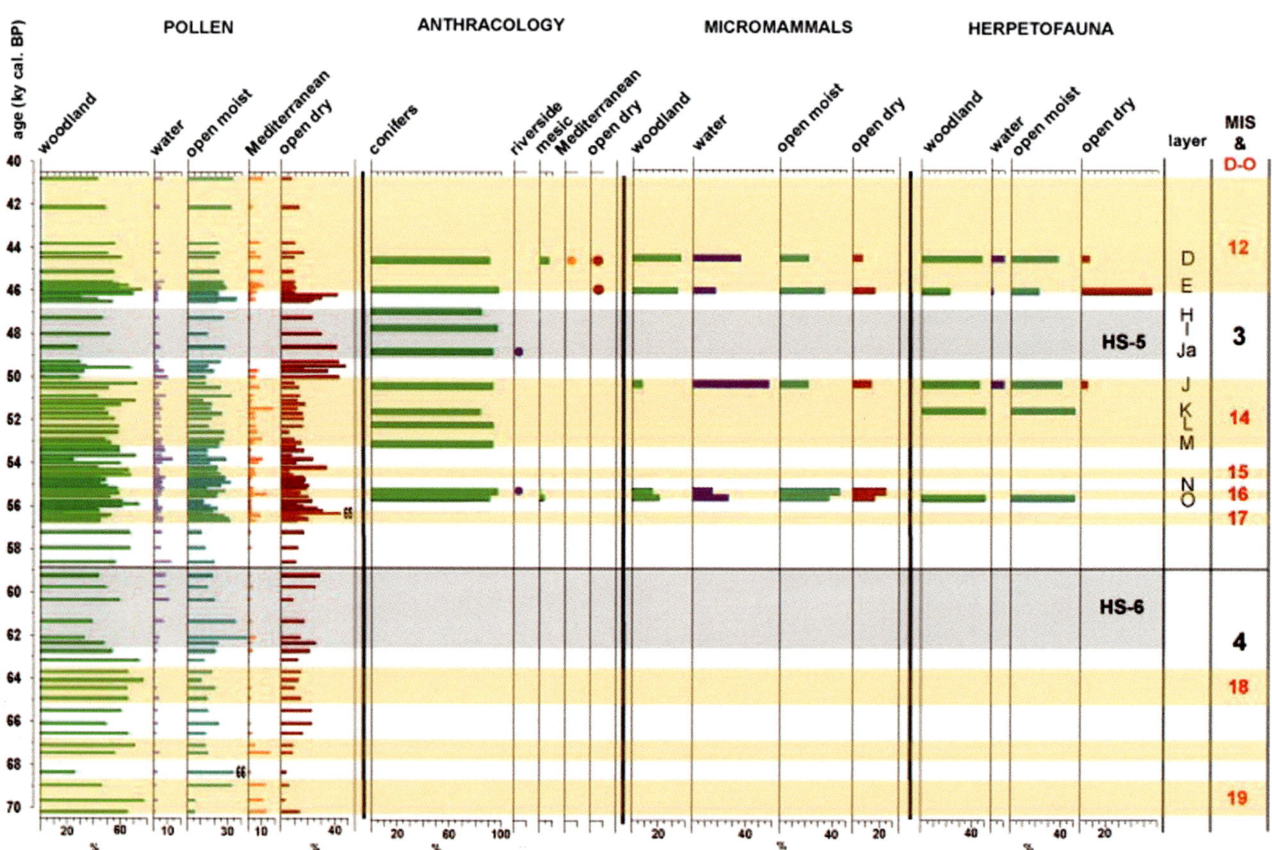

Figure 3. The biostratigraphy record of the *Abric Romaní* and the habitats identified by the disciplines dedicated to paleoenvironmental and paleoecological reconstruction.

fore the predominant category in all archaeological levels of the site. However, cores and retouched objects are scarce in the record, not reaching significant percentages in most of the archaeological levels except level O, where we documented 170 cores.

In terms of raw materials, the most used is chert, in different varieties (Fig. 4, D), followed by quartz and limestone, and there are a few in quartzite, porphyry, granite and schist. Lithic raw apcaptation is local and semi-local in a perimeter around the shelter ranging from a few hundred metres to 20 km.

Changes in the strategy for raw materials provision within the same environment are observed throughout the sequence. The clearest example is chert; this raw material is dominant throughout the sequence but the percentage changes from one archaeological level and another. In the case of level I, this raw material has very low percentages (level I = 50%) compared to the rest of the sequence. Secondly, there are levels that have significantly higher percentages (F, G, L, O), reaching values of up to 90%, and even monopolising all knapped objects, such as level H. This would reflect the ability of human groups to select the most appropriate strategy from the possible alternatives for supply raw material at any given time.

Morphotechnical analysis of the cores and knapped products has allowed the different types of operative sequences performed in the Middle Palaeolithic levels of the site to be reconstructed: tested cores left without late transformation, hierarchical centripetal cores, Levallois method (essentially recurrent centripetal), discoid method, polyhedral morphologies and fragments or flakes with some isolated retouch without any predetermined organisation or schema. The distribution of the different strategies is not homogeneous on all levels. Thus, in the upper levels (level E) there is a tendency for hierarchical strategies (Fig. 4, C). However, in the intermediary levels (levels I, J, K, L, M) there is a preference for non-hierarchical models. At lower levels O and P the existence of hierarchical strategies is identified again, with a high number of cores and knapped products that show the use of the Levallois method. In terms of the production sequences, there is an almost exclusive operating standard. Denticulate morphologies dominate in all levels, especially in the lower levels (90%) (Fig. 4, A). For this reason, after the first studies of the lithic industry, based on the liste-types, the *Abric Romani* sequence was ascribed to "Mousterian of denticulates".

Large surface excavation has allowed studies on the spatial distribution of lithic assemblages to be carried out (Fig. 4, E). These studies have permitted reconstruction of the spatial distribution of the lithic technical activities and in particular, of movement and transport of raw materials between the lithic activity areas identified within the site. The spatial dimension of the operative sequences shows an anthropic differentiation in different lithic activity areas of the living floors, particularly in the levels made of large lithic assemblages quantity, with spaces that act as convergence points for the different operating processes. By analysing the spatial distribution of the lithic remains in a large part of the sequence of *Abric Romaní* we have been able to document a very different use of the space, indicating highly complex organisation and activity area contemporaneity in the Neanderthal living floors. Secondly, these studies have also provided diachronic and synchronic data, several episodes of independent occupation being documented for the same level, which we have identified based on the recycling of artefacts.

A functional analysis of the use-wear lithic assemblage using a scanning electron microscope has been carried out on a sample of flakes and retouched objects from all archaeological levels in the sequence. The results show that the pieces in which traces of use-wear have been identified were used mainly for transforming animal biomass in butchery activities and in some isolated cases, for technical activities related to transforming vegetable remains (mainly wood).

5. The fauna

The skeletal remains of fauna are abundant throughout the sequence of *Abric Romani*. A total of 13 different taxa have been identified, although deer (*Cervus elaphus*) and horses (*Equus ferus*) are the most common animals in all levels of the stratigraphic sequence. Aurochs (*Bos primigenius*) and chamois (*Rupicapra pyrenaica*) are also present, the former in the lower part of the sequence and the latter at higher levels. The presence of specimens of rhinoceros (*Stephanorhinus hemitoechus*) has also been documented at various levels, although through few remains. At level E a femur of an unidentified proboscidea was recovered. Despite the high prominence of her-

Figure 4. Lithic industry at *Abric Romaní*. A. Chert retouched objects (denticulate tools); B. Pseudo-Levallois lithic flake in limestone; C. Bifacial centripetal cores (discoid and Levallois) in chert; D. Flake and laminar flake in chert; E. Lithic reassemblages in chert, quartz and limestone.

bivores in all levels, some carnivore remains have also been recovered (Table 1). These are most abundant in the upper part of the sequence (up to level E) where a cave environment allows the presence of these animals to be associated with the establishment of occasional dens. Apart from the natural intrusion of carnivores in levels B and O, remains of *Lynx sp.* and *Felis silvestris* have been documented, respectively, with cut marks and which are the result of the contribution and use by Neanderthals.

In terms of taphonomy, the most abundant modifications in the bone assemblage are those related to anthropic use: cut marks and fractured bones. Cremation has also been found very often but it could be related to specific deliberate activities. However, it can be said that cremation was possibly carried out using different processes ranging from preparing food to clearing the floor of the living floor. Carnivore modifications are almost absent from the faunal assemblage.

In addition to the diversity, it seems clear that deer and horses were an important part of the diet of the Neanderthals during the settlements at *Abric Romaní*. The assemblage stands out for the presence of high survival items: craniums, jaws, diaphysis fragments of long leg bones. The first studies established that this representation was due to the different ways prey was transported. According to this model, deer was transported whole and the axial skeleton of larger animals was left where it was found. Current research indicates that the selective transportation process carried out by Neanderthals was highly complex and variable in terms of anatomy and did not simply involve abandoning the axial skeleton of large animals. Thus, for example, the scarce rhinoceros remains or the single proboscidea remain in level E, seems to be the result of this decision. The low presence does not mean anything more than selective transport of the skeleton of these animals, undoubtedly related with the profitability of the contribution to the camp of one party or another.

The faunal record for the *Abric Romaní* shows that Neanderthals were active hunters and that they used complex strategies to catch and transport the carcasses of large ungulates. The low presence of carnivores and their modifications in the assemblage suggests that these animals were not much competition for the Neanderthals. These human groups also developed an intense intake of the entire carcass and combined with the use of fire, they left few items that could be a target in order to be ravaged by carnivores.

	A	B	C	D	E	F	G	H	I	J	K	L	M	N	O	P
Ursus sp.		X											X		X	
Canis lupus		X			X											X
Panthera leo spelaea									X							
Panthera pardus				X												
Lynx sp.	X	X			X											
Felis silvestris	X	X											X		X	
Crocuta crocuta	X	X			X								X			
Proboscidea indet.					X											
Stephanorhinus hemitoechus								X					X		X	
Equus ferus	X	X	X	X	X	X	X	X	X	X	X	X	X	X	X	X
Cervus elaphus	X	X	X	X	X	X	X	X	X	X	X	X	X	X	X	X
Bos primigenius					X				X	X	X	X	X	X	X	X
Rupicapra pyrenaica	X	X		X	X	X	X	X		X					X	

Table 1. Main fauna taxa in the archaeological levels of *Abric Romaní*.

Figure 5. A wood imprint located in level N. The imprint is clearly defined aswood and seems to have been modified, as it does not have any type of branch.

6. Wood imprints

The wood record at *Abric Romaní* represents a particularly unique case, as the context is a prehistoric habitat. Wood remains have been identified in all of the levels excavated in the large surface excavation (from H to P), its use for various activities being documented; as fuel, the wood imprints are documented as charred firewood on the combustion strucutres or as accumulated reserves; for structural or architectural applications (Fig. 5); for wooden objects; and for tools. The fossils are preserved under very special conditions related to the drip of water from the shelter roof. Both charred wood and imprints formed/buried very quickly by calcium carbonate precipitation.

The study of this exceptional record and the possibility of associating it with the other elements of the living floor a various large surface archaeological levels have great potential to generate new interpretations, providing information on the ways of life and social organisation of the domestic space of the Neanderthals. The methodology for studying these remains is based on analysing the morphology and stratigraphic and spatial position. The preservation of wood in the form of imprints, charred wood and charcoal allows us to interpret, for the first time, how firewood was gathered, the formats collected and how it was used.

The fuel used for household maintenance consisted mainly of Scots pine and different sizes and shapes were used. According to data provided by the characterization of the firewood in the level M, the sample from which is the largest and best studied so far, there are two fuel collection methods. Collection would be based on dead wood, therefore, that which occurs physiologically (twigs) would be collected directly, immediately and systematically with little investment and effort while larger firewood that occurs more traumatically (branches and logs) require a greater investment of effort to find and transport, which is offset by the higher performance of these items. Different patterns of fuel use have also been observed, according to the spatial distribution pattern: especially the distance between the wall of the shelter and the human occupation/s density.

7. Combustion structures

The record on fire use at the *Abric Romaní* is further evidence of the exceptional state of preservation of the archaeological assemblages and, particularly, the possibility to study archaeological structures in the record on ancient human groups like the Neanderthals. The combustion structures have been repeatedly documented in the archaeological levels excavated and their spatial documentation in a large surface excavation allows uncommon problems in the Archaeology of the Neanderthals. Use of fire is an activity that is repeated in the levels excavated in the shelter and their spatial record can be allow a comparaison analogue with the use of fire in others prehistoric and current hunter-gatherer (contemporaneous) localities. Studying the combustion structures of the *Abric Romaní* indicated the existence of a number of intra-occupational episodes in every archaeological level. The spatial distribution of the combustion structures could indicate the juxtaposition of the different activity areas around the fire use (heart related activity areas). The juxtaposition of distinct activity areas is a guide for estimating the site structure in the archaeological record (types of settlement, number of occupants, etc.).

The spatial documentation combustion strucutres in the *Abric Romaní* record supports the argument that the Neanderthals used fire for different purposes. The inventory of the combustion structure documented at *Abric Romaní* exceeds 200 and these include a range of construction techniques. The most common combustion structures (>80%) are flat and without stones. There are also flat combustion structures with stones; within concavities with carved tails; in small pits with burned stones and sediments; in re-excavated holes. In our opinion, many of these combustion structures could be considered special fire use activity areas.

The spatial distribution of most of the flat combustion structures can be described by their distance from the shelter wall according to the each archaeological level. In level I we documented combustion strucutres with accumulations of faunal and lithic remains (hearth related assemblages) without any relationship between them. However, there are 8 combustion structures connected by a few refitted lithic and faunal remains which describe a circle. The combustion structure assemblage in level J shows two modal distances from the shelter wall. One places the use of fire within 0 to 3m of the wall and the other places the combustion strucutres between 6 to 9 metres. Level N combustion strucutres has been arranged based on the principle that certain group of these combustion structures, which are one metre apart, are the inner zone of the site structure during the prehistoric settlement in the rock-shelter. This inner zone does not have any lithic or faunal remains and the combustion strucutres are less than 2 metres from the shelter wall. The other combustion structures in level N are distributed into two arches to 5 and 9 metres respectively from the inner zone of the settlement. Level O contains a large number of combustion structures. There are combustion structures in concavities with burned rocks and very few fauna remains; and combustion structures with lithic industry between 6 and 12 metres from the shelter wall. Large combustion structures are superimposed close to the shelter wall and have elementary hearths 1 metre apart and contain fauna remains and knapped lithic artefacts.

The study of micro-artefacts, microstructures and other residue from the molecular scale is relatively limited and is one of the next challenges of the *Abric Romani* research team. Another challenge for archaeological researchers is to characterise the combustion strucutres that have no lithic artefacts or fauna remains. Among the micro-remains, incorporated during the fire use determined in the *Abric Romani* combustion structure record, there are coprolites, calcium oxalate, fibre remains, pigments, etc. The thermal modification of the combustion structure sediments, based on the modification of calcite by heat and the combustion residues rich in charcoal, indicates fire use in which low temperatures are reached. Charcoal-rich sediments contain little ash. The low temperatures estimated are based on observing the size of elementary hearths too, observed in the stratigraphic sections of the combustion structures. These are charcoal lenses 20cm in diameter with a matching rubification band of the same size. This size, measured in meridional stratigraphic profiles of these elementary hearths, indicates use of fire in which fuel is limited. There are also combustion structures with large carbonaceous lenses and a rubification band of more than 40 cm but these are less common in the *Abric Romani* combustion structure record.

Josep Maria Vergès*,**, Andreu Ollé*,**

La Cansaladeta

Introduction

The site of La Cansaladeta is situated in the Roixeles canyon, a natural pass carved in the Pre-Coastal Catalan mountain range by the Francolí River, which connects the Tarragona coastal plain with the interior depression of Conca de Barberà. The archaeological deposit is located in the upper part of a fluvial terrace, approximately 45-50 metres above the river, at the foot of a small, almost dismantled rock shelter formed in the Middle Triassic limestones (*Muschelkalk* deposits) at 260 metres a.s.l.

Members of the Department of Prehistory of the URV discovered the site in 1998. In 1999 a first excavation was carried out, aimed at assessing the site's potential. Excellent results brought its integration in the research project "Paleoenvironmental evolution and prehistoric settlement in the Francolí and Gaià Rivers" in 2002 (Angelucci *et al.*, 2003, 2004). Since then archaeological fieldwork is conducted annually.

Stratigraphy

The sedimentary deposit is 16 metres thick. It is composed of a significant succession of alluvial deposits, covered by hillside deposits product of mass wasting dynamics under the influence of gravity forces. The alluvial sequence, noticeable in the fluvial terrace at 45-50 m, starts with different sized blocks and gravels transported by the river. After that, from bottom to top, there is an alternation of alluvial gravels and sands, alternating with occasional depositions of limestone blocks coming from rocky walls. The last phases of alluvial accumulation consist of sandy layers assorted with substantial blocks. A rubified paleosol is present at the end of the sedimentary cycle opening a steady phase. In the upper part, the alluvial deposit is cut by erosive processes occurring after the river bed was filled and downcut by the river. Subsequent to that, hillside deposits were piled, forming a limestone breccia in silty loamy matrix.

The archaeological material appears on the top of the alluvial accumulation, close to the limit with the foothill deposits (Fig.1). The most ancient evidences of human activity have been found at level M, where lithic assemblages were recovered in a sandy layer superimposed on a limestone breccia. However, the first traces of importance regarding human occupation have been documented at level L and K. During this period, the relative height of the site in relation to the bed river protected it from the main stream. The developed paleosol indicates Mediterranean environmental conditions. Also, at that time, the rock shelter had still preserved its brow, since that level contains cryoclastic breccia materials originally coming from that part.

These elements point to colder and wetter climate conditions, prior to the formation of the paleosol.

Afterwards, the erosive action of the river affected the rock shelter stratigraphy. Archaeological levels J and I belong to this phase. Low-energy alluvial deposits from the river flooding, and cultural layers result of human occupation during periods with no depositional processes from the watercourse, compose the sedimentary sequence.

Later, when the river started to downcut the underlying bedrock, its influence on the rock shelter sedimentation sequence gradually disappeared. After a transition phase, corresponding to level E, the predominance of colluvial hillslope materials and rocks from the wall is documented. This is observed in levels D, C, B

* IPHES, Institut Català de Paleoecologia Humana i Evolució Social, C/ Marcel·lí Domingo s/n (Edifici W3), Campus Sescelades, 43007 Tarragona, Spain

** Àrea de Prehistòria, Universitat Rovira i Virgili, Fac. de Lletres, Av. Catalunya 35, 43002 Tarragona, Spain

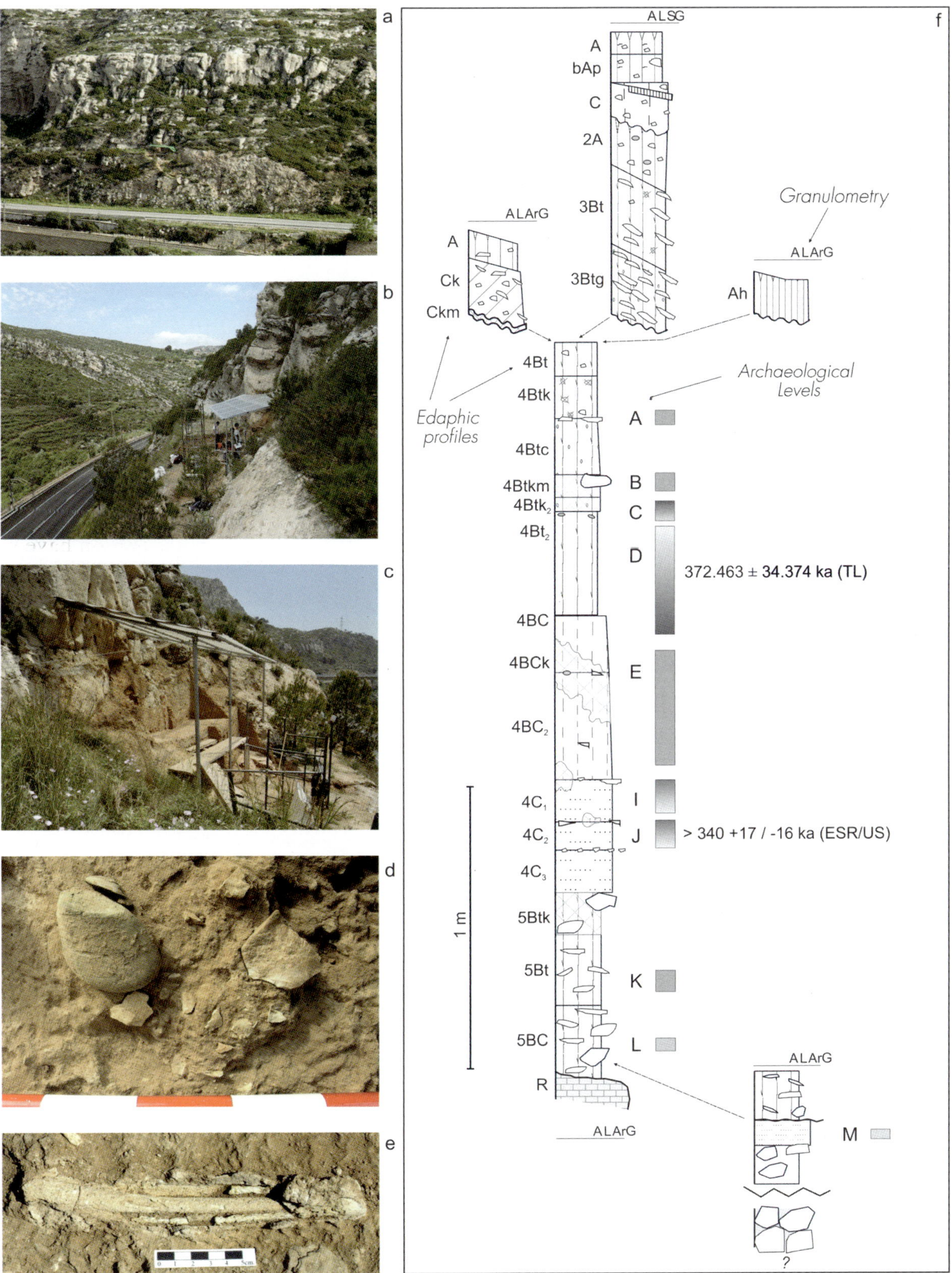

Figure 1. A. Location of La Cansaladeta site (on the centre), on the top of the fluvial terrace ±45-50 m. of the Francolí River; B and C. Overview of the excavated areas. D. Lithic assemblages in situ, level J (hornfels pebble and flint flakes); E. Altered bone, level K; F. Stratigraphic sequence (modified from Angelucci *et al.*, 2004).

and A, which compose a thick edaphological sequence, the result of a large and steady geomorphological period, probably developed in Mediterranean climate conditions.

Chronology

One of the first chronological proxies is the fluvial terrace situated on the top of the sequence that has been ascribed as Final Lower /Early Middle Pleistocene. Another key element providing a relative chronology is the presence in level L of an *Hystrix refosa* tooth, a kind of porcupine that became extinct around 500,000 years in the Iberian Peninsula (G. Cuenca, *pers. com.*). On top of that, two numerical dates are available: one ESR/US date on a rhinoceros tooth fragment from level J, that yielded a minimum age of 340,000 ± 17,000/16,000 years BP (C. Falguères, *pers. com.*); and another date by thermoluminiscence method on burnt flint form on level D, 372,000 ± 34,000 BP. Accordingly, occupations at La Cansaladeta site can be situated in a chronological span from 300,000 to 500,000 years BP (Angelucci *et al.*, 2004; Ollé *et al.*, 2008).

Archaeological record

Almost all the archaeological materials of La Cansaladeta site correspond to lithic assemblages (7575 items, 94.8% of the total), whereas faunal remains represent the remaining 5.2%. Lithic and faunal assemblages have been retrieved at 8 of the 10 archaeological levels, while the other two levels (B and A) only had lithic material.

Lithic assemblages

Raw materials employed for knapping activities can be found both in secondary position on the alluvial deposits of Francolí river at the bottom of the site where they probably were procured, and also in primary position within a minimum catchment area with a radius of 10 km.

Flint was largely the most common rock type used in around 82% of the artefacts, followed by hornfels (7.5%), quartzite (3.3%), and other rock types such as limestone, agate, granite, and lidite, with percentages lower than 1%. Flint, from Eocene deposits, appears as nodules of irregular morphology, slightly rounded by fluvial erosion, with a heterogeneous structure and abundant cracking. The rest of the raw material comes from pebbles and cobbles of fluvial origin. Its morphology, in cases such as the quartz, the quartzite and the lidite, is derived from the original geological formation, the *Buntsandstein* conglomerates.

All the raw materials, except the granite, have been used as blanks for knapping stone objects. Granite, hornfels, quartzite and limestone have been used to make hammers or anvils. The presence of all sized cores, flakes, other debitage waste-products, and some refitting, indicate that most of the *chaîne opératoire* took place at the campsite.

The lithotechnique assemblage presents a large homogeneity between levels (Fig.2). Unipolar core reduction strategy, together with orthogonal and opposed bipolar core flaking strategies, has been documented. Also centripetal core reduction has been detected, which is poorly standardised. Flint characteristics caused different knapping accidents that, in the end, have influence on the exploitation process. Likewise, the small size of quartz, quartzite, and lidite restricted the length of the lithic reduction sequence, and favoured knapping on an anvil. On the contrary, the large size and homogeneity furnish hornfels pebbles as the chosen raw material to shape large tools or flaked big blanks.

Flakes are the most abundant debitage products. Due to the above-mentioned flint characteristics, many of them have irregular morphology and present a lot of knapping accidents. Direct percussion with a hard hammer contributes to increase the knapping accidents percentage, and makes bulbs and marked scars on the core surfaces that restrict the reduction dynamics. Because of that, most of the debitage products are shaping out or preparation flakes with cortical backs.

Along the whole sedimentary succession, retouched pieces have a very low frequency, and the morphology variability is scarce. Denticulate objects dominate (notched, denticulate points, *épines* and denticulate scrapers).

Technical procedures observed at La Cansaladeta lithic assemblages make it difficult to ascribe it to a particular technological complex. Nevertheless, the presence of large tools characteristics of Mode 2 (such as cleavers, and picks) is significant, although they are sporadic and limited to the lower levels. On the other hand, reduction techniques aimed at getting debitage products with a prede-

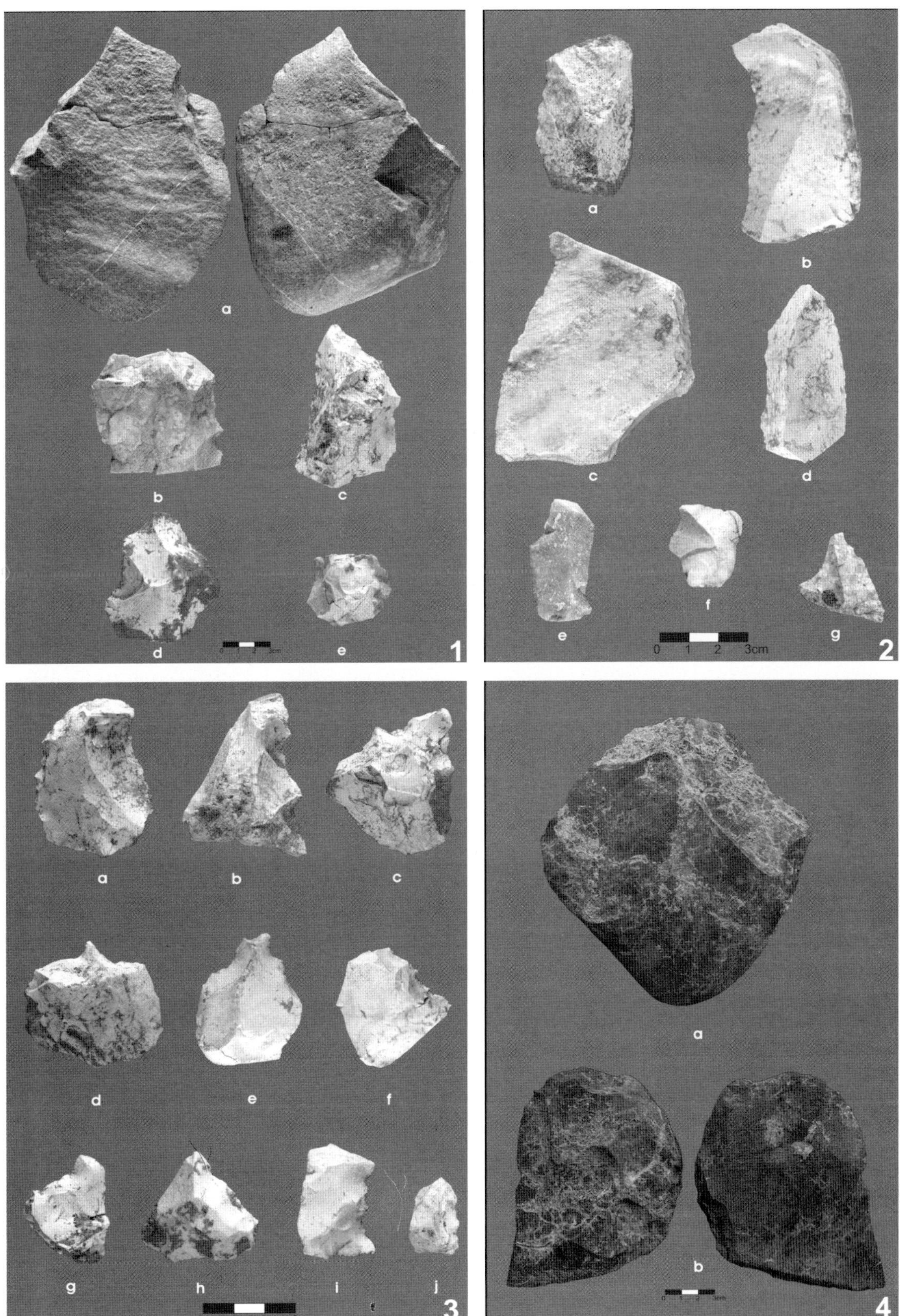

Figure 2. 1. Cores (a, from level K, hornfels; b, c, e, from level J, flint; d, from level D, flint); 2. Flakes (a,b,d, from level D; c, e, f, from level J; g, from level K; all made of flint except g, made of quartzite); 3. Retouched flint flakes (a,b,c,d, from level D; e,g,h,I, from level K; f, from level J; j, from level L); 4. Large tools on hornfels, from level J.

termined morphology (such as *Levallois*) are not documented, and retouched flakes do not show any standardized or regular configuration. Thus, the available data, broadly interprets the lithic assemblage of La Cansaladeta as Acheulean, a collection where large sized tools are clearly in the minority.

Faunal remains

Animal remains were recovered from eight levels, being levels J, K and L, those that gather the vast majority of the faunal record. The osteological collection is characterized by two main trends: the small size of the fossils, and its intense postdepositional alteration. Obviously, the assemblage represents only a small percentage of the whole animals set that might have been deposited during the occupations. This fact limits the information that archeofaunal remains can provide. Nonetheless,different taxa have been identified: *Leporidae* remains at levels I, J, K, and L; *Cervidae* bones at levels K, and L; one *Equidae*, one *Rhinocerotidae* and one fish remains at level J; as well as the above-mentioned porcupine at level L. Some of these bones present butchering cut marks and intentional breakages that have an anthropic origin.

Fire is responsible for the most common alterations in La Cansaladeta faunal assemblages (specially al levels D and L). With some exceptions, intensity of burning damage has been rather medium and did not reach maximum degrees of white calcined bones. This heat alteration has also been identified in lithic artefacts (especially at levels C and D, and to lesser extents, at levels E, J, and K), as rubified areas, fine fire cracks and thermal debris. Although no charcoal fragments or hearths were documented at the site, the amount of burned items, and their iteration along the stratigraphic sequence, suggests that they were the result of human activity rather than natural fire effects.

Fontanals, Marta **' *
Vergès, Josep Maria *' **
Morales, Juan Ignacio*

La Cativera (El Catllar, Tarragona). A Pleistocene-Holocene interface site in southern Catalonia

The Cativera archaeological site (El Catllar, Tarragona) (Fig 1), is in a small open shelter on the left bank of the Gaià River, roughly 70 m above sea level. The shelter, at the base of a Miocene calcarenite wall, is 23m wide, with a maximum height of 3 m and a current depth of at least 3 m.

Stratigraphy and chronology of occupations

The stratigraphic succession is approximately 2 m deep, divided into 8 archaeological levels, identified from base to top as A, B, Bb, C1, C2, C3, C3b and C4, the 7 geoarchaeological units distinguished on the basis of sedimentary and pedological criteria (Fig. 1). The top section, including levels A, B and Bb, consists of a calcareous breccia with a silty-loam matrix built up from fragments of the ceiling and fine sediment on the slope. The sedimentation of the middle and base part, corresponding to the rest of the archaeological levels, is originated in the cyclical alluvial processes associated with the activity of the Gaià River (Angelucci, 2003, 2005).

Charcoal sample datings are consistent with the stratigraphic sequence, and situate the site's chronocultural sequence between the final stages of the Pleistocene and the start of the Holocene

* IPHES, Institut Català de Paleoecologia Humana i Evolució Social, C/ Marcel·lí Domingo s/n (Edifici W3), Campus Sescelades, 43007 Tarragona, Spain

** Àrea de Prehistòria, Universitat Rovira i Virgili, Fac. de Lletres, Av. Catalunya 35, 43002 Tarragona, Spain

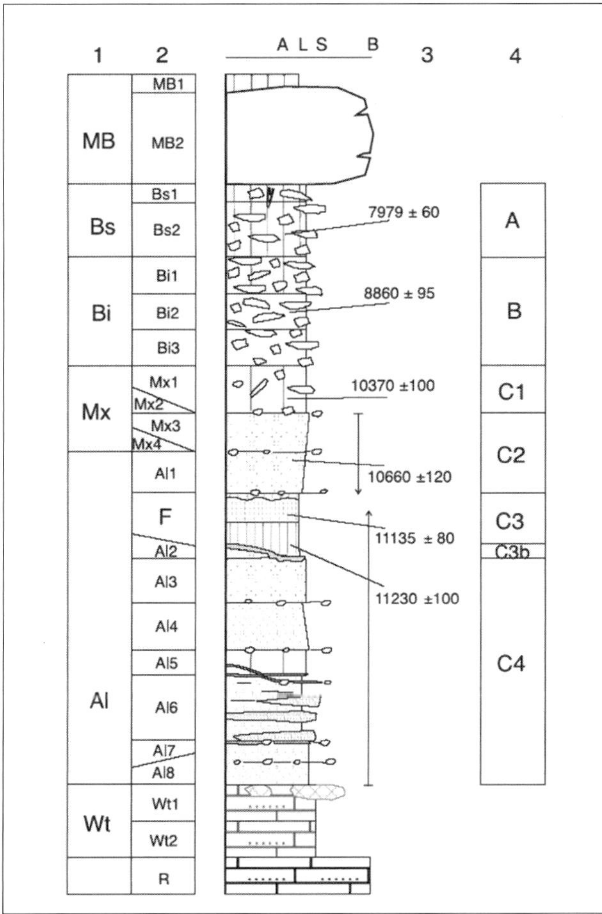

Figure 1. Frontal view of the Cativera deposit.

Level	Lab. Ref.	Material	C14 BP Data
A	MAD-4645BIN	Ceramic	4645± 316
A	AA-23367	Charcoal	7979 ± 60
B	AA-23368	Charcoal	8860 ± 95
Bb	Beta-281623	Charcoal	8230± 40
C1	AA-23369	Charcoal	10370 ± 100
C2	AA-23370	Charcoal	10660 ±120
C3	AA-23371	Charcoal	11230 ± 100
C3b	AA-23372	Charcoal	11135 ± 80

Table 1. La Cativera site datings.

Archaeological material

The archaeological items found on all levels consist of lithic industry, iron oxides –not documented on level A–, marine and terrestrial malacofauna, charcoal, fauna and mobile art on level C4. However, there are significant typological differences between the material on level A and the rest of the archaeological levels. The flint and limestone lithic material is by far the most abundant on the levels, although the latter material is in a much smaller proportion. Flint is only involved in the tool production and configuration sequences, while limestone is functionalized directly, without modification. Despite this homogeneity in the use of raw materials through the levels, Level A is predominated typologically by notches and denticulates, and thus referred to as configured items with simple reduction sequences intended for flakes (Fontanals *et al.*, 2009), while in the rest of the sequence, the exploitation systems are predominantly aimed at producing blade-like products, the majority of which were endscrapers and blade/backed blades (Morales *et al.*, 2012, 2013). This profile seems to indicate that in all the occupations, the raw materials were supplied from the terraces of the Gaià River, quite close to the settlement. This source was abundant but generally did not provide good quality material. The average length of the items was never more than 15 cm, and less than 10 cm in the case of good knapping material (Fontanals 2001). Abundant remains of marine mollusc fauna were found at the site, no doubt influenced by its proximity to the coast. To date, 18 different species have been documented. This variation is particularly broad on levels B and Bb, where specimens were clearly used for at least three differentiated purposes: consumption (*Mytilus galloprovincialis* and *Patella caerulea*), ornaments (*Dentalium vulgare* and *Cyclope sp.*) and as a container for ochre (*Glycimeris insubrica* and *violascens*). This differentiated use of marine mollusc fauna is less obvious on level A, where the documented species, judging by their features, seem to have been brought to the site for consumption, as indicated by the presence of *Patella caerulea* and *Cerasthoderma glaucum*, the latter quite abundant, unlike level B, although other secondary uses must not be excluded, as in the case of *Pecten jacobeus* and *Insubrica Glycimeris*, despite the absence in this case of traces of ochre inside the valves found in assemblage B. Items from several species of terrestrial mollusc fauna have also been documented. On level C3, 21 *Cepaea nemoralis* shells suggest the use of this species as a food source.

The faunal record is quite scarce on all levels and the recovered remains are poorly preserved. This is probably due to the high acidity of the sediment in the rock-shelter and post-depositional taphonomic disturbances to the archaeological remains, mainly caused by roots (Allué et *al.*, 2000). Nevertheless, various skeletal parts of *Leporiade* and *Cervidae* taxa were identified on levels A, B and Bb. Despite the above-mentioned bias in the record due to poor preservation, the number of *Leporidae* items is clearly much higher than others, permitting the assumption of its priority for consumption. Remains of burned wood fuel have been recovered throughout the sequence, although the sample is only representative on the levels excavated horizontally. Several species have been identified, many of them common to levels A, B and Bb, such as *Pinus sp, Pinus alepensis, Juniperus and* Quercus *ilex/coccifera*. Their differing degrees of presence on each level and the presence/absence of other species, such as the presence of *Acer sp* on level A alone and the abundance of conifers and *Juniperus sp* on levels B, Bb and C1, are proof of climate variations between the different occupation periods.

Different evidence of the use and processing of iron oxide has been documented in these series, with the exception of level A. Fragments of this mineral have been found, mostly burned or impregnated in the surface of different species of marine mollusc fauna, a considerable number of endscrapers and some natural limestone blocks. It also appears in patches in the sediment. The use of this mineral has also been detected on level C4, where remains of staining material concentrated in the centre of a limestone pebble has been identified, with a set of straight and curved red lines connected physically.

Conclusions

The chrono-cultural sequence in the Cativera rock shelter has provided reference data for the study of the cultural processes between the Late Glacial and the early Holocene in north-eastern Iberia. This period has been subject to reinterpretation since the emergence of new archaeological records which, in conjunction with the revision of existing assemblages and datings, permits the construction of a scenario in which the apparent persistence of micro-blade techno-complexes until the start of the Holocene overlaps with the few sauveterroid records, coinciding with the Pleistocene-Holocene transition and an increasingly numerous and better defined sets of notches and denticulates, evidence of a clear temporal and cultural break. The background to this cultural and chronological discontinuity can only be interpreted with new archaeological data and their social, economic and demographic interpretation.

Manuel Vaquero *,**, E. Susana Alonso Fernández **, Ethel Allué **, James L. Bischoff***, Francesc Burjachs**,****, Josep Vallverdú**

Cinglera del Capelló sites (Capellades, Barcelona)

Cinglera del Capelló is a 1.5 km long travertine scarp on the right bank of the Anoia River, Capellades, Anoia District, Barcelona Province. At this point, the Anoia River cuts through Catalonia's pre-coastal mountain range in a gorge (Capellades Narrows), a natural link between the inland districts of the Ebro Depression and the Catalonian Pre-Coastal Depression. There are

* Àrea de Prehistòria, Universitat Rovira i Virgili, Avinguda Catalunya 35, 43002 Tarragona
** Institut Català de Paleoecologia Humana i Evolució Social (IPHES), Escorxador s/n, 43003 Tarragona
*** US Geological Survey, ms/470, 345 Middlefield Rd, Menlo Park CA 94025
**** Institució Catalana de Recerca i Estudis Avançats (ICREA), Barcelona

several rock shelters in the travertine wall, many of which contain evidence of prehistoric occupation. Most of these sites were first discovered and excavated by Amador Romaní in the early 20th century (Bartrolí *et al.*, 1995). Many only contain material from late prehistory, but in some cases, documented sequences contain Palaeolithic and Mesolithic occupation levels. The latter are the focus of the *Abric Romaní-Cingles del Capelló* research project, begun in 1983 and still in progress. The most important of these sites is undoubtedly Abric Romaní, the subject of another article in this volume and therefore not discussed here. This paper presents three other shelters in the *Cinglera* area which have been excavated in recent years: Balma dels Pinyons, Balma de la Costa de Can Manel and Abric Agut (Fig. 1). The sequences documented at these sites mainly cover the second half of the Upper Pleistocene and the start of the Holocene. They provide information about the occupation of *Cinglera* during the Upper Palaeolithic and Mesolithic, thus complementing the *Abric Romaní* stratigraphy and permitting the reconstruction of the sequence of environmental and cultural changes for the period from 100 to 7 ky BP, i.e., from the bottom of Romaní to the top of Agut (Bartrolí *et al.*, 2008, Vaquero *et al.*, 2013.).

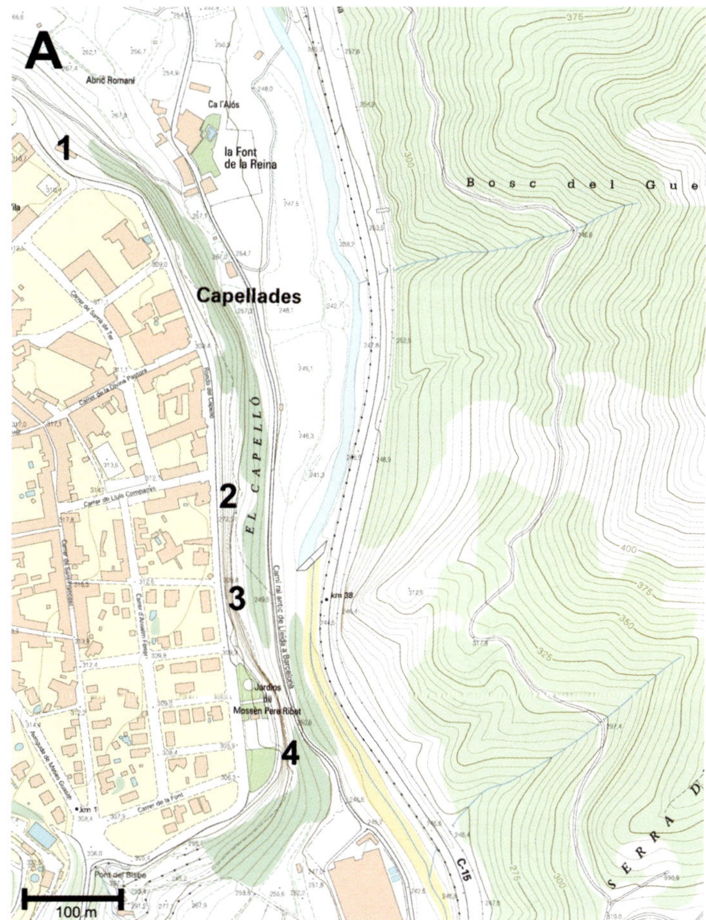

Figure 1. Location of Cinglera Capelló sites (A) and overview of Cinglera (B). 1. Abric Romaní, 2. Balma dels Pinyons, 3. Abric Agut, 4.Balma de la Costa de Can Manel.

1. Balma del Pinyons

This site was discovered by Amador Romaní. In 1905 he carried out the first excavation, only at the top of the sequence, and identified an archaeological level with several stone items. Between 2000 and 2001, a 3 x 2 m test pit (Vaquero, 2004) documented a sequence at least 6 m deep, dated by several methods (U/Th, luminescence, C^{14} AMS) at between ca. 52 ky BP and the start of the Holocene (Table 1-3).

The stratigraphic sequence includes sedimentary deposits which are not linked to their formation by precipitation of water-borne calcium carbonate. These levels indicate quite different conditions from the predominant climate in the sequences found in the majority of the Cinglera sites. The following units have been distinguished, listed in an upward sequence (Fig. 2):

- Unit 7 (2 m). Succession of layers of travertine with a dome morphology, interstratified with sands and gravels.
- Unit 6 (0.5 m). Red silty sands. Contains archaeological level C, dated at 43,185 to 41,745 cal BP.
- Unit 5 (0.8 m). Poorly stratified travertine, gravel and sand.

Site	Lab. Cod.	Stratigraphic level	U ppm	$^{234}U/^{238}U$	$^{230}Th/^{232}Th$	BP date years	BP date years corrected
Agut	00-43	4.4	0.84	2.90	15	7731 ± 370	
Agut	00-51	4.4	1.00	2.27	17	9376 ± 453	
Agut	00-50	4.6	0.98	2.42	16	9875 ± 390	
Agut	00-113	4.6	0.90	2.59	30	10863 ± 326	
Agut	00-263	4.6	1.2	2.48	9	10905 ± 375	9995 ± 650
Agut	01-135	4.8	1.41	2.68	3	14274 ± 200	11064 ± 1480
Agut	00-63	4.8	1.93	1.76	11	13633 ± 527	12672 ± 1200
Can Manel	01-136	1	1.3	2.85	40	12700 ± 160	
Can Manel	01-134	1	0.6	2.71	3	11900 ± 1600	
Can Manel	00-262	2	1.1	2.62	4	13600 ± 700	
Can Manel	07-20	5	0.55	2.44	17	33742 ± 260	
Can Manel	07-8	6	0.7	2.37	46	35954 ± 239	
Can Manel	07-7	Base	0.6	2.33	7.6	39388 ± 264	
Pinyons	00-259	1	0.9	2.37	228	8800 ± 600	
Pinyons	00-258	1	0.6	2.87	4	9000 ± 2000	
Pinyons	00-257	5	1.0	2.15	143	32800 ± 1000	
Pinyons	02-15	7	1.7	2.29	96	48100 ± 1300	
Pinyons	02-16	7	0.8	2.26	35	52700 ± 1900	

Table 1. Uranium series dating of travertine samples from Agut, Can Manel and Pinyons.

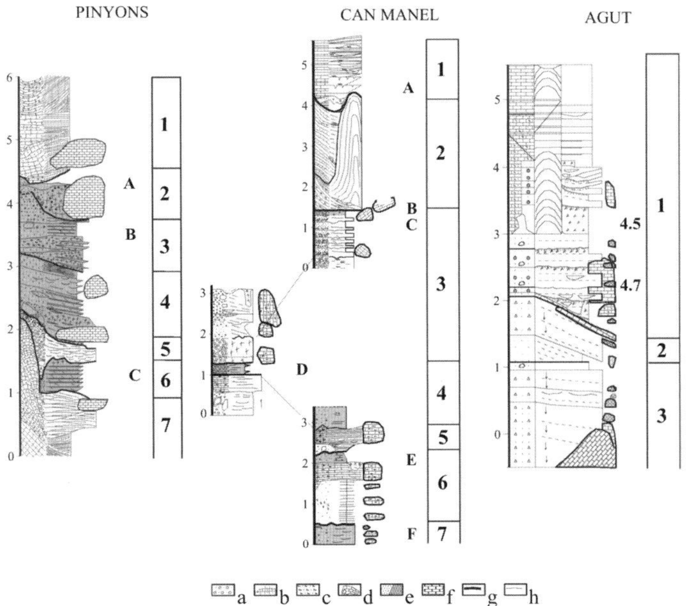

Figure 2. Lithostratigraphic columns in Pinyons, Can Manel and Agut, showing stratigraphic units described in the text and the archaeological levels. a. Travertine, conglomerates and carbonate sands; b. Bryophyte bioconstruction; c. Travertine and angular gravel; d. Algal laminated travertine; e. Red sands and silts; f. Stalagmitic dome; g. Boundary surfaces; h. Unit limits.

- Unit 4 (0.8 m). Red silty sands, carbonate sands, gravels and blocks.
- Unit 3 (1.2 m). Poorly stratified red silty sands, carbonate sands and weathered gravels. Includes archaeological level B.
- Unit 2 (0.4 m). Red silty sands and fallen blocks. Archaeological level A is at the top. Unit 1 (1.7 m). Laminated and stratified travertine.

In this sequence, three horizons with evidence of human occupation have been identified, although their archaeological content is quite poor in general and composed exclusively of lithic artifacts and charcoal. The bone record has not been preserved. Level A corresponds to the description by Amador Romaní at the top of the site, immediately below the early Holocene travertine. The excavated area was almost completely plundered by clandestine diggers, and only a few isolated items were recovered. The second archaeological level (level B) was identified at the top of unit 3. It yielded a small assemblage of lithic remains, with evidence of an *in situ* knapping sequence, although some of the material seemed to be in a secondary position. The lack of diagnostic elements precludes an accurate chronocultural estimate beyond its attribution to the Upper Palaeolithic on the basis of a few blade elements and the radiometric data. There is somewhat more abundant material on level C, whose technological and dating features suggest its attribution to the Middle Palaeolithic. In any case, the available data indicate quite sporadic and ephemeral human occupations throughout the sequence.

2. Balma de la Costa de Can Manel

Unlike most Cinglera sites, this shelter was not documented by Amador Romaní. It was discovered as a consequence of the new Capellades Archaeological Park. Excavations between 2003 and 2006 consisted an 18 m^2 survey which yielded a stratigraphic sequence at least 9 m deep. As in the case of Pinyons, this survey did not reach the base of the site. U/Th and 14C AMS dating indicate that this sequence lies between *ca.* 12 and *ca.* 39 ky BP (Table 1 and 3). The following stratigraphic units were differentiated (Fig. 2) :

- Unit 7. Poorly stratified red silty sands lying directly above a dome-shaped travertine layer. Includes archaeological level F.
- Unit 6 (1.5 m). Carbonated micro-stratified sands, travertine with fallen blocks and red silty sands. Includes archaeological level E, with two AMS 14C dates, between 29,805 and 31,485 cal BP.
- Unit 5 (0.5-1 m). Stratified carbonate sands and gravels with blocks and travertine blocks.
- Unit 4 (0.4 m). Stratified carbonate sands and gravels with red silty sand. Includes archaeological level D, dated at 18,645 to 18,050 cal BP.
- Unit 3 (2.5 m). Poorly stratified gravels, carbonate sands and well stratified blocks and gravels, carbonate sands and travertine with blocks. The top section contains a micro-stratified layer of red sands with blocks in which archaeological units B-C were found, with two AMS 14C dates which define a chronological range span from 13,940 to 14,880 cal BP.
- Unit 2 (2.5 m). Set of dome-shaped travertine layers.
- Unit 1 (1.5 m). Carbonate sands interrupted by a palaeosol rich in organic microaggregates. The upper part consists of a set of well-stratified travertine layers. Includes archaeological level A.

Site	*Stratigraphic level*	*Lab. Cod.*	*Date BP years*	*Material*
Pinyons	3	MAD- 4600R.SDA	(OSL) 19962 ± 1402	Sandy sediment
Pinyons	4	MAD- 4599BIN	(TL) 23702 ± 1591	Brunt sandy sediment

Table 2. Optically stimulated luminescence (OSL) and thermoluminescence dating of sediment samples from stratigraphic units 3 and 4, Balma dels Pinyons.

Six archaeological units (A-F) have been identified in this sequence. However, with the exception of levels B-C, the number of items tends to be small and composed almost entirely of lithic remains. As in Balma dels Pinyons, faunal remains were not preserved in most of the archaeological units, with some exceptions such as sea shell fragments (Fig. 3.2).

Level A was identified as a result of a stratigraphic analysis in one unexcavated sector of the site, and thus did not provide any information. The lithic assemblage on levels B-C is relatively abundant and is partly consistent with the radiometric data suggesting its attribution to the Upper Magdalenian, with the presence of sidescrapers, burins and denticulates in the retouched assem-

Figure 3. Archaeological remains found at Balma de la Costa de Can Manel. 1. Flint bladelets from level F. 2. Fragments of seashells from level E.

blage. However, other features of the industry such as a near-complete lack of laminar knapping methods are unusual in an Upper Palaeolithic assemblage. Level D, with an early Magdalenian chronology, has not yielded any evidence to clarify its cultural attributes, although laminar knapping is better documented here than in the upper units. Finally, U/Th and 14C AMS dates attribute the two lowest levels to different periods of the Early Upper Palaeolithic. However, the lack of diagnostic elements in this case also prevents a more accurate chronocultural identification (Fig. 3.1).

3. Abric Agut

The history of archaeological work at this site dates back to 1910 when Amador Romaní conducted the first excavations (Vidal, 1911-1912), followed by a second dig soon afterwards, in 1914. On the basis of this early work, it was attributed to the Mousterian, maintained despite subsequent excavations and reviews of the material by several experts. In the 1950's, E. Ripoll and H. Lumley (1964-1965) carried out a short excavation at the site and attributed its lithic industry to a Denticulate Mousterian, similar to that documented at the nearby Abric Romaní site. Meanwhile, the human teeth found during excavations by Amador Romaní were, upon analysis, considered typically Neanderthal (De Lumley, 1973).

The results of a new excavation in 1976 headed by L. Freeman, E. Ripoll and H. Lumley did not change the previous assessments, although they did highlight unusual data for the Middle Palaeolithic contexts such as the abundance of rabbit in the faunal record (González Echegaray and Freeman, 1998). Under the *Abric Romaní-Cingles del Capelló* project, in 1985 a test pit was dug in the eastern sector of the site, which did not bring to light anything new with respect to what was previously known. None of this work led to the questioning of the Middle Palaeolithic adscription of this site, most of which had been excavated by 1999. Only one sector at the southern end of the shelter was left to dig, which in any case did not contain the entire original stratigraphic sequence, as the upper levels had only appeared in the northern half of the site, excavated entirely by Amador Romaní. The results of the work between 1999 and 2001 permitted a reinterpretation of the archaeological sequence in this shelter. This work focused on a roughly 35 m^2 area at the SW edge of the site (Fig. 4). The deposit, approx. 3.7 m deep, was divided into three main units, from bottom to top (Vaquero *et al.*, 2013.):

- Unit 3 (1.3 m.). Stratified gravels, carbonate sands and blocks above basal fallen blocks.
- Unit 2 (1 m.). Stratified carbonate sands and gravels with fallen blocks up to the top.

Figure 4. Overview of excavated area in Abric Agut during the 1999 dig.

- Unit 1 (3 m.). Travertine, gravel, carbonate sands and organic-rich lutites with dome-shaped travertine at the top. All of the archaeological units (4.5, 4.7a, 4.7b and 4.7c) are in this unit.

Uranium-Thorium and 14C AMS dates (Tables 1 and 3) indicate that the chronology of the archaeological levels is between 10,200 and 11,600 cal BP (Vaquero *et al.*, 2002), thus refuting the site's previous attribution to the Middle Palaeolithic. In addition to the consistency of the radiometric data, other aspects of the archaeological record support its attribution to a quite different context from the Middle Palaeolithic.

On the one hand, the charcoal record is quite different from the Middle Palaeolithic material documented in Abric Romaní (Allué, 2002). In Abric Romaní, pine is virtually the only identified species throughout the entire sequence, while the charcoal at Abric Agut corresponds to a wide variety of taxa. The taxa identified in the three analyzed archaeological units were: on level 4.5, *Acer, Populus/Salix, Prunus, Rhamnus cathartica/saxatilis* and *Sambucus;* on level 4.7b, *Juniperus, Acer, Populus/Salix, Prunus, Rhamnus cathartica/saxatilis*, and on level 4.7c, *Juniperus, Acer, Hedera, Populus/Salix, Prunus, Rosaceae/ Maloideae, Rhamnus cathartica/ saxatilis, Rhamnus cf. pumila* and *Sambucus*. The absence of pine is particularly noteworthy as this taxon was detected in the pollen analysis and is virtually the only species documented in the anthracological record from previous periods at other Cinglera del Capelló sites. This may be related to a significant increase in moisture. The presence of *Juniperus* at the base levels, especially

Site	*Stratigraphic level*	*Acheological level*	*Ref. Lab.*	*BP radiocarbonic data years*	*Years data Cal BP*	*Material*
Agut	1	4.7a	OxA-10049	9185 ± 60	10500 –10235	Charcoal
Agut	1	4.7a	OxA-10064	9660 ± 110	11250 –10700	Charcoal
Agut	1	4.7c	OxA-10050	10085 ± 60	11975 –11355	Charcoal
Agut	1	4.7c	OxA-10051	9895 ± 60	11600 –11200	Charcoal
Agut	1	4.7c	OxA-10074	10060 ± 65	11960 –11315	Charcoal
Can Manel	3	C	Beta-184712	12300 ± 60	14880 –13960	Charcoal
Can Manel	3	C2	Beta-184713	12290 ± 60	14875 –13940	Charcoal
Can Manel	4	D	Beta-198058	15190 ± 60	18645 –18050	Charcoal
Can Manel	6	E	Beta-209792	25700 ± 220	31045 –29805	Charcoal
Can Manel	6	Eb	Beta-209793	26770 ± 240	31485 –30950	Charcoal
Can Manel	6	Fsup	Beta-221914	29420 ± 250	34655 –33380	Charcoal
Pinyons	6	C	OxA-11249	37900 ± 500	43185 –41745	Charcoal

Table 3. 14C AMS datings for Agut, Can Manel and Pinyons. Stuiver *et al.*, (2000) was followed for the 2σ calibration.

in 4.7c, could be related to its tendency to colonize open space. This taxon tends to disappear at higher levels, giving way to deciduous species.

Anthracological analysis showed some differences from the pollen data (Vaquero *et al.*, 2006 and 2013), with quite similar results for the three sublevels of unit 4.7, characterized by the presence of Mediterranean and deciduous taxa along with riparian arboreal taxa, indicative of moist conditions. The identified arboreal taxa were *Pinus, Juniperus, Quercus ilex*, deciduous *Quercus, Corylus, Ulmus* and *Salix*. An increase in shrub species (*cf. Erica, Buxus, Phillyrea, Rhamnus*) was also detected, as well as an increase in *Asteraceae* and *Chenopodiaceae*. In archaeologically sterile unit 4.6, there is a degree of deterioration of the thermo-mesophylous tree layer and an increase in conifers. Mountain taxa such as *Betula* and *Abies* appear, with locally persistent forests of pine, holm oak and deciduous oak along with hazel, elm and willow. The herbaceous vegetation suggests meadows of grasses, Asteraceae and sagebrush. Finally, unit 4.5 shows cold conditions in which the thermomesophylous taxa are scarce and the forests are primarily pines.

The faunal associations differ from the usual in Mousterian sites. Rabbit (*Oryctolagus cuniculus*) is the most widely represented animal in all the archaeological units, quite common at Mesolithic sites on the Mediterranean side of the Iberian Peninsula. No cut marks were found on the rabbit bones, but the high percentage of burnt items and breakage patterns point to humans as the main agent responsible for the formation of the assemblages (Ibáñez, 2005). Other identified faunal taxa were *Cervus elaphus, Capra pyrenaica, Canis lupus* and two turtles of an undetermined species. Several species of birds were documented, including *Alectoris sp., Nucifraga caryocatactes, Pyrrhocorax sp.* and *Tyto alba*.

The lithic assemblages are characterized by the predominance of flint (70-80%), followed by limestone (10% to 20%) and much more occasionally, other materials such as quartz, sandstone, granite and porphyry. While flint was only identified in reduction and configuration sequences of tools on flake, the rest of the material is largely associated with the introduction of cobbles used as hammerstones or crushers, without any intentional modification. However, reduction sequences on limestone and granite are also documented. Limestone was used exclusively to shape pebble tools. This raw material usage pattern does not necessarily reflect the type of material available in the immediate environment, as flint is scarce around the site, and significant concentrations are only found 5 km away in the Anoia alluvial formations, north of Capellades. The rest of the raw materials are strictly local, especially limestone, which

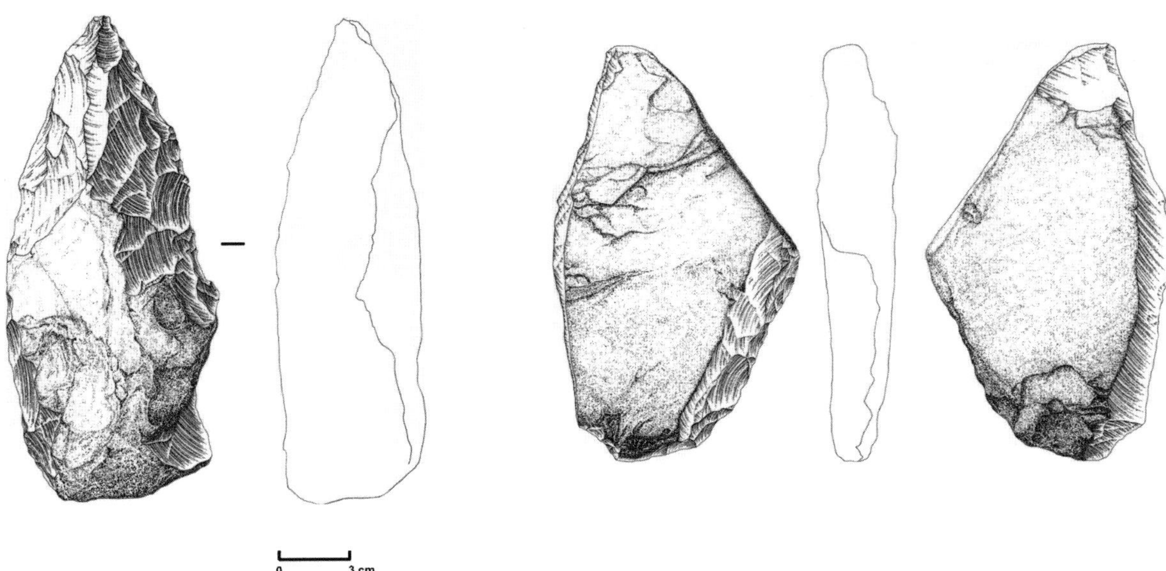

Figure 5. Large format items on cobble from Abric Agut level 4.7.

is abundant in the alluvial deposits at the foot of the site. The scarcity of quartz is also curious, given that outcrops of this raw material are close to shelter and could be easily collected from the alluvial deposits and the hillside nearby. These supply strategies are similar to those documented at the nearby Middle Palaeolithic Abric Romaní site.

The exploitation methods seem to have been aimed at systematic flake production. No evidence has been found to suggest blade-like strategies. Indeed, blade cores are completely lacking and the proportion of blades is very small (barely 3%). Core analysis shows a predominance of bifacial centripetal methods, including strategies that do not involve a hierarchy of flaking surfaces (in the line of the discoidal knapping) and those based on the definition of a preferential flaking surface. The latter fits perfectly in the Levallois knapping context. The cores are generally very small, suggesting maximised exploitation of their potential. The distribution of the tools into typological groups shows that more than half of them are denticulates. Within this group there is a balanced representation of notches and denticulates, although the former are more numerous. There is a significant presence of worked cobbles, almost all shaped by unifacial removal, including a pick found on level 4.7c (Fig. 5). The rest of the identified typological groups (retouched flakes, sidescrapers, endscrapers, borers and items with flat retouch) are only occasional. There is a particularly significant lack of typical Upper Palaeolithic artefacts. However, a comparative study of the Mesolithic denticulates from Abric Agut and from the Middle Palaeolithic at the Abric Romaní site suggests some differences between the two sets, with a few technical features that characterize the Mesolithic denticulates (Vaquero, 2006) such as inverse removals in a large percentage of the items and a tendency to configure distal trihedrons. The "Middle Palaeolithic" aspect of this industry explains its initial definition when radiometric dating was not available.

It is important to note the presence of fire-related structures on level 4.5 and also in the units of level 4.7. The record is better preserved on level 4.5, which a considerable number of refits generally characterized by short connection distances. The units in level 4.7 underwent more disturbances due to water flow dynamics. Items bearing signs of water abrasion or covered with carbonated concretions are much more abundant. There is also a slight under-representation of small tools. These disturbances seem to be more frequent in the areas furthest from the shelter wall. However, the discovery of refits on these units as well and the preservation of fire-related structures suggest that the original spatial relationships were not completely distorted by post-depositional disturbances.

The palaeoenvironmental, technological and subsistence data at hand show that the chronology and culture of this site does not correspond to the Middle Palaeolithic as previously claimed, and must lie within the framework of the macrolithic industries characterized by a predominance of denticulates. These assemblages, grouped as Mesolithic macrolithic or Mesolithic of notches and denticulates, are frequent in the early Holocene sequences on the Mediterranean side of the Iberian Peninsula, and bear a resemblance to a trend found elsewhere, such as the Cantabrian coast, southern France and Portugal. In the northeast quadrant of the Peninsula alone, this macrolitic context embraces several assemblages including level C at Balma Guilanyà (Casanova and Pizarro, 2004), level 4 at Balma Margineda (Guilaine *et al.*, 1995), level A at Cativera (Allué *et al.*, 2000), levels SG and ASG at Font del Ros (Pallares *et al.*, 1997), level II at Roc de Migdia (Yll *et al.*, 1994), level 10 at Sota Palou (C.R.P.E.S., 1985), level 2 at Cova del Filador (García– Argüelles *et al.*, 2002) and level Sup at Molí del Salt (Vaquero *et al.*, 2004). The recurrence of this macrolithic episode across a wide geographical area and its chronological coherence suggests that it was not a short-term phenomenon linked to the functions of the occupations or the availability of raw materials. On the contrary, it seems to be a well-defined stage in the cultural sequence at the start of the Holocene.

Julià Maroto*

Localities of Reclau

Localities of Reclau

Geographic location

Localities of Reclau are located in the municipality of Serinyà, in the Pla de l'Estany district (province of Girona), to the northeast of Catalonia and the Iberian Peninsula.

It is 4 km north of Banyoles and 1 km south of the village of Serinyà, on the eastern side of the C-66 motorway. It forms part of the right bank of the Serinyadell stream and the travertine ledge, with the site located approximately 60 m to the east of the motorway. Localities of Reclau are currently part of the Parc de les Coves Prehistòriques de Serinyà (Fig. 1).

Geological location

The Reclau prehistoric caves are located in the lacustrine zone of Banyoles. This unit is defined as a moderately depressed sector in the central section of the province of Girona. It is located in a strip that marks the point of contact between two clearly distinct units of relief: the Catalonian Transversal System and the Empordà Depression.

However, despite the abundance of plio-quaternary lacustrine materials in the area, the travertines on which the Reclau caves are located are not lacustrine and consist of carbon deposits characteristic of rivers or springs, known as cascade travertines (Julià, 1980; Brusi *et al.*, 2005).

Localities of Reclau are located on the western edge of the Usall plain. This is an almost horizontal structural plain that extends between the Fluvià River to the north and the basin of the Banyoles Lake to the south. It is oriented north-south and measures approximately 5 km long by 3 km wide. To the west, it borders on the end of the Eocene relief of the Transversal Catalonian Range; to

* Àrea de Prehistòria, Universitat de Girona, pl. Ferrater Mora, 1, 17071 Girona. julia.maroto@udg.edu

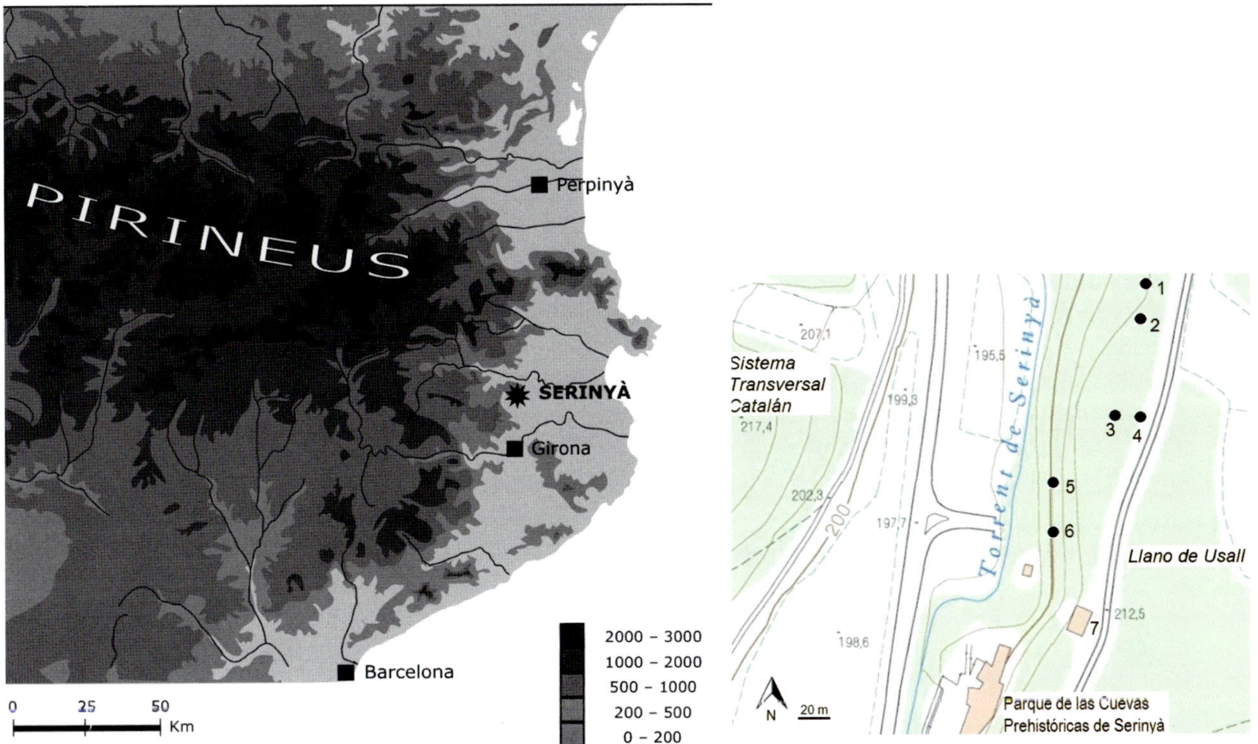

Figure 1. Geographic location of Serinyà and the Reclau caves. 1: Reclau Viver; 2: Pau; 3: Cau del Roure; 4: Outer Zone of Cau del Roure; 5: Mollet; 6: Mollet III; 7: Arbreda.

the east on a system of mounds and plains from the Pliocene, which form part of the Empordá Depression. The Usall plain is formed of a Plio-quaternary lacustrine limestone, covered by fersialithic clay soil (*terra rossa*).

Description

Localities of Reclau are actually complex cascade travertine structures whose morphology forms caves, and that have in turn undergone karstification (Brusi *et al.*, 2002, 2005).

On the western edge of the cave site, crossing from south to north, is the Serinyadell, a tributary of the Ser River. The caves are located on the western edge of the Usall plain. This sector, is significantly affected by the river channelling of the Serinyadell; during the end of the Middle Pleistocene this stream of bicarbonate-rich water (today the Musoga stream), which originated from a spring in the Usall plain, leveraged this ideal topographical feature to build cascade travertine deposits.

The rapid evolution of this flow of water created a travertinization front that is very simple as a whole, but highly complex in its detailed geometry. The travertine cascade facies on one side, which are continuously modified by the processes of erosion and by the migration of the active flow, resulted in the combination of different deposit and erosive morphologies. The general growth of the different morphologies built a ledge that sheltered a series of cavities at its base that were of sufficient size to facilitate human occupation. However, these cavities and the high degree of porosity of the cascade facies, also represented a new element of complexity in the evolution of the deposit, because the hollows allowed the development of brechoid facies, terrigenous fill, and also the formation of interior castings of travertinization that evolved in the opposite direction from the exterior slope of the structure. Likewise, the processes of karstification, secondary travertinization, and later recrystalization of conduits and cracks were common (Brusi *et al.*, 2005).

The travertinization process took place at least between 215,000 and 134,000 years ago (Maroto *et al.*, 2012).

Today, the caves are practically filled and a significant percentage of their original roofs have collapsed. For this reason, the current morphology of the caves is quite different from their original shape. Only the Reclau Viver cave conserves part of its primitive morphology and shows us what it would have been like during the first human occupation.

The fill of the Reclau caves is essentially detritic and is made up of clay, silt, or sand with varying granulometry and percentages, frequently accompanied by travertine blocks and pebbles, often in abundance, from the walls and ceilings of the cavities. In the case of some of the bases, as in layer 1 of the Mollet cave, the deposits were the result of precipitation of the calcium carbonate, which is the same process that was responsible for the formation of the site itself.

The main caves of the site are arranged along a travertine cliff approximately 200 m long, 50 m wide, and with an elevation of slightly more than 10 metres (Fig. 1). The Arbreda, Reclau Viver and Mollet caves are the sites that have been conditioned to allow visitation, and are also the ones that have been excavated most extensively. Excavation has recently been resumed in the Cau del Roure and Mollet III caves, and the same is planned for the Pau cave within the next few years. Another cave has a more modest archaeological record: the Arbreda II cave. Lastly, another eight caves are sterile or almost sterile (Soler *et al.*, 2001).

There are two clearly distinct types of vegetation at the site. Mediterranean holm oak predominates on the very rocky travertine slop, also with some oak and parasol pines. There is a gallery forest beside the Serinyadell, made up mainly of ash, poplar, aspen, willow, and elm. Between these two is a very moist meadow with rushes, mint, and wild violets (Soler *et al.*, 2001).

History of archaeological studies

In the 1940s, Josep M. Corominas began the archaeological study of the Reclau caves. Prior to this, there had been no known archaeological interest. The first cave in which he worked was the Reclau Viver, which was excavated between 1944 and 1948. During this time, he also carried out some excavations in the Mollet and Pau caves.

In 1958, he resumed excavation in the Mollet cave.

Between 1972 and 1974, there was enormous excavation activity: Mollet, Mollet III, la Arbreda, Pau (sectors Cau d'en Paquito and Pau III), Arbreda II, Cau del Roure and once again, Pau (sector Davant Pau).

Between 1972 and 1973, a large sunken cavity filled with sediment was discovered.

The materials from the excavations of J.M. Corominas, with a few exceptions, are in the collection of the Museu Arqueològic Comarcal de Banyoles.

From 1975 to 1987, the Centre d'Investigacions Arqueològiques de Girona (initially under the responsibility of the Girona Regional Council, and later the Generalitat de Catalunya) carried out annual excavations in Arbreda.

In 1996, archaeological work was resumed in the Reclau caves, but this time under the direction of the Universitat de Girona. That same year saw the creation of the Parc de les Coves Prehistòriques de Serinyà, and excavation has continued until today (Soler *et al.*, 2001).

Mollet cave

Location, description, history

The Mollet cave is a small cave located, in a south-north direction, between the Arbreda and Reclau Viver caves, in the lower section of the travertine cliff, at an elevation of approximately 200 masl (Fig. 1). It is a cave which is open to the west and currently measures approximately 9 m north to south, by 3 m east to west, although the layout is somewhat artificial, because the visible walls are a combination of the cascading travertine of the area with unexcavated sediment concretion. The roof is significantly eroded, although the north end remains intact, where a small area slightly larger than 3 m^2 is totally closed, creating the sector that has been called "racó" (Fig. 2).

This cave was excavated in the years 1947-1948, 1958 and 1972 by Josep M. Corominas, with the collaboration of Eduard Ripoll and Lluís Pericot in 1958 and Miquel Oliva, Josep M. Bedoya and Josep Canal in 1972 (Maroto *et al.*, 1987). A large part of the sedimentary fill in the cave was excavated during these campaigns. Between 2001 and 2005, and in 2010 and 2011 excavation work resumed under the direction of J. Maroto. Recent campaigns have consisted of the partial excavation of layer 5, the only layer that was partially preserved, in order to classify and interpret it.

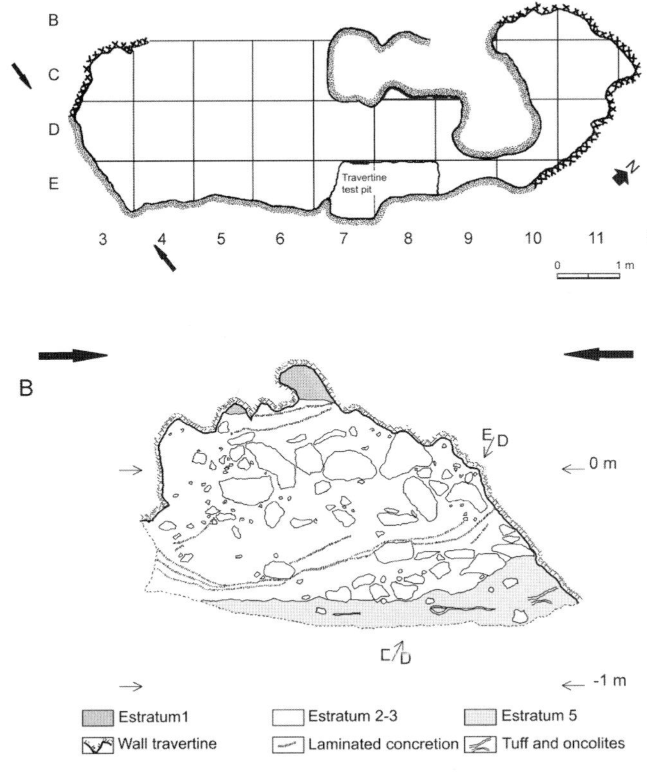

Figure 2. Mollet cave A: Floor plan indicating the excavation grid. B: stratigraphic cross-section.

Stratigraphy

Although most of the sedimentary deposit was removed by the work carried out prior to 1972, it was possible to reconstruct the stratigraphy based on the data from recent excavations, in conjunction with the data from the earlier excavations (Corominas, 1948; 1958; Ripoll and Lumley, 1965; Lumley, 1971; Mir and Salas, 1976; Villalta and Estévez, 1977; Soler, 1986). The thickness of the fill was as much as 3.5 m, although in a test pit that has been conserved in one of the marginal areas, it is only 1.60 m (Fig. 2). From ceiling to base, it would consist of:

- Layer 1. Red clay. Holocene. Early Neolithic.
- Layer 2. Brown clay with travertine blocks. Upper Pleistocene. Upper Palaeolithic (Early Aurignacian).
- Layer 3. Brown clay with travertine blocks. Upper Pleistocene. Middle Palaeolithic (Mousterian).
- Layer 5. Yellowish calcified silty sand (equivalent of travertine sand) with laminated tuffs and oncolithic gravel. Middle Pleistocene. Large mammals.

The nomenclature of the levels defined by Henry de Lumley (Ripoll and Lumley, 1965; Lumley, 1975) has been maintained. For this reason, there is no layer 4, because it corresponds to a local facies that cannot be generalized within the fill.

On the other hand, in the west sector (the external sector), layer 5 is not covered by layer 3, but rather by travertine constructions (tuff deposits) that connect with the roof and the external cascade threshold. The current visible configuration of the shelter is therefore later than the deposition of layer 5 (Maroto *et al.*, 2012).

Layer 1

The upper layer contains minimal archaeological material, with only a few lithic ornamental and malacological elements, and a small quantity of ceramics. It also contains human remains, and on the whole appears to correspond to an Early Neolithic burial (Tarrús, 1986).

Layer 2

Layer 2 also contains few archaeological remains, although it is not as poor as the preceding layer.

Dating of a bone sample indicates an age of 33,780 ± 730 BP (OxA-3728) (Maroto *et al.*, 1996).

The lithic production is knapped imported silex and consists of 2 good cores, one a double-ended laminar prism and the other a single-ended laminar pyramid, as well as a decent number of sheets and flakes. The number of retouched tools is very small, but a few Dufour bladelets can be observed. The technology and morphology of the pieces correspond to Early Aurignacian; based on dating, they could be from the Classic Aurignacian (Soler, 1986; Maroto *et al.*, 1987; Maroto, 1994).

The ornamentation is represented by a deer incisor, with a perforation in the root.

The mammal species identified (with caution and a certain degree of reservation due to the difficulty of correlating the materials from previous excavations to those of the actual levels) are: *Canis lupus*, *Vulpes vulpes*, *Ursus arctos*, *Felis sylvestris*,

Lynx cf. *spelaeus*, *Oryctolagus cuniculus*, *Lepus* sp., *Erinaceus europaeus*, *Equus ferus*, *Equus hydruntinus*, *Cervus elaphus*, *Bos primigenius*, *Capra pyrenaica* and *Rupicapra rupicapra*. Rabbit remains, which are the most abundant, appear to present some anthropic marks (Maroto *et al.*, 1996).

Layer 3

Rich in lithic industry, this layer contains the Mousterian artefacts defined and studied by H. de Lumley and E. Ripoll (Ripoll and Lumley, 1965; Lumley 1971), and analysed later by different authors.

Its age places it in the classic Upper Palaeolithic, because it is later than the last travertine construction facies, and prior to the start of the Upper Palaeolithic.

The lithic industry is mostly knapped quartz (64.5%), followed by quartzite and subvolcanic rock. There are different cores with varying morphology, including some knapped edges as well as some products using the Levallois method, which are not numerous, but nonetheless significant. The tools include abundant racloir, followed by denticulate tools and indentation tools (Maroto *et al.*, 1987).

With regard to fauna, with the aforementioned reservations, the following large-mammal species may be cited: *Ursus spelaeus*, *Palaeoloxodon antiquus*, *Equus ferus*, *Equus hydruntinus*, *Cervus elaphus*, *Rangifer tarandus* and *Bos primigenius*. As always, the rabbit (*Oryctolagus cuniculus*) is abundant.

Exterior tuff deposits

The overlying tuff deposits on layer 5, and that connect to the existing roof of the shelter and the cascade threshold indicate a U-Th age between ca. 163 ky and 134 ky; the most recent coincides with the outermost part of the cascade facies (dating done by Ramon Julià in the Institut de Ciències de la Terra Jaume Almera, Barcelona, CSIC) (Maroto *et al.*, 2012).

Layer 5

The lower layer has a paleontological association that is rich in large mammals.

The results obtained using uranium-series dating 215 ky indicate an approximate age of 215 ky (Ref. Lab. 3103: 215.092 +12.926/-11.668) (Maroto *et al.*, 2012).

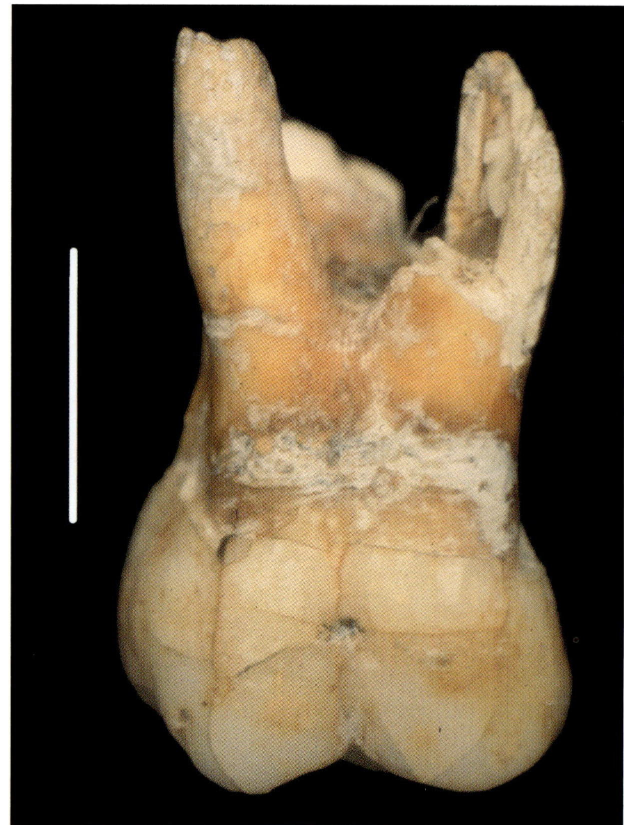

Figure 3. Mollet cave, layer 5. First molar (M1) upper right, human; mouth view. Scale 10 mm.

It contains very few elements of anthropic activity: some quartz lithic remains and a few burned travertines. However, it is rich in animal remains that were not contributed by humans. In addition to the presence of carnivores and ungulates, the human molar found in the 1972 excavation campaign belongs to this level.

The tooth in question is an upper right premolar of a juvenile, with morphological and morphometric characteristics that match those of Pre-neanderthals and Neanderthals (Cortada and Maroto, 1990) (Fig. 3).

The list of fauna that corresponds to this association, which includes this human molar (*Homo* sp.), includes 12 other species of medium and large mammals (one lagomorph, seven herbivores, and four carnivores), the most abundant of which is the spotted hyena (*Crocuta crocuta*) (Fig. 4). Namely: *Canis lupus*, *Vulpes vulpes*, *Crocuta crocuta*, *Ursus* sp., *Oryctolagus cuniculus*, *Equus* gr. *mosbachensis-ferus*, *Equus* cf. *hydruntinus*, *Stephanorinus hemitoechus*, *Cervus elaphus*, *Dama* sp., *Capreolus capreolus* and *Bos primigenius*.

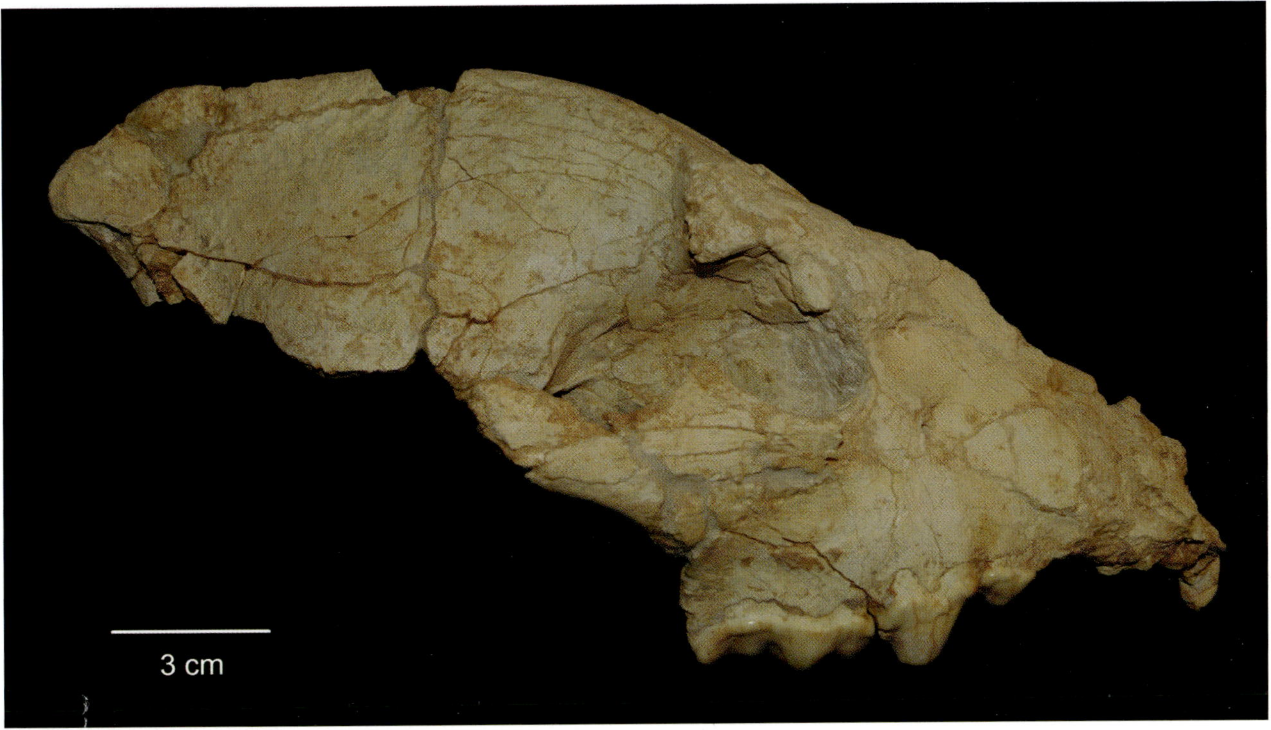

Figure 4. Mollet cave, layer 5. Skull of a spotted hyena (*Crocuta crocuta*), right side view.

On the other hand, the microvertebrates represent a total of 14 taxa (two amphibians, two scaly reptiles, one insectivore, two chiroptera, and seven rodents), the most abundant of which is *Iberomys brecciensis.* These are the following: *Pelodytes* cf. *punctatus*, *Bufo* cf. *bufo*, *Lacerta* s.l., *Vipera* sp., *Erinaceus europaeus*, *Myotis* gr. *myotis-oxignathus*, *Miniopterus schreibersii*, *Arvicola* sp., *Iberomys brecciensis*, *Microtus jansoni*, *Microtus arvalis*, *Terricola* cf. *atapuerquensis*, *Apodemus sylvaticus* and *Eliomys quercinus* (Maroto *et al.*, 2012).

The association of large mammals appears to have been the result of the accumulation produced by the most abundant carnivore, the hyena, which probably used the cave as a den.

For microvertebrates, the main agents of the accumulation of remains were nocturnal birds of prey, with the exception of the chiroptera, which may be an *in situ* accumulation.

This association of vertebrates suggests a forest landscape that was both open and moist at the same time, with mild weather conditions, probably corresponding to an interstadial period, which, based on the U-Th age, concordant with the micro-mammal study, could correspond to a moderate oscillation within the isotope stage 7 (MIS7) (Maroto *et al.*, 2012).

Mollet III cave

Location, description, history

The Mollet III cave is located between the Arbreda and Mollet caves, approximately 15 m south of the latter, and in the bottom of the travertine slope (Fig. 1).

The site is actually a shelter formed by a wall with a visible north-south length of approximately 18 m, only very partially covered. As a result of the excavation, it is divided into different sectors: West Extension North Sector, North Sector, Balk, Central Sector, and South Sector.

It was discovered in September 1972 by Josep Canal, who came across a human jawbone on the surface. A few days after this find, Josep M. Corominas began his excavation, with the collaboration of J. Canal. The excavation would extend from 30 September to 24 November 1972, and was immediately followed, on 26 November, by a new intervention, that of Anna Mir and Ramon Salas, representing the Quaternary Ecology Section of the CSIC of Barcelona, under the direction of palaeontologist José F. de Villalta, who installed a grid on the balk that day. They proceeded with a painstaking excavation, but only for one week in

April and another in July 1973, descending 25 cm (Maroto, 1980).

In July 1975, taking advantage of the intervention in the Arbreda cave, the sections of the visible cuts were drawn and the topographical floor plan of the site was carried out.

In 2013, excavation of the balk was resumed, by Alba Solés, Neus Coromina and Sònia Ramió. One of the objectives of this new intervention is to better contextualize the finding of a cranial vault from the Upper Palaeolithic, which, as a hypothesis, is thought to come from a burial.

Archaeostratigraphy

Based on the excavation diary of J.M. Corominas and the oral indications of the excavators themselves, Maroto (1980) interpreted the archaeostratigraphic correlation between the different sectors.

Likewise, using this data and the studies that have been conducted on the materials, three distinct archaeostratigraphic layers may be identified, all poor in terms of material culture, but not with regard to skeletal remains.

Recent prehistory

The upper layer, consisting of reddish clay, was between 60 and 100 cm thick.

It corresponds to several ceramic periods, that appear to have been found mixed together. There is ceramic from the Roman, Iberian, Late Bronze, Early-Medium Bronze, Chalcolithic and Early Neolithic periods.

Of these periods, the most significant are the Chalcolithic and Early-Middle Bronze, which provided a series of burials accompanied by fragments of vessels and other funerary offerings, that are rather poor. These burials were probably located in the spaces that would have been created between the large blocks that fell during the Holocene, and could be either individual or collective (Tarrús, 1978, 1986; Toledo, 1990). Vives (1986) interpreted them as secondary, while Agustí (1998), as successive. During the excavation, J.M. Corominas identified a grave sealed with a large sandstone slab.

A human humerus in this layer was recently dated at 4115 ± 35 BP (GrA-47329) (Soler *et al.*, 2013), which confirms that at least part of the burials are Chalcolithic.

E. Vives (1986) and B. Agustí (1998) carried out an anthropological study, although the sample studied by the two researchers was did not match exactly. The remains are highly fragmented, which complicates study and interpretation (fragmentation affects 88.4% of the sample). From the synthesis of the two studies, the presence of at least 9 adults, 2 adolescents, and 5 juveniles (2 between 6-8 years and 3 between 3-6 years of age) may be deduced.

Upper Palaeolithic

The second layer, with brown clay, has a thickness between 40 and 80 cm and corresponds to the Upper Palaeolithic, specifically, the Gravettian.

Direct ^{14}C AMS dating, published recently (Soler *et al.*, 2013), demonstrated that a human cranial vault is from this set. The cranial vault was excavated by J.M. Corominas in 1972, but there was reasonable doubt as to whether it corresponded to the ceramic level or the Gravettian layer. It was found in the North Sector, between 0.60 m and 1.00 m deep.

Likewise, the dating (22,330 ± 90 BP, GrA-43783) verified the Gravettian age of the set.

The cranial vault includes most of the front bone, both parietal bones, the occipital bone, and a fragment of the posterior side of the temporal bone. Soler *et al.*, (2013) estimated a female between 40-45 years of age, but it is important to emphasize that both are approximate estimations because the remains provide little diagnostic evidence.

Several elements of personal ornamentation were found in the same layer. On one hand, 10 perforated deer canines (Maroto, 1980). And on the other, 17 malacological fragments. 12 *Dentalium* sp., 1 *Glycymeris* sp. perforated, 1 *Nucella lapillus* perforated, 1 *Phalium* sp. perforated, 2 fragments of *Acathocardia* (classified by Josep Escortell). Some of these elements are clearly dyed red; likewise, J.M. Corominas in his excavation log, noted the presence of reddish coloration of the sediments. All of this, and based on the precedents of the abundant presence of decorative elements in the funerary structures from the Upper Palaeolithic, led Soler *et al.*, (2013) to consider the possibility that the cranial vault and the jewellery belonged to a disturbed Palaeolithic grave from the Gravettian age, although in reality, they acknowledged that they did not identify graves, structures, or anatomical connections of human remains in the excavation.

The lithic industry is poor, but highly characteristic, with an abundance of abrupt retouching (including several Gravette points) and a large presence of scrapers and burins. All of the retouched pieces are on imported silex (Maroto, 1980; Soler, 1986).

Bone industry is represented by a burned punch.

The large and medium-sized mammals in this set identified by J. Estévez (1979) include: *Equus ferus*, *Equus hydruntinus*, *Cervus elaphus*, *Rupicapra rupicapra*, *Bos primigenius*, *Sus scrofa*, *Lepus* sp., *Oryctolagus cuniculus*, *Erinaceus europaeus*, *Vulpes vulpes*, *Canis lupus* and *Lynx spelaeus*.

Middle Palaeolithic

The third layer, with calcified silt, was excavated only 40 cm and only in some places; it is

Figure 5. Outer zone of Cau del Roure. Excavation of layer 3 (2013). Access to Cau del Roure is near the person located furthest in the back.

not known whether the base of the deposit was reached at any point.

As excavation has been minimal, the recovered sample is poor; there are only 8 retouched tools on lithic flakes, all quartz. However, based on the technical and morphological characteristics of the lithic industry as a whole, as well as the absence of silex, it has been attributed to the Mousterian period (Maroto, 1980).

The large and medium-sized mammals in this level identified by J. Estévez (1979) include: *Equus ferus*, *Equus hydruntinus*, *Cervus elaphus*, *Bos primigenius*, *Lepus* sp., *Oryctolagus cuniculus*, *Erinaceus europaeus*, *Ursus spelaeus* and *Crocuta crocuta*.

Cau del Roure

Location, description, history

The Cau del Roure is located in the upper part of the travertine slope that forms the Reclau caves, halfway between the Arbreda and Reclau Viver caves. It is a small cave, closed and with a vertical access, with an interior area of approximately 4 m x 2 m. It is located at an elevation of approximately 210 masl (Fig. 5).

It was discovered and excavated in 1973 by Josep M. Corominas, who opened a test pit 2.40 m deep.

The second intervention was in 1978 by Jordi Barris, who sketched the site and sampled the fill, recovering remains of micro-mammals that were studied by Gabriel Alcalde (Alcalde, 1983; Barris, 1983).

Archaeostratigraphy

Different studies were conducted based on the materials found by J.M. Corominas. An archaeostratigraphy with three layers was synthesized from these studies.

The first layer contained medieval and Roman materials (Barris, 1983).

The second, human remains, corresponded to at least six individuals, three adults and three juveniles (Agustí, 1998), and some archaeological materials, essentially from the Chacolithic period. The cave was said to have functioned as a burial cave during that period (Tarrús, 1978, 1986; Toledo, 1990).

The third layer contained material with few distinguishing characteristics, but with no ceramics. Barris (1983) attributed it to the Palaeolithic.

Recent work

The Universitat de Girona (J. Maroto) in conjunction with the Institut Català de Paleoecologia Humana i Evolució Social (IPHES) (E. Allué, F. Rivals and M. Vaquero) have undertaken a project aimed at determining the importance of this site. Interventions were carried out in September 2012 and September 2013 (Rufí *et al.*, 2014).

After the mixed sediment that occupied the test pit was removed and sifted, it was observed that the borehole had reached the base of the sequence and that the remaining layer, with an approximate area of 3.6 m^2, had a thickness of 1.40 m. The start of the new excavation focused on a long narrow area, covering approximately 1 m^2, in order to normalize the cross-section of the test pit. This criterion was followed to determine the stratigraphy and study the fill, before starting the extended excavation. A single homogeneous sedimentary matrix was observed in this fill, which corresponded to the third archaeostratigraphic layer. The two upper layers were therefore completely removed by J.M. Corominas.

With regard to the findings of the recent excavation, there is an absence of ceramics and the lithic industry is poor. Nevertheless, significant decorative elements were recovered: three sea snails from the species *Nucella lapillus*, two of them perforated and with traces of ochre. Likewise, six human remains were found, both cranial and post-cranial (all small in size) and that correspond to a provisional minimum of three individuals. As regards large mammals, there was no domestic fauna and the taxa represented were (*Equus ferus*), the common deer (*Cervus elaphus*), wild boar (*Sus scrofa*), wolf (*Canis lupus*), fox (*Vulpes vulpes*) and an undetermined felid (Felidae). Also of note was the presence of abundant remains of rabbits, micro-mammals, birds, reptiles, amphibians, and continental gastropods, which are not resedimented.

This layer was dated using ^{14}C AMS. One of the datings corresponding to the upper part determined a date on the order of 20,000 BP. The other dating, of the lower part determined a date on the order of 34,000 BP. The remarkable difference between the two numerical results is still pending justification, along with the association with human remains and the archaeological remains, and the interpretation of all of these findings (Rufí *et al.*, 2014).

Outer Zone of Cau del Roure

Location, description, history

In the Outer Zone of Cau del Roure, an open-air deposit has been documented, discovered from a borehole made approximately 10 m to the east of Cau del Roure itself, in a depressed area bordered on the north by a constructive front of travertine facies (Fig. 5).

Excavation was carried out in September 2012 and September 2013 (the same team that was working in Cau del Roure). A regular area called Test Pit A, corresponding to an area of 8 m x 3 m (Rufí *et al.*, 2014) was marked off.

Stratigraphy

The stratigraphic sequence is the following:

- Layer 1: reddish clay layer (*terra rossa*), with no pebbles or blocks. Highly bioturbated due to the action of roots.
- Layer 2: reddish clay layer (*terra rossa*), with blocks of travertine. This layer is distinguished from the previous one only due to the block, because the sedimentary matrix is the same. To the west, it narrows and disappears, and increases in thickness to the east.
- Layer 3: sandy, carbonated layer that includes caliche-type carbonate crusts. This caliche is post-sedimentary, edaphic in origin, and can be found on the ceiling, as well as in the middle and in the base of the layer. It contains numerous skeletal remains and few elements of lithic industry. The base travertine formations already begin to appear underneath, in the western zone of the test pit.

Layer 1

The findings in layer 1 include the significant presence of remains of large mammal fauna, with large bovines and horses predominating, which, due to the degree of fossilization as well as the morphometric characteristics, could be said to be Palaeolithic. These remains came from lower layers as a result of bioturbation. Also, there is a small number of lithic elements and several sandstone chips, as well as ceramic fragments and other elements from historical periods.

Layer 2

In layer 2, which is also bioturbated, many unidentifiable remains of fauna were recovered, although many could be identified as cervids and equids. These animal remains also came from the underlying layer. A small number of elements of lithic industry were found, as well as a few ceramic fragments, mostly rolled and with no distinct shape, from different historical periods.

Layer 3

Layer 3 contained abundant remains of large fauna, with very little lithic industry. Many of the fauna remains are large and are of significant anatomical interest. The taxa identified correspond to the spotted hyena (*Crocuta crocuta*), bear (*Ursus* sp.), wolf (*Canis lupus*), fox (*Vulpes vulpes*), aurochs (*Bos primigenius*), common deer (*Cervus elaphus*), boar (*Sus scrofa*), horse (*Equus ferus*) and rabbit (*Oryctolagus cuniculus*), with the auroch and horse most prevalent for the time being. In terms of lithic industry, there are a small number of quartz, hornfels, quartzite, and sandstone.

One sample of constructive facies, taken from the travertine front located to the north of the test pit, was dated by Ramon Julià, at the "Jaume Almera" Institute for Earth Sciences in Barcelona, using the U-Th method, and the results indicated 165,000 years, which indicates a *post-quem* chronology for layer 3. This would therefore fall between the end of the Middle Pleistocene and the end of the Middle Palaeolithic, due to the presence of hyena and based on the lithic industry.

The fauna in layer three are well preserved, with a decent proportion of bone remains that are relatively intact. The absence of anthropic cut marks and fractures, and the presence of marks that indicate the intervention of carnivores, suggest that this material corresponds to an accumulation made by the large carnivores (as in the case of a hyena den). Obviously, the finding of lithic objects confirms human presence at the site, but their direct relationship with the fauna remains cannot be guaranteed or that they are resedimented. This lithic industry is not especially indicative, although the raw materials that were documented are customary of the Middle Palaeolithic of the Reclau caves, and the absence of silex, as well as the presence of hyena rule out assignment to the Upper Palaeolithic (Rufí *et al.*, 2014).

Xosé Pedro Rodríguez *,**,
Robert Sala *,**

Palaeolithic Settlements in the Congost de SantJulià de Ramis (Girona)

Approximately five kilometres to the north of the city of Gerona lies the "Congost de Sant Julià de Ramis" (Fig. 1).This is where the Ter River has carved out a narrow ravine through the Sant Julià Mountains (which form part of the last foothills of the Rocacorba Range) and Sant Miquel Mountains (within the Les Gavarres Massif). This narrow ravine connects the plains of the region of Gerona and those of El Empordà. It is in this area, which has a surface area of some 15 km^2, that a whole series of prehistoric sites have been discovered, including several Palaeolithic settlements dating from the lower to the upper subdivisions of that period (Canal and Carbonell 1989) (Fig. 1). Specifically, Costa Roja and Mas d'en Galí are open air sites dating from the early Lower Palaeolithic; Montaspre, also an open air site, has provided Acheulean materials; Pedra Dreta and Can Garriga are dated to the beginning of the Upper Pleistocene and have provided materials corresponding to the early Middle Palaeolithic; the lithic tools found at the open air site of"Cruilla de Cornellà" also belong to the Middle Palaeolithic. Materials from the Upper Palaeolithic have also been found in this area, namely at Cau de les Goges (Solutrean) (Pallarés and Werner 1920), Can Vicenç (Solutrean) (Riuró 1945) and Cova de les Goges (Magdalenian). In addition, epipalaeolithic materials have been found at Abric del Bosquetó. The investigation of this area goes back to the end of the 19th century, with Cau de les Goges being discovered in 1899 and Cova de les Goges in 1889.

In addition to this dense concentration of sites within such as small area, another relevant fact that is well worth mentioning is the discovery of faunal remains at some of these sites. Specifically, the horse and rhinoceros remains were found at Pedra Dreta, Cau de les Goges contained the remains of mammoths, horses, red deer, wild cats and rabbits; the finds made at Cova de les Goges included the remains of bovids, red deer, foxes and lynxes, while goat and red deer remains appeared at Abric del Bosquetó.

Perhaps the most noteworthy sites of the Sant Julià de Ramis region are Costa Roja, Pedra Dreta and Can Garriga. Costa Roja is an open air site with lithic industry on the surface and is located on a hillside on the left bank of the Ter River right at the entrance of the "Congost". The site lies at around 100 metres above the present bed of the Ter River and has been related with the T4 (García, 2005). Of the 207 objects found in 1980, the most noteworthy are the flakes, which were produced using non-complex strategies (Garcia, 2005). In the configuration sequences there is a significant presence of chopping tools (Fig. 2.1-2). As is commonly found at the sites on or around the Ter River, quartz is the dominant raw material. In general, the appearance of the industry found at this site is markedly archaic, with no evidence of any predetermination with respect to the reduction process (Canal and Carbonell, 1989). In 1978 194 artefacts with a number of characteristics similar to those of Costa Roja were found on the surface at the Mas d'en Galí site in the Medinyà area (Garcia, 2005). No morphotypes characteristic of Mode 2 have been found at any of these sites.

The Pedra Dreta site, which lies where the La Garriga Torrent joins the Ter River, is an ancient and completely collapsed travertine rock shelter (UTM: 486.156, 4.653.147). The site was excavated in 1976-1977 and again in 1991 (Carbonell and Mora 1984; Rodríguez *et al.*, 1995). The archaeological material found includes the remains of large mammals, lithic industry and some charcoal. Among the materials recovered in 1976 special mention must be made of two molars of *Equus sp.* and an upper right D3 of a rhinoceros. Most of the materials come from a salvage excavation carried out in 1991: 184 bone remains (quite fragmented and many of them burned) and 688 lithic objects (Rodríguez *et al.*, 1995) (Fig 2.8-10). At Pedra Dreta quartz is the most used raw material (66.1%), followed by porphyry (18.9%) and quartzite (9.7%). At this site very few retouched objects have been found (1.6%), so much so that it would seem obvious that the purpose here was the systematic production of flakes, with operational sequences involving the predetermination of the final

* IPHES, Institut Català de Paleoecologia Humana i Evolució Social, C/ Marcel.lí Domingo s/n. Campus Sescelades, (Edifici W3), Tarragona 43007

** Area de Prehistoria, Universitat Rovira i Virgili (URV), Av. Catalunya 35, Tarragona 43002

Figure 1. Location of the Palaeolithic sites of the Sant Julià de Ramis region. 1: Abric del Bosquetó, 2: Can Garriga, 3: Cova de les Goges, 4: Pedra Dreta, 5: Campdorà, 6: Costa Roja, 7: Sant Vicenç, 8: Cau de les Goges, 9: Cruïlla de Cornellà, 10: Mas d'en Galí.

products being frequently used (Fig. 2. 9). Reduction products constitute 93.5% of all the objects recovered during the 1991 digs (Rodríguez *et al.*, 1995). The data available is not sufficient for us to safely assert the existence of a close relationship between the lithic objects and the faunal remains, but it is likely that this site was used for butchery purposes. We have two radiometric dating (uranium series) which delimit the human occupations of Pedra Dreta: the lower travertines dated at 92±4 ky and the upper at 88.15 ±4 ky. This means that human occupations took place at around 90 ky (Giralt *et al.*, 1995).

Can Garriga is an open air stratigraphic site located a short distance from Pedra Dreta (UTM: 486.070, 4.652.964). Discovered in 1986, the site lay alongside the N-II trunk road, meaning that part of the record, without doubt, has disappeared (Mora *et al.*, 1987). An emergency dig was carried out during the year of its discovery. A few years later, in the spring of 1991, another emergency dig was undertaken in light of the imminent destruction of the site due to the upgrading of the N-II trunk road and the connection thereof to the A-7 Motorway (Rodríguez *et al.*, 1995). The site lay a few metres from the left-hand bank of the Ter River on the slopes of a small hill at 70 metres above sea level and 22 above the present river bed (Fig. 1).

The site's sedimentary dynamic is characterised by the alternation of periods during which it was affected by glacial activity, which deposited sands, and periods of stability, during which small ponds and travertines were formed. These travertines present an extremely significant lateral variation. The 1991 excavation enabled the documentation of four technological assemblages resulting from the different occupations of this open air riverside site at a time when the Ter River had already found its present course (Fig. 3). The human occupations occurred as and when the travertines retreated. The sedimentary dynamic of the site could be explained in the following way (Fig. 3). A travertine, the lower part of which is dated at 128.8 ±6.5 ky and the upper part at 112.2 ±7.5 ky, formed over a terrace of the Ter River (Terrace II' following Pallí 1982). The next feature discovered was the presence of a traction, or alluvium, level caused by the surface runoff from the La Garriga hill. Lithic material in secondary position appeared in this level (five objects recovered in 1991 and 90 in 1986). A travertine dated at 107.6 ky then formed above this. Almost simultaneously we came across an archaeological level in pedogenic clays (paleosol), containing quite a dispersed lithic industry (24 objects found in 1991). Volcanic particles were found on top of this level which, on analysis, indicated an inverse magnetic polarity attributable to the Blake episode (dated at 118 ky) (Giralt

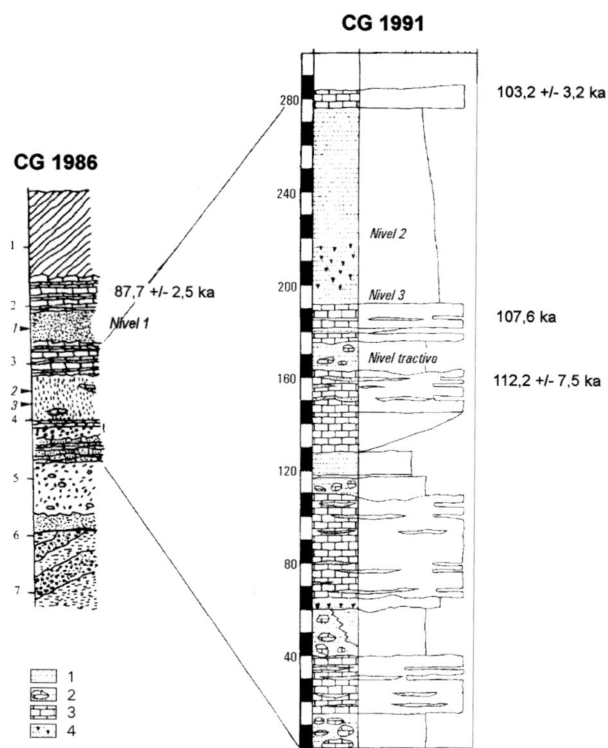

Figure 3. Can Carriga stratigraphic columns. On the left, the column created in 1986 (Mora *et al.*, 1987), and on the right that generated in 1991 (Giralt *et al.*, 1995). The 1991 column does not include either level 1 or travertine 1, pointed out in the 1986 column. Legend (for the 1991 column): 1, sands. 2, sands with travertine nodules. 3, travertine. 4, sands with volcanic particles.

et al., 1995). Another archaeological level (level 2), made up of clays and sands, was deposited on top of the level containing the volcanic particles. Lenticular formations of travertine, dated at 103.5±3.2 ky, appeared at the top of this second anthropic level. Archaeological level 1, which also consists of clays and sands, was found on top of these. Finally, a travertine terrace dated at 87.7±2.5 ky appeared. Levels 1 and 2 provided few objects during the 1986 campaign, but were found to be the most prolific material-wise in the 1991 dig, with 300 and 130 pieces respectively. In general, the entire Can Garriga archaeological site can be correlated to episode 5 and the occupations of levels 1 and 2 would have occurred between 107 and 90 ky.

None of the levels present paleontological remains, except for the small record of malacofauna and two fragments of indeterminable and burned diaphsis. Natural bases of limestone were found in level 1, with these having been intentionally brought to the site, as were slabs of travertine, which also appear to have been intentionally introduced into the archaeological level. The most important of these associations consists of a speleothem measuring 270 x 190 x 30 mm, six fragments of travertine and seven boulders (six of them limestone and one granite). This accumulation of blocks and boulders cannot have been the result of geological phenomena. In level 1 a group of syenite boulders was found with signs of percussion in their centres, which could indicate their use as anvils (Rodríguez *et al.*, 1995).

The two levels richest in material (1 and 2) present a notable similarity with respect to the representation of the structural categories, but with some differences that may be due to the purposes for which they were used (Rodríguez 2004) (Fig. 2.3-7). The raw materials came from areas close to the site, namely the terraces of the Ter River. In level 1 of the Can Garriga site quartz (61%), quartzite (10.7%), hornfels (8%) and porphyry (7.3%) are the most habitual raw materials. The rest is distributed between 9 scarcely-used materials. In level 2, quartz is the most preponderant (71.5%) followed, in this case, by porphyry (10%), quartzite (6.9%) and hornfels (5.4%). Other token materials found are syenite, sandstone, granite and limestone. In both levels the most common category of objects are flakes, which amounted to 60% (excluding the fragments, abundant in both levels). The production methods include centripetal reduction with preconfiguration of the end products (Levalloisian), although the majority of the cores respond to orthogonal and centripetal strategies (Fig. 2.3-5). Similarities also exist in the type of artefacts configured: chopping tools are scarce (two in level 1 and one in level 2) and the presence of flake-based instruments is noteworthy (Fig. 2.6-7). Almost half the retouched flakes found in level 1 are denticulate and a third side scrapers. In level 2 the most frequent types are the denticulate scraper and the simple lateral side scraper.

The lithic operational sequence is more complete in level 2. This is because in level 1 there is low presence of cores (3%), above all of the most used raw materials (fundamentally quartz). On the other hand, there are cores of other raw materials from which no products have been recovered. Despite this, there is evidence of the production of flakes and of the configuration thereof on the site itself. Evidence exists of the entire production process from its initial phases (with a notable presence of cortical by-products) through to the final phases (shown by a practically exhausted quartz core). One of the hypotheses put forward is that the level 1 record is the result of short occupations, with the performance of reduction activities (above all of tools configuration, although maybe also of flakes production), and probably the processing of faunal resources involving a simple or-

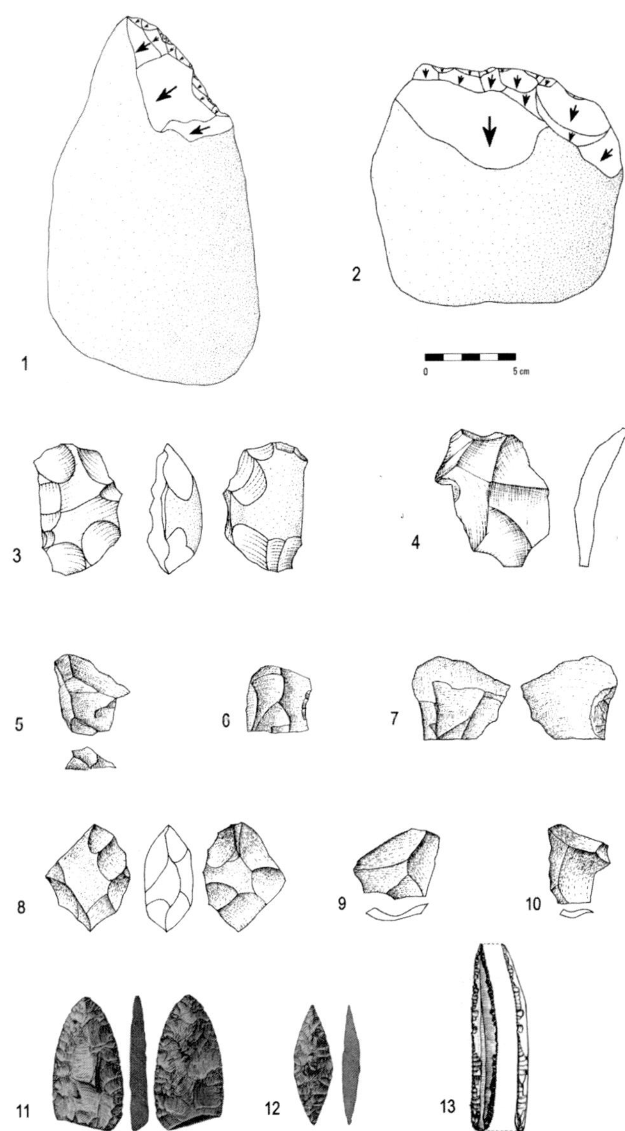

Figure 3. Lithic industry of the Congost de Sant Julià de Ramis sites. 1 and 2: Sandstone chopping tools, Costa Roja (García 2005), 3-7: Materials from Can Garriga (Rodriguez 2004), 3: Centripetal bifacial hornfels core (level 1), 4: Levalloisian flake in metamorphic rock, 5: Quartz flake (level 2), 6: Notch in quartzite with marginal retouch (level 1), 7: Quartz side scraper (level 1). 8-10: materials from Pedra Dreta (Rodríguez *et al.*, 1995), 8: Centripetal bifacial porphyry core, 9: Levalloisian flake in porphyry, 10: Porphyry flake. 11 and 12: Solutrean foliate flint projectile points from Cau de les Goges (Pallarés and Wernert 1920), 13: Backed flint projectile point (Sant Vicenç).

ganisation of the space. Level 2 would be the result of less habitual occupations, but also with the carrying out of raw material extraction and product configuration processes (Rodríguez 2004).

Both Pedra Dreta and Can Garriga would correspond to occupations at the beginning of the Upper

Pleistocene with a Mode 3 lithic technology using the local lithic resources (Rodríguez *et al.*, 2004).

Human occupations in Congost de Sant Julià were continuous throughout the end of the Upper Pleistocene, with Mode 4 technology sites of which Cau de les Goges, with Solutrean materials (Fig. 2.11-12) and Cova de les Goges, attributed to the Magdalenian being the most noteworthy (Pallarès and Wernert 1920). The latter, which has now disappeared, was, following its discovery as an archaeological site, excavated on three occasions since the end of the 19th century, during which it provided a scarce and non-definitional industry, with burins, end scrapers and bladelets, which was attributed to the Magdalenian (Pallarès and Wernert, 1920; Canal and Carbonell, 1989). In Cau de les Goges a level rich in charcoal remains was described, which was laterally widened to provide two archaeological layers. The complete archaeological ensemble was rich in the remains of fauna and lithic industry, characterised by the presence of the invasive Solutrean flat retouch and notched projectile points. The most noteworthy fauna found was *Elephas primigenius, Equus caballus* and *Cervus elaphus* (Pallarès and Wernert, 1920). At the beginning of the 20th century these sites were the most outstanding sources of Upper Pleistocene archaeology and served to show the presence of the morphotypes typical of the Solutrean prior to the discovery of the large regional sequences. Nowadays, given that these are sites with individual levels, they do not play such an important role in general reconstructions, although they are of interest with respect to the reconstructions of human paleoecology.

There is no doubt that this high density of Palaeolithic sites within a relatively small area is related with the strategic location of Congost de Sant Julià, which functions as a thoroughfare that connects the Gerona plain and the Empordà region.

Joan Garcia *, **, ***, ****,
Eudald Carbonell **, ***, *****,
Xosé Pedro Rodríguez **, ***,
Robert Sala **, ***

The Ter River basin in the Lower Palaeolithic: Cau del Duc, Puig d'en Roca and La Selva (Northeast Catalonia)

Abstract

The Lower Palaeolithic sites of the Ter River basin have been exhaustively investigated since the beginning of the 1970s. The fact that most of them are surface sites and devoid of fauna has focused attention on the study of their lithic industry. The most important of the Ter basin sites have been revisited in order to compile an evolutionary outline of these industries: Puig d'en Roca (I-II, Excavació, III and IV), Cau del Duc de Torroella de Montgrí and La Selva (Puig d'Esclats, Casa Nova d'en Feliu and Can Burgès). The presence of Mode 1, 2 and 3 sites on the lower (T2), middle (T3) and upper (T4) terraces of the Ter River and in the alluvial Pleistocene deposits of the Onyar, together with the absolute dates of travertine and volcanic levels between about 350 and 85 ky, enable to defend the settlement continuity within the region between the Middle Pleistocene and the early Upper Pleistocene.

Keywords: Lower Palaeolithic; lithic technology; Mode 1; Mode 2; technical traditions.

1. Introduction

The watercourses associated with the Ter River and its tributaries in the Girona region were occupied by hominin communities throughout the Lower Palaeolithic period. With the exception of the Cau del Duc de Torroella de Montgrí cave (Baix Empordà), in the Ter River there are generally open-air sites without stratigraphic context which preserve superficial lithic industry and de-

* Corresponding author: Joan Garcia. e-meil: jgarc338@xtec.cat. tlf: 699855077

** IPHES, Institut Català de Paleoecologia Humana i Evolució Social (IPHES), C/ Marcel·lí Domingo s/n, Campus Sescelades URV, Edifici W3, 43007, Tarragona, Spain.

*** URV, Universitat Rovira i Virgili, Àrea de Prehistòria, Avinguda de Catalunya 35, 43002 Tarragona, Spain.

**** UOC, Universitat Oberta de Catalunya (UOC), Avinguda del Tibidabo 39–43, 08035 Barcelona, Spain.

***** Visiting professor, Institute of Vertebrate Paleontology and Paleoanthropology of Beijing (IVPP).

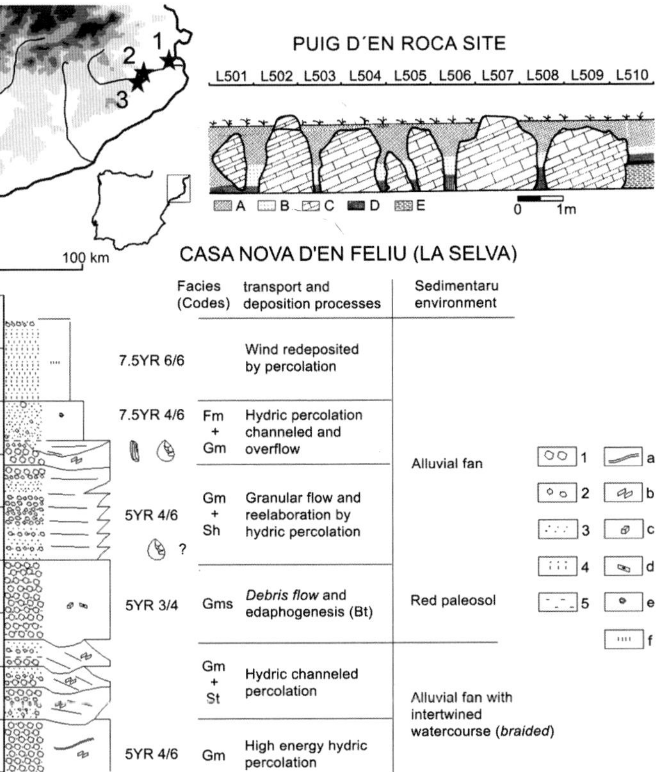

Figure 1: Location of Cau del Duc de Torroella de Montgrí (1), Puig d'en Roca (2) and La Selva (3) and the stratigraphic sequences of Puig d'en Roca Excavació (in Carbonell *et al.*, 1988) and Casa Nova d'en Feliu, La Selva (prepared by J. Vallverdú). Captions: A: superficial clays, B: clay with detritic elements, C: sandstone blocks, D: clays without detritic elements, and E: yellowish marls. 1: blocks, 2: gravels, 3: sands, 4: sands and silts, 5: clays, a: affected by oxy-reduction, b: clasts imbrication, c: medium polyhedral aggregation, d: coatings of sands cemented over the clasts, e: granular aggregation, and f: low density.

void of faunal remains. Due to these limitations, the study of the lithic objects is the only empirical instrument that enables us to investigate the palaeoeconomic relations of the hominins and the chronology of the occupations. To create a contextual benchmark framework of the Lower Palaeolithic sites and their industries within this region, we have focused on those sites whose lithic record provides us with the most information, as is the case of the Cau del Duc de Torroella de Montgrí, Puig d'en Roca and La Selva complexes (Fig. 1).

One of the main problematic which has had an influence on the discovery and subsequent study of the Lower Palaeolithic in Catalonia has been the lack of recognition of this type of surface findings finding records. In the early 1970s, the Associació Arqueològica de Girona began to revise the archaeological discoveries, of which the aforementioned sites form a significant part, and assigned them to the Lower Palaeolithic (Canal and Carbonell, 1979). Scientific works carried out on the terraces of the Ter River (Canal and Carbonell, 1978), in the Freser (Carbonell *et al.*, 1976), in La Selva and in the Montgrí (Canal and Carbonell, 1989) began the vindication of the Lower Palaeolithic in Catalonia and ended with the creation of the Girona School of Palaeolithic archaeologists (Garcia *et al.*, 2009). The publication of "El Paleolític a les Comarques Gironines" on the occasion of the visit of the experts of the 9th International Congress of Prehistoric and Protohistoric Sciences (UISPP) held in Nice in 1976 represented a milestone in the onset of the systematic study of this type of technocomplexes (Canal and Soler, 1976; Canal and Carbonell, 1978, 1989). The archaeological field works carried out in the 1970s at Reclau Viver in the Serinyà complex, in particular at Mollet Cave and Cau del Duc del Montgrí, as well as the excavations at Puig d'en Roca and the archaeological prospections at La Selva resulted in the accumulation of thousands of lithic records and highlighted the importance of these technocomplexes when studying the first settlement in the Northeast of the Iberian Peninsula. A series of synthetic work carried out over the last thirty years have highlighted the importance of these types of records (Canal and Carbonell, 1978, 1989; Mora and Carbonell, 1987; Rodríguez and Lozano, 1999; Rodríguez, 2005; Rodríguez *et al.*, 2003/2004; Carbonell and Rodríguez, 2007-2008; Garcia, 2008, 2010, 2011).

2. The sites

Puig d'en Roca is a complex of open-air sites (Puig d'en Roca I-II and IV) with lithic industry in stratigraphic context and in secondary position (Puig d'en Roca Excavació and III), situated on small promontories rising above the left-hand bank of the Ter River to the northeast of the suburbs of Girona (Carbonell *et al.*, 1988; Canal and Carbonell, 1989). The different sites are distributed over small hills above terraces 3 (T3) and 4 (T4) of the Ter (Pallí, 1976). A test pit carried out between the reddish clays preserved by the sandstone blocks of the Rocacorba formation, immediately below T4, resulted in the recovery of the Puig d'en Roca IV lithic industries, consisting of 323 pieces (Fig. 1). Furthemore, Puig d'en Roca I-II, which is situated on the highest part of these promontories, provided a total of 1,136 lithic objects. An archaeological test pit called "Puig d'en Roca Excavació" was carried out in this same sector and it provided an abundant lithic record of around 5,000 objects (Fig. 1 and Tab. 1). At Turó de la Bateria (Puig d'en Roca III), which is located to the east of Puig d'en Roca Excavació, some 300 pieces were found in surface. These discoveries led to an archaeological test pit being conducted in 1987, which increased the collection to 455 pieces (Serra *et al.*, 1981; Garcia, 2008, 2011, 2011) (Tab. 1). Subsequent excavations carried out in 2007 on this same promontory have contributed new materials with characteristics similar to those already documented (Rosillo *et al.*, 2008).

On the other hand, Cau del Duc de Torroella de Montgrí is a large cave that forms part of the karst system of the Montgrí Massif, where erosive diagenetic processes carved out the cavity (Pericot and Pallarés, 1931). When the field work was carried out in 1976, the finds, which included 6,071 lithic objects, were recovered in a secondary position in a level of reddish sands preserved between the interstices of the cave floor (Soler, 1982) (Tab. 1). Furthemore, more than 120 archaeological sites in the La Selva depression have provided an abundant superficial industry. This has been recovered during a series of systematic prospections undertaken between 1976 and the first half of the 1980s. These finds were discovered in reddish alluvial clays deposits and the most important of these sites are Puig d'Esclats, Casa Nova d'en Feliu and Can Burgès (Garcia, 2008, 2010, 2011) (Fig. 1 and Tab. 1).

3. The lithic industry

3.1. *Raw materials*

The predominant raw materials procurement at the sites associated with the Ter River basin involves the local supply of the rocks. Their use depends exclusively on the availability within

Site	Quartz		Quartzite		Porphyry		Hornfels		Sandstone		Limestone		Others		Total
		%		%		%		%		%		%		%	
Puig d'en Roca Excavació	2078	83,5	83	3,3	139	5,6	66	2,6	-	-	17	0,7	106	4,3	2489
Puig d'en Roca III	238	52,4	88	19,3	43	9,4	30	6,6	39	8,6	3	0,6	14	3,1	455
Cau del Duc de Torroella de Montgrí	449	42,1	140	13,1	105	9,8	230	21,6	35	3,3	53	4,9	56	5,2	1068
Puig d'Esclats	1184	83,2	155	10,9	30	2,1	2	0,1	7	0,5	4	0,3	41	2,9	1423
Casa Nova d'en Feliu	1567	74,1	322	15,2	99	4,7	11	0,5	31	1,5	2	0,1	82	3,9	2114
Can Burgès	1256	73,7	200	11,7	75	4,4	11	0,6	58	3,4	1	0,1	105	6,1	1706

Site	Manuports		Knapped pebbles						Flakes		Flakes				Total
			Indet.		Tools		Cores				Cores		Retouched		
		%		%		%		%		%		%		%	
Puig d'en Roca Excavació	186	7,4	110	4,4	206	8,3	243	9,8	1299	52,2	10	0,4	435	17,5	2489
Puig d'en Roca III	15	3,3	8	1,7	29	6,4	173	38,1	198	43,6	23	5,0	9	1,9	455
Cau del Duc de Torroella de Montgrí	-	1,5	13	1,2	24	2,2	72	6,7	858	80,4	85	8,0	-	-	1068
Puig d'Esclats	-	2,4	5	0,4	73	5,1	261	18,3	673	47,3	323	22,7	54	3,8	1423
Casa Nova d'en Feliu	-	1,1	1	0,1	58	2,7	259	12,3	1298	61,3	389	18,4	86	4,1	2114
Can Burgès	-	1,9	1	0,1	24	1,4	202	11,9	1249	73,2	174	10,2	22	1,3	1706

Table 1. Raw materials and categories of lithic objects (the fragments found at Puig d'en Roca Excavació have been omitted and with respect to Cau del Duc the lithic industry studied by Rodríguez in 2005 has been considered).

the immediate surroundings of the settlements. In these sites, a specialisation in the knapping of quartz was produced. Quartzite and hornfels are the other most commonly represented materials, while there is extremely scant presence of other rocks. Quartzite was used as a secondary rock at Puig d'en Roca I-II, III, IV and Excavació and the La Selva complex, while hornfels was preferred at Cau del Duc de Torroella de Montgrí (Tab. 1). Despite the predominant use of quartz, at Puig d'en Roca Excavació and Cau del Duc sandstone and hornfels were usually used for the configuration of pebble tools, while porphyry was reserved for developing the Levallois operational sequences (Rodríguez and Lozano, 1999; Rodríguez *et al.*, 2003/2004). At the La Selva complexes quartzite was chosen to the configuration of large size pebble artefacts, above all picks and handaxes (Garcia, 2008, 2010, 2011). At Puig d'en Roca I-II and IV, quartz was indistinctly used in most of the configuration and knapping processes. However, quartzite and in some cases porphyry and hornfels were preferred for the configuration of pebble tools and for the knapping of cores using more complex reduction strategies (Tab. 1). Complete operational sequences that include all the technical categories are documented at the sites.

3.2. *Configuration operational sequences*

At Puig d'en Roca Excavació, Cau del Duc and La Selva, the configurated elements account for more than 20% of the total remains (Carbonell, 1985; Rodríguez, 2005; Garcia, 2008, 2010, 2011). The proportion of pebble tools to flake tools shows a pre-eminence with respect to the configuration of the retouched tools at all the sites. At Cau del Duc and Puig d'en Roca IV, and above all at Puig d'en Roca Excavació, I-II and III, it is the pebble tools which, unlike at the La Selva complexes, outnumber the flake tools (Carbonell, 1985; Rodríguez, 2005) (Tab. 1). Both the pebble tools and the retouched flakes are unifacial, while the cores are usually bifacial. In the pebble shaping sequences a certain systemisation in the activation of dihedrons (especially chopping-tools) can be observed (Fig. 2). Whenever picks and handaxes appear in the records, they always do so in a far more sporadic way. At Puig d'en Roca Excavació, Cau del Duc and La Selva handaxes and cleavers are rare but very significant, while picks are more common at all the sites (Fig. 3). It is important to point out that the types of blanks generally used for the configuration of these large size instruments was the river pebble, although in the case of the handaxes these were knapped using large flakes.

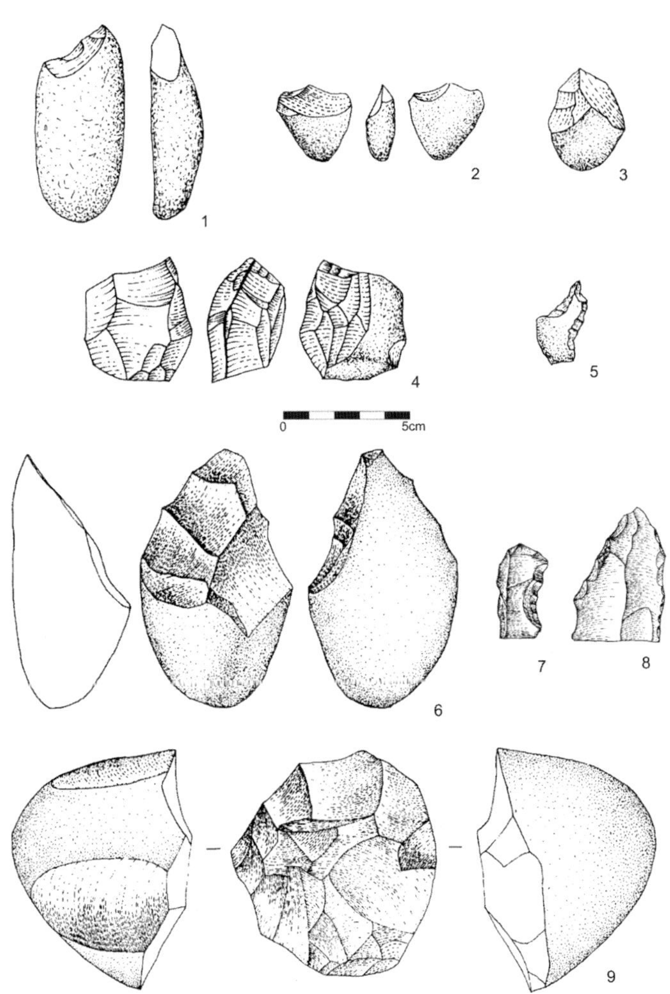

Figure 2. Drawings of the lithic industry of Puig d'en Roca Excavació (1-5) and Cau del Duc de Torroella de Montgrí (6-9). 1-3: choppers and chopping-tools, 4: opposed bipolar bifacial porphyry core, 5: denticulate point, 6: sandstone pick, 7: denticulate quartz tool, 8: porphyry point, and 9: centripetal bifacial limestone core (drawings by X.P. Rodríguez, in Rodríguez and Lozano, 1999 and Rodríguez *et al.*, 2003/2004).

With respect to the flake tools, the denticulate and concave dihedrons (notches) predominate at the majority of the sites, given the fact that they are the most common at Puig d'en Roca Excavació, the La Selva technocomplexes and, above all, at Puig d'en Roca III and IV. In contrast, more continuous segments (side scrapers) have been found at Puig d'en Roca I-II and Cau del Duc. Individualised analysis by archaeological complexes has enabled us to differentiate between Puig d'en Roca III and Excavació, given that the denticulate and notched tools were

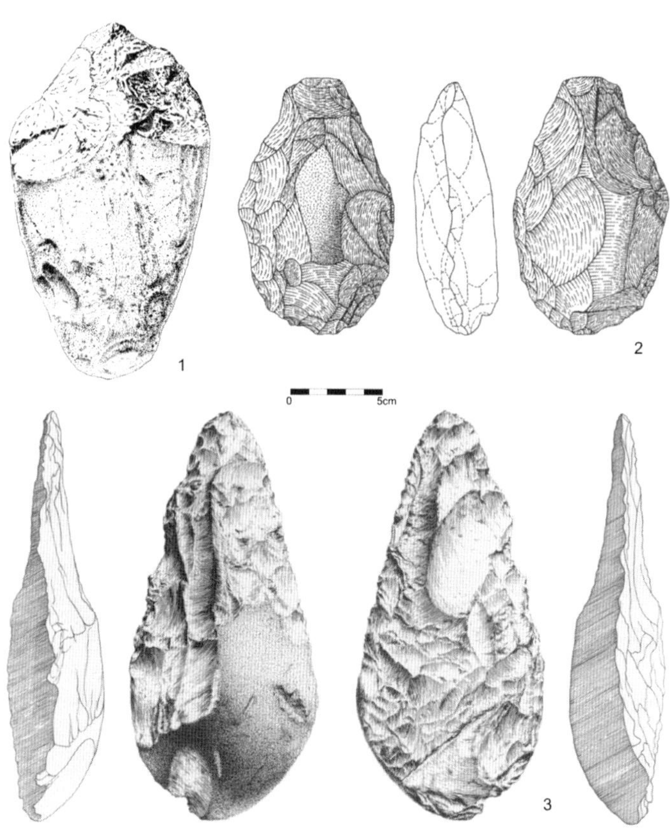

Figure 3. Drawings of configured artefacts from the La Selva complex. 1: quartzite pick from Puig d'Esclats (drawing by N. Sanchiz, in Canal and Carbonell, 1989), 2: quartzite handaxe from Puig d'Esclats, 3: large quartzite handaxe from Cellera de Ter (drawing by S. Barrera, in Canal and Carbonell, 1989).

preferred by the hominins of Puig d'en Roca III, while trihedrals (points) were the tools of choice for those of Puig d'en Roca Excavació (Fig. 2). Among the La Selva sites the structure observed is very similar, except for the greater number of handaxes at Puig d'Esclats and of denticulate and notched tools at this site and at Casa Nova d'en Feliu.

3.3. *Knapping operational sequences*

Special mention must be made of the uniformity that exists between the knapping systems and their representational percentage of Puig d'Esclats and Casa Nova d'en Feliu and between those of Puig d'en Roca III and Cau del Duc. The availability of the raw materials did not determine the knapping systems given the fact that poor quality rocks, such as quartz, were used for the Levallois method. Despite this, whenever this type of reduction was carried out at the different complexes, the tendency was to selectively introduce more suitable materials for the knapping process, such as quartzite, porphyry or hornfels (Tab. 1). Frequently represented at Cau del Duc de Torroella de Montgrí are the reduction sequences related with the massive longitudinal knapping with abruptly angled extractions in the transversal and/or sagittal planes of the core and, just as at La Selva, the Levallois cores are very significant. At Puig d'en Roca Excavació, on the other hand, it is the non-Levallois unifacial and bifacial cores with centripetal extractions which predominate. Unifacial and bifacial cores with lineal knapping systems, either orthogonal or opposed, also abound. At Puig d'en Roca I-II and IV the same tendency as that at the Excavació conmplex is detected, with a preponderance of centripetal and multidirectional unifacial and bifacial strategies. However, at the second of these sites a significant increase and generalisation of the polyhedral multidirectional systems, and in particular of others such as the centripetal multipolar bifacial, among which the discoidal stand out, is detected (Rodríguez, 2005) (Fig. 2).

The presence of Levallois cores at Cau del Duc de Torroella de Montgrí and La Selva has been interpreted as a feature of technological development (Garcia, 2008, 2010, 2011). The flakes found at these sites usually present high indices of bifaceted and multifaceted butts and ridges on the dorsal surface wich would be related with this system. On the contrary, the trifacial and multifacial strategies knapped using disorganised and unsystematic reduction methods (polyhedral cores) are detected, above all, at the Puig d'en Roca and La Selva sites. At these sites, the flakes are characterised by the presence of unfaceted or unifaceted butts, cortical dorsal surfaces and a reduced presence of ridges and flake scars. At Puig d'en Roca Excavació the centripetal strategies were systemised, while at Puig d'en Roca III the unipolar is the most frequent. At Puig d'Esclats and Casa Nova d'en Feliu it is the centripetal knapping strategies that are the most recurrent, while at Can Burgès the opposed bipolar is the most used. The most significant associations are those linking Puig d'en Roca Excavació with the centripetal unifacial and bifacial knapping processes, and those that associate Cau del Duc with the orthogonal unifacial and bifacial systems (Fig. 2). Although bifacial reduction carries more weight in the knapping activities, a significant increase in trifacial, multifacial and especially unifacial reduction can be observed. Whenever flakes were chosen for extracting new products variability increases, as bifaciality was preferred in the La Selva and Puig d'en Roca Excavació technocomplexes, while more unifaciality is documented at Puig d'en Roca III.

4. Discussion

The sites analysed share some of the same technological structures within the regional evolutionary *continuum*, which have been associated with technological traditions inherent to the different regions of Northeast Catalonia (Garcia, 2008, 2010, 2011). At all of them there exists a specialisation in the use of quartz, although a different selection of rocks can also be observed, which is evidenced at Puig d'en Roca Excavació in the use of sandstone and hornfels for the configuration of pebble tools and of porphyry for the knapping of cores (Fig. 2 and Tab. 1). Likewise, at this site a significant presence of pebble tools is observed, namely a very low number (less than 2%) of handaxes and cleavers, a predominance of trifacial and multifacial knapping strategies and an absence of Levallois cores. Puig d'en Roca III and IV have relatively synchronic records showing similar technological traits, although not a single handaxe or cleaver has been found. This does not apply to Puig d'en Roca I-II, which presents a number of more archaic features, such as the absence of handaxes and cleavers and a significant increase of pebble tools, at the same time as retaining the importance of disorganised and multifacial and polyhedral knapping systems.

Between Cau del Duc de Torroella de Montgrí and La Selva and other sites in the Ter River basin such as Cau del Duc d'Ullà, Can Garriga, Pedra Dreta, Can Rubau and La Jueria we also find technological similarities, with a drop in the number of pebble tools and a significant presence of Levallois cores and flakes in the first two sites. Can Garriga, Pedra Dreta, Can Rubau and La Jueria also stand out from the rest due to the increase undergone by the retouched artefacts and to the high level of standardisation of the lithic industry. Of all these sites, Cau del Duc de Torroella de Montgrí and d'Ullà are those which present the most analogies. The geographical proximity of these caves and the fact that they share the same ecological and geological environment would explain the noteworthy connections that exist with respect to the raw materials and the knapping systems used, of which the Levallois stands out. Furthermore, the percentages of flakes and retouched tools are extremely high and similar between both sites. Despite this, it is also possible to point out certain differences, such as the absence of handaxes, cleavers and cores at Cau del Duc d'Ullà.

The presence of Levallois cores and/or flakes on the one hand, and of trifacial and multifacial knapping strategies on the other, are two criteria that enable us to differentiate the industries on a technological and chronological level. One group of sites would be composed of Cau del Duc de Torroella de Montgrí and the La Selva complex, together with other Ter Basin sites such as Cau del Duc d'Ullà, Can Garriga, Pedra Dreta, Can Rubau and La Jueria, while the other group would consist of Puig d'en Roca I-II, Excavació, III and IV. Another chronological differentiation criteria would be the number of pebble tools found at the sites, which enables us to separate them into a first group comprised of Puig d'en Roca Excavació, IV, Cau del Duc de Torroella de Montgrí, La Selva and, above all, Puig d'en Roca I-II and III, where these are quite abundant, and a second group composed of other sites in the Ter River basin like Cau del Duc d'Ullà, Can Garriga, Pedra Dreta, Can Rubau and La Jueria, where hardly any, or even none, have been found (Garcia, 2008, 2010, 2011) (Figs. 2 and 3).

Despite the fact that the presence of pebble tools might be related with the functionality of the settlements, the disappearance and progressive replacement of these artefacts by retouched flakes marks an evolutionary line that would enable a diachrony between the sites to be established. Based on this criterion, the first group would be older and have more archaic technological structures, while the second would be more recent and produce a more developed record. The presence of Mode 2 operational standards such as handaxes and cleavers is extremely scarce at the sites. Within the Ter Basin, only at Cau del Duc de Torroella de Montgrí (3.1% of the total record), Puig d'en Roca Excavació (less than 2%) and La Selva (less than 1%) have been found in a low number, meaning that despite being highly significant their presence is practically token, while at the other sites none of these morphotypes have been found (Fig. 3). The absence or scarcity of handaxes at coeval regional sites has been interpreted as a transfer of their potentiality to that of the unifacial uniangular (Carbonell *et al.*, 1992) or as the existence of different technological traditions (Garcia, 2008, 2010, 2011).

5. Conclusions

The geoarchaeology of the terraces of the Ter middle basin, where the hominin occupations are spread among the upper (T4), middle (T3) and lower (T2) terraces of this river and among the alluvial Pleistocene deposits of the Onyar River (La Selva), suggests continuous hominin settlement throughout the Lower Palaeolithic. The occupations of Puig d'en Roca III and IV are situated in the stratigraphic sequence in the pediment that links up with the terrace at +20 metres and lies below the basaltic flow of Pla de Dalt-Jueria (prior to the 317±4.9 ky) (Lewis *et al.*, 1998). Within this regional context, continuity with respect to the population of the more recent Middle Pleistocene is represented in the paleosoil of Pla de Dalt-Jueria, on top of the basaltic flow, between 350 and 200 ky.

Cau del Duc de Torroella and d'Ullà, with a significant part of the sediments having been deposited during the Riss and with the last sedimentary contributions being accumulated during the initial phases of the Würm, would have to be attributed to this same period (Estévez, 1979). Based on the dating by the U-series method provided by a sample of the stalagmitic sheet, an absolute date was obtained that puts the age of the lowest stratigraphic layer at prior to 350 ky (Rodríguez *et al.*, 2003/2004). On the other hand, also using the U-series method, Tissoux (1999) obtained a date of 135+10/-9 ky for the stalagmitic levels that seal the stratigraphic package of Cau del Duc d'Ullà. Therefore, the occupations of these caves took place across a time span between 350 and 135 ky. During the early Upper Pleistocene, the continuity of the occupation of the Ter Basin occurs in the hominin settlement of Can Garriga (Giralt *et al.*, 1995).

The technical characteristics of the main sites of the Ter Basin point to a series of more archaic technological structures in Puig d'en Roca I-II, which would correspond to Mode 1. Within the context of this river basin, this technology would be related with the importance of the trifacial and multifacial strategies and an absence of the Levallois method, as well as of handaxes and cleavers. Puig d'en Roca Excavació, III and IV, with their more complex and developed technology, would be adscribed to Mode 2, where the Levallois method and handaxes and cleavers appear and/or increase, although only a small number of these are documented. One theoretical explanation for the absence or scarcity of handaxes at the coeval sites of the Ter Basin is based on the "transfer theory", which justifies the substitution of their morphodynamic potentialities by those of other instruments such as the pick (Carbonell *et al.*, 1992). Apart from the fact that this substitution could also be due to the different functionalities of the settlements, another more culturally-based interpretation put it down to the existence of differentiated technological traditions (Garcia, 2008, 2010, 2011).

At Cau del Duc de Torroella and La Selva, as well as at other sites in the Ter Basin such as Cau del Duc d'Ullà, La Jueria and Pedra Dreta, the increase in the standardisation of the industries and the gradual disappearance of the pebble tools (a good number of which still remain at Cau del Duc de Torroella and La Selva) and of handaxes and cleavers, would situate them in the Mode 3 evolutionary line. Other sites linked with the Ter Basin, such as Can Garriga and Can Rubau, where a higher level of standardisation of the lithic assemblage can be appreciated, would be ascribed to this same technical mode (Canal and Carbonell, 1989; Rodríguez and Lozano, 1999). In these cases, the sporadic presence of pebble tools can be interpreted as a regional persistence of archaic technical traditions that were being gradually replaced by the production of retouched tools.

Joaquim Soler Subils, Narcís Soler Masferrer, Alba Solés Coll, Xavier Niell Ciurana*

Cova de l'Arbreda from the Middle Paleolithic to the Neolithic

Situation of Cova de l'Arbreda

Cova de l'Arbreda is a cavity formed by travertine from the municipality of Serinyà (el Pla de l'Estany, Girona) (Fig. 1, with UTM coordinates 479077.64m E and 4667647.45m N, datum WGS84). It is one of a series of cavities of the same kind that are opened up along a travertine cliff in an area known as Reclau. Of these caves, in addition to Cova de l'Arbreda Reclau Viver, Mollet cave, Mollet III cave, d'En Pau cave and Cau del Roure are of interest in terms of Prehistory. They are all very close to one another and have been collapsed and masked with vegetation with the passing of time.

* Institut de Recerca Història, Universitat de Girona, Facultat de Lletres, Plaça Ferrater i Mora, 1 17071 Girona, joaquim.soler@gmail.com

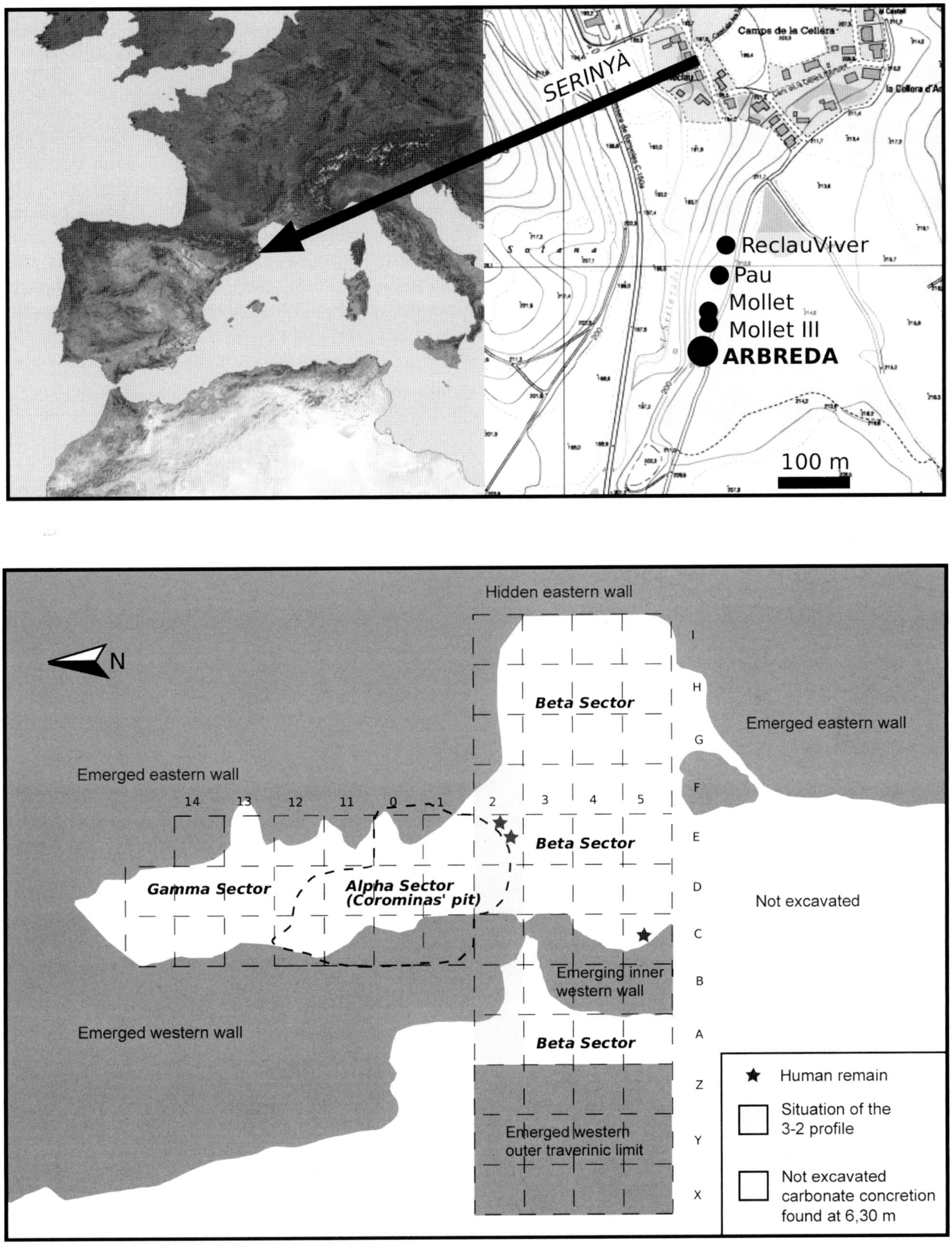

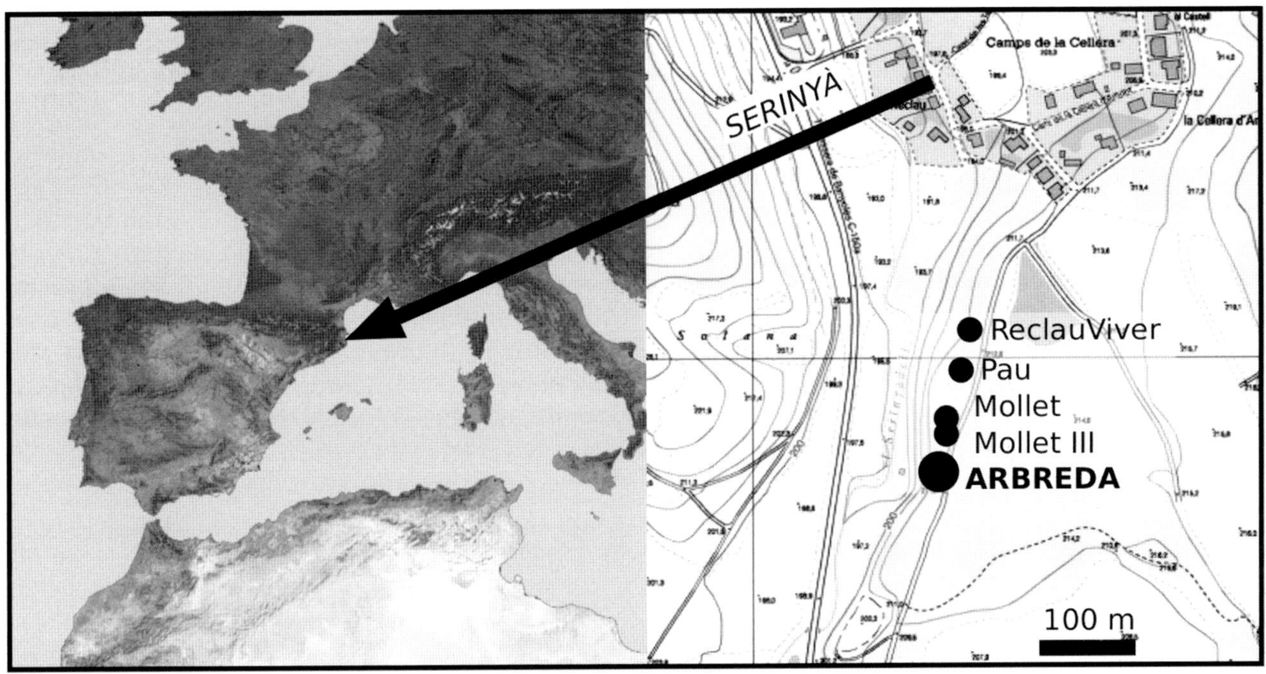

Figure 1. Location of Cova de l'Arbreda.

The Reclau (meaning cornered, protected place) area is long and narrow. A small stream, the Serinyadell, marks its western boundary while on the right, a narrow fluvial terrace separates it from the travertine slope where the cavities open up, on top of which the Usall plain is located, 10 m higher.

This plain, followed to the north by the Martís plain, is the old bed of a lake from the Plio-Pleistocene that left about 15 m of lacustrine travertine that is now very weathered and covered in clay. Erosion of surrounding land permitted the old underground springs that at one time had fed it to form the cascade travertine cliffs on its western and northern banks, where the sites are located. At present time the Serinyadell is fed almost exclusively by the springs that formed the cavities in the past and that still flow by its bed today. From the U/Th dating values obtained from the travertine of Cova de l'Arbreda, we know that the travertine in Reclau area was forming 250,000 years ago. Today, highly eroded, it simply forms a slope, a hill, and the cavities, the majority of which have collapsed, are hidden in the vegetation.

For thousands of years, the Reclau cavities provided nomad hunters with refuge but they were also occupied by cave hyenas and bears. During the Holocene they were used as graves and were less commonly settled. Arbreda is the cave that was habitable for the longest time, as its stratigraphy, which goes from the Middle Paleolithic to late Prehistory, is the most complete of all of the sites at Reclau (Soler Masferrer, 1999, Soler Masferrer *et al.*, 2009). Arbreda, Mollet and Mollet III contain Middle Paleolithic; Cova de l'Arbreda, Reclau Viver, Pau and, to a lesser extent, Mollet III and Mollet, Upper Paleolithic. All of them preserve remains of post-Paleolithic occupations. In general, they were abandoned after the Solutrean until the Neolithic and at the moment, Magdalenian has not been found in any of them. However, Upper Paleolithic hunters intensely occupied Bora Gran d'En Carreras, an open rock shelter in Plio-Pleistocene conglomerates on the other side of the Serinyadell, downstream from the Reclau site.

Excavations of Arbreda cave

Josep M. Corominas, doctor and archaeologist, who had worked at the Bora Gran site and taken part in Lluís Pericot's excavations of this site in 1944 and 1945, discovered the archaeological interest of the Reclau area between these dates and 1973 and totally or partially excavated all of the sites, starting with the Reclau Viver cave.

About 300 m south of this site, he was intrigued at different times by a small cavity in the travertine, called Cova de l'Arbreda, in which there was barely room for a couple of people, but the boreholes he made seemed unpromising. Finally, in 1972, he continued making boreholes from the inside, firstly through the travertine blocks and in the clay along almost 9 m. and as result he exposed the long stratigraphy of Cova de l'Arbreda that enriched the Upper Paleolithic that had been discovered previously in Reclau Viver cave (Soler and Maroto, 1987).

Josep M. Corominas called this borehole the Alfa sector and started two more adjacent boreholes. The northern borehole began two metres higher than elevation 0 and he stopped it at that levelCorominas called it the Gamma sector. The second was called Beta sector. It was opened to the south of Alfa sector in a lower area. It reached a depth of almost 2m. These sectors were protected by a cover from the beginning and the cuts have been kept in good condition.

In 1975 excavation of the Beta sector was resumed and continues today, when a depth of up to 7 m has been reached (9.60m in the profiles next to the Alfa sector). From the outset, the excavation, mainly directed by the same team, currently from the Universitat de Girona, has applied the same method and coordinated the same categories of objects. Cova de l'Arbreda has been protected with a new large cover and the rest of the sites at Reclau have been adapted for visitors and currently form the Serinyà Prehistoric Caves Park, which allows them to be shown to the public with aspects of the life of prehistoric man. The results of the excavation campaigns are published regularly (Soler Subils *et al.*, 2012).

Cave morphology

At present time It is difficult to get an idea of what Arbreda was like during Prehistory because it collapsed. To the east, on the edge of the Usall plain, there is a massive wall from which water fell from the Usall plain and calcareous formations were deposited. Those made it expand towards the west, forming the ceiling of a shelter. The high part of that massive wall is only visible today in the Gamma sector, where excavation was carried out and in the eastern edge of the Beta sector (Fig. 1). Part of the ceiling has been preserved over Alpha sector from this initial morphology as a shelter, we believe that Cova de l'Arbreda, became a cave through the merging of the edge of the shelter with a western wall that rose up from the ground in the places where water fell from the western edge of the ceiling. In accordance with this hypothesis, Arbreda could have been a long gallery running north to south with a high, permanent wall to the east, a ceiling, which could have been incomplete, and finally an unsteady wall to the west, which probably formed throughout various episodes of activity. It is the same model presented by the Reclau Viver cave, which is smaller but much better preserved. The collapse of Arbreda started from the south and west and reduced the space available to occupants, especially those of the Upper Paleolithic, who were increasingly cornered to the east. After the Evolved Aurignacian a large part of the ceiling fragmented and large blocks fell, forcing the Gravettian and Solutrean settlements to occupy the spaces between the them. After the Solutrean, a final collapse of the roof caused prehistoric nomads to lose interest in the cave.

Chronostratigraphy and prehistoric occupations of Cova de l'Arbreda

Once the springs that had formed it left the large gallery that we have imagined, it started filling in, which in general was done continuously. However, two major solutions of continuity were detected that establish three major geological divisions in the sequence.

The first division is between the Holocene filling (section A) of the Pleistocene (section B), which was eroded, in some areas at least, before the start of the Holocene. The latter covers, with varying thicknesses, all the sectors excavated. It is *terra rossa*, highly pure, very plastic red clay, accompanied only by worn travertine blocks. This clay comes from the decomposition of travertine blocks covering the Usall plain and must have been dragged from there by rainwater.

Section A contains some archaeological materials, the majority from the Neolithic, and human remains, which seems to suggest a burial function, taking advantage of the residual cavities in the travertine and the spaces protected after the collapse of the majority of the roof. Cardium pottery fragments indicate the presence of the Early Neolithic in the Beta sector, while elements typical of the Middle Neolithic have been found in the Gamma sector.

Under this red clay we found the Pleistocene sediment (section B), lighter and sandy, separated from section A by a line of erosion. It consists of clay and sand formed by small travertine particles and nodules, with small minerals and karst pebbles. There is a very high number of travertine fragments and calcareous concretions of all sizes, generally angular, making excavation difficult during the entire Upper Paleolithic. This is in addition to the large blocks that fell from the ceiling. A second line of erosion splits section B into two units: B.1 (upper) and B.2 (lower). Finally, a concretion followed by practically sterile silt closes the sequence, for now.

From the Pleistocene sediment we have distinguished several archaeological levels corresponding to the Upper and Middle Paleolithic, generally due to the differences in density and nature of the archaeological materials rather than the differences in the sediment or other geological criteria. We understand that, in general, these levels were formed over a long period of time, where individual occupations cannot be distinguished. However, in some cases, other intensive concentrations as a result of long or very close occupations were detected. We have named these levels, from top to bottom, A to N (Fig. 2). We will now go on to describe them and summarise the radiometric results available, adding some that are being published for the first time here (levels B, C, D and E).

Level A. The last Paleolithic evidences

In some places, as soon as it starts, the Pleistocene sediment contains Solutrean. In others, such as the Beta sector, it could be preceded by a practically sterile section of varying thickness, which we call level A. Some evidence suggests the passing of people from the Magdalenian.

Level B. Upper Solutrean

The first truly identifiable archaeological occupation is very poor in lithic industry and fauna. However, it contains some Solutrean notched points of Mediterranean type , short and wide, with abrupt notched retouch. It therefore corresponds to the Upper Solutrean, which is also found in Reclau Viver cave and d'En Pau cave. In 1987, a dating of 17,320±290 BP (Gif-6418), using conventional radiocarbon dating was obtained for level B (Delibrias *et al.*, 1987).

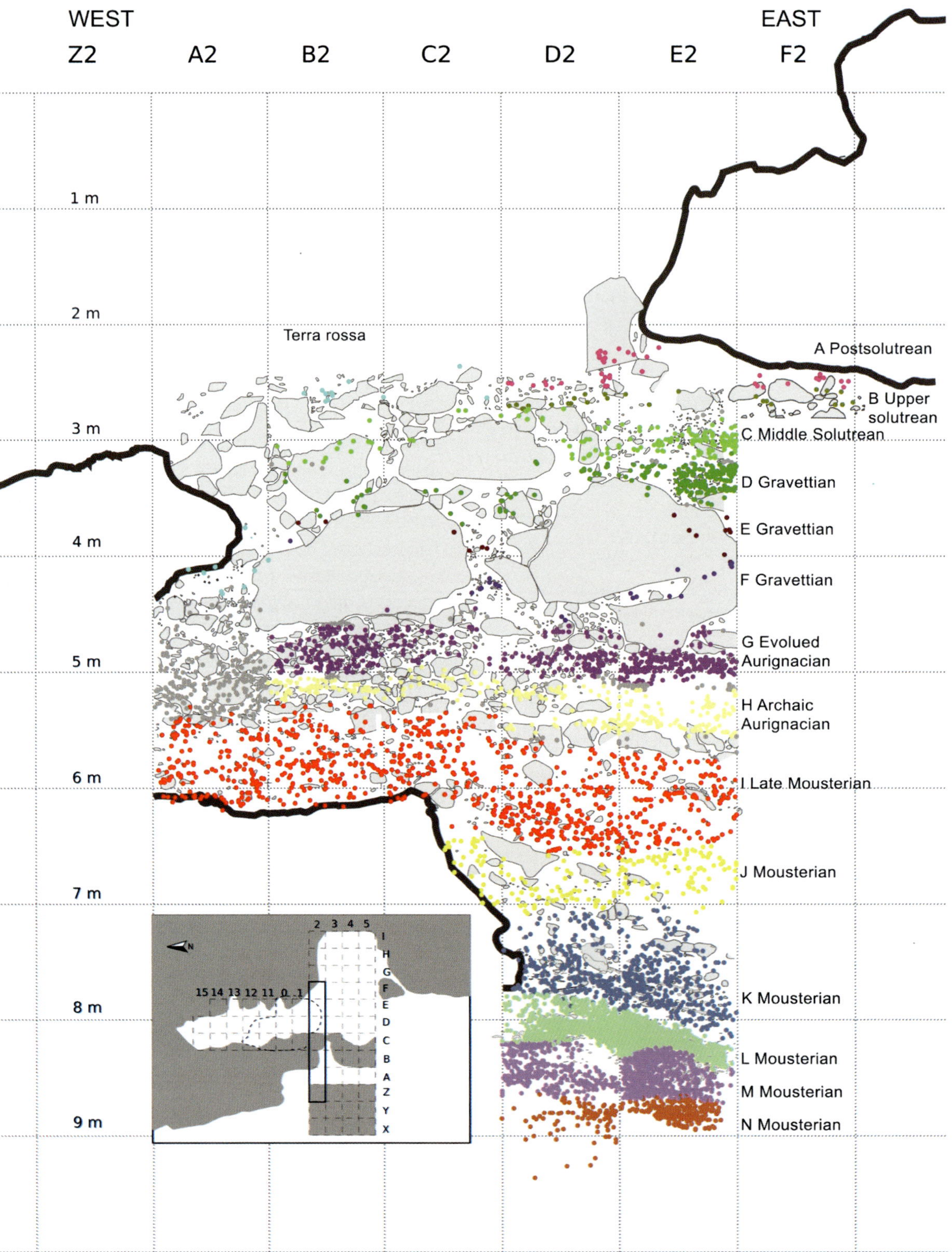

Figure 2. Stratigraphy of Cova de l'Arbreda with specification of the archaeological levels. The range of coordinated objects plotted belong to squares 2 and the profile 2/3.

This and other dating values for Cova de l'Arbreda obtained in 1987 at the Gif-sur-Ivette laboratory for lower levels are perfectly coherent with the stratigraphy but always exaggeratedly young, a problem also suffered by the first dating values obtained in Reclau Viver. New AMS dating values have been obtained for both sites that correct them. For level B we now have a new AMS value obtained from a deer phalanx with cut marks that attributes an age of 18,860±80 (GrA-47320) to it.

Level C. Middle Solutrean

Below is a level that is much richer in lithic industry and fauna. The origin of the majority of this level is anthropic and generally comes from horse and deer. Their bones were crushed to extract the bone marrow and left in the form of large chips. Many pebbles cracked by fire could have been used to boil them (Maroto and Terradas, 1986). On this level, the bone remains are larger and better preserved. The industry is well defined by the presence of flat retouched bifacial pieces, including asymmetric tanged points or Serinyadell points, which also characterise similar occupations in Reclau Viver cave and d'En Pau cave (Fig. 3). These industries have the highest percentage of flat retouch of all the Solutrean sites in the Iberian Peninsula (Fullola, 1979). To ascertain its absolute age, until recently we only had one result from Gif-sur-Yvette (17,720±290 BP, Delibrias *et al.*,,1987). Now a new dating of cut marks has given it a date of 19,480±80 BP (GrA-47330).

Level D. Gravettian

Below, among the large ceiling blocks detached after the Evolved Aurignacian, there is a section that is poorer in archaeological evidence, which we call level D. In previous publications it appears as Solutrean because a few fragments with flat retouch appeared on its ceiling. Now it should be attributed, its lower section at least, to the Middle Gravettian and we have a first radiocarbon dating obtained from a horse femur with cut marks, which returned a value of 22,630 ± 100 (GrA-47323). Perhaps this is poor evidence belongs to the Late Gravettian, which in Reclau Viver cave appeared with great richness and variety (Soler Masferrer and Soler Subils , 2013). From this result, and after carefully observing the range of coordinated objects and studying the materials, it has been concluded that this level should probably be subdivided in the future.

Level E. Gravettian

This occupation, widespread across the majority of the Beta sector, was concentrated towards the north east, where it was thick and dense, in the form of a high concentration of ash, lithic industry and fauna of anthropic origin among the blocks that had fallen from the ceiling. Its industry is characterised above all by the presence of many backed edged blades and points, or Gravette points. The flint is far much variedthan during the Solutrean, a detail that suggests very different origins of the raw material. We had a dating of 20,130±220 BP (Gif-6420, (Delibrias *et al.*,,1987) but now we have three new dating values. We published one of them recently, which was obtained from a chip with cut marks using the ultrafiltration method, which has returned a value of 25,780±210 (OxA-21669) or 26,100±210 (OxA-

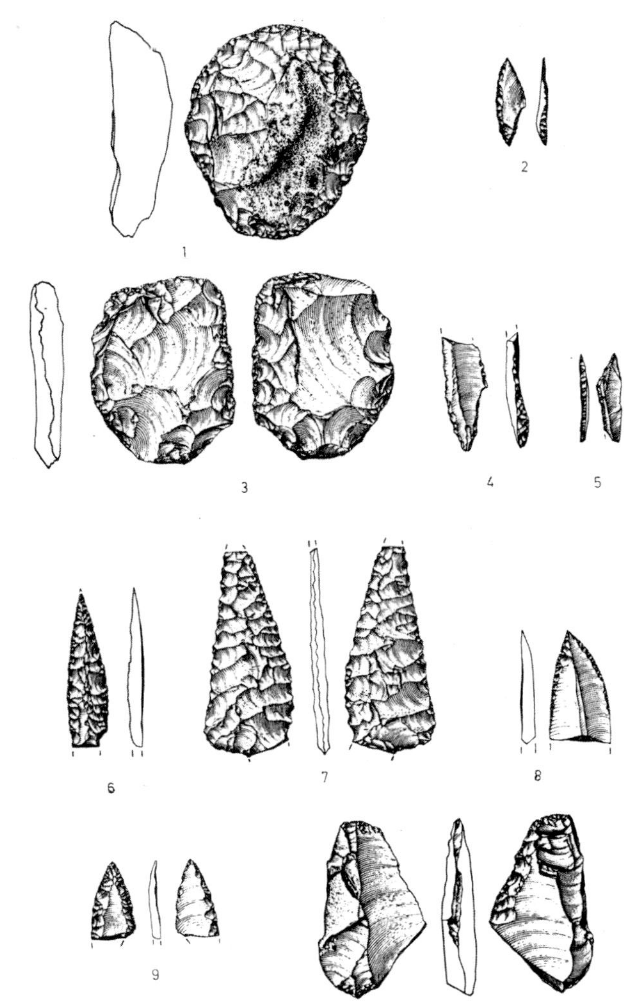

Figure 3. Solutrean lithic industry, levels B and C.

21668) (Wood *et al.*, 2014). A new AMS radiocarbon dating specifies an age of 24,840±120 (GrA-57326) and a third, AMS of a chip, provides another unpublished date of 25,240±120 (GrA-47351).

Level F. Gravettian

Among the large travertine blocks the archaeological remains become scarcer but a Gravettian level can be identified. We recently published two ultrafiltration results for deer remains: 28,280±290 (OxA-21782) and 28,260±280 (OxA21781) (Wood *et al.*, 2014).

Level G. Evolved Aurignacian

Below the base of the large blocks is evidence of intense occupation that spread throughout the Beta sector, as it was still protected by a large ceiling. In this level we excavated large hearths made of sandstone from the nearby tertiary lands on the right of the Serinyadell stream, which had been fragmented by the activity of fire. One block had been used to cover the inside of a small cookingtray that could have been used as an oven. The fauna remains, always anthropic, were very fragmented and dominated by deer. Palynology and anthracology analyses indicate a relatively warm climate with thermophile plant species, so we can assume a greater expansion of forests than during the Gravettian and Solutrean, both belonging to the colder times of the last glacial period (Burjachs and Renault-Miskovsky, 1992). The majority of the lithic industry is knapped in blackish grey flint from the Corbières massif, between the French Eastern Pyrenees departments and the Aude, 130 km from Serinyà. It is a highly microlith industry, with small cores in the shape of carinate scrapers or multiple burins from which tiny laminar flakes have been obtained, which have been retouched using semi-abrupt direct or inverse retouch and, in general, direct on one side and inverse on the other. They are 5-6 mm long and account for 80 to 90% of retouched tools. The rest are burins made using cross-lateral strikes, scrapers and a few racloirs. In contrast to the microliths of the flint industry, the material used to make the majority of the retouched tools, here we find a discoid quartz core 25 cm in diameter. As in the other Upper Paleolithic levels half of the industry is knapped on local stone, quartz dominating. The bone industry, consisting of rhomboid bone points with an oval section, which is also typical of the Evolved Aurignacian, more specifically from the period known as Aurignacian II by D. Peyrony (Fig. 4). This occupation does not exist in any other site at Reclau and in the Spanish Mediterranean a similar period is only known in Beneito cave (Iturbe and Cortell, 1992).

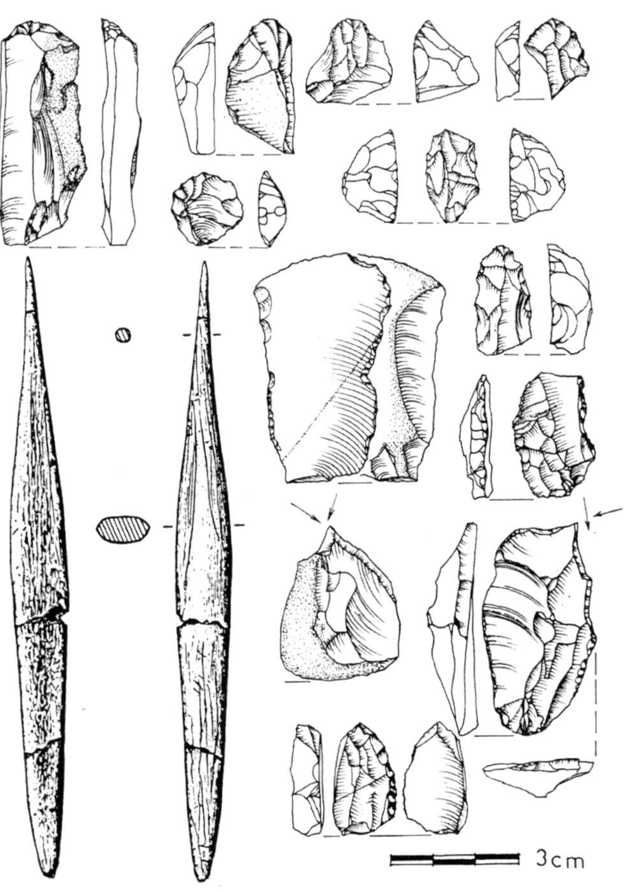

Figure 4. Evolved Aurignacian lithic and bone industry, level G.

The first radiocarbon dating obtained from this level returned a value of 22,590 ± 290 (Gif-6421, Delibrias *et al.*, 1987) and led us to assume a long duration of the Aurignacian in the eastern Pyrenees (Sacchi *et al.*, 1996). However, a new carbon dating of > 28,800 (Beta-85551), despite its lack of specificity, brought us to the dates typical of Aurignacian II or Late Aurignacian (Soler and Maroto 1993). Recently we obtained three dating values based on the ultrafiltration method. The first is a direct dating of a typical rhomboid spear from the time, which characterizes this level perfectly and this has returned a value of 32,100 ± 450 BP (OxA-21783). The other two results were obtained from chips with cut marks and returned ages of 32,250 ± 450 (OxA-21667) and 32,750 ± 450 BP (OxA-21666) respectively (Wood *et al.*, 2014). A dating on charcoal returned the value 30,950 ± 220 (OxA-19935) (Maroto *et al.*, 2012).

Level H. Archaic Aurignacian

This is what we call the level below the Evolved Aurignacian level. This level contains several occupations, which we imagine are quite close to one another in time. They correspond to the Archaic Aurignacian or Proto-Aurignacianand and are characterised by many alternate semi-abrupt retouch flakes or Dufour bladelets, from pyramidal or prismatic cores, only curved along the length and much bigger than those of the Evolved Aurignacian. They are accompanied by cores, burins and large flint flakes, rarely retouched, in the form of Aurignacian blades. The retouched tools are almost exclusively made of flint from the the Corbières massif (Ortega *et al.*, 2005). Among the bone industry we found three bone points with a split base of different sizes, which are the only ones found in the Spanish Mediterranean, apart from the one in Reclau Viver cave. They could be part of the Archaic Aurignacian or from a sporadic Classic Aurignacian occupation towards the top of the level. AMS dating values were obtained for the top of the level, around ten centimetres above the underlying Mousterian, which returned dates around 38,000 BP (Bischoff *et al.*, 1989, Hedges *et al.*, 1994, Maroto *et al.*, 1996). They are very old dates for the Archaic Aurignacian, and although they were positively compared with similar ones from Castillo cave (Puente Viesgo, Cantabria) and from Abric Romaní (Capellades, Anoia, Barcelona), questions were raised about their validity (Zilhão and d'Errico, 1999). We subsequently explained that the samples were taken from places that were undoubtedly part of level H and in an industrial context that did not raise any questions (Soler *et al.*, 2009). We recently published ultrafiltration results for the bone industry and fauna remains with anthropic signs from level H that, curiously, provided more recent dates: 34,800±760 (SANU-29017), 35,900±860 (SANU-29019), 35,700±830 (SANU-29016), 31,900±530 (SANU-29014), 33,800±500 (OxA-21674), 35,850±700 (OxA-21665), 36,000±700 (OxA-21784), 35,900±650 (OxA-21664) (Wood *et al.*, 2014)

Level I. Late Mousterian

Below the Archaic Aurignacian, in the same geological section, B.1, where the levels described up until now are located, comes level I, corresponding to the Late Mousterian. It is a typically Mousterian industry and completely different from the Archaic Aurignacian industry. It hardly contains any flint; almost all of the industry is knapped in local stones, the same as that used during all the Mousterian levels. A clear and sudden rupture is detected between the Mousterian and Aurignacian of Arbreda that does not present arguments for a cultural transition.

The top of level I is anthropic, rich in industry and fauna. The industry includes Châtelperronian points, but we cannot talk about a level or occupation of this facies, which should present a laminar technique, bone industry and decorative objects like other Upper Paleolithic cultures, which are completely absent from level I.

The first dates obtained from this period put the level at around 40,000 BP (Bischoff *et al.*, 1989) and sustain that, in addition to being sudden, the replacement of Neanderthal man by anatomically modern man must have been fast (Maroto *et al.*, 1996). We have recently obtained new radio carbon dating results using the ultrafiltration method applied to the fauna remains with anthropic signs that offer a less clear visionof the chronology of level I : 32,100±450 (OxA-21663), 32,300±450 (OxA-21703), 39,200±1.000 (OxA-21704), 44,400±1.900 (OxA-21702), 37,300±800 (OxA-21662) (Wood *et al.*, 2014). Another dating on charcoal has returned the date of 38,350±400 (OxA-19994) (Maroto *et al.*, 2012).

Towards the bottom of this level I, the fauna remains of non-anthropic origin increase, basically cave bears. The artifacts, although still abundant, are more dispersed. We interpret it as evidence of short occupations that were alternated with hibernating ursidae, that could have distorted human occupations.

We establish the lower limit of level I coinciding with an eroded surface at around 6.30 m and which splits section B into units B.1 and B.2. This line also coincides with another concretion surface in the west of the Beta sector and the base of an accumulation of stalagmites.

The Alfa sector and the northeast part of the Beta sector of level I and the underlying level J are altered by phosphate paragenesis.

Level J. Mousterian

In this level the Mousterian industry is present throughout but identifiable fauna of clearly anthropic origin is very scarce. However, cave bear remains are abundant; we have referenced hundreds of milk teeth, found whole skeletons of newborn. In a similar depth in the Alfa sector the skeleton of an old bear with very worn teeth had been found. Level J has also provided a tooth of a *Homo Neanderthalensis*. Level J is where now the excavation of the Mousterian levels of Beta sector is located, more specifically at 7 m deep. At the moment, we only know of lower levels in the Alfa sector after the regularisation we did between this profile and the Beta 2/3 profile 2/3 (Fig. 2).

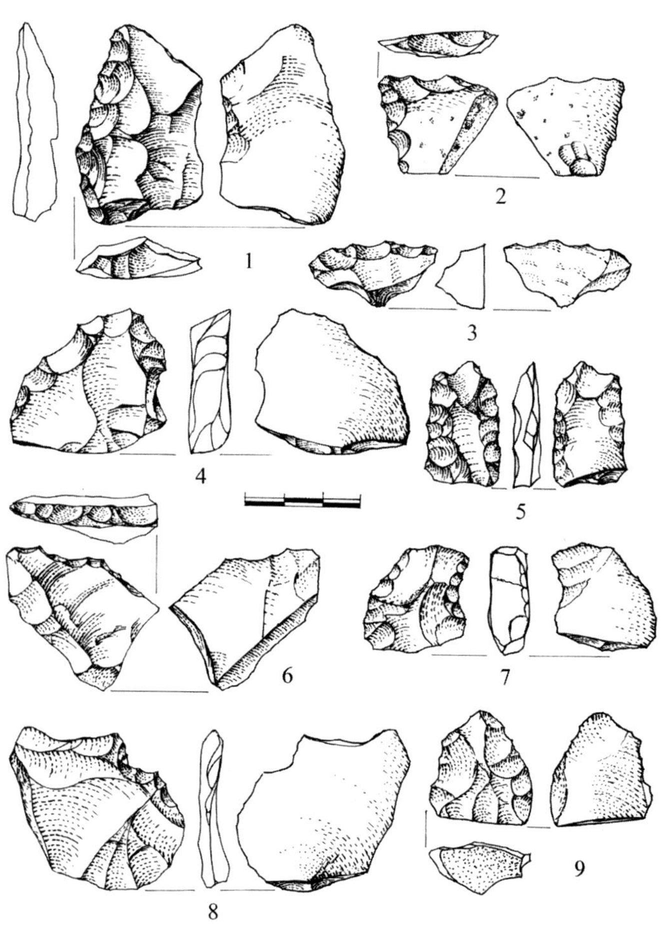

Figure 5. Mousterian industry from level M, frame E2, at 8.55 m deep.

Level K. Mousterian

As in level J and the base of I, we interpret this level as a result of alternating short occupations by humans and ursidae. The archaeological materials are affected by a precipitation of manganese that clearly distinguishes them from those belonging to higher levels and also from the lower levels, from which they are separated by a clear solution of continuity: a thick black line of sediment with a high level of manganese that closes the level along with a very poor section about 15 cm thick.

Level L. Mousterian

An extraordinary concentration of fauna remains of anthropic origin and lithic industry indicate the presence of level L, in a context of calcareous sand and gravel, with hardly any finer sediment. The ursidae occupations have disappeared. The only regularisation of the profile between the Alfa and Beta sectors and total excavation of at least half a square metre in frames D2 and E2 has provided thousands of coordinated objects. We believe that this density is not only a consequence of repeating human occupations; the rises in the underground water levels might also have intervened, washing the sediment and concentrating the objects. There are a few rolled objects but most of them preserve fresh edges. The level ends with calcareous concretions.

Levels M and N

Below is another l high concentration of industry and fauna in which two large levels can be distinguished, M and N (Fig. 5). Level N has provided two *Homo Neanderthalensis* molars, which seems to have come from two individuals. Ursidae occupations have not been detected.

Calcareous concretion at the base and underlying silt

The lower level, N, lies on a calcareous concretion that seems to be formed by water running down the western and northern walls. At the top, in the form of a gap, it encloses industry and fauna. Its thickness is very uneven. In E2, which was dug to cement the base of a metal structure, they reached a depth of at least 60 cm. D2 is thinner and below it there is a mixture of yellowish grey silt which is, so far, sterile (section C).

	Quartz	Quartzite	Cristal	Porphiries	Hornfels	Silexs	Radiolarite	Sandstone	Other	TOTAL %	TOTAL (n)
I FINAL MOUSTERIAN	76,5%	8,0%	0,1%	5,1%	3,4%	4,3%	0,6%	0,8%	1,3%	11,1%	1582
blanks	167	54		27	25	28	2	5	3	311	
fragmented blanks	218	48	1	19	21	18	2	2	4	333	
indeterminable	808	21	32	32	7	22	5	5	12	912	
pebbles and fragmented pebbles	18	3	2	2			1		2	26	
J MOUSTERIAN	77,7%	10,0%	0,3%	2,6%	2,7%	3,0%	0,3%	16,0%	2,2%	27,6%	3670
blanks	706	150	3	40	52	35	5	16	25	1032	
fragmented blanks	969	139	7	34	36	59	3	11	25	1283	
indeterminable	1048	61	1	21	11	19	4	17	18	1195	
pebbles and fragmented pebbles	128	17				1		3	11	160	
K MOUSTERIAN	76,6%	11,1%	0,6%	1,6%	2,3%	3,8%	0,2%	0,0%	2,8%	9,3%	1237
blanks	185	62		10	13	16		3	13	302	
fragmented blanks	467	61	8	6	13	24	1	3	16	599	
indeterminable	282	14		4	3	7		5	6	321	
pebbles and fragmented pebbles	14						1			15	
L MOUSTERIAN	76,7%	9,3%	0,2%	2,2%	5,5%	2,8%	0,3%	0,8%	2,2%	29,3%	3891
blanks	1186	208		64	122	68	4	18	50	1710	
fragmented blanks	1236	123	5	15	78	47	9	4	27	1544	
indeterminable	502	28	1	6	13	4		7	7	568	
pebbles and fragmented pebbles	60	4		1				1	3	69	
M MOUSTERIAN	78,2%	8,8%	0,1%	3,9%	4,7%	1,2%	0,2%	1,5%	1,5%	8,6%	1138
blanks	386	67	1	37	43	11	2	14	9	570	
fragmented blanks	307	28		4	8	2		3	4	356	
indeterminable	150	4		2	2					158	
pebbles and fragmented pebbles	47	1		1		1			4	54	
N MOUSTERIAN	80,1%	10,2%	0,5%	3,5%	2,0%	1,2%	0,2%	1,2%	1,2%	13,2%	1759
blanks	590	100	4	39	19	13	1	12	14	792	
fragmented blanks	511	57	4	13	13	5	2	4	3	612	
indeterminable	240	15		8	4	3		1	3	274	
pebbles and fragmented pebbles	68	7		1				4	1	81	
ALL MOUSTERIAN LEVELS	77,5%	9,6%	0,3%	2,9%	3,6%	2,8%	0,3%	1,0%	2,0%	100,0%	13277
	Quartz	Quartzite	Cristal	Porphiries	Hornfels	Silexs	Radiolarite	Sandstone	Other	TOTAL %	TOTAL (n)

Table 1. Table of all of the Mousterian industry from all the Middle Paleolithic levels of Cova de l'Arbreda.

Chronology of the Mousterian levels

Apart from the Late Mousterian (ceiling of level I), whose nature and age we have discussed, the entire sequence of Mousterian levels show very similar behavioural cultures (Duran and Soler 2006). The lithic artefacts are always knapped in local rock (table 1), quartz dominating overall. Small products based on discoid and Levallois cores and others that use the ventral side of thick flakes as a production surface are obtained. Some of the supports produced are transformed into racloirs and denticulate tools.

The animal species documented (*Cervus elaphus*, *Equus ferus* and *Equus hydruntinus*, *Bos primigenius*, *Capra pyrenaica*, *Bison priscus*, *Sus scrofa*, *Oryctolagus cuniculus*, *Lepus europaeus*, *Ursus spelaeus*, *Canis lupus* and occasionally, *Vulpes vulpes*, *Crocuta crocuta*, *Castor fiber* and *Elephas*) suggest a diverse environment and wide catchment area but do not help us to definitively decide the chronology.

Two dating values from the Uranium series on the stalagmites found at the base under level N specify an age after 140,000 that is compatible with the range of fauna identified and with the cultural character of the lithic industry.

Joan Daura *, Montserrat Sanz*

Cova del Gegant (Sitges, Barcelona)

Location and description

Cova del Gegant (Sitges, Barcelona) is a cave located in the Garraf Massif (NE Iberian Peninsula), on the cape of Punta de les Coves (UTM Zone 31T, Abscisa 397159.04 m E, 4564171.74m N) facing the sea and to the west of the delta generated by Riera de Ribes. Cova del Gegant is currently accessible both from the sea and from above, via a vertical shaft located over the Main Gallery (GP).

Cova del Gegant is actually formed by a subterranean network (Fig 1), which includes Cova del Gegant and the adjacent Cova Llarga or de la Trompeta (CL), to which it is connected by a very narrow passage (GL-T). Cova del Gegant is the most important and consist of a principal chamber (GP1+GP2) with a length of 22 m and two side galleries (GL) almost in parallel, one closer to the sea (GL1) and the other, more interiorly (GL2).

Although there are previous studies (Masriera, 1975, Martínez *et al.*, 1985, Mora, 1988; Martínez *et al.*, 1989; Daura, 2008) focused on the stratigraphy, the sequence of Cova del Gegant is currently defined based on a total of 8 episodes from the Upper Pleistocene (Episodes 1-3) to the Holocene (Epsiodes 4-7) (Daura *et al.*, 2010. Episode 0 is placed at the base, represented by level XVI, which is characterised by a thin layer of endokarstic deposit of red clay. Above it is Episode 1, documented in a large part of the cave (GP1-GP2, GL2) and which corresponds to level V and probably also to level XVIII, but not documented in GL1. This is followed by Episode 2, represented by level IV (GP), XIIb (GL2) and VIII (GP). Levels XXIV and XXVII, documented in the GP, also correspond to this moment whereas as level XV of GL1 could be associated to this time and levels XVII and XVa, which are preserved as a small concretion only, could probably also be associated. Episode 3 is formed by levels II and IIb (GP, GL2) and by level XVa and part of levels IX and XVII (GL2 and GL1). Fig 1-B shows these correlations, some of which are tentative.

As regards the Holocene levels, Episode 4 is the oldest (Bronze Age), represented by levels

* Grup de Recerca del Quaternari (GRQ) – Seminari Estudis i Recerques Prehistòriques (SERP). Dept. Prehistòria, H. Antiga i Arqueologia. Facultat de Geografia i Història. Universitat de Barcelona. C/Montalegre, 6-8.08001 Barcelona.
[J. Daura: jdaura_lujan@ub.edu; M. Sanz: grq@ub.edu]

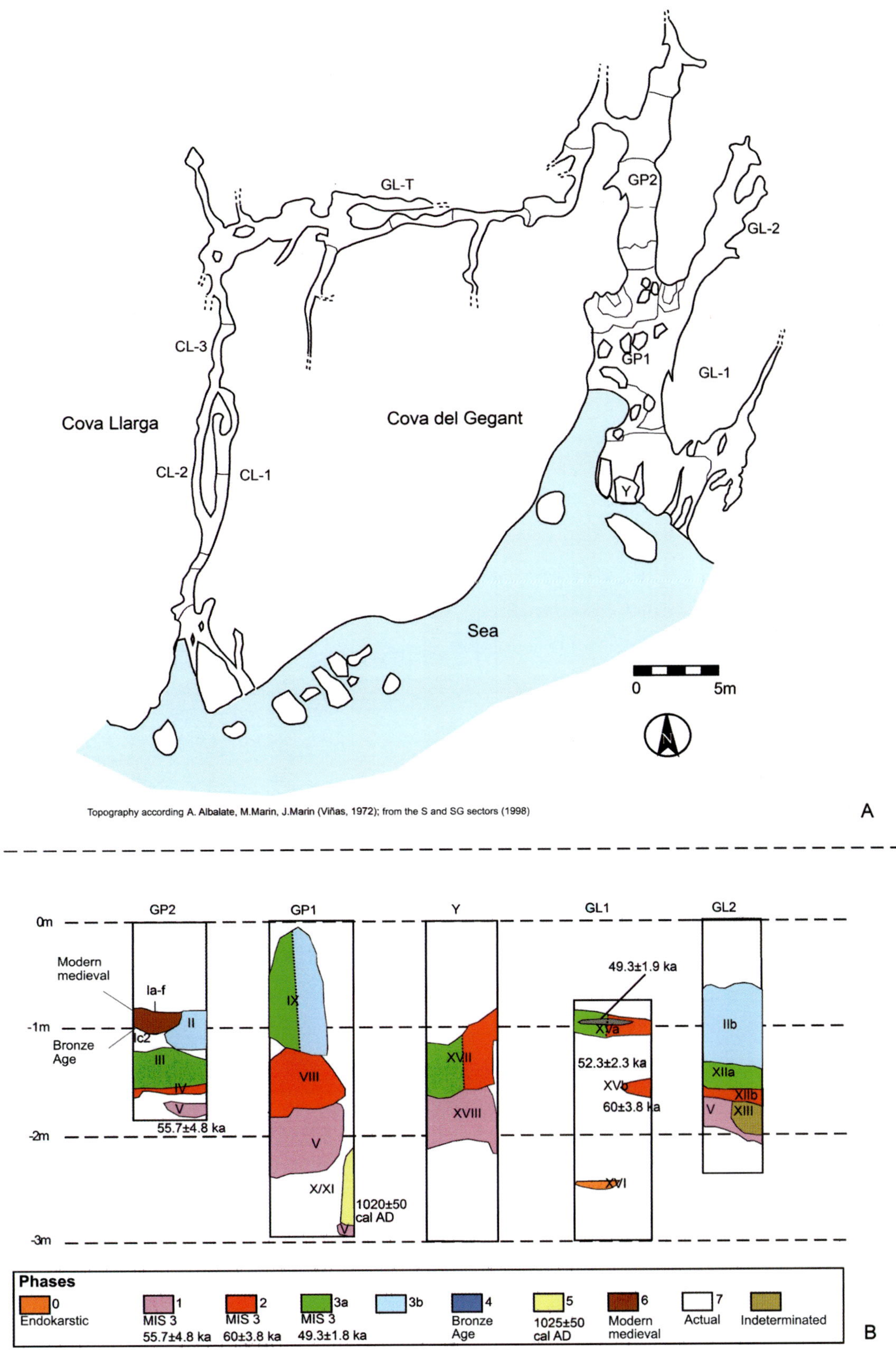

Figure 1. A: Plan site of Cova del Gegant. B: Stratigraphy and chronology.

Carnivora

Canis lupus
Cuon alpinus
Crocuta crocuta
Felis silvestris
Ursus arctos
Vulpes vulpes
Meles meles
Panthera pardus
Lynx pardinus

Lagomorpha

Oryctolagus cuniculus
Lepus capensis

Anura

Pelobates cultripes
Bufo sp.
Bufo bufo
Bufo calamita
Anura indet.
cf. *Rana*

Galliformes

Alectoris rufa
Coturnix coturnix

Apodiformes

Apus apus

Columbiformes

Columba livia s. oenas

Proboscidea

Proboscidea indet.

Primates

Homo neanderthalensis

Artiodactyla

Bos/Bison
Capra pyrenaica
Cervus elaphus
Sus scrofa

Rodentia

Microtus arvalis
Microtus agrestis
Terricola duodecimcostatus
Terricola aff. *pyrenaicus*
Iberomys cabrerae
Apodemus sylvaticus
Eliomys quercinus
Hystrix cf. *vinogradovi*

Passeriformes

Anthus spinoletta
Emberiza calandra
Coccothraustes coccothraustes
Pyrrhocorax pyrrhocorax
Pyrrhocorax graculus
Corvus monedula
Pinicola enucleator
Pica pica
Turdus viscivorus
Fringilla coelebs
Carduelis chloris
Delichon urbica
Corvus corone

Perissodactyla

Stephanorinus hemitoechus
Equus ferus
Equus hydruntinus

Chelonia

Testudo hermanni
Emys sp.

Squamata

Lacerta cf. *lepida*
Timon cf. *lepidus*
Malpolon monspessulanus
Rhinechis scalaris
Serpentes indet.
Colubrinae indet.
Vipera sp.

Chiroptera

Myotis myotis
Myotis sp.
Miniopterus shreibersi
Rhinolophus ferrumequinum

Procellariiformes

Puffinus puffinus

Strigiformes

Athene noctua
Tyto alba
Strix aluco

Table 1. Faunal assemblage from Cova del Gegant according to the data collected from various authors Viñas, 1972; Viñas and Villalta 1975; Estévez, 1979; Mora, 1988; Cerdeño, 1990; Martínez, 1990; Santafé and Casanovas, 1993; Blain, 2005; Daura *et al.*, 2005; Fèlix *et al.*, 2006; López-García *et al.*, 2008; Daura, 2008; Sanz, 2013 and Samper-Carro and Martínez-Moreno, 2014). For the micro-fauna we have used the latest review from López-García *et al.*, (2008). For birds we have included the review by Sánchez Marco (2005), which does not include modern species that have probably been infiltrated.

VI and Ic2 (GP, GL2) and to which level XXV (GP2) has been added recently. Episode 5 corresponds to an erosive transgression that emptied part of the deposit and accumulated beach sand, corresponding to level VII, X and XIf (Iron Age – Middle Age). Episode 6 is the most recent sediment with levels Ia-f (Middle Age –Modern). Finally Episode 7 corresponds to current sea erosion.

Fauna remains and lithic industry

Cova del Gegant has provided a significant collection of fauna remains, particularly from GL1, GL2 and GP2. The most relevant data so far comes from GL1, where it is possible to establish a unified taxonomical list of recovered species. Table 1 shows all of the data available for this part of the cave based on studies of large mammals (Viñas, 1972; Viñas and Villalta 1975; Estévez, 1979; Mora, 1988; Cerdeño, 1990; Martínez, 1990; Santafé and Casanovas, 1993; Blain, 2005; Daura *et al.*, 2005; Fèlix*et al.* 2006; López-García *et al.*, 2008; Daura, 2008; Sanz, 2013; Samper-Carro and Martínez-Moreno, 2014). For the micro-fauna we have used the latest review from López-García *et al.*, (2008 and 2011). For the birds we have used the review from Sánchez Marco (2005), which does not include modern species that have probably been infiltrated.

The most common species among the carnivore fauna remains is hyena (*Crocuta crocuta*), which dominates the assemblage. Many coprolites have also been recovered, which along with taphonomic traces of bone remains, demonstrate that the cave was mainly used as a den. Felids, although fewer in number, are also well represented, particularly by leopard (*Panthera pardus*) and lynx (*Lynx pardinus*), as canids by wolf (*Canis lupus*) and fox (*Vulpes vulpes*) and bear (*Ursus arctos*) are also present, albeit fewer in number.

However, the assemblage is dominated by equids (*Equus ferus* and *Equus hydruntinus*), followed by other large herbivores, such as large bovids (*Bos primigenius*) or the rhinoceros (*Stephanorhinus hemitoechus*), taxa that are associated to open spaces. Species related to Mediterranean environments, such as *Sus scrofa* or rocky areas, such as *Capra*, are virtually testimonial.

In this respect, the micro-fauna remains correspond to taxa associated to open spaces (Alcalde, 1986; López-García *et al.*, 2011) that, along with the large vertebrates and chronological period within which the site is located, could be related to the presence of the now submerged coastal plain. Bird remains (Sánchez, 2005) also document an open environment with running water, probably marked by the presence of the delta and the river Ribes, less than 1km from the site.

So far, Cova del Gegant has provided few lithic remains, totalling around 100 remains in the entire site, which come from previous excavations (Mir, 1975; Martínez *et al.*, 1985; Martínez *et al.*, 1989) and current excavations, although the majority of the lithic remains come from GL1. The assemblage is dominated by retouched objects (37%-NR 25), followed by lithic flake (32%-NR 22), flake fragments (16%-NR 11), knapped remains (12%-8) and cores (3%-NR 2) (Mora, 1988).

Human remains

In Cova del Gegant three human remains of Neanderthals are identified (Fig. 2) (Daura and Sanz, 2011-2012). The first (Gegant-1) corresponds to a mandible, formed by three fragments that make up the majority of the mandibular corpus, the alveoli from the third left molar to the first right molar. The fact that it almost does not have a chin, the rear positioning of the mental foramen and the size clearly assign this specimen as Neanderthal (Daura *et al.*, 2005). From this mandible it has been possible to establish a sequence of 52 mitochondrial DNA base pairs, allowing the fossil to be generally identified as Neanderthal; this confirms the anthropological analyses previously carried out (Arsuaga *et al.*, 2011). Similarly, the human fossil has been dated directly using U-Th dating, returning an age of 52.3±2.3 ky. The sediment that fills GL1, from where the mandible comes, is dated at between 49.4±1.8 and 60.3±3.8 ky, a chronology that is fully consistent with the age obtained directly from the human fossil and from the proposals made for the biostratigraphy (Daura *et al.*, 2011).

A second Neanderthal remain was recovered from the same site (Gegant-2). It is a permanent lower side incisor from the 1974-75 excavations (Rodríguez *et al.*, 2011; Sanz, 2013). The study of its morphology and size shows that this tooth

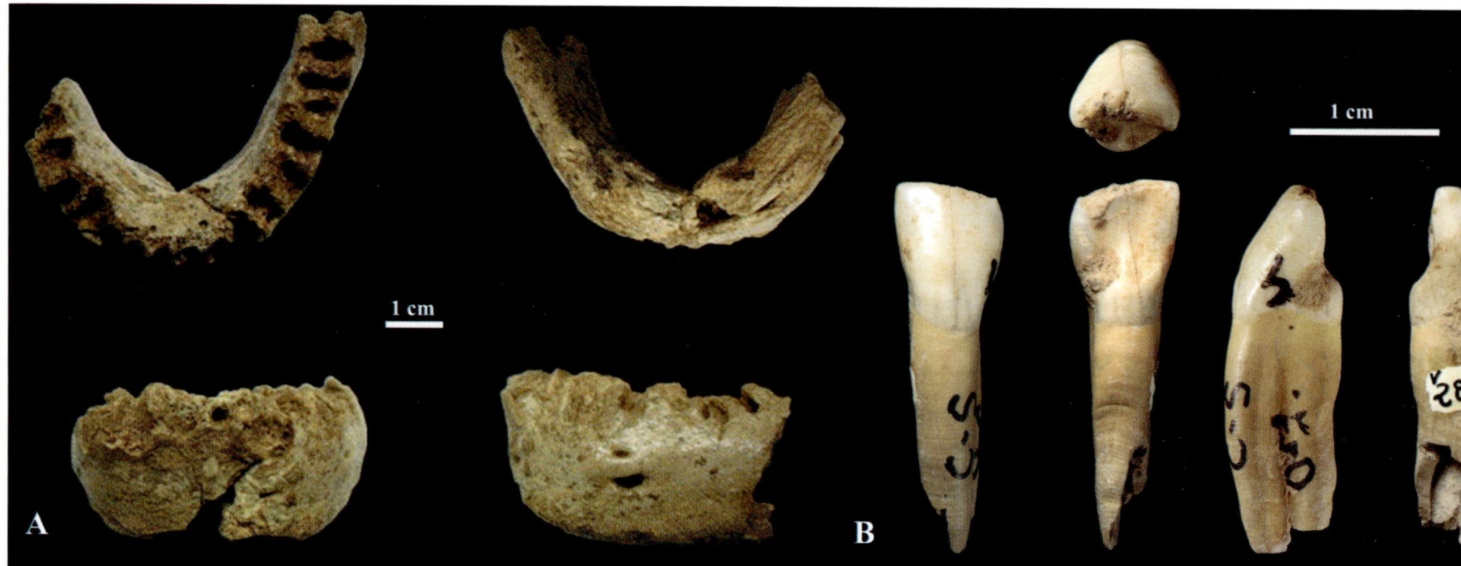

Figure 2. Neanderthal mandible (Gegant-1) (A) and incisor (Gegant-2) (B) from Cova de Gegant.

is clearly Neanderthal but it is difficult to associate the mandible and the tooth, as although they both come from the same gallery, they are from different individuals. The mandible (Gegant-1) would be from an adult and the tooth would be from a subadult aged between 8 and 10 years old (Rodríguez *et al.*, 2011).

Finally, the third remain (Gegant-3) from the 1985 campaign corresponds to the germ of a permanent central incisor (Martínez *et al.*, 1985, 1989; Martínez 1990). This remain comes from the excavation of GL2 and was found in a level with black sand (level IV of 1985; level B of 1989, Vb3 and V cof 2010).

Therefore, from Cova de Gegant we have three Neanderthal human remains from three individuals. The first, a mandible from GL1 (Gegant-1) from an individual over 15 years old, the lower incisor (Gegant-2) also from GL1,from an individual between 8 and 10 years old and finally the germ of a incisor (Gegant-3), from GL2, possibly from a younger individual than the aforementioned.

Acknowledgements

This article is the result of the research project *Humans, carnívors i medi natural durant el Plistocè al massís del Garraf-Ordal i curs baix del riu Llobregat*, within the SERP project funded by 2014SGR-108 and 2010ACOM00061 (Generalitat de Catalunya), HAR2011-26193 (MICINN). J. Daura funded by the Juan de la Cierva programme. The fieldwork was funded by the Servei d'Arqueologia i Paleontologia de la Generalitat de Catalunya.

Montserrat Sanz*/ Joan Daura *

Cova del Rinoceront (Castelldefels, Barcelona)

Location and site description

Cova del Rinoceront (Castelldefels, Barcelona) is located in the Garraf karstic massif (North-eastern sector of the Iberian Peninsula), in an abandoned limestone quarry at 25 metres a.s.l. (UTM Zone 31T, 412969.78 E, 4569650.51 N), and approximately 1 km from the current coastline. Today, the morphology of the site is modified by quarrying and the rehabilitation works of the rocky slope where the cave is located (Sanz *et al.*, 2011; Terrado *et al.*, 2013).

From the original karstic conduit only an approximate area of 5-6 m^2 remains, while the original entrance has been completely destroyed. Archaeological fieldwork has been focused on the excavation and sampling of the deposit preserved in stratigraphic position and sieving the sediments accumulated at the foot of section.

Stratigraphy and chronology

At Cova del Rinoceront eight sedimentary layers have been grouped into three main lithological units (Daura, 2008).

From base to top:

- Unit III, comprising layers VIII and VI, is composed of silty-sandy facies separated by an accumulation of subangular gravels (layerVII).
- Unit II corresponds to the middle unit of the stratigraphic sequence and is composed of layer V formed by a breccia with large boulders, and layer IV characterized by gravels and granules almost without matrix.
- Unit I is the upper unit and it is composed of layers I, II and III, characterized by breccia deposits with large-sized clasts and boulders. Finally, the deposit was sealed by a speleothem flowstone (Fig. 1).

Cova del Rinoceront chronology spans from 83 ky to 220 ky, since a thorough chronological study is still in progress. U/Th samples obtained on the speleothem flowstone have provided a minimum age for the deposit; the average of the two samples taken has yielded a date of 83.8 ± 5.9 ky BP. TL dating from level I have provided a date around 87 ky. Although it was obtained by the additive dose method, this date is consistent with results from the stalagmite flowstone. Finally, other U/Th dates were obtained from speleothems formed in the cavity walls, indicating a maximum age for the site, ranging from 218 ky to 261 ky. Results allow us to establish that the site presents a chronological range from 250 ky to 85 ky, which correlates with isotopic stages 5 to 7.

Faunal remains and lithic assemblages

The most abundant archaeological evidences in the site are faunal remains (large and small), lithics, and other bioarchaeological indicators (coprolites, charcoals, etc). Lithic remains are scarce (NR=22) and do not allow us to infer any technological or typological assumption, although the small size of the artefacts should be highlighted (Daura *et al.*, 2005).

The most remarkable evidences are large vertebrate remains. Levels I and II were completely excavated between 2003 and 2010, while works in level III are currently being carried out. The concentration of bones in levels I and II is extremely high and some skeletal elements are articulated. Also cranial and postcranial bones are present; however ribs and vertebrae are low in number, the

* Grup de Recerca del Quaternari (GRQ) – Seminari Estudis i Recerques Prehistòriques (SERP). Dept. Prehistòria, H. Antiga i Arqueologia. Facultat de Geografia i Història. Universitat de Barcelona. C/Montalegre, 6-8.08001 Barcelona.
[M. Sanz: grq@ub.edu; J. Daura: jdaura_lujan@ub.edu]

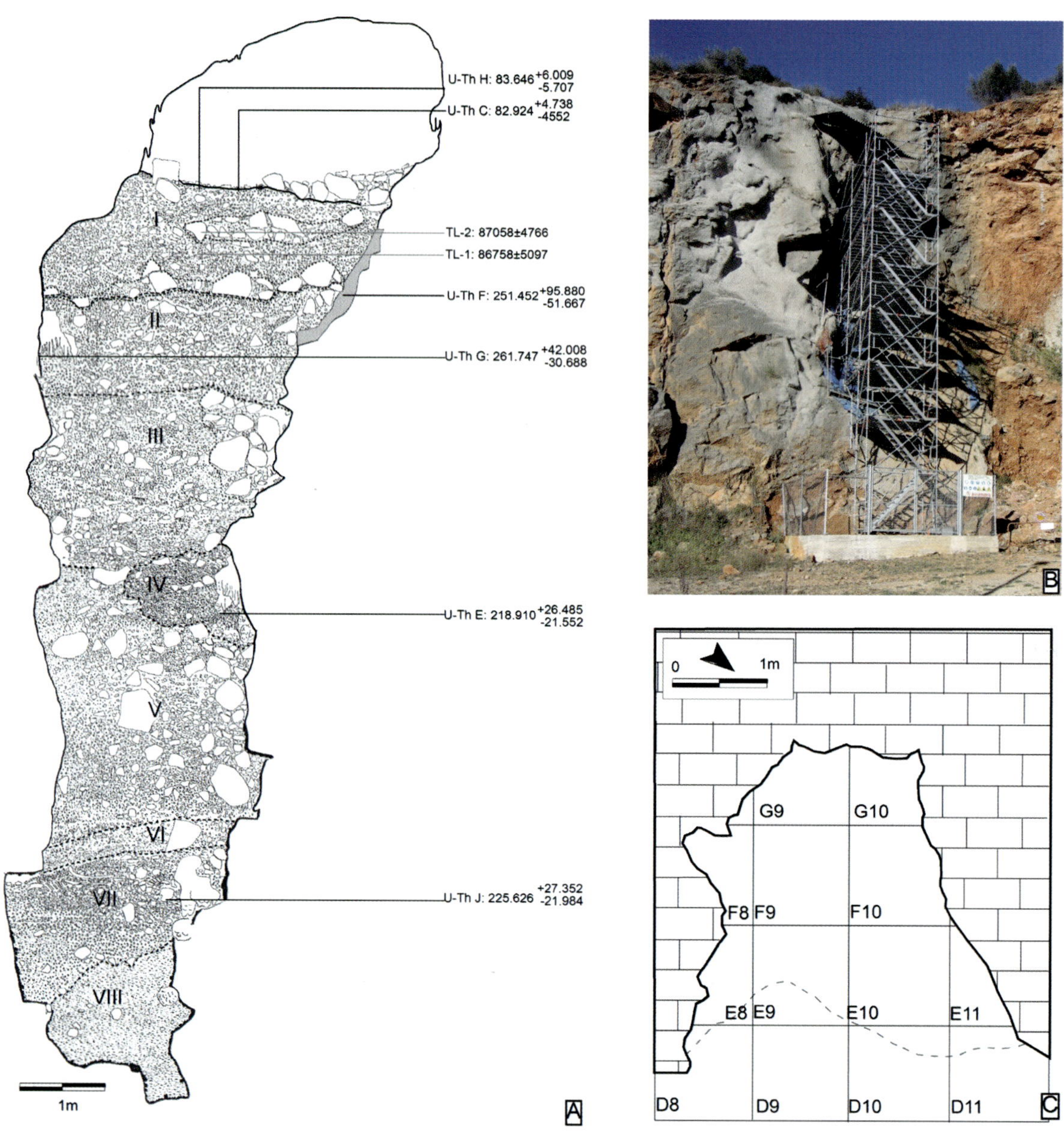

Figure 1. Cova del Rinoceront. A: Stratigraphy and chronology. B: General view of the site at the present time. C: Site plan.

same as isolated teeth. **Carnivores are plausibly the main agents responsible for carcass modification**, whereas it has not been possible to establish the association between faunal remains and lithic artefacts (Sanz, 2013).

One of the most noteworthy facts relies on the high accumulation of deer *Haploidoceros mediterraneus* in levels I and II which represent the dominant species of the ungulate group (MNI=12). Other taxa are less represented: *Capra sp.* (NMI=5), *Cervus elaphus* (NMI=1), *Bos/Bison* (NMI=1) and carnivores such as *Lynx pardinus* (NMI=4), and a shed tooth from *Ursus arctos* (NMI=1). Finally, both levels have remains of *Testudo hermanni*, in large amounts at level III and at the fallen sediments (Daura *et al.*, 2006) where other species, such as *Stephanorhinus hundsheimensis*, were also documented (Sanz, 2013).

Cervidae *Haploidoceros mediterraneus*

One of the most relevant discoveries in levels I and II from Cova del Rinoceront has been the identification for the first time in the Iberian Peninsula of the genus *Haploidoceros* (Fig. 2), defined by Croitor *et al.*, (2008) on the basis of preliminary remains identified as *Euctenoceros mediterraneus* (Bonifay, 1967) in the French site of Lunel-Viel. Previously, at Cova del Rinoceront two cervidae species had been identified (Daura, 2008; Daura *et al.*, 2010), although in the identification of fallow deer not all the defined criteria were recognized (Sanz, 2006). Only the recent restoration allows the certain identification of genus *Haploidoceros* (Sanz *et al.*, 2014). This is a small size cervidae, smaller than the present-day red deer, whose antlers are the most diagnostic element. The antler shape is characterised by a sickle-shaped tine curving backwards and sideways with a long frontal beam. The identification of this taxa at the Cova del Rinoceront in Castelldefels demonstrates its persistence at least until MIS5, since it has been identified in MIS7 and 9 in the south of France, where Croitor et al., (2008) proposed that its presence on the other side of the Pyrenees was the result of the expansion of well-established Iberian Peninsula populations that became endemic on that area.

Thus far, remains from Cova del Rinoceront are dated at marine isotopic stage 5, while on other more recent sites in the same area (from MIS4 and MIS3), this genus has not been documented, indicating that climate changes could have had some sort of responsibility for its extinction.

Finally, the absence of this genus is surprising in similar contexts on the Iberian Peninsula, given the high number of remains (NR=718) and individuals (NMI=19) at Cova del Rinoceront. For the moment, we can speculate that its probable absence in the fossil record could respond to three main causes: a wrong taxonomic identification caused by the high fragmentation level of the Cervidae remains; an absence of diagnostic elements such as antlers; or the overlapping of certain metric traits with other deer.

Acknowledgements

This paper is the result of the research project *Humans, carnívors i medi natural durant el Plistocè al massís del Garraf-Ordal i curs baix del riu Llobregat* carried out by SERP and funded by 2014SGR-108 (Generalitat de Catalunya), HAR2011-26193 (MICINN). J. Daura was supported by the Postdoctoral programme Juan de la Cierva (MICINN). Fieldwork has been funded by Servei d'Arqueologia i Paleontologia de la Generalitat de Catalunya and Ajuntament de Castelldefels.

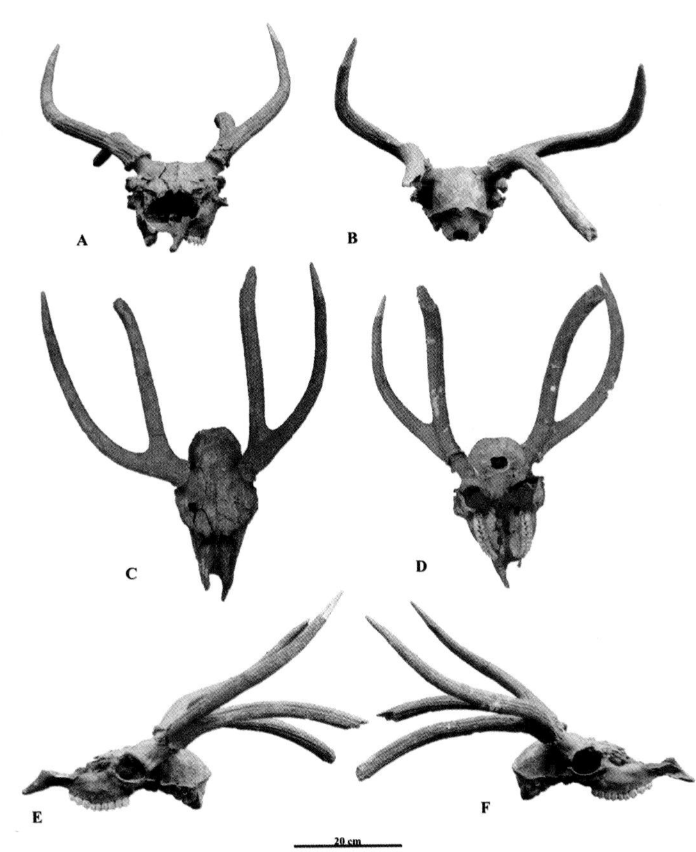

Figure 2. Skull of *Haploidoceros mediterraneus* (individual #2413): A. Anterior view. B: Posterior view. C: Dorsal view. D: Inferior view. E-F: lateral views.

Josep Maria Vergès* ,**, Xosé Pedro Rodríguez* ,**

Els Vinyets (El Catllar, Tarragona)

Location and excavation history

Els Vinyets site, in the municipality of El Catllar, is located on the right bank of the river Gaià, 75 metres above sea level and 7 km from the river mouth (UTM X: 359.843, Y: 4.560.957). It was discovered by chance in 1991 by Josep Zaragoza Solé, who noticed lithic industry one of the cuts below the excavations for extracting clay, used to build the dam on the river Gaià (1975-1980). Shortly after the discovery of the site, the first archaeological excavation was carried out, in June 1991, of a surface area of 21 m^2 (Fig. 1). Subsequently, in 1995, a second excavation was carried out, extending the area excavated in 1991 by 8 m^2 and exploring an area located 50 metres to the west.

Stratigraphy

The archaeological levels are located in a sedimentary sequence of more than 15 metres, which is part of the +20 m terrace of the river Gaià, consisting of alluvial silts and clays with small discontinuous layers of gravel, which is where the lithic industry appears (Fig.2). More specifically, three levels with archaeological materials have been documented (NI, NII and NIII), exclusively with lithic industry elements, located 12 to 13 metres deep. Three palaeosols are also documented, the third of them at the base of level NII.

Lithic industry

The lithic assemblage recovered at Els Vinyets in stratigraphic context amounts to 318 elements. Of these, 67 come from level 1, 196 from level 2 and 18 from level 3. Another 37 pieces were re-

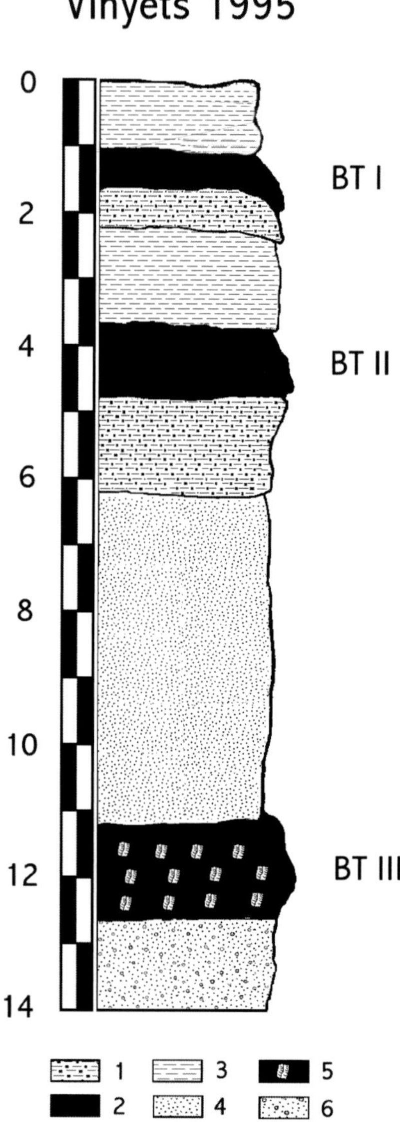

Figure 1. Stratigraphic sequence of Els Vinyets, 1: Clays, silts and fine sands 2: Palaeosol, 3: Clays and silts, 4: Fluvial sands and silts, 5: Archaeological levels, 6: gravel colluvium, probable terraces of the river Gaià.

* IPHES, InstitutCatalà de Paleoecologia Humana i Evolució Social, C/ Marcel.lí Domingo s/n. Campus Sescelades, (Edifici W3), Tarragona 43007

** Area de Prehistoria, Universitat Rovira i Virgili (URV), Av. Catalunya 35, Tarragona 43002

covered without stratigraphic context. Given the similarity observed between the lithic industry from the different levels, a joint study of all of the material was carried out (Rodríguez, 2004).

Flint is the most commonly used raw material, with 92% of elements. The remaining 8% is distributed among quartzite, quartz and limestone. The majority of the flint objects have a yellowish patina and some show rolling and concretion. The flint was taken from the alluvial deposits of the river Gaià. They are small nodules, which conditions the knapping and results in an industry that in general, except for a few cases, does not exceed 30 mm.

The 318 artefacts include six Natural Bases and eleven First Generation Negative Bases (1GNB), three of which are clearly configured items (tools made by retouching a nodule) and three are 1GNB

Figure 2. General view of Els Vinyets site and details of the excavation. Flint lithic industry: 1: Nodule with denticulate removals, 2: Denticulate flake, 3: Notch, 4: Flake, 5: Endscraper.

for exploitation (cores to obtain flakes). The rest include three objects that were in principle 1GNB for exploitation but were then configured to be used as instruments (BN1GC). The three 1GNB exploited as cores are similar in size and morphology (with a cubic trend). In addition, the three cores are almost exhausted. The raw material was exploited following a bifacial strategy with linear orthogonal knapping. We have also found two 2GNB for exploitation, that is, cores on flakes. One of these pieces, with concretion, shows linear unipolar knapping, whereas the direction of the removals cannot be clearly identified on the other one.

The lithic category with most items is the Positive Bases (flakes), which make up 34.9% of the total, whereas the Second Generation Negative Bases of Configuration (retouched flakes) accounts for 25.2% of the objects. We have also counted 33.6% of fragments and 1% of pieces that cannot be determined. The presence of a PB with the morphology of a small preconfigured point indicated the existence of a knapping strategy aimed at preconfiguring products. However, while the linear-orthogonal strategy is well represented by objects from all of the structural categories, the same does not apply to the knapping strategy, which implies preconfiguration, represented only by flakes. As a result, it is highly probable that preconfigured objects were not produced in Vinyets.

The PB have mainly non-cortical (86%) and unifaceted (55%) butts. However, there is a noteworthy number of PB with bifaceted butts (9%). The dorsal surfaces are mainly non-cortical (77%). The significant number of bifaceted and multifaceted butts coincides with the characteristics of cores, with orthogonal knapping and cubic morphology, with alternating use of the exploitation surfaces.

The instrument configuration processes are extremely important in this record: these artefacts (1GNBC and 2GNBC) account for almost 40% of the lithic material that can be identified (excluding the fragments). Particularly noteworthy is the high number of retouched flakes (2GNBC). The configuration of the instruments mainly focuses on creating dihedral edges on one side or in the transversal sector of the object. This type of configuration appears in 38 instruments (48.1%). There is also a large proportion of denticulate tools (19%), concave dihedral tools (16.5%), and trihedral tools (16.5%). In terms of tipology, the retouched flakes included 15 points (7 of them denticulate), 13 notches, 10 side scrapers and 9 endscrapers (Fig. 1).

Conclusions

The small number of lithic objects seems to indicate low intensity occupations, dedicated to configuring instruments on flakes, previously obtained using, above all, simple unipolar and orthogonal knapping. However, there is also evidence of more complex methods, albeit sporadic.

The stratigraphic position in relation to the terraces of the river Gaià and the characteristics of the sedimentary sequence could indicate a late Middle Pleistocene chronology. The lack of morphotypes typical of Mode 2 and the use of exploitation strategies to make flakes with predetermined morphologies place the lithic record of Vinyets in the Mode 3 (Rodríguez *et al.*, 2004).

Josep Vallverdú*,**,***, Palmira Saladié*,**,****, Antonio Rosas*****,*** , Rosa Huguet*,**,***, Isabel Cáceres**,*, Antoni Pineda**,*, Andreu Ollé*,** , Marina Mosquera**,*, Antonio Garcia-Tabernero*****, Almudena Estalrrich*****, Ángel Carrancho******,******, Juan José Villalaín******, Didier Bourlès********, Régis Braucher********, Anne Lebatard********, JaumeVilalta*,**, Iván Lozano-Fernández*,**, Lucía López-Polín*,**, Elena Moreno*,**, Josep Maria Vergés*,**, Isabel Expósito*,**, Jordi Agustí*********,*,**, Eudald Carbonell*,**,***,**********, Ramón Capdevila*.

El Barranc de la Boella (La Canonja, Tarragona, Catalonia, Spain)

1. Location and Researchs History

The el Barranc de la Boella (literally Boella Creek) site (la Canonja, Tarragona, Catalonia, Spain) is situated in the Northeast of the Iberian Peninsula, 3 kilometres inland from the Mediterranean coast close to the city of Tarragona. The site lies on the terrace system of the Francolí River, which is, in turn, related with the Neogene Gavarres – Constantí interfluve and the Pleistocene *bajada* (merging of several alluvial fans) of the Reus depression. In the second series of the geological map produced by the Spanish Geological and Mining Institute (IGME), the Constantí – Gavarres interfluve is described as a Quaternary calcrete in reference to the Pliocene-Pleistocene limit. With respect to Gavarres – Constantí interfluve, the memoir of this map describes one terrace of the Francolí River above + 60 metres of the Francolí River.

The terrace system within which the Barranc de la Boella site is located was partially buried by the bajada deposits from Reus Depression origin. This area abounds in quarries for the extraction of gravels which have exposed a number of significant outcrops that have enabled us to confirm the existence of the Early Pleistocene terraces of the Francolí River in this area delimited between Constantí – Gavarres interfluve and the Pineda Beach (near the Cape of Salou). The terraces system of Middle and Late Pleistocene age at the lower Francolí River valley is located between the Gavarres – Constantí interfluve and the city of Tarragona where it joins the Mediterranean (Fig. 1).

The first reports on oldest prehistoric artefacts discovered within the geographical area involved the finds made on Early Pleistocene terraces at the foot of Constantí – Gavarres interfluve and Pineda Beach. Many of the sediments that make up the deposits of the terraces of the Francolí River were transported from the Ebro Depression with rocks rich in chert (Bartonian and Lutetian), which lend themselves

* Institut Català de Paleoecologia Humana i Evolució Social (IPHES), Campus Sescelades, (Edifici W3), Universitat Rovira i Virgili (URV). Carrer Marcel.lí Domingo s/n. 43007 Tarragona, Spain.

** Àrea de Prehistòria, Departament d'Història i Història de l'Art, Facultat de Lletres, UniversitatRovira i Virgili (URV). Avinguda de Catalunya, 35. 43002 Tarragona, Spain

*** Unidad Asociada al CSIC. Museo Nacional de Ciencias Naturales (MNCN), Consejo Superior de Investigaciones Científicas (CSIC). Calle José Gutierrez Abascal, 2. 28006 Madrid, Spain

**** GQP-CG, Grupo Quaternário e Pré-História do Centro de Geociências (uI&D 73 – FCT)

***** Departamento de Paleobiología, Museo Nacional de Ciencias Naturales (MNCN), Consejo Superior de Investigaciones Científicas (CSIC). Calle José Gutierrez Abascal, 2. 28006 Madrid, Spain

****** Laboratorio de Paleomagnetismo. Departamento de Física, Escuela Politécnica Superior - Edificio A1, Universidad de Burgos (UBU). Avenida Cantabria s/n. 09006 Burgos, Spain

******* Área de Prehistoria. Departamento de Ciencias Históricas y Geografía. Edificio I+D+I. Universidad de Burgos (UBU). Plaza Misael Bañuelos s/n 09001 Burgos, Spain

******** Aix-Marseille University, CEREGE, CNRS UM34, F-13545 Aix-en-Provence, France

********* Institució Catalana de Recerca i EstudisAvançats (ICREA)

********** Visiting professor, Institute of Vertebrate Paleontology and Paleoanthropology of Beijing (IVPP), Beijing, China

* Corresponding authors: jvallverdu@iphes.cat; psaladie@iphes.cat

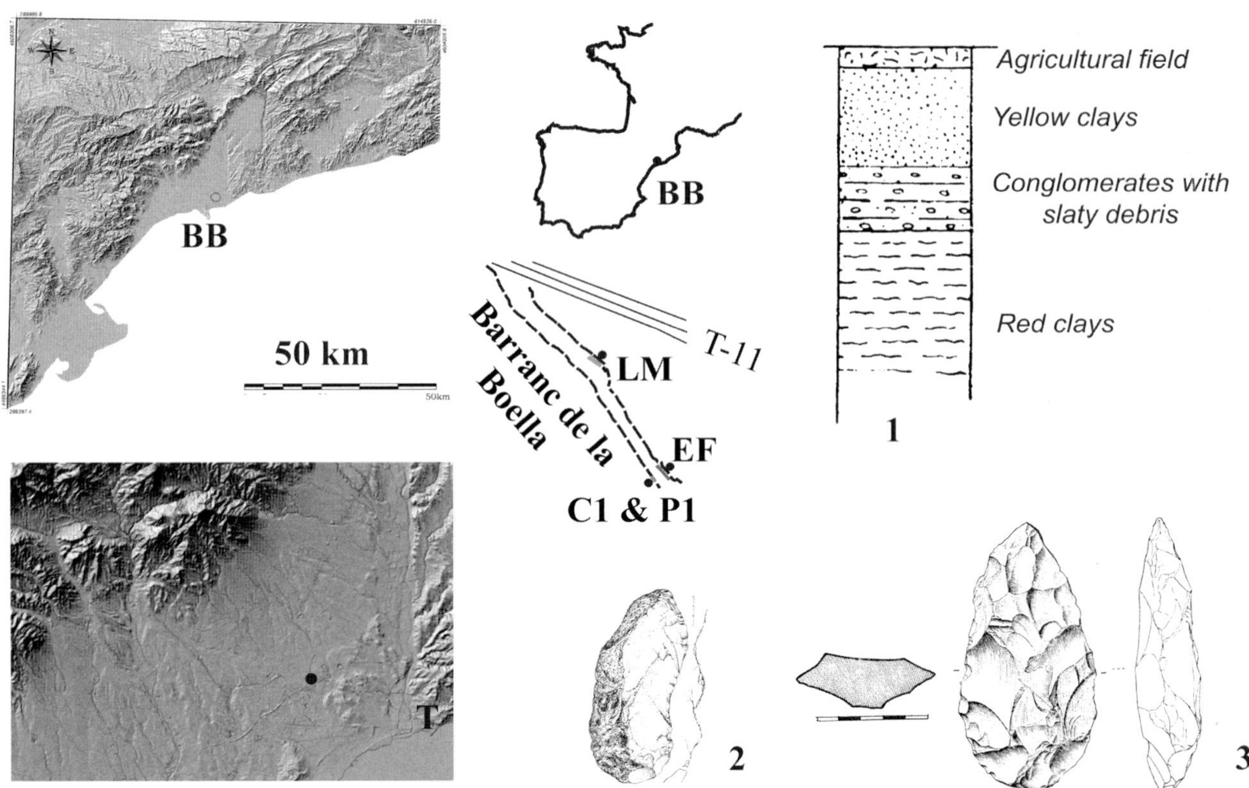

Figure 1. El Barranc de la Boella (BB) is situated in the Northeast of the Iberian Peninsula in the basin of the Francolí River. In the digital model of the terrain, courtesy of Miquel Vilà of the Geological Institute of Catalonia, the elevation of the surface area of the upper terraces can be observed to the northeast of the black spot (which is where the el Barranc de la Boella sites are located), with the elevations of the miopliocene between the black spot and the city of Tarragona (T) also being shown. The Barranc de la Boella sites are pit 1 (C1) alongside profile 1 (P1), pit 2 (LM, la Mina) and pit 3 (EF, el Forn). The stratigraphic column represented in 1 shows the stratigraphy reproduced by Marin (1933). The lithic industry shown in 2 is a reproduction of an atypical artefact found next to the remains of proboscideans (Vilaseca, 1973) in which Dr Vilaseca observes artificial, not natural fractures. The lithic industry shown in illustration 3 is the Constantí black flint hand axe documented in 1909 (Gibert, 1909).

extremely well to lithic industry, were frequently brought down with them. The provenance of a cordiform hand axe (Gibert, 1909) is attributed to the Constantí area, and for many years it was considered as the oldest proof of the presence of human beings in Catalonia, although the exact location of the find has never been known (Fig. 1: 3). Another piece reported from the past, which is worth mentioning only because it occurred close to Tarragona, is the identification, by Harlé, of a molar of *Elephas meridionalis*, details of which were also published by Marià Faura i Sans (1920). Once again, the exact location of the find is not known, and it is only described here due to its having been found in some gravel quarries administered by the Tarragona Port Authority.

The first paleontological and archaeological finds made in the area around la Canonja and in the Barranc de la Boella are mentioned in the explanatory note of the first series of 1:50000 IGME maps directed by Agustí Marín (1933). In this map, and in the accompanying explanatory note, the outcrop of el Barranc de la Boella was considered to be a paleontological Pliocene site due to the presence of *Rhinoceros* sp., *Cervus* sp. and *Equus caballus* Lin., which were found within a stratum composed of red clays (Fig. 1: 1). This note also describes the discovery of *Helix* sp. in the sand and clay deposits of el Mas Boella on top of the stratum of red clays, which were dated as Upper Pliocene. In the section dedicated to prehistory of the memoir of this map, it is noted that prehistoric lithic implements had been found in la Canonja. Years later, Dr Salvador Vilaseca published details of the discovery of abundant lithic industry remains at la Boella within a stratigraphic context. The remains of the lithic industries were found in a number of large gullies close to Reus Airport (Vilaseca, 1954). These archaeological remains were discovered in clayey strata that had settled on top of some conglomerates that had, in turn, settled on top of the red clays described above. Dr Vilaseca named this prehistoric site close to Reus Airport la Boella and proceeded to describe it archaeologically based on the prehistoric pottery and archaic lithic industry he found there at a depth of approximately 1.5 metres. On the other hand, this area, at the foot of the Constantí – Gavarres interfluve, contains numerous surface archaeological sites, with many of these considered as Middle Palaeolithic on the archaeological inventories of the Generalitat de Catalunya. However, only one publication exists that is dedicated to these surface sites and in it les Gavarres and their industries are classified as "*campiñoides*" (Vilaseca and Capdevila, 1968).

In 1970 Ramón Capdevila accidentally discovered the remains of large herbivores at Barranc de la Boella. J. F. de Villalta i Comellas identified them as *Elephas (Archidiskodon) meridionalis* and in 1973 Dr S. Vilaseca published this as Barranc de la Boella site. Together with the discovery of these remains of proboscides, Dr. S. Vilaseca described the finding of flint fragments, which he classified as atypical artefacts (Vilaseca, 1973). In the paragraph that precedes this classification of the atypical flint artefacts Dr. S. Vilaseca insists on admitting that "..., no site or discovery whatever is known that may be attributed to the Lower Palaeolithic which can provide the necessary scientific guarantees" within Southern Catalonia Archaeology. Dr. S. Vilaseca describes this lithic industry in minute detail and arrives at the conclusion that it includes dubious pieces of flint, meaning that the flakes they bear may well be natural, and mentions one flake is clearly artificial (Fig. 1: 2). In this respect he points out that the existence of the Lower Palaeolithic in Tarragona is suggested by the aforementioned Constantí hand axe, details of which were published in 1909 (Gibert, 1909), although he does express his doubts as to its provenance. However, he then goes on to suggest that more evidence exists regarding the Lower Palaeolithic by pointing out other discoveries, made in Reus, of ancient stone axes, or the Middle Palaeolithic industries found at el Forn d'en Sugranyes (Reus), details of which he himself published (Vilaseca, 1952).

Living, as he did, in the town of Reus meant that Dr. S. Vilaseca had known about Barranc de la Boella for many years. In his summary of 1973 he distinguishes the discoveries made at the site of la Boella (Vilaseca, 1954) from those of the Barranc de la Boella. He also used this study to highlight the contribution made by his friend, the palaeontologist Josep Ramón Bataller, to the explanatory note of the geological map of 1933 (Marín, 1933; Bataller, 1935). Much of the information provided by this mapping of the 1933 received the backing of the Geological Institute of Catalonia, created by the Junta de Ciencias de la Mancomunitat de Catalunya in 1914, under the direction of M. Faura i Sans. Josep Ramón Bataller and Salvador Vilaseca worked as assistants to M. Faura i Sans and had to leave this geological mapping project unfinished in 1924.

Dr S. Vilaseca describes the Barranc de la Boella finds in a chapter dedicated to Quaternary fauna and not to the Palaeolithic in his 1973 publication. The finds are situated on both margins of the creek close to the buildings (Mas Boella) that gives its name to this municipal district of la Canonja. The fossils are described as coming from the clays, but the illustrations show that the finds are located in the conglomerates and the sands above the reddish clays. The stratigraphy of the Barranc de la Boella is described as having a total thickness of almost 7 metres.

The current archaeological project began with a preventive survey dig in 2007. A torrential flow caused the banks of the creek to collapse at the same point where Dr S. Vilaseca and R. Capdevila discovered the bone remains published in 1973. During this survey a significant number of faunal remains and lithic industry made from chert and other rocks (schist, sandstone, etc.) was documented (Vallverdú *et al.*, 2009; Saladié *et al.*, 2009). The discovery of lithic industries at Barranc de la Boella associated with the proboscide confirmed the evidence of lithic industries that had been so prudently presented by Dr S. Vilaseca 35 years earlier. During those 35 years the concept of Spanish Prehistory went from doubting the existence of the Lower Palaeolithic on the Iberian Peninsula to providing direct proof of the first human inhabitants of Europe dating back to 1 Ma. The investigations carried out in Barranc de la Boella as of 2008 were included in the archaeological excavations project called "*Evolució paleoambiental i poblament prehistòric a les conques dels rius Francolí, Gaià, Siurana i rieres del camp de Tarragona*". To date the fieldwork have been concentrated on 3 pit excavations. Pit 1 (C1) contains the 9 m^2 dig of 2007 and stratigraphic profile 1 (P1) on the right-hand bank of the creek. Pit 2, or la Mina (The Mine) (LM), is situated 180 metres upstream from Pit 1 locality and covers an area of 25 m^2. Pit3, also known as el Forn (EF), is situated on the opposite bank to Pit 1 locality and also covers a surface area of 25 m^2. During the 2013 excavation fieldwork the actions planned to be carried out in Pit 3 were totally completed, with the dig reaching the clays (Neogene) making up the basal layer. On the other hand, with respect to LM we have carried out an extremely partial exploration with only 4 m^2 having been excavated without reaching the clays.

The most recent fieldwork has managed to test the value of the cultural and paleontological succession of the Barranc de la Boella record. The available existing fossil record and the results of the stratigraphic research might be considered sufficient for establishing the patrimonial and scientific value of the site. The team participating in this project are those represented in this text as authors. The next research challenges involve the exploration of the deposits laid down prior to the Jaramillo Subchron (< 1Ma) and also of those deposits in which we hope to find archaeo-paleontological remains dating back to the beginning of the Middle Pleistocene (0.5-0.78 Ma). Therefore, at Barranc de la Boella it is our intention to investigate the temporal continuity of the first human occupations of Europe prior to and during the transition from Early Pleistocene to Middle Pleistocene (1.5 to 0.5 Ma). Within the Eurasian context, the first human occupations have, to date, been seen as biological dispersions fed by different migratory currents, rather than a colonisation based on the adaptation of the human settlements on the Eurasian continent (Dennell, 2003). Finally, the industries of El Barranc de la Boella confirms the existence Acheulean technocomplex during the Early Pleistocene in Europe.

2. Geological Context and Stratigraphy

The geology and stratigraphy of El Barranc de la Boella can be described as an incised valley fill encaised in the +60-metres terrace of the Francolí River system. The basal lithostratigraphic units of this incised valley fill is interbedded with the + 50-metre terrace deposits.

The incised valley fill of the Barranc de la Boella has been characterised in 4 principal outcrops with a thick of 9 metres and 6 lithostratigraphic units have been determined (Fig. 2). In units I to III negative polarity has been determined in a high number of samples. The change of polarity has been measured in the samples of the base of unit IV of profile 1 (Fig. 2). The magnetostratigraphy of the top section from unit IV to unit VI shows a normal polarity. The determination of *Mammuthus meridionalis, Hippopotamus antiquus, Mimomys savini* in the biostratigraphy of unit II indicates that the inverse polarity determined in units I, II, III and in the basal part of IV corresponds to the Matuyama chron (> 0.78 Ma) and to late Early Pleistocene (1 –0.78 Ma) of the temporal geological scale.

The botton of the unnit I consists in an erosive unconformity that covers miopliocene clays (unit 0) and has a variable thickness to 1.5 metres of beds with well stratified, imbricated and clast supported schistt gravels set in azoic reddish muds. Unit I also contains, albeit less frequently, greenish grey massive sandy beds with fine graded gravels within lenticular scours. On occasion, and on top of unit 0, there are discontinuous lag deposits which contain limestones and flint as well as the schists and other lithologies in which igneous rocks predominate. Unit II overlay unit I in erosive unconformity and has a variable thickness of up to 2 metres. Unit II contains poorly stratified beds made from medium gravel-sized schist matrix supported by green-grey sands. The top of unit II is dominated by poorly stratified beds of massive greenish-grey sand and granules and fine graded gravels in scours. In addition to the schists, in the lithology of the gravels found in unit II sandstones, weathered limestones, rounded flints and other igneous rocks (granitoids) are also less frequently found. The sand and gravel beds of the top layer of unit II are impregnated with yellowish bands of cryptocrystalline segregations and also by carbonaceous laminated muds , especially in the Forn outcrop. Unit II contains fossils in different layers: in C1 and LM 2 levels have been determined; and up to 6 levels have been determined in El Forn. Unit III contains massive greenish muds and has a regular thickness of 2 metres. This unit is extremely mottled by brown and reddish cryptocrystalline segregations, and it is also the unit in which 1 archaeo-paleontological level has been determined in C1 and in EF. Unit IV consist in tabular green sandy muds and scours and channels filled with imbricated schist gravels, and lenticular bodies of matrix supported carbonated nodules by green muds. Its thickness is quite regular and reaches a maximum of 2 metres. The top of unit IV contains calcium carbonate rhizomes at la Mina outcrop. Unit V has a thickness of up to 3 metres in pit 2, which rapidly thins out towards EF and desapears in pit 1. Unit VI merges with unit V in EF in a conglomeratic petrocalcic horizon that has continuity with the petrocalcic horizons which exist on top of the deposits of the alluvial fans of the Reus Depression. These deposits of the Reus Depression have been dated from the second half of the Middle Pleistocene using the Uranium series technique.

3. The Archaeo-Paleontological Record

The most abundant bone remains found in the prehistoric localities are those of the large herbivores located in the lithostratigraphic units II and III (Tab. 1). The species identified at the different locations ex-

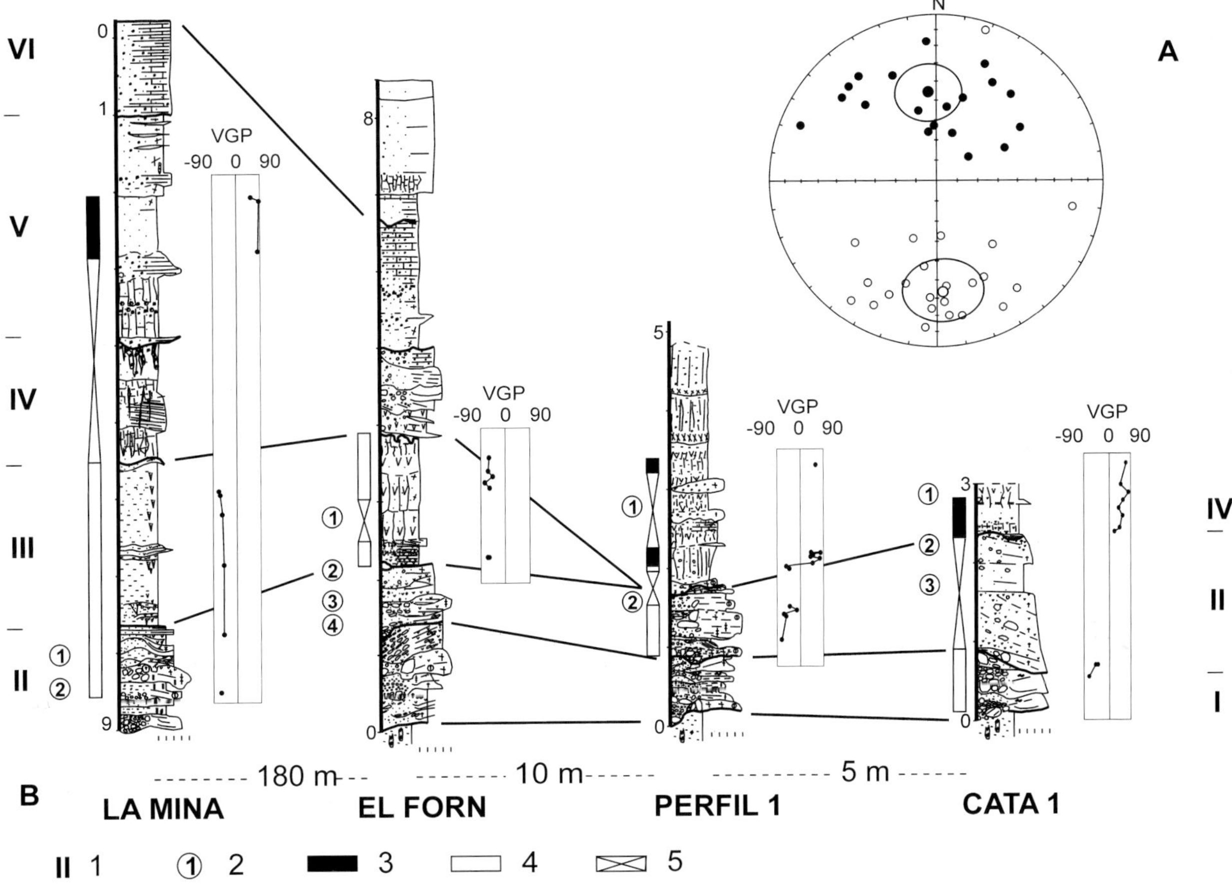

Figure 2. Paleomagnetic samples and stratigraphic correlation between the Barranc de la Boella localities.
A. The number of samples with a characteristic component for projecting the paleomagnetic direction within an equal area. The solid circles are projections within the normal polarity in the lower hemisphere and the blank circles are the projection within the reverse polarity in the upper hemisphere.
B. Correlations between stratigraphic units based on lithostratigraphic and magnetostratigraphic measurements and observations. Key: 1, lithostratigraphic unit; 2, archaeo-palaeontological level; 3, normal polarity; 4 reverse polarity; 5, undetermined polarity.

cavated are *Mammuthus meridionalis*, *Hippopotamus antiquus*, *Stephanorhinus* cf. *hundsheimensis*, *Equus sp.*, Cervidae, *Ursus* sp., *Panthera* cf. *gonbaszoegensis*, *Hyaenidae*, *Macaca sylvanus*, *Mimomys savini* and *Victoriamys chalinei*. Found alongside the bones were the abundant remains of the coprolites of a large bone crushing carnivore, possibly a type of hyena.

The most noteworthy faunal remains found in level 2 of C1 are those of *M. meridionalis* (n=549), which pertain to a single individual of around 30 years of age. Both of the animal's tusks were recovered together with its upper and lower molars (Fig. 3). The remains of ribs, vertebrae and skull fragments were found scattered around the tusks and teeth and the two scapulas, one of them totally fragmented, possibly as a result of being trodden on by other mammoths. Found together with these dental and bone remains was the most significant collection of lithic industry discovered at the site complex to date (n=125).

The composition of the faunal materials and of the lithic industry can, in accordance with the classification of site types established by Leakey (1971), to be related with those of a "butchering site" where the carcass of a large herbivore was processed. Although there is no doubt that the Hominidae ate meat, it has not been possible to establish how they accessed carcasses. In the level immediately below (level 3) more remains of *M. meridionalis* were found; these mainly comprised dental elements (2 tusks, 4 molars) and skull fragments. No lithic industry associated with this animal was found in this level. However, this discovery confirms that this is an area that was habitually frequented by these animals, which possibly came to the channels and pools to drink.

	Centre de Convencions		EL Forn							La Mina		
Archaelogical Level	2	3	1	2	3	4	5	6	7	1	2	3
Cervus sp.			x	x	x	x		x			x	
Dama cf. *vallonetensis*	x	x	x	x	x	x	x			x	x	x
Megaloceros savini			x	x	x	x					x	
Equus cf. *stenonis*		x	x	x	x	x	x			x	x	
Bovini indet.				x	x	x				x		
Hippopotamus antiquus			x	x	x	x	x			x	x	x
Stephanorhinus hundsheimiensis			x	x	x	x			x			
Mammuthus meridionalis	x	x		x	x	x					x	
Sus scrofa			x									
cf. Pachycrocuta brevirostris					x							
Ursus sp.						x				x	x	
Canis sp.											x	
cf *Panthera gombaszoegensis*											x	
Macaca silvana											x	
Castor sp.						x						

Table 1. The table shows the species present in the different archaeological levels of the three locations excavated in El Barranc de la Boella. All of the levels pertain to lithostratigraphic unit II, except for level I of El Forn, which forms part of unit I.

Figure 3. Image of the tusks of *Mammuthus meridionalis* and other skeletal elements found in level 2 of the pit 1 (P. Saladié/IPHES).

Figure 4. a) Schist pick found in level 2 of the pit 1 locality. b) Cleaver discovered in level 2 of el Forn. c) Chopping tool found in la Mina. (A.Ollé/IPHES).

Figure 5. Hyena coprolite found in la Mina in spatial association with a flake of chert (P. Saladié/IPHES).

In pit 3, el Forn locality, taxonomic diversity is high and similar in all the archaeo-paleontological levels (Tab. 1). The most commonly found skeletal elements are the most robust due to their higher mineral density, such as teeth, horns, antlers and the fragments of the diaphysis of the long bones. In pit 3, la Mina locality, complete bones are less abundant, which seems to be due to the increased activity of Hominidae and carnivores with respect to the bones found throughout the entire sequence known to date. The activity of the carnivores has been identified by way of the bite marks, the consumption of the epiphysis of the long bones and the presence of long splinters of bone showing signs of digestion. These modifications, together with the presence of coprolites (Fig. 5), would appear to indicate the presence of a large type of hyena, perhaps *Pachycrocuta brevirostris*, although so far no skeletal remains of these animals have been found at this site.

Evidence of Hominidae activity is barely visible. In general, the surfaces of the bones found at the three sites excavated in el Barranc de la Boella are in poor condition. This makes it impossible for us to accurately identify any possible cut marks. Despite this situation, the presence of Hominidae is evident at all three sites due to the presence of lithic industry. At el Forn this is abundant in levels 1 and 2 and disappears in the levels below these.

The lithic industry in the Barranc de la Boella record most of the pieces are made of chert, although schist, quartz, granite and quartzite were also used. All of the raw materials are locally available.

The lithic collection of the level 2 at pit 1 locality contains three hammerstones and seven fractured cobbles, which may suggest they were used either for striking or as striking platforms. The three existing cores show a unipolar and, occasionally, centripetal reduction. The rest of this lithic industry located at level 2 of the pit 1 locality consists of 45 complete flakes, 37 fractured flakes and fragments of flakes. Finally, the lithic assemblage contains only 8 retouched flakes, in the form of notched and denticulate implements. Also associated with this collection was a large-format tool: a pick made from a thick flake of schist (Fig. 4a). It must be pointed out that 11 refit groups were identified in this lithic collection, thereby proving its integrity.

The EF unit II (levels 2, 3 and 4) assemblage is composed of 104 items, including three hammerstone; 11pebbles and fractured pebbles mainly made from schist and one unipolar quartz core. The group of artefacts made from chert includes seven cores, 46 flakes, 14 broken flakes and six retouched flakes (denticulates). The assemblage also contains one cleaver made from a massive schist flake (split cobble) (Fig. 4b).

In the LM assemblage, with 81 pieces found to date, sandstone and granite hammerstone have also been identified, together with several pebbles and cores from different types of rock. A. LM contains pebble and core technology with three schist choppers and two chopping tools, one of quartzite and the other of porphyry (Fig. 4c). The chert artefacts are almost as common (25 flakes, 21 flake fragments and seven retouched denticulate flakes).

4. Conclusions

The fossil associations of the Barranc de la Boella were distributed in a flooded habitat situated at the confluence of a torrential tributary watercourse and the Francolí River. Against this backdrop the hominines accessed the carcasses of large animals that had become trapped or stranded in pools or channels, as documented in recent studies (Haynes, 1981). These animals also being accessed by carnivores have also been documented. A long mammoth bone found in EF shows significant perforations in its epiphyses caused by the consumption thereof by carnivores. These modifications point, almost without doubt, to the presence of *Pachycrocuta brevirostris* in this area during the Early Pleistocene.

We cannot know for sure whether the animals were obtained actively, perhaps by being pursued and driven into the boggiest places or whether the carcases were accessed following the accidental or natural deaths of the animals. The record of the late Early Pleistocene TD6-2 shows that the hominines of this time actively hunted large and potentially extremely dangerous animals such as rhinoceros or aurochs (Saladié *et al.*, 2011), which is why we can assume that the same strategies were also used in and around the Barranc de la Boella. However, it is possible that other methods were used to obtain the animal resources provided by mega-herbivores such as *M. meridionalis* or *H. antiquus*. The sites used for butchering individual large herbivores have been described as part of the foraging strategies of modern hunter-gatherers. This analogy would suggest that the hominines that occupied the area in and around Barranc de la Boella localities and, by default, the hominines of that time, were towards the top of the food chain, a claim also indicated by the record of level TD6-2 of Gran Dolina (Sierra de Atapuerca) (Saladié *et al.*, 2014) and by all the other Lower Pleistocene collections of the Sierra de Atapuerca (Huguet *et al.*, 2013). The El Barranc de la Boella record also confirms the capacity of these hominines to use and obtain animal resources in the European ecosystems of the late Early Pleistocene by means of different strategies.

Finally, mention must be made of the discovery of elements characteristic of an early Acheulean technology in the pit1 and EF locations, whereas these have not been found yet in LM. These Acheulean components consist of large cutting tools manufactured in schist and represent standardised morphologies such as the pick and the cleaver, and they are accompanied by an assamblage collection of smaller chert instruments, the most noteworthy of which are small– and medium-sized flakes, some of them retouched (denticulate tools). It is important to point out that the large cutting tools from level 2 of the Pit 1and el Forn represents one of the oldest evidences of the early Acheulean in Europe.

The goal of archaeological investigation at Barranc de la Boella site over the next few years will be to develop a research project based on the established documentation. This fieldwork will be one of the key factors in the acquisition of diaphanous and well founded archaeological records in order to participate in the debate regarding the origin, autecology and paleoecology of the first settlers of Eurasia. This oportunity was opened by Dr Salvador Vilaseca at Barranc de la Boella when he produced his daring description of an artificially reduced stone object found there together with the faunal remains of a proboscide. This paradigm has been recognised 40 years later and we must now acknowledge his honest stance with respect to the facts observed regarding the material culture of our most distant predecessors.

Acknowledgements

The team that conducted the archaeological research and excavation of the El Barranc de la Boella site would like to acknowledge the interest shown by the Municipal Council of La Canonja with respect to the funding and presentation to the public of the fieldwork and research carried out since 2007 to the present day. The Archaeological Service of the Department of Culture of the Regional Government of Catalonia is authorising and subsidising the fieldwork via a programme of investigative archaeological projects. The following Spanish state public administrations are contributing towards the investigation and research programmes: central government, Ministry for the Economy and Competitiveness (MINECO) (CGL2012-36682; CGL2012-38358; CGL2012-38434-C03-03 and CGL2010-15326) and the Ministry for Science and Innovation (MICINN) (HAR2009-7223/HIST); the Regional Government of Catalonia, Agency for Management of University and Research Grants (AGAUR) (2009SGR –324, 2009PBR-0033 and 2009SGR-188); and the Regional Government of Castile and Leon (BU1004A09).

Manuel Vaquero *,**, E. Susana Alonso Fernández **

Moli Del Salt (Vimbodí I Poblet, Tarragona)

The Molí del Salt site is located in the village of Vimbodí i Poblet (Conca Barberà Region, province of Tarragona), at 490 meters a.s.l., on the left bank of the Milans, a small tributary of the Francolí river. Its UTM coordinates are X=336532.5 Y=458446.5 (ETRS89 system). It is a rockshelter open in the Upper Oligocene conglomerates and lutites formations, common along the eastern borders of the Ebro basin. The site was first mentioned in the works of Salvador Vilaseca (1953), who cited it as a surface lithic scatter. The existence of a stratified deposit was not determined until the 1990s. The first archaeological excavation was carried out in 1999. This fieldwork consisted of a test pit of 3 m^2 that revealed a complete stratigraphic sequence. After positive results, a research project was undertaken in 2001 and is still in progress today. The excavated area has been extended from the first excavations up to 70 m^2 of the current excavation area (Fig. 1).

1. Stratigraphy and chronology

The stratigraphic sequence is 2.5 meters thick (Fig.2). Two main human occupation phases have been distinguished, separated by fallen blocks from the collapsed ceiling. The earliest phase corresponds to the Late Upper Paleolithic (units B and A), and the most recent to the Mesolithic (Sup level). The lowermost section of the sequence corresponds to Upper Paleolithic levels. It is the most relevant from an archaeological point of view and it was deposited in an interior context of the rockshelter. The Mesolithic level was formed outside in an open-air context instead when the rockshelter had disappeared as a consequence of the filling processes and the collapse of the ceiling. It was developed adjusting to the slope topography. These are the main stratigraphic units identified, from bottom to top:

– Unit B. It is 75 cm thick of gravels and brown and dark yellow sand layers and is directly superimposed over the lutites of the substrate. It is a succession of lenticular layers subdivided into two levels (B1 and B2). Sedimentary processes could be related to diffuse surface runoff water. There is an important increase in the thickness of the layers towards the top of the deposit. At the moment, the only data available corresponds to the test pit excavated in 1999, and because of that the information is relatively scarce in comparison with that from upper levels.

* Area de Prehistoria, Universitat Rovira i Virgili, Avinguda Catalunya 35, 43002 Tarragona
** Institut Català de Paleoecologia Humana i Evolucio Social (IPHES), Escorxador s/n, 43003 Tarragona

Figure 1. General view of the site.

- Unit A. It is composed of around 70 cm of silty and sandy thick layers poorly stratified. This unit includes three archaeological levels (A1, A and Asup). The prevailing sedimentary process is the mechanical weathering of sandstone from the rockshelter walls and ceiling. In the upper part (level Asup) there are the first conglomerate blocks collapsed from the ceiling. Unlike unit B, the appearance is very homogeneous, what could be related to biological weathering. This unit has been excavated extensively between 2001 and 2013, being the one that has yielded more information.
- On top of unit A a collapse episode is registered where large conglomerate boulders fell down and subsequently were incorporated into sand and red silt deposit. These deposits appear mainly in the sector closer to the wall of the rockshelter.
- Superficial level (Sup). It is composed by dark gray sands, poorly stratified, and attached to conglomerate blocks from the previous unit. It has a variable thickness that increases toward the distal part of the deposit where it reaches 20 cm. Sands show an aggregate structure in a kind of biological excremental fabric that suggests very intense bioturbation processes. Mass wasting slope processes would be the dominant agent in the formation of this unit. Archaeological evidences correspond to the Mesolithic of Denticulates and Notches.

A radiocarbon ^{14}C/AMS series of 14 dates have been obtained (tab. 1). Most of the radiocarbon dates belong to levels Asup and A, where fieldwork between 2001 and 2013 has been focused, whereas the lowermost level (Unit B) and the top of the deposit are still poorly dated. For unit B there are only two dates available that situate this unit between 15300 and 13590 cal BP. Although no radiocarbon date is available for the base of unit A (level A1), it has been thought that this unit would have a chronological range between 13800 and 12670 cal BP. These results situate the main archaeological sequence development (units A and B) at the end of the Pleistocene. Level Sup, solely according to the radiocarbon date available which indicates a chronological span between 9110 and 8710 cal BP, would correspond to the beginning of the Holocene. Altogether, the collapse of the rockshelter ceiling would be situated around the Pleistocene – Holocene boundary.

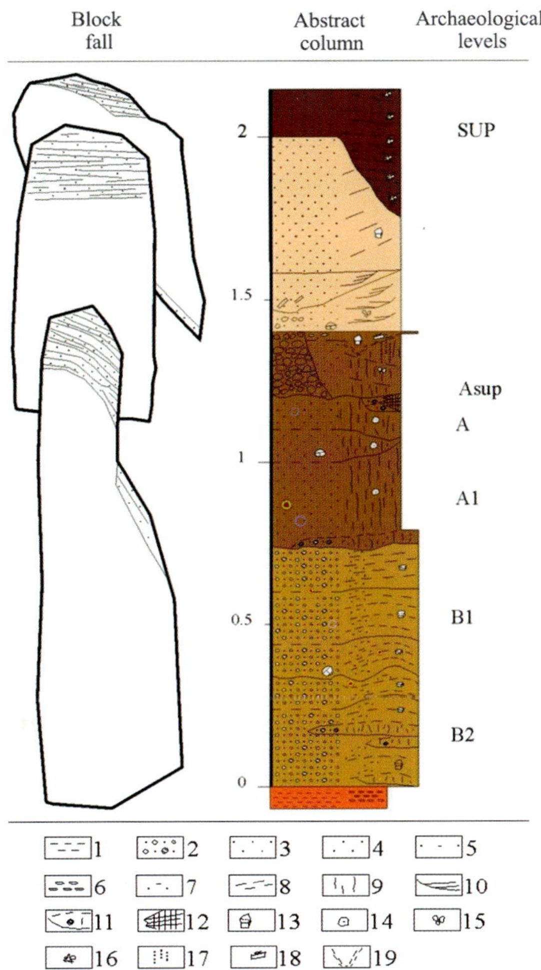

Figure 2. Lithostratigraphic sequence of Molí del Salt, according to Vallverdú and Carrancho (2004). Lithology: 1. Clay. 2. Gravel. 3. Silt. 4. Sandstone. 5. Sand-Clay. Sedimentary structure: 6. Nodular. 7. Graded. 8. Plane not paralleled. 9. Massive. 10. Channel. 11. Lenticular massive. 12. Hearth. Edaphic traits: 13. Polyhedron. 14. Microaggregates. 15. Particular. 16. Crumbly rock. 17. Pseudomycelia. 18. Calcitic *pendents*.

During the following sections we will present a brief synthesis of the results obtained regarding different aspects of human behaviour, particularly in the units corresponding to the Upper Paleolithic period. The main traits of the Mesolithic level, slightly poorly preserved and less significant from a behavioural point of view, have been exposed in previous publications (Vaquero, 2004 and 2006).

2. Exploitation of animal and botanical resources

Concerning animal resource exploitation, rabbit (*Oryctolagus cuniculus*) is the most represented species at every level of Molí del Salt (Allué *et al.*, 2010; Ibáñez and Saladié, 2004); it reaches more than 90% of the bones identified. Other documented species are: ibex, red deer, wild boar, lynx, fox and badger. Some remains from birds have also been identified, particularly in the lower section of the sequence (unit B2), most of them belong to the subfamily *Perdicinae*. This faunistic spectrum, and especially the predominance of rabbit, is common in the Upper Paleolithic record of the Mediterranean coast of the Iberian Peninsula and show subsistence strategies based on the exploitation of the close surrounding areas of the site.

All the anatomical parts of rabbit have been identified which means that these animals were transported whole to the site, although some skeletal parts, such as vertebrae and ribs, are comparatively less represented (Allué *et al.*, 2010: 14). Most of the bones, especially long limb bones, which contain more marrow quantity, appear fractured on both edges. This breakage pattern is typical from human consumption, which implies that rabbits were carried and consumed by humans rather than being the result of natural transportation or another predator's action. Cutmarks are other data that support the anthropogenic character of the bone assemblage. Their presence has been identified at different anatomical parts (humera, femora, tibia, coxal bone, mandibles, etc.), indicate, by their characteristics and location, different actions relating to defleshing, disarticulation and skinning.

Macromammals (ibex, deer, and wild boar) show a much more selective introduction. Concerning the skeletal representation, not all the parts are present in the archaeological deposit which means that animals were not entirely transported to the site but there was a previous selection process elsewhere and only some portions were carried. Ibex and deer show a predominance of appendicular skeletons, whereas axial and cranial parts are less represented. Conversely, wild boar has been identified especially from teeth and mandible fragments. Likewise in the case of rabbit, cutmarks and anthropic breakage in macromammal bones evidence the human activity. Also, it cannot be ruled out that some of these remains were transported to the site as raw material to make artefacts. Moreover, different evidences of bone industry have been recovered. There is an assemblage of up to 48 bone artefacts, also there are bone fragments that seem to correspond to waste

Level	Lab. ref.	Material	Years ^{14}C	Years cal BP (2σ)	Years cal BC (2σ)
Upper	Beta-173335	Bone	8040 ± 40	9110-8710	7160-6760
A upper	Beta-179599	Charcoal	10840 ± 50	12890-12690	10940-10740
A upper	Beta-179598	Charcoal	10990 ± 50	13050-12730	11100-10780
A upper	Beta-221912	Charcoal	11060 ± 70	13130-12770	11180-10820
A upper	Beta-221913	Charcoal	10850 ± 70	12950-12670	11000-10720
A upper	Beta-235268	Charcoal	10920 ± 60	12990-12710	11040-10760
A	Beta-235267	Charcoal	11000 ± 60	13080-12720	11130-10770
A	Beta-277000	Charcoal	11230 ± 50	13270-13030	11320-11080
A	Beta-277001	Charcoal	11440 ± 60	13500-13180	11550-11230
A	Beta-284214	Charcoal	10940 ± 50	12990-12710	11040-10760
A	Beta-284212	Charcoal	11770 ± 50	13790-13550	11840-11600
A	Beta-284213	Charcoal	11800 ± 50	13800-13560	11850-11610
B1	GifA-101037	Charcoal	11940 ± 100	14070-13590	12120-11640
B2	GifA-101038	Charcoal	12510 ± 100	15300-14540	13350-12590

Table 1. ^{14}C/AMS radiocarbon dates from Molí del Salt. Radiocarbon dates have been converted to calendaric dates by means of the calibration curve CalPal 2007 – Hulu.

products from the fabrication process as well as unfinished artefacts. This data would confirm that bone tool fabrication would have taken place in the same site.

Concerning the exploitation of botanical resources, the study of wood charcoal has allowed the identification of the following taxa: *Pinus sylvestris*, *Juniperus*, *Acer*, *Betula*, *Corylus avellana*, *Prunus*, *Rhamnus cathartica/saxatilis*, Rosaceae/Maloideae and *Sambucus*. Among charcoal of genus *Prunus*, 3 different varieties have been documented, which correspond to different species: *Prunus avium/padus* (cherry tree), *Prunus spinosa/mahaleb* (mahaleb cherry/St Lucie cherry) and *Prunus spinosa/amygdalus* (blackthorn). Apart from the use of wood as fuel, it cannot be ruled out that some of the identified species had other uses, like fruit consumption. This consumption of wild fruits would be supported by the finding of charred seeds, although in a very low quantity. The identified taxa are blackthorn (*Prunus spinosa*), hawthorn (*Crataegus*) and rose hip (cf. *Rosa*) (Allué *et al.*, 2010). Resources identified at Molí del Salt, both animal and botanical, indicate the exploitation of the surrounding environment of the site, in the context of a broad spectrum economy. Site location in a transition context between the mountain environment of the Prelitoral Mountain Range and the plain of the Ebro Basin is particularly suitable for that subsistence strategy. Framed on this economic strategy, there are certain evidences that confirm movements to relatively far away places from Molí del Salt. Apart from lithic raw material, which will be commented on in the following section, marine shells are the objects that show a major mobility range. There have been

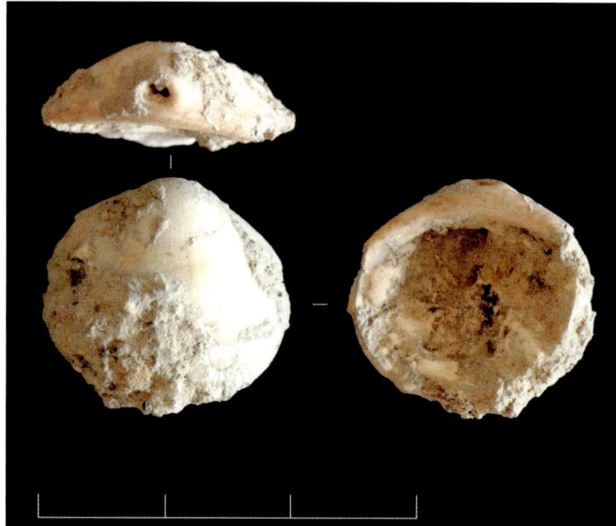

Figure 3. Perforated marine shell found in unit A of Molí del Salt.

documented specimens that correspond to different species (*Pecten jacobaeus*, *Glycymeris glycymeris*, *Cyclope* sp., *Dentalium* sp.), that suggest movements up to the coastline (situated around 36 km away in a straight line at the present time), or contacts with populations living closer to the Mediterranean sea. These shells arrived to Molí del Salt, not for being consumed, but they were used as personnel ornaments. Most of them are perforated, which indicates that they were used as pendants or beads (Fig. 3).

3. Lithic industry

Knapping and the use of stone tools were usual as the large quantity of lithic artefacts recovered in every level demonstrates. Most of the lithic industry has been worked on flint, a raw material particularly abundant in the Conca Barberà region, and also in the evaporitic Paleogene formations documented on the marginal sectors of the Ebro Basin. The use of other rocks such as limestone, schist, hornfels or sandstone was quite unusual and is related, in general, with the use of pebbles for different tasks (as hammer, work surfaces, blank for graphic representations, etc.). In the lithic assemblages of Molí del Salt different types of flint coming from different sources of procurement have been identified, which suggest quite diversified procurement strategies. Most of the flint present typical characteristics from Conca Barberà region (Soto *et al.*, 2011 and 2013). Nevertheless, there are also others varieties coming from outcrops outside the region, such as the Ulldemolins, 15 km from Molí del Salt, that have outstanding qualities for knapping. Along the archaeological sequences some evolutionary trends on raw material provisioning suggest significant modifications in the mobility strategies. Flint from Ulldemolins show higher percentages at the earliest levels (unit B), but its representation decreases towards the upper part of the sequence. This tendency culminates at the Mesolithic level, when raw procurement strategies show a more local character. These changes can be interpreted in the context of the reduction of exploitation territories as long as we approximate to the end of Paleolithic.

Tool production is made following different knapping methods (García Catalán, 2007; García Catalán *et al.*, 2013), which cause a wide morphological variability, both among cores and among products. Blade production is well represented, although it is not dominant in any level. Cores for systematic blade debitage are slightly frequent and the blade percentage represents, in general, 20% of blanks. However, even though blade debitage is not the majority, a tendency to produce elongated flakes can be observed. Often, these products are obtained from unipolar cores or bipolar cores with hierarchical structures that are characterized by a well defined flaking surface opposite to another one that is not knapped. Finally, other more expedient knapping methods are also documented, oriented to the production of short flakes from discoidal or polyhedral cores.

Regarding lithic retouched artefacts typology, endscrapers are the best represented group on the whole sequence, especially at the upper levels where they reach percentages of almost 40%. Other types of the toolkit show lower percentages but are well represented too, as backed elements (points and blades), denticulates, truncations, burins and borers. However the typological group distribution show significant changes through the sequence, emphasizing differences between unit B and unit A already detected in regards to raw material procurement. Thus, Unit B is characterized by the high percentage of truncations, the most represented tool that reach values of 27% and 22% at levels B2 and B1, respectively. Then, the toolkit is composed by endscrapers (20% and 19%), denticulates (12% and 16%) and backed artefacts (13% and 12%). The absence of burins at these lower levels should be highlighted. On the contrary, Unit A shows an abrupt decrease of truncations that are reduced to values around 5%, while endscrapers slightly increase, until they reach the percentage of almost 40%. Denticulates and backed artefacts do not show significant changes. It can be stressed that the presence of burins increase significantly with regard to unit B, with a maximum of 10% in unit A.

This typological representation is characteristic of Late Upper Paleolithic assemblages in the Mediterranean coast of the Iberian Peninsula. In particular, the similarities between Unit A of Molí del Salt and other sites from South Catalonia of similar chronologies, such as Font Voltada, Els Colls, El Filador, l'Hort de la Boquera, La Cativera, Picamoixons or Cova del Vidre, can be remarked. In the same chronological context we can include other resembling archaeological assemblages, though they still don´t have available dates: Sant Gregori, Balma de la Vall, l'Areny or Cova de les Borres. On the contrary, they are less parallel cases for Unit B. The predominance of truncations is not very usual in the Late Upper Pleistocene sites, even though it has been recognized in other cases with similar chronologies to the assemblages of Molí del Salt: layer 5+6 of the Vestibulo chamber of Nerja Cave, level I of the inner sector of Tossal de la Roca and the upper levels of sector 2 of Cova Matutano (Vaquero, 2004).

Functional analysis has confirmed that endscrapers were specially used for hide working. Use-wear analysis has documented traces corresponding to the working of both fresh hide and dry hide, which suggest that the whole process was carried out in the site. Nevertheless, endscrapers were not the only tool used in hide working, since characteristic use-wear has been also identified in others tools such as truncations, denticulates and unretouched flakes. Backed elements were used as projectile points just as scars and impact fractures have demonstrated. Another activity documented is defleshing work, which use-wear has been identified mainly in unretouched flakes. It seems strange that functional analysis do not have documented certain activities that have already been confirmed by other evidences such as work on vegetal materials, bone tool making or engraving.

Recycling and reusing of artefacts have recently been documented at Molí del Salt. This technological behaviour probably has a significant impact on the composition of Paleolithic lithic assemblages. One way to document recycling is to identify intentional modifications in objects that have had no alteration when they remained abandoned at the site, which allows us to differentiate two moments of the artefact history, one previous and one posterior, to the alteration. This is the case of burned lithic artefacts, where it can be recognized when they were retouched after the heat damage (Fig. 4). At Molí del Salt this practice has been well documented (Vaquero et al., 2012) and it has been calculated that at least a 7.5% of artefacts were made of recycled blanks. Recycling is mainly associated to artefact used in domestic context (endscrapers, denticulates, borers), which demonstrates its expedient character and its capacity to attend to immediate needs in the context of daily activities.

Figure 4. Tools retouched after fire damage. White lines indicate the location of the retouched edges. Differences of colour and patina could be noticed between retouched and unretouched surfaces.

4. Portable art.

The discovery of portable art pieces has been one of the most relevant aspects of the archaeological record from Molí del Salt (García Díez and Vaquero, 2006), since the scarcity of artistic evidences has traditionally been one of the main anomalies of Catalan Paleolithic. Except for some decorative motifs on bone industry, only existed only two engraved slabs from Sant Gregori, a parietal engraving from Cova de la Taverna and the parietal paintings of Cova de la Moleta de Cartagena. In Molí del Salt up to 13 pieces of portable art have been found, all engraved. Regarding the blank used, 9 cases are schist slabs, 3 are of limestone, and the one remaining corresponds to a bone fragment. Both the schist and limestone are abundant in the surroundings of the site. Schist slabs used as blanks are bigger and can reach 30 cm long, while the engraved limestone pebbles are 6-7 cm. As they are bigger and offer plane surfaces which are suitable as graphic spaces, schist slabs show more complex representations, combining several figures in the same slab and engravings on one or two surfaces. Except two slabs (one out of stratigraphic context and another one found in uncertain context), the rest of the evidences have a clear stratigraphic attribution. Most of them correspond to Unit A, except the last slab found so far that comes from the top section of Unit B.

Concerning the motifs represented, the importance of figurative representations, basically animal figures, should be stressed. Eight pieces show these kind of figures, either exclusively or in combination with schematic motifs. In total, 18 figures have been recognized, most of them corresponding to undetermined zoomorphic representations, although it has been possible to identify depictions of cervids, horses and bovines, as well as one human figure. It is worth mentioning the discrepancy between animals engraved and the species identified in the faunal assemblage, where until now, no remains of horse have been found. Representations were made with fine incision. In some cases zoomorphic figures are incomplete, and also there is no interest to represent anatomical internal details, even though in one case the infilling of the internal part of the animal figure with transversal lines to imitate fur animal has been documented. From a stylistic point of view the slenderness of figures is remarkable, particularly in the case of some pieces found in Unit A. This trait can be observed in limbs, trunk, and especially animal neck enlargement.

Considering the combination of figures in the same piece, interesting differences have been observed. Slab no. 1 shows five depictions, two in the upper surface and three in the lower one, without noticing any criteria in its apparently random arrangement. Also, slab no. 1 has a broad thematic diversity, with unusual motifs at Molí del Salt, such as the human figure or a bovine head. On the other hand, other pieces such as slabs no. 3 and no. 4 show a coherent pattern, both in their thematic content and in their figures arrangement. It should be pointed out, that slab no. 3 (Fig. 5) includes the same two zoomorphic partly overlapped depictions represented in each of its surfaces. The figure on top corresponds to a cervid and presents a deeper engraving, whereas the figure beneath shows less marked lines and has a much more complicated taxonomical attribution. Even though both figures express a tendency towards slenderness, this characteristic is more accentuated in the figure underneath. In spite of having a large graphic space, this composition is not situated in the centre of the available surface but moved to the upper edge of the slab. The reiteration of the same composition pattern in both slab surfaces indicates that the graphic sequence was not improvised but responds to a well-defined spatial planning composition, which in turn suggests a solely representation moment probably made by just one individual.

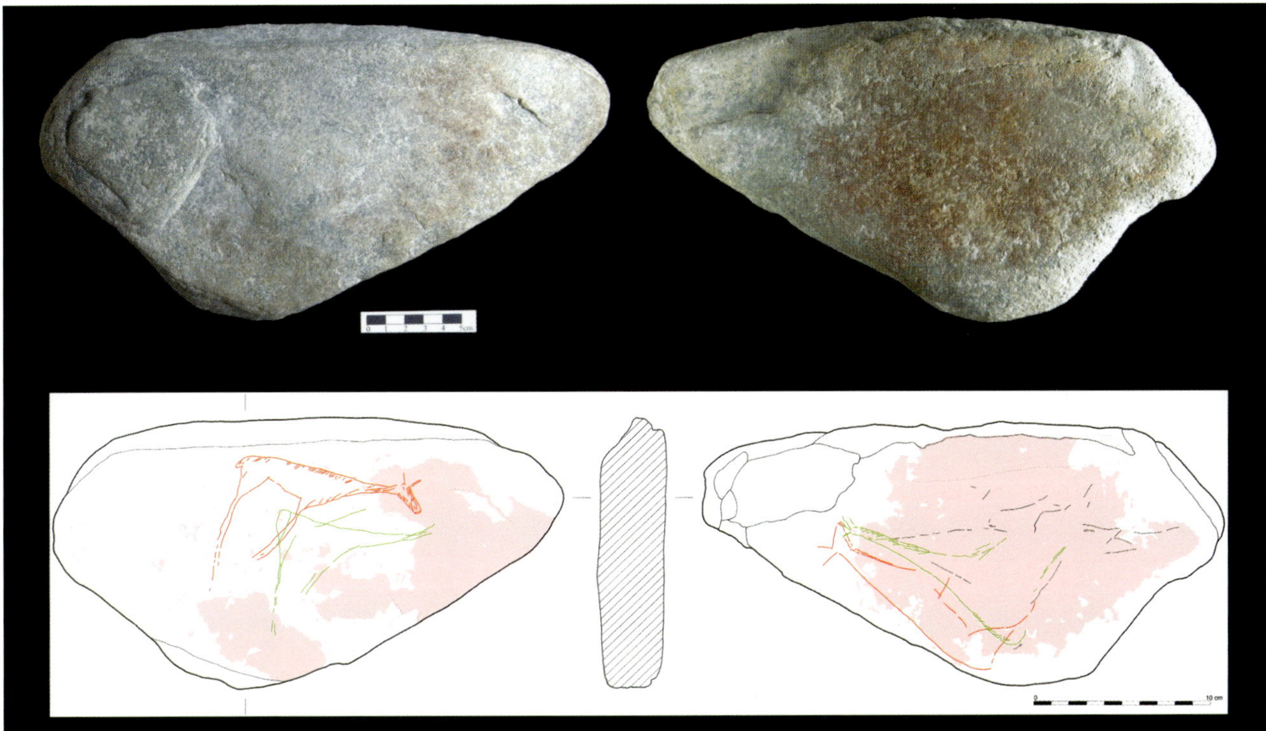

Figure 5. Schist slab with zoomorphic representations engraved at both surfaces.

Regarding the functional context of the portable art representations, it should be noted that some of the engraved pieces were used at different activities. For example, slab no. 3 has both surfaces impregnated with red pigment, which indicates that was used as a working surface for ochre processing. Slab no. 4 presents scars, especially in one of its surfaces, as a consequence of being used as a working surface. Another example could be slab no. 2 that after being engraved was knapped on both surfaces and used as a hammer. These evidences indicate that portable art pieces, or at least some of them, would not have had exclusively a symbolic meaning, but they were daily objects used in domestic activities.

Jordi Rosell*,**, Ruth Blasco***, Florent Rivals*,**,****, María Gema Chacón*,**, Hugues-Alexandre Blain*,**, Juan Manuel López*,**,*****, Andrea Picin, Edgard Camarós*,**, Anna Rufà*,**, Carlos Sánchez*,**, Gala Gómez*,**, Maite Arilla*,**, Bruno Gómez de Soler*,**, Guillermo Bustos*,**, Eneko Iriarte*******, Arthur Cebrià*, **

Cova del Toll and Cova de les Teixoneres. Moià, Barcelona

The Coves del Toll complex is situated around 4 km east of the municipality of Moià (Bages, Barcelona), in the valley of the spring of Mal (Fig.1). The complex is composed of a series of karstic duct-like galleries developed on limestone of Neogene origin (Collsuspina formation). It is situated at 760 metres a.s.l. and its coordinates are 41° 48' 25" N and 2° 09' 02" E. The archaeological site was discovered at the end of 1940s, when several members of the Grup Muntanyenc from Barcelona and the Grup Espelològic del Moianés were exploring the cave and found very well preserved Neolithic pottery. During the 1950s the first archaeological excavations were carried out, both in Cova del Toll conducted by J.F. de Villalta and M. Fusté, and in Cova de les Teixoneres conducted by J. de C. Serra Ràfols, all sponsored by a local businessman S. Oller (Fig.1). Fieldwork at both caves consisted of different regularly placed test trenches that brought to light relevant Pleistocene sequences which were sealed by Neolithic and Bronze Age levels (in Cova del Toll), or by a stalagmite crust (in the case of Cova de les Teixoneres).

The relevance of the discoveries entailed their inclusion in the visits of the Vth Congress of INQUA, held between Madrid and Barcelona in 1957 (Serra *et al.*, 1957). Afterward, fieldwork was interrupted and only occasionally some were analytical studies done such as lithic industry analysis by H. de Lumley (1971). At the beginning of 1970s, the archaeological excavation was resumed at Cova del Toll by J. Guilaine and M.A. Petit. The main goal was to establish a Neolithic periodization aimed at being the reference for the northeastern area of the Iberian Peninsula. However, after two years the cave was abandoned again. Something similar happened with Cova de les Teixoneres. In the middle of 1970s, M. Castellví started fieldwork again on that site looking for Quaternary fauna in Catalonia (Castellví, 1974).

It wasn't until the end of the 1990s when Professor D. Serrat and A. Cebrià decided to uncover the old test pits from Cova del Toll which had been filled by sediments from the same cave

* Àrea de Prehistòria, Universitat Rovira i Virgili (URV), Avinguda de Catalunya 35, 43002 Tarragona, España.
** IPHES, InstitutCatalà de Palaeoecologia Humana i Evolució Social, C/ Marcel·lí Domingo s/n (Edifici W3), 43007 Tarragona, España.
*** The Gibraltar Museum, 18–20 Bomb House Lane, Gibraltar.
**** ICREA, Institució Catalana de Recerca i EstudisAvançats, Barcelona, España.
***** Sezione di ScienzePreistoriche e Antropologiche, Dipartimento di StudiUmanistici, UniversitàdegliStudi di Ferrara, C. so Ercole I d'Este, 32, 44100 Ferrara, Italia.
****** NeanderthalMuseum, Talstrasse 300, 40822 Mettmann, Alemania
******* Departamento de Ciencias Históricas y Geografía, Universidad de Burgos, Villadiego, s/n, 09001Burgos, España.

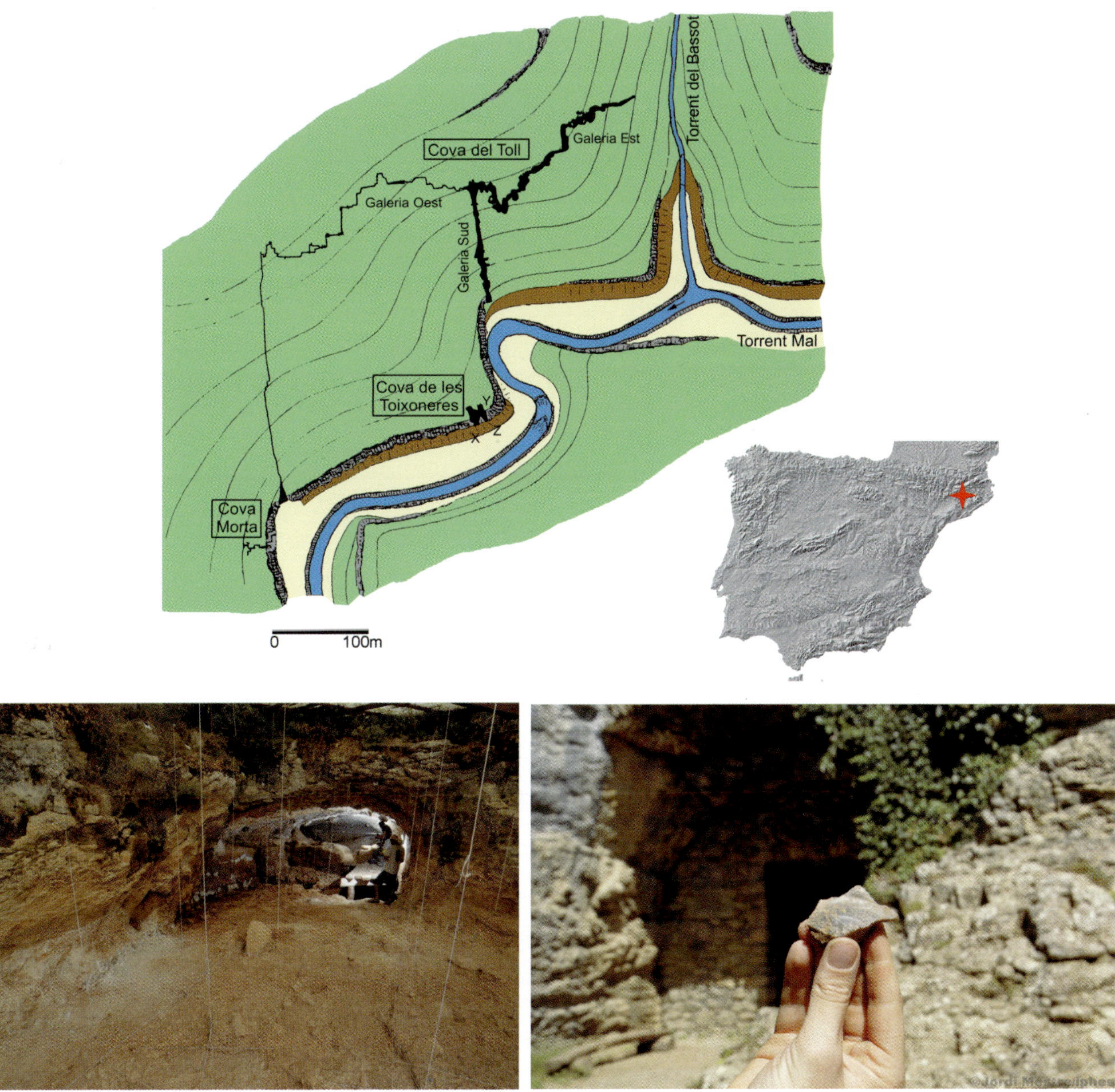

Figure 1. Location of the Coves del Toll and Teixoneres and map of the karst. Left, Cova de les Teixoneres. Right, detail of a lithic artefact found in Cova del Toll and photographed next to the entry.

after several flooding episodes occurred in 1982. This work motivated the contact with IPHES (Institut Català de Paleoecologia Humana i Evolució Social) in 2003 and enabled the beginning of the current research project.

Cova del Toll is approximately 2 km long and is composed of a series of galleries known as South Gallery, East Gallery and West Gallery. The current entry is situated in the South gallery, a rectilinear duct, about 130 m long and 3-4 m wide, that joins at the end with the other two galleries where a small creek runs. The South gallery is the most interesting from an archaeological standpoint. During the 1950s the first researchers elaborated the following stratigraphy in the gallery entrance: upper deposit (0.5 -1 m thick) from Neolithic and Bronze periods (level 1); a deposit of coarse-grained sand and gravel of 25-30 cm of thickness (level 2), probably originated in the last moments of Pleistocene; and underneath a deposit of more than 9 metres thick of Pleistocene sediments with abundant faunal remains (Tab.1). Serra and colleagues (1957)

Level	Chronocultural period	Stratigraphy		Faune	Pollen	Paleoenviroment
		Thickness	Sediment			
A	Bronze Chalcolithic Neolithic	60 cm 30 cm 30 cm	Sandy loose matrix	*Bos taurus, Capra hircus, Ovis aries, Cervus elaphus, Equus caballus, Meles meles, Vulpes sp., Oryctolagus cuniculus*		Mild and moist
B	Pleistocene	20 cm	Red compact clays	*Linx pardina, Felis sylvestris, Meles meles, Equus caballus, Cervus elaphus*		Cold and moist
C	Pleistocene	-	Interspersed sands			
D	Pleistocene	20 cm	Red sandy clays	*Ursus spelaeus, Hyaena spelaea, Canis lupus, Meles meles, Linx pardina, Cervus elaphus, Capreolus capreolus*	*Pinus* (49%)	
E	Pleistocene	20 cm	Clay with abundant hyena coprolites	*Hyaena spelaea*	Pine forest	
F	Pleistocene	30 cm	Red compact clay interspersed with gravels	*Ursus spelaeus, Hyaena spelaea, Cervus elaphus, Capreolus capreolus, Sus scrofa, Erinaceus europaeus, Talpa europaea, Apodemus sylvaticus, Plecotus auritus*		
G	Pleistocene	25 cm	Laminated clay	*Ursus spelaeus*		
H	Pleistocene	35 cm	Angular gravel in loose clay matrix	*Ursus spelaeus, Canis sp., Hyaena spelaea, Felis spelaeus, Felis sylvestris, Linx pardina, Meles meles, Oryctolagus cuniculus, Castor fiber, Microtus nivalis, Bison priscus, Bos primigenius, Capra ibex, Rupicapra rupicapra, Cervus elaphus, Sus scrofa, Equus caballus, Rhinoceros tichorhinus*		Very cold and moist
I	Pleistocene	20 cm	Red compact clays	*Ursus spelaeus, Hyaena spelaea, Equus caballus, Bison priscus, Rhinoceros mercki, Hippoppotamus major*		Cool conditions
J	Pleistocene	40 cm	Very compact dark clays with angular gravels	*Ursus spelaeus*		
K	Pleistocene	120 cm	Sandy loose clays with large boulders collapsed from the ceiling of the cave	*Ursus spelaeus, Sus scropha, Talpa sp., Equus caballus, Rhinoceros mercki*		Environment flooded with water
L		70 cm	Clay. Sterile			
M		40 cm	Sandy clays. Contains fauna			
N		200 cm	Coarse-grained sands with laminations of clay and manganese. Contains fauna.			

Table 1. Stratigraphic details from Cova del Toll (Source: Bergadá and Serrat, 2001).

described relevant accumulations of cave bear (*Ursus spelaeus*) on that lower level, thus Cova del Toll now has one of the most important collections of this species in the Iberian Peninsula. Remains of other large carnivores such as hyena (*Crocuta crocuta*), cave lion (*Panthera leo spelaea*), and wolves (*Canis lupus*), were found, and also small carnivores such as lynxes (*Lynx pardina*), wildcats (*Felis silvestris*), foxes (*Vulpes vulpes*) and badgers (*Meles meles*) were identified. Among ungulates Serra cited the presence of rhinoceros (*Stephanorhinus etruscus*), horses (*Equus ferus*), red deer (*Cervus elaphus*), roe deer (*Capreolus capreolus*), wild boar (*Sus scrofa*) and rabbit (*Oryctolagus cuniculus*). On the lower levels, Serra and others (1957) pointed out the presence of hippopotamus (*Hippopotamus* sp.), which would situate the base of the sequence around the final of the Middle Pleistocene. Presently, part of these collections is deposited in the Natural History Museum of Barcelona (Ciutadella Park). Unfortunately, much of them remain in private ownership or have been lost.

The current research project in this cave started in 2004. The main aim is to produce data regarding the behaviour of large carnivores during the end of the Middle and Upper Pleistocene, as well as bringing light to their interaction with Middle Paleolihic human groups. One of the first stages has been to obtain dating information. Recently, several cave bear teeth were sent to the Biomolecular Stratigraphy Laboratory of the School of Mining Engineering of Madrid and dated by amino acid racemization. Results situate level 4 in a chronological span between 57.9 and 69.8 ky (Refs. LEB 12755-12757).

From an archaeological standpoint, the cave was interpreted in the 1950s as a hibernation cave bear shelter alternating with carnivore dens. However, the discovery of a Mousterian lithic tool in level 4, besides several cave bear bones with anthropic cutmarks, suggests that human groups also visited the cave occasionally. The characteristics and intensity of the human occupation at the cave is one of the priorities of the current project.

The other cave at the same karstic system is Cova de les Teixoneres, situated at 50 m from Cova del Toll. Teixoneres is a U-shape cave with a main entrance oriented towards the south providing access to chamber X. From this chamber there is a 30 m long and 6-8 m wide corridor that connects to the east with chamber Y, which was completely emptied during the 1950s. A narrow passage in the south part communicates chamber Y with the smallest space of the cave, chamber Z, which also has an exit towards the south.

Originally, cave deposits were sealed with a stalagmite crust (Level 1) of 20-40 cm thickness. This crust has been dated by U/Th to 17 ky (Tissoux *et al.*, 2006). Underneath there are several levels of lutites (Level II and III) with clasts of different sizes that have provided a large amount of faunal

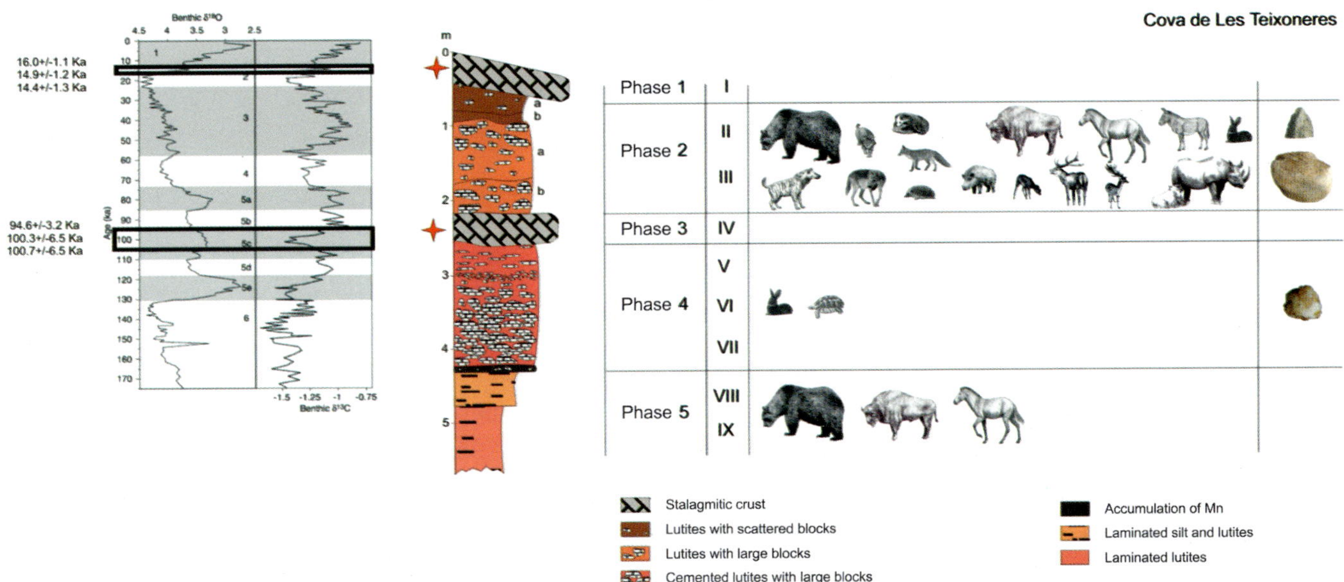

Figure 2. Stratigraphic context of Cova de les Teixoneres.

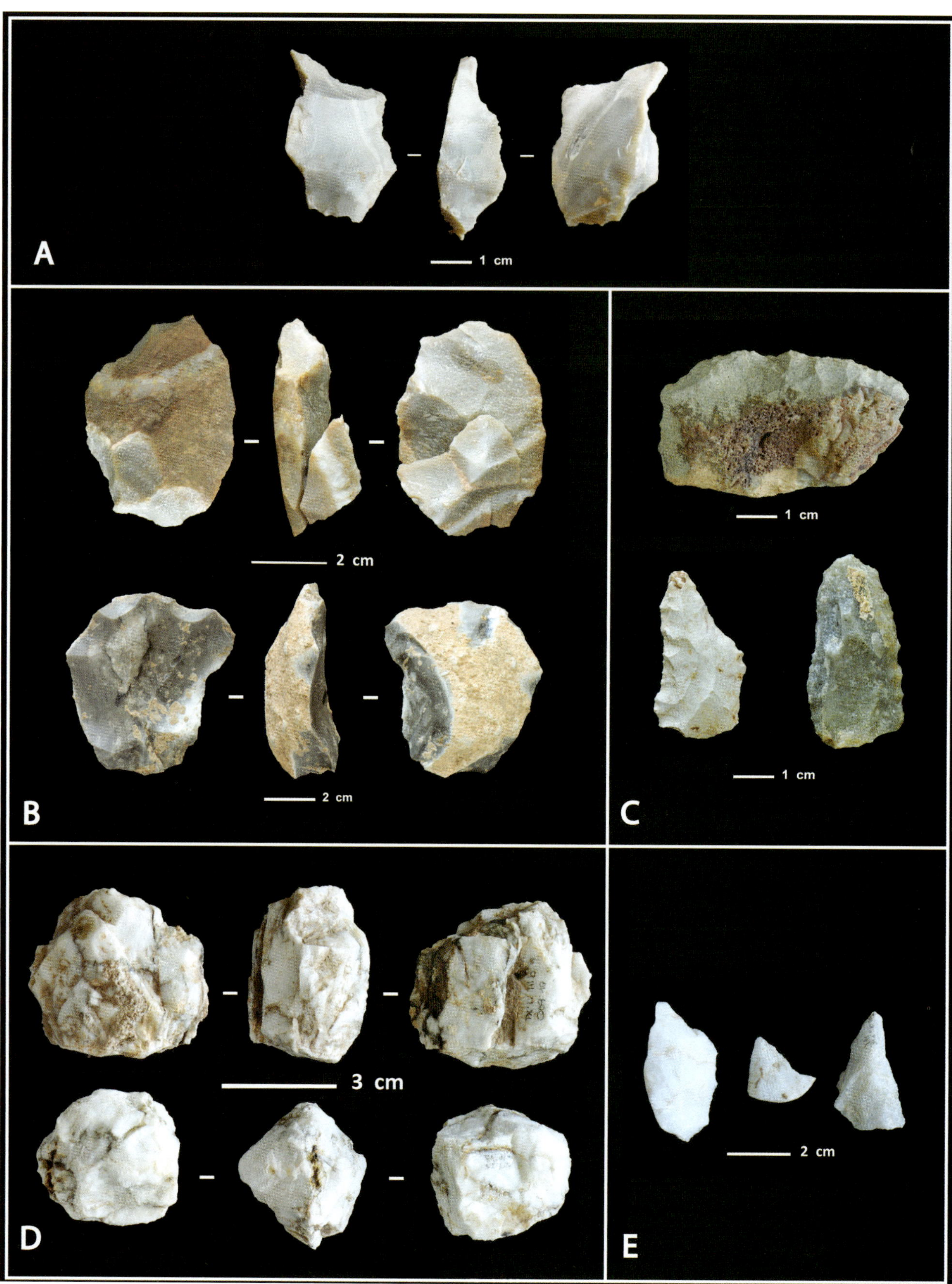

Figure 3. Detail of some lithic artefacts recovered at Teixoneres cave.

assemblages, as many of carnivores as of ungulates and other animals: *Ursus spelaeus*, *Canis lupus*, *Vulpes vulpes*, *Crocuta crocuta*, *Lynx spelaea*, *Meles meles*, *Stephanorhinus hemitoechus*, *Equus ferus*, *Equus hydruntinus*, *Bos/Bison*, *Cervus elaphus*, *Capreolus capreolus*, *Sus scrofa*, *Lepus sp.*, *Oryctolagus cuniculus* and *Testudo hermanni* (Fig. 2). Initially the cave was interpreted as a hyena den with occasional events of human occupation. Recent excavations have corroborated this idea for levels II and III on the basis of the discoveries of great numbers of carnivore and ungulate bones with chewing marks. Nevertheless, extended excavation at chamber X shows a major human frequency on those levels, especially under a large heap of collapsed boulders that separates level II and III. These occupations are evidenced by the presence of hearths, quite desestructured in some cases, surrounded by abundant lithic assemblages and faunal remains with clear anthropogenic marks (cremation, cutmarks and intentional breakage).

Lithic industry, typical from Middle Paleolithic technocomplexes, is worked on varied raw materials, some of them locally available (quartz and limestone), and others from farther places (chert, quartzite and hornfels) (Fig.3). This dichotomy between autochthonous and allochthonous materials also appears in core reduction strategies. Thus, debitage strategies on local materials preferably consisted of orthogonal or discoidal debitage and the whole "chaine opératoire" took place on the site. Conversely, materials procured in remote sources are obtained from Levallois strategies, and the debitage products mainly correspond to end-products. Flakes, cores shaped out in their last exploitation debitage, and retouched artefacts, particularly point and side scrapers are frequent. Concerning the fauna related with this human occupation, a high varied of taxa has been identified. Ungulates of different sizes (aurochs, horses, red deers and roe deers) appear together with small prey, such as leporids and tortoises. The faunal assemblage is very fragmented and frequently corresponds to upper and lower limbs, whereas the axial skeleton is rarely represented.

The general characteristics of lithic and faunal assemblages suggest the expeditious nature of human occupations in the cave. Judging from the reduced dimensions of the occupied area, the groups would be composed of few individuals. All this data seems to indicate that Cova de les Teixoneres would have occasionally been visited by human groups in transit along seasonal movements around these territories. This reasoning would fit with a major frequency on the use of the cave by large carnivores: cave bears during hibernation and others predators during breeding. From the spatial standpoint, the main difference between human groups and carnivores is found in the occupied area. Whereas hominids seem to prefer the main entrance area (chamber X), carnivores like the innermost sector as shelter (Rosell *et al.*, 2010). Based on available data, a general dynamic in the cave can be proposed. It seems likely that carnivores would have established their dens/shelters more or less constantly; these periods would have been interrupted by small groups of hominids visiting the cave sporadically. All these activities would have been developed in a context of climatic oscillations, always during a cold period, dominated by a forested landscape (López-García *et al.*, 2013).

Underneath level III there is another stalagmite crust dated around 90-100 ky (Level IV)(Tissoux *et al.*, 2006). Lower levels (V-IX) present two dynamics clearly differentiated. The upper section (levels V-VIII) is composed of lutites and clasts, with similar characteristics to levels II and III. The lower section (level IX) corresponds to fluvial facies related with the spring of Mal. Although these levels have not been thoroughly explored yet, they possess abundant archaeological remains.

In summary, Cova del Toll and Cova de les Teixoneres represent two relevant sites for the study of the Pleistocene in Central Catalonia. These caves can potentially provide an accurate data set to enhance our knowledge of the Middle and Upper Pleistocene in that area, both from a paleoecological and a cultural point of view.

Acknowledgements

This research is funded by projects CGL2012-38434-C03-03, CGL2012-38358, CGL-BOS-2012-34717 and HAR2010-18952-C02-01, sponsored by the Secretary of State of Research, Development and Innovation of Spain. Ruth Blasco has a postdoctoral fellowship in the programme Beatriu de Pinós-A of Generalitat de Catalunya, cofunded by Marie Curie Actions, EU-FP7. Edgard Camarós has a FI predoctoral fellowship of the Generalitat de Catalunya, cofunded by the European Social Fund. Anna Rufà has a FPU predoctoral fellowship funded by the Secretary of State of Research, Development and Innovation of Spain. We acknowledge Jordi Fábregas for his comments.

Kenneth Martínez [a,b], Joan Garcia *, [a,b,c]

The Mode 1 lithic industry of Vallparadís (Terrassa, Catalonia)

Abstract:

The Vallparadís site contains a long archaeological sequence dating to between the late Early Pleistocene and the first half of the Middle Pleistocene. Levels 10 and 10c (unit EVT7) have yielded abundant macrofauna and Mode 1 stone tools calibrated by paleomagnetism and by biostratigraphy to the upper limit of the Jaramillo subchron (0.98 Ma) and by ESR/U–series to 0.83 ± 0.13 Ma. The industries, elaborated from local raw materials, are small in size. The *chaînes opératoires* used for lithic production are poorly elaborated and are based on a bipolar on an anvil knapping technique. Retouched tools include notches, becs, scrapers and denticulates on small pebbles, clasts, fragments and flakes as well as a large single chopper. Based on the techno-typological comparison with other known Early Pleistocene sites in Europe, it has been proposed that these sites share a single technology with a variability range. Successive migratory episodes with biological and cultural exchange and independent evolution during the Early Pleistocene would imply the possibility of the development of regional technological traditions in Europe.

Keywords: Early Pleistocene; Mode 1; Vallparadís; first Europeans; lithic technology.

1. Introduction

The Vallparadís site (Terrassa, Barcelona) has helped expand the knowledge of the first human settlement in Europe during the Early Pleistocene (Martínez *et al.*, 2010). The combination of biostratigraphic, paleomagnetic and radiometric analyses (ESR/U–series and OSL) place the main archaeological level (level 10 or unit EVT7) at the upper limit of the Jaramillo subchron, approximately at 0.98 Ma (Martínez *et al.*, 2010, 2014; Duval *et al.*, 2011, 2012; Lozano-Fernández *et al.*, 2013) (Fig. 1). The site has also led to new lines of investigation, such as the proposed continuity in the human population of Europe between 1.4–1.2 Ma until the Matuyama–Brunhes limit (0.78 Ma) (Garcia *et al.*, 2011; Bermúdez de Castro *et al.*, 2013). The debate in regard to the moment, hominin species, and causes that made possible the first expansion of hominins throughout Eurasia is focused on the hypotheses that associate it with the same migratory behaviour as other African mammal species (Dennell 2004; Agustí *et al.*, 2009). Or those that point to the evolution of a series of unique adaptive strategies among certain hominin groups that gave them the capacity to leverage new resources, exercise new roles within the African ecosystem and expand beyond it (Carbonell *et al.*, 2010).

The presence of hominins outside Africa can be traced back practically to 2 Ma, which would explain the presence of Mode 1 industry in the first Eurasian deposits. The human fossil remains found at Dmanisi and Atapuerca (Sima del Elefante TE9) show a series of archaic forms of the first hominins who emigrated from the African continent (Rightmire *et al.*, 2006). Current studies even propose the existence of complex phylogenetic relations among the human remains found in Africa, Europe, and Asia, which point to specific evolutionary processes among Eurasian hominins, instead of a succession of migratory waves arriving directly from Africa (Martinón-Torres *et al.*, 2007; Bermúdez de Castro *et al.*, 2011; Bermúdez de Castro and Martinón-Torres 2013).

During the Early Pleistocene, Europe may have been populated repeatedly with the arrival of new immigrants from the regions of the Middle East, along with the groups settled in the refuge areas in southern Europe (Dennell and Roebroeks 2005; Dennell 2010; Dennell *et al.*, 2011; Stewart and

* Corresponding author: Joan Garcia. e-meil: jgarc338@xtec.cat. tlf: 699855077

[a] IPHES, Institut Català de Paleoecologia Humana i Evolució Social (IPHES), C/ Marcel·lí Domingo s/n, Campus Sescelades URV, Edifici W3, 43007, Tarragona, Spain.

[b] URV, Universitat Rovira i Virgili, Àrea de Prehistòria, Avinguda de Catalunya 35, 43002 Tarragona, Spain.

[c] UOC, Universitat Oberta de Catalunya (UOC), Avinguda del Tibidabo 39–43, 08035 Barcelona, Spain.

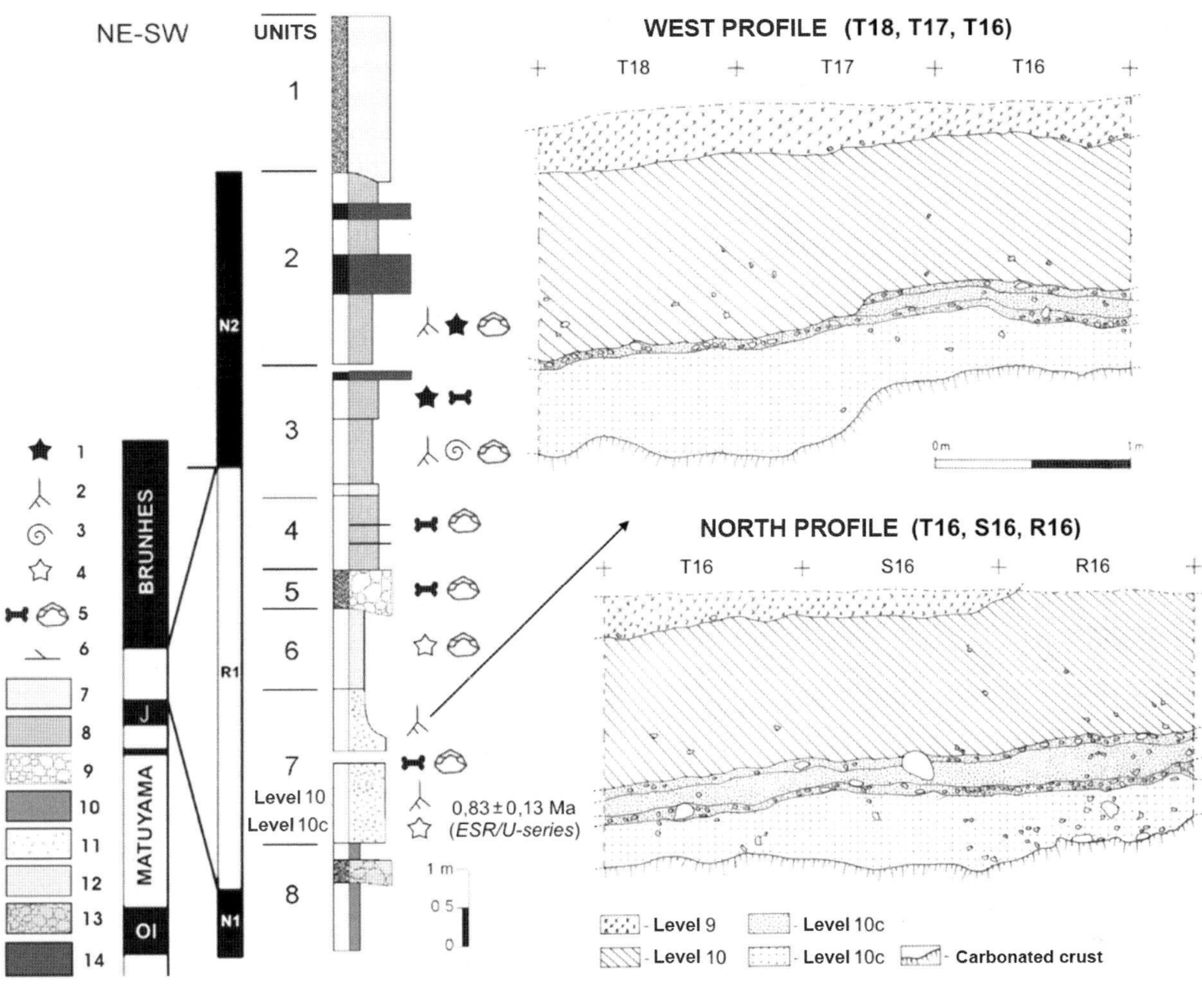

Figure: 1. Stratigraphic cross-sections of levels 10 and 10c (unit EVT7) in Vallparadís, in relation to the magnetostratigraphy and dating by ESR/U–series: (1) organic material and fossil wood remains, (2) root marks, (3) gastropods, (4) traces of CaCO3, (5) units with archaeological remains, (6) crossed lamination, (7) Late Pleistocene terrace, (8) clay and silt with gastropods, (9) unit EVT5, (10) reddish clay and silt, (11) unit EVT7 (levels 10 and 10c), (12) brown clay and silt, (13) conglomerate and (14) paleosoil (stratigraphy drawn by M. Gómez, M. Felipe Frias and R. Ibáñez).

Stringer 2012). The arrival of hominins in Europe may have occurred during periods of glacial-interglacial transition, when the landscape was open and weather conditions improved. These climate conditions obtained repeatedly during the Early Pleistocene (Leroy *et al.*, 2011), which means that the European populations in the refuge areas in the south could have come into contact repeatedly with other populations from Asia. This would explain the complex evolution observed among the hominin fossils from the Early and Middle Pleistocene (Martinón-Torres *et al.*, 2007; Dennell 2010; Bermúdez de Castro *et al.*, 2011). This model would also explain the persistence of populations in Eurasia that are culturally and genetically interrelated. They maintained a series of technological and adaptive patterns that were shared throughout the Early Pleistocene until the expansion of the Acheulean in Europe, approximately 650 ky ago (Garcia *et al.*, 2013a).

2. Lithic industry

2.1. Raw materials

The raw materials used by the Vallparadís hominins came from the same sedimentary matrix of the archaeological levels, which include the presence of small centimetre-sized clasts and river pebbles made of quartz, lydite and sandstone. The outcroppings of these rocks are found in the Sant Llorenç del Munt Range, 6 km from the site, in Eocene and Oligocene conglomerates, sandstone from the Buntsandstein, slate and metamorphic rocks from the Paleozoic, and in the case of flint, in paleogenic evaporitic formations. Natural erosion and transport processes included these materials in the sediments of archaeological levels 10 and 10c (EVT7). The exploitation sequences were mainly developed on small pebbles and clasts of quartz, flint, lydite and quartzite, while the other materials (limestone, sandstone, hornfels, granite and jasper) are documented in lower quantities.

	Manuports		Hammerstones		Anvils		Pebble tools		Cores		Flakes		Flake tools		Debris		Total	
Level 10																		
Quartz	5		2		1		125		513		1178		250		6355		8429	79.4
Flint	-		-		2		41		249		244		165		659		1360	12.8
Lydite	1		-		-		27		92		79		65		422		686	6.4
Quartzite	13		11		4		8		4		12		14		36		102	0.9
Limestone	1		-		-		3		2		5		2		4		17	0.1
Sandstone	3		6		-		-		-		-		-		3		12	0.1
Granite	4		-		-		-		-		-		-		-		4	0.1
Hornfels	2		-		-		-		-		-		-		-		2	0.1
Jasper	-		-		-		-		-		-		1		-		1	0.1
Total	29	0.3	19	0.2	7	0.1	204	1.9	860	8.1	1518	14.3	497	4.7	7479	70.4	10613	
Level 10c																		
Quartz	-		-		-		4		21		36		10		-		71	50.4
Flint	-		-		-		-		22		13		16		-		51	36.2
Lydite	-		-		-		-		5		1		5		-		11	7.8
Quartzite	-		2		-		2		2		-		1		-		7	4.9
Hornfels	-		-		-		1		-		-		-		-		1	0.7
Total	-		2	1.4	-		7	4.9	50	35.5	50	35.5	32	22.7	-		141	
Total levels 10/10c	29	0.3	21	0.2	7	0.1	211	1.9	910	8.5	1568	14.6	529	4.9	7479	69.5	10754	

Table 1. Lithic industry at Vallparadís according to tool types and raw materials.

Quartz, flint and lydite were used in the knapping and retouching sequences, sandstone were used as anvils and for the configuration of the single documented chopper and quartzite was preferred for the percussion objects (hammerstones and anvils) (Garcia *et al.*, 2013a) (Table 1).

2.2. *Hammerstones and anvils*

Although few in number, the hammerstones and anvils, all made from quartzite, sandstone and flint river pebbles are significant. These objects present extractions, percussion marks or fractures related to theses marks that demonstrate that they were selected and manipulated by hominins (Fig. 2). Specifically, 21 spherical objects (13 made of quartzite, 6 of sandstone and 2 of quartz) with clear percussion and depression marks have been interpreted as hammerstones. Another 7 flat river pebbles (4 of quartzite, 2 of flint and 1 of quartz) have been interpreted as possible anvils, as they present percussion and depression marks concentrated in the central areas of their plane surfaces and on their edges. The river pebbles of this size and raw material do not naturally form part of the deposit. In addition to these objects, there were 29 manuports, which corresponded to large-sized quartzite objects, which, although they did not present traces of percussion or fractures, were probably brought to the deposit by hominins (Garcia *et al.*, 2013a) (Table 1).

2.3. *Knapping sequences*

One of the main technical characteristics in the knapping strategies of Vallparadís is the systematic use of small clasts and river pebbles (98.4% of the cores measure 2-5 cms), on which short knapping sequences were developed (Garcia *et al.*, 2013a) (Table 1). The rest of the cores (11, 1.1%) were knapped using non-orthogonal methods (unipolar and centripetal). One of the notable strategies was the bipolar on an anvil knapping technique, which strongly determines the morphology and technical characteristics of the flakes, the prevalence of fragments and debris and surely the low percentage of cores that were identified (Fig. 2). The cores were knapped without any prior preparation of the percussion plane, striking the natural surface of the support directly. Many of these cores conserve marks from the impact of the hammerstone and the counter-impact of the anvil.

The bipolar on an anvil knapping technique generated different core morphologies depending on the knapping intensity. The following morphologies have been identified from least to most intensely exploited: 1) cores with a single knapping plane located on the longest side edge, on which a series of consecutive removals were carried out, reducing the width of the core, 2) cores with a single knapping plane that follows the perimeter of the core, creating a circular or tabular morphology, 3) pyramidal cores, whose proximal bases correspond to the surface in contact with the anvil, and with the distal pointed extremities corresponding to the percussion plane, and 4) cubic or polyhedral cores generated by multipolar removals (Fig. 2).

Some cores and flakes were generated by hand held knapping, through the application of bifacial and unifacial unipolar centripetal methods. The volumetric model of the documented centripetal cores is flat-convex, with a cortical surface that serves as a percussion plane. The volume reduction process is carried out by radial and unifacial centripetal removals. Six cores, three made of quartz and three of flint correspond to this model. Bifacial centripetal knapping has also been identified at the site in five quartz cores. The one that shows the most developed knapping has a wavy edge along three-quarters of the perimeter, which is separated into two opposing knapping surfaces. The remaining segment presents a single removal (Fig. 2). Apart from these cores, some flakes were also produced by the use of centripetal methods, which include some *débordant* flakes. Another five cores (four quartz and one flint) have three abrupt isolated unipolar extractions, which also demonstrate the use of hand held knapping. Lastly, there are two retouches of quartz flakes obtained using a unidirectional hand held sequence.

The flakes generated are small, carinated and with square morphologies, with an average length of 17.3 mm. The majority present partially or totally cortical surfaces, both on the butt (56.7% of the flakes) and the dorsal side (62.1%). The vast majority of the flakes have platform butts and counter-butts (58.1%) as opposed to a few cases with pointed butts (4.9%) and linear butts (1.5%), which is a characteristic of those with bipolar on an anvil knapping technique (Fig. 3). There was a high percentage of flakes with longitudinal fractures, with Siret dorsal fractures predominating. Other knapping accidents produced by the counter-strike of the anvil are also significant. The abundance of flakes with cortical dorsal surfaces and/or platform butts suggest the predominance of the initial knapping phases. Likewise, the small size of

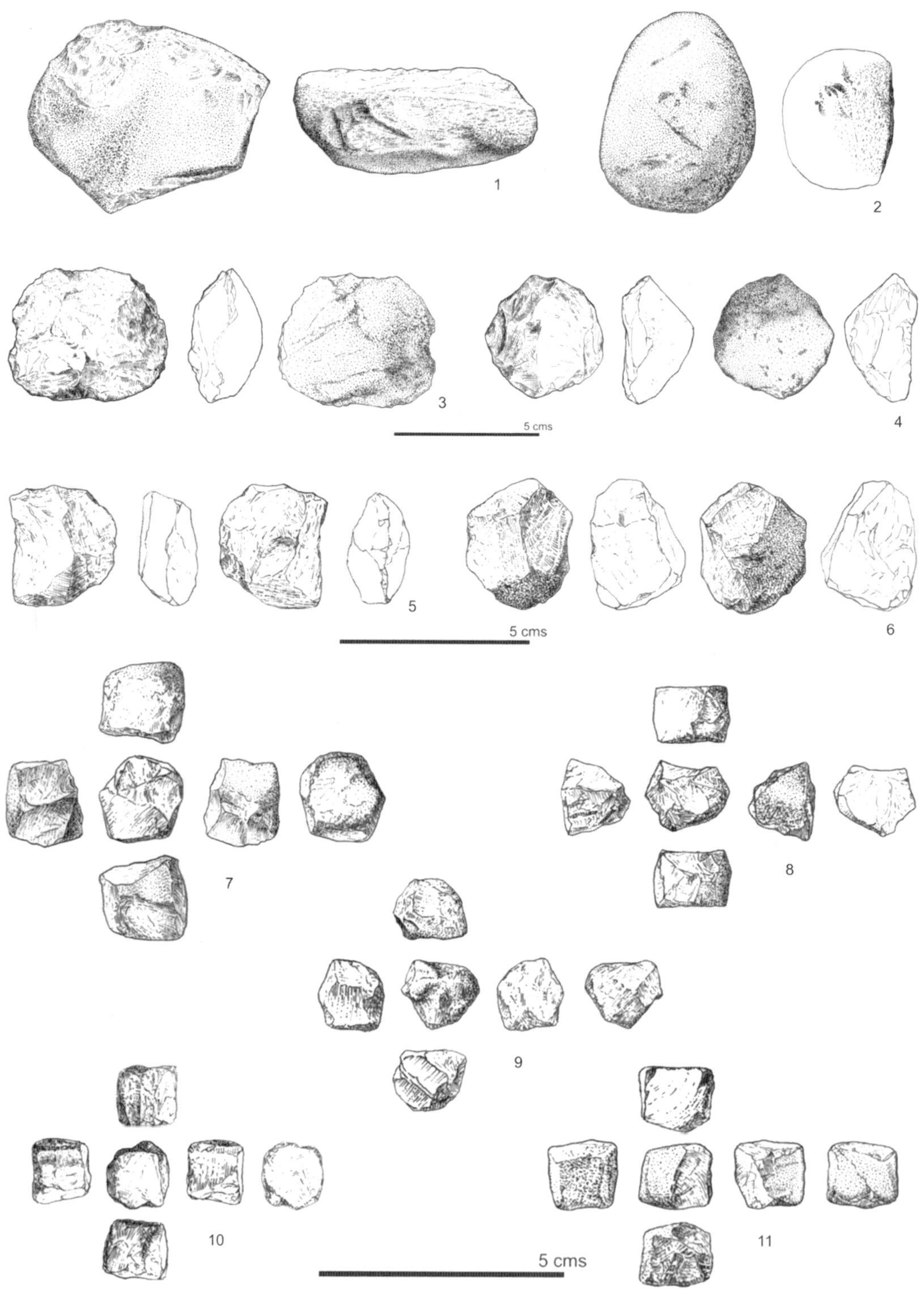

Figure 2. Anvil, hammerstones and cores: flint anvil (1), quartzite hammerstone (2), unifacial centripetal cores made of quartz (3) and flint (4), bifacial centripetal quartz core (5) and bipolar on an anvil cores made of flint (7) and quartz (6 and 8-11) (drawn by N. Sanchiz).

the cores suggests the use of short knapping sequences. The lithic assemblage contains technical elements from all knapping phases, from entirely cortical flakes to completely exhausted cores.

2.4. *Configuration sequences*

A single large configured artefact has been documented, a sandstone chopper with a configured edge with three consecutive removals. Other large objects show isolated extractions, without forming active edges or standardized shapes. Unlike these large tools, the lithic record includes a significant quantity of small retouched flakes, fragments and small clasts and pebbles (529 retouched objects, 4.9%) (Garcia, *et al.*, 2013a) (Table 1). Most of the retouched tools are unifacial and show retouching that affects less than half of the perimeter of the object. Their dimensions (21.2 mm) are larger than the flakes (17.3 mm), but should still be considered small. More than half of the tools show semi-abrupt retouching (>45°) and deeply affect the edges. Notched tools (34.9% of the retouched tools), becs (27.7%), scrapers (18.9%) and denticulated tools (16.3%) are the most numerous, but there are also some denticulated tools associated with distal notches (1.9%) and points (0.3%) (Fig. 3).

The denticulate edges are convex or rectilinear, and the standardization of the retouching varies considerably. The configuration type of the tools is also affected by the depth of the retouching, which ranges from very deep to marginal. Although there is a tendency towards abrupt and semi-abrupt edges, oblique retouching was used to configure edges with significant cutting power. The length of the retouched edges varies and most are located at the proximal or distal ends. Notched tools tend to be composited, unifacial and deep, although there are some supports with double notches, with angles that range between simple and abrupt. Most of the scrapers present discontinuous or marginal retouching, although some have regular and continuous retouching that affects the entire perimeter of the support. Scrapers with retouched series of rectilinear and convex delineation are similarly represented. Many scrapers are concave and have continuous edges configured by regular and abrupt retouching.

The assemblage of retouched objects includes certain different morphotypes with recurring technical characteristics. These include the becs, configured with double notches, sometimes with a notch associated with a denticulated edge or with continuous retouching, similar to a scraper, or with converging denticulate edges that form a dihedral or trihedral. The becs are generally configured on the opposed edge to the percussion plane of the support, or on the thicker part of the flake, fragment or clast. This configuration may have been done in order to reinforce the active edge of the tool. Another less-common model is the lateral semi-abrupt denticulated tool, or the marginal scrapers associated with a distal notch. In these cases, the notches are simple and show an angle superior to 75°. These tools were made on supports with square or rectangular morphologies (Fig. 3).

3. Discussion

The lithic industry at Vallparadís shows a series of common technological patterns shared with other assemblages from the Early Pleistocene in Spain (Orce and Atapuerca) and a margin of variability and/or technological evolution among them (Garcia *et al.*, 2013a). The shared technical elements correspond to: 1) a local selection of raw materials, 2) preference for a type of rock for the development of the knapping sequences, either quartz in Vallparadís, flint in Orce and chert in Gran Dolina TD6, 3) specialisation in the use of quartzite and sandstone river pebbles as hammerstones, anvils and large tools (choppers), 4) the recurrence of orthogonal knapping strategies, bipolar on an anvil knapping technique at the Orce and Vallparadís sites, and hand held knapping at Gran Dolina TD6, with some examples of on an anvil knapped quartz cores (Carbonell *et al.*, 1995, 1999; Toro-Moyano *et al.*, 2009; Barsky *et al.*, 2010; Ollé *et al.*, 2013), 5) the minor presence of unifacial and bifacial centripetal methods at Orce, Gran Dolina TD6 and Vallparadís, which in some cases are deduced only based on the presence of typical flakes generated by these methods, and 6) the reduced presence of large shaped objects such as choppers or chopping-tools.

The knapping sequences are characterised by the use of unipolar, bipolar and multipolar orthogonal strategies, with anvil in Orce and Vallparadís and occasionally at Gran Dolina TD6, where hand held systems are most frequent, with cores for obtaining large flakes. As at Orce and Vallparadís, the bipolar on an anvil knapping technique is also common to other Eurasian Early Pleistocene sites, such as Dmanisi in Georgia, 'Ubeidiya and Bizhat Ruhama in Israel,

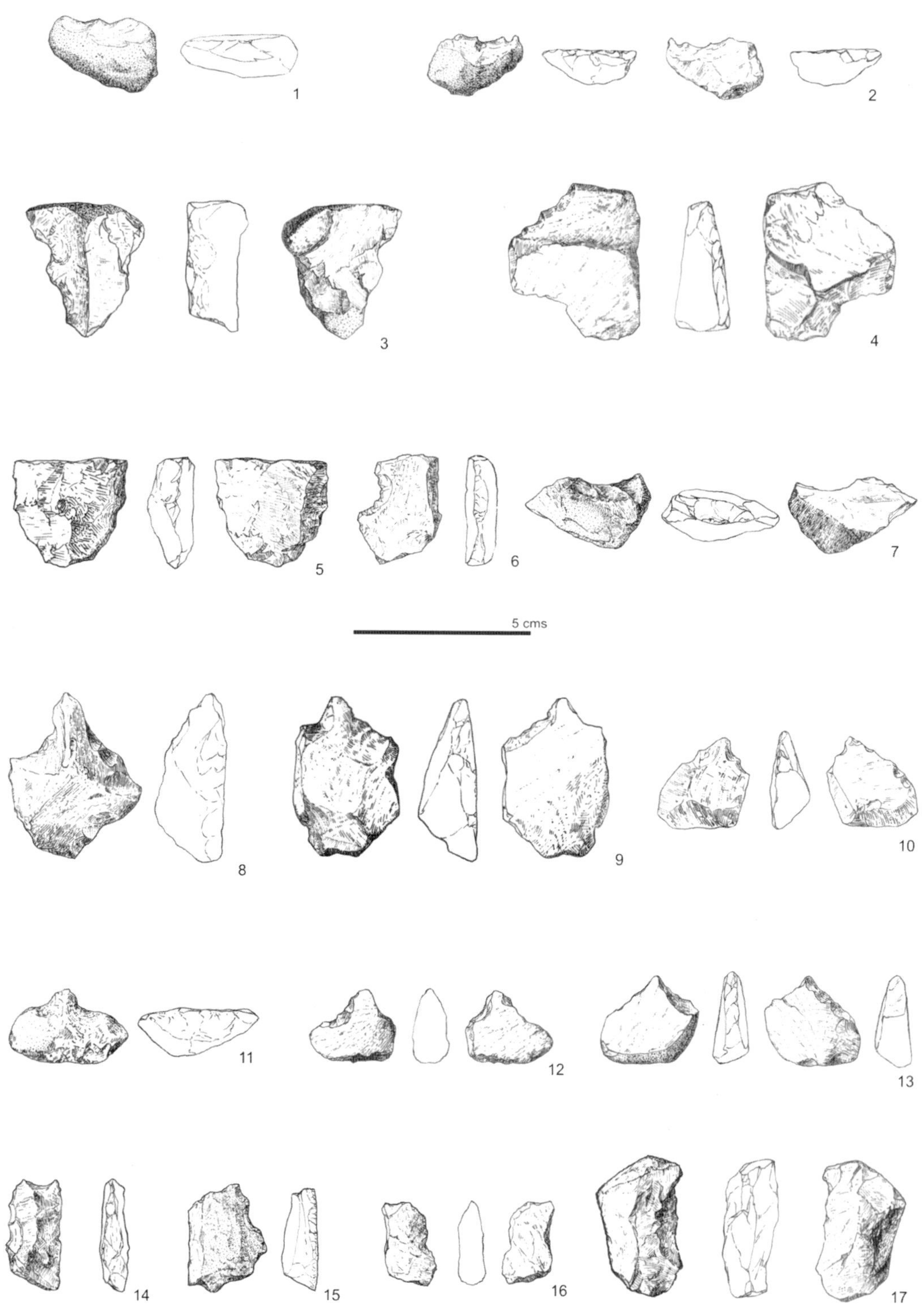

Figure 3. Retouched tools and flakes: on lydite (1), denticulate tools on flakes of quartz (2 and 5), jasper (3) and quartzite (4), notched tools on quartz flakes (6 and 7), becs on flakes (8) and cobbles (11) of quartz and flint (9-10 and 12-13), distal notched tools associated with lateral retouches on flakes of flint (14) and quartz (15 and 16) and quartz flake (17) (drawn by N. Sanchiz).

Ca'Belvedere di Monte Poggiolo in Italy, Pont de Lavaud in France and Untermassfeld in Germany. The main difference lies in the fact that the retouched tools are present at Vallparadís and Gran Dolina TD6, but have scant representation at the sites of Orce and Sima del Elefante TE13 and TE14. They are also minimally represented at Dmanisi, Pirro Nord, Pont de Lavaud, Lunery-Rosières, Lézignan-le-Cèbe, Le Vallonnet and Untermassfeld (Garcia *et al.*, 2013a). However, after the Jaramillo, they became more widespread in the lithic assemblages, as in the case of Vallparadís and Gran Dolina TD6.

Despite the chronological proximity between Gran Dolina TD6 and Vallparadís (Duval *et al.*, 2012), there are differences between the types of retouched tools. Both sites are characterised by the presence of notched and denticulated tools, although at Vallparadís the common tool is the bec and at Gran Dolina TD6 there is a greater variety of types, with scrapers represented the most. Given their chronological proximity, these differences in the types of retouched objects in Vallparadís and Gran Dolina TD6 do not appear to be related to technological evolution; rather they probably have to do with functionality and intensity of the occupations. Even the generalized selection in Vallparadís of small clasts and pebbles for the knapping sequences may not be conditioned solely by the available resources, but also by a technological tradition adapted to the low quality of the knapping of small supports (Garcia *et al.*, 2013a). In the area of the Vallparadís stream, there are secondary deposits of raw materials in which hominins may have obtained supports that were larger than the ones that were used.

4. Conclusions

Thanks to the data from Vallparadís (Martínez *et al.*, 2010; Garcia *et al.*, 2012), dated by ESR/U-series and OSL, magnetostratigraphy and biostratigraphy at the upper limit of the Jaramillo subchron (0.98 Ma), in addition to the sites from the Early Pleistocene on the Iberian Peninsula (Orce and Atapuerca), we have an archaeological sequence that covers the entire period between 1.4–1.2 Ma until the Matuyama-Brunhes limit (0.78 Ma). This data suggests continuous human occupation of the Iberian Peninsula throughout this time interval (Garcia *et al.*, 2011; Duval *et al.*, 2012; Parés *et al.*, 2013). Based on the technological characteristics of the industries of the sites on the Iberian Peninsula, we can associate them as belonging to European Mode 1, with a variability margin (Garcia *et al.*, 2013a). The lithic technology documented at Vallparadís and the rest of the European sites is based on a series of knapping systems based on orthogonal methods, both anvil and hand held knapping exploitations, and in the retouched objects in the form of denticulated and notched tools. Lithic assemblages with flakes and small retouched tools are also present at other sites such as Ca'Belvedere di Monte Poggiolo, Kozarnika cave, Untermassfeld and Ain Hanech (Garcia *et al.*, 2013a). The margin of variability of European Mode 1 would be expressed with the presence of centripetal knapping methods and retouched objects, such as scrapers or becs.

The hominin fossil evidence suggests different evolutionary processes, which, along with technological variability, may indicate the presence of different human groups that maintained evolutionary traits and technological traditions over time. The exchanges between populations within Europe would have given rise to a metapopulation that contained groups that shared the same technological substrate (Mode 1), defined by tools with a high degree of functional effectiveness obtained using short *chaînes opératoires*. Similarly to genetic processes, the Mode 1 industry would be differentiated territorially and/or chronologically, resulting in the technological variability observed. These first human groups were able to sustain continuous occupation on the Iberian Peninsula and expand towards northern Europe during temperate climate periods (Garcia *et al.*, 2013b).

5

MEDITERRANEAN BASINS. CENTRE

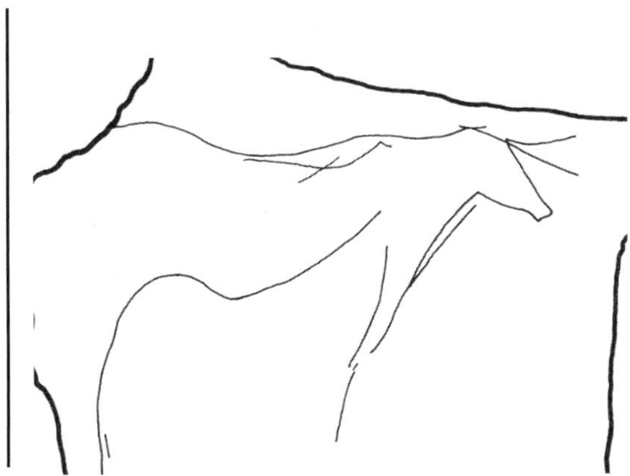

Site	Map numbering
Abric de El Pastor	56
Cova del Bolomor	57
Casa Corona	58
El Collado	59
Cova Beneito	60
Coves Santa Maira	61
Cova Foradà	62
Cova Negra	63
Cueva de la Cocina	64
La Cueva Negra del Estrecho Río Quípar	65
El Salt	66
Cova e les Cendres	67
Malladetes	68
Cova Matutano	69
Parpalló	70
Sima de las Palomas del Cabezo Gordo	71
Tossal de la Font	72
Tossal de la Roca	73

C.M. Hernández*, B. Galván*, C. Mallol*, J. Machado*, F.J. Molina**, L. Pérez***, J.V. Morales****, A. Sanchís*****, P. Vidal****, A. Rodríguez******

Abric de El Pastor in the Neanderthal Occupation of the Alcoy valleys, Alicante (Spain)

Abric de El Pastor is a Middle Palaeolithic site located in the Miocene limestone hills forming Serra Mariola in the mountains of Alicante, at 820 m above sea level. It is located on the right bank of the ravine Barranc del Cinc, on the upper part of the hillside, facing north-east and with a surface area of nearly 60 m^2. It is an ancient karst tube formed in a bed of conglomerate limestone, in the Tortonian bioclastic calcirudites.

1. M. Brotons' excavations

The first archaeological excavations in Abric de El Pastor were carried out in 1953 by M. Brotons, a bookseller from Alcoy interested in the local archaeology and who received technical advice from Professor F. Jordá for his work, as reflected in the documentation held in the C. V. M. Municipal Archaeological Museum. This consists of numerous letters dealing with methodology with recommendations about the excavation and the treatment of the archaeological record, also of historiographical interest because of references to the Middle Palaeolithic in Mediterranean Spain; in addition to the excavation logbook, stratigraphic sketch, inventory and drawings of the finds.

The stratigraphic notes and some photos have been able to determine that the excavated area was in the central part of the rock-shelter and only affected the upper part of the deposit (about 50cm). Brotons thought he had reached the end of the sequence. Indeed, it was generally believed that the excavation had exhausted the potential of the deposit, which had yielded rich lithic and faunal assemblages.

2. Current research in Abric de El Pastor

The study of the site re-started in 2005 with an examination of the objects found by Brotons and a new series of excavations, initially aimed at establishing their stratigraphic context and the chrono-cultural sequence, as far as its state of conservation permitted, within a full pluri-disciplinary study of the Neanderthal occupation of the mountains of Alicante (Galván *et al.*, 2007-08, 2008; Morales and Sanchís, 2009; Molina *et al.*, 2010).

The lithic assemblage recovered by Brotons is abundant and varied (2,430 pieces), formed by varieties of detritic flint from the surroundings of the site (Molina *et al.*, 2010). Complete *chaînes opératoires* were identified, above all Levallois, and even several refits were achieved. This attests knapping *in situ* and the integrity of the lithic assemblage (Galván *et al.*, 2008). The retouched elements form a large proportion of the assemblage (n = 543) with a predominance of side-scrapers and a significant group of pointed objects (n = 64), of which 27 display diagnostic impact fractures (Fig. 1a and b) (Galván *et al.*, 2007-08). The archaeozoological record from the old excavations is formed by a faunal assemblage with an anthropic origin, with a choice of prey consisting mainly of ibex, red deer and horses, as well as the Mediterranean tortoise, which was a common resource (Morales and Sanchís, 2009).

* U.D.I. de Prehistoria, Arqueología e Historia Antigua. Grupo de Investigación Sociedades Cazadoras Recolectoras Paleolíticas. Universidad de La Laguna

** Dpto. de Prehistoria, Arqueología, Historia Antigua, Filología Griega y F. Latina. Universidad de Alicante.

*** Dpto. de Historia e Hª del Arte, IPHES. Universitat Rovira i Virgili

**** Dpto de Prehistoria y Arqueología. Universidad de Valencia

***** Museo de Prehistoria de Valencia. S.I.P.

****** Dpto. de Prehistoria, Historia Antigua y Arqueología. GEPEG. Universidad de Barcelona.

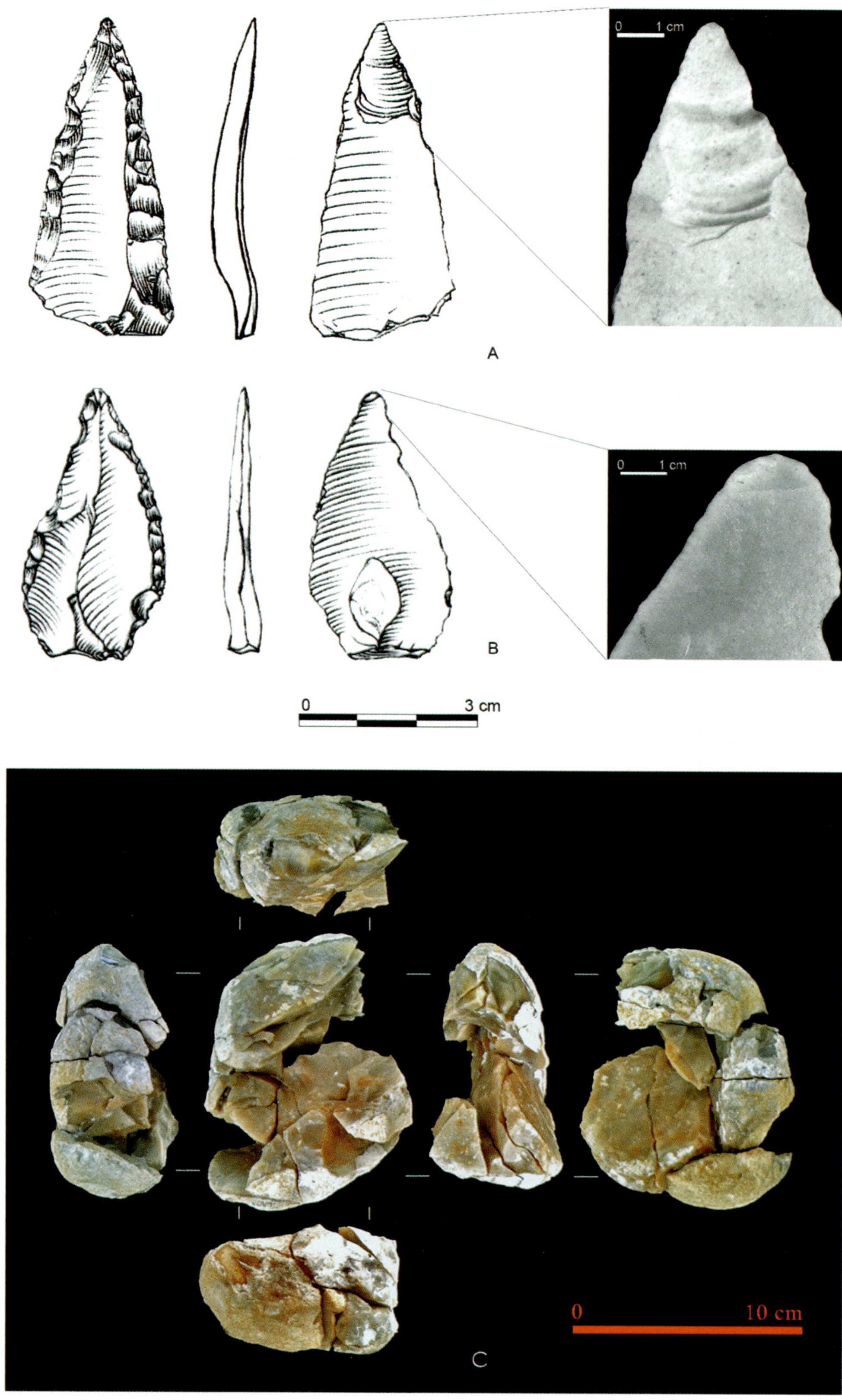

Figure 1. Lithic material: a and b, pointed artefacts with impact fractures from the Brotons collection; c: refit in Mariola-type flint, from SU IVb, demonstrating the almost total reduction of a block.

2.1. The stratigraphic sequence

The current excavations cover an area of 42 m^2 (70% of the total surface area). The sedimentary sequence uncovered to date is 1.5m thick and has been divided into six stratigraphic units, according to macroscopic and micromorphological textural parameters (Fig. 2a and b). The main origin of the sediment is the disgregation of the conglomerate bed with cobble-stones and quartzitic fossil limestone gravel that outcrops in the rock-shelter. The matrix consists of micritic calcite in a good state of conservation, with little evidence of solution. In general there is very little clay, which is only present as fine coverings and filling the porosity. From top to bottom, the sequence is as follows:

- SU VI: This has only been identified in a stratigraphic sounding; it is still in the process of being excavated and its thickness is unknown. It is a silty-sandy sediment, with 40% of clasts and gravel, very similar to the following unit. It has yielded a dense accumulation of materials (flint, fauna and charcoal) and several hearths, next to the wall of the rock-shelter (Fig. 2b).
- SU V: This has also been identified in the stratigraphic sounding. The silty-sandy sediment, with a proportion of gravel similar to SU VI, is about 25cm thick. It displays evidence of illuviation and repeated reducing-oxidising processes, indicating a regime of greater humidity than in upper layers (Fig. 2b).
- SU IV: Identified all over the excavated area, with a mean thickness of about 70cm, it consists of seven sub-units in which discontinuous layers of cobble-stones (IVa, IVc, IVe and IVg) alternate with clayey-sandy silts, sand and fine-grained gravel (IVb, IVd and IVf). Several remains of human occupations, probably of a short duration, have been discriminated in it (Machado *et al.*, 2013) (Fig. 2a and 2b).
- SU III: This stratigraphic unit has equally been recognised all over the excavation area, with a thickness varying from 3 to 12cm. It consists of rounded gravel with no matrix, which suggests a period of sub-aerial exposure, in which the rock-shelter was affected by run-off processes. The archaeological remains are very scanty (Fig. 2b).
- SU II: This is a relict sediment occurring in the north-west sector of the excavated area, truncated by SU I. Its calcitic matrix, cemented in places, contains a large number of solution cavities and its appearance is powdery, due to abundant spots of organic material. The archaeological evidence in this unit is limited to a faunal assemblage associated with a hearth.
- SU I: Several episodes of Holocene sedimentation, in which six sub-units (Ia to If) have been discriminated, are all in an erosional contact with the Pleistocene deposit. They fill large hollows (4m in diameter), connected with animal-herders' use of the rock-shelter. They contain Middle Palaeolithic remains in a secondary position, from the erosion of the upper part of the Pleistocene sequence, some of which is conserved as breccia, adhered to the wall up to 0.7m above the modern surface (Fig. 2a).

Most of the remains retrieved by Brotons must have come from SU I, whose characteristics coincide with this researcher's description of his Level A, although he did not realise this was a Holocene layer with Palaeolithic objects in a secondary position. His excavations also partially affected the stratigraphic units II, III and IVa.

2.2. Hearths

The excavations at Abric de El Pastor have been able to study one hearth in SU II, two in IVa, three in IVb, one in IVc and five in IVd, as well as further evidence in SU VI. In general, they occupy the centre of the rock-shelter, near the entrance and beneath the line of the overhang. They vary from 0.3 to 1m in diameter. The ash has only been conserved minimally, as shown by micromorphological analysis and FTIR, and therefore these hearths are recognised by their thermal impact on the substrate, whether it is rocky or sandy. They played a structural role in the organisation of the area (Machado *et al.*, 2013) and are characterised by a very rich anthracological record attesting the use of a wide range of plants in the activities connected with the fires (Vidal, per. comm.).

2.3. Human occupations

The excavation over the area of SU IV has made it possible to recognise certain aspects of the dynamics of the occupation by the groups who lived in the rock-shelter. SU III and II are archaeologically very poor and affected by Brotons' excavation and the animal-herders' activities. Similarly, SU V and VI are only known partially in the sounding. However, the

Figure 2. a) Stratigraphic sequence SU I to IVd. b) Stratigraphic sequence in the sounding from SU IVd to VI.

objects found in SU IVa, IVb and IVc are evidence for between four and six brief occupations of low intensity (Machado *et al.*, 2013). The absence of thermo-altered flint in these units susceptible to dating by TL has not allowed a chronological determination, and therefore it can only be said that they are older than 75 ± 10ka, the result of a TL determination for materials in the Brotons collection (N. Mercier, per. comm.). All these occupations are very similar in the use of the space (central hearth or hearths, activities around them and an empty space at the back of the rock-shelter). However, they are different in terms of the importance of the activities carried out. In SU IVa and IVc, animal processing predominated, especially the consumption of *Testudo hermanni*, whereas knapping tasks are practically unknown. In contrast, these tasks predominate in IVb (Fig. 1c). SU IVd, currently being excavated, reflects a similar pattern, although with a larger number of hearths.

Acknowledgements

This communication forms part of the research being carried out in the framework of the project: I+D+I HAR2012-32703, *The disappearance of Neanderthal groups in the central region of Mediterranean Iberia. A methodological proposal for an approach to the historical process and the palaeo-environmental background* (MINECO-FEDER).

We would like to thank Camilo Visedo Moltó Archaeological Museum, Alcoy Town Corporation and the General Directorate for Cultural Heritage of the Government of Valencia for their support of the archaeological research.

Josep Fernández Peris*, Virginia Barciela**, Ruth Blasco***, Felipe Cuartero****, Laura Hortelano*****, Pablo Sañudo******

Bolomor Cave (Tavernes de la Valldigna, Valencia, Spain)

Location and geographical context

Bolomor cave is located on the southern slope of the Valldigna valley, on the right bank of Bolomor Canyon, near the Valencian town of Tavernes de la Valldigna. Valldigna is a flat-bottomed valley with an east-west orientation. The river Vaca runs through the valley, nourished by the springs of the nearby limestone massifs.

The cavity, about 100 m above sea level, is part of the series of karst forms along the northern side of the Mondúver massif, opposite the limestone alignments of the Sierra de Les Agulles and the Sierra de Corbera. The coast lies northeast of the site, almost perpendicular with the valley, whose base extends almost at sea level. The cave was formed by the intense karstification and fracturing of the Santonian limestone in a northeast-southwest direction. It is located on a vertical cliff that forms part of the southern flank of the tectonic depression of the Valldigna. It has a surface area of approximately 35 × 17 m (600 m^2). Its Universal Transverse Mercator (UTM) coordinates are scale 1:25,000: ETRS89 and area 30N 737919E 4329998N, according to sheet no. 770-4 of the National Geographic Institute.

Valldigna is located in one of the wettest areas of Valencia, with a typical Mediterranean climate and an annual rainfall of over 700 mm. The regional to-

* SIP (Servei d'Investigació Prehistòrica), Museu de Prehistòria, Diputació de València, C/Corona, 36, 46003 Valencia, España. E-mail: josep.fernandez@bolomor.com

** Departament de Prehistòria, Universitat d'Alacant, Carretera de Sant Vicent del Raspeig, S/N. 03690 Sant Vicent del Raspeig, España. E-mail : virginia.barciela@gmail.com

*** The Gibraltar Museum, 18-20 Bomb House Lane, PO Box 939, Gibraltar. E-mail: rblascolopez@gmail.com

**** Departamento de Prehistoria y Arqueología, Universidad Autónoma de Madrid, Laboratorio de Arqueología Experimental, Campus Cantoblanco, 28049 Madrid, España. E-mail: felipe.cuartero@uam.es

***** Departament de Prehistòria i Arqueologia, Universitat de València. Blasco Ibáñez, 28 46010 Valencia, España. E-mail: lahorte25@hotmail.com

****** Universitat Rovira i Virgili (URV), Campus Catalunya, Avinguda de Catalunya, 35, 43002 Tarragona, España. E-mail: pablo.sanudo@bolomor.com

pography plays an important role in this record: the mountains advance towards the sea and block the humid winds from the northeast, thus favouring rainfall.

The vegetation surrounding Bolomor Canyon has adapted to summer droughts and is evergreen type with small, leathery leaves. No more than 100 years ago, Mondúver was covered by a dense holm oak wood, but today, crop fields and shrubs, including rosemary, thyme, *Cistus* and *Chamaerops*, predominate. The holm oaks have disappeared as a result of a long process of degradation. However, Bolomor Canyon is a magnificent example of a vegetation refuge in which flowering ash (*Fraxinus ornus*), laurus (*Viburnum tinus*), Mediterranean honeysuckle (*Lonicera implexa*), sarsaparille (*Smilax aspera*), Mediterranean buckthorn (*Rhamnus alaternus*), Cade juniper (*Juniperus oxycedrus*) and Phoenician juniper (*Juniperus phoenicea*) grow as representatives of the ancient Mediterranean forest.

History of excavations and development of research

The importance of the cavity as an archaeological and paleontological site was recognized in the 19th century in the references of Juan Vilanova i Piera in 1868. However, it was geologist Leandro Calvo who provided specific data, including a brief description of the stratigraphy (more details are given in Barciela *et al.*, 2013). The inhabitants of Valldigna at the time already knew about the cavity and for the inhabitants of the village it was where the "*Cementerio de los Moros*" was located. During the first half of the 20th century, various naturalists and researchers visited the cavity. These included Henri Breuil, who deposited the first materials extracted from the cave at the *Institut de Paleontologie Humaine* of Paris in 1913. Then, the *Comisión del Colegio de Doctores* of Madrid explored the cavity in 1923 in search of human remains. However, from 1930, the thick sheet of stalagmites at the base of the cave was mined, affecting a significant part of the archaeological site. This work mainly destroyed the central half of the sedimentary filler, exposing an important sequence over 14-m thick. For this reason, the current excavation is being carried out in the side and central cores, creating an artificial division of the site in the areas of excavation depending on the geographic orientation: the Western, Eastern and Northern sectors.

Since the end of the 1980s, the syntheses of the Middle and Lower Palaeolithic in Valencia highlighted the significant research opportunities that this site could offer. But it was not until 1989, that the current phase of systematic research and excavation began, co-directed firstly by Fernández Peris and P. Guillem Calatayud and directed by J. Fernández Peris since 2008 through the Prehistoric Research Service (SIP) of the Regional Council of Valencia and the Ministry of Culture of the Regional Government of Valencia.

Stratigraphy, paleoclimatic phases and dating

The sedimentary filler in the cave of Bolomor mainly consists of colluvial allochthonous material, which has been deposited through open channels in the walls and ceilings. In addition to these contributions are local gravitational contributions from clastic rock landslides or weathering processes. The sedimentary series that rests on the cretaceous rock starts with thick lithochemical levels in the form of stacked sheets of calcite. In these, layers of pure crystallized carbonate alternate with others that include detrital rock without fauna remains. This deposition covers the whole floor of the cavity from the entrance to the innermost point with castings adapted to an irregular topography and stalagmite formations from clastic rock drops. New materials are stacked over this first layer of filling with a subhorizontal overhang and variable thickness depending on the location (between 4 and 8 m).

The karstic deposition of Bolomor cave presents paleoclimatic implications that come from the data based mainly on the sedimentology (Fumanal, 1993, 1995; Guillem, 1995, 1996; Martínez Valle, 1995, 2001; Fernández Peris, 2007). These values translate into a sequence that is summarised from base to ceiling in four paleoclimatic phases (Fig. 1):

- Bolomor phase I (levels XVII, XVI and XV): This is a baseline sequence corresponding to a mild climate cycle with a certain level of humidity, at least seasonally, during which materials from external areas accumulated and sediment brecciation is recorded. Level XV offers a gradual separation of the connection. This is the base with the introduction of materials that were weathered in areas at a certain distance from their final point of disposition. The coeval atmosphere seems to have been mild (without the harshness of active physical weathering of the surroundings) and wet, at least seasonally, allowing the dissolution-concretion of carbonates in the environment. Dating of level XVIIa was obtained by amino acid racemisa-

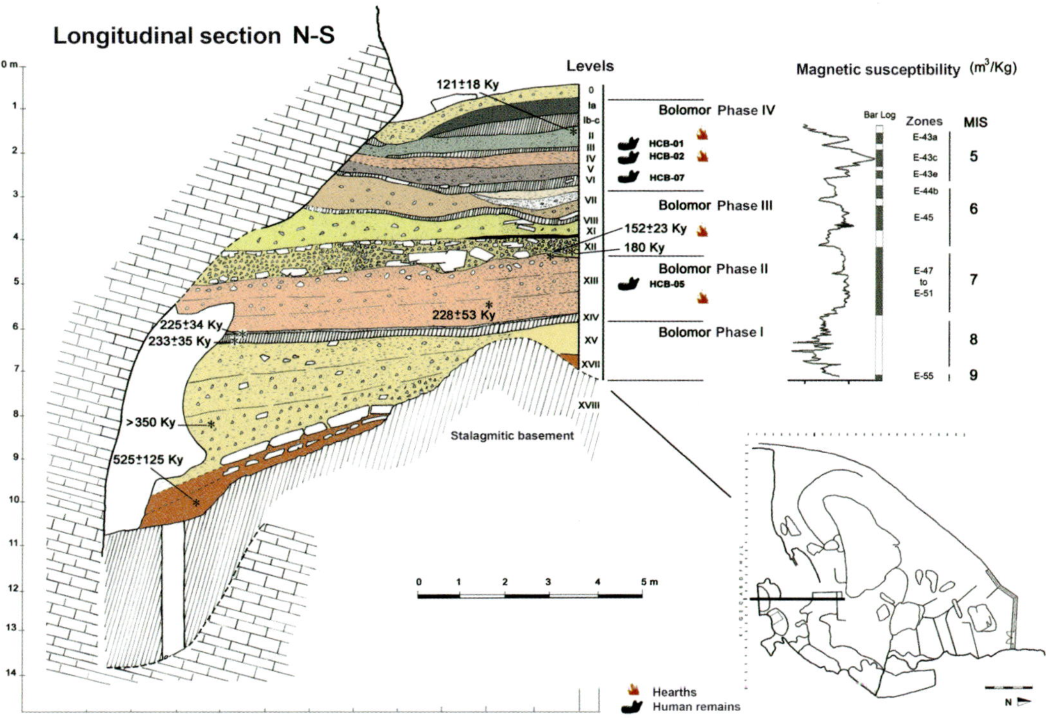

Figure 1. Stratigraphy and dating of Bolomor cave (Tavernes de la Valldigna, Valencia, Spain).

tion (AAR) of 525±125 ky[1] of the enamel of a tooth belonging to the *Equus ferus*. The magnetic susceptibility analyses are rejuvenated at the baseline, relegating it to MIS 9 (Ellwood, unpublished). More samples from level XVII are being analysed using AAR at the Biomolecular Stratigraphy Laboratory of Madrid.

- Bolomor phase II (levels XIV and XIII): This was a climatic period with interstadial characteristics, mild-warm and seasonally very wet, which caused periodic flooding of the cave. A gradual but very pronounced change in the climatic conditions is marked by the installation of level XIVa and b. The environmental parameters changed significantly and the previous severe manifestations remitted completely, giving way to the action of gentle water streams that introduced certain material and a probable differentiation of soil horizons, given that the vertical migration of carbonates in this unit is evident. It was a mild-warm phase and seasonally very wet. Net contact with the next level (XIII) suggests that the overhead stalactite covering collapsed. Two dating values were obtained for level XIV using thermoluminescence (TL): 233±35 ky and 225±34 ky[2]. And at level XIII, the AAR dating values provided a chronology of 228±53 ky[3]. Therefore, Bolomor Phase II is placed within MIS 7.

  For level XIV, two thermoluminescence (TL) dating values were obtained: 233±35 ky and 225±34 ky[4]. In level XIII, the AAR dating values provide a chronology of 228±53 ky[5]. Therefore, Bolomor phase II is situated within the MIS 7.

- Bolomor phase III (levels XII to VII): This was a climate episode with cool and wet os-

1 Dating performed by G. Belluomini, Dipartimento di Scienzedella Terra from La Sapienza University, Rome.

2 Dating performed by W. Stanska-Prószzynska and H. Prószzynska-Bordas, Sedimentology Laboratory at the Facultyof Geography and Regional Sciences, University of Warsaw, Poland.

3 Dating performed byT. Torres, Biomolecular Stratigraphy Laboratory, Madrid.

4 Dating performed by W. Stanska-Prószzynska and H. Prószzynska-Bordas, Sedimentology Laboratory at the Facultyof Geography and Regional Sciences, University of Warsaw, Poland.

5 Dating performed by T. Torres, Biomolecular Stratigraphy Laboratory, Madrid.

cillations, which gradually evolved towards a harsher and drier situation (level XII). Then, this situation seems to have remitted, with a mild and very wet climate finally setting in (level VIII-VII). In level XII, AAR dating values were obtained that put it in an approximate chronology of 185 ka[3]. It is therefore placed between the late MIS 7 and MIS 6.

- Bolomor phase IV (levels VI to I): This represents the upper section of the sequence with mild and wet oscillations typical of the last interglacial period. It formed a globally mild period, with slightly accentuated cool periods (levels VI to III), which led to the accumulation of small rock fragments as a result of weathering of the cavity's dome by the action of cryoclastic processes. High humidity caused partial flooding of the cave and brecciation of the sediment. Also, a climate entailing cyclic conditions seems to have been widespread; that is, there were even cooler periods (levels VI, V-IV-III) during which small subangular detrital material accumulated and was then disrupted, giving way to a flow of constant and highly carbonated streams that brecciated the ceiling of levels VI, III and Ic. In general, it was a globally mild period with slightly accentuated deteriorations, during which high and oscillating levels of humidity persisted. This phase is linked to MIS 5e. An absolute dating of 121±8 ka[2] was obtained via TL for level II.

M. P. Fumanal's sedimentology studies were continued by Brooks B. Elwoood of Louisiana State University. He obtained a magnetic susceptibility event curve (MSEC) that covered the entire chronostratigraphy. The correlation with the sedimentary cycles was satisfactory and added higher paleoclimatic value to it. Magnetic susceptibility (MS) relates the magnetic properties preserved in the sediments of Bolomor cave with the paleoclimate estimates and correlations with other sites. Using MS and cyclostratigraphy (CS) presents a paleoclimatic structure based on this method (MSEC) through graphic correlation with the marine oxygen isotope record (MIS). In Bolomor cave, this study included a temporary continuous sequence from MIS 9 to MIS 5e.

The fauna record

The fauna identified at Bolomor cave has resulted in the identification of 20 species of macromammals; the distribution throughout the sequence and relative frequencies indicate the development of slight changes to the environment surrounding the site.

The biostratigraphic sequence is mainly characterized by the presence of red deer (*Cervus elephus*) and wild horse (*Equus ferus*), and more occasional records at certain times of species such as aurochs (*Bos primigenius*), fallow deer (*Dama sp.*) tahr (*Hemitragus sp.*), megaloceros (*Megaloceros giganteus*), steppe rhinoceros (*Stephanorhinus hemitoechus*), wild boar (*Sus scrofa*), Barbary macaque (*Macaca sylvanus*), wild ass (*Equus hydruntinus*), elephant (*Palaeoloxodon antiquus*), hippopotamus (*Hippopotamus amphibius*) and beaver (*Castor fiber*) (Table 1). The presence of carnivores in the cavity is sporadic, both in anatomical representation and frequency in the bone record. Fossil remains of *Ursus arctos*, *Ursus tibetanus*, *Canis lupus*, *Panthera leo*, *Lynx pardina*, *Vulpes vulpes* and *Meles meles* have been identified (Martínez Valle, 1995, 2001; Sarrión and Fernández Peris, 2006).

It is also important to highlight the presence of small animals such as rabbit (*Oryctolagus cuniculus*), hare (*Lepus* sp.), birds (*Passeriformes, Galliformes, Corvidae, Columbidae, Phasianidae, Anatidae*), tortoise (*Testudo hermanni*) and occasionally fish (*Salmonidae*), throughout the sequence. The proportion and relative frequencies vary from level to level (e.g., Blasco *et al.*, 2013; Sanchís Serra, 2010). Human consumption of small prey, in the form of cut marks, cremation, deliberate fracturing and human bite marks have been identified throughout the sequence. In some cases, the proportion of these animals exceeds 60% in MNI, as is the case in sub-level XVIIc (Blasco *et al.*, 2013) (Fig. 2).

Micro-vertebrates

The micro-fauna sampling performed by Guillem (1995, 2001) provided a total of 1,124 individuals from 12 species of micro-mammal (insectivores and rodents) for the western sector of the site: *Erinaceus europaeus* (common hedgehog), *Sorex minutus* (Eurasian pygmy shrew), *Sorex sp.*, *Neomis sp.* (tailed shrew), *Crocidura suaveolens* (lesser white-toothed shrew), *Talpa europaea* (mole), *Sciurus vulgaris* (squirrel), *Eliomys quercinus* (garden dormouse), *Allocricetus bursae* (hamster), *Arvicola sapidus* (water vole), *Microtus brecciensis* (Cabrera's vole) and *Apodemus sp.* (field mouse). None of the species found in Bolomor indicate extremely cold conditions, which coincides with a peri-Mediterranean environment that softens Quaternary climate oscillations. *Allocricetus bursae*is the taxon that is most closely connected to dry and cold con-

NISP*	Ia	Ib-c	II	III	IV	V	VI	VII	VIII	XI	XII	XIII	XV	XVIIa	XVIIc
Macaca sylvana					1						2		1		
Carnivora indet.	2	3		2	5	1						2	1		
Ursus arctos				2	1	1									
Canis cf. *lupus*	2				2							2		4	
Vulpes vulpes					2										
Panthera leo spelaea					3										
Lynx pardina					2						1				
Meles meles		3													
Castor fiber										2	2				
P. antiquus	2				4	2					1	2		2	2
S. hemitoechus		1		1						3	6	2	3	8	1
Equus ferus	28	4	1	5	65	2				2	165	11	41	77	56
Equus hydruntinus	3	2	1		16										
H. amphibius	4	2		3	46	2									
Sus scrofa	17	1		7	115	3									
Cervidae indet.	20	4	1	4								1	5		
Megaloceros giganteus										2	5		2	10	8
Dama sp.	9	3	1	2	91	6				4	17	5	4	27	13
Cervus elaphus	271	18	7	55	647	18	3			55	325	51	50	177	132
Bos primigenius	146	11	12	61	213	16	3		1	2	35	2	1	24	22
Capridae indet.	36	2	4	5		19	1					5	7		
Hemitragus bonali										16	4	12	23	28	6
Hemitragus cedrensis	4	1	1	4	121	2									
Oryctolagus cuniculus	167	28	5	52	789	297				262	135	182	1156	620	457
Lepus sp.		1						1						5	
Passeriformes					25						13			5	9
Galliformes					19						8			8	
Phasianidae					24									18	10
Anatidae														4	
Cygnus olor											1				
Anas sp.					29						21				16
Aythya sp.					34					202					
Corvidae					20										
Pyrrhocorax sp.					6										
Columba sp.					34										
Strigidae					1										
Aves indet.	32	3			17	18						2	22		
Testudo hermanni	465	10	9	67	526	84				4		4	4		
Bufo sp.					4									1	
Pisces					2					1					

Table 1. Number of specimens identified throughout the stratigraphic sequence of Bolomor cave. *NISP = Number of Identified Specimens. The data on levels Ia, Ib-c, II, III, V, VI, VIII, XIII and XV were extracted from Fernández Peris (2007) and the data on levels IV, XI, XII, XVIIa and XVIIc were taken from Blasco (2011). The data on *Lepus sp.* were extracted from Sanchís and Fernández Peris (2011).

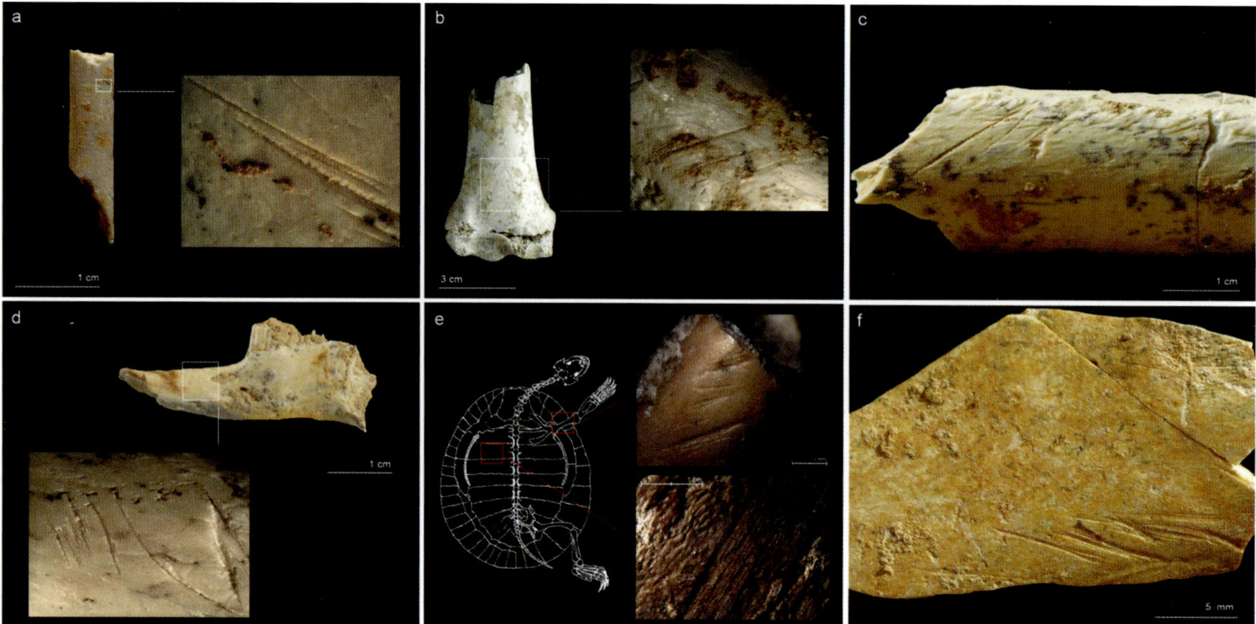

Figure 2. a) Cut marks on a rabbit (*Oryctolagus cuniculus*) tibia from sub-level XVIIc; b) cut marks on a swan (*Cygnus olor*) tibia from level XII; c) cut marks on a red deer (*Cervus elaphus*) femur from sub-level XVIIc; d) cut marks on a rabbit (*Oryctolagus cuniculus*) jaw bone from sub-level XVIIc; e) cut marks on tortoise (*Testudo hermanni*) remains from level IV; f) cut marks on a long bone from a large animal from level IV.

ditions, along with the *Sorex minutus*, which had environmental requirements like those of the current Medio-European, along with the *Erinaceus europaeus* and *Talpa europaea* that penetrate certain Mediterranean environments inhabited by the *Microtus brecciensis*. The rest of the species were ubiquitous and related to strict requirements, such as the formation of woods (*Sciurus vulgaris*) or the presence of waterways (*Arvicola sapidus*).

Micro-mammal remains recovered from Bolomor cave were mainly introduced by small carnivores (*Vulpes vulpes*) depositing droppings in the cavity and by owls (*Strix aluco*) regurgitating the parts of the prey that their stomachs could not digest (hair, bones, etc.).

Other biotic remains

The presence and malacology study of small bivalve seashells contributes to the assessment of possible changes to the coastline and their relationship with climatic oscillations. The origin of these elements could be deposition in the form of pellets by seabirds (cormorants, shearwaters, storm petrels, seagulls, etc.) that feed on fish and shellfish. These small molluscs were documented at levels V, VII, XII, XIII, XIV and XV of the sequence, and their characteristics indicate moments of mild climate and greater proximity to the sea (Fernández Peris, 2007). This documentation also includes remains of teeth and fish spines (level I, IV and XI). Other inland molluscs (snails), such as the *Rumina* and *Melanopsis*, indicate a wet environment in their corresponding levels (I, IV, VIIb and XIIIc). Unfortunately, the sediments of Bolomor cave have been pollen sterile so far (Dupré and Carrión, 2001). However, the presence of fossilised seeds throughout the sedimentary sequence of the cavity has allowed us to carry out paleocarpology analyses. These have documented the presence of two plant species: *Celtis australis* (European nettle tree) and *Prunus spinosa* (blackthorn). Both species must have colonised different places. The European nettle tree requires a certain level of humidity in the ground and is usually associated with elm woods, while the blackthorn is common in oak woods. The *Celtis australis* could be part of the elm wood that would circle the riverside of the Vaca (Bolomor phases II and IV) (Fernández Peris, 2007). Furthermore, the *Prunus spinosa* would have been associated with an oak wood that could run along the depression of the Valldigna and occupy the shade of the mountains, at least during the cooler periods of the MIS 5e (Bolomor phase IV).

The recovery of thermo-modified plant remains in the form of charcoal also allowed study of the plants using anthracology. Remains have been recovered from the levels in which anthropic combustion structures have been identified (levels II, IV, XI and XIII). They are currently being analysed.

The lithic industry

The lithic industry of Bolomor is a lithic flake assemblage or techno-complex pertaining to the Middle Palaeolithic. There is little variety throughout the sequence and it is marked by the occupational characteristics of each level. However, the industries seem to have taken on a certain level of complexity in the most recent periods of the sequence, when occupation also seems have been more intense (Fernández Peris, 2007). In this respect, it is difficult to establish elements of change in the manufacturing of the knapped tools and their relationship with behavioural aspects. The main raw materials used were flint, limestone and quartzite. These came from sea, colluvial and fluvial stones from the immediate surroundings of the site and from more distant areas, such as the Xùquer basin and the Serpis basin (around 15 km from the site) (Fernández Peris, 2007; Fernández Peris *et al.*, 2008).

The technological characteristics of the industry allow it to be defined as not Levallois, not faceted and not laminar, consisting of a wide range of highly retouched lithic flake tools. There are no bifaces, cleavers, trihedral or knapped stones in the any of sequences. In general, the lithic record reflects a techno-complex of small flakes (presence of non-laminar microliths), scrapers, denticulate and varied retouched tools. The pieces show intense reuse in the higher levels (Fernández Peris, 2007; Cuartero, 2008). Macro-tools consisting of a wide range of flake formats made of limestone, without retouching or with simple retouching, are documented in some levels only. This applies to level XII, where the lithic assemblage is almost exclusively large limestone flake with little transformation.

Hearths

The excavations carried out to date have provided remains of fire use in levels II, IV, XI and XIII (Fernández Peris *et al.*, 2013) (Fig. 3). In the first level, possible ash castings between gaps have been documented; these are the result of hearth cleaning that was done in preparation for new fires. In level IV, the remains of four hearths were found, which left evidence in the form of reddish thermo-modified sediment (rubefaction layer). One of them includes stones thermo-modified at their bases. Level XI falls within MIS 6 and contains six simple hearths without internal structures. As indicated by the analyses and reproductions in progress, the hearths seem to correspond to short combustions (Fernández Peris *et al.*, 2007). Finally, two hearths have been documented in level XIIIc. Both have clear internal structures, which show that the area and the structures were prepared before the fires were lit. *Focus* 1 was built on base of blocks or *dallage de pierre* of varying sizes and calcareous origins. These structural blocks appear in direct contact with the layer of carbonaceous sediment and are connected to the thermo-modified sediment. The preparation of *focus* 2 was different. It is located inside a depression or basin with blocks that run along the edge of the deepest side, with some at the bottom. This basin is 76-cm long by 41-cm wide, with a maximum depth of 5 cm compared to the flat area; it is higher at the southeast end and its depth decreases towards the northwest, where the depression is very shallow. We obtained a dating based on amino-acid racemisation of molluscs collected in the surrounding area of the hearths that gives a chronology of 228±53 ky. This makes it the oldest controlled use of fire in the Iberian Peninsula and in Southern Europe (Fernández Peris *et al.*, 2013).

The Palaeoanthropology

The human fossils in Bolomor cave published to date comprise six pieces of bone and tooth. Some of the remains were found during the sieving of disturbed sediment by the quarry work carried out in the 1930s, and others have been recovered in the excavation process and, therefore, have a clear stratigraphic location. The human fossil assemblages found comprise a very small and fragmented sample in which dental elements dominate over postcranial elements (Arsuaga *et al.*, 2013):

- HCB 01: Fibular shaft measuring 48.7 mm corresponding to an adult. This remain was recovered through systematic excavation of level III (MIS 5e), with an *ante quem* dating of 121±18 ky.
- HCB 02: Lower left molar (M_1) corresponding to a child (around 5 years old). It was found in level IV (MIS 5e), with an *ante quem* dating of 121±18 ky.
- HCB 03: Upper right deciduous molar (dm^2) corresponding to a 6–9-month-old

Figure 3. Hearths at Bolomor cave: a) hearths on level IV (c. 130 ky); b) hearths on level XI (170 ky); c) hearths on level XIII (250 ky) undergoing excavation; d) fine flake *focus* I, level XIII; e) *focus* I section level XIII.

baby. It was recovered from the sediment modified by the quarry work.

- HCB 04: Lower left canine (C_1) very similar to modern humans. It came from the sediment disturbed in level I sub, wherein intrusive modern day elements have been documented.
- HCB 05: Upper left canine (C^1) with a very similar morphology to the dental remains from Sima de los Huesos in Atapuerca (Burgos, Spain) and from Krapina (Croatia). This piece was found in the clearance of Ia-Sub XIII in contact with the clearance of XIII. The gap attached to it could be located in level XIII.
- HCB 06: Fragment of parietal bone (22 × 18 mm) with a coronal suture. This was recovered from the sediment modified by the quarry work.
- HCB 07: Fragment of parietal bone (109 × 116 mm) from the sediment modified by the old quarry work at the site. The gap in the parietal bone could be related to the carbonated sediment from level VI, putting it in the MIS 5e with a dating of around 130 ky. It is currently being studied and the findings published.

All of the pieces, except HCB 05, could be assigned to MIS 5; of these, HCB 03, HCB 04 and HCB 06 could be more modern, as they were located in a clearance context with some post-Palaeolithic items. Specimen HCB 05, however, given the sedimentologic characteristics associated with it and where it was found (Clearance XIII), is related to levels XII-XV and its location in MIS 7 cannot be dismissed. This remain is metrically different from the Neanderthals and is well related to the canines from Sima de los Huesos, in Atapuerca (Burgos, Spain), and Krapina (Croatia). According to Arsuaga and collaborators (2013), even the less common traces (presence of the entoconulid of the M_1 or lack of structural details in C^1), are frequently found in European human fossils from the Middle Pleistocene. Therefore, it might be attributable to the *Homo heidelbergensis-Homo neanderthalensis* lineage.

Acknowledgements

Bolomor excavation is part of the archaeological excavations program of Servicio de Investigación Prehistórica (SIP) (Museo de Prehistoria de Valencia) under the authority of Diputación de Valencia (España). Research project is financed by the Ministry of Science and Innovation CGL-BOS-2012-34717. Ruth Blasco is a Beatriu de Pinós-A post-doctoral scholarship recipient from Generalita de Catalunya and co-finaced by the European Union through Marie Curie Actiones, FP7.

Javier Fernández-López de Pablo*
Magdalena Gómez Puche**
Marco Aurelio Esquembre Bebia***

Casa Corona (Villena, Alicante, Spain)

1. Location

The site of Casa Corona is located in the town of Villena, close to the administrative border between the provinces of Alicante and Albacete, 80 km from the coast (UTM 680306 4282783, zone 30N, Datum ETRS 89, 502 m.a.s.l). The site lies at the centre of a broad natural corridor known as the Villena-Caudete plain, with an average altitude of 500 m.a.s.l. Quaternary materials, continental aeolian formations, endorheic lagoons and ponds dominate the landscape. The site covers the top of a partially cut Late Pleistocene dune (Fig. 1).

The site was discovered in 2006 by the staff of the Archaeological Museum of Villena. In 2008, the company Arpa Patrimonio S.L. excavated the site over three months, in a rescue program resulting from the construction of the Madrid-Alicante AVE high-speed rail network (Fernández-López de Pablo *et al.*, 2013). In 2013, a new excavation phase was started as a part of a multi-year fieldwork program coordinated by the IPHES. In this chapter, we will synthesize the results obtained on the Early and Late Mesolithic occupation phases (Fig. 2) from the 2008 excavations. In addition, we will complement this synthesis with new stratigraphic information from the 2013 excavations.

2. Stratigraphic record and occupation phases

The 2013 excavations have characterized the succession of litho-stratigraphic units that form the site's sedimentary context. From the bottom to top:

- SU 303: a 3 m deep stratum of pale-yellow consolidated siliceous sands form the base of the archaeological stratigraphy which lacks archaeological materials. From a geomorphological and sedimentary point of view, it corresponds with a continental dune dated to the Late Upper Pleistocene (Fernández-López de Pablo *et al.*, i. p.) (Fig. 2 and Table 1). This correlates with the SU 127 from the 2008 Arpa Patrimonio S.L. Excavations (Fernández-López de Pablo *et al.*, 2013).

* Institut Català de Paleoecologia Humana i Evolució Social (IPHES) jfernandez@iphes.cat
** Institut Català de Paleoecologia Humana i Evolució Social (IPHES) mgomez.puc@gmail.com
*** Arpa Patrimonio S.L. Avenida Rodalet 23A. San Vicente del Raspeig C.P.03690. (Alicante). arpapatrimonio@gmail.com

Figure 1. Aerial photograph of the site after the 2008 excavation. The Pleistocene dune (light brown) is exposed after the excavation of the plough soil. In the south (dark grey) there is a dried inter-dune depression pond. The black square indicates the area where the Early and Late Mesolithic features were located.

- SU 301: Dark greyish-brown sandy and semi-compacted stratum with a variable depth ranging from 30-40 cm. It lies in gradual contact over the SU 303. Its upper limit has been post-depositionally disturbed by agricultural uses. It corresponds with an Early to Middle Holocene paleosol formed into a small talweg at the top of the dune. The SU 301 overlies most of the combustion structures and presents archaeological materials of the different ceramic and preceramic occupational phases. This corresponds with the SU 101, 102 and 103 of the Arpa Patrimonio S.L. Excavations.
- SU 300: light-brown unconsolidated plough-soil stratum of 20-40 cm depth. It overlies SU 301 and contains archaeological materials from different periods.

The Early (Notches and Denticulates Mesolithic) and Late Mesolithic structures and archaeological deposits have been documented at the northern sector of the site, which extends up 565 m^2. This sector also records archaeological materials of subsequent occupation phases. That is the case of 6 Chalcolithic and partially conserved pit -structures (one of them is the remaining part of a hut); and a pit that contained an Early Post-Cardial Neolithic ceramic ware.

The two oldest occupational phases (Early and Late Mesolithic) have yielded 16 combustion structures and two burial pits. The combustion structures are hearth pits that cut the stratum of Late Upper Pleistocene sands (SU 303). Their average dimensions are 0.7 m in diameter and 0.2 m in depth (Fernández-López de Pablo *et al.*, 2011). The sedimentary fill of the hearth pits is formed by carbonaceous sediment of burnt sands containing fire-cracked stones, lithic artefacts, burnt land snails and faunal remains.

The radiocarbon dates obtained from two combustion structures indicate different occupational phases (Table 1, Fig.3). The chronology of the combustion structure 4 (SU 142) is the oldest one (Beta-330866, 10312 ± 40 BP). Its calibration ranges overlap the Younger Dryas. Thus, its chrono-cultural attribution should correspond with the Epipaleolithic or Epimagdalenian (in a broad sense). In contrast, the combustion struc-

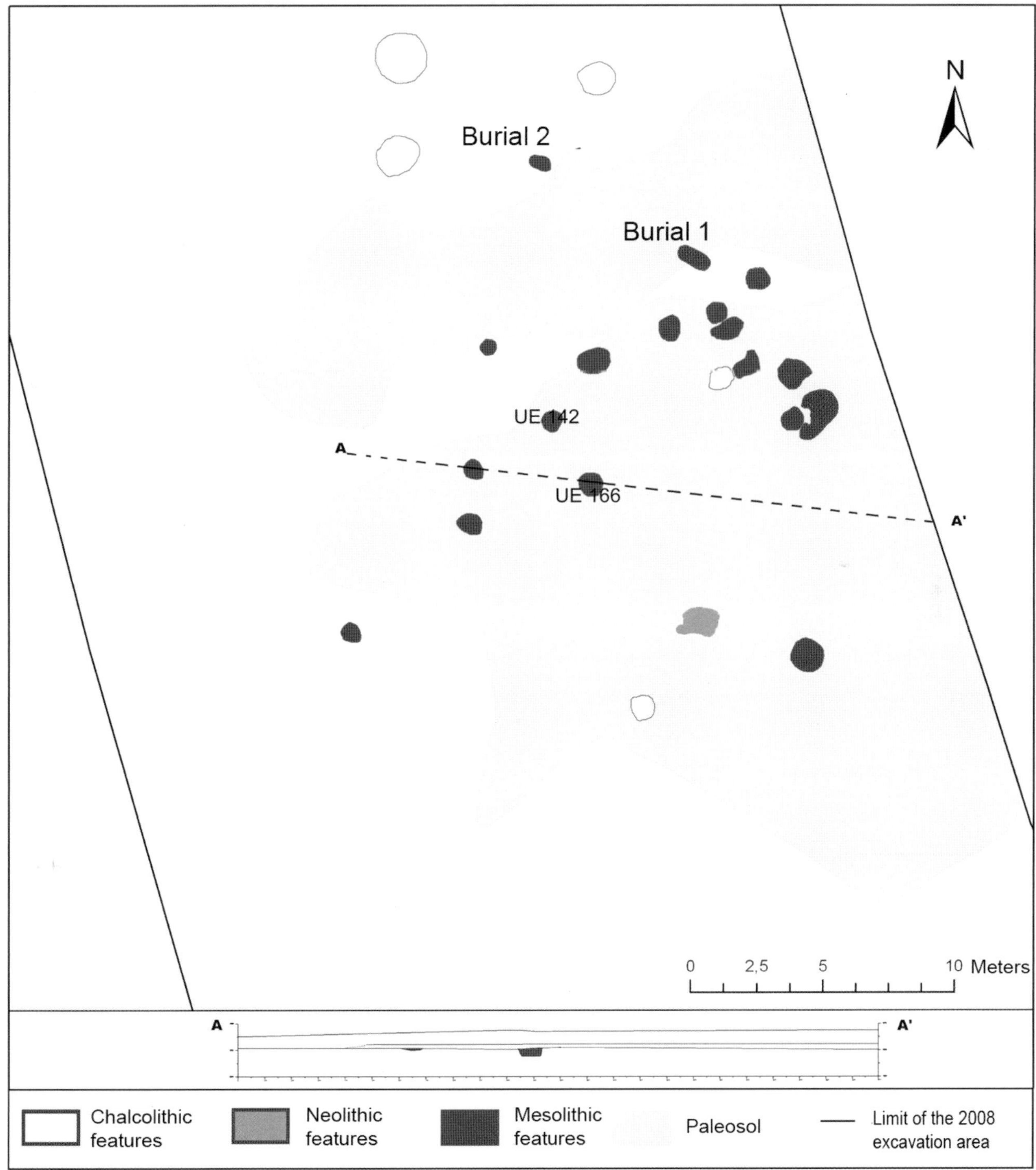

Figure 2. Cumulative plan of the northern sector with the location of the dated features.

ture 8 (Beta-323497, 8520±50) is dated during the Early Holocene, in the Boreal chrono-zone and the Early Mesolithic period. New radiocarbon determinations are needed to establish the chronology of the remaining combustion structures.

In addition to the combustion structures, the 2008 excavations uncovered two burial pits containing two primary inhumations: the first one, known as burial 1, is the burial of a woman aged 35-40 years old; and the second one, is the primary interment of a child aged 12-18 months (Fernández-López de Pablo *et al.*, 2013). The radiocarbon dates on individual samples of bone collagen gave a very similar chronology; burial 1 (Beta-272856, 7070 ±40) and burial 2 (OxA-V-2392-27, 7116 ±32 BP). The calibration ranges of both radiocarbon dates partially overlaps the 8.2 kyr cal BP cold event. Finally, a radiocarbon date on a shell lip fragment of a land snail recovered in the filling sediment of burial pit 1 (UE 128) yielded an Early Holocene age (Beta-330865, 8898±40). Such a chronology is placed into the time window defined by the radiocarbon dates of the combustion structures UE 142 and UE166. In turn, that date confirms our previous observations about the fact that the filling sediments of the burial pits incorporated debris of previous Mesolithic occupations.

Despite the long occupational sequence, the record of lithic artefacts is quantitatively discrete.

Context	Affiliation	Sample	Lab. Ref	Method	^{14}C BP age	2 σ Cal BP age
UE 142	EPIMAG	*S. candidissima*	Beta-330866	AMS	10312±40*	12383-11960
UE 128	EM	*S. candidissima*	Beta-330865	AMS	8898±40*	10190-9892
UE 166	EM	*Quercus* sp.	Beta-323497	AMS	8520±50	9551-9454
Burial 2	LM	Human bone	OxA-V-2392-27	AMS	7116 ±32	8007-7886
Burial 1	LM	Human bone	Beta-272856	AMS	7070 ±40	7972-7800

Table 1. AMS radiocarbon dates of different archaeological features at Casa Corona. (**) corrected ^{14}C dates after the subtraction of 210 years of local limestone effect (Yanes *et al.*, 2013).

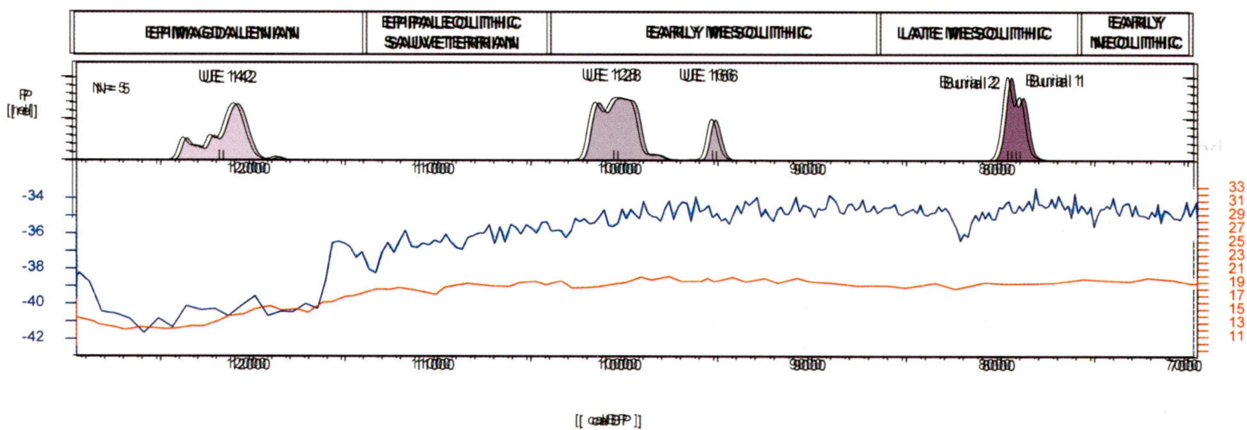

Figure 3. Average probability of calibrated radiocarbon distributions of Casa Corona obtained with CalPal (Weniger and Jöris 2004) and the Intcal13 calibration curve (Reimer *et al.*, 2013). Up: Periodisation model of the Iberian Mediterranean region during the Postglacial (Aura *et al.*, 2011); Bottom: In blue ^{18}O variations from the Greenland GISP2 ice see core (Stuiver, Grootes 2000). In red: Sea Surface Temperature estimation from the Alborán Sea (Cacho *et al.*, 2001).

A total number of 3,322 lithic artefacts are associated with both Mesolithic occupation phases, just 29 of them are retouched. The Early Mesolithic phase is characterized by flake *debitage* and the selection of thick flakes to be transformed in notched and denticulated tools. On the other hand, the Late Mesolithic phase presents 12 geometric microliths: 11 trapezes with step retouch and a "Cocina" type triangle. However, the evidences of blade *debitage* are meaningless so far (1 core and 76 bladelets).

On the other hand, 8 pierced *Columbella rustica* shells with dorsal perforation have been recovered. This species of marine gastropod is common in many ornamental assemblages dated between the Early and Late Mesolithic periods in the Iberian Mediterranean region (Álvarez, 2008).

3. Paleoecology

The Upper Vinalopó valley contains two lake deposits –the Villena lagoon and the Salinas Playa lake– placed at 4 and 15 km away from Casa Corona. Both palaeoenvironmental records provide different chronological resolution about the local vegetation and the responses of hydrological systems responses to Pleistocene-Early Holocene transition climate changes and, particularly, the Bond events. Thus, the study area offers a unique opportunity of correlating the palaeoenvironmental dynamics inferred at the natural deposits with the chronological framework of the human occupations during the Postglacial period (Fernández-López de Pablo *et al.*, 2011a).

The first occupation of Casa Corona was coeval to the Younger Dryas, an episode of climatic deterioration that is well defined in the pollen record of the Villena lagoon. The pollen zone D2 reflects a significant increase on the *Artemisia* and *Ephedra* taxa, associated with a general decrease in the tree pollen (Yll *et al.*, 2003).

In the Villena lagoon, the beginning of the Holocene corresponds with pollen subzone 3, characterized by the increase of tree pollen, mainly pine, and the abrupt decrease of the *Pseudochiazea* and *Chenopodiaceae* taxa, thus, reflecting more temperate environmental conditions. According to the ostracod assemblages of the Salinas playa lake (Roca and Julià 1997), the Early Mesolithic occupations at Casa Corona were coeval to the lacustrine phase 2, which witnessed short-term fluctuations with the alternation of permanent and ephemeral water bodies.

On the other hand, the stable isotope analysis of $\delta^{13}C$ and $\delta^{18}O$ of *Sphincterochila candidissima* land snail shells from different combustion structures of Casa Corona and Arenal de la Virgen sites provide additional information on the paleovegetation and paleoathmospheric conditions at the time of the human occupations (Yanes *et al.*, 2013).

The land snail specimens of the SU 142, dated by radiocarbon during the Younger Dryas chronological span, present a $\delta^{13}C$ and $\delta^{18}O$ isotopic composition that indicate dryer and colder palaeoenvironmental conditions than those reported in the specimens recovered from the SU 166 and 128, dated during the Early Holocene (Yanes *et al.*, 2013).

4. Subsistence

The vertebrate zooarchaeological remains are badly preserved at the Casa Corona site due to taphonomic biases. The site's sedimentary context –dominated by siliceous sands– and the combustion processes, explain the bad preservation of bones, most of them very small (<1cm) diaphyseal fragments. At both Mesolithic phases, only 12 individuals have been identified at taxonomic level (Morales 2008). The presence of three *Bos primigenius* remains is qualitatively significant. On the other hand, amongst the small prey, we have identified remains of lagomorphs and turtles (*Emididae/ Bataguridae*). Such a taxonomic spectrum is consistent with the zooarchaeological information from other Mediterranean open-air Mesolithic sites located on coastal wetlands such as El Collado (Fernández-López de Pablo *et al.*, i.p.).

Unlike vertebrates, land snails are very well represented in the 14 Mesolithic combustion structures at Casa Corona (Fernández-López de Pablo *et al.*, 2011a). Two edible land snail species clearly dominate the land snail assemblages: *Sphincterochila candidissima* (90,67%, n=2844) and *Iberus alonensis* (4,23%, n=116). The biometric analyses based on the maximum width of the *S. candidissima* specimens show that immature individuals were not represented in the malacological assemblages. The spatial association of both species with the combustion structures at Casa Corona and the neighbour site of Arenal de la Virgen uncover a systematic exploitation pattern of this class of invertebrate resources during the Early and the Late Mesolithic periods. The seasonal ethology of both species, which hibernate and aestivate underground or in crevices, suggest that the gathering and consumption took place during the spring and/or fall seasons.

The palaeodietary evidence, based on stable isotope $\delta^{13}C$ and $\delta^{15}N$ data of bone collagen from the burials, provides complementary information about the Late Mesolithic subsistence patterns (Fernández-López de Pablo *et al.*, 2013). The human remains present $\delta^{13}C$ (-19.3 and -18.5) and $\delta^{15}N$ (8.4 and 11.6) values compatible with a diet based on terrestrial resources. There is not a clear isotopic signal suggesting a minimal contribution of marine or fresh water proteins. However, the child individual presented a slightly higher $\delta^{15}N$ value, due to the breastfeeding effect.

5. Funerary record

Two Late Mesolithic burials containing the human remains of two individual inhumations were located northwards of the area delimited by the combustion structures (Fig.4). The distance between both burials is of 7 m, which, in addition to their radiocarbon age overlapping, indicates that they were part of the same cemetery.

The identification of the burial pits from the beginning of the excavation process has allowed the documentation of the individual's position regarding the funerary space as well as their relationship with other Mesolithic occupation remains.

Burial 1 is a primary individual interment of an adult woman aged 35-40 years. The skeleton has a poor state of preservation due to the acidity of the soil. However, the epiphyses of the long bones as well as the vertebral bodies are preserved, and were placed in a supine position with the legs flexed and the face towards the left. The skeleton is oriented in a NE-SW direction.

The position of this individual in the burial-pit, with the upper extremities flexed into the abdominal region and the shoulders hunched, is forced. The thorax is open, indicating that there was enough space around it for this to happen during the stages of decomposition. However, the position of the clavicles indicates a lack of space during decomposition. At the same time, the pelvis is totally closed, and the lower extremities flexed, still leaning against the wall of the grave itself.

All these evidences –the persistence of narrow joints, the forced position of the shoulders and the location of the right arm with respect to the ribs– seem to indicate that this individual had been wrapped in a shroud. A pierced shell bead of *Columbella rustica* was likely deposited as a grave good. The grave pit was filled after the cadaver deposition. The filling sediments contained residues of previous Mesolithic occupations such as burnt land snails, charcoals, lithic debris and small dyaphesal fragments of faunal bones.

Burial 2 is a primary individual interment of a child aged 12-18 months. The skeleton also has a poor state of preservation. The individual was placed in a supine position and oriented NW-SE. The skull is raised, with the jaw closely articulated and vertebral arches inside, denoting a position forced by the presence of a perishable object (not preserved) such as a pillow under the skull. Such an arrangement allowed the face of the individual to look towards the left shoulder, which leaned in a higher position than the right one. The orientation of the humerus denotes a forced position of the shoulders. The ribs on the right side belong to a closed thorax. Everything seems to reveal that the dead individual was placed in the pit wrapped.

A flint blade, deposited by the side of the right femur, is the only grave good clearly documented. In addition to this item, some burnt land snails and lithic debris were randomly found across the burial pit fill, as well as small fragments of charcoal and burnt bones.

6. Perspectives

There are different reasons that make of Casa Corona a key site for progressing in the knowledge of the open-air sites in the Iberian Mediterranean region into its palaeoecological and cultural contexts.

First, because the geomorphological context of the site on the top of a continental dune located at the centre of a valley, the alluvial and colluvial sed-

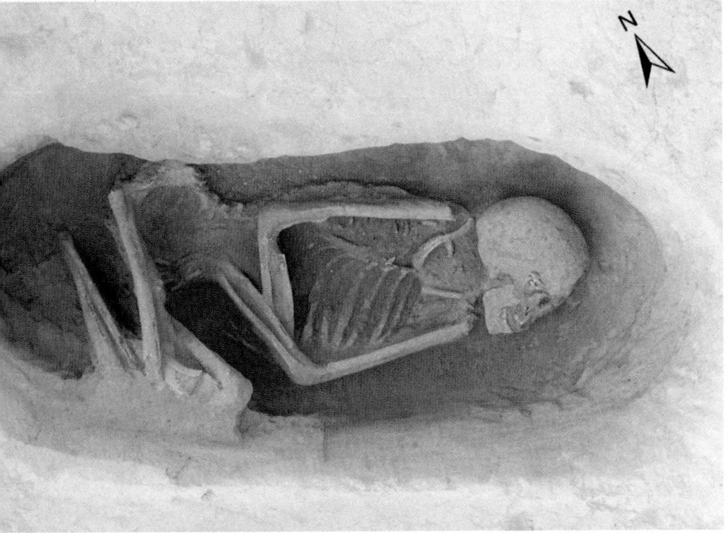

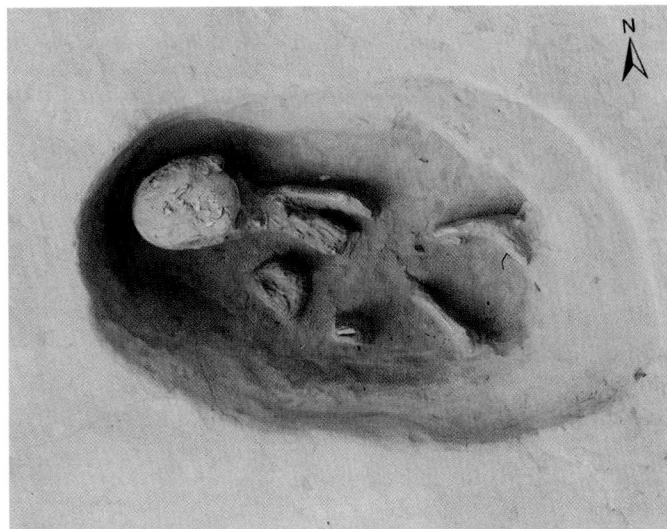

Figure 4. Late Mesolithic burials of Casa Corona.

imentary processes were not responsible for the site's formation. Thus, the resulting archaeological record of the human frequentations to this site has generated an extensive palimpsest with different occupation phases.

The oldest known occupation is dated during the Younger Dryas, thus, establishing an *ante quem* chronology for the dune formation. Afterwards, along the Early Holocene, the site witnessed different frequentation episodes that generated an archaeological record composed of different combustion structures. Finally, during the Late Mesolithic, the site witnessed short funerary activity. Considering the site's long occupational sequence, the identification of chronologically narrower occupation events on the basis of micro-spatial and micro-stratigraphic analyses is our main aim in future works.

Also, the study of new lake records should improve the available palaeoenvironmental information and its chronological resolution on a local scale. Both research lines would enhance the interpretation of the impact of the late Pleistocene and Early Holocene environmental changes on human settlement areas.

Finally, we would like to stress the relevance of the site for the knowledge of the last Late Mesolithic episodes and the Neolithisation process. In the central Iberian Mediterranean region, the radiocarbon dates of the human burials of Casa Corona (Fig. 4) fill the 7 centuries chronological gap between the last Late Mesolithic contexts and the first Early Neolithic sites. The location of new Late Mesolithic burials and its interdisciplinary palaeoanthropological study are two of the main objectives of the new phase of excavations at the site started in 2013.

José Aparicio Pérez *

El Collado (Oliva-Valencia)

1. Introduction

Around 9,000 BC, a small group of maybe five or six humans with obvious signs of kinship installed their abode a crag or rock shelter near the present day Oliva, in an area known as El Collado, where they remained for about 3,500 years until the middle of the 6th millennium BC.

After the excavation work, which began in 1987, we were able to complete the subsequent research process with archaeological, anthropological and radiocarbon analyses. The comprehensive anthropological study was led by Dr. Domingo Campillo Valero, Head of the Palaeopathology and Palaeoanthropology Laboratory at the Barcelona Archaeological Museum, and involved a large team of anthropologists, radiologists, restorers and photographers who studied the purely bone-related aspects such as teeth, illness and palaeopathologies, food science/eating habits, etc., using conventional and also advanced methods such as isotopic analysis (VV.AA, 2008: 179-344). The archaeological and historical analysis was conducted by the undersigned (VV.AA, 2008: 28-91 and 347-359).

The chronology defined by archaeological methods was initially backed up by four radiocarbon datings, as well as others. Two important aspects must be noted. Firstly, exploration of the site was not exhausted and much of what remains is still buried under tons of fertile soil dumped there by the property owner, Mr. Bolinches.

Secondly, the site was completely disfigured from its original configuration during the occupation. Weathering processes underway from its abandonment until its discovery certainly altered it, but a much greater impact was undoubtedly caused by subsequent human action including its transforming into cropland with staggered horizontal contoured terraces, and the use of rock from around the site, either loose or dug from limestone outcrops.

On the basis of this assumption and the remains in the vicinity, we believe that this human settlement was established beneath a limestone crag with a shelter-like concavity inside or nearby, with an easterly aspect, i.e. facing the Mediterranean Sea, which during the period was probably slightly higher than its current level, with a marsh, fen or aigua-moll covering what is now the coastal plain. The site is on the slope of a terminal elevation of a low-lying mountain range, a few hundred metres above current sea level and about seven kilometres in a straight line from the coast, a little more than one metre above the start of the marsh. A basal concavity in the same place as the site, inside the probable gap in the cliff or shelter, proof of its existence, facilitated their installation on this steep hillside, which ends at a saddle or collado (hence the name) overshadowed by Montanyeta de Santa Ana, a hill between the site and the marsh.

2. Chronology

We shall first clarify the chronology used as the basis for the subsequent considerations.

Long before radiocarbon dating became available, we defined the chronology of this settlement on the sole basis of archaeological data, i.e. derived from the lithic material and on the basis of our own structure of the Mesolithic. Later, following anthropological studies, Dr. Campillo Valero became concerned abut this issue and arranged for two radiocarbon analysis to be conducted on human bones from burial site XIII.

More recently, following further dental analyses, further datings were suggested to assist confirmation of the previous dates, which we accepted in order to dispel any shadow of doubt, although it had never crossed our minds to question the authenticity and chronology of the human remains (Tab 1 and 2).

* Arqueólogo. Director de la Sección de Estudios Arqueológicos y Prehistóricos de la Real Academia de Cultura Valenciana. Académico C. de la Real de la Historia. joapa2005@hotmail.com P.O.BOX 2260. En 46080 VALENCIA

The subsequent analyses were also conducted in the Radiocarbon Dating Laboratory, Faculty of Chemistry of the University of Barcelona, under Dr. Joan S. Mestres, with the following results:

Burial XIII (Campillo Individual XIII), from layer 4 of LEVEL II, equivalent to layer 3 of the first excavation, was performed between 7649 and 7570 BC. Burial IV, also from layer 3, was around 8690 BC, and burial VI, from the same layer, was from 8080 BC. Given that the grave was accessed from layer 2 or at least the first layers of Level II –due to the dismantling or disturbance of layer 1 and its mixture with other material during the farming and terracing operations, this layer or level can be dated as no earlier than the middle of the 6th to the start of the 7th or the middle of the 8th

	ID	DATING	UNCERTAINTY	CALIBRATION 2δ cal. A.C
BURIAL XIII	UBAR 280	7570	160	6804-6066
BURIAL XIII	UBAR 281	7649	120	6799-6234

Table 1. Datings for burial XIII.

	ID	DATING	UNCERTAINTY	CALIBRATION 2δ cal. A.C
BURIAL IV	UBAR 927	8690	100	8188-7551
BURIAL VI	UBAR 928	8080	60	7299-6780

Table 2. Datings for burials IV and VI.

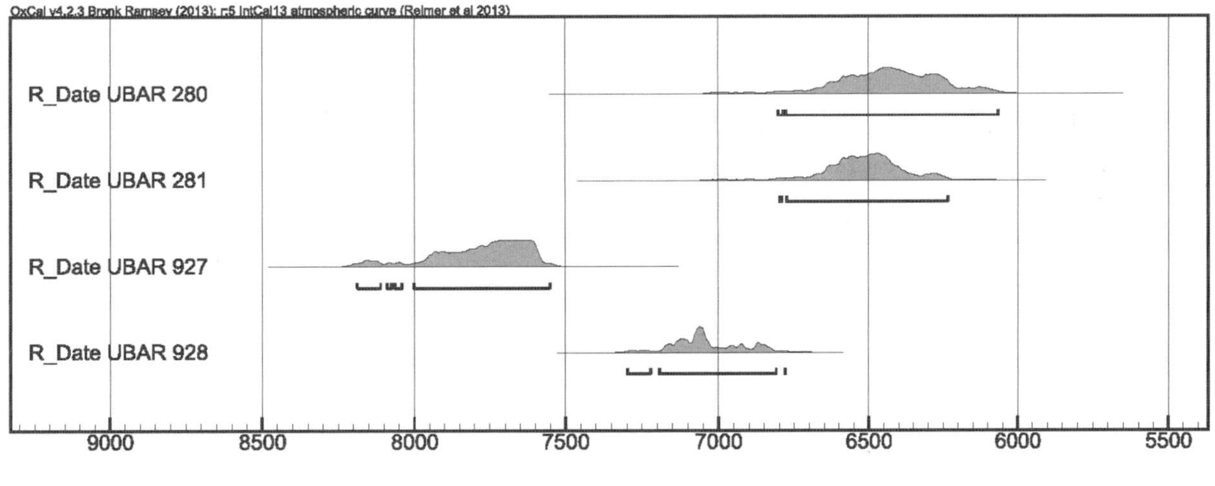

Figure 1. Comparative chart of calibrated dates.

millennium BC. With the 1000 year period from the middle of the 8th to the middle of the 9th millennium BC designated to layer 3 or Level III, the basal m-r or terra rossa layer can be attributed to the previous period, which ended around 8500 BC.

The following graph shows the calibrated datings (Fig. 1).

We shall now see if this chronology is feasible on the basis of the lithic material.

3. Lithic material

Conscientious washing and sieving allowed us retrieve almost all the archaeological material contained in the soil matrix at the site, consisting of tools, artefacts and lithic remains, just one bone tool, mastological and mollusc fauna, haematites or ochre and ceramics.

The lithic material was essentially flint and stone (see detailed inventory in Table 3).

Accordingly, focusing on the flint material, 11,887 items were found (see table), which may seem large but in our opinion is not so, bearing in mind the volume of sieved earth and that 11,204 are debitage flakes and flakelets, leaving 683 tools as such, including 125 cores and 278 blades and bladelets. Tools thus only comprise 4.98% of the flint material, an obviously low figure which indicates the low specific weight of stone tools in the daily activities at this site, with the exception of a certain type.

This is undoubtedly a microlithic assemblage, despite these being substrate items, sidescrapers, denticulates, retouched flakes, or those of Palaeolithic origin– endscrapers or burins, with the occasional larger format item amongst them. This feature is characteristic of the postulated period.

The stone tools and their grouping, together with the soil features, the anthropological remains with their respective radiocarbon datings and the faunal remains allow us to structure the industrial, environmental and cultural sequence of the site in the following manner.

Level IV and layers 4 and 5 correspond to the initial settlement which left traces, m-r and red

Figure 2. Stratigraphic section.

FLINT	Sup. All	Iª. Sup. B1-2-T	SEASON I						Iª AI-B-T- BII-BIII				IIª N-I	SEASON II.. N-II								IIª N-III B-E XIII	IIª N-III	IIª N-IV	TOTALS
			Sup	C1	C2	C3	C4	C5	C1	C2	C3	C4		C1	C2	C3	C4	C5	EIX	EXII	EXIII				
CORES	52	2	6	5	7	5	2	1	15				1	4	5	4	2		2	4		2	4	2	125
ENDSCRAPERS	2	3	2	4	6				3	2			1	2	3								1	1	30
MICRO SCRAPERS	3	1	4	1	5	6			6	2			1	2		2	1			2		2		1	39
BURINS	4	4	1	2	3	5	1		4		3		2	4	1		1				1	2		1	39
MICRO BURINS	2		7	1	1	1			5		1			2						1					21
BACKS & BACKED EDGES		1				2							1											3	7
STRANGLED BLADES /BLADELETS		1			1				3	1															6
GEOMETRICS	3		4		1				4			1			1										14
POINT WITH NOTCHES	2	6	1		1				8		1	1	2		1	2	1				1	1	2		30
SIDECRAPERS	5	2	10	2	8	3			16				2	3	2		2		1	1				1	58
AWLS/DRILLS		1		1	1	1				1		2	1	1	1								1	1	12
BLADES/BLADELETS	36	17	42	14	40	11			50	2	7	1	6	14	2	4	4		3	8		4	2	11	278
FLAKES	576	980	980	616	1.195	567	15	9	1.702	529	274	205	187	701	366	316	410	48	83	549	167	206	213	310	11.204
VARIOUS	12		3		2	1					2			3									1		24
TOTALS	697	1.018	1.060	646	1.271	602	18	10	1.816	537	288	210	204	736	382	328	421	48	89	565	169	217	224	331	11.887
STONE	1	23	56	38	70	19	5	3	42	34	12	4	1	6	8	4	12	V.	1	2	2	2		2	347
OCHRE				1													7							1	9
B/C				13						23															36
TOTALS	1	23	56	52	70	19	5	3	42	57	12	4	1	6	8	4	19	V.	1	2	2	2		3	392

LEGEND: SUP = Superficial T = Embankment E = Burial B- E= Deep burial N = Level C = Layer B/C = Clay/Pottery V= Various

Table 3. Overview of retrieved material.

basal earth, as shown in the stratigraphic section (Fig.2).

This period corresponds to Mesolithic I-B (10,000-8,500 BC), chronologically after Mesolithic I-A which in turn followed the Late Magdalenian. One endscraper, 2 burins, 1 microscraper, 3 blades and backed blades, 1 geometric, 1 point with notches, 1 sidescraper, 3 borers/drills and 12 bladelets confirm the above.

Level III and Layer 3 correspond chronologically to Dyras III, (8,500 – 7,500 BC), while technological and culturally they corrspond to the Mesolithic II or "Sauveterr" in our structure. This level has yielded 1 endscraper, 6 micro-endscrapers, 2 microburins, 8 burins, 2 backs and backed blades, 3 points with notches, 3 sidescrapers, 2 borers/drills and 20 blades and bladelets.

The Mesolithic III-A took place between 7500 and 6500 BC, during the Pre-boreal – with a slight increase in cold spells within a general trend of rising temperatures, lower rainfall and more frequent widespread droughts. During this period, snail collection became widespread in the hinterland areas, with snail and shell middens in coastal areas. This period corresponds to Level II and Layer 2, which yielded 13 endscrapers, 9 microscrapers, 8 burins, 1 microburin, 2 blades/bladelets with opposite notches, 2 geometric blades, 2 points with notches, 10 sidescrapers, 3 borers/drills, 44 blades and bladelets and over 2,000 flakes and flakelets. The first dated burial (individual IV) in this period took place around 6,740 BC.

Level I and Layer 1 correspond to the Boreal period, 6.500/6.000 BC and the start of the Atlantic, from 6000 to 5500 BC in this area. The former was accompanied by a considerable rise in the sea level as temperatures rose and the icecaps melted, which triggered a new marine encroachment, the Versilian in the Mediterranean, accompanied by the submergence of coastal areas and changes in the coastline and the landscape, while local rainfall remained low. The coastal wetlands were reactivated and invaded much of the Gulf of Valencia. Individual 6 was buried around 6,130 BC.

Level I and Layer 1 yielded 8 endscrapers, 8 microscrapers, 8 burins, 6 microburins 1 blade/backed blade, 3 flakes/strangled flakelets, 10 points with notches, 20 sidescrapers, 2 borers/drills and 70 blades and bladelets. The superficial Atlantic layer yielded 2 endscrapers, 4 microscrapers, 1 burin, 7 microburins, 4 geometric, 1 point with notches, 10 sidescrapers 42 blades and bladelets. Individual XIII lived during the Atlantic.

4. Human remains

We have reached the following conclusions from a study by Dr. Campillo Valero (Aparicio, 2008) and his team: 15 individuals were located in the excavated material. It is unlikely that all of them were buried, as we do not know if the zone marked as the perimeter of the site includes the entire original site area or whether part of it was either removed by erosion or the above-mentioned farmwork, and also because ultimately it became impossible to fully excavate the subsoil.

However, it is reasonable to assume that not all those who lived at this site were buried here, even if we accept that the earliest date corresponds to the first burial, i.e. from the 2nd century of the 7th millennium BC. Considering that during the 1,300 year period, assuming that the occupation was seasonal and that the group or community was small, at least 200 or 250 people may well have died here in this period, which begs the question what happened to the rest? This issue is impossible to resolve on the basis of the data at hand. Perhaps in the future, if a full excavation of the subsoil can be completed, the permanent or seasonal nature of the site will be ascertained and, if others are found nearby, we might be able to find an answer.

From the first layers of level II, either above or within level III, and on level II, the corpses were placed in shallow graves, with dimensions that matched the volume of the remains. In the case of 1, the volume was quite small as it was a bundle of bones; even smaller in the case of X where only a skull and a few bones were buried. In conjunction with the discovery of other remains scattered across the site, this suggests that some of the buried remains were disintegrated when the graves were opened or stumbled on, or the floor was dug up for some purpose. Their shallow nature was presumably due to crushing by the inhabitants and their continuous heavy pressure on the floor.

A large rock with a sloping lateral surface was used in the burial of Individual 11, discovered when the pit was opened. The corpse had been placed leaning against this rock and was thus in a near-vertical position.

The lack of several bones in the case of skeletons still in anatomical connection is not easy to explanation, with the exception of number XIII, which lay beneath an olive tree which we had to remove to excavate the area beneath. When digging the hole for this tree, the bones of a lower limb were scattered across the terrace and then disappeared as a result of crushing or weathering.

Some of the skeletons were deliberately protected by stones on or around them, as in the case of II, III and IV, VI, XIII and large rocks in the case of XIV. Almost all were laid on their left side except for VI and V and possibly III, which were lying on the right. In all cases, the legs were folded, the hands were placed together with the arms placed on the upper or lower chest.

Perhaps the most noteworthy aspects of the anthropological analysis are the following: The disinterred individuals or graves revealed: one 9 month old perinatal; 2 sub-adult juveniles aged 15-18; 1 young adult aged 18-20; 6 adults, 3 of them aged 20-25, 1 aged 30-35, and 2 aged 35-40; and 2 mature individuals over 45 years of age. The average age of death is thus 29 years, with 58.33% to 66.66% in the 20 to 40 year range. We may thus conclude that neither infancy nor puberty were the most critical period, in this case situated between 15 and 25 years– the average age amongst the prehistoric populations of the time. The exact causes of death could not be determined, however we did detect few cases of caries and frequent –but resolved– injuries.

We were able to determine the sex of 6 males and 3 females, with another 2 doubtful. The average male height was 1636 cm and 1554 cm for women, quite tall in comparison with contemporary and later data, particularly in the case of the females.

The anthropological features include a mesocephalic component with brachycephaly, quite rare in Spain and absent in compared series which are later in most cases, with a doubtful evolutionary process. Differences also occur in the skull, which is more robust in this case, accentuating the head. These individuals have low eye sockets and broad faces, suggesting a link to the Central European Mesolithic and subsequent remains from the Valencia region, an aspect which should be considered in studies of a possible indigenous evolution.

The mandible is narrower than might be expected, especially considering the large, robust teeth which in the anthropological study seem reminiscent of Neanderthals. This would be consistent with the sub-nasal prominence, interpreted as a persistent archaic feature which underscores the possible Neanderthal lineage and also opens up a suggestive line of research which we wish to begin immediately. The large number of Wormian bones points to probable consanguinity, and endogamy as a useful social aspect.

Dental features and other elements found at the sites lead to the conclusion that plants formed a minor part of the diet while there was a high consumption of animal protein, either marine or terrestrial. Analysis of middens Cuerda and Gasull has led to the suggestion that shells were consumed as well.

On the other hand, after the initial anthropological studies, Dr. Subirà –an efficient and constant collaborator with a highly skilled team of collaborators– studied the diet on the basis of stable isotopes (Subirà *et al.*, 2003, García *et al.*, 2006). These studies concluded that protein intake of animal origin, both marine and terrestrial, only formed 25% of the diet, with little difference between sexes –both were omnivores– although there were some differences in minor dietary preferences amongst individuals (Chimeno *et al.*, 1992). However, this begs the question that, if animal protein intake was only 25%, there is no evidence of other products which increased it and plant intake was low, what was the food source which completed the rest of their diet? This is a very difficult question which remains in the air.

A list of species which formed the terrestrial meat diet has been published elsewhere (VV.AA., 2008). This list reflects the range available in this area according to other studies. The aquatic species certainly included turtles, whose shells were found in abundance on all levels at the site.

5. Conclusion

The following historic reconstruction is based on the aforementioned details: Around 9,000 BC, a small group of people, probably five or six, moved from a relatively close settlement to what was probably a shelter or recess at the foot of a limestone cliff on a hillside near the modern day town of Oliva. Their aim was to exploit the surrounding territory which included marine resources –the coastline was quite nearby at this time– and land resources as well –in the surrounding plains and mountains there were herds of different quadrupeds, despite the deleterious effects of environmental changes caused by the Interglacial. The sea at the time was a source of fish, Cardium edule and some other species, while the coastal plain was not yet a swamp. Their lithic technology was inherited from the Magdalenian but limited to common types– scrapers, burins, backs and backed blades. The use of bone had been abandoned.

These individuals may have arrived from one of the other sites nearby which were abandoned in this period, such as Cova Foradá or El Capurri, both in the Oliva municipality, or from the site in Camp de Sant Antoni, barely 500m away in a straight line.

Between 8,500 and 7,500 BC, their stone tools underwent technological changes, gradually incorporating geometric items for hunting or fishing – arrows or spears in the former case, harpoons in the latter.

After 7,500 BC, geometric items became widespread and something extraordinary happened: they begin to bury their dead, in the case of these small communities, perhaps amongst individuals who had close blood or kinship ties. The dead had to be protected– they were no longer regarded as inert, worthless refuse but the remains of loved ones. Society became humanised and anthropocentrism began– human beings –men and women– were now at the centre of their world and indeed the world of all, by now a widespread concept and sentiment. This conceptual progression was also linked to human representations in the local Levantine prehistoric art, where it first appeared, coinciding with the burial phenomenon. This small human group did not consume large amounts of seafood or animal products, nor did they need many stone tools for hunting or fishing, reflected in the items accumulated found throughout the occupations of the site.

Around 6500 BC, the sea level began to rise slowly and flooded the entire coastal area up to the base of the slope at the foot of the cave, transforming the area into a great marsh or fen that contained abundant lagoon molluscs and turtles. The geometric tools became diversified and new types appeared.

In the middle of the 6th millennium, higher –now intense– rainfall probably forced the occupants to abandon the site and search for a new cave or perhaps huts on the plain. We believe they moved to the foot of the slope alongside the marshy plain, as a Neolithic or perhaps Protoneolithic site containing a midden and hand-made pottery has been excavated recently in this area, now in the urban heart of Oliva.

Elisa María Domènech Faus*; Mª Mercè Bergadà Zapata**; José Antonio Riquelme Cantal***; José Luis Vera-Peláez; Mª Carmen Lozano-Francisco****; Consuelo Roca de Togores Muñoz*****; Rachel Wood******

The Upper Paleolithic From Cova Beneito (Muro, Alicante, Spain)

1. Introduction

Cova Beneito opens in a powerful package of gray dolomites around l'Altdels Volcadors (Serra Benicadell). Placed 650 meters above sea level and is oriented west-southwest. It is a large rock shelter, whose overhang has detached and the left wall unbolts in a cavity of 6x8 meters.

From 1980 to 1990, work on the cavity revealed a long sequence with different levels attributed to Mousterian, Middle and initial Upper Paleolithic (Iturbe *et al.*, 1993).

In 1993, we proceeded to review the interior north and east profiles in order to complete the sedimentological and palynological studies. The excavation of 1994 clearly displayed the differential contact between the C units, sterile from an archaeological point of view, and the first layers of the Mousterian horizon (Domenech, 2005).

In 1999, a new stage began with the excavation of the south profile, in danger of collapse, and near the entrance of the cavity. Following the recent documentation review and materials provided at that time, three Paleolithic phases were differentiated: Gravettian, Solutrean and Solutrean-Gravettian.

From that moment on, an open exterior sector is posed under the great shelter protection. In this new step, the main lines of research have focused on the verification of the actual settlement dimensions in order to complete the stratigraphic sequence, paleoenvironment, and paleoeconomics studies, for example, analysis of occupancy levels and obtaining reliable absolute dating.

2. The Excavation In The Rock Shelter Exterior

Archaeological work in the new sector allowed for outlining the boundaries of the occupation area during the Upper Paleolithic, a fact which proves the existence of a settlement of hunters more significant than assumed in previous studies during the late twentieth century. As it progress-

Figure 1. Stratigraphic section from Cova Beneito.

* Ajuntament de Muro d'Alcoi, Placeta Molina, 4, Muro d'Alcoi-03830 edomenech@vilademuro.net; Museu Palau Comtal, El Pla s/n, Cocentaina-0382 patrimoni@cocentaina.org

** SERP. Departament de Prehistòria, Història Antiga i Arqueologia. Universitat de Barcelona. C/ Montalegre 6-8, Barcelona- 08001 bergada@ub.edu

*** Universidad de Córdoba,Departamento de Geografia y Ciencia de la Tierra, Plaza del Cardenal Salazar, 3, 14003- CÓRDOBA, jriquelme@uco.es

**** Gaia Museum S.L., Avda. María Victoria Atencia s/n, 2901-MÁLAGA gaiadidactica@gmail.com

***** MARQ Museo Arqueológico de Alicante Pza. Dr. Gómez Ulla s/n Alicante-03013 SPAIN crocat@diputacionalicante.es

****** AResearchSchool of Earth Sciences, Australian National University, Canberra, 0200, Australia; ResearchLaboratory for Archaeology and the History of Art, University of Oxford, Oxford OX1 3QY, United Kingdom rachel.wood@anu.edu.au

es in breadth and depth, large blocks that define the occupation area appear, especially around the Solutrean and Solutrean-Gravettian. In addition, several areas of combustion have been located where flint has been treated, as well as preferred knapping zones, with a presence of large traces of preparation.

The obtained sequence begins with a superficial level of medieval and Bronze Age materials. Followed by a minor sterile layer, then level II is developed. This one was tentatively attributed to Solutrean-Gravettian period, according to absolute dating and by analogy with other data obtained in the interior excavation. The level's bellows are III and IV, which allowed for dating and outlining of some parts, is ascribed to the Solutrean, but was difficult to define given the scarcity of retouched, and especially the absence of, diagnostic spare parts. Upper Paleolithic sequence is ended in the V exterior level with clearly Gravettian industries.

2.1. Stratigraphic sequence, sedimentary evolution and Paleoenvironment

In 2009, the sedimentary record studies restarted and focused on the exterior of the cave in the field called "Excavation I", the north profile, with an output of more than two meters (Fig. 1). The aim of the current research focuses on the analysis of the filling formation, the human occupations interaction with the environment, and finally the postdepositional evolution of the site and the components that comprise it. Thus, it will be possible to frame Cova Beneito data in the Upper Paleolithic evolution in the Iberian-Mediterranean area.

The methodology we used involved the stratigraphic-sedimentary field description and application of micromorphology levels V to I; although the data presented here are still quite preliminary (Domenech *et al.*, 2012).

Figure 2 a. The stratigraphic sequence of Cova Beneito. Excavation Sector I. Northern Profile. b. Detail of the falling blocks from level III. c. Micromorphological sample from north profile.

This record begins with level V, Gravettian of carbonated clayey, silty sand blocks and pebbles. Its formation process responds with a colluvial depositional period characterized by block falls, mainly located at the ceiling level; almost in contact with the overlaying level IV. This brought a change in the general shelter morphology. Subsequently, there was percolation of carbonated water and saturation of sedimentary fill.

Below, the level IV is attributed to the Solutrean. It has a silty sand clays matrix, pebbles and blocks with erosional contact respect to the level III; corresponding with a colluvial process less marked than level V. This horizon has obtained an absolute dating of 18,275 ± 175 ky BP setting this stretch of sequence. To relate the paleoenvironment episodes documented with Upper Pleistocene chronostratigraphic scale used globally, dating has been calibrated by CalPal 2007_HULU program (Weninger *et al.*, 2004) with the purpose of placing it between 22,580-21,380 ky calBP. Therefore, it was possible to ascribe it to the GS-2c period, categorized by cold, but not severe, weather conditions. Subsequently, an erosive process occurs. Following this hiatus, begins the sediment reactivation with Solutrean level III. This one has presence of pebble, blocks and silty clays, also caused by a colluvial process and block falls. The conditions of this deposit are more stringent and cold than the others from level IV. This second drop of blocks, produce another important change on the roof shelter morphology.

The level II is related to the Solutrean-Gravettian cultural period. Furthermore, it has silty clays with sand, whose depositional conditions are different from those of previous levels. It corresponds to a process of diffuse gullies, with minor competence and continual slow movement of the laminar type. This level is dated in 16,180 ± 140 ky BP that correspond to the calibration range of 19,820 and 18,900 ky calBP, which would correlate with the moist and fresh episodes of GS-2b.

Finally, an erosive process that ends with the silting Holocene colluvial fill type, level I, pebbles with silty clays sands with abundant remains of plant origin, in which a tank weathering occurs through today.

2.2. Absolute dating

The absolute dates collected for Upper middle Paleolithic phases were obtained by Thermoluminescence, ^{14}C and Accelerator mass spectrometry (AMS) (Table. 1). The first, were achieved in the radiochemical dating laboratory from the Universidad Autónoma de Madrid. Samples for AMS and ^{14}C dating were sent to the laboratory of the University of Uppsala. (Domenech *et al.*, 2012)

There is corresponding dating of skeletal remains excavated in the Gravettian levels during the 1999 season. In this sample, no bone was found with marks as they eroded surfaces and concretions. Furthermore, from the 64 selected remains only 4 contain> 0.5% N, and of these, only three can be dated through collagen.

To identify bone with sufficient collagen, the nitrogen content was measured by using an Elemental Analyzer adapted to Isotope-ratio mass spectrometry (IRMS), driven in continuous flow mode (Brock *et al.*, 2010.2013). Collagen extraction was attempted only on those containing more than 0.5% nitrogen. This process was followed by the protocol of treatment with an acid wash to demineralize, exogenous removal of carbonates and humid acids, followed by gelatinization, filtration and ultrafiltration (Vivaspin 15,30 KDA molecular weight) (Brock *et al.*, 2010). The lyophilized samples were burned in the EA to allow the measurement of the carbon and nitrogen stable isotope. The radiocarbon years were measured with the Accelerator Mass Spectrometer.

The dates have been calibrated with IntCal 13 curve (Reimer *et al.*, 2013) in Oxcal v4.2. (Bronk, 2009). From the data obtained, we must mention two circumstances. The first is related to samples with quality assurance indicators outside the ac-

LEVEL II	Ua-32243 16180±140 BP (bone)
LEVEL III	Sample A MAD-3916 TL 18025±1623 BP Sample B MAD-3917 TL18167±1631 BP
LEVEL IV	Ua-32244 18275±175 BP (charcoal sediment)

Table 1. Absolute dates for the exterior excavation.

Sample	Context	Yield (mg)	Yield (%)	% C	δ13C	δ15N	C:N	OxA-	Date (BP)	Error	Calibrated date (cal BP, 95,4% probability)	
											From	To
BEN-7	Lev. 42	6,59	0.7	42.1	-19.6	6.5	3.2	X- 2366-7	25150	200	29675	28730
BEN-16	Lev. 40	13,5	1,3	44,5	-18,4	5,4	3,5	21842	23730	180	28208	27522
BEN-29	Lev. 32	12,5	1,5	46,2	-18,6	4,5	3,3	21843	23180	160	27719	27183
BEN-8	Lev. 42	5,1	0,5									

Table 2. The Gravettian dating results for the levels from 1999 campaign.

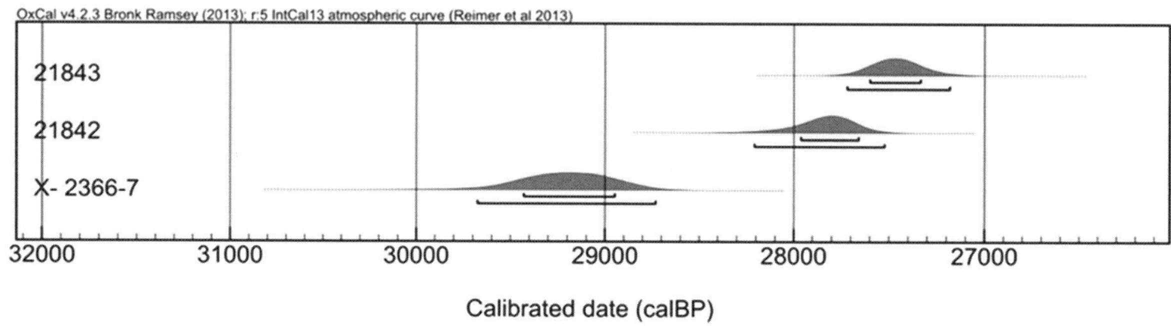

Figure 3. Compared graphics for the radiocarbon dates.

cepted archaeological collagen-OXA-X 2366-7 range, which contains 0.7% collagen (only 1% difference acceptable). The second is the high amount of C: N of 3.5 dating ref. OXA-21842 accepted, for instance the index is usually between 2.9 and 3.4. Nonetheless, these samples are only slightly outside the acceptable ranges. Additionally, the consistency of three dates dismisses both limitations (Table 2) (Fig. 2).

2.3. *Typology and lithic technology*

The overall lithic remains in the levels attributed to Upper Paleolithic have posted a total of 7,609; of those 226 have been used as a blank for the retouched pieces, representing 2.9% of the total. For the technological study (Table 3), 4,209 remains were selected.

For the typological study, the retouched artifacts have been included in five major groups: scrapers, burins, flat retouched and abrupt retouched tools, microburin and fractured pieces. Also, another various group, composed by simple retouch objects, retouched fractures, denticulate and borers, among others (Table 4).

The three groups best represented in the Solutrean and Solutrean-Gravettian, II and III / IV levels are scrapers, abrupt retouched artifacts and various; while in the Gravettian, level V, highlight the abrupt retouched stone tools (Fig. 3). Nonetheless, the two groups reflecting the qualitative differences are flat retouched and fractured pieces. The first, connects to levels II and III / IV; although neither the diagnostic characteristics pieces of these phases appear. While the second links to levels III / IV and V, with similar percentages and parts with resembling morphological type characteristics.

The artifacts with abrupt retouch are significant in the Gravettian, among which are the gravettes and bladelet with dejected edge, including double truncation bladelet linked with the presence of microburin. The various group soffers greater variability in the Solutrean levels with significant retouched tools and borers.

The archaeological and technological analysis of the three units, in progress, documents the existence of various knapping processes in the production of two types of utensils, blades and flakes.

	Level II	Levels III-IV	Level V
Scrapers	27,66% (13)	19,32% (23)	10% (6)
Burins	8,51% (4)	8,40% (10)	12,66% (7)
Flat retouch	4,25% (2)	3,36% (4)	-
Microburin	-	1,68% (2)	-
Abrupt retouch	14,89% (7)	24,37% (29)	45% (27)
Chipped pieces	6,38% (3)	13,44% (16)	13,33% (8)
Divers	38,29% (18)	29,41 (35)	20% (12)

Table 3. Totals of lithic evidence analyzed.

	Level II	Levels III-IV	Level V	TOTAL SAMPLE
Total sample	1403	4629	1577	7609
Technologic analysis	837	1759	620	3216
Retouuuch pieces	47 (3,3%)	119 (2,57%)	60 (3,80%)	226 (2,9%)

Table 4. Typological features of Cova Beneito.

In blade manufacturing, several methods were used to obtain elongated tools with measurements and diverse morphologies. Among them are identified knapping methods by applying standard methods of volumetric operation; as well as bipolar knapping using the anvil technique, similar to the manufacturing of chipped pieces. These productions were virtually unchanged throughout the sequence, with a peculiar proliferation of bipolar knapping in Solutrean-Gravettian and Gravettian levels.

Major changes are observed in flakes manufacturing between different chrono-industrial phases. The Levallois method is clearly defined in Solutrean-Gravettian and Solutrean periods used for making armor with flat retouch. In addition, the presence of exploited cores without prior shaping is observed. The raw material used was flint and limestone.

2.4. *Zooarchaeology*

The material used has provided a total of 8,537 bone fragments, pooled in two levels, Solutrean and Solutrean-Gravettian. Of those, 2,132 (24.97%) have been determined, while the remaining 6,405 (75.03%) residues have not been attributed to any species due to its high degree of fragmentation.

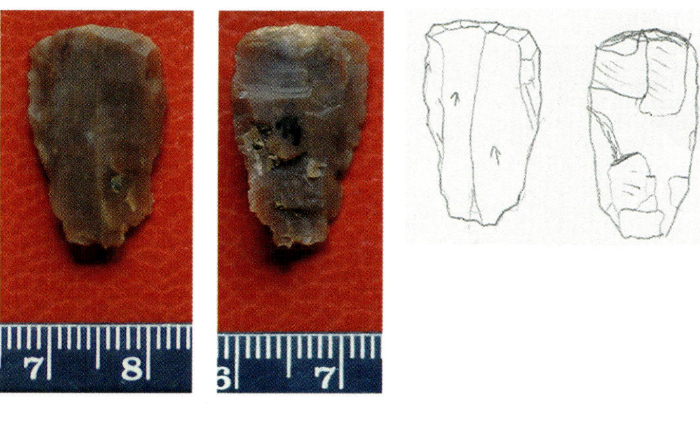

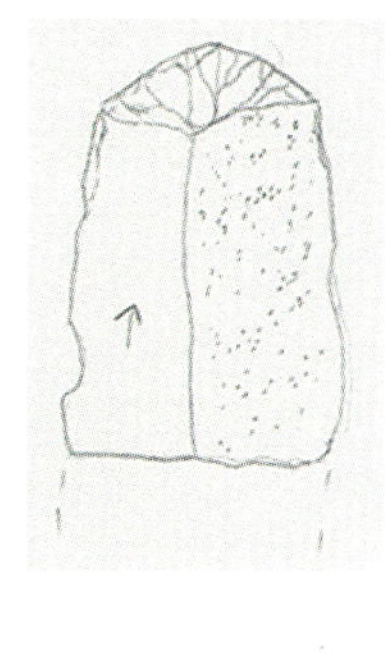

Figure 4. Retouched materials. Level V.

Solutrean level

This level has provided a total of 1,234 bone fragments, only 225 (18.23%) have been identified both anatomically and zoologically, forming the number of identified specimens (NISP). The identified mammal species are:

Equus sp. (horse)

A carpal (semilunar) belonging to an adult has been identified.

Cervus elaphus (deer)

Similar to the horse, the deer is also represented by a single bone fragment, in this case a 3rd phalanx.

Capra pyrenaica (mountain goat)

The mountain goat has provided a total of 8 certain bone fragments (3.56%), representing a minimum of 2 individuals (12.5%). Age cohorts are represented, both juvenile and adult. The anatomical detail is marked by the presence of a greater number of head skeletal portions, followed by the appendicular.

Oryctolagus cuniculus (rabbit)

The rabbit is the best species represented in the analyzed set a total of 215 fragments determined (95.56%) corresponding to a minimum of 12 subjects (75%).The skeletal portions better represented are the appendicular, followed by the cranial and axial. The bones are fractured and, in most cases, burned so is difficult to propose an intrusion. Fractures on rabbit bones indicate modalities that can only be attributed to human intervention (Pérez, 1992).

Solutrean-Gravettian Level

The corresponding recovered bone material at this level rises to a total of 7,303 fragments. From this pooled, have been recognized anatomically and zoologically 1,907 (26.11%) of them, that conform the numbers of identified specimens (NISP).The documented mammalian species at this level are as follows:

Equus sp. (horse)

The horse has provided a total of 37 specific fragments (1.94%) representing a minimum of 2 individuals (1.79%) adults. Skeletal fragments best represented are appendicular, followed by the cranial and axial. This is the third most important ungulate species in the site. In the1st phalanx a longitudinal fracture is observed, from which is possible to obtain the bone marrow. Although the identified material has been scarce, some measures have been obtained, particularly from teeth. The measurements acquired are within the variation of this species in the southeast peninsular (Martínez, 1996).

Cervus elaphus (deer)

This species is represented by a total of 48 specific fragments (2.52%) expressing a minimum of 4 individuals (3.57%).The only age cohort found is the adult. The anatomical analysis has shown the prevalence of appendicular skeletal parts, followed by the cranial and axial. The bone material studied is highly fragmented, responding to butcher process and bone marrow removal (Pérez, 1992). Finally, we note the presence of 1st and 2nd phalanx digested, the first partially and the other entirely, implying the presence of carnivores in the cavity.

Capra pyrenaica (mountain goat)

The mountain goat is the best represented ungulate on the site. A total of 78 bone fragments (4.09%) have been recorded; these represent a minimum number of 6 individuals (5.36%). Age cohorts represented are both juvenile and adult, with undistinguishable dominance of one over the other. In this case, the anatomic elements are marked by the presence of a greater number of appendicular portions, continued by cranial (which shows the number of isolated teeth) and axial. Frequently, there is presence of fire traces in the bones. Furthermore, in this case, bitten short bones (patella) and digested (1st phalanx) by carnivores have been found. The identification of these scarce carnivore marks would suggest, possibly a timely existence of these taxa in the cavity. This situation would be directly related to a temporary occupation by man.

Sus scrofa (wild boar)

Its presence in the bone sample is particularly uncommon. Currently, we only have identified a fragment belonging to the 1st phalanx, possibly next to an adult individual at this age.

Oryctolagus cuniculus (rabbit)

It is the best represented species in the bone assemblage with a total of 1,740 determined fragments (91.24%) corresponding to a minimum number of 97 individuals (86.61%). The most abundant skeletal portions are the appendicular, after the cranial and axial one. The bones are fractured, and in most cases, burned, so an intrusion is not recorded. In addition to the presence of several cut marked bone, we have found rare evidence indicating how small carnivores or raptors, transported some rabbits into the cavity, documented by the finding of a humerus with small carnivore bites. Nonetheless, there is an overwhelming amount of fragments showing clear human activity. The fractures found on rabbit bones from Cova Beneito, except a few of them as we mentioned above, indicate modalities that can only be attributed to human intervention

Lepus granatensis (hare)

Like the wild boar, the hare bone sample is especially sparse. Only a fragment of femur belonging to an adult individual has been identified.

Pardina Lynx (lynx)

Finally, this carnivore is represented by a total of 2 bone fragments (0.11%) belonging to the same adult (0.89%). The determined bone portions belong to appendicular skeleton. The scarcity of bones does not allow for many insights. Nevertheless, the fractured humerus recovered could point to the hunting and consumption by man. It is the only certain carnivore bone sample.

The bone sample recovered in Cova Beneito belonging to the Solutrean and Solutrean-Gravettian levels indicate the unclear differences between periods. This statement is based on the presence of different taxa species, as well as the hunting and consumption activity by human groups occupying the cavity in both periods. The continued presence of man in some sites could be a rising point in the same occurrence of carnivores, and therefore a decrease in its role as accumulators of bones. This fact, together with specialization in hunting rabbits, deer and mountain goat, will continue this pattern throughout the Upper Paleolithic period in the peninsular south.

The abundance of rabbits, in the levels analyzed, should not overestimate their intake as food, as the hunting of one deer or a mountain goat would be the equivalent biomass to a high number of rabbits. Subsequently, the archaeological record indicates hunting animals with different biomass levels change their treatment in terms of cutting and consumption. For ungulates, anatomical parts would be consumed near the place of capture, while others would berelocated to settlements, because midsize and large prey cannot be totally consumed immediately. On the other hand, rabbit stalking, permits use of a different model for its availability throughout the year as adjusted biomass meat to daily needs of a person.

2.5. Malacological Study

Paleontological study was performed on fossils and organic remains of mollusks obtained in the 1999 Upper Paleolithic excavations deposited in the MARQ and 2001-2005 campaigns.

In 1999, 16 species of mollusks have been identified, six belong to terrestrial lungfish found in their natural habitat; two fluvial *(Melanopsis lorcana* and *Theodoxus baeticus)*, eight marinas, six bivalves (*Glycymeris insubrica, Pecten maximus, Pecten jacobaeus, Chlamysvaria, Cerastoderma edule* and *Acanthocardia* sp.); a gastropod (*Nucella lapillus*) and a *scaphopoda* (*Antalisina equicostatum*) between the chrono-cultural sections from Solutrean to Gravettian. In all cases, it can be said that the mollusks have been used for a symbolic purpose. In the case of fluvial gastropod *Melanopsis lorcana* shell, has an anthropogenic hole to wear as a necklace, or other ornament. Similarly, with the shell *Insubrica Glycymeris*, the umbo is perforated, possibly for use it as a pendant. In the 2001-2005 campaign, 17 species of the terrestrial pulmonary have been identified and as in the previous case were found in their natural context; along with three marine species, one gastropod *(Littorina obtusata)* and two bivalves *(Pecten maximus* and *Pecten* sp.)

Knowing the specific features of the cave, out of the reach of the tides during the studied periods, it can be said that all the fauna found there were collected at the sea or beach level by man and transported to the cavern; except *Melanopsis lorcana* and *Theodoxus baeticus* which came from a nearby stream, also collected by man.

Regarding the paleobiogeography of the species under study, it can be said that all mollusks found currently belong to the Mediterranean, with the exception of *Nucella lapillus* and *Pecten maximus*. The first one, during the Gravettian, exclusively Atlantic, comes from Portugal. The second one, located in the Solutrean levels, can be found nowadays in the Atlantic and Alboran Sea, but not in Alicante. The presence of cold-water species in these latitudes is consistent with the glacial maximum in the case of Solutrean and Gravettian, and is included in this Würm glacial cold period. This is the logical explanation for the existence of these species in Cova Beneito through these chronocultural segments from the end of Upper Pleistocene.

The free swimming (FS) mollusks (Pilgrim and scallops) live on mobile funds, along with the sandy-muddy paleoenvironment (SMU) (gastropod mollusks, bivalves and scaphopods from benthic infralittoral floor). Their presence demonstrates how human population living in Cova Beneito throughout the beginning and middle of the Upper Paleolithic had a common coast line with sand, mud or clay, which indicates mobile backgrounds, with an almost entire absence of rocky coast species. The exception is the *Nucella lapillus,* Gravettian single copy, attesting the presence of an obstacle, or rocky reef, on the Alicante coast during this chrono-cultural segment.

It should be mentioned, regarding the malacofauna found at the site during the Upper Paleolithic, that almost all mollusks found were used for symbolic purposes. Most of them have holes in the umbo or lugs (for the case of shells from bivalves and scallops, respectively) to be used as beads and earrings;gastropods, such as *Lorca Melanopsis, Nassarius gibbosulus, Nassarius corniculus* and *Theodoxus baeticus,* with roughly spherical holes near the labrum, resemble a string of beads. In other cases, the gastropods appear polished all around, outer labrum and columella, such as the shell of *Nucella lapillus.*

The presence of Scaphopods is dominated by *Antalisinae quicostatum* species, drill holes, or anthropogenic punctures, were discovered in specimens. Nevertheless, these tusk shaped shells were used as necklace or jewelries beads, since they show two holes one oral and another aboral. These shells, which were used as symbolic ornaments, can be picked up on the beach, and generally have a bright white color. They are present in all chrono-cultural segments studied in Cova Beneito.

Where do the mollusks of these excavations come from? They emanate from the sandy-muddy infralittoral (SMU) paleoenvironment and are free swimming (FS) bivalves. The most logical explanation would be that the shell collectors had gathered on the beach, tide level, with valves already disjointed, but given the fragmentation of the shells of pectinidae, *a priori* hypothesis cannot dismissed.

Regarding *Littorina obtusata,* it comes from the same tide level, the supralittoral and mesolittoral levels, so their gathering could be straight from the rocks on the Alicante coast during the Solutrean. On the other hand, they could also have been collected directly from the beach, likewise in the tidal zone.

2.6. *Study of a tooth*

In the case of dental research, here is outlined the study of one tooth found in level III, from the Solutrean period on Cova Beneito (Fig. 4).

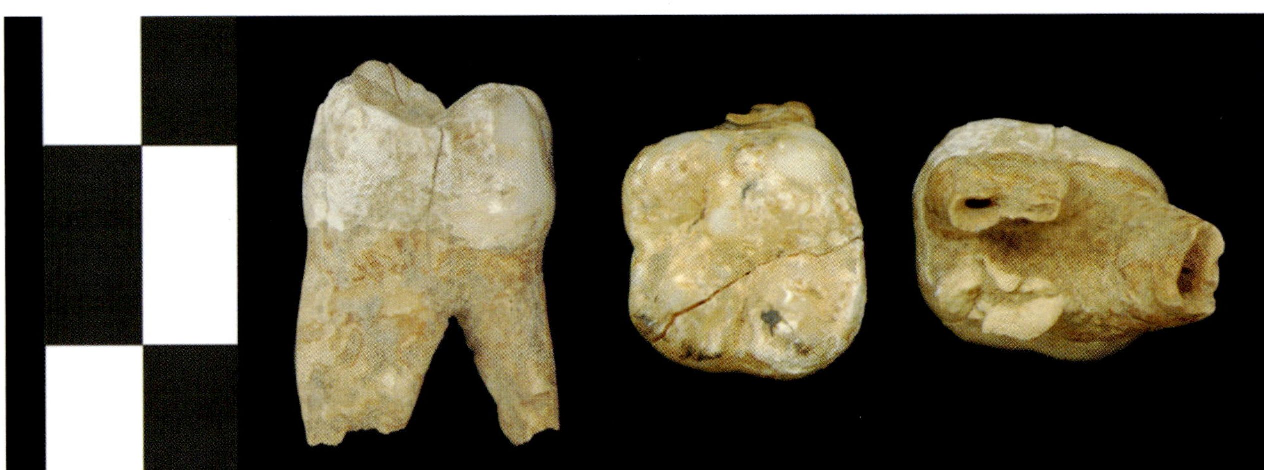

Figure 5. Tooth located at Level III.

Radiological techniques, specifically Scanning Electron Microscopy, were used to examine the formation of roots, and the pulp chamber, for information about diet.

The tooth sample corresponds to a left upper second molar (27) of the permanent teeth, which belonged to a 12-year-old preadolescent of indeterminate sex. It shows slight wear on the occlusion surface. Through microscopic traces of wear analysis (pits and striations), high density of enamel micro-striations with a flat trend have been observed, related to a diet mostly based on very abrasive vegetable consumption without an elaborate processing, such as in populations of similar chronology.

J. Emili Aura Tortosa *

Coves de Santa Maira (Castell de Castells, Alacant)

Les Coves de Santa Maria are located at the sun-trap of serra d'Alfaro (1166 m), at the head of the Girona river. The cavity is configured around a breach inclined to the NW opening in the rocky wall of the Eocene reefs sandstones in the external Prebetic at an altitude of 600 m above sea level, 14 m above the current riverbed, and 25 km from the coast. Its denomination includes two sectors: the Boca Oeste (SM-W) and the lower entrance, called Corral del Gordo (CG), as that was its role until recently.

1. Lithoestratigraphy and Chronology

The correlation between the lithoestratigraphic sequences of the mentioned sectors is included in Fig.1

The description from the base to the top of the sedimentary sequence is the following:

In CG, the known sequence starts with Unit GCII, corresponding to a sandy-silty section with little presence of human activity, in accordance with the micro morphology analysis (Verdasco, 2002). According to the encompassed materials and radiocarbon dating, it was formed between the Last Maximum Glacial and the Younger Dryas, dating between 24 -13 ky cal BP.

The upper unit CGI, is placed discordantly in respect to the CGII. It is of Holocene origin and corresponds to a Neolithic "fumier" against the wall; radiocarbon dating places it in the Atlantic Period (6.7 - 6.1 ky calBP).

Five sedimentary units have been identified at the west entrance. A large share of the upper deposits were formed from fallen materials due to gravity, as water action is weak or absent according to the sedimentological analysis made by Jesús F. Jordá.

Unit SM5 was deposited at the end of OIS2, during GI-1 (13.5 – 13 ky calBP), and it is formed by centimetric thick laminations of mixed colors which rest on a speleothem.

Unit SM4 is formed by shales with sands, little gravel and small limestone pebbles of less than 3cm. Unit 4 basis could be related to the end of Younger Dryas, while the upper sequence corresponds to the Pre-Boreal, dating between 11-3 - 10.2 ky calBP.

Unit SM3 presents a remarkable dip towards the inner part of the cavity. Five sub-units have been identified with a similar grain size and a variable coloring. Pebbles and big limestone blocks appear on the basis, separate from unit 4. Radiocarbon dating places it at the Boreal (10,2 - 9,5 ky calBP).

Unit SM2 has an irregular geometry with remains of organic laminations; it shows erosional contact over the lower unit.

Unit SM1 presents a chaotic appearance, tabular geometry and it is strongly erosive over the underlying unit.

The three upper units present important processes of bioturbation linked to rodent activity and their predators.

* (jeaura@uv.es). Dept. de Preshistòria i Arqueologia. Universitat de València.

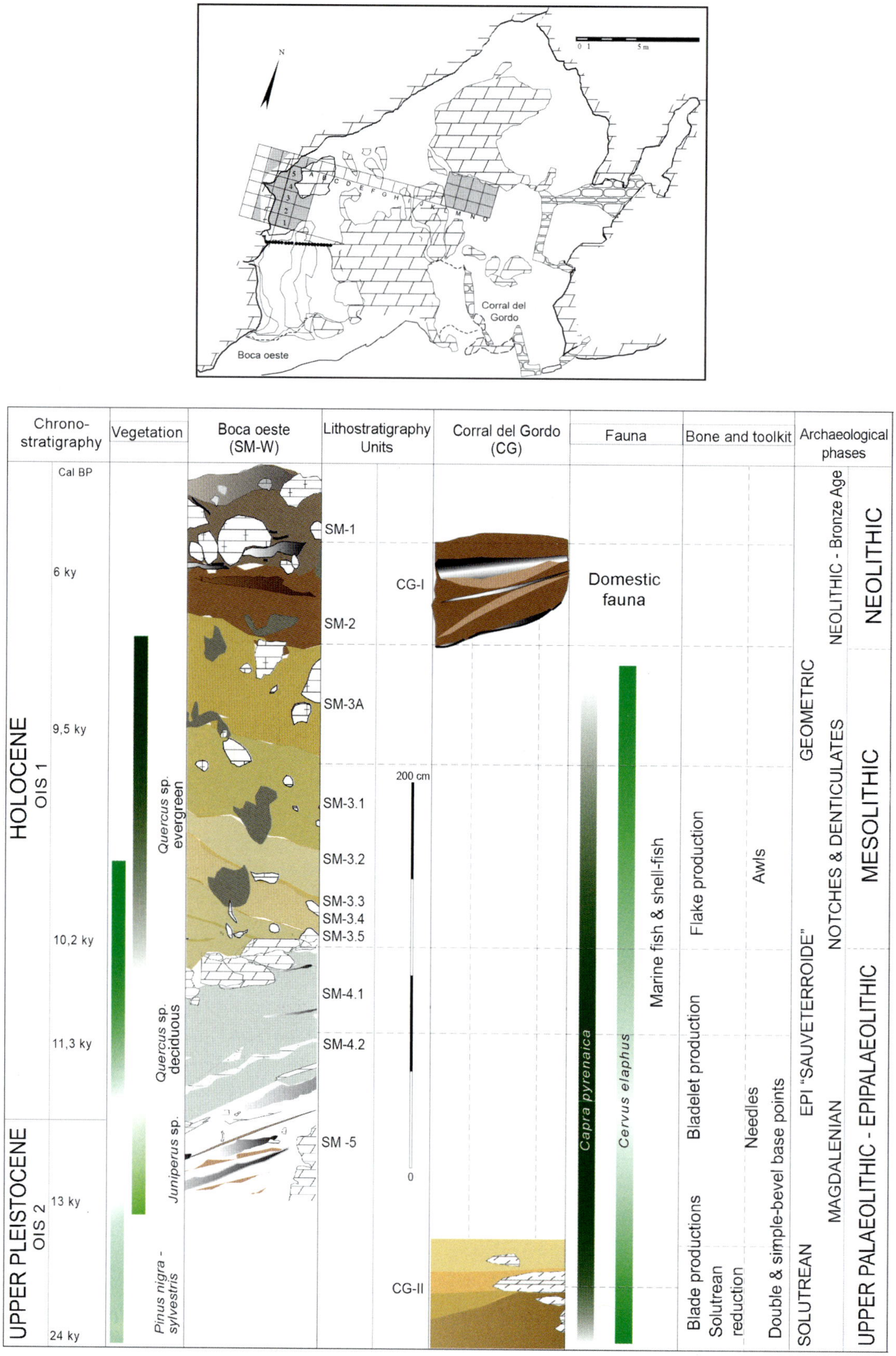

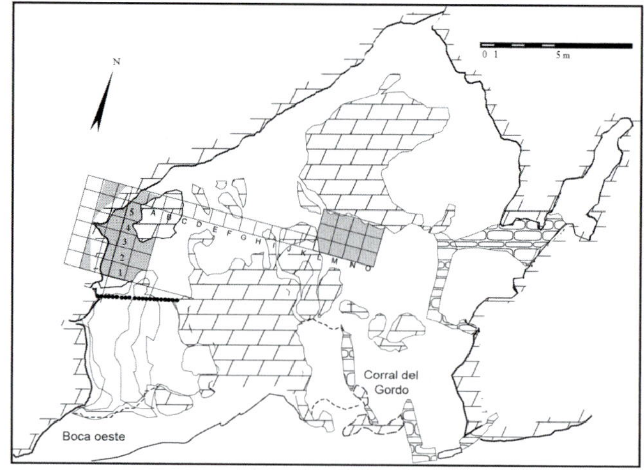

Figure 1. Coves de Santa Maira. In the upper part, planimetry of the archaeological site. At the bottom, chronoestratigraphy, lithoestratigraphy and archaeological stratigraphy of the sedimentary sequences of Boca Oeste (SM-W) and Corral del Gordo (CG) sectors.

2. Paleoenvironment

Anthracological remains studied by Y. Carrión (2005) show that in the cavity´s environment open vegetation existed with a predominance of *Pinus nigra/sylvestris* during a large part of MIS2. During GI-1, *Juniperus* sp. reached an important presence, causing an increase of *Quercus* sp. (deciduous and evergreen) during the Pre-Boreal and highlighted during the Boreal (Fig. 1). Riparian species (cf. *Salix– Populus*) and thermophile species (cf. *Olea europaea*) also show an increase from the Holocene.

Changes of marine species brought to the site could have a paleogeographic reading. Thus, until the Pre-Boreal, bivalves species correspond to a sandy substrate –mainly *Pectinidae* sp. and *Cardídae* sp.– while from Boreal, they are made of rocky substract (*Mytilus* sp.). On the other hand, icthyofauna shows an increase in species linked to estuaries (sea breams and mullets) during the Boreal. These variations reflect the eustatic changes of the coastal morphology.

The identified herbivores are common in other mid-mountain places and in this chronology; however, carnivores allow a certain serial numbering. he skull of de *Cuon alpinus*, whose direct dating proves its permanence during MIS 2 and apendicular remains of *Panthera* sp., come from the basal third of CGII. *Lynx pardina* has been identified in both sectors, and *Felis silvestris* and *Vulpes vulpes* are more common as the Holocene advances.

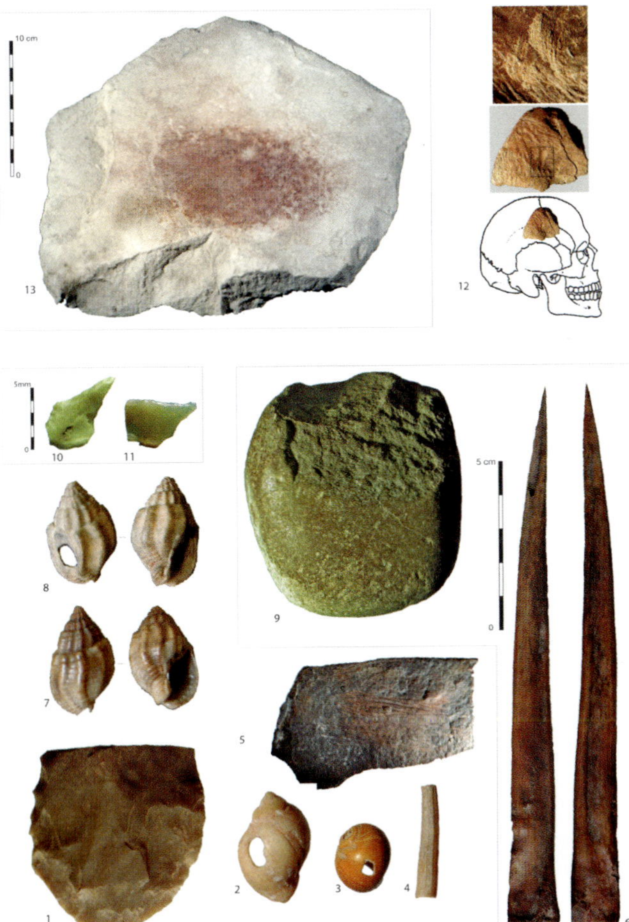

Figure 2. Coves de Santa Maira.1: Solutrean broken foliaceus; 2-4: personal ornaments; 5: oxide platelets with repeated incisions; 6: awl; 7-8: personal ornaments; 9: pebble with percussion and polished marks; 10-11: retouched micro-flakes, usedas projectile; 12: human skull fragment with anthropogenic marks; 13: pebble used for ocher enhancement;(n 1 - 4 Solutrean CG-II; n 5-6 Epipalaeolithic, SM-4; n 7-13: Denticulate-notches Mesolithic, SM-3).

3. Techno-economical features

In Fig. 2 a selection of variables is included, attempting to summarize changes of the use of the cavity along the MIS 2 and the Early Holocene.

Occupations of the CGII, dated between 24-23ky-calBP, contain Solutrean diagnostic elements –heat treatment and bifacially retouched leaf points– and high blade productions. A second occupation episode (CGII 5-2), dated between 17-13 ky calBP, shows a clear increase of micro-blade productions. In both cases, consumption and abandonment phases are registered, contrasting the reduced number of lithic blanks and by-products to pendant ornaments. The bone points collection is small: only double and mono-bevelled based points.

The top dating of CGII is linked to the ones of the bottom of the known sequence for SM-W, although both sectors appear quite different. In the lithic productions of SM5 and SM4, there is a higher diversity of raw materials including the use of limestone. An integrated production is now recognized whose supports will be used for two large tools groups: scrapers –truncated pieces and microliths. The by-products remains are numerous, being documented throughout the technical process.

The identification of domestic industry on bone –needles and awls– contrasts with a limited use of the antler. Another remarkable feature of these occupations is the recorded ocher working: from the collecting of raw material to the processing pebbles (Fig. 2: 5 and 13).

From the Boreal, occupations located in SM3 become more episodic with moments of little ‘carnivore´ contribution (Morales, 2013). This change coincides with a lithic industries break, blade and bladelet productions being drastically reduced for the benefit of flakes, frequently over limestone (Miret, 2007). The input of flat edges from the river and the use of slappers and pebbles suggest new working processes, including ocher processing. Except for some retouched micro-splinters, projectiles have not been identified and bone industry is limited to punches (Aura *et al.*, 2006).

From an economic point of view, *Capra pirenayca* and *Cervus elaphus* are the basic species –in this order–. In the MIS 2 occupations, few remains of *Equus* sp. are identified and as the Holocene advances, forest-environment species are incorporated (*Rupicapra rupicapra*, *Capreolus capreolus* and *Sus scrofa*).

SM-W has also provided information about the use of vegetables and the transport of marine mollusks and fish to inland sites (Aura *et al.*, 2005). These resources, together with the lagomorphs, have established tendencies and make up the sense of formulations such as intensification and diversification for the Iberian final Palaeolithic and Mesolithic.

4. Human remains

In the thick unit SM3 "loose human remains" have been identified with anthropogenic processing and depleting marks of at least three individuals according to the study of Mª P. de Miguel (Fig. 2: 12) (Aura *et al.*, 2009).On the other hand, the only evidences of the Early Holocene identified in CG correspond to a set of human and charcoal remains concentrated in an area of less than 1m^2. Its dating places them at the end of the Boreal. This sudden appearance of human remains and burial rites in the Mesolithic start-up constitutes an emergent feature at a regional level, accompanied by direct evidences of relationships with the coast which is also confirmed by the isotope analysis of human remains (Salazar-García *et al.*, 2014).

José Aparicio Pérez*

Cova Foradà (Oliva. Valencia)

1. Introduction

Cova Foradà is located in the west part of a low hill that, together with others, forms part of the set called Muntanyetes de Oliva, the last foothills of Serra de Mustalla over the coastal floodplain of the Gulf of Valencia, in the town of Oliva, Valencia. The setting where it lies is called Racó de Gisbert.

This opened in the limestone rock of the karstic system of Serra de Mustalla, offering two openings: the western one is the entrance, and the eastern one was opened after the beginnings of the Holocene when the vault broke in the deeper part of the cavity. The name refers to this structural particularity, meaning *holey cave*.

At the time of its discovery as an archaeological site in the early 1970s, the cave appeared to be a small cavity, rather like a shelter, about 6m deep and 7m wide. The reason was an inner weathering of the limestone rock which produced the subsidence of the back vault that we pointed out, and also the subsidence of the front, or entrance, vault in a length of about 25 m and a width of around 20 m. The back blocks remained unchanged due to handling and extraction difficulties, while the blocks of the western vault had been rolled to the bottom of the ravine in order to take advantage of the rock for lime processing in a furnace, installed for this purpose, which still maintains its infrastructure *in situ*.

The importance of *Cova Foradà* de Oliva as an archaeological site was proved after the findings during 39 years of research and studies.

First of all, a powerful and thick stratigraphic sequence must be pointed out (Fig. 1) which, apart from minor remains on the surface, offers a

* Arqueólogo Director de la Sección de Arqueologia y Prehistoria de la Real Academia de Cultura Valenciana. Académico C. de la Real de la Historia. P.O. BOX. 2260-46080 VALENCIA joapa2005@hotmail.com

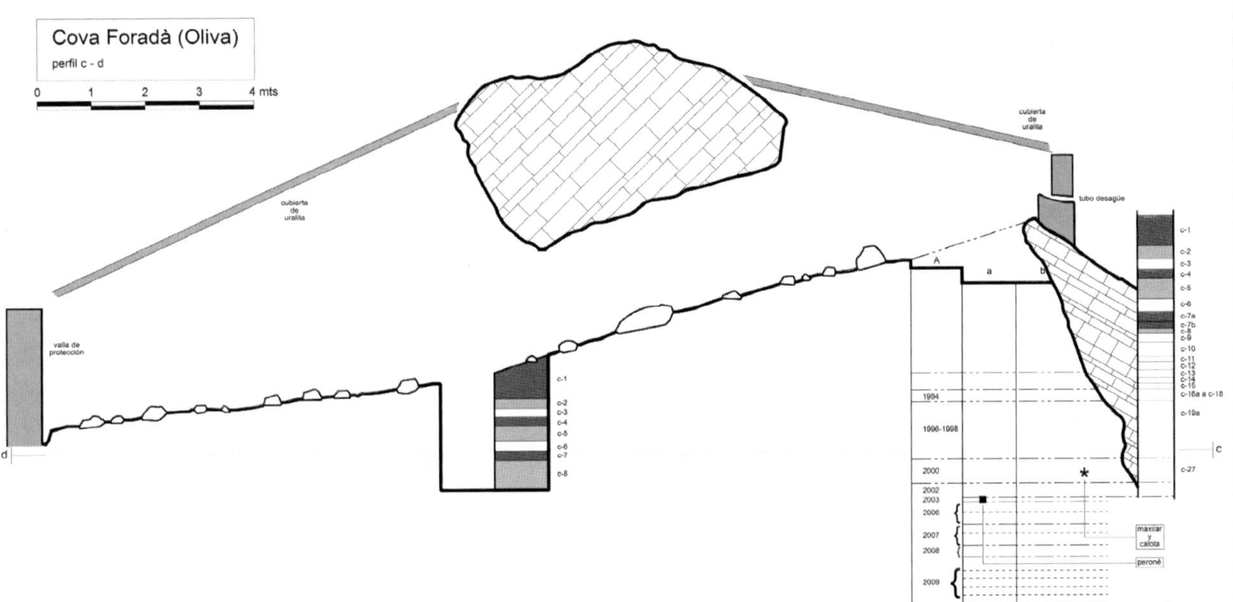

Figure 1. Section with the stratigraphy.

continuity to life that start in the first levels of the Mesolithic, take roots in the Paleolithic, and whose density and capacity could lead to the extent of the Middle Paleolithic despite the lack of clear dating. Even so, there is a possibility of finding former occupations of the cavity by going deeper, without reaching the bedrock or the sterile riverbed.

Between the Mesolithic and the Mousterian we find, without a solution of continuity, the whole sequence known as Upper Paleolithic, Magdalenian, Solutrean and Gravittean-Aurignacian, not having the thickness of Parpalló but with a large quantity of discoveries, taking into account the small surface in which the activity took place.

From early Leptonian, Mousterian starts with many lithic and faunal discoveries, just like in former levels, differentiating from Parpalló by the presence of the Middle Paleolithic which is nonexistent in the cavity of Gandía. The difference with *Cova Negra* de Xàtiva is also significant because of the lack of Upper Paleolithic levels.

The singularity of the Middle Paleolithic levels is determined by the anthropological discoveries corresponding, at least for the moment, to three individuals among whom one, the CF10, matches with a Neanderthal specimen with a whole skull, a large part or the complete rib cage, vertebrae and ribs, maybe many of the upper limbs and some yet to be identified from the lower limbs.

At this point, we have decided to intensify the investigation of the whole archaeological site, an essential requirement, adding to the anthropological studies already done and those which are being done currently, such as faunal, edaphic, lithic, palynological, environmental, economical, etc., which are more and more necessary in order to reach a holistic vision about the site´s activity.

2. Ecosystem

The most remarkable feature of the territory's ecosystem is the bio-diversity, as it participates, at present, in four environments: the maritime, due to the proximity to the coast, although we can´t forget the fluctuations along the Pleistocene and the Holocene; the mountain, with the whole Serra de Mustalla that we pointed out; the inner aquatic, due to the presence of the river Bullens whose drains run at the foot of the hill where it is located; and the mentioned Serra, located between the municipalities of Oliva and Pego, which also feeds the Las Aguas gap, marsh, or lagoon depending on the time of the year. The ecosystem is clearly reflected in the remains of the consumed fauna which have been recorded in the archaeological activities in the cave which we will mention later.

The richness of this ecosystem explains the permanence and continuity of this cavity's habitat, frequented during the Middle Ages, the Iberian Age, the Bronze Age, and consistently from the Mesolithic to the Middle Paleolithic, despite not knowing the moment of the first occupation due to the impossibility of reaching the bottom of the cavity.

3. Archaeological Activities

The explorations made in 1975 brought together a batch of lithic material found by an amateur archaeology group which delivered it to us for examination. We observed that, for the most part, the material belonged to the Middle Paleolithic or Mousterian.

In 1977 we made the first dig campaign, digs which are still being performed. In 2013 we carried out the XXX campaign.

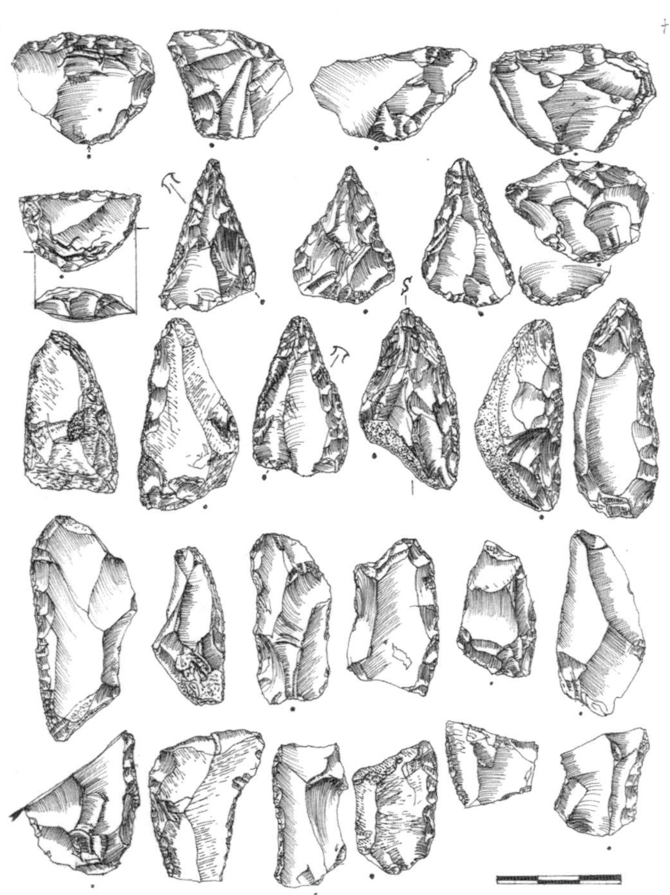

Figure 2. Lithic tools from the Mousterian level.

However, the first years were discouraging. The first campaign confirmed the existence of Mousterian levels, powerful and rich, both in industry and fauna, but a certain number of signs made us suspect of the contamination on the mentioned levels in the western part –charts E and D, 8 and 9 respectively of those first activities–, confirming the first dating with C14, done at the CSIC, showing the existence of Magdalenian levels. Digging in the range of charts K, J, I, H, G, F, E and D, 7, 8, 9, also in the west part, as well as the removal of levels, very deep into this part when digging charts I11, I12 and I13, fully confirmed this fact. Such an intense removal could be ascribed to treasures hunts in the Middle Ages, an activity that awakened an interest in this whole area and which we thought corresponded to the site´s entire surface.

Given these circumstances and as a last option, we considered that if the large existent blocks in the east part, irremovable for their dimensions, corresponded to the wrecked vault, they would seal and correctly preserve the sedimentation and its archaeological content in the deeper part of the cavity. This comes from the Bronze Age as, among the blocks, the existence of burials was detected, confirming the dig and the dating with C14 of the CSIC.

The digging of charts A 12-13 and 14; a 12-13, 14, 15 and 16; b 12, 13, 14 and 16 and c 12, 13, 14 and 15 confirmed our hypothesis, and behind a thick humus layer of 50cm, among the blocks and under their layers with the burials´ remains, fruitful archaeological levels arose, both in thickness and in content, exceeding all our hopes.

The digging´s continuity as we have pointed out, has allowed us, through the thirty campaigns done since 1988, to configure a powerful and rich stratigraphy (Fig. 1) from the Mesolithic to the Lower Mousterian, established as follows: Mesolithic I with the line coast within the economical limits and the subsistence area –Mesolithic I with the line coast pushed away and outside the limits –Magdalenian with plenty of significant bone industry –Solutrean with Parpallean cutout points –Medium Solutrean –proto-Solutrean –Aurignacian –Gravettian and Mousterian (Fig. 2).

Currently, the survey is in full Mousterian, with plenty of material and extraordinary fauna but without signs of the proximity of the cavity´s base, thus the necessity to follow up with a survey to reach the bottom area, the initial settlement, and in such a way finish the survey, starting later with digging in extension from this area, is necessary.

The discovery of human remains in the Mousterian level increased the interest and the richness of the content, reinforcing the protection fence with a cover over the unprotected sedimentation by the vault.

4. Human Remains

In the year 2000, during the XX digging campaign, we foundin layer 28 and chart C14/C15, a piece of human jawbone and a piece of skull, both studied by D. Campillo; M.E. Subirà; E. Chimenos; A. Pérez and S. Vila (see Cypsela, nº 14, pages 143-148, Barcelona, 2002), whose conclusions were the following: "The pieces definitely match two individuals, an adult and a child".

The neurocranium fragments are not-excessively swelled, and there is a small fragment corresponding to a very developed *torus frontalis* due to its morphology and thickness.

The preserved fragment of the jawbone, although is damaged, affirming that both the alveolar process and the nostril are quite broad, as well as its vestibule. The teeth are bulky and show in the x-ray the existence of a moderate taurodontism. All the arguments expressed are consistent with a Neanderthal diagnosis, probably a female.

In the digging campaign in 2010, it was decided to continue with the digging of charts C-14 and C-15 where in the year 2000 some remains of a jawbone and skull fragments of a Neanderthal were removed. This is why the digging team joined forces with the anthropologists M. Eulàlia Subirà and Jordi Ruiz, both belonging to the Unitatd'Antropologia Biològica of the Universitat Autònoma de Barcelona (UAB), and who in the last years have conducted the study of human remains of the cave in coordination with Gala Gómez Merino and Carlos Lorenzo from the Institut de Paleoecologia Humana I Evolució Social (IPHES), Tarragona.

On 9 August, the remains of quite a complete skull of a Neanderthal were discovered. In the following days, the chances of discovery of the upper part of a Neanderthal skeleton that included the skull to the first sacral vertebrae rose.

The discovery is important because the skeleton was very complete and the bone joints were in close anatomic connection, that is to say with connections among the bones similar to those while alive, with no displacements at all. In most Neanderthal discoveries in caves, the remains are limited, fragmentary, and scattered, with signs of having been moved and eaten by predators. The different digging campaigns in the cave have proved the presence of hyenas which alternated with the Neanderthals in the use of the cavity.

The digging was really slow at every moment because the bones were immersed in calcareous formations. This is why it was decided to extract the whole cemented block, including the immersed remains, for later digging in a laboratory.

The fossils' condition is very delicate. They are quite fragile and are cemented into a block of a very carbonated sediment. This is why, before being dug in the laboratory, they were submitted to a computerized axial tomography (CAT) and other image treatments in order to know the preservation condition of the bone remains, facilitating in this way the block´s digging in the laboratory. To extract and clean the remains from the block, mechanical equipment under binocular loupe was used. The treatments started, and are still continuing, in the Restoration Laboratory of the IPHES in Tarragona headed by Gala Gómez Merino, which has the necessary facilities for dealing with this type of bone material,. Furthermore, corresponding samples for later studies were taken.

Once the bones are unlocked, the anthropological study, headed by Dr. M. Subirá of the UAB in coordination with the IPHES members, will take place.

Together with the study of human remains, complete paleontological, sedimentological, antracological and palynological studies will also be handled, and the existent dating number will be expended by the C14 or by using other means which the C14 cannot reach. Dr. Eudald Carbonell has promised his complete collaboration from the IPHES and his management.

5. C14 Dating

We now offer the dating set obtained throughout these years from the different remains subjected to the corresponding analysis.

Cova Forada (Oliva)		
C-575	9.645 ± 327	12.081-10.000
	7.695 ± 327	10.101-8.050
Cova Forada (Oliva)		
C-277	12.500 ± 800	16.855-12.871
Layer 7. Son. I	10.550 ± 800	14.905-10.921
Cova Forada (Oliva)		
C-276 ó C-126	11.500 ± 1.000	16.127-10.787
Layer 4. Son. I	9.550 ± 100	14.177-8.837
CSIC-1492	6.196 ± 34 BP	
Charcoal		5.279-5.046 BC
Layer 2, part E o back part.		
CSIC-1493	5.633 ± 31 BP	
Charcoal		4.533-4.363 BC
Layer 1, superficial Part E o back part.	16.960 ± 100 BP	
UBAR-935 / CNA 089		
Fauna bones	16.960 ± 100 BP 18.133	18.355-18.255
Marjal de Pego (essential on the eco-system next to the cavity)	[14 Samples UBAR]	
	From 1.660 ± 50 to 10.120 ± 460 = 13 samples	
UBAR-45	28.240 = 1 sample	

Table 1. C14 Dating.

6. General Conclussions

As formerly explained, *Cova Foradà* de Oliva constitutes one of the most complete archaeological sites and therefore, one of the most important to the study of Prehistory on a national level. In our autonomous region, it is possible that the site might be one with the largest stratigraphy comparable to the total of the strata of *Cova Negra* (Xàtiva) and *Cova del Parpalló*, (Gandia). It is one of those places which seems to acquire a larger extent after each archaeological exploration campaign –taking place regularly since 1977–. This particular site, so named because of becoming a crossing cavern after its vault´s partial detachment, quintessentially embodies the prototype of a Prehistoric site.

Cova Foradà is one of those places which will always provide news. Among its countless virtues, it has a stratigraphic richness that makes the cave exclusive, and this is something just a few sites can maintain. Although early Medium Paleolithic strata have been reached in the last campaigns, the fact that the basal rock has still not been achieved is an opportunity that may bring many surprises.

Among the exhumed remains, prolific and abundant lithic tooling points out consistent morphologicality with the different periods represented by the stratigraphy. It also appears that a large quantity of fauna remains: some heavy mammals, but above all little rodents, among which the rabbit stands out due to its abundance. Coprolites, and other vestiges related to the periods of animal occupation combined with human groups, have also appeared.

However, this cavity is famous for the discovery of Neanderthal remains, among which the half-fossilized body of an individual is a highlight, and up to now represents one of the most important discoveries added to other remains formerly found in our Peninsula.

The vestiges of this specimen appeared in 2010, in a small niche emerging naturally from the east wall at the bottom part of the cave, about 7m deep from the reference point –0–. They were immediately set, the whole skull, part of the face, some vertebrae and part of the rib cage. All these bone vestiges were almost petrified by the action of the carbonate exchanging and the incipient mineralization inherent to such ancient remains. They were part of a concrete block in which mineral and bone parts were a whole.

As it was the only way to recover the set without damaging it, the entire dug block had to be extracted by removing part of the cavity´s stone support. In order to be transported and studied in a place with the necessary means for the objective, a box-nest was prepared to make movement and handling easier.

Thus, the petrified remains of the Neanderthal body were moved to the IPHES laboratory, in Tarragona, where the restoration team could start a micro-digging, which still continues today, to separate the human parts from the mineralized matrix.

Formerly, in the year 2000, a fragment of an upper jawbone had appeared, being attributed to a Neanderthal individual by the anthropologist team headed by Dr. Eulalia Subirà.

The different studies done on this bone piece gave very significant data of anthropologic and pathological nature which provided new proofs about the traditions of these societies. The use of sticks to palliate the pain produced by different processes of gingivitis was recorded and the results were published in a prestigious scientific magazine.

Throughout the years, there have been many studies covering a complete investigation of the archaeological site´s sequences. Samples of the different grounds were taken, the slopes deposition sequences were delimited, C14 dating was done, samples for palynological studies were kept, remains of presumably extinct animals were collected, vestiges of remote human activity were recorded and, in short, connections between all these discoveries were sought.

During 2011 and 2012, some ashes and coal from two fireplaces with an estimated dating close to 100,000 years was recovered, and recently in 2013, a limestone piece was identified as a probable bear head with traces of parallel incisions resulting from a human-induced action, this will give rise to future studies as the piece is considered to be related to some ritual or symbolic activity.

V. Villaverde*, P. M. Guillem**, R. Martínez-Valle**, A. Eixea*

Cova Negra

Location and background archaeological research

Cova Negra is located on the left bank of the Albaida River after it passes through the Estret de les Aigües, in the town of Xàtiva (Valencia, Spain). Cova Negra is a clearly visible cavity. Its large dimensions, 18 metres wide and approximately 18 metres high at the entrance, and 25 metres long, provide enough light and offer good conditions for habitability (Fig. 1).

J. Vilanova i Piera was the first to identify Cova Negra as an archaeological site. He cited it in his work "Origen, naturaleza y antigüedad del Hombre" in 1872 and included in one plate an illustration of one molar of *Equus* which was recovered at the site.

G. Viñes conducted the first systematic archaeological fieldwork, between 1928 and 1933. Little data was obtained from this works, although a hu-

* Departament de Prehistòria i Arqueologia. Universitat de Valencia
** IVACOR. Generalitat Valenciana

Figure 1. General view of Cova Negra.

man parietal bone was discovered and subsequently studied and assigned to the Neandertal species by M. Fusté. Materials recovered during the course of the excavations were enough to corroborate the relevance of the site and propitiate one preliminary attribution of the lithic assemblages to the Mousterian period. Additionally, the possibility that in the upper part of the deposit could be Capsian materials was suggested.

Between 1950 and 1957, the Servicio de Investigación Prehistórica resumed fieldwork campaigns after a first evaluation and revision of Viñes' results carried out by F. Jordá. In the course of this work, besides F. Jordá, D. Fletcher, E. Pla, V. Pascual and J. Alcacer also participated. Results led to the same chronocultural attribution, although the upper part of the sequence was now ascribed to the Lower Aurignacian.

Finally, between 1981 and 1991, excavations were undertaken, again directed by V. Villaverde and aimed at clarifying the stratigraphy and addressing the nature of occupation, since from the previous campaigns, the information available only allowed a general interpretation of the recovered lithic assemblages and the faunal remains.

As G. Viñes pointed out in one of the few publications concerning his excavations, Cova Negra presents severe disturbances and has been affected by numerous removals. Its location in a crossing point, its systematic occupation, and the loose consolidation of the sedimentary deposit have facilitated all these alterations that seriously affect the interpretation of its stratigraphy and chronology.

In 2013, a new stage of archaeological fieldwork was set up, aimed once again at specifying the chronological issues of the deposit and deepening the nature of the lower level occupations, barely excavated in the campaigns from 1980 to 1991. These new works have been favoured by relevant progress made in the Paleolithic period in a regional context, mainly through data sets provided by excavations carried out at Cova del Bolomor (Tavernes de la Valldigna), El Salt (Alcoi) and Abrigo de la Quebrada (Chelva). Furthermore, revision of the chronological sequence proposed in the 1990s has become necessary, particularly in the light of new biostratigraphic data.

Because these works are currently in progress and the new seriation proposal has not yet been published, in the present text we will refer to the already published results, referring only the general traits that we continue reviewing.

Stratigraphic sequence and chronology of the deposit (Fig. 2)

The current interpretation of the stratigraphic sequence from Cova Negra comes from the work of M.P. Fumanal. Succinctly, it comprises 15 levels grouped in six sedimentary phases. Hereafter, we will describe their main characteristics:

- Cova Negra Phase A. It is the first depositional phase represented by level XV, more than one metre thick. This is an allochthonous level of fluvial origin. This phase corresponds to a floodplain where clay materials were seasonally deposited in the cave by the overflow of the Albaida River. Consequently, the riverbed would be higher above than the present time, which in turn means that processes of terrace formations and down

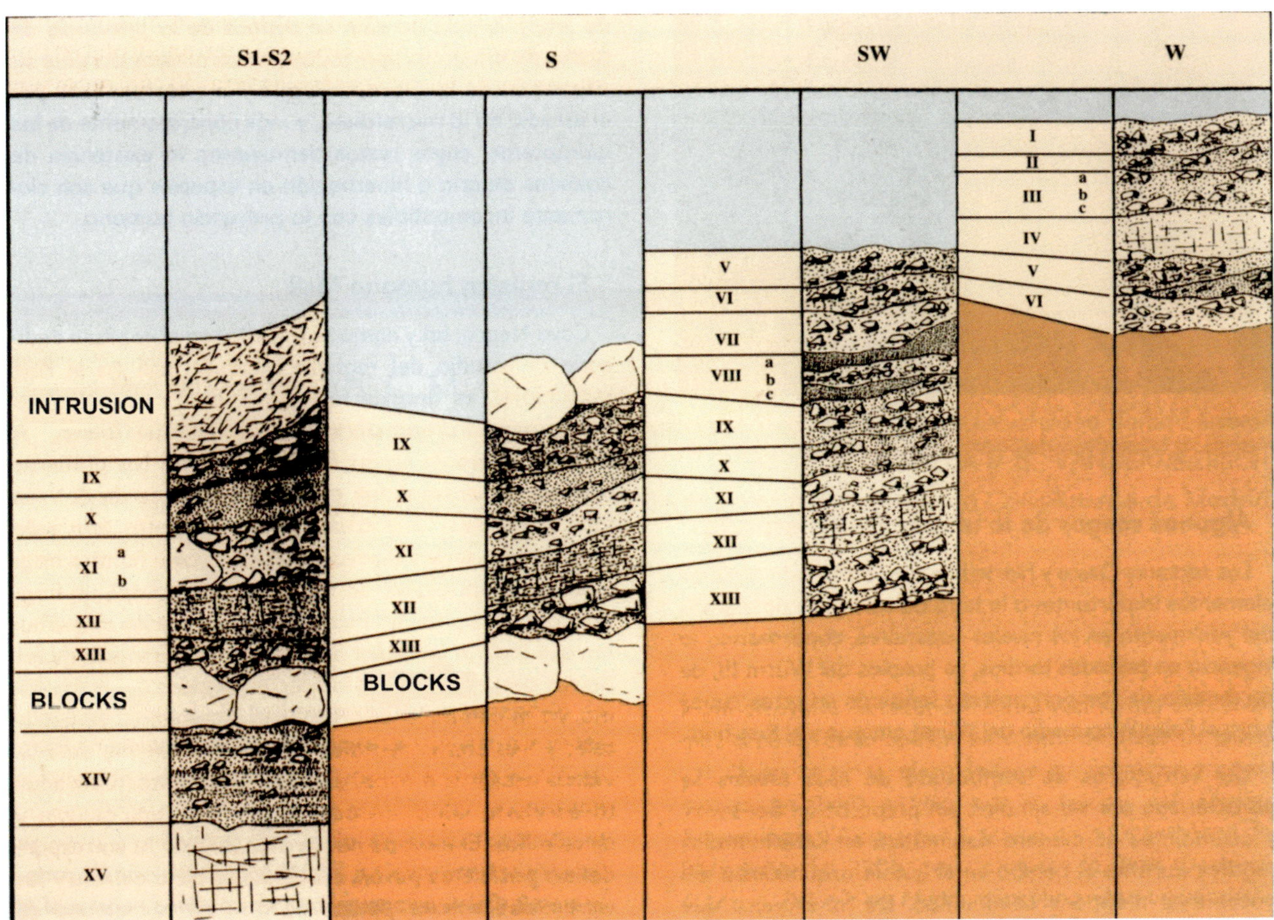

Figure 2. Cova Negra. Stratigraphic profile comparing different sectors excavated during the 1980s.

cut of the river would have started at that time. From a paleoclimatic point of view, the absence of cold climate conditions indicators should be mentioned. Phase A is archaeologically sterile due to the flooding episodes that did not allow permanent human habitation of the site.

- Cova Negra Phase B. This phase corresponds to levels XIV and XIII and possesses a totally different sedimentary characteristic compared to the previous phase. Along 170 cm, materials are accumulated in a yellow, loose sandy matrix that incorporates a discrete frequency of very altered coarse fraction on the base. This fraction increases towards the top of the deposit as a result of frost weathering processes. In between Phase A and Phase B there was an episode of ceiling collapse, indicating the first cold sign, where large blocks probably fell because of previous dissolution processes occurring in conditions of high moistness, which had already weakened the cave dome. Human occupation happened sporadically and is associated with an increase in the organic components. One TL dating on the sediment corresponding to the base of level XV, gave the result of 117± 17 ky BP.
- Cova Negra Phase C corresponds to level XII and represents an interruption of the previous conditions. There is an almost total reduction of pebbles and gravels and an absolute dominance of fine-grained fraction, with a clay component that contrasts sharply with the sandy component of the limestone where the cave is situated. These conditions indicate a slightly rigorous climate with seasonal humidity pulses allowing soil formation processes typical of a warm climate. Sediment of Level XII has been dated by TL obtaining a chronological range between 107± 16 ky and 96± 14 ky.

- Cova Negra Phase D. After an abrupt contact, a new accumulation with different traits occurred. It has been interpreted as an erosive phase. This phase includes levels XI to V and its thickness ranges between 90 and 130 cm. The most characteristic feature is the persistent inclusion of angular clasts, fractured under cold environmental conditions, with milder pulses and variable degrees of humidity. A more rigorous climate is observed at levels XI, IX (very pronounced), VII and V. This cold trend decreases at level X (more sharply), VIII and VI (with possible anthropic influences). Therefore, at this phase there is a rhythmic oscillation on climatic conditions, where the effects of deterioration periods are mitigated intermittently, but always inside the dominant cold stage. TL dating obtained on thermoaltered flint from level VIII, gave 255 ± 20 ky and 206 ± 23 ky, also from level V there is a result of 235 ± 21 ky. Additionally, ^{14}C dating from level V provided a radiocarbon date greater than 28.7 ky and less than 34.4 ky.
- Cova Negra Phase E. It can be observed clearly in the west sector profile, where it represents a clear interruption compared to the previous phase. It corresponds to level IV that, after an abrupt contact (hiatus or erosive phase), is composed of an alteration level where a paleosol has preserved a clayed horizon, enriched secondarily by carbonates in the form of millimetre-sized nodules of $CaCO_3$. Climatic conditions of this episode within a morphogenetic calm correspond to warm temperatures and seasonal rainfall where weathering erosion processes are replaced by gentle soil formation. This phase is 30 -35 cm thick in this sector. Two TL dates of sediments exist providing ages of 53.8 ± 8 and 50 ± 8 ky BP.
- Cova Negra Phase F. This phase culminates the sedimentary and climatic sequence of Cova Negra. It is characterized by rigorous climatic conditions. This phase comprises levels III to I averaging around 60 cm thickness. It corresponds to a significant environmental aridity stage. Mechanical erosion prevails again, but clasts now have sharp edges. The end of this phase coincides with a superficial and disturbed level of variable thickness that includes abundant materials from Middle Paleolithic and some artefacts from Upper Paleolithic. These evidences seem to correspond to final periods of the regional Upper Paleolithic and, at least in the area excavated in the 1950s and the 1980s, they represent low intensity occupations, indicating that human occupation of the cave was interrupted during a relatively long period.

Several factors have influenced the chronological interpretation of the sedimentary and climatic data described so far. First, the influence of the research tradition that from the initial work assigned the deposit to Würm chronology based on the study of faunal and lithic assemblages. Also, the identification of advanced traits on some lithic artefacts from the upper level contributed to support this chronological hypothesis. However, the excavation system in the 1950s clustered different levels in the same artificial unit with too much thickness. Finally, the limited knowledge of chronostratigraphic and paleoenvironmental issues in a regional context permitted this chronological proposition to be maintained. Accordingly, during the 1980s and 1990s, Phase A was correlated to the interglacial period Riss/Würm or the beginning of Würm (OIS 5e or 5d), considering that TL dating obtained supported this chronology. Phase B was related with subphases OIS 5 d-b, or stadial Würm I. Following the same logic, Phase C was assigned to OIS 5a, or interstadial Würm I-II. Taking into account its more rigorous climatic conditions, Phase D was associated with OIS 4, or Würm II, dismissing both TL dates on thermoaltered flint and ^{14}C radiocarbon dates from level V. Finally, Phase E, with interstadial characteristics, was assigned to Würm interstadial, while the upper section of the sequence equivalent to Phase F, characterized by aridity and climatic rigour, would suggest a correlation with Heinrich 3 and 4 climatic events, considered a demonstration of the persistence of Middle Paleolithic until OIS 2. Ultimately, most of the archaeological sequence in Cova Negra was placed at the beginning of Upper Pleistocene, while its end would correspond to the Middle Paleolithic period that would have continued until late chronologies contemporaneous with the beginning of the Upper Paleolithic in other regions.

This proposal is currently being reviewed in the light of new biostratigraphic indications provided by the revision of the faunal assemblages and the chronological implications derived from the fauna collection study. Furthermore, contributions from relevant sites such as Bolomor, el Salt and Quebrada have improved advances in the knowledge of regional chronological and biostratigraphical context. In 2013, new archaeological fieldwork started again in Cova Negra allowing a reconsideration of the stratigraphic sequence on the site, particularly concerning the postdepositional processes that affected the upper layers, and also providing a more precise sedimentary correlation of the levels at the different sectors of the site.

It should be stressed that much of the upper section of the site presents a mixture of different deposits that refers to the Upper Paleolithic and, probably, to a classical Middle Paleolithic, corresponding to OIS 3 and 4. This interpretation is supported not only by lithic materials and some bone industry recovered during cleaning tasks on disturbed levels at the south sector (that can be clearly assigned to Gravettian, Solutrean and Magdalenian periods), but also by archaeological materials retrieved in the 1950 and 1980 campaigns of the same chronology, and some others Middle Paleolithic artefacts such as a Soyons point, which refers to late Middle Paleolithic in south-eastern France. This alteration of the upper levels was already pointed out by Viñes in his work in the 1920s, and, together with the pronounced slope towards the exterior of the cave, explains the presence of recent materials in most of the levels excavated in the 1950s, since this disturbed level, in some parts reaches, more than one metre of thickness.

Bearing in mind the available biostratigraphic data and the existing information about lithic industry, a new chronological interpretation for the cave deposit can be proposed. Succinctly, it seems that Phase F in Cova Negra should be subdivided in two sections: the upper part, variable in thickness and completely disturbed, which can be assigned to different periods of the Upper Pleistocene; and some levels, in primary position and separated by an abrupt contact, which could be assigned to the Middle Pleistocene or the beginning of the Upper Pleistocene. The identification of *Microtus breccensis* has been determinant to support this interpretation. According to that proposal, the other phases of the sequence at Cova Negra should be correlated with Middle Pleistocene, and they beginning should not be situated far from OIS 7.

Concerning the chronological evaluation formulated in previous works, a necessary change of perception should be assessed. This will have partial consequences in some other issues, such as the nature of the occupation of the cave and the evaluation of the human remains recovered, as well as a review of the archaeological materials from the campaigns of Viñes and Jordá.

The human fossil record

The human remains of Cova Negra are some of the richest Middle Paleolithic collections in the Iberian Peninsula and their study has been published in recent works (Arsuaga *et al.*, 2007). Some part of the collection corresponds to disturbed levels and its chronology remains uncertain. However, other remains were recovered during excavations in the 1950s and their position in the sequence can be assigned imprecisely to the upper half of the deposit that corresponds to phases D, E and F. Only one mandibular fragment associated with one molar could be referred to phase C or D.

Figure 3. Cova Negra. Right upper central incisor, mandibular fragment and right lower second deciduous molar.

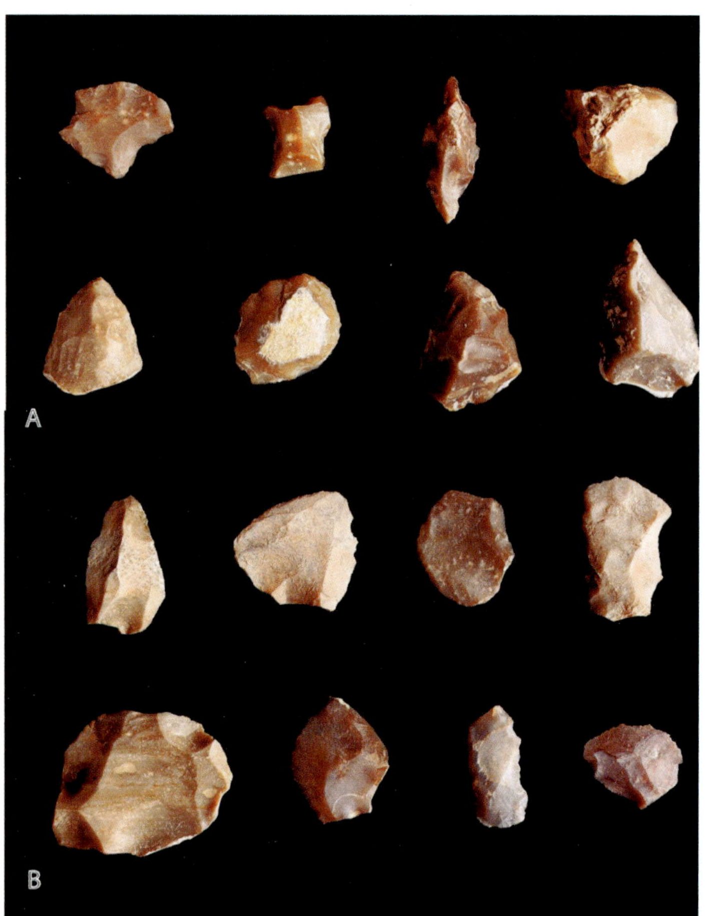

Figure 4. Cova Negra. A. Quina industry from lower levels; B. Levallois industry from upper levels.

The total number of remains recovered until now comes to 26. From the excavations of G. Viñes there are two parietals. One occipital, one incisor, one mandibular fragment associated to one deciduous molar, two femora, one radius, one fibula and two metatarsal bones were recovered at the excavations carried out by F. Jordá. Also, during the excavations undertaken by V. Villaverde, nine cranial fragments, corresponding to right and left parietals, one deciduous molar, one premolar, and one molar were retrieved. Also, we should add the unpublished human remains from the campaign in 2013, one parietal fragment, one cranial fragment, one premolar and one incisor.

In total, according to its position in the sequence and its morphological characteristics, a minimum number of seven individuals can be established: two adults, one juvenile and four infants.

Taking into account the position of the remains in the sequence and the relation of some of them with the superficial disturbed level, it is difficult to establish a chronological attribution. Nevertheless, considering the new chronological proposal, we can recognize this collection as one of the most important evidences of the oldest Neandertal human remains in the Iberian Peninsula, with a similar chronology to the neighbour sequence of the Bolomor site.

All the remains that were assigned to a level or layer in the Viñes and Jordá campaigns correlate with OIS 6 and 5. It should not be ruled out that some human fossils associated with the disturbed level could even correspond to OIS 4 or 3.

The morphological traits do not result discordant with the proposal that moves the chronology of the collection to the end of Middle Pleistocene.

The significant representation of infant individuals should also be stressed, especially considering the lack of these kinds of evidences in other assemblages with similar chronology along the European recent Middle Pleistocene and the beginning of Upper Pleistocene.

Characteristics of the lithic industry

In the sequence of Cova Negra two different flaking methods have been observed: discoidal debitage and Quina retouch associated with the earliest phases (phases A, C and the lower part of D), and Levallois debitage identified in the latest phases (phases F, E and upper part of D). In any case, in phase B Levallois debitage has also been recorded in a representative proportion (Fig. 4).

From an industrial point of view, retouched material is dominated by sidescrapers that reach very high percentages in the whole sequence. Plane and wide blanks predominate in the upper levels, the presence of deviated and transversal sidescrapers should also be highlighted, while thick sidescrapers with Quina and semi-Quina retouch, together with sidescrapers with bifacial retouch, sidescrapers with thinned back and *limaces*, are present in Quina and discoidal assemblages.

Flint is the prevailing raw material, although some fine-grained quartzite and limestone materials with good flaking qualities exist too. In general terms, the low representation of cores is remarkable, as well as lithic debris and scars from retouching. This data, associated with a high proportion of retouched materials, indicates a limited representation of the initial phases of debitage and a large presence of the final stages of the *chaîne opératoire*. These circumstances reinforce the idea of short-term occupations focused on the exploitation of some resources, including previously knapped lithic materials.

Faunal assemblages and their paleoenvironmental and chronological implications

Keeping in mind the complete sequence, it is possible to assess jointly the faunal remains recovered in the campaigns of the 1950s and 1980s, although the inherent constraints of the 1950 fieldworkshould be taken into account considering both the excavation system and the NW-SE dipping orientation.

Cervidae are present along the whole sequence and are represented by three species: red deer (*Cervus elaphus*), fallow deer (*Dama* sp.) and roe deer (*Capreolus capreolus*). Red deer is particularly abundant in the lower levels. It is medium sized and has morphological traits close to the *simplicidens* type from the beginning of the Upper Pleistocene. Fallow deer also appear along the entire sequence, although with a moderate representation. Its anatomical proportions refer to the inferior limited proportions of *Dama dama geiselana* from the end of the Middle Pleistocene and beginning of the Upper Pleistocene. The remains of roe deer are less numerous, and are limited to some of the upper levels.

Goat is also abundant in the upper levels. Its bones could be assigned to two species: tahr (*Hemitragus* sp) and ibex (*Capra* sp). Tahrs from the lower levels of Cova Negra belong to the species *Hemitragus bonali*, however the specimens of the upper levels (II-III) present minor dimensions and morphological traits characteristic of the species *cendrensis*, a well-represented species in the southeast of France, from the end of the Middle Pleistocene and the beginning of the Upper Pleistocene. The large amount of tahr in Cova Negra also reinforces its chronological attribution to the final of Middle Pleistocene and beginning of the Upper Pleistocene.

Equidae, in the same way as other species mentioned above, are also present in the whole sequence, with values that vary substantially among levels. Horse (*Equus caballus*) is best documented species, whereas other remains of small sizes classified as *Equus indet*. might correspond to European ass.

Other identified species, although with few remains, are auroch (*Bos primigenius*), narrow-nose rhinoceros (*Stephanorinus hemitoechus)*, an undetermined rhinoceros, and wild boar (*Sus scrofa*).

Regarding carnivores, up to eight species have been identified in recent campaigns: grey wolf (*Canis lupus*), dhole (*Cuon alpinus*), fox (*Vulpes vulpes*), lynx (*Linx pardina*), leopard (*Panthera pardus*), wildcat (*Felis silvestris*), brown bear (*Ursus arctos*) and hyena (species undetermined). In addition, the presence of lion (*Pantera spelea*), macaque (*Macacus silvana*) and straight-tusked elephant (*Palaeoloxodon antiquus)* registered in the campaigns of the 1950 should be included. Also, on the lower levels, there are abundant coprolites, probably from hyena.

Finally, among the small mammals the presence of abundant remains of lagomorphs, especially European rabbit (*Oryctolagus cuniculus)*, should be included, and a reduced number of hare (*Lepus capensis*), and beaver (*Castor fiber*), are documented at levels IX, III and II.

Among the groups of birds, the number of species represented is very high, reaching 33 species. The most represented are rock dove (*Columba livio/oenas)*, chough (*Pyrrhocorax)*, and red-legged partridge (*Alectoris rufa*).

Materials from the 1980's campaigns enable us to specify trends at phases D, E and F in Cova Negra. On the one hand, there is progressive increase of caprines, dominated bytahr, and a gradual decrease of horses and *bovinae*. Regarding *cervidae* species, they are relatively abundant in levels IV and V, levels, where the *bovinae* also gain importance. In relation to the most meaningful species from an environmental point of view, we can only cite the wild boar, present at levels V and IIIb, the roe deer, present al level IIIb, the narrow-nose rhinoceros, documented at level IIa, and the beaver, present at levels IIIa and II.

The above mentioned species do not facilitate going deeply into the environmental characteristics associated with these tendencies. Only the large number of horses at level VI can be pointed out to indicate the existence of open landscape, combined with forested areas suitable for deer. In the same way, roe deer could confirm the presence of a certain forested prairie. Levels V and IV, where an increase of deer and a decrease of horses and *bovinae* is registered, could correspond to moments of forested area expansion. Level IIIb has a low number of deer, while tahr remains increase. This last species is associated with cool and moist climatic conditions, something that is consistent with the presence of roe deer in the same level, as well as the presence of brown bear, typical of forested habitats. Meanwhile, at level IIIa, the presence of narrow-nose rhinoceros could be signalling the existence of relatively extent open spaces. Finally, level II presents a high percentage of caprines, where tahr is dominant, but brown bear and beaver are also present. In any case, that the presence of carnivores could be responsible for the accumulations in the cavity and that their actions could distort the faunal spectrum should be taken into consideration. Also, the proximity of the river could explain the presence of gallery forest formations close to the cave, being shelter for particular species.

Analyses of microfaunal remains have helped to refine the previous conclusions and above all to specify the chronology of the deposit. On the basis of the taphonomic study over remains recovered, it has been possible to establish that nocturnal birds of prey and carnivores were the main accumulator agents of rodents and insectivores. Specifically, the study of murid molars, which have better supported the postdepositional alterations, has enabled establishment not only of the presence of fox, strix and owl at different levels on the sequence of Cova Negra, but also to associate these accumulations to a lower or higher intensity of human occupation and several factors responsible for postdepositional alterations. In total, microfaunal remains from the 1980 campaigns rose 24,044 units. Distribution by sectors and levels is not equal, since lower levels present larger quantities, while the upper ones, corresponding to the west sector, are the ones with fewer remains. These differences are related to inherent transport factors considering the layers' arrangement, but they are also associated with the different human occupation intensity, which was already mentioned.

The location of Cova Negra, close to the Albaida river, origin of a large number of insects, and its latitude and altitude, provided, during cool oscillations of the Early Würm, different populations of Quiroptera shelter in the cave. A total of 15 different species have been documented in recent excavations deposits. Among the most significant remains there are deciduous teeth, distal epiphysis, not fused to diaphysis, and fetuses that refer to the moment of raising the young by colonies of some species such *Rhinolophus ferrumequinum* (Greater horseshoe bat), *R. euryale* (Mediterranean horseshoe bat), *R. mehelyi* (Mehely's horseshoe bat), *Myotis daubentonii* (Daubenton's bat), *M. nattereri* (Natterer's bat), *M. myotis* (greater mouse-eared bat) and *Miniopterus schreibersi* (common bent-wing bat).

Because of the calm that these species need in their reproductive cycle, their presence in the cave only could be explained if human occupation had very low intensity, which becomes significant data in order to interpret the nature of the occupation by Neandertal populations.

On the other hand, the presence of very old adults together with infants seems to indicate the existence of hibernation colonies of particular species, such as *Rhinolophus* and *Plecotus*, since both, after the end of the winter period and in the same winter, a certain mortality rate occurred at these ages.

All these *Quiroptera* species as well as rodents, build chronostratigraphic sequences that allow the comparison of Cova Negra with other Middle and Upper Pleistocene archaeological sites in a regional context, and also provide key information to envisage the climatic conditions developed during the formation of levels where they appear. Thus, at levels XIV and XIII (Cova Negra phase B) the presence of species that need moist and cool conditions has been registered, although the identification of *Sorex* sp., *Sorex minutus* and *Allocricetus bursae* might indicate a slight nuance of this cold. Level XII (Cova Negra phase C) presents a typical association of mild and moist environmental conditions. There, the insectivores disappear and the relation between murids and voles is typical of mild environmental conditions. Levels XI to V (Cova Negra phase D) present some associations pointing to an evolution from cold and moist to cold and dry conditions, alternated with some mild oscillations. In that sense, levels XI and IX are characterized by the equilibrium between voles and murids, with the presence again of *Sorex minutus*, while at level X insectivores disappear, indicating an amelioration of temperatures. Level VIII has a substantial postdepositional alteration caused by fire, whereas levels VII to V have low number of remains. Climatic characteristics of Level IV (Cova Negra phase E) cannot be defined from microfaunal remains either, since they have poor representation. Meanwhile, at levels III to I (Cova Negra phase F), *Sorex* disappears, *Allocricetus bursae* persists and there is a proportion between murids (39.5) and voles (26.3), indicating drier climatic conditions. In any case, it should be noticed that *Quiroptera* associations reflect mild climatic conditions, typical of the Mediterranean climatic zone at the present time.

From a biostratigraphic point of view, the absence of *Terricola duodecimcostatus* and *Microtus arvalis* in Cova Negra, species that are documented in the Upper Pleistocene deposits of El Salt and Abrigo de la Quebrada, and the relevant presence of *M. Brecciensis*, point to a Middle Pleistocene chronology for the Cova Negra deposit. On the other hand, the reduced length of *Allocricetus bursae correzensis* m1 and the presence of *Arvicola* aff. *sapidus* in Cova Negra, as well as its morphological characteristics suggest late phases of the Middle Pleistocene, without ruling out the inclusion of levels II to III at the start of the Upper Pleistocene. Level I, being very thick and disturbed, would incorporate Upper Pleistocene materials, both from the Middle Paleolithic and the Upper Paleolithic.

The nature of the occupation of the Cova Negra site

The information regarding spatial information is limited to the data provided by the excavations of the 1980s in the west sector and also, some general inferences can be made from the quantification of materials recovered in campaigns in the 1950s. In general terms, occupations in the lower half of the sequence, as well as in the upper section of the sequence, were short-term and spaced between long periods of abandonment. In any case, findings density is particularly low at Cova Negra Phase B (levels XIV and XIII).

Data available from the level III west sector refine the occupation system. Within an area around 12m^2 different ashen spots, associated with fire-cracked stones and rubified sediments were located. These very simple hearths overlapped, creating a real palimpsest that, in turn, imply repeated occupation patterns in a level without a high density of lithic and faunal remains. In fact, some bones show complex superpositioning taphonomic processes. Specifically, data of carnivore toothmarks and anthropogenic cutmarks, suggesting a rapid succession of episodes of human and carnivore occupation. Short-term occupation, associated with accumulations of hunted animals and consumption activities around hearths, were followed by abandonment episodes and reoccupation of the cave by carnivores, responsible both for the scavenging of the food leftovers discarded by Neanderthals and for the incorporation of new faunal remains consumed, particularly tahr bones (*Hemitragus* sp.).

The construction of simple hearths, a low quantity of animals, especially herbivores, and the partially represented reduction sequence of lithic materials, indicate a model of short and sporadic occupations occupying relatively limited surface areas. In this case, an ellipsoidal area, close to the west wall of the cavity and delimited by large fallen blocks, where organic remains and human occupation evidences are concentrated.

This spatial pattern is repeated in the whole cave. Profiles exposed in different archaeological campaigns allow us to notice how accumulations of hearths and organic depositions are concentrated at particular points varying along the sequence. The use of the space was always restricted to relatively limited surface areas. The number of faunal remains recovered at sectors excavated in the 1950's campaigns corroborates the same pattern. Density of bone findings at level IIIB is 17.5 items per m^2, and that of lithic remains is 2.5 per m^2.In the 1950's campaigns, Level III, excavated in a total surface of around 130 m^2, yielded a bone density of 1.9 items per m^2, and 3.9 items per m^2 of lithic remains. Ultimately, the anthropic evidences show spatial variations that also validate a short-term spatially variable occupation pattern concentrated in the most sheltered area of the cave, the southwest sector. This data, that suggests small groups of hominids, is completely consistent with the existence of carnivore accumulations of large and small herbivores, and the repeated presence of colonies of bats for hibernation and raising their young in the cave.

Oreto García Puchol*, Joaquim Juan Cabanilles**, Sarah B. McClure***, Josep Lluís Pascual Benito****, Bermat Martí Oliver *****, Manuel Pérez Ripoll******, Joan Bernabeu Aubán*******, Salvador Pardo Gordó********, Lluís Molina Balaguer*********, Yolanda Carrión Marco*********, Agustín Diez Castillo**********

The Last Hunter-Gatherers in Cueva de la Cocina (Dos Aguas, Valencia, Spain)

1. Presentation

J. Fortea (1973) characterised the "facies Cocina" of the Geometric Epipalaeolithic, attributed to the "Tardenoid" tradition, based on the outstanding archaeological record obtained at the eponymous site of Cueva de la Cocina. This large cave, measuring 20 x 15m, is at 405m a.s.l., in the last foothills of the Sierra del Caballón, between the River Júcar and the coastal plain of Valencia. It is situated in a valley with difficult access (La Canal), at the modern base of Ventana Ravine, which forms part of the drainage of the valley through a vertical exit to the Jalón Ravine. A large lithic assemblage including nearly two thousand geometric armatures, a hundred portable art objects consisting of plaquettes with engravings and remains of paint (geometric linear art) (Fig. 1), and a series of painted motifs on one of the cave walls, interpreted by L. Pericot (1945) as Levantine art and by J. Fortea (1974) as geometric linear art, have captured attention at this key archaeological site for understanding the socio-ecological dynamics of the last hunter-gatherers and first farmers in the western Mediterranean.

Figure 1. Engraved plaquette (geometric linear art) from L. Pericot's excavations.

Research at Cueva de la Cocina goes back to the 1940s, when L. Pericot carried out a series of excavations from 1941 to 1945. The last year's fieldwork provided the fullest stratigraphic sequence by including Neolithic levels in the upper part of the deposit (Pericot 1945). Cocina's international recognition came when J. Fortea (1973) examined the remains from the 1945 season as part of a wider study of the micro-blade and geometric lithic assemblages of the last hunter-gatherers on the Mediterranean side of the Iberian Peninsula. He interpreted the archaeological sequence at Cocina

* Investigadora Programa Ramón y Cajal. Departament de Prehistòria i Arqueologia. Universitat de València. oreto.garcia@uv.es
** Museu de Prehistoria de València –S.I.P.–. joaquim.juan@dival.es
*** Department of Anthropology. The Pennsylvania State University. sbm19@psu.edu
**** Museu de Prehistoria de València –S.I.P.–. josep.ll.pascual@uv.es
***** Museu de Prehistoria de València –S.I.P.–. bernat.marti@dival.es
****** Departament de Prehistoria i Arqueologia. Universitat de València. manuel.perez@uv.es
******* Departament de Prehistoria i Arqueologia. Universitat de València. juan.bernabeu@uv.es
******** Departament de Prehistoria i Arqueologia. Universitat de València. salvador.pardo@uv.es
********* Departament de Prehistoria i Arqueologia. Universitat de València. lluis.molina@uv.es
********** Departament de Prehistoria i Arqueologia. Universitat de València. yolanda.carrion@uv.es
********** Departament de Prehistoria i Arqueologia. Universitat de València. agustin.diez@uv.es

in four phases, two initial Mesolithic phases (A and B, corresponding to Levels I and II in Cocina) and two Neolithic phases (C and D, or Levels III and IV), where the latter were interpreted in terms of the neolithisation of the Mesolithic substrate. At the same time, Fortea began a series of annual excavations that lasted from 1974 to 1981. The results were presented in a brief summary that anticipated their potential interest (Fortea *et al.*, 1981). However, most of the documentation obtained in L. Pericot's excavations and Fortea's fieldwork has never been published.

2. New Research Perspectives

A full study of the site within the context of neolithisation in Mediterranean Iberia has been started with the project HAR2012-33111. Several significant aspects of this process converge in Cueva de la Cocina. A recent programme of radiocarbon dates situate the Mesolithic sequence between the mid seventh millennium and first half of the sixth millennium cal BC (Juan Cabanilles and García Puchol 2013; Perrin *et al.*, i.p.). When calibrated, the most recent dates overlap slightly with the oldest dates for the first Neolithic occupations in the central-southern part of Valencia (obtained at such sites as Mas d'Is and En Pardo).

The Mesolithic sequence is characterised from bottom to top by a regular and standardised flint blade technology which follows a pattern that is common to the late Mesolithic in the western Mediterranean (Castelnovian, upper Capsian) and aimed to made trapezoidal geometric projectiles using the micro-burin technique (Binder *et al.*, 2012; García Puchol and Juan Cabanilles 2012). In the initial phase (Cocina 1 or Phase A, second half of the seventh millennium cal BC) asymmetrical trapezes with abrupt retouching and concave edges predominate, whereas on the turn of the sixth millennium, Cocina or Muge-type triangles with concave sides increase in numbers (Cocina II or Phase B). In this way, the site was visited repeatedly over nearly a millennium, within a mobile strategy of territorial use, possible connected with coast-interior movements as suggested by the significant number of malacological and ichthyological remains. However, the hunting of ibex, and also red deer and wild boar, was the main form of subsistence procurement.

Lithic reduction and food-processing are the main daily activities documented in the material record. In addition, Cocina has yielded an ensemble of Mesolithic portable art objects that is unique in Iberia, and should be regarded as reflecting the symbolic world of the pre-Neolithic groups. Their presence might evoke the particular significance of the place/cave as a special social space. The confirmation of the age of a burial partially excavated in the 1943 season, at the base of the sequence, would add new elements to this interpretation. The hearths described by the excavators would have been the focus of the domestic and social area, located in the front half of the cave.

The Neolithic levels at Cocina reflect a series of poorly-defined occupations yielding some im-

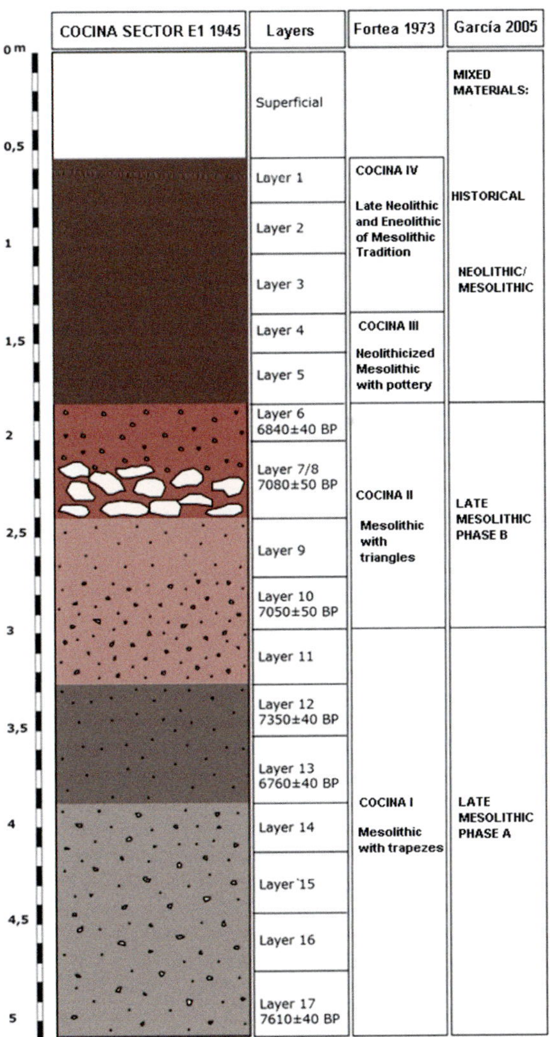

Figure 2. Chrono-cultural sequence at Cueva de la Cocina, after J. Fortea and O. García-Puchol. Ideal stratigraphic section in Sector E1 based on L. Pericot's excavation logbooks.

pressed cardial sherds, characteristic of the earliest Neolithic in the region (second half of the sixth millennium cal BC), overlying the Mesolithic levels. Later visits in the Chalcolithic and Bronze Age have also been documented. J. Fortea proposed an explanation based on the neolithisation of the local population with the introduction of certain Neolithic technological elements, such as the pottery, but hardly any changes in subsistence strategies until the Chalcolithic. A recent reappraisal of the same sector studied previously by Fortea and Pericot (Sector E1 in 1945), focusing on the techno-typological assessment of the lithic assemblage from a diachronic approach (García Puchol 2005) has returned to Pericot's observations and impressions about stratigraphic differences between the levels with pottery and the previous Mesolithic layers. The hypothesis to be tested in the new re-examination of the data, through a programme of chrono-stratigraphic and bio-archaeological analysis, relates to the interpretation of a break between the Mesolithic and Neolithic or the identification of continuity in the terms proposed by Fortea (Fig. 2).

The expansion of the earliest Neolithic towards inland Valencia is marked by finds of a small number of impressed potsherds at sites in the Caroig massif and Sierra del Caballón (including Cueva de la Cocina) and rock paintings classed as Early Schematic Art, reminiscent of decoration on the impressed ware (Martínez Rubio and Martorell Briz 2012). These elements attest the Neolithic advance in a region where a well-structured Mesolithic population existed just a short time before, according to the available radiocarbon dates.

The research described here has been carried out in the framework of the project "MESO COCINA: the last hunter-gatherers and the neolithisation paradigm in the western Mediterranean" (HAR2012-33111) funded by the Ministry of the Economy and Competitiveness of the Government of Spain, and the ANR research program "The last hunter-gatherers of Western Europe" (PI: Pierre Allard).

Michael Walker*†, Mariano López-Martínez**†, María Haber-Uriarte***†

Cueva Negra del Estrecho del Río Quípar (Caravaca de la Cruz, Murcia, Spain)

Cueva Negra is 10 km S of Caravaca de la Cruz, lying at 740 m a.s.l. (metres above sea level) and 40 m above the R. Quípar where it flows northwards out of a gorge ("Estrecho") below the hamlet of La Encarnación (Fig. 1). The large rock-shelter contains a noteworthy depth of Pleistocene sediments cursorily explored in 1981 (Martínez-Andreu *et al.*, 1989). It lies in Upper Miocene (Tortonian) biocalcarenite rock on the right-hand side of the narrow gorge through which the R. Quípar Gorge descends before joining the R. Segura which reaches the Mediterranean Sea 110 km

* Departamento de Zoología y Antropología Física, Facultad de Biología, Universidad de Murcia, Campus Universitario de Espinardo Edificio 20, 30100 Murcia, España. Correo electrónico: mjwalke@gmail.com Tfnº: 34-620-267104

** Calle Pintor Joaquín 10-4º-I, 30009 Murcia, España. Correo electrónico: marianolopez@hotmail.com Tfnº: 34-630-408806

*** Departamento de Prehistoria, Arqueología, Historia Antigua, Historia Medieval y Ciencias y Técnicas Historiográficas, Facultad de Letras, Universidad de Murcia, Campus Universitario de La Merced, Calle Santo Cristo 1, 30001 Murcia, España. Correo electrónico: mariahaber@pi-ma.es Tfnº: 34-629-756183

† Directores de la excavación, *MUPANTQUAT, Murcian Association for the Study of Palaeoanthropology and the Quaternary, Asociación Murciana para el Estudio de la Paleoantropología y del Cuaternario*, http:www.mupantquat.com (Museo Arqueológico de Murcia, Avenida Alfonso X El Sabio 7, 30008 Murcia, España), toda correspondencia a: Secretario de MUPANTQUAT, M.López Martínez <info@mupantquat.com>

† Grupo de Investigación E005-11 de Ciencias Experimentales de la Universidad de Murcia, "*Quaternary Palaeoecology, Palaeoanthropology and Technology*" (Inv.Resp., Dr.J.S.Carrión García, Departamento de Biología Vegetal, Facultad de Biología, Universidad de Murcia, Campus Universitario de Espinardo Edificio 20, 30100 Murcia, España)

E of the site that nevertheless is but 75 km N of the southern Murcian coast. Systematic excavation began in 1990 and 25 field seasons have taken place. For some years neither the chronology nor the complexity of the Pleistocene geology were understood correctly. Inaccuracies and mistaken interpretations in earlier publications were corrected in the 2013 revision (Walker *et al.*, 2013) that supersedes them all and significant aspects of it are summarized here (earlier publications cited here are preceded by indicating they contain some unreliable information, usually a chronological attribution that is too young, sometimes incorrect faunal assignation, occasionally a geological error).

The 5 m-deep Pleistocene sedimentary fill (Fig. 2) is assigned by magnetostratigraphy to the Matuyama magnetochron >0.78 Ma (Scott and Gibert, 2009). Optically-stimulated sediment luminescence implies >0.5 Ma and mammalian biochronology indicates >0.7-<1 Ma (Walker *et al.*, 2013): e.g. the extinct Arvicolid rodents *Mimomys savini*, *Microtus* (*Iberomys/Terricola/Pitymys*) *huescarensis huescarensis*, *Pliomys episcopalis*, *Allophaiomys* (*Microtus/Euphaiomys*) cf. *chalinei*, *Stenocranius* (*Microtus*) *gregaloides*; the extinct Cervids *Megaloceros* aff. *savini* and *Dama* cf. *nestii vallonnetensis*; the Rhinocerotid *Stephanorhinus* cf. *etruscus*; the Equid *Equus altidens*, etc. Sediment micromorphology shows the fill represents near-horizontal, gradual, intermittent fluviatile accumulation (Angelucci *et al.*, 2013) with no significant horizontal or vertical discontinuities (*pace* Jiménez-Arias *et al.*, 2011). Mammals, birds (including waterfowl), reptiles and amphibians corroborate pollen (Carrión *et al.*, 2003) typical of mild (MIS-21), damp, fluvio-lacustrine environments. Anne Eastham identified >60 bird species (Walker *et al.*, 1998) implying nearby biotopes of (1) lakes and rivers with temperate woodland, (2) open mixed woodland, (3) open grassland and

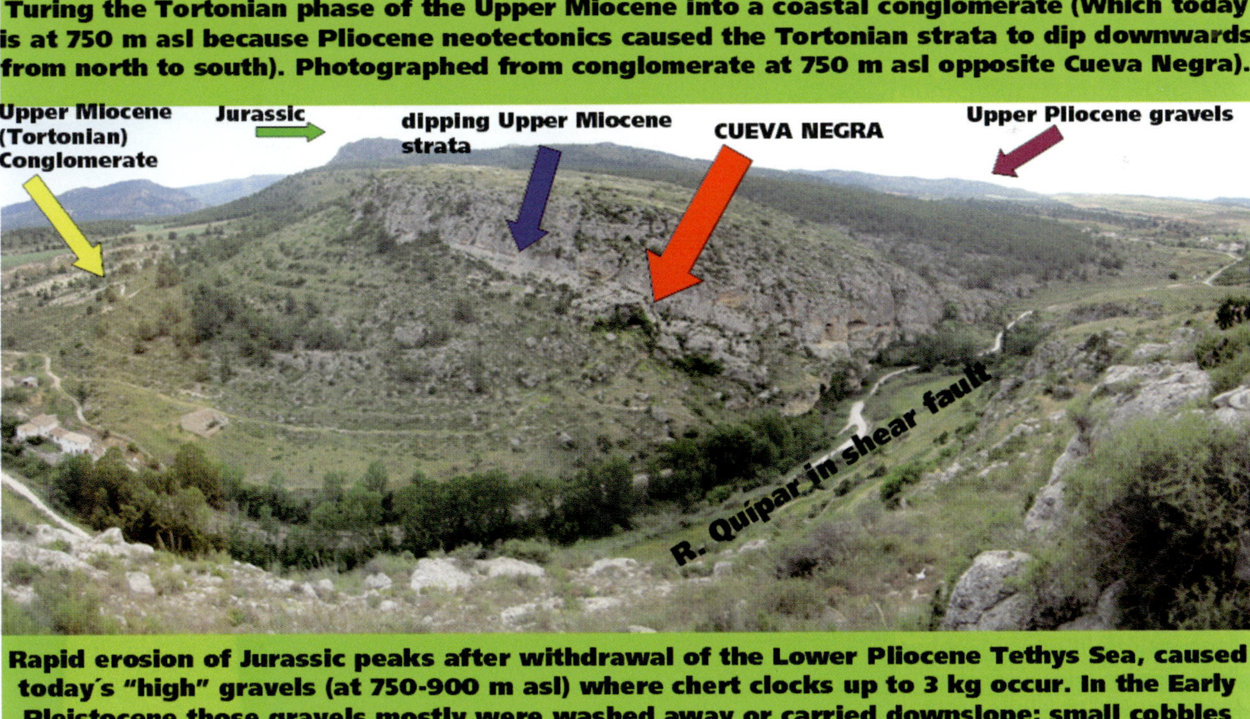

Figure 1.Cueva Negra del Estrecho del Río Quípar in its surroundings.

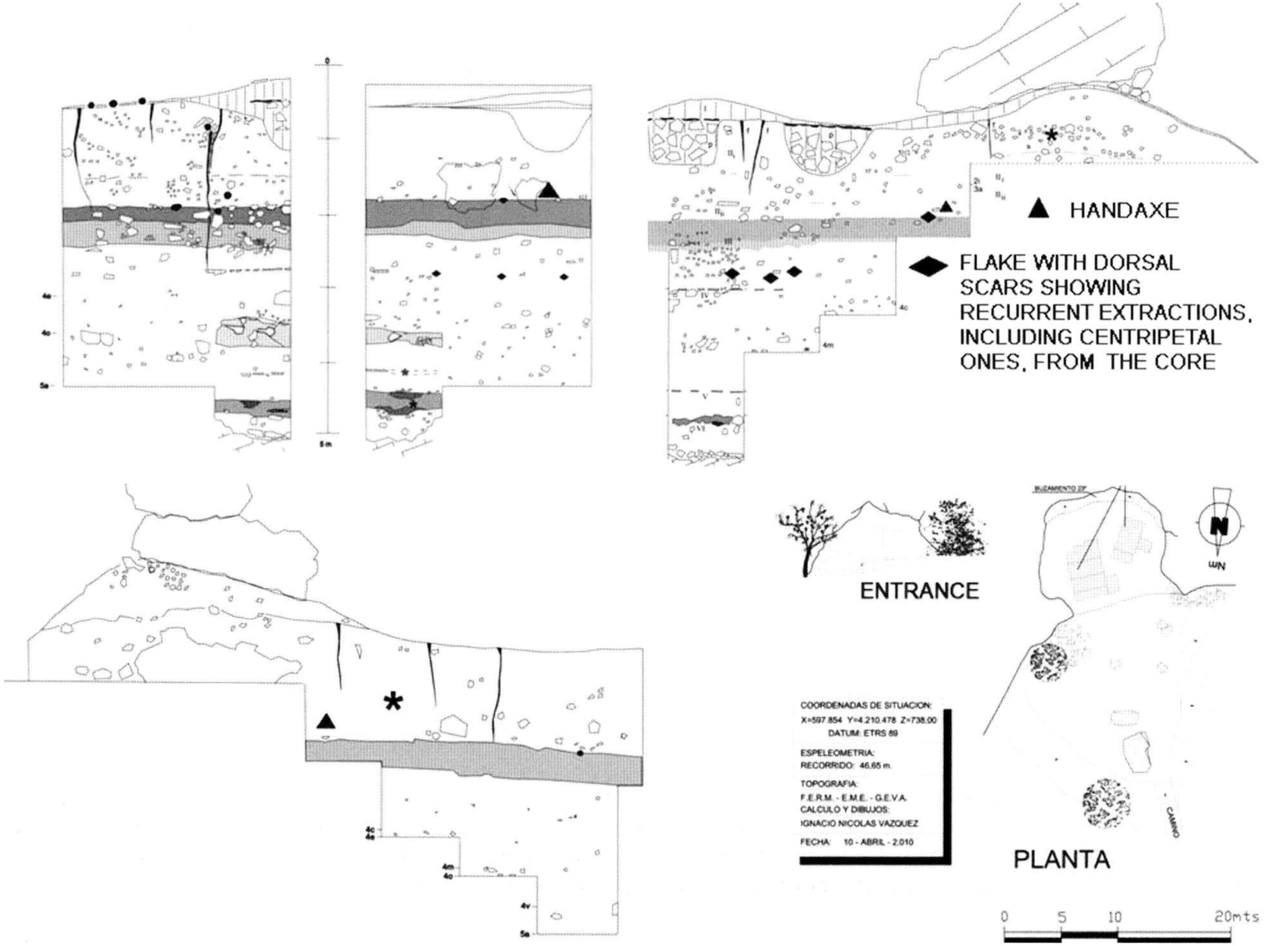

Figure 2. Cueva Negra del Estrecho del Río Quípar: Plan and sections.

heath, and (4) craggy mountainsides. That suggests the site was frequented owing to its well-favoured position in surroundings with noteworthy biodiversity, though it may have been taken over by birds whenever flooding required mammals to abandon the cave, perhaps seasonally.

Cueva Negra "pre-Neanderthal" (*Homo* cf. *heidelbergensis*) teeth (Fig. 3) give several measurements (Table 1) outwith modern ranges; e.g. large antero-posterior measurement at the neck, or cervix, between crown and root (cervical vestibulo– or bucco-lingual dimension), typical in Neanderthals and archaic humans and often interpreted as a "buttressing" adaptation to using front teeth as a vise. Extreme tooth wear (attrition) of Cueva Negra front teeth, exposing dentine and the pulp– or root canal (rendering lingual crown height unreliable and uninformative) is also typical of Neanderthals and archaic humans, perhaps caused by using front teeth as a vise; in modern humans tooth wear and exposure of dentine occurs mostly on crowns of back teeth, only rarely on front teeth. One incisor tooth crown has a "shovel" form (a broad vertical scoop) on its internal (lingual) surface; "shovelling" is common on Neanderthal incisors. A canine tooth with occlusal attrition that exposed the pulp canal has a root that is much longer than in modern humans though comparable in length with some Neanderthal canines (e.g. from Grotte d'Hortus). The two premolars lack transverse crests and are thus unlike Neanderthals (though 17% of Sima de los Huesos premolars lacks them also).

The most important findings at Cueva Negra concern human activity ca. 0.Ma. Two aspects are of especial interest. First, undoubted evidence of fire has been uncovered (Fig. 4), sealed within a 4.5 m-deep layer of sediment 5 m back from the present entrance, perhaps still further back 0.8 Ma if rock overhanging the entrance has undergone erosion since then. Geoarchaeological investiga-

Figure 3. Cueva Negra del Estrecho del Río Quípar: Hand-axe, human teeth.

tions of the sediment suggest combustion (Angelucci *et al.*, 2013) and recent geochemical analysis supports that. Since 2011 excavation has found both thermally-altered, lustreless chert, with pot-lid fractures and conjoined splintering caused by thermal shock to both nodules and artificially-struck flakes, and also charred burnt animal bone and white calcined fragments showing conjoined lengthwise long-bone spalling typical of circumferential shrinkage after thermal volatilization of organic components (Walker *et al.*, 2013). Recent taphonomical analysis and electron microscopy of bone fragments attribute discolouration to burning, not to post-depositional mineral staining, and both Fourier Transform infrared spectroscopy and electron spin resonance analysis of chert and bone imply firing temperatures ca. 550°C (Walker *et al.*, in preparation).

A fire-place is not a hearth. The Cueva Negra humans could have brought glowing brands left by a forest fire into the cave to *establish* and *tend* a fire where rain or wind would not put it out. They may well have been less afraid of fire outside than other animals they saw fleeing from it (which could have led them to play with fire in order to drive animals towards natural death-traps, such as swamps, enabling dismemberment and roasting). This does not mean they could *reproduce* or *control* fire; there is a dearth of archaeological evidence for hearths or fire-pits before 0.5 Ma.

Nevertheless, fire ca. 0.8 Ma supported hominin cognitive versatility, techno-manual dexterity, and palaeoeconomic extractive behaviour in long-vanished Western European palaeoecological and palaeobiogeographical contexts. Cueva Negra exemplifies those aspects; Palaeolithic finds imply resources were exploited as far away as 40 km downstream and 30 km upstream from the site (Zack *et al.*, 2013). That range is unsurprising given that ≥1.3 Ma early humans had begun migrating into Western Europe from northern Africa or western Asia, and therefore they could not have been congenital stick-in-the-muds even though, plausibly, their preferred habitats were localities with abundant biodiversity to hand (cf. ! Walker *et al.*, 2006).

The excavated Palaeolithic assemblage includes a bifacially-flaked "Acheulian" limestone hand-axe, though it mostly consists of small chert, limestone or quartzite artifacts (<60 mm long), knapped on site, often by bipolar reduction or repetitive centripetal flaking of small discoidal ("Levallois") cores, and often showing marginal retouch that is mainly steep-angle (>50°) and sometimes abrupt ("Mousteroid"), and very occasionally invasive or semi-invasive low-angle (<30°) (from the hand-axe to very small chert flakes <30 mm long). Serrated, notched or denticulate edges occur, and pieces bearing one or two large notches are common.

Some flakes and several flattish or laminar subrectangular fragments were knapped to give steep abrupt ("Mousteroid") edge-retouch (Fig. 5). Steep retouch on a piece of flattish laminar chert can transform its perpendicular edge to give an acute angle useful for cutting or scraping. It is plausible to see that as being very different indeed from abrupt retouch of "scrapers" in most Mousterian assemblages where steep retouch applied to thin feathered flakes could spare them from accidental breakage by snapping during use or may have been applied to resharpen a cutting tool. Well-formed feathered flakes with striking platforms and bulbs of percussion are fairly uncommon at Cueva Negra, whereas small fragments of laminar chert abound. Many of the small artifacts seem to have much in common with those from the penecontemporaneous Cat-

Figure 4. Cueva Negra del Estrecho del Río Quípar: Deep layer with thermally altered remains.

Table 1 Cueva Negra fossil human teeth by type, metre-square, layer and spit (right), and measurements taken (below)	right mandibular permanent medial incisor B1i(1)	left maxillary permanent lateral incisor B2f(1-2)	left maxillary permanent canine C3e(2c)	right mandibular anterior premolar C2e(3ñ)	left mandibular anterior premolar C1a(1-2)	anterior permanent tooth root C4g(2c)
incisoapical height	23,0 mm	25,2 mm	27,2 mm	21,9 mm	22,9 mm	no crown
mesiodistal crown dimensión	5,7 mm	7,6 mm	7,0 mm	11,8 mm	6,2 mm	no crown
buccolingual crown dimensión	7,9 mm	9,6 mm	7,8 mm	8,0 mm	7,6 mm	no crown
buccal crown height	7,7 mm	9,6 mm	8,2 mm	9,4 mm	10,4 mm	no crown
lingual crown height	6,1 mm	unreliable	unreliable	unreliable	unreliable	no crown
buccal height of root	15,3 mm	7,9 mm	19,0 mm	14,3 mm	14,6 mm	22,5 mm
mesiodistal dimension at neck	5,4 mm	5,8 mm	6,5 mm	4,6 mm	5,5 mm	7,3 mm
buccolingual dimension at neck	7,7 mm	7,8 mm	8,0 mm	7,7 mm	7,0 mm	8,1 mm
maximal mesiodistal dimension of root	5,0 mm	5,3 mm	5,3 mm	3,7 mm	5,0 mm	5,5 mm
maximal buccolingual dimension of root	8,3 mm	8,7 mm	8,0 mm	6,5 mm	6,9 mm	7,6 mm

Table 1. Cueva Negra fossil human teeth by type, metre-square, layer and spit (right), and measurements taken (below).

alan site of Vallparadís (Martínez *et al.*, 2010) and from the Italian site of Isernia La Pineta, rather than with assemblages ≥1 Ma from Atapuerca and Orce.

From a descriptive viewpoint of stone-knapping techniques the assemblage may be called "Acheulo-Levalloiso-Mousteroid" (Walker *et al.*, 2006; Walker *et al.*, 2013; Zack *et al.*, 2013); this descriptive techno-methodological approach can be uncoupled, viewed epistemologically, from prescriptive ontological typologies influenced by relative chronological inferences drawn tautologically from conjectural "culture history" and pseudo-evolutionary conjectures about Palaeolithic technology.

Once freed from the dead hand of traditional perspectives, other aspects of the assemblage come to the fore. Several small retouched artifacts seem to fall into overlapping groups, in contrast to some other Spanish Early Pleistocene assemblages that have been called "Oldowan" due to perceived similarity to African ones; the term is inappropriate at Cueva Negra because, unlike typically Oldowan artifacts in Africa, nearly all those excavated at Cueva Negra are <60 mm in size. Steep retouch is seen on many pointed pieces; some are flattish pieces and could be regarded as fine points, "awls", or "perforators", whereas others resemble thick "Tayac points" described often in Middle and early Late Pleistocene European assemblages. Pointed artifacts include "becs", small chunks of chert from each of which there projects incongruously a delicate elongated tiny spur, or "beak" (fancifully bringing to mind a small bird head with its beak). There are also many steeply-keeled fragments; some resemble steep scrapers on short stumpy cores, whereas others, knapped into elongated keeled planoconvex shapes resembling garden slugs ("limaces") may be called "proto-limaces". Beaks and slugs could be interpreted as convergent steep scrapers, or where both ends are pointed they could be envisaged as thick double points. However, researchers at 0.7 Ma Isernia La Pineta argue that its beaks and slugs are what were left behind after their reduction by bipolar knapping to remove extremely small flakes used as unretouched tools, backing their argument up with microscopical use-wear analysis and experimental knapping (Crovetto, 1994; Crovetto *et al.*, 1994; Peretto, 1994; Peretto *et al.*, 2004).

Flakes produced by bipolar knapping occur at Cueva Negra, though they are yet to be quantified because quantification of bipolar elements depends on whether carinated pieces with notches, spurs (beaks) and planoconvex double-ended slug-shaped pieces, were outcomes, first and foremost, of bipolar core-reduction to remove usable flakes, or whether, instead, they were primarily fashioned intentionally for use as implements themselves. The two possibilities need not be mutually exclusive because comparable pieces have been interpreted as implements, sometimes supported by microscopical use-wear analysis; an extensive literature exists with references to "limaces", "becs" and "microperforators" from Pleistocene and Holocene lithic assemblages Europe, Africa, and North and South America.

Most Cueva Negra artifacts are "expedient", frequently of "informal" shape, implying "opportunistic" or "eclectic" technological behaviour. They bring to mind the different blades of a Swiss knife. It is perhaps unsurprising that retouch is seen as often on stone fragments as on well-made flakes struck from prepared discoidal cores by recurrent repetitive centripetal flaking, given that at 0.8 Ma secant-plane control of knapping was in its infancy worldwide. It should be borne in mind that such cores are known from 1.3 Ma in Africa (de la Torre *et al.*, 2004) where hand-axes have even greater antiquity (1.7 Ma) and that both of these involved bifacial flaking albeit with different formal secant-plane implications (asymmetrical and symmetrical, respectively), though more eclectic informal ("Oldowan") tool-making continued alongside them. Extraction of regular flakes by recurrent repetitive centripetal flaking of prepared discoidal cores is demanding in both cognitive and technical terms (Coolidge and Wynn, 2005); the putative flakes are, as it were, "hidden" from view (like the yolk inside a hen's egg, so to speak), and "unimaginable" simply from looking at the external shape of the stone before the reduction sequence begins. Evidence at Cueva Negra of both bifacial hand-axe production and recurrent repetitive centripetal flaking of prepared discoidal cores, together with a diverse range of small artifacts, implies manual dexterity, technical aptitude and cognitive versatility.

This raises the question of how those who frequented Cueva Negra 0.8 Ma perceived and exploited their surroundings, particularly where they obtained raw materials for stone tools. Two different matters are relevant. First, how far were the different possibilities of different rocks perceived? Secondly, were outcrops available then that nowadays afford suitable stone?

The hand–axe shows 30 fresh bifacial extractions on a flattish limestone cobble with some cortex still present and a similar cobble had 15 unifacial fresh extractions along one side. Both probably were obtained from fluvio-lacustrine gravels, though X-ray diffraction and petrography indicate that their grey-blue micritic limestone (94% calcite; 6% quartz) originated in Lower Jurassic (Lias) rocks (Walker *et al.*, 2006). An unworked cobble from Cueva Negra is a dismicrite containing 10% quartz, radiolarian fragments, and filamentous planctonic fragments, characteristic of Middle Jurassic (Dogger) strata. Lower and Middle Jurassic beds are exposed in mountainsides upstream from the site. Another unworked limestone cobble from the site lacks quartz, being oolitic sparite (oosparite). Two limestone cobbles from a small conglomerate outcrop 0.8 km E of the site also lack quartz, one being composed of cryptocrystalline limestone pellets of organic faecal origin, the other of sparite cement with microscopical fossils.

The aforementioned conglomerate outcrop is an Upper Miocene (Tortonian) marine conglomerate, containing complete Ostreid and Pectinid sea-shell fossils, that was an inshore Tethys Sea deposit of cobbles and stones eroded out of the nearby mountainside and later cemented by $CaC0_3$ when intense Upper Pliocene and Early Pleistocene neotectonic activity lifted up the mountains and their erstwhile sea-shore to its present height of 750 m a.s.l. (the Tortonian strata dip strongly to the SW and 0.8 km away lie at 730 m a.s.l. below Cueva Negra; the steep dip was not taken into account in some early publications, leading to mistaken interpretations). The cemented cobbles and stones are of limestone, chert and quartzite; several were taken at Cueva Negra and at the outcrop Palaeolithic artifacts have been picked up similar to those of the rock-shelter, including a small prepared discoidal chert core. The chert raw material includes eroded frangible tabular nodules derived from chert blocks or slabs of sub-parallelepiped shape. They are best described as "fissible" (Stein, 1981: 537) because hammering on them often fails to elicit conchoidal fractures or produce feathered flakes with well-developed convex bulbs of percussion. If hammering does not simply shatter the chert blocks into very small chips and fragments, it may split them open along fissible flat planes defined by internal structure or impurities, and produce flattish sub-rectangular laminar fragments available for modifying as tools.

Loose chert cobbles and blocks (some upto 0.3 m across weighing 5 kg) abound <5 km S of Cueva Negra from 770 up to 890 m a.s.l. on the flanks of mountains from whose crags of Jurassic limestone chert was eroded. Massive continental lateral erosion took place in the Upper Pleistocene and initial Pleistocene, leaving high-altitude vestiges of an erstwhile vast gravel spread 100-120 m thick ("raña"; "glacis") containing conglomerate bands, the base of which lies ca. 45 m above the river today (Walker *et al.*, 2013; Zack *et al.*, 2013). Later on, much of that ancient gravel was displaced both laterally and longitudinally and redeposited, owing to ongoing Early Pleistocene erosion induced by falling base level as uplift continued. The process gave rise, in two or perhaps three depositional cycles, to horizontally-bedded outcrops of gravels and fluvio-lacustrine conglomerate that abound at relative heights of 5-25 m above the river today. These outcrops often include noteworthy fossil vestiges of local lakes. The matter is complicated by unequal uplift of the sides of the active longitudinal shear fault along which the R. Quípar runs (unequal uplift saved the Cueva Negra sediments from riverine erosion), and by unequal spatiotemporal activity of those faults normal to it which probably determined development or drainage of hanging lakes upstream in the upper Quípar valley (where it is called the Rambla de Tarragoya). In short, there is a wealth of possible secondary or even tertiary sources of eroded Jurassic chert, but just which were available to Cueva Negra chert-knappers called out for forensic research.

There are also a few small primary chert outcrops. One is of radiolarite ca. 40 km downstream from the rock-shelter where a radiolarite scraper was found in 2013. Another is of light-brown tabular chert at Río Caramel, a tributary of the R. Guadalentín that joins the R. Segura near Murcia; the upper Quípar is separated by a watershed from the Guadalentín river system. It has not been possible yet to determine whether light-brown chert at Cueva Negra came from the outcrop. At high altitude on the watershed itself there is a very small outcrop of biogenic chert that probably formed in a freshwater Pliocene lake, which has the unusual frondose cactus-like form not unlike that of East African Lake Magadi flint; at least one flake at Cueva Negra may well have come from the outcrop. Primary chert outcrops seem not to have been exploited intensively.

Most Cueva Negra chert originated in Jurassic rock strata, albeit obtained from secondary or even tertiary gravel or conglomerate accumulations. Which ones? Petrographically the cherts look much alike. Might help come from chemical finger-printing of chert? Thanks to collaboration with the University of Arizona help came from the laser-ablation inductively-coupled plasma mass-spectrometry of trace elements present in several of the Earth's crustal rocks (Sc, V, Cr, Co, Zn, Ga, Ge, Rb, Sr, Y, Zr, Nb, Cs, Ba, La, Ce, Pr, Nd, Sm). Chert samples were taken from a number of outcrops for comparison with chert from Cueva Negra (Zack *et al.*, 2013).

Multivariate factorial analysis of the data show most chert fragments analyzed from Cueva Negra resemble chert sampled at the Tortonian conglomerate 0.8 km to the E (Fig. 6). A few Cueva Negra fragments more closely resemble samples from fluvio-lacustrine gravel outcrops upstream in the Rambla de Tarragoya as far as the headwaters of the valley (where we even picked up a "proto-limace") ca. 25 km S of the site. Plausibly, variation in trace-element composition cherts that had formed at separate localities or times in the Jurassic is reflected in compositional differences between outcrops of gravels that received chert nodules eroded from the mountainsides nearest by. Some of those cherts were taken to Cueva Negra. Trace-element characterization indicates how far humans ranged.

Research at Cueva Negra throws new light, including fire-light, on the cognitive versatility, manual dexterity and technical aptitude of early humans ca. 0.8 Ma in S.E. Spain. They exploited their surroundings in a competent fashion that implies precise knowledge and accurate awareness of what was available for survival. Research continues both in the field and laboratory at this intriguing late Early Pleistocene site.

Acknowledgements:

We thank all research collaborators named in the text or references as well as palaeontologists Drs. A. Ruiz Bustos, J. van der Made, X. Murélaga Beirucua and archaeologists Drs. D.A. Roe and I. Martín-Lerma for their kind help.

B. Galván*, C.M. Hernández*, C. Mallol*, J. Machado*, A. Sistiaga*, F.J. Molina**, L. Pérez***, R. Afonso*, M.D. Garralda****, N. Mercier*****, J.V. Morales******, A. Sanchís*******, A. Tarriño********, J.A. Gómez*********, A. Rodríguez**********, I. Abreu*, P. Vidal******

El Salt. The Last Neanderthals Of The Alicante Mountains (Alcoy, Spain)

Since 1986 archaeological investigations have been conducted at the site of El Salt (Alcoy, Alicante) attempting to deepen the knowledge of its Paleolithic record from an integrated multidisciplinary perspective. The aim is to understand the MIS 3 Neanderthal population in the central region of the Iberian Mediterranean. The research comprises a wide range of studies, including analysis of site formation processes and the application of archeostratigraphic methods in the dissection of archaeological palimpsests (Machado *et al.*, 2011) with the aim of recognizing and describing settlement patterns, activity areas and the role played by environmental factors.

This enclave is located in a mountain area which has yielded several Middle Paleolithic sites in caves, rock shelters and open-air surfaces. All of them are between the Middle Pleistocene (Abric Pastor) and the end of MIS 3. Some of these places have provided a broad and diversified archaeological record, suitable to address one of the most controversial issues in current Paleolithic research: Neanderthal disappearance.

Despite many studies that have tried to address this phenomenon in Eurasia, macro-regional approaches have not solved the problem, demonstrating the need to promote regional research. In fact, an increasing number of late Middle Paleolithic deposits are reflecting significant variability. In this sense, current research in the Iberian Peninsula offers a complex scenario for the final stage of the Middle Paleolithic and the early Upper Paleolithic (Zilhão *et al.*, 2006; Jennings *et al.*, 2011; Baena *et al.*, 2012; Maroto *et al.*, 2012).

Research by our team in El Salt has recently provided data in conflict with previous models advocating persistence of the Neanderthal population in the Iberian Peninsula. This leads to questioning the role of Iberia as a refuge area for the last Neanderthals groups (Mallol *et al.*, 2012; Wood *et al.*, 2013; Hernández *et al.*, 2013; Garralda *et al.*, i. p. and Galvan *et al.*, i. p.).

This paper summarizes the current state of investigations, with particular attention to the time frame, the sedimentary and paleoenvironment framework, and archaeological indicators, in order to recognize and sequence the context of Neanderthal occupations in the Alicante Mountains during MIS 3.

The site of El Salt

The site is located at the head of the Serpis River, 680 meters above sea level at the confluence of courses and Barchell Polop, two small tributaries. It is now an outdoor locality of about 300 m^2situated at the foot of a 38 m-high limestone wall covered with travertine (Fig. 1b).

The wall corresponds to a thrust fault of Paleocene limestone over Oligocene conglomerates that led to the installment of a large travertine

* U.D.I. de Prehistoria, Arqueología e Historia Antigua. Grupo de Investigación Sociedades Cazadoras Recolectoras Paleolíticas. Universidad de La Laguna
** Dpto. de Prehistoria, Arqueología, Historia Antigua, Filología Griega y F. Latina. Universidad de Alicante.
*** Dpto. de Historia e Hª del Arte, IPHES. Universitat Rovira i Virgili
**** U.D. de Antropología Física. Facultad de Biología. Universidad Complutense de Madrid
***** UMR 5060 CNRS-Université de Bordeaux
****** Dpto de Prehistoria y Arqueología. Universidad de Valencia
******** Museo de Prehistoria de Valencia. S.I.P.
******** Dpto. de Geografía, Prehistoria y Arqueología. Universidad del País Vasco
********* Agencia Estatal de Meteorología. Valladolid.
********* Dpto. de Prehistoria, Historia Antigua y Arqueología. GEPEG. Universidad de Barcelona.

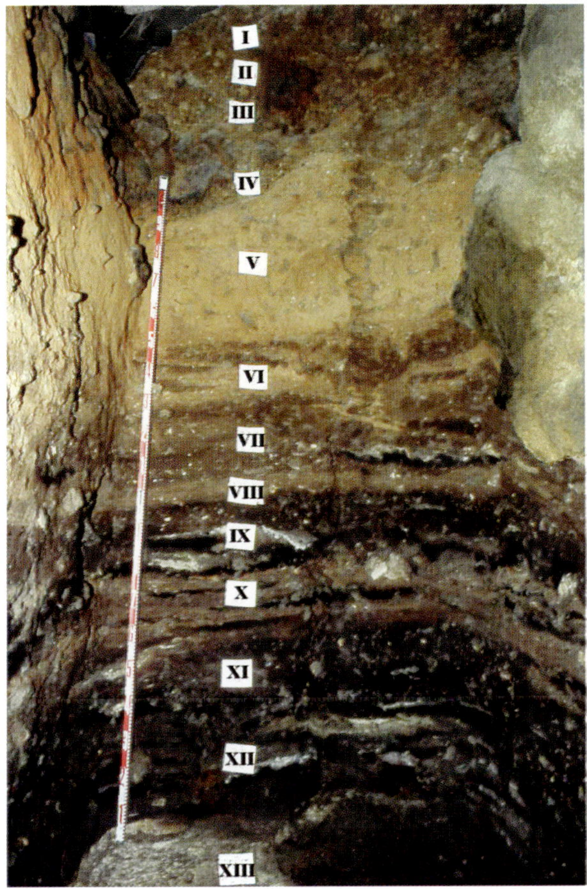

Figure 1. a) Stratigraphic sequence, b) Overview of the site.

formation stretching more than 2.5 km at the foothills of Sierra de Mariola. It is a vast travertine construction linked to the Barchell River. The watercourse was blocked by the limestone, forming a lake whose waters would spill over the tall wall in the form of cascades and waterfalls. This paleolake has been identified by the existence of paleolacustrine travertine and limestone sediments resting on Miocene marls in the area above the site, known as "Cases del Salt".

The space occupied by humans at the bottom of the wall was sheltered by a large travertine overhang, which at times of maximum development covered almost the entire excavated surface. The onset of the projection still remains in place and several associated fallen blockshave been found on the ground about 8 and 10 m away from the wall. The blocks are stratigraphically correlated with the archaeological sequence, indicating that the falls occurred throughout the Neanderthals occupation period.

The human occupation surface next to the wall was relatively flat, with water from the travertine system possibly flowing downhill at about 13 m from the wall, forming ramps and stepped platforms down to the river. In sum, El Salt exhibits a strategic position amidst various biotopes (plain, mountain, river valley, springs and a lacustrine-marshy environment). It is immersed in a mountainous area rich with a diversity of resources.

General description of the archeostratigraphic sequence and chronological framework:

The archeosedimentary deposit of El Salt is 6.3 m thick. It was initially studied by P. Fumanal, who distinguished 13 lithostratigraphic units (Fumanal, 1994) (Fig. 1a). Subsequent work led to subdivision of the sequence into 5 segments, according to their macroscopic textural features, as well as their archaeological content. The description of each segment is presented below, from base to top:

1. **Unit XIII:** This is a lithochemical layer of unknown thickness (>0.50 m), it is archaeologically sterile, dated at the top by J. Bischoff (J. Geol. Survey, USA) to 81.5 + / – 2.7ky and 80.1 + / – 4 ky (MIS 5a) using the Th / U method. It represents a subhorizontal platformat the foot of the fault and has been exposed in different parts of the site. The archaeological deposit rests on this platform. To date, the only evidence of human activity associated with this unit consists of a small area of the platform exhibiting thermal alteration (subcircular, 0.60 m diameter) at the top of the unit, in direct contact with overlying SU XII.
2. **Units XII to IX:** This segment has an average thickness of 1.5 m and is characterized by dark brown, loose, fine sands containing abundant combustion residues.

   These units yielded an accumulation of large travertine blocks, weighing several tons, along with a large number of smaller sized-blocks, interpreted as the first episode of overhang collapse. The accumulation rests directly on the platform (SU XIII).

   On the other hand, Units SU XII to IX are characterized by the presence of frequent combustion features, many of them have been identified as structures; simple hearths of various sizes (0.20 to 1 m diameter). They are primarily located near the travertine wall. These features are usually associated with rich archaeological assemblages composed by abundant anthropogenic faunal remains, lithic objects and limestone pebbles with marks of use. This segment of the archeosedimentary deposit represents a dense palimpsest of recurrent human occupations. Preliminary results of our integrated studies point to the existence of activity areas, these correspond to the generic model of "hearth-related assemblages" (Vaquero and Pastó, 2001; Dorta *et al.*, 2010).This part of the sequence has been dated by thermoluminescence (TL) to between 60.7 +/- 8.9 and52.3 +/- ky (Galvan *et al.*, i. p.).
3. **Units VIII to Lower V:** The thickness of this segment ranges between 1.5-2.8 m and is composed of silty and sandy clay. It is characterized by a gradual decrease in archaeological evidence. For instance, only seven combustion features were documented, compared to 54 hearths in SU IX and X. There is also a significant decrease in the lithic and faunal record.

   Another accumulation of large blocks was identified at the top of SU VI, indicating further roof collapse. This segment has bring in TL dates of 52.3 + / – 4.6 ky to 47.2 + / – 4.4 ky. Lower SU V has been dated by OSL to 45.2 + / – 3.4 ky (Galvan *et al.*, i. p.).
4. **Upper Unit V:** Only 0.50 m of sediment has been preserved, as this unit was partially truncated by an erosive episode of Holocene age. It comprises generally massive sandy silts, capped by a gravelly deposit (the top 0.20 m).This unit is archaeologically sterile except in the mentioned upper coarse part, where two flint blades were found together with several undiagnosed small lithic objects and a small combustion feature. The sterile segment of the unit has been dated by OSL to 44.7 + / – 3.2 ky (Galvan *et al.*, i. p.).
5. **Units IV to I:** This is 1.3 m thick segment consisting of an accumulation of pebbles and gravel in a silty clayey matrix. This Holocene deposit is in erosional contact with the one above. It contains reworked materials of different time periods; mainly late Upper Paleolithic, Epipaleolithic / Mesolithic and early Neolithic.

Human Occupations Older Than 50 ky (Su XII To Ix)

In general, human populations in El Salt seem to respond to a pattern of short duration as manifests different temporal indicators, mainly inferred from the spatial distribution of hearth, units of raw material and lithic refitting. Therefore aspects as the presence of clearly delineated accumulations around combustion structures, with little interaction among them are interpreted as inferred from the relations between their respective materials, the incompleteness of the operational chains, quantitative shortages and unidirectional of refit-

Figure 2. Structure of SU combustion Xa. Plan and profile

ting. The evidence supports recycling of lithic or the importance of geogenic against anthropogenic sediment inputs.

At microstratigraphic scale, there is a low proportion of anthropogenic elements versus geogenic and biogenic soil material (detrital sand, humified organic matter and animal excrements).

The position of the thermally altered objects associated with the combustion structures are basic to establish relationships of synchrony or diachrony among the materials constituting the archaeological palimpsests. Field observations and experimental work have enabled us to determine that the black layers of combustion structures from El Salt were produced by the carbonization of organic matter in the soil on which the fires were made (Mallol *et al.*, 2013). The surfaces of these layers correspond to human occupation surfaces. Consequently, they become fundamental archeostratigraphic landmarks for the study of archaeological site formation processes.

From a diachronic perspective, the remains of combustion exhibit spatial recurrence. The hearths were preferentially located near the travertine wall. Hearths were simple (fire made on the ground), large (1 m diameter) and small (0.60 - 0.20 m). They are often found in clusters.

The combustion structures studied (54) (Mallol *et al.*, 2013) show very good states of preservation (Fig. 2). Some were found intact, including a millimeter-thick layer of calcitic ash with a pseudomorphic cellular structure corresponding to pine wood. . Others are dismantled and display structural features that suggest trampling. According to the latter, the phytolith content and lipid analysis data, the black layers of the studied hearths, which range in thickness from 1 to 3 cm, have a low degree of thermal alteration (<400°). Microscopically, they are mainly composed of soil organic matter (SOM; humified leaves, stems, roots, woody tissue, amorphous organic particles, fungi and spores) in a sandy matrix bioturbated by worms and abundant microfaunal bone and coprolite fragments of different animals, as well asseed coats from the fruits of *Celtis sp.* The representation of flint microflakes, charcoal and bones of meso and macrofauna in the black layers is low and reflects weak anthropogenic impact. The overlying and underlying sediment has a lighter color due to the scarcity of microscopic charred plant remains.

The study of travertine thermal alteration, limestone, flint and fauna reveals that they reached temperatures of 700 °C and 800 °C. Nevertheless the midrange for heat modification is around the 450 °C-500 °C, according to the type of hearths documented in these archaeological units.

In this part of the sequence, episodes of abandonment in the overall context of the stratumhas been perceived despite its homogeneous appearance; its recognition during the excavation process is highly difficult. This has been made possible by a multianalytical approach based on the study of the horizontal and vertical distribution of the soil by the use of GIS, the micromorphological analysis of archaeological series associationsand sedimentary lipid markers due recognition, as well as the presence / absence of chemical markers of human presence. Integrated treatment of this information has isolated these episodes of abandonment from the identification of small levels concerning 1 and 3 cm thick throughout the intervention area.

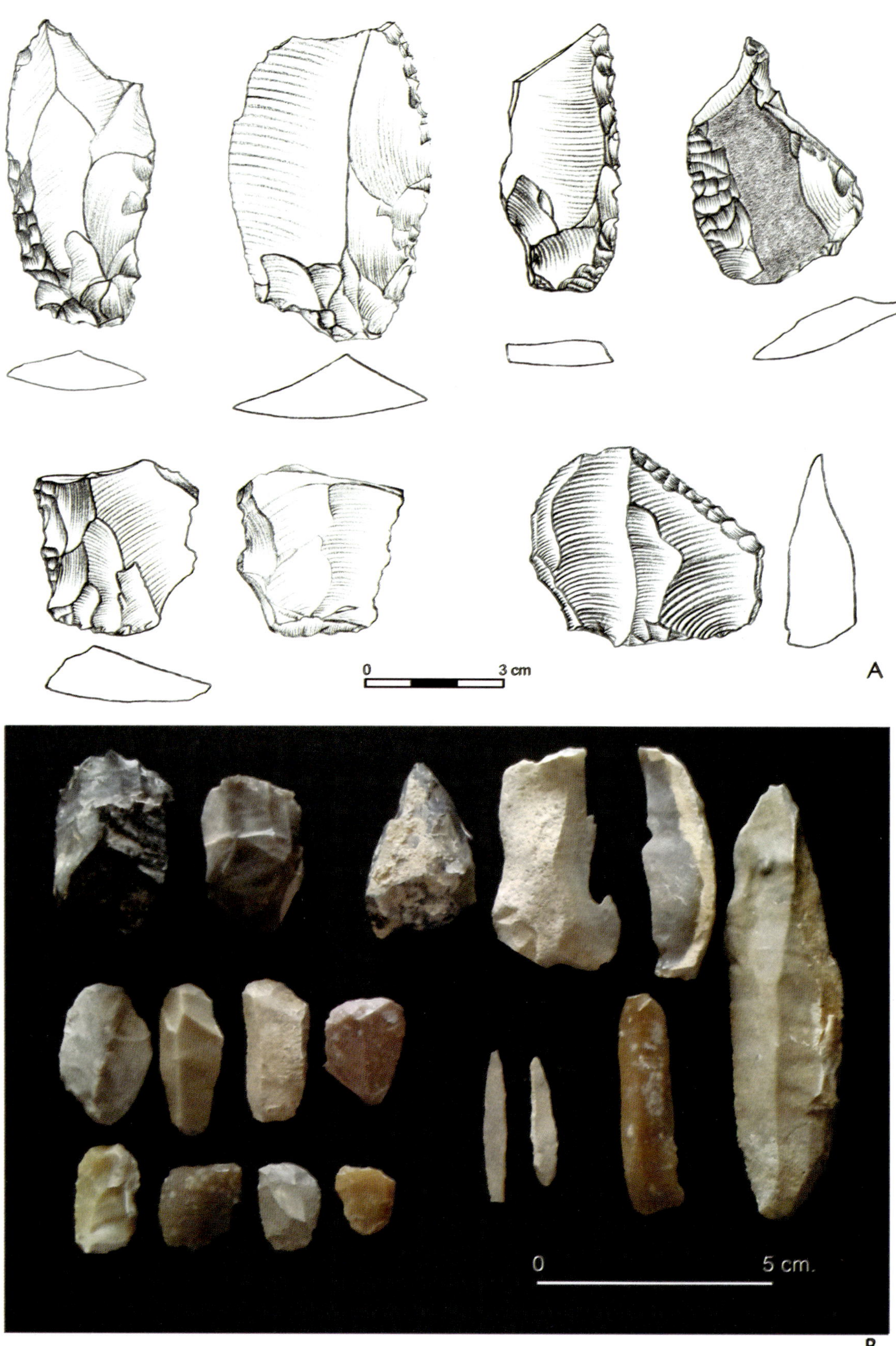

Figure 3. Lithic industry. A) Middle Paleolithic. B) Upper Paleolithic.

The remains of 50 ky previous occupations reflect, although not exclusively, diversified and preferential use of local resources. The lithic raw materials, hunting registration and identified fuels, show a minimum holding territory that is confined to Alcoy valleys environment, characterized by its high biodiversity and accessibility to supply distances around 10 km.

Flints found in El Salt comes mostly from siliceous formations identified in Mesozoic and Cenozoic levels of the Alicante Prebaetic system, formed in marine platform environment (flint-type Mariola, Upper Campanian- Maastrichtian) or reef / toward reef (flint type Serreta-ilerdean or Beniaia, probably ilerdean). The Serreta type is the most widely used not only in this field, but in all places, from the Middle Paleolithic to the Neolithic (Molina *et al.*, 2011). Its acceptance occurred in the Oligocene detrital deposits, where the blocks freed by erosion and resedimented result easier to collect with the technology of Neanderthal groups. During conducted geoarcheological surveys it has been possible to locate capturing areas of this lithological variety with signs of Middle Paleolithic exploitation in Penella. This site is located on the northern slope of La Serreta and Aigüeta Amarga, both within 3 to 5 km radio from El Salt (Molina *et al.*, 2011).

Several tools, retouched or not, were added to the site already configured, while some were collected and reused in the settlement itself. Knapping processes have also been identified, usually ascribed in the Levallois methods and linked to the development of subsistence activities (butcher and vegetable processing, as well as leather and wood working in different states) (Rodríguez *et al.*, 2002) and repair actions of cutting edges (Fig. 3a). A comprehensive set of limestone pebbles with different traces of human manipulation (staking, linear impacts, cuts, wear and fractures) interpreted in the clearest cases as hammers, anvils and retouches increases the evidentiary record concerning to highlighted activities.

The faunal assemblage performs similar pattern to other deposits of the Iberian Mediterranean lift from MIS 3, characterized by exploitation centered on goats *(Capra pyrenaica)*, deer *(Cervus elaphus)* and horses *(Equus ferus* and *Equus hydruntinus)*. Along with these and in a timely manner, we have identified a use of small prey (lagomorphs, *Oryctolagus cuniculus)*.Nonetheless, most of all Leporidae of El Salt relates to the contribution of raptors. Similarly, the presence of bovine *(Bos primigenius)*, turtles *(Testudo hermanni)* and carnivores is timely. Particularly of the latter a unique carnivore dental remaining indeterminate has been recognized, without any evidence of its action on the bone assemblage.

Traces of defleshed bone and intense fracturing reflect faunal exploitation in order to exploit all possible nutrients. The discarded after consumption are distributed throughout the excavation area. There is especially an accumulation near the travertine wall, where the size of the fragment also decreases compared to the outer zone. In the same way, thermal alteration is another constant phenomenon in all archaeological faunal linked to heated waste management and the use of residues as fuel. Our experimental studies helped to raise the possibility that some of the material provided in previous occupations is affected unintentionally by different combustion events made after its deposit.

Neanderthal occupations after 50 ky

This period is represented by the stratigraphic units VIII to lower V and its main feature is the progressive decrease of human impact, compared to the significant increase of geogenic processes in the formation of archaeological sedimentary deposit (Galvan *et al.*, i.p.).

In the stratigraphic unit VIII four combustion structures have been identified and only three in the SU VII, despite widely excavated area (40 m^2). The lower incidence of hearths across this deposit stretch entails a coarser distribution of the materials, without recognizing clear accumulation as described for the oldest sedimentary units. The faunal and lithic record, especially the limestone pebbles with traces of human manipulation also show a gradual downsizing of resources (Galvan *et al.*, i.p.).

At the roof of SU VI a second episode of falling blocks from the big rock shelter overhang is recognized, which marks a turning point not only in the sediment dynamics, also significantly limited since anthropogenic contribution. From this unit, the only evidence of fire is represented by anthracological remains (less abundant than in the previous segment). The lithic, faunal remains, limestone, and travertine also present thermal alteration marks. This reinforces the idea of a gradual and steady process of decline in the Neanderthal footprint at the site among 52.3 + / – 4.6 ky BP and 45.2 + / – 3.4 ky BP, coinciding with the end of Heinrich 5event.

The upper section of this sequence displays sedimentological traces indicative of an abrupt change. Indeed, the SU V is lithological different from the rest of the deposit. It is configured as a massive sand calcite layer, very fine, fresh and well-sorted to fossilize blocks and mega blocks from the collapse originated during the second episode of roof collapse.

This unit must be combined with a high sedimentation rate, given the fresh state of the sand calcite derived from the breakdown of rocky bed and massive structure that presents an assemblage. According to the chronostratigraphic framework provided by TL dates, this process may be hypothetically associated with severe aridification described for the central region of the Iberian Mediterranean during the H5 (Sánchez-Goñi and Harrison 2010).A dry or semi-dry climate context is consistent with the interruption of travertine and limestone bedrock. Both would be subject to a recurring solution and precipitation under humidity conditions. Added to this is the identification of authigenic gypsum crystals in SU VI and V as evidence pointing to the mentioned arid or semi-arid conditions.

In this framework is ascribed the finding of six dental remains(I^1 right, P^3 right, P^4 right, M^1 right, M^2 right and third molar remains, also right) located at the base of the SU V lower in a proper Middle Paleolithic archaeological context (Fig. 4). Its morphometric study has attributed a Neanderthal right hemimaxilla to a young individual (Garralda *et al.*, i.p.). The chronology of these fossils falls be-

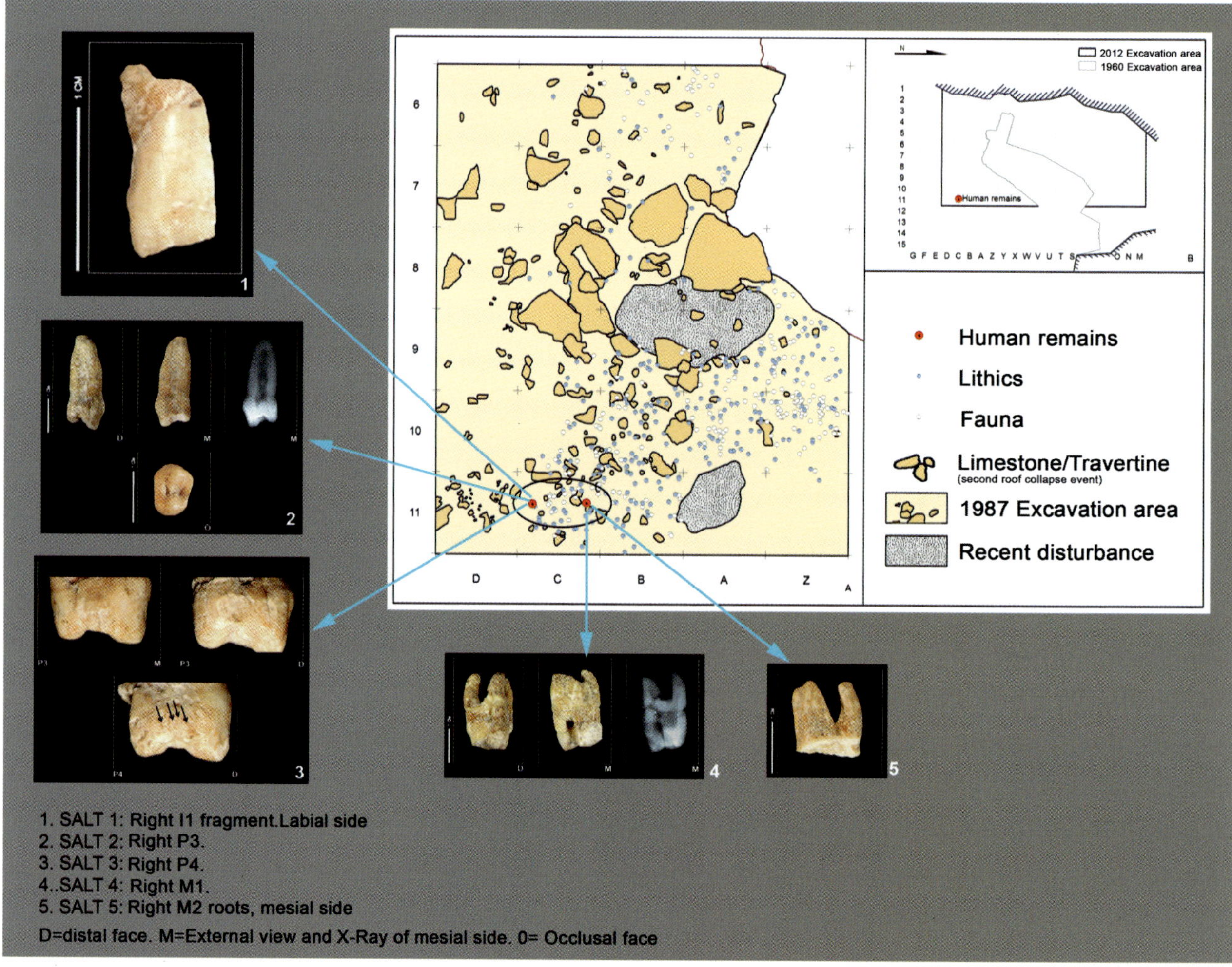

1. SALT 1: Right I1 fragment.Labial side
2. SALT 2: Right P3.
3. SALT 3: Right P4.
4..SALT 4: Right M1.
5. SALT 5: Right M2 roots, mesial side
D=distal face. M=External view and X-Ray of mesial side. 0= Occlusal face

Figure 4. Neanderthals human remains. Plan showing the location of the teeth remains (SU V lower).

tween 47.2 + / – 4.4ky (base of SU V lower) and 45.2 + / – 3.4 ky (roof SU V lower). This suggests that they represent some of the last Neanderthals in the region.

The Upper Su V: The Disappearance Of Human Occupation Evidence From The Middle Paleolithic

This unit has been identified only in the upper zone of the site, along the travertine wall. Its thickness exceeds 0.60 m in some places. These are subhorizontal beds and fine silts and very fine sands with massive structure and diffuse contacts. Specifically some facies of coarse sand and gravel (1-3 mm), with small blocks of limestone (10 cm) scarce and isolated within the thin deposit of this unithave been documented. The entire assemblage goes in the slope direction and out of the wallpackage. Its contacts to wall and roof are fuzzy. The OSL dating of the sediment is 44.7 + / -3.2 ky.

This deposit has been excavated in an area of about 30m^2, and throughout its development any evidence of human occupation has not been located.

At the roof of this unit, in diffuse contact, continues a deposit of about 0.30 m thick and a denser heterometric texture, consisting of silt, coarse sand and gravel. It incorporates lots of fragments and small blocks of limestone and travertine platelets. This deposit thins towards the wall and nozzle in the course of the slope, but its components do not show a preferred orientation. It was excavated in an area of 10 m^2 where it has been able to recover a small lithic assemblage composed by two laminar and some technologically undifferentiated flakes, next to small structure of combustion associated to abundant and dispersed anthracological material (about 700 units) under study. These few elements, sparsely diagnostics from the technological and typological point of view, constitute the first evidence of human presence after the discontinuity described above.

In neighboring Cova Beneito (Muro de Alcoy, Alicante) Middle Paleolithic sequence also crown a thick sterile deposit, similar to that referred to in the El Salt on which subsequent stratigraphic units assigned to early Upper Paleolithicare developed.

This pattern of discontinuity has been described in other Iberian sites (Mallol *et al.*, 2012), suggesting the existence of a depopulation of southern peninsular territory after the Neanderthals' disappearance and before the first signs of the presence of anatomically modern humans groups.

El Salt subsequent to Middle Paleolithic

El Salt archeosedimentary sequence ends with a powerful erosive deposit where, 37 lithostratigraphic facies evidencing the succession of different erosion processes have been recognized. The first, very energetic and fast, hit part of the Pleistocene sedimentation. Nonetheless, subsequent events of variable energy, partially removed the gravel deposit itself, as the channel morphology show in the different layers that comprise it.

The clasticfraction of this deposit filled the karst system of El Salt with sediment. Its output abroad took place after the reactivation of the water circulation. This led to the opening of a cavity in the upper third of the travertine wall and expulsion from their sediment content.

The lithic record provides no doubts about the presence in El Salt of Magdalenian materials, Epipaleolithic / Mesolithic in the sequence (Fig. 3b). Between laminar and microlaminar cores there are diagnostic examples by standardization in the blank obtaining; thus as by the use of soft hammer and pressure flaking. A number of macroutensils are related to macrolithic denticulate facies typical of Mesolithic between the IX and early VIII millennium BP. Bipolar cores and *ecaillées* from the Gravettian and the Solutrean of Hispanic Mediterranean are also present in this data. The most problematic issue is to attribute specific materials to the early stages of the Upper Paleolithic, especially consideringits current redefinition after the controversy between the Aurignacian and the Gravettian (De la Peña, 2013) and the recent detection of anearly Upper Paleolithic in determinate, well described in Cova Gran (Martinez *et al.*, 2012).

The record seems to reveal a ceramic(continuous or discontinuous) occupation that can be bound between the Neolithic IA and the Bell-Beaker horizon transition (5500-2500 BP). The existence of fragments from large containers, especially amphora-like indicate El Salt could have some habitat stability. The transition of Bell-Beaker pottery is providing the *terminus post quem* for the deposition of gravels, being newer material enclosed therein.

Acknowledgments

This article is part of the research undertaken in the project I + D + I HAR2012-32703: *The disappearance of Neanderthals groups in the central region of the Iberian Mediterranean. A methodological proposal for approaching the historical process and paleoenvironmental framework.* (MINECO-FEDER).

Thanks to Camilo Visedo Moltó Archaeological Museum, to the Excmo. Ayuntamiento de Alcoy and the General Direction of Cultural Heritage of the Generalitat Valenciana the support to archaeological research.

Valentín Villaverde*, Didac Román**, Rafael Martínez-Valle***, E. Badal*, P.M. Guillem***, M. Pérez-Ripoll*, M.M. Bergadà****, C. Real*, M. Borao*

Cova de les Cendres

Cova de les Cendres opens to the sea at the cliffs of Punta de Moraira, 60m above sea level. It is a cavity of a certain extent, consisting of an outdoor space with a high vault presenting lots of cenital detachment blocks, particularly on its south wall, and another indoor space reached through a narrowing between the vault and the sedimentary filling of the surface whose final part is partially loaded by the sedimentation (Fig. 1). The archaeological excavation performed in this archaeological site have always been carried out in the inner part, reaching a surface of about 600 m^2.

Figure 1. Cova de les Cendres. The cave´s view.

H. Breuil visited and identified the place as an archaeological site in 1913. However, the first archaological activities were carried out by E. Llobregat in 1974 and 1975 obtaining an important archaeological sequence especially relevant concerning the Neolithic. From the revision of the materials by J. Bernabeu and the identification of a harpoon and several pieces of Paleolithic typology, the possibility of the archaeological site to conserve Pleistocene chronology levels emerged, which is why a survey was practiced in 1981. These activities confirmed, with new materials, the importance of the Magdalenian levels and demonstrated the interest of the archaeological work. After some surveys in later years, the archaeological activities focused on Pleistocene levels have continued from 1995 until now.

Archaeological activities of Pleistocene levels started with a stratigraphic survey in squares A-17

* Departament de Prehistòria i Arqueologia. Universitat de Valencia.
** Departament de Prehistòria i Arqueología. Universitat de Valencia. TRACES UMR-5608. UNiversité de Toulouse-Le-Mirail.
*** IVACOR. Generalitat Valenciana
**** SERP. Universitat de Barcelona.

and B-17, which has continued up to now (Villaverde *et al.*, 1999)advancing the filling features in the two sectors in which the excavation was further developed (Villaverde *et al.*, 2010).In sector A, in the area in which the excavation of Neolithic levels was made, the extension covers between 10m² and 12m², depending on the levels. All the same, the packages corresponding to the Upper Magdalenian have been studied while the archaeological excavation of the Lower and Medium Magdalenian was taking place. In sector B, the archaeological work area has fluctuated between 7m² and 9m² and, although part of the Magdalenian levels was conserved at some points, the storage pits and the Holocene erosions contribute to the information being primarily limited to the Solutrean and the Gravettian.

Pleistocene stratigraphic sequence

The Paleolithic stratigraphic sequence of Cova de Cendres contains a total of 9 levels including, from the roof to the wall, Magdalenian, Solutrean and Gravettian occupations. These packages have a thickness of 3 meters, without reaching the filling basis (Fig. 2). The most recent Pleistocene level is in an erosive contact with the first Neolithic level. Therefore, the stratigraphy presents a sedimentary *hiatus* from the Epigmagdalenian to the geometric Mesolithic. The Holocene sequence goes from level I to VII with a thickness of 3.5 m and includes a rich sequence of different periods of the Neolithic, the Transition of Bell Beaker Culture and the Bronze Age.

Level VIII remains only in some areas, as a great deal of the Neolithic contact with the Pleistocene sequence is preceded by erosive processes. In addition, during the ancient Neolithic, silos were practiced in some areas of the cavity affecting different Magdalenian levels depending on the importance of the previous Holocene erosion. Where itis preserved it has a thickness of 5-7 cm , a red brown color and a high-limestone, cobble, sand, gravels, fraction of little size with the presence of small slabs. Its cultural adhesion is uncertain as the archaeological activity was always done on a very small surface.

Level IX has an unequal thickness reaching 30-40cmin some areas. The structure is massive and includes a few medium to large-sized blocks. It has erosive contact with regard to the underlying unit that sometimes remained totally dismantled. It encloses materials of the Upper-final Magdalenian. Two complete datings have been obtained, one in squarE-13, with a result of 12,740 ± 100 BP, and other in square A-17 with a result of 13,320 ± 170 BP, in this case through traditional C14 and several charcoals, so it is much less reliable.

Level X is preserved in a few areas, as has been pointed out, as a consequence of the Holocene erosions, the Neolithic silos, or the erosive process previous to the deposition of level IX. The structure is lamninated and sterile in archaeological terms. The formation seems to be a consequence of flood processes of the cavity, with deposition of fine sediment stored in calm conditions, probably carried by soft streams from the highest areas of the cavity. It is important to point out that the stratigraphy presents a very strong dip line from the entrance to the back, promoting this type of processes in high-humidity stages.

Figure 2. Cova de les Cendres. Right-sagittal stratigraphic profile of square A-17. Levels XI to XVIA.

Level XI is light-brown in color and includes plenty of little and medium-sized limestone cobbles and gravels of bu-angular to angular morpohology, with a variable thickness of between 10cm and 25cm. It coincides with an intense settlement stage and many charcoals and bone remains are included in its matrix. It presents a laminated structure enclosing several consecutive combustion structures in the sector where it was excavated, protected by the peripheral position of several large-sized blocks, certainly favoring the preservation. The package has been dated on different squares. They correspond for sure to this stage the following dating: 13,220 ± 50 BP, 13,120 ± 60 BP, 13,280 ±50 BP and 13,350 ±50 BP, all of them obtained via the AMS system from a single charcoal. The materials correspond to the Upper Magdalenian with many harpoons and other pieces of antler and bone industry.

Level XII is in an erosive contact with the former and includes two sub-levels. The higher one –A–, with a thickness of about 10cm, is grayish brown in color made by clayey silty sands enclosing limestone pebbles; the lower one –B–, with a thickness of about 24 cm, it is also in erosive contact with the former. Its structure is laminated with a clayey silty texture, a variable color and a presence of limestone fraction of a varying size on its base. The industry corresponds to the Medium and Lower Magdalenian. Its excavation has only been carried out in a survey of a small area but different dating have been obtained via AMS system confirming this attribution: 13,400 ± 50 BP, 13,690 ± 120 BP, 14,510 ± 50 BP, 14,850 ± 100 BP, 15,630 ± 60 BP and 16,030 ± 60 BP.

Level XIII is also in erosive contact with the former; it´s grayish brown color and laminated structure with a variable morphology and thickness in lateral terms, encloses different combustion structures and pulsations of rich coarse limestone, medium and small-sized. Its thickness reaches 35-40cm with a marked dip towards the back of the cavity. The dating obtained via AMS are numerous and confirm its attribution to the Evolved Solutrean with the following results: 16,790 ± 60 BP, 17,210 ± 60 BP, 17,230 ± 130 BP, 18,750 ± 130 BP and 18,920 ± 180 BP.

Level XIV is blade-structured and in erosive contact with the former, alternating orange and blackish lands, as a consequence of the human settlement processes. The coarse material is moderated, with a small size. The thickness presents important lateral variations, with dislocation phenomena and erosive scars which seem to have a post-depositional origin that is difficult to evaluate, as in some areas it is not preserved. A dating corresponding to the level, as it has been removed directly from the profile, has provided a result of 20,200 ± 80 BP. It is therefore the Middle Solutrean, although its industrial mark is conditioned by the narrowness of the excavated surface and the difficulty of the underlying level splitting. In addition, the identification on the archaeological works is difficult.

Level XV presents similar conditions to the former, with a lower thickness and it is also very affected by post-depositional movements. The contact with the XIV is normal but erosive with the XVI. The color is grayish and has a clayey silt sedimentary component. Two datings place it between the 20,800 ± 110 BP and the 21,230 ± 80 BP, indicating a settlement stage of the Lower Solutrean.

Level XVI constitutes at the moment the basis of the archaeological sequence. The thickness is high and to descriptive effects it has been divided in three. The sub-level XVI-A reaches 10-15cm of thickness. It is light brown color and with a massive structure; sub-level XVI-B is of laminated structure, with a loamy component and marked black and light beige variations; its contact with the underlying sub-level is in line with a pulsation of a greater proportion of medium-sized limestone and cobbles; and sub-level XVI-C is also laminated structure, with very pronounced color alternations, loamy and the base seems to be in line with a larger presence of coarse fraction and a block of a certain size. It has only been excavated in a small area, so its features should be specified in greater detail in the future. The thickness reaches 20cm. The three sub-levels have provided materials of a clear adhesion to the Gravettian and are well dated, with the following results: 21,880 ± 100 BP, 23,350 ± 100 BP, 23,860 ± 100 BP, 23,920 ± 100 BP, 24,080 ± 150 BP, 24,240 ± 220 BP, 25,600 ± 140 BP and 25,850 ± 260 BP.

Features of the industries

Lithic industry of the Upper Magdalenian at Cova de les Cendres is characterized by micro-blade group predominance –62,4%–. Burins –7,9%–, scrapers –7%– and edge-retouched pieces –6,7%– also reach certain importance, but with values far from the micro-blade group. The rest of the typological groups are below 4% and the presence of chipped pieces is hardly mentioned.

In the micro-blade group, backsides are thin and direct in almost 90% of the cases, and little blades pointed trough the retouch are the 19.3% of the group and 12% of the total retouched. We could add to these pieces a large deal of little bladelets presenting a natural pointing, with just one retouched edge that does not reach the distal extreme –9.6% of the micro-laminar group and a 6% of the total retouched–. Furthermore, bladelets with reverse retouches reach a high percentage -17.4% of the micro-laminar group and a 1.9% of the total– some of them being pointed.

Another fact to be pointed out is the small size of the micro-laminar tooling, a large amount of pieces being classified as very microlithic A, 15% of the 140 retouched little blades –types 84 to 91– are under 10mm, and 65% are not larger than 15mm, showing us the smallest micro-blade tooling of the Upper Paleolithic and the Regional Mesolithic.

As for bone industry, its richness must be pointed out, both for the tooling and manufacturing wastes. Among the recovered pieces, the large amount of harpoons is especially interesting (Fig. 3), many of them were recovered in the levels corresponding to this period and some pieces are out of context or integrated into Neolithic levels as a consequence of the silos made during this stage. In total, there are 20 pieces representing one of the most important sets of all of the Iberian-Mediterranean coast. Harpoons offer an important variability in typometrical and morphological terms: the lengths are between 73 mm and 163 mm, 12 pieces are made of horn and 8 are made of bone, the oval section –10 models–, quadrangular –5–, flat –3– and round –1–, and the barbs number is between 2 and 12. On the other hand, the bases do not present variations with respect to the shaft, showing only in some cases simple or double extremity bevel. Only some lateral swelling can be pointed out, previous to the first barb. Finally, except for one case, the barb do not exceed the base width, giving them quite a different appearance from the Cantabrian Magdalenian harpoons (Román and Villaverde, 2012).

Most of the harpoons correspond to level XI –11 models–, another 3 correspond to level IX and the rest do not have a defined stratigraphic context.

The rest of the bone industry is composed by batons, needles, points of single or double bevel, some points *à base raccourcie* and many broken point fragments. The ornament is also plentiful, the most part through the drilling of gastropods, mainly *Theodoxus fluviatilis*, and through bivalve´s shells and atrophied deer´s canine teeth.

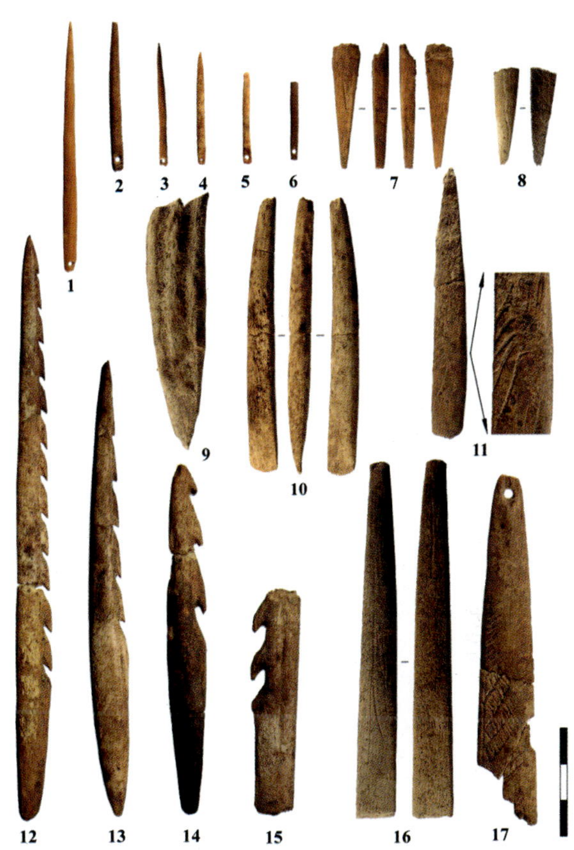

Figure 3. Cova de les Cendres. Upper Magdalenian bone industry.

As the Medium and Upper Magdalenian records in Cova de les Cendres are limited to the survey's information, the existent one is restricted. The lithic industry is dominated again by the micro-laminar group, but with a greater share of scrapers over burins. In addition, there is an average percentage of substrate pieces. Inside the micro-laminar group, the presence of bladelets with inverse and direct retouches and the existence of truncated pieces of backside stand out, allowing a distinction from the higher levels. The presence of points of single bevel and batons deserve to be highlighted, some of them with curvilinear and angular decoration (Villaverde *et al.*, 2010 and 2012).

In the current state of the investigation, only the fact that inside level XII it is possible to establish a micro-laminar stage between the Medium Magdalenian and Upper Solutrean can be pointed out; the distinction of the Badegoulianin Parpalló is significant in regards to the Lower Magdalenian. In any case, it is necessary to wait for the results of the current archaeological activities to precise this part of the sequence in more detail.

From this moment and in sector B, the sequence of Cova de les Cendres presents really complex sedimentary conditions determined by the identification of many erosive processes in the form of fairways and buckets, level thickness, and inclination differences as a consequence of the presence of a stalagmite flow projected in the left sagittal part of sector B causing a dipping of the packages opposite to the sector´s general trend, and a high level of bioturbation. All these circumstances make it very difficult to establish, during the excavation process, the stratigraphy detail. This problem affects levels XIII, XIV and XV.

These reasons explain why the information related to Solutrean is evaluated on global terms, without specifying the features of the diachrony that the assessment of the obtained information suggests or the assessment of the attribution of industry in levels XIV and XV I as just an attempt partly conditioned by the absolute chronology and some quality pieces.

In level XIII, related to Evolved Solutrean, the recovered material exceeds the 5,200 lithic remains, although the number of splinters is very high –64.8%–. While flakes are the main support, the negative dorsal mainly bladed and the balance between full production flakes and the beginning of exploitation and preservation show that the operational chain is intended for the procurement of laminar supports. However, this circumstance is not contrary to the fact that 45% of the flakes have been retouched mainly for the manufacturing of scrapers, burins and pieces with one or both edges retouched.

Laminar flakes reach much more measured values, less than blades, but their presence is significant and probably linked to a small raw material, conditioning the length of the obtained supports. The restructuring by retouch is high, especially in the lower half of the package where they involve 39.4% of the supports. A high percentage of the supports correspond to the full production stage –70%–.

Strictly blade supports reach a value slightly higher than laminar flakes, especially in the lower half of the package. The consistency of the blade production is significant in quantitative terms: the 56.4% of the pieces are blade and the 87.2% collecting the pieces over laminar flakes and bladelets. Most part of pieces correspond to the full production stage –about the 80%–. As in the former supports, the sizes are small and the selection of elongated supports correspond very precisely to the manufacturing of shouldered points.

Micro-laminar supports have very similar quantifications to the blades, and they mainly correspond to the full production stage –70/80%- This part of the production is essentially linked to the retouched little blades and shouldered points.

The cores are well recorded, with a great presence of the ones made on nodule, dominating the exploited in one or two opposite directions.

As for the retouched material, totally296 pieces are collected adding another 73 with retouches of use. The Solutrean set brings 12 laurel leaves points which are present along the whole package, 15 shouldered points, some of them broken, and 7 *pointes à face plane*. Altogether this represents 11.4% of the retouched material. The Solutrean flat-retouch is limited to 20 pieces, 6.4%.

Among the most classic Solutrean pieces, it´s worth noting the presence of a pedunculate point of bifacial retouch, covering just the dorsal face. The parallel of this piece in Parpalló and Ambrosio show that we are not at the end of the evolved Solutrean. Other significant pieces are a willow leaf, a unifacial point similar to the Badegoule type, and an elongated and narrow laurel-leaf point with thin denticulate edges.

Shouldered points present an important size variation. They are produced from high-quality laminar supports; the co-existence of a large format, with lengths between 4 and 6 cm and widths between 1 and 1.2cm, and other small format, between 2 and 3cm long and .6 and 0.8cm wide, can be seen.

The rest of the industry is characterized by a scraper index –15.5– higher than the burin index –9.1–, a large number of pieces with one or two edges retouched –29.4– as well as chipped pieces –10.1– and a considerable presence of micro-blade tooling –7.4– especially in the higher part of the level.

Finally, one of the most interesting novelties of this package is the richness of the bone industry (Fig. 4) and the ornament industry. The number of perforated mollusks comes to 70 pieces, with 14 different recorded species, although the *Theodoxus fluviatilis* concentrates the highest proportion of the specimens –42.8%–. As for the bone and antler industry, we have 19 pieces with a predominance of double antler or bone points –6 specimens–, a rounded basis point, three of polygonal basis, a flat point, two points a single bevel, two perforated needles, two double thin points, one punch and an unclassifiable fragment.

The information obtained in Cova de les Cendres suggests the inclusion of the level XIII industry into the *Solutreo-Gravettian* (Villaverde *et al.*, 2010).

With regard to levels XIV and XV, it is possible that the presence of some *pointes à face plane* could indicate the existence of a Middle or Lower Solutrean stage, although with the information currently available it is not worthwhile to go forward with this subject.

The industrial description of the Gravettian in Cova de les Cendres has been made from the information provided by the survey that is currently being extended through the excavation of sector B (Villaverde and Román, 2004). Although it is possible to observe some differences from the sequential point of view in the carving processes, especially between sub-level XVI-A and the two remaining, XVI-B and XVI-C, and more particularly in the importance of the blade carving, the limited nature of the set –2,088pieces– does not give much importance to this face. We will just comment on the higher proportion of flakes in sub-level XVI-A and a larger presence of micro-blade supports in sub-levels XVI-B and XVI-C. The laminar supports of the three sub-levels present very similar alteration by retouching percentages: 40-45% of the blades and 35-40% of the bladelets. Blades are perfectly positioned between 20 and 35mm, reaching a maximum of 45mm, while bladelets are between 13 and 32 mm.

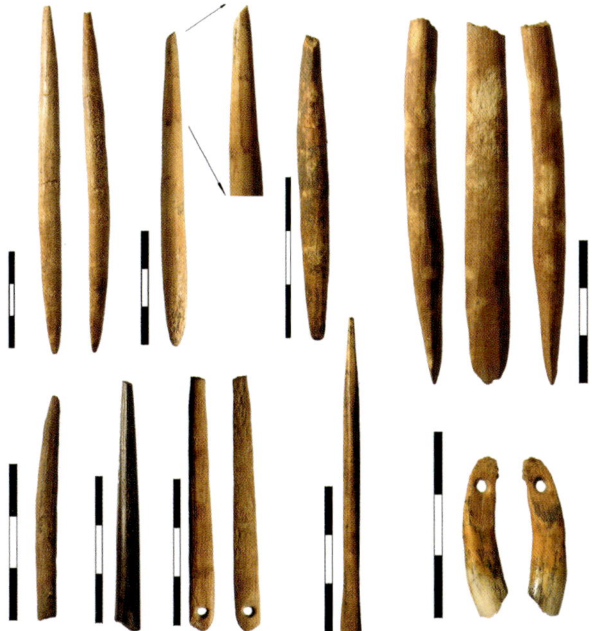

Figure 4. Cova de les Cendres. Bone Industry of the Evolved Solutrean.

The retouched material presents a predominance of the micro-blade group –26.5%–, ahead of the backed group –19.6%–, amongst them Gravette and micro-Gravette points can be highlighted. The presence of Cendres-type points is significant, made from a slight modification of blades with a certain format and a natural direction. Pieces with retouched edges and chipped pieces have a good presence, reaching 11.8% of the retouched. It´s also worthwhile highlighting that burins beat the scrapers, the flat ones and those with flint knapping on truncated pieces standing out.

As for the bone industry, it´s worth while highlighting its richness, although the typology is focused on double points of round-basis or polygonal points. Among the ornaments we find two species of marine gastropods (*Fossarus ambiguus* and *Littorina obtusata*), several *Dentalium sp.*, and two deer´s atrophied canine teeth, one perforated and other with a groove for the suspension.

Fauna: economic and paleoenvironmental implications

Fauna of Magdalenian levels at Cova de les Cendres (Martínez Valle, 1996) presents a high percentage of rabbit remains. This fact, common in most part of the Upper Paleolithic archaeological sequence and the whole area of the Iberian Mediterranean, is particularly important at the moment of establishing models of economic behavior of the human groups at that time. The evaluation of the recovered materials related to a level XI combustion structure at Cendres is significant in this regard. 95% of the remains correspond to this specimen and the most part of the long bones present cut marks from humans. It´s very possible, as almost every bone has chipping marks -jaws, ribs, vertebrae, scapula, pelvis, all the long bones and even some metatarsus- that these marks are related to meat procurement for its preservation through drying techniques (Villaverde and Madrínez Valle, 1995).

Considering the rest of the recorded species, deer is the best represented with a domain of remains belonging to infant, young and sub-adult individuals. The goat is also present, in a much smaller remains number, as well as the horse, and among the carnivores, the lynx, the fox and the wildcat. The enhancement of lynx remains, whose consumption can be seen from the marks, is a feature that will have continuity along the whole sequence. Finally, the presence of some seal remains must be pointed out.

In level XI, *Microtus arvalis* denotes the development of fresh weather conditions (Guillem, 1996). These same features emerge from the study of the bird fauna, where the record of *Pyrrhocorax graculus*, considered as a clear sign of fresh weather conditions, is a highlight.

During the Solutrean, and compared to the former levels, a decrease in the contribution of bone remains to the archaeological site seems to take place, and an increase of the marks made by carnivores and nocturnal birds is recorded. The Solutrean sample analyzed is composed of 6,953 bone remains where the rabbit prevails just as in the former levels –Figure 4–.

The macro-mammals fauna is dominated by the red deer followed by the goat and, in smaller percentages the horse, the auroch, and some carnivores. Red deer hunting is focused on the adult individuals, good size males predominating, and goats and horses, where adults also prevail.

The richness of carnivores´ remains is surprising, especially those of the lynx, whose remains present again torn marks and fractures similar to those observed on herbivores bones indicating human consumption.

The information provided by the Gravettian levels at Cova de les Cendres is especially relevant because it constitutes one of the contributions to this period at Mediterranean level.

First of all, the importance of the hunting and the consumption of small prey in the Gravettian period of the Mediterranean area is determined, particularly the *Orictolagus cuniculus* (Pérez Ripoll, 2004).Their percentage values are similar to the ones of the rest of the Upper Paleolithic sequence. Secondly, the information of Cova de les Cendres offers a higher diversity of the consumed fauna as the most significant novelty with regard to the known information in other archaeological sites of a similar chronology. Thus, as in other sites a clear predominance of red deer and goat remains can be seen, with total values overtaking 80% of the recognized macro-fauna, in the levels of Cova de les Cendres the predominance of these two species is nuanced, as other species like the horse, the auroch and the wild boar reach a certain presence. This information may indicate both a less detailed model than in later periods and a different occupation rhythm of the cavity, with sojourns of shorter duration. Finally, in view of the modest sample analyzed, it´s difficult to determine the ages of the hunted prey, except for indicating that the hunting of sub-adult individuals in Cendres was occasional, with a higher incidence in young and adult individuals.

The Gravettian sequence of Cova de les Cendres has not provided any micro-mammal taxon of very cold weather as the environmental requirements of the analyzed species are included in the bio-climatic thermo-Mediterranean and supra-Mediterranean levels (Tormo, 2010). The best represented specie in every Gravettian sub-level is *Apodemus sylvaticus*, followed by *Terricola duodecimcostatus* and *Microtus cabrerae*.

On the basis of sub-level XVI-C a domain of *Apodemus sylvaticus*is observed, and together with *Eliomys quercinus* would indicate the presence of Mediterranean deciduous forests and scrubland areas. The high percentage of microtinos which require on its biotope open spaces plenty of vegetation and a certain degree of edaphic humidity is also important. In Central Gravettian, an increase of humidity from the remarkable presence of *microtinosis* is seen, above all due to the emergence of *Arvicola sapidus*. The lack of *Crocidura russula* also confirms the existence of wet weather conditions. In the higher part of sub-level XVI-A a decrease of humidity seems to be recorded due to the disappearance of *Arvicola sapidus* and *Terricola duodecimcostatus*. The increasing of arboreal stratum of the black pine and the undergrowth, to the detriment of open spaces, interpreted in the antracological study, is consistent with the recorded species in this level.

Antracological data evaluation

In Cova de les Cendres during the Gravettian-an absolute predominance of Mediterranean pine remains of cold ecology is recorded, such as the *Pinus nigra* together with junipers and shrubs like woody fabaceae, labiates, etc. The most thermopile plants like the Aleppo pine –*Pinus halepensis*- or the *Quercus*, both deciduous and evergreens, have few remains.

The current distribution of these pine species and their ecologic features allow an interpretation about the environmental conditions at the end of MIS3. If we consider the altitude and the latitude where the archaeological sites of the eastern coast are located, we can postulate that the *Pinus nigra* would be on the lower limit of its distribution area, so the average annual temperature could lie between 14°C and 12°C at best, and the rainfalls about 400-600 mm in view of the absence of hydrophilic plants. Also, Mediterranean pines are perfectly adapted to the summer drought because they store a large quantity of water in the trunk.

During the Solutrean a similar flora to the Gravettian is recorded, but the taxa proportions change. The charcoals show an open landscape ruled by junipers and woody fabaceae, although black pines are still the dominant trees. The pine forest reduction may indicate a decrease in precipitations, opposite to the situation in Cova de les Cendres regarding to the continuous curve of evergreen *Quercus*, so it is difficult to choose one of the two options in view of the high tolerance of this flora that is really well-adapted to the Mediterranean droughts.

Finally, during the Magdalenian period the vegetation used by human groups is still the one of the black pine forests which during the Late Glacial were recovered at the expense of the junipers and the fabaceae scrubs. It is worth noting the continuous curve of evergreen *Quercus*, the presence of some deciduous Q. and sporadically, some Aleppo pine (*Pinus halepensis*). This group of plants could be the prelude of a gradual weather improvement of the Late Glacial (Villaverde *et al.*, 2010).

Valentín Villaverde*

Cova de les Malladetes

Location and background

Cova de les Malladetes –Malladetes cave– is in the Mondúver massif, in the Barx municipality. This small cave measuring approx. 135 m² has three NW-facing apertures: the main mouth, another tiny aperture and a small East facing aperture. Its high location, 600 m asl, provides commanding views of the Barx *polje* and the Valldigna depression. The first archaeological work conducted at the site dates back to the period between 1946 and 1949, when excavations by the Prehistoric Research Service were led by Ll. Pericot and F. Jordá. A substantial area was dug, divided into 19 sectors covering more than two-thirds of the potential space. The base of the infill, 4.90-5.50 m below the surface, was reached in the central sections (D, E and F). Less progress was made in others, only reaching 3.15 m in sectors A and B, 3.40 m in sector I and even less depths in the others. The material retrieved from these digs has only been studied partially. F. J. Fortea's Ph.D thesis included an analysis of the packages at the top of the sequence detected in the first test pit excavated in 1946 and sectors F, G and I (Fortea, 1973). This study assessed the Epigravetian and its relationship to the Neolithic. More recently, P. de la Peña (2013) did the same with research focused on the Gravetian. Her study, also part of a Ph.D. thesis, included the 1946 test pit, sectors E, D, F, G, H and I, and the East pit excavated by F.J. Fortea and F. Jordá in 1970 (Fortea and Jordá, 1976). I. Davidson's 1980 Ph.D. thesis included the study of the fauna from the same test pit (Davidson, 1989). The East test pit, located in the sectors corresponding to sectors L and M, along with another in the western part of the cave, adjacent to sector C, formed the second stage of the Malladetes excavations. In this case, the main results were published in 1976 by the authors of the excavation. These two test pits facilitated the sedimentological definition of the infill, a palynological study and a pal-

* Departament de Prehistòria i Arqueologia. Universitat de València.

aeoclimatic interpretation of the sequence by M.P. Fumanal (Fumanal, 1988) and M. Dupré (Dupré, 1988).

Major stratigraphic and palaeoenvironmental features (1970 dig) (Fig1.)

The East test pit shows a stratigraphic evolution that was decapitated at the top when three layers in this sector were excavated in 1949. The detailed description is compulsory reading as this site, scarcely 2 km from Parpalló, has a clear correspondence with the infill of the latter site and permits its sequence to be compared with the other earlier location, with less stratigraphic detail of the infill (Fortea and Jordá, 1976).

Level XIV, the base of the infill, is 30-35 cm deep. Little anthropogenic evidence is limited. This level has a massive sedimentary structure, a fine fraction of clayey-silt sand and clear signs of gelifraction. It has a very pale brown colour. The site was formed under intense cold, with an input of autochthonous material under fluctuating humidity. The pollen record shows scarce arboreal vegetation, corroborating this description.

Level XIII corresponds to more moderate and moister conditions, with heavy runoff. There is

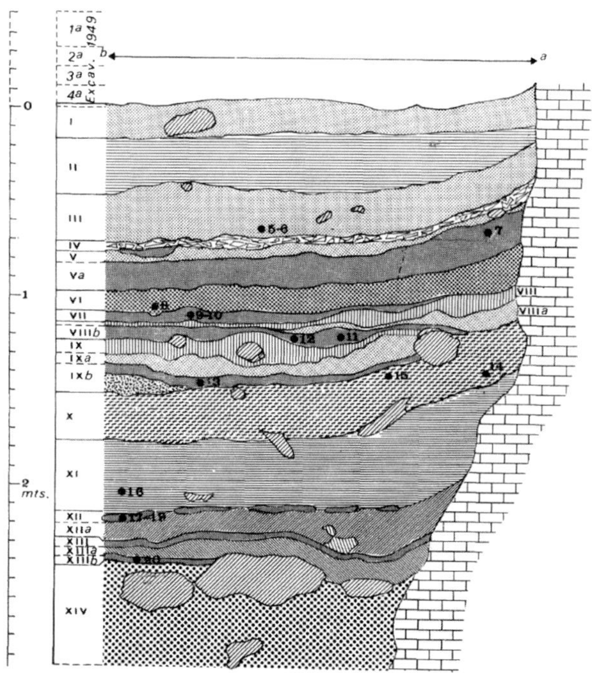

Figure 1. Malladetes cave. Stratigraphic profile of eastern test pit, 1970. (Fortea and Jordá 1976).

little anthropogenic evidence on this level as well. The vegetation shows the presence of a few thermophilic taxa.

Level XII shows a clear decrease in the coarse fraction, in response to runoff erosion facilitated by winter rainfall. The shallow depth might indicate a deceleration of the sedimentary buildup. This level has been dated at 29,690 ± 560 BP. Anthropogenic material remains scarce. There is more arboreal vegetation, primarily pines.

Level XI presents abundant evidence of gelifraction. It is approx. 25 cm deep, also with little evidence of human presence. The vegetation is indicative of low humidity.

Level X shows a change from the previous pattern. It is also roughly 25 cm deep. The coarse fraction has angled edges which indicate a phase of frequent but not intense cold, under semiarid conditions. It is associated with the start of a more intense human occupation. The lack of arboreal taxa corroborates the harsh climate.

Level IX, 20 cm deep, marks a slight impoverishment of the occupation. The coarse fraction still has sharp edges and the sand fraction is larger. It shows signs of intense cold, seasonal rain and little vegetation cover.

Level VIII, 15 cm deep, has a large coarse fraction, with strong signs of occupation in the form of ash and burned material. It is similar to level XI, with less intense freezing in winter. The cold conditions are reflected in the vegetation, with a decrease in *Oleaceae* and the arboreal fraction.

Level VII is shallow (approx. 5 cm) with a massive structure and a moderate coarse fraction. This level marks a crisis in the occupation. The formation indicates slightly damp and moderately cold conditions, or an infill of the gaps in the coarse fraction by the fine fraction from the level above.

In **Level VI**, 15 cm deep, the coarse fraction is not particularly large, with a calcium carbonate crust and a rounded appearance. There is a new intensification of its occupation, dated at 21,710 ± 650 BP. This level seems to reflect cold conditions, less intense than the previous level, with gentle runoff. There is a larger proportion of arboreal pollen.

Level V, 15 cm deep, dark grey-brown, has been dated at 20,140 ± 460 BP. The coarse fraction has a highly evolved aspect with a secondary limestone layer. Its features suggest a more moderate climate with a better rainfall distribution.

Level IV corresponds to a uniform thin (5cm) brown layer with many angular platelets, indicative of gelifraction and a harsh, dry climate. It is archaeologically sterile. No pollen from thermophilic plants has been detected.

Level III is 25 cm deep. It has a massive structure, a brown colour and a moderate presence of coarse fraction. Moisture conditions seem to have favoured the vegetation cover which slowed runoff. It has been dated at 16,300 ± 1,500 BP. The vegetation reflects these conditions, with a large proportion of arboreal vegetation.

Level II is 20 cm deep. It has a brown colour, asmaller percentage of coarse fraction and no aggregate in the fine fraction. It suggests fresh conditions with little moisture. The vegetation cover is stable with the presence of hygrophylous taxa.

Level I, with a partially disturbed upper section, was not studied sedimentologically by M.P. Fumanal.

Industrial sequence and cultural features

The interpretation of the Malladetes infill is primarily based on the analysis of the stone industry found in test pits excavated in 1970 by Fortea and Jordá. This work and subsequent papers mentioning the site (Aura *et al.*, 2006, Villaverde, 2013) also considered data from the excavations in 1940s. However, the difficulty of correlating some sectors with others and certain inconsistencies in the sequential distribution of materials, especially in the Solutrean sequence and higher levels, makes this correlation purely indicative. The start of the Malladetes sequence, as shown in levels XII-XIV, yielded a poor lithic record in both the 1940's excavations and the 1970's test pits, with the exception of a small batch of bone items (Fig. 2) whose typology –three broad-based spear tips made from antlers and two bone awls– brings the Evolved Aurignacian to mind. The dating for level XII is generally consistent with this designation, as is the lack of Gravettian-type items. In this period there was little human presence at the site but no lack of carnivore material.

A comparison between Level XI, linked by Fortea to the previous levels, and the adjacent sectors must include some of the backed items. As suggested by P. de la Peña, this could mark the start of the Gravettian sequence at the site. The period spanning level X to level VIII contains a rich lithic assemblage with technical and typological features that can be correlated with the Gravettian. Specific features include the presence of backed items with a relatively good representation of Gravettes and microgravettes or bladelets as well as the blade and microblade knapping technique with unipolar and bipolar cores. Splintered items, interpreted in some cases as cores used to remove splinters, are also present.

Figure 2. Malladetes cave. Broad based Aurignacian points.

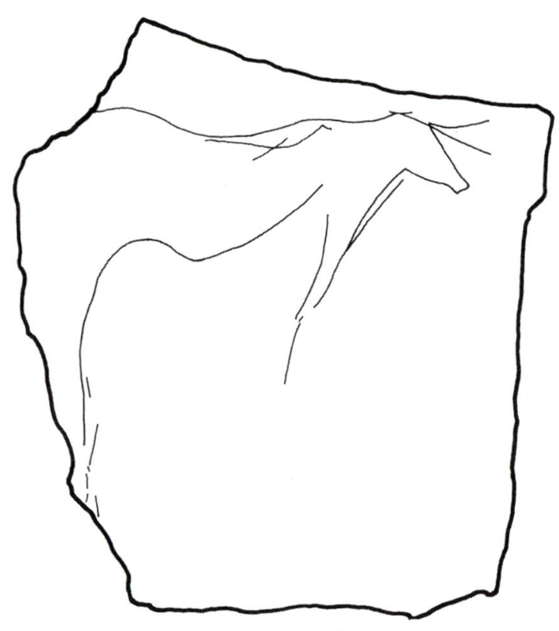

Figure 3. Malladetes cave. Traced uro engraved on Gravettian plaquette (layer 13, sector D).

This layer was the source of two major discoveries in the 1940's excavations. Firstly, the only figurative engraving found at the site (Fig. 3) was found in layer 13 of sector D. One face of the limestone *plaquette* shows an incomplete bovid, with straight horns and a clearly narrowing mouth, engraved with simple, shallow lines. The rump articulated with the foreleg creates a characteristic narrowing effect found in the early phases of the Mediterranean artistic sequence. Although its correlation with the 1970's stratigraphy is difficult, it can definitely be attributed to the Gravetian on the basis of the associated material. Secondly, layer 12 of Sector E yielded important material including a human infant occipital, reconstructed from numerous fragments (Fig 4). This human fossil is associated with several charcoal rests and deer antlers, all in a small recess in the wall forming the boundary of the sector. A sample of the charcoal, collected and preserved in association with the remains, was identified as *Pinus nigra* and dated at 25,210 ± 1120 BP. This is one of the few remains from this chronology located on the Iberian Peninsula, with traits of anatomically modern human populations (Arsuaga *et al.*, 2012).

The period corresponding to levels VI-III is separated from the previous section by a poorly defined level detected in the 1970 excavation, and is difficult to correlate with the 1940's material. Nevertheless, it shows a series of characteristic features found in Iberian Solutrean facies. The first Solutrean presence at this site, identified by a *pointe à face plane*, seems to have been during the Lower Solutrean. The dating obtained for this level is not inconsistent, although there is a large degree of indetermination. Bifacial retouch –without the characteristic features of the evolved Solutrean– permits the attribution of this part of the sequence to the Middle Solutrean. Sterile level IV may cor-

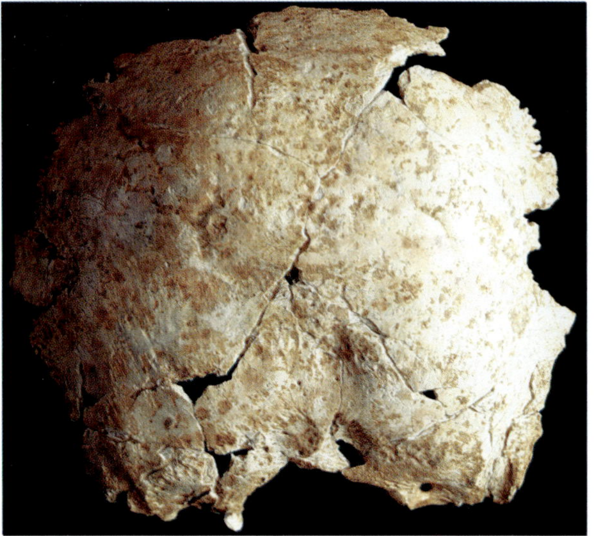

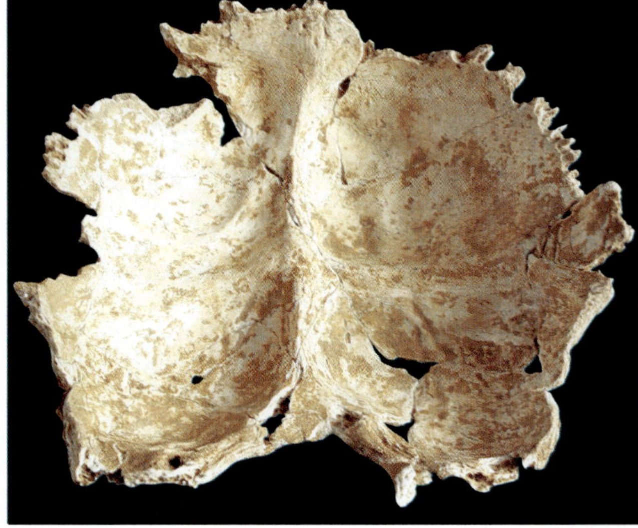

Figure 4. Malladetes cave. Gravettian infant occipital (layer 12, Sector E).

respond to the start of the Upper Solutrean at the Parpalló site, while levels III and II show the typical typological evolution in the Solutrean-Gravettian. Level I is difficult to classify as it contains Solutrean-Gravettian material but, as indicated above, was partially stripped and also contained mixtures of material.

Considerations in recent years suggest that the top of the Malladetes sequence may well include not only Holocene material but also Magdalenian or Epimagdalenian levels, as suggested by some of the items from this phase. More detailed analysis is required for further clarification.

A Reference model for the Upper Magdalenian of the Mediterranean flank of the Iberian Peninsula. Cova Matutano (Vilafamés, Castellón, Spain)

C. Olària*

Summary: The Matutano Cave completes our perspective of the upper-late Magdalenian on the Mediterranean flank of the Iberian Peninsula, evolving in four occupation stages with absolute chronology, habitation structures and a remarkable representation of portable art in all stages.

Keywords: Magdalenian Epimagdalenian, portable art.

Site and location

This site is located within a town, Vilafamés (Castellón), 40°06'50" north and 3°38' east of the Madrid meridian, on the National Mapping Institute's "Vilafamés" Map 616" (E/1:50.000).

The cave is on the western slope of a mountain, *Tossal de la Font*, at the end of the *Les Altures de les Contestes* range composed of Dogger Jurassic limestones which left a karst system with intricate underground networks.

Matutano Cave is 351 m asl, roughly 6 km inland from the coast. Interestingly, this cave is at the rear of a house which was once an oil mill entered from the northwest. This construction disturbed the lip and the upper levels of the cave, which was used as a pen. Its 105m^2 are distributed in a single space (Fig 1).

Opposite the site is a flat area, *Pla de Vilafamés*, an endorheic basin dating from the Pleisto-Holocene and defined as an authentic *polje*, which currently holds water like a lagoon.

Occupation phases

Matutano IV

The first occupation of the cave, probably seasonal, from spring to early autumn, was during the initial Upper Magdalenian. Its absolute chronology is (I-11312): 13.960 ± 200 BP– (UGRA-225): 13.370 ± 260 BP. The climate during this period was cold and wet. This phase includes Levels 5 and 6 of Sector 1 and Levels 6 and 7 of Sector 2. The open landscape included herbaceous vegetation alternating with small conifer forests. The identified living structures include small sub-circular hearths, post holes and cists. The most numerous fauna was rabbit, followed by a considerably smaller number of hare and deer. Remains of goat, horse, wildcat and wolf were also found. There was a low presence of hedgehogs. Bird remains are from partridge, hazel grouse, bustard, chough, dove, little owl and blackbird. The malacofauna includes marine taxa– *Pecten jacobeus*, *Crastoderma*, *Turritella*, *Cerithium* and parts of *Cardiidae*. No terrestrial taxa were found. The fish fauna remains are probably mullet. The lithic industry in this phase was clearly predominated by burins, along with the presence of large flakes used to obtain end-scrapers, a remarkable presence of denticulates and

* Univeristat Jaume I. Laboratori d'Arqueologia prehistòrica. olaria@uji.es

Figure 1. Outside view next to oil mill, and fracture lip. Photo Jordi Mestre.

sidescrapers and a significant use of simple retouch along with retouch with burin. No abrupt retouch has been found in the analyzed lithic assemblage. The bone industry is characterised by the presence of harpoons and spears on deer antler. The presence of perforated needles has been detected in this phase. Tool decorations are linear and geometric votes. The manufacturing technique on the bone objects was found to be by rotation. The majority of the tools are classified as borers. There is a surprising amount of traces of red ochre on this bone industry. Other stone tools include hammers, retouchers, smoothers and sheets of red sandstone. The only adornments are *Pecten jacobeus* and *Cerastoderma edulee* pendants, bored by rotation.

There is also a remarkable presence of portable art, superficially engraved or "graffitied" pebbles bearing figurative representations of zoomorphic horse heads and unidentified hindquarters along with linear strokes, all with abundant remains of ochre.

Matutano III

The second occupation, quite possibly seasonal –spring and autumn–, is from the early-full Upper Magdalenian. Its absolute chronology is between (UGRA-208): 13,220 ± 270 BP and (UGRA-201): 12,460 ± 180 BP, a milder, moist climatic interphase. This phase was identified on Levels 4 and 5 of Sector 2 and Levels 5 and 6 of Sector 3 (Fig. 2). In this meadow landscape, there was a significant increase in coniferous forests and a moderate presence of Evergreen oak. The identified occupation structures include hearth floors, holes for posts or props and aligned stones which formed low partitions leading out from the cave wall, used as dumps for ash and other waste. Here as well there was an intense presence of rabbit and a smaller proportion of hare, while the presence of other species is higher. There was an increase in the number of hunted partridges, followed by rock pigeon. Amongst the malacological remains, there was a significant collection of *Pecten* followed by *Glycimeris*. Terrestrial taxa were scarce, with the exception of Sector 3 where there was a notable presence of *Iberus*. Unidentified vertebrae of marine fish fauna have also been found. The lithic industry continued the former traditions, with a predominance of burins. The base material was smaller, with a tendency to use blades. There was a significant presence of simple retouch and burin

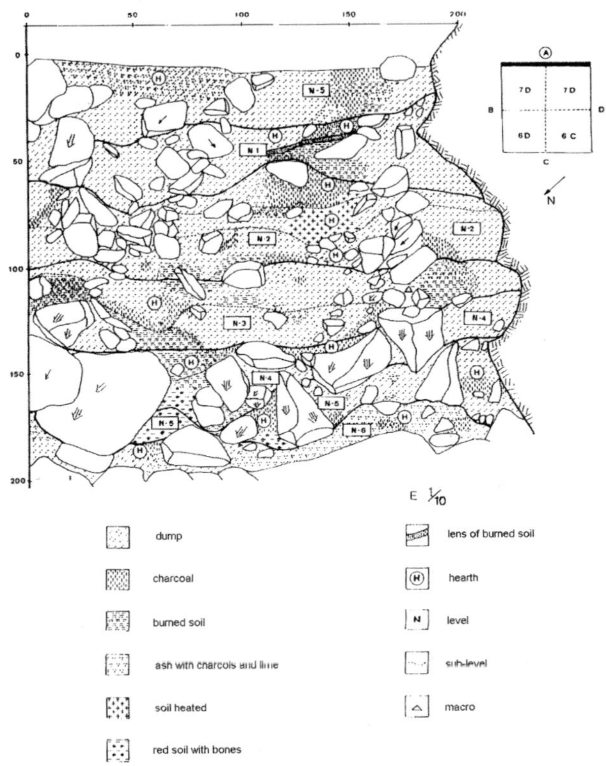

Figure 2. Stratigraphy of section A from Sector 3.

retouch. Abrupt retouch began on backed blades. In the bone industry, the use of deer antlers was reduced and replaced by bone, and there was also a decline in harpoons. The stone industry yielded quite similar materials to Phase IV, retouchers, smoothers, hammerstones and sandstone slabs. Zoomorphs, particularly fawns and deer hindquarters, were still etched on pebbles. Ornaments were limited to shells such as *Glycimeris* with remnants of ochre, perforated by rotation and abrasion.

Matutano II

This level is the third occupation of the cave, probably seasonal (March to October). This Phase corresponds to an evolved Upper Magdalenian. Its absolute dating is (I-11326):12,390 ± 190 BP. The climate was moderately warm and moist, with a considerable increase in tree cover. Domestic structures correspond to medium sized hearths, in some cases adjacent with floors, as well as post holes for props and cists. The diversity of fauna species was greater, particularly notable in increased deer hunting and a significant presence of hedgehog. The bird fauna includes the red-legged partridge, rock partridge, bustard, a significant presence of raptors such as the Lammegier vulture, imperial eagle and golden eagle, and also native species such as the rock pigeon and the red billed chough. The mollusc fauna consisted of marine species *Pecten* and *Naticarius*, while the only inland species detected on Level 3 was *Iberus*, while vertebrae of unidentified fish species fauna were found. In the lithic industry, there was a considerable increase of abrupt blades, backed bladelets, abrupt retouches, backed points and undifferentiated abrupts. The bone industry included spears, harpoons, burnishers, perforated items and grooved decorations. The stone industry featured the presence of retouchers in Sector 3, sandstone slabs and few hammerstones. The portable art included figures representing horse and bovid heads and hindquarters, as well as drawn lines, while the adornments were still *Glycimeris* and *Pecten jacobeus* pendants with traces of ochre.

Matutano I

The fourth occupation of this site, considered to be annual, with an intense hunting season between March and October. The absolute dates are (UGRA-244): 12,520 ± 350 BP, (UGRA-241): 11,590 ± 150 BP and (UGRA-243): 11,410 ± 610 BP, from the end of the Upper Magdalenian or Epimagdalenian. The climate was warm and moist, and the landscape had a greater tree cover along with rangelands and scrub, alternating with grassland in open areas. This Phase corresponds to the surface level and Level 1 of Sector 1, Levels 1, 2 and 3 of Sector 2, and the surface level and

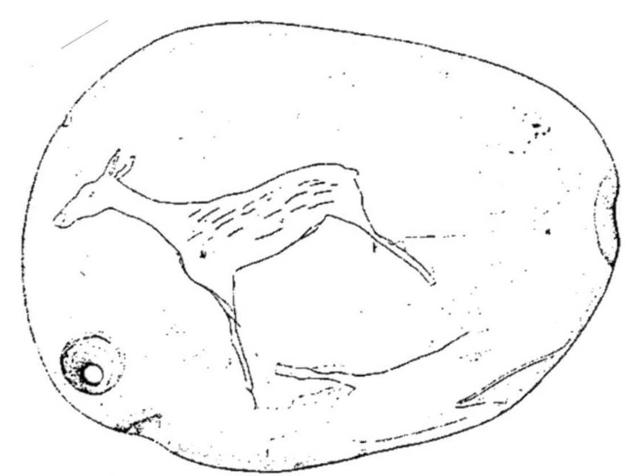

Figure 3. Pebble from Level 4, Sector 2, perforated and engraved with a doe or fawn.

Levels 1 and 2 of Sector 3. The habitation structures were identified by large hearths and low walls used as partitions and spatial divisions. The fauna remains include a broad species diversity and specialized deer hunting. The bird fauna is predominantly partridge followed by great bustard and pheasant, and just one crow. Marine molluscs were primarily *Pecten*, *Glycimeris* and *Cerastoderma*, while terrestrial molluscs were *Iberus Pseudo fachea* and remains of *Rumina*. The fish fauna vertebrae might be from *Mugil* sp. The lithic industry includes a significant number of abrupts, an abundance of abrupt retouches and few burins, with a wide diversity of typological groups. The bone industry included spears and punches on antlers, although the majority were manufactured on bone, particularly in the case of domestic tools: burnishers and wedges. The stone industry showed an increase in the number of hammerstones, retouchers, smoothers and sandstone slabs. Portable art on pebbles included linear motifs and schematic zoomorphs (Fig. 3), while adornmets were made from *Glycimeris* and *Detalium*.

Conclusions

Cova Matutano is an interesting settlement from the end of the Upper Palaeolithic. It completes our knowledge of this period on the Mediterranean coast of Iberia (Olària, 1999) and the overall development of the Upper Magdalenian at Mediterranean sites such as Tossal de la Roca (Cacho, Jordá *et al.*,,i.p., 2001) and Cendres (Villaverde, Martínez, *et al.*, i.p., 1999), amongst others. Its interesting range of portable art provides added interest to this chrono-cultural framework from the initial Upper Magdalenian to the Epimagdalenian (Olària, 2008).

J. Emili Aura Tortosa*
Valentín Villaverde Bonilla**

Cova del Parpalló (Gandía, Valencia)

1. Presentation

The publication of this text coincides with the centenary of the authorization by the la *Junta Superior de Excavaciones y Antigüedades (Real Orden de* 17-10-1914) to excavate at the Parpalló and Calaveres sites requested by H. Breuil.

Unfortunately the global situation prevented him from undertaking the work. A year earlier, Breuil dug a shallow test pit, following the notes drafted by J. Vilanova i Piera, and yielded the first decorated plaquette with engravings. In 1927, Luis Pericot García joined the University of Valencia after a brief period in Paris, coinciding with the establishment of the Servei d'Investigació Prehistòrica of Valencia. He promoted and undertook three seasons of excavations between 1929 and 1931 in conjunction with the service's first director, I. Ballester Tormo.

The first results published by Pericot confirm the importance of Parpalló, a site that had already received some attention since the last 30 years of the 19th century. In the first stage, a deep sequence of 7-9 metres was organized into two large episodes (Magdalenian and pre-Magdalenian levels), noting some issues to be taken up in subsequent work. This was southern Europe's first documented a Palaeolithic Art painted and engraved plaquettes and identified a complete evolution of the Solutrean and Magdalenian. This initial information suggested connections with the Franco-Cantabrian region, with Levantine Art and with North Africa (Pericot, 1942).

Breuil was very interested in having a reference site in the Mediterranean region of the Iberian Peninsula, as reflected in his numerous references to Pericot's work at Parpalló included in the 1937 reissue of his study of "Les subdivisions du Paléolith-

* jeaura@uv.es Dept. de Prehistòria i Arqueologia. Universitat de València.
** valentin.villaverde@uv.es. Dept. de Prehistòria i Arqueologia. Universitat de València.

ique supérieur et leur signification". Iberia's role as a bridge between Europe and Africa was already a central topic of discussion in wich any new data becoming argument for the dissemination processes, its routes and its scope. In this context, Parpalló joined the restricted list of sites used in the first half of the 20th century as a basis for organizing the Upper Palaeolithic sequence in Europe.

A comprehensive monograph on the work in Parpalló was finally published in 1942, coinciding with the global conflict. The World War once again delayed the impact of the results and gave rise to certain misgivings about the sequence and evolution of Parpalló, which have been clarified by various reviews of the material which began in recent decades and are still underway.

Most of the authors who have worked with the material found at Parpalló coincide on two outstanding qualities: its ongoing validity due to its ability to open up new perspectives, and the cumulative nature of results which need to be checked with new sequences. The last 30 years of the 20th century marked a turning point in our understanding of this site. Palaeoeconomic studies and the first radiocarbon datings by I. Davidson coincided with a review of the lithic industries at Parpalló and its regional context by J.M [a]. Fullola Pericot. These results gave rise to an initial profile of the economic system and the regional settlement in the Mediterranean area (Davidson, 1989), while an outline of regional relations with the Palaeolithic in the Cantabrian area and southern France was based on a sequence ranked into three major technological complexes: Gravettian, Solutrean and Magdalenian (Fullola, 1979).

Archaeological seriation, primarily based on typological data, new perspectives in palaeoeconomics, radiocarbon chronology and the regional relationships, steered several revisions of the Gravettian (J. L. Miralles), the final evolution of the Solutrean (V. Villaverde, J. L. Peña and Mª. J. Rodrigo) and the Magdalenian (J. E. Aura). More recently, a revision of the Upper Solutrean by from a technological perspective (Tiffagom, 2006) has begun to extend to the first Magdalenian indications in the Badegoulien facies. Another outstanding contribution has been a technological and functional analysis of Magdalenians endscrapers (Jardon, 2000).

Changes in material culture have often been linked to evolutionary processes in graphic expressions on decorated plaquettes and more recently, on the cave walls itself. Work by J. M. Arias, E. Portell and A. Velasco, supervised by V. Villaverde, began the process of updating the documentary material and reappraising the site's artistic sequence. We should also mention the related study of part of the ornamental material (B. Soler), the study of human remains (J.L. Arsuaga, I. Martínez) and colouring materials (Roldán *et al.*, 2013).

2. Stratigraphy and chronology

Cova del Parpalló –Parpalló Cave– lies on the southern flank of Montdúber, 440 m asl and

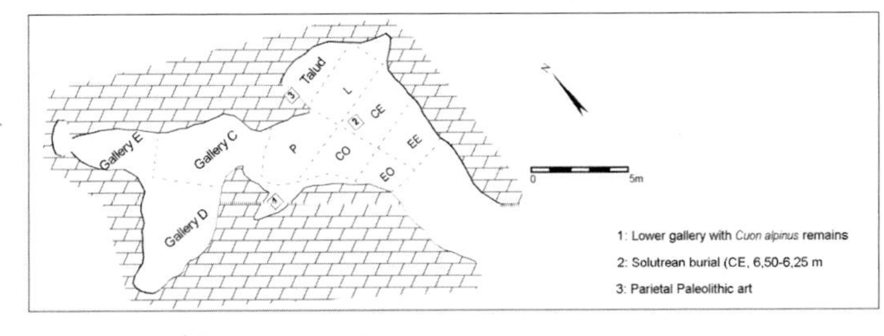

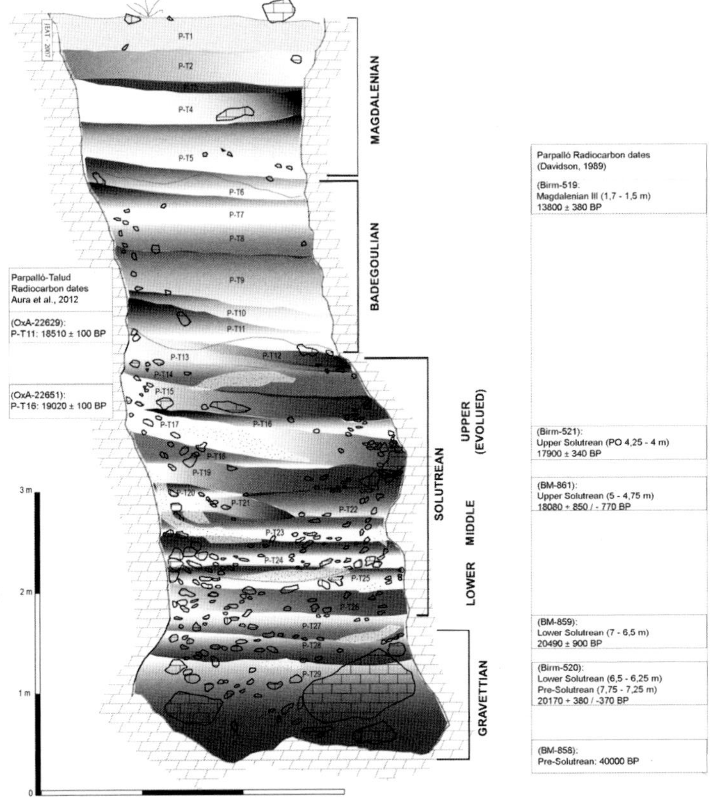

Figure 1. Cova del Parpalló. Stratigraphy of the Talud sector, reconstructed from graphics by L. Pericot (SIP archive), showing levels, radiocarbon datings and main archaeological divisions.

roughly 9 km from the current coastline. The only documented stratigraphy worth a tentative reconstruction is the "Talud". This sector was excavated during the final season (1931) with the stratigraphic section exposed. In conjunction with the data from the previous digs, this led to two changes to the previously used excavation procedures, as the layers were no longer 25 cm thick as mentioned in the monograph, and their profile was irregular, giving rise to different orientations and slope angles (Fig. 1).

Analysis of the photographic series held at the Prehistory Museum of Valencia identified three possible discordant contacts in the Talud stratigraphy, including changes in the dip of the levels, a decrease in the coarser fraction from ceiling to wall, and the detection of cross laminations in the central package. Although this is a limited reconstruction, it is of undeniable interest, as it permits the description of four major episodes that match the main archaeo-stratigraphic divisions (Aura, 1995). The description of these four episodes from wall to ceiling is as follows:

I Massive, horizontal disposition with large angular blocks at the base and whitish nodules. Contact with the following section is erosive and corresponds to layers 29 to 27, which encompass material from the Gravettian and the early Solutrean.

II Graphic documentation shows that this is the most complex section of the stratigraphy. It is a succession of layers whose lenticular arrangement and orientation are reminiscent of an encrusted basin geometry. The coarse fraction is smaller than the section below and contact with the section above is brusque. It corresponds to layers 26 to 11-12, with Solutrean materials.

III Fines, lighter in colour and cobbles scattered more or less horizontally. Coincides with layers 11-12 to 6 and includes Badegoulien material.

IV Massive sedimentation and scattered cobbles. The top of the section is obscured by what seems to be mudflow. Corresponds to layers 5 to 1, with Magdalenian materials.

These layers are presumed to match palimpsests of human occupations, whose rates of accumulation match what is known from other sites. This aspect is also worthy of analysis in the regional settlement context. The density of the anthropogenic material is uneven, with clear differences between the above-mentioned sections. In the Talud sector, a rate of 10 retouched tools per m^3 of sediment is only surpassed after the full Solutrean, with more variable ratios during the Upper Solutrean (8 to 88 retouched objects per m^3), and up to 260 items in the Badegoulien occupations and 350 retouched tools during the Magdalenian. Recently, it has been able to identify a paleontological context in a gallery wall located archaeological sequence in which quite complete remains of a dhole are associated with several skeletal parts of *Capra pyrenaica* bearing bite marks and fractures. Unfortunately, this context could not be dated and we do not know its chronological position with respect to the early Gravettian occupations.

The series of radiocarbon datings by I. Davidson using collagen samples of bone and antler reappraised the age of the regional solutreanization process and a more southerly dating for a Magdalenian assemblage. New datings for Talud, in this case bone pre-treated with ultrafitration, ages the previous results by 0.5 to 1 ky (Fig. 1).

3. Archaeological sequence and techno-economic transformations

The four sedimentary sections and densities are discussed for the Talud section match the techno-complexes described for Parpalló: a Gravetien level at the wall, followed by a thick Solutrean deposit, and a Magdalenian layers in which has identified an initial block related to the Badegoulien.

a) The first human occupations correspond to groups of anatomically modern humans who, on the basis of documentation from the nearby Malladetes site (Villaverde *et al.*, 2010), are presumed to have manufactured Gravettian tools. These occupations are below 7.25 m and have a low density of anthropogenic material, which contrasts with the quality of the raw material employed in regular, well-sized blade products to manufacture a number of endscrapers, Gravettes, microgravettes and backed bladelets. The occasional blade produced with a hard hammerstone, with convergent preparation found in the final stages of the Gravettian. The bone industry is limited to awls and double points with a rounded base. The position of the Gravettian and early Solutrean at the Parpalló site, its radiocarbon chronology and the relationships between the two techno-complexes are open to conjecture, delimiting debate about a critical episode in which new technical traditions were formed.

b) Heat treatment of flint, pressure retouch, bifaciality and tanged points are the most characteristic features of the Solutrean (Fig. 2). Its evolution at the Parpalló site and also at Malladetes has been used as a basis to build a chronological model for the Iberian Solutrean.

- A Lower Solutrean level was defined between 7.25 and 6.25 m, characterized by flat faced points and the disappearance of tools manufactured with abrupt retouch. The human occupations still have a low density of material and a radiocarbon chronology amongst the oldest Solutrean dates.
- The Middle Solutrean is situated between 6.25 and 5.25 m. This period documents heat treatment and flat pressure retouch applied to bifacial lanceolates points; primarily laurel-leaf blades with a convex base and asymmetrical items, although flat faced points have not disappeared completely at this stage. Faceted Solutrean and laminar knapping are the basic techniques, with an increase in bone tools, still focused on double points with a rounded base and the first items with a polygonal base, mostly in bone.
- The Upper or evolved Solutrean coincides with one of the most complex sections of the Parpalló sequence. Pericot identified an evolutionary process between 5.25 m and 4 m, summarized in the replacement of the barbed and tanged points produced using Solutrean retouch by shouldered points with abrupt retouch, the incorporation of bone industry parallel to the disappearance of stone points. This section has been revised in several papers, all of coincide in the proposal of a sequence detailed in several horizons:

Figure 2. Cova del Parpalló. Solutrean lithic and bone industry.

- Upper or evolved Solutrean I (5.25 to 4.75 m) in which Solutrean reduction, heat treatment and pressure retouch techniques are joined by a new morphotype: barbed and tanged points;
- An evolved Solutrean II or Solutrean-Gravetian I is described above this general level (4.75 to 4.50 m), in which there is a substantial decline in Solutrean features parallel to an increase in blade production used to shape shouldered points.
- An evolved Solutrean III or Solutrean-Gravetian II (4.50 to 4.25 m), in which the above features are refined.
- Finally, a Solutrean-Gravetien III or final level (4.25 to 3.50 m) is added to the evolved Solutrean III, at the expense of the first Magdalenian level described by Pericot. In this section there is a substantial drop in shouldered points and a significant increase in antler simple bevel points.

This seriation has sought to describe the transformation of the Solutrean at the Parpalló site, although its impact undoubtedly spread beyond the regional sphere (Aura and Jorda Pardo, 2013; Villaverde *et al.*, 1998). Moreover, the possible incongruence between a long-term Solutrean evolution and the presence of a bone industry –a characteristic Magdalenian feature– can only be resolved by analyzing its incorporation in the context of acculturation-relationship processes between groups which were already fully Magdalenian to the north and still Solutrean further south. When added to this sequence, the first radiocarbon datings lent weight to the perspective that in Parpalló –and also in southern Iberia as a whole–, the Solutrean remained persistent, which directly affects the analytical framework of the early Magdalenian technocomplex.

The Solutrean-Magdalenian "transition" (Aura *et al.*, 2012) is another critical point in the Parpalló sequence. As with the early Solutrean, there was a significant drop in the number of sequences that record this period, possibly caused by erosion linked to the Lascaux interstadial. The assessment of the impact of these processes on the archaeostratigraphy and radiocarbon chronology of the earliest Magdalenian is currently under review.

Pericot identified the first four stages of the French Magdalenian in Parpalló on the basis of changes in bone points, focusing on the shape of the bases and also decorative motifs (Fig. 3). However, a revision of the lithic and bone industries from the first 3.50 m of the sequence has identified Badegoulien traits in the early Magdalenian lithic industries (part of Pericot's Magdalenian II and III), confirmed by technical, typological and decorative convergences with the French Badegoulien bone industries.

The Parpalló-Talud lithic industries have facilitated the description of two major episodes with different productions and typologies.

c) An early Magdalenian on Badegoulien facies has been described above level 3,50 m on Talud layer 11, in fact a "Parpalló type" of Badegoulien, characterized by lithic production aimed at short, broad flakes and blades which were used in turn to produce tools bearing evidence of continuous sharpening. Endscrapers, sidescrapers, notch-denticulates and raclette are the most common tools. Bladelets and microflakes are scarce in Parpalló due to the recovery techniques that were used, however there are several types of cores (on carenated endscrapers, burin-cores and others) which point to small-sized microflake production.

The typological and technomorphological evolution of this Badegoulien at the Parpalló site has been divided into two phases: Badegoulien A (Talud layers 11 through 9) and Badegoulien B, (layers 8-6). Bone industry, primarily using deer antler, show a significant increase and a degree of continuity with the end of the Solutrean. The presence of spears with a long, often concave single bevelled edge, double tips and rounded bases, and some flat tips and rods are the most common types. There are two significant incised decorations: broad bevelled herringbone decorations of the Le Placard type, and a second group of motifs that was largely concentrated into the Badegoulien B, consisting of arms, angles and zigs-zag compositions.

The datings obtained with prior ultrafiltration applied to bone samples situate start of the Badegoulien phase in Talud at 18.5 ky BP. This result has triggered debate about the above-mentioned Solutrean persistence model, the scope of which extends beyond the site itself.

d) The last episode described for the Talud sector corresponds to the Magdalenian blade-

Figure 3. Cova del Parpalló. Magdalenian lithic and bone industry.

microblade knapping industries. These productions are the basic component of industries which included large percentages of microliths tools and a significant presence of burins. The only dating for Pericot's Magdalenian III (section 1.70-1.50m) is around 14 ky BP, nearly 2000 years after the current datings for Cendres' Lower Magdalenien.

The bone industry in this block is also manufactured from antler material that was prepared using grooving technique. Points and rods are the predominant groups, with an increased variation of base material (pointed, rounded, single and double bevelled edges) and sections, primarily angular (square-rectangular and triangular) in larger numbers than round sections in some layers. This toolkit, widely distributed in other sites, included barbed points after 14 – 13.5 ky BP.

The Parpalló sequence probably continued into historic periods, as material attributed to the Mesolithic, Neolithic and even Roman times has been found here (Aura, 1995).

4. Human remains

In addition to the material in the Vilanova i Piera collection, which is probably from the top levels or the upper galleries and thus has an uncertain chronology, Pericot's excavations also discovered scattered human remains in the Magdalenian levels consisting of at least 3 individuals and one burial in the central-east sector which corresponds to the deep levels of the Solutrean, although logically, the burial could have been undertaken from the upper levels.

It is unclear whether the remains were in a grave or covered with piles of stones and earth. The published description only mentions the discovery of a skull and a humerus fragment, possibly from the same individual. The identification of stones around the body, extended to slabs and remnants of a home that could coat the skull, are the only known elements on their context. However, the material found between layers 6.50-6.25m included two tibia whose biometric dimensions suggest that they may be from the young female buried in Parpalló.

5. Parietal and portable art: the importance of the sequence

The collection of portable art in Parpalló is one of the reference points for European Palaeolithic art. The site has contributed more than 5000 decorated plaquettes which span the entire Palaeolithic sequence (Villaverde, 1994). This is particularly important bearing in mind the scarcity of pre-Magdalenian figurative references elsewhere in Iberia. The collection is enriched with bone items bearing Solutrean and Magdalenian figurative representations, along with the documented rock art on the north wall of the main chamber in the area bounded to the west by the Talud sector.

Many of the decorated plaquettes were painted, with and without engraved, which heightened the importance of the collection.

Diachronically, the first plaquettes are from the Gravettian. This is a set of items with figurative representations. In some cases their cultural designation is dubious, while the position of two items in the sequence leaves no doubt about their dating, as they show similar conventions to an item with an identical chronology in the neighbouring Cova de Les Malladetes, thus confirming this chronology for the first known figurative portable art in the Spanish Mediterranean region.

Analysis of the technical and stylistic components of these items in comparison with those at the start of the Solutrean sequence has found a high degree of congruence throughout this long period. This coherence includes the conventions used to draw limbs and heads, body proportions and the articulation of the different parts of the depicted animals. The legs are drawn in three ways on these levels: arched legs, legs drawn with three strokes and legs drawn with two parallel lines which diverge at the extremities. Within the diversity of the zoomorphs in this phase, the heads show solutions with a greater chronological precision: disproportionately small goat heads with long curved horns, combined with details of the ears; a trilinear convention in the depiction of female deer heads, and a falling termination in equine noses. Finally, a narrowing body in the contact area between the belly and the forelimbs, associated with body predominated by juxtaposed anatomical parts and scant attention to naturalistic articulations, and a larger proportion of straight biangular perspectives in depictions of the extremities, as well as massiveness and a tendency for disproportion are all characteristic traits of this early phase of pre-Magdalenian art.

The techniques include the use of double engraved line and a well documented use of paint, including a variety of colours and combinations with engrave. Red, obtained from iron oxide, and black, both organic and mineral, in this case manganese oxide, have been detected in a recent study of the pigments from these periods (Roldán *et al.*, 2013).

The above-mentioned parietal engraved horse can be linked to this phase on the basis of its stylistic features and its position in the sedimentary infill. The association with the barbed sign helps to confirm the "unity" of the early pre-Magdalenian graphic phenomenon in South-western Europe. The differences of these plaquettes from the rest of the Solutrean sequence, allow the possibility of organizing the pre-Magdalenian art, distinguishing between an old and a more recent phase, associated with the most advanced period of the Middle Solutrean and the evolved Solutrean. This proposal is based on the quantitative entity of the 2481 Solutrean platelets found at the Parpalló site, which includes 386 zoomorphs, well distributed between the earlier phase and the period corresponding to the more recent pre-Magdalenian art. The fact that 64 painted zoomorphs (95.5% of zoomorphs in this technique) correspond to pre-Magdalenian art is also indicative of the importance of the art from this period in the Parpalló sequence (Fig. 4).

The distinctive traits include the abandonment of the biangular perspective of legs, a greater attention to the articulation of the body parts, and with regard to technique, multiple and repeated strokes. Some of the representations of head and legs not only serve to profile the features of this phase, but also to draw parallels with the scope of

Figure 4. Cova del Parpalló. 1: pre-Magdalenian portable art; 2: Magdalenian portable art.

SE France: a triangular start to feet, prolonged in a linear stroke, and goat heads that are open at the top, with horn insertions drawn with two strokes in this space.

Mention should also be made of the importance of scenes and animations in both pre-Magdalenian phases, including the well-known examples of a fawn drinking from a doe, a doe with two associated fawns and a lynx lunging at the neck of a ibex. The lynx and the two possible dholes found on Middle Solutrean platelets are amongst the few exceptions to an iconography heavily influenced by the importance of deer, ibex, aurochs and horses. Rectangles, cross-hatching and strip lines are signs that became frequent in the recent pre-Magdalenian.

The Magdalenian cycle in Parpalló began with a quite impoverished phase with abundant figures drawn according to somewhat archaic conventions, and soon gave way to a type of art in which the most characteristic feature is its lack of connection to prevailing contemporary trends in the Cantabrian and Pyrenean areas.

There are few features that permit the figures from these stages to be distinguished from the more recent pre-Magdalenian, although some aspects do show noticeable differences and nuances in the proportions, the articulation of the anatomical parts, a greater attention to internal details and a more detailed execution of the morphology. This change affected the depiction of deer ears, replacing the trilinear convention with V-shaped ears or, in some Upper Magdalenian items, with naturalistic ears, in some cases executed from a single angle perspective. The same details are seen in several figures which either have an absolute profile or a more naturalistic style including details of auroch horns, deer antlers, eyes, mouths and sex, as well as more attention to the correct perspective. There are also elements with a clearly pictographic component, seen most clearly in the depiction of a young animal. The decline of the use of paint in the zoomorphs was accompanied by the appearance of composite lines and a rich succession of highly complex variations of signs, some with precise indications of their chronology, such as cross-hatching with internal divisions.

Wild boar, found on a *plaquette* showing three individuals, a partridge, a duck, an otter and several canids are particularly interesting species as they all appear in the Parpalló collection of Magdalenian art but are generally rare in Palaeolithic art.

Recent discoveries of Magdalenian portable art in the Mediterranean area has shown a tendency towards stylization at the end of the regional artistic cycle, which seems to have prevailed over a more proportioned, detailed component in the Upper Magdalenian.

Michael Walker*†, Mariano López-Martínez**†, María Haber-Uriarte***†

Sima de las Palomas del Cabezo Gordo (Torre Pacheco, Murcia, Spain)

This vertical cave system was formed by karst solution of a Triassic marble hill overlooking the Mediterranean. In 1991 a spelaeologist descending the 18-m deep entrance shaft (Fig. 1) extracted a fossil (SP1) which, once cemented breccia was removed, comprised Neanderthal maxillae connected to the mandible, with almost all their adult teeth. Subsequent systematic excavation (Walker *et al.*, 2012a) uncovered 3 undisturbed Neanderthal partial skeletons (SP96, SP92, and a child, SP97) with several skeletal parts in anatomical position (including cranio-mandibular articulation, femoro-pelvic articulation, elbow, rib-cage, vertebral column, shoulder girdle, foot bones, etc.), Mousterian Palaeolithic artifacts, and animal bones (some charred), all lying deeply in a cemented rock tumble within the upper part of an 18-m deep wall of brecciated sediments that was left exposed by miners after they took out most of the shaft's sedimentary fill ca. 1900. SP96 and SP97 have crania and mandibles, unlike SP92. Because SP1 had lain near SP92 it might be SP92's head. Excavation uncovered SP96 lying with elbows flexed and hands touching the forehead. Computer-assisted tomography revealed hand-bones in breccia adhering to the forehead of the SP97 child (Walker *et al.*, 2012b) which lay underneath SP96, perhaps its parent. The position of the upper extremities implies intentional arrangement before rigor mortis had set in; it is recorded at some other Mousterian sites (Defleur, 1993).

Individual articulated skeletons are very important indeed because they enable far better precise and accurate estimates of body size and

---

* Departamento de Zoología y Antropología Física, Facultad de Biología, Universidad de Murcia, Campus Universitario de Espinardo Edificio 20, 30100 Murcia, España. Correo electrónico: mjwalke@gmail.com Tfn°: 34-620-267104

** Calle Pintor Joaquín 10-4°-I, 30009 Murcia, España. Correo electrónico: marianolopez@hotmail.com Tfn°: 34-630-408806

*** Departamento de Prehistoria, Arqueología, Historia Antigua, Historia Medieval y Ciencias y Técnicas Historiográficas, Facultad de Letras, Universidad de Murcia, Campus Universitario de La Merced, Calle Santo Cristo 1, 30001 Murcia, España. . Correo electrónico: mariahaber@pi-ma.es Tfn°: 34-629-756183

† Directors of the excavation, *Murcian Association for the Study of Palaeoanthropology and the Quaternary, MUPANTQUAT* web-site http:www.mupantquat.com (Murcia Archaeological Museum, Avenida Alfonso X El Sabio 7, 30008 Murcia, Spain), all correspondence to MUPANTQUAT Secretary M.López Martínez <info@mupantquat.com>

† Murcia University Experimental Sciences Research Group E005-11 "*Quaternary Palaeoecology, Palaeoanthropology and Technology*" (c/o Dr. J. S. Carrión García, Department of Plant Biology, Biology Faculty, Murcia University, Campus Universitario de Espinardo Edificio 20, 30100 Murcia, Spain)

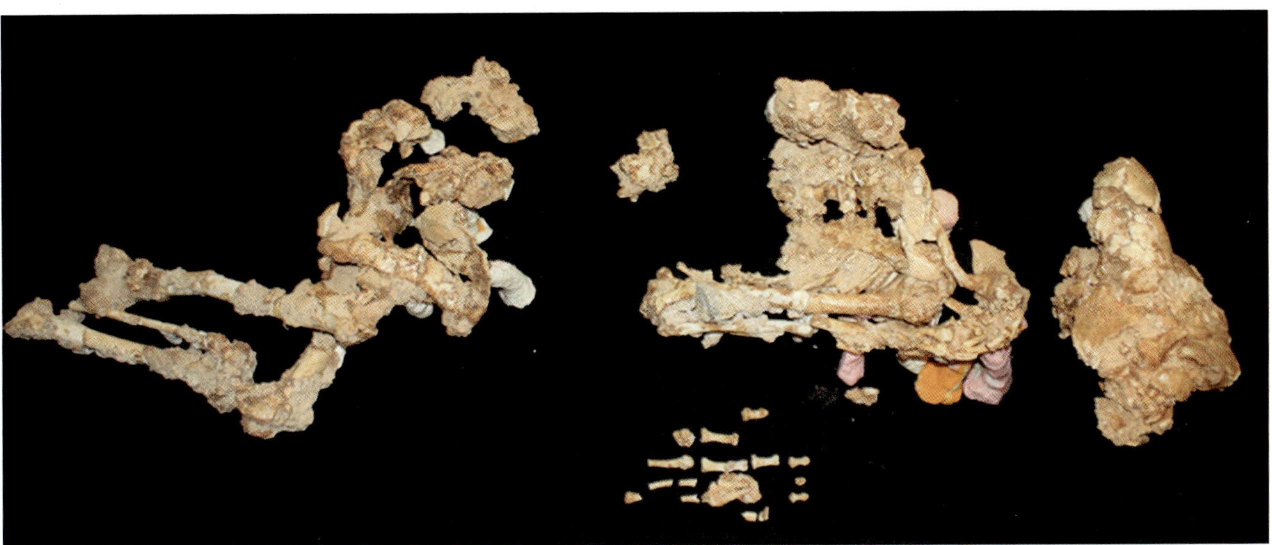

Figure 1. Neanderthal skeleton SP 96 ("Paloma").

proportions than estimates derived from pooled statistical analyses of a given bone type (e.g. femur, tibia, or humerus) from an assemblage of bones from different people who may well not be identifiable individually in it. SP96 was a short Neanderthal woman ("Paloma") <20 years old, with the typically female wide greater sciatic notch of the pelvic basin which underwent post mortem distortion (that "virtual" reconstruction will correct from tomographs). The skeleton is about 85% complete which permits precise and accurate morphological measurements for estimating body proportions (e.g. crural index, etc.) which are undoubtedly Neanderthal and robust ("hyperpolar"). Remarkably, its stature is one of the shortest known for Neanderthal adults (Walker *et al.*, 2011a).

The child skeleton SP97 lay underneath "Paloma" (her child?). Also short in stature, SP92 was probably <25 years old (Walker *et al.*, 2011b). Short, too, was the owner of SP77, a femoral head from looser sediment that had banked up against cemented rock tumble and contained scattered Neanderthal remains, including mandibular fragments of a baby, a child, and an adolescent female (Walker *et al.*, 2010a; Walker *et al.*, 2008); this sediment contained lenses with signs of burning. Fragments of 3 more Neanderthal mandibles were found sieving rubble left by miners. Neanderthal finds include many teeth and bone fragments. In all, at least 9 Neanderthals are represented at the site. The excavated Neanderthal remains correspond to a time about 50,000 years ago; different scientific methods, Fig.2, give estimates implying >40,000-<60,000 (U-series, TL, ^{14}C: for details, see Walker *et al.*, 2012b). Palaeopalynology indicates cool moist conditions though with persistence of species ill-adapted to resist frost (Carrión *et al.*, 2003), and a time before the cold Heinrich 4 episode may be inferred.

Excavated with the SP97 child were the only articulated bones of large animals found at the site so far, viz., two sets of horse ankles (calcaneum, talus, cuboid), one group, cemented by $CaCO_3$ to SP97's skull, had undergone burning, the other, unburnt, beneath SP97's trunk, included additionally a distal tibial fragment, and a third horse talus lay underneath SP97. Two leopard metacarpal bones lay near SP97's skull and 2 leopard hind-paws, with metatarsal and phalangeal bones in anatomical articulation, lay 0.5 m from SP97's skull in a similar level; no doubt preserved thus by the same process that maintained anatomical connexion in the 3 skeletons. It is unlikely horse ankles and leopard paws were fortuitous accumulations, given absence around SP97 of other body parts of those species. A heavily burnt leopard temporal bone found in mine rubble implies Neanderthal intervention; a large premolar tooth implies presence of cave hyaenas. Flakes and spalls from flint-knapping lay close to SP97. The site has provided some carefully prepared Levallois points on flat triangular flint flakes with finely-retouched

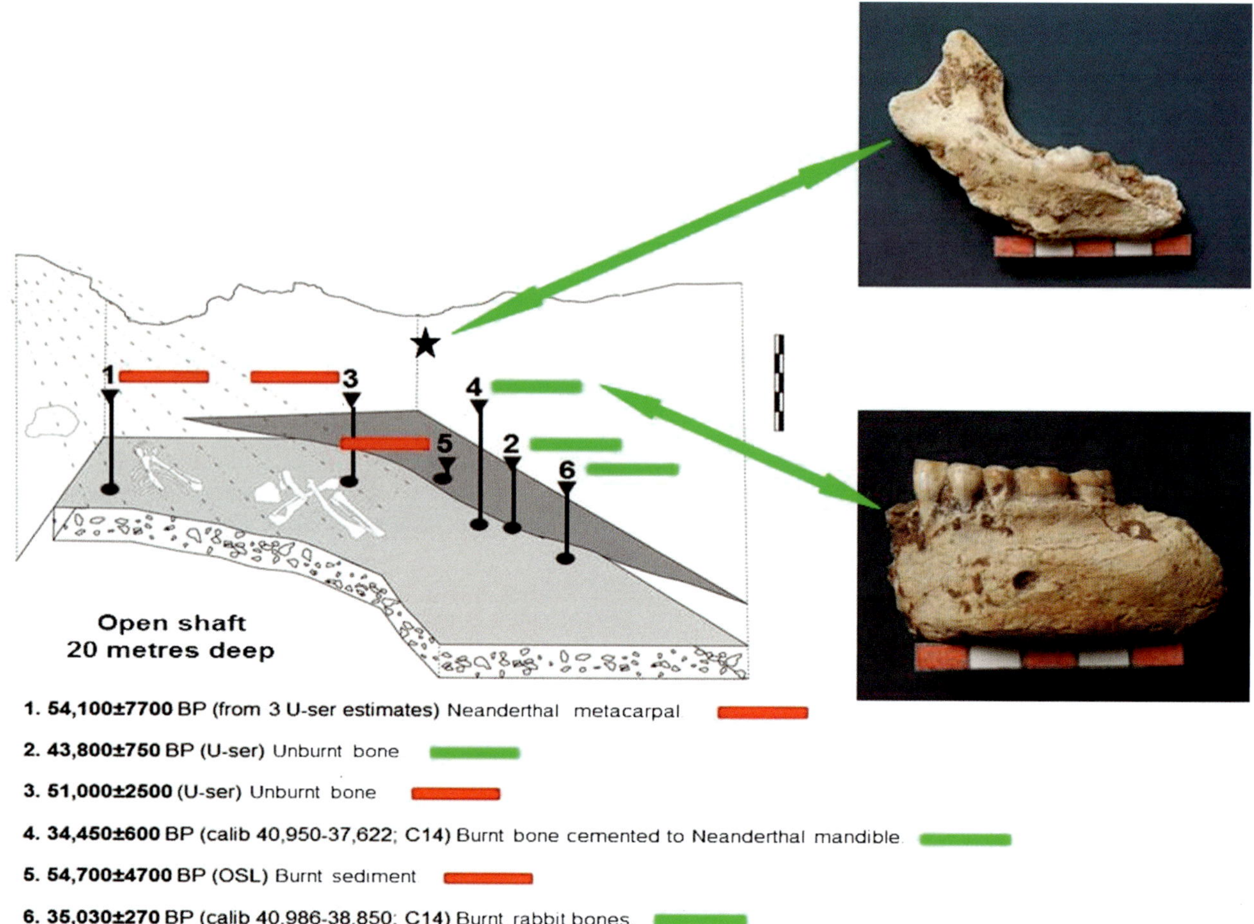

Figure 2. La Sima de las Palomas del Cabezo Gordo: Stratigraphical position of articulated Neanderthal skeleton SP 96 ("Paloma") within cemented rock tumble (broken lines) and situations of dated materials and two other Neanderthal mandibles (see Walker *et al.*, 2012a).

margins, surely effective for hunting with thrusting spears. Flint outcrops are unknown on Cabezo Gordo. Some flint quite likely came from a hydrothermal outcrop inspected ca. 25 km to the S though it is hardly the source of the bulk of the Palaeolithic assemblage. Despite lack of clear-cut signs of intentional interment, large stones might have been thrown over SP96, SP92 and SP 97 to deter leopards and hyaenas from disturbing the corpses. This is a prosaic interpretation.

Rarely are Neanderthal skeletons uncovered in anatomical connection. When animals die their soft parts decompose quickly, aided and abetted by various organisms (carnivorous animals or birds, insects, saprophytic fungi, bacteria, etc.), after which skeletons come apart. Long before they can get buried by natural deposition of sediment, wind and rain may scatter bones where carnivorous animals and birds have failed (exceptionally, skeletons of creatures trapped in caves or swamps escape from being scattered). At La Sima de las Palomas 3 articulated skeletons from 50,000 years ago lay close together. It raises a conjecture that behavioural or cultural impingement occurred, implicating individuals *other* than the 3 deceased. Maybe it is an instance of Neanderthals attending to their dead, albeit with a prosaic motive.

The 3 Neanderthal skeletons and the rock tumble over them lay on a thin bed of extraordinarily hard conglomerate, though it contained some Palaeolithic artifacts and charred bone fragments. Beneath it coarse sediment has been excavated to a depth of 2 m so far, containing many bones of red deer, horse and other herbivores, many of which are charred, as well as rabbits and other small animals, including mandibular fragments of two porcupines (*Hystrix brachyura*: Rhodes *et al.*, 2013). Tortoise seems to have played a part in the diet (Morales-Pérez and Sanchis-Serra, 2009). Characteristically Mousterian flint artifacts are present. Several smooth rounded cobbles were undoubtedly brought by Neanderthals to the site from stream gravels in the plain below. Being larger than some hammer-stones from the site they might have been used to pound or grind minerals (perhaps haematite; the Cabezo Gordo marble contains veins of magnetite and other iron ores) or foodstuff. Vegetable food at La Sima de las Palomas is suggested both by phytoliths discovered in calculus on some Neanderthal teeth (Salazar-García *et al.*, 2013) and two examples of dental caries (Walker *et al.*, 2010b).

Andreu Ollé*,**, Palmira Saladié*,**, Josep Vallverdú*,**, Isabel Cáceres**,*, Jan van der Made***, Isabel Expósito*,**, Francesc Burjachs****,*,** Lucía López-Polín*,**, Carlos Lorenzo**,* Maria Bennàsar*,**, Domingo Carlos Salazar-García*****,******, Carme Olària*******,********

La Cova de Dalt del Tossal de la Font

Geographical location

The cave of Tossal de la Font is situated in a complex structural karstic formation located on one slope close to the town of Vilafamés, 25 km north of Castelló de la Plana. Its dimensions reach more than 2 km of interior paths (Castelló, 2003), and it is developed in Jurassic brecciated dolomites.

The site of Cova de Dat del Tossal de la Font is on the upper section of this karstic system. Its UTM coordinates are (ETRS89) 30N X=751380, Y=4444419, at 357 metres a.s.l.

Background research

Archaeological fieldwork conducted on the site between 1982 and 1987 uncover an important karstic filling from the Upper Pleistocene (Gusi *et al.*, 1983; 1987), as well as a set of Holocene occupations (Gusi and Aguilella, 1998). The Pleistocene evidences retrieved, whose date was estimated around 90,000 years old, included a full faunal list and a restricted lithic assemblage, besides two human fossils assigned to Neanderthals (Arsuaga and Bermúdez de Castro, 1987; Arsuaga *et al.*, 2001), and a tooth frag-

* Institut Català de Paleoecologia Humana i Evolució Social (IPHES), C/ Marcel·lí Domingo s/n (Edifici W3), Campus Sescelades, 43007 Tarragona-Spain.
** Àrea de Prehistòria, Universitat Rovira i Virgili (URV), Av. Catalunya 35, 43002 Tarragona-Spain.
*** Dpto. de Paleobiología, Museo Nacional de Ciencias Naturales, C.S.I.C., José Gutiérrez Abascal 2, 2800****** Madrid-Spain.
**** Institució Catalana de Recerca i Estudis Avançats (ICREA).
***** Dept. of Archaeology, University of Cape Town (Cape Town, South Africa).
****** Research Group on Plant Foods in Hominin Dietary Ecology, Dept. of Human Evolution, Max-Plank Institute for Evolutionary Anthropology (Leipzig-Germany).
******* Laboratori d'Arqueologia Prehistòrica, Dept d'Història, Geografia i Art, Universitat Jaume I (UJI). Campus Riu Sec, 12071 Castelló de la Plana-Spain.
******** Servei d'Investigacions Arqueològiques i Prehistòriques. Diputació Provincial de Castelló (SIAP). P.O. 31******. E-12080 Castelló de la Plana-Spain.

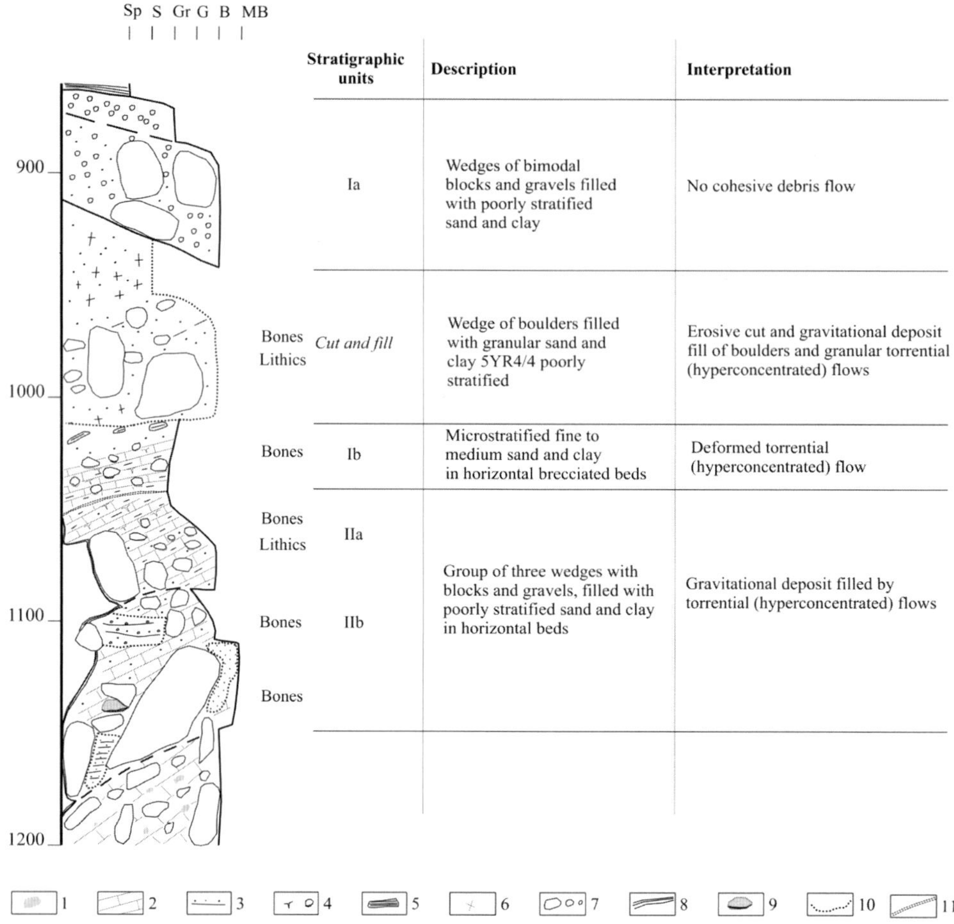

Figure 1. Synthetic log of the Pleistocene talus cone deposits from Tossal de la Font. Legend: 1, fenestral porosity; 2, cemented zone; 3, horizontal stratification; 4, cracking with decarbonation and load structures under clasts; 5, fragments of stalagmites; 6, massive to crudely stratified deposit; 7, blockss and gravels; 8, micro laminated stalagmite layer; 9, microlaminated stalagmite empty; 10, secondary unconfromity; 11, listric fissure.

ment (Olària *et al.*, 2007). Between 2004 and 2012, in a collaborative research initiative among UJI, SIAP and IPHES, a second period of archaeological fieldwork was carried out on the site. The main aims were: (I) to review the Pleistocene deposit stratigraphy; (II) to date it; and (III) to extend the excavation area, increasing the available data in order to enhance the paleoenvironmental context, the taphonomic processes, and the contextualization of zooarchaeological and technological remains found in the first period of excavations (Saladié *et al.*, 2010).

The ultimate depletion of the fertile deposit, the big effort required to reach it, the increasing cementation of the same deposit, and the reiteration of the fossils appearing, led to the end of this second period of fieldwork in 2012 (Gusi *et al.*, 2013).

The stratigraphic sequence

The fossiliferous deposit that presents a major tilt and limited lateral continuity is situated on the cave entrance, just a few metres from the access, and fills a narrow fringe between the cave wall and a talus cone originated by large endokarstic boulders.

The archaeopaleontological units have been established considering the different deposits accumulated through fissures and marked by decarbonation. Two big sets have been identified. In each of them gravitational sedimentation on high slopes has been produced. The entrance deposits have limestone boulders mixed with sandy clay, probably coming from the breccia cemented with large boulders and speleothems that indicate the closing of the point of entry. Each unit has this chemical deposit on its top (Fig. 1).

The most abundant paleontological record is on unit IIa. This unit presents a truncated stalagmitic crust that appears transformed in clasts at unit IIb. These sedimentations and emptying processes characterize the filling of that cave-fissure, where a steep slope and mass wasting movements played a key role in the opening of new points of entry and in the creation of the space to collect breccia deposits with embedded macrovertebrates and lithic remains from the Upper Pleistocene.

Although no new human remains have been recovered, the section of the old level E. where they appear in, located in the original publication (Gusi *et al.*, 1983: 17) clearly corresponds with unit IIa.

Pending on new results, U/Th dates are available for two breccia sealed by stalagmitic crusts and situated on top of unit IIa: 61,846 ±585 years BP and 56,014 ±484 years BP. The beginning of the isotopic stage 3 can be quite an accurate chronological assignation for this unit, since both dates are allegedly from the same stalagmitic crust.

The archaeological record

On the first campaigns, the identification of several rodent species allowed the site to be placed in a chronological framework between the late interglacial Riss-Würm and the beginning of Würm glacial stage (Gusi *et al.*, 1987). At the most recent campaigns, in unit IIa, *Iberomys brecciensis* has been identified,a characteristic species of the Middle Pleistocene that existed until the Upper Pleistocene.

Apart from micromammals, and unit IIa always being the richest and most diverse regarding bone assemblages, the faunal list includes: *Lynx spelaea, Felis sylvestris, Crocuta crocuta, Equushydruntinus,* Rhinocerotidae, *Sus scrofa, Cervus elaphus, Capra/ Hemitragus* sp., Bovinae indet., Chelonia and *Oryctolagus cunniculus*. *Cervus elaphus* is by far the best represented taxa, and is also the species that shows more variability in the representation of skeletal parts. Distal parts of limbs predominate in faunal assemblages. They are segments that often appear anatomically connected, or located at a few centimetres. Both the rest of the appendicular bones and the axial skeleton are under-represented, and display a more scattered spatial distribution.

Anthropogenic activity over faunal remains is very scarce. Some red deer bones with cutmarks, relating with defleshing activities and intentional bone breakage have been identified (unit IIa).

Carnivore activity, on the contrary, is well represented, and can be traced through different marks such as punctures, pits, scores, crenulated and jagged edges, digested bones. Gnawed marks primarily appear over red deer bones indicating the action of a big predator, such as a hyena, lion, or bear. Some leporid remains also show punctures and scores pointing out chewing activities of carnivores such as lynx or fox (Fig.2, k-n).

Human remains

The three human fossils recovered (Fig. 2, o-p) are a distal fragment from a left humerus, a fragment of right coxal and a fragment of tooth. The part that has been preserved in the humerus (CTF-1) corresponds to a third distal that has the whole joint and displays several characteristics that makes it alike to the European Middle Pleistocene populations represented at Sima de los Huesos and also to the Neanderthals (Arsuaga *et al.*, 2001). From the coxal fragment (CTF-2) only the upper part of the femoral joint remains and part of the ischial spine. Although their fragmentary conditions do not allow the distinction of taxonomic traits, the presence of a very pronounced supra-acetabular groove and the thickening of the greater sciatic notch edges should be stressed. The tooth fragment (CTF-3) corresponds to a maxilar molar from a child.

Lithic industry

The available lithic assemblage is very scarce. In total, there are 8 small flint artefacts, 2 from unit Ic and f and 6 from unit IIa (Fig.2, a-j). Half of these tools are simple flakes. Among retouched flakes there are two points, one sidescraper and one denticulate sidescraper. Half of the artefacts have developed patinas, but they surfaces do not display other postdepositional modifications visible (such as erosion or false retouch). One of the flakes shows fine cracks from heat damage. Finally, an single artefact of quartzite, a broken pebble with evident marks of being used as hammerstone has been recovered.

Little can be said about the tecnhnotypological characterization of the lithic assemblage, beyond to roughly assigning it to a Mousterian context. Neither is there enough data to infer occupational interpretations based on lithic assemblage. Nevertheless, the collection has a great taphonomic value, since it ap-

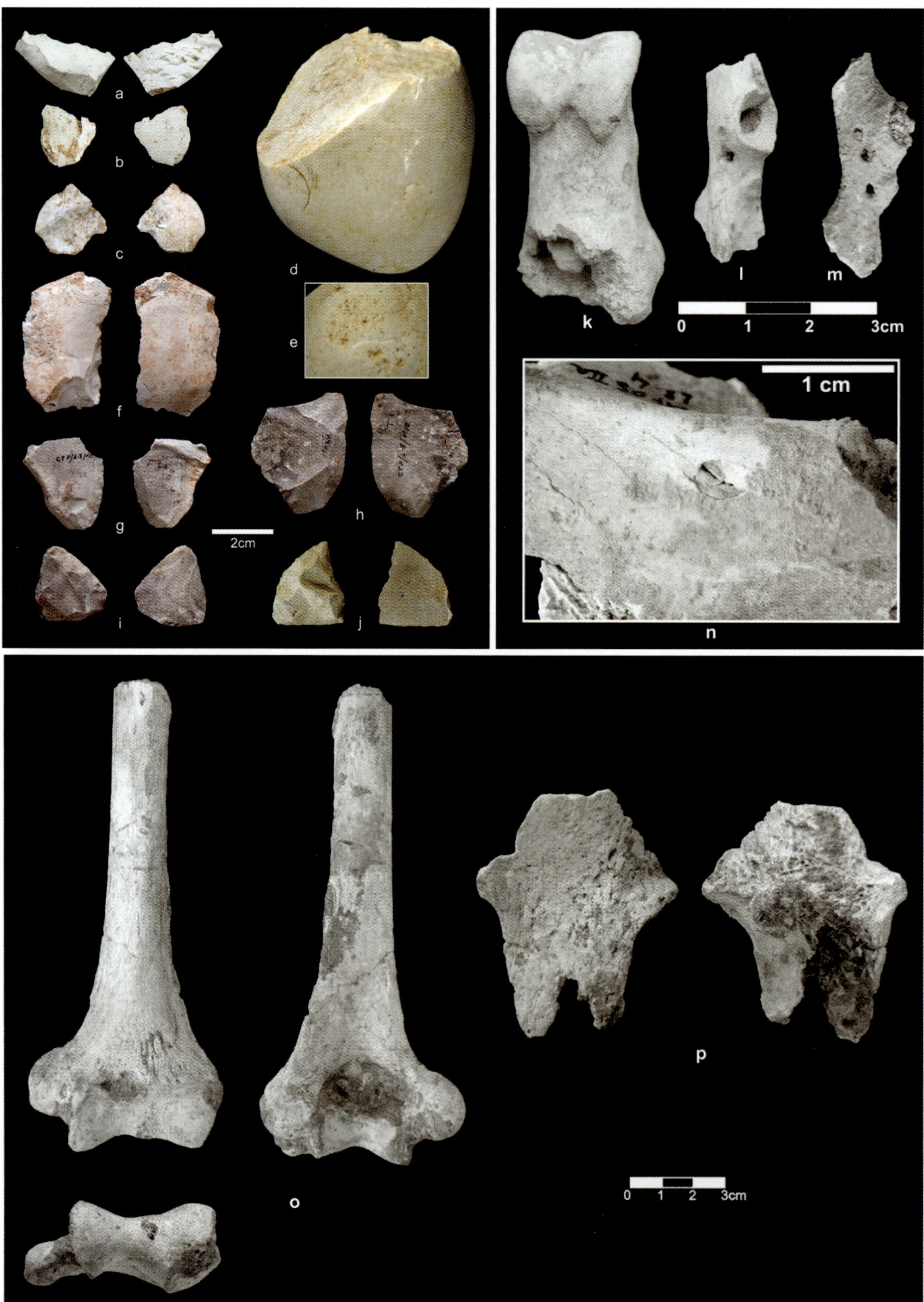

Figure 2. Flint flakes from unit Ic and f (a,b) and from unit IIa (c,e); Retouched flint flakes from unit IIa; denticulate side-scraper (f), sidescraper with marginal retouch (g) and points (i, j); quartzite pebble broken (d), and with percussion marks (e), unit Ic and f; red deer phalanx with a vacuum in its proximal part, unit Ib (k); punctures over coxal bones produced by a small size carnivore (l and m: units Ic and f, and IIc and f, respectively); puncture provoked by a big size carnivore over a vertebra from a medium size animal, unit IIa (n); fragment of human humerus CTF-1 (o); and fragment of human coxal bone CTF-2 (p).

pears closely related with fossils, and demonstrates the development of human activities in the cave itself or in the immediate surroundings of the cave entrance.

Concluding remarks

The information gathered led us to interpret that fossils in Tossal de la Font are in secondary position. This location was the result of short distance transportation, since there is low occurrence of modifications that could indicate friction over the substrate such as trampling, rounding and abrasion marks on bone surfaces. The fossil association responds to the addition of different events, each of them could include in turn several causes of death and taphonomic processes. In the case of Tossal de la Font, the result is that fossils present a twofold history, one biostratinomic due to exokarstic factors and another fossildiagenetic one caused by endokarstic agents. The first one is characterized mainly by carnivore action and, to a lesser extent by hominid action over some carcasses. The second one can be observed by the presence of dissolution, chemical corrosion produced by the sediment, and also generalized processes of cementation and formation of breccia deposits.

Carmen Cacho*, Jesús Jordá Pardo**

El Tossal de la Roca

The archaeological site of Tossal de la Roca is situated in Vall d'Alcalá (Alicante), at 640 m.a.s.l. and 20-25 km away from the present coastline. This west oriented rockshelteris situated in a mountainous area in a foothill on the left bank of the Penegrí creek, one of the small tributaries that configures the short current network of the Serpis River fluvial system.

The archaeological sequence, excavated by our team between 1981 and 1999, ranges from the Late Upper Pleistocene (end of OIS 2) to the first third of the Holocene (beginning of OIS 1). It has a discontinuous sequence that spans from Upper Magdalenian to the Mesolithic with trapezes documented in two different areas of the rockshelter. The interior sector (Fig.1) contains several Upper Magdalenian levels (III and II int), and Final Magdalenian (I int), whereas the exterior sector includes diverse occupations from the Notched and Denticulates Mesolithic (II b and II a ext.) and Geometric Mesolithic (I ext.). Radiocarbon dates have provided, the following chronological span for the stratigraphic units, from bottom to top: 17200-16310 cal BP (level III int.), 15550-14040 cal BP (level II int.), 13780-13580 cal. BP (level I int.), 10550-9410 cal. BP (level IIb ext.), 9510-8640 cal BP (level IIa ext.), 8560-8230 cal BP (level I ext.) (Cacho and Jordá 2009: 222-227; Jordá and Cacho, 2008).

Palynological and antracological analysis as well as micromammal studies from Tossal de la Roca indicate that level III (int.) developed in temperate and moist climate conditions, conversely, cold and arid conditions are documented for level II (int.); vegetation cover is reduced to conifer at both levels. In the upper part of level II and especially at level I (int.), a significant climate change is reflected, pointing at milder and moister climatic conditions that contribute to an open environment vegetation development and to a large variety of species, where *Quercus* gain importance at the expenses of conifers; other thermophilic taxa as *Juglans*, *Ulmus*, *Betula* are documented. From level IIb (ext.) there is a great advance of the Mediterranean forest (oak forest) with a remarkable presence of *Quercus*, which becomes the prevailing species in the subsequent periods (levels IIa and I ext.), together with the increase of other taxa indicative of some humidity.

* Departamento de Prehistoria. Museo Arqueológico Nacional. Serrano 13. 28001 Madrid. Spain.

** Departamento de Prehistoria y Arqueología. Universidad Nacional de Educación a Distancia. Senda del Rey 7. 28040 Madrid. Spain.

Figure 1. Stratigraphy of the interior sector. Tossal de la Roca.

Rabbit is the most frequent species of Tossal, as it happens in other Mediterranean Magdalenian sites, but considering its low energetic value it should be considered as a complementary diet intake, ibex hunting and, to a lesser extent deer hunting, being the main nutritional food source. From the Geometric Mesolithic, deer consumption increases over ibex, and new species such as chamois or wild boar are incorporated. According to the taphonomic study, ibex and deer hunted during the Magdalenian occupations would have been partly consumed in the hunting place and only some of its portions would be transported to the site. This behaviour will change in the Notched and Denticulates Mesolithic period and even more during the Geometric Mesolithic when the entire prey was carried to the site. Besides this prevailing species, other resources were consumed such as partridges and some fish such as trout and eel during the Magdalenian period, together with the gathering of some fruits and leguminous plants during the Mesolithic occupations (Cacho, 1995: 95-96).

Lithic industry is overwhelmingly made of flint from the close surrounding, approximately in a radius of 4 km of distance. Technological study from the Upper Magdalenian levels reveal reduction strategies with predetermined debitage from standardized cores (prismatic), and also a flexible system (amorphous core) that adapts to the characteristics and quality of raw materials. Both strategies are oriented to bladelets production, lately transformed by pressure debitage on backed bladelets. Retouched artefacts assemblage from these stratigraphic units show a clear predominance of tools made from bladelets, with a large typological variety at level III. Also to be noted is the presence of some scalene triangles. Endscrapers are the second most relevant type of this assemblage, while burins, mainly dihedral, appear in a very low proportion (Cacho and Martos, 2004: 100-101).

After the Late Magdalenian characterized by an increase of endscrapers and a low diversification of tool made from bladelets, there is a hiatus in the Tossal de la Roca sequence that will start again with level IIb in the outside sector, assigned to the Notched and Denticulates Mesolithic. Lithic industry from that stratigraphic unit, dated between 10580 and 9390 cal BP, reflects significant changes in regard to the Late Magdalenian. On the retouched artefact assemblages, bladelets tool decreases at the same time that short endscrapers increase, but the appearance of notches and denticulates in large proportion (20-40%) is the most outstanding change. These artefacts are always very thick and present a typical retouch known as *Campiñoide* (direct-abrupt/ stepped and bifacial) in most cases. From a technological point of view these lithic assemblages (levels IIb and Ia ext.) configure a flake industry –where in turn flakes are used as core-like flakes–, in addition microblade tools are really scarce limited to little projectile points for hunting. This flake industry with thick notched and denticulates artefacts persist during the Geometric Mesolithic, where trapezes on bladelets are manufactured (Cacho and Jordá, 2009: 230-233).

Bone industry is scarce and appears rather fragmented. In the Magdalenian assemblages the presence of assegai should be stressed, some bone points and one needle, but the most relevant artefact is a complete bone harpoon. This has four insinuated teeth though not totally exempt, and a straight base without any kind of retaining mechanism. Similar harpoons to the one of Tossal de la Roca have appeared on other Upper Magdalenian records from the Mediterranean coast of the Iberian Peninsula such as Matutano or Cendres (Cacho and de la Torre, 2005: 259-261; Cacho *et al.*, 2001: 85-87). On Mesolithic levels bone industry is very limited and only consists of some bone points and some spatula.

Figure 2. Decorated slab from Tossal de la Roca.

Without stratigraphic context, several slabs with zoomorphic representations where cervids and caprines depictions prevailhave been recovered, almost always isolated, although there are some overlapping cases (Fig.2). Schematism is one of the most characteristic traits of this representations, especially on limbs, whereas in the design of head and neck some anatomical details are incorporated (Cacho and Ripoll, 1987: 54). In addition, one pendant on bone spatula with geometric decoration has been recovered (D'Errico and Cacho, 1994).

As a novelty, traceology studies have suggested that partridge wings could be used as personal ornaments during the Magdalenian period (Sánchez and Cacho, 2010).

The most relevant contribution of Tossal de la Roca is the multidisciplinary study of one of the most complete archaeological records from the Upper Pleistocene and the beginning of the Holocene in the Mediterranean coast of the Iberian Peninsula. Research on this site situated in a regional context enables assessment of the environmental transformations which occurred at this transitional period which forced the last hunther-gatherer populationsinto a steady adaptation process. This process would have implied major territorial control and deep transformations of food resources procurement strategies, technology, and artistic expression (Cacho and Jordá, 2009: 233-234).

6

SOUTHERN MEDITERRANEAN COAST, GUADALQUIVIR RIVER AND BETIC INTRAMONTANE BASINS

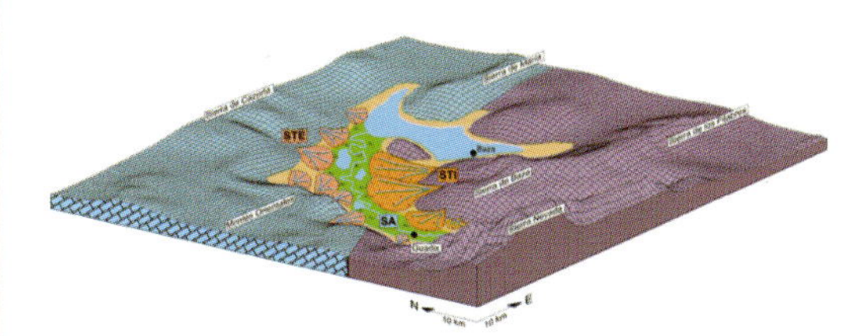

Site	Map numbering
El Aculadero	74
Ardales	75
Bajondillo	76
Cueva Ambrosio	77
Cueva de Nerja	78
Cueva and abrigo del Ángel	79
Cueva del Boquete de Zafarraya	80
Cuenca de Guadix – Baza and Conjunto de Orce	81
Las Grajas de Archidona	82
El Pirulejo	83

Manuel Santonja*,
Alfredo Pérez-González*

El Aculadero (Puerto de Santa María, Cádiz)

1. Initial assessment of El Aculadero and the 1973 – 1980 excavation campaigns

The El Aculadero site, located in the northernmost corner of the Bay of Cádiz (southern Spain), was initially discovered and surveyed by Claude Viguier in collaboration with Claude Thibault, under the supervision of François Bordes. The first publications interpreted this discovery as the first clearly European Oldowan site (Bordes and Viguier 1971; Bordes and Thibault 1977), comparable to the known sites in the North Africa Casablanca region.

El Acudalero was excavated from 1973 until 1980 under the leadership of Claude Thibault and Ángeles Querol. Their main objectives were to confirm the absence of Acheulian technocomplex in the site and thoroughly study of the stratigraphic sequence. The 127 m^2 opened only yielded lithic material in quartzite (91%) and other rock –schists, quartz, flint and limestone–, all found on the same level as the pebble industry.

The assemblage consisted of 934 varied knapped pebbles –in some cases probably elementary cores–, 573 retouched flakes, 133 cores, and 1160 flakes and fragments (Querol and Santonja 1983). The tools on flake consisted of pieces with generally non-intense retouch, although some 60 items were defined as sidescrapers or denticulates. There were no Acheulean tools –neither bifaces, nor cleavers, nor trihedral pics–. The most significant exploitation schemes in the cores were discoidal (45 items) and in some cases Levallois (Fig. 2).

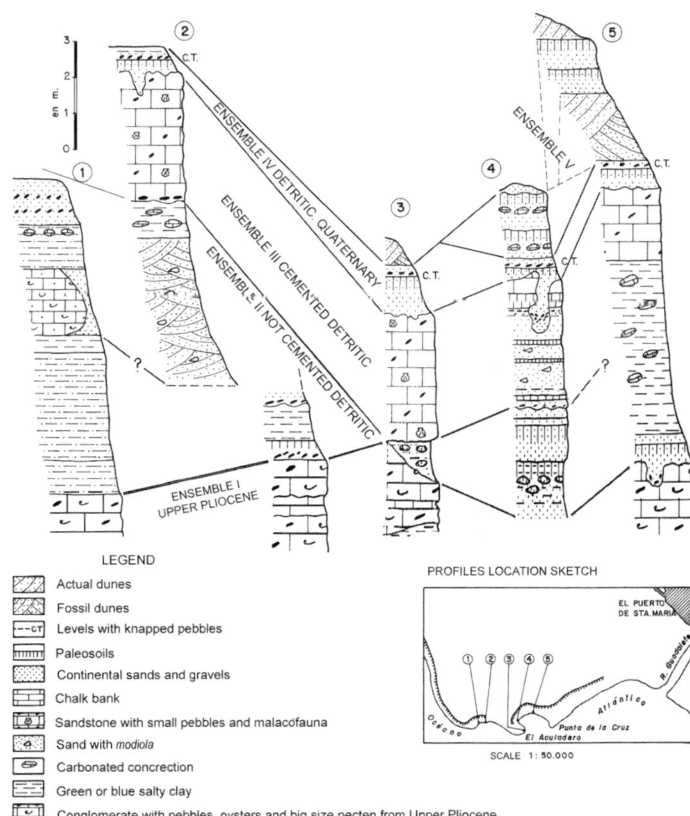

Figure 1. Plio-Pleistocene stratigraphic sections on the El Aculadero seacliff (Querol and Santonja 1983, cf. fig. 6, p. 23). Continental units IV and V are deposited on marine units bed I, II and III (columns 3, 4 and 5). El Aculadero site (CT) is located at the bottom of the continentals units IV and V.

The presence of tools indicated that this was not exclusively spot of primary raw material captation (Querol and Santonja 1983). However, the lack of debris and the low ratio between products and knapped blank –two flakes per three cores– indicated poor conservation of the initial ensemble, which may have partly disappeared due to erosion processes. However, the deficit of flakes, particularly non-cortical flakes, may be due to their deliberate transfer to more specialized sites (Santonja and Pérez González 2010).

* Centro Nacional de Investigación sobre la Evolución Humana. (CENIEH); 09002 Burgos. manuel.santonja@cenieh.es

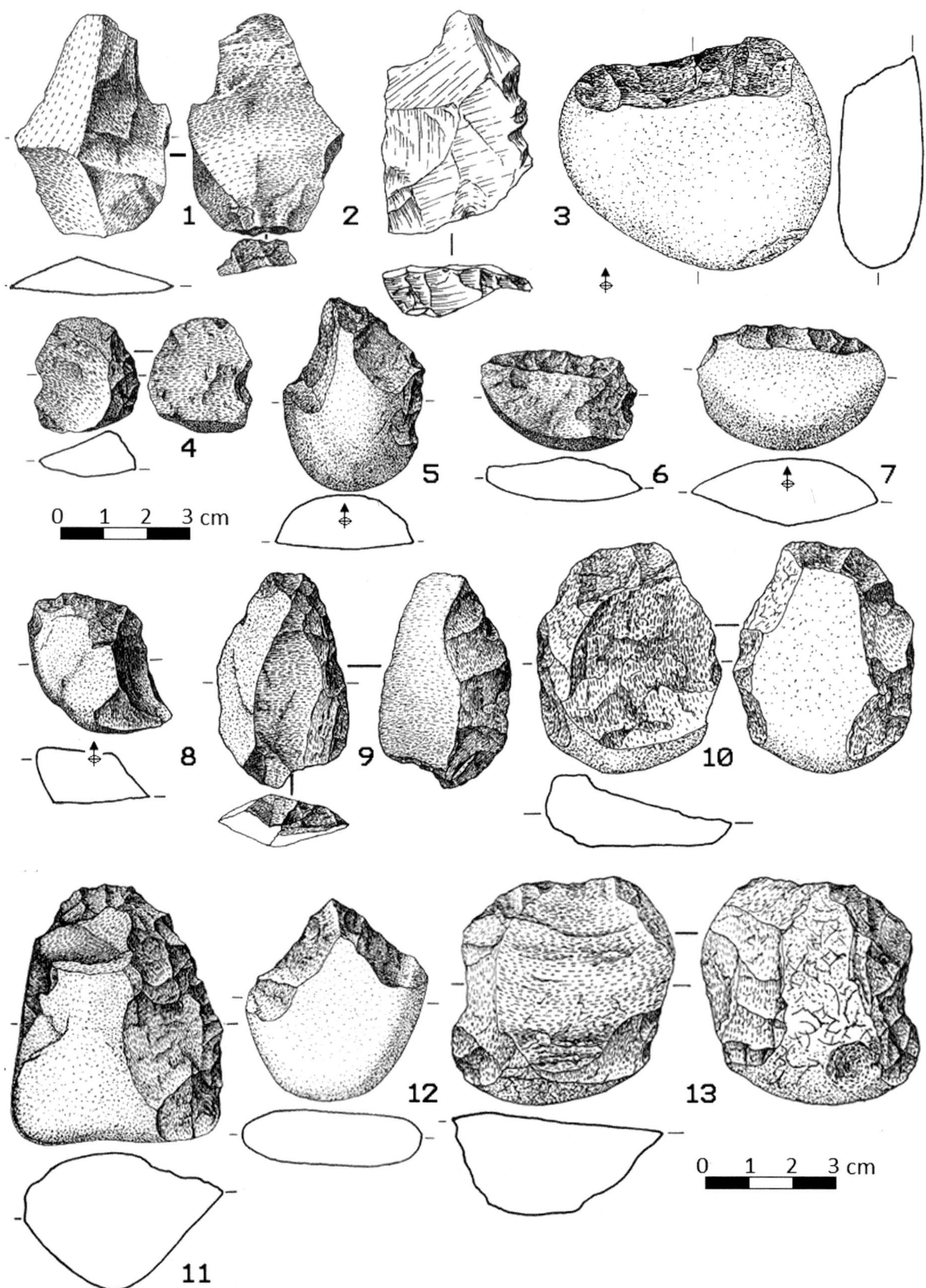

Figure 2: 1: Levallois flake. 2: Retouched Levallois flake. 3 and 11: Sidescraper on pebble. 4 and 6-9: Sidescrapers. 5: Denticulate. 10 and 13: Levallois cores. 12: pointed pebble-tool.

In 1983, findings from the study of this industrial assemblage led to the suggestion that the technology employed here was comparable to that observed in the Iberian Middle Pleistocene sites. A new stratigraphic interpretation was particularly focused on the highly erosive contacts between the Pliocene sea levels and the location of the site in the stratigraphic sequence (Fig. 1). These discontinuities suggested that the correct age could be in the second half of the Middle Pleistocene (Querol and Santonja 1983: 244-246).

2. Interpretations of the Lower Palaeolithic in this area since 1983

Studies in recent years have detected Acheulean series including handaxes and cleavers on terraces of the Guadalete River such as Laguna de Medina (Giles *et al.*, 1996). Other terraces of the same river have yielded Acheulean ensembles attributed to the Middle Pleistocene, a comparable situation to Spain's Central *Meseta* (Plateau), where Acheulean industries range chronologically from MIS 13 to MIS 6 (Santonja and Pérez-González 2010a).

On the other hand, several assemblages with similar industrial series to El Aculadero have been reported in the vicinity of the Bay of Cadiz and further west. The number of such sites has gradually increased, and in some cases have been proposed ages near the end of the Middle Pleistocene (Giles *et al.*, 1994). At some of these sites, a Mousterian-like development of tools on flake has been found along with discoidal cores and knapped pebbles of the El Aculadero type.

3. El Aculadero dating

In the El Aculadero stratigraphic sequence, continental units (UIV and UV) are superimposed on others (UI, UII and UIII) of a marine origin or influence (Fig. 1). The site is located on a quartzite and quartz– gravel level at the base of Unit IV (CT, Fig. 1). This level, along with an underlying sandy level, form a cover-glacis layer which also contains a red soil developed on the sandy layer from before or after the level containing the pebbles and industry (Querol and Santonja 1983).

In this edaphic-sedimentary context, four samples were taken for optically stimulated luminescence dating (OSL) –additive dose method–, in 2-10 µ grain size of the mineral fraction. The Radiochemical Dating Lab at the Autonomous University of Madrid provided the following results (Santonja and Pérez-González 2010):

- *Sample D*: Collected from the yellow sand level on the paleosol developed, in the lowest part of UIV. A red deposit (2.5 YR 4/8) with fine-medium grain sand and silt-clay content (33%). Dated at 110507 ± 7481 BP.
- *Sample* C: From the cemented dune above the pebble and industry level. This well preserved dune can be clearly identified with Zazo's Unit 11 (Zazo *et al.*, 1983). A medium grain sand deposit with scarcely clay-silt fraction (<2%), light brown colour (7.5YR 6/4). Dated at 62914 ± 5094 BP.
- *Sample B*: Collected in the north of the excavation site, in medium to fine sands with less than 22% silt + clay, brown colour when moist (7.5YR 5/4). Its stratigraphic position is equivalent to the basal part of the top of UV (Section 5, Fig 1). Dated at 40493 ± 2434 BP.
- *Sample A*: Recent dune consisting of loose sand, to top of UV (Section 5, Fig 1), light brown colour when moist (7.5 YR 6/4). Fine to medium grain sand and almost no silt + clay fraction (<1%). Dated at 7000 + 466 BP.

These four samples permit an objective estimation of the age of the site, situated between samples D and C. The results concur with others conclusions. For Zazo (1989: 119, Fig. 3), the continental materials on the El Puerto de Santa María seacliff are later than the Trafalgar marine episode, dated by Th/U at 100 ky BP. This chronology matches the OSL date of 110.5 ± 7.5 ky BP in the UIV sands affected by pedogenesis which led to a well-structured and rubefacted soil during a warm episode, probably corresponding to the Eemian interglacial. If this edaphogenesis did affect the level containing gravels and industry, the age of the site would be no less than 110 ky BP. Otherwise it could be subsequent to the Eemian interglacial. OSL dating of Sample C, collected from the cemented dunes, was 62.9 ± 5.0 ky BP, marking then the youngest limit of the El Aculadero industry.

5. Conclusions

The OSL dating presented herein defines the age of the El Aculadero site as either in the Eemian interglacial, which ended around 110 ky BP, or in the MIS 4, before c. 63 ky BP. These results rule out not only the earlier datings of the industry, but also the postulated modern ages including the Holocene.

On the Atlantic coast of southern Iberia, a group of comparable sites to El Aculadero have been recorded, all characterized by retouched tools on flake along with shaped pebble tools. At El Aculadero, the first stages of production are well documented, while at other sites the sub-phases of full production and consumption, represented by significant percentages of retouched tools suggest a more varied range of activities. All of these sites have a common technological identity. This is a local Middle Palaeolithic facies, stretching along a timeline starting in the initial Upper Pleistocene or perhaps earlier. On the basis of known data, it is later than the Acheulean sequences on the Guadalete terraces.

Pedro Cantalejo*, Jose Ramos**, Gerd-Christian Weniger***, Martin Kehl ****
Maria del Mar Espejo*****

Cueva de Ardales, Province of Malaga

The Ardales cave (UTM 337.110/4.082.540) is located in a mountain called Cerro de la Calinora 565 m a.s.l. near the village of Ardales about 50 km north of the Mediterranean coast. It was discovered in 1821 after an earthquake exposed a cave entrance previously sealed by colluvial deposits. From 1852 on, the cave was opened to local tourism without recognizing its prehistoric finds. It was Henri Breuil who recognized the Palaeolithic heritage during a visit in 1918 and who first studied the rock art of Ardales cave (Breuil 1921).

The site then lost attention for decades. After a time of scientific standstill, research restarted in 1990 (Ramos *et al.*, 1992). A detailed complete documentation of the artistic inventory was finished after more than 10 years of study in 2005 (Cantalejo *et al.*, 2006). From 2011-2013, first limited excavations where conducted in the entrance area (Fig. 1) and coring outside the front of the cave took place (Ramos *et al.*, 2014). The site is a multi-branched karstic system that is separated into five areas: Area I (Sala del Saco), area II (Sala de las Estrellas), area III (Galería de los Laberintos), area IV (Calvario) and area V (Galerías Altas). This later area was discovered in 1981 by speleologists. It is a separate cave system above the main cave area. Today the Galerías Altas are accessible only by a narrow fissure that can be reached from the Galeria del Arquero by climbing vertically about 18 m high. The natural entrance to this area was probably sealed by a slide in the late Holocene. Coring outside of the original entrance area of the Galerías Altas in 2011 provided evidence for such an entrance. This part of the cave has not yet been analysed systematically. But, burials from Copper Age and Palaeolithic rock art have been recorded from short expeditions into the Galerías Altas. By sealing off the entrance, prehistoric surfaces including dispersed artefacts and burials have been conserved perfectly.

The galleries of Ardales cave have a total extension of more than 1,500 m. The cave is accessible today via a system of stairs, which was constructed by its first owner Doña Trinidad Grund in the mid-

* Ayuntamiento de Ardales-Cueva de Ardales. Avenida de Málaga 1, 29550 Ardales, Málaga, España, pedrocantalejo@gmail.com
** Universidad de Cádiz. Facultad de Filosofía y Letras. Avda. Gómez Ulla s.n. 11003 Cádiz. jose.ramos@uca.es.
*** Neanderthal Museum. Talstr. 300, 40822 Mettmann, Germany; weniger@neanderthal.de
**** University of Cologne, Institute of Geography. Albertus-Magnus-Platz, 50923 Cologne, Germany; kehlm@uni-koeln.de
***** Cueva de Ardales. 29550 Ardales, Málaga, España. Investigadora, Grupo PAI-HUM-440, mariadeespejo@gmail.com

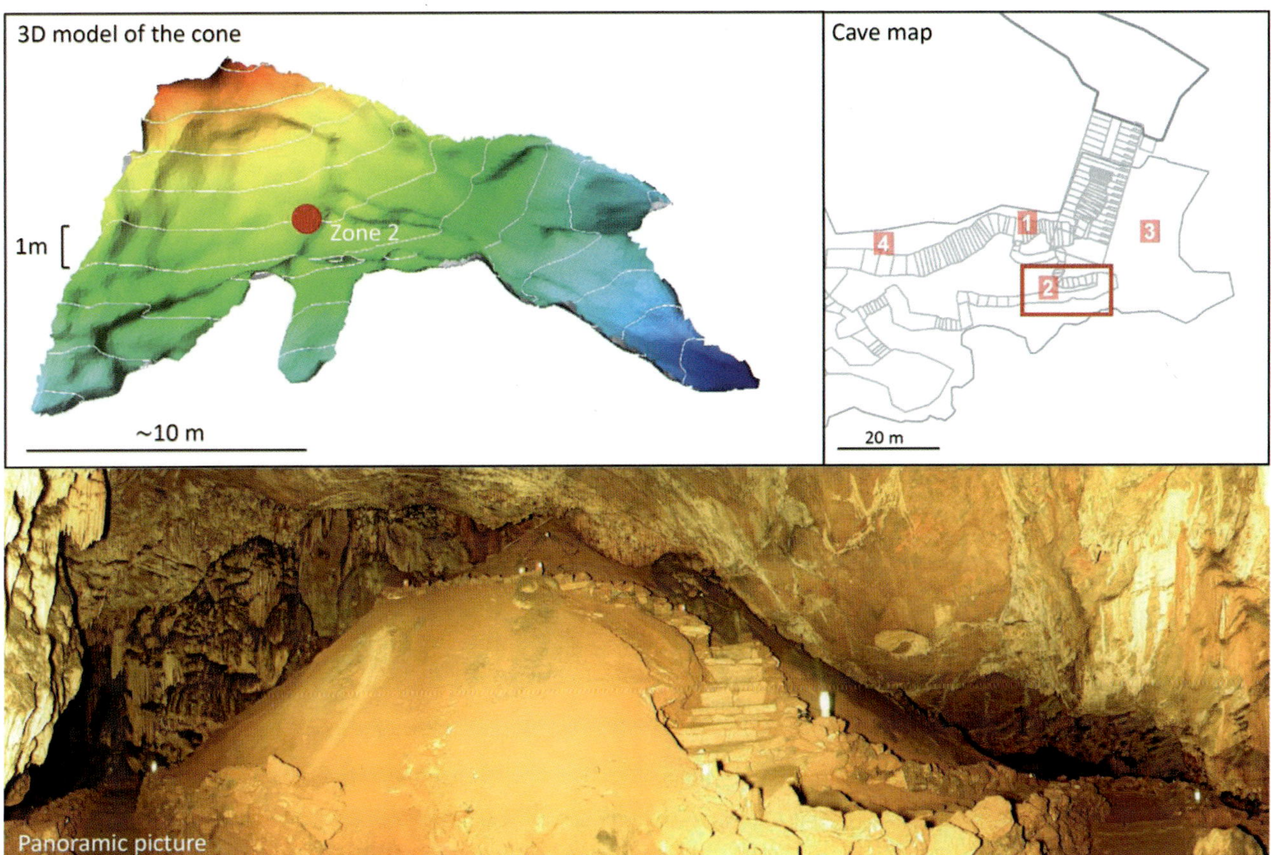

Figure 1. The entrance cone of Ardales cave. Test excavations are marked by red figures (1-4). The red square marks Zone 2 with a multi-layered stratigraphy.

dle of the 19th century. The stairs were cut into a steep sediment cone that stretches over 20 m from the opening of the cavity down to the Sala de Estrellas (Fig. 1). The cone is the result of frequent sediment deposition from the slope above the cave entrance.

Ardales cave is outstanding in Southern Iberia for its numerous examples of paintings and engravings from the Upper Palaeolithic. Breuil described in his first analysis about 20 animal figures from 10 panels. Until today, 1010 pictorial artefacts have been described from 252 different sites (Cantalejo *et al.*, 2006 and 2014 b). These include 787 signs, 106 unclassified motifs, 98 animal figures, 10 human figures and 9 hand stencils – positives as well as negatives. All kind of surfaces were used for artistic expression: walls, ceilings, grounds, speleothems and blocks. Within the animal representations cervids dominate (64%) followed by equids (26%), others are statistically of minor importance. From the cervides 85% represent females. Two depictions of birds, including a flamingo (Fig. 2), one reptile and a fish are noteworthy.

The chronology of the rock art is divided by stylistic analysis into three stages. The initial phase is supposed to represent a Gravettian chronology followed by the middle phase equal to the Solutrean and a final phase attributed to the Magdalenian. Beside the pictorial artefacts an important number of additional finds linked to the human use of the cave have been conserved. These are stone or bone tools placed near the panels with rock art, which might have been used for engravings, paste of red and brown pigments, stone containers used as pigment palettes (Fig. 3) and stone lamps used for artificial lighting (Fig. 4). To date 13 artefacts probably linked to the artificial illumination of the cave were found. Beside mobile stone lamps, immobile lamps made by reshaping of stalagmite bases and very limited micro combustion areas indicated by small heaps of charcoal are documented (Cantalejo *et al.*, 2014 a). A research program for residue analysis by Raman

Figure 2. Engraving of a flamingo scanned with a structured light scanner (Breuckmann SmartScan).

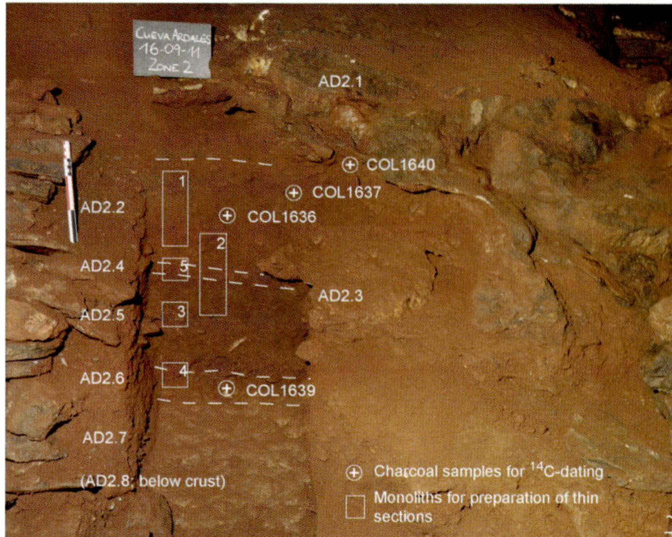

Figure 3. Profile of Zone 2. The bottom of the sequence immediately above the third stalagmitic crust is dated to 15,945 ± 60 yrs BP. The top of sequence is dated to 3,718 ± 40 yrs BP (all dates uncalibrated).

spectroscopy and radiocarbon dating of charcoal of these items is in progress.

Limited test excavations conducted from 2011-2013 at the entrance cone give first results for the absolute chronology of Ardales cave. The entrance cone of the cave (Fig. 1) was originally covered by a stalagmitic crust that was partly destroyed during the construction work of the stairs in the 19th century. In archaeological zone 2 (Fig. 1 and Fig. 5) a multi-layered stratigraphy could be recognized. Below the first and the second stalagmitic crust sediments belonging to the Holocene could be detected together with a small number of ceramics, lithics and fragments from a human cranium. Three radiocarbon dates from charcoal (COL 1640: 3,718 ± 40 yrs BP; COL 1637: 3,621 ± 35 yrs BP; COL 1636: 3,885 ± 36 yrs BP) indicate a chronology for the Copper Age. Below the second crust Pleistocene sediments were found. A radiocarbon date from a charcoal sample immediately above the third crust (COL 1639: 15,945 ± 60 yrs BP) suggests a Solutrean age. Bone fragments and a burin were associated with the sample. Sediments continue below the third crust. Manual drilling was performed using a soil auger, which reached a depth of 35 cm below the crust. The chronology of the sequence is supported by pollen analysis that indicates from the third crust to the top an increase of temperature and humidity (Ruiz Zapata and Gil García 2014).

The Holocene occupation of the cave is further supported by radiocarbon dates from test excavations of zone 4. Here charcoal samples from a nearby combustion feature indicate the same chronology as the upper part of zone 2. In zone 3, two charcoal samples gave results of more than 50 kyrs BP. The very small test excavation gave an additional result from a bone fragment of *Felis silvestris* of Holocene age (COL 2011.1.1: 5,562 ± 48 yrs BP). The contradicting dates need further sampling and expansion of the test excavation. Confirmation of a Middle Palaeolithic chronology would be in agreement with the observation that during the remodelling in front of the cave for the construction of the entrance building lithic artefacts of Middle Palaeolithic technology were discovered. Additionally, 200 m downslope of the actual cave entrance a Middle Palaeolithic surface

Figure 4. Top part of a stalagmite that was struck from the stalagmite, turned around and then used as lamp.

site La Cucarra has delivered a rich lithic assemblage.

The recent test excavations in the entrance cone of Ardales cave give new insight into the human occupation of the site. A Holocene and late Pleistocene occupation could be confirmed. Due to the steep topography of the entrance hall no suitable space for an occupation was available in the mouth of the cave in prehistoric times. Only in front of the cave or inside at the foot of the steep cone plane surfaces were available. A study of lighting conditions by ray tracing gives evidence that the cone area inside the cave was basically without day light in prehistoric times (Hoffmeister *et al.*, i.p.). Occupation and movement in the cave was possible only with the help of artificial light by fire or lamps. The number of finds that document artificial illumination in the cave represent an important sample for further analysis. Holocene occupation was probably linked to burial activities, while Pleistocene occupations were probably related to art activities. A great number of surface finds like lithics and other artefacts as well as human bones and animal bones are still in original position. Some of them are coated by thin stalagmitic layers. The ongoing study of their distribution in relation to the network of paths and items of rock art will give important insight into the human use of the cave. The blend of a rich record of rock art distributed over the whole interior with an excellent surface preservation of many areas of Ardales cave are a most valued resource for the study of past human behaviour.

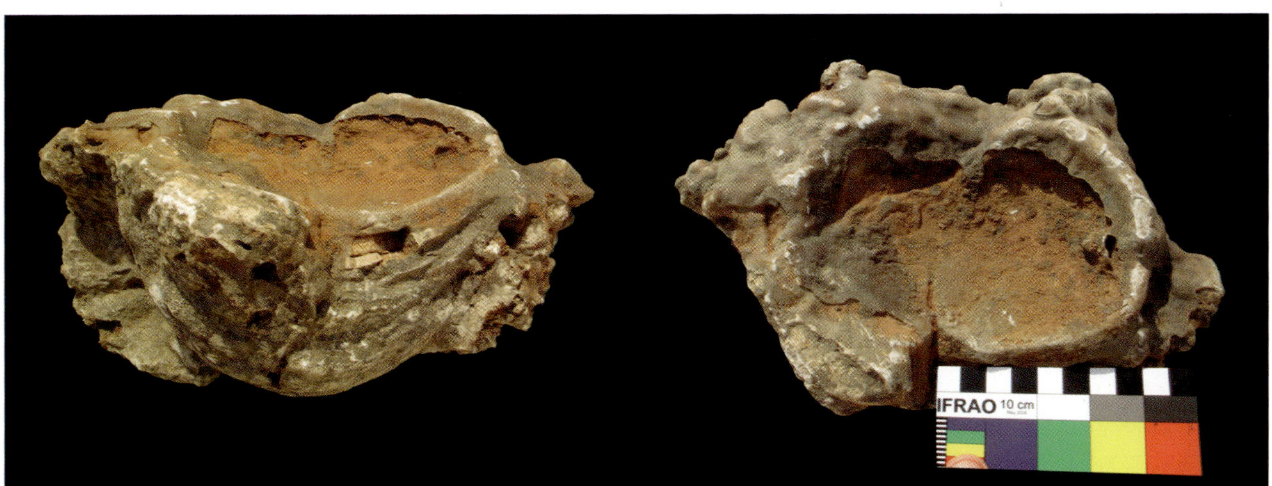

Figure 5. Top part of a stalagmite that was used as container for pigment.

Miguel Cortés Sánchez*,
María D. Simón Vallejo**

Bajondillo cave (Torremolinos, Malaga)

Abstract

Bajondillo cave is an archaeological site with a sequence that ranges between *c.* MIS 7 and V millennium BP, with occupations from the Middle Palaeolithic, Upper Palaeolithic and late prehistoric period. The data obtained from its sedimentary deposits and paleogeographic analysis of the western area of the bay of Malaga are essential for understanding the paleo/climate-environmental evolution of the coast of Malaga during the recent Quaternary period. The archaeological sequences permit the chronoculture of the recent Quaternary period in the south of the Iberian Peninsula to be established.

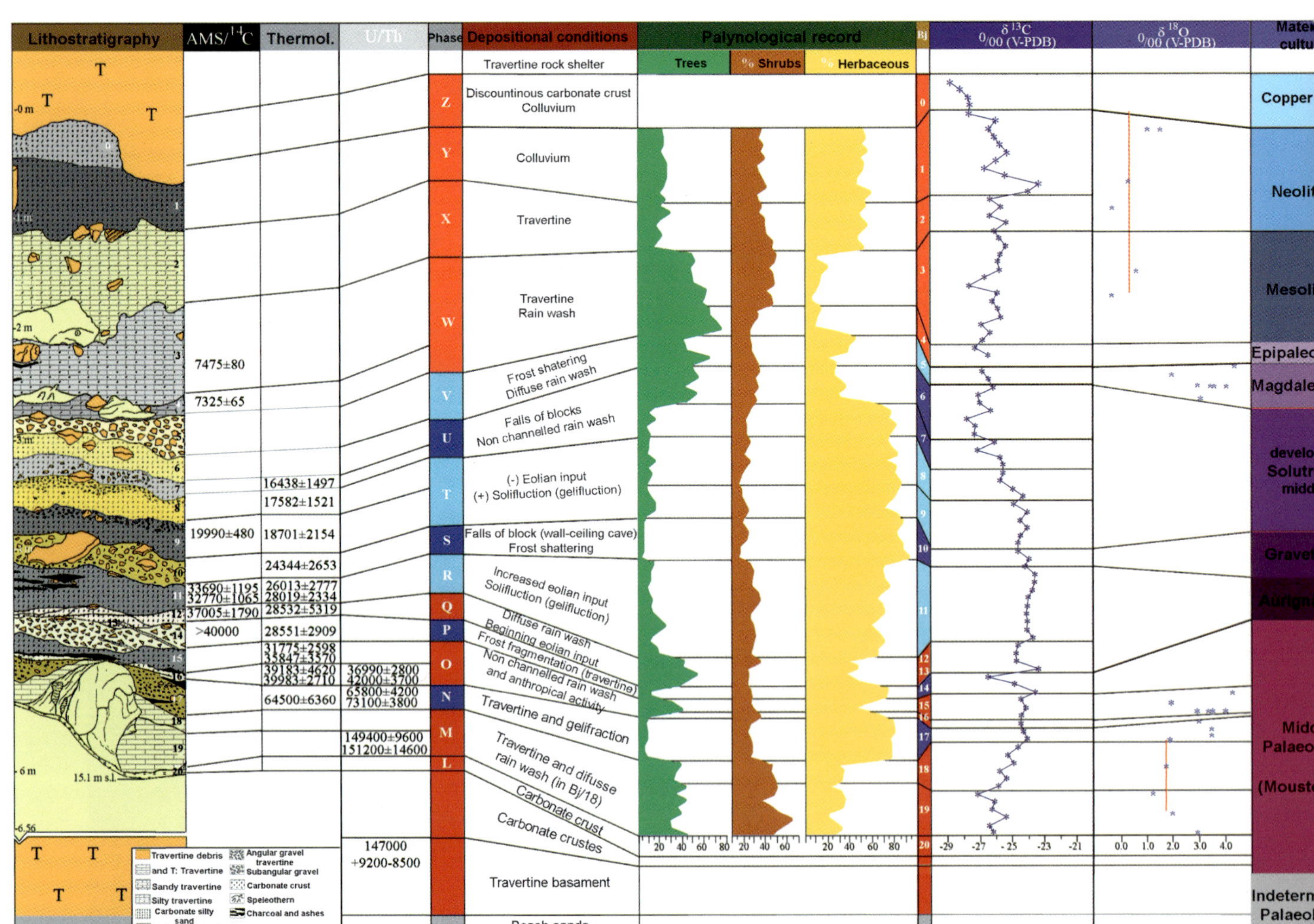

Figure 1. Bajondillo cave: Overview of records from the chronostratigraphical sequence.

* Prehistory and Archaeology Department. Faculty of Geography and History, University of Seville, c/. Doña María de Padilla s/n. 41004. Seville. mcortes@us.es

** Archaeological Museum of Frigiliana, c/. Cuesta del Apero, 10. 29788-Frigiliana (Malaga) (Spain). simonmd63@gmail.com

Figure 2. Lithic industries, marine molluscs and barnacles.

Keywords: Recent Quaternary period. Chronocultural sequence. Middle Palaeolithic. Upper Palaeolithic. Neolithic

Introduction

The western sector of the bay of Malaga has a morphosedimentary record of the different periods of the Neogene-Quaternary period that permits the geomorphic sequence of the north eastern foothills of Sierra de Mijas to be established (fan delta; erosion and sedimentary shaping, as cones and alluvial fans; river terraces; travertine construction and coastal deposits or coastal benches), the reference geographic framework for the populations that used this area as an area for gathering resources, mobility, etc.

Bajondillo cave is currently located in the area where the best microclimate conditions of the bay of Malaga converge. It has wide and guaranteed availability, from season to season and from year to year, of environmental resources, for example, springs, raw materials for knapping or the development of a rich ecotone (mountain range, proximity to the river mouth and estuary), which explain the use of the area by Neanderthals and modern human beings.

From a tectonic point of view, the area can be considered essentially stable since the mid-Middle Pleistocene, so that the impact of the glacio-eustatic dynamic during the recent Quaternary period can be analysed, which designed similar coastlines to the current (Holocene) and others up to 8-10km away, *c.* 21-18ka (all dates BP).

Bajondillo was discovered (1989) in the travertine construction in Torremolinos during construction work that destroyed areas of the upper sedimentary section (Bj/0-Bj/9). The site was excavated to an average of around 13m^2, reaching a maximum stratigraphic depth of almost 6m. The western profile was subsequently surveyed in 2000 and 2002, obtaining different chronological and paleo-environmental information (Fig. 1).

The sequence possibly started in MIS 7 and shows the typical climate-environmental dynamic of a coastal influence and the recent Quaternary period. The area never experienced the profound effects of other more northern sequences and allowed a shelter to exist where various species of thermophile are quartered.

Figure 3. Lithic industries. Middle Palaeolithic (Bj/17 to Bj14).

Sequence

Bajondillo has 20 archaeological layers whose chronological sequence has been established by 27 dating processes (^{14}C/AMS, TL and U/Th) of 13 levels (Fig. 1). The travertine where the cavity is located is deposited by constant contact with beach sands at a time that has not yet been well defined but probably within an advanced-late phase of the Middle Pleistocene, perhaps MIS 7, the cavity being filled at the base by a lithochemical plug at the bottom of the cavity, sealed with a stalagmite crust (Bj/20) on which a detrital deposit started to be deposited between MIS 6 (Bj/19) and Early Helocene.

The earliest archaeological evidence documented is two knapped chopping tools and some lithic tools below Bj/20 and >150ka (Fig. 2.16).

***Middle Palaeolithic* (Bj/19-Bj/13), *c.* 150-38/28.5ka.** From an economic point of view, the Neanderthal populations took advantage of an ecotone which retains an important tree-shrub cover and incorporates a wide variety of vital resources (water, biotic and abiotic). The Mousterian lithic industries developed Levallois production techniques, predominant, but also discoid, among others, with the presence of ramification and miniaturization.

Bj/19-Bj/18 (sedimentary episode [ES]/M) deposited under humid and mild conditions (Fig. 2.1-9). It is noteworthy that, along with large fauna (deer and aurochs), consumption of marine molluscs is also documented (Fig. 2), in a similar age (*c.*150ka) to the oldest documented in the world (Cortés *et al.*, 2011), in this case by modern humans.

Bj/17-Bj/15 (ES/N-O) indicate colder conditions with fluctuations in humidity. The lithic industry at these levels presents a variety corresponding to Typical Mousterian (Fig. 3).

Bj/14 (ES/P), in a colder and drier context, Mousterian of Denticulate assemblages tools are deposited.

***Upper Palaeolithic* (Bj/13-Bj/5. Fig. 4).** The oldest are detected in the section Bj/13-Bj/11(ES/Q-E), generated in a less cold and dry context than in Bj/14. The industry can be attributed to the Aurignacian (fig. 4A). The technological change compared to the Middle Palaeolithic is abrupt, the disappearance of the last techno-cultural examples from the Middle Palaeolithic seems to occur, as in the rest of the sites in the south of the Iberian Peninsula, with the epigonal occupations of the Middle Palaeolithic, as a phenomenon of collapse, rapid and synchronous disappearance with the development of the Mediterranean Aurignacian in *c.* 30-28/AMS-28.5ka/TL.

B/10(US/S), generated under cold and drier conditions than in Bj/11, it contributed Gravettian industries (*c.* 26-21.5 ky/TL) (Fig. 4B).

Bj/9-Bj/6 deposited in a wet and cold context (US/T), followed by a mild and humid one (US/V), and they contributed industries typical of the Solutrean (fig. 4C). The earliest full Iberian Solutrean phase (Bj/9) and *c.* 21-19/AMS/21.5-18,1/TL ky with the presence of artefacts with flat retouch. Bj/8-Bj/6 present evolving Solutrean industries (*c.* <19/AMS/18-16/TL ky) with notched pieces and high percentages of burins, many of them with truncated retouching.

Bj/5(US/V), deposited in wet and cold conditions. There are no diagnosis objects to define it but it falls within the advanced-final Late Glacial Maximum, perhaps *c.* 13-12ka.

Bj/4-Bj/3(ES/W) deposited in the Holocene and chronologies corresponding to the Epipaleolithic and Mesolithic.

Bj/2-Bj/0(US/X-Z) are attributable to late prehistoric period (Neolithic-Chalcolithic), *c.* 7.5-5ka. The Neolithic seems fully formed, with agricultural activities that leave their mark in the form of seeds of cultivated species, sickle elements or leaving their mark in the pollen record.

Bajondillo also has functional studies of collections from the Middle Palaeolithic, of phytoliths, raw materials for knapping or a fragmented example of portable art.

Systematic archaeological surveying around Bajondillo (20km^2) has allowed us to locate outcrops of lithic raw materials similar to some industries recovered at the site.

Conclusions

The formation of the travertine that gives rise to Bajondillo is earlier than MIS 6 (Bj/19), perhaps the warm MIS 7 period.

The coastal strip, whose variable amplitude was dependent on the glacio-eustatic dynamic of the bay of Malaga, is part of the subsistence territories, at least from the end of the Middle Pleistocene. This effect should undoubtedly be correlated with the high suitability of the environment and high availability of mineral and food resources in the geographical area defined by the travertine deposits of Torremolinos, the southern slopes of Sierra de Mijas and the river Guadalhorce; a geographical area that seems to offer sufficient resources for the territory to be integrated and visited, for more than 150 thousand years, in the core of the subsistence and mobility strategies of the hunter-gather communities (neanderthals and modern human beings) and subsequently crop-livestock farmers.

From MIS 6 and up until 36/38 ky, levels (Bj/19-Bj/14) are deposited with c. Mousterian industries, from which time we find technology systems from the Upper Paleolithic, at least Aurignacian, Gravettian and Solutrean, with some regional peculiarities.

Since it was discovered, the site has degraded quickly, which puts the record kept under serious threat.

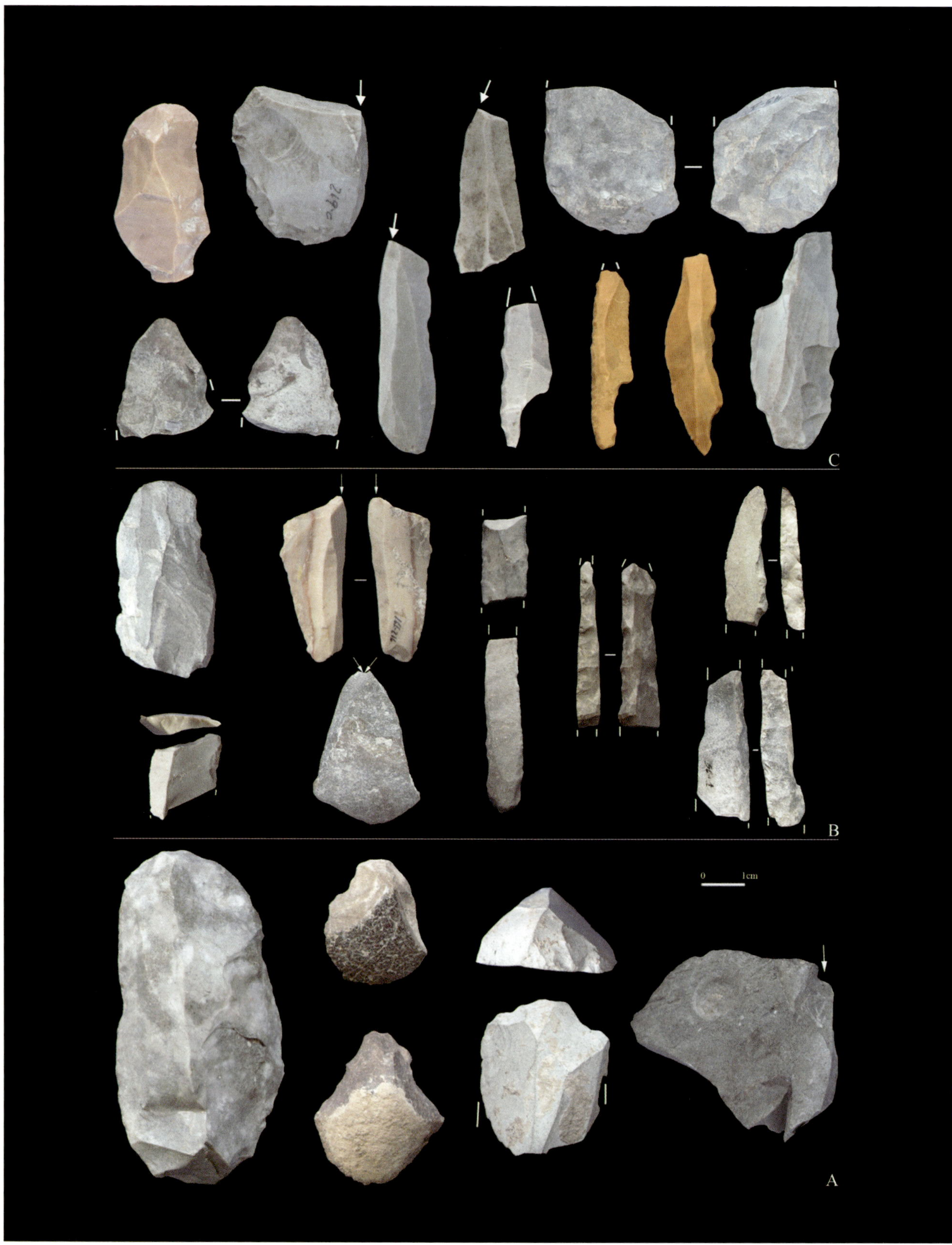

Figure 4. Lithic industries. Upper Palaeolithic (Bj711 to Bj/6).

Sergio Ripoll López,
Francisco J. Muñoz Ibañez*

The Solutrean Station of The Cueva de Ambrosio (Vélez Blanco, Almería, Spain)

Abstract: The last investigations made during the excavation of the different levels at this important site of study the Solutrean in the southeast of the Iberian Peninsula, have permitted us to make some precisions on its chronostratigraphic position in the Upper Pleistocene. The calibration of a new radiocarbon date for level IV (Upper Solutrean) and six other new dates (five of them AMS) for level II (Final Upper Solutrean) allow us to place these two cultural phases between the Greenland Stadial GS3 (end of OIS 3) and the end of the Greenland Intersatial GI 2, with a greater occupation of level II after the Heinrich Event H2, agreeing with the intersadial that come just before the last glacial maximum (GS 2). This new data clearly modifies the dates existing before, making the whole record much older. On the other hand, the discovery of decorated panels with engravings and paintings, recovered from Upper Solutrean sediments, allow us to place these representations, with great precision, in the Medium Solutrean (level VI) that must be placed between the GI 5 and the GI 3. The excavation of the area that we call the microstratigraphy, included in level II (Final Upper Solutrean or Evolved Upper Solutrean), has provided 21 double layers of hearts, one of them with a stone structure and thousands of very typical solutrean flint implements that include the characteristic barbed and tanged points, shouldered points and leaf points. The investigations carried out in the Laboratorio de Estudios Paleolíticos with these arrowheads, show that they must be thrown with a bow.

Key words: Solutrean, rock shelter, radiocarbon dates, southeastern Iberian Peninsula.

1. Introduction

When Breuil was digging in 1911 with Motos on a remote site in the southeast of the Iberian Peninsula, he could never have imagined that almost 100 years later the levels of occupation that fill this huge cavity would still not be clear. The work carried out by E. Ripoll in the 1960´s could not complete the stratigraphical sequence either, and the long excavation campaigns run by S. Ripoll from 1981 to the present, could not achieve this objective (real campaigns for digging: 1981,1982, 1983, 1986, 1990 1992, 1994 and 2002).

Figure. 1 Location Map and picture of The Cueva de Ambrosio (Almería, Spain).

* Laboratorio de Estudios Paleolíticos. Departamento de Prehistoria y Arqueología. Universidad Nacional de Educación a Distancia. Senda del Rey, 7. 28040 Madrid (Spain) sripoll@geo.uned. es, fjmunoz@geo.uned.es

2. Geo-Archaeology

The site is placed in the southeast edge of the external areas of the Betic Mountains (Fig1). The neogen sediments where the cave opens are limestone rocks of the Upper Burdigalian-Lower Langhian, made by biomicritasalgales rich in fossil remains, sometimes loamy, that integrate redeposit rests of the close mentioned materials; they surface in east to west direction belts and they are affected by post-mantle tectonics, although they are not raid by any other mode.

The Cueva de Ambrosio is located at the head of the Moral stream, on a peak 1,060 m above sea level. The mentioned limestone rocks are affected by a deep fracturing which conditions their geometry and the processes acting over them. The orientation is S-SW and the dimensions are a maximum of 15m high in the entrance and 17 m to the inside part of the shield´s edge.

3. Chronostratigraphy

The stratigraphy sequence of the Pleistocene deposits are composed by two clear lithostratigraphic units (Jordá and Carral, 1988). The lower one is made by thin-sterile materials produced by mud-flow from the inside of the karst that constitutes the beginning of the cavity´s sedimentation without reaching the rock´s substrate. The upper one is made by high energy deposits resulting from gelifraction processes with insertions of deposits mainly from human activity related to the Solutrean occupational levels of the shelter – Ambrosio II: Upper Evolved Solutrean; Ambrosio IV: Upper Solutrean; Ambrosio VI: Medium Solutrean (Fig.2). This unity presents an alternation of high energy sands and conglomerates in the roof, and ends in a cemented fracture which filled the sequence until a subsequent breakdown occurred.

In order to place Ambrosio´s sequence in the cronoestratigraphic scale, the radiocarbon dating obtained until this moment have been calibrated to sigma 2 probably 95%– through the calibration curve calPal 2007 Hulu, included in the program calPal (March Version 2007) (Weninger *et al.*, 2007). Also, to place it in the cronoestratigraphic and archaeological context of the Upper Pleistocene in the Southern Peninsula, we have integrated our dates in the set of radiocarbon dating coming from other sites with a similar chronology (between 27000 and 19000 years BP). We have considered 30 valid dating subjected to

Figure 2. Statigraphic profile view with the three Solutrean levels during the 1986 campaign.

the calibration through the calPal 2007 Hulu curve (Weninger *et al.*, 2007). The taken dates come from the southeastern Mediterranean sites in the Peninsula (Malladetes, Parpalló, Cova Beneito, Ratlla del Bubo, Cendres) (Villaverde *et al.*, 1998, 1999; Villaverde, 2001), southern Mediterranean (Nerja and La Pileta) (Aura *et al.*, 2006; Sanchidrián *et al.*, 2001) and Portuguese Atlantic (Buraca Grande, Vale Boi, Caldeirao, Lagar Velho, Salemas, Lapa da Rainha and Vale Almoinha) (Bicho, 2004; Pettit *et al.*, 2002).

The problem arises when comparing the three first dates of the Ambrosio sequence achieved by the usual procedure of the 14C (Ripoll, 1988) with the eight recently obtained, not only the conventional ones (3) but also the AMS ones (5), five of them already published (Ripoll, 2006) and other four unpublished. The first ones are markedly more recent than the second ones, as can be seen in schedule 1.

Level	Culture	Sample	Procedure	Cod.	¹⁴C (BP) Data)	cal. BP Data (2 σ; 95% prob.)	Ref.
Ambrosio II	(SSE)	Charcoal	Conventional	Gif-7276	16500 ± 280	20500 –19140 calBP	Ripoll,1988
Ambrosio IV	SS	Charcoal	Conventional	Gif-7275	16620 ± 280	20540 –19260 calBP	Ripoll,1988
Ambrosio VI	SM	Charcoal	Conventional	Gif-7277	16590 ± 1400	23180 –17020 calBP	Ripoll, 1988
Ambrosio II Generic	(SSE)	Charcoal	Conventional	Gif-9883	19250 ± 70	23570 –22490 calBP	Ripoll, 2006
Ambrosio II Layer 1	(SSE)	Charcoal	AMS	GifA-95576?	20150 ± 200	24550 –23550 calBP	Ripoll, 2006
Ambrosio II Layer 1	(SSE)	Charcoal	AMS	GifA-95577	19950 ± 210	24320 –23400 calBP	Ripoll, 2006
Ambrosio II Layer 2	(SSE)	Charcoal	AMS	GifA-A-II.2	19170 ± 190	23630 –22310 calBP	Ripoll, unpublished
Ambrosio II Layer 4	(SSE)	Charcoal	Conventional	Gif-A-II.4	19110 ± 90	23450 –22330 calBP	Ripoll, unpublished
Ambrosio II Layer 6	(SSE)	Charcoal	AMS	GifA-A-II.6	19300 ± 190	23680 –22440 calBP	Ripoll unpublished
Ambrosio II Layer 9	*(SSE)*	Charcoal	*AMS*	*GifA-A-II.9*	*13740 ± 140*	*ANÓMALA*	Ripoll unpublished
Ambrosio IV	SS	Charcoal	Conventional	Gif-9884	21520 ± 120	26270 –25230 calBP	Ripoll, 2006

Table 1. Radiocarbon dating.

The most ancient date of the three first ones (Gif-7277) presents a clear defect of precision, so it should be excluded in a strict analysis; as for the other two, they are consistent with each other, although they do not match with those obtained recently. When every date has been found in the same laboratory with a difference of almost 20 years, we finally choose the recent ones as they

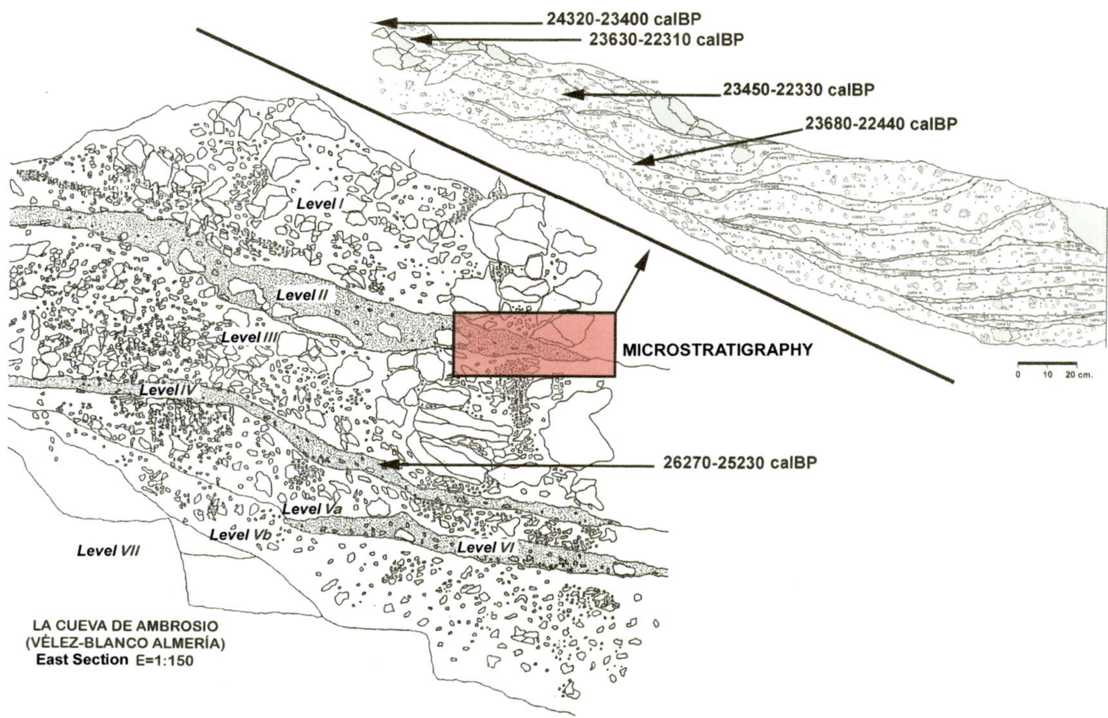

Figure 3. Stratigraphic profile with specific dating of every level.

come from a clearly defined and registered archaeological context (Fig. 3.).

Among the eight dates recently obtained, one of them (GifA-A-II.9) is clearly anomalous inside the sequence, so it will not be taken into account. The other six dates of the level Ambrosio II were obtained in a microstratigraphy constituted by an overlapping of prehistoric bonfires, and among them soft reversals can be seen, probably due to the nature of the dated coals, that, unfortunately, have not been subjected to an anthracology study before being dated. However, they present a good cluster; therefore they can be considered as a whole dating the Ambrosio´s Solutrean Upper Evolved. The date of the level Ambrosio IV offers no problem at all, and allows a precise dating of the Upper Solutrean. Unfortunately, in this new dating-series we do not have any of lower level, Ambrosio IV, that contains materials of the Medium Solutrean.

The level Ambrosio IV (Upper Solutrean) is located in the beginnings of the cold stage *Greenl and Stadial* 3 GS 3) (Björk *et al.*, 1998), in a moment in which the temperature of the Alboran´s Sea fluctuated between 11° C and 14° C (Cacho *et al.*, 1999, 2001), during the first half of the EH 2. At a regional scale, the level Ambrosio IV(Fortea and Jordá, 1976) is placed between the date of the Upper Solutrean of Malladeted and the most ancient of the Medium Solutrean at Vestíbulo de la Cueva de Nerja (NV. 9).

The level Ambrosio II (Upper Evolved Solutrean) develops during the second half of the GS3 and the event of Heinrich 2 (H 2), a moment in which the lowest temperatures of the Alboran´s Sea take place during the Final Upper Pleistocene, around 10° C, and ends during the warm inter-stage of the *Greenland Interstadial* 2 (GI 2) (Björk *et al.*, 1998), with Alboran´s sea temperatures of 12° C (Cacho *et al.*, 1999, 2001). Regionally, this level is placed in a fork defined by the dating of the Solutrean artistic expressions at Cuevas de Nerja and La Pileta (Sanchidrián *et al.*, 2001), and the dating of the Upper Solutrean at Nerja in the southern Mediterranean sea (Aura *et al.*, 2006) and other Portuguese (Bicho, 2004; Pettit *et al.*, 2002) and Valencian sites (Villaverde *et al.*, 1998, 1999; Villaverde, 2001).

4. Mediterranean shouldered points

Both Cueva de Ambrosio and Cova Parpalló articulate the industrial sequence of the Extra Cantabrian Solutrean, as they are the only sites with plenty of lithic assemblage and especially Solutrean points (Muñoz, 2000).

In the Medium Solutrean (Level IV) the Solutrean tools are marked by the consolidation of the bifacial knapping, prevailing novaculite laurel above the points of flat-side that still maintain an important weight. At the end of this period, a tendency to peduncle in novaculite laurel can be seen; their morphologies adopt a typology of transition between the novaculite laurel subtype "H" fins points (Smith, 1966) and peduncles. Bifacial Solutrean pieces are detected in the archaeological register for the first time. They are drafts of novaculite laurel whose fabrication process would not be completed.

In the Upper Solutrean (Level IV), flat-side points are still present, although in an occasional way. The novaculite laurel, which maintain their importance in the whole tooling of plane retouch, get smaller and thinner and sometimes have a rectilinear edge. In the Solutrean arrow points, the idea of peduncles technical is settled, timidly tested at the end of the former stage. Thus, fins points and peduncles become the distinctive tooling of this period, after the firsts drafts made at the end of the Medium Solutrean. The last type of arrow point representing this period is the Mediterranean notch point, with increasing importance on the whole of arrow points.

In the Upper Evolved Solutrean (Level II), the plane-invasive retouch loses its preeminence in favour of the abrupt retouch. The novaculite laurel are still present, although their number is significantly reduced. Although the fins points and peduncles are still important, the most remarkable tooling in all this period is the Mediterranean notch point, outnumbering any other arrow point of the Solutrean group. In addition, the tooling on little leaves presents a remarkable advance in regard to the former period.

The functional and experimental research done on fins points and peduncles and notch points of abrupt retouch show their use as arrow points, which means that the appearance of the bow and arrow technique could be traced back to the beginning of the Upper Solutrean in the ex-Cantabrian region of the Iberian Peninsula (Muñoz 2000; Muñoz and Márquez 2006; Muñoz *et al.*, 2012), (Fig. 4).

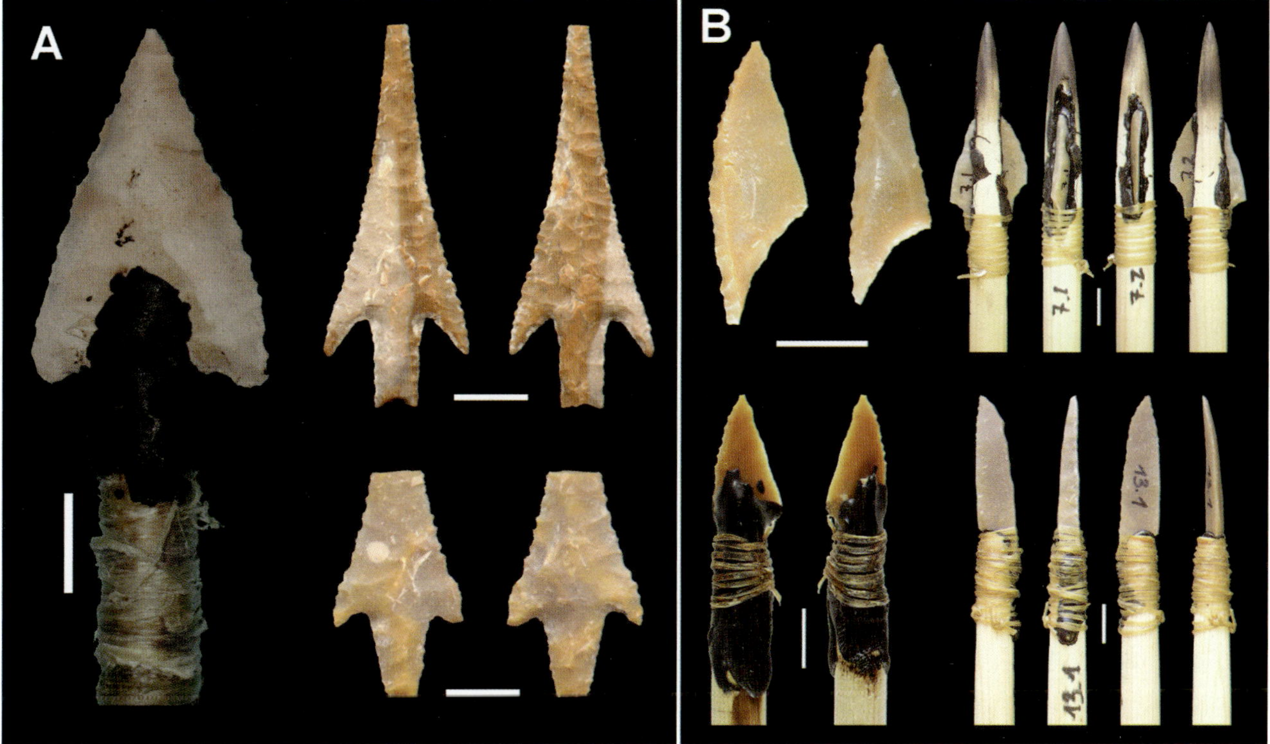

Figure 4. Upper Solutrean and Upper-Evolved Solutrean Points. A: Fins points and peduncles and fastening proposal in arrow shaft. B: Abrupt retouch of notch points and fastening proposal in arrow shaft.

5. Taphonomy

According to traditional interpretations assuming that all the taxa related to lithic industries appearing in an archaeological site are the consequence of human intervention, the marrow accumulation of Ambrosio could be considered an example of an archaeological site for specialized hunting of lagomorphs, as they constitute more than 90% of the recognized individuals.

However, the taphonomic research shows that they had a varied contribution made by birds, carnivores and humans. A small number of lagomorphs died of natural causes due to the falling of blocks from the shelter´s roof. Considering all these circumstances and calculating the amount of meat they could bring to the site, Ambrosio was actually not a hunting lodge specialized in rabbit hunting, because other animals like the horse, the goat, or the deer provided more meat.

The analysis shows that all the ungulates, as well as foxes, were meat processed by humans. After these were taken apart, carnivores would occupy the shelter scavenging offal of what was left. This shows that human occupation was not continious, so in certain moments the site was abandoned, facilitating carnivores benefiting from the waste they left.

Among the ungulates there is a diversified strategy over the goat, the horse and the deer. However, the analysis of seasonality has observed different hunting strategies.

A diversified hunting exists of the deer, the horse and the goat in the most benign seasons for the Medium and Upper Solutrean, and other more specialized hunting of the goat in the hardest moments of winter.

The duality of these two hunting strategies seems to be conditioned by resource availability. The goat would be the only animal hunted in winter because its adaptability to a variety of means allowed it to live in an immediate environment to Ambrosio during the hardest weather conditions of the year. On the other hand, the deer and the horse went to lower valleys in winter, and during the most benign seasons they climbed to Ambrosio´s environment to take advantage of the mountain pastures.

Figure 5. View of the set of panel II in which we have identified a total of 26 engraved and painted figures.

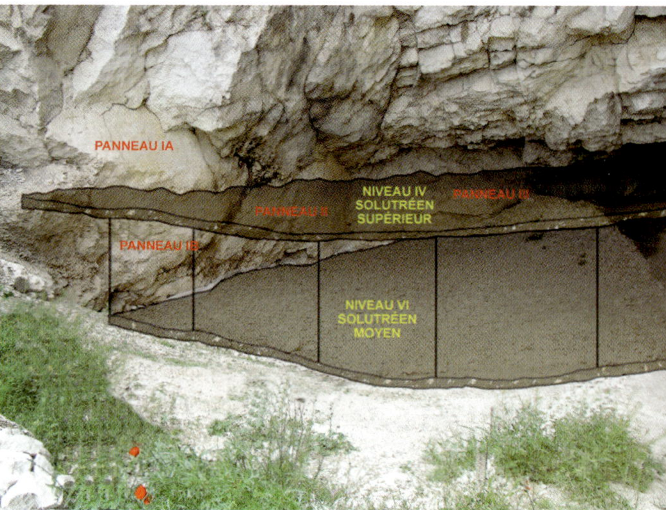

Figure 6. All the representations of Ambrosio are covered by archaeological levels. Its position, perfectly established, allows dating the set with great precision in two different cultural horizons. Panel IA is located in the Upper Solutrean, while panel IB and panel II, where the figure subject of this text is placed, match up to Medium Solutrean.

6. Prehistoric Rock Art

The archaeological site gave us a great surprise on 10 September 1992, when we found the first carved figures of Ambrosio cleaning a smooth surface where the reference point 0 is placed. Up to now, we have identified 35 representations engraved and/or painted, mainly zoomorphous including equidae, although there are also a bird, a bovine and some idiomorphs (Fig. 5). However, the remarkable figures are the incredible horse painted in red ochre, left-oriented and of a length of 92cm, and an immensely realistic, engraved and painted human face.

Nobody could imagine that in a shelter in the southeast of the Iberian Peninsula parietal representations could exist, and besides that, they were covered with sediments from the different archaeological levels. Rare are the seasons in which we find parietal representations covered by archaeological levels that allow a precise dating, and this is the case of Ambrosio. Although panel I is today outdoors, at the time it was covered by the intact levels placed a few centimeters to the left, which were removed by uncontrolled diggers, as well as the natural breakdown of the trench cuts opened by E. Ripoll in the 1960´s (Fig. 6).

All the levels filling the shelter reached a power of 4.97 meters, and would be covering all the embellished surfaces. Panel I-A would be covered by Fini Pleistocene levels on its upper level, as well as by the strata I (sterile), II Upper-Evolved Solutrean with an updated dating that ranges from 19250 and 20150 BP and III (sterile), being made from the occupational ground corresponding to level IV, or Upper Solutrean, with a new dating of 21520 ± 120 BP.

On the other side, panels I-B, II and III, which have a lower position respecting the former descriptions, would be covered by level IV, Upper Solutrean and by level V (sterile), and would have been made from the cultural horizon of the Medium Solutrean, which is much more ancient than the human level formerly described and that has a radiocarbonic dating of 23180 calBP.

In a region where Paleolithic paintings are really poor, even non-existing, these representations are surprisingly classic. The Cueva de Ambrosio is one of the few places with absolutely dated parietal Paleolithic art in the Iberian Peninsula. It is also located in the Mediterranean area where the placards collection of Parpalló (Valencia) (Pericot 1942; Villaverde 1994) are always mentioned, and we can also find outdoor figures as the place is a shelter, not a deep cave without natural lighting. These parietal figures offer great interest due to the importance, the artistic quality and the location in the southeast of Spain, and are certainly higher than the ones presented in the few sets of Paleolithic Art of the Mediterranean area.

The discovery of these figures fills the vacuum existing in this area in the geographic dispersion of quaternary-parietal art in the Iberian Peninsula, only represented by hammering equidae of Paleolithic style in Piedras Blancas (Almería) (Martínez 1986/87).

In Europe there are only four Paleolithic sites with the characteristics of an absolute dating, as the representations are covered by archaeological levels, and one of these is the cave of La Viña (Asturias), where some naturalistic representations covered by Medium-Evolved-Cantabrian Magdaleniense levels were found (Fortea 1981 and 1990). In the year 2001 the discovery of several parietal representations in the Parpalló (Valencia) was announced (Beltrán 2002). Although nowadays these figures are at a great height, respecting to the current ground, at the time they were covered by the archaeological levels dug by Professor L. Pericot in the 1930's (Pericot 1942); these are an equidae, a goat and several disjointed lines, as well as a quadruped in red ochre located above the area where Pericot's Medium and Upper Solutrean were placed. In the cave of El Mirón (Cantabria), some non-figurative representations have been found, covered by the archaeological levels of Medium-Cantabrian Magdaleniense (García *et al.*, 2012).

In the grotto of La Tête du Lion in France (Francia) (Combier 1972 and 1977), pictorial representations were not properly covered by the strata, but the systematic excavation carried out in the paintings base provided the tooling, "pencils" and charcoals used to make them allowed the dating. From this moment on, the figures set found in Ambrosio will be added.

The frequent discoveries of Prehistoric art stations outdoors or in archaeological sites, like in the present case, will introduce important changes on the ideas generally assumed referred to the geographical distribution, both for Paleolithic and post-Paleolithic art. The imposed schedules by important investigators have provoked these areas to be taken into account as exceptions contradicting objective pragmatisms, easily handling, and that marginally incorporated too many updates which later remained outdated because of the non-resolution of the real problem. Abnormal assumptions were accepted and increased, forcing us to make a revision of these problems admitted up to now as undisputed. These issues must be deeply addressed in scientific meetings that shed light on the distribution and dating of Peninsular Paleolithic art.

7. The Solutrean in the south of the Iberian Peninsula

The Solutrean in the Iberian Peninsula has a great industrial polymorphism that is reflected in the remarkable differences between the Cantabrian and the ex-Cantabrian areas. These two areas would be limited by an imaginary axis going from Portugal to the southeast of France via Madrid. The main reasons to mark the existing differences are essentially industrial and typological, as in other aspects, like the artistic, they offer many common points. These dissenting points arise to a greater extent at the end of the Solutrean, with the existence or the absence of the plane retouch over notch's points, as well as the existence or the absence of fins points and peduncles which start to appear in the cultural period of the Upper Solutrean, although at Parpalló they appeared in the Medium Solutrean.

Inside the extra-Cantabrian area, the Catalan Solutrean in the archaeological sites of L'Arbreda, ReclauViver, El Cau de les Goges, Davant Pau, etc., offers a certain originality, due to the presence of the plane retouch over notch points as well as other points with an incipient peduncle; together with other features, it could be considered different from the rest of the Spanish Mediterranean, but at the same time it is difficult to "accommodate it into the classic sequence" (Soler, 1986).

The fauna in almost every archaeological site is mainly dominated by lagomorphs (*Oryctolagus cuniculus*), related to goats, deer and equidae, as well as other mammals; the proportion of this composition varies in order of the environment of the seasons. .

Traditionally, the Solutrean has been considered one of the best known periods of the cultural sequence of the Spanish Mediterranean Paleolithic. However, while it is true that there are lots of archaeological sites with some integrated pieces of the Solutrean group, just a few have an enough representative industrial series to precise the exact moment of the occupation. This is the case of the Cave El Parpalló in Valencia and Cueva de Ambrosio in Almería. Only a few sites have a complete and updated study including all the range of analysis that allow fixing its chronostatigraphic position.

J. Emili Aura Tortosa*, Jesús F. Jordá Pardo**

Cueva de Nerja (Maro, Nerja, Málaga)

Introduction

Cueva de Nerja is a large cave with thick archaeological deposits in its outer chambers: Vestíbulo Hall, Mina Hall and Torca Hall. It also contains an important ensemble of Palaeolithic and Neolithic art in its inner chambers and varied documentation of funerary practices attributed to the Palaeolithic, Epi-Palaeolithic and Neolithic periods.

Located in the extreme south-west of Europe, on the coast of the Alborán Sea, this region has yielded some of the oldest evidence of the use of marine resources by humans. The mutual visibility of southern Europe and North Africa has led to proposals about the existence of relationships between both shores during the Palaeolithic, from simple formal and technical convergences.

The data used in this description come from the project directed by Professor F. Jordá Cerdá between 1979 and 1987 about the Palaeolithic and Epi-Palaeolithic in Cueva de Nerja (Aura *et al.*, 2002, 2010). The bibliography lists the most important texts and recent articles.

Stratigraphy and chronology

The sedimentary sequence in the deposit, obtained by correlating the lithostratigraphic and archaeological sequences in Mina (NM) and Vestíbulo (NV) Halls, consists of twelve stages of sedimentation and erosion corresponding to seven litho-stratigraphic units separated by five stratigraphic discontinuities (Jordá and Aura, 2009) (Fig. 1). These litho-stratigraphic units have been precisely placed on the Upper Pleistocene chronostratigraphic scale by a series of radiocarbon determinations calibrated with the curve CalPal 2007 HULU, using the CalPal software (2013 version). From top to bottom, the chronostratigraphic sequence is as follows (Jordá and Aura, 2009):

- Nerja Stage 1 (Unit 1, Levels NV13, NV12 and NV11). Located in NV, this unit overlies a thick speleothem and comprises autochthonous detritic sedimentation which took place between 29,940 and 28,480 cal BP, at the end of the OIS 3a, at a time that coincided with the end of Heinrich event 3 (H3), which would cover the GS 5and GI 4. It includes Gravettian industrial remains. In its base level (NV13, coprolites attributed to *Crocuta crocuta spelaea* indicate the absence of humans in the cave at the start of the sedimentary record (Arribas *et al.*, 2004). This unit may tentatively be associated with at least a part of the basal levels in NM (NM19, NM18 and NM17).
- Nerja Stage 2: A stratigraphic hiatus detected in NV and estimated to have lasted about 3000 years, caused by an erosive process related to GI3 and the start of GS3.
- Nerja Stage 3: (Unit 2, Levels NV10, NV9 and NV8). Detected in NV, these are deposits with characteristics of a cold but not extreme climate, dated from 25,6 to 20 cal BP. The sedimentation in the two lower levels (NV10 and NV9) is associated with GS3. An erosive contact has been recognised between NV9 and NV8, and the formation of NV8 also took place in a slightly cold and wet climate, which became drier towards the top of the level. This internal hiatus in Unit 2 may be related to the GI2, while its upper section (NV8) can be linked to the GS2c, in the Last Glacial Maximum. The archaeological materials are Solutrean.
- Nerja Stage 4: A stratigraphic hiatus caused by erosive processes together with a possible absence of sedimentation, which led to the non-existence of as much as 4000 years in the record in NV. It corresponds to the cold pulse at the start of the GS2a.

* Departament de Prehistòria i Arqueologia, Universitat de València, Avda. Blasco Ibañez 28, E-46010 València, Spain. (jeaura@uv.es)

** Laboratorio de Estudios Paleolíticos, Dpto. de Prehistoria y Arqueología, Facultad de Geografía e Historia, Universidad Nacional de Educación a Distancia, Paseo Senda del Rey 7, E-28040 Madrid, Spain. (jjorda@geo.uned.es)

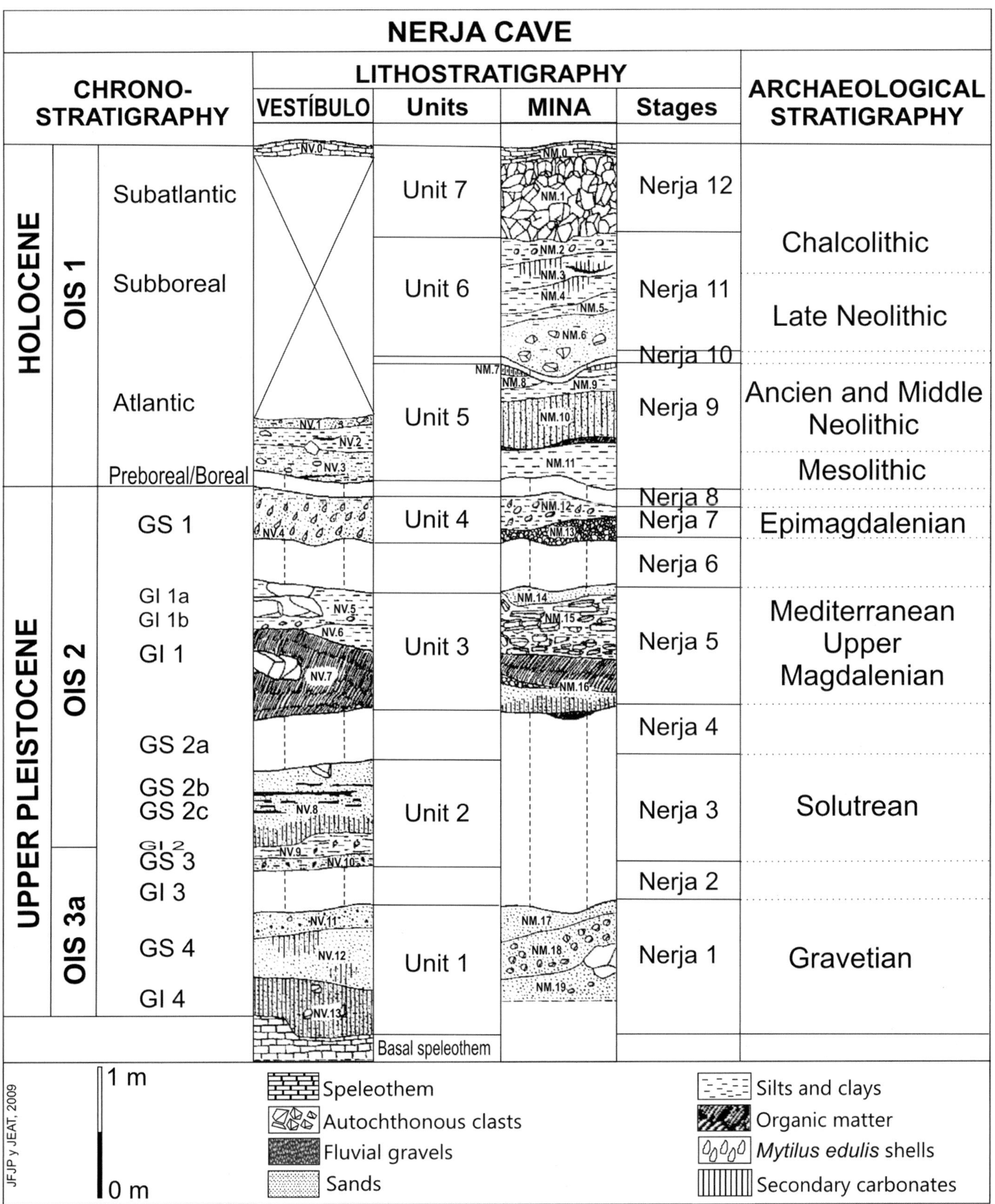

Figure 1. Cueva de Nerja. Chronostratigraphy, lithostratigraphy and archaeological stratigraphy in the sedimentary sequences in the Vestibule and Mine Halls.

- Nerja Stage 5: (Unit 3, NV7, NV6 and NV5; NM16, NM15 and NM14). Detected in NV, NM and NT, this unit is dated between 14,820 and 13,600 cal BP, coinciding with the GI or Late Glacial period, with mild climate conditions. Level NM15, characterised by a large accumulation of cryoclasts reflects one of the coldest moments in the sequence at Nerja and might be correlated with the GI1b. Nerja Stage 5 finished with the sedimentation in NM14 and NV5, with temperate characteristics, during the GI1a. This unit contains a Mediterranean upper Magdalenian occupation.
- Nerja Stage 6: A fluvial erosive phase which removed 600 years from the record, between GI1a and GS1.
- Nerja Stage 7 (Unit 4, NV4, NM13 and NM12). It is characterised by a large accumulation of remains of *Mytilus edulis* forming an anthropic shell midden in NV (Jordá *et al.*, 2011a). This unit developed from 12,950 to 11,360 cal BP, coinciding with the GS1 and the beginning of the OIS1, in the early Holocene. It contains remains of an Epi-Magdalenian occupation.
- Nerja Stage 8: An erosive phase responsible for a stratigraphic hiatus that lasted for a little less than 3000 years in the lower Holocene.
- Nerja Stage 9: (Unit 5, NV3, NV2 and NV1; NM11 to NM7). The base of this unit has yielded a few remains of the geometric Mesolithic and is located in the time between 8530 and 7920 cal BP, in the climate optimal in the mid-Holocene, at the base of the Atlantic chrono-zone. The middle and top section of the unit corresponds to levels with early and middle Neolithic materials, dated between 7490 and 6820 cal BP, in the middle-late part of the Atlantic chrono-zone.
- Nerja Stage 10: An erosive phase detected in NM.
- Nerja Stage 11: (Unit 6, NM6 to NM2). Deposits with late Neolithic materials, dated between 6910 and 5050 cal BP, in the last part of the Atlantic chrono-zone and the start of the Sub-Boreal, in the mid-Holocene. Chalcolithic levels are found at the top of this unit, which in Torca Hall is dated to 4820-3600 cal BP (Sub-Boreal).
- Nerja Stage 12: (Unit 7) Breccia and speleothems formed in the late Sub-Boreal and early Sub-Atlantic, during a temperate pulse in the upper Holocene.

Palaeogeography, palaeotemperature and palaeoenvironment

The study of the palaeogeographic evolution of the area around Cueva de Nerja reveals marine transgression in which several episodes can be identified in connection with the human occupations inside the cave (Jordá *et al.*, 2011b). During the GS2b (Between 20 and 19 ky cal BP), in the Last Glacial Maximum, the coastline was at –120m, which left a coastal strip uncovered extending over 4.5 km from the modern shore. After this time, the general warming and ice melt caused sea level to rise. This, in the GS2a, coinciding with the H1 (between 16.5 and 16 ky cal BP), the coastline was at –90 m, and 3.5 km from the modern position, whereas in the GI1 and GS1 (between 14 and 12 ky cal BP) the sea was at –70 m and 3 km away. The rise in level continued until it stabilised at –50m in the Pre-boreal and Boreal (from 11 to 8.5 ky cal BP), with the sea 1km away from the modern shore, and it rose again in the Atlantic and Sub-boreal with the sea level at –20 m and the shore 400m away from its current position.

A correlation has been proposed between the high resolution curve of the Sea Surface Temperature (SST) provided by the MD95-2043 core in the Alboran Sea (Cacho *et al.*, 2001) located to the south-east of Nerja with the different stages of sedimentation recorded inside Cueva de Nerja (Jordá *et al.*, 2011b): Nerja 1, with a SST between 10 and 14°C (last cold episode in the OIS 3a); Nerja 3, with a SST between 12 and 13°C (GS3, GI2 and GS2c); Nerja 5, with SST between 12 and 14°C (Late glacial or GI1); Nerja 7, with a SST reaching a minimum of 12°C (GI1 or Younger Dryas); Nerja 9, with a SST between 18 and 20°C (Atlantic); Nerja 11, with a SST between 18.5 and 19.5°C (Atlantic and Sub-Boreal); and Nerja 12, with SST about 18 or 19°C (Sub-Boreal/Sub-Atlantic).

The anthracological study for NV was able to propose the evolution in the palaeovegetation around the cave (Aura *et al.*, 2010). In the late OIS3 (Nerja 1), charcoals of *Pinus nigra* and *P. pinea* predominate, together with ligneous Fabaceae and several kinds of shrubs like juniper and rockrose. The area where the two pine species meet is between the Meso-Mediterranean and Supra-Mediterranean bio-climatic zones, in areas with a mean annual temperature of between 8 and 15°C, which reflects the conditions around Nerja in the Gravettian, with a regime of low precipitation: an annual mean of about 400-600mm. In the Last Glacial Maximum (GS3 to GS2), the Solutrean levels (Nerja 3), the same vegetation community existed with a tendency towards a reduction in black pine and an expansion in Fabaceae and other shrubs and low plants, with a similar proportion of stone pine to the previous period. In this way, the coastal strip around Nerja displayed Meso-Mediterranean conditions, although the black pine at higher altitudes indicates a colder vegetation type. In the Late Glacial period or GI1 (Nerja 5), the anthracological studies indicate an improvement in the climate with a decrease in black pine, and the presence of the Aleppo pine and *Quercus*. It was an open shrub vegetation, dominated by ligneous Fabaceae and with stone pine located probably in the coastal strip. During the Epi-Magdalenian occupation (Nerja 7) in the Younger Dryas and early Holocene, the species diversified, with the appearance of warmth-loving trees such as *Olea europaea*, mastic, the strawberry tree, box and flax-leaved daphne among the shrubs, while the Fabaceae are still well-represented, black pine continues to decline and a decrease in stone pine is also noted. These typical conditions of the thermo-Mediterranean bio-climatic zone appear to establish themselves on the coast around Nerja from the Epi-Magdalenian onwards. The improved climate of the Late Glacial period continued in the emerged areas during the GS1, while the sea water maintained its stadial conditions, allowing the entry of cold-tolerating Atlantic species.

The archaeozoological study also provides palaeoclimate and palaeogeographic data for the late Pleistocene and early Holocene (Aura *et al.*, 2010). Its results indicate that aurochs, horses and chamois were marginal species, while ibex continued to expand throughout the sequence, only surpassed in the number of remains by rabbit, most of which had an anthropic origin. Red deer was relatively important in the Pleniglacial, while wild boar is found from the Late Glacial period onwards.

At the base of the sequence, coprolites of *Crocuta crocuta spelaea* are associated with osseous remains of *Equus* sp., *Bos* sp. and red deer (Arribas *et al.*, 2004). Small carnivores (lynx, wild cat, fox and possibly wolf) are not common and appear throughout the sequence.

In the base unit was also found a single remain of *Testudo hermanni* identified in NV, which can be added to the turtles (*Emys orbicularis* and *Mauremys leprosa*) identified in NM during the Pleistocene-Holocene transition (Morales and Sanchís, 2009).

The earliest evidence of marine mammals is found at the base of Unit 2: two remains of *Phoca vitulina*. During the Late Glacial period (Nerja 5 and 7) the monk seal has been identified, as well as dolphins (Delphinidae and *Delphinus delphi*). In NM, the remains of two whale barnacles have been found. Their host was *Eubalena australis*, and the entry of this whale in the Mediterranean poses palaeo-climate issues (Álvarez *et al.*, 2014).

Nerja contains one of the most complete invertebrate, bird and marine fish records in the south of Europe (Aura *et al.*, 2002): thousands of remains of molluscs, fish, echinoderms, crustaceans, cephalopods and sea birds. The data provided by NV allows an analysis of trends over time. This in Nerja Stages 1 and 3, marine molluscs make up less than 20% of the total, and continental gastropods dominate in all the assemblages, coinciding with the practical absence of fish, echinoderms and sea birds. At the top of Nerja 3 (upper Solutrean) this trend is inverted, so that after this time marine molluscs predominate together with an extraordinary number of fish remains, in both Nerja 5 and Nerja 7 units. During the Last Glacial Maximum occupations, several mollusc species indicating cold conditions have been classified (*Pecten maximus*, *Nucella lapillus*, *Littorina obtusata*, etc.). In the Late Glacial levels, *Pinguinus impennis* has been identified, as well as guillemot and the little auk. These coincide with fish species that now have a northern distribution (*Melanogrammus aeglefinus* and *Pollachius pollachius*) (Rodrigo, 1991).

Techno-economic transformations

Changes in the surroundings of Cueva de Nerja were closely tied to the impact of eustatic oscillations around the continent. Their variations conditioned the size of the emerged land and movements along the main route of communication on the Mediterranean seaboard of Iberia: the coastal corridor. These palaeogeographic changes affected the possible procurement of resources and lithic raw material, as reflected by the composition of the tools and the palaeo-faunal and palaeo-botanical assemblages (Aura *et al.*, 2010). Thus, the variations in the density of remains, in the technology and typometry of lithic implements, and in the terrestrial and marine origin of the biotic remains attest aspects of the site history, and also of the distribution and economy of the Palaeolithic hunter groups who lived in one of the southernmost parts of Europe.

The techno-economic data provided by Cueva de Nerja can be arranged in three main cycles, with some internal details:

– The first corresponds to the full Glacial occupations, dated in NV to between 30 and 20 ky cal BP. Their main common trait is a careful blade production (select raw materials and mean length of 50-70mm) obtained from prismatic and flat cores with unipolar reduction series on their widest face. The presence of unweathered cortex indicates the raw material was procured in a primary position, at a distance of over 30 km from the site, and certain diversity has been seen in the flint groups, while jasper and rock crystal reach their highest percentages.

After this first characterisation, the descriptors used in Fig. 2 indicate that the density of materials, fauna and tools are able to discriminate two episodes corresponding to Units 1 and 2.

- The Gravettian occupations (Unit 1) have yielded the lowest density of lithic objects (150-800 per cubic metre of sediment excavated), basically documenting the phases of use and abandonment (Fig. 2). The lithic projectiles are limited to narrow points, backed in some cases, and a few bone points, found in low densities (3 points/m^3). Among the adornments, some gastropod species now have an Atlantic distribution area (cf. *Littorina*). The taphonomic study of the fauna has identified a carnivore occupation at the base of Unit 1, but the presence of remains with an anthropic origin from NV13 onwards. The most outstanding trait of these assemblages is the mean percentage of lagomorph remains and the high proportion of red deer, which has been linked to the size of the coastal strip. Marine fauna is scarce, limited to a few remains of fish and molluscs, in comparison with the large number of terrestrial gastropods.
- The Solutrean occupation (Unit 2) has yielded a greater density of lithic remains (900-1200 remains/m^3) in which all the phases have been documented, from manufacture to use and repair. Blade production is still important, but from NV9 onwards Solutrean reduction methods and heat treatment increase significantly, coinciding with the presence of leaf-shaped points and pieces with flat retouching. In the upper section (NV8 and NV8/s) a decrease in blade production is noted and an increase in backed micro-blade tools, obtained from differentiated productions. The increase in the number of broken and fire-altered projectiles is considerable, made both from lithics (uni and bifacial leaf-shaped points) and from bone and antler, mainly points with a rounded base (4 points/m^3). The objects of adornment are still made mostly from gastropods. Finally, terrestrial fauna displays an increase in ibex and lagomorphs, and a smaller diversity of species that is partly compensated by the identification of four remains of seals (*Phoca vitulina* and *Monachus monachus*). At the top of Unit 2, coinciding with the end of the Last Glacial Maximum, the percentage of marine fauna and pine nuts increases (Badal, 2001).
- Although a hiatus is found between both episodes, the techno-morphological and typological traits indicate significant continuity between the Gravettian (NV13-NV11) and the so-called Solutrean A (NV10), and objects similar to those in Vale Comprido have been identified (Fig. 3).

– The second of the cycles corresponds to the late Glacial occupations, dated between the end of the H1 event and the Younger Dryas (15-11.5 ky cal BP). These are occupations conserved in the three outer chambers in the cave (Vestíbulo, Mina and Torca), and have yielded a greater density of lithic remains (1200-1800 remains/m^3) and diversity of resources exploited (Fig. 2).

One common element in these occupations is the manufacture of lithic tools from flint cobbles collected in a secondary position, above all on beaches, according to their shape. Polished cortex is seen on 20% of the knapped lithic materials and many of these cortical fragments are altered thermally. Several thick-grained rocks (limestone, quartzite and metamorphic stone), obtained from cobblestones, were used as well as flint, and macro-lithic tools were made with them.

The reduction systems were aimed at obtaining blades and bladelets (20-35 mm mean length) and the different productions can be associated with the flint quality. The best quality raw materials were used for the most regular blade products, using a soft hammer, whereas a hard hammer was mostly used for more robust and irregular blades and bladelets, in

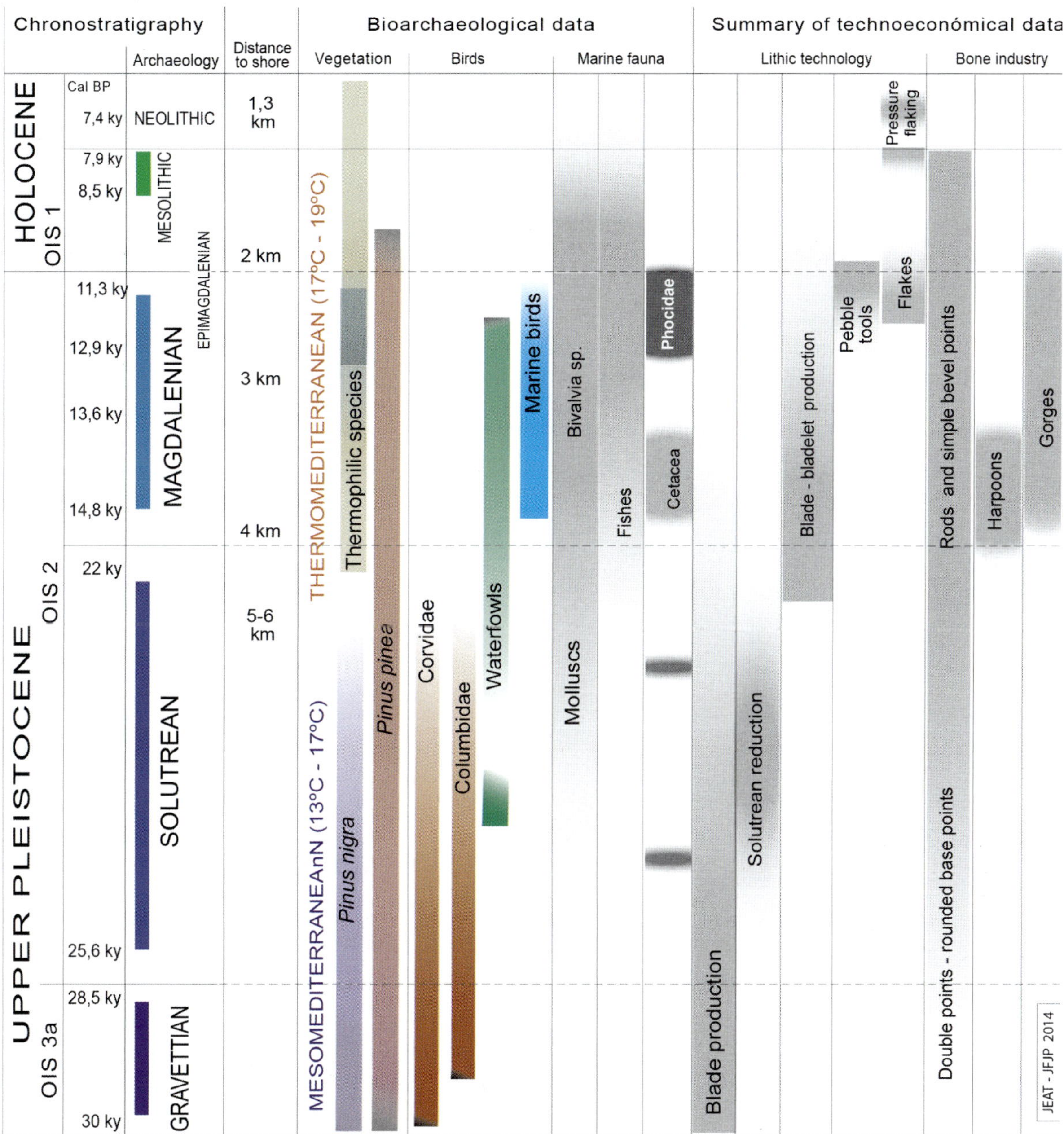

Figure 2. Cueva de Nerja. Summary of bio-archaeological and techno-economic data in the Upper Palaeolithic, Epi-Palaeolithic and Mesolithic occupations.

raw materials of a poorer quality. Most of the micro-blades are regular, some made from a flake blank, while others, according to their cross-section and profile, could have been extracted from burin-cores and nucleiform endscrapers. A production of short and elongated flakes has also been identified, using cores with a natural back and a uni and bi-polar reduction system. Many of the Magdalenian domestic tools (endscrapers, retouched pieces, notches...) are products shaped from blade cores.

The osseous assemblages in these occupations display greater variability and also density (from 6 to 40 pieces/m^3, depending on the sector and level). They are dominated by pointed objects, especially double thin and short points, thought to be gorges or straight fish-hooks. The five harpoons and over half the needles come from the Magdalenian levels, while the flat points, the chisels and remaining needles come from the Epi-Magdalenian occupations. Manufacturing waste indicates that

Figure 3. Cueva de Nerja. 1-9 Solutrean lithic industry; 10, 13-14, Gravettian lithic industry; 11, pierced and broken *Lynx pardina* canine tooth; 12: cirripede carina (*Pollicipes pollicipes*) with suspension notches (1-9: NV10-NV8; 10-12: NV13-NV11).

Figure 4. Cueva de Nerja. 1-2, knapped cobbles from the shell-midden; 3-4, Epi-Magdalenian bone industry; 5, cobble stone with geometric engravings; 6-9 upper Magdalenian bone industry (1,2 and 3: NV4; 4: NM13; 5: NM16: 6-9: NV7-NV5). Top right: remains of marine fish from level NV4.

bone was used to make the thin points and needles, whereas antler was used for the points, most of the harpoons and the chisels (Fig. 4).

The changes in the toolkit are accompanied by a clear reorientation towards exploiting the marine environment. In addition, the differences in the marine species that are seen between the chambers also raise questions about the duration and seasonality of the occupations. Contrasting with the diversity in the marine species, the capture of land mammals was still directed towards ibex, with the structural complement of rabbit.

Within this second cycle, two episodes can be established that unite both sequential and functional elements.

The first corresponds to the Mediterranean upper Magdalenian (with harpoons) occupations (15-13.5 ky cal BP: NV7-NV5 and NM16-NM14). A careful blade production, the highest densities of lithic and bone remains in the whole sequence and five harpoon fragments are some of its specific traits. Objects of ornament are sill made from shells and some pierced teeth; above all from *Cyclope neritea*, *C. pellucida* and *Theodoxus fluviatilis*.

Marine fauna now becomes more common: molluscs, echinoderms, coastal and estuary fish and marine mammals. These occupations have provided the largest numbers of remains of cetaceans and whale balanoids These indicate a use made of beached animals, whose size would determine whether they were taken to the cave or not: cranial remains and vertebrae in the case of dolphins, portions of skin and meat in the case of the whales.

The second episode represents evolution in Magdalenian technical systems and is dated between 13 and 12.5 ky cal BP, at the time of the Younger Dryas. The lithic assemblages reflect an increase in more expedient production and the presence of a significant macro-tool assemblage made from cobbles: hammer-stones, knapped cobbles, grinders and millstones transmit the processing of a wide range of resources and new ways of using the site (Fig. 4). The bone assemblage is restricted to some points, chisels and gorges, while ornments are made from *Cyclope neritea*, together with *Nucella lapillus* and *Trivia arctica*.

The marine fauna becomes even more abundant, and one of the oldest shell-middens on the continent accumulated (NV4). Together with the bivalves, the number of fish remains and migratory character of some species marks some differences from the Magdalenian occupations. Among the mammals, the large number of monk seal remains (Pérez and Raga, 1998) is only second in importance to ibex and is much larger than the number of red deer remains.

– After another hiatus, the third cycle corresponds to the middle Holocene and its main justification is its date within the Atlantic chrono-zone, as it corresponds to two different periods: Late Mesolithic and Neolithic. These are occupations with a low density of lithic remains and an unequal standard of documentation.

The Mesolithic could not be isolated stratigraphically, as intrusions and Neolithic pits seriously affected it. However, some lithic products (flakes), morphotypes (trapezes, micro-burins and Montbani-type blades) and short-life radiocarbon dates indicate human presence in the cave between 8.5 and 7.9 ky cal BP, although not with the density of the previous periods (500-700 lithic objects/m^3).

Finally, the Neolithic is dated to between 6.9 and 5 ky cal BP and has yielded a similar density of remains (about 600 remains/m^3). Short-life dates indicate a gap of several centuries after the Mesolithic, with the sudden appearance of pottery, domestic species and new lithic reduction systems: pressure knapping associated with the heat treatment of the cores. The osseous industry also exhibits new morphotypes (spoons, tubes, ovicaprine punches) made by fracturing the bones. At the time of this third cycle, *Columbella rustica* became widely used as an object of adornment on both shores of the Mediterranean.

Palaeolithic art and burials

Several references exist to Palaeolithic burials in Cueva de Nerja, while in recent Prehistory the cave was repeatedly used as a necropolis. In 1963-64, four "Solutrean" burials were excavated in the Vestíbulo Hall. However, a direct radiocarbon determination for a remain belonging to Individual 1 or A, indicated a Neolithic age. In 1982, an Epi-Palaeolithic burial was excavated in Torca Hall. The individual was identified as a female. In 1984, some phalanges and metatarsals were recovered in NV, for which a tentative age of 18-12 ky BP was proposed, according to which these burials could correspond to Palaeolithic. Apart from these descriptions of articulated remains, "isolated human bones" have been found in Palaeolithic and Epi-Palaeolithic levels, coinciding with a general trend observed in Mediterranean regions after the Late Glacial period.

In the deposits in Mina and Vestíbulo Hall, a few portable art objects have been found: plaquettes and cobblestones with linear incised motifs and a naturalistic representation of a bird, as well as pieces of ochre and tools connected with its processing. This kind of evidence is more common in the Solutrean and Epi-Magdalenian occupations, with which most of the Palaeolithic art inside the cave has been associated. The recent publication by J.L. Sanchidrián of the use of hollows and *Pecten* sp. valves as possible points of illumination, indicates a close correlation between the occupations in the outer chambers and the use of deep parts of the cave in the full Glacial period.

The inner chambers are known as the Tourist Galleries and the High Galleries. These two decorated areas are differentiated topographically, but also by the number of motifs and iconographic themes they contain. In the former, most of the simple signs are associated with a few animal figures (horses, ibex and deer). They are pre-Magdalenian in age, possibly beginning in the Gravettian. In the latter galleries, a mono-thematic composition is known as the "Shrine of the Dolphins". Animals and linear motifs have been described in other parts of the cave too, including a black linear phase, largely of Holocene age.

Cecilio Barroso Ruiz *, Anne Marie Moigne **, Miguel Caparrós *****, Vincenzo Celiberti **, José García Solano ***, Guadalupe Monge ****, Antonio Monclova *

The Acheulian at Cueva and abrigo del Ángel (Lucena, Córdoba)

Introduction

Cueva and abrigo del Angel is a Middle to Upper Pleistocene site situated in the south of the Iberian Peninsula, in the municipality of Lucena (Córdoba, Spain). It is located in the Sierra de Aras (also named Sierra de Araceli), at 620 metres a.s.l. Its coordinates are 37° 24' 22" Lat. - 4° 24' 59" Long. The archaeological fieldwork started in 1995. Until 2014, the General Administration of Cultural Heritage from the Junta de Andalucía has approved seven campaigns on this site.

Geological setting

The lithostratigraphic series of the Sierra de Araceli belong to the External Meridional Subbetic Domain of the Betic Cordilleras, and comprises materials from the Triassic to the latest Quaternary period. Triassic materials are represented by red, green and bluish-purple clays that become masses of gypsum on the top of the sequence. These Triassic materials do not appear at the surface of Araceli massif directly, although they probably constitute the base of the stratigraphic series (López Chiclano, 1985). On the contrary, two chronostratigraphic units are well represented both in the Sierra and in the surrounding mountain:

a) Mesozoic unit that comprises mainly limestones, dolomites and carbonated marl from the Jurassic-Cretacic period. It is the most relevant relief of the sierra, affected by various faults and diaclases, as the result of which important karstification processes have given rise to the formation of sinkholes and cavities, such as Cueva del Angel.
b) Cenozoic unit composed by marl, biocalcarenite and most recent detrital sediments; it has very sharp contact with the former unit. Miocene deposits are composed of more than 100 metres thick of white and green marls and biocalcarenites, whereas the Quaternary period is well represented in vast clay plains resting on the top of the above mentioned materials, corresponding to fluvial, glacis and piedmont deposits.

* Fundación Instituto de Investigación de Prehistoria y Evolución Humana. Plaza del Coso 21, 14900 Lucena (Córdoba, España) email: barroso.cecilio@gmail.com
** Muséum National d'Histoire Naturelle. Centre Européen de Recherches Préhistoriques de Tautavel.
*** Departamento de Prehistoria y Arqueología. Universidad de Granada.
**** Departamento Cristalografía, Mineralogía y Q.A. Facultad de Química. Universidad de Sevilla.
***** Département de Préhistorie, Muséum National d'Histoire Naturelle, 75013 París, France.

Concerning its geomorphological structure, the Mesozoic Unit presents an alternation between soft and hard deposits that give a stepped landform to the northwestern sector of the Sierra de Araceli. The loamy soils are often cultivated and the harder ones support scrubland formations. On the other hand, the Cenozoic unit has a morphology of very eroded domes, also cultivated, that appear as very extensive outcrops (López, 1985).

J/K section stratigraphy

Transverse stratigraphic profile in J/K zones is the most relevant area discovered so far at the Cueva del Angel. It goes from sector 5 to the middle area of sector 8 (Fig.1) and is 365 cm thick. This profile includes great archaeological and paleontological material that consists mainly of faunal remains, mostly burned, and lithic assemblages, especially worked on flint.

Furthermore, secondary calcite precipitations fill any little hollow in the whole profile in a homogeneous and accentuated way. These precipitations are typical of the vadose zones of every karst system and come from the alternation of moist and dry periods. In humid periods, water rich in bicarbonate predominates and subsequently is completely filtered by percolation processes along the profile. Whereas in dry periods evaporation prevails and consequently carbonates precipitate again provoking the cementation of the entire stratigraphic profile. Once more these alternations of moist and dry periods conditioned the formation of several generations of speleothem layers that will cover any vacuolar porosity (Monge, 2012).

At the J/K profile, twenty stratigraphic levels have been established (Fig.1) based on the observation and description of their particular traits. Levels have been differentiated on the base of the following categories: lithology, colour, texture, consistency, fine-grained structure, coarse fraction proportion, porosity and bioturbation. Also, the presence of anthropic features in each level has been taken into account (Table 1).

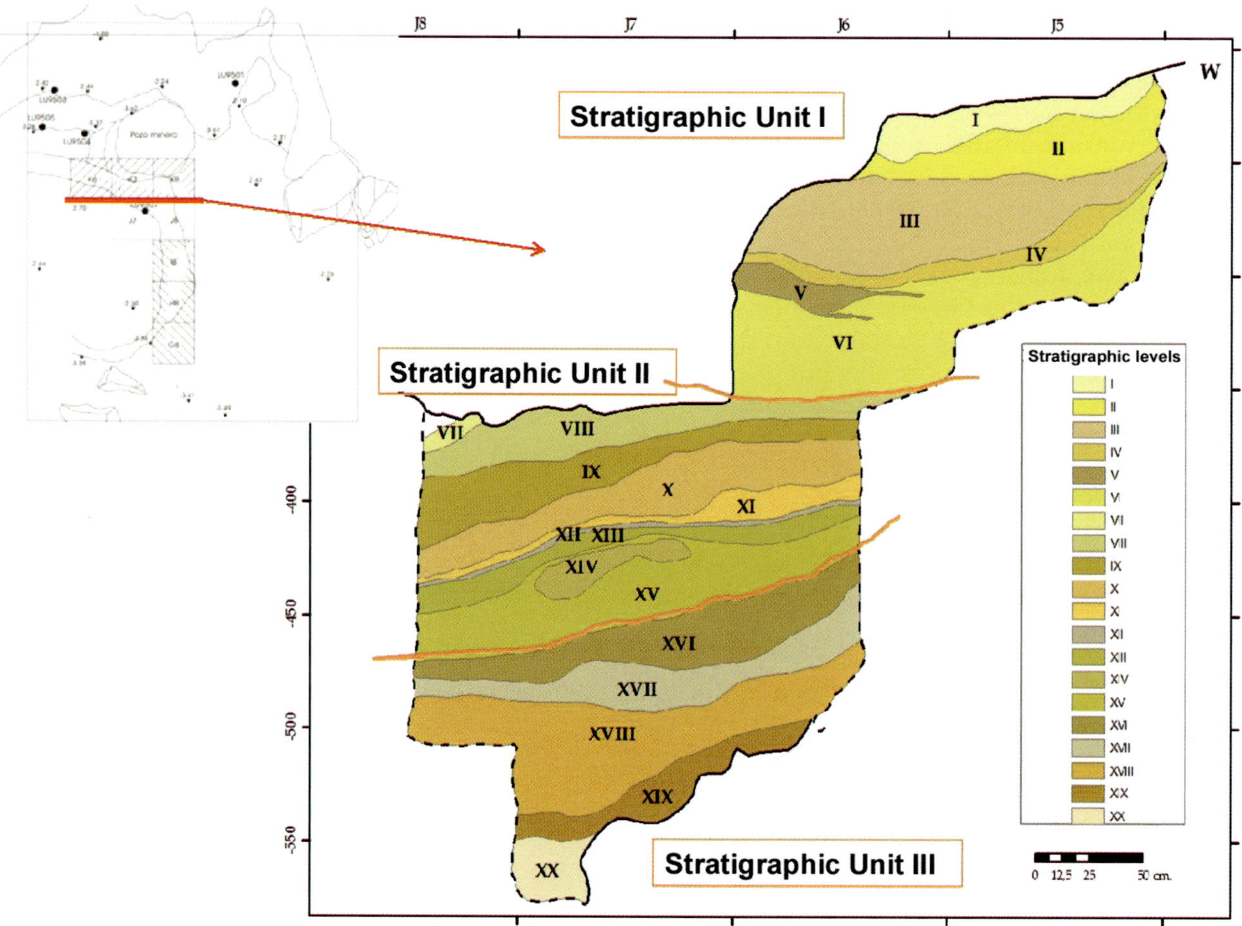

Figure 1. Stratigraphic profile of J/K zone.

Stratigraphic levels	Depth (cm)	Munsell Colour	Texture	Structure	Consistency	Porosity	Coarse fraction/ fine-grained fraction (%)	Anthropic features
I	208-250	Pinkish gray (7'5 YR 7/2)	Loamy*	Blocky	Soft to hard	Low	20/80	Scarce
II	214-258	Very dark greyish brown (10 YR 3/2)	Loamy	Granular	Soft to hard	Low	1/99	Slightly abundant
III	240-300	Dark reddish brown (7'5 YR 4/2; 5 YR 3/2)	Loamy	Granular	Hard	High	20/80	Slightly abundant
IV	249-307	Pinkish gray (5 YR 6/2)	Sandy loam	Blocky	Loose	High	0/100	Scarce
V	294-318	Pinkish gray to dark brown (5 YR 6/2; 7'5 YR 4/2)	Loamy	Platy	Soft	_	0/100	Scarce
VI	253-355	Dusky red (7'5 YR 3/2; 2'5 YR 3/2)	Loamy	Granular	Soft	Low	1/9	Slightly abundant
VII	364-381	Red (2'5 YR 5/7)	Sandy loam*	Granular	Soft	_	0/100	Scarce
VIII	348-390	Dark brown to dark reddish gray (7'5 YR 3/2; 5 YR 4/2)	Sandy loam	Granular	Soft	Low	30/70	Very abundant
IX	363-422	Dark brown to dusky red (7'5 YR 3/2; 2'5 YR3/2)	Sandy loam	Granular	Hard	Low	50/50	Very abundant
X	374-434	Dark reddish brown (7'5 YR 4/2; 5 YR 3/2)	Clay loam	Granular	Soft to hard	Low	40/60	Very abundant
XI	386-436	Pale red (2'5 YR 6/2)	Sandy loam*	Granular	Hard	Low	5/95	Scarce
XII	398-438	Gray (2'5 Y 5/0)	Sandy loam*	Granular	Soft	_	1/99	Scarce
XIII	400-449	Pinkish gray (5 YR 6/2)	Sandy loam*	Granular	Hard	Low	20/80	Scarce
XIV	416-443	Pinkish gray (7'5 YR 7/2)	Sandy loam	Granular	Hard	_	20/80	Very abundant
XV	405-470	Pale red to pink (2'5 YR 6/2; 2'5 YR 8/4)	Sandy loam	Granular	Hard	Low	40/60	Very abundant
XVI	423-480	Pale red (2'5 YR 6/2)	Loamy	Granular	Hard	_	30/70	Slightly abundant
XVII	436-493	Pinkish gray (7'5 YR 7/2)	Loamy*	Granular	Hard	_	30/70	Slightly abundant
XVIII	462-539	Pinkish gray to pale red (5 YR 7/2; 2'5 YR 6/2)	Silt loam	Blocky	Hard	_	20/70	Slightly abundant
XIX	494-550	Reddish brown (5 YR 5/4)	Silt loam	Granular-Blocky	Very hard	_	1/9	Slightly abundant
XX	546-580	Reddish brown to pink (5 YR 5/4; 5 YR 7/4)	Silt loam	Granular	Plastic	_	20/50	Slightly abundant

Table 1. Descriptive characteristics of the stratigraphic levels.

Looking at the arrangement of the stratigraphic levels, one of the most noticeable facts is the strong dip direction that levels VII to XV have towards the east (see Fig.1), as well as the small but abundant fractures that dominate in the speleothem system situated in the excavation area of the karst complex and provoke the vertical displacement of some speleothems regarding others.

Furthermore, the small cavity (Covacha del Angel) as much as its extension in the sinkhole (Sima del Angel), are part of a fault, in turn integrated in a major fault system on the Sierra de Araceli. Consequently, it seems evident that tectonic processes have occurred once the archaeological record had been deposited. This point has been made quite certain because the original roof and walls from the original cavity are absent, although their existence has been registered in the present floor with frequent speleothem structures. Neither should we exclude a suction effect produced by the sinkhole itself on sediments and gravitational blocks, since it is obvious that both parts of the karst system, the small cave and the sinkhole, were connected in the past.

The twenty stratigraphic levels present a subhorizontal arrangement or dipping towards the east (levels VII to XV) with convex morphology that suggest postdepositional collapse phenomena (Monge, 2012).

The colouration of all levels varies between different tones of brown, gray, pinkish and reddish, with a loamy to sandy loam texture, according to USDA (Staff, 2010), and a remarkable granular soil structure. Concerning the consistency it is very heterogeneous because it varies according to how each level has been affected by secondary calcite precipitations. Porosity is non-existent or very scarce (if it exists, is always vacuolar), and contacts between levels are neat. The percentage of coarse fraction, as well as the frequency of archaeological material, present major variability. Considering these two variables, three big stratigraphic units have been differentiated (see Fig.1).

The upper unit (I) comprises levels I to VI, and it extends from top (–215 cm) to –350 cm thick. It presents little archaeological material and also scarce and scattered coarse fraction. The prevailing texture is loamy and exhibits different types of structure: blocky, granular and platy. Porosity is quite variable (always of vacuolar type), and brown and reddish are the dominant colour.

The middle unit (II) develops from –350 cm to –450, includes levels VII to XV and comprises a large amount of burned bones lithic tools and abundant coarse fraction from carbonated origin. Its colours vary among brown, grey and reddish. Although in a global concept this unit is a breccia deposit, considering the fraction lower than 4 mm, the dominant texture is sandy loam with fine subordinated granulometry; the structures of all levels is granular and its scarce porosity–when present- is of vacuolar type. This unit is the most homogeneous of the three units defined.

The lower unit (III) develops from –450 cm to the base of the deposit, includes levels XVI to XX. The prevailing colours vary between pinkish grey and reddish brown. Its texture is sandy loam and much more fine-grained in the bottom part; no porosity has been observed and its structure varies between granular and blocky. This unit presents the lowest proportion both of archaeological material and coarse fraction that again appears disperse. Considering these two descriptive characteristics, which are the ones that reflect a major variability, Unit III is very similar to Unit I.

Archaeological site description

The site is situated in Mesozoic karstic unit of the Sierra de Araceli, and downcut in the Lías dolomitic limestone formation in the External Meridional Subbetic Domain; its description presents some complexity.

The site is located in the southwestern slope of the sierra, at around 100 metres high regarding its base, so it cannot be considered a real mountainous site.

The archaeological site presents three differentiated, although interconnected, parts. Firstly, the "platform", an open-air area that would have been the remnant of a cave that probably collapsed before hominids came to this place. Archaeological excavations were undertaken in this area in 1995. Located a few metres from the platform, there is a small cave of approximately 60 m^2 that still has not being excavated, although it was looted in the past. And finally, the sinkhole situated beneath the small cave and the platform. It presents a narrow morphology with vertical 100 metres depth walls. It is filled at the bottom with substantial detrital accumulations that from a 70 m high dejection cone. In 2009, a 30 metre long tunnel was drilled connecting the exterior, almost the base of the sierra, with the inner part of the sinkholes, in order to further study and better understand the nature of the human occupation and also to open the place to tourism in the future.

Fieldwork excavations

The first archaeological campaign at Cueva del Angel was undertaken in 1995-1996 authorized by the regional government. From these years until 2014, the General Direction of Cultural Heritage of Junta de Andalucia has authorized seven archaeological campaigns on the site: two short and very specific campaigns in 1995-1996; other two short archaeological excavations in 2002-2003; two campaigns in the context of a research project (2005 and 2008), and lately, one new fieldwork excavation in 2013. The archaeological fieldwork has been funded, mainly by the municipality of Lucena, as well as by Consejería de Cultura and Cuevas and Sima del Angel Foundation.

Until 2013, the archaeological excavations have been focused at the platform sector. The excavation area has been partitioned into a system of Cartesian coordinates of 1 m^2 squares with letter and number axes. The following zones have been excavated: J7, K5, K6, K7, K8, F8, G8, H8, I8 and J8. In 1996 a mining well (L7/L8) from the end of XVIIIth century was discovered. It has 2 m diameter and 5 m depth and the refreshing of its profiles has uncovered a sedimentary sequence along five grid units, all of them situated in the transversal axis of J/K sector. At the present time, excavation has also started in the longitudinal axis in the grid units of the number eight.

The platform area has less than 300m^2, where at least 100 m^2 are Pleistocene deposits, the rest correspond to limestone outcrops and especially speleothems (stalagmite, wall speleothem, etc.) which indicates that a closed cavity existed in the past and subsequently –at an undetermined moment– the roof and walls of the cave collapsed leaving the inner part exposed to open air. It has been hypothesized that on the north wall there could have existed traces of a kind of ceiling configurating some rockshelter-like form where hominids installed a hearth of more than 3 m in diameter. This perfect place for shelter and the rich faunal and botanical environment in the surroundings of the site, favoured the permanence of the Acheulean occupation in this place.

Spatial and taphonomical analysis of faunal assemblages, as well as typological and technological studies of lithic industry recovered at the platform area have raised the hypothesis that this space was used for skinning, fracturing, disarticulation, filleting and defleshing animal food transported to the site by hominids, and then cooked on fire and consumed there. Knapping is also documented in this place and is represented by non-modified flakes used as knives. Lithic tools present few variety, sidescrapers predominate (typical for fur working), and notches and denticulates have a very low percentage. Bifacial pieces have pointed shape edges; in some cases this pointed extremity is broken due to the impact of breaking bones. Truncations, burins and endscrapers are anecdotic. It is worth mentioning that all this lithic type distribution is closely related with the specific economic activity developed on the site, and that would explain the absence of numerous typologies typical from the Acheulean toolkit.

In 2013, the archaeological excavation in the sinkhole was undertaken by means of 6m^2 test pit. Previously, a geophysics survey using electronic tomography was done. This survey determined the presence of a 10 m deep deposit with Holocene and Pleistocene origins. In 1 m^2 of the test pit more than 800 fragments of human bones have been recovered. All of them belong to Homo sapiens and are associated to Neolithic, Chalcolithic and Bronze Age pottery. It has been proposed as a preliminary hypothesis that these human remains were discarded at the sinkhole.

Stratigraphy in the J/K sector

The sedimentary deposit is more than 5 m thick; so far 20 stratigraphic units (SU) have been identified without reaching the bedrock at the base. SUII, SUIII, SUXVI and SUXVII are the levels that contain more paleontological and archaeological materials. In the remaining stratigraphic units, although the presence of bones and lithic industry is evident, they are less abundant. No abandonment episode has been detected at any level, which reinforces the hypothesis of an intense and continuous occupation of the site.

Paleontological remains

At the present times, an amount of approximately 8000 fossil bone remains compose the paleontological record of the Cueva del Angel. Bone density per m^2 is very high; it almost doubles the lithic industry density.

The bone assemblage is very rich, being represented at every one of the 17 excavated levels. The most important taxonomic groups found in the faunal spectrum are large mammals; medium-sized and small mammals although appreciable are scarcer.

Fossil record has good conservation without evidence of weathering alteration or biological or chemical postdepositional processes. It is characterized by a high degree of fossilization, a recurrent presence of small concretion, big fragmentation and an extended occurrence of bone cremation. The main biases of the collection are due to the previous selection of the species that lives on the biotopes surrounding the site. In the order of *Perissodactyla*, the horse of Cueva del Angel (*Equus ferus*) (Fig.2) presents similar characteristics to the pre-Würmien horse of the Iberian Peninsula. *Stephanorhinus hemitoechus* corresponds to an evolutionary stage of the second half of the Middle Pleistocene. The presence of *Dama* indicates a record previous to the beginning of the last Glaciation. In that context, *Capra* only appears on the base of the sequence and could be the oldest species of the Iberian Peninsula. There are also Mediterranean taxa represented: *Equus hydruntinus, Cervus elaphus, Bos primigenius* and *Palaeoloxodon antiquus*. One of the particularities of the fossil assemblage is the good representation of Sus *scrofa*, this species is generally scarce in the Middle Pleistocene records; also, the presence of *Bison pricus* has been documented in one of its southernmost locations in Europe. Carnivores are represented by 4 taxa: *Ursus arctos, Canis lupus, Felis silvestris* and *Lynx pardinus spelaeus*. This Iberian type lynx ought to be used as a transition form in the anagenetic southern lineage.

The best represented taxa in the fossil assemblage are *Equus, Bos/Bison* and *Cervus*. All of them appear in the whole sequence. Large species present a vari-

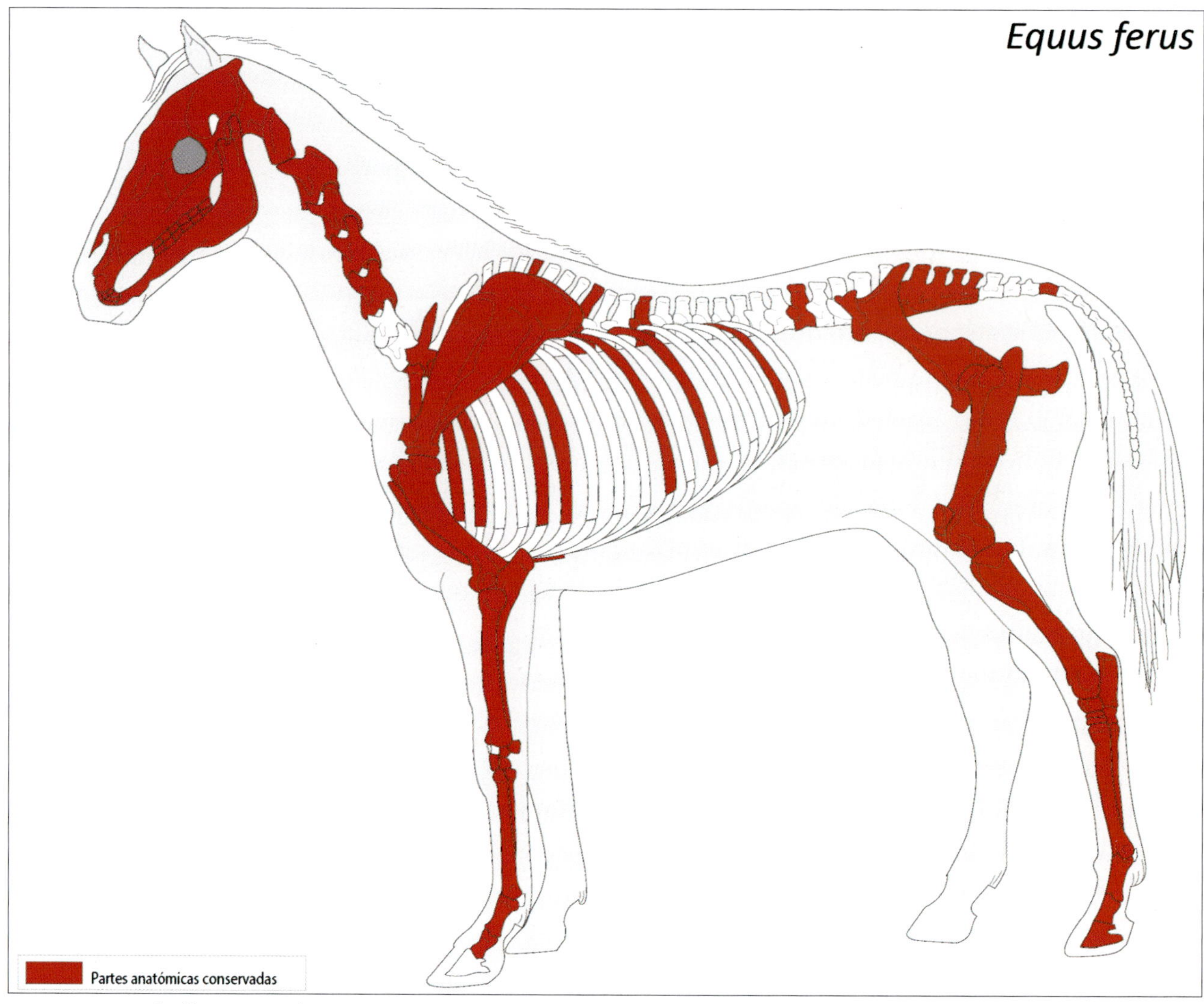

Figure 2. Equid silhouette indicating anatomical parts transported to the site by hominids

able proportion always bigger then cervids number, although this last species remains constant. Regarding the mortality profile, adults compose the most abundant group, while juveniles are only a few, except in the case of *Stephanorhinus*, characterized by major presence of infant individuals. The presence of carnivores is very discrete in the whole collection as well as their evidences on bone remains. Conversely, a large proportion of cutmarks has been documented and intentional breakage patterns that point to an anthropogenic origin for explaining the accumulation of faunal assemblages. The action of carnivores would be limited to the scavenging of bones previously discarded by humans.

Skeletal representation of large and medium mammals is mainly composed by long bones, cranial remains (basically mandibles) and, to a lesser extent, hip bones. The axial skeleton is more scarce and mainly represented by ribs. The presence of joints is very punctual, whereas the presence of phalanx is slightly higher. This differential preservation does not respond to the bone nature that can suggest alteration and postdepositional destruction processes, but is the product of anthropic action. Anatomic representation of large and medium-size mammals is very regular along the whole sequence and it is the result of a specific strategy oriented to bone marrow exploitation. The distribution pattern showed by cutmarks, the skeletal representation and the absence of consumption patterns typical from carnivores, indicate a primary access by hominids over the animals' carcasses of the three prevailing species. Taking into account the large proportion of adult animals, all the evidences point to well developed hunting strategies

(Gaudzinski and Roebroeks, 2000). Nevertheless, the anatomic representation of *Sus*, *Palaeoloxodon* and, probably *Stephanorhinus*, indicates secondary nutrient sources. Thus, the meat supply comes primarily from cinegetic strategies, with a secondary access over certain small preys. Carcasses are generally dismembered and cut into pieces in the hunting place and then the parts with more nutritional value are transported to the site. Among others, highly splintered long bones and cranial remains are the most represented, also with a regular presence of phalanx indicatives of the bone marrow extraction. For instance, the skeletal representation of cervids is quite complete along the whole sequence.

Butchering and fracturing evidences suggest that all the carcasses processing and exploitation, from skinning and evisceration to filleting and periosteum scraping has been documented. The presence of retouchers on different bones of cervid, horse and auroch evidenced the use of lithic industry in situ. Bone marrow exploitation is one of the main activities recurrently documented with the same pattern along the whole sequence. Its use is systematic, as recursive fragmentation method of hemimandible, first phalanxes, hip bones, scapula and even calcaneus demonstrate. Food production strategies follow hardly the same pattern along the whole stratigraphic sequence.

Paleoecological context

A preliminary paleoclimatic indicator of the environment of the site is provided by the herpetofauna assemblage of the Cueva del Angel, which is characterized by the presence of taxa typical of the Mediterranean domain (Barroso *et al.*, 2011; Barroso *et al.*, 2012). *Blanus cinereus* is the best squamous represented; ars the genus *Chalcides* also appears, large size lizards such as *Timon lepidus* and several small species, such as genus *Podarcis* and *Lacertidae* ind., among others. Snakes are represented by colubridae *Coronella* sp. and *Malpolon monspessulanus*, and probably cf. *Hemorrhois hippocrepis*.

Chelonia remains correspond to *Testudo hermanni*, one species that nowadays is only present in the Catalan region, although until the Upper Pleistocene it had a wider geographical distribution in the Iberian Peninsula as their presence in Zafarraya Cave demonstrates (Barroso and Bailon, 2003). Amphibia taxa represented are *Bufo bufo, Bufo calamita, Discoglossus* (indet.) and *Alytidae* (indet.). The two first species are currently widely distributed in the Iberian Peninsula where they occupy a great diversity of habitats.

The present geographical distribution of the majority of these species has a climatic threshold linked to temperature and summer insolation: average annual temperature greater than 10° C, minimum average temperature of summer months greater than 21° C and average annual insolation of between 2500 and 3000 hours.

Among the large mammal remains present at the Cueva del Angel, large herbivores are the most represented taxonomic group, while the presence of carnivores although appreciable is more modest, and the presence of rabbits is very scarce (Barroso *et al.*, 2011; Barroso *et al.*, 2012). The faunal assemblage is dominated by the horse *Equus ferus*, followed by large bovids *B. primigenius*/ *B. priscus* and cervids *C. elaphus* and *D. dama* with, although less abundant, a good representation of the suid *S. scrofa*, the rhinoceros *S. hemitoechus*, the brown bear *U. arctos* and the lynx *L. pardinus spelaeus*. The elephant *P. antiquus* and the wolf *Canis lupus* are scarce while the Ibex Capra sp. is practically inexistent. Given the latitude of the site and the average size of the species identified, smaller than the ones of Northern Europe specimen, the collection correlates with those from the end of the Middle Pleistocene. This assemblage in the Cueva del Angel corresponds to an accumulation of anthropic origin during a long period, and is not necessarily representative of a palaeo-biodiversified ambient, although the abundance of large hypsodont herbivores, associated with cervids and boars, reflects a mixed environment of wooded grasslands, probably with a more humid climate than today.

Lithic industry

Lithic assemblage of the Cueva del Angel recovered along seven archaeological campaigns, sum sup more than 5000 coordinated pieces and with a precise stratigraphic position (Fig. 3). However, aimed to better characterize the industry collection, some pieces come from the early cleaning operations of disturbed sediments which covered the site prior to excavation. Lithic artefacts are abundant in the whole stratigraphy; no level is sterile of that archaeological material, which indicates a continuous process of occupation of the site (Barroso *et al.*, 2012).

The lithic assemblage is relatively well preserved, although some flint pieces are desilicified and, around a third part of the artefacts have evidences of fire exposition.

Figure 3. Lithic industry: A. Endscraper on flake. B. and C. Flint bifacial sidescraper. D. and E. Double tool: denticulate lateral sidescraper and flint transversal sidescraper. f. Discoidal core with centripetal removals. G. Bone retoucher (pictures by V. Celiberti).

Flint, quartzite and limestone are the three main raw materials employed. Flint is overwhelmingly dominant (more than 97%). It is very abundant in the same region where the Acheulean habitat is located. However, the basic procurement area are the fluvial terraces of the Genil River, 14 km from the site; for that reason, raw material comes on the form of pebbles and only occasionally as tablets and blocks, originally from siliceous stratified levels in limestone. Only 2% of the industry has been knapped in quartzite, whose close procurement areas are the fluvial terraces of the Guadalquivir domain, 40 km north. Limestone knapping is solely sporadic or opportunistic; it represents around 0.47%. Both quartzite and limestone come in the form of pebbles.

All the elements of the *chaîne opératoire* are represented in the lithic assemblage of the Cueva del Angel: entire rocks and pebbles (*manuports*), as well as percussion tools, knapped pebbles –although extremely rare–, bifacial elements and all the debitage products, cores, flakes, knapping waste products and retouched tools. The typological representation of the lithic industry remains quite steady along the whole stratigraphy (Tables 2 and 3).

Levels	Tools. retouched	Han axes	>2 cm flakes	<2 cm flakes	Lame/ small lame	Cores	Debris	Choppers & chopping tool	nº	%
I	64		148	168	10	25	269		684	12,28
II	30		64	33	4	1	21		153	2,75
III	63		118	41	9	8	60		299	5,37
IV	109	4	293	169	12	17	142	1	747	13,41
V	47		55	20	2	5	22	1	152	2,73
VI	61	2	166	87	6	5	233		560	10,05
VII	30		85	31	5	3	36	1	191	3,43
VIII	26		65	21	2	7	18		139	2,49
IX	67		210	146	15	12	144		594	10,66
X	51	1	130	46	9	3	75		315	5,65
XI	18	1	64	10	2	3	16	1	115	2,06
XII	27		74	23		3	22		149	2,67
XIII	38	1	98	38	3	5	89		272	4,88
XIV	13	1	59	24	2	3	40		142	2,55
XV	107	1	237	96	8	17	111		577	10,36
XVI	23		31	8	3	2	22		89	1,60
XVII	8		49	6	1	2	8		74	1,33
XVIII	2								2	0,04
IND	45	35	67	12		151	8		318	5,71
TOTAL	829	46	2.013	979	93	272	1.336	4	5.572	100
%	14,9	0,8	36,1	17,6	1,7	4,9	24,0	0,1	100	

Table 2. Lithic tool categories identified.

Artefact types	Nº	%	Group	Nº	%
Endscraper	14	2,0	Upper Paleolithic type	42	6,1
Burin	13	1,9			
Drill	2	0,3			
Truncated piece	13	1,9			
Clactonian notch	59	8,6	Notched tools	143	20,8
Shoulder retouched	41	6,0			
Multiple notch	4	0,6			
Bec	16	2,3			
Doble bec	1	0,1			
Lateral denticulate	15	2,2			
Transversal denticulate	7	1,0			
Lateral sidescraper	294	42,9	Sidescrapers group	490	71,4
Transverse sidescraper	85	12,4			
Double sidescraper	76	11,1			
Triple sidescraper	9	1,3			
Convergent scraper	26	3,8			
Points	3	0,4	Points	11	1,6
Quinson point	4	0,6			
Protolimace	2	0,3			
Tayac point	2	0,3			
TOTAL	**686**	**100**		**686**	**100**

Table 3. Groups of retouched tools on flakes.

Non-modified flakes are largely the dominant category of the assemblage (53.7% of the total). They are mostly larger than 2 cm (36.1%), while the smallest ones often coming from retouched tool, are less numerous (17.6%). Traceological analyses have not been systematically done yet in the lithic collection of the Cueva del Angel. However some use-wear traces and irregular notches have been observed, which prove their use as knives. Handaxes and thick tools on flakes are also present along the whole sequence. They alternatively appear in small or medium size. More than one third of handaxes are made of flint, some in quartzite and very few of limestone. Handaxe tools were configured mainly on flakes or fractured pebbles, and some still have more or less cortical residue. Almost all of the handaxes show relatively thin pointed extremities, but with a low degree of convergence and oval, lanceolated, subtriangular and cordiform morphologies. The assemblage of large tools also includes a single chopper and a trihedral pick, both in quartzite. Most of the cores were knapped from flint and some from quartzite. These large primary supports would have been reduced on the site by intense *debitage* and, consequently the identification of original core supports is made difficult by the intensity of the reduction process. Operational schemas were directed towards progressively smaller blanks as volumes were repeatedly reduced using the flake-core technique. Most of the cores present low average dimensions and numerous removal negatives.

Out of the analyzed cores (272), almost half were found in a precise stratigraphic position. Their frequency represents 5% of the total lithic material within the stratigraphy. Recurrent unipolar flaking, flaking on alternate surfaces and bifacial discoidal flaking are the main techniques employed at the site. Bifacial discoidal flaking has been most commonly observed for quartzite pieces, while the recurrent unipolar appears mainly in flint pieces. Concerning technological analysis a specific technique aimed to thinning blanks that may relate to Kostienky type thinning has been well documented. This recurrent unipolar reduction produce very thin flakes from natural or prepared platforms previously obtained from convex or planar extraction surfaces. Recurrent orthogonal reduction where each successive recurrent knapping sequence is followed by a change in striking platform (direction) –provoking exploited surfaces to sometimes become in turn striking platforms– is developed combining the production of centripetal or even partial discoidal flakes. This technique also occasionally produces blades and/or bladelets. A few pyramidal cores are present, whereas Levallois flaking methods are absent on the site.

There is an almost total absence of cortical flakes, in contrast a large number of artefacts of the Kombewa type have been recovered, thus one cannot rule out the possibility that part of the raw materials were introduced into the site as large flakes or preconfigured cores, with the initial reduction stage knapped out of the archaeological site. The abundance of *éclat débordant* and *éclat outrepassé* illustrates intentional systematization in maintaining convex exploitation surfaces. Final knapping stages have produced small or very small flakes, smaller than 2 cm long.

Small retouched tools are abundant along the stratigraphy and have been produced from flakes. Lateral sidescrapers represent the dominant typological group (75%), with lateral single sidescrapers being the most numerous (more than 290 pieces over a total of 294). Transverse side scrapers are also well represented, although double sidescrapers and composite scrapers show a low frequency. Sidescrapers most often present direct retouch, sometimes inverse or bifacial; retouch are thin, semi thick or flat, with 10% of the scrapers shaped by semi-Quina and Quina retouch. Edge morphology was most often convex, and sometimes rectilinear and concave.

Notched tools (notches, denticulates and becs) are the second most numerous retouched tools, representing 21% of the total. In this group denticulates, retouched notches and single Clactonian pieces are the most frequent types, whereas single denticulates and becs are less frequent. At least, two convergent-edge denticulates may be assimilated to Tayac points.

Combined Upper Paleolithic tool types are less frequent, they represent barely more than 6%. Within this group, endscrapers, burins and truncations are the most numerous. Pointed tools in general are scarce, and include Tayac points, four Quinson points and two proto-limaces.

One of the outstanding characteristics of the Cueva del Angel industry is the frequency of flakes and retouched tools with thinned edges. Such thinning is observed on support bases but also on their lateral and distal edges. Another specific technological trait is the removal of flakes from the retouched tool edges, which produces a very characteristic morphology rarely observed in others sites. This could be a distinctive hallmark of the Cueva del Angel industry.

Knapping patterns at the Cueva del Angel reflect exhaustive, well standardized and economic use of relatively fine quality materials. Early phases of knapping are not represented in the assemblage since initial shaping was performed outside of the cave, probably on the catchment area where a singular branching operational schema was practiced. This schema was based on repeated application of recurrent unidirectional, often radial, knapping from prepared striking platforms. This economical method sometimes produced cores with a morphology akin to Levallois forms. Raw material procurement is essentially local, which is a typical characteristic of the Acheulean and Mousterian technological behaviour around other sites in Western Europe.

The Cueva del Angel lithic assemblage appears to fit well within the regional diversity of well developed final Acheulean industry, and its technological particularities can be interpreted as one more expression of the regional variability already observed at other sites of the Iberian Peninsula,as elsewhere in Western Europe at the end of the Middle Pleistocene.

Dating

During the first archaeological campaign in the platform of Cueva del Angel, the geologist Joaquín Rodríguez Vidal, carried out a first sample selection aimed at dating. Samples were taken from calcite flowstones to be dated by U/Th. The seven samples taken were processed at the Institut de Paléontologie Humaine in Paris by members of the team of C. Falguères (Botella *et al.*, 2006). Some of the samples were taken to obtain geological ratings (LU9501, LU9502, LU9503, LU9505 and LU9506), and two were aimed to date the Pleistocene deposit (LU9504 and LU9507). At these moments, and after a deepened knowledge of the site, it has been detected that none of the samples are reliable, because there is no certain attribution to secure location in the topography. Thus all the results have been rejected, including the sample LU9504 that gave a result of 121+11/-10 ky (SU VIII) and has been used as a chronological indicator for the faunal and lithic assemblages of the site. Currently, new dating is being undertaken by Alfredo Pérez and C. Falguères.

Conclusions

The significant use of fire is one of the most remarkable characteristics of the site. Around 90% of the faunal bone remains are burnt. Mineralogical changes experimented by fossil bones have been recently investigated (Monge *et al.*, 2014). Eighteen samples of fossil bones from J/K sector have been analyzed. In the light of analysis and subsequent studies, the existence of different thermal events of anthropic origin has been proved, not only based on the colour spectrum but also in the increase of the cristallinity of the phosphated phases and the apparition of authigenic rare phosphates as the whitlockite. Besides, diagenetic processes have been observed, including phosphate authigenic. Also, the presence of secondary calcite has been established and manganese oxide precipitations. The analytical evidence indicates that reached temperatures ranged 650°C to 700°C, in the large stratigraphic units I and II. So far, no analysis has been done in unit III, thus it is not clear that fire existed or not at that moment. It is clear that meat roasting was one of the most frequent activities, although some smoking strategies aimed at better preservation of the foodcannot be ruled out (Patou-Mathis, 1996). On the other hand, the large degree of fragmentation and the absence both of epiphyses and spongy tissues could indicate the use of bones as fuel (Costamagno *et al.*, 2005; Théry-Parisot *et al.*, 2005).

The stratigraphic continuity of the sequence with neither sedimentary hiatus nor human abandonment episodes (Barros *et al.*, 2011), the low carnivore intervention, together with the continuous use of fire and the persistence of butchering patterns, suggest a long, intense and continuous occupation of the site. Cueva del Angel would be a place where most of the daily activities took place and also would act as central point from where all the logistic strategies of raw material procurement would occurred. The faunal spectrum and the skeletal representation indicate the exploitation of a rich and varied ecological niche.

Concerning the lithic industry, the tool typology, the technology, etc., fit well within the regional diversity of a well developed final Acheulean industry in the European continent. Knapping patterns at the Cueva del Angel reflect exhaustive, well standardized and economic use of raw materials. It has been observed that raw materials came to the site as preconfigured cores, probably being preliminary flaking done in the procurement area. Ninety-five percent of cores were knapped on flint. Recurrent unipolar flaking, as well as bifacial discoidal flaking are quite significant. Cores were almost depleted, which give rise to small size flakes. After analyzing 272 cores with a reliable stratigraphic context, the presence of Levallois flaking method should be ruled out, as we already mentioned in 2006, when the studied lithic assemblage was composed of 667 pieces (Botella *et al.*, 2006).

In the first years of research at Cueva del Angel, lithic assemblage from its upper levels was assigned to a Late Acheulean and to a Mousterian of Acheulean tradition periods. Conversely, in recently published papers (Barroso *et al.*, 2011; Barroso *et al.*, 2012), when the excavation had progressed and sufficient lithic material had been recovered, it was determined that no changes occurred along the whole sequence, the typometry of pieces present the same values, handaxe typology and size alternate indistinctly along the sequence, sidescrapers typology and retouched over them does not change and core typology and exploitation remains the same. In other words, from the base to the last occupation level, the same techno typological pattern continues, and that corresponds exclusively to an Acheulean industry, excluding completely the presence of Mousterian industries.

The presence of Acheulean industries in the Iberian Peninsula is basically confined to the fluvial ambience of major rivers. These industries are made with quartzite cobbles (choppers, cleavers, pics, handaxes, etc...) and, technologically are far from the one encountered at Cueva del Angel. Probably, industries from fluvial terraces respond to a different scheme of raw material procurement and transformation developed in the same place, whereas industry from Cueva del Angel responds to a unitary scheme composed by the habitat and the procurement area. Inhabitants of Cueva del Angel made an extraordinary use of small tools as flakes, also typologically diverse sidescrapers were common. In the future, further dating of levels with lithic industry on fluvial terraces as well as Acheulean levels in caves, will help to ascertain the relationship between both contexts. At the moment, the reference sites that can be compared with Cueva del Angel are Galería in Atapuerca (Carbonell *et al.*, 1999), Cova del Bolomor (Fernández Peris, 2007) and Galeria Pesada (Marks *et al.*, 2012).

Regarding the chronology, the rejection of dates used so far prevent the establishment of a precise chronological framework of the Cueva del Angel, but there is no doubt that the analysis currently being done will age considerably the date of 120 ky years available so far.

Cecilio Barroso *, Miguel Caparrós **, Deborah Barsky ***, Anne Marie Moigne ****, Antonio Monclova *

Boquete de Zafarraya cave: A Neanderthal site in southern Iberia

Introduction

Boquete de Zafarraya cave (hereinafter C.B.Z.) is in the Alcaucín municipality, Málaga Province (southern Spain). It is 1020 m asl, facing S-E at the foot of a cliff, with a steep slope below it. The coordinates are: 36° 56` 58``N – 4° 7`40`` W.

This cave in Sierra de Alhama overlooks an extremely irregular landscape of limestone ranges and very narrow valleys boxed in between them. Scarcely a few dozen metres away, however, the landscape opens onto the mountain pass, Boquete de Zafarraya, which at 900 m asl connects the Mediterranean coast with inland Andalucia (Fig. 1). This landscape mosaic is completed by the 22 km² Zafarraya polje, formed from an intra-montane depression of karst and tectonic origin filled with basically Quaternary sediments, powerfully contrasting with its surroundings by its extensive subhorizontal landscape (Barroso, C. *et al.*, 2006).

The prehistoric Boquete de Zafarraya cave site was discovered by a member of this team (C.B.R.) in 1979. During the first stage of the archaeological excavations (1981-1983), led by C. Barroso and F. Medina Lara, we discovered levels containing Mousterian industry, a rich and varied quaternary wildlife and two quaternary Neanderthal fossils (Zaf. 1) and (Zaf. 2) (Barroso *et al.*, 1983; Barroso *et al.*, 1984.). The second archaeological stage at the site continued from 1990 to 1994. B.Z.C. is the last vestige of a cave which collapsed and whose morphology has been heavily affected by powerful slope erosion. At the mouth, a large arch-shaped porch rises 30 metres, measuring approx. 10 metres at the base. On the north wall there is a narrow 22 m long gallery, barely 2 m. in the widest sections, developed from a fault plane. The cave is in stratified pisolitic and pseudo-oolitic limestone. This gallery is the source of the quaternary deposit. The infill was preserved by the carbonation processes inside which cemented much of it, preventing the intense erosion which took place throughout the area, heavily affected by the steep slope.

Neanderthal fossils

B.Z.C. is perhaps one of Iberia's most important sites of *Homo neanderthalensis* fossils (Bar-

* Fundación Instituto de Investigación de Prehistoria y Evolución Humana. Plaza del Coso 21, 14900 Lucena (Córdoba, España) email: barroso.cecilio@gmail.com

** Départment de Préhistorie, Muséum National d'Histoire Naturelle, 75013 París, France

*** Departement d'història i història de l'Art. Universitat Rovira i Virgili.

**** Muséum National d'Histoire Naturelle. Centre Européen de Recherches Préhistoriques de Tautavel.

Figure 1. Neanderthal *Capra pirinaica* hunting scene in Boquete Zafarraya (author: Antonio Monclova Bohorquez).

roso *et al.*, 2006 b). There are at least 9 individuals (2 children, aged 14 months to 12 years and 7 adults, four almost 20 years old and two aged 25 and 30, and one undetermined). There is a notably poor representation of infants and a heavy adult mortality. The most surprising feature, however, is the "significant" presence of Neanderthal bones (16 fossils) in a cave which was visited sporadically by these hominids, who spent very short periods there, computed as a few days each time at the most judging by spatial analysis of the lithic industry and the fragments of animal bones bearing obvious signs of anthropic manipulation. Anatomically, the fossils include:

Cranial elements: 2 mandibles (Zaf. 2 and Zaf.4-5-18) (Fig. 2) and 5 separate teeth (Zaf. 12 Zaf. 16, Zaf. 20, Zaf. 23 and Zaf. 24).

Mandible Zaf 2, discovered in 1983, was initially attributed to a *Homo sapiens neanderthalensis* male aged between 25 and 30. The jawbone is practically intact, with 13 teeth preserved. This jawbone was studied in depth by Maria Antoinette de Lumley, who established the phylogenetic position of Zafarraya Man in the group of so-called "classic" Neanderthals. Zafarraya retains some features described for the Ante-Neanderthals, particularly amongst those discovered in Banyoles and Montmaurin, although no features permit their connection to modern populations. Mandible Zaf. 4-5-18, discovered in 1990 and 1992, is broken into 3 pieces, with evidence of fire exposure, related to the presence of a Mousterian hearth in the quadrat Q-18. All three fragments are from an adult mandible. The proportions and morphology are comparable to Zaf. 2.

Upper limbs: 1 scapula (Zaf. 6), 1 humerus (Zaf. 22).

The specimen discovered in 1990 is the lower half of the glenoid cavity of a right scapula. Its blackish surface evidences exposure to fire and, like other human remains, is associated with the hearth in quadriculate Q-18. Comparison with the Krapina scapulae shows it is amongst the variations attributed to males.

Humerus Zaf. 22 was discovered in 1992 at the rear of the gallery on a disturbed superficial level, and thus lacks stratigraphic context. Morphological and metric analysis has attributed this fossil to the Neanderthal group, although certain parameters such as maximum length, minimum perimeter and poor robustness are also present in modern humans. Morphologically, the humerus matches the Neanderthals from Cova Tossal de la Font and Grotte d' Hortus. The proportions indicate that this was a fairly robust and unequivocally female Neanderthal.

Lower limbs: 3 femurs (Zaf. 1-15 and 16), 1 tibia (Zaf. 27) 1 coxis (Zaf.17) and 1 foot phalange (Zaf. 3).

Femur Zaf. 1 was found during the 1982 digs. Only the upper half of a right femur was preserved, in which part of the upper epiphysis and the upper half of the 225 mm long diaphysis can be appreciated. The femoral head and trochanters were broken. The initial study (see note) attributes this to a Neanderthal adult male aged 30-49 years. It has a relatively strong size ratios for a Neanderthal, measuring 159 cm to 162cm in height. The medial bone fragmentation and the large splinter extracted from the diaphysis are clearly anthropogenic. Metric and morphological analysis concludes that Zaf. 1 is distinct from Neanderthal femurs in the lack of a vertical incurvation. On the other hand, the cortical thickness, antero-posterior flatness of the shaft and the lack of a posterior pilaster are comparable to Neanderthals. The less pronounced muscular relief than other fossils suggests that these were less robust individuals than the classic Neanderthals populations in southwest France and the Middle East.

Femurs Zaf. 15 and 26 (Fig.2).

Found heavily fragmented and burned in the Q-18 hearth during the 1990-1992 excavations. Zaf. 15 preserves the shaft of a left human femur. Both the anterior and posterior faces have been reconstructed from 11 fragments. Zaf. 26 retains part of the diaphysis of a right femur, reconstructed from 9 fragments. Its robustness is quite different from Zaf.1: Zaf. 15 and 26 have slender shafts and weaker anteroposterior and transversal diameters than Zaf.1. The major difference in strength between the three femurs could reflect sexual dimorphism, with FAZ. 1 belonging to a slim male individual while the other two femurs are from two females.

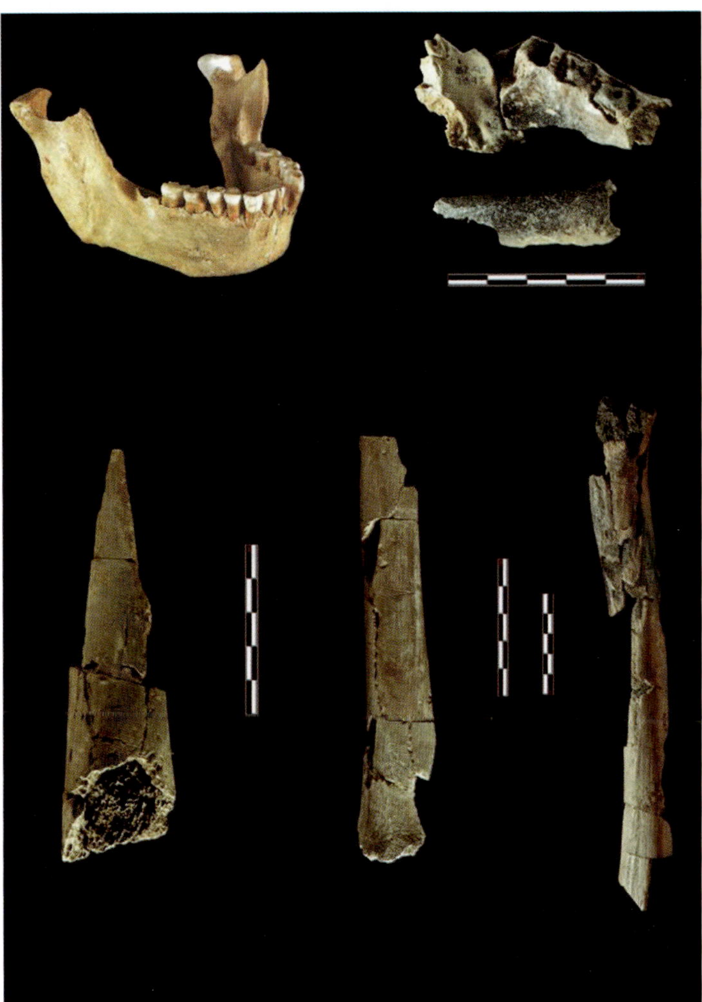

Figure 2. Neanderthal fossils in Boquete de Zafarraya cave. From Left to right A: Mandible Zafarraya 2 (photo. Cecilio Barroso Ruíz), B: Burnt mandible 4-5-18, C: Burnt Femur Zafarraya 26, D: Burnt Tibia Zafarraya 27, E: Burnt femur Zafarraya 15 (B, C. D and E: photos. Rafael López Gómez.

Zaf. 27, a right human tibia (Fig. 2), consists of 10 burned fragments found in the Q-18 hearth. The lower half of the shaft and a fragment of the upper half have been preserved. It seems to be from a graciles individual, whose overall proportions suggest an adult female, with the diameter in the midsection of the shaft close to the Ferrassie 2 individuals, attributed to a female, and smaller than those of the Chapelle-aux-Saints tibia, attributed to a male.

The phalanx of the right foot (Zaf. 3), located during the 1983 dig, is incomplete, although it may be attributed to a proximal phalanx of the second toe of the right foot. Its morphological and metric characteristics suggest that this may be Neanderthal phalanx. It belongs to an adult, as the overall dimensions of the head are comparable to the homologous Shanidar 8 phalanx, attributed to a female. The coxis (Zaf.17) was located during the 1992 dig in quadrat Q-18, on the edge of the pit that shaped the Mousterian hearth. It is well preserved and permits the examination of the symphysis face, the horizontal and descendant branches of the pubis. The break at the branches is old and covered with concretion. It is attributed to a male individual estimated to have been 20-21 years old.

Thorax: 1 rib (Zaf. 19).

This human right rib appeared in the 1992 dig in the context of the Q-18 hearth. It is from a right C7, two-thirds of which are well preserved. It is characterized by its thickness, slight helical torsion and faces angled obliquely at the base, which probably gave the bottom of the rib cage an open form, contrary to modern men. It is attributed to an adult Neanderthal male.

Mousterian industry

A rich and stone tool industry has been collected from all seven distinct Archeostratigraphical Units (AU) attributed to the Mousterian (Barroso *et al* 2006 c.) The global assemblage comprises 813 items; mostly knapped in flint as well as some quartzose-sandstone. Lithic raw materials were collected from primary and secondary sources not exceeding 12 km away. Outcrops situated some 11 km away provided the finest flint and were preferred to other nearby sources. The assemblage is well preserved overall but some flakes display post-depositional edge damage. Patina attributed to fire exposure is observed on only 17 items.

The lithic type distribution per-AU varies significantly according to occupation intensity and the extension of excavated surfaces but no noteworthy technological or typological differences are detected within the sequence. Knapping waste (L> 2 cm) dominates the assemblage and the average flake/core ratio is 23. This core deficiency is to be put into relation with the paucity of small-sized flakes and flakes with residual cortex, all suggesting that much of the knapping and shaping occurred off-site.

Many of the 539 knapped items (flakes, blades, points) were obtained by Levallois production methods (194 pcs., Levallois technological index excluding pseudo-Levallois points= 36%). No important variation in the Levallois index is observed within the sequence: the entire assemblage is Levallois dominant. A ratio of 1 Levallois product for every 2 to 3 standard products is constant regardless of the raw material used. Levallois flakes are numerically prevalent (161 pcs.) compared to blades (25 pcs.) and points (8 pcs.).

Recurrent centripetal is the most common Levallois method attested from flakes and cores, although lineal, unipolar recurrent and bipolar methods have also been identified. A few symmetrical preferential flakes reflect a final phase of recurrent centripetal Levallois schemes with dorsal surfaces bearing traces of their core's prepared convex surface. The Levallois flakes often present prepared, facetted platforms (LevFI = 48,6, FI = 16,6).

Among the 23 cores unearthed at the site, only 4 are clearly of Levallois conception: 3 centripetal recurrent and 1 unipolar recurrent. A further three cores present convex extraction surfaces analogous to Levallois-type production strategies. Alternative core reduction modes appear nonstandardized, mainly because the matrices are exhausted. These are uni, bi and multi-directional and polyhedral. Most cores are knapped from flint nodules rather than flakes and the assemblage includes only three double ventral flakes and two cores on flakes.

Blades were mostly made from the finest flint and their overall index is quite low (BI = 8,1%). Elongated supports were rarely obtained by methods other than Levallois (NLevBI =5,5%, LevBI= 12,8%). Use of a soft percussion instrument is only sporadically recognized. The BDZ industry is further characterized by a high frequency of core-edge flakes (Fr.: *éclat débordant*) and pseudo-Levallois points, both typically obtained during different phases of Levallois and discoid core surface convexity maintenance.

Nearly one quarter of the flakes > 2 cm are retouched into various tool types. While no selectivity of supports is evidenced, the Levallois typological index is to be considered elevated (41,4 %). The retouched toolkit includes: Mousterian points, scrapers (42%), some notched tools (30 %), trimmed and truncated instruments, as well as some Upper Paleolithic types. Quina retouch is rare and there are no handaxes and only one chopper-like tool.

Given the techno-typological features outlined above, the stone industries from the Boquete de Zafarraya Mousterian levels are ascribed to a *Levallois dominant typical Mousterian*.

Large animal vertebrates

The faunal remains found at the Zafarraya cave site (Barroso *et al.*, 2006) provide information about various aspects of the Neanderthal lifestyle. First, the list of fauna matches a fresh episode in the middle of the last glaciation. The abundance of *Cuon alpinus* and *Panthera pardus* (Fig. 3) is unusual at European sites, permitting its comparison with caves in the Basque Country. The vast majority of the sites where panther (245 remains, 10 individuals) or dhole are well represented have been dated in the Hengelo episode. *Ursus arctos* (Fig 3), *Crocuta crocuta*, *Felis silvestris*, *Lynx pardina* and *Vulpes vulpes* form the classic range of Upper Pleistocene carnivores. The herbivores do not point to a specific biochronology except for the apparently robust horse, attributed to *Equus c. germanicus* which became extinct 30,000 years ago. A substantial majority is mountain fauna, particularly goats (78% of the identified remains) and fallow deer, which are associated with their usual predators: panther, lynx and dhole. The frequent meso– to supra-Mediterranean environment has been described on the basis of palynological analysis as cold and very dry for a herbaceous steppe stratum with a few pines. The sedimentological sequence dated between 49 and 38 ky corresponds to several alternations of more or less moist climates with a homogeneous vegetation throughout the Mousterian occupation of the cave. The microfauna also describes a colder climate than today at 1000 m asl. The cave provided shelter for these large mammals on several occasions. The 46 archaeo-stratigraphic units defined from the sedimentary sequence, along with evidence of humans and carnivores, clearly show an alternation in the occupations.

The remains of aurochs, deer, wild boar and horse indicate that hominids frequented the Zafarraya polje moorland where these animals were present. Some of the rodents and small birds also came from these moist wooded areas.

The faunal remains from the different levels suggest a concomitant presence between carnivores and Neanderthals, with several possible scenarios. There may have been mutual periodic exclusions in which Neanderthals were replaced

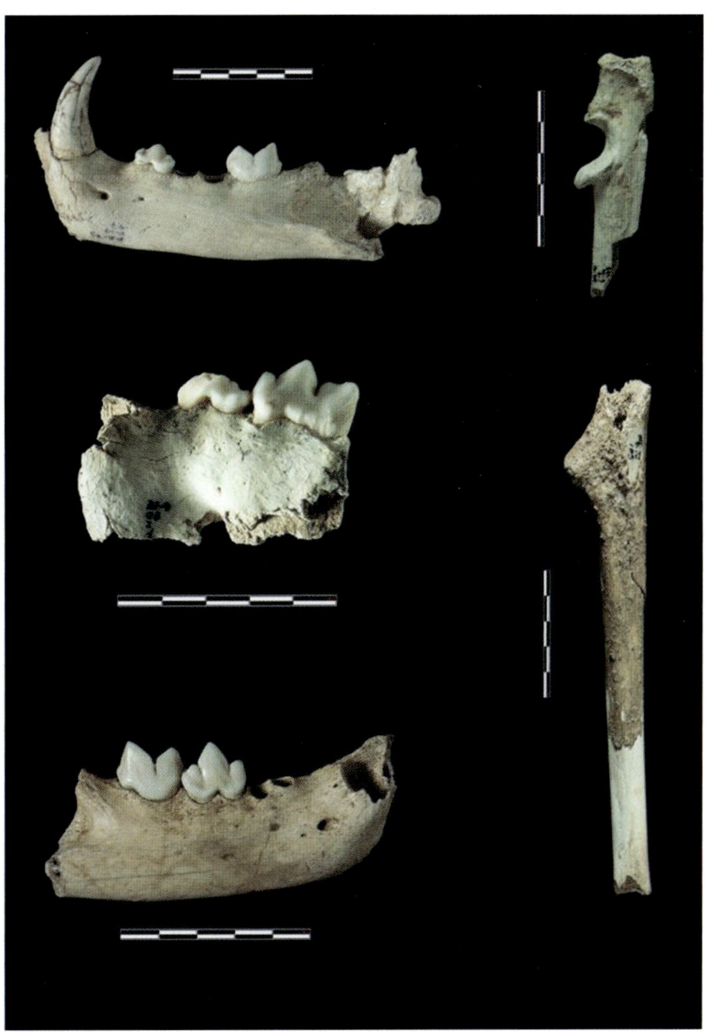

Figure 3. Carnivore fossils in Boquete de Zafarraya cave. From left to right o A: *Panthera Pardus* mandible, B: *Linx pardina* ulna, C: *Panthera pardus* maxillary, D: *Panthera Pardus* mandible, *Ursus arctos* ulna (Photos: Rafael López Gómez).

by carnivores or vice-versa as the cave occupants. Another scenario is that these two types of predators were not mutually exclusive and may have coexisted, or perhaps the presence of carnivores might even be a direct consequence of the humans. The analysis of different interventions by panthers, lynx and dholes suggests a more intense involvement by the former, which is also consistent with the number of individuals at all levels. The presence of dholes on the upper levels of the infill is more sporadic and their remains show greater pressure by predators. Skeletal representation of goats indicates that the carcasses were brought to the site, although the bias is not uniform in all levels. The abundant remains of this species (2667 items in the stratigraphy) show all stages of impact by carnivores on virtually every part of the skeleton. However, carnivore marks are associated with evidence of anthropological activity. Evidence of carnivore activity is particularly notable on the bones of other carnivores such as dholes, but also on the remains of a hyena and also a bear discovered on the low levels of the infill, on the "levels containing panther". Deer and wild boar were probably prey for large carnivores. Human activity is visible on many goat items. Like the large carnivores, Neanderthals frequented the cave when hunting goats in this area. The high numerical presence of juveniles indicates the hunting season, which ran from spring to summer. Goat butchering is attested by the numerous cut marks on skulls, phalanges, axial skeletons and long bones. Deliberate fracturing of the jaws and long bones is quite common. Other species such as deer, from a much broader area, were also carried intact to the cave, and similarly have numerous marks and deliberate, systematic breakage. In this case, evidence of human activity predominates over the marks of small carnivores, which are superimposed on the cut marks. The carcasses of large herbivores such as aurochs, horses and wild asses (*Equus hydruntinus*) are quite incomplete. They may have been dismembered previously, with the most nutritious parts brought to the site. Evidence of carnivore impact on these remains is generally weak.

The fossil association on the archaeological levels of Boquete de Zafarraya cave is indicative of frequent occupation by Neanderthals in summer, at the same time as carnivores exploited the cave. The mortality of juvenile deer and carnivores coincides with that of juvenile capridae, clear evidence of intervention by carnivores and humans at the same time. The considerable anthropic presence at the Zafarraya site, evidenced by the stone tools found in every archaeo-stratigraphic unit, seems to have posed no impediment to panthers frequenting this cave. The abundance of goats and rabbits in the environs must have proved a particular challenge for both groups.

Palaeoecology

The Zafarraya cave environment was generally inhabited by rock-dwelling species of large mammals directly related to the morphology of this landscape, as well as other species more characteristic of woodlands, areas with abundant water, the polje, sheltered zones and mountain areas with lush vegetation, all propitiated by higher moisture levels than the current local conditions. The best represented carnivore species in Zafarraya cave are dholes and leopards (Fig. 3), both rare at most European Pleistocene sites (all the more so in caves at this altitude). The dhole, typical of the warmest periods of the Eemian interstadial, is robust, closer to the currently species found in semi-desert and mountain landscapes, where it hunts in groups. The leopard occupied several environments including forests and abrupt areas such as Zafarraya where herbivores hunted medium-small sized herbivores. Hyena and fox, more robust than the Mediterranean fox, were scarce while the lynx was slightly more numerous. Bears, lynx and weasel were quite robust, indicating a temperate climate. Of all the carnivore taxa, only brown bear, bobcat and lynx are characteristic of forest habitats, while the rest were more or less ubiquitous (Barroso *et al.*, 2006e; Monclova *et al.*, 2012.).

The mountain goat is the most abundant herbivore in Zafarraya Cave, probably a preferential prey for Neanderthals, dholes and leopards. Relatively gracile, this goat is different from the larger pre-Würm species and the Mediterranean goats associated with Mousterian sites. The continuous presence of deer indicates that it was hunted during summer in the polje woods near the cave. Chamois seek winter refuge in forests when the peaks and pastures are covered with snow, but in Zafarraya they appear in more benign periods, probably because the moister climate at the time reduced the snow cover in the higher areas. The auroch appears frequently throughout the Pleistocene on the Iberian Peninsula. Its minor presence in Zafarraya could be associated with flooded areas in the cave near the polje. Wild boar are usually quite rare in the Pleistocene, and while scarce in Zafarraya, they show a preference for forested and, more particularly, wet areas. Horses, also rare, are represented by the robust *Equus caballus germanicus*, known in Western Europe during the first half of the last glaciation. Its relative absence could be related to the site's elevation. The wild ass, frequent since the last interglacial and typical of the Mediterranean region since the beginning of the Middle Pleistocene, could survive in rugged areas like Zafarraya (Monclova *et al.*, 2012).

Given that the few mammal taxa at Zafarraya reduce the representativity of the cenograms, in some of them data from several archaeo-stratigraphic units have been used to clarify the site's environmental and climatic evolution. On the basis of the preferences shown by different taxa for open/closed, wet/dry environments, these cenograms point to a moist climate which only underwent minor variations throughout the stratigraphic sequence. The lack of a dividing line between the data on the large and small body mass of all Zafarraya mammals indicates that the habitat was closed. When carnivores (average sized species) are removed from the analysis, a dividing line does appear between macro– and micro-mammals, indicative of the presence of open spaces on the edge of the forests in a temperate and permanently moist climate.

Evidence of a closed environment not far from the rocky cave landscape, in a climate tending to be moist, matches the polje. The various biotopes around Zafarraya formed a landscape mosaic in which different forest fauna taxa coexisted with other inhabitants of more open and even more humid environments such as streams and wetlands, which only retreated to the polje in the driest periods. Through the successive archaeo-stratigraphic units in Zafarraya, an abundance of hypsodont animals alternated with braquidonts, an indication of mountain + grassland or forested environments, respectively.

The climatogram drafted to compare Zafarraya's major archaeo-stratigraphic units clusters species by their ecological affinities (giving priority to the moisture gradient). It illustrates the climate trend through the sedimentary infill of the cave as the fauna composition changed in the stratigraphic sequence. Some results are difficult to interpret. While the goat/deer or bison/deer ratio reflects variations in the intensity of the cold at many Mousterian sites, the altitude of the Zafarraya site hinders this pattern, and thus the continued presence of goats does not necessarily indicate variations in the intensity of the cold but rather oscillations linked to the presence or absence of other species. Similarly, although the presence of horses might indicate alternating colder or drier climates, here they are not only rare but their remains are associated with archaeo-stratigraphic units with highly uneven moisture levels according to other records. In ungulates, neither chamois nor aurochs show variations related to the frequency of the presence of deer in the stratigraphic sequence, while the presence of wild boars, usually associated with increased moisture, does match the increase in deer and chamois, also in a moister period (Monclova *et al.*, 2012). Finally, variations in the proportions of the macromammals through the Zafarraya stratigraphic sequence seem to confirm a moist, temperate climate, cooler than today, with a wetter initial phase when the forests spread, but generally characterized by Mediterranean conditions. The various Neanderthals occupations occurred during the more or less fresh and more or less temperate periods, always at the start of or during the summer, when leopards and dholes arrived.

Taphonomy

The taphonomic and zooarchaeological analysis of Zafarraya cave gave rise to a proposed model in which the Neanderthal occupants of the cave became specialist hunters of goats, the most abundant species in the record (Barroso and de Lumley, H. 2006). However, the wide diversity of herbivore prey that inhabited the environment and the parallel presence –and continued occupation– of carnivores and Neanderthals prevent this model from fully reflecting the interaction between the two. Their overlap in the cave may have occasionally led to competition for food resources in the environs. The interactions between Neanderthals, carnivores and herbivorous prey has been the subject of a recent study (Caparros *et al.*, 2012).

There are three possible scenarios: 1) Neanderthals predominated over carnivores and excluded them from the surrounding ecological system, or vice versa. 2) Once the Neanderthal and carnivore niches overlapped, one excluded the other from the immediate ecological environment. 3) Once the two niches overlapped, neither was able to exclude the other and they coexisted. In order to determine which of the three was most likely, we studied the overlapping Neanderthal/carnivore occupation of the cave from the perspective of their interaction with the herbivore prey items and also their competition for *Capra*, the most abundant resource.

Using the zooarchaeological analysis and the known ecology of the taxa which fed in the vicinity of the cave, a path analysis (Wright, 1968) was applied to the faunal data to define the likely fauna acquisition strategies by Neanderthals and carnivores. Initially, the applicable scenario seems to be a complete overlap of the Neanderthal and carnivore niches, both cohabiting the cave environment. The analysis shows that: 1) Although the continued presence of *Capra* made it a prey for both groups, *Panthera* was the main predator, alternating with the Neanderthals in the cave occupation. 2) *Rupicapra* was overwhelmingly hunted by *Panthera* and rarely by Neanderthals. 3) Neanderthals were the main accumulators of *Cervus*, hunted at some distance from the cave and probably scavenged by the carnivores. 4) Large herbivores such as horses and aurochs were hunted by Neanderthals and secondarily by carnivores.

In the vicinity of the cave, *Panthera* was clearly more efficient than the Neanderthals, who were excluded when this carnivore was present (*Capra* and *Rupicapra* remain in the record). The large herbivores that roamed the Zafarraya polje probably offered good opportunities for cooperative hunting by Neanderthals (accumulation of *Cervus* and others). If there was indeed coexistence, as evidenced by scavenging, it must have been during short periods of random or seasonal occupation.

Dating

Following the discovery of the B.Z.C. site, preliminary studies were presented in several publications, where the age of the Mousterian levels were estimated to be more recent than other Middle Palaeolithic sites in the region. This first estimate was based on a biostratigraphic study which compared rodent populations found in the Zafarraya sediments and those in Cariguela. This latter site was considered contemporary to "Würm II", permitting the inference that Zafarraya could be the "Würm II-III" or "Würm III" interstadial. In 1989, Barroso *et al.*, forwarded the open hypotheses that the Zafarraya fossils might represent Europe's last Neanderthal populations. The first series of radiocarbon datings from the Mousterien levels of B.Z.C. were presented in 1995 (Hublin *et al.*, 1995). Two methods were used, C-14 (based on the acid fraction and the collagen) and the U-Th method, using herbivore bone samples. The ages for C-14 (collagen) ranged from 29.8 $\pm$ 0.6 ky (Gif-9140-II) and higher levels of 31.8 $\pm$ 0.55 ky (Gif/LSM-9140-I) level 8, while the acid fraction, for the same samples gave 23.6 $\pm$ 1 $\pm$ 0.1 ky and 22.0 ky. The U-Th ages are stratigraphically consistent, ranging from 25.1 $\pm$ 1.3 ky on level I-3 to 31.7 $\pm$ 3 ky on level I-8. Level D, the location of one of the Neanderthal fossils (Zaf. 2), was dated by U-Th at 33.4 $\pm$ 0.2 ky. These absolute dates showed that between 30 ky and 33 ky BP, groups of Neanderthals survived the pressure of A.M.H. in a sort of "refuge" at the southern extreme of Iberia. The hypothesis of the "last Neanderthals" in Zafarraya thus seemed to be confirmed at this site, which gave rise to the paradigm. A new set of absolute datings began almost a decade later using several methods (Michel *et al.*, 2003, Michel *et al.*, 2006). C-14 datings (AMS) of 20 charcoal samples by ORAU yielded quite mixed results because the collection methodology for the 1996 samples was not excessively rigorous. Samples from stratigraphic sections in grids which were never dug, the source of the problem were: Q-9, P-9, R-9, P-20 and R-1. These samples, with the exception of R-16, yielded aberrant dates.

The charcoal samples located and extracted from the stratigraphic sections under controlled conditions during the dig were: P10395, Oxa-9001, P10397, P10398, Oxa-9002 and P10400. This methodological control makes these samples highly reliable with respect to their spatial location and stratigraphic context.

Eight faunal remains were chosen for C-14 (AMS) dating, although half the samples were rejected due to lack of collagen. The samples at depths from 168 cm to –171 cm yielded three ages ranging from (OxA 8411) 26.36 ± 0.44 ky (Z6d) to (OxA 8999) 33.3 ± 1.2 ky (Z8os). A sample from –223 cm yielded an incongruous dating, (OxA 9000) 30.65 ± 0.65 ky (Z69os). U-Th alpha spectrometry was applied to 25 herbivore teeth. The results were not conclusive, as six ranged chronologically from 29,300 + 1.4-1.3 (Z4cem) to 39,700 ± 2.2 (Z126os) at depths between –133 cm and –239 cm. Eight of the samples were between 40.9 ± 1.3 ky (Z2os) and 60 + 3.7-3.6 ky (Z205os) at similar depths.

The U-Th thermal ionization mass spectrometry (TIMS) was applied to 9 samples, two of which were invalidated. The remaining 7 showed a range between 16.88 ± 0.535 ky (Z6d.a) at 171cm and 53,345 ± 5,025 (Z696e) at –133 cm. At the same depth, alpha spectrometry dated the –170 cm samples at 31.6 ± 203 and for –133cm, at 32.8 + 0.201 –0.2 ky. The obvious contradictions prevent conclusive results from being reached.

The ESR (EU, early uptake) and ESR (LU, linear uptake) method was used with 6 horse and goat teeth. The result was (Z62) 24 ± 0.3 ky (EU) and 24 ± 0.4 ky (LU) at –165cm, while the oldest (Z126) 44 ± 0.5 ky (EU) and 45 ± 0.6 ky was from –178 cm. The weighted mean of the most consistent results yielded by this method, i.e. above 30 ky, is 35 ± 0.3 to 39 ky ± 0.3 ky. The age of Neanderthal mandible Zaf. 2 could not be defined by high resolution gamma spectrometry direct dating due to its low uranium content. The imprecise conclusion was that it must be at least 42 ky old.

The final conclusion was that the results showed a chronological range from 30 ky to 45 ky, thus leaving the possible late age of Neanderthals in southern Spain unresolved.

In 2013, an article was published on the Zafarraya datings based mainly on the calibration of the 2006 AMS dates (Michel *et al.*, 2013, (Table 1). Samples OxA-7117 were 7 metres from Neanderthal jaw Z-2 (found at a depth of –194 cm, and in the same stratigraphic unit D, with a calibrated C-14 age of 38.7 ky to 44,117 ky. In 1995, level D level was dated at 33.4 ± 0.2 ky, which proved fundamental in consolidating the theory of the last Neanderthals in Zafarraya.

Sample OxA-9002 is from UF35 (-213 –218 cm), the floor of the Neanderthal occupation where several human remains were found: Zaf.4-

SAMPLE	LABORATORY Nº	DEPTH (cm.)	DATA (C-14 ky BP)	DATA (C-14 cal. ky BP)
Q-14, 3 UE31	P10395	– 182	FAILED	–
P-11, 70 UG36 D	OxA– 7117	– 194	36,9 ± 3,0	38,700 – 44,117
Q-14,1 UE34	P10398	– 210	FAILED	–
R-16, 1 UE?	OxA-9002	– 217	34,6 ± 0,8	38,763-40,604
Q-17, 202 UG42 E	OxA-7120	– 234	30,9 ± 1,3	34,038 – 36,839
Q-18, 167 UG42 E	OxA-7135	– 235	14,93 ± 0,09	18,262 – 18,489
Q-17, 3 UG44	P10400	– 240	FAILED	–

Table 1. Charcoal samples in precise stratigraphic context, with AMS radiocarbon dating. Both uncalibrated ages (BP) and calibrated ages (cal. BP) are shown, as per Michel, V 2013.

5-18, Zaf.15, Zaf.16, Zaf.27, Zaf.17 and Zaf.19. This level has been dated at 38,763 to 40,604 ky. Both this and the previous data seem quite reliable, allowing the Zafarraya Neanderthal fossils to be dated between 38.7 ky and 44 ky.

The most recent publication on this issue (Wood *et al.*, 2013), present results from Zafarraya. The author applied extremely strict protocols such as ultrafiltration pretreatment (AF) of bone collagen to prevent contamination of the processed samples. Previously, the nitrogen content (% N) of the selected bone sample is measured to determine the collagen content, which is used to decide whether or not to radiocarbon date the sample.

Two stages were used in the Zafarraya analysis. In the first stage, bone samples previously dated by C-14 (AMS) at the ORAU (OxA-8024, OxA-8999, OxA-9000, OxA-8411) with results published in Michel *et al.*, 2003 and Michel *et al.*, 2006.) were chosen. Only sample Z8os, which was subject to the AF protocol, yielded a dating of 33.3 ± 1.2 ky. The rest had a low % N and were rejected. In the second stage, 29 bone samples from the stratigraphy were analysed. Only two had an acceptable %N, ZAF2 (0.8) and ZAF5 (1.5). and 0.8 Another three samples, ZAF3 (0.7) ZAF7 (0.6) and ZAF8 (0.6), were on the borderline. The AF protocol was applied to these samples, yielding results in ZAF2 (46.3 ± 2.5 ky) and ZAF7 (49.3 ky). The latter, almost on the threshold of the method, showed an age greater than 46.7 ± 0.7 ky, i.e., roughly 13,000 years older.

The work by both Michel and Wood underscores the age of the Mousterian levels at Zafarraya, between 38.7 ky and 49.3 ky.

Only 6 out of 33 analysed samples contained a % N that would permit collagen to be obtained, and only three of these specimens could be dated, less than 10% of all the selected samples. This methodology was also used at other sites along the Mediterranean coast: Les Cendres (3 samples), Mallaetes (2 samples), El Niño (23 samples), Quebrada (9 samples), Sima de las Palomas (1 sample), El Salt (43 samples), Nerja (25 samples) and Gorham's Cave (73 samples), all with negative results.

These newer results clearly question not only the chronological framework on which the evidence of the Middle Palaeolithic in the Spanish Mediterranean was based, but also the very existence of the last Neanderthals in their "refuge" in southern Iberia. This paradigm is thus now under serious challenge, and the existence of these late hominids is difficult to sustain at present. After Zafarraya, Gorham's Cave was presented as further near-indisputable proof for the paradigm, however in the light of the data provided above, this can no longer be sustained. Other challenges or scenarios must be investigated to explain what seems to have been a "depopulation" of southern Iberia from 40 ky until the arrival of the Gravettian groups.

THE LOWER AND MIDDLE PLEISTOCENE IN THE GUADIX-BAZA AND ORCE BASIN

Introduction and geological context

Robert Sala Ramos*

The Guadix-Baza region spans a large area in south-eastern Iberia. It was a vast intramontane endorheic basin between the Miocene and the end of the Middle Pleistocene, when regional tectonics led to the formation of the Guadiana Menor River which drained the former lake system. The first hominins who settled in Western Europe occupied this area at a time when the Guadix sub-basin was crossed by a hydrological system, descending from Sierra Nevada and Sierra de Cazorla and flowing into a lake in the Baza sub-basin in the eastern part of the region.

This 3,000 km^2 basin lies between the Internal and External Zones of the Betic Range. The Cenozoic infill was initially composed of marine

* Universitat Rovira i Virgili. Institut Catala de Paleoecologia Humana i Evolucio Social.

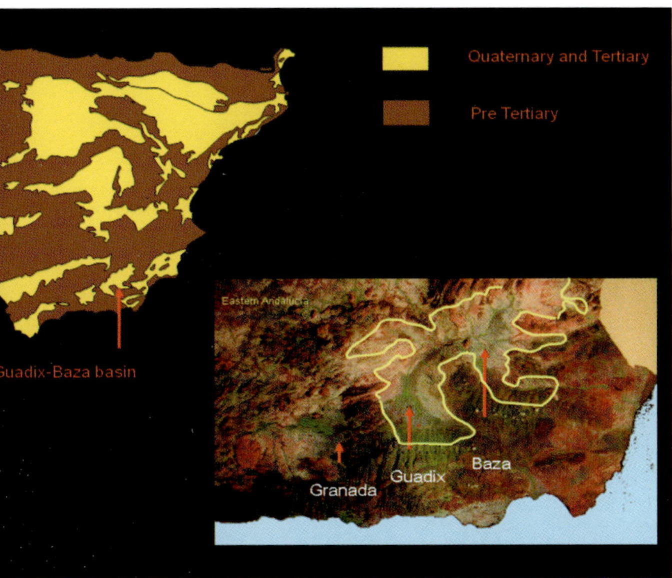

Figure 1. Geological map of the Iberian Peninsula and location of the Guadix-Baza basin. (© Oriol Oms).

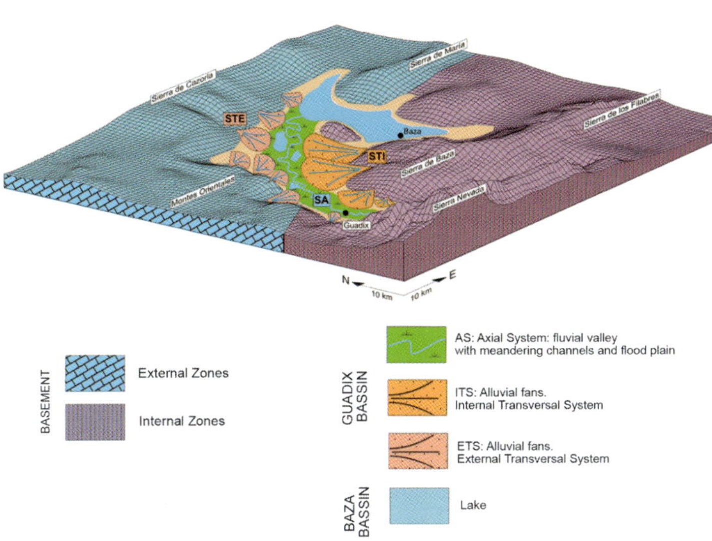

Figure 2. Palaeogeography of the ancient Guadix-Baza river-lake basin at the time of the first human settlement in Orce (© César Viseras, Viseras *et al.*, 2006).

sediments, and covered during the upper Miocene by continental deposits. The Orce sector is at the north-eastern end of the basin, with outcrops of Pliocene and Pleistocene alluvial and lacustrine sediments assigned to the Baza formation (Vera *et al.*, 1984, Soria *et al.*, 1987; García 1997, Oms *et al.*, 2009). The area contains many palaeontological and archaeo-palaeontological records spanning the same period and beyond, including remains from the Upper Pleistocene and the Holocene.

Three sites in the Orce municipality have an Early Pleistocene record, with evidence of the oldest known human presence in Western Europe. They are providing deep knowledge about primitive human adaptation to the continent and the evolution of these hominins' behaviour. These three sites, Venta Micena, Barranco León and Fuente Nueva 3, lay on the south-eastern shore of the ancient Baza Lake. The former contains a purely palaeontological record while the other two contain evidence of the earliest known human presence in Western Europe.

Most of this chapter focuses on these three sites. However, in order to provide a clearer vision of the prehistoric wealth and importance of the entire region, we have also included four other sites in the Guadix-Baza basin which testify to the diachrony of human evolution in this territory.

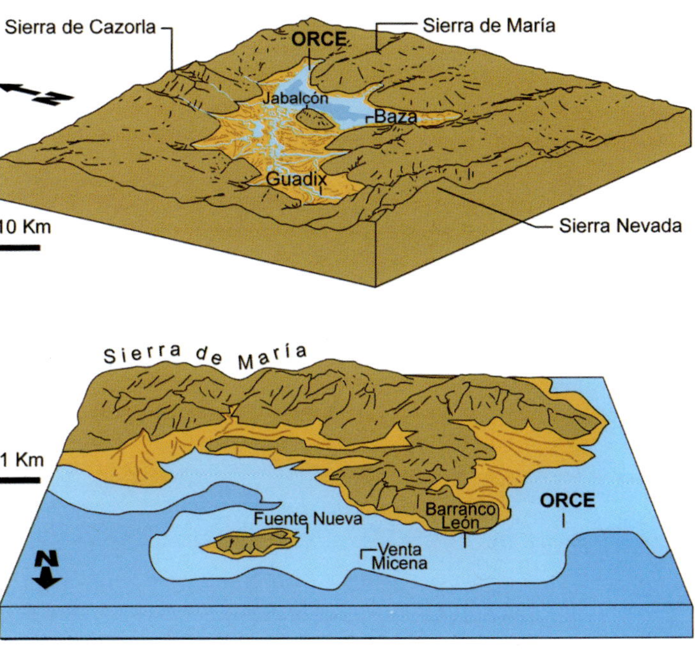

Figure 3. Reconstructed geomorphological and palaeoecological location of the three main Orce sites (© Oriol Oms).

Bienvenido Martínez Navarro*,**,***, María-Patrocinio Espigares Ortiz****,*****, Sergio Ros-Montoya****,*****, Paul Palmqvist ****

1. Venta Micena

Since the discovery of site of the Venta Micena in 1976, and after nearly four decades of continuous survey and research, the region of Orce (Guadix-Baza Basin, southeastern Spain) has provided one of the most important Early Pleistocene collections of large mammals from the European continent.

The Venta Micena stratum is an 80-120 cm thick horizontal layer of micritic limestone whose outcrop can be followed for more than 2.5 Km along the surface (Palmqvist *et al.*, 2008a). Until now, more than 17.000 fossil bones have been unearthed at this site.

The chronology of the site has been obtained by combining paleomagnetic data with the biochronological evidences. It is placed within the *Allophaiomys ruffoi* Zone, located below the *Allophaiomys* aff. *lavocati* Zone (ex. *Allophaiomys bour-*

Figure 4. Panoramic of Venta Micena during the field season of 2005.

* ICREA, Barcelona, Spain
** Institut Català de Paleoecologia Humana i Evolució Social-IPHES, C/ Marcel.lí Domingo s/n, Edifici W3, Campus Sescelades, 43007 Tarragona, Spain
*** Àrea de Prehistoria, Universitat Rovira i Virgili, Avda. Catalunya 35, 43002 Tarragona, Spain
**** Departamento de Geología y Ecología, Universidad de Málaga, Campus de Teatinos, 29071 – Málaga, Spain.
***** Museo de Prehistoria y Paleontología, 18858 – Orce (Granada) Spain

gondiae Zone) and above the *Mimomys oswaldoreigi* Zone (Oms *et al.*, 2000; Agustí and Madurell, 2003). The large mammal assemblage from Venta Micena is different in composition and younger than the ones from the Italian sites included within the Tasso faunal unit in the Upper Valdarno (Rook and Martínez-Navarro, 2010, and references there in). However, Venta Micena and the Georgian site of Dmanisi, dated around 1.8 Ma (Lordkipanidze *et al.*, 2007), show important similarities between both assemblages, such the presence of the bovid species *Soergelia minor* (Moyà-Solà, 1987; Vekua, 1995; Buhksianidze, 2005) which is also present at the Greek site of Apollonia-1, named there *Soergelia brigittae* (Kostopoulos, 1997), and at Italian site of Argentario (Martínez-Navarro *et al.*, 2012). Given that this species is not recorded in the latest Late Villafranchian assemblages, it suggests an earlier age for the Spanish site. Therefore, it is possible to conclude that Venta Micena is situated above the Olduvai subchron, with an age around 1.5±0.1Ma. This chronology is also supported by new data based on ESR methodology (Duval *et al.*, 2011).

The study of the bone assemblage from Venta Micena has helped to detect, among the members of the Late Villafranchian fauna, the presence of African origin species, such as the sabre-tooth *Megantereon whitei* and the mega ungulate *Hippopotamus antiquus* (Martínez-Navarro, 1991; Alberdi and Ruiz-Bustos, 1985; Martínez-Navarro and Palmqvist, 1995; Palmqvist *et al.*, 2007; Martínez-Navarro, 2010). However, it is worth noting that the large mammal assemblages from the Orce sites are basically composed of Holarctic origin species, including equids, rhinos, bovids, cervids, and most of the carnivores, with a faunal list composed by 21 species of large mammals (Table 1).

Taphonomic study of Venta Micena shows that most herbivore remains come from carcasses of ungulate prey selectively hunted by hypercarnivores (coursers *Homotherium latidens* and wild dog *Lycaon lycaonoides*; ambushers *Megantereon whitei* and jaguar *Panthera* cf. *gombaszoegensis*) and scavenged afterwards by the giant bone-cracker hyena *Pachycrocuta brevirostris*.

Modifications produced by the tooth of this hyena follow specific patterns of bone consumption for

Figure 5. Accumulation of bones in the Corte III excavation area of Venta Micena.

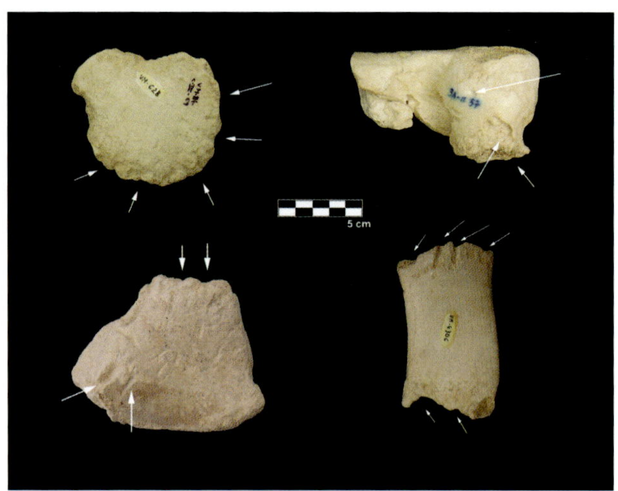

Figure 6. Tooth marks on bones from Venta Micena.

each anatomical element of the ungulate skeleton. Pits, scores, furrowing and crenulated edges are present in a great number of elements, and the analysis of the fracture edges in long bones are consistent with fractures produced when bones are fresh. These features, together with the conservation pattern of anatomical regions in the bones allow us to confirm that *Pachycrocuta* was the main accumulator agent of this site. Some taphomonic biases, that support this interpretation, has been detected in the assemblage as: (a) the kleptoparasitism of ungulate carcasses by *Pachycrocuta*; (b) the transport of ungulate prey as whole carcasses or anatomical parts, depending on the size of the species scavenged; and (c) the selective fracturing of bones as a function of their marrow contents and mineral density.

Ecomorphological inferences allowed to classify ungulate species as grazers in open environment (*Equus altidens, Hemitragus* cf. *albus, Bison* sp., *Praeovibos* sp., *Hippopotamus antiquus*), mixed feeders (*Hemibos* aff. *gracilis, Soergelia minor, Metacervocerus rhenanus* and *Mammuthus meridionalis*) and browsers in forested habitat (*Stephanorhinus* aff. *hundsheimensis* and *Praemegaceros* cf. *verticornis*). The comparison of the abundance of these ecological categories with those present in modern communities show that the fauna of Venta Micena inhabited a mixed environment with a predominance of open plains in the surroundings of a lake fed by hydrothermal waters, similar to the Rift Valley in East Africa.

The presence of several human remains at Venta Micena has been proposed since the discovery in 1982 of the skull fragment VM-0, a small and problematic piece that was classified as *Homo* sp.(Gibert *et al.*,,1983). However, after a long polemic on the supposed human affinities of this fossil, it was concluded that it belonged to a female of a ruminant without cranial appendages, horn cores or pedicels (Martínez- Navarro, 2002). At the moment, no other clear human remains or other evidence of human activity have been found at the site of Venta Micena (Espigares, 2010). Nevertheless paleoecological study of this assemblage, based on combined taphonomic, biomechanical, ecomorphological and biogeochemical approaches, has provided compelling evidence on the environmental context inhabited by the first human populations that dispersed in Western Europe.

VENTA MICENA
Ursus etruscus
Lycaon lycaonoides
Canis mosbachensis
Vulpes praeglacialis
Pachycrocuta brevirostris
Megantereon whitei
Homotherium latidens
Panthera gombaszoegensis
Lynx sp.
Meles meles.
Mammuthus meridionalis
Stephanorhinus aff. *hundsheimensis*
Equus altidens
Hippopotamus antiquus
Bison sp.
Hemibos sp. aff. *H. gracilis*
Soergelia minor
Praeovibos sp.
Hemitragus albus
Praemegaceros cf. *verticornis*
Metacervocerus rhenanus

Table 1. Large mammals lists from Venta Micena (after Martínez-Navarro, 1991; Martínez-Navarro *et al.*, 2010, 2011, and references therein).

Robert Sala Ramos*
Leticia Menéndez Granda*,
Sergio Ros Montoya**, Isidro Toro Moyano***

2. Barranco León

Human activity during the Early Pleistocene at Orce has been well described at two sites on the south-eastern edge of the old Baza lake basin. Barranco León and Fuente Nueva 3, first excavated in the 90's, are two well known sites which have been largely responsible for much of what we know about early human settlement in Western Europe more than one million years ago. Since 2009, the sites are currently under study by a multi-disciplinary, multi-institutional team led by the Catalan Institute of Human Palaeoecology and Social Evolution. The Barranco León site (UTM 548.400 / 4.175.340, 975 m a.s.l.) is located about 3 km from the village of Orce, on the María-Vélez highway. It is located in a north-south gully, at the foot of Sierra Umbria, and ends at the Vélez glen. This area has been well known since the 1980s thanks to the abundance of palaeontological remains (Anadón *et al.*, 1987). The site was discovered in 1983 during a survey in search of micromammals, although it was only in 1992 when A. Arribas did a lithostratigraphic study of the site and discovered the importance of archaeo-palaeontological level BL5 (now level D). This led J. Gibert to apply to the Government of Andalusia for permission to conduct an initial excavation in 1995. Early work

Figure 7. Excavation at the Barranco León site (© Jordi Mestre. IPHES).

* Universitat Rovira i Virgili. Institut Català de Paleoecologia Humana i Evolució Social
** Departamento de Geología y Ecología, Universidad de Málaga, Campus de Treatinos, 29071 – Málaga, Spain. Muso de Prehistoria y Paleontología, 18858 – Orce (Granada) Spain.
*** Museo Arqueológico de Granada.

brought to light several stone tools and remains of horses and hippopotami (Turq *et al.*, 1996). In 1999 and 2000, a new team led by G. Martínez and I. Toro resumed systematic excavation at the site, headed by I. Toro after 2001. The final dig prior to the new research project was in 2005. Since 2010, a new team led by the Institute of Human Palaeoecology and Social Evolution has been responsible for research in the Orce region. A total area of roughly 200m^2 has been excavated at Barranco León in the course of all this work.

2.1. Stratigraphy and dating

The main archaeological record at the Barranco León site is concentrated in detrital horizons lying on dark clayey and sandy facies which form the basis of the excavation. Above these clay facies there are firstly autochthonous carbonated gravels linked to unchannelled bedload inputs. Resting on these gravels are massive sands with floated cobbles plus fauna and industry. In addition, canaliform fine gravels culminate in material with low-angle cross stratification. The sand facies overlie massive levels with medium and fine gravels decreasing in thickness, fining eastward, suggesting that the direction of the input was oblique (SW-NE) to the current canyon, which is more N-S. The channelled facies gave rise to erosive bases with soft cobbles from the lower units (sand and clay below). These channelled facies derive laterally, eastward to fine sands corresponding to the channel bank containing *in situ* archaeological material. The current project has highlighted the existence of such fine sediments and the good preservation of the anthropic record therein. The top of this fluvial sequence consists of silty, sandy facies rich in organic matter from the marsh-lake environment. There are several hydroplastic deformations which had a considerable effect on the sand+gravel channel facies.

The part of the Barranco León sequence containing the anthropogenic occupation thus shows alternating lake and channel and bank levels, indicating different transgressive and regressive phases in the level of the lake and the human occupation of a channell bank close to that lake. Palaeomagnetism and Electro Spin Resonance (ESR) datings situate Barranco León between 1.2 and 1.4 million years (Oms *et al.*, 2000; Duval *et al.*, 2012), while the mammal biochronology and the more recent dating suggests it is closer to the lower end of this range (Toro *et al.*, 2013).

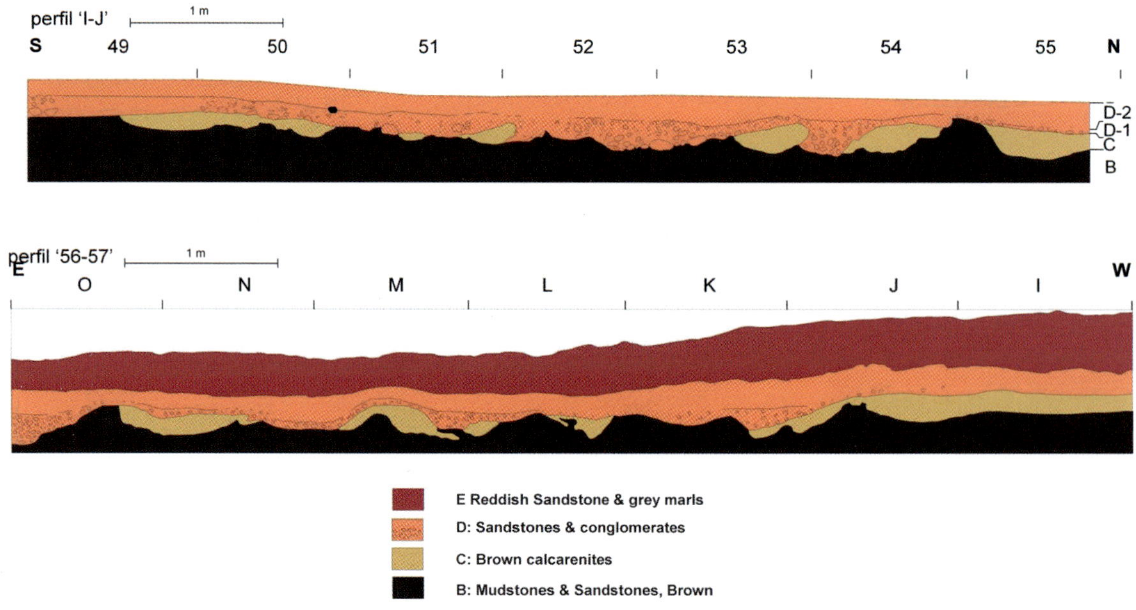

Figure 8. Barranco León stratigraphic sequence (© Oriol Oms).

Robert Sala Ramos*, Leticia Menéndez Granda*, Patrocinio Espigares**, Isidro Toro Moyano***

3. Fuente Nueva 3

The site's UTM coordinates are 522.490/ 4.174.885, on 1:50,000 Army Sheet 23-28. Discovered in 1991 by Alain Bocquet, there have been several emergency excavations and systematic digs in 1993, 1994 and 1995. Systematic annual excavations took place from 1999 to 2003, as well as in 2005 and 2006. As in Barranco León, the current project began in 2010. In all, roughly 75 m^2 have been excavated in two main areas- the majority in the northern part while the area in the south-west quarter is roughly half the size of the other.

3.1. Stratigraphy and dating

The stratigraphic sequence containing evidence of anthropogenic activity at this site starts at the bottom with a whitish basal limestone package (level 1) and a nodular and/or brecciated appearance, in irregular contact with the next level. The sequence continues with a level composed of green-grey clay (level 2), then grey-green carbonated clay and white silt (level 3), followed by another level of brecciated limestone (level 4) whose irregular surface caused by erosion and brecciation facilitated the formation of pockets which include the clays on level 5. The entire sequence is affected by numerous slikensides which have led to the discovery of fossils in a vertical position. Above and to the west there is a thin layer of dark brown clay (level 6), below a layer of greenish-brown sludge on levels 7-11, which are followed by the limestone ceiling.

Figure 9. Excavation at Fuente Nueva 3 (© Jordi Mestre. IPHES).

The aforementioned distinctive levels can be distinguished within the two main upper and lower units of the fossil record. Many of them contain archaeo-palaeontological remains which, for the purpose of clarifying the anthropic activity here, can be assigned to the following individual horizons or levels. In addition to these levels, there are at least two more at a higher level, identified in an extension of the 2013 excavation area. Recent work has increased the number of units containing lithic industry. In addition to Units 1, 2 and 5, where human activity was previously described, remains have been exhumed in technical units 3 and 7, which also contain significant archaeological and palaeontological material. In order to fine-tune the definition of the possible horizons of human activity and/or carnivores, we are currently subdividing Unit 5. This unit –basically greenish loamy sands and shales– can be locally subdivided into 5a, 5b and 5c. At some points, these subdivisions cannot be detected due to the lack of calcrete nodules (one of the indicators), the size of the bones or the shape of the layers, heavily affected by irregularities in the ceiling of Unit 4. The latter factor means that some –or all– of the three subunits can be hard to identify. They are distinguished by the following features:

– 5a contains a large amount of palaeontological remains with varying degrees of al-

* Universitat Rovira i Virgili. Institut Català de Paleoecologia Humana i Evolució Social
** Departamento de Geología y Ecología, Universiad de Málaga, Campus de Teatinos, 29071 – Málaga, Spain. Museo de Prehistoria y Paleontología, 18858 – Orce (Granada) Spain.
*** Museo Arqueológico de Granada.

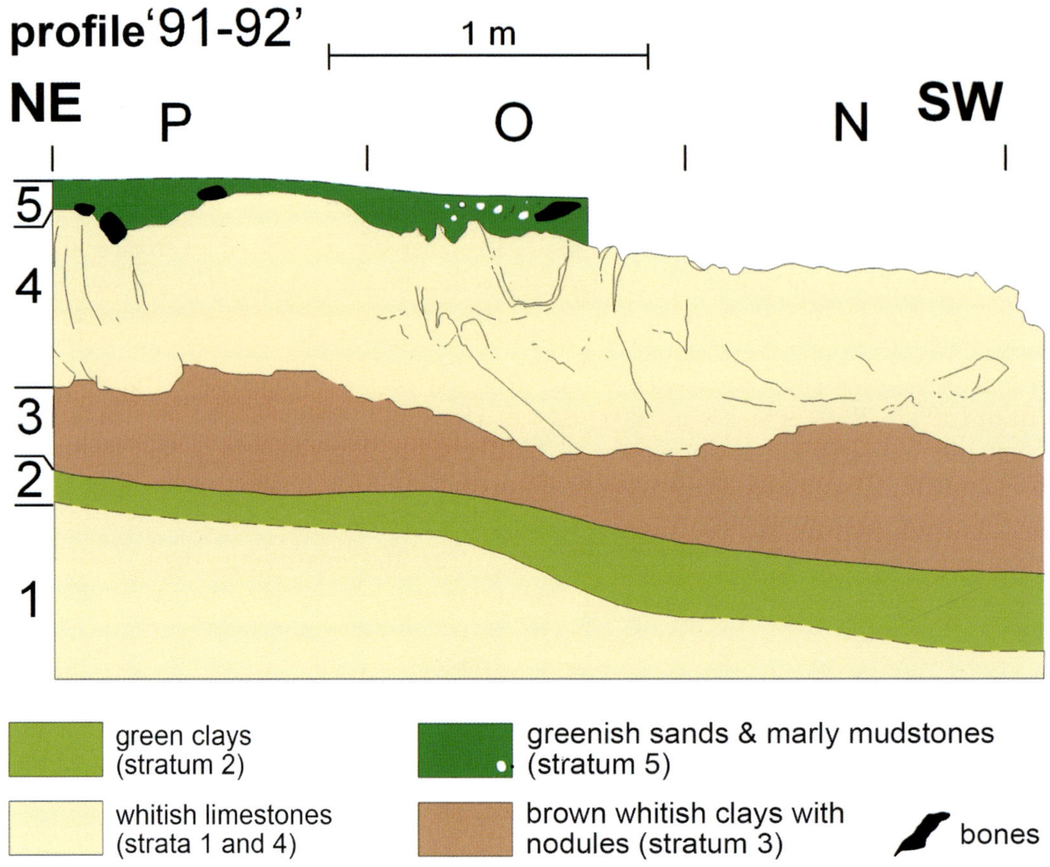

Figure 10. Fuente Nueva 3 stratigraphic sequence. (© Oriol Oms).

teration, forming a mass of mainly disarticulated bones (e.g., in the case of the main proboscid tusks).

- 5b is a distinctive level due to the large amount of reworked calcrete nodules.
- 5c has few nodules, but does contain 'the' complete, articulated skeleton of a *Mammuthus meridionalis*.

In the coming years we plan to complete a geological and sedimentological reconstruction to facilitate an integrated 3D view which will be useful not only as a geologic framework for the units containing lithic industry and palaeontological remains, but also to understand the genesis of the site (or at least the agents and natural factors involved). The latest ESR datings from equid teeth are 1.2Ma BP for the fertile levels at this site (Duval *et al.*, 2012).

María-Patrocinio Espigares Ortiz*,**, Sergio Ros-Montoya*,**, Paul Palmqvist*, Bienvenido Martínez Navarro***,****,*****

4. The faunal assemblage of Barranco León

The archaeopaleontological site of Barranco León, dated 1.4 Ma (Toro-Moyano *et al.*, 2013) shows a typical Late Villafranchian assembblage, mostly composed of large mammal species: eight carnivores (one ursid, three canids, two mustelids, one hyaenid, and one felid), one proboscidean, three perisodactyls (two equids and one rhinocerotid) and five artiodactyls (one hippopotamid, two cervids and two bovids) (Table 1). Carnivores are represented only by isolated teeth from adult individuals and are scarcely recorded, whereas herbivores represent the greater part of the bones unearthed.

It is especially important the record of a first deciduous molar of early *Homo*, specimen BL02-J54-100, which was found in direct association with lithic artefacts and large mammal bones. It represents the oldest anatomical evidence of human presence in Western Europe. This finding,

Figure 12. Third metatarsal of *Equus altidens*.

Figure 11. Antler of *Praemegaceros aff. Verticornis* (© Sergio Ros).

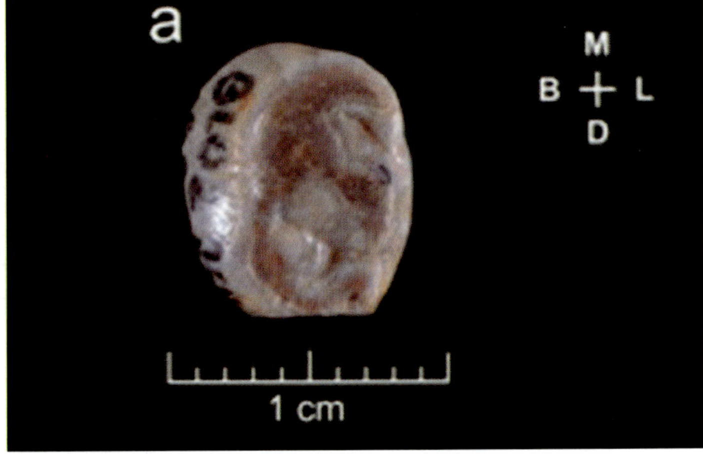

Figure 13. Occlusal view of a first deciduous molar of *Homo* sp. recorded at Barranco León (Toro-Moyano *et al.*, 2013).

* Departamento de Geología y Ecología, Universidad de Málaga, Campus de Teatinos, 29071 – Málaga, Spain.
** Museo de Prehistoria y Paleontología, 18858 – Orce (Granada) Spain
*** ICREA, Barcelona, Spain
**** Institut Català de Paleoecologia Humana i Evolució Social-IPHES, C/ Marcel.lí Domingo s/n, Edifici W3, Campus Sescelades, 43007 Tarragona, Spain
***** Àrea de Prehistoria, Universitat Rovira i Virgili, Avda. Catalunya 35, 43002 Tarragona, Spain

combined with the important lithic tool assemblage, confirms that Western Europe was colonized less than 0.5 Ma after the first expansion of *Homo* out of Africa.

From the paleontological point of view this assemblage is very similar to that documented in the nearby localities of Fuente Nueva-3 and Venta Micena. The absence of *Soergelia minor*, a middle sized, mesodont bovid recorded at Venta Micena, and the presence of the new species of Asian origin *Equus sussenbornensis* suggests a process of aridification during the late Late Villafranchian, previous to the arrival of the classical Galerian species.

It is remarkable the record of megaherbivores, proboscideans are practically absent from this site while hippos are very abundant. This difference with Fuente Nueva-3, where elephants are one of the best represented species, was probably due to the different sedimentary environment in both sites, a palaeochannel for Barranco León and a swampy area for Fuente Nueva-3.

In addition to the lithic artefacts and the human tooth, abundant cut-marks and percussion marks, that evidence bone fracturing for accessing marrow contents, have been identified in this site. Cut marks localized on the diaphyses of the major limb bones may be related to defleshing activities. Evidences of disarticulation and evisceration were inferred by cut marks recorded in metapodials, vertebrae and internal surface of ribs. The skeletal elements bearing cut marks are mainly included in the large size category (340-907 kg). Fractured bones show frequently spiral fractures, impact points and flaking produced when they were broken by percussion (Espigares *et al.*, 2008; Espigares, 2010).

Evidence of carnivore activity is scarce and consists mainly of scores and pits located in metapodials and carpal/tarsal bones. Comparative taphonomic analyses of this assemblage with the pattern of modification of bones by *Pachycrocuta brevirostris* developed in Venta Micena, reveal, a similar morphology of the tooth marks than that produced by this hyaenid. Presence of *P. brevirostris* in Barranco León is supported by the record of abundant coprolites and some isolated teeth, although anthropic activity predominates in Barranco león with a punctual and secondary access of carnivores to these areas.

Barranco León D
Homo sp.
Ursus sp.
Canis mosbachensis
Lycaon lycaonoides
Vulpes cf. *praeglacialis*
Pachycrocuta brevirostris
cf. *Homotherium* sp.
Meles meles
cf. *Pannonictis* sp.
Mammuthus meridionalis
Stephanorhinus hundsheimensis
Equus altidens
Equus suessenbornensis
Hippopotamus antiquus
Bison sp.
Hemitragus albus
Praemegaceros cf. *verticornis*
Metacervocerus rhenanus

Table 2. Faunal list (large mammal species) for the archaeological levels of Barranco León (Oms *et al.*, 2000; Martínez-Navarro *et al.*, 2003, 2010; Palmqvist *et al.*, 2005; Toro *et al.*, 2013 and references there in).

María-Patrocinio Espigares Ortiz*,**, Sergio Ros-Montoya*,**, Paul Palmqvist*, Bienvenido Martínez Navarro***,****,*****

5. The faunal assemblage of Fuente Nueva-3

The archaeopaleontological site of Fuente Nueva-3, dated 1.2-1.3 Ma (Martínez-Navarro *et al.*, 1997; Oms *et al.*, 2000; Martínez-Navarro et al., 2010, Duval, 2011), show a typical Late Villafranchian assemblage, similar to that of Venta Micena and is mostly composed of large mammal species: nine carnivores (one ursid, three canids, three mustelids, one hyaenid, and one felid), one proboscidean, three perisodactyls (two equids and one rhinocerotid) and six artiodactyls (one hippopotamid, two cervids and three bovids) (Table 1).

Figure 14. Semi-complet skeleton of *Mammuthus meridionalis*.

It is interesting the absence of *Soergelia minor*, a middle sized and mesodont bovid that is recorded at Venta Micena, and the presence of new immigrants of Asian origin, especially *Equus sussenbornensis* (Alberdi, 2010) and *Ammotragus europaeus* (Moullé *et al.*, 2004). Both species are typical grazers and inhabited open environments, which suggests a process of aridification during the late Late Villafranchian, previous to the arrival of the classical Galerian species.

Figure 15. Hemimandible of *Stephanorhinus hundsheimensis* together with some ribs and fragment bones from large mammals.

Two archaeopaleontological ensembles have been described in this site: the Upper Level and the Lower Level. The faunal composition of both is the same, the main differences are located in the abundance of lithic artefacts associated with skeletal remains of large mammals (Toro *et al.*, 2011), more abundantly represented in the Lower than in the Upper Level, which suggests a marginal occupation of the latter by the hominins and a difference in the preservation of the anatomical parts. Other intriguing difference is the abundance of *Mammuthus meridionalis* remains in the Upper Level, including a semi-complete carcase and five tusk, as well as abundant molars and tooth fragments.

In addition to the lithic artifacts, there is evidence of anthropic modifications on the bones'

* Departamento de Geología y Ecología, Universidad de Málaga, Campus de Teatinos, 29071 – Málaga, Spain.
** Museo de Prehistoria y Paleontología, 18858 – Orce (Granada) Spain
*** ICREA, Barcelona, Spain
**** Institut Català de Paleoecologia Humana i Evolució Social-IPHES, C/ Marcel.lí Domingo s/n, Edifici W3, Campus Sescelades, 43007 Tarragona, Spain
***** Àrea de Prehistoria, Universitat Rovira i Virgili, Avda. Catalunya 35, 43002 Tarragona, Spain

surface, cut and percussion marks were identified in skeletal elements mainly included in the large size category (340-907 kg). Cut marks located on the diaphyses of the major limb bones and on the external surface of the ribs may be related to defleshing activities. There are also cut marks on a pelvis fragment and several metapodials, which were probably produced during the disarticulation of these elements. Finally, there is also a scrape mark which was probably originated during the removal of the periosteum before fracturing the bone. Fracturing patterns in the skeletal elements indicate that fresh bones were broken mainly by percussion. As a result, they show spiral fractures, impact points and flaking (Espigares *et al.*, 2008; Espigares, 2010).

Evidence of carnivore activity on the cortical surface is scarce and consists mainly of scores and pits. However, the presence of carnivores in the Upper Level will probably increase in the near future, because more than a 150 coprolites of *P. brevirostris* have been documented, which show the intense activity of the giant hyenas during the time of deposition of this level, that has provided the oldest evidence of a probable direct competition between *Homo* and *Pachycrocuta*, the two major bone modifying and accumulating agents during Early Pleistocene times in Eurasia. The evidence lies in the finding of an incomplete skeleton of *M. meridionalis* surrounded by 34 coprolites and 17 lithic artifacts. The skewed spatial distribution of these elements, the physical characteristics of the coprolites and the absence of the elephant limbs and cranium suggest that both hominins and hyenas scavenged the carcass of this megaherbivore, following a sequence of consumption in which the hominins arrived first, dismembered and transported the limbs, and probably also the cranium, and later the hyenas consumed the rest of the elephant carcass (Espigares *et al.*, 2013).

Fuente Nueva 3
Ursus sp.
Canis mosbachensis
Lycaon lycaonoides
Vulpes cf. *praeglacialis*
Pachycrocuta brevirostris
Felidae indet.
Lynx sp.
Meles meles
Pannonictis cf. *nestii*
Mustelidae indet. (small size)
Mammuthus meridionalis
Stephanorhinus hundsheimensis
Equus altidens
Equus suessenbornensis
Hippopotamus antiquus
Bison sp.
Ammotragus europaeus
Hemitragus albus
Praemegaceros cf. *verticornis*
Metacervocerus rhenanus

Table 1. Faunal list (large mammal species) for the archaeopaleontological levels of Fuente Nueva-3 (Martínez-Navarro *et al.*, 1997, 2003, 2010; Oms *et al.*, 2000; Palmqvist *et al.*, 2005; Espigares *et al.*, 2013 and references therein).

Deborah Barsky *,**, Robert Sala **,*, Isidro Toro ***, Leticia Menéndez Granda*, **

6. The Lithic industry from Barranco León and Fuente Nueva 3

The Barranco León and Fuente Nueva 3 sites have yielded some of the best preserved and most numerically rich Oldowan stone tool assemblages so far to have been discovered in Eurasia. The industries, excavated *in situ* from each stratigraphical sequence, are found in clear association with the remains of large and medium-sized herbivores and carnivores (Espigares *et al.*, 2013). The unearthing of this exceptionally rich accumulation (BL=;1 722 pcs.; FN3= 1 264 pcs.) provides the opportunity to analyze one of the oldest known and most comprehensive lithic series in a rigorously controlled archeological, stratigraphical and chronological situation. Ongoing excavations and interdisciplinary studies considerably enlarge potential interpretations of the paleo-environmental context reigning at the time of the appearance of the first inhabitants of Western Europe, some 1,4-1,3 Ma (Toro-Moyano *et al.*, 2010 a, 2010 b). The technological, typological and traceological features of the Orce assemblages are thus founded on a coherent and exceptionally complete data-set which is still increasing in pace with the progression of excavations and research. In future, spatial analysis of the archeological remains will add yet another horizon to what is presently known of the behavior and cognitive levels of the hominins frequenting the Orce paleo-lake basin.

The lithic assemblages and their raw materials

Only subtle differences are highlighted between the lithic assemblages from BL and FN3 and the two industries are considered to be largely analogous. Both of the toolkits were manufactured from local flint and limestone and they clearly belong to an Mode 1 tradition. Accordingly, they present a low degree of standardization: there are no handaxes, cleavers nor picks and the few existing secondary knapped flakes are attributed to cores rather than to retouched tools (Barsky *et al.*, 2013, 2014). Knapping waste, mainly in flint, is composed of abundant and small-sized flakes. While cores are relatively scarce, all elements of the various reduction and use schemes identified at the sites are represented in the assemblages, proving that these activities were practiced *in situ*. In addition, a considerable proportion of the larger-sized limestone instruments bear marks of intensive use attributable to percussive or pounding activities. These voluminous tools include non-modified cobbles and blocks marked by traces of percussion and/or breakage impacts. Interestingly, there is a dimensional and functional dichotomy that appears to be rooted in the selective use of the two local raw materials: flint and limestone. These rocks are accessible in the immediate vicinity of the sites. These are the only kinds of rocks identified in the industries to date. Hominin raw material sourcing patterns were, therefore, strictly local.

Both bipolar on an anvil and hard hammer methods were used for flake production and sometimes both techniques are recognizable on a single core. The use of bipolar on an anvil knapping is attested by clearly identifiable stigma on some of the cores (opposite impacts/negatives) and some flakes display prognostic traces; such as bullet-like morphologies or opposite impact points on their ventral surfaces. Experimental knapping has confirmed that this method is particularly well adapted to small flake production from tiny, cube-shaped flint matrixes identical to those found near the sites. It should be noted, however, that meter-sized flint blocks were probably also available from the outcrops and in secondary situations close by.

The assemblages (particularly BL) also comprise large, quadrangular, flat limestone slabs displaying percussion stigma on their surfaces. Peripheral breakage with opposite impact points

* Institut Català de Paleoecologia Humana i Evolució Social
** Universitat Rovira i Virgili
*** Museo Arqueológico de Granada

are observed on these slabs, buttressing evidence for their use as anvils. Indeed, anvils would have been necessary both for bipolar reduction of stone and to effectively break some of the larger-sized bones. The industry equally includes the corresponding "anvil fragments" attesting that these activities were carried out on-site. The high item breakage ratio is explained by the force of the blows needed to carry out these activities, and also by the mediocre quality of much of the flint and the limestone.

The flint

Flint, outcropping from Dogger limestone formations located 5-15 Km to the south, was introduced mostly as flat, slightly rolled nodules originating from secondary deposits in the immediate vicinity of the sites (Turq *et al.*, 1996; Toro Moyano *et al.*, 2010 a; 2010 b). The scarcity of cores relative to flakes as well as a paucity of cortical elements may be related to the morphology of these brute flint nodules (intense breakage, partially covering cortex), but may also indicate that some of the knapping was carried out away from the sites. A few, larger-sized flakes were re-knapped; principally on their ventral surfaces. This could signal an *ad hoc* behavioral response to competition with other large carnivores present in the landscape and a need to expediently produce small, sharp-edged flakes for rapid and efficient meat acquisition. However, none of the flaked flakes correspond unambiguously with stereotyped retouched tools, such as notches, scrapers or denticulates (Barsky *et al.*, 2010, 2013; Toro-Moyano *et al.*, 2010 a, 2010 b, 2011). These *secondary knapped flakes* could be linked to bipolar on an anvil production (Zaidner, 2013).

Core platforms were not prepared (facetted) and the plane surfaces of removal negatives most often served as platforms; giving way to polyhedral core forms. Knapping episodes were relatively long and the flint cores are generally maximally exploited. The bulk of the flakes correspondingly display unidirectional or orthogonally oriented removal negatives on their dorsal surfaces and smooth striking platforms. Small, cube-shaped cores with opposite removals show crush marks typically produced by this method. A few, somewhat enigmatic products (essentially at FN3) are attributed to *pieces esquillées*: they likely result from extracting flakes by bipolar method on an anvil using blows effectuated from a summital crest.

Figure 16. Top: small, elongated flint flake (BL 2013.D1.G49 nº 1). Bottom: limestone macro tool (BL 2011 D1.G51.16) with bipolar breakage and flat impact removals on the upper extremity (Photos Jordi Mestre. IPHES).

The limestone

This raw material was collected from local alluvial sources and also from the substructure of the sites themselves. Different kinds of limestone outcrop in the immediate vicinity of the sites and was most probably transported there by water or even locally mined, displaced and collected by hominins: procurement was strictly local in all cases. Most of the archeological limestone cobbles display slightly rolled surfaces and are loosely compacted, indicating short-distance transport. The cobbles, blocks and stones have bearing on anthropic activities that are somewhat difficult to evaluate, especially since, in some instances (especially at BL), surface alteration impedes adequate readability of the material. In any case, careful study of the limestone (Barsky *et al.*, in progress) reveals that hominins displaced, gathered and used it in different ways that are linked to criteria such as morphology, volume, weight, and petrographic quality. The widely variable nature of the limestone excavated from the archeological contexts has given way to a number of interpretations. At BL, for example, a fossil alluvial bed traversing the site in its southeastern extremity and contemporary to the occupation likely provided the main source of the limestone cobbles. This alluvial level is visible throughout the extension of the *Barranco* and could also have provided some fragmented flint nodules which erode out of an outcrop upstream.

Contrastingly, fine grained siliceous limestone outcrops abundantly around the FN3 site and could have been opportunistically collected- or even locally mined. Limestone cobbles from other (yet to be localized) alluvial sources were also recovered and brought to the site.

The presence of mediocre quality and poorly compacted or excessively large limestone items in the sites may therefore be at least partially explained by its introduction by natural forces: alluvial at BL and erosive at FN3.

Siliceous limestone was preferentially used for controlled flake extraction and also for the manufacture of some loosely configured macro tools. The latter group includes chopper-like instruments and a few poorly standardized heavy-duty scrapers (as defined by Leakey, 1971). All of these macro instruments bear visible traces of use; mainly accidental removals and crush marks on their crests. At Barranco León, a few of the tools with abundant fracture angles (de la Torre and Mora, 2005) and removal negatives display a polyhedral morphology consistent with a sub-spheroid morpho-type. In any case, the differential quality of the limestone did not always prevent hominins from making some use of even the poorest quality rocks (Fig. 17, bottom right). The assemblages also contain a few considerably well-struck limestone flakes whose presence, alongside some organized core forms (orthogonal, multiplatform), indicates a dual functionality for the limestone: percussion and debitage.

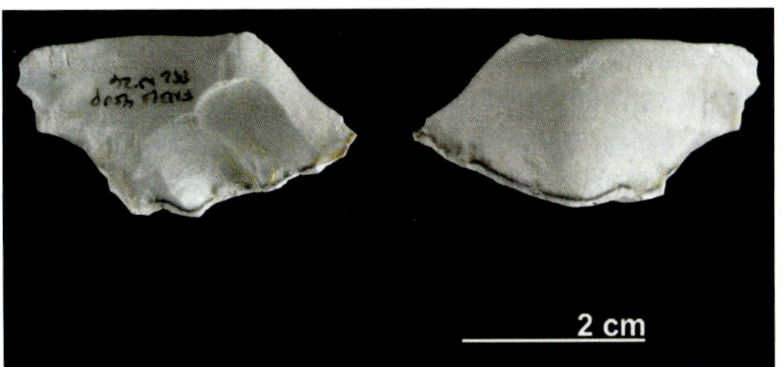

Figure 17. Top: small flint flake (FN3 2013.Nivel superior. T92.nº 26) with a cortical striking platform. Bottom: macro limestone tools (left: FN3 2010.R92 nº 98 and right: FN3 2011.P88. nº 28) with lateral unidirectional removals and crush marks on the edges (Photos Jordi Mestre. IPHES).

Compared with flint, limestone matrixes often show a lower degree of transformation. The majority of each limestone assemblage is in fact made up of used or slightly modified cobbles and blocks, a large number of which have traces of percussion. The corresponding flakes are bigger than those in flint (3-4 cm).

The anthropic nature of the traces on the tools is underlined by the consistency with which they are found to be localized in specific areas on the tools, in accordance with their shape and size. The kinds of traces documented vary considerably in both intensity and morphology. They include: accidental removal negatives, surface scarring, stigmata, irregular retouch, crushing, polish, bipolar breakage impacts, cupula, striations, facetted breakage and fracture angles (Barsky *et al.*, in progress). This trace variability on the limestone macro tools surely indicates that a wider range of activities was being carried out at the sites than previously attributed to Mode 1 hominin groups and constitutes a focus of ongoing research efforts.

Synthesis

The BL and FN3 industries, largely analogous, fall within the variability of the Oldowan or Mode 1 techno-complex *sensu lato*: local raw material procurement, poorly standardized cores and flakes and very few large or small intentionally shaped items. We underline however that, for each of these defining characteristics the industries show some 'progressive' features that could suggest some kind of continuity or evolutionary trend consistent with a move towards more complex technological behavior. This increase in innovative behavior could have been transmitted by progressive social integration (cultural transmission). We may highlight some of the more significant characteristics underlining the relative sophistication of the hominins present at the paleo lake Baza over a million years ago, such as: a comprehensive knowledge of the potential uses for the raw materials available to them, a clear functional dichotomy established upon this petrographical familiarity applied to optimize its potential, the systematic use of orthogonal knapping strategies for flake production, the capacity to adapt their flake knapping strategies to compensate deficiencies in rock quality, the presence of a few loosely configured macro tools, including heavy-duty scrapers and sub-spheroids, and, finally, a variability of on-site tasks (yet to be defined) is made manifest by the wide range of traces left on their tools.

J.M. Jiménez Arenas*

7. Huéscar-1

The Huéscar-1 archaeo-palaeontological site (HU-1, 940 m.a.s.l.) is in the north-eastern sector of the Guadix-Baza intramontane basin, 4 km from Huéscar on the left bank of Barranco de las Cañadas ravine. The site was first excavated under A. Mazo, then by M.T. Alberdi (1986). Surface surveys were conducted by the Sabadell Institute of Palaeontology in the early 80s and again in 2003 by a team led by B. Martínez Navarro. The most productive work in palaeontological terms was the 1986 dig, particularly test pit , while from an archaeological perspective it was the 2003 survey, the only one to detect human presence in the form of stone knapping. Five levels have been defined at HU-1. The three levels containing vertebrates are, from bottom to top, Level 2, composed of superposed sand lenses, which decrease in grain size upwards, yellowish conglomerates, plus carbonates and flint clasts and occasionally Keuper hyacinths of Compostela; Level 3, composed of massive carbonate silts (carbonation increasing upwards) with mottled ochre and millimetric plant residues; and Level 4 composed of yellowish microconglomerates and sands. The published (Alonso Diago *et al.*, 2003) faunal list consists of the following taxa: **Pisces:** *Leuciscus pyrenaicus*; **Reptilia:** *Emydidae* indet.; **Aves**: cf. *Tachybaptus ruficolis*, *Anas crecca*/*A. querquedula*, *Anas platyrhynchos*, *Anas clypeata*, *Anas strepera*, *Anas* sp., *Netta rufina*, *Aythya ferina*, *Aythya nyroca*, *Aythya fuligula*, *Aythya* sp., *Perdix perdix*, *Crex cres*, *Bubo bubo*; **Soricidae**: Soricidae indet.; **Rodentia**: *Eliomys quercinus*, *Apodemus* sp., *Paraethomys meini*, *Castillomys crusafonti* ssp., *Mimomys savini*, *Microtus* (*Pitymys*) *gregaloides*, *Microtus* (*Microtus*) *brecciensis*; **Lagomorpha**: *Oryctolagus* sp., *Lepus* cf. *L. granatensis*, Leporidae indet.; **Carnivora:** *Canis etruscus*, *Crocuta crocuta*, *Vulpes* sp., *Vulpes prae-*

* Dpto. de Prehistoria y Arqueología, Universidad de Granada, Campus de Cartuja s/n (Granada) 18071

Figure 18. Knapped flakes from Huéscar-1. Left: flake found *in situ* on the bed, near Section cut 1. Right: flake found on the surface on the rockfall face. Adapted from Martínez Navarro *et al.*, 2006.

glacialis; **Proboscidea:** *Elephas antiquus*, probably the earliest record of that species in Europe; **Perissodactyla:** *Equus altidens, Equus sussenbornensis, Stephanorhinus hundsheimensis*; **Artiodactyla**: *Bison cf. schoetensacki, Capra* sp., *Cervus acoronatus, Dolichodorycerus savini, Sus* cf. *scrofa, Hippopotamus maior*.

There is an extraordinary number of waterfowl remains which, together with the nature of the deposition, suggest that this was a shallow delta lake. The most common taxon amongst the large mammals is the genus *Equus*. Taphonomic studies have revealed that the accumulated bones, mainly oriented in a N-S direction, show no evidence of alteration by carnivores (neither predators nor scavengers) and few traces of weathering. On the other hand, they do show many marks caused by traction. We can therefore infer that at least part of the large mammal association –perhaps with the exception of *Hippopotamus*– was transported by flowing water that built up in a shallow delta lake environment. The chronology proposed on the basis of palaeomagnetism (below the Brunhes-Matuyama polarity inversion) and the composition of the faunal assemblage is ~900 ky. The lithic industry consists of three flakes, attributable to the Oldowan or Mode 1, with clear percussion bulbs and no evidence of retouch on their active edges. Two of them "were found on the north side of the stream, about 3 metres from where they had become detached from the rockface, the other *in situ*, partially adhered to the sediment between sections A and B excavated by Mª. Teresa Alberdi" (Martínez Navarro *et al.*, 2006:55).

J.M. Jiménez Arenas*

8. Cúllar Baza-1

The Cúllar Baza-1 site (CB-1, 965 m.a.s.l.) is in the northeastern sector of the Guadix-Baza intramontane basin, 2.5 km SE of Cúllar. The three fieldwork seasons (1973, 1975 and 1986), were directed by A. Ruiz Bustos, M. Botella and M.T. Alberdi respectively. The chronology of CU-1 has been defined as ~720 ky on the basis of palaeomagnetism, the biostratigraphic interpretation of the vertebrate association and the stone industry. The stratigraphy was first defined by Ruiz Bustos (1976) and subsequently revised by Alonso Diago *et al.*, (2001) and Torrente Casado (2010). On the basis of the latter author (with additional reference to the denomination in Alonso

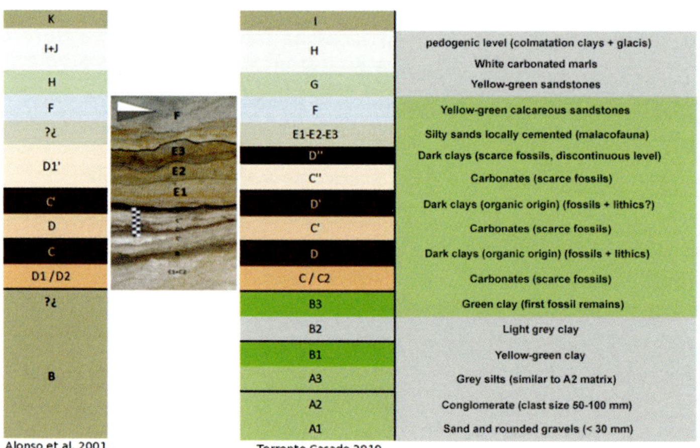

Figure 19. CB-1 stratigraphy. Left, as proposed by Alonso Diago *et al.*, (2001). Right, as proposed by Torrente Casado (2010). The stratigraphic column is in the centre. Adapted from Torrente Casado (2010).

Diago *et al.*, 2001), ten levels can be distinguished in CU-1. The three sub-levels on Level D –the most archaeo-palaeontologically significant– are, from bottom to top, D (C) –black or brown-green clays and silts, with major plastic tectonic deformations, D' (C') –black, massive clayey silt, and D'' composed of massive, carbonated dark brown sandy silt (D1').

The published faunal list contains the following taxa: **Pisces:** *Leuciscus pyrenaicus*; **Reptilia:** *Acanthodactylus* cf. *erythrurus*, *Blanus cinereus*, *Chalcides* indet., *Chalcides* cf. *bedriagai*, *Lacerta* sp., *Lacerta* cf. *lepida*, *Lacerta* (*Podarcis*) indet., *Natrix* sp., *Rhinechis scalaris*, *Scindidae* indet., *Testudo* sp. *B*, *Timon* cf. *lepidus*; **Insectivora**: *Sorex* sp., *Neomys* sp., *Crocidura* sp.; **Rodentia:** *Apodemus* aff. *sylvaticus*, *Cricetulus* (*Allocricetus*) *bursae*, *Elyomis quercinus*, *Microtus* (*Microtus*) *brecciensis*, *Arvicola mosbachensis/A. cantiana*; **Lagomorpha:** *Lepus* cf. *granatensis*, *Oryctolagus* cf. *cuniculus*; **Carnivora:** *Canis etruscus*, *Crocuta crocuta*, *Vulpes* sp., *Vulpes praeglacialis*; **Proboscidea:** *Mammuthus trogontherii*; **Perissodactyla:** *Equus altidens*, *Equus sussenbornesis*, *Stephanorhinus etruscus*; **Arctiodactyla:** *Bison* cf. *schoetensacki*, *Capra* sp., *Cervus acoronatus*, *Dolichodorycerus savini*, *Sus* cf. *scrofa*. The most common taxon amongst the large mammals is the genus *Equus*. The site's sedimentology permits the inference of several major palaeogeographic aspects, with nine sedimentary environments (four suggested by Alonso *et al.*, 2001) which, depending on the depth of the water, are more reductor environments with a greater amount of organic matter (marsh or lake edges) or more open, oxygenised lake environments with a greater input of alluvial matter. The most fertile archaeo-palaeontologicals levels are probably from swamp or lakeside contexts. There is no evidence of taphonomic abrasion, fractures or incisions, or heavy weathering. In contrast, carnivore bite marks, by both hunters and scavengers, are present. The presence of coprolites also indicates *in situ* activity by hyaenids. Small numbers of articulated elements have been found on all levels. The random

* Dpto. de Prehistoria y Arqueología, Universidad de Granada, Campus de Cartuja s/n (Granada) 18071

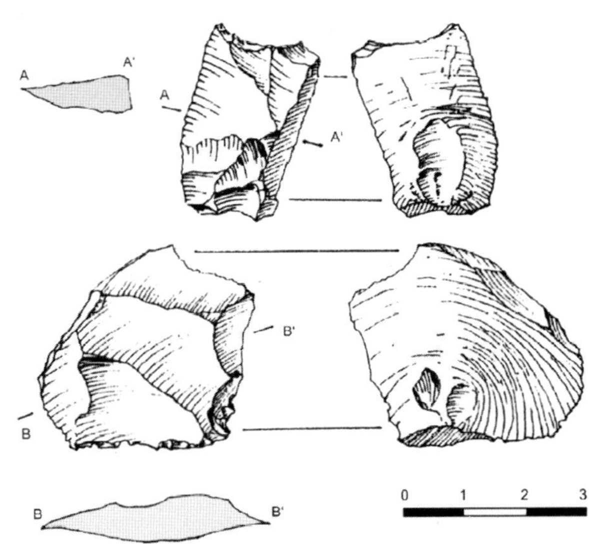

Figure 20. CU-1 lithic industry. Flakes discovered in 1986 excavation. Adapted from Vega Toscano (1989) and Bonadonna Alberdi (1989).

distribution of the elements suggests that there were no significant alluvial remobilization episodes. The mortality profile of the species shows an L shape, suggesting catastrophic or seasonal-attritional mortality on and near the lake banks or marsh areas in a hot, dry climatic context. The meagre lithic industry catalogue consists of a quartzite chopping tool, a metamorphosed dolomite chopper and five manuports in the same rock (1973 excavation), at least two pieces of flint and several worked pebbles (1975 excavation, now misplaced) and nine manuports and two flint flakes (1986 excavation). This assemblage has been assigned to Oldowan or Mode 1 on the basis of both typological (presence of *chopper, chopping tool* and flakes) and technological criteria (use of hard hammer, lack of retouch).

J.M. Jiménez Arenas*

9. Solana del Zamborino site

The Solana del Zamborino (SZ) archaeo-palaeontological site, 992 m a.s.l., is in the western sector of the Guadix-Baza intramontane basin, 7 km from Fonelas. This is a terminal level of the Guadix formation. The three fieldwork seasons in 1972, 1973 and 1976 were led by M. Botella.

Six levels have been described, three of which contain archaeological and palaeontological remains: from bottom to top, Level A, composed of clays (A_1 -grey plastic clay, $A2_1$ -green clay), silt ($A2_2$ -grey silt) and sand ($A2_3$ -very fine sand); Level B, the richest level in fauna and tools, where three types of material have been distinguished, equivalent to lateral changes in facies, very fine-grained black clay (B_1), sandy loam (B_2) and greenish grey clay (B_3); and Level C, with two chronological periods (C1 and C2), and within them, lateral changes of facies ($C1_1$ -greenish-grey clay with very fine polyhedral structure, $C1_2$ -very fine sands, difficult to follow, $C2_1$ -prismatic black clay with violet patches, $C2_2$ -green clays with a polyhedral structure, $C2_3$ -sand and silt, $C2_4$- similar clay to $C2_2$, with carbonated nodules).

The vertebrate faunal association consists of: **Reptilia:** *Lacerta* sp., *Testudo* sp., Anura indet.; **Insectivora**: *Sorex* sp., *Crocidura* sp.; **Rodentia**: *Eliomys quercinus* cf. *quercinus*, *Eliomys quercinus* cf. *lusitanicus*, *Allocricetus bursae colombierensis*, *Arvicola sapidus* (*A. cantiana*, según A. Ruiz Bustos), *Microtus brecciensis*, *Apodemus* cf. *flavicollis*; **Lagomorpha**: *Oryctolagus cf. cuniculus*, *Lepus* sp.; **Carnivora**: *Canis cf. lupus*, *Panthera* (*Leo*) *spelaea*, *Lynx* cf. *pardina*, *Felis sylvestris*; **Proboscidea**: *Mammuthus trogontherii* (present only in level A), *Elephas antiquus* (levels B and C); **Perissodactyla**: *Equus caballus torralbae* (present in levels A, B and C),

* Dpto. de Prehistoria y Arqueología, Universidad de Granada, Campus de Cartuja s/n (Granada) 18071

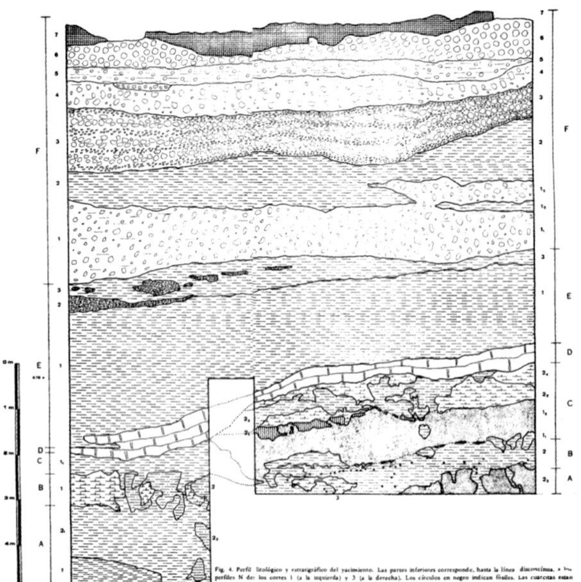

Figure 21. SZ site stratigraphy. Adapted from Casas *et al.*, (1976).

Stephanorhinus hemitoechus; **Arctiodactyla**: *Cervus elaphus, Capreolus capreolus, Dama* sp., *Bos (Bos) primigenius, Bos (Bison) priscus, Hippopotamus* sp., *Sus scrofa*; **Primates**: *Macaca* sp.

The archaeo-palaeontologicals levels have been linked to lake and marsh environments in which the different lithologies correspond to seasonal variations in the water level under a warm, moist climate regime. The predominant taxa are *Equus* and *Bos*. The lithic industry consists of more than 1,500 items. Amongst the raw materials, there is an abundance of quartzite and quartz tools but less flint items. Most of the items are retouched, some with soft hammerstones. The most abundant types are scrapers, notches and denticulates, and also the three characteristic Acheulean or Mode 2 formats, i.e., handaxes, cleavers and trihedrals, as well as cores and choppers. All of this led Botella *et al.*, (1976) to frame it in the Mediterranean Late Acheulean. However, Level A has a major feature: a lack of denticulates, a drastic reduction in sidescrapers and a lack of Acheulean types. In conjunction with the replacement of *E. antiquus* by *M. trogontherii*, this suggests a hiatus between Level A and the others with a palaeontological and archaeological record.

One outstanding aspect of SZ is the large amount of charcoal and the presence of a structure interpreted as a hearth. The circular distribution of the cobbles and the heat disturbance to their inner faces are the main arguments for this interpretation. The chronological interpretation of this site has been reignited in recent years since the proposal of SZ as the source of one of Europe's oldest evidence of handaxes (720 ky, Scott and Gibert 2009). However, this dating has been seriously questioned since several errors have been detected in the interpretation of the archaeological assemblage (generically framed in an early Middle Palaeolithic context) and significant discrepancies between the faunal list and the original list referred to by the authors of the aforementioned article, with taxa omitted or altered in an attempt to make the faunal assemblage consistent with ages deduced from magnetostratigraphy (Jiménez-Arenas *et al.*, 2011). From an archaeological –both typological and technological– and palaeontological perspective, the Solana del Zamborino site should therefore be attributed to a well advanced point in the Middle Pleistocene (400-300ka).

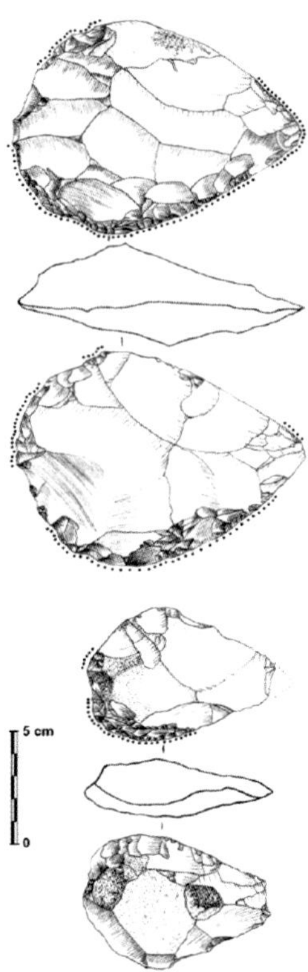

Figure 22. Handaxes found at Solana del Zamborino. Above: chordate handaxe found on the surface. Below: handaxe from Level B. Spots indicate where it was retouched with a soft hammer. Adapted from Botella *et al.*, (1976) and Jimenez-Arenas *et al.*, (2011).

Juan Manuel Jiménez Arenas*,
Ignacio Martín-Lago*,**

10. Cueva Horá (Darro, Granada)

Horá Cave is 2.5 km from Darro, in the final eastern foothills of Sierra Harana, 1,217 m a.s.l. Discovered by H. Obermaier in 1916, several excavations have been undertaken since the middle of the 20th century under J. Spahni (1956), M. Pellicer (1957) and M. Botella (1977-1985).

The cave is in a limestone block separated from the main range by a major N-NE/S-SE fault. Although this site is called a cave, in fact it is morphologically a shelter with two entrances, one facing SE and the other NW. On the steeply sloping floor there are many limestone blocks which have fallen from the roof and the retreating entrance canopy. Excavations headed by M. Botella at the entrance documented at least 61 levels (I-LXI) in more than 14 m of sedimentary infill, all containing traces of human presence according to the authors.

Only the sequence containing Levels I to XIX, the first three metres of infill, have been published to date. These levels were grouped into six set of strata which showed that the corresponding palaeoclimate occurred between two warm, humid periods. The first three strata were deposited in a cold and somewhat wet context, while the fourth (levels VIII-IX) coincided with the warmest and wettest period. The fifth set (levels X-XII) was the coldest and driest stage, while the sixth (levels XIII-XVII) was similar to the wettest climatic phase. The cave infill has been inserted chronologically in the Würm. However, the stratigraphic sequence poses several problems for its chronostratigraphic analysis. These issues, as well as criticism of the designation of micromammal species, has had played a decisive role in the attribution of this cave to a specific period in the Upper Pleistocene. The faunal list consists of the following taxa: **Rodentia**: *Eliomys quercinus*, *Allocricetus bursae*, *Microtus arvalis agrestis*, *Microtus* cf. *dentatus*, *Microtus (Pitymys) duodecimcostatus*, *Arvicola* sp., *Pliomys lenki*, *Pliomys episcopalis*, *Apodemus sylvaticus*; **Carnivora**: *Lynx pardina*, *Canis lupus*; **Perissodactyla:** *Equus caballus* cf. *germanicus*, *Equus hydruntinus*, *Stephanorhinus hemitoechus*; **Artiodactyla**: *Cervus elaphus*, *Bos* o *Bison* sp., *Capra pyrenaica*. The principal taxon, *Equus*, clearly predominates over the others. The lithic industry has not been fully analysed to date, as only partial studies of some of the archaeological levels have been conducted. Overall, flint is the most commonly used raw material in this industry. The upper levels have been classified techno-typologically as a typical

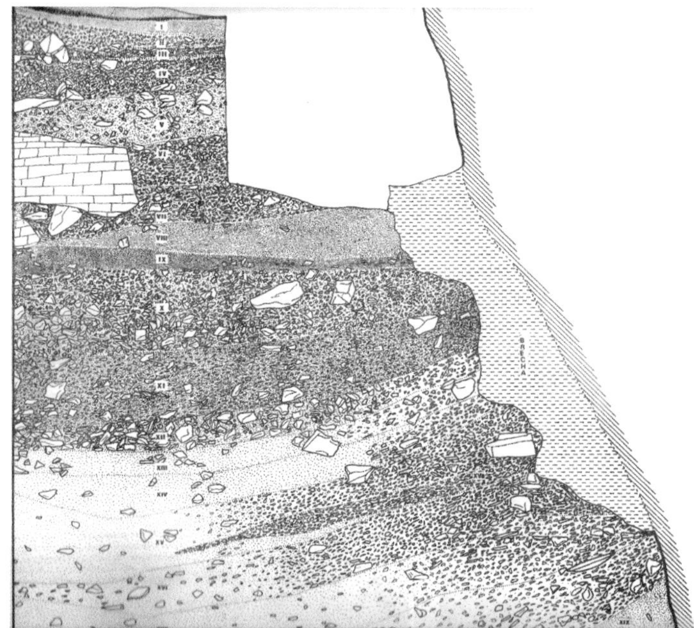

Figure 23. Horá Cave stratigraphy (cut 7). Adapted from Botella and Martínez (1979).

* Dpto. de Prehistoria y Arqueología, Universidad de Granada, Campus de Cartuja s/n (Granada) 18701.
** Delegación Territorial de Educación, Cultura y Deporte en Granada, Paseo de la Bomba, 11 (Granada) 18071

Mousterian with a weak Levallois knapping and non-Levallois facies, rich in sidescrapers (Levels I-XIX, XXII, XXV and XXVI), while the lower levels (XLVIII, IL and L) were previously associated with Southern Late Acheulean (Botella *et al.*, 1984). However, analysis of Levels LV and LVI, the oldest studied to date, has led us to the conclusion that Horá Cave could be associated with non-Levallois Mousterian facies predominated by sidescrapers and denticulates, with few handaxes, an indication of its conservative nature in comparison with previous traditions. This industry is comparable to those found at other sites in southern Iberia such as Levels D and E in Carigüela Cave, and Levels I-XIII in Angel Cave.

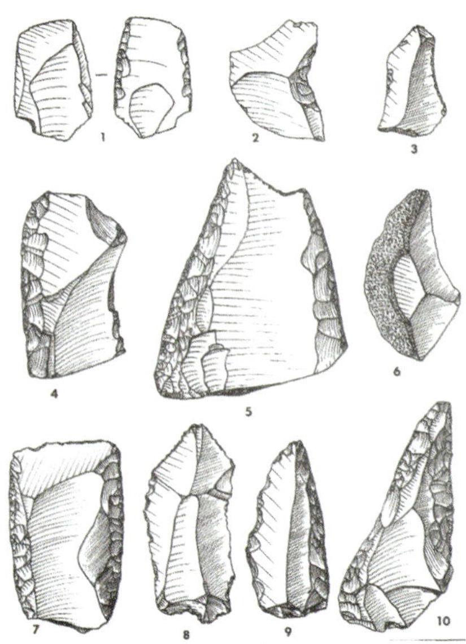

Figure 24. Lithic industry from the base level of Horá Cave. Adapted from Botella and Martínez (1979).

The Las Grajas de Archidona cave (Malaga, Spain)

Isidro Toro Moyano*, Juan Manuel Jiménez Arenas**

1. Introduction

Situated in the south of the Iberian Peninsula right in the geographical centre of Andalusiain the north of the province of Malaga, the cave lies less than one kilometre to the west of the town of Archidona.

An extremely powerful regional landscape feature, this is a huge rock shelter (Fig. 1) located at an altitude of 775 metres above sea level. The mouth of the shelter is 66 metres wide, 40 metres deep and 30 high from canopy to floor, which is uneven, quite steeply sloped and covered with large clasts that have broken away from the canopy. In the central section, which is higher, there is a small cave, and the wall of the shelter features numerous hollows and protuberances.

Figure 1. The Las Grajas de Archidona cave.

The shelter was used in the more recent past as a fold for livestock. Between 1972 and 1976 it was the scene of a series of systematic archaeological digs carried out under the direction of Professor Benito del Rey of the Prehistory Department of Salamanca University (Benito del Rey, 1976).

* Museo Arqueológico de Granada. Carrera del Darro 41-43. 18010 Granada. isidro.toro@juntadeandalucia.es

** Departamento de Prehistoria y Arqueología Universidad de Granada. Campus Cartuja. 18003 Granada. jumajia@ugr.es

The shelter was found to contain diagrammatic cave drawings in and on some of the hollows and protuberances and a necropolis consisting of artificial caves dug out around the threshold of its mouth.

In 2009 the General Directorate of Cultural Heritage of the Regional Government of Andalusia helped to start a programme to study the materials recovered during the aforementioned archaeological digs and to publish the findings. This year has seen a continuation of the programme with the general research project entitled "Las Grajas Archidona. Human Settlements, Cultures, Faunas, Floras, Climates and Landscapes during the Middle and Late Pleistocene Central Andalusia".

2. The Cave. Geological Context.The Archaeological Site

The Archidona Mountains are located in the central-western part of the Béticas Ranges, within the area known as the Mid-Subbética. These mountains form part of the series of early to middle Lias limestones with a dolomite base upon which successive layers of white bioclastic and oolitic limestone have been laid down to reach a thickness of approximately 200 metres.

The Lias limestones display the affect of speleogenesis due to chemical dissolution or atmospheric phenomena that have resulted in the existence of numerous rock shelters, caves, chasms and other types of cavity and of a karst landscape that is partially plugged by detritic and calcitic deposits.

The entire system, shelter, cave, hollows and protuberances forman immense archaeological site that has revealed an extensive record encompassing both ancient and recent prehistory.

The archaeological digs were carried out over sixteen square metres in the eastern area of the shelter next to its wall. This area revealed a stratigraphic column composed of nine levels which, although all of them contained archaeo-paleontological remains, level 6 stands out for its greater wealth of finds (Fig. 2).

3. The Fossil Record

1. The paleontological record

Although it has not been studied in its entirety, partial details have been published showing the presence of five macromammaland many micromammal species, especially Chiroptera, with the remains of Cheloniiand several species of herpetofauna also being found (Tab 1).

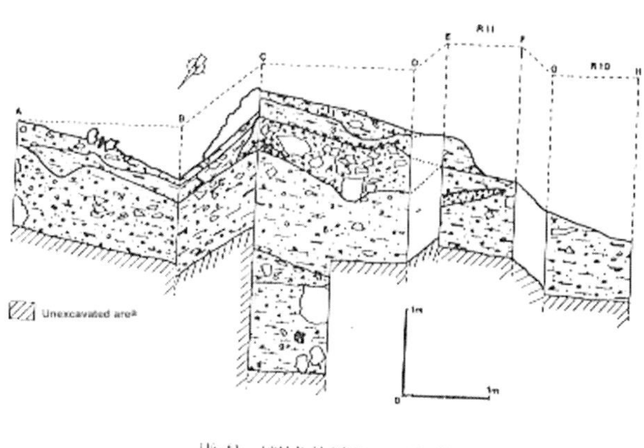

Figure 2. Cross-section (from Sevilla, 1988) showing the stratigraphy.

	Species
Order Carnivora	Carnivora indet.
Order Perissodactyla	*Equus caballus*
Order Artiodactyla	*Bos* sp.
	Capra sp.
	Cervus sp.
Order Lagomorpha	*Oryctolagus* sp.
Order Insectivora	*Erinaceus* sp.
	Talpa sp.
	Sorex sp.
	Crocidura cf. *russula*
Order Rodentia	*Allocricetus bursae*
	Microtus brecciensis
	Apodemus sylvaticus
	Eliomys querquinus
	Arvicola cf. *sapidus*
Order Chiroptera	*Rhinolophus ferrumequinun*
	Rhinolophus euryale
	Myotis myotis
	Myotis emarginatus
	Myotis cf. bechsteini
	Papistrellus papistrellus
	Papistrellus savii
	Papistrellus kuhlii
	Plecotus austriacus
	Eptesicus serotinus
	Miniopterus schreibersi
Order Chelonia	*Emys orbicularis*
	Testudo aff. *hermanni*
Order Anura	*Discoglossus pictus*
	Bufo cf. bufo
	Bufo calamita
	Rana ridibunda
Order Squamata	*Lacerta cf. lepida*
	Lacertidae indet.
	cf. Blanus cinereus
	Coronella sp.
	Cf. Malpolon monspessulanus
	Cluber/Elaphe
	Vipera sp.

Table 1. List of fauna found in the Las Grajas cave (from Espigares and Ros, 2011).

From the taphonomic and archaeo-zoological point of view (Espigares and Ros, 2011), a presence of mostly medium– to small-sized species can be observed. The analyses of the cortical surface have clearly shown the presenceof cut marks related with the processing of the carcasses of the animals for obtaining energy resources. The skeletal elements were found to have been systematically fractured, above all the long bones of the extremities, for the purpose of extracting the bone marrow. Furthermore, the presence of a significant number of elements showing evidence of charring has been documented.

There is a paleoenvironmental and paleoclimaticinterpretation (Sevilla, 1988, Sevilla *et al.*, 2012), that indicates a "dry Iberian" or southern climate, a climate that was slightly cooler and wetter than it is today with less noticeable differences between winter and summer.

The chronology of the record (more specifically that of level 6) is established as being halfway through the Middle Pleistocene during a cold period, with this observation being based on the analysis of the morphology and the size of a series of rodent fossils found at the site. We believe that this cold period could correspond to isotopic stage 8 (between 303,000 and 245,000 years ago).

2. *The Lithic Industry*

The raw materials used to support this industry are of local and semi-local origin, the majority of which consists of flint of variable quality, limestone and quartzite. Both the flint and limestone are mainly used for reduction, with the quartzite being associated with percussion. Outcrops of flint and limestone are found in the Jurassic formations of the Archidona Mountains, whereas the nearest quartzite is found at a distance of approximately 6 kilometres from the shelter.

This is a uniform site from the technical point of view. All the elements of the different phases of the shaping process (hammer stones, cores, flakes and other reduction debris) are present to a greater or lesser extent. This uniformity extends to the effects of the "chaine operatoire" (operational sequence), with all the phases thereof being present. The "chaines operatoires" are intense and, in many cases, result in the total reduction of the core.

Reduction is predominantly carried out using a hard hammerstone, although the use of soft hammerstones is also detected for the manufacture of tools and retouching.

The composition of the site is dominated by the flakes and debris left behind by the reduction and retouching processes.

The condition of the material found is good and features fresh sharp edges, with cases of double patination due to exposure to the air or rolling being practically non-existent.

Large pebbles, nodules and tablets are all used as supports. The cores show signs of recurrent and orthogonal unipolar reduction, with final phases of discoidal reduction (unifacial or bifacial) and some pyramidal cores with centripetal projections.

With respect to the flakes, several categories may be observed: Cortical flakes (Type I), namely flakes whose whole upper face is completely covered with the cortex of the stone (*primary flakes*), extremely cortical flakes (Type II), partially cortical flakes (Type III) and non cortical flakes (Type IV).

Tools make up approximately 10% of the finds. These are, fundamentally, flat scrapers, with smaller quantities of denticulate tools and notches; some scratchers and burins, and a few reverse knives. Another of the objects found at this siteis an excellent hand axe manufactured in good quality flint, the cortex of which has been retained on its base and lower face, and which is finished in an extremely careful mannerusing a soft hammerstone around its entire edge (Benito del Rey, 1982).

Likewise, there are a number of elements that would appear to have been manufactured using pressure reduction with prior heat treatment.

The retouch is semi-abrupt or abrupt, and there are also Quina and semi-Quina type retouches, with there being fewer examples of the flat type. With respect to direction, direct retouch dominates.

4. Conclusion

In conclusion, we feel we can safely say that what we have here is an industry based on flakes of a Mousterian appearance typical of the archaic Middle Palaeolithic. These lithic finds dating from halfway through the Middle Pleistocene are flake-based industries, with a low Levallois index, an abundance of scrapers, the presence of denticulate tools and the absence or presence of hand axes, albeit always in very low amounts, and are well documented in the Iberian Peninsula.

Las Grajas de Archidona presents one of the oldest examples of the human occupation of caves in the south of the Iberian Peninsula, that is, more than 300,000 years ago. Its fossil record, which would cover the whole of the Middle and Late Pleistocene and Holocene periods, provides information of exceptional value for understanding the behaviour of the hunter-gatherer societies that populated Andalusia through out this long period of time, and the way they relate with and use the resources around them.

Miguel Cortés Sánchez*, María Dolores Simón Vallejo**, Francisco José Jiménez Espejo***, José Antonio Riquelme Cantal****

El Pirulejo. A Late Glacial campsite in the Subbetic Sierra (Cordoba, Spain)

Summary. The richness and diversity of the record at the El Pirulejo site makes it one of the most important Late Glacial archaeological sequences in southern Iberia. An interdisciplinary project has contextualized Solutrean and -more particularly- Magdalenian levels on the basis of a technological analysis of the material culture and a study of symbolic expressions as well as economic and environmental aspects.

Keywords. Late Glacial. Solutrean. Magdalenian.

El Pirulejo (Priego, Córdoba) was discovered in 1988 and excavated by M.D. Asquerino in an 8m2 area (fig. 1). After his death, his research team summarized the main discoveries (Asquerino 1991, Cortés *et al.*, 2008.).

Palaeoenvironmental data

El Pirulejo is in the Subbética Range of Cordoba, near the Salado River, a tributary of the Guadalquivir, on an ecotone where several biotopes come into contact (700-1200m asl). The abundant biotic and abiotic resources probably played a role in its choice as an anthropogenic site during the Late Glacial. The site is located in a cave at the foot of a travertine cascade which was filled with sediment during the Late Glacial-Early Holocene. The pollen record depicts a landscape generally dominated by oaks and a remarkable presence of thermophilic taxa, some still persistent (myrtle, wild olive or mastic) and others relict (chestnut and walnut). Herbaceous steppe formations and heathland appeared at the end of the early Bölling/early Dryas, in a relatively dry and somewhat cold climate. Montane pine forests formed at high altitudes on the surrounding mountains (Pandera and Magina) with Lusitanean oak woods in shady areas and moist valleys. During the Bølling-Allerød Late Glacial Interestadial, a significant rise in temperatures and humidity encouraged the growth of riparian forests (alder, birch, willows and elms) and *Quercus* sp. (Holm and Lusitanean oak), especially at the end of the period, accompanied by today's xerothermophyllous maquis. In the early Holocene – around 10ka calBP– there was a significant increase in the cover of Holm and Lusitanean oak woods. Pollen data define a refuge for mesophilic species (chestnut and walnut) during the Late Glacial and a similar type of vegetation -thermophilic faciation of Betic and basophilous Holm oak woods- maintained down to the present day without major changes.

Chronocultural sequence

Indeterminate Upper Palaeolithic, (P/6). Possibly a Solutrean level given its position between level P/5 and the underlying travertine rock, attributed to c. 19 ky BP, although it has scarcely been explored.

Evolved Solutrean s.l., (P/5). Scarcely explored, although it is known to contain highly indicative elements from this period (foliaceous lithic retouched points).

Mediterranean Middle Magdalenian (P/4). Lithic industries defined by high percentages of microflake tools with little diversification and a predominance of inverse retouch, a lack of geometrics, a clear predominance of burins over endscrapers and other groups. The available dating (P/4D, ca. 14.4ka BP) and technical features match the MMM/MSM-A attributes defined by several authors (see Cortés et *al.*, 1998 and references therein) for the Magdalenian sequence

* Departamento de Prehistoria y Arqueología. Facultad de Geografía e Historia, Universidad de Sevilla, c/. María de Padilla s/n. 41004. Sevilla. mcortes@us.es

** Museo Arqueológico de Frigiliana. c/. Cuesta del Apero, 10. 29788-Frigiliana (Málaga). simonmd63@gmail.com

*** Departament of Biogeosciences. Japan Agency for Marine-Earth Science and Technology (JAMSTEC).Natsushimacho, 2-15, 237-0061 – Yokosuka (Japan). fjjspejo@jamstec.go.jp

**** Departamento de Geografía y Ciencias del Territorio. Universidad de Córdoba. Plaza Cardenal Salazar, s/nº. 14071-Córdoba. jriquelme@uco.es

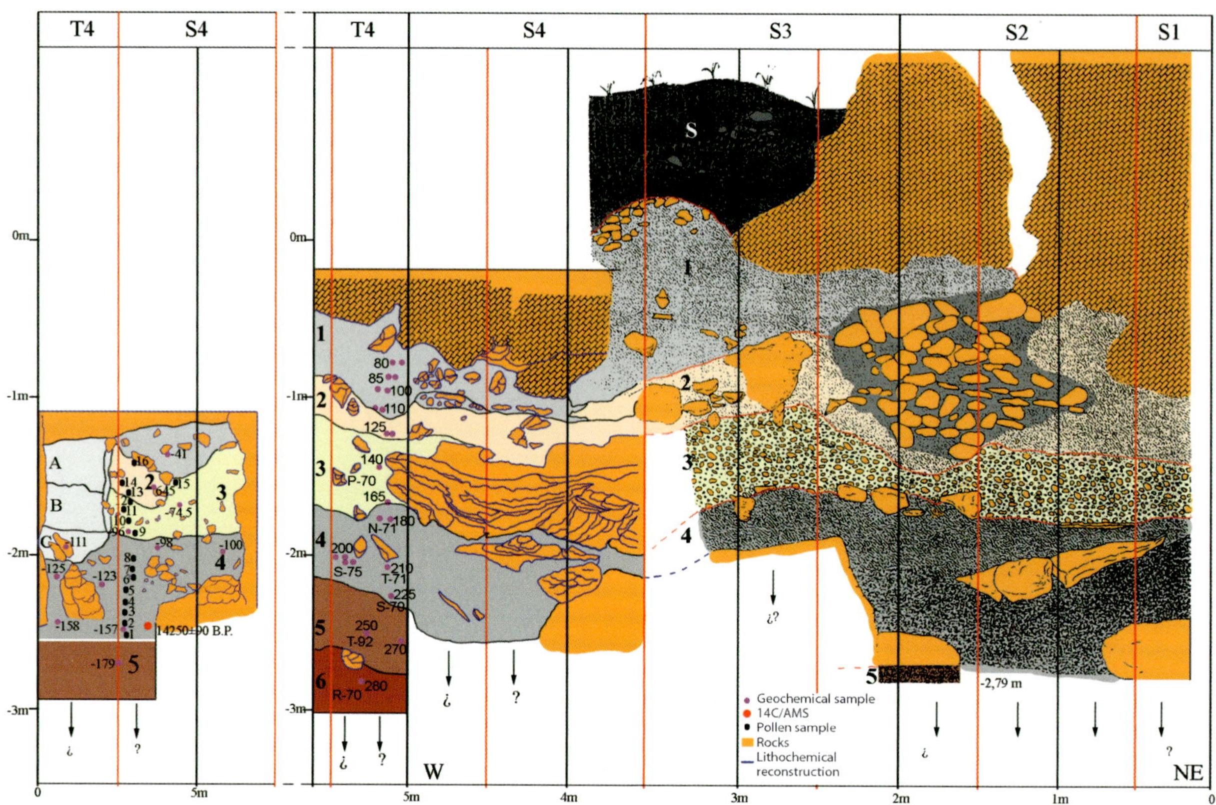

Figure 1. El Pirulejo. Stratigraphy.

in Mediterranean Iberia. The artefacts on organic matter include a semi-cylindrical rod decorated with incised motifs, similar to items found in more northern areas (fig. 2). To date, level P/4 is the only one with a ^{14}C/AMS dating: 14,250 + 90 BP (Poz-21164, charcoal) or 17,458 ± 257 cal BP.

Mediterranean Upper Magdalenian (P/3). Scalene bladelets and a geometric shape (isosceles triangle), a novelty which has also been found in a much smaller assemblage than the one available for P/4. The number of bladelets with inverse retouch is much smaller.

Mediterranean Final Upper Magdalenian (P/2). Sharp decline in archaeological material and disturbance to the site due to post-palaeolithic structures.

Bronze Age. Funerary structures.

Contemporary-Modern Era. Heterogeneous deposits and materials.

There is also an assemblage of highly symbolic objects, ochre, personal ornaments and Palaeolithic mobile art. The latter includes a remarkable series on hard animal matter (P/5-P/3) including an outstanding semi-cylindrical rod (P/4) with an incised motif and clear parallels with Parpalló cave and the Lower-Middle Magdalenian in the Cantabria-Pyrenees area. The other motifs are simpler- individual oblique lines or a cross designed using deep incisions.

The portable art from El Pirulejo includes 20 platelets with ochre, 24 engravings (P/5-P/3), 15 of them in P/4. The iconography includes zoomorphs of a goat (1) deer (2) and indeterminate graphics (7). There are few signs (triangles, cross, zigzag and spindle).

The material used as ornaments includes 2 fluvial and 20 marine molluscs which, given the location of the site (> 80 km from the coast), points to a mobile/exchange network amongst groups in southern Iberia during the Late Glacial.

Economic aspects

The analysed faunal assemblage is predominated by rabbit, followed by ungulates and a few carnivores (table 1).

Figure 2. Worked lithic industry (1-6), platelet with portable art depicting a goat from P/4 (7), decorated semi-cylindrical rod fragment from P/4 (8).

The taphonomic data (alteration by heat, fracturing or marks) point to a basically anthropogenic source of the rabbit remains. Death patterns show that with only one exception, all the deer were adults. However, all age groups of ibex have been found, with a predominance of juveniles-adults, along with infant and juvenile wild boars. No seasonal patterns have been detected in their capture. Many ungulate fragments bear signs of intense thermal alteration and defleshing. Carnivore species, mainly recognizable from jaw and teeth remains, are scarce throughout the sequence. The lynx and bobcat remains are broken and burned, indicating that they were hunted and consumed. The inorganic resources show that El Pirulejo was a strategic residential campsite in the Sub-Betic area. Some of these resources were secondary acquisitions in the local area, including cobbles and platelets washed downstream on the Salado or Ophites River 500m away, for use as hammerstones, anvils, grinders and portable art, while flint had to be obtained from further away. This strategy is evidenced by the near-absence of patina on the material, as the reduction and pre-shaping of the cores was done elsewhere. Other types of rock (galene or rock crystal) and seashells (from > 80km away) also support the idea of socio-economic networks and mobility circuits between the coast and the inland amongst the hunter-gatherers of Andalusia during the Late Glacial-Early Holocene.

Palaeoanthropology

In addition to anthropological remains from the Bronze Age, there is also some material from level P/4 (teeth and skulls). Mitochondrial genetic analysis of two identified individuals has found similar

	P/5		P/4		P/3		P/2	
Taxon	NRD	MNI	NRD	MNI	NRD	MNI	NRD	MNI
Cervus elaphus (deer)	3.11	8.00	0.89	0.94	0.58	1.06	2.91	4.95
Capra pirenaica (ibex)	5.78	12.00	2.80	2.13	2.10	2.85	1.43	2.97
Rupicapra rupicapra (chamois)	-	-	0.05	0.24	-	-	-	-
Sus scrofa (wild boar)	0.44	4.00	0.11	0.47	0.21	1.06	1.49	2.97
Oryctolagus cuniculus (rabbit)	90.67	76.00	96.07	96.26	96.99	93.59	93.79	86.14
Lepus granatensis (hare)	-	-	-	-	0.04	0.36	0.19	1.98
Mustela nivalis (wessel)	-	-	-	-	0.24	0.36	-	-
Lynx pardina (lynx)	-	-	0.01	0.24	024	0.36	0.19	0.99
Felis silvestris (bobcat)	-	-	0.03	0.24	-	-	-	-
Vulpes vulpes (fox)	-	-	0.01	0.24	-	-	-	-
Carnivora sp.	-	-	0.03	0.24	0.02	0.36	-	-

Table 1. Percentage of mammals (%) in each of the defined archaeological levels.

results to other Palaeolithic individuals. Sample 2PI coincides with the consensus sequence, the most common in European populations (20%), while 1PI shows a combination of mutations 16182C-16183C-16189C, only present in one individual from Macedonia. These are the only data currently available for Late Glacial human populations in Andalusia.

Synthesis

El Pirulejo is an exceptional site that contains relevant information about the end of the Palaeolithic in southern Iberia. It is also the oldest Magdalenian record available for this region, and is helping to complete knowledge about the context prior to the widespread use of harpoons. It is also the first site to permit a detailed characterization of the occupation of the interior of this region during the Late Glacial, as to date, the best known sites have been in coastal areas with a heavy economic dependence on marine ecotones (e.g. the Bays of Málaga and Algeciras).

However, El Pirulejo is just one example of a settlement process that must have been much more intense judging by evidence from other less well known sites such as Mármoles, Murciélagos, Nacimiento and El Duende, and parietal art sites in the Malaga hinterland (Ardales and Pileta).

All this information shows that Late Glacial hunter-gatherer populations in southern Iberia were not restricted to coastal areas, evidenced by famous sites such as Nerja, Hoyo de la Mina and Gorham. El Pirulejo and other sites in the Guadalquivir River basin show that southern Iberia's main river system played a key role in these populations' mobility and subsistence in the Betic hinterland. Indeed, there has been a remarkable increase in knowledge about the settlement of inland Iberia during the Late Glacial since research projects began to focus on sites from this era. El Pirulejo definitely shows that Magdalenian technocultural innovations were fully assimilated in inland Andalusia as well, following a similar pattern to other Iberian sites. El Pirulejo is therefore probably an example of the territorial articulation in the Late Glacial linked to the Guadalquivir River system and the exploitation of resources in the Betic area.

7
STRAIT OF GIBRALTAR

Site	Map numbering
Abrigo de Benzú	84
Giraltar: Gorham and Vanguard cave	85

José Ramos*, Darío Bernal*, Eduardo Vijande*, Juan Jesús Cantillo*, Antonio Barrena*, Salvador Domínguez-Bella*, Joaquín Rodríguez Vidal**, Simón Chamorro***, Juan José Durán****, Manuel Abad**; David Calado*****, Blanca Ruiz Zapata******, María José Gil García******, Ignacio Clemente*******, Paloma Uzquiano********, Mila Soriguer*, Antonio Monclova*, Jesús Toledo*, Sergio Almisas*

The Benzu rockshelter (Ceuta). Stratigraphic sequence and record of Hunter Gatherer societies of marine resources with Mode 3 technology in North Africa

Location, stratigraphy, chronologies

The Benzu rockshelter (Ramos *et al.*, 2008; Ramos *et al.*, eds., 2013) is located in the North-African area of the Strait of Gibraltar, Ceuta. It is situated 230 m from the current coastline, 63 m.s.n.m., close to Algarrobo stream and Ballenera Bay.

It is located in Dolomitic marble Alpujarrides of the Triassic Age, with an abrupt typography and almost vertical walls. It has lost a part of its superior cover due to collapsing. Its dimensions are about 15.52 x 6.2 m, with a visor cover. In the southwest end there is a little cave with Neolithic settlements. The archeological deposit has got a surface of about 61.1m2 with a power higher than 5.50 m of cemented carbonates sediment, with calcareous Geological divide and interspersed levels of sediment of calcites. Laterally this thickness reduces up to 1m. Ten strata have been identified, and seven of them have human occupation evidences of the Middle and Upper Pleistocene (Fig. 1).

During the cold stages of the Quaternary, sea-level fell more than 120m, generating a huge platform that is immersed today. The immediate territory of the rockshelter offered the possibility to access large resources: marine, hunting, plants, water sources, lithic.

Several studies about micro morphology and bio-erosive processes in the environment of the Benzu rockshelter show that its erosive process would be previous to human occupation, before e.i.9.

The investigation has been directed by J.Ramos and D.Bernal (University of Cádiz), and researchers belonging to different institutions have participated, also Co-operation agreements between University of Cádiz and the City of Ceuta have been developed. The studies have been done with the authorization of the Ministerio de Cultura.

The results of dates have been: level 7 (Th/U, IGM: ±70 ky), level 5 (OSL, Shfd 020136: 168 ± 11 ky), level 3b (Th/U, IGM: 173 ± 10 ky), and level 2 (OSL, Shfd 020135: 254 ±17 ky). In this way, the sediment and archeological sequence is previous to 70Ka and the register of the first human occupation of the rockshelter is before 250 ky.

Due to the peculiar characteristics of the site, a specific technology has been used; this has

* Universidad de Cádiz, jose.ramos@uca.es, dario.bernal@uca.es, eduardo.vijande@uca.es, jesus.cantillo@uca.es, antonio.barrena@uca.es, salvador.dominguez@uca.es, mila.soriguer@uca.es, anmonc@terra.es, jesustoledo86@gmail.com, seralmcru@alum.us.es
** Universidad de Huelva, jrvidal@uhu.es y Universidad de Atacama, manuel.abad@uda.cl
*** Instituto de Estudios Ceutíes. Ceuta, schamorrom@wanadoo.es
**** Instituto Geológico y Minero de España. Madrid, jj.duran@igme.es
***** Instituto Português do Património Arquitectónico. Faro. Portugal, dcalado@ippar.pt
****** Universidad de Alcalá de Henares, blanca.ruiz@uah.es, mjose.gil@uah.es
******* Institució Milá i Fontanals, CSIC. Barcelona, ignacio@bicat.csic.es
******** Universidad Nacional de Educación a Distancia (UNED), p_uzquiano@hotmail.com

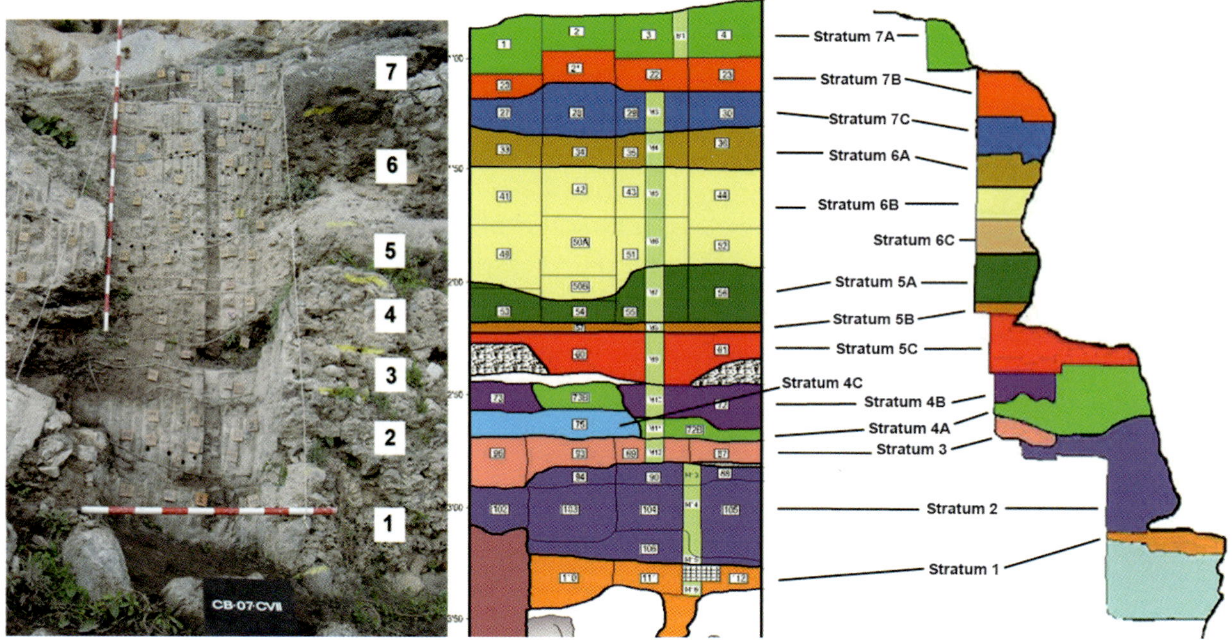

Figure 1. The Benzu rockshelter. Stratigraphic profile.

permitted the removal of blocks that have been finished to dig in laboratory with a micro spatial control of the products (Domínguez-Bella *et al.*, 2012).

Pollen, anthracology, terrestrial and marine fauna

Pollen analysis has shown that the territorial vegetation was mainly constituted by Cedrus and, in a minor extent, by Pinus. *Quercus*-p, *Olea*, *Ceratonia* and waterside elements, such as *Alnus*, *Salix* and *Ulmus*, have been developed. The shrubby herbaceous has mainly been constituted by steppe elements (*Artemisia*, Asteraceae and Chenopodiaceae). The shrub layer, with Ericaceae and *Juniperus*, did not have an important role. This composition shows Mediterranean characters conditions, primarily dry, with pathways of water which are more or less permanent and ponds which favor the development of waterside and aquatic taxa. Throughout the sequence, oscillations and changes in tendency to the decrease of the humidity rate occurred. A cyclicity happened with the installation of a forest including warm and Mediterranean elements together with a varied shrubby herbaceous vegetation and a high representation of waterside taxa and aquatic elements.

The Anthracological data have documented plant taxa: Erica sp., in strata 4, and Fabaceae in strata 2. These two taxa have good flammable properties and could be used as fuels.

The terrestrial fauna consists of 3,362 bony fragments of medium-sized mammals and splinters, as well as pieces of humerus diaphysis of medium-sized ungulates. They were deposited as a consequence of human activity. Several areas of activity and possible consumption places in 4, 5 and 6 strata have been documented. There are lots of bony fragments presenting burned and deliberate fractures. Bovine ungulates and other medium-sized herbivorous predominate.

The marine fauna is documented with 144 fragments, showing an exploitation of coastal resources, underlining the presence of malacofauna –mainly Patélidos molluscs– in all the stratigraphic sequence. There is a clear predominance of the Gastropod Class faced with the Bivalvia, noticing the group of the non-spiraled gastropods and in particular the Patellidae family, followed by *Siphonariidae*, being *Siphonaria pectinata* the greatest exponent. In this way, there are specimens of Patella sp., among others. Referring to bivalves, its representativeness is attested to by the presence of some remains of the species *Tapes decussatus* in level 6, and others belonging to *Glycimeridae* family. Remains of ictiofauna vertebrae in level 5a are registered –possibly from the *Sparidae* family.

Lythic technology

From strata 1 to 7, 36,092 samples have been analised. The raw materials basically come from the immediate environment of the site, underlining the compact sandstones –61.71%–, in the face of the red radiolarites rocks –36.37%–. There are other minority lithologies that would set a certain mobility of the human groups that frequented Benzú.

There is a predominance of rests of carve –35,322 samples– in the face of refinished products –763–. 523BN1G-Cores, 11,648BP-Flakes and 23,151 ORT-Others rests of carve have been documented. There is a remarked presence of levallois technique and Centripetal-Multipolar Core. Among flakes, the internal ones are the most representative, as well as those from the levallois technique. Tipometric Analysis show that flakes –95.76%– dominate over blades –4.24%–, with a significant presence of small-sized types. Among the retouched products-BN2G, scrapers dominate over notches, denticulates and points –Fig.2–. Five Operational Technique Indirect scheme have been documented: 1-Longitudinal, 2-Unipolar, 3-Centripetal, 4-Bipolar, 5-Multipolar, that show the technique process of the lithic production.

The functional study has documented traces of use in almost the 20% of the lithic rests analyzed. The wood working is documented in every archaeological level with more frequency than the activities for meat production and/or leather. However, in level 3 butchering is the most representative activity, and it is the only level where scraping of a hard material from animal origin is documented. There is a significant presence of thermal damage. The use of shrink fitting in an instrument is obvious in level 4.

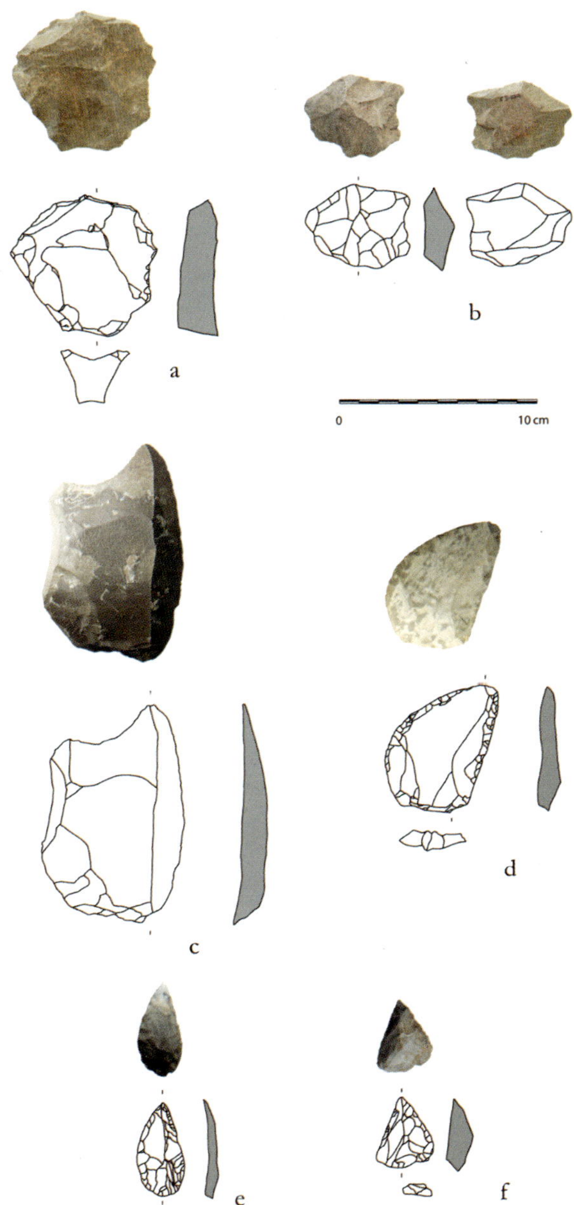

Figure 2. The Benzu rockshelter. Carved lythic products. a-b: Centripetal-multipolar Core; c: BP– Levallois Flake; d: BN2G.Scraper; e-f: BN2G-Points. (a-b: Strata 1, c-d-e-f: Strata 4 a).

Conclusions

The Benzu rockshelter was a place where Hunter gatherer societies of marine resources usually went, doing activities in a seasonal residence with production and consumption processes.

We discuss the register and documentation of leveraging practices of marine resources –fish and mollusks–. Species next to the coast have been collected, being an important resource and one of the most ancient evidences of fishing and shell fishing practices by prehistoric society.

The lithic assemblage is clearly mode 3, therefore Middle Paleolithic.

The use of fire related to processes of prophylaxis and cleaning has been proved.

In conclusion, there are no significant technical differences within the sequence. The technical systems of production and working show different ways of life based on hunting, collecting and exploitation of marine resources.

Clive Finlayson*, Ruth Blasco*, Joaquín Rodríguez-Vidal**, Francisco Giles Pacheco***, Geraldine Finlayson*, José María Gutierrez****, Richard Jennings*****, Darren A. Fa*, Jordi Rosell******,*******, José S. Carrión********, Antonio Sánchez Marco*********, Stewart Finlayson*, Marco A. Bernal*****

Gibraltar excavations with particular reference to Gorham's and Vanguard Caves

Gibraltar (36°07'13"N 5°20'31"W) is located at the southern end of the Iberian Peninsula, at the eastern end of the Bay of Gibraltar. It is a small peninsula being 5.2 km in length, 1.6 km in maximum natural width and about 6 km^2 in total land area. This peninsula forms part of the northern shore of the Strait of Gibraltar, linking the Mediterranean Sea and the Atlantic Ocean (Fig. 1). Currently, the Rock of Gibraltar includes 213 catalogued cavities, at least 26 catalogued as containing archaeological deposits. Among these, Gorham's Cave is perhaps the most referenced in the research and general literature; however, there are other significant Pleistocene archaeological sites, as Vanguard Cave, Devil's Tower Rock Shelter, Forbes' Quarry, Ibex Cave and Beefsteak Cave, among others.

Early developments

The history of cave research in Gibraltar goes back to the 18th Century.The Reverend John White, brother of the famous Gilbert White of Selborne, who was chaplain at Gibraltar during the 1770s, collected many zoological specimens and kept detailed records, corresponding regularly with his brother and other famous zoologists of the day, in particular Thomas Pennant and Daines Barrington. White wrote a *Fauna Calpensis*, the first detailed zoological account of Gibraltar, which was sadly never published, with the manuscript now lost (Mullens, 1913).

Interest in the geology, pre-history and natural history of Gibraltar during the 19th and early 20th centuries

Great interest and excitement about the geology and prehistory of Gibraltar was generated during the 19th Century following the discovery of rich deposits of bone breccia, as well as bones and human artifacts in caves in the limestone of the peninsula. The material recovered was considered to be of such great importance that it attracted the attention of famous names of the day, for example Sir Hugh Falconer and George Busk. As early as 1846 James Smith, who was an officer stationed in the Garrison of Gibraltar and who had become an active member of the Gibraltar Scientific Society, published a paper "*On the Geology of Gibraltar*" in the *Quarterly Journal of the Geological Society of London* (Smith, 1846).

Gibraltar, being a military fortress, acted as a magnet which concentrated individuals who would otherwise not have come to the area. The knowledge accumulated and disseminated by these officers was crucial in highlighting the uniqueness of Gibraltar and the surrounding areas of Spain. Among them, Lieutenant Colonel Willoughby Verner was an intrepid explorer with an insatiable passion for collecting and classifying birds and birds' eggsVerner was also interested in prehistory. In 1911 he had heard of a cave with paintings in the Ronda area in southern Spain and was responsible for making known the exist-

* The Gibraltar Museum, 18-20 Bomb House Lane, PO Box 939, Gibraltar.
** Depto. Geodinámica y Paleontología, Facultad de Ciencias Experimentales, Campus del Carmen, Universidad de Huelva, 21071 Huelva, Spain
*** Gibraltar Caves Project, 18-20 Bomb House Lane, P. O. Box 939, Gibraltar
**** Museo Histórico Municipal de Villamartín. Avda. de la Feria s/n, 11650 Villamartín, Cádiz, Spain
***** Research Laboratory for Archaeology, University of Oxford, New Barnett House, 28 Little Clarendon Street, Oxford OX1 2HU, UK
****** Àrea de Prehistòria, Universitat Rovira i Virgili (URV), Avinguda de Catalunya 35, 43002 Tarragona, Spain.
******* IPHES, Institut Català de Paleoecologia Humana i Evolució Social, C/ Marcel·lí Domingo s/n (Edifici W3), Campus Sescelades, 43007 Tarragona, Spain
******** Department of Plant Biology, University of Murcia, Campus de Espinardo, 30100 Murcia, Spain
********* Area of Neogene and Quaternary Faunas, Institut Català de Paleontologia, Campus de la UAB, Cerdanyola del Vallès, Barcelona, Spain

ence of La Cueva de la Pileta and its Palaeolithic Cave Art. The eminent prehistorians Professor H. Obermaier and L'Abbé Henri Breuil learnt of the existence of the cave and visited it with Verner in 1912. The relationship between Verner and Breuil developed from this contact and is another example of the fortuitous way in which discoveries were often made. Breuil, who was Professor at the Institut de Paléontologie Humaine de Paris, visited Gibraltar in 1914 at Verner's instigation and, while walking along the north-eastern side of the Rock, commented to Verner that the brecciated talus he had observed should prove fruitful in investigating the existence of prehistoric Man at Gibraltar (Verner, 1919).

Breuil returned in 1917 and examined the brecciated talus. At the time he was in the war service of the Naval Bureau and the French Embassy at Madrid and was employed on several occasions as courier between Madrid and Gibraltar (Breuil, 1922). He found animal bones and Mousterian implements but was prevented from exploring further by a military policeman. He returned yet again in 1919, on this occasion with a Governor's permit to excavate. He found conclusive evidence of use of the site by "Palaeolithic Man" (Breuil, 1922). At Breuil's instigation, Miss Dorothy Garrod conducted detailed excavations of the site between November 1925 and January 1927 –her results included the discovery of fragments of the skull of a Neanderthal child. Gibraltar's second Neanderthal had been found, a few hundred metres from the 1848 find in Forbes' Quarry. The discovery is indirectly attributable to Verner– without his initial discovery of La Pileta and contact with Breuil, the latter might never have visited Gibraltar.

Perhaps the individual most responsible for bringing Gibraltar's caves and deposits to the forefront of scientific research was Captain James Brome, Governor of the Military Prison on Windmill Hill, Gibraltar, between April 1863 and December 1868. His investigations were so detailed and thorough that it prompted scientists such as Falconer and Busk to visit Gibraltar and examine the Rock's rich deposits. When Brome arrived in Gibraltar, the scientific community had begun to recognize the importance of Gibraltar's palaeontological deposits, especially the bone breccias. He took up the appointment of Governor of the Military Prison on Windmill Hill, Gibraltar. Windmill Hill is an ancient wave-cut platform at the southern end of the Gibraltar peninsula and it is here that a system of fissure caves (known as

Figure 1. Location of Gibraltar at the southern Iberian Peninsula (top) and the present-day Rock of Gibraltar showing the location of Gorham's (A) and Vanguard Cave (B) on its east face: (A1, A2) Stratigraphic sequence of the outer area of Gorham's Cave; (B1, B2) new excavations at the Upper part of the stratigraphic sequence of Vanguard Cave.

the Genista complex) is to be found. The largest and most important of the system is Genista I which was discovered by Brome. He used convict labour to excavate this deep fissure, which yielded large quantities of bone some of which are thought to be the oldest so far found in Gibraltar. Brome was a thorough researcher and gained the respect of scientists of the day with whom he corresponded and to whom he sent most of what he collected in Gibraltar. The bulk of Busk's paper (Busk, 1868) on the Gibraltar bone finds is a verbatim account of Brome's discoveries.

The Neanderthal finds

The year 1848 saw many momentous events in European politics, but it was also an archaeological watershed. Another momentous event, although unrecognised at the time, was the recognition and curation of a fossilised human cranium found during work at Forbes' Quarry, Gibraltar (Busk, 1865; Broca, 1869; Sollas, 1907). Although, technically speaking, the child's skull from Engis in Belgium was the first known discovery of a Neanderthal fossil, some 18 years earlier, its features were less obviously distinct from those of a modern human, and it was over a hundred years before its importance was recognised. In the case of the Forbes' Quarry discovery, the unusual morphology of the face and vault alone could have been enough to alert an educated observer to its possible significance, but instead fate decreed that today we discuss "Neanderthal Man" (*Homo neanderthalensis*) rather than "Calpican Man" (*"Homo calpicus"*) (King, 1864; Keith, 1911). So it was that on the 3rd of March, 1848, a Captain Edmund Flint, secretary of the Gibraltar Scientific Society (at this time renamed the Gibraltar Museum Society) presented a human skull to this body of essentially military officers. The minutes of the meeting simply read: *"Presented a human skull from Forbes' Quarry, North Front, by the Secretary...".* Flint had been in charge of the society's museum since the 5th June, 1844, and his efforts were recognized in the minutes of 3rd October, 1849.

Nobody took much notice of the skull which was promptly put away in the Society's museum. The skull was in fact that of a Neanderthal but this was not realized until eight years later when another was found in the Neander Valley in Germany. Brome sent the skull to England with his extensive material from the Genista Caves. This material was being examined by Falconer and Busk. In 1864, Busk visited Gibraltar and went to Forbes' Quarry with Lieutenant Alexander Brown. There they found the matrix in which the skull had been embedded. It was then that Busk pronounced the skull: *"to be of a human being of the lowest known organization somewhat analogous to the Neanderthal"* (Busk, 1868), a view supported by Falconer: *"This human skull yielded by the Rock, appears to us to point to a still higher antiquity of man than even those found in the valley of the Vezere in the south of France. In fact, it is the most remarkable and perfect example of the kind now extant"* (Murchison, 1868).

The skull was exhibited at the meeting of the British Association in Bath in 1859. Busk subsequently presented the skull to the Royal College of Surgeons in 1868 – it caused a sensation and became known as the Gibraltar Skull. The skull was examined by Professor Sollas and Dr. Sera of Naples and Professor Keith of the Hunterian Museum and it was stated to be of a woman who may have lived 200,000 years ago (Duckworth, 1911). Recently, as part of his research on George Busk (Gardiner, 1999), Professor Brian Gardiner located a review paper by Cook (1997), which referred to two neglected publications of Busk from 1864. These provide further information on the Forbes' Quarry discovery, and show that Busk was remarkably prescient in identifying some key morphological features of the fossil – in fact he was the first to note the midfacial projection and inflated cheekbones which are now considered one of the most distinctive of Neanderthal characters. As these sources were apparently unknown to Sir Arthur Keith when he described what was known of the early history of the specimen (Keith, 1911), we quote some of the pertinent material from these papers. On the 16th July 1864, Busk wrote a short communication in *The Reader* (Busk, 1864) entitled "Pithecoid Priscan Man from Gibraltar". Near the end he stated of the Forbes' Quarry cranium: *"Its discovery also adds immensely to the scientific value of the Neanderthal specimen, if only as showing that the latter does not represent, as many have hitherto supposed, a mere individual peculiarity, but that it may have been characteristic of a race extending from the Rhine to the Pillars of Hercules: for, whatever may have been the case on the banks of the Dussel, even Professor Mayer [a contemporary sceptic regarding the Neanderthal find] will hardly suppose that a rickety Cossack engaged in the campaign of 1814 had crept into a sealed fissure in the Rock of Gibraltar."*

In the *Bath Chronicle* Busk (1864) described the fossil in more detail, making morphological comparisons with "Negro", Australian and Tasmanian crania. He stated: *"The cranium in question, we understand, was originally deposited in a museum of natural curiosities, which at one time existed at Gibraltar, but which it is to be much regretted has of late years been allowed to fall into a state of confusion and neglect [...] Its extraordinary peculiarities fortunately struck the notice of Dr Hodgkin in a visit paid by that ethnologist to Gibraltar in the course of last year, in company with Sir Moses Montefiore, and it was at his instance that Captain Browne [Brome?], with his eminent zeal in the cause of science, was induced to procure its being forwarded to us for examination and description. [...] it was dug up in the course of some excavations being made in what is termed "Forbes Barrier", which is situated near the entrance into the fortress from the neutral ground or mainland. [...] the Gibraltar skull exhibits not only several of the striking peculiarities of the neanderthal [sic] calvarium but also many others, which from the imperfect condition of that famous specimen, are altogether wanting in it [...] In general outline the Gibraltar cranium viewed in profile, bears a strong resemblance to that from the Neanderthal, except that the sapraorbital [sic] projection is not quite so great. The forehead is equally receding, and the great depression in the hinder part of the cranium is equally remarkable in both [...] One consequence of the great breadth and convexity of the nasal process of the maxillary bone, combined with the increased width of the nasal opening, is, as it were, to throw forward the entire nasal framework, whilst at the same time the canine fossa [...] is entirely filled up, the central portion of the bone rising in a uniform curve on either side, so that the central part of the countenance projects in a very remarkable manner ".*

It was the virtual absence of information on the skull and the circumstances of its discovery that led to Dr. W.L.H. Duckworth's (Cambridge University) visits between 1910 and 1912. His stated objective was: *"to learn from personal observation and inquiry , so much as might be possible about the circumstances of the discovery of the now classical 'Gibraltar Skull' "* (Duckworth, 1911). Duckworth found very little – the site had been extensively quarried and the cave's depth reduced (Duckworth, 1911). To make matters worse, a rock fall during Duckworth's visit sealed off the cave completely.

The skull is today in the Natural History Museum in London, transferred from the Royal College of Surgeons. A cast is exhibited in the Gibraltar Museum. Forbes' Quarry is the subject of a research and conservation project by the Gibraltar Museum. As we have already discussed, a second Neanderthal skull was found much later, in 1926. Dorothy Garrod found the fragmented skull of a child in Devil's Tower Rock Shelter and took it back to England along with all the material collected from this Mousterian Rock Shelter. This skull is also in the Natural History Museum in London.

Today, Forbes' Quarry is nearly stripped of Pleistocene sediments, but there are lingering pockets of a cemented, shelly sand which, to judge from the remaining matrix on the fossil, may relate to the provenance of the cranium. However, it will only be by direct age estimates using techniques such as Electron Spin Resonance on tooth enamel, or Gamma Ray dating on the whole cranium, or OSL on the matrix, that we will eventually determine whether the Forbes' Quarry Neanderthal dates from the earlier or later part of the Late Pleistocene. The neighbouring site of Devil's Tower produced the partial skull of a Neanderthal child in 1926 (Garrod *et al.*, 1928), and has greater potential for further excavation and discoveries. It preserves much more Pleistocene sediment than Forbes' Quarry, and it is possible to relate that sediment to the previous excavations.

Neanderthal archaeological sites

There are several other sites in Gibraltar which preserve evidence of Neanderthal occupation. One, Ibex Cave, lies high up on the eastern face of the Rock, while four others lie to the southeast, close to the sea near "Governor's Beach". The present beach mainly consists of fine limestone blast debris from military tunnelling operations, but there are also cemented remnants of more ancient beaches which presumably accumulated during Oxygen Isotope Stage (OIS) 5. The caves are named (from the south) Bennett's, Gorham's, Vanguard and Boat Hoist. Three of these caves (Ibex, Gorham's and Vanguard) have been excavated since 1994 as part of the Gibraltar Caves Project and the project PalaeoMed.

Gorham's Cave

Gorham's Cave was discovered in 1907 by Captain A. Gorham of the 2nd Battalion Royal Munster Fusiliers, who opened up a fissure at the back of the cavity which bears his name. Subsequently, for convenience, both the cavern and the system of fissures came to be known as Gorham's Cave.

The cave appears to have been forgotten after 1907, although it may have been visited sporadically by military speleologists. However, on 16 March 1945, Lieutenant George Baker Alexander, R.E., a graduate geologist from Cambridge University, arrived in Gibraltar and conducted a thorough geological survey of Gibraltar at this time, concluding with the production of a new geological map of the region (Rose and Rosenbaum, 1990). Alexander became the first person to excavate Gorham's Cave, along with his companion, Lt. Monke. Both set out to excavate the upper layer of the site. Alexander's work, how-

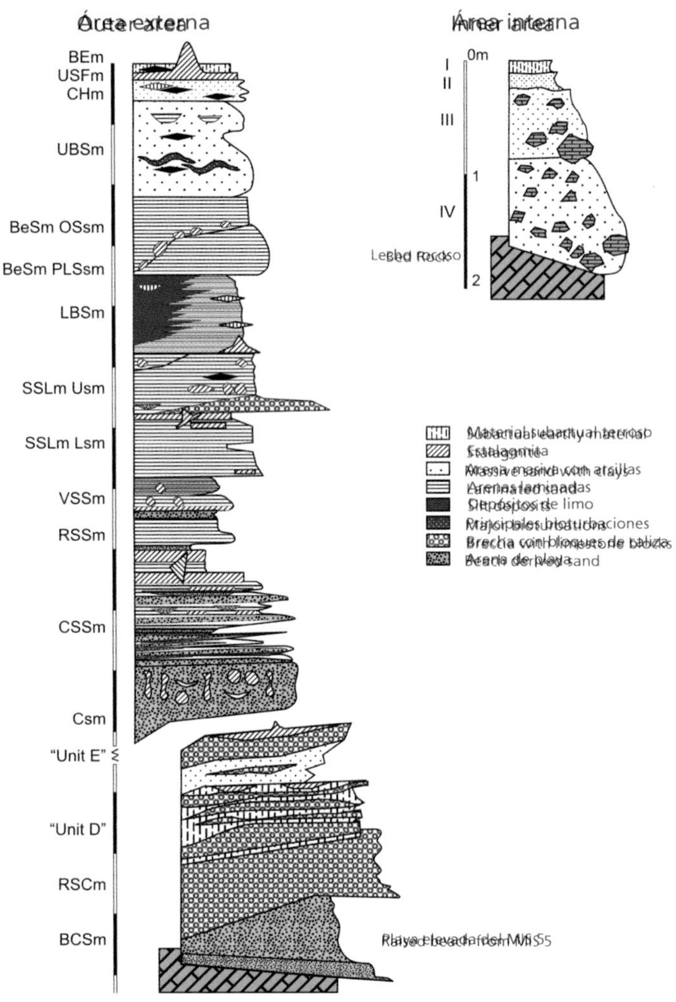

Figure 2. Stratigraphic profile of Gorham's Cave: Schematic profile of the outer sector (middle area of the cave) modified from Collcut (2013) in Barton *et al.*, (2013) (left) and stratigraphic profile of the inner sector (right).

ever, was not viewed well by the Gibraltar Museum Committee of the day. At about the same time (spring of 1948), the then governor, Sir Kenneth Anderson, presumably on the advice of Padre Brown, stopped further digging and wrote to the British Museum asking them to continue any further explorations. However, the British Museum had no staff available and the governor's letter was forwarded to Prof. Dorothy Garrod at Cambridge University, who had excavated Devil's Tower Rock Shelter in 1927–28. She was unable to undertake the work, and asked Dr John D'Arcy Waechter, fellow of the British Institute of Archaeology, Ankara, to fit the work in with his own programme in Turkey.

Waechter's excavations represented the first large-scale excavations in Gorham's Cave and established that it contained a record spanning perhaps 100 kya of Middle Palaeolithic, Upper Palaeolithic and Holocene occupation (Waechter, 1951, 1964). Waechter reported the presence of ancient hearths at various levels in the cave, and of faunal material throughout the sequence, dominated by the remains of ibex, rabbit and many species of bird. Unfortunately, many aspects of Waechter's excavations were never properly recorded or published, and much of the material he recovered has since disappeared. On the other hand, Waechter's stratigraphic sequence of layers running approximately horizontally east-west must have been simplified considerably compared with the complex reality which has since been observed.

The second phase of systematic excavations was carried out by a joint team from the Natural History Museum, London, led by Dr Christopher Stringer, and the British Museum, London, and by Ms Jill Cook, who visited Gibraltar in 1989. After preliminary excavations, the work developed as the 'Gibraltar Caves Project', jointly directed by the Gibraltar Museum and the Natural History Museum, London. Work until 1997 focused on the outer part of the cave, which had previously been excavated by Waechter (1951, 1964). Since 1997, the project direction has expanded to include the Museo de El Puerto Santa María and the University of Huelva. It is at this stage that the excavations in the inner part of Gorham's Cave commenced; their first results were published by Finlayson *et al.*, (2006).

The excavations in the outer area have been recently described by Barton *et al.*, (2013), shedding light on the sedimentary formation of the cave with a stratigraphic sequence of more than 16 m in thickness (Fig. 2). This sequence is composed mainly of earthy materials covering a cemented beach-rock deposit which presumably accumulated during OIS 5. The nature and sedimentary structures of the sediments filling the cave show a massive aeolian accumulation related to transgressive coastal dunes that migrated during OIS 3 highstand substages and/or cold, arid periods (Jiménez-Espejo *et al.*, 2013). The stratigraphic series include dark-brown organic-rich silty clay, grey sand and irregularly bedded yellowish-brown sand, brown-black organic-rich clay with whitish gritty phosphatic lenses and interbedded, massive, homogeneous, coarse brown sand (Collcut, 2013).

Radiocarbon dates of between *ca.* 29 and 51 kyr BP were obtained for UBSm.7 and BeSm.1; nevertheless, the dates from the underlying LBSmff.1–5 (*ca.* 42 and 56 kyr BP) seem to suggest that most charcoal fragments could have been derived from lower down the sequence (Higham *et al.*, 2013). The single-grain (SG) optically stimulated luminescence (OSL) chronology and the Bayesian age model yielded an age of MIS 5 near the base of the stratigraphy (119,300±14,800 kyr for CSm; Rhodes, 2013a).

The excavations in the inner area exposed an area of ≈29 m^2 of bedrock and a stratigraphic sequence formed by four archaeological levels (IV–I from bottom to top; Fig. 2). The stratigraphic composition is different from that of the other sectors, displaying local rock falls, aeolian dust and mainly karstic clay (Finlayson *et al.*, 2006). The sedimentary deposit is thinner (<2 m) than that of the outer area due to the higher position of the cave substrate. Levels I and II correspond to Phoenician and Neolithic horizons, respectively. Level III (mean depth of ≈60 cm) is subdivided into a basal Solutrean (IIIb) and an upper Magdalenian (IIIa) horizon. A distinctive feature of the middle part of this level is the high proportion of fallen fragments of angular limestone and speleothem. Levels III and IV are clearly differentiated by their textural composition, since level III consists of sandy sediment with dark brown clay in a sandy matrix, while level IV is characterised by a beige-coloured pure clay horizon (Finlayson *et al.*, 2006).

Figure 3. Mousterian tools from Level IV of Gorham's Cave.

Regarding lithic assemblages, the outer stratigraphic sequence is consistent with the Middle Palaeolithic techno-complexes in its middle and lower part. The knapping technique mainly follows discoid reduction sequences, although a significant increase in laminar flakes coming from bipolar Levallois cores is observed at SSLm.5–6. The last moments of the Middle Palaeolithic seem to be represented by a Levallois point from UBSm.4, as CHm.5 is the first attributed to the Upper Palaeolithic (Barton and Jennings, 2013). In the inner area, level IV corresponds to a Mousterian techno-complex (Giles Pacheco *et al.*, 2012; Shipton *et al.*, 2013; Fig. 3). All the lithics from this level – in flint, sandstone, limestone and others – are made from autochthonous raw materials from the fossil beach deposits near the caves and from the levels of flint immersed in the Jurassic units of the Rock. The characteristics of the assemblage indicate discoidal and Levallois reduction methods. Some cores show unipolar orthogonal and opposite bipolar reductions. The tools from Level IV show a predominance of sides-crapers and denticulates. Notches and abrupt retouches are also represented. The metrics of the flakes seem to be conditioned by the size of the pebbles, especially in the case of flint, since the nodules in the beach breccias are small. In contrast, the technology from the overlying Level III is characteristic of the Upper Palaeolithic, with diagnostic pieces attributable to the Solutrean and Magdalenian (Giles Pacheco *et al.*, 2012).

Palaeobotanical (charcoal and pollen) samples from Gorham's Cave have revealed a diverse Mediterranean landscape during the Middle and Upper Palaeolitihc, covering the stratigraphic sequence of the cave (Carrión *et al.*, 2008). Inferred vegetation types include oak, pine, juniper and mixed woodlands and savannahs, grasslands with heaths, heliophytic matorrals, phreatophytic formations (such as wetlands and riverine forests) as well as a thermomediterranean coastal scrub. The macro-mammals do not show marked fluctuations through time, as they appear taxonomically constant through the stratigraphy with a predominance of two ungulate species – *Cervus elaphus* and *Capra ibex* (Currant *et al.*, 2013a). Only the presence of grey seal (*Halichoerus grypus*) can be interpreted as punctual evidence of a cold phase in CHm (D unit in Waechter, 1951, 1964). At least 33 taxa of amphibians and reptiles have been recovered, including 24 in the inner area, including newts, toads, frogs, tortoises, turtles, lacertid and scincid lizards, geckos and several snakes (Blain *et al.*, 2013). In the outer area, the largest assemblage comes from LBSmcf.11 and involves 21 species. The most frequent specimen is the western spadefoot toad (*Pelobates cultripes*; Gleed-Owen and Price, 2013a). Regarding small mammals, five species show predominance along the sequence – *Oryctolagus cuniculus*, *Apodemus sylvaticus*, *Eliomys quercinus*, *Microtus brecciencis* and *Terricola* (*Microtus*) *duodecimcostatus* (López-García *et al.*, 2011; Price *et al.*, 2013). The inner chamber also has an important representation of *Myotis myotis* (López-García *et al.*, 2011). The outer area has yielded a significant large assemblage of bird species, with at least 90 species (seabirds, ducks, birds of prey, partridges, waders, pigeons, swifts, crows and small passerines), which were registered by Cooper (2013a). Put together with recent finds in the inner chambers (Sánchez-Márco, in prep.) the total Pleistocene avifaunal list for Gorham's Cave is currently at 142, the highest recorded in any Palaeolithic archaeological site. The fossil birds from Gorham's and Vanguard Caves have been used in the quantification of the habitats outside the cave (Finlayson, 2006) and data from birds, amphibians, reptiles, micro-mammals and intertidal molluscs have been used in climate reconstruction at scales down to seasonal (Finlayson, 2006; Ferguson *et al.*, 2011; López-García *et al.*, 2011; Blain *et al.*, 2013) Finally, Finlayson *et al.*, (2012) showed an association involving the direct intervention of Neanderthals on the wing bones of raptors and corvids, which was interpreted as evidence of extraction of large flight feathers (Fig. 4).

Vanguard Cave

Vanguard Cave, located on the southeast face of the Rock of Gibraltar, is one of four caves which make up the Gorham's Cave complex. Vanguard Cave shows a stratigraphic sequence which is less complex than that of Gorham's Cave (Fig. 1). It contains 17 m of deposits, mainly composed of massive, coarse-to-medium sands intermixed with tabular-to-lenticular units of silts and silty sands (Macphail and Golberg, 2000). Most of the Vanguard sediments are calcareous, with little diagenesis. In the upper area of the cave, the sands are interdigitated with black humic clays, showing evidence of phosphatisation. However, the sediment deposits at Vanguard are generally less phosphatic and organic, and exhibit fewer diagenetic

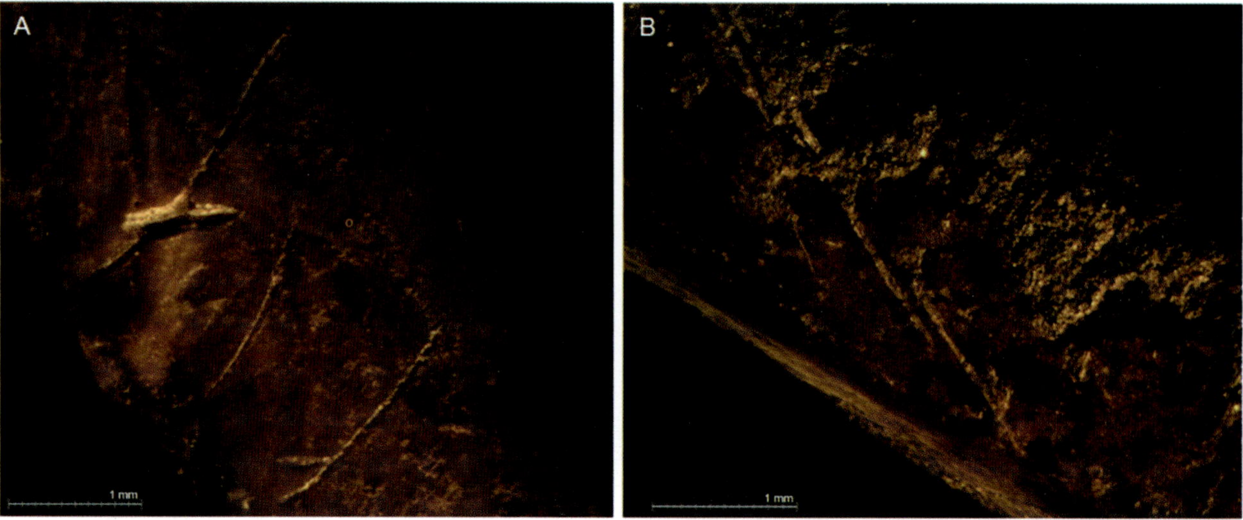

Figure 4. Examples of cut-marks on corvid wing bones from the Middle Palaeolithic levels of Gorham's Cave: (A) Proximal diaphysis of *Pyrrhocorax pyrrhocorax* humerus (GOR'96 NO. 299); (B) proximal diaphysis of *Pyrrhocorax graculus* ulna (GOR'00/B5/NIV/57). Images taken from Finlayson *et al.*, (2012).

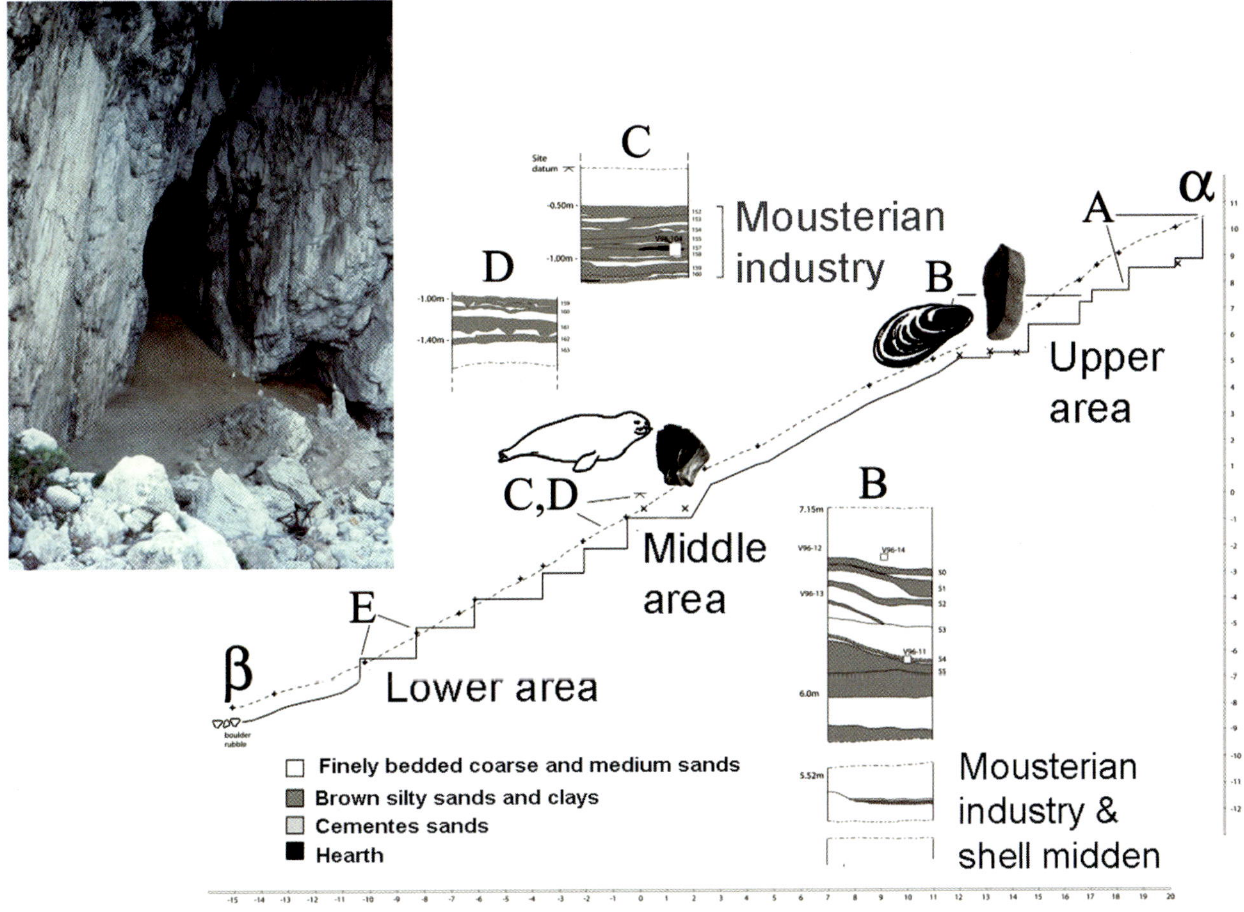

Figure 5. Section of Vanguard Cave showing excavation areas along the dune deposit. Graph taken from Stringer *et al.*, (2008).

changes compared to Gorham's Cave (Macphail *et al.*, 2013).

Five main excavation areas (A–E) were established at different heights of the dune, with A being the highest area and E the lowest one (Fig. 5; see Stringer *et al.*, 2008 and Macphail *et al.*, 2013 for more details). Sectors A and B are described as Upper area, C and D as Middle area and E as Lower area. From these areas, sediment samples were collected for optically stimulated luminescence (OSL). Quartz OSL data, including single-grain (SG) measurements, indicate that much of Vanguard Cave was filled around the time of OIS 5 (Rhodes, 2013b). This age estimation is older than the OSL chronology reported by Pettit and Bailey (2000), but for Rhodes (2013b), this is primarily due to a difference in dose rate estimation. The OSL date from the uppermost part of the sequence yielded an age of 75 kyr (when the cave was practically silted). This age was obtained from breccia fixed in the wall of the cave; however, erosion phenomena could have altered some superficial sand layers, generating new earlier deposits.

Macroscopic analyses of charcoals indicate very little evidence of taxonomical change, with an arboreal landscape apparently dominated by warm-climate vegetation. *Pistacea* sp. and *Olea* sp. are registered as thermophilous indicators along the sequence, since both species are located within thermo-Mediterranean bioclimates (<600 m.a.s.l.; Ward *et al.*, 2013). The examination of the reptile and amphibian assemblages carried out by Gleed-Owen and Price (2013b) yielded a minimum of 17 species in the middle excavation area. A core of four species, including western spadefoot toad (*Pelobates cultripes*), stripeless tree frog (*Hyla meridionalis*), Moorish gecko (*Tarentola mauritanica*) and worm lizard (*Blanus cinereus*), was detected at Vanguard Cave. Of these, *B. cinereus* is obligate thermophile, *T. mauritanica* does not tolerate extreme cool environments and *H. meridionalis* is restricted to meso-Mediterranean biomes with an overall dry climate. On this basis, the herpetofaunal remains suggest a remarkable environmental stability, with thermophilous species that are currently restricted to southern Europe (Gleed-Owen and Price, 2013b). A total of 73 bird species have currently been identified from Vanguard Cave (Cooper, 2013b; Sánchez-Marco in prep.) and are the subject of ongoing ecological and biogeographical analysis.

Macro-mammals show little variation, indicating environmental stability during the deposition period. The Middle area is characterised by the presence of ibex (*Capra ibex*), red deer (*Cervus elaphus*), wild boar (*Sus scrofa*) and bear (*Ursus arctos*), as well as evidence of marine mammals (seals and dolphins). Almost 50% of bones show human-induced damage (e.g. cut-marks, percussion marks) affecting ibex, red deer, wild boar and seal, and only 3% bear carnivore tooth-marks (Currant *et al.*, 2013b). In addition to the terrestrial fauna, two monk seal fossils (*Monachus monachus*) show human alterations on a proximal phalanx and a scapula (Stringer *et al.*, 2008). In association to terrestrial and marine mammals, molluscan shells such as *Mytilus galloprovincialis, Callista chione, Acanthocardia tuberculata, Patella vulgate, P. caerulea* and a few barnacles (*Balanus* sp.) are widely documented.

The study of the lithic artefacts reported by Barton (2013) comes from the Upper and Middle areas of the cave and shows clear assignation to the Middle Palaeolithic techno-complex. Lithic industry suggests little variation through the sequence, with little change in the dominance of quartzite over finer-grained cherts. This reflects the more common availability of this material in comparison to other raw materials. Limestone from the cave bedrock was often used to make artefacts, representing a significant expedient behaviour. For Barton (2013), the low diversity of raw material and the limited range of tools in the assemblages are concordant with a succession of short-term human occupations at the cave.

Currently, new fieldwork is being carried out at the Upper part of the sequence. Our aim is to determine the complete stratigraphic sequence of the cave, developing a new programme of dates, and to deepen our understanding of Vanguard Cave during the Neanderthal occupation phases (see Fig. 1-B1, B2 for the new excavation).

8
CENTRAL PLATEAU

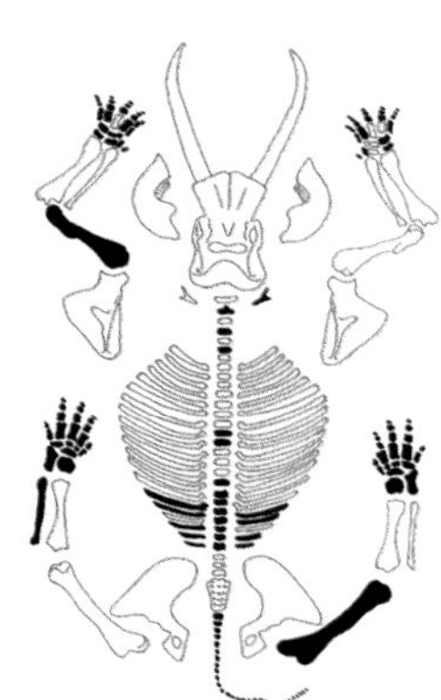

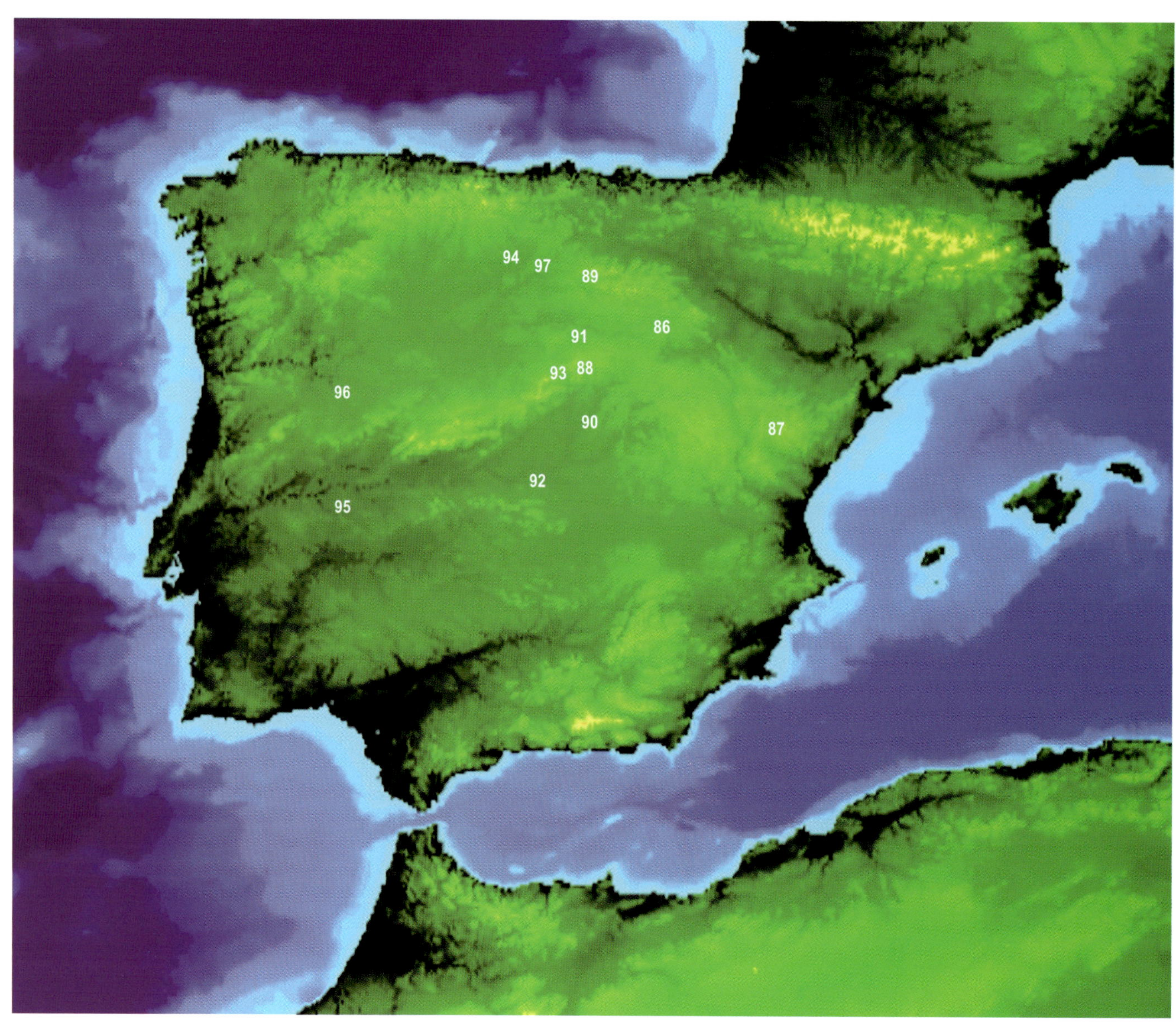

Site	Map numbering
Ambrona and Torralba	86
Cuesta de la Bajada	87
Jarama VI	88
Conjunto de Atapuerca	89
Manzanares and Jarama	90
La Peña de Estebanvela	91
Pinedo	92
Pinilla	93
San Quirce	94
Cueva de Maltravieso, Cueva de Santa Ana, Cueva de el Conejar, Vendimia and El Millar	95
Siega Verde	96
Valdegoba	97

Manuel Santonja*, Alfredo Pérez-González*, Joaquín Panera**, Susana Rubio-Jara**, Carmen Sesé***, Enrique Soto***, Laura Sánchez-Romero*, ****

Ambrona and Torralba archaeological and palaeontological sites, Soria Province

1. Discovery and early research

The Torralba and Ambrona sites (Santonja *et al.*, in: Santonja and Pérez-González, 2005 (eds.): 18-39) are 150 kilometres north east of Madrid on the watershed between the Ebro, Duero and Tagus Rivers, in the southern part of Soria Province. This is a strategic transit zone between the highlands of the Iberian *Meseta* (plateau) and the Jalón River Valley. An oblique perspective generated by a digital terrain model shows the two sites between reliefs drained by tributaries of the Atlantic slope Duero and Tajo Rivers. To the east, the clear outline of the Jalón River canyon, which flows into the Ebro and eventually into the Mediterranean (Fig. 1).

1.1. *First work by Marquis of Cerralbo (1909-1916)*

The discovery of both sites began with the detection of large elephant bones in 1888 at the Torralba railway station. Between 1909 and 1913, Enrique de Aguilera y Gamboa (1845-1922), the 17th Marquis of Cerralbo, excavated over 2000 m^2 in Torralba. From 1914 to 1916, he continued his work at the Loma de los Huesos in Ambrona site, 2.5 km to the north. His results had a great impact at the time and drew visits by leading researchers. Cerralbo's conclusions, paradoxically from a creationist's ideological perspective (Santonja and Vega, 2002), conjugated the key aspects around which the site was later interpreted –organised hunting of elephant herds by a group of human settlers on the banks of a lake– and provided a glimpse of the potential importance of these sites for the study of human behaviour (Isaac, 1977: 3-4).

1.2. *Research resumed by F.C. Howell (1960-1963)*

In Spain after the Civil War, in 1936, Lower Palaeolithic research was abandoned almost entirely. Only occasional visits to international congresses awakened memories of Torralba and Ambrona and spurred individual initiatives such as the palynological studies by J. Menéndez Amor and F. Florschütz in 1959 and 1963, which focused on the Middle Pleistocene chronology of the sites (Santonja and Vega, 2002).

Contacts between Luis Pericot and Clark Howell at the Panafrican Prehistory Congresses led to the recommencement of the research work, nearly 50 years later of the Cerralbo's work. Howell proposed systematic full-cover, multidisciplinary excavations for Torralba and Ambrona. By the end of the decade, research into the African Pleistocene had implanted this model, but in 1960 it was a novelty in Europe.

When this work began, the Torralba site was estimated to cover approximately 3800 m^2 (Howell *et al.*, 1962), of which over 2000 m^2 were to be preserved, of which 1026 m^2 dug between 1961 and 1963 (González Echegaray and Freeman, 1998). Loma de los Huesos in Ambrona was estimated to cover roughly 6000 m^2, of which 1243 m^2 were excavated in 28 weeks during the 1962 and 1963 digs (Howell, 1965). Both sites were studied by the same team –K.W. Butzer, E. Aguirre, P. Biberson and L.G. Freeman– who used a similar methodology and reached common conclusions. Butzer's geological survey attributed an identical age and formation processes to both sites and defined a morphosedimentary unity, the "Torralba Formation", which integrated the strati-

* Centro Nacional de Investigación sobre la Evolución Humana. (CENIEH); 09002 Burgos manuel.santonja@cenieh.es
** IDEA (Instituto de Evolución en África), Museo de los Orígenes, Plaza de San Andrés 2, 28005 Madrid.
*** Departamento de Paleobiología. Museo Nacional de Ciencias Naturales. Madrid.
**** Escuela Interuniversitaria de Posgrado en Evolución Humana, Universidad de Burgos. C/ Juan de Austria 1, 09001 Burgos.

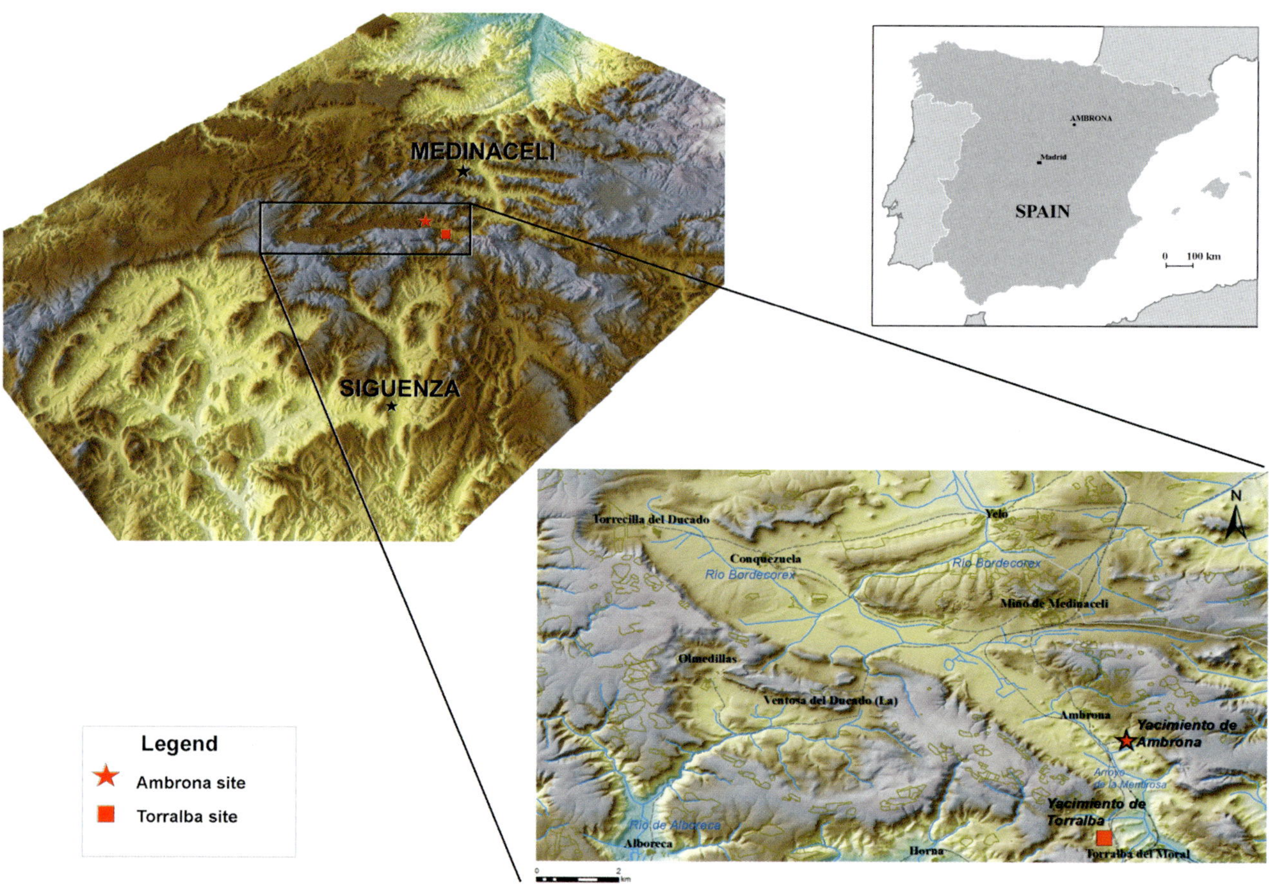

Figure 1. Geographic location of the Torralba and Ambrona sites in the south of Soria province, 150 km NE of Madrid (Spain). Both sites are in the valley of La Mentirosa arroyo Rivulet, also known as Mansegal, a tributary of the Jalón River which flows into the Ebro. The Bordecorex stream flows into the Duero River, while south of Olmedillas and Ventosa del Ducado, the river network flows into the Henares River (Tagus basin).

graphic sequences of the two sites, described at the time as twin (Butzer, 1965).

The published studies of the lithic tools, all preliminary, interpreted the industry at either sites as early (Freeman, 1975) or middle (Biberson, 1964) Acheulean. Biberson and Aguirre also noted the existence of worked bone, an issue debated subsequently and pending a systematic review (Domínguez-Rodrigo, in Santonja and Pérez-González (eds.), 2005: 282-287).

This first research stage led to an interpretation of the sites which in some general aspects matched Cerralbo's imaginative foresight. The Mansegal or La Mentirosa stream valley connected the highlands plateau of the North with the Ebro Basin, and was probably a corridor frequented by herbivores during their seasonal migration (Butzer, 1971). The presence of these herds led groups of hominins –in a display of premonitory behaviour– to burn the vegetation in order to drive them into swampy zones where weeds and mud hampered the animals' movement. In these conditions would have been easy to kill them, dismembered in nearby spaces and prepared for consumption (Howell, 1966).

1.3. The Howell-Freeman period (1980-1983)

The complete aperture of East Africa to Pleistocene research led Howell to interrupt his Spanish work in 1963. The large interdisciplinary teams which started to work at African sites proved decisive and triggered profound changes to the methods used in Palaeolithic archaeology from the 1970's onwards. In this context, the interpretations of Torralba and Ambrona were reviewed by Binford, who found no arguments in support of organized hunting, expressed doubts about the presence of fireplaces and questioned whether the areas containing bones had remained in a primary position. Even in the absence of different data from those published by Howell and his team, Binford suggested that natural agents and trampling by elephants had caused intense modifications (Binford, 1987).

The debate was in full swing when a new phase of research at Ambrona began in 1980. With the addition of 207 m^2 dug by E. Aguirre in 1973, by the start of the 1980 season, almost 1450 m^2 had been excavated at Ambrona. During this stage, under the joint leadership of Howell and Freeman and the management of M. Almagro –responsible for channelling relations with the Spanish government and facilitating funding for the project under the Spain-US Cultural Cooperation Programme–, an additional 1267 m^2 were dug in 203 days. By 1983, 2717 m^2 of the estimated 6000 m^2 of the Ambrona site had been excavated. In addition, work continued on the hillside opposite Loma de los Huesos (Camp North). Here, although published references are quite vague (Howell and Freeman, 1982), we know that a little over 200 m^2 were dug, 55m^2 in 1963 and 162 m^2 in 1981 and 1983, according to unpublished documents held at the Numantine Museum in Soria.

The Ambrona assemblage remained attributed to Butzer's "Torralba Formation", with new aspects in the stratigraphic interpretation (Howell *et al.*, 1995), primarily the differentiation of two members, the "Lower complex" and the "Upper complex". The former included the characteristic concentrations of megafauna –particularly elephant– and Acheulean industry. An intermediate occupation was defined in the central part of the site, with fauna and sporadic industry considered close or equivalent to Camp North, where deer, aurochs and elephant were recorded along with some Acheulean handaxes. At the "Upper Complex", on the levels of alluvial and colluvial origin, a more frequent and more evolved lithic industry than the Lower complex was detected, also identified as Acheulean. Scarcely any elephant remains were detected, replaced in importance by *Equus* (Howell *et al.*, 1995).

At the end of this stage, the older interpretations of Ambrona's Lower complex were accepted with certain nuances. The faunal remains were basically regarded as residue from deliberate hunting activity and the processing and consumption of the food. The hominins had also shifted substantial portions of this prey to their base camps, whose location was imagined –in the absence of evidence– to be on high ground overlooking the area, "overlooking the valley" (Freeman, 1994).

2. Current state of research at Torralba and Ambrona

2.1. *Digs from 1990 to 2000 and subsequent work*

The controversy over the nature of these sites continued into the late 1980's, and the published information was still insufficient to be able to test the hypotheses proposed in the light of the previous excavations. Substantial unknowns still remained about the general sedimentary processes and also the microstratigraphy and the spatial distribution of the remains.

It was known for certain that there were still large unexcavated areas in Ambrona and probably in Torralba as well. Consequently, in 1990 –following an excavation permit granted to E. Carbonell in 1988 which was not continued and there are no known results– another project headed by M. Santonja and A. Pérez-González was begun using geoarchaeological, taphonomic, and techno-economic methods. In summary, its aims were to understand the morphodynamic and sedimentary processes in order to contextualize the megafauna assemblages and interpret the human activity in this area (Santonja, 1989).

An initial stage between 1990 and 1991 ascertained the basic features of the local geomorphological evolution and situated the sites in a geological framework at the local and regional scale (Pérez-González *et al.*, 1991).

Annual digs were conducted at Ambrona from 1993 to 2000, focused on the "Lower complex", with 688 m^2 excavated. In Torralba, work was hampered by the large volume of waste material from previous excavations dumped on the site itself, and thus only limited test pits were dug (Santonja *et al.*, in Santonja and Pérez-González (eds.), 2005: 104-123).

In 2001, a vertical electrical sondage was lowered into a sinkhole in Jurassic dolomites 200 m NE of Ambrona, where Pleistocene fauna was recorded. In 2001 and 2002, samples were removed for magnetostratigraphy as well as dating by luminescence and aminoacid racemisation (Parés *et al.*, in Santonja and Pérez-González (eds.), 2005: 190-199; Falguères *et al.*, 2006).

Finally, in 2013 the National Human Evolution Research Centre (CENIEH) began fresh digs focused initially on the middle stratigraphic member –partly equivalent to the Upper Complex of Howell (Pérez-González *et al.*, in: Santonja and Pérez-González, 2005 (eds.): 176-199)–, in Ambrona and Torralba.

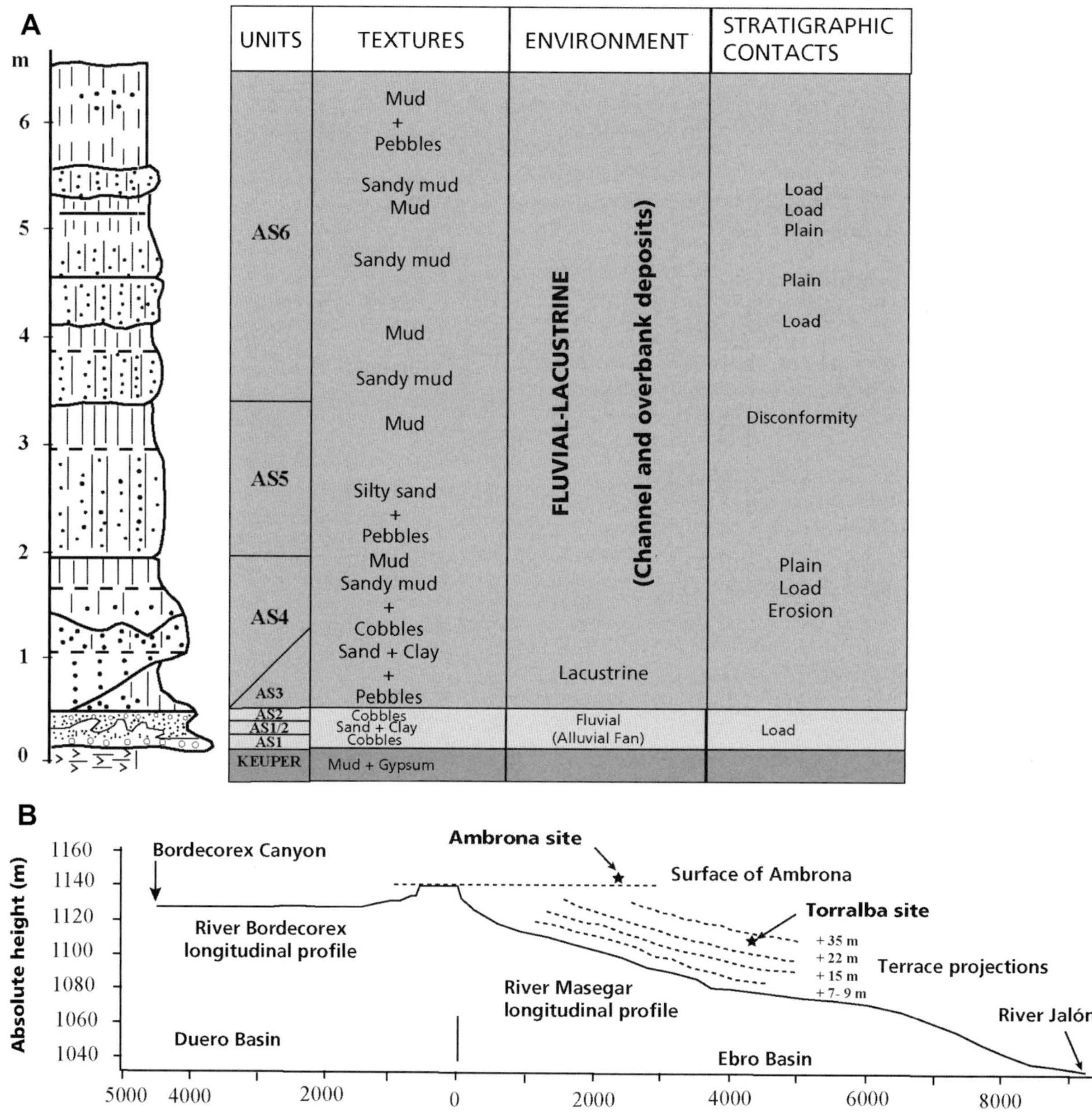

Figure 2. A: Stratigraphy of Ambrona, lower and middle members, in the central sector of Loma de los Huesos. B: Relative geomorphological position of the Torralba and Ambrona archaeological sites.

2.2. *Results from Ambrona and Torralba sites between 1990 and 2000*

2.2.1. Geomorphology and chronology of the sites

Ambrona is at the bottom of the karst valley or polje between Torralba, Ambrona and Conquezuela, while Torralba is in the valley of the Mansegal, built up from the bottom of the polje and set on the + 35 m terrace of the current valley (Pérez-González *et al.*, in Santonja and Pérez-González (eds.), 2005: 176-199). A cut and fill phase of the Mansegal stream, and another of the +35 m terrace development and subsequent incision on this terrace separate the two sites (Fig. 2b), categorically invalidating hypotheses which merged their stratigraphies in a single unified sequence (Butzer, 1965).

The chronological distance between Ambrona and Torralba has also been checked by numerical dating. The middle stratigraphic unit of Ambrona has been dated at c. 350 ky by ESR/U series (Falguères *et al.*, 2006), suggesting an age of around 400 ky for the lower unit of this site. In the case of Torralba, OSL datings currently in press (N. Mercier) indicate around 200 ky, similar to the 220 ky and 240 for U series (Howell *et al.*, 1995), obtained on a +20-25 m terrace (comparable to Torralba) in the nearby Alto Henares area. This reinforces the geomorphological interpretation which refutes the contemporaneity of the sites and instead suggests a sequence of occupations in the area. The Torralba site at the bottom of the Mansegal River valley is close to MIS 7 (243-192 ky), while the lower and middle stratigraphic units of Ambrona correspond to MIS 11 (424-375 ky) and MIS 10 (374-338 ky) or 9 (337-301 ky) respectively, in positions related to the small ponds and the drainage network which developed at the bottom of the Conquezuela polje.

2.2.2. Ambrona stratigraphy

The stratigraphic units defined in Ambrona correspond to fluvial and fluvio-lacustrine environments (Pérez-González *et al.*, in: Santonja and Pérez-González, 2005 (eds.): 176-199), each one with a different preservation potential for remains. A systematic, integrated stratigraphic interpretation has been proposed for the site, which we have called "Ambrona formation", consists of the lower, middle and upper members. Excavation campaigns from 1993 to 2000 were carried out in the lower member, that includes the following levels (Fig. 2a):

- A fluvial (AS1) and another fluvio-lacustrine level (AS4) which contains the highest density of lithic and faunal remains, albeit in a derivative position, partly brought from outside the preserved site.
- Level AS3, composed of mud built up at the bottom of a shallow pond with occasionally input via small channels. This level has the best conservation conditions for industry and fauna remains, mainly found in a primary position.
- Other minor levels in the lower stratigraphic unit are of a fluvial nature (AS1/2 and AS2). At the top of this unit is the fluvio-lacustrine level AS5. The presence of archaeo-palaeontological remains is sporadic in all these cases.

All these levels were mapped, defining the vertical and horizontal relationships of the stratigraphy across more than 400 linear metres. While AS1, AS5 and AS6 are spread across almost the entire site, other levels cover smaller areas, resulting in different stratigraphic sequences in each zone. Thus, in the Central and Western sectors there are several areas where AS1/2, AS2 and AS3 are absent and the AS4 level lies directly in contact with AS1.

The middle member of the Ambrona formation (AS6) includes fluvio-lacustrine deposits in the Central and Western Sectors and fluvial deposits in the Eastern Sector. The latter are rich in lithic industry and they also contain fauna. In some cases they occur in overbank facies, accumulated in low energy conditions which enabled the remains be found in an almost primary position. The Ambrona formation is completed by the upper member (AS7), composed of channelled and edaphized facies. It is archeologically and palaeontologically sterile.

2.2.3. Ambrona palaeontology

The results from the 1990-2000 stage almost coincide with those obtained previously, with some further details, particularly about birds and small vertebrates. The mammal association identified between 1993 and 2000 (Sesé and Soto, in: Santonja and Pérez-González 2005 (eds.): 258-281) is the following: *Crocidura* sp.; *Microtus* (Iberomys) *brecciensis*; *Arvicola* aff. *sapidus*; *Apodemus* aff. *sylvaticus*; *Oryctolagus* sp.; *Canis lupus* cf. *mosbachensis*; *Panthera* (*Leo*) cf. *fossilis*; *Palaeoloxodon antiquus*; *Stephanorhinus hemitoechus*; *Equus caballus torralbae*; *Cervus elaphus*; *Dama* cf. *dama*; *Capreolus* sp. and *Bos primigenius*. Other taxa identified previously in the lower Ambrona member must be added to this list (Howell *et al.*, 1995): *Vulpes* sp., *Crocuta crocuta* aff. *praespelaea and Megaloceros* aff. *savini*.

In the middle member, almost the only species recorded to date from the 1993-2000 excavations is *Equus caballus* and very occasional remains of *Palaeoloxodon antiquus*.

The presence of avian fauna is recorded (Sánchez Marco, in: Santonja and Pérez-González 2005 (eds.): 248-257): *Anser anser*; *Tadorna ferruginea*; *Tadorna* sp.; *Anas acuta*; *Anas strepera*; *Anas* sp.; *Mergus merganser*; Anseriformes indet.; *Fulica* cf. *atra*; *Otis tarda* and *Vanellus vanellus*; A herpetological sample (Martínez-Solano and Sanchiz, in: Santonja and Pérez-González 2005 (eds.) : 232-239) includes: *Bufo bufo*; *Bufo calamita*; *Discoglossus* cf. *jeanneae*; *Hyla arborea*; *Pelobates cultripes*; *Pelodytes punctatus*; *Rana perezi*; *Rinechis scalaris*; *Natrix* sp.; Lacertidae and Colubridae indet. There was also some ichthyologic remains (Perea and Doadrio, in: Santonja and Pérez-González 2005 (eds.): 240-247) of *Chondrostoma arcasii*.

The macromammal series is considered characteristic of the advanced but not final Middle Pleistocene, with more modern elements than the peninsular faunas from early Middle Pleistocene sites such as Cúllar de Baza I (Granada) or Buenavista, Campo de Tiro and Polígono Industrial (Toledo), characterized by *Mammuthus trogontherii*. The micromammals show a similar chronology. The morphology and size of *Microtus* (I.) *brecciensis* teeth imply a previous age to those found in late Middle Pleistocene populations of the same species. The presence of a relatively large form of the *Arvicola* aff. *sapidus* species indicates a more modern phase than the fauna from Cúllar de Baza I, with *Arvicola mosbachensis*. The evolutionary stage of the Ambrona microfauna corresponds to the third ensemble of Middle Pleistocene associations defined by Sesé and Sevilla (1996), which include fauna such as that found in Áridos.

2.2.4. Palaeoenvironments

In addition to the study of the fauna and nanofauna –ostracods–, palynology and biomineralizations –phytoliths– have provided information about the environmental conditions when the deposits of Ambrona formation were accumulated (Baltanás *et al.*, 2005; Ruiz Zapata *et al.*, 2005; Pinilla *et al.*, 2005, in Santonja and Pérez-González (eds.), 2005: 200-231). All the conclusions indicate the existence of climatic constants which were comparable to the current conditions, albeit with certain nuances.

The macromammals from the lower member of Ambrona indicate a good representation of forest environments and open lands, with meadows and areas with abundant water in relatively warm and moist climatic conditions. Birds confirm the proximity of wetlands, flooded zones and shallow water bodies. Some species like the common goose and lapwing denote flat or gently undulating grassland. Taxa such as swamphen, coot and northern pintail require thick patches of vegetation around water bodies. The swamphen, a sedentary animal, is incompatible with very low temperatures. The herpetofauna corroborates these interpretations and indicates that the conditions were similar to today, with a more or less contrasted seasonality, less dry summers and less wet springs and winters, with slightly higher winter temperatures.

Locally, the presence of ostracods as *Leucocythere* cf. *mirabilis* in several levels indicates a lake system in oligotrophic conditions. The taphocenosis found in the ostracods is similar to current conditions in shallow ponds and lakes in southern Europe. Sometimes, *Heterocypris salina* became predominant at Level AS6 (middle member), suggesting a drier and colder period, a trend also suggested by the dominion of *Equus caballus* in replacement of *Palaeoloxodon antiquus*.

The silicophytoliths in the lower member suggest a temperate climate. The diatoms are often epiphytes, indicating a frequency of aquatic plants. Biominerals are less abundant at the top of the lower member due to the changed environmental conditions. Silicophytoliths are more abundant, but with many spicules and diatoms reduced to the *Amphora* genus, reflecting quite stressful environmental conditions for microorganisms. The reduction in the number and variety of biominerals is greater in the middle member: virtually all are silicophytoliths and almost all C3 grasses. *Hantzschia amphioxys*, a species that can survive in a wide range of saline environments, predominates amongst the diatoms. There are almost no biominerals at the top of AS6, suggesting that the lake may have dried up.

Pollen analysis describes vegetation mainly consisting of pine (*Pinus*), juniper/sabine (*Juniperus*) and grasses (Poaceas). The riparian taxa such as alder (*Alnus*), willow (*Salix*), elm (*Ulmus*) and characteristic swamp species (Cyperaceas, Ranunculaceas, *Typha*...) were present. Temperate trees such as deciduous oak (*Quercus*), birch (*Betula*), chestnut (*Castanea*), hazel (*Corylus*) and walnut (*Juglans*) were also detected. These results corroborate the predominance of a milder climate than today's conditions at the time of the lower member accumulation.

2.2.5. Human presence

The technical characteristics of the lithic industry and the sources of the raw material have fostered debate about the mode and intensity of the site's use. With regard to bone industry, recent studies (Domínguez-Rodrigo, in: Santonja and Pérez-González, 2005 (eds.): 282-287) do not support the hypothesis suggested primarily by

Aguirre and Biberson about an intense transformation of elephant bones by shaping and retouch. The possibility that the fragments corresponding to the tip of infantile elephant tusks found at both sites deriving from any kind of manufacturing has also been rejected (Villa and d'Errico, in: Santonja and Pérez-González, 2005 (eds.): 288-305), arguing that they broke off naturally in the course of the elephants' lives.

To understand the significance of the Ambrona lithic industry, we must take into account its taphonomic history (Santonja *et al.*, in: Santonja and Pérez-González, 2005 (eds.): 306-333). AS1 and AS4, the richest levels in the lower member, are fluvial deposits with a degree of energy. The industry they contain is not in a primary position, having been dragged from its original positions in the immediate vicinity of the site. This material and the fauna found on the same levels was carried and classified by size by the watercourse. The technological imbalance in the series from AS1 and AS4 are not due to any palaeoeconomic or functional factors but rather to the natural process which formed record. On AS3, however, the industry is mainly in a primary position, albeit with some items deposited along the small streams leading to the pond. It is very low-density and essentially contains final elements of *chaînes opératoires* with little or no shaping, such as non-retouched flakes selected by size and form, and also bifacial macrotools brought from outside and left on the site.

EXCAVATED AREAS IN THE LOWER STRATIGRAPHIC MEMBER OF AMBRONA IN 1993-2000	LITHIC INDUSTRY
Level AS1: 535m^2. Only 35m^2 complete. Only the surface of the level in the rest	235 items, including 9 handaxes and 5 tools. Density in 35 m^2: 5 items/m^2, 1 handaxe/5 m^2 and 1.25 tools/m^2 (= 5 items/4 m^2)
Level AS3: 250 m^2	72 items, including 2 handaxes and 17 tools Density in 250 m^2: 1 item /3.5 m^2; 1 handaxe/ 125 m^2 and 1 tool/15 m^2
Level AS4: 379 m^2	339 items, including 1 handaxe and 56 tools. Density in 379 m^2: nearly 1 item/m^2;1 handaxe in 379 m^2 and 1 tool/7 m^2

Table 1. Excavated areas and lithic industry in the Lower Stratigraphic Member of Ambrona.

The industry at AS1 and AS3 can definitely be ascribed to the Acheulean technocomplex, as with the other levels in the lower stratigraphic member, given that in AS4, hydraulic factor is responsible for the deficit in medium and large format of lithic items, which explains the absence of bifacial tools.

The industry in AS6, previously defined as a more advanced Acheulean type than the lower levels (Howell *et al.*, 1995), is characterized by the lack of true handaxes and cleavers, the development of retouched tools on flake and the presence of Levallois debitage (Fig. 3). This level corresponds to the early Middle Palaeolithic (Santonja and Pérez-González, 2006).

2.2.6. Ambrona palaeoeconomy

The study of the sedimentation processes has enabled us to establish significant differences in relation to the meaning of the presence of remains in each stratigraphic context. A unified interpretation of the site, accepted until 1993, now seems inappropriate. The process by which the sequence was built up is a millenarian time period, but each level also comprises a major diachrony. Consequently, interpretations contextualised in short time intervals can only be applied to specific stratigraphic and spatial units. Moreover, they are obviously only meaningful for each case in point, and may differ even in areas that are part of the same level.

The low lithic density suggests that human activity did not reach great intensity in the lower stratigraphic member. Although the small amount of Acheulean evidence in the surrounding area supports this interpretation (Rodríguez de Tembleque, in: Santonja and Pérez-González, 2005 (eds.): 334-

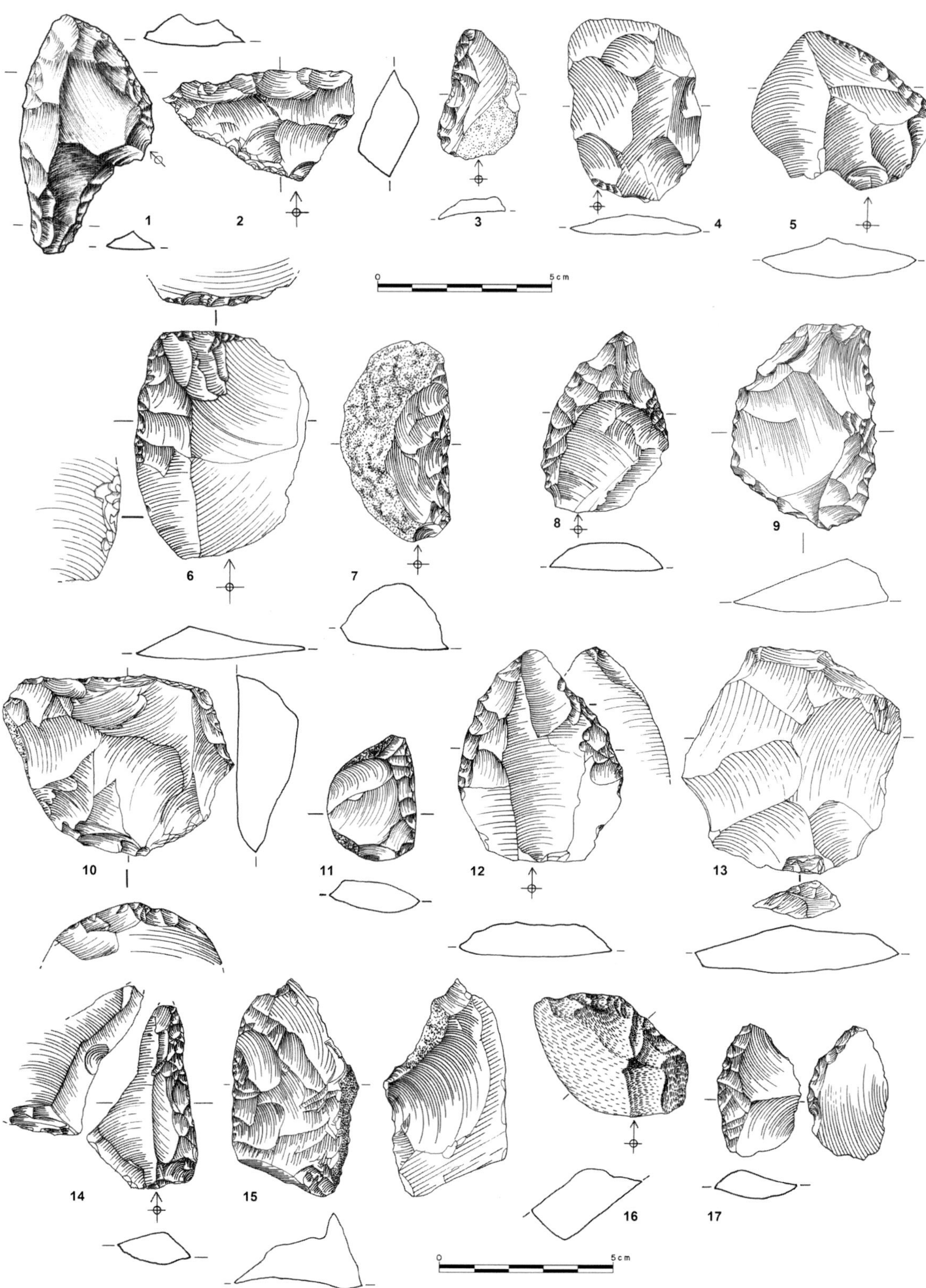

Figure 3. Lithic industry of the middle member of Ambrona site. Various sidescrapers: convergent pedunculate (1), angled-convergent (10), alternate angled-convergent (17), alternate with partial low retouch (6), doubles (8 and 12), concave (3), straight opposite a cortical back (11), sub-transversal straight (5), straights with invasive retouch (7 and 14 on *débordant* flake), straight with stepped retouch and Kombewa removal on ventral face (15) and sub-transversal convex (16). Denticulates (2 and 9). Levallois flakes (4, 12 –sidescraper– and 13). Flint, except for 8 (lidite) and 16 (quartzite).

351). Under these circumstances it must be stressed that the Ambrona area was a recurrent point of attraction for several millennia, given that lithic industry has been recorded on all levels in the lower member. The general pattern for the procurement of raw material coincides in all of them, and it must also be noted that both the flint and the quartzite used here was brought from elsewhere, in the case of the flint, from sources up to several dozen kilometres away (Freeman, 1991; Parcerisas, 2006).

The relationships between fauna –particularly elephants– and humans has not been established in all cases. The low incidence of freshly broken bones and cut marks indicates that human groups did not play a major role in the accumulation of these fauna remains. Current studies of the behaviour patterns of herds of elephants and other herbivores eloquently define the environments where remains of these animals build up in Africa: around ponds and springs, and during prolonged droughts (Haynes, 1991).

A natural scenario such as the one indicated in the previous paragraph is what we propose for Ambrona (Villa *et al.*, in: Santonja and Pérez-González, 2005 (eds.): 352-381). The concentration alpha at Level AS3, mainly consisting of a well-circumscribed adult elephant carcass, has been studied in depth (Fig. 4). This case provides an example of an individual which died from natural causes and was buried in mud, without evidence of human intervention. The presence of lithic industry and the few recorded cut marks indicates that the Palaeolithic groups only acted in the site in a marginal way on the fauna.

2.2.7. Torralba

Work at Torralba between 1990 and 2000 has been much more limited than in Ambrona (Santonja *et al.*, in: Santonja and Pérez-González, 2005 (eds.): 104-123). Nevertheless, stratigraphic checks, numerical dating and reviews of the industry confirm that this is an Acheulean site situated chronologically toward MIS 7 (*vid.* § 2.2.1).

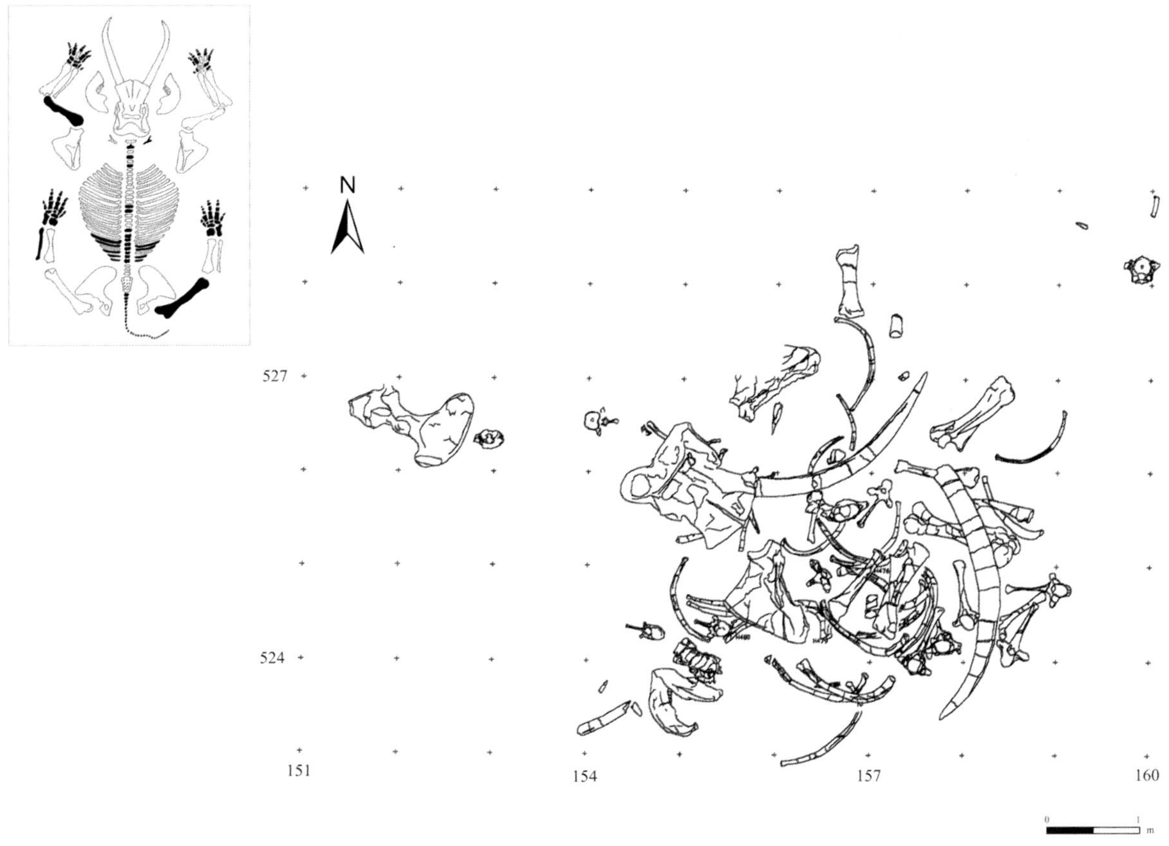

Figure 4. Remains of adult male *Palaeoloxodon antiquus* scattered across less than 60 m^2 on Level AS3, Central Sector. Excavation campaign of 1995. Bones not detected in the excavated assemblage marked in black (upper left).

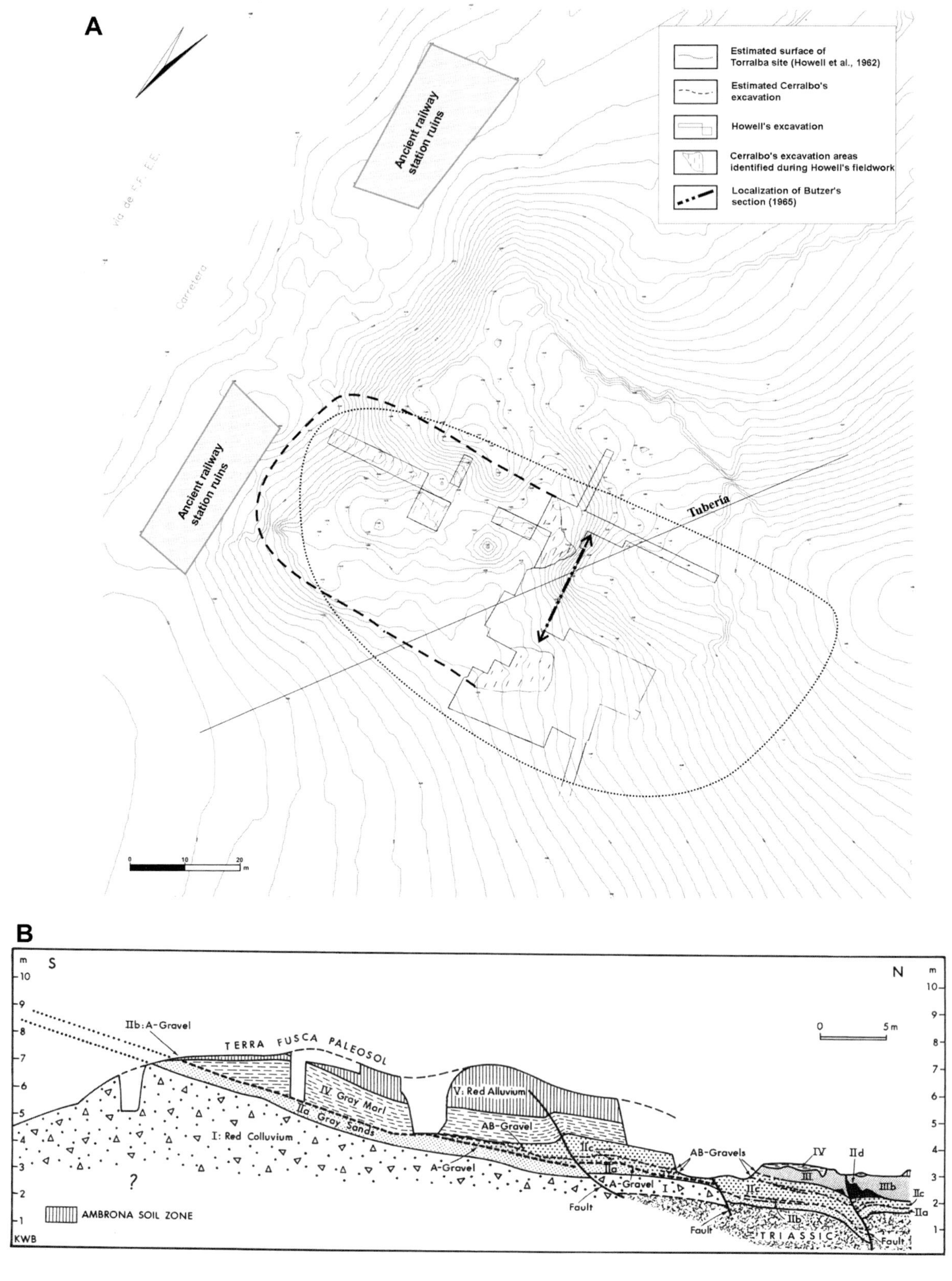

Figure 5. A: Torralba site. Zone partly dug by the Marquis of Cerralbo (1909-1913) and areas excavated by F. C. Howell (1961-1963). Equidistance of level curves: 25 cm. B: Torralba: composite stratigraphic profile (adapted from Butzer 1965).

The oldest formations on which the Torralba Pleistocene deposits lie are, as in Ambrona, red clays and gypsum from the Keuper and Triassic-Jurassic carbonate deposits. Despite the large area of the site, the only detailed stratigraphy is the N-S section in the western sector of the site (Fig. 5a), published by K.W. Butzer (1965). This is a composite profile (Fig. 5b) which starts with up to 3-4 m deep red colluvial facies lying on the Keuper. These deposits disappear to the north and the sequence continues with gray sand facies, interspersed with angular and sub-angular gravel with a carbonate composition, sized 1-3 cm along the major axis, reaching a maximum depth of 1 m in the northern half of profile. At the top there is a fairly continuous unit of grey-green marl, somewhat more sandy at the base, with a maximum depth of roughly 2 m. Above these facies, of a shallow lacustrine nature, there is a red alluvial-colluvial deposit, between 0 and 1.5 m deep. In this sector, the Pleistocene and Keuper levels are affected by reverse faults with movements of more than one metre.

The above-mentioned river sand and gravel facies contain the main concentrations of fauna and industry found during the excavations by Cerralbo and Howell. The evidence of fluvial rolling found on the fauna and industry is typical of this type of context, and implies movement or disturbance of some intensity (Sánchez-Cervera *et al.*, e. i. p.). The former interpretation of some of the Torralba stratigraphic units (Freeman and Butzer, 1966; Freeman, 1994) as occupation sites thus seems irrelevant, as they did not take into account the fact that these deposits were built up in fluvial contexts with enough energy to move the material. The same is true of the findings of the taphonomic studies of the Torralba fauna (Díez *et al.*, 1985), which assumed the unitary nature of the assemblages on each level, which is are inconsistent with the secondary position (non-autochthonous) of the remains.

The composition of the Torralba macrofauna closely resembles Ambrona, although there is a clear imbalance in the frequency of certain representative taxa such as *Equus* and *Elephas*. A parallel of any greater scope would be premature at this stage, given that only a few taxa –including *Equus* (Prat, 1977), poorly represented in the lower member of Ambrona– have been studied in depth, and the microfauna and small vertebrates –except for birds (*Tadorna ferruginea*; *Mergus serrator*; *Anatidae* indet. and *Porphyrio porphyrio*)– are still largely unknown also at Torralba.

In Torralba, the lithic industry has a density of less than 1 item per m^3 throughout the levels excavated by Cerralbo and Howell. As in Ambrona, such low frequencies suggest low-intensity human presence and interventions.

The raw material collection patterns are also similar to those observed in Ambrona. The presence of cores and flakes shows that in Torralba, quartzite and flint blocks brought from elsewhere were exploited. But the lack of cortical flakes suggests also that the material brought to the site may have been previously scabbled. Similarly, the lack of cores used to produce the flake supports for handaxes and cleavers indicates that this toolkit was already configured when it was brought to the site (Sánchez-Cervera *et al.*, i.p.).

The handaxes and cleavers on flake set lets us include Torralba in the Acheulean technocomplex. However, progressive technological items have also been observed, such as handaxes and cleavers with retouch (bifaces support of tools), making further work necessary to check for technological traditions which may be ascribed to the Middle Palaeolithic, as in the case of Ambrona. In the general context of the European Acheulean, it is important to stress the presence of true flint *hachereaux*, since there is a clear tendency to link these items closely to the availability of quartzite. In the light of the numerical chronologies now available, Torralba is one of the most recent Acheulean sites in southern Europe.

Manuel Santonja*,
Alfredo Pérez-González*

Cuesta de la Bajada (Teruel): an early Middle Palaeolithic site

1. Discovery and excavation

Cuesta de la Bajada (CB hereafter), situated on the left bank of the Alfambra River upstream from Teruel, was the first open air Middle Pleistocene site to be excavated in the Aragón Region. The identification of fauna and stone tools by Etienne and Nicole Moissenet prompted an initial survey and assessment in October 1990. Between 1991 and 1994, three brief excavations in a 30 m^2 area focused on the most accessible zone, now called the Western Sector (SO), which yielded basic information about the site and its environs (Santonja and Pérez-González 2001). Subsequently, a thick accumulation of sterile sediment in the East Sector (SE) was removed, leaving a new surface of 350 m^2 ready for excavation, of which 92 m^2 were dug in successive campaigns between 1999 and 2011(Santonja *et al.*, e.i.p.). The working methodology, which has remained constant since 1990, has adopted an essentially geoarchaeological approach with the participation of a large multidisciplinary team.

2. Geology and chronology

The Alfambra River flows through Cuesta de la Bajada, overlap in the lower section of the site terrace, which show syn-sedimentary thickenings of over 60 m caused by subsidence of the rocky substratum of Pliocene carbonates and gypsums in this valley sector. This terrace is in a central location on the Alfambra 10 fill-strath stepped terraces, with relative heights given in relation to the current river level at +2-3 m (T10, present-day floodplain), +6 m (T9), +13-15 m (T8), +20-25 m (T7), +30-35 m (T6), +40-45 m (T5), +50-53 m (T4, Cuesta de la Bajada site terrace), +65-70 m (T3), +90-95 m (T2), and +103-104 m (T1).

At CB there have been frequent lateral changes to the sedimentary facies, a quite common phenomenon in fluvial environments. In CB-SO, we identified four successive floors of poorly stratified gravels containing large concentrations of fauna and lithic industry, all in non autochthonous positions (Santonja *et al.*, 2000). In CB-SE, which is located in an upper stratigraphic position, we recorded a sequence of fine sediments built up in a pond environment. In this case, the archaeo-palaeontological materials are basically in a primary position. These deposits are in a small depression caused by deformation, located between a cyclical sequence of gravel bars and floodplain silts. At the bottom is a massive level with massive gravel (G) that lacks any archaeological record, successively followed by levels CB3, CB2 and CB1 with 1.5 m thickness (Fig. 1). The composition of the base level CB3 is sandy with high percentages of clays. Level CB2 has a greater presence of gravels (1-3 cm) and granules (2-4 mm) at the base, along with finer sands toward the top. The more recent Level CB1 also consists of a fining-upward sequence with a massive internal structure, albeit with a much finer texture, with granules and pebbles at the base and clays towards the top. Units CB3, CB2 and CB1 are capped with a 1 m-thick series of floodplain facies, denoted level P. All these levels correspond to low-energy sedimentary environments.

A multidisciplinary study about the chronology of archaeological level CB3 was conducted using single-grain OSL and ESR dating in sedimentary quartz at the CENIEH lab (Burgos), multigrain aliquot OSL (Institut de Recherche sur les Archéomatériaux, Bordeaux), ESR/U series on *Equus* teeth (IPH, Paris), and also Amino Acid Racemization (AAR) analysis on *Equus* teeth (Biomolecular Stratigraphy Laboratory ETSIM, Madrid). According to these datings, the age of the Cuesta de la Bajada site ranges between 250 ky and 450 ky. Considering other dates obtained in nearby river formations, the most likely age of this site is MIS 8 or prior (Santonja *et al.*, submitted).

* Centro Nacional de Investigación sobre la Evolución Humana. (CENIEH); 09002 Burgos manuel.santonja@cenieh.es

3. Palaeontology and environment

The faunal assemblage recorded to date this site is as follows (Blain, in preparation); Sesé and Soto, in Santonja *et al.*, 2000):

– Herpetofauna:

Alytes obstetricans; Pelodytes punctatus; Bufo bufo; Bufo calamita; Hyla arborea; Pelophylax perezi; Anura indet.; Lacertidae indet.; *Coronella* cf. *girondica; Vipera* sp.; Ophidia indet.

– Micromammals:

Lagomorpha: *Oryctolagus* cf. *cuniculus;* Soricomorpha: *Crocidura* cf. *russula;* Rodentia: *Eliomys quercinus, Apodemus* cf. *sylvaticus, Cricetulus (Allocricetus) bursae, Microtus brecciensis, Microtus* cf. *duodecimcostatus* and *Arvicola* aff. *sapidus.*

– Macromammals:

Carnivora: *Canis lupus;* Proboscidea: *Elephas (Palaeoloxodon) antiquus;* Perissodactyla: *Stephanorhinus* cf. *hemitoechus* and *Equus chosaricus;* Artiodactyla: *Cervus elaphus, Bos primigenius, Rupicapra rupicapra* and *Capra* sp.

Almost all these species – rodents, elephant, rhinos, bovids, canids and caprids – are represented by isolated remains. *Cervus* is most frequent, but *Equus* is by far the most abundant genus. From a palaeoecological perspective, there are different palaeoenvironments. Among themselves: *Arvicola* aff. *sapidus* inhabited the proximity of watercourses with riparian vegetation; *Microtus* inhabited moist and wet soils. All the species indicate developed vegetation, and most are typical of open landscapes, although *Eliomys quercinus* and *Apodemus* cf. *sylvaticus* are not abundant, suggest the existence of wooded areas nearby.

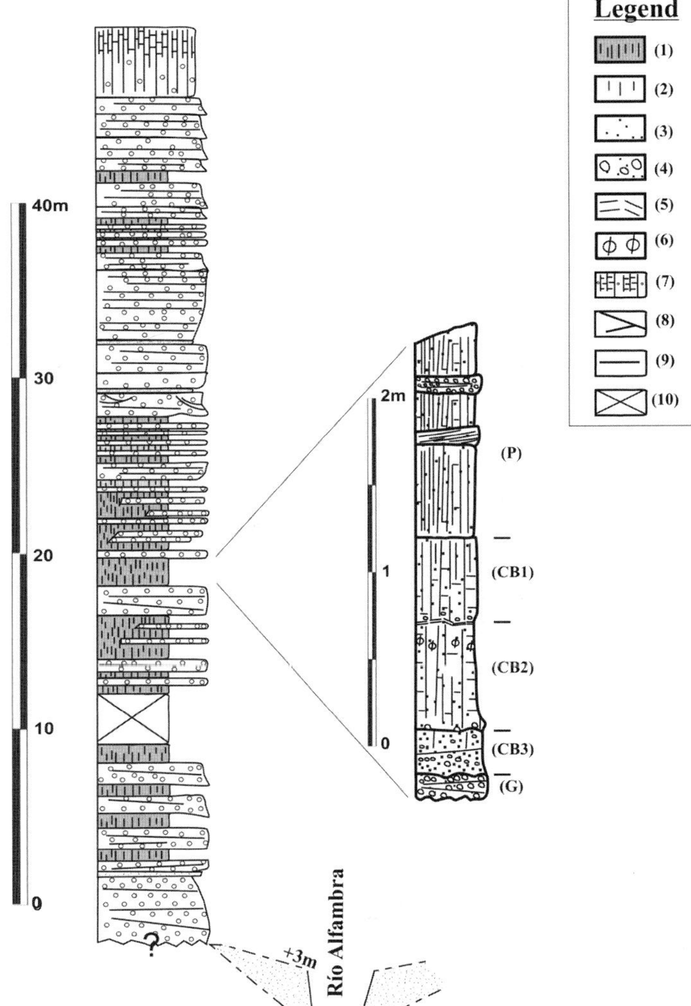

Figure 1. Stratigraphic section of the Alfambra River terrace T4 and details of the sequence G, CB3, CB2, CB1 and P at the Cuesta de la Bajada site. Key: **(1)** Mud. **(2)** Clay and silt. **(3)** Sand and granules. **(4)** Gravel. **(5)** Oxidation level. **(6)** Carbonate concretions. (7) Colluvial and soil. **(8)** Cross-stratification. **(9)** Stratification contact. **(10)** Covered.

4. Lithic industry and human activity

The raw materials used at Cuesta de la Bajada was flint in some cases, more commonly silicified limestone, present in the Alfambra River's alluvium, and also quartz and quartzite, which must have been brought from the Guadalaviar River basin, 2 km away. Local ordinary limestone was also used in an almost natural state, in some cases as anvils or hammers.

The lithic industry in the two sectors of CB was identical, both technologically and typologically. In SO, the worked material, dragged along alluvial environments, evidences a degree of size-based selection, and some sections of the operational chains are missing or infra represented. By contrast, in SE, the knapping process is fully represented: hammerstones, raw material which was only tested, cores, all phases of flake production, debris and retouched tools. The cores were managed relatively frequently by means of orderly removal systems –polyhedral, Quina, discoidal and sometimes, Levallois–. In some cases, however, there is evidence of random and low intensity exploitation, adapted to the size and shape of the blank.

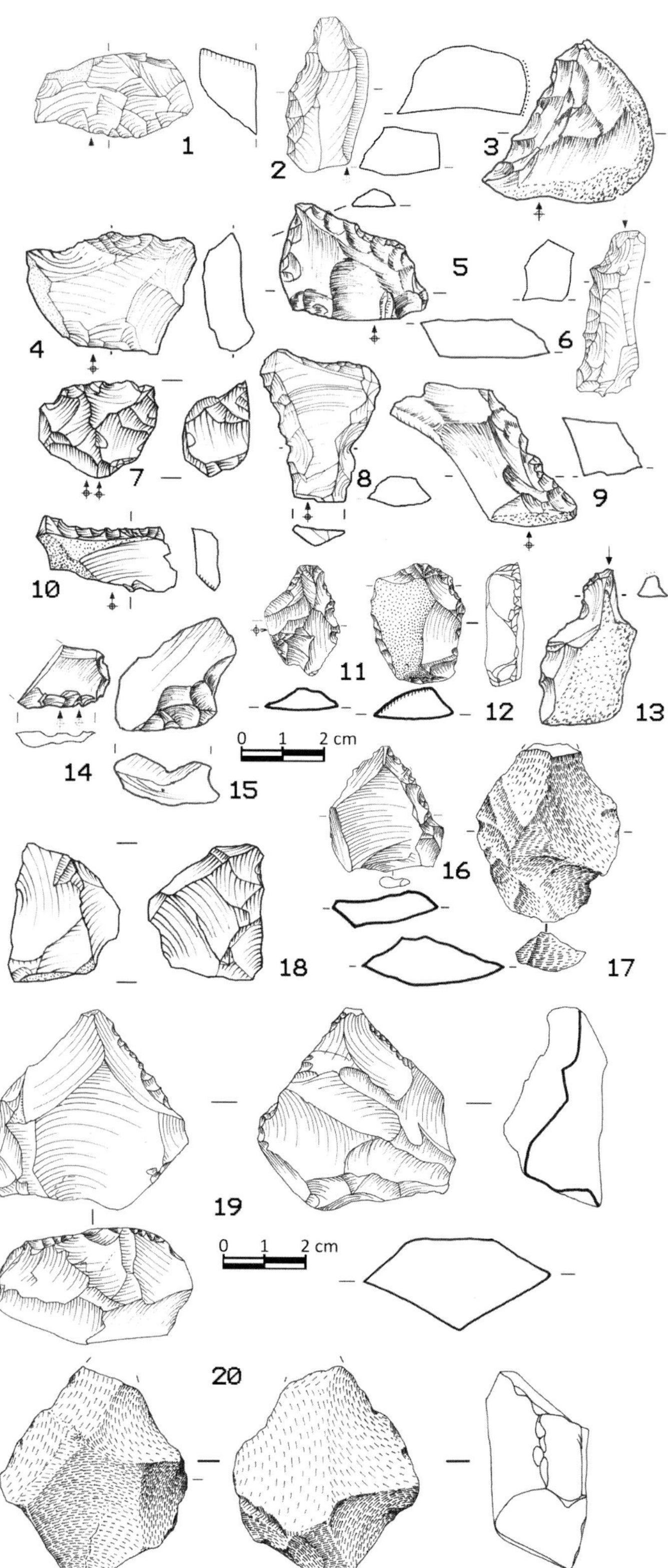

Figure 2. Cuesta de la Bajada lithic industry. Sidescrapers (1-10); endscrapers (11-13); flakes from tool retouching (14-15); Levallois flakes (16-17); Levallois cores (18-20).

None of the assemblages contained any macrotools (handaxes, cleavers, large retouched flakes or trihedral pics). The retouched toolkit matches Mousterian patterns, with a large percentage of sidescrapers and denticulates (Fig. 2). In the light of the dated chronologies, the CB industry should be framed in the European context of the early Middle Palaeolithic.

Human activity took place in the general framework of the Alfambra floodplain, either on one of the small channels that ran through it or in relation to the ponds in the shallow depressions caused by surface deformation due to subsidence in the area. In SE, green fractures and numerous cut marks were detected, particularly on long bones of horses and in some cases deers, indicative of systematic human intervention on these animals.

Acknowledgements

To all our colleagues who participated in the research and excavation of Cuesta de la Bajada: Carmen Sesé and Enrique Soto –National Museum of Natural Sciences–, H. Blain –IPHES, Catalonian Institute of Human Palaeoecology and Social Evolution– (Palaeontology); Manuel Domínguez Rodrigo, José Yravedra and Rebeca Barba Egido –Prehistory Dep., Complutense University, Madrid– (Taphonomy); Blanca Ruiz Zapata –University of Alcalá de Henares– (Palynology); Ch. Falguères –Institute of Human Palaeontology, Paris–, Lee Arnold and Mathieu Duval –CENIEH–, T. de Torres and José E. Ortiz (Biomolecular Stratigraphy Laboratory, School of Mines and Energy, Complutense University, Madrid), N. Mercier – Centre de Recherche en Physique Appliquée à l' Archéologie, Bordeaux University– (Geochronology); Giacomo Gillani, Eduardo Méndez, Joaquín Panera, Susana Rubio, Juan R. de Tembleque and Borja Sánchez-Cervera (Excavation and Archaeology); Raquel Rojas Mendoza (Lithic drawings and Conservation treatments).

Jesús F. Jordá Pardo*, Marta Navazo Ruiz**, J. Carlos Diez Fernández-Lomana**

Jarama VI (Valdesotos, Guadalajara, Castilla – La Mancha)

Introduction

Work in the Upper Jarama Valley (Valdesotos, Guadalajara, Castilla-La Mancha) began in 1983, when a team led by Dr. Francisco Jordá Cerda discovered the Jarama I and Jarama II sites. In 1985 and 1988, systematic excavations were conducted at Jarama II as part of the *Prehistoric Research in the Upper Jarama Valley (Valdesotos, Guadalajara)* project, accompanied by archaeological surveys in the Jarama canyon in 1988 which located a new archaeological cave site, Jarama VI, excavated between 1989 and 1993 under the same project. Jarama II yielded lithic and bone industries attributed to the Magdalenian along with a sperm whale ivory statuette depicting a glutton and also several Chalcolithic burials (Adán *et al.*, 1995). In 1992, an emergency dig at Jarama I permitted the recovery of a lithic assemblage attributable to the Magdalenian (Adán *et al.*, 1995).

Stratigraphy and chronology

Jarama VI, 822 m asl, is a Rock Shelter 23 m above the left bank of the Jarama River, located amongst the Cretaceous karstified dolomites on the S boundary of the Spanish Central Range. It faces N and is partially infilled by sediment. Its lithostratigraphic sequence consists of several units resting on the bedrock (Adán *et al.*, 1995, Jordá Pardo 2007) (Fig. 1). The lowest unit (JVI.3), a cryoclastic deposit containing lithic and bone remains, is well preserved throughout its area and sealed by an intermediate unit, JVI.2, which has an erosive contact and is structured into three sub-units consisting of sands and luttites of obviously fluvial origin. The lower sub-unit (JVI.2.3) is sterile, alternating between sands and luttites deposited by floods. The intermediate silty sub-unit (JVI.2.2) is a floodplain facies containing archaeological remains, scattered locally around a small hearth. The top sub-unit of this unit (JVI.2.1) consists of clayey sands with interspersed clasts and abundant archaeological material. The upper unit (JVI.1), separated from JVI.2 by a diastem, consists of gelifracts and reddish sands and silts due to sheet-flood sedimentation, with quartzite, slate and quartz pebbles of anthropogenic origin at the base. Less than 4 m^2 of this unit is preserved. It contains abundant archaeological material. The sequence culminates with breccia and speleothems (JVI.K).

In 1992, three conventional ^{14}C dates situated the lower units in a range between 41 and 30 ky cal BP (Beta-56639 and Beta-56638), with the upper unit between 29.6 and 26.8 ky cal BP (Jordá Pardo 2001, 2007), although there are doubts about the representativity of the latter (Beta-56640) (Fig. 1). In 2008, AMS ^{14}C dates with ultrafiltration was performed in collaboration with the Oxford Radiocarbon Accelerator Unit on samples of bone fragments bearing anthropogenic marks. Only 3 of the 30 analyzed bones could be dated, two of which (OxA-X-2290-56 and OXA-21714) revealed infinite ages beyond 50.2 for unit JVI.1 and 47 ky BP for unit JVI.2, while the third date (OxA-X-2310-22) for subunit JVI .2.2 was 49.4 ± 3.7 ky BP (Wood *et al.*, 2012). At the end of 2010, a fieldwork was conducted at Jarama VI along with researchers from the Neanderthal Museum and University of Cologne in order to collect several samples, some of them for luminescence dating (IRSL). The results are consistent with the ORAU datings, situating the occupations at beyond 50 ky BP (Kehl *et al.*, 2013).

Lithic industry

The raw material employed here was primarily quartz and quartzite, followed by flint and rock

* Laboratorio de Estudios Paleolíticos, Departamento de Prehistoria y Arqueología, Universidad Nacional de Educación a Distancia. Ciudad Universitaria. Paseo Senda del Rey 7, E-28040 Madrid, Spain; jjorda@geo.uned.es

** Área de Prehistoria, Departamento de Ciencias Históricas y Geografía, Universidad de Burgos. Plaza Misael Bañuelos s/n, E-09001 Burgos, Spain; mnavazo@ubu.es; clomana@ubu.es

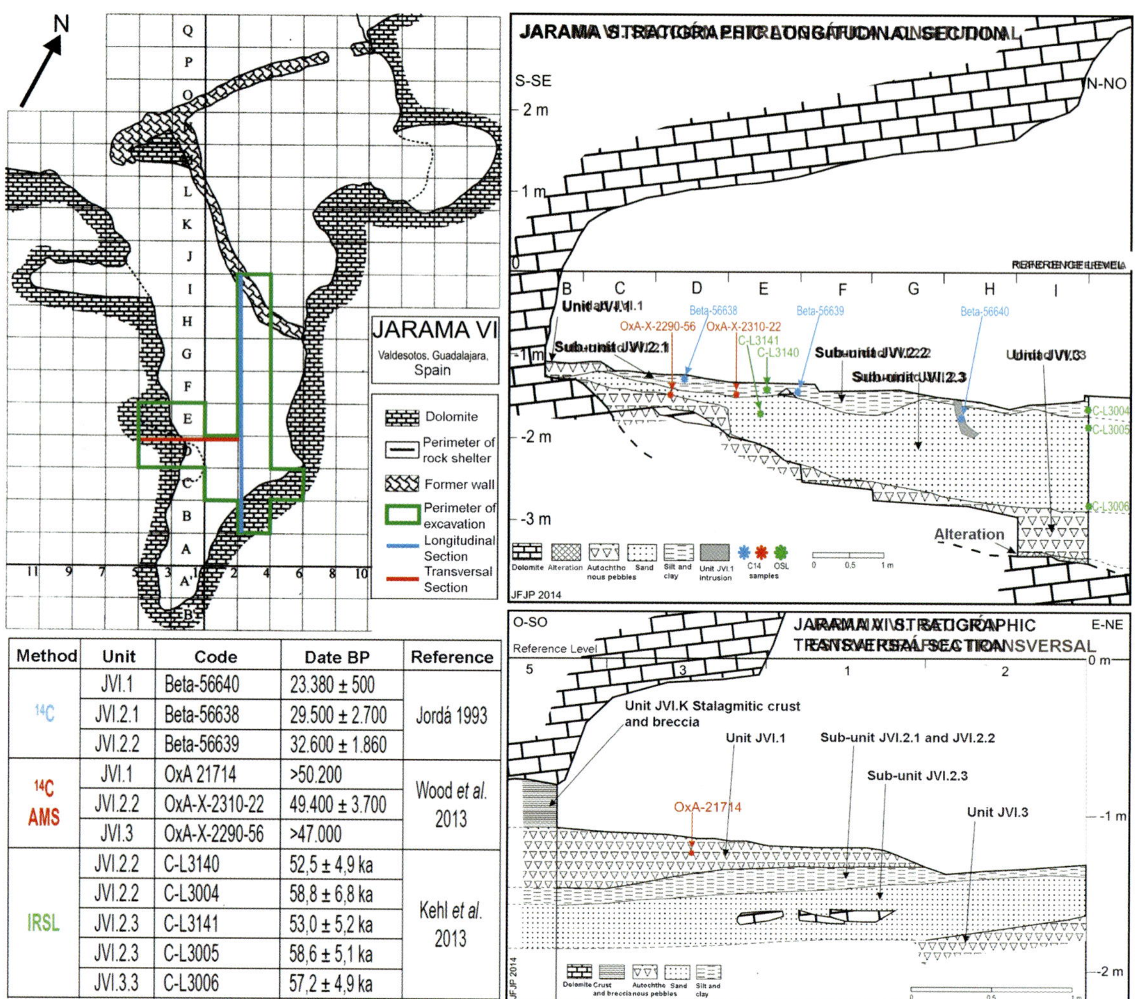

Method	Unit	Code	Date BP	Reference
^{14}C	JVI.1	Beta-56640	23.380 ± 500	Jordá 1993
	JVI.2.1	Beta-56638	29.500 ± 2.700	
	JVI.2.2	Beta-56639	32.600 ± 1.860	
^{14}C AMS	JVI.1	OxA 21714	>50.200	Wood *et al.* 2013
	JVI.2.2	OxA-X-2310-22	49.400 ± 3.700	
	JVI.3	OxA-X-2290-56	>47.000	
IRSL	JVI.2.2	C-L3140	52,5 ± 4,9 ka	Kehl *et al.* 2013
	JVI.2.2	C-L3004	58,8 ± 6,8 ka	
	JVI.2.3	C-L3141	53,0 ± 5,2 ka	
	JVI.2.3	C-L3005	58,6 ± 5,1 ka	
	JVI.3.3	C-L3006	57,2 ± 4,9 ka	

Figure 1. Jarama VI. Plan of the rock shelter, showing the excavated area, longitudinal and transversal stratigraphic sections and dating table (illustrations and production, J.F. Jordá).

crystal. The former were brought to the cave as cobbles, while the flint arrived already shaped in the form of flakes and retouched flakes. Quartz, quartzite, sandstone, shale and limestone pebbles were also found in the cave but not considered to be part of the technological assemblage.

Differences in the operational chains were detected, depending on the type of raw material. The quartz and quartzite cores were in the early stages of reduction, the vast majority on pebble. Only three flint items were found in the whole sequence, all exhausted cores on flake. Discoidal reduction is the most common system.

The aim of the reduction was to produce small and micro-sized material (flakes and retouched items). Butts and dorsal faces have cortex, indicating that they were in the early stages of reduction. The flint flakes and retouched flakes have the same size but lack cortex. The best represented types are denticulates and notches in JVI.1 and JVI.3, and sidescrapers in JVI.2. The material includes allochthonous flint sidescrapers whose edges were sharpened at the campsite, while the local materials were used to manufacture denticulates and notches. Other documented types include endscrapers, becs, burins and points (Fig. 2).

The technological characteristics of Jarama VI suggest expeditious knapping of local materials, indicating these groups' adaptability to local resources. On the other hand, flint was an allochthonous material and was therefore part of a more complex mobility strategy. This material was fully exploited, and the items were already knapped when they arrived at the site. We interpret the presence of pebbles as a

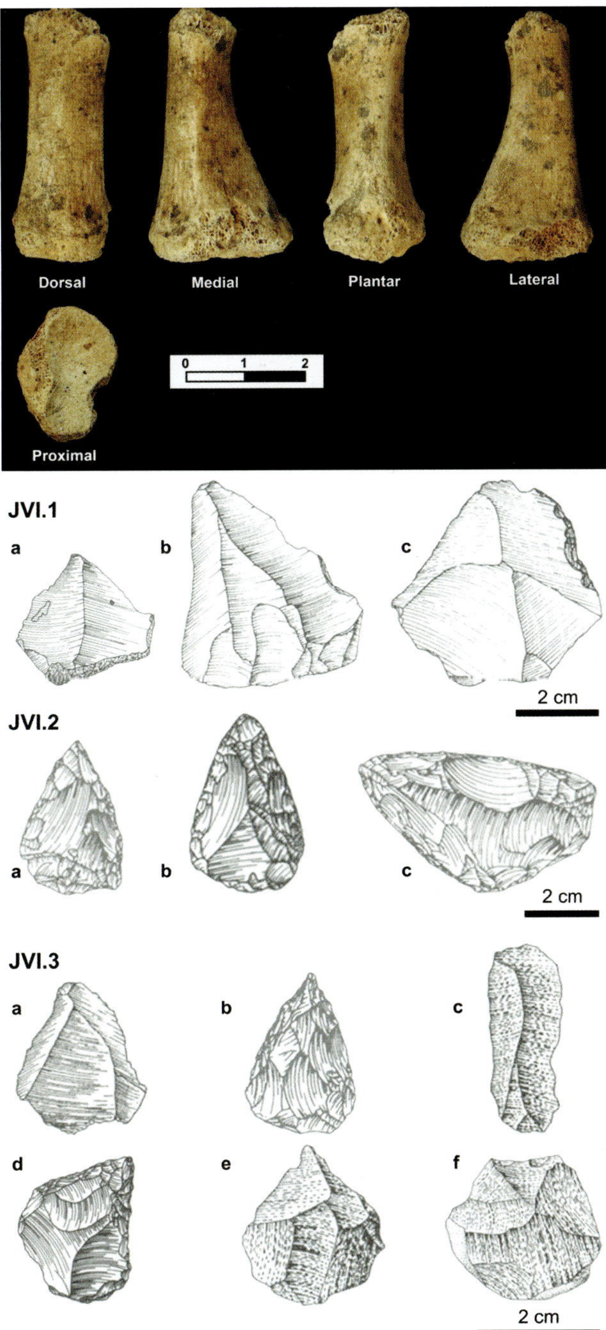

Figure 2. Jarama VI : Human metatarsal (photos and montage, C. Lorenzo) and stone tools from units JVI.1 (a, flake; b and c, retouched flakes), JVI.2 (a, point, b and c convergent sidescrapers) and JVI.3 (3a, c, e and f, flakes, b point, c sidescraper) (illustrations B. Márquez, flake montage, M. Navazo and A. Benito).

reserve of raw material, which in strategic terms suggests that there was prior planning for the requirements of these groups, a strategy that was repeated in the different occupation phases of this shelter.

Fauna

Unit JVI.2 unit has provided a near-complete adult human first metatarsal bone (Fig. 2). Although the species is difficult to diagnose, its context, morphology and dimensions permit its attribution to *Homo neanderthalensis*. The surface shows clear signs of action by a carnivore (depressions and grooves) (Lorenzo *et al.*, 2012). Other more modern human remains (*Homo sapiens*) have been identified on the surface of the site.

Skeletal remains from microvertebrates (*Pliomys* cf. *lenki, Microtus arvalis, Microtus agrestis, Apodemus sylvaticus and Apodemus flavicollis*) are abundant in all units at Jarama VI. Beaver, rabbit, several species of birds and some amphibians are also present. None of the above taxa show evidence of hunting or human consumption. Herbivores predominate over carnivores in all units, although the minimum number of individuals is small in all cases. Deer, goats, large bovids and horses, generally adults, are predominant.

Analysis of the bone surfaces has found indications of rapid burial with minimal pre– or post-sedimentary alterations. We have found little evidence of exposure to the air, but somewhat more to roots and trampling. Several zones contain bones with signs of abrasion, dissolution and crusting. Moisture is evidenced by the presence of manganese on bones as well as cracks caused by environmental changes.

Long bones, the main category, bear signs of fresh breakage, epiphysis removal and abundant percussion and cut marks. Incisions suggest that defleshing was the main activity. Very few bones were burned. Several were used as retouchers. Remains bearing carnivore bite marks (probably from wolves and foxes) occur in small numbers. Overlapping marks show that these animals always had access to the prey after the hominids as marginal scavengers, without prolonged habitation in the cave. They left a coprolite and half a dozen digested bones.

Conclusion

The three archaeosedimentary units at Jarama VI seem to reflect short but repeated occupations by mobile groups of Neanderthals who used the cave in activities associated with the consumption of medium-sized herbivores obtained in the local environs in a temperate climate during OIS 3.

Carbonell, E.[a,b,c]; Huguet, R.[b,a,c,*]; Cáceres, I.[a,b]; Lorenzo, C.[a,b,d]; Mosquera, M.[a,b]; Ollé, A.[b,a]; Rodríguez, X.P.[a,b]; Saladié, P.b,[a] ; Vergès, J.M.[b,a]; García-Medrano, P.[b]; Rosell, J.[a,b]; Vallverdú, J.[b,a,c]; Carretero, J.M.[e,d]; Navazo, M.[f,g]; Ortega, A.I. g,h; Martinón-Torres, M.g; Morales, J.I.[b,a]; Allué; E.[b,a]; Aramburu, A.[i]; Canals, A.[a,b,n,] Carrancho,A.[f]; Castilla, M.[e]; Expósito, I.[b,a]; Fontanals, M.[b,a]; Francés, M.[e]; Galindo-Pellicena, M.[d,j]; García-Antón, D.[a,b]; García, N.[d,j]; Gracia, A.[d,k]; García, R.[e]; Gómez-Merino, G.[b,a]; Iriarte, E.[e]; Lombera-Hermida, A.[b,a]; López-Polín, L.[b,a]; Lozano, M.[b,a]; Made van der, J.[l]; Martínez, I.[d,k] ; Mateos, A.[g]; Pérez-Romero, A.[e]; Poza, E. [d,j]; Quam, R.[m,d]; Rodriguez-Hidalgo, A.[b,a,n]; Rodríguez, J. [g] Rodríguez, L.[e]; Santos, E.[e,d]; Terradillos, M.[k]; Bermúdez de Castro, J.M.[g]; Arsuaga, J.L.[d,j]

Sierra de Atapuerca archaeological sites

Introduction

Sierra de Atapuerca (Burgos, Spain) is a mid-altitude karst range characterised by the subterranean morphology concentrated on its south-western flank (San Vincente Hill, 1085 m asl). This multilevel karst system, an inactive legacy of old base levels formed during the Plio-Pleistocene, is linked to palaeo-upwelling of the Pico River. It consists of three main levels of sub-horizontal ducts which are interconnected by spaces and sinkholes, now hanging +90 m, +70 m and +60 m above the present bed of the Arlanzón River (Ortega *et al.*, 2013, 2014). Only 4.7 km of the accessible ducts in this system are known at present. Around 50 completely infilled cavities have been identified (Ortega, 2009), some of which became exposed when a cutting for a mine railway line between Monterrubio de la Demand and

a Àrea de Prehistòria, Universitat Rovira i Virgili (URV), Avinguda de Catalunya 35, 43002 Tarragona, Spain.
b Institut Català de Paleoecologia Humana i Evolució Social (IPHES), C/ Marcel.lí Domingo s/n e Campus Sescelades URV (Edifici W3), 43007 Tarragona, Spain.
c. Unidad asociada al CSIC. Departamento de Paleobiología, Museo Nacional de Ciencias Naturales. Calle José Gutierrez Abascal, 2. 28006 Madrid, Spain.
d Centro Mixto UCM-ISCIII de Investigación sobre Evolución y Comportamiento Humanos, c/Monforte de Lemos, 5, 28029 Madrid, Spain.
e Laboratorio de Evolución Humana (LEH), Dpto. de Ciencias Históricas y Geografía, Universidad de Burgos, Edificio I+D+i, Plaza Misael Bañuelos s/n, 09001 Burgos, Spain.
f Área de Prehistoria. Dpto. de Ciencias Históricas y Geografía, Universidad de Burgos, Edificio I+D+i, Plaza Misael Bañuelos s/n, 09001 Burgos, Spain.
g Centro Nacional de Investigación sobre la Evolución Humana (CENIEH), Paseo Sierra de Atapuerca, 09002 Burgos, Spain
h Grupo Espeleológico Edelweiss, Excma, Diputación Provincial de Burgos, Paseo del Espolón s/n, 09071 Burgos, Spain
i Departamento de Mineralogía y Petrología, Facultad de Ciencia y Tecnología, Universidad del País Vasco/EHU, c/ Sarriena, s/n, 48940 Leioa, Spain
j Departamento de Paleontología, Universidad Complutense de Madrid, Avenida Complutense s/n, 28040 Madrid, Spain.
k Área de Paleontología, Departamento de Geología, Universidad de Alcalá de Henares, 28871 Alcalá de Henares, Spain.
l Museo Nacional de Ciencias Naturales (MNCN). Calle José Gutierrez Abascal, 2. 28006 Madrid, Spain.
m. Department of Anthropology, Binghamton University (SUNY), Binghamton, NY 13902-6000, USA.
n. Equipo Primeros Pobladores de Extremadura, Casa de la Cultura Rodríguez Moñino. Avda. Cervantes s/n, 10003 Cáceres, Spain
* Corresponding autor: Institut Català de Paleoecologia Humana i Evolució Social (IPHES), C/ Marcel.lí Domingo s/n e Campus Sescelades URV (Edifici W3), 43007 Tarragona, Spain. E-mail address: rhuguet@iphes.cat

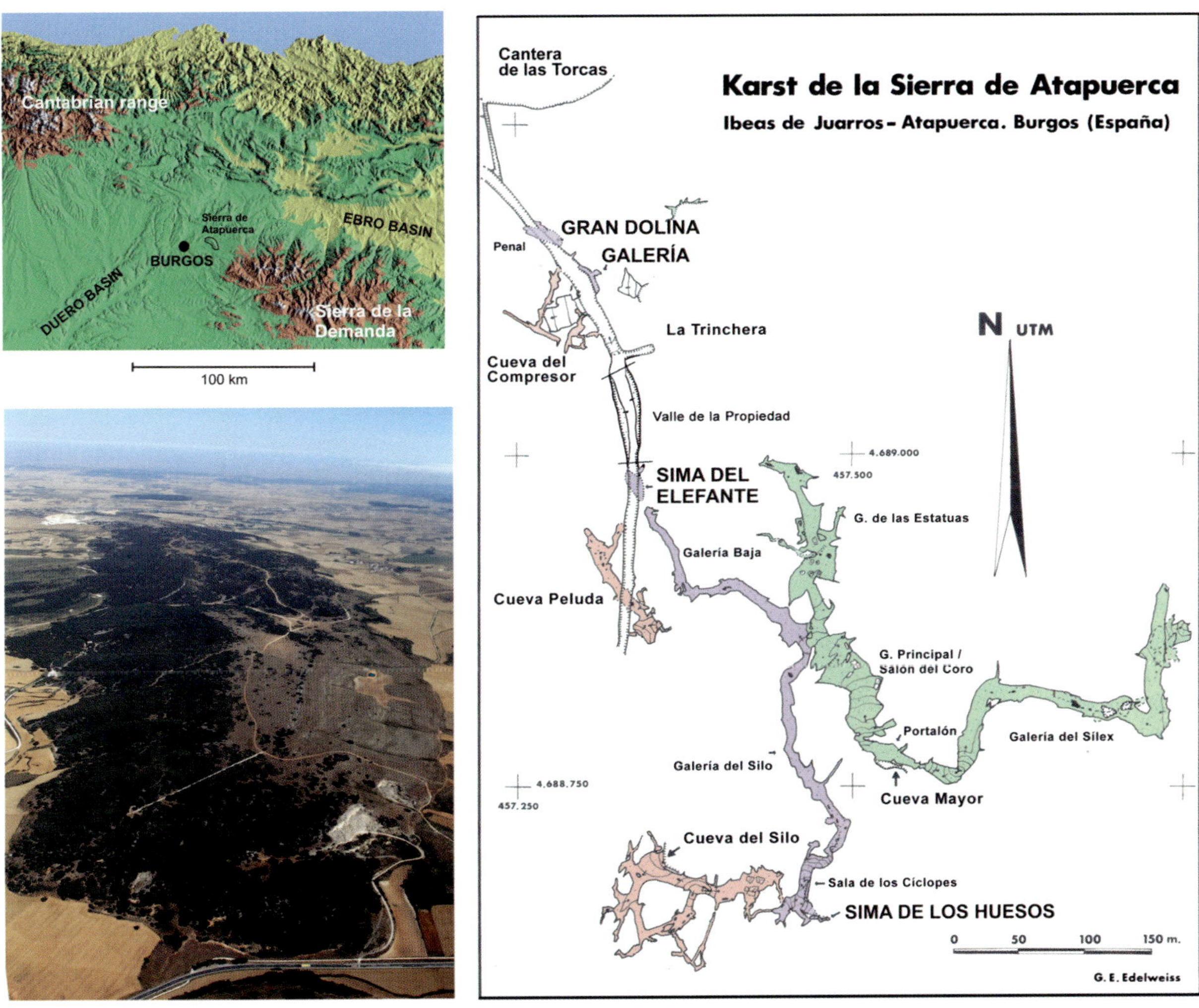

Figure 1. Location of Sierra de Atapuerca sites. Karst map based on original topography by Edelweiss Speleological Group, adapted from Ortega (2009). Green: top level of karst, purple: middle level, pink: bottom level.

Villafría was dug in the late 19th century (Ortega *et al.*, 2012). Other cavities remained hidden, although in the course of hundreds of thousands of years, they have been visited by successive settlers in the Sierra de Atapuerca area. Apart from the sites within the karst system, open air campsites with evidence of activity by human groups have been recorded on the slopes and moors around this low mountain range. Sierra de Atapuerca and its occupations are one of Europe's most important sources of ancient human fossils. They were declared a World Heritage Site by UNESCO in 2000. In this chapter, we will review the research that has been underway at the Sierra de Atapuerca sites for more than thirty years. The excavations and subsequent analysis of several sites, both caves and open air campsites, have found evidence of occupations by hominins groups in different periods, from 1.3 million BP to less than 3,000 years ago. Digs at Sierra de Atapuerca have focused on four different sectors: *Trinchera del Ferrocarril*, *Cueva Mayor*, *Cueva del Mirador* and the open air karst zone. Listed in chronological order of human occupation, the cave sites are *Sima del Elefante*, *Gran Dolina*, *Galería*, *Sima de los Huesos*, *Portalón* and *Mirador*. The outdoor sites include *Hotel California*, *Hundidero*, *Fuente Mudarra* and *Valle de las Orquídeas* (Fig. 1).

Trinchera del Ferrocarril

As its name suggests, the *Trinchera del Ferrocarril* (Railway Trench) is an artificial trench dug during the construction of a mine railway. In plan, the trench is a 500 metre long arc running N-S through the southern part of the Sierra. The primarily limestone walls of the cutting, no more than 20 metres high, contain sectioned cavities which had been filled with sediment of different origin. Three of these cavities –from south to north *Sima del Elefante, Gran Dolina* and *Galería*– have been defined as archaeological sites.

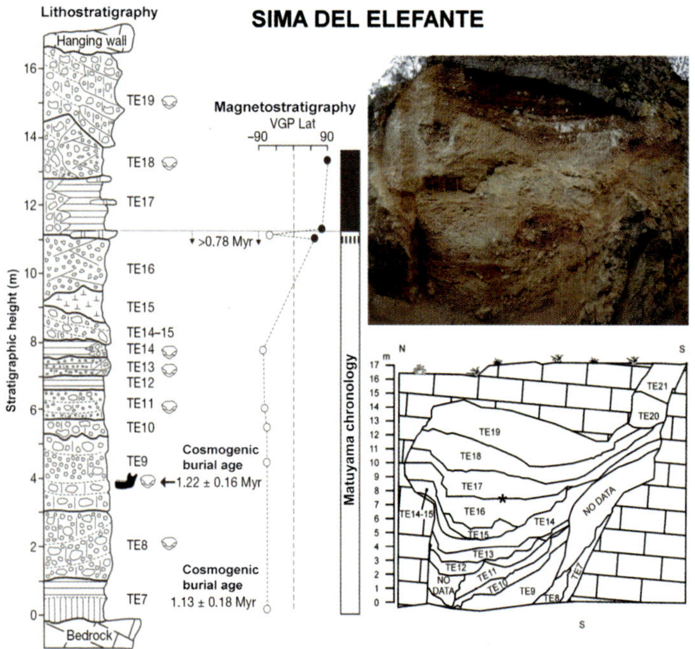

Figure 2. Stratigraphic section of Sima del Elefante. Asterisk marks position of Matuyama-Brunhes inversion. Height in metres from *Trinchera del Ferrocarril* floor. Synthetic stratigraphy shows location of U-Th and cosmogenic nuclide datings (Rosas et al., 2006; Carbonell et al., 2008).

Sima del Elefante

The *Sima del Elefante* site is the southernmost cave in the Trinchera del Ferrocarril. The first archaeo-palaeontological work here was in 1986 under Prof. Emiliano Aguirre, consisting of a test pit to determine the characteristics of the infill, its archaeological potential and a rough chronology for the sedimentary deposits. Systematic excavation of the site began in 1996, and has continued uninterrupted down to the present day across a 32 m^2 excavation area.

The stratigraphic succession at Sima del Elefante is 15 m wide, with a 25 metre thick and with high degree of heterogeneity due to lateral and vertical lithological changes. The sedimentary deposit is divided into 21 units, grouped in turn into three sedimentary phases. Phase I is the lowest in the sequence, from TE7 to TE14. Phase II contains units TE15 to TE19, inclusive. Finally, the most recent Phase III comprises Units TE20 and TE21 (Rosas *et al.*, 2001, 2006) (Fig. 2).

Palaeomagnetic analysis has detected polarity changes at the basis of unit TE17. Sediments below this unit from TE16 to TE7 have reversed polarity and have been assigned to the Matuyama subchron (> 780 ky) (Parés *et al.*, 2006). This is consistent with the results from the analysis of the U/Th uranium series of a stalagmite sample in the TE16-TE17 contact area, which shows a chronology of more than 400,000 years. Analysis of cosmogenic cores shows that the age of sublevel TE9c in Sima del Elefante is 1.22 ± 0.16 Myr (Carbonell *et al.*, 2008). These dates are consistent with biochronological data (Rofes and Cuenca-Bescós, 2006; Cuenca-Bescós and García 2007; García *et al.*, 2008).

On the basis of biochronological material, more recent units containing archaeo-palaeontological records of the site (TE18-TE19) have been attributed to the second half of the Middle Pleistocene, around 250-350 ky (OIS 9-8) (Rosas *et al.*, 2006, Lopez-García *et al.*, 2011). However, uranium series (U/Th) analysis of a stalagmitic crust from the roof of level TE18 has yielded two datings, 307 ± 19 ky and 255 ± 12 ky (Bischoff pers. comm.). These results suggest that level TE18 was formed during OIS 9 and 7, and that the chronology of TE19 is more recent than 255,000 ky.

Lower levels have yielded a rich faunal association including small animals such as birds, lagomorphs and beavers, as well as medium and large sized animals (Sánchez Marco, 2004; Cuenca-Bescós and García, 2007; García *et al.*, 2008; Van der Made, 2013) (Tab.1). The climatic and environmental reconstruction on the basis of faunal analysis indicates that the landscape around Sima del Elefante through the lower sequence (Lower Pleistocene) included open habitats dominated by moist, wooded areas, large areas with permanent water (Rosas *et al.*, 2006, Blain *et al.*, 2010 ;). In the upper units, equids remains are predominant, although remains of other herbivores and carnivores have also been found (Rosas *et al.*, 2001; Van der Made, *et al.*, 2003, 2013. Cuenca-García and Bescós, 2007) (Tab.1). For these units, the suggested landscape is a moist forest with open spaces and possibly drier and colder conditions than the Lower Pleistocene units (Rosas *et al.*, 2006; López-García *et al.*, 2011).

Evidence of human activity has been documented in the Middle Pleistocene units and also in the oldest units of Sima del Elefante. By 2013, 127 lithic artefacts had been located (Fig. 3).

To date, 86 stone artefacts have been recovered from the Lower Pleistocene Phase I units (TE7-TE14). The main raw material is chert (72.1%) of both Cretaceous and Neogene origin. Three quartz objects and some artefacts in Cretaceous limestone have also been found. All the raw materials could have been found within a 2 km radius of the site. The most represented categories are related to knapped products (flakes and flake fragments). However, there is a significant percentatge (34.9%) indeterminable objects. due to the poor preservation of the Neogene chert. Only four cores (one of them a core fragment) have been found amongst the Lower Pleistocene assemblage. These cores bear evidence of short knapping sequences, based on longitudinal removals. The knapped products have different morphologies but are generally small, averaging 32 x 30 x 9 mm for complete flakes. We have also found a few knapping products with centripetal removals. Retouched tools have only been found in units TE13 (n=3) and TE14 (n=1). These retouched flakes are slightly larger than the average non-retouched items, and have been classified as sidercrapers (n=2) and notches (n=2). In 2013, a chert flake was unearthed in unit TE8, the oldest evidence of human activity found to date in Atapuerca. In the Lower Pleistocene units, no pebble tools, handaxes or cleavers have been found. This assemblage has been assigned to Mode 1 (Carbonell *et al.*, 2008; Ollé *et al.*, 2013). Some of the faunal remains (0.6%) from these lower units (TE7-TE14) bear signs of anthropogenic modifications (cut marks and breakage). Most of the remains with cut marks are from ungulates, specifically deer and bison. We have also identified human activity on small animals such as birds, rabbits and turtles (Blasco *et al.*, 2011, Huguet, 2013). These marks are found in all anatomical areas, from the appendicular skeleton through the axial skeleton to the skull. Some ungulate long bones were fractured by hominins in order to access nutritional resources inside the bone. The distribu-

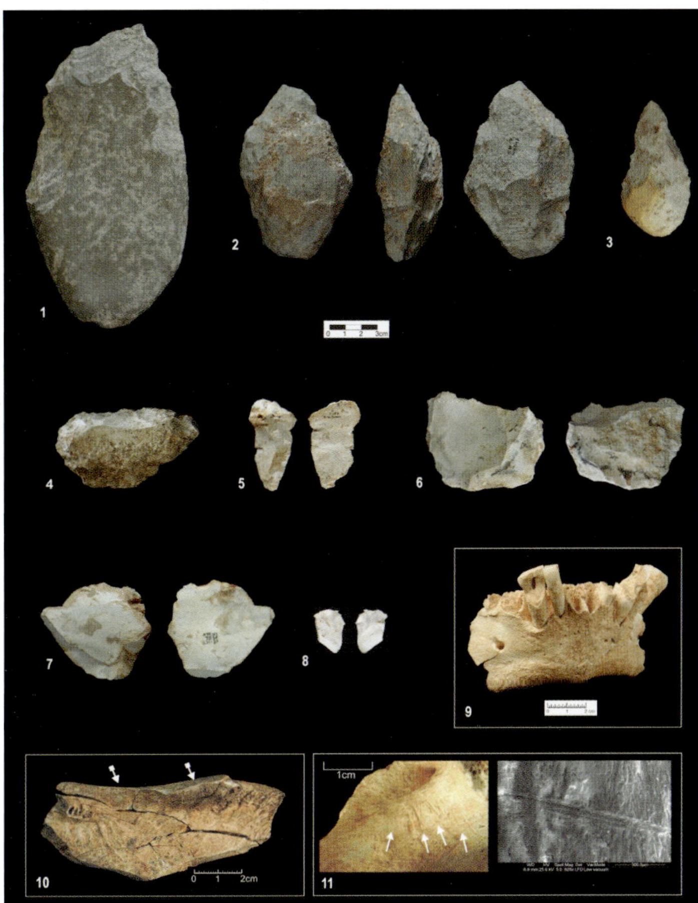

Figure 3. Archaeo-palaentological material from Sima del Elefante. 1: Cleaver-like tool (Unit TE18, Sandstone). 2: Sandstone handaxe (Unit TEsup), 3: Quartzite point (TEsup), 4: Retouched flake (sidescraper) of Neogene chert (TE19), 5: Retouched flake (sidescraper) of Cretaceous chert (TE13), 6: Cretaceous chert core (TE9c), 7: Cretaceous chert flake (TE9c), 8: Cretaceous chert flake (knapping debris) (TE9c), 9: *Homo* sp. mandible (TE9c), 10: Macromammal bone with evidence of fresh fracture (arrows) (TE9c), 11: Left, cut marked bovid vertebra (TE9c); right, electron microscope detail of cut marked bovid mandible (TE9c)(Photos: A. Ollé/J.Mestre/R.Huguet/IPHES).

	TE19	GIII	GIIb	GIIa	TD10.1	TD10.2	TD10.3	SH	TD8	TD7	TD6.1	TD6.2	TD6.3	TD5	TD3-4-5?	TD3-TD4	TE14	TE13	TE12	TE11	TE10	TE9	TE8	TE7
Equus cf. *hydruntinus*		x	x		x	x																		
Capreolus priscus					x	x	x																	
Stephanorinus cf. *hemioechus*	x	x	x	x	x	x	x																	
Bison sp. (small)		x	x	x		x	x																	
Cervus elaphus priscus	ssp.	x	x	x	x	x	x																	
Equus ferus	x	x	x	x	x	x	x																	
Dama dama clactoniana	ssp.	x	x	x	x	x	x																	
Hemitragus bonali		x	x	x																				
Megaloceros solilhacus sspp.		x	x	x																				
Bison schoetensacki	x				x																			
Praeovibos cf. *priscus*										x														
Mammuthus sp.												x										cf.		
Cervidae indet.																			x	x	x	x	x	
Cervus elpahus cf. *acoronatus*									x		x	x	x		x	x								
Eucladoceros giulii									x			x	x			x								
Hippopotamus									x								x							
Stephanorhinus etruscus									x	x	x	x	x	x	x	x	cf.							cf.
Sus scrofa									x			x			cf.							sp.		
Bison cf. *voigtstedtensis*									x		x	x	x	x	x	x	sp.		sp.			sp.		
Macaca					x				x			x										x		x
Equus altidens									x	cf.	cf.	x	x	x	cf.	x	cf.	cf.				cf.		cf.
Dama vallonnetensis									x	x		x	x	x	x	x	x				x	x		x
Mustelidae indet.					x																			
Martes martes								x																
Mestela putorius		x	x	x		x		x																
Muestela nivalis		x	x	x				x																
Canidae indet.	x				x																			
Cuon alpinus europaes		x	x	x	x																			
Canis lupus				x	x	x		x																
Felis sylvestris		x				cf.		x																
Panthera sp.						x		x																
Panthera leo	sp.	x	x	x	x	x	x	x																
Vulpes vulpes	x	x	x	x	x	x	x	x																
Ursus sp.					x		x		x	x														x
Hyaena sp.									x	x														
Ursus deningeri	sp.	cf.																						
Lynx pardinus spelaeus		x	x	x				x																
Meles meles			x	x	x			x						sp.										
Homoterium sp.							x							x										
Canis mosbachensis									x			x	x	x		x								
Vulpes praeglacialis												x	x	sp.		sp.								
Crocuta crocuta									x	x	x	x	x	x		ssp.								
Panthera gombaszoegensis									x					x		x			x			x		
Mustela palerminea												x		sp.						x		x		
cf. *Baranogale antiqua*																			x			x		
Lynx cf. *issiodorensis*																			x	x		x		
Lynx sp.						x				x		x	x	x		x	cf.				x	x		
Pannonictis cf. *nestii*																						x		
Canis sp.(*arnensis/mosbachensis*)																	x	x	x	x	x	x		
Vulpes cf.*V. alopecoides*																	x		x		x	x		
Ursus dolinensis											sp.	sp.	sp.	x		x	x							

Table 1. Stratigraphic distribution of carnivores, ungulates, sub-ungulates and primates at Atapuerca Pleistocene sites (from Rodríguez *et al.*, 2011; van der Made, 2013).

tion and location of the cut marks and fractures indicate that human groups had different activities in the butchering chain. The identification of these activities shows that hominins had primary access to some of the animals that they consumed. The bird, rabbit and carnivore remains found in anatomic connection in the lower units of Sima del Elefante indicate an excellent state of conservation of the fossils found in this cave. However, macromammal remains are scarce and fragmentary. If hominins had processed their prey inside the cave, we would expect to find a large number of anatomical elements of their prey, but the anatomical representation of animals indicates otherwise. The faunal remains thus suggest that most of the anatomical assemblage is the result of low intensity occupations, possibly located near the cave entrance (Huguet *et al.*, 2007).

The units in Phase I of the sedimentary infill generally have similar dynamics to the anthropic record recovered to date. However, special mention must be made of level TE9c (1.22 ± 0.16 Ma). At this level, in addition to indirect evidence of human presence, three hominin fossils were found: a mandible, a phalanx and a humerus fragment. These remains were provisionally attributed to *H. antecessor* (Carbonell *et al.*, 2008, Bermúdez de Castro *et al.*, 2010a), however after a comparative morphological analysis of the mandible, Bermúdez de Castro *et al.*, (2011) concluded that its attribution to any known taxon is unclear, and thus suggested that it should be referred to as *Homo sp.* Along with these human remains, faunal remains with signs of anthropic intervention and 33 stone objects were found.

Units TE18-TE19 at this site (Middle Pleistocene) have yielded 41 artefacts, the majority from unit TE19 (n=36). Only one stone tool has been found on TE18, along with four objects whose exact origin is unknown, as they were taken from the stratigraphic section in this part of the sequence. Middle Pleistocene material includes a considerable use of sandstone (39.3%) followed by quartzite (34.1%) and Neogene chert (24.4%). Knapped products, retouched flakes and hammerstones predominate in this lithic assemblage, along with four cores. The predominant knapping strategies are unifacial and unidirectional, but there is also evidence of centripetal knapping in some products. To date no evidence has been found on these levels of the use of knapping methods involving a predetermined morphology of the products, such as Levallois or discoidal, for example. Most of the configured tools were found in unit TE19. The largest proportion of morphotypes are sidescrapers and denticulates. There is also a large unifacial pebble tool from TE18, with a similar morphology to a cleaver. A sandstone handaxe was found on TE Sup, as well as a point and a cleaver, both knapped with quartzite. The lithic industry found on the Middle Pleistocene levels has been tentatively ascribed to Mode 2 (Acheulean). The faunal remains found in these upper units have not been analyzed in depth due to the poor state of the material, although a preliminary list of fauna has been drafted (Table 1). However, Rosas *et al.*, (2004) have presented several working hypotheses concerning the origin of the fossil assemblage in unit TE19, including the possibility that this unit acted as a trap for animals attracted by water or fresh grass. The presence of the taxon *Ursidae* might be related to the use of the cave for hibernation.

Gran Dolina

The *Gran Dolina* site (TD) is an 18 metre thick cave infill. Its stratigraphic succession was initially divided into 11 units, TD1 to TD11 from base to top (Gil and Hoyos, 1987; Parés and Pérez-González, 1999. Pérez-González *et al.*, 2001), which were later revised slightly (Rodríguez *et al.*, 2011) (Fig. 4). The first systematic archaeological excavations were carried out between 1981 and 1989 in a 30 m^2 area on level TD10 level. Between 1990 and 1991, work focused on TD3-4, the earliest levels with evidence of human activity. A 9 m^2 test pit initiated in 1993 confirmed the presence of palaeontological material at every level of Gran Dolina, except for endo-karstic infills on TD1-2.

The results of this test pit led to the start of the horizontal excavation of Gran Dolina from 1996 onwards, which covered an area of more than 95 m^2 (Fig. 5). In 2001, excavation began on a series of overhangs in the western part of this site due to the threat of their collapse. This work recovered material from levels TD4 to TD10. At present, level TD10.3 (approx. 90 m^2) is being excavated horizontally along with the overhang of TD3-4 (approx. 8 m^2).

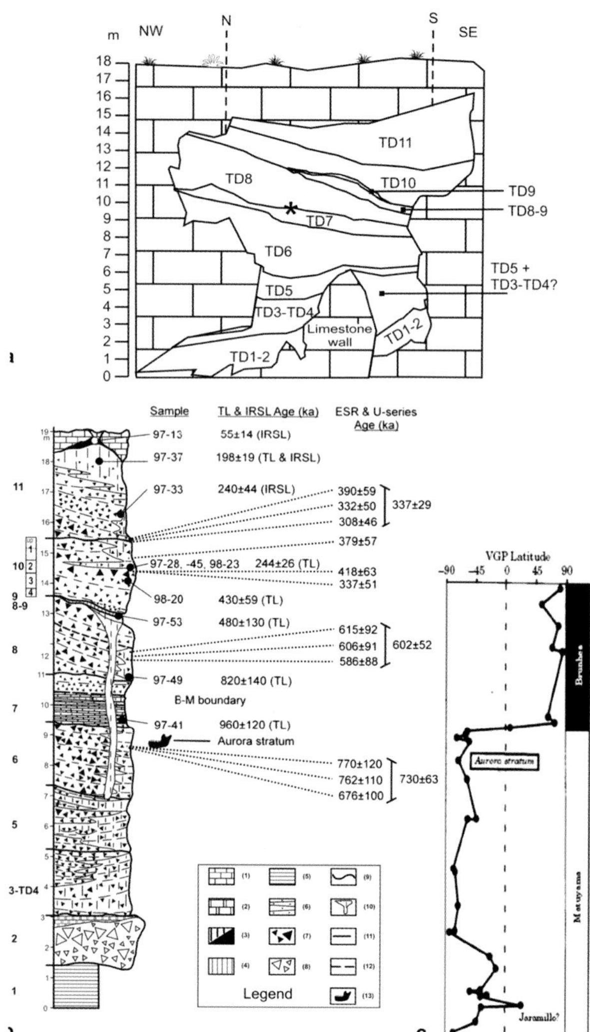

Figure 4. a. Stratigraphic section of Gran Dolina. Asterisk marks position of Matuyama-Brunhes boundary. Height in metres from Trinchera del Ferrocarril floor; b. Synthetic stratigraphy shows location of TL, IRSL and ESR/UTh datings, from Falguères *et al.*, (1999); Berger *et al.*, (2008) and Falguères *et al.*, (2013). Legend: (1) Mesozoic limestone from Gran Dolina roof; (2) speleothem (3) mudstone, clayey silt/terra rossa; (4) bat guano; (5) laminated silty clay; (6) calcilutites and calcarenites; (7) gravel and cobbles and clast flow (8) position of fallen cobbles; (9) principal stratigraphic discontinuity; (10) secondary discordance and silt-sand-clay infill; (11) Matuyama-Brunhes boundary; (12) disappearance of *Mimomys savini* and first appearance of *Iberomys brecciensis*; (13) Position of *Aurora* stratum; c, Palaeolatitude of virtual geomagnetic pole of Gran Dolina stratigraphic section. Each point is a mean Fisher direction of individual samples. The Matuyama-Brunhes boundary is in stratigraphic unit TD7 (Parés and Pérez-González, 1999). Figure modified from Ollé *et al.*, (2013).

The Lower Pleistocene record

Over 1,300 faunal remains of herbivores and carnivores (Table 1) have been recovered from unit TD3-4. Amongst the latter, the most frequent is the bear species *Ursus dolinensis* (García and Arsuaga, 2001). These animals used the cave regularly for hibernation, as evidenced by numerous remains and claw marks on the walls. However, this pit was a natural trap for ungulates which died when they fell in. Predator activity around these herbivore carcasses was uncommon. Some of the faunal remains show cut marks, and anthropogenic fractures suggest that human groups entered the cave to exploit the fallen ungulates and thus had primary access. Carnivore tooth marks have also been documented. Remains of felines (*Panthera gombaszoegensis*) and small dogs (*Canis sp.*) suggests that these predators may have been responsible for the tooth marks (Rosell, 1998; Huguet *et al.*, 2013). A small collection of tools, primarily quartzite, has been recovered from this sedimentary deposit. The objects show simple working sequences, essentially reduced to obtain flakes from unipolar strategies and rough configuration of cobble choppers (Carbonell *et al.*, 2001, Rodríguez, 2004). Unit TD5 shows different types of operation. The remains documented from this unit have different origins. On the one hand, carnivores were quite active. One of the most important taxa are hyaenids, which occupied the unit as a den, with documented remains of their prey and also some coprolites. In unit TD5, some of the remains also arrived by gravitational processes (Huguet, 2007; Saladié, 2009). In subunit TD6.3, remains of hyena (*Crocuta crocuta*) and their prey bearing numerous tooth marks and modifications during digestion permit the inference that these animals used the site as a den (Fernández-Díaz, 2013). In both units (TD5 and TD6.3) occupation by hyaenids alternated with ursids, which used the cave to hibernate. Hominins also occupied the cave, alternating with both carnivores to a lesser extent than at the next level up (Saladié, 2009, Fernández-Díaz, 2013).

Subunit TD6.2 is the result of an anthropogenic assemblage where a large collection of archaeo-palaeontological remains was found, including more than 180 hominin remains. Thermoluminescence and simulated infrared luminescence dating for this assemblage is 960 ± 120

Figure 5. Horizontal excavation of level TD10, 2007 dig (Photos: J. Mestre/IPHES).

ky (Berger *et al.*, 2008). Palaeoenvironmental and palaeoclimatic studies indicate that overall, unit TD6 corresponded to a period with an interglacial climate, holartic vegetation and abundant resources (García Antón, 1998; Cuenca-Bescós *et al.*, 1999. Burjachs, 2002; Rodríguez *et al.*, 2011).

The human remains found in unit TD6 at Gran Dolina were assigned to a newly described species, *Homo antecessor,* which was proposed as the last common ancestor of modern humans and Neanderthals (Bermúdez de Castro *et al.*, 1997). During the last decade, the TD6 human hypodigm has increased, permitting advances in the taxonomic and phylogenetic characterization of this species. *H. antecessor* has a number of features suggesting its "modernity", such as a cranial capacity of more than 1,000 cc, a modern tooth growth pattern (Bermúdez de Castro *et al.*, 2010b) and a modern face in both its aspect and its growth forms (Bermúdez de Castro *et al.*, 1997, Lacroix *et al.*, 2013.). The TD6 hominins also shared some features of the postcranial skeleton with *Homo sapiens* (Carretero *et al.*, 1999). Several features which were hitherto considered typical and unique to the Neanderthal lineage have been identified in the TD6 human remains, including humerus (Bermudez de Castro *et al.*, 2012) and, more particularly, teething (Martinón-Torres *et al.*, 2006, 2007; Gomez-Robles *et al.*, 2007, Martinón-Torres *et al.*, 2007). Recent studies suggest that *H. antecessor* may be a European lineage of Asian origin, close to the divergence point between *H. sapiens* and *H. neanderthalensis* (Martinón-Torres *et al.*, 2007, 2011, , Bermúdez de Castro and Martinón-Torres 2013).

Zooarchaeological analyses have detected frequent cut marks and anthropogenic bone breakage on the remains found at this level (Fig. 6), indicating that the hominins who occupied TD6.2 actively accessed the prey that they brought to Gran Dolina (Saladié *et al.*, 2011). Remains of *H. antecessor* are amongst their prey. This is the oldest case of anthropogenic cannibalism known to date (Fernández-Jalvo *et al.*, 1996), which current stratigraphic evidence suggests took place over a long time sequence (Carbonell *et al.*, 2010). Anthropogenic modifications to *H. antecessor* and deer on level TD6.2 suggest that the butchering process was the same for both taxa, and that the remains were also discarded on the floor of the habitat in the same way. In this context, the consumption of infants and immature individuals was common. This age profile is similar to the one associated with episodes of intergroup aggression in chimpanzees. These parallels permit cannibalism in TD6 to be linked to low-risk attacks on individuals, possibly in order to defend and expand the resource provisioning territory against other neighbouring groups (Saladié *et al.*, 2012).

The *H. antecessor* remains also show certain peculiarities, such as the lack of activity by carnivores and better preserved axial and brittle bones than the other animals in the assemblage. This feature seems related to the different types of occupation that took place during the formation of TD6.2 and the episodes of cannibalism. This investigation suggests that the Lower Pleistocene hominins were at the top of the food chain and were able to control the competition that might arise from other groups of congeners or other predators in the same ecological niche (Saladié *et al.*, 2014). In this regard, Huguet *et al.*, (2013) propose that the groups of hominins which inhabited Sierra de Atapuerca during the Lower Pleistocene had a high degree of control over their territory and its resources.

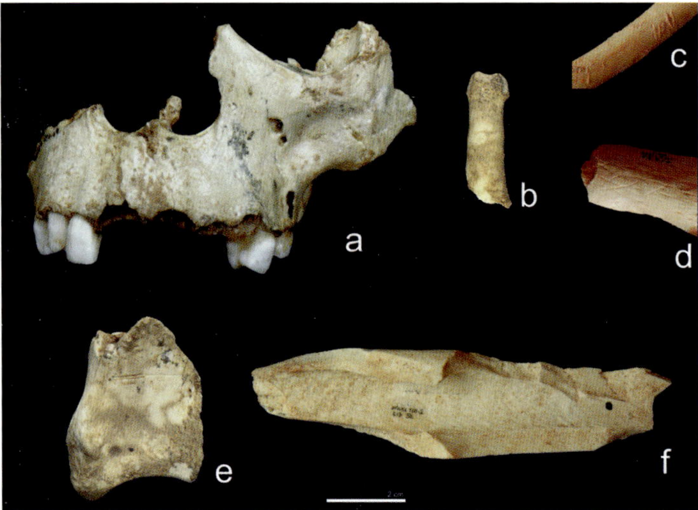

Figure 6. a) *Homo antecessor* jaw with percussion stigma. b) *H. antecessor* proximal phalanx with cut marks. c) *H. antecessor* rib processed during corpse defleshing. d) Striations on *H. antecessor* tibia fragment produced while Achilles heel was being cut. e) Equine phalanx with cut marks produced during skinning. f) Deer radius with removals during fracturing to access bone marrow (Photos: P. Saladié/ IPHES).

Evidence of the stone tools in this assemblage is much more representative numerically than the above-mentioned units (Fig. 7) (Carbonell *et al.*, 1999, Rodríguez, 2004, Ollé *et al.*, 2013.). For the first time, there is a full range of suitable rocks for working in the Atapuerca area. Chert -both Neogene and Cretaceous- is the predominant material, followed by quartzite, quartzarenite, sandstone, quartz and limestone. A degree of planning can be observed in the way these resources were managed, with all stages of the lithic production chains present (hammerstones, cores, flakes, retouched flakes and knapping debris). The reduction strategies are varied (longitudinal unipolar, centripetal and occasionally bipolar on anvil), and all seem to be aimed at the systematic production of small and medium format artefacts. This is the first point in the Atapuerca sequence where retouch is used systematically to make tools in the form of denticulates, notches and, to a much lesser extent, sidescrapers. To date, the only evidence of large-format tools is a single sandstone chopper.

Level TD7 marks a major shift in the dynamics of the cave. This level consists of limestone gravel, giving way laterally to silt. The action of water thus seems to mark the overall dynamics of the cave in this period. This level has only yielded remains of *Stephanorhinus etruscus* and *Praeovibos* in anatomical connection, suggesting that the natural trap in the roof of the cave was reactivated (Rosell and Blasco, 2009). The only lithic item recovered is a small quartz flake.

The Middle Pleistocene record

In the Gran Dolina sedimentary succession, the Matuyama-Brunhes palaeomagnetic boundary is located at the top of unit TD7 (Parés and Pérez-González, 1995, 1999). The Middle Pleistocene archaeo-palanteological fossil record in Gran Dolina therefore consists of units TD8, TD8-9, TD9 and TD10. Each of these units has specific features which show that the cave was sometimes used by carnivores as a den and in others, as a base for Preneandertal occupations.

The palaeomagnetic data combined with ESR and uranium series situate unit TD8 at the beginning of the Middle Pleistocene, *circa* 600 ky BP (Falguères *et al.*, 1999, 2013; Parés and Pérez-González, 1999). This unit contains a large, diverse range of ungulates and carnivores, predominantly fallow deer (*Dama vallonnetensis*) and occasional remains of carnivores (Table 1). The sample of fallow deer remains is characterized by the presence of appendicular and cranial items, with abundant carnivore tooth marks. They bear no signs of anthropogenic action and there is no lithic industry. According to Blasco *et al.*, (2011) these features suggest that the primary agent involved in this accumulation of ungulates were hyaenids. However, several factors do not fully correlate with some of the features traditionally used to define these carnivores' dens. In TD8 there are no immature carnivores, marks related to the final stages of carnivore consumption (e.g., intensive bone chewing, diaphyseal cylinders or hollowing), there is a low proportion of coprolites, an absence of an attritional mortality profile, and also many whole bones. According to Blasco *et al.*, (2011), this variation in the composition of the assemblage from what might be expected in a den is because the assemblage in TD8 might not be the exclusive result of the cave's use as a hyaenid den, but rather the product of the combination of several types of occupations, in the course of which it was occasionally accessed by other carnivores as well. Units TD8 and TD8/9 are currently a hiatus in the presence of anthropic activity in Gran Dolina. This is the only section with no evidence of material culture, as four lithic industry items have been found in the unit immediately above (TD9) (Ollé *et al.*, 2013), making this the first unit in Gran Dolina with evidence of human activity in the Middle Pleistocene, dated by TL at 480 ± 130ka.

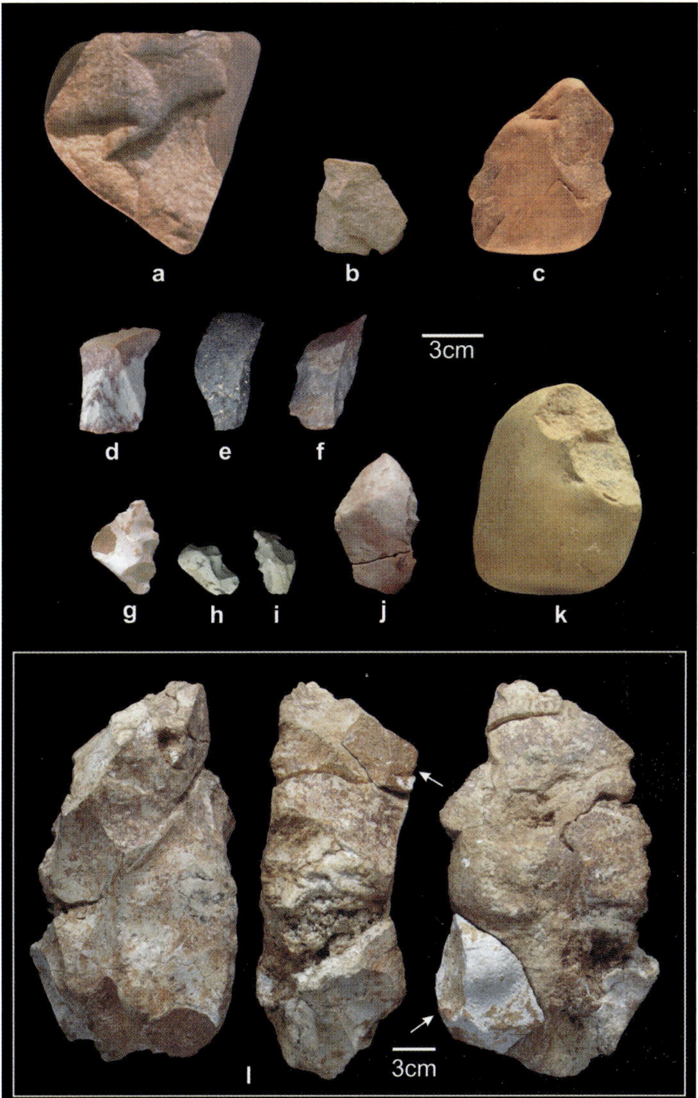

Figure 7. Lithic industry from TD4 (a-c) and TD6.2 (d-l). a) quartzite unipolar core; b) quartzite flake; c) quartzite chopper; d, e, f) quartzite flakes; g, h, i) retouched flakes (denticulates) in Cretaceous chert; j) quartzite retouched flake -refit of 2 items-; k) sandstone chopper; l) large Neogene chert core, with refit of 2 flakes (white flecks) (Photos A. Ollé/IPHES).

TD10 has the largest accumulation of archaeological remains in the entire Atapuerca complex. This unit is divided into 4 lithostratigraphic sub-units, identified from base to top as TD10.4 to TD10.1. The top two units (TD10.1 and TD10.2) are now fully excavated. Both sub-units have yielded large concentrations of archaeo-palaeontological material, with approximately 120,000 faunal remains and 35,000 lithic items recovered to date. This density of material shows an intense occupation of Sierra de Atapuerca by Preneandertal groups. The high level of activity by these hominins is confirmed by the different assemblages generated by occupations with a similar chronology at the nearby Galería and Sima de los Huesos sites. Geochronological tests of TD10 to date include a TL dating of 430 ± 59 ky for the top of subunit TD10.3, and a series of ESR/UTh datings including two for TD10.2 (418 ± 63 and 337 ± 51 ky), one for the base of TD10.1 (379 ± 57ka) and an average of 337 ± 29 ky for its top. However, a slightly discordant average TL date (244 ± 26 ky) has also been obtained for the lower part of unit TD10.2. The archaeo-stratigraphic sequence ends with an archaeologically sterile unit (TD11) dated between 240 ± 44 ky and 55 ± 14 ky (Falguères *et al.*, 1999. 2013, Berger *et al.*, 2008).

Figure 8. Lithic industry from TD10. a) centripetal chert core (TD10.2); b) unifacial centripetal core in quartzite (TD10.1); c) large bifacial tool in sandstone (TD10-2); d) small quartzite handaxe (TD10-1); e) quartzite double sidescraper (TD10-1); f) quartzite sidescraper (TD10-1); g) Cretaceous chert sidescraper (TD10-1); h) sandstone denticulate (TD10-1); i) Cretaceous chert denticulate; j) quartzite point (TD10-1) (Photos: A.Ollé/IPHES).

The technology of subunits TD10.2 and TD10.1 is characterized by diverse, standardized operating sequences and tool configuration (Fig. 8). Centripetal flake removal methods are predominant, along with some hierarchical cores and a somewhat predetermined size and shape in the products. The presence and degree of configuration of large standardized tools (handaxes and cleavers) is less than the assemblage documented at the Galería site, and instead there is a higher incidence of tools on small flakes which are moreover morphologically diverse and standardized. The rich archaeological level documented at TD10.1 could therefore reflect a local evolution from Mode 2 (Acheulean) to Mode 3 (Mousterian) in Sierra de Atapuerca. Finally, the top section of TD10.1 clearly shows a gradual decrease in the use of Gran Dolina. Technologically, it seems to follow the transitional trends identified in the rest of TD10.1.

In fauna, TD10.2 is a clear case of specialized hunting focused on the exploitation of bison (*Bison sp.*), as approximately 95% of the NISP (Number of Identified Specimens) and MNE (Minimum Number of Elements) correspond to these animals. In contrast, in sub-unit TD10.1 there is a broad spectrum of prey (Blasco *et al.*, 2013, Rodríguez-Hidalgo, in progress), with a predominance of ungulates such as deer and horses (Table 1) and also other animals such as small prey and a few carnivores (Blasco *et al.*, 2010, 2013). The information gathered from the analysis of the sub-units in TD10 excavated in their entirety to date suggests a wide variety of preneandertals' subsistence strategies at the end of the Acheulean.

Galería

The *Galería* site is 50 m south of Gran Dolina. It is divided into three sections: the central section (TG) linked to the north with a hall known as *Covacha de los Zarpazos* (TZ) and to the south with a vertical conduct known as Trinchera Norte (TN). The first archaeological works at the Galería site began in 1976. Systematic, excavations were developed from 1982 to 1995. From 2002 until 2010 the works were focused on TZ. Since then, the excavations have focused on sector TG-TN. Nowadays, the excavation area affects to more than 40m². The sedimentary infill at Galería consists of five lithostratigraphic units, identified from bottom to top as GI to GV (Pérez-González *et al.*, 1995, 2001). Archaeologically sterile Unit GI is the oldest, and consists of *facies* from the interior. Units GII and GIII are rich in lithic and faunal remains. Units GIV and GV ultimately clogged this cave. While the latter were initially sterile, in the latest work phase GIV has yielded over 100 items including stone tools and faunal remains (Fig. 9).

The Matuyama-Brunhes transition has been detected in GI, at the base of Galería (Pérez-González *et al.*, 1999). TL, IRSL and ESR datings for units GII to GIV (Berger *et al.*, 2008, Falguères *et al.*, 2013) suggest that it was formed between 500 and 250 ky. The speleothem that seals unit GIV in the central sector of TG has been dated at 118 +71/-49 ky and 200 ky by means of uranium-series and ESR respectively (Grün and Aguirre, 1987, Falguères *et al.*, 2013).

Galería has provided important evidence of human occupation, with a rich Mode 2 or Acheulean lithic assemblage associated with abundant faunal remains (Ollé *et al.*, 2005, 2013, Cáceres *et al.*, 2010, Cuenca-Bescós *et al.*, 2010, Rodríguez *et al.*, 2011, García-Medrano *et al.*, 2013). Two human fossils, a mandible and a skull fragments have been attributed to *H. heidelbergensis* (Bermúdez de Castro and Rosas, 1992; Arsuaga *et al.*, 1999a). (Fig. 10).

The lithic items in Galería were produced from 7 types of raw material, all found within 2 to 5 km of the site (García-Antón *et al.*, 2002.

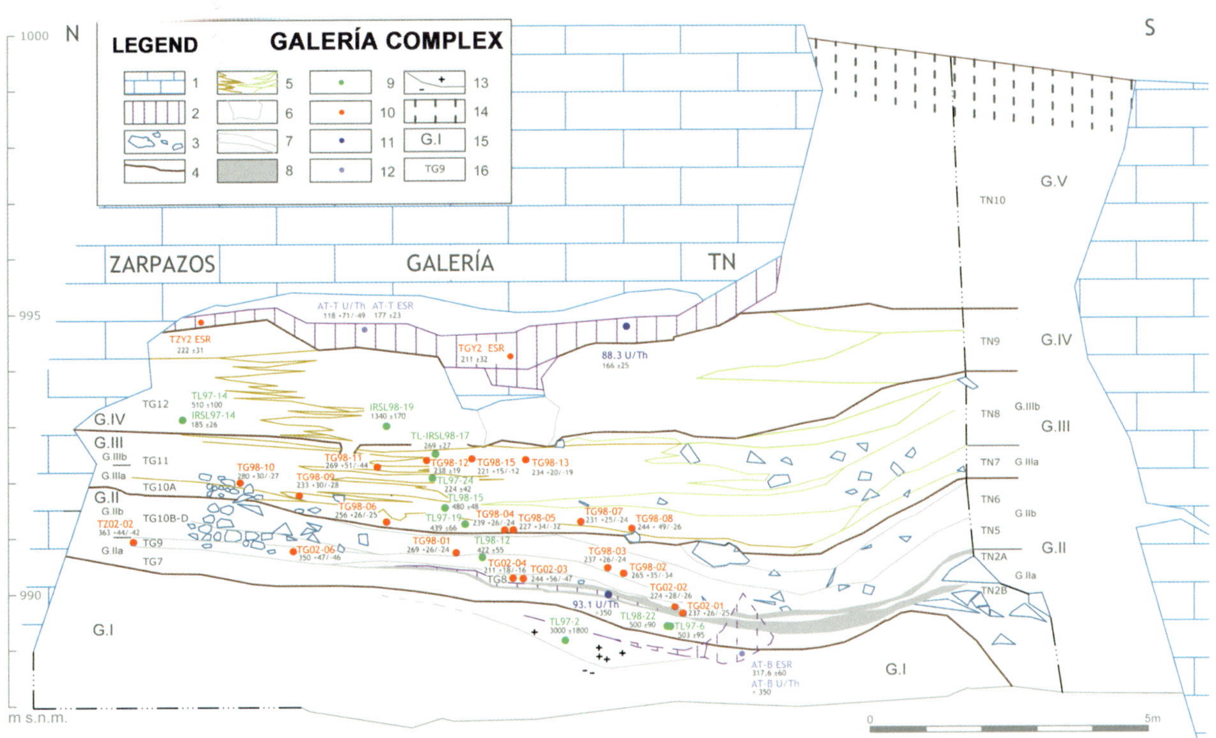

Figure 9. Galería stratigraphic sequence, showing location of luminescence, ESR and Useries samples. Legend: 1) Upper Cretaceous limestones and dolomites (Galería cave wall); 2) Speleothems; 3) Limestone blocks and cobbles; 4) Main stratigraphic unconformities 5) Lateral facies variations, from clay loam to gravels (left side of figure) and from gravels to breccia (right); 6) Cut and fill; 7) Limit of GII Unit layers; 8) Bat guano level; 9) Luminescence samples (Berger *et al.*, 2008); 10) ESR samples (Falguères *et al.*, 2013); 11) U/Th samples (Bischoff, published in Falguères *et al.*, 2013); 12) U/Th and ESR samples (Grün and Aguirre, 1987); 13) Matuyama-Bhrunes reversal (Pérez-González *et al.*, 1999); 14) Soil; 15) Allostratigraphic levels; 16) Archaeopalaeontological levels.

Figure 10. Above: General view of renewed Galería excavation (J.Mestre/IPHES). Centre (left to right: quartzite handaxe from TG07; quartzite cleaver from TN2B; quartzite sidescraper from GSU11 (Photo: P. García-Medrano/A. Ollé/IPHES). Below (left to right): Long bone fragment of medium-sized animal from GSU10 with cut marks interrupted by carnivore tooth marks; deer sacrum with carnivore tooth marks from TN6 (Photos: I. Cáceres/IPHES).

García-Antón and Mosquera, 2007). Neogene chert is most abundant, followed by quartzite and sandstone. Other material such as Cretaceous chert, limestone, quartz and schist, have a minority presence. The operative chains are highly fragmented and the knapping sequences are mainly allochthonous. The knapping inside the cave was aimed to solve specific requirements, and was highly expeditious. Most of the artefacts were produced outside the cave (Mosquera, 1995, Carbonell *et al.*, 2001, Ollé, 2003; Ollé *et al.*, 2005, 2013, García-Medrano, 2011, García-Medrano *et al.*, 2013, 2014; Terradillos, 2010; Terradillos and Rodríguez, 2012). The best represented exploitation methods are multipolar centripetal and unipolar longitudinal, reflected by products and cores. Also, other strategies such as multipolar orthogonal have been documented. Knapped products are the most common structural catergory. Large cutting tools are well represented, although the small and medium formats are predominant (scrapers, denticulate and tips) (Carbonell *et al.*, 2001). In the earliest levels (GIIa), the large tools are mainly made on quartzite cobbles, while from GIIb onwards, the large tools are made on Neogene chert and sandstone flakes (García-Medrano, 2011, García-Medrano, *et al.*, 2014).

The main uses of the tools were for butchering, although work on hides and, to a lesser extent, plant material has also been identified (Márquez *et al.*, 2001. Ollé, 2003). The majority of the faunal remains in Galería are from herbivores, with a major presence of deer, horses and, in smaller numbers, bovines and rhinoceros. Carnivore remains are scarce, (Rodríguez *et al.*, 2011) (Table 1). Galería also has a good representation of micromammals (Cuenca-Bescós *et al.*, 2010) and birds (Sánchez Marco, 1999).

The most part of herbivores anatomical representation are axial and cranial elements, with few remains from the appendicular skeleton. These skeletons are from 219 individuals of all ages, with a slightly greater abundance of immature than adult and senile individuals.

These remains show abundant evidence of carnivore intervention (tooth marks) and less human intervention (cut marks and fractures). Nevertheless, the faunal association at Galería does not match the expected pattern of an assemblage originated by hominins or carnivores. The taphonomic features suggest that Galería did not meet the environmental conditions appropriated to the establishment of human occupations, nor was it used as a carnivore den (Cáceres *et al.*, 2010). The origin of this accumulation was the vertical conduct in TN, which acted as a natural trap for herbivores. Fallen animals attracted the attention of carnivores and hominins alike to exploit these meat resources (Díez *et al.*, 1999. Huguet *et al.*, 2001. Cáceres,

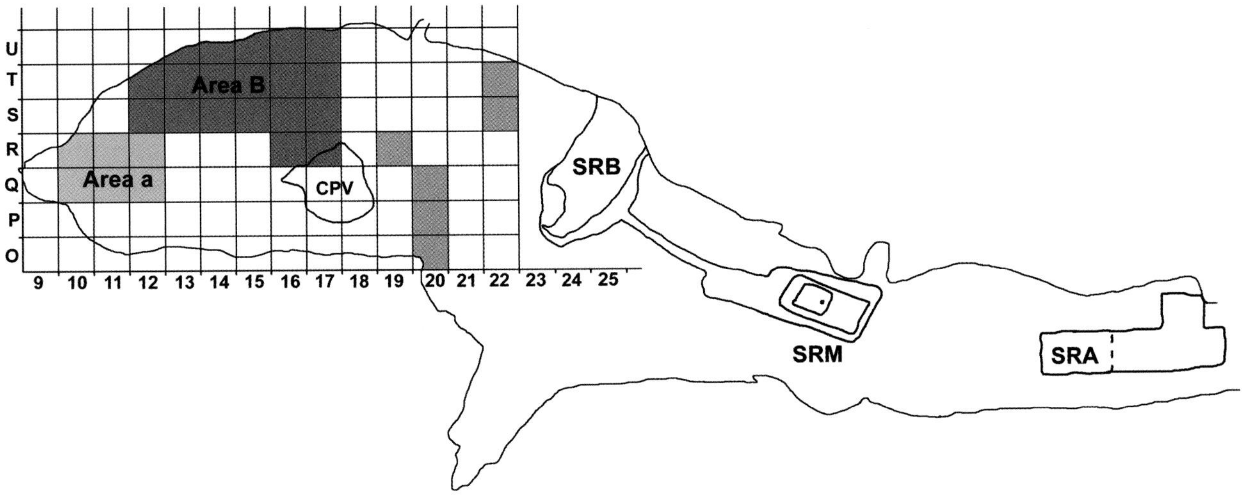

Figure 11. Sima de los Huesos plan showing location of each excavation area (Arsuaga *et al.*, 1997b).

2002; Cáceres *et al.*, 2010). Carnivores, mainly canids, prioritized the *in situ* carcass consumption, sometimes with secondary access to the carcasses left by the humans. On the other hand, hominins usually had a primary access and processed the animals in order to transport them out from Galería in either skeletal segments in the case of large animals or whole animals when permitted by their weight. This type of strategy suggests that these preneandertals had a deep knowledge of the environment and a good planning and organizational capacity.

Cueva Mayor

The entrance to the complex known as *Cueva Mayor-Cueva del Silo* (Martín-Merino, 1981) is less than a kilometre from the Trinchera del Ferrocarril sites. There have been several sedimentary infill chronologies in this complex which have yielded archaeo-palaeontological remains.

Sima de los Huesos

The *Sima de los Huesos* site lies inside the Cueva Mayor-Cueva del Silo karst system (Arsuaga *et al.*, 1997a). Sima de los Huesos (SH) is roughly 500 metres from the entrance to Cueva Mayor, at the bottom of a 13 metre vertical shaft. There are two parts to this cave: the ramp and the site itself. The former consists of an approx. 10 metre long ramp on a 30 ° slope which descends to a small chamber 5 metres below. The second part consists of a roughly 8 metre long by 3 metre wide chamber. Three stratigraphic test digs have been conducted on the ramp, named SRA (Sima Ramp Upper Test), SRM (Sima Ramp Middle Test) and SRB (Sima Ramp Bottom Test) (Fig. 11). Two excavation areas have been distinguished in Sima de los Huesos (Area A and Area B).

The Sima de los Huesos stratigraphy has been studied by Arsuaga *et al.*, (1997a), Bischoff *et al.*, (2003, 2007) and Sala (2012) (Fig. 12). It is summarized in the following units or episodes, listed from bottom to top:

Episode 1

The lowest unit in Sima de los Huesos consists of a layer of clayey marl, observed at the base of the SRA, SRM, SRB and Sima de los Huesos stratigraphic sequences. In Sima de los Huesos, above these marls there is a layer of water-borne sand and silt (Bischoff *et al.*, 2007).

Episode 2

Consists of breccia and plastic clays of different colour. This unit contains layers of sterile red clay, clay breccia with bear and human bones, and fossil-bearing yellowish brown clay breccia. These are the levels where human remains were found alongside carnivore remains.

Episode 3

The final sedimentary unit consists of a speleothem on the ramp which covered the previous deposits. Throughout the ramp, the speleothem is covered by a layer of dark brown clay up to 20 cm thick, which includes a dark layer of bat dung. Bischoff *et al.*, (2003, 2007) conducted several SRA datings of the speleothems in Episode 3, which covers the entire fossil assemblage. Bischoff *et al.*, (2007) estimated a minimum age of 530,000 years for the speleothem. New analyses are currently underway to confirm this chronology and the stratigraphic relationship between the speleothem and the human fossils.

Sima de los Huesos has yielded the world's largest and most comprehensive assemblage of human fossils from the Middle Pleistocene, with approximately 5,000 items recovered to date from at least 28 individuals. Most are adolescents or young adults, with very few children or senile individuals. The human representation from Sima de los Huesos includes every part of the skeleton (Arsuaga *et al.*, 1997b). These fossils have been attributed to a single biological population inserted amongst the hominin ancestors of the Neanderthals, the species *Homo heidelbergensis* (Arsuaga *et al.*, 1993, 1997b).

Morphologically, the fossils from Sima de los Huesos exhibit many primitive features that are not present in Neanderthals (Arsuaga *et al.*, 1993, 1997b). They also bear some derived Neanderthal traits in the facial skeleton (Arsuaga *et al.*, 1997b), teeth (Martinón-Torres *et al.*, 2012) and postcranial bones (Carretero *et al.*, 1997; Arsuaga *et al.*, 1999b, Bonmatí *et al.*, 2010).

Mitochondrial DNA analysis of samples from a Sima de los Huesos *H. heidelbergensis* femur shows that this group of hominins is genetically closer to the Denisovan population that lived in Siberia 40,000 BP than the Neanderthals (Meyer *et al.*, 2013).

The current working hypothesis is that the Sima de los Huesos site was generated by a deliberate accumulation of corpses by other humans (Arsuaga *et al.*, 1997a, Arsuaga and Martínez,

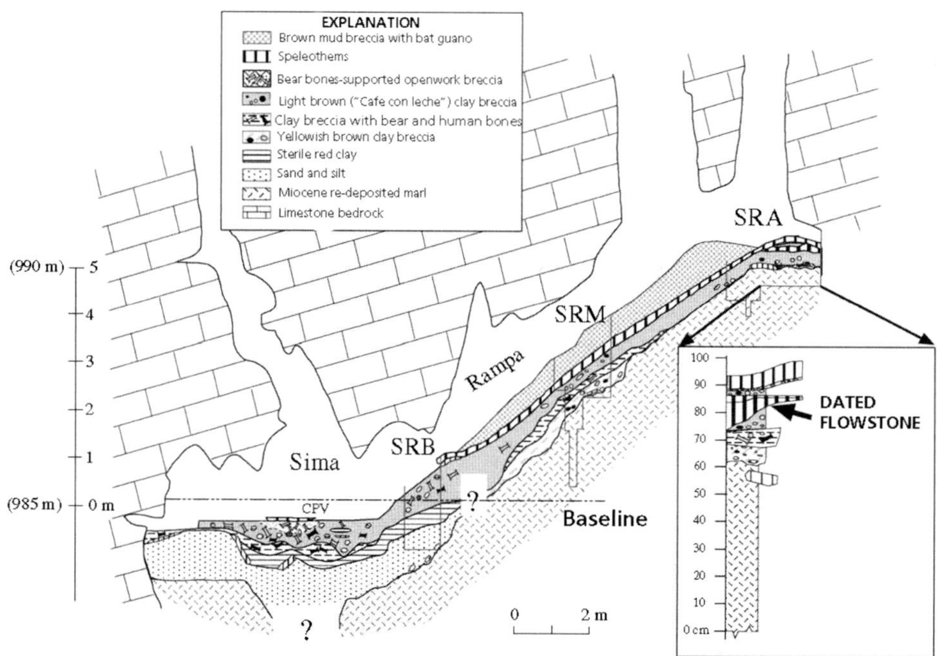

Figure 12. Stratigraphic diagram of Sima de los Huesos and stratigraphic column of Upper Sima Ramp (SRA) (Bischoff *et al.*, 2007).

2004). Although the distribution of these individuals' ages at death does not show the attritional profile expected of a cemetery, there are many feasible explanations for the deliberate accumulation of corpses with the age distribution found here (Arsuaga and Martínez, 2004). In Sima de los Huesos, no herbivore remains have been found alongside the human and carnivore fossils, and only one lithic item has been recovered (Carbonell *et al.*, 2003). Due to the unique context of this handaxe, Carbonell *et al.*, (2003) argue that this might be evidence of symbolic behaviour in this Middle Pleistocene population (Carbonel and Mosquera, 2006). In addition to the human remains, Sima de los Huesos has also yielded numerous remains of carnivores and mammals (Cuenca-Bescós *et al.*, 1997, Cuenca-Bescós and García 2007, García *et al.*, 1997, García, 2003) (Tab.1).

El Portalón

El Portalón is one of the current entrances to the Cueva Mayor-Cueva del Silo karst system, approx. 1040 m asl. It never became fully clogged by external sediment. The large, well-preserved stratigraphic sequence (over 9 metres) of this entrance porch is an exceptional site for the study of recent prehistory (the last 10,000 years) as it documents a wide range of human activities during this period. Almost nothing has been published about the excavations in the late 1960's and 70's. Fresh work by the Atapuerca Research Team in 2000 discovered a much broader stratigraphic sequence than the previously known strata, which has been divided into two major sedimentary units (Fig. 13). The lower unit (Upper Pleistocene) contains a significant palaeontological record but very few traces of human activity in the form of small flakes. The upper unit

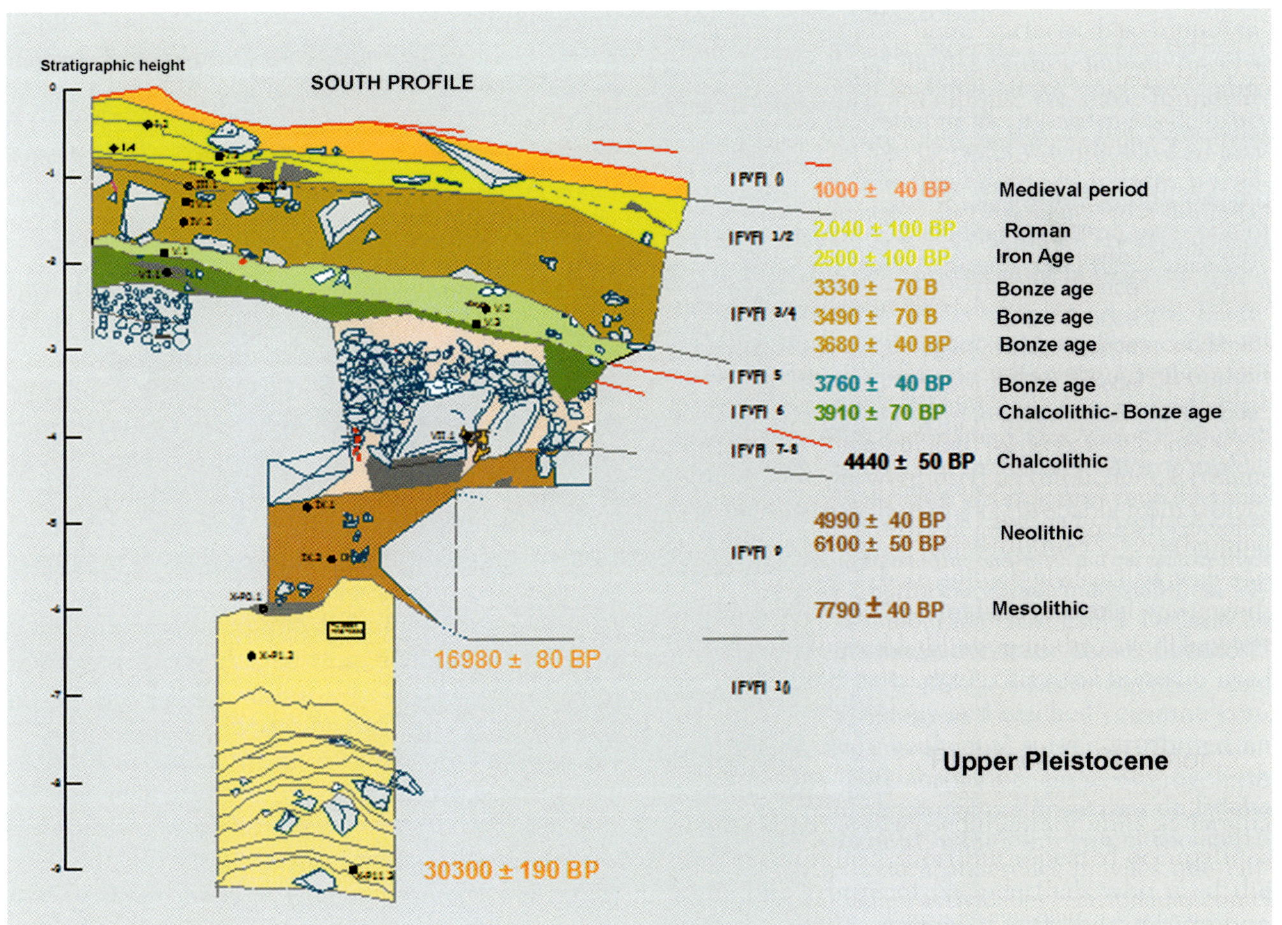

Figure 13: Stratigraphic column of Portalón South profile showing radiocarbon dates and associated cultural periods (modified from Carretero *et al.*, 2008).

(Holocene) has a homogeneous sediment with abundant evidence of material culture. Its human occupations are Medieval, Roman, Iron Age, different stages of the Bronze Age, Chalcolithic, Neolithic and Mesolithic. The relevance of this new sequence in Portalón is due to the paucity of information about the Upper Palaeolithic, Mesolithic and Neolithic in inland Iberia, particularly on the Northern Plateau (Carretero *et al.*, 2008).

Although Portalón occupations in the Middle Ages, the Roman Empire and the Iron Age were sporadic, surprising material has been found, including an Almohad gold coin from the 13th century, the only one known is this region (Pérez-Romero *et al.*, 2010, 2013). The Bronze Age occupation (2nd millennium BC) was intense, with thousands of pottery shards from everyday materials- plates, bowls, pots, large jars, cheese containers and pitchers. Some of the items were etched and decorated with great care, an indication of the intentions and identity of the manufacturer and the special nature of the ceramics, probably related to prestige or ritual. There are also dozens of items in bone, antler and ivory (Alday *et al.*, 2011) used in everyday activities (spatulas, spoons, astonishing needles and awls) and personal or ritual adornments (buttons, necklace beads of various types, awls with special features, arrowheads and others). Polished, perforated shells have also been found amongst these ornaments. There are many stone items manufactured for agricultural purposes such as sickle blades, grindstones, flakes, small cutters, polished stone axes, loom weights and hammerstones for carving. Not many metal (bronze) items were found, apart from some square headed punches and a magnificent flat axe. The economy was based on livestock grazing, agriculture, and to a lesser degree hunting, hence the thousands of remains of domestic and wild animals (e.g. horse, cow, sheep, goat, dog, deer, pig wild boar, fox, beaver, and a few birds) (Galindo-Pellicena *et al.*, 2014) (Fig. 14).

During the Chalcolithic (3rd millennium BC), Portalón was used as a "Sanctuary" or burial ground for humans. The numerous large-format stones in the cave were rearranged to form burial mounds in which the corpses and ritual objects were placed. Although many of these burials were later disturbed by Bronze Age peoples, the intact body of a 6.5-7 year old child buried in a pit-like structure made from stones was found in 2012. Ceramic objects were placed around the head, chest, knees and feet, and a near-complete skeleton of an immature ungulate lay at its foot. The excellent state of preservation facilitated the detailed study of the teeth and bones in the skull, face, arms and legs (Castilla *et al.*, 2014). Anthropological analysis has revealed that this child might have suffered from both rickets and scurvy in at least two different periods of his/her short life. The signs of these diseases on the teeth and bones identify the first episode between the age of 18m months and 3 years, precisely the period when children are being weaned and start to add other food sources to breast milk. Abnormal curvature of the long bones may be related to rickets at an age when the subject was still crawling or learning to walk. Other signs on the bones show a second episode at 4-5 years which cannot be linked to weaning. It might be related to a lack of vitamin C due to a monotonous diet based on cereals and lack of vitamin-rich food such as fruit and vegetables. Analysis of old DNA from human and animal remains found in Portalón is making a significant contribution to major scientific debates. A recent genetic analysis of adult human bones from Portalón (Sverrisdóttir *et al.*, 2014) has revealed, much to our surprise, that these Bronze Age shepherds still lacked the genetic mutation which now allows us to properly digest milk lactose as adults, and thus use it as a source of calcium and vitamins. Since the current populations on the Iberian Peninsula have a high frequency of this mutation, it follows that this trait was probably selected very quickly in populations which did not have it. This study has allowed us to look a little further into the causes of selection of this adaptation, perhaps related to famine periods which were probably frequent in prehistory. When crops failed, the heavy consumption of dairy products would have been a good alternative, which may have led to episodes of strong natural selection for lactose tolerant individuals, i.e. people who could properly and comfortably digest these products. Genetic analysis of cow remains from Portalón (Anderung *et al.*, 2005) has corroborated ancient contacts between the peoples of North Africa and Iberia across the Strait of Gibraltar. A typical mitochondrial genetic strain of African cattle (Haplotype T1), which was thought to have arrived in Europe during

Figure 14. Examples of archaeological remains found on some of the Portalón levels. (Photos and montage L.E.H.).

the Muslim expansion in the 8th century, found in an early Bronze Age cow from Portalón, shows that the arrival of this haplotype is much older than previously thought, thus corroborating archaeological evidence of contact between the two continents across the Strait in recent prehistoric times at least. Remains from Portalón initially attributed to domestic cattle on the basis of size and shape include one which contains Uro (wild bull) DNA, which might also be evidence that these animals were not only hunted but also that there was deliberate cross-breeding between wild and domestic animals. Genetic analysis of horse remains from Portalón has also contributed to the debate about possible local episodes of domestication of these animals on the Iberian Peninsula (Lira *et al.*, 2010).

Although the Neolithic levels (IV-V millennium BC) are yet to be fully excavated, they will no doubt yield surprising results. At present, information is only available from one test pit, which has nevertheless yielded a wide range of typically Neolithic ceramic typologies with Boquique decorations, incised motifs filled with red paste, bottles with conical bases and broad handles, personal adornments including a ring and two bracelets in marble, bone tools including an awl made from a deer metapodial, geometric implements and flint backed blades.

Portalón's large stratigraphic sequence and its long palaeontological and archaeological record is also being used in major studies of the climate and environmental patterns in the Upper Pleistocene and Holocene (Ruiz-Zapata *et al.*, 2003, López-García *et al.*, 2010; Martínez-Caught *et al.*, 2014), as well as geophysics and new geochronology techniques applied to the archaeological record (Carrancho *et al.*, 2013).

The abundance, richness and variety of materials from Portalón is indicative of the diversity of activities and events that took place at this exceptional site during recent prehistory. (Fig. 15)

El Mirador cave

El Mirador cave (Ibeas de Juarros, Burgos) overlooks the southernmost flank of Sierra de Atapuerca at an altitude of 1,033 m asl, with commanding southerly views across the Arlanzón River valley. The mouth of this karst cavity is now approximately 23 m wide and 4 m high, penetrating some 15 m inwards. Its current shelter-like form is due to the collapse of part of the roof. It is part of the Sierra de Atapuerca karst system, although a possible connection to the Cueva Mayor system and the cavities along Trinchera del Ferrocarril is yet to be confirmed. It is probably an old karst window filled by sediment which collapsed when the slope retreated. Outside there is a rockfall of large blocks, indicating ongoing degradation of the lip until quite recently. In 1970, a small test pit dug by the Edelweiss Caving Group (Ortega and Martín, 2012) unearthed Bronze Age remains. This work was not continued, and the site was looted by poachers in the following years. Excavation by the Atapuerca Research Team began in 1999. In the following 9 years, a 20 metre deep test pit was dug in a 6 m^2 area in the centre of the zone now sheltered by the roof, in order to ascertain the archaeological potential of the site. In 2009, excavation began in two new sectors, 100 and 200, at the NW and NE ends of the cave respectively, in contact with the current wall. These sectors are

Figure 15. General view of excavation on Portalón level 7/8 in 2012. (Photos J. Trueba/Madrid Scientific Films).

not being dug vertically but in steps, following the line of the cave roof. The main aim of this work is to document the inward retreat of the cave and also the stratigraphic variations between its different areas.

The 20 m profile explored in the 1999-2008 survey consists of 14 metres of Pleistocene deposits and 6 metres of Holocene material. The Pleistocene deposit (MIR51) has the following stratigraphic succession, listed from base to top (Fig. 16):

MIR51/4. 12 metres of metric and decimetric blocks with virtually no sedimentary matrix in between. The result of the collapsed roof.

MIR51/3. A shallow, archaeologically sterile level composed of wind-borne sediment, mainly lying on the limestone blocks. This level has been dated at 12,480 ± 40 BP (15,060-14,700 cal. BP 95%).

MIR51/2. This centimetric deep level covers MIR51/2, and differs basically in its archaeological contents: remains of a hearth, lithic and fauna material along with evidence of human activity. It has two datings, 11,470 ± 40 BP (13,510-13,230 cal. BP 95%), and 11,610 ± 40 BP (13,640-13,360 cal. BP 95%), from charcoal samples extracted from material burned in the hearth.

MIR51/1. Roughly 2 metres deep, formed by large blocks fallen from the roof. This level only contains palaeontological remains, mainly wolf.

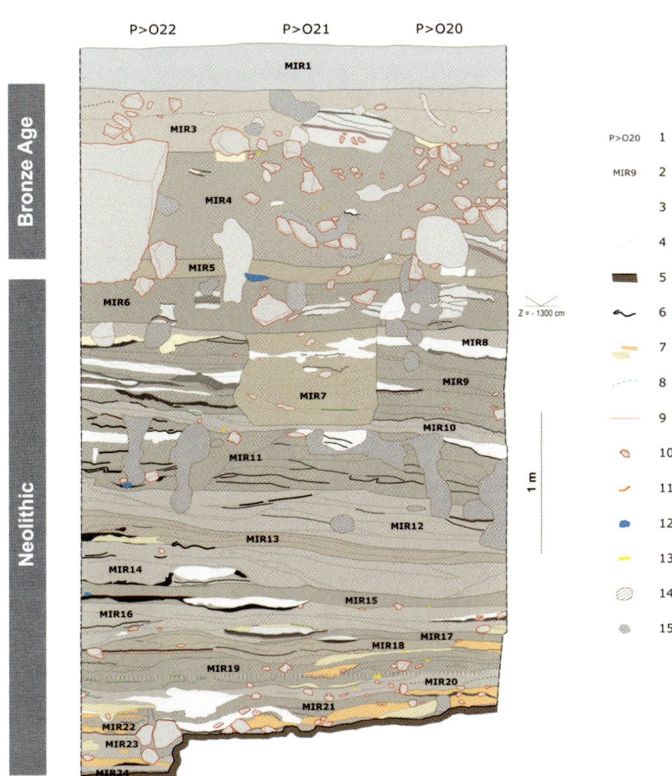

Figure 16. El Mirador: cross-section of the Holocene sequence, south wall of test pit. 1 squares, 2: unit names, 3: unit boundaries, 4: facies boundaries, 5: top of Pleistocene succession, 6: charcoal accumulations, 7: ash accumulation (distinct facies), 8: ash layers, 9 burnt sediment (rubefaction); 10: limestone fragments, 11: potsherds; 12: lithic artefacts; 13: bones; 14: sub-current burrows; 15: ancient burrows.

A Holocene sedimentary layer rests directly on top of MIR51/1, four metres of which correspond to Neolithic occupations between the last third of the 6th millennium and the first half of the 4th cal BC[1]1, MIR24 to MIR6 (Vergès *et al.*, 2008), while the remaining two metres are from the Middle Bronze Age, MIR4 and MIR3A (Vergès *et al.*, 2002), between the 2nd and 4th quarter of the 2nd millennium cal BP. This part of the Bronze Age is also represented in sector 100 by levels MIR103 to MIR105. All these levels were essentially formed as a result of the cave's use as a livestock pen. They contain items from domestic and agricultural activities and areas use as habitats. Intense livestock farming left a sedimentary layer, basically dung, which was piled together and burned at regular intervals in order to reduce the volume and eliminate parasites. This left an alternation between unburned layers of manure and nodules of ash from burned dung, a feature of this type of site.

In the central test pit, archaeologically sterile level MIR5 is only a few centimetres deep, generated by natural sedimentation between the middle of the 4th millennium BC and the second quarter of the 2nd millennium cal BC. Burials from the same period as MIR5 have been found in sectors 100 and 200, in contact with the cave wall, showing that in fact the cave was not abandoned but rather transformed into a burial site. (Fig. 17).

1 The dates for the Pleistocene levels are shown in years BP, while those for the Holocene are presented in calibrated years BC. This lack of uniformity reflects the annotation system used most frequently by researchers for each of the periods.

The oldest evidence of burials has been dated at around the second quarter of the 3rd millennium cal BC, during the Chalcolithic. Remains of at least 22 individuals have been identified (MIR203), laid in a small natural chamber and accompanied by a small number of objects: smooth hemispherical bowls, fractured deer antlers and river shell valves. Cannibalism, probably of a ritual nature, has been documented in relation to this phase of the cave's use for burials in the final third of the 3rd millennium cal BC, i.e., at the start of the Bronze Age. Skeletal remains of six individuals bear evidence of having been defleshed, fractured, cooked and eaten (Cáceres *et al.*, 2007). The remains were found in a small hole dug in the middle Bronze Age levels (MIR4), indicating that they were collected and buried hundreds of years after their death, once livestock farming resumed here.

The final stage of this site's use as a burial cave is marked by a single burial (MIR106) of a young male who was placed on one of the rock ledges inside the cave, contextualised chronologically in the second quarter of the 2nd millennium cal BC, i.e., the Middle Bronze Age.

A large part of the cave roof collapsed in a relatively short period, probably at the start of the Late Glacial. As a result, a 12 metre deep level (minimum, since the excavation did not reach the base) was deposited without time for exogenous sediment to become lodged between the rocks. We do not know whether it was connected to the outside prior to this point, or whether the cave had been occupied. Exogenous input of essentially wind-borne sediment began after this massive collapse, and formed a level (MIR51/3) which covered the layer of blocks. Upper/Late Magdalenian hunter-gatherer groups established sites on top of

Figure 17. Upper left: aerial view of El Mirador cave (J.Mestre/IPHES). Upper right: stratigraphic section of Neolithic series. Lower left: ovicaprine remains in partial anatomic connection from level MIR-14. Lower right: Individual Bronze Age burial (MIR-106) (J.Vergès/IPHES).

this level (MIR51/2). Their occupations left a minor archaeological record, perhaps because of their brevity, and had no continuity. A new episode of rockfalls from the cave roof (MIR51/1) covered these remains and left an uneven floor with many gaps. From this point until the arrival of Neolithic settlers, the cave was occupied by wolves which used these gaps between the rocks as dens.

The first documented occupations of the cave by Neolithic groups were around the last third of the 6th millennium cal BC. From the outset and throughout the Neolithic (MIR24 to MIR6), it was repeatedly used as a habitat and a livestock pen, primarily for sheep and goats (Vergès *et al.*, 2008). This dynamic continued until the middle of the 4th millennium cal BC, with only variations in the material culture, primarily ceramics. The use of El Mirador as a pen then ceased and a period of apparent abandonment began.

Between the second quarter of the 3rd millennium and the second quarter of the 2nd millennium cal BC, El Mirador was used once again as a burial cave. Group burials, ritual cannibalism and individual burials associated with different periods have been documented. Extensive excavation will allow us to discover whether the differential treatment of the corpses and the different types of burial reflect different funeral traditions, or whether they evolved together.

Immediately after the last documented burial, the use of El Mirador as a pen resumed with exactly the same livestock handling features as the Neolithic period. This continued until at least the last quarter of the 2nd millennium cal BC (Vergès *et al.*, 2002), when the stratigraphic succession was interrupted, most probably by the removal of sedimentary material from the cave. Decontextualized items point to the continuation of human activity in the late Bronze and Iron Ages, and also most probably in historic times as well. In fact, the cave was still used by shepherds in the 20th century.

Open air sites

The Upper Pleistocene in Sierra de Atapuerca is well documented outside the above-mentioned caves. Archaeological surveys conducted between 1999 and 2003 (Navazo and Carbonell, 2014) discovered 31 open air campsites. During this work, 314 km2 were inspected around the Trinchera del Ferrocarril sites to ascertain how Upper Pleistocene groups of hunters and gatherers organized their daily lives. Once the campsites were discovered, the area and location of each one was analysed in depth to define those which contained archaeological material in a good state and analyse their stratigraphy. The most recent open air site in Sierra de Atapuerca, *Valle de las Orquídeas* -Orchid Valley- (Mosquera *et al.*, 2007) was excavated in 2000 and 2001. In 2004, work commenced on the *Hundidero* site (HU) in 2004 (Navazo *et al.*, 2011.), where up to four different occupation levels were identified. In 2006 a test pit was excavated at another site, *Hotel California* (HC) which ended in 2010 with five detected archaeological levels. Work is currently under way at *Fuente Mudarra*, where three archaeological levels have been found so far. The data obtained to date show that Sierra de Atapuerca was occupied by groups of Pleistocene hunter-gatherers from at least 70 ky until to 27 ky BP. Datings from Hundidero are 70.556 $\pm$11,011 BP (TL) for the oldest level and 30,221 $\pm$ 3,636 BP for the most recent (Benito-Calvo, et al., 2005). Middle Palaeolithic stone implements have been found on each of the four archaeological levels, with more than 50 tools made from local raw material. (Fig. 18).

Hotel California datings (Arnold, *et al.*, 2013) show that the oldest occupation in this area was around 71.0 $\pm$+5.6 ky and the most recent 48.2 ky $\pm$3.3 ky BP. A 24 m^2 test pit –larger than Hundidero– was dug at this site, which obviously yielded much more lithic material: up to 2,000 items, all manufactured from local raw material. Material from the first test pit at Fuente Mudarra in 2011 yielded datings which match the most recent period at Hotel California.

As a result of the work done so far, we know that Neanderthal groups lived in Sierra de Atapuerca during Isotope stages 4 and 3. The chronology of the assemblages under excavation in the Trinchera del Ferrocarril is older than the Neanderthal open air sites. This space should be interpreted as a large archaeological site in which each campsite is a location interrelated with the rest, i.e., like a house with several rooms. Hunter-gatherers controlled and occupied all the Sierra environments. Sites have been found in the

Figure 18. View of Hundidero site during excavations (Photos: M. Navazo).

lowest-lying areas on river terraces, on hillsides and above, on the moors. It stands to reason that different activities were done in each one, with the hillsides most likely to have the greatest habitational stability.

Local raw materials were used to make the stone tools (Navazo *et al.*, 2008). The most widely used material at Hundidero, Hotel California and Fuente Mudarra is overwhelmingly Neogene chert (generally more than 90% of all assemblages), followed by Cretaceous chert and quartzite. The sources of the Neogene chert were secondary deposits in the Sierra. In fact, almost all the campsites around Sierra de Atapuerca are located on secondary deposits of Neogene chert.

The technological features observed at all three sites show that the main aim was to manufacture products through the reduction of a core. The flakes were used directly or in the configuration of series. The most widely employed structural category is flake (BP), followed by retouched flake (BN2GC). Cores only outnumber retouched flakes at 3 of the 31 sites. Typometric analysis shows a predominance of small-sized flakes (Bagolini, 1968). As with the retouched flakes, in most cases these flakes have non-cortical, unifaceted platform butts and non-cortical dorsal faces. Retouched flakes are larger than simple flakes, although both are small-format. Denticulates are the best represented morphotype, followed by sidescrapers and many abrupts. A few more points and burins were found at sites on high ground than on terraces, where more points were found. Orthogonal knapping was the predominant reduction system in the case of pebble cores, and centripetal knapping in the case of cores on flake. In general, there was little or no preparation of cores prior to the removal process, and little complexity in the knapping strategies. The minimal presence or absence of cortex on the butts and dorsal faces of items seems to be due to the type of raw material available at these locations. Since these were secondary deposits, the chert blocks were already broken and in many cases lacked a patina. Moreover, the fact that the vast majority of butts were platform and unifaceted seems to be due to the predominant weight of the initial knapping sequences in these assemblages.

Visits to the Pleistocene settlements in this study area, located in all the geomorphological units, coincided with the formation of terraces T9 (+19-30 m) to T12 (+8-10 m) (Pérez- González and Benito-Calvo, 2014). There were sites on high ground, associated with sinkholes, on colluvions, river terraces and caves. This diversity shows that the campsites were chosen on basis of the availability of basic subsistence resources, and that the groups adapted their movements to the distribution of food and other resources. The resources required for these groups' survival were animals, plants, stone and water. During the final third of the Upper Pleistocene, Atapuerca Neanderthals lived in an altitude range between 902 and 1,086 m asl, where the climate was not excessively harsh, and exploited both the moors and the river terraces. We have documented 15 sites on moors and upland zones, 12 on river terraces (some associated with ponds, etc.), and four on hillsides (Fig. 19). Our analysis of the assemblages suggests that all sites seem to have been visited for short but recurrent periods of time, except for the four sites on steep hillsides which may have had a more stable occupation pattern. Several occupation levels have been identified at the Hundidero and Hotel California campsites, corroborating their reoccupation during thousands of years. Most of these sites are spread across a large area, which may be due to several factors. Firstly, the dynamics of the occupations, with repeatedly visited sites. Secondly we must bear in mind the disturbances to the assemblages caused by farming practices. Experimental observations of disturbance by ploughing in the same area (Navazo and Díez, 2008) have found that the surface area of archaeological sites on tilled farmland tends to expand while the density of their archaeological record decreases. They also completely lose their spatial and stratigraphic matrix.

Valle de las Orquídeas is an open air site from the end of the Upper Pleistocene (Mosquera *et al.*, 2007). It is located at the top of Sierra de Atapuerca, south of Alto de Matagrande (1,078 m), at the head of a valley connected to a broad exokarst formation somewhat like a sinkhole, with water at the base available to the wildlife and humans who inhabited this area.

During the 2000 and 2001 field seasons, we excavated an 18 m^2 area which yielded 306 lithic items associated with *terra-rossa* deposits (Fig. 20). Two TL dating of this *terra-rossa*, the base of the analysed stratigraphic sequences, showed an age of 27,507 ± 2,295 years BP and 29,955 ± 2,319 years BP. Most of the items are in Cretaceous chert, which is found in the form of small nodules encrusted in the Sierra crevasses. Highlights include four quartzite hammerstones, 56 cores, 44 retouched cores on flake and 158 simple flakes. Reduction was predominantly unifacial centripetal, primarily aimed at producing denticulates, notches and sidescrapers, although other curious discoveries include two denticulate points, two atypical scrapers, one possible burin and two retouched blades. This industrial assemblage is technologically homogeneous and reflects a typical Middle Palaeolithic technical undercurrent, as well as some Upper Palaeolithic features.

Valle de las Orquídeas may well represent the last of the stages in human evolution that has remained undiscovered in Sierra de Atapuerca: the cultural and biological transition between Neanderthals –the presumed occupants of the upper levels of Sima del Elefante and Galería de las Estatuas– and modern humans, the early settlers of the stage represented by the Mirador and Portalón caves.

Conclusions

This chapter is an overview of more than 30 years of research at the Sierra de Atapuerca sites. This work has proved the importance of this large archaeological-palaeontological complex for the study of human evolution, not only in Europe but also at the global scale. Europe's longest Pleistocene stratigraphic sequence has been documented at two of the sites in the Trinchera del Ferrocarril, Sima del Elefante and Gran Dolina. The archaeo-palaeontological remains found at these sites deposits prove that groups of hominins (*Homo sp.*) inhabited Western Europe at least 1.3 M years ago. The hominin remains found on more recent levels of the Lower Pleistocene sequence (TD6.2) led to the proposal and profiling of *H. antecessor*, a human species which inhabited Western Europe at the end of the Lower Pleistocene. Analysis of these human remains has also detected evidence of the oldest known episode of cannibalism. A Mode 1 lithic assemblage has been found in association with these *H. antecesor* remains, where the full range of workable lithic resources available in the Atapuerca area was used and, for the

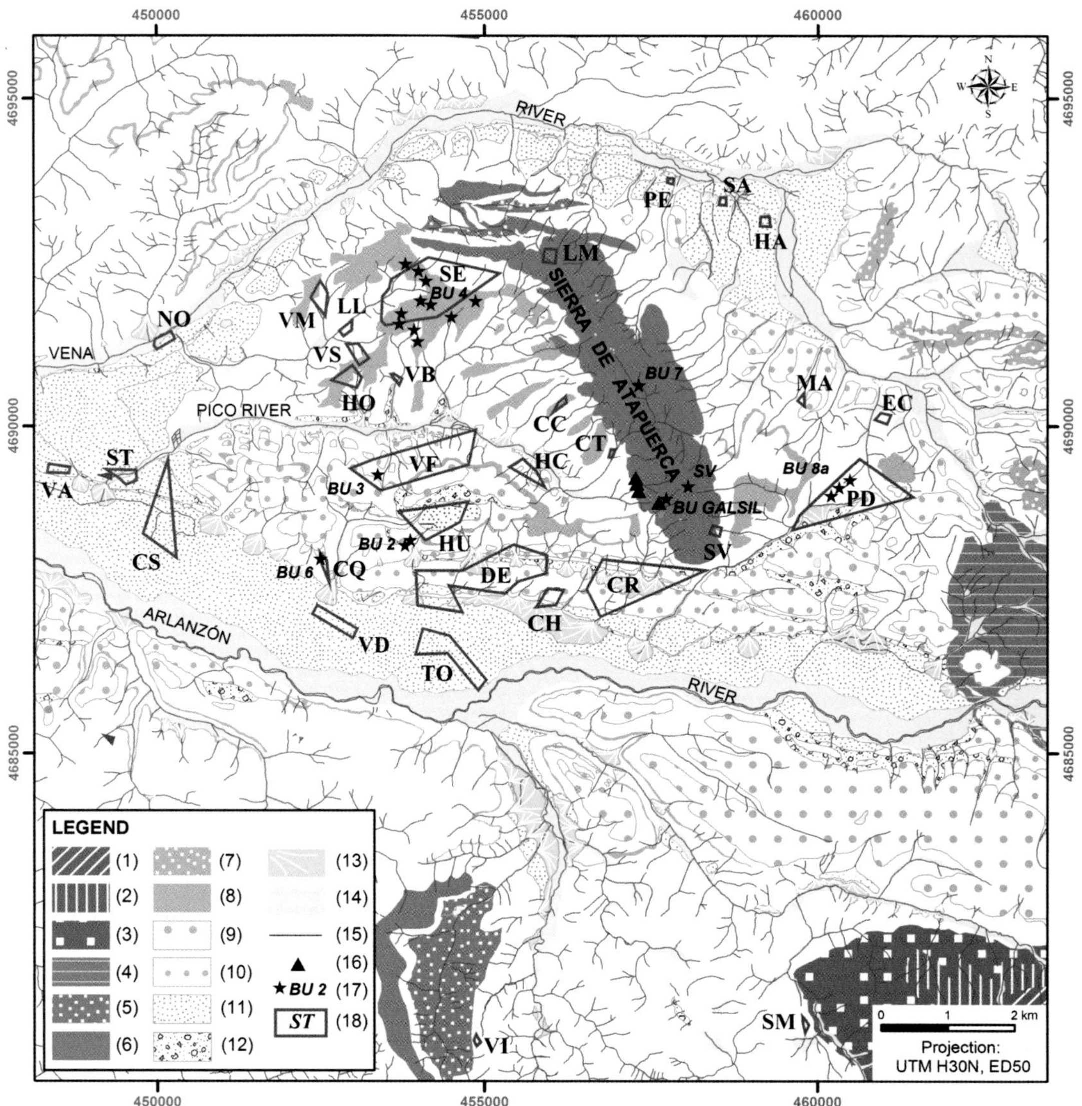

Figure 19. Geomorphological map of the study area (1): Cambrian (metasandstones and slates); (2): Carboniferous (conglomerates, sandstones and slates); (3): Triassic (conglomerates and sandstones); (4): Lower Cretaceous (limestones and quartzite conglomerates); (5): Lower Cretaceous siliciclastic detritic sediments; (6): Upper Cretaceous (limestones and dolostones); (7): Middle Miocene sediments with quartzite conglomerates; (8): Middle Miocene limestone with chert nodules; (9): Lower Pleistocene terraces; (10): Middle Pleistocene terraces; (11): Upper Pleistocene terraces; (12): colluvial deposits; (13): cones; (14): floodplain and valley floor; (15): drainage network; (16): Palaeo-archaeological sites in Sierra de Atapuerca endokarst system [1. Gran Dolina, 2. Galería, 3. Sima del Elefante, 4. Cueva Mayor]; (17): sampling in primary chert outcrops; (18): archaeological occurrences. (From Navazo and Carbonell 2014; produced by A. Benito-Calvo).

first time in the sequence of these sites, the systematic use of retouch in tool manufacture. The archaeological remains recovered from the various Lower Pleistocene levels at Atapuerca provide evidence that the human groups from these chronologies were active hunters, that they were at the top of the food chain and that they had a high degree of control over their territory and its resources.

After a gap in the evidence of human presence –but not the palaeontological record–, a new phase in the human occupation of the Sierra began approx. 500,000 years ago, evidenced

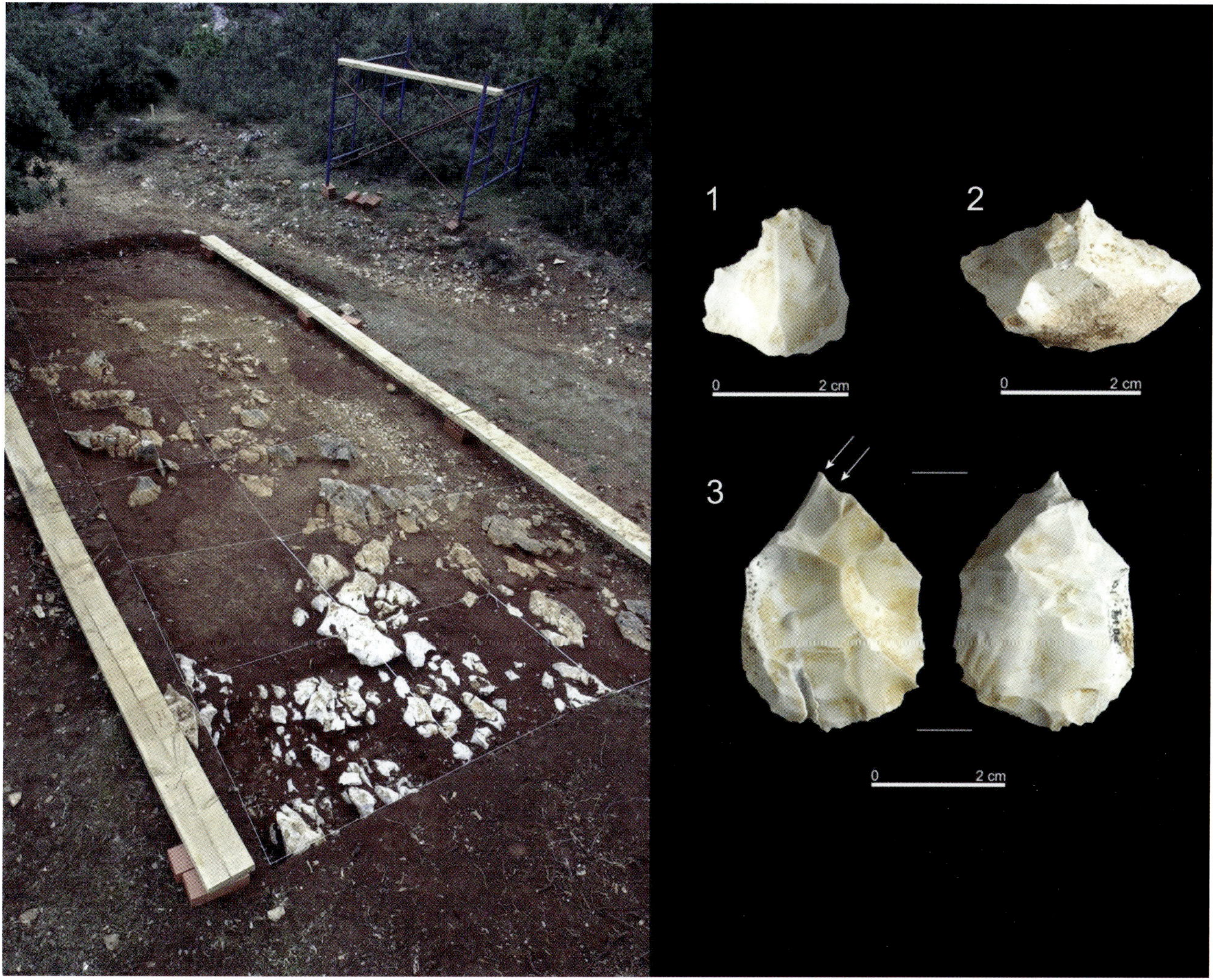

Figure 20. El Valle de las Orquideas site (Sierra de Atapuerca, Burgos). 1: Convex denticulate, 2: Épine 3: Possible burin. (Photo: EIA).

in Galería, Sima de los Huesos and the upper section of Gran Dolina. The record from these sites has proved essential for the study of the hominins (*H.heidelbergensis-Preneandertals*) who inhabited Europe between 500 and 200 ky BP. Sima de los Huesos has yielded the world's largest, most extensive and complete collection of human fossils. These remains from a single population have provided the oldest genetic material of a fossilized human species sequenced to date. The presence of this population at the bottom of Sima de los Huesos has been interpreted as a deliberate accumulation of corpses by other humans, and also as the oldest recorded symbolic behaviour. The density of the material retrieved from the sites in the Trinchera del Ferrocarril suggests an intense occupation of Sierra de Atapuerca by *H. heidelbergensis-Preneandertal* groups, a wide range of developed subsistence strategies, and good capacity for planning and organization, reflected in the features of their Mode 2-Acheulean lithic tools.

Outside the karst caves, our work at Sierra de Atapuerca has made a significant contribution to knowledge of the human groups which inhabited the area during the Upper Pleistocene. Some of these open air sites –Hundidero, Hotel California and Fuente Mudarra– have provided information about the lives of the Neanderthals groups which lived in the Sierra during Isotope stages 4 and 3. Campsites have been found in low lying areas and river terraces, on hillsides and on moors, and it stands to reason that different activities were done at each one, with the hillsides most likely to have had the greatest habitational stability. At one of the open air campsites –Valle de las Orquídeas–, some of the retrieved stone material has been linked to the cultural and biological transition between Neanderthals and modern humans.

In recent decades, studies of the Portalón and Mirador sites have contributed important information about the human groups which inhabited the Sierra during the Holocene, due to the scarce information about the Mesolithic and Neolithic on the Iberian Peninsula's Northern Plateau or *Meseta*.

The archaeological record from both sites (Portalón and Mirador) has shed light on the everyday lives of the Bronze Age groups (2nd millennium BC) in this area. Their domestic chores and agriculture and livestock-based livelihoods are reflected in the archaeological record and the use of the cave as a pen. During the Chalcolithic, both caves began to be used as burial chambers. Cannibalism, probably ritual, has been documented at the Mirador Cave, in connection with this burial phase. Analysis of old DNA from Portalón has shown that the Bronze Age shepherds still lacked the necessary genetic mutation to properly digest lactose in milk. This site has also yielded archaeological records from the Neolithic, Iron Age, Late Roman Empire and the Middle Ages.

The almost constant presence of human groups in this range of hills since the Lower Pleistocene (1.3 Ma) shows that the area has been a rich source of resources necessary for the reproduction and survival as groups of several hominin species which lived in and around Sierra de Atapuerca.

Acknowledgements

We thank everyone who has collaborated in any capacity in the excavation and research work at the Sierra de Atapuerca sites. Our fieldwork is funded by the Castilla-León Regional Government and the Atapuerca Foundation, and our research work is supported by the Spanish Government's Ministry of Economy and Competitiveness (MINECO) under the "Sierra de Atapuerca V Pleistocene and Holocene" Project CGL2012-38434-C03, as well as by the Government of Catalonia, under projects SGR 2014-899; SGR 2014-901 and SGR 2014-900. J.I.M. has a pre-doctoral grant (FI) from the Government of Catalonia; A.H.L, M.G.P., M.T.B. and L.R. have all received pre-doctoral grants from the Atapuerca Foundation. A.R-H has a pre-doctoral grant (FPI) from MINECO CGL2009-12703-C03-02).

Manuel Santonja*, Susana Rubio-Jara**, Joaquín Panera**, Alfredo Pérez-González*

The Palaeolithic in the Manzanares and Jarama River valleys (Madrid)

1. Geological setting and time frame

The largest known concentration of Palaeolithic sites on the Iberian Peninsula is in the deposits on the middle and lower terraces of the final section of the Manzanares River, from San Isidro in the heart of Madrid to its confluence with the Jarama River –a 22 km long valley–, and the middle section of this river (Fig. 1). In the last decade, data on the Pleistocene human occupation of this area has been updated significantly, further highlighting its relevance to the European Lower Palaeolithic.

In the River Jarama valley, a sequence of 19 terraces has been identified between +8 m and +190 m, along with another one containing 13 levels in the Manzanares River valley between +4-5 m and +95 m (Pérez-González and Uribelarrea 2002). The Palaeomagnetism has detected and located the Matuyama-Brunhes inversion in the Jarama between the end of the formation of the terrace +60-65 m and before began to incise the next terrace at +50-55 m (Pérez-González *et al.*, 2013). To the south and east of Madrid, these rivers lie on Miocene gypsum and salt rocks which, when dissolved, left overlapping terraces in the Jarama valley below the relative +40 m level, with the more recent levels above the older ones, giving rise to the Complex Terrace of Arganda (hereinafter CTA) which are up to 40-50 m deep, formed by successively stacked fluvial sequences identified in ascending order as Arganda I, II, III and IV. The first three of these units are equivalent to the +30-32 m, +23-24 m and +18-20 m terraces, respectively. The combination of numerical datings obtained by aminoacid racemization, with the evolutionary state of the microvertebrae and the climatic implications of the herpetofauna, place Arganda I in MIS 11 and Arganda II in MIS 9-8. These chronologies have also been assigned to the correlated terraces (Panera *et al.*, 2011).

In the River Manzanares valley, the +25-30 m terrace has been attributed to MIS 11-13 on the basis of the presence of *Megaloceros savini* at the Transfesa site (Fig. 1). Downstream, the terraces formed over evaporitic rocks (+25-30 m, +18-20 m and +12-15 m at least) are affected by the synsedimentary subsidence resulting in a huge thickness increase of tens of meters. All these terraces form the Complex Terraces of Butarque (hereafter CTB). Numerical dating of TL, OSL and AAR place the visible bottom of the CTB, in the +18-20 m level, around MIS 6-5d, the intermediate section in MIS 5b-5a, and the top in MIS 4. For level +12-15 m, datings have yielded 40.2 ± 5 ky and 39.7 ± 2.7 ky, while level +8 m is attributed to 26.7 ± 3 ky and 26 ± 2 ky (Silva *et al.*, 2013; Panera *et al.*, 2014).

In both valleys, knapped stones have been found on terraces from the first half of the Middle Pleistocene; however the recorded lithic assemblages start to become numerous on the +30-32 m terrace in the River Jarama valley and +25-30 m terrace in the River Manzanares valley. Acheulean technology, with large cutting tools (LCT) is confirmed in the second half of the Middle Pleistocene, from MIS 11 at least. The Middle Palaeolithic is well identified between the late MIS 6 and IS 8 of MIS 3, and the Upper Palaeolithic is identified in MIS 2. On the platform which defines the watershed between the two valleys, flint and opal outcrops were subject to anthropic exploitation, probably throughout these periods.

2. Remarkable sites

2.1. *San Isidro and the start of prehistoric research in Spain*

The discovery of worked stone tools in sand and clay deposits at Tejar de las Ánimas (San Isidro Hill, Madrid) marked the beginning of the Prehistory in Spain. Edouard de Verneuil (1805-1873), Louis Lartet (1840-1899) and Spanish geologist Casiano de Prado (1797-1868) identified the first tools in 1862, making this site the first milestone in the Peninsular Palaeolithic (Santonja and Vega

* Centro Nacional de Investigación sobre la Evolución Humana. (CENIEH); 09002 Burgos.. manuel.santonja@cenieh.es

** IDEA (Instituto de Evolución en África), Museo de los Orígenes, Plaza de San Andrés 2, 28005 Madrid.

2002). San Isidro is located in the +25-30 m of the Manzanares River, with more than 15 m depth, with a typical fluvial series at the bottom, followed by gravel bars, sand with gravel and silt horizons containing Acheulean tools and fauna remains.

This site immediately became an emblematic point of reference for the Manzanares valley, although some of the items attributed to San Isidro, which began in 19th century collections and are now preserved in leading museums, might in fact have different origins. However, the source of series collected by Pérez de Barradas, published in 1940 towards the end of his palaeolithic research, has been confirmed, and enables the industry from the lowest levels of San Isidro, some associated with elephant remains (*Palaeoloxodon antiquus*), to be defined as Acheulean.

Since 1917, José Pérez de Barradas (1897-1980), under the initiative and supervision of Hugo Obermaier (1879-1946), began an intense research project in Manzanares River. Initially accompanied by Paul Wernert (1889-1972), he spent 15 years discovering and studying numerous sites until 1931. Pérez de Barradas defined the Quaternary geological synthesis of the Manzanares, published in the 1924 edition of Obermaier's *Fossil Man*. Pérez de Barradas was also responsible for successive interpretations of the sequence, from 1924 onwards based on the ideas of Breuil, postulating two distinct *phyla* –biface industries and flake industries. In 1940, Palaeolithic research in Madrid ceased after the Spanish Civil War and under the Franco dictatorship. Therefore Pérez de Barradas' ideas were not updated. When renewed work began in the 1970s, the methods had undergone profound changes and the previous results lacked validity.

2.2. *Elephants and humans*

In the Acheulean context, the +25-30 m terrace and the CTB in the Manzanares River, yielded sites with a single individual elephant –*Palaeoloxodon antiquus*– possibly in association with lithic industry, although almost all these cases were old and incompletely documented locations. The most characteristic sites are San Isidro, Orcasitas and Transfesa (Santonja *et al.*, 2001).

Mariano de la Paz Graells (1808-1898) wrote an accurate description of his work at San Isidro in 1847 and 1850 on two sets of elephant bones –both adult males– found close to each other in distinct stratigraphic positions (Pérez-González and Uribelarrea 2002). The first one included at least the two tusks, a tibia and part of a jawbone. The second ensemble consisted of a near-complete set of remains from another individual, with some of the bones in a "concordant" position. Graells' detailed stratigraphy places this 1847 discovery on a "sandy clay" level immediately below the deep layer of "plastic blue clay" which contained the remains excavated in 1850. This level yielded the cleaver on flake published in 1863 by Verneuil and Lartet, and other knapped stone items (Santonja and Vega 2002).

At the +25-30 m Manzanares terrace of Orcasitas (Fig. 1) was excavated an area with the skull and the tusks of a 45 year old *Palaeoloxodon antiquus* in 1959. It was lying on an 80 cm deep layer of loam included in a section of "loamy sand", beneath another of "clayey sand". In 1958, in the Transfesa company quarry, also in the +25-30 m terrace, unearthed many remains of other two elephants, both adult males, the largest measuring 4-5 m in height. The fossils lay on a gravel layer covered by loams with fine gravels. These remains were scattered across the 70x20 m area. Some of the long bones were broken, but no details are available about the nature of these fractures. Acheulean industry was present at both the Orcasitas and the Transfesa sites, but the published information does not provide any basis to establish relationships with the fauna (Santonja *et al.*, 2001).

At least 17 of the open sand quarries in the CTB have yielded proboscidean remains dating from MIS 6 to MIS 5. They have also yielded numerous worked stones and fauna associations which have been attributed biostratigraphically to the Middle and Upper Pleistocene. The former is characterized by the presence of *Palaeoloxodon antiquus*, *Bos primigenius* and *Dicerorhinus hemitoechus*, and the second by *Megaceros* cf. *giganteus*, *Mammuthus* cf. *intermedius* and *Coelodonta antiquitatis* (Sesé and Soto 2002). The large number of proboscidea has been linked to the geographical and environmental situation of the lower section of the Manzanares River, a major ecological corridor in the well-documented Mediterranean climate of this period which included several months of summer drought. The surrounding ecosystems were characterized by sparse vegetation cover, which was favourable for herds of large mammals to gather on the banks of the lower Manzanares during the arid summer (Panera *et al.*, 2014).

Scarce information is available about most of these discoveries, although interactions between hominins and megafauna have been documented in four cases, Arenero de Rojas, Arriaga IIa, PRE-

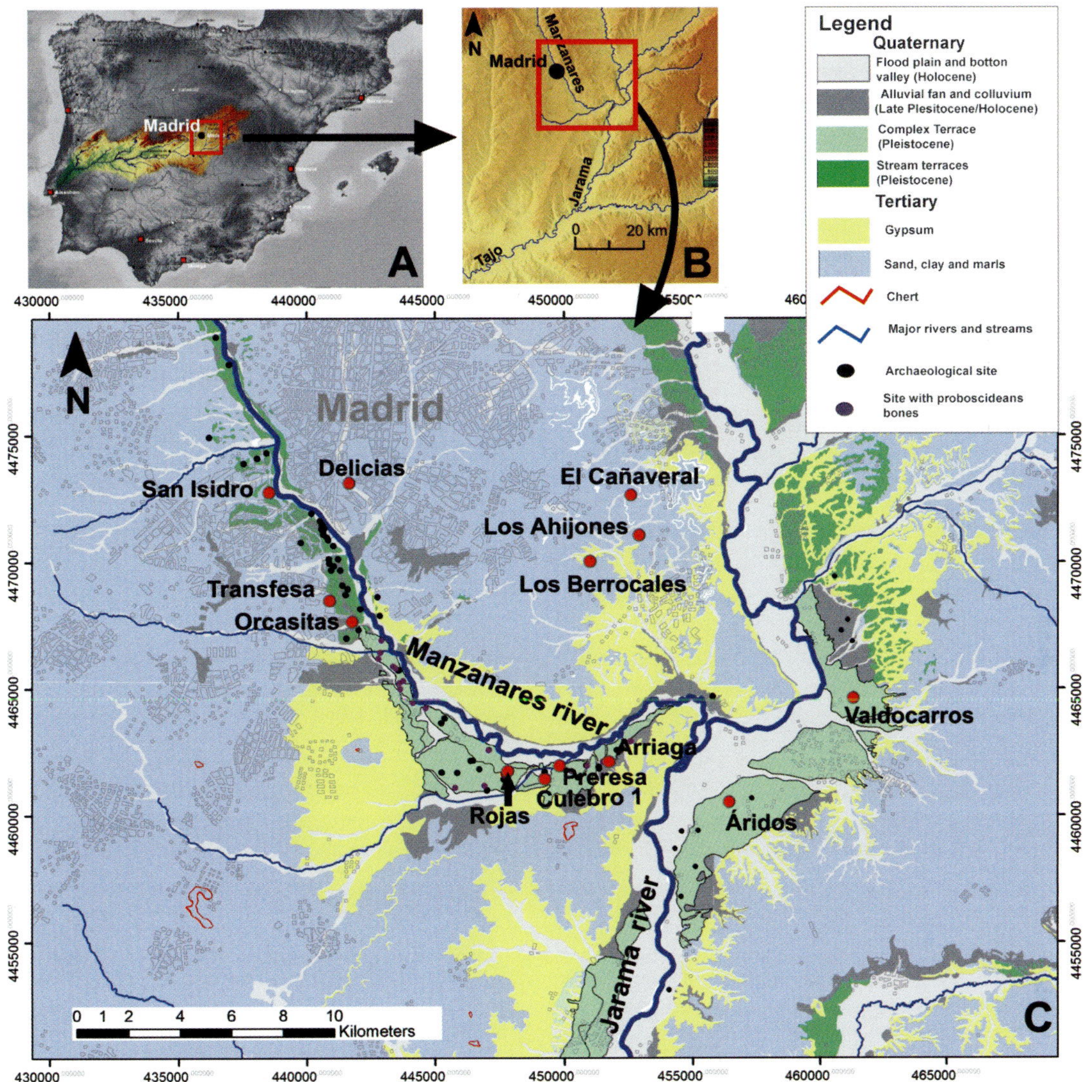

Figure 1. **A** Location of the Tajo River Basin in the Iberian Peninsula. **B**. Relief of the Manzanares and Jarama Valleys (generated from the DEM SRTM-3, source: NASA). **C**. Geological sketch of the Manzanares and Jarama Valleys around Madrid City and position of the sites cited in the text and other important archaeological localities.

RESA, and EDAR Culebro 1. In Europe, more sites in Lower Palaeolithic than Middle Palaeolithic contexts have been found with evidence of this type of exploitation. In the CTB, however, at least these four sites prove that between MIS 6 and MIS 5, mega-herbivores were exploited by human groups. This also shows that there was no major change in subsistence strategies with respect to these mammals between the Middle Pleistocene and the first part of the Upper Pleistocene. In the Jarama and Manzanares valleys, a considerable number of sites have been found to contain Acheulean lithic industry associated with elephant remains (San Isidro, Transfesa, Áridos 1 and Áridos 2). At a later time, the Mousterian groups recorded in the CTB had provided and exploited these animal resources in a similar way to the Acheulean groups.

2.3. Áridos Acheulean sites in the Jarama River valley. Acquisition of resources from elephants and small animals

Áridos 1 and Áridos 2 (Santonja *et al.*, 1980), are located in the Arganda I unit of the CTA, in the Jarama River valley. Áridos 1 yielded part of an adult female *Palaeoloxodon antiquus* skeleton scattered across the preserved 50 m^2 area of the site. The remains were resting on a consolidated palaeosurface and covered by overbank facies sediments. Despite their disturbance and weathering due to subaerial exposure, they were quite complete. 331 flint and quartzite items with no evidence of drag, of which 1/5 was refitted, are associated. This lithic industry was scattered with a distribution that coincided with that of the remains of elephant (Fig. 2). The assemblage was essentially flakes from the maintenance of at least two handaxes and knapping of 19 other flint nodules, as well as four hamerstones and five large worked quartzite cobbles. Quartzite is common in the Jarama valley, what explains immediate uses such as hammers and short production chains, in contrast to patterns observed in the case of flint.

Another subsequent occupation was identified in Áridos 1, also in a floodplain context. In less than 4m2, separated from the elephant scapula by a few centimeters of fine sediment, an exceptionally varied concentration of small or medium-sized animal species was recorded, in most cases represented by the remains of a single individual, *Alosa* sp., *Anguilla anguilla*, *Chondrostoma* sp., *Leuciscus cephalus*, *Barbus* sp., *Carassius carassius*, *Emys orbicularis*, *Rinechis scalaris*, *Timon lepidus*, *Anas platyrhynchos*, *Anas clypeata*, *Alectoris graeca/rufa*, *Perdix paleoperdix*, *Columba oenas*, *Columba palumbus*, *Corvus monedula*, *Turdus pilaris*, *Turdus iliacus*, *Dendrocopos major submajor*, *Oryctolagus* cf. *lacosti*, *Lepus* sp. and *Castor fiber*. The repeated appearance of bones in anatomical connection precludes their identification as regurgitated pellets. Conversely, the presence of two flint microflakes from a sharpened tool allows us to raise that at least some of them could be anthropically processed remains.

The evolutionary stage of the Áridos 1 micromammals led to an estimated age of the site, which coincided with the recent AAR numerical dating of Arganda I at 379.7 ± 45.0 ky (López, 1980; Panera *et al.*, 2011). The Áridos 1 herpetofauna indicates that the climate was similar to the current conditions, with a little more rainfall (Blain *et al.*, e.p.).

Áridos 2, in a similar stratigraphic position to Áridos 1 and roughly 150 m NE, was also excavated in 1976. This site contained connected remains of another *Palaeoloxodon antiquus*, in this case a large

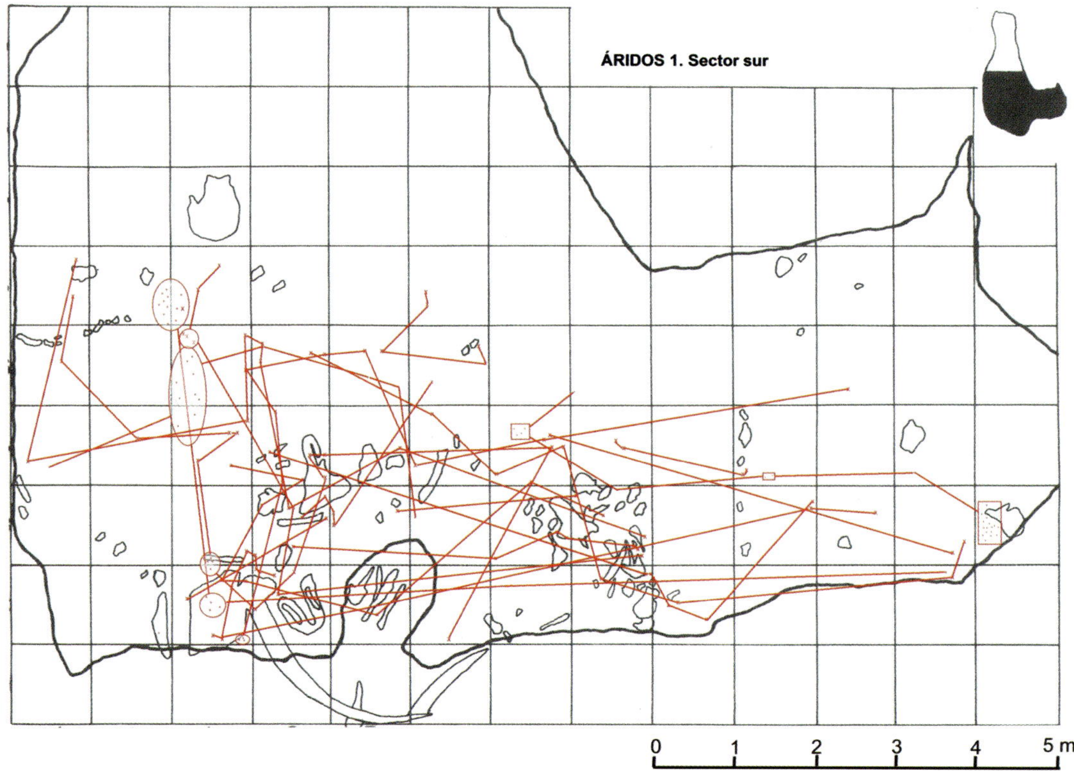

Figure 2. Dispersal of elephant remains in the southern area of Áridos 1 site. Refitting items or pieces that belong to the same knapped blank are connected by lines. The distribution of lithic industry is related to the remains of elephant.

and very old male, aged 45-50 years. Work in the gravel pit only preserved about 12 m^2 of the original area, where a central part of the skeleton was found in connection. The remains lay on an ancient floodplain, covered and partially eroded by gravels and sands. Human intervention, which did not reach to disconnect this axial part of the skeleton, was evidenced by 34 associated lithic items in flint and quartzite –knapped products, a biface and a cleaver on flake– and the presence of cut marks and impact by heavy stone tools –the recorded biface and cleaver or similar items– on the scapula and a rib. Hyaena bite marks were also detected on the humerus, while the cut marks on the ventral surface of a rib suggests primary access by hominins (Yravedra *et al.*, 2010).

2.4. *Valdocarros: repeated Acheulean occupations of a former meander*

The archaeological site is in the upper third of the Arganda II stratigraphic unit. It consists of three sedimentary episodes named –from bottom to top– I, II and III. Valdocarros I and III are large floodplains then disconnected from the main stream (Fig. 3). Valdocarros II is an abandoned meander with four layers, fining upwards from silt to silty-clay each one, 30-50 cm thick and several tens of meters wide. Each layer buries an archaeological level, from bottom to top, 1, 2, 3 and 4 respectively. Neither erosional nor current structures have been identified, showing a very low-energy environment. The weak to absent soil profile development, few distinct traces of bioturbation and well preserved of fossil record, suggest a relatively high rate of burial of archaeological levels 1, 2, 3 and 4 in Valdocarros site. A total of 18 m^2 have been excavated in Valdocarros I and 836 m^2 in Valdocarros II. AAR dating has yielded 245 ± 47 ky and 262 ± 07 ky, consistent with the evolutionary stage of the micromammals (Panera *et al.*, 2011; Sesé *et al.*, 2011). In the association of amphibians and reptilians recorded at levels 2, 3 and 4 of Valdocarros II, a rapid climate change has been detected which might correspond to the transition from MIS 8 to MIS 7 (Blain *et al.*, 2012).

The fauna is generally fragmented and disjointed, with a similar distribution to the lithic industry. *Cervus elaphus* is the best represented species

Figure 3. **A**. *Bos primigenius* and proboscidean remains at PRERESA site. **B**. Fragment of diaphysis, green-bone fracture. Close-up of the notches which occurred as a result of percussion and cut marks on proboscidean bone.

amongst the 2,750 remains of large mammals, followed by *Equus caballus*, *Bos primigenius* and to a smaller extent, *Capreolus sp.*, *Dama sp.*, and *Elephas sp.*, as well as a small number of carnivore remains (*Felix sp.*, *Canis lupus* and *Vulpes vulpes*). The hominins –who probably shifted the carcasses over short distances (Yravedra and Domínguez-Rodrigo 2009)– seem to have been the main agent involved in accumulating the macrovertebrate remains.

In Valdocarros II, the knapping work was mainly related to core reduction and on some levels to shaping and resharpening handaxes. The sample consists of 3009 worked items and 1119 pebbles, likely *manuports*. Roughly two thirds of the former are flint, one third quartzite and the rest quartz. Judging by the production schemes identified on the cores, quartzite was used more often in short *chaînes opératoires* (unifacial and bifacial), while flint was used in long *chaînes opératoires* (multifacial and discoidal). Levallois and discoidal schemes are under-represented. Handaxes predominated in the large tool category, although cleavers on flake and pebble-tools have also been documented. The retouched tools include abundant denticulates, many flakes with elementary retouch and sidescrapers.

The abandoned meander at Valdocarros II was occupied on at least four different occasions under different climate conditions. Hominins returned repeatedly, probably attracted by the combination of the proximity of a major river, shelter provided by the meander depression and the dense vegetation.

2.5. *PRERESA: first evidence of the use of proboscidean marrow*

The PRERESA site is in the lower segment of the River Manzanares valley. Stratigraphically it is roughly 5.5 m from the top of the CTB, between two river sequences deposited during the second half of MIS 5, as indicated by the 84.126 ± 5.633 OSL dating. This is consistent with the evolutionary level of the mammals. Of the 255 m^2 excavated area, 36 m^2 contain the most intense concentration of industry and fauna (Panera *et al.*, 2014).

The herpetofaunal association indicates a similar Mediterranean climate to the present day, or even warmer, with four dry months in summer and early autumn, more abundant rains in spring and winter, less continentality and higher winter temperatures (Blain *et al.*, 2013). The micromammals indicate the presence of forested landscapes and abundant riparian vegetation which provided a transition to more open areas with shrubs and wet meadows (Sesé *et al.*, 2011a).

The macromammal remains (*Elephas* sp., *Bos primigenius*, *Dama* sp., *Cervus elaphus*, *Capreolus capreolus*, *Equus* sp., *Vulpes vulpes*, *Lynx pardinus*, *Meles meles* and *Canis lupus*) are in good condition, and show little impact of carnivores and net evidence of human activity on the large animal bones, including elephants (Fig. 4). It is remarkable the presence of a considerable part of a *Bos primigenius* skeleton scattered across roughly 120 m^2. In addition, 82 bones of a single elephant were spread across 130 m^2. Cut marks, green-bone fractures and percussion marks were detected on the elephant remains, the first case in which they have been able to be associated with the exploitation of these taxa' bone marrow (Yravedra *et al.*, 2012).

The lithic assemblage consists of 754 pieces, all flint except for six quartz items, of which only 182 are more than 3 cm long, with 75 exceeding 5 cm. The flint *chaîne operatoires* are complete. Cores were exhaustively exploited. Short operative chains prevail, as well as flakes with greater width than length. There is a notable absence of macrotools and a small proportion of retouched flakes. The presence of knapping debris and refits shows that at least some of the tools were prepared *in situ* from flint pebbles introduced to the site (Rubio-Jara, 2011).

2.6. *Manzanares-Jarama interfluve: exploitation and flint supply area in the Middle and Upper Pleistocene*

One of the Iberian Peninsula's largest concentrations of siliceous outcrops –flint and opal– is on the Manzanares-Jarama interfluve. Archaeological surveys in recent years have found that these resources were exploited from the Middle Pleistocene to the Holocene.

Numerous Upper Pleistocene Mousterian sites have been found in the area known as **El Cañaveral** (Fig. 1). Flint was collected on outcrops of large blocks measuring 50 to 200 cm, as well as in colluvial deposits where 10-20 cm nodules were selected. Flakes were produced in the same zone where the raw material was selected, resulting in large areas with a predominance of early stages of production, represented by abandoned cortical flakes, cores and knapping debris (Baena *et al.*, 2011).

At **Los Ahijones** (Fig. 1), 14 *in situ loci* have been located in a 550 ha area. Several of these are Palaeolithic, Acheulean and Mousterian, and they have been linked to this utilization of the Miocene flint resources (Bárez *et al.*, 2011). Their age ranges between the second half of the Middle Pleistocene and the start of the Upper Pleistocene. At the

Figure 4. Aerial view of the Valdocarros site. The main excavated area in Valdocarros 2 is in blue color. The Valdocarros 1 surface was staked out by trenches and sondages.

Charco Hondo I site, more than 1,500 items were recovered in a 6 m² area, predominantly cortical and ordinary flakes and biface preforms.

The **Los Berrocales** (Fig. 1) area has yielded Lower and Middle Palaeolithic industrial assemblages in stratigraphy. Three sites have been dug. The **Langostillo** site, linked to the exploitation of large flint boulders, contains a big concentration of waste knapped elements, and with all stages of the operational chain represented, including retouched items (Manzano *et al.*, 2011).

2.7. *Upper Palaeolithic*

The work of Pérez de Barradas attributed lithic assemblages found on the +8 m terrace of the Manzanares River valley to the Solutrean. Recent researches in several sections of this terrace have yielded new Solutrean lithic discoveries, all in secondary position, with two TL numerical datings: 26.7 ± 2.9 ky and 26 ky ± 1.7 ky (Domínguez *et al.*, 2009; Gil Ortiz and Callejas 2009).

H. Obermaier and P. Wernert excavated a site at Madrid's Las Delicias train station in 1917. This site was initially attributed to the Acheulean, although recent revisions have interpreted it as also Upper Solutrean, with characteristic bifacial foliated points (Alcaraz *et al.*, e.p.). Las Delicias is on the left bank of the River Manzanares valley +16-20 m above the present valley floor but in a semi-endorheic area disconnected from the terrace system. The identified industry indicates that this was a knapping zone for the flint that outcropped on the adjacent hillside. The presence in the River Manzanares valley of a Solutrean workshop of this nature, probably from the Upper Pleniglacial (MIS 2), near the Last Glacial Maximum, indicates an organized occupation of the Central Iberian plateau in these chronologies, given that if there were specialised knapping sites, there also must have been consumption zones nearby.

C. Cacho*, J. A. Martos*, J. Jordá-Pardo**, J. Yravedra***, M. Ruiz****, L. Zapata*****, C. Sesé ******, B. Avezuela**, J. Valdivia*, P. Ortega*******, D. Arceredillo********

La Peña de Estebanvela

La Peña de Estebanvela is a rock shelter (1,065 metres above sea level) excavated in the Miocene conglomerates. It opens up to the south east along the right bank of the river Aguisejo, a tributary of the Riaza. It nestles in the south east sector of the Duero basin, in a mountainous landscape delimited to the south by the foothills of the Sistema Central (Sierra de Ayllón) and to the northeast by the southern edge of the Sistema Ibérico. To the west it meets the plains of Aranda de Duero and to the east, the Almazín basin, which connects to the Ebro through the Jalón valley, giving it a privileged strategic position.

It was discovered in 1992 during surveying work led by Fernando López Ambite to draw up an archaeological map of the area. The Rock Shelter was clogged with sediment and discovered thanks to the materials found in a ravine that had washed away part of the cavity filling.

Between 1999, when work started, and 2009 ten excavation campaigns were carried out under two research projects funded by the Castilla y León regional government, and since 2004, with the collaboration of the CSIC.

Peña de Estebanvela is currently the main research reference for the Magdalenian in the Meseta. Its stratigraphic sequence has undergone extensive chronostratigraphic control. The radiocarbon dating values obtained, the widest for the geographical range analysed, have allowed the definition of the chronological framework of the late Upper Pleistocene in this area to progress.

1. Stratigraphy and dating values

Six levels, from wall to ceiling, have been identified and are chronoculturally attributable to the Middle Magdalenian (VI and V), Upper Magdalenian (IV and III) and the late Magdalenian (II and I) (Cacho *et al.*, 2007: 53-64). The sedimentology

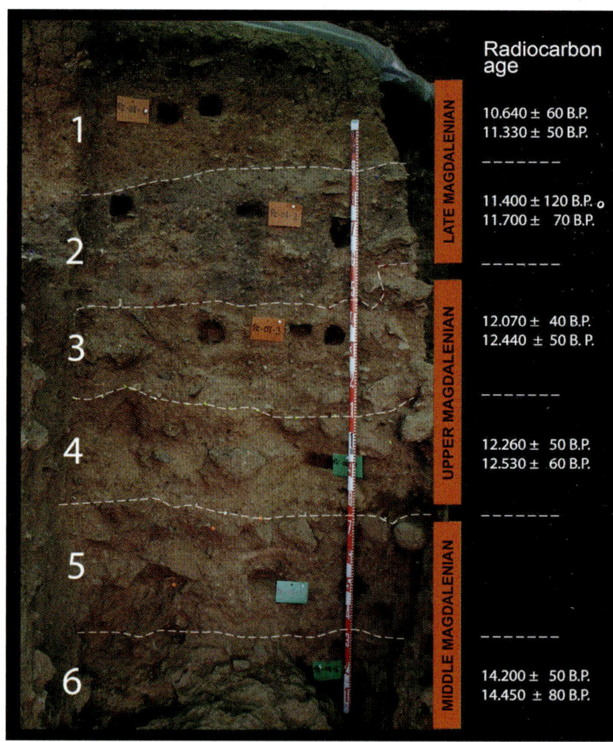

Figure 1. Stratigraphy and radio carbon dating values of La Peña de Estebanvela.

* Departamento de Prehistoria. Museo Arqueológico Nacional. Serrano 13. 28001 Madrid. Spain.
** Departamento de Prehistoria y Arqueología. Universidad Nacional de Educación a Distancia. Senda del Rey 7. 28040 Madrid. Spain.
*** Departamento de Prehistoria. Facultad de Geografía e Historia. Profesor Aranguren, s/n. 28040 Madrid, Spain.
**** Grupo de Investigación Arqueobiología. Instituto de Historia. CSIC. Albasanz 26-28. 28037 Madrid. Spain.
***** Área de Prehistoria. Universidad del País Vasco. Tomas y Valiente s/n. Apdo. 2111. 01006 Vitoria-Gasteiz. Spain.
****** Museo Nacional de Ciencias Naturales. MNCN-CSIC. José Gutiérrez Abascal 2. 28006 Madrid. Spain.
******* Departamento de Prehistoria, H. Antigua y Arqueología Facultad de Geografía e Historia. Universidad de Salamanca
******** Departamento de Geología. Área de Paleontología. Universidad de Salamanca.

conditions and the radiocarbon dating values put the stratigraphic sequence at the end of the Upper Pleistocene.

The series starts with sedimentation of level VI (17,770–17,190 cal BP), at the start of GS 2a, of cold conditions before a slight warming that comes before Heinrich event 1 (H1). Then a time lapse of around 2,000 years is detected, which corresponds to GS 2a before H1, of cold conditions but evolving towards warm conditions, for which we do not have radiocarbon dating values, although level V, in apparent continuity with level VI and which has not been dated, must fall within this time period. Levels IV and III, with seven valid dating values and whose cumulative probability curves for the calibrated ages overlap almost entirely, are placed within the interval between 15,150 and 13,890 cal BP. Therefore, these levels must have been deposited between the last cold period of GS 2a (Older Dryas), the first half of the warm period GI 1e (Bölling) and the cold period GI 1d (Older Dryas). However, given the characteristics of the sediment and the geographic and topographic location of the site, we favour sedimentation for both levels during GI 1e of warm conditions. The sequence continues with level II, whose dating values calibrated with a high probability put it in the range of 13,720–13,100 cal BP, during the warm period GI 1c (Alleröd). Above this level, the development period of level I falls between 13,300 and 12,610 cal BP, from the cold oscillation of GI 1b (Alleröd) to the start of GS 1 (Younger Dryas) of cold conditions.

Finally, following sedimentation of level 1, post-depositional processes of cold conditions take place, which are responsible for the cryoturbation that affects levels I and II; these processes occurred during GS 1 (Younger Dryas) (Jordá Pardo and Cacho 2013: 75-92).

2. Paleoenvironment framework

The information available, basically deduced from the association of micro-mammals, is irregular throughout the sequence, due to the fact that the largest volume and surface area of the sediment excavated is concentrated in the top section. In fact, level I is the only level that has a large enough record to make paleoenvironmental interpretations. It stands out for its diversity in terms of micro-mammals, 15 of the 16 taxa identified at the site (one erinaceidae, three soricomorpha, four chipotera, seven rodents and one lagomorpha), and for containing the highest minimum number of individuals. From this assemblage it may be inferred that the climate would have been warm and wet, like today's. The association also suggests various types of environment: woodland edges, scrublands with wet grasslands and scrublands with dry grasslands. The landscape would not be very different (although perhaps with more plant coverage) from the one that exists around the site today, where the river Aguisejo, framed by riverside woodlands, would facilitate the different environments.

There is no species at the site that indicates a harsher climate than today's. Rather, there are elements with a clear thermophile character, such as *Apodemus sylvaticus* and *Eliomys quercinus* which are relatively abundant in the assemblage of level I and some taxa that have a clear preference for the Mediterranean climate, such as *Crocidura russula, Microtus duodecimcostatus* and *Oryctolagus cuniculus*, which is the most abundant mammal in level I (Sesé 2013: 17-23; Laplana *et al.*, 2011). *Microtus oeconomus* is the only Euro-Siberian element found so far, although it only indicates cold weather conditions when it is very abundant (Sesé 2005: 190). This is not the case of La Peña de Estebanvela where, although present in almost all of the levels in the sequence (levels I, III, IV and V), the number of individuals is always small; one in the first three levels and two in the last.

3. Exploitation of the territory and seasonality

From the zooarchaeology and taxonomic analyses it may deduced that the Magdalenian groups exploited the different habitats of the immediate surroundings of the site: open environments (*Equus ferus, Equus hydruntinus*), woodlands (*Capreolus capreolus, Cervus elaphus, Lynx pardinus*), rocky (*Capra pyrenaica)* and mountainous (*Rupicapra pyrenaica*).

In the upper levels (I-III), with a larger archaeological record, lagomorphs dominate. The most common species of macro-mammal is the goat, followed by the horse. To a lesser extent, deer, chamois, roe and boar also appear, in addition to some carnivores, such as the lynx. From the taphonomy study it may be concluded that the prey hunted was transported whole to the site, regardless of its size, a capture pattern arising in the surrounding area not exceeding 10 kilometres, where they were skinned, the flesh was removed, they were taken apart and consumed in full (Yravedra and Andrés 2013: 230). The scarcity of burned bones suggests that if the meat were cooked it must have been done after the flesh had been removed and that the fat of the axial and epiphysis elements was not used. The lack of thermal alternations in the fauna also indicates that waste removal strategies were not followed.

The ungulate hunting process is selective; prey aged between 4 and 6 years, complemented by some baby and young individuals. This strategy has some advantages, such as higher quality of the meat and a higher probability of success, as young individuals, which are solitary, do not have group protection. Seasonality, established based on the ungulates from levels I to III, indicates two periods for accumulating prey in the annual cycle: spring – early summer and autumn, coinciding with calving periods (higher vulnerability) and mating season (addition of more individuals) and a shelter usage pattern that mirrors this activity throughout the sequence (Arceredillo 2013: 204).

The charcoal identified indicates the use of wood, mainly willow, as fuel for fires. Its dominant presence reflects an intensive and recurrent use of the riverside. Although they have not been recovered, Magdalenian groups would have access to a large number of edible fruit and nuts (cherry, sloe, hazelnut and apple) that could have been part of their diet (Ruiz-Alonso *et al.*, 2013. 118-119). Use of riverside resources is complemented by fishing, which is demonstrated by the presence of *Salmo trutta* vertebrae (Perea and Doadrio 2013: 136-138). Birds must also have been consumed, although there are no cut marks or direct evidence of human intervention on the bone remains found to date (Sánchez Marco 2013: 153-154). Other charcoal samples from La Peña de Estebanvela could indicate use of certain plant resources for uses not related to diet, such as young willow or hazelnut branches for basket making.

4. Lithic assemblages and bone industry

The operating sequences identified in the lithic assemblages show no significant differences throughout the sequence. Lithic production is aimed at obtaining laminar flake products almost exclusively from flint obtained from the immediate surroundings (in an arc of about 20 km), although quartzite, quartz and rock crystal are also present.

The core reduction strategies focus on preparing and then manufacturing plano points via parallel or convergent flaking from one or two striking platforms. The result is dome-shaped cores. Flaking is sometimes performed on convex or carinate surfaces, resulting in dome-shaped cores. In addition to these unipolar or two opposing striking platform systems, a third system is detected, which follows a reduction process based on either of these two reduction sequences and finishes by incorporating successive surfaces and platforms. In some cases, this third system is linked to a more opportunistic laminar flake objects and in others, to a desire to maximise the core reduction possibilities.

The most common type of retouched assemblages in levels I and II are blades and short scrapers. In addition, there is also a significant presence of denticulate retouch in the top level. In level III, and even more so in level IV, burins start to gain a certain level of representation but scrapers and above all, single, double or direct fine retouch back-edge blades are still more common. Finally the two lowest levels reflect a change in typology as burins exceed scrapers. This, in addition to the wider variety of raw materials, suggests a techno-typology transformation process, which would have to be evaluated properly when we have a larger record from levels V and VI (Martos *et al.*, 2013: 383-384).

The bone industry is relatively small; it is almost always quite fragmented and has been preferentially prepared on bone. Tools for day-to-day life stand out, mainly awls and needles, in this case with repairs on the hole and the shaft that indicate heavy use, probably for working skins. The small number of spears throughout the sequence could be because this type of tool was made of another material that is difficult to preserve, such as wood, or a hunting strategy that does not require them.

5. Personal ornaments and portable art

In total 53 decorative items have been recovered, all of them except one from the top section of the sequence (18 in level I, 9 in level II, 35 in level III and 1 in level IV). The absence of these in the lower section could be related to the smaller amount of

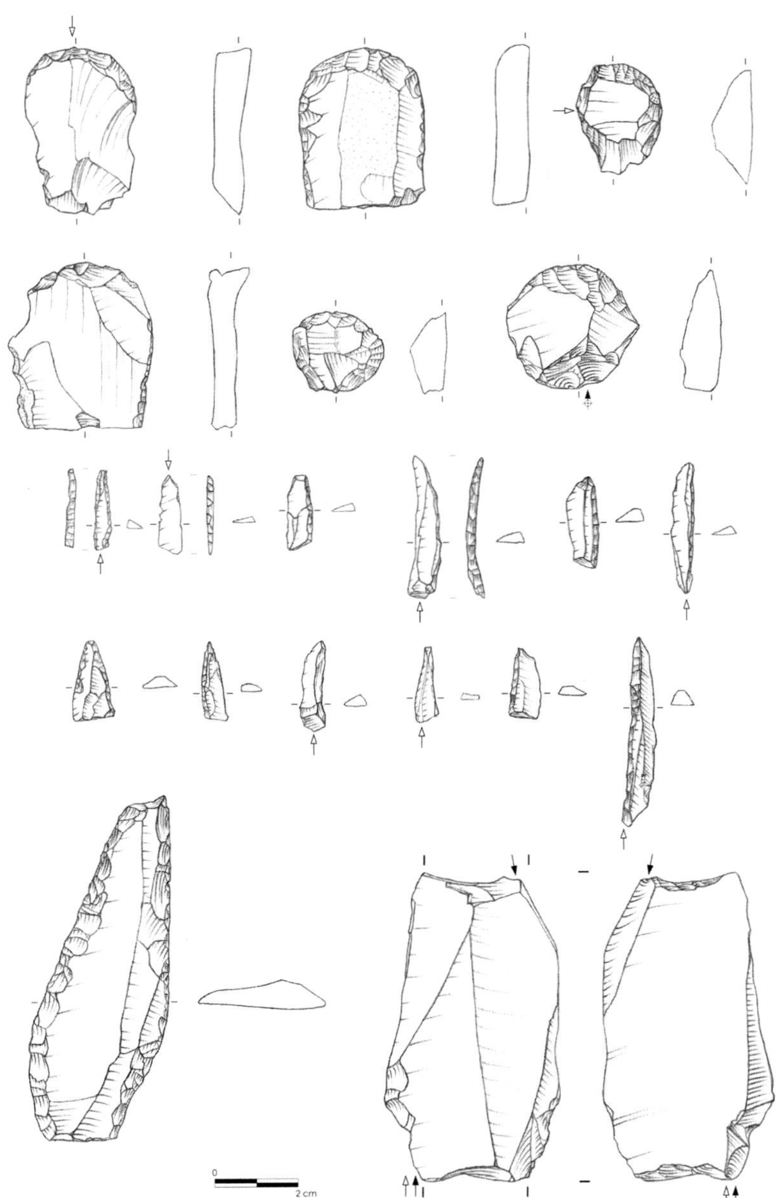

Figure 2. Lithic industry from level I of La Peña de Estebanvela.

sediment excavated. They have been made on gastropods (*Cyclope neritea, Trivia arctica, Trivia pulex, Littorina obtusata, Nassarius reticulatus, Theodoxus fluviatilis*), except for three stunted deer canines (*Cervus elaphus*) and a fourth on sepiolite. The use-wear analysis shows significant wear that refers to its constant use in the life of these Magdalenian groups.

The upper levels also contained an assemblage of 43 pieces of portable art made on small, flat, long stones, all of them shale. The art is geometric and has been made using fine incisions. Notches and zigzags are also present but the motif that is repeated throughout the assemblage is a pattern consisting of two opposing sets of parallel lines perpendicular to the largest axis of the support. Only two pieces are not geometric and include configurations of horses superimposed, on one of them, over these decorations (Cacho *et al.*, 2012: 51).

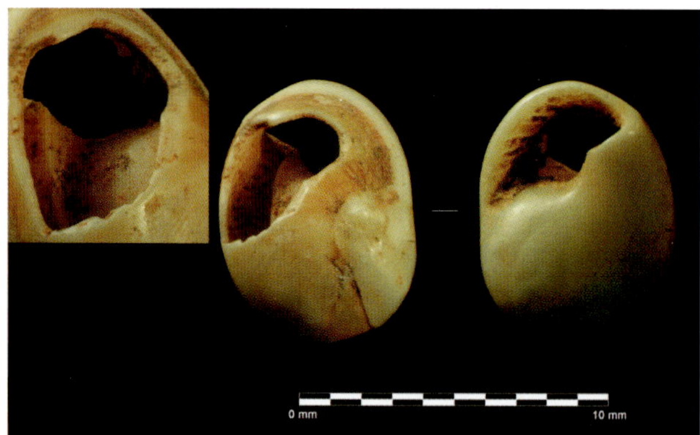

Figure 3. Decorative items on *Cyclope neritea* from level IV of La Peña de Estebanvela.

Figure 4. Decorated shale stone from level II of La Peña de Estebanvela.

6. Layout and functionality of the settlement

The analysis of the space based on the record from the latest campaigns has detected concentrations of materials of particular interest for finding out about the layout of the space. The most obvious is a crescent-shaped structure discovered in level III, in the central sector of the site, where several cores and debris and small flakes have been found and which has been interpreted as a knapping area (Ortega 2013: 526-527). In the same level, but in the eastern sector, a concentration of flint was found in an area where the compact calcareous sterile sediment comes into contact with the archaeological deposit. It is worth pointing out that the sterile sediment had been deliberately cut out of this sector. The pieces are arranged on it, almost stacked, in a small area of around 25cm^2. The entire assemblage is made from the same type of opaline, of excellent quality and uncommon in the lithic repertoire of the site. It mainly consists of large cores, barely shaped, with one or two extractions and good sized decortication flakes back to back. We consider that this concentration could be interpreted as a space that was for storing or stockpiling raw material.

In the eastern sector of level II, attributed to the end of the Magdalenian, three hearths were excavated (Cacho *et al.*, 2007: 236-237). They are flat-bottomed pit hearths surrounded by blocks. Two of them are slightly larger than one metre in diameter and are filled with a 10 to 15 cm layer of ash. The presence of lithic or fauna remains inside is negligible, the main reason for ruling out their use for domestic tasks like cooking or transformation and treatment of lithic raw materials. Furthermore, the presence of a large number of boulders (quartzite, quartz and limestone) with thermal fracturing, which demonstrates that they were heated, points to activities related to using these hearths to accumulate heat.

7. Contextualising the sequence of La Peña de Estebanvela in the Magdalenian of the inland Iberian Peninsula

Despite the advances made in the research over these years, it is not easy to contextualise the series of La Peña de Estebanvela in the chronocultural sequence of the inland Iberian Peninsula due to the small archaeological record known to date.

The sequence begins with level VI, whose radiocarbon dating values indicate a middle Magdalenian. The Vergara Rock Shelter (level 5d) (Deza, Soria) has returned similar dates, with which it can be related because the topology of its industry is similar to that of the interior units of Peña de Estebanvela. Level VI can also be linked to the lithic series of the Alejandre Rock Shelter, although it has a slightly earlier date (Utrilla and Blasco 2000:

21). On the southern slope of the Sistema Central, and quite close to La Peña de Estebanvela, is the Jarama II site (Valdesotos, Guadalajara), which does not have any C14 dating values. Its archaeological record is not significant enough to contextualise the sequence in this region (Adán and Jordá Pardo 1989). Monte Rock Shelter (Vellón, Madrid) has radiocarbon dating values that are close to the lower unit of La Peña de Estebanvela and its industry could be attributed to the start of the Magdalenian but it cannot be accurately evaluated until the details have been published (Vega *et al.*, 2008). In Meseta Sur there are another two sites, in the province of Cuenca, which given their dating values could be considered contemporary to level VI of La Peña de Estebanvela, Buendía and Verdelpino (level Vb), but their industries differ in the large number of burins and the presence of fine direct retouch blades, which are not present in level VI of La Peña de Estebanvela (Cacho and Pérez Marín, 1997; De la Torre *et al.*, 2007; Moure and López, 1979).

Human occupations of the Segovia Rock Shelter represented in levels III and IV are placed in an advanced period of the Upper Magdalenian, according to radiocarbon dating values; this fact is also supported by the lithic repertoires, which show a gradual increase in burins compared to scrapers. So far no parallels are known for the industries in these levels of the Meseta.

Levels I and II seem to belong to the same cultural period, with a lithic industry characterised by a large number of blades and a significant presence of points, followed by scrapers, the majority short. These characteristics, along with a significant proportion of large retouched blades, like at the end of the Magdalenian in the French Languedoc and Provence (Escalon de Fonton et Onoratini 1979), and the presence of needles that are not present in the archaeological record of Aziliense, put these levels in the end of the Magdalenian. In Henar valley is La Peña del Diablo 1 (Cetina, Zaragoza) with contemporary radiocarbon dating values (Utrilla *et al.*, 2006) to levels I and II of La Peña de Estebanvela. Its lithic industry shows significant differences with the site in Segovia, as burins dominate over scrapers, but here the number of back-edge blades and the number of points is not as significant as that of level I of La Peña de Estebanvela. The lithic series of Dehesa del Tejado (Béjar, Salamanca) (Fabián 1997) could belong to the same period, although it does not have a geoarchaeological context such as radiocarbon dating. Detailed technology studies are required for the industries attributable to this period of the Magdalenian, which could be compared with the data provided in this respect by La Peña de Estebanvela.

8. Final considerations

Today, despite the gaps in the Magdalenian panorama of the inland Iberian Peninsula, we have evidence that these lands were occupied throughout the different stages of the Magdalenian, from the early Magdalenian to the late Magdalenian, as happens in the surrounding area (the Cantabrian coast, the Mediterranean side and the Atlantic coast). These settlements not only occurred in the warmer climates, as happens in level I of La Peña de Estebanvela (according to the micro-mammal and herpetofauna studies), but also during the cold phases, as is the case of the Alejandre and Vergara shelters in Soria, in the Dryas I.

Regarding the exploitation model of the territory, we only have data for La Peña de Estebanvela, which indicates recurrent use of the immediate surroundings for hunting ungulates and some carnivores, trout fishing and possible gathering of wild fruit and nuts.

The clearest indications we have that these Magdalenian groups from the inland Iberian Peninsula had contact with other geographical areas are limited to La Peña de Estebanvela. A number of sea gastropods transformed into decorative objects were found here. These gastropods come from the Atlantic or Mediterranean coast. This implies movement of these Magdalenian groups to these areas in order to collect them but they could also have been obtained through exchanges with other groups that frequented these coastal areas. Further evidence of contact is found in the portable art in this Rock Shelter in Segovia, whose most characteristic motif is well represented in some sites in the French Pyrenees - Gourdan (Haute Garonne), Espelugues (Haute Pyrenées) or Rhodes (Ariège) – or further away from the Meseta, such as Pages (Lot) and Dufaure (Landes). There is even a similarity in its portable art with more remote sites, such as Rochedane near the Swiss border, which would indicate long-distance contact of these Magdalenian groups from the south of the Duero valley and would reflect common symbolism at the end of the Pleistocene.

Manuel Santonja*, Alfredo Pérez-González*

The Acheulean Pinedo site (Toledo), in the middle Tagus River basin

1. Discovery and study of Pinedo

The first research at Pinedo (Toledo) was conducted during the methodological renewal process begun in the early 1960's at Spain's oldest Palaeolithic sites. This revived interest in the discipline coincided with excavations by Clark Howell at Torralba and Ambrona sites in Soria Province (1961-1963), and was evidenced in regional studies and in other monographic research such as Gándaras de Budiño (Pontevedra) by E. Aguirre, and Pinedo itself, begun by Máximo Martín Aguado. This work helped to trigger the start of modern research into the early Palaeolithic following the drastic cut following the Civil War (Santonja and Vega, 2002).

A gravel pit opened on one of the middle terraces on the right bank of the Tagus River, immediately upstream from Toledo, permitted the identification of a lithic industry assemblage, one of the largest on the Iberian Peninsula. According to the results obtained by Martin Aguado and subsequent excavations between 1972 and 1976 by A. Querol (Querol and Santonja, 1979), the density of knapped stones in this sector of the terrace (30 ha) was approximately 50 per cubic meter in the set of levels of gravels and sands, with an average depth of 3-4 metres. This was possibly a retention phenomenon which occurred in the river alluvia immediately upstream from Toledo's Palaeozoic threshold, facilitating the buildup in this area of faunal remains and several million of worked items.

2. Stratigraphy and chronological elements

The Pinedo terrace (+25-30 m, Fig. 1) is in a lower-middle position in Toledo's Tagus sequence, which consists of 13 levels at relative heights ranging from +3-5 m to +125 m. Palaeomagnetic dating situated the start of the Brunhes chron (c. 780 ky BP) on the +60 m terrace (Pinilla *et al.*, 1995). Recent pIRIR datings of the Pinedo terrace (Lopez-Recio *et al.*, 2013) have indicated 292 $\pm$17 ky, towards the end of MIS 9. The fauna recorded at Pinedo *Lepus* cf. *europaeus*, *Oryctolagus cuniculus*, *Equus* sp., *Cervus elaphus*, *Bos* sp., *Palaeoloxodon antiquus* e *Hippopotamus amphibius* (Sesé *et al.*, 2000) is consistent with this date.

3. General features of the Pinedo Acheulean industries

The Pinedo industry was found in a secondary depositional context, in medium-energy conditions. It was generally typified by an abundance of pebble- and macro-tools –handaxes, cleavers and trihedrals– which fully match the Acheulean technocomplex (Fig. 2). Pieces with a less specific configuration led Pinedo to be inserted in an early stage of the Iberian Acheulean. Some of them may be interpreted as preforms, partially confirming the use of this area as a 'workshop'(Freeman, 1975). However a certain percentage of well-finished artefacts which were abandoned after use is linked to specific activities which took place on the river floodplain. Localized concentrations on the fluvial levels of Pinedo are definitely accumulations in secondary position, composed of remains from sites with different functionality.

4. Other Acheulean sites on the middle course of the river Tagus in Toledo

At other spots near Pinedo on the same terrace, identical sites have also been found which have expanded the area of remains in the immediate environs of Toledo (Pérez-González and Silva, 2009). The most important site is Cañete Bajo, ten kilometers upstream from Pinedo on the opposite bank of the Tagus. It has a similar density of lithic industry, together with fauna. It is also in secondary position, particularly in bed load deposits.

* Centro Nacional de Investigación sobre la Evolución Humana. (CENIEH); 09002 Burgos. manuel.santonja@cenieh.es

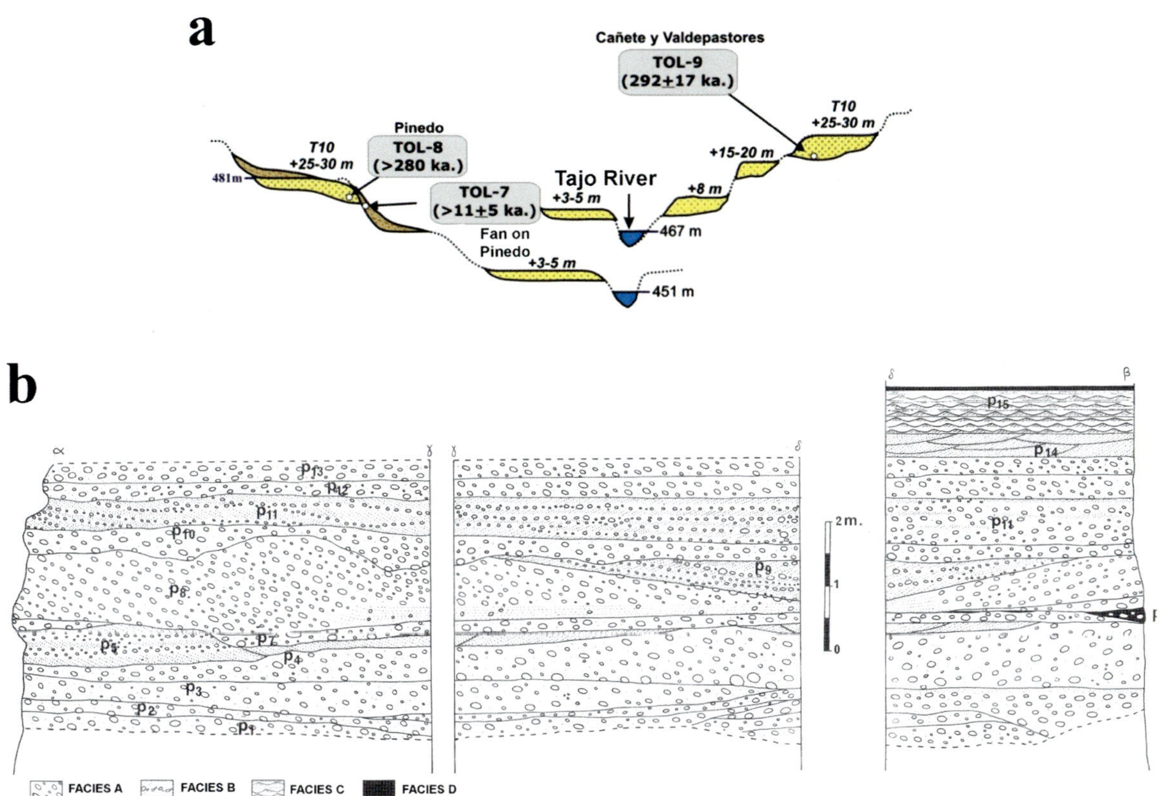

Figure 1. a) Diagram of the position of the +25-30 m Tagus terrace upstream from Toledo at the Pinedo site (right bank) and the Cañete Bajo site (left bank). According to López-Recio *et al.*, 2013b) Lateral sections produced by excavations on the Pinedo terrace. Facies A: Gravels with a coarse sand matrix. Facies B: Sets consisting of coarse sands with cross-laminations and gravel levels. Facies C: Fine sands with small-scale cross-stratifications and parallel laminations; Facies D: Massive silts and clays. According to Pérez-González and Díaz Martín, in Querol and Santonja 1979.

In addition to Pinedo and Cañete Bajo, other sites further upstream including La Flamenca in Aranjuez and Arroyo de los Huesos in the Añover de Tajo district (Rodríguez de Tembleque, 2005) have helped to show that human presence and activity on the Tagus Valley floor was intense around MIS 9.

Further west along the Tagus River, in the Talavera de la Reina district, there is a similar sequence of terraces to the Toledo area (Pérez-González and Silva, 2009), with Acheulean industry on several levels, probably dating from the beginning of the Middle Pleistocene (Rodríguez de Tembleque, 2005). Locations containing Acheulean sites have been identified in the Valdecañas reservoir and the Gébalo River. All of these series include handaxes and cleavers on flake. They confirm extensive human occupation along the middle course of the Tagus river.

The most important site in this latter sector is Puente Pino (Alcolea de Tajo, Toledo), possibly pre-dating Pinedo, on the +40 m terrace. Nine excavation campaigns were conducted between 2001 and 2011(Rodríguez de Tembleque *et al.*, 2010). The main level at Puente Pino is at the top of a fluvial sand deposit. It does not seem to have undergone significant movement. It only contains lithic industry, consisting of over 10,000 pieces in a 35 m^2 area, including a large component of microflakes and knapping debris. This assemblage is mainly in a primary position.

The Acheulean nature of the Puente Pino industry is manifested in the importance of the shaped tools –handaxes, cleavers and trihedral pics– ac-

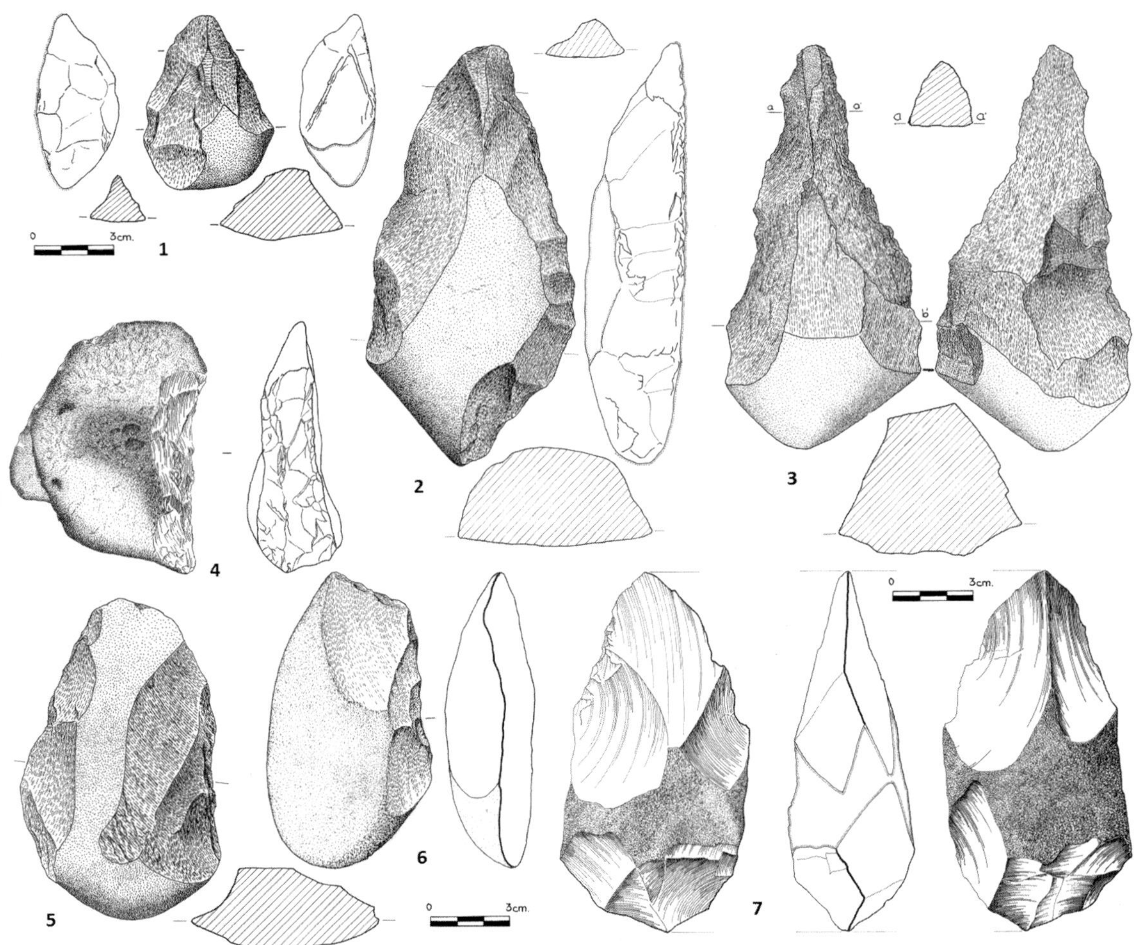

Figure 2. Small trihedral pic (1); trihedral pic (2-3); Quina sidescraper (4); *hachereaux* –type 0 (5) and type I (6); amygdaloid handaxe (7); small tools on flake: abrupt scraper (8); *tranchet* (9); denticulates (10 and 11); angled convergent scraper (12) and *bec* (13). 4, 7 and 9 are made in flint, the rest are quartzite.

companied by a non-standardized quartzite toolkit comparable to Pinedo, and an exploitation of cores with bifacial, multipolar and discoidal patterns, generally without hierarchical extraction surfaces.

The composition of the industry suggests that this site, on the bank of a small watercourse near its confluence with the river, was used for knapping and other activities, i.e., that the tools were produced and used on the same spot. Both the strategic location of Puente Pino and the existence of successive occupation levels suggests repeated visits, perhaps seasonal, over a long period.

Baquedano, E*., Márquez, B*., Laplana, C*., Arsuaga, J. L**, Pérez-González, A***.

The Archaeological sites at Pinilla del Valle (Madrid, Spain)

Introduction

The archaeological sites at Pinilla del Valle, to the north of the Autonomous Community of Madrid, are an exceptional location for learning about the evolution of the behaviour of human groups from the Middle Pleistocene to the Holocene. In Calvero de la Higuera, a headland of about 3.5 hectares, a number of sites of different origin and meaning covering a wide timespan are concentrated (Fig. 1).

Camino Cave was the first site to be discovered, in 1979 (Alférez *et al.*, 1982). Subsequent excavations carried out by the UCM team that discovered it resulted in the documentation of a significant fauna assemblage in the Pleistocene filling and two hominid molars belonging to *Homo neanderthalensis*.

Since 2002 a multi-disciplinary team led by the Regional Archaeological Museum of the Autonomous Community of Madrid has been managing the project. As a result of their work, another four sites –Navalmaíllo Rock Shelter, Buena Pinta Cave, Ocelado Rock Shelter and Des-Cubierta Cave–have been discovered on the same headland, another two in another promontory situated half a kilometre to the west –Toconal Cave and Carrión Cave– and finally, another open Acheulean site north east of Calvero de la Higuera (Márquez *et al.*, 2008).

Geographical and geological context

The Calvero de la Higuera sites are located in the upper valley of the river Lozoya in the Sierra de Guadarrama, a mountain range running NE-SW. Its general structure is pop-up and it is part of the Spanish Sistema Central (Pérez-González *et al.*, 2010).

The Lozoya valley is a tectonic depression (pop-down) running in the same direction as the pop-up of the Sistema Central, which is delimited to the north by the Carpetanos mountains, the highest peak of which is Peñalara (2428m), and to the south by Cuerda Larga. The bottom of the valley is situated at approximately 1100m.

From a geological point of view, it is part of the Complejo Esquisto-Grauváquico of the central Iberian Peninsula. However, the pop-up of the valley of the river Lozoya was formed in the Alpine orogeny. The oldest exposed rocks are gneisses, leucogranites, adamellites, granitoids, migmatites and, to a lesser extent, schists and quartzites. There are also late dykes in quartz, lamprofid and porfid.

Above the metamorphic rocks there are outcrops of sands, clays and carbonates, sandstones and bedded Late Cretaceous dolostones. On the latter, karstic processes have developed, such as a limestone pavements and dolines on the outside and Rock Shelters and caves on the inside. The Pinilla del Valle sites are associated with these types of processes (Pérez-González *et al.*, 2010). The Cretaceous materials contain invertebrates (brachiopods, echinoderms and rudists) and vertebrates (sharks, rays and fishes), which sometimes appear as reworked elements in the fillings of the karst forms in the valley (Hontecillas *et al.*, 2012). The marine sequence ends with a few dozen metres of sands, clays and gypsums in a marine-continental environment. Continental Paleogene materials are deposited in erosive unconformity.

The most recent Quaternary deposits are widely represented in the Lozoya valley. In the Peñalara massif, Late Pleistocene moraines associated with

* Museo Arqueológico Regional, Plaza de las Bernardas s/n, 28801-Alcalá de Henares (Madrid-Spain). E-mail: enrique.baquedano@madrid.org; belen.marquez@madrid.org; cesar.laplana.conesa@madrid.org.

** Centro Mixto UCM-ISCIII de Evolución y Comportamiento Humanos, Avda. Monforte de Lemos 5 – Pabellón 14, 28029-Madrid (Spain). E-mail: jlarsuaga@isciii.es

*** Centro Nacional de Investigación sobre la Evolución Humana (CENIEH), Pº Sierra de Atapuerca s/n, 09001– Burgos (Spain). E-mail: alfredo.perez@cenieh.es

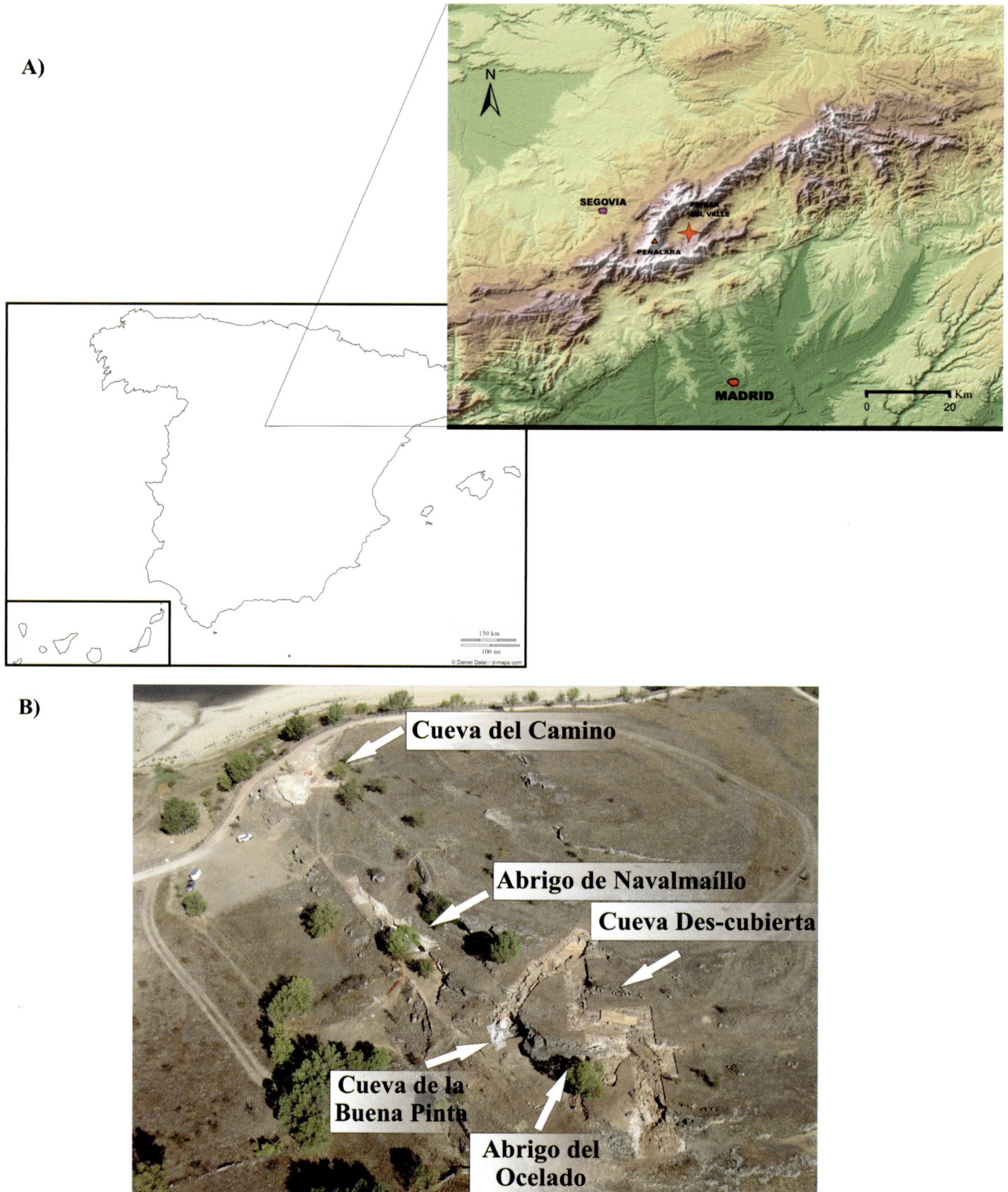

Figure 1. (a) Location of the sites at Pinilla del Valle the upper valley of the river Lozoya (Madrid) (b) Location of the main sites at Calvero de la Higuera (Modified by Pérez-González *et al.*, 2010).

cirques have been preserved. Other deposits are peat lands and screes and colluvial solifluidal layers of fine hillside materials (Pedraza 1994, Pedraza *et al.*, 2003).

In the central sector of the Lozoya valley there are fluvial deposits made up of blocks, gravel, sand and silt-clay, alluvial fans, terraces and alluvial plains.

The Calvero de la Higuera sites (1110m) are associated with cavities developed on an Late Cretaceous carbonate rock slope, inclined a few degrees towards the river Lozoya, which flows W-E along the valley. The Lontanar and Valmaíllo streams split the relief of the Calvero de la Higuera slope, leaving Camino Cave, Navalmaíllo Rock Shelter, Buena Pinta Cave, Ocelado Rock Shelter and Des-Cubierta Cave hanging (Pérez-González *et al.*, 2010).

The Calvero de la Higuera sites

Camino Cave

As mentioned earlier, Camino Cave was discovered in 1979. Nowadays, the ceilings of the cave are collapsed and broken up. The first excavations were carried out by Professor Alférez's team from 1980 to 1989. From 2002 new excavations were undertaken at the site, which lasted through to 2009.

In 2002 the area had been almost entirely excavated and it was difficult to establish lithic-stratigraphic relations between the sectors of the site. The bottom of the sequence consists of allochthonous siliceous facies formed by a fluvial terrace of gravel rod, sand, sandy mud and clay deposited by the Valmaíllo stream. This terrace has been TL dated using grains of quartzite at 140.4 ± 11.3 ky BP. Towards the top of the sequence and after partial emptying of the terrace facies, sand, loamy sand and silt facies with carbonate fragments from the karst dolostones are deposited. These facies contain the main fossil deposits, with TL dating values for level 5 of 90.9 ± 7.8 and 91.6 ± 8.1 ky BP (Pérez-González *et al.*, 2010), and amino acid racemization dating values of 94.4 ± 20.6 ky BP (Torres *et al.*, 2014), which put this accumulation in the MIS 5b.

The collapse of the ceiling and the apparent disappearance of the cave morphology at this site are related to the incision processes of the fluvial network, the action of the cold and disturbance and external erosion from MIS 4 to the Holocene (Pérez-González *et al.*, 2010).

Camino Cave has been divided into 4 sectors: North, Central, Diaclasa Roja and South (Arsuaga *et al.*, 2010). The highest concentration of fossils at the site is in the North sector, where 7 stratigraphic levels have been distinguished (numbered from 3 to 9) (Pérez-González *et al.*, 2010; Arsuaga *et al.*, 2011, 2012). Level 5 contains more than 53% of the NISP of macrofauna and presents a wider biodiversity. In 1982 and 1984 two molars –one right $M^1$and one right M^3, respectively– belonging to the same individual were found in this level, who in principle was identified as an ante-Neanderthal (Alférez *et al.*, 1982, Alférez and Roldán 1992), but they were later assigned to the *Homo neanderthalensis* species (Gómez Robles *et al.*, 2007, Martinón-Torres *et al.*, 2007, 2008, Quam *et al.*, 2009, Arsuaga *et al.*, 2011, 2012).

This site preserves one of the most complete MIS 5 fauna assemblages in the Iberian Peninsula. The association of large mammals from the North, Central and Diaclasa Roja sectors stands out for an abundance of carnivore remains. The spotted hyena (*Crocuta crocuta*) is the most abundant species with adult and young specimens and many coprolites. The site also contains, but in a lower number, *Ursus arctos, Canis lupus, Vulpes vulpes, Panthera leo, Lynx pardinus, Felis silvestris, Mustela putorius* and *Mustela nivalis.*

In these sectors, ungulates are represented by 6 species of Artiodactyla (*Dama dama geiselana, Cervus elaphus, Capreolus capreolus, Bos primigenius, Rupicapra rupicapra, Sus scrofa*) and 2 Perissodactyla species (*Equus ferus*¸ *Stephanorhinus hemitoechus*). Camino cave stands out for having the largest accumulation of fallow deer remains (*Dama dama*) in the Iberian Peninsula (Alvarez-Lao *et al.*, 2013).

The presence of young hyena remains and the high frequency of coprolites, bite marks and digested bones are indicative that the cave was used as a den by this species. The carnivore / ungulate ratio and bone fracturing patterns lead to the same interpretation. Anecdotal presence of lithic industry at the site should not be interpreted as a sign of human activity but as the result of it entering the cave via natural processes (Arsuaga *et al.*, 2012). The study of the age of the fallow deer at the time of death has concluded that hyenas occupied the cave for almost the entire year, with a small gap between May and June (Álvarez-Lao *et al.*, 2013).

The microvertebrate record is, as in the case of large mammals, one of the most complete from the Late Pleistocene in the Iberian Peninsula, with 49 species identified. The richness of the associations of microvertebrates at this site is due to several factors (Laplana *et al.*, 2013). Firstly, the intense sampling carried out at the site over the ten excavation campaigns. Secondly, the location in the upper valley of the Lozoya in areas of both Mediterranean and Euro-Siberian influence, surrounded by peaks of over 2000m, which increases rainfall. Thirdly, the diversity of the habitats surrounding the site as a consequence of the marked altitude gradient in the valley. And finally, small age differences in the fillings of the different sectors of the site, which translate into differences in their associations of microvertebrates.

Regarding the diachrony of the different sectors of the site, the stratigraphic criteria and biochronological dating coincide to establish a sequence in which the oldest sediments are located in the North sector and the most modern in the South sector, with an intermediate age for the Central and Diaclasa Roja sectors. The only dating obtained for the South sector returned a date of 74.5 ± 6.3 ky BP, in the limit between MIS 5 and MIS 4 (Pérez-González *et al.*, 2010). The Palaeoclimatic reconstruction based on successive associations of herpetofauna (Blain *et al.*, 2014) have allowed warm conditions to be inferred for the site in general, typical of the MIS 5, with some colder oscillations, the last and coldest of which is related to the transition from MIS 5 to MIS 4.

Navalmaíllo rock shelter

Discovered in 2002, Navalmaíllo rock shelter is a large cavity located 100m south of Camino Cave. As it collapsed after it had been occupied, its presence was not visually evident.

The main sequence of the site, from top to bottom, consists of a 40cm-thick Ap soil horizon, followed by at least two colluvium deposits approximately 1m thick. Under these units is another (level D) with large dolostones that fell when the ceiling collapsed. Surrounding these blocks is brown clay sediment injected from the underlying level F. The top in this level is highly deformed due to the weight of the fallen blocks. The main occupation of the site was developed in level F (Arsuaga *et al.*, 2011; Baquedano *et al.*, 2011-2012).

Two TL dating values have been obtained for this level, 71.6 ± 5.0 and 77.2 ± 6.0 ky BP, which indicate an age in the MIS 5a or early MIS 4 (Pérez-González *et al.*, 2010). A much older dating, 234.9 ± 65.3 ky BP, obtained through amino acid race-

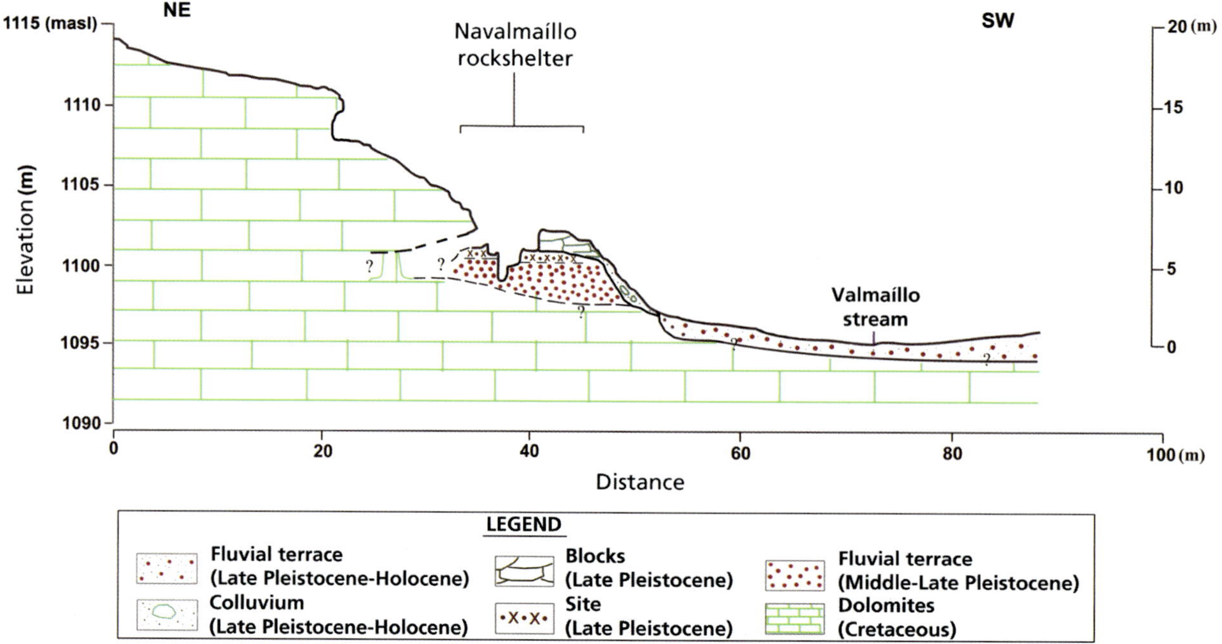

Figure 2. Relationship between the terraces and deposits in Navalmaíllo rock shelter, including the deposits with Neanderthal settlements (modified from Pérez-González *et al.*, 2010).

mization (Torres *et al.*, 2014) has been artificially aged by the heat of a medieval lime kiln excavated inside the shelter. When level F was occupied, the valley next to the Valmaíllo-Lontanar alluvial system would have been vertically very close to the settlement. Under level F there are at least 2m of gravel and siliceous sand allochthonous fluvial facies deposited by the Valmaíllo stream (Fig. 2).

The association of large mammals in levels D and F has only been studied in part. The majority of the fauna remains studied belong to medium-to-large animals. Provisionally, the taxa represented include *Dama dama, Cervus elaphus, Bos primigenius, Equus ferus, Stephanorhinus hemitoechus, Vulpes vulpes, Oryctolagus cuniculus, Lepus* sp. *Chelonia* indet (Arriaza 2011; Huguet *et al.*, 2010; Baquedano *et al.*, 2010; Baquedano *et al.*, 2011-2012).

The preliminary taphonomic studies show a high frequency of fresh bone fractures. A number of fragments show impact marks, hammerstone marks and cut marks, which indicate a high level of anthropic activity (Baquedano *et al.*, 2011-2012, Márquez *et al.*, 2013). The low presence of axial skeleton elements indicates selective transport of prey by hominids from the place of procurement to the place of consumption.

The presence of carnivores is irrelevant in the Navalmaíllo Rock Shelter and it seems that when they had access to prey, this was in a secondary way. The carnivores in Navalmaíllo probably accessed the site in search of remains abandoned by the hominids.

There is a clear presence of hearths in level F, α and β. Micromorphology studies of the hearths in levels α and β indicate post depositional processes that slightly shifted the remains (Goldberg and Mallol 2006). As it has only been partially excavated, there is no evidence of any remains of the nearest combustion structure from which the excavated hearths could have come. Regarding the hearths in level F, five have been found so far, which seem to have a bimodal system, where the smallest are nearest to the wall and the largest are further away from it (Baquedano *et al.*, 2011-2012).

Regarding the lithic industry, in Navalmaíllo rock shelter several levels contain Mousterian industry: so far, levels D, F, H, α, β, γ and C. Level H has only been excavated in part, in a small area in the north of the Rock Shelter. Levels α, β, γ have been documented in part in two points in the north and south of the Rock Shelter. Level C is still being studied.

From 2002 to 2013, in level F, which as mentioned earlier contains the main settlement of the Rock Shelter, more than 11,000 pieces of lithic industry were recovered. Fifteen types of raw material were documented, although six account for the highest percentages of use: quartz, flint, quartzite, porfid, rock crystal and sandstone. Approximately 77% of the tools are made of quartz. The products made of the different raw materials are similar (Márquez *et al.*, 2013).

The majority of these materials can be found in the surrounding area of the sites, from gravel deposits from the Lontanar and Valmaíllo streams and the river Lozoya. As flint does not appear in these deposits or in the Cretaceous facies of the valley, they might have come from Cretaceous or Miocene outcrops in the Duero basin, to the north, or from the Madrid basin, to the south.

There are hardly any traces of the use of a soft hammerstone for knapping tools but a hard hammerstone is frequently used, as well as bipolar knapping on an anvil. In this respect, the presence of pink porfid anvils has been documented in the site.

The main knapping techniques used in Navalmaíllo Rock Shelter were bifacial and unifacial combined with centripetal techniques, unipolar-longitudinal, orthogonal, Levallois and discoid. The rock crystal and flint cores are those that are most frequently knapped using a bifacial-centripetal technique. The majority of the materials were knapped in the site, the operating sequence being complete in general, expect for perhaps flint and sandstone.

The largest flakes were usually chosen for retouch. Among the retouched objects, denticulate tools are the most common, followed by notches and racloirs (Fig. 3).

A noteworthy characteristic of the Mousterian assemblage at Navalmaíllo is that the tools are small in general. The intention to make small products is clear if we look at the abundant presence of small cores. The shortage of raw materials can be ruled out as the reason behind this behaviour, as there are plenty of these materials in the environment, expect for the aforementioned flint, the source of which is yet unknown. Use-wear analyses could shed some light on the use of the small knapped products in Navalmaíllo.

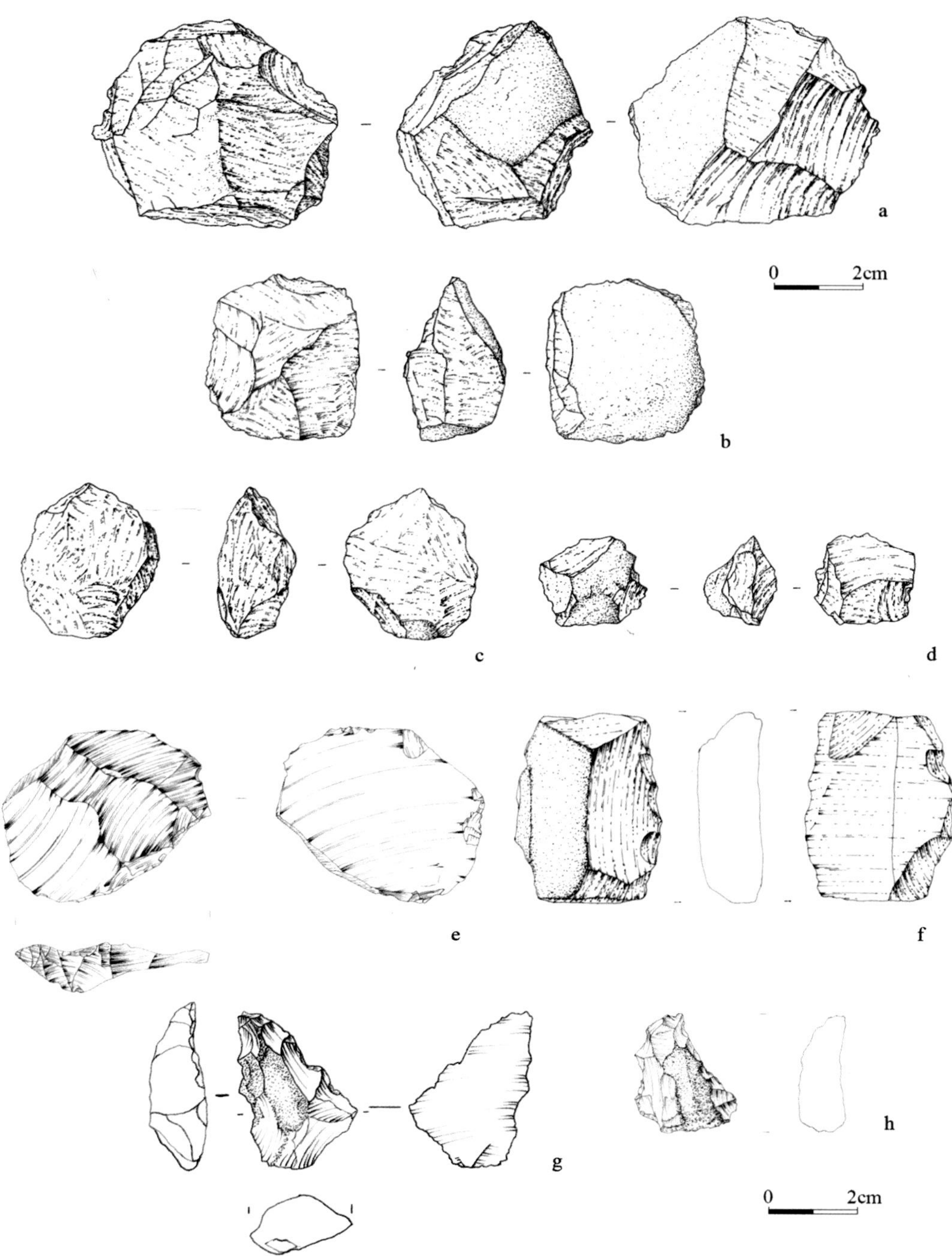

Figure 3. Lithic industry at Navalmaíllo rock shelter: a) Trifacial quartz core; b) Unifacial centripetal quartz core; c) Bifacial centripetal core; d) Quartz micro-core; e) Levallois flake; f) Sandstone denticulate tool; g) Flint denticulate points; h) Retouched flint flake (Modified by Márquez *et al.*, 2013).

Buena Pinta Cave, Ocelado rock shelter And Des-Cubierta Cave

Buena Pinta Cave was discovered in 2003 as a result, as in the case of Navalmaíllo Rock Shelter, of the surveying work undertaken by the excavation team. Located a few metres south of Navalmaíllo rock shelter, it is a small gallery with an elliptical section of phreatic origin measuring 10 m long, which at the time it was discovered was completely filled with sediment. This gallery is 7-8m above the Valmaíllo stream.

Two main units have been distinguished; one Holocene at the top, which covers the deposits from the Pleistocene. We have C14 AMS (2 sigma) dating values for the Holocene unit between 5,740-5,610 and 1,940-1,800 cal BP. Level 3 of the Pleistocene unit has a TL dating value of 63.4 ± 5.5 ky BP, which would put it in MIS 4 (Ruiz Zapata *et al.*, 2008, 2012). Recently, Torres *et al* (2014) presented an older dating of 85.5 ± 11.9 ky BP for the same level of Buena Pinta Cave, obtained using amino acid racemization.

The excavations performed to date reveal an extremely complex network of facies in the Pleistocene unit, all of which are autochthonous. Their stratigraphic relations have not yet been well defined (Baquedano *et al.*, 2011-2012). However, it can be said that fauna remains modified by the activity of large carnivores have been documented at all levels. Like Camino Cave, hyenas used the cavity as a den (Huguet *et al.*, 2010; Baquedano *et al.*, 2011-2012). According to the preliminary data available, the assemblage of large mammals documented at this site is similar to that recovered in Camino Cave, in terms of conditions of preservation and the species present (Arsuaga *et al.*, 2011). The same does not occur with the microvertebrate species, particularly, micromammals. In this case, there is a marked contrast with the associations in Camino Cave due to the presence of species adapted to cold climates in Buena Pinta Cave, such as the tundra vole (*Microtus oeconomus;* Sevilla 2012) and the steppe pika (*Ochotona pusilla;* Laplana *et al.*, 2009) and others, not present in the former. This data suggests colder formation conditions for the site than in Camino Cave, which coincides with the climate interpretation for the palynological sequence (Ruiz Zapata *et al.*, 2008).

In contrast to Camino Cave, evidence of human activity has been detected based on the presence of lithic industry, which is more abundant in the lower level (5) and outer level (23) of the cave. However, the percentage of bone remains is always significantly higher than the presence of lithic remains, human presence at this site being sporadic.

Quartz, as happens in the Calvero de la Higuera sites, is the material preferred for making tools. Flakes that have not been retouched are the most common, followed by fragments. The cores at Buena Pinta Cave have been unifacial, bifacial or trifacial unipolar longitudinal knapped and less frequently, orthogonal bipolar and opposing bipolar. In general, they are partly formed. As happens in Navalmaíllo Rock Shelter, denticulate tools stand out among the retouched pieces and the use of bipolar knapping on an anvil has also been documented (Baquedano *et al.*, 2011-2012).

In Buena Pinta Cave two molars assigned to *Homo neanderthalensis* have been found in level 3 of the site (Huguet *et al.*, 2010).

In Ocelado rock shelter, a small gallery a few metres south of Buena Pinta Cave, fauna remains have appeared; these include, once again, hyena remains, which lead us to think of a small den.

Finally Des-Cubierta Cave was discovered more recently (2009) and is therefore still being studied. It is a long gallery that runs NW-SE at the top of Calvero de la Higuera. It contains fillings with lithic materials and fauna remains that cover a chronological period from the Middle Pleistocene to the Late Pleistocene. In the oldest levels of this site, Laplana *et al.*, (2013) describe an association of unique micromammals compared to those known in the centre of the Iberian Peninsula, with species in this site that reach the southern end of their distribution during the Middle Pleistocene, such as *Microtus vaufreyi* or *Microtus agrestis*.

The appearance of various *Homo neanderthalensis* child remains are noteworthy.

Conclusions

The Pinilla del Valle sites assemblage represents an almost continuous record of the final stages of the Middle Pleistocene, represented in some sectors of Des-Cubierta Cave, and the majority of the Late Pleistocene, with the succession of Camino Cave-Navalmaíllo rock shelter-Buena Pinta Cave - more modern levels of Des-Cubierta Cave. Its significant paleontological record (pollen, carbons, vertebrates) allows us to specify cold climates and environments that would serve as a framework for the Neanderthal settlements in a mountainous region like the Sistema Central. The study of the archaeological record at the Pinilla del Valle sites also allows us to know the characteristics of these settlements, how the hominids adapted to their environment and how they interacted with it. The fact that they are sites with different functions gives added interest to the assemblage.

Some of the sites also have anthropological remains, all of which belong to the *H. neanderthalensis* species. By continuing with the excavation work over the next few years, we will undoubtedly be able to extend the time frame represented at the Pinilla del Valle sites and increase the archaeological and paleobiological record, thereby helping to enhance our knowledge of this chronological period in the centre of the Iberian Peninsula.

Acknowledgments

This study has been conducted in the framework of the S2010/BMD-2330 project funded by the R and D activity programme for research groups of the Ministry of Education, Youth and Sports of the Autonomous Community of Madrid. We are grateful to the Ministry of Employment, Tourism and Culture of the Autonomous Community of Madrid for the funding. The General Foundation of the University of Alcalá executes financial management of the project. The authors would also like to thank Mahou-San Miguel S.A. for its work as sponsor, and to the Peñalara Nature Reserve, Pinilla del Valle Town Hall and Canal de Isabel II for their collaboration. .Finally, we would like to thank the Pinilla del Valle excavation team for its work, without which this publication would not have been possible.

Marcos Terradillos-Bernal*,**, J. Carlos Díez Fernández-Lomana*, Jesús-Francisco Jordá Pardo***, Alfonso Benito-Calvo****, Ignacio Clemente*****, Alexandra Hilgers******

San Quirce (Palencia, Spain), a Middle Paleolithic site on the northern plateau

1. Introduction and Background

Surveys were conducted in the 1980s and 1990s to identify prehistoric occupations in the middle reaches of the Pisuerga River between Alar del Rey and Astudillo (Palencia) (Arnaíz, 1990), which resulted in the recovery of many Paleolithic series.

San Quirce was the only excavated site. It was discovered during the preparation of a gravel pit. The terrace was cut and three profiles were surveyed, measuring 35 m (east) and 40 m (north). Excavation was conducted in two areas, with 19,537 lithic artefacts recovered along with two small hearths attributed to the Acheulean period (Arnaíz, 1996).

The current research team resumed the excavations in 2009 in the context of a new survey and research project in the Pisuerga River valley. To date there have been three excavations.

2. Context

The San Quirce Paleolithic site is located in the extreme north of the Duero Basin (UTM: X = 392.828, Y = 4.720.122, Z = 861 m. using H30N, reference system ETRS89) on a river terrace +22- 23 m (T9). The context is of great interest since it is located in a strategic contact area between the Cantabrian Mountains and the Northern Plateau. Terrace T9 consists of gravel bars and a clay matrix, mostly by illuviation. Four major stratigraphic units were identified: Colluvium (I), colluvium (II), floodplain at the distal end of an alluvial fan (III) and river terrace deposits (IV) (Fig. 1).

We have obtained an OSL dating sequence between 74 ± 16 ky in sandy flood deposits (profile E in the quarry and lateral variation of level III) and 154 ± 18 ky in the area excavated on level III

* Área de Prehistoria. Universidad de Burgos mterradillos@hotmail.com, clomana@ubu.es
** Fundación Atapuerca
*** Dpto. de Prehistoria y Arqueología. Universidad Nacional de Educación a Distancia
**** Centro Nacional de Investigación sobre evolución Humana (CENIEH)
***** Institució Milà i Fontanals-CSIC
****** Institute of Geography – University of Cologne

(samples SQ1 and SQ4 measured at the University of Cologne Institute of Geography).

3. Palaeolithic archaeological record

An assemblage of 651 lithic technology items from level III at San Quirce has been identified. Raw material gathered in the proximity of the site included quartzite (85.5 %), quartz (11.7 %) and allochthonous flint (2.1 %) brought from more than 15 km away.

The main features of the quartzite knapping are: highly homogeneous, fine grain, high resistance to fracture and resorted small cracks in 70% of cases, invisible from the cortex, which generated a large percentage of fractures.

There is a major presence of hammerstones and *manuports* (12.5 %) and flakes (68.9 %). There is a small proportion of cores (8.1 %), characterized by low complexity and lack of predetermination. The cores are medium to small size with a length of 61 mm and a weight of 147.5 g. These dimensions and the large number of final negatives suggest high knapping intensity. Reduction methods are varied, primarily unifacials, unipolar with orthogonal angles. Only 58 retouched artefacts were documented, 72% on flake. These are small items (mean 57 mm). Only three bases measure more than 10 cm. The tools lack a complex knapping system, and are very specialized, as denticulates prevail in tools on pebble (43.7 %) and also on flake (78.6 %). Small trihedrals and worked pebbles have also been identified, while Acheulean morphotypes such as handaxes or cleavers are absent (Fig. 2). Edge production is concentrated mainly on flakes (67.6 %); therefore the edges are mainly sharp and rough. The retouched edges of the tools only reach 21 % of the entire perimeter. 21 lithic refits have been identified, all on quartzite. The maximum distance between cores in the same group is 535 cm. Numerous traces of use are preserved. These tools were used for processing meat, hides, wood and vegetable fibres. Among the 313 items recovered in 2009, 13 tools were identified as having been exploited in butchery activities (meat used as a food resource and hides as raw material for manufacturing other products), 21 tools and one small sharpened quartz flake linked to woodworking, 13 tools used on vegetable fibres, while 3 quartzite pebbles bore signs of use as hammerstones (Clemente-Conte *et al.*, 2012). Signs of crushing and scraping plant material suggests the production of rope.

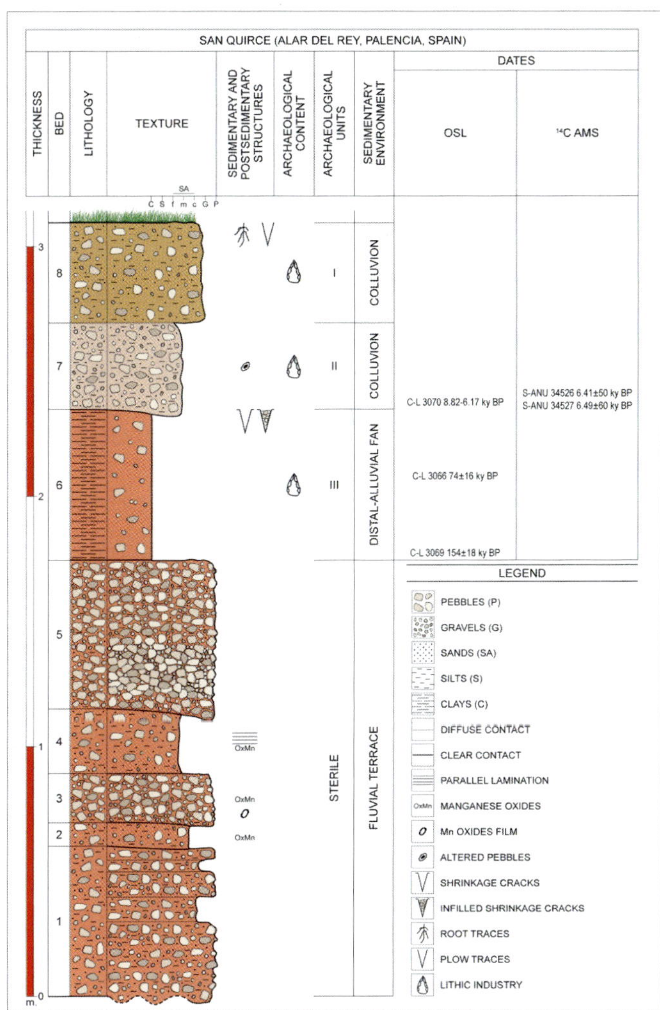

Figure 1. Overall stratigraphy of San Quirce.

The San Quirce lithic repertoire resembles Mode 3, albeit characterised by particular circumstances (speed of production and a unique tool mode, see Terradillos, 2010: 346; Terradillos and Díez 2012). San Quirce has become a highly relevant open air site on the Iberian Peninsula since it contains a Paleolithic assemblage which has been preserved in-situ, composed of a broad technological repertoire in which numerous refits and traces of use have been identified.

4. Holocene occupations

After the Palaeolithic occupations, at the start of the colluvium formation which sealed it (level II), we recorded four superimposed combustion structures alongside a charred post hole. Datings (^{14}C) for two carbon samples were 7,450-7,250 calBP and 7,520-7,280 calBP (Australian National

University), confirming dates previously obtained by OSL (range 6.17 - 8.82 ky, sample SQ5, Institute of Geography, University of Cologne). Structures were not accompanied by any other ceramic or lithic item which would have allowed permitted the description of these Holocene populations.

5. Conclusions

This site is unique on the Northern Plateau due to the extraordinary conservation of its Middle Palaeolithic lithic record. This has facilitated the analysis of its technology, spatial distribution and uses. San Quirce contains a rich and varied record which shows how its space was occupied, mainly for meat consumption and work on plant resources.

This is a reference site in the search for evidence of Neanderthal patterns, cultural exchanges (learning, shared space) and resource administration (food, deferred consumption, differential deposition of objects ...).

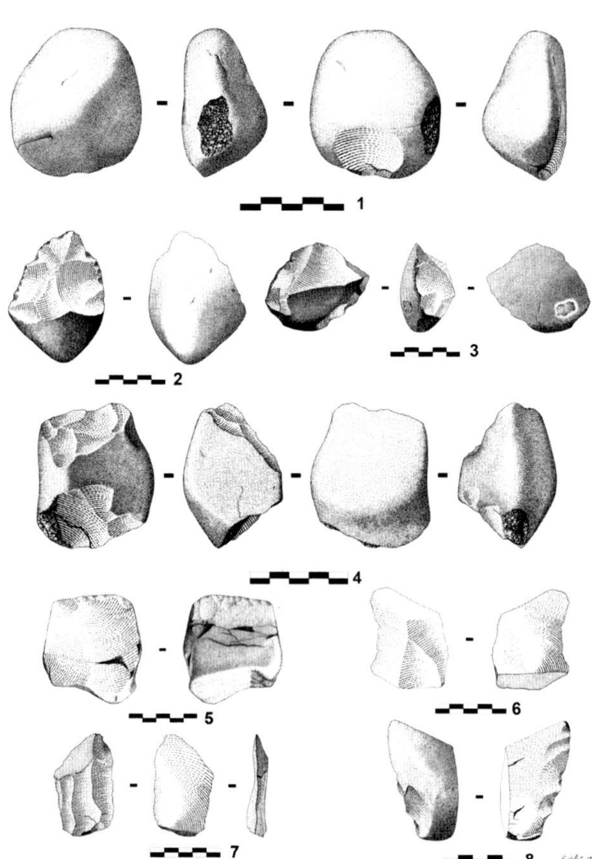

Figure 2. Lithic industry from San Quirce level III 2009. Quartzite. 1: Pebble with fractures and stigmas; 2 and 3: Pebble tool; 4 and 5: Pebble core; 6 and 7: Flakes; 8: Denticulate on flake.

Technologically, the tool repertoire at San Quirce varies significantly from the main Middle Palaeolithic sites. The lithic assemblage lacks great complexity, it is highly specialized in light denticulates produced with little power and characterized by fast production and poor cutting ability. Large handaxe and cleaver morphotypes, Levallois and Quina methods are all absent from the record. Neither the strictly Acheulean nor Mode 3 traditions have been distinguished. San Quirce cannot be included in the developed models of Mode 1 and Mode 2. Instead, it must be contextualised in a Mode 3 characterised by the particular circumstances of this assemblage.

During the digs in the 1990s, San Quirce stood out on account of its small outdoor hearths, presumably Palaeolithic. Carbon dating of a depression has shown that the larger hearth (over two metres) is from the Holocene. This team has also identified another three circular hearths measuring 40x30x3 cm, 20x15x3 cm (L9) and 35x25x3 cm each (M9), which might be Palaeolithic, although caution is advisable pending new datings.

Only a small part of the San Quirce Neanderthals campsite has been dug to date. Its archaeological record contains an unusual variety of evidence of work with wood and vegetable fibres.

Acknowledgments

MT-B has been the beneficiary of a fellowship from the Cátedra Atapuerca (Fundación Atapuerca and Fundación Duques de Soria). This research is part of project Order EDU/940/2009 from Education Department of the Castilla y León Regional Government.

VENDIMIA, MILLAR, CUEVA DE SANTA ANA, CUEVA DE MALTRAVIESO AND CUEVA DE EL CONEJAR

Antoni Canals*,**,***,†, Victoria Aranda***, Nova Barrero***,****, Lucía Bermejo***,*****, Paolo Donadei***, Isidoro Campaña***,***** Francisco J. García***, Dolores Megías***, Juan Marín***, Mario Modesto***,*****, Abel Morcillo***, Ana Rabazo***, Antonio Rodríguez-Hidalgo*,***, Eudald Carbonell*,**,***.

1. Santa Ana cave, Cáceres (Extremadura)

Santa Ana cave is located on the grounds of the CEFOT Troop Training Centre #1, Cáceres province, at the base of two hills, Alcor del Roble and Alcor Santa Ana, from which it takes its name (37°N x = 547193.1375737764 y = 9296013.12126188). The southeast-facing entrance porch, now sunken, is near Santa Ana Creek. Geologically, the cave is in Caceres *Calerizo*, a limestone structure on the large granite Cáceres peneplain covered by the characteristic Berrocale landscape. It is surrounded to the northeast by the quartzite outcrops of the Cáceres Ranges and to the south by the Salor and Ayuela Rivers which flow past the foot of the San Pedro Range. These and other neighbouring zones form a cultural unit defined as the "Cacereño Complex". There are three caves in the Calerizo zone: Maltravieso, El Conejar and Santa Ana. The first two extend inside the Calerizo complex, while Santa Ana is the only one on the mountain crests that separate the Calerizo limestone from the adjacent granite zone. Alcor de Santa Ana and Alcor del Roble are easily accessed from the Salor River wetlands, where the Vendimia and El Millar open air sites are located. Crossing the nearby Gamellas Pass, the visitor leaves the mountain zone, crosses the Calerizo and arrives at Rivera de Marco, the natural outlet to the Guadiloba River across the Vegas del Mocho terraces. The presence of caves in a territory facilitates the establishment of fixed points with rapid access to a wide range of scattered resources such as plant and animal biomass, and raw material for toolmaking. In Calerizo, all these resources are concentrated in a small area. Moreover, the water table surfaces inside Santa Ana cave, forming a small lake. Archaeological work between 2000 and 2013 defined the general stratigraphic sequence of the site (Fig. 1). From the information gathered to date, the whole cave seems to have been affected by major post-sedimentary and taphonomic processes. Unfortunately, a large-scale cut and fill destroyed most of the sediment at the entrance, and the cone which clogged the interior has been affected by erosion and drag. The test pits are located at the entrance and inside the cave. This is where a rich palaeontological level was discovered in 2012, albeit without associated cultural material, which opens up new archaeological perspectives as it does not seem to have been affected by the aforementioned sedimentary processes.

Geological problems affecting the sediments have prevented the collection of palaeomagnetic and biostratigraphic data or reliable radiometric dating. The Institut de Paléontologie Humaine in Paris (IPH) has only been able to analyse the speleothem that closes

* Institut Català de Paleoecologia Humana i Evolució Social. C/ Marcel·lí Domingo s/n – Campus Sescelades URV (Edifici W3). 43007 – Tarragona – SPAIN.
** Àrea de Prtehistòria. Universitat Rovira i Virgili. Avda. Catalunya, 35,43002 Tarragona.
*** Equipo Primeros Pobladores de Extremadura. Casa de Cultura "Rodríguez Moñino", Avda. de Cervantes, s/n. 10005 CACERES – SPAIN.
**** Museo de Nacional de Arte Romano de Mérida. C/ José Ramón Mélida, s/n. 06800, Mérida.
***** CENIEH. Paseo Sierra de Atapuerca, s/n, 09002 Burgos, España
† Corresponding author. acanals@iphes.cat

Cueva de Santa Ana
(Cáceres, Extremadura)
Stratigraphic columns

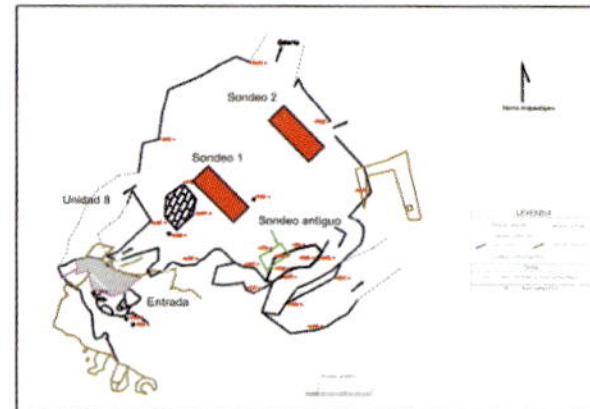

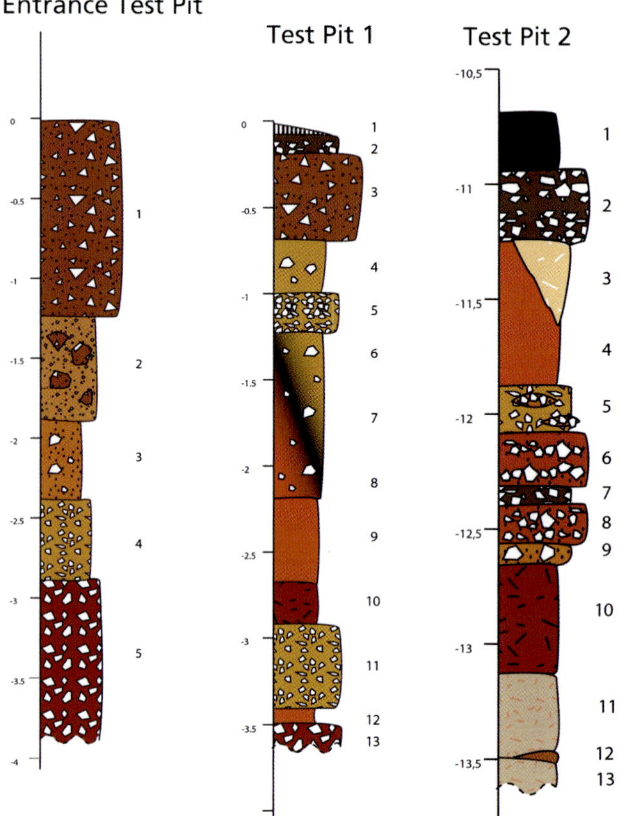

Figure 1. Santa Ana cave. Stratigraphic sequences defined in surveys. Entrance: Level 1 is a sedimentary breccia composed of angular fragments, agglutinated by natural cement with a clay matrix, with large-format archaeological objects, primarily handaxes. Levels 2, 3, 4 and 5 alternate a sequence of coarse/decimetric gravel and more or less sandy silt. Test pit 1: begins with a speleothem. Level 3 is a breccia, and levels 4 to 13 alternate gravels, clays and silts; Test pit 2: a layer of black clay covers the sequence (1), which contains modern materials, a layer of gravel (2), silt (3 and 4), a gravel sequence (5,6,7,8) and sandy loam (9). Levels 10 and 13 contain red clay and palaeontological material.

the complete sequence at the cave entrance, dated at 130,000 ± 8,000 BP (230Th/234U). The most outstanding feature of the stone tools from Santa Ana cave (Fig. 2) is the presence of the first three technical modes, with a clear predominance of Mode 2. Handaxes predominate in the Santa Ana assemblage. Many of the butts still have the original cortex or unmodified areas which facilitates their comprehension. Despite tapho-sedimentary problems, this material is exceptionally well preserved. Abundant water or moisture in the sediment precipitated a thin layer of calcite which protected it against erosion and corrosion, and traceology analysis has found extraordinary marks from the tools' usage on meat and wood.

The palaeontological assemblage from the cave, anthropised judging by the cut marks, spans a wide range of species with a possible time range from 600,000 to 200,000 BP. The carnivores include *Ursus sp.*, wolf (*Canis lupus*), badger (*Meles meles*), Iberian lynx (*Lynx pardinus*), fox (*Vulpes vulpes*) and hyena (*Crocuta crocuta*). Coprolites and bones of these animals have been found, indicating stable occupation. Herbivores include rhinoceros (*Rinhocerontidae sp.*), deer (*Cervus elaphus*), horse (*Equus cf. ferus*), aurochs (*Bos sp.*) and wild boar (*Sus scrofa*). The rich variety of species in Santa Ana cave provides an important insight into the biodiversity of the Calerizo area. In conjunction with Maltravieso and El Conejar caves, this is a unique assemblage in SW Iberia. The Santa Ana cultural record, characterized by large format Acheulean tools, cannot be inserted in any specific or intra-site context at present due to the lack of well-preserved occupation levels, nor an extra-site context due to the lack of regional comparison (dated stratigraphies).

Cueva de Santa Ana

(Cáceres, Extremadura)

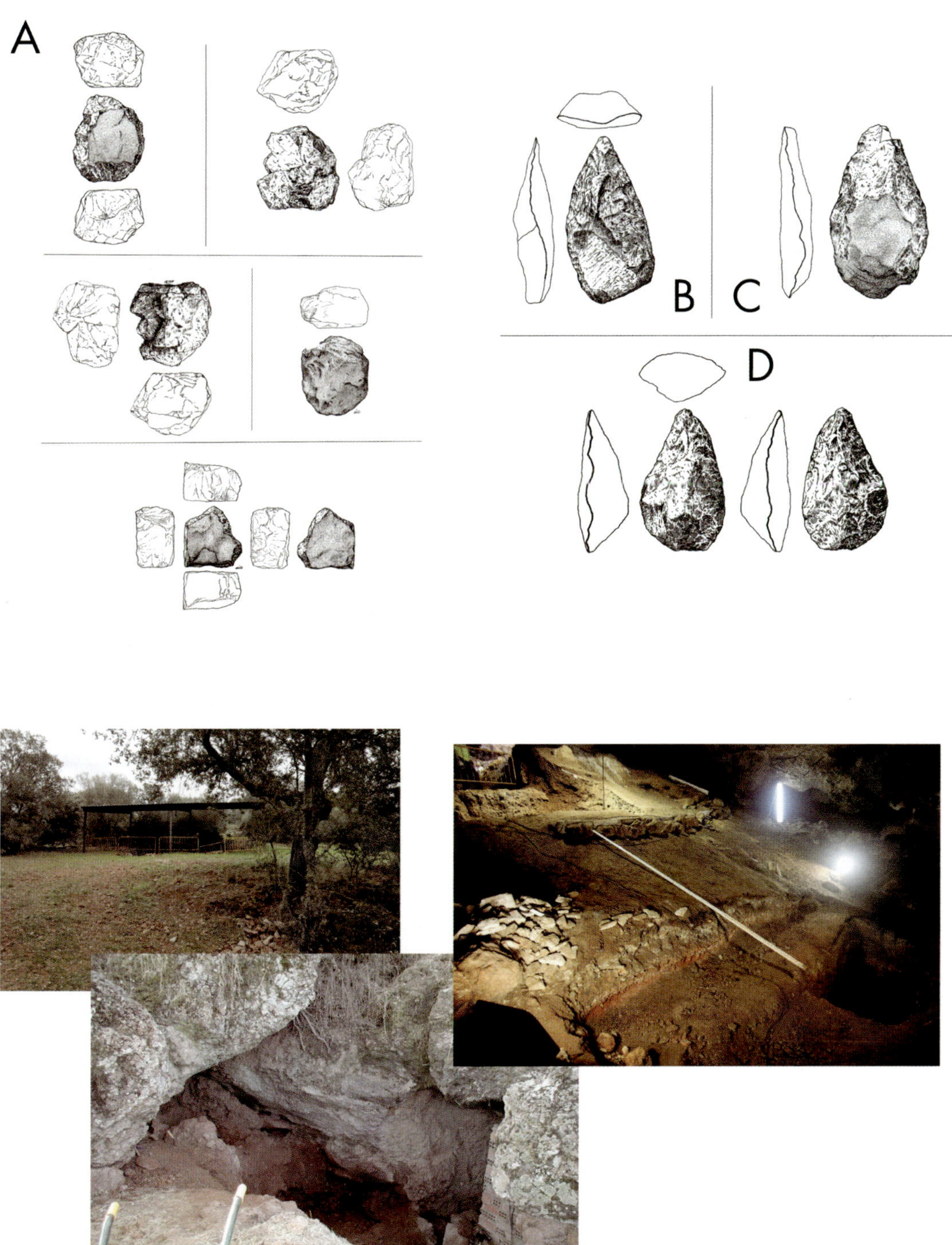

Figure 2. Santa Ana cave: A) quartz stone industry from the entrance test pit. B and C) quartzite handaxe from the entrance pit D) quartz handaxe from the test pit 1. Photos show current cave entrance and interior, with test pits 1 and 2 (top to bottom).

Antoni Canals*,**,***,†, Victoria Aranda***, Nova Barrero***,****, Lucía Bermejo***,*****, Paolo Donadei***, Isidoro Campaña***,***** Francisco J. García***, Dolores Megías***, Juan Marín***, Mario Modesto***,*****, Abel Morcillo***, Ana Rabazo***, Antonio Rodríguez-Hidalgo*,***, Eudald Carbonell*,**,***.

2. Maltravieso cave, Cáceres (Extremadura)

Maltravieso cave (37N x=550590.8801250727 y = 9295773.420866288) is a unique example of karst in urban areas. This natural structure was used recurrently by the human communities which inhabited the Caceres Calerizo area from at least the second half of the Middle Pleistocene until the Bronze Age. This cave system, which also includes Santa Ana and Conejar caves, is part of the "Cacereño Complex", an inclusive unit composed of two

Cueva de Maltravieso
(Cáceres, Extremadura)

Stratigraphic sequence

Sala de las chimeneas

Sp S FgB
0,50
0
?

FACIES DESCRIPTION	DEPOSIT	LEVEL
Altered speleothem	Alluvial	Cn1
Gravels and sand red clay with sheet stratification		
Red sand clay with humic content and clast altered		
Gravels and red lens-shaped clay sands stratification		
Archaeological level	Rock fall	A
Blocks partially infilling by red clay, bad stratification, chemical corrosion, bones and lithic industries		B
Red and yellow stratified clay		C

Figure 3. Maltravieso cave. Stratigraphic sequence in Chimney Room: the base (C) is a package of stratified silt, unit B is poorly stratified but contains a thin archaeological level identified as a floor. Level A, the only archaeological level, forms the upper part of this sequence. It consists of almost 20 cm of yellow silt. Above it there are a few levels of cross-stratified gravel. The sequence concludes with a disturbed speleothem. The photos show a general view of the Chimney Room and a detail of the stratigraphy of the central cone.

* Institut Català de Paleoecologia Humana i Evolució Social. C/ Marcel·lí Domingo s/n – Campus Sescelades URV (Edifici W3). 43007 – Tarragona – SPAIN.

** Àrea de Prehistòria. Universitat Rovira i Virgili. Avda. Catalunya, 35,43002 Tarragona.

*** Equipo Primeros Pobladores de Extremadura. Casa de Cultura "Rodíguez Moñino", Avda. de Cervantes, s/n. 10005 CACERES – SPAIN.

**** Museo de Nacional de Arte Romano de Mérida. C/ José Ramón Mélida, s/n. 06800, Mérida.

***** CENIEH. Paseo Sierra de Atapuerca, s/n, 09002 Burgos, España

† Corresponding author. acanals@iphes.cat

different palaeoecosocial units: mountains -the Caceres Calerizo and the surrounding low hills-, and wetlands –the flat, open terrain between Caceres and Malpartida de Cáceres– containing two Middle Palaeolithic open air sites, Vendimia and El Millar. These two environments provide a varied set of biotic and abiotic resources. Maltravieso (Fig. 3) was discovered in 1951, and the cave paintings were found by Carlos Callejo five years later. Despite the interest generated by these paintings, the first archaeological excavation was only conducted by the *First Settlers of Extremadura* team in 2001. After removing the main debris, particularly the material resulting from the circulation trench dug by Martín Almagro Basch in 1960, work began on Chimney Room, Bones Room and Discovery Room. The former two yielded lithic industry and fauna remains, while the only human remains were from a Neolithic necropolis and the Bronze Age.

Excavation in the Chimney Room has revealed a stratigraphic sequence (Fig. 3) with 4 levels. The base is a package of heavily laminated red and yellow silt. The second stratigraphic unit contains a package of limestone blocks infiltrated by red sand-clay. This unit is poorly stratified and contain a thin archaeological level (level B). Level B has been identified by a micromorphological study of the soil. Archaeological level A is a sedimentary package deposited on top of the second stratigraphic unit, composed of layers of yellow silt. Level A is 20 cm deep. The stratigraphic profile continues upwards with gravel and red sand-clay with a red lenticular stratification, covered by a thin layer of red sand-clay with humic content and altered limestone clasts, and then another gravel layer with red sand-clay in a horizontal stratification. The stratigraphic succession ends with an altered speleothem.

The archaeological material recovered during the 2005 and 2006 excavations is entirely from Level A (Fig 4), dated by 14C at 17,840 ± 90 BP (Poz-30469 MTV-2006-SCH-L29-48). Highlights include various symbolic objects, two perforated shells and an etched bone, along with a wide variety of taxa. The Perissodactyla include remains from 2 types of equid (*Equus ferus* and *Equus hydruntinus*). The Artiodactyla are from *Bos/Bison sp.*, *Cervidae* indet. and *Sus scrofa*. The identified carnivores include remains of *Ursus sp.*, *Lynx pardinus*, *Vulpes vulpes* and *Felis silvestris*. The assemblage is completed with remains from *Oryctolagus cuniculus* and indeterminate bird species. Almost all of these remains have cut marks.

The lithic industry, manufactured from local quartz and flint exogenous to Caceres Calerizo, evidences high flake production, while the retouched material includes a raclette –an item with direct, semi-abrupt peripheral retouch and an irregular outline– on a débordant flint flake, a carenated endscraper on a fragment and notches, one possibly on flake –albeit broken– and another on the right proximal side of a flint flake. The Bones Room is a homogeneous sedimentary assemblage affected by post-sedimentary alluvial and re-sedimentation processes. The unit is sealed by a stalagmite slab dated by the IPH (Institut de Paléeontologie Humaine, Paris) at 117,000 BP, which rests on another slab dated at 183,000 BP. The archaeological level has yielded 814 faunal remains from a wide variety of species and at least 13 taxa. Ungulates predominate amongst the macromammals, along with a considerable number of carnivore remains. *Leporidae* remains are the most abundant in this assemblage. Despite the heavy fragmentation of the remains, it is estimated that there are at least 304 items, mostly from *Leporidae* (53%), followed by deer (13%), *C. crocuta* (9%) and equids (6%). The lithic industry, consisting of 128 objects, is all on quartz found *in situ*. Each part of the operational chain is present in this assemblage with Mode 3 morpho-technological features. The Discovery Room, now exposed due to the destruction of the cave, only yielded human remains from the necropolis identified when the cave was initially discovered. It is currently being analysed and dated. According to currently available data, Maltravieso cave was occupied from the Middle Pleistocene onwards, and left a number of recorded events -from Neanderthals activity in the Bones Room to *H. sapiens* in the Chimney Room- related to the symbolic use of the site, evidenced in both the archaeological record and paintings, particularly hands. Finally, the funerary use of the site in the Holocene illustrates the "permanent" presence of human communities in the Calerizo area. Unfortunately, *First Settlers of Extremadura* is engaged in an administrative conflict with the Government of Extremadura's Heritage Directorate-General, specifically with the Technical

Cueva de Maltravieso
(Cáceres, Extremadura)

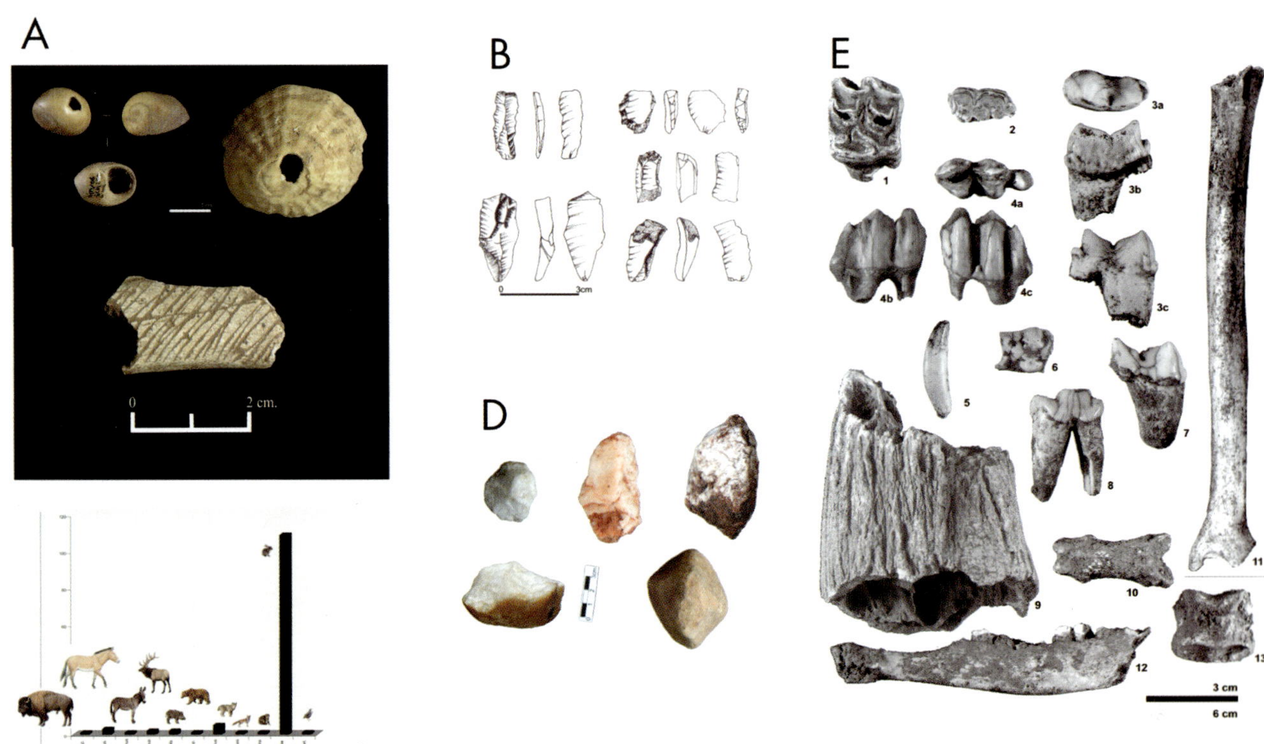

Figure 4. Maltravieso cave: A) Chimney Room. Perforated shells and etched bones; B) Chimney Room lithic industry; C) Chimney Room taxa; D) Bones Room lithic industry; E) Palaeontological material from Bones Room and from the clearance of the cave sediment: 1) M1/2 sin. *Equus cf. hydruntinus*; occlusal face. 2) M1/2 dext. *Equus cf. hydruntinus*; oclusal face. 3) M1 sin. *Crocuta crocuta*; a-b ocusal, buccal and lingual faces. 4) M3 sin. *Dama dama cf. clactoniana*; a-c occlusal, lingual and buccal faces. 5) Cx sin. *Lynx pardina*; lingual face. 6) M3 dext. Sus *scrofa*; occlusal surface. 7) M1 sin. *Crocuta crocuta*; buccal face. 8) P4 sin. *Crocuta crocuta*; lingual face. 9) *Bos primigenius* bone core, dorsal face. 10) *Ursus* first phalanx, dorsal face. 11) Tibia sin. *Lynx pardina*, anterior face. 12) Mandible ext. *Dama dama cf. Clactoniana*, lingual face. 13) Second phalanx sin. *Equus cf. Caballus*, dorsal face.

Services Department over the conservation and scientific use of the cave. In 2008, the D.G. closed the cave definitively, and is currently drafting a regulatory framework to protect the artwork and prevent any other type of action at the site.

Antoni Canals*,**,***,†, Victoria Aranda***, Nova Barrero***,****, Lucía Bermejo***,*****, Paolo Donadei***, Isidoro Campaña***,*****, Francisco J. García***, Dolores Megías***, Juan Marín***, Mario Modesto***,*****, Abel Morcillo***, Ana Rabazo***, Antonio Rodríguez-Hidalgo*,***, Eudald Carbonell*,**,***.

3. El Conejar cave (Cáceres), new data for the Palaeolithic- Neolithic transition in inland Iberia

El Conejar cave, 444 m asl, is on the edge of Cáceres city (37N x=550332.5869994011 y=9296593.467214169) in a Carboniferous limestone formation, one of the concentric layers that comprise the Cáceres syncline. The cave is roughly 17m in diameter, with a phreatic morphology, chimneys and exposure to the open air following the lateral collapse of the walls. It shows heavy fracturing along its lines of structural weakness, resulting in blocks and large slabs falling from the ceiling. In addition to this room, the cave consists of two narrow corridors, currently sealed. The geological sedimentation and erosion process shaped a space with varying depths. The first excavations were in 1916 by archaeologist and ethnographer Ismael de Pan (del Pan 1917), but work was not resumed until the early 1980's, when the University of Extremadura conducted several test pits at the entrance and the central-eastern area. In 2000, the *First Settlers of Extremadura* team began a new dig in the cave as part of their research into prehistoric occupations in the Caceres Calerizo area. Initial surveys recovered a large amount of archaeological material including stone tools, hand-made and wheeled pottery, and metal. An erratic block of breccia was also recovered, which contained bone material, pottery and charred cereal grains (identified as wheat). This exploration also identified preserved breccia hanging on the wall. Between 2000 and 2003, systematic excavations focused on undisturbed sedimentary deposits. A small excavation area was prepared in the so-called Intermediate Breccia at the lowest level of the eastern sector, near the 1980's pit. Bone material, mainly rabbit, coals and some lithic piece was recovered. Subsequently, the work will focus on other brecciated deposit located in the wall opposite the entrance of the cave (Superior Gap). During the excavation process lithic industry, wildlife and coals documented. Work focused on another brecciafied area on the wall opposite the entrance (Upper breccia). Lithic industry, fauna and charcoal was documented during the excavation.

In 2009, work resumed in El Conejar cave on the Upper Breccia (BS) and the East Sector in the Holocene Upper Breccia (BSH). Ceramic material was found in the stratigráfic section.

The stratigraphic sequence (Fig. 5) found in these carbonated deposits in the course of the successive archaeological work is the following:

Upper Breccia (BS) (Fig. 6): raised several metres above the current floor, varying between 2.5m and 0.5m in depth, 6m long and up to 2m wide. The stratigraphy contains the following levels:

- Level 1 (BS1). Silt and red clay base, 0.4m-1m deep, linked to a common process of influx of fines and fossil material throughout the cave.
- Level 2 (BS2). Cemented breccias of limestone clasts, in greater abundance towards the base of this Level, increasing from 0,4m-1m deep towards the archaeological East. Above the breccia in the archaeological West (quadrat D25), there is a small speleothem level which seals it, probably related to a chimney.

* Institut Català de Paleoecologia Humana i Evolució Social. C/ Marcel·lí Domingo s/n – Campus Sescelades URV (Edifici W3). 43007 – Tarragona – SPAIN.

** Àrea de Prehistòria. Universitat Rovira i Virgili. Avda. Catalunya, 35,43002 Tarragona.

*** Equipo Primeros Pobladores de Extremadura. Casa de Cultura "Rodíguez Moñino", Avda. de Cervantes, s/n. 10005 CACERES – SPAIN.

**** Museo de Nacional de Arte Romano de Mérida. C/ José Ramón Mélida, s/n. 06800, Mérida.

***** CENIEH. Paseo Sierra de Atapuerca, s/n, 09002 Burgos, España

† Corresponding author. acanals@iphes.cat

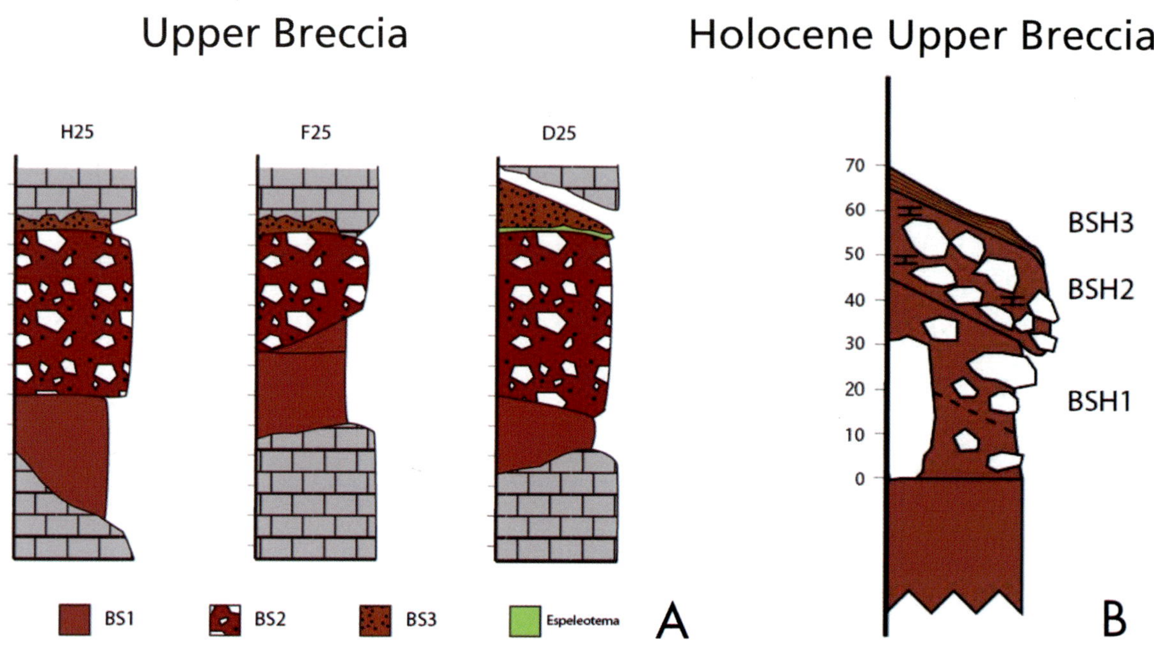

Figure 5. El Conejar cave: stratigraphic sequences of the Upper Breccia and Holocene Upper Breccia.

- Level 3 (BS3). Coarse, cemented dark reddish-brown sands, maximum depth 10cm, resulting from sporadic alluvial flows which filled the gaps in the blocks.

Holocene Upper Breccia (BSH) (Fig. 6): in the archaeological East sector, topographically at a higher level than the Upper Breccia (BS), marking the cave's infill during the Holocene. Consists of three levels with a dip towards the archaeological SE:

- Level 1 (BSH1). Contains a conglomerate of clasts immersed in a silty-clay matrix, 0.4m deep, dipping towards the archaeological South.
- Level 2 (BSH2). Consists of a breccia of clasts and a silty-clay matrix, maximum depth 0.35m, shallower to the South.
- Level 3 (BSH3). Laminated and cemented clays without clasts, the result of a speleothem drip, moulded to the top of the previous Level, reaching a maximum depth of 0.10m, shallower to the South.

As a result of the archaeological work, we can confirm that the only preserved elements are the Upper Breccia and the Upper Holocena Breccia, two *in situ* archaeological levels, discontinuous and in differentiated topographic situations. Fauna and lithic industry have been found in the Upper breccia, along with charcoal, used to obtain a radiometric chronology of 8220±40 BP (Beta – 154490 sample CC-00-H27-1). The lithic industry is technically standardised. The operative chain is relatively short. It consists of the immediate, expeditious production of flakes using non-hierarchical methods. The raw material selected by the communities is predominantly local, e.g., quartz and quartzite, easily accessible and suitable for knapping. Flint is present at the site from the Upper Palaeolithic onwards. Its allochthonous origin is indicative of territorial expansion during the process of its collection. The faunal remains, cut marks,

Cueva de El Conejar (Cáceres, Extremadura)

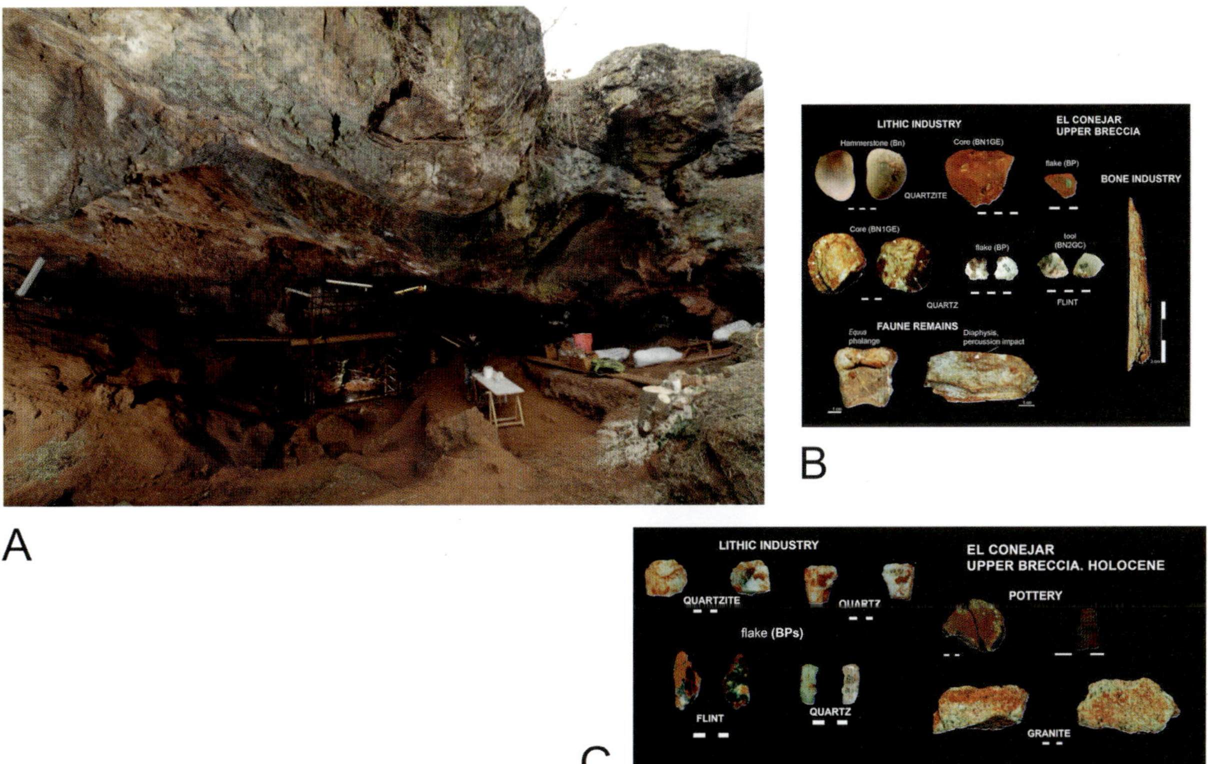

Figure 6. El Conejar cave: A) current entrance porch. Centre: Upper breccia. Right, outside the photo, Holocene Upper Breccia ; B) Main Upper breccia material; C) Main Holocene Upper Breccia.

burned bones and heavy fragmentation of the assemblage suggests an anthropogenic origin. The archaeological record in the Upper breccia points to an occupation in the Mesolithic, a transition period between the last hunter-gatherer groups and the first productive societies (cropping and grazing). This helps to establish chronological parameters in the transition from the Palaeolithic to the Neolithic in Extremadura, and contextualize them with those in the rest of the Iberian Peninsula.

Work on the Upper Holocena Breccia (BSH) is less advanced. The material found to date differs from the Upper Breccia (BS). The presence of many ceramic fragments situates this site in the Holocene. Current results of the fauna assemblage shows the presence of farm animals such as goat and sheep. The presence of charcoal here as well will permit its accurate dating and contextualisation in the Palaeolithic-Neolithic transition in Iberia and Europe.

Antoni Canals*,**,***,†, Victoria Aranda***, Nova Barrero***,****, Lucía Bermejo***,*****, Paolo Donadei***,Isidoro Campaña***,*****, Francisco J. García***, Dolores Megías***, Juan Marín***, Mario Modesto***,*****, Abel Morcillo***, Ana Rabazo***, Antonio Rodríguez-Hidalgo*,***, Eudald Carbonell*,**,***.

4. Vendimia open air site, Malpartida de Cáceres (Extremadura)

The Vendimia site (Fig. 7 and 8) (37N x=549402.5331505185 y=9284871.401430668), in the Malpartida de Cáceres municipality, is near the "Los Barruecos" ecological reserve, in the geomorphological context of a granite batholith related to a stream in the Salor River basin. Following several surveys and test pits, systematic excavations were conducted between 1999 and 2003 in a 78 m^2 area, with 2,164 lithic items found. The spatial distribution of the lithic material shows natural water-related processes determined by the orography. The stratigraphic sequence contains several units: shallow topsoil, a unit composed of coarse sand with a clay matrix, a silt layer covering the archaeological layer, and finally the bottom layer of medium sands with a clay matrix containing the clasts and the lithic industry. This level, an archaeological palimpsest, lies directly on granite.

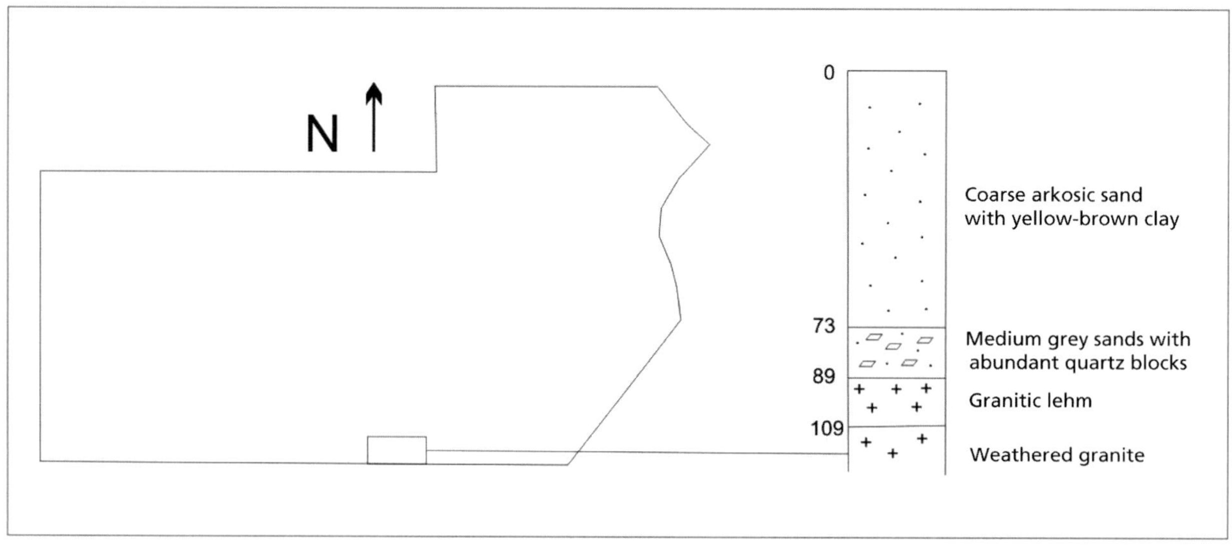

Figure 7. Vendimia site: plan and section of sedimentary infill.

* Institut Català de Paleoecologia Humana i Evolució Social. C/ Marcel·lí Domingo s/n – Campus Sescelades URV (Edifici W3). 43007 – Tarragona – SPAIN.

** Àrea de Prehistòria. Universitat Rovira i Virgili. Avda. Catalunya, 35,43002 Tarragona.

*** Equipo Primeros Pobladores de Extremadura. Casa de Cultura "Rodíguez Moñino", Avda. de Cervantes, s/n. 10005 CACERES – SPAIN.

**** Museo de Nacional de Arte Romano de Mérida. C/ José Ramón Mélida, s/n. 06800, Mérida.

***** CENIEH. Paseo Sierra de Atapuerca, s/n, 09002 Burgos, España

† Corresponding author. acanals@iphes.cat

Vendimia open-air site (Malpartida de Cáceres, Extremadura)

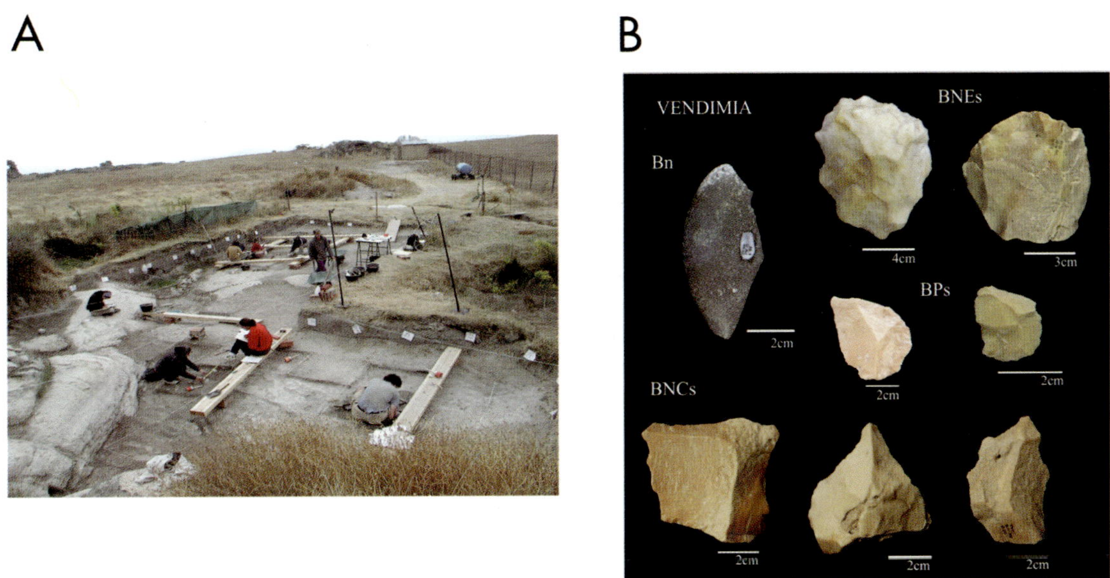

Figure 8. Vendimia site: A) overview of the site; B) principal materials found on the site.

The predominant material is quartz and to a lesser extent quartzite. The quartz collection model was based on intensely aggregated secondary deposits, the result of dismantling adjacent to the primary outcrop. The rest of the primary material was found somewhat further away, but also of local origin. The morphotechnical analysis found every part of the technical operative chain. The lithic assemblage is assigned to technical Mode 3 or Mousterien. The knapping strategies are characterised by centripetal and Levallois removal, with pre-configured and hierachised cores, notches, sidescrapers and denticulates, generally medium and small sized.

This site is interpreted as a point of reiterative exploitation and use of biotic and abiotic resources. Its situation in a potentially strategic ecological location, with the necessary plant and animal biomass resources, met the conditions required by the hunter-gatherer societies who exploited this environment recurrently.

The Salor River wetlands, near Calerizo de Cáceres and the Santa Ana, Maltravieso and Conejar Caves, are part of the "Cacereño Complex", a cultural unit with a high diversity of resources which human communities exploited from the end of the Lower Pleistocene.

Antoni Canals*,**,***,†, Victoria Aranda***, Nova Barrero***,****, Lucía Bermejo***,*****, Paolo Donadei***,Isidoro Campaña***,*****, Francisco J. García***, Dolores Megías***, Juan Marín***, Mario Modesto***,*****, Abel Morcillo***, Ana Rabazo***, Antonio Rodríguez-Hidalgo*,***, Eudald Carbonell*,**,***.

5. El Millar open air site, Cáceres (Extremadura)

El Millar (Fig. 9) is in the Cáceres municipality (29N, X: 721.439 ; Y: 4.368.539. Z: 370 m.), in the Salor River wetlands, like the Vendimia site. Systematic excavation, which began in 2000, is still in progress. The delimited area covers 91 m^2, divided into two sectors: north (49 m^2) and south (42 m^2). This site is a Quaternary alluvium deposit, with mainly quartz and quartzite cobbles deposited on the valleys and floodplains of the main river basin. These deposits now correspond to accumulations of fine detrital material with some interbedded gravels and boulders.

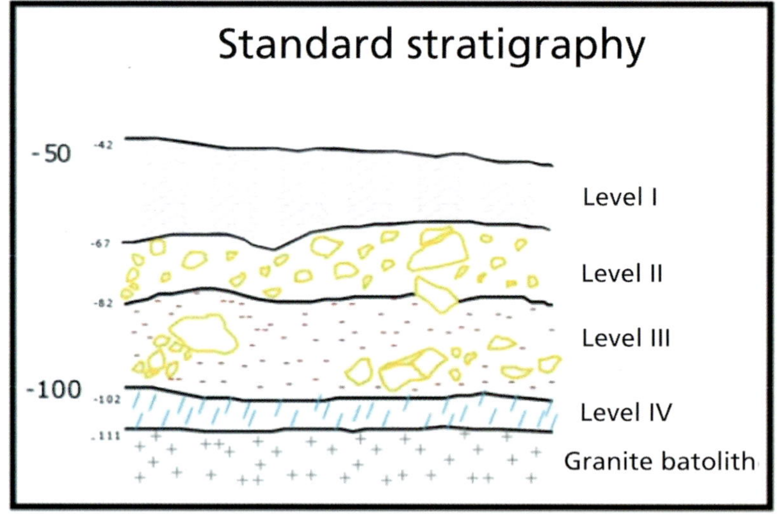

Figure 9. El Millar: site and standard stratigraphy. The sequence includes the following levels: NI) current floor with erratic archaeological material; NII) archaeological palimpsest based on alluvium; NIII) homogeneous package with scattered materials, probably from level II; NIV) Sterile granitic lehm, result of batholith decomposition.

* Institut Català de Paleoecologia Humana i Evolució Social. C/ Marcel·lí Domingo s/n – Campus Sescelades URV (Edifici W3). 43007 – Tarragona – SPAIN.

** Àrea de Prehistòria. Universitat Rovira i Virgili. Avda. Catalunya, 35,43002 Tarragona.

*** Equipo Primeros Pobladores de Extremadura. Casa de Cultura "Rodíguez Moñino", Avda. de Cervantes, s/n. 10005 CACERES – SPAIN.

**** Museo de Nacional de Arte Romano de Mérida. C/ José Ramón Mélida, s/n. 06800, Mérida.

***** CENIEH. Paseo Sierra de Atapuerca, s/n, 09002 Burgos, España

† Corresponding author. acanals@iphes.cat

The sedimentary sequence of this site was initially interpreted on the basis of a stratigraphic section exposed during gravel quarrying. This stratigraphy shows a succession of geological levels from granite bedrock to the first level, composed of large (>10 cm) subangular pebbles with a sandy-clay matrix. The quartz and quartzite pebbles are from the reactivated outwash deposits, evidenced in the stratigraphy by a succession of alluvia, with an initial phase in which erosive alterites are dragged away, leaving the substrate exposed. In a second phase, the alluvium elements are dragged along intertwined channels, with finer material appearing as well, transported by diffuse lamellar flows which ultimately cover the surface of the glacis. This phase is predominated by the buildup, and may have been caused by a rise in the base level of the streams. The next stage shows a buildup period, a drop in the base level and the erosion of part of the previous level by means of runoff. This site contains lithic tools but no palaeontological remains (Fig. 10). Different methodologies were used to dig the two sectors. The deposit was regarded as a palimpsest in the design of the north sector's excavation. We noted the coordinates of all modified items, discarded the natural and unmodified material, and did not take into consideration any sedimentary or taphonomic data. The southern section was excavated using two different methodologies, noting the coordinates for all lithic material, modified or not:

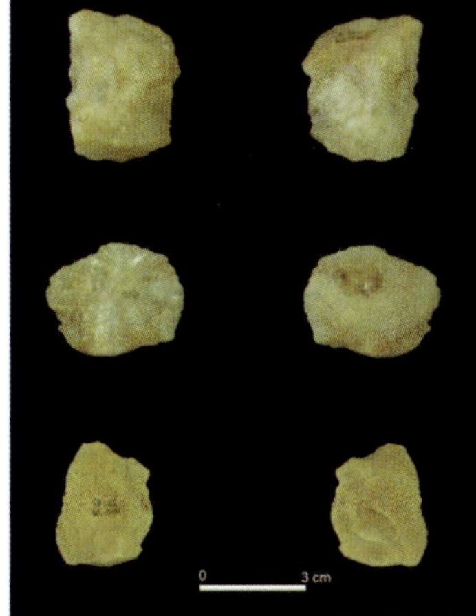

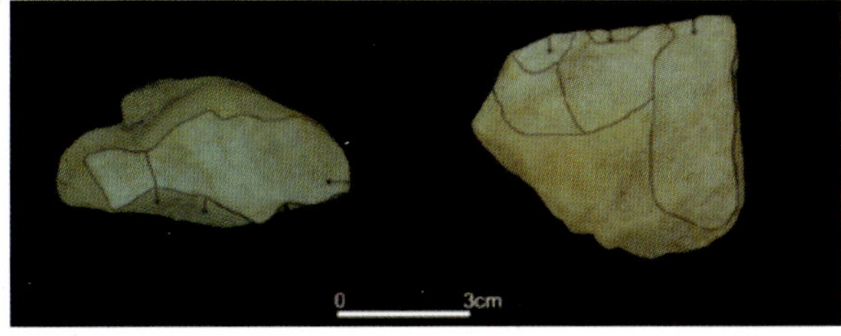

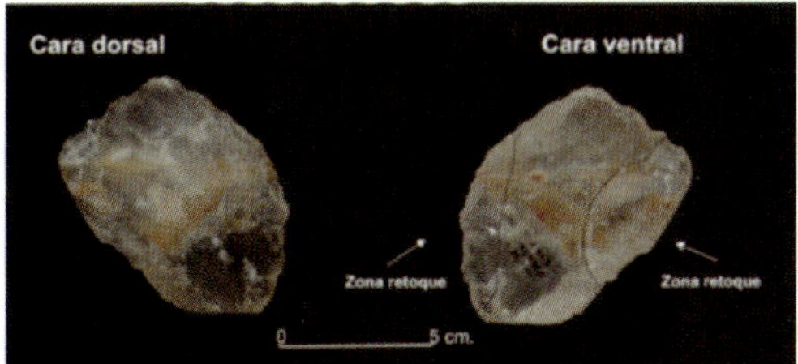

Figure 10. Millar: technical categories and worked items in quartz and quartzite, the local raw material.

the stratigraphic terraces and the boundaries between layers of alluvia. In this case we wanted to profile the cultural palimpsest on the basis of the taphosedimentary processes in order to define a diachronic criterion for the deposit. The results of this study are under evaluation.

A morpho-technical analysis of 828 items found in a 14 m^2 area, excavated between 2004 and 2007, found that 97.1% were in various types of quartz and the remaining 2.7% in quartzite. Ranked by structural categories, simple knapping products included 411 whole flakes and 166 broken flakes, with the butt retained in 125 of them, followed by 114 fragments and 105 retouched items.

There were 6 natural bases and 75 cores, all worked on different types of quartz, with flakes used for bipolar knapping on an anvil in 5 cases. Of the 70 cores knapped on natural fragments, semi-eroded fragments or cobbles, 36 were worked on an anvil and 34 freehand. A wide range of knapping strategies were detected with regard to faciality, direction and disposition of removals. We recorded 49 unifacial cores, predominantly unipolar unifacial, followed by bipolar unifacials and multipolar unifacials. Bifacial knapping was found in 19 items, predominantly orthogonal multipolar, although centripetal multipolar (discoidal *sensu* Lato) and the Levallois technique (Boëda, op. cit.) were also present but in smaller amounts. The assemblage is completed with bipolar handaxes, bipolar longitudinal opposed and longitudinal unipolar handaxes. Finally, the least represented strategy (7 items) was multifacial multipolar orthogonal knapping. It is important to note that most of the cores were in an initial stage of exploitation

Of the 104 shaped items, 93 were retouched flakes and 11 configured directly on natural fragments, semi-eroded fragments or pebbles. Most of them are milky quartz, with retouched translucent quartz also represented. In contrast, the presence of quartzite, hyaline and cryptocrystalline quartz are testimonial in this category. The majority show unifacial, marginal and extremely marginal retouch. Continuous retouch and denticulates are the best represented categories, and indeed could be said to characterize this assemblage, although a large number of items, characterized by irregular, marginal retouch, could not be assigned to a specific morphotype. These items were classified as doubtful retouch. The El Millar site, unlike Vendimia, is in an open area where cultural objects were accumulated as a result of alluvial processes which prevent the identification of any primary or recurrent type of occupation. El Millar is at the lowest part of a small basin which drains a large marauding area containing abundant lithic resources (from dikes in the granite).

Rodrigo de Balbin Behrmann*,
José Javier Alcolea González*

Siega Verde

1. Introduction

The site of Siega Verde was discovered in 1989 by Manuel Santonja Gómez, who was at that time the director of Salamanca Provincial Museum. His archaeological surveying in the area caused him to find an engraved horse, which led on to the discovery of many other figures, which were studied by a team from the University of Alcalá de Henares. The site was included in the list of UNESCO World Heritage sites in 2010 as an extension of the prehistoric rock art sites in the Côa Valley in Portugal.

Its recognition as an ensemble of Palaeolithic engravings opened a totally new line of research for understanding hunter societies in the interior of the Iberian Peninsula. Until that time, these groups were not known nor sufficiently understood.

Early evidence of open-air engravings had not been studied in depth. The first site to be found was Mazouco, Freijo da Espada à Cinta, in 1981, on the banks of the Aldeadávila Reservoir, on the River Douro. This large reservoir must still possess a large number of similar engravings under its waters. This site was published by a team from the University of Porto.

The second open-air site to be discovered was Domingo García in 1982, in countryside to the south of Segovia, opposite the Central Mountain Range, in an area with schist outcrops that continue as far as Ávila, with dispersed and quite damaged remains. It displays a few Palaeolithic figures and a large number of post-Palaeolithic figures in an ensemble of extraordinary interest, not only because of the wealth and variety of depictions but because of the graphic continuity in a place used over many thousands of years.

The third site, discovered in 1983, was Fornols Haut, in French Catalonia, in the Pyrenees under Canigó Mountain. It is clearly a high altitude site, like Piedras Blancas and Domingo García, ideally located to watch over the territory. What is still conserved today consists only of small remains of ungulates and birds, suggesting that there must once have been more.

The fourth ensemble was Piedras Blancas, in the mountains of Almería, near Sierra Nevada, at 1,300m above sea level, on a hill overlooking the Bay of Almería. The figure published by Julián Martínez in 1987 was accompanied by others we found in 2005 and which he included in his communication at the Salamanca meeting (de Balbín, 2008). It is undoubtedly a large site with numerous engraved figures.

After this, Siega Verde was found, on the banks of the River Águeda, a tributary on the left of the Douro and near the Portuguese border, 60km in a straight line from Côa. It is located in the town of Villar de la Yegua, opposite Castillejo de Martín Viejo, in Salamanca, 15 km downstream from Ciudad Rodrigo.

It had been discovered and its study was under way before we knew of the impressive ensemble at Côa. Even so, our team always believed in the importance of Siega Verde as the driving force for a reflection on the interpretation of Palaeolithic Art in southern Europe (Alcolea and de Balbín, 2003 a and b, 2006 a and b; de Balbín, 1995; de Balbín and Alcolea, 1992 a, 1994, 1999, 2001, 2002, 2005 a; de Balbín *et al.*, 1994, 1995, 1996 a and b; de Balbín and Santonja,1992) and as a criterion on which to base the chronology of the whole Douro.

The discovery of the site of Côa was made known in 1992. It is the largest site of this type and the one to receive most attention in the mass media. As it is larger than the other sites, the final study has been more complex. It is on the banks of the River Côa, a tributary of the Douro from the west, 60 km in a straight line from the River Águeda at Siega Verde. Its sequence is very long and its relationship with Siega Verde is very intense, but

* Universidad de Alcalá de Henares. rodrigo.balbin@uah.es,. javier.alcolea@uah.es

not unique. These two, together with Mazouco and Sabor, form the central core of Palaeolithic art on the Douro, although it is possible that more sites will be found. It also possesses deposits that have been carefully excavated, and these are a vital chronological and cultural point of reference for open-air Palaeolithic art. A similar excavation project was proposed for Siega Verde, but did not go ahead because of administrative problems.

The model of open-air art was established and the discoveries that have been made are the result of greater or lesser surveying of the terrain, which has advanced more and been more successful on the Portuguese side of the border than on the Spanish side.

Further to the north and south of the Douro basin, and within it, sites of the same age and art have continued to be found: on the River Sabor, near Côa, on the River Tua, in Tras os Montes, in Zézere and Ocreza, in the Tagus and in the Guadiana basin, like the site of Molino Manzanez in Cheles. To these can be added some of the Tagus engravings which had long been known, in San Simao, Gardete and Fratel, where most of the depictions are post-Palaeolithic although others are clearly in an earlier style. In all cases, the succession of engravings belonging to different styles and periods is a defining factor.

The fact is that Mazouco was the trigger for an understanding and appreciation of open-air Palaeolithic art, but it is equally true that representations practically in the open-air had been known for a long time, as at Cap Blanc in the Perigord, and the sites on the River Nalón in Asturias and on the Nansa in Cantabria. It is also true that in the Iberian Peninsula, many sites are known in rock-shelters nearly in the open-air, such as Ambrosio, Cieza, Vero, Tarifa and Gibraltar, in all regions. These may be a link between caves and the outside, indicating the possibility of using surfaces in nearly all situations.

Individuals in the Upper Palaeolithic did not restrict themselves when choosing places in which to express their messages.

2. The site and its figures

Siega Verde is a continuous site, on the banks of the River Águeda, in a medium and not too rugged part, with schist bedrock and located in a general area where the river later enters the granite zone until it reaches Arribes del Duero. It rises in the Central Mountain System and flows north to the Douro, parallel to the Portuguese Côa.

The artistic representations are located on blocks of stone by the side of the river, which does not carry much water except in times of flood, depending on the rain and snow regime. The outcrops are predominantly vertical in the south and centre of the site, and horizontal-zenithal in the north, which produces different topographic situations which are used in different ways and contain groups of figures of different kinds.

The southern area is where the first figure of a horse was found, in isolation in an area with hardly any other engravings. This absence is almost certainly because a water mill was built, like so many others on interior rivers, and stones in the surrounding area were used as building material, emptying a large area between the mill and the horse.

From this point, the valley narrows, with vertical walls on the left bank, until the first homogeneous decorated area is reached, covering the whole central part of the site.

This is the location of the best ford across the river, and was also used to build a bridge over the river in the twentieth century. One of its supports was raised on one of the most important engraved rocks in the ensemble, indicating the preference for the best place to cross the river.

The right bank is usually more rugged than the left side, and its outcrops are more sloping and heterogeneous. This may be the reason why its surfaces display few old engravings, with the exception of the last engraved rock at the site, which is at the northern end of the right bank, with a horse, and which seems to have moved, by either natural or artificial causes. Here, and on the opposite side, the ensemble finishes with engraved horses, the same image as was used at its start.

The northern end possesses more animated and varied figures, on zenithal surfaces that normally allow smaller sizes for the images. Whether or not that is the reason, the animals represented are usually smaller than they generally are in the central zone, they form clearer scenes and move the different parts of their body more.

To date, 443 engravings have been discovered, 241 animals, 3 anthropomorphs, 165 non-figurative motifs and 34 indeterminate; mostly Palaeolithic and some later ones, belonging to what we

Figure 1. View of the site of Siega Verde towards the south, from the road bridge.

call Style V, and they are distributed along a length of 1km. The engraving techniques are incision and pecking, the former used mainly for cervids and the latter mostly for horses.

Most of the figures are animals: horses, bulls, stags, ibices and some extinct species like the giant deer and woolly rhinoceros, as well as others now disappeared from the region, like bison and reindeer. Few characteristic signs are known, but there are numerous lines that are difficult to define.

The engravings are distributed in 29 ensembles and 91 panels, and paint has almost completely disappeared although some small remains suggest that it was more common and possibly abundant in the lifetime of the site. The remains are iron and manganese oxides, silicates and phosphates, and it may be proposed that both engravings and paintings were produced, as in most cave sites. This relationship also exists in the organisation of site, which is organised linearly following the river, which articulates it. In caves, this system arises naturally because of the arrangement of their galleries and passages, creating a similar discourse to this exterior site.

3. Chronology

From the start, we proposed a chronology for both Siega Verde and Côa that would begin in at least the Gravettian and continue until the end of the Upper Palaeolithic. This chronology was based on the criteria of A. Leroi-Gourhan and was equivalent to his Styles II, III and IV. It was found to be effective and was generally accepted with the excavations at the site of Fariseu, on the banks of the River Côa, some time after our proposal. The excavations there, carried out by the CNART team discovered stratigraphy next to a wall engraved with the characteristic motifs at the site, which had been produced precisely from the levels dated in the Gravettian.

Siega Verde possesses early phases in its decoration, equivalent to those determined at Côa as explained above. criteria, they were not the most important phases at the site, as this would take place later in the Magdalenian, in Leroi-Gourhan's Styles III and IV. The centre of the site contains figures that can be situated precisely in the Style III to IV transition, and the time advances discreetly towards the north, with more animated figures that indicate a full Style IV in this area. This means that the main body of engravings at the site can be dated between 17,000 and 13,000 BC.

There is a general custom of interrupting Palaeolithic art at the end of the Pleistocene Ice Age, creating an artificial frontier between Palaeolithic and post-Palaeolithic representations. We believe this is an artificial and unfounded division, and therefore we have developed the concept of a Style V, a connection between the Pleistocene and Holocene in artistic terms. This is characterised by the continuity in certain animal images and the progressive predominance of more or less schematised human forms. The most representative animals are red deer and ibices, with some new motifs, such as fish and characteristic signs.

At Siega Verde, the late Palaeolithic forms are not very well developed, unlike at its twin site of Côa, where this period is very well represented. However, in Style V, the Portuguese site possesses a large number of figures, certified chronologically by the excavation at Fariseu and the portable objects found there, and above all on the banks of the Douro, immediately to the north of Côa. The number of representations at Siega Verde belonging to that time is smaller, as is logical at a smaller site, but they are found in significant numbers, sometimes superimposed on the Palaeolithic figures, and they decrease in size to about 5cm.

We do not believe that Côa and Águeda are so complementary as to have been produced by the same artists, but it is true that the oldest phases are found almost only at the Portuguese site, the intermediate phases in the Spanish ensemble, and the last phases are shared, with Siega Verde seemingly the smaller brother.

Research at Siega Verde succeeded in characterising open-air Palaeolithic art in southern Europe. Thus, the clearly ancient age of the representations and techniques at Siega Verde were determined. Compared with our understanding of art inside caves, a development was established in a discourse similar to the caves, with similar forms at the same times. In each case, we understood the figures as the graphic manifestation of human groups living in the Spanish Plateau during the whole upper and final Würm. Also, as in the caves, we saw the different open-air sites were similar but independent from each other. They ap-

Figure 2. Panel 32 displaying the figures of three bulls, a horse, a canid and a horseshoe-like sign.

peared to be graphic markers, with representations intended to be seen and not hidden (Bueno and de Balbín, 2009), as they were displayed in an open public place, not a secret one. The time of their execution was also established, in a middle-late stage in Upper Palaeolithic art, of which the presence of extinct fauna was illustrative but not necessary. These were some of the conclusions reached in the 1990s and which have been confirmed by new studies and discoveries.

At the start, open-air art was included in a special chapter, creating its own area for this form, different to what was produced inside caves. For some authors, one of the supports for this artificial difference was the technique used, mostly discontinuous pecking. This claim is too simple and un-nuanced to be relevant. In the first place, techniques do not indicate an absolute chronology, neither in caves nor in the open air. They are used indifferently depending on the needs of expression and they change with time for different reasons. The use of pecking rather than incised engraving has no chronological implications, and nor does the former technique define art in the open air.

Pecking is the most common technique during the main phase at Côa, although incised engraving is also employed, and it is the most common at Siega Verde in its main phase, which in fact is later than that at Côa. At that same time, Domingo García displays more incised engravings than pecked ones, and Molino Manzánez only possesses incised engravings. Each site reflects a technical choice that depends on its cultural and spatial organisation, not simply on the time when the figures were produced. It should also be borne in mind that what we can see today is only a fossil of what there used to be, and we are drawing excessive conclusions from a part of reality. The number of figures visible now is not the original number and the engravings would not always have been produced alone but accompanied by paintings in a significant proportion.

Pecked engravings are more common in the open air than in caves, among other reasons because schist is a more appropriate rock for this technique. They are conserved better in this rock and when they were made they would have possessed an additional advantage in that the schist surface is darker than its interior, because of patination, and this would produce a colour difference with a pictorial effect. The difference may not have lasted very long, but would be sufficient at the time of creating the artistic work.

Caves also contain pecked engravings dated in early periods, although in smaller proportions and the technique is used when needed, just as in the open air. Pecking is not unique to the exterior, nor a dating method, nor an indicator of cultural regions or styles.

It is true that the open-air forms are particularly indicative, as they exhibit the same as caves belonging to the same period. There are not many cave art sites in the Iberian Plateau, although around the edge of the Central Mountains some examples are Los Casares, La Hoz, La Griega and El Reno. Significant comparisons should be made according to styles and periods, and in this way Siega Verde in its main phase is much closer to Los Casares than to nearby Côa, even though they are both open-air sites.

4. Assessment

Based on Siega Verde and the other sites that have been discovered, a model of the situation and occupation of the territory has been constructed which has fundamentally changed the ideas we held about Palaeolithic groups and their graphic activity.

The discovery of outside Palaeolithic art has opened a conceptual door towards an understanding of an area which until then was nearly unknown. This is the interior of the Iberian Peninsula, a large area often thought to be depopulated or lacking in any ancient evidence of importance, such as Palaeolithic graphic activity. A few caves were known, it is true, but the scarcity of limestone hills inland was the reason for the rarity of Pleistocene artistic forms in the area.

Palaeolithic Art has been, and often still is, associated with caves, ever since the discovery of this human cultural form. The models created since then uncritically assumed the need for an underground, deep, difficult, isolated and mysterious setting for the art, and such a context must necessarily have been a shrine. Often, when we do not understand a phenomenon, as frequently occurs in Prehistory, we mechanically regard it as religious or votive. This is exactly what happened to Palaeolithic graphic forms, discovered inside caves and the necessary consequence of religious beliefs and actions, within a place consecrated for them.

However, caves are not places devoted to cults, they are not shrines, but places where the human groups lived and shared all the possible aspects of their existence. Altamira, Tito Bustillo and La Pasiega, to give some of the best known examples, possess deposits where people lived their lives, ate, drank, made tools, maintained a sex life and defecated, in the immediate surroundings of the artistic representations. This does not seem to be the best way to define a shrine.

Indeed, many of the sites used to define Palaeolithic art as a deep cave art are not in the interior of the caves, and this is the case of the three sites mentioned above. In La Pasiega the most important decorated area in Gallery B is above the habitation deposit, which has been excavated. The most important habitation deposit in Tito Bustillo is in Zone XI, which also contains the largest artistic representations in the whole cave. In Altamira, before its interior was altered by the building of concrete walls in the 1950s, its most representative ensemble, the famous Sistine Chapel of Palaeolithic Art, was only 20m from the entrance. When the cave was open, with a long horizontal entrance, daylight would have reached the chamber painted with the famous bisons.

There was already evidence that Palaeolithic Art did not need the mysterious darkness, but it was not interpreted correctly. There was equally evidence that the depictions were available to the whole group, but it was not understood appropriately.

Palaeolithic Art in the open air has supplied us with the right way to interpret the meaning of these figures correctly, beginning with Siega Verde and what this first great site of this kind to be published and interpreted has signified. It is not in caves or large rock surfaces, but on limited surfaces that depend on the structure, erosion and fracturing of the schist.

Figure 3. Panel 89 situated in the north border of the site, displaying a bear chasing two running horses.

The art usually appears on the banks of rivers or in high and dominant places, always by the side of paths, occasionally near dwellings, as at Fariseu in Côa. In Siega Verde, Zézere, Cheles, Quinta da Barca and Penascosa the engravings are also by the easiest place to cross the river. The figures were made to be seen.

It might be said that caves and the open air are the products of the same way of thinking and the same cultural tradition during the same periods of time, and their differences are due mainly to the kind of rock surface and their spatial location. What the open air tells us has helped us to understand the cave phenomenon.

In his time, A. Leroi-Gourhan proposed an interpretation of Palaeolithic graphic activity based on spatial organisation, the relationship between figures and with the panels in which they were presented, the general location of the cave and the frequency of the different types of representations. In the open air, the spatial arguments are easier to follow and differentiate, but ultimately they demonstrate the reality of what was proposed for caves: a discourse arranged in panels and groups, which may be followed topographically along a cognisable route, above all in places like Siega Verde. The inner and outer spaces are organised according to a logical discourse and an understandable sequence, with graphic formulae, thematic actors, associations and scenes, which changed with time.

Outside artistic ensembles, including Siega Verde, occupy a space which did not end in the Palaeolithic, but which often continued in use until the Age of Metals, or if you like, until Romanisation. Many of these Palaeolithic sites possess a continuation in what has been called Style V, the morphological and conceptual continuation after Palaeolithic Art, and the introducer of Levantine and Schematic forms. Siega Verde displays a significant sample of that style, and Côa even more. Open-air sites have given us another gift: proof that the naturalistic graphic system did not finish with the end of the Ice Age, but continued until the start of written history, partly changing the actors in the images, who became increasingly human.

The places marked in the Upper Palaeolithic by the people who occupied the land were still significant, occupied and marked, and nobody abandoned them. The continuity of art as a graphic marker brings to mind a corresponding long-lasting human continuity and a cultural descent from the Palaeolithic that lies at the foundation of the new material forms and the new periods that we call Mesolithic, Neolithic, Chalcolithic, and Bronze and Iron Ages.

At the same time as Upper Palaeolithic cultures existed around the edges of Iberia the groups inside the peninsula carried out a similar activity, they were almost certainly in contact with their near neighbours but not dependent on them.

Siega Verde has taught us many things, to which lessons from other discoveries and other studies can be added. There is a before and after Siega Verde in Palaeolithic Art research, because it was its publication that demonstrated it belonged to the Palaeolithic style, the continuity of graphic systems, their public nature, the continuous occupation of inland regions and the need to understand art as less mysterious and religious, enormously enlarging the distribution map of the Pleistocene symbolic world. Siega Verde was not alone, but it was the start of an interpretation that has changed old concepts and which faces the future positively.

J. Carlos Díez Fernández-Lomana*, Jesús F. Jordá Pardo**, Diego Arceredillo Alonso*

Valdegoba Palaeolithic site (Huérmeces, Burgos)

Introduction

Valdegoba, a set of three caves, was discovered scientifically in 1980. The central cavity, which contains an archaeological deposit heavily disturbed by furtives and karst reactions, was excavated in 1987-1991 and 2006. The cave faces NW, overlooking the Úrbel River valley, 28 km from Burgos and 930 m asl. Its maximum dimensions are 21x14x5 m. Nestled on the southern edge of the Cantabrian mountain range, it sits 35 m above the river, its base level, on a narrow Turonian limestone canyon.

Stratigraphy and chronology (Fig. 1)

Analysis of the four test pits in the cave (Díez *et al.*, 1988; 1988-89) revealed the lithostratigraphic sequence of the site, composed of the following lithostratigraphic units, from bottom to top: – Unit A: Speleothems at the base of the sequence.

- Unit B: Deep layer of reddish clay that fills the entire cavity. Its massive, disorganized appearance and the mixture of granulometric populations shows that it was transported in mass, as in a mud flow. – Unit C: Fragments of stalagmite concretions and small speleothems, without continuity throughout the cave, originating in concretions which fell from the walls and roof, and speleothems which grew at certain points in the cave.
- Unit D: Clast deposits with abundant Middle Palaeolithic technological material along with bones of large mammals and *Homo neanderthalensis*. It has eroded the previous level, and its origin is due to gravitational collapse of autochthonous clasts due to cryoclastic processes and sheet-flood which provides fine detritic material. Its unstructured composition suggests subsequent movement of this material, e.g. slow mud flow which left an erosive scar on the underlying deposits.
- Unit E: Speleothem, spread throughout the cave, which sealed the sedimentation process. Only residue attached to the walls is left. At some points there is a sequence consisting of breccia produced by the cementation of material from the roof of unit D and a stalagmitic cortex which is connected to the roof at some points by small columns.
- Unit F: Separated from the rest of the sequence by a deep erosive scar. It includes mixed material from the levels below. This level was formed during a period of karst reactivation, with intense erosion and a subsequent remobilization of material from the units below. Several stalagmite crusts were analysed with Uranium series by James Bischoff. The one on Level 1 (Unit A) was in equilibrium, and its age is therefore older than 350 ky. The ones on Level 7 (unit E) which sealed the site were aged due to contamination by detrital Thorium, which led Bischoff to consider the dates (95 and 73 ky BP) unreliable. In 2005, the team led by Trinidad Torres produced dates for several bones from unit D on the basis of amino acid racemization. Level 6 yielded 93.26, 106.02 and 117.78 ky BP. On level 5, the dates were 72.59 and 138.74 ky BP, for level 4, 121.86 BP. Two bones from Level 5 (unit D) were dated by ^{14}C with prior ultrafiltration at the University of Oxford (ORAU). One of them could not be dated while the other yielded an uncalibrated date: 48,400 ± 3,300 BP (OxA-21970), close to the threshold of the technique.

* Laboratorio de Prehistoria. I+D+i. Universidad de Burgos. Plaza Misael Bañuelos s/n. 09001 Burgos. clomana@ubu.es;

** Laboratorio de Estudios Paleolíticos, Departamento de Prehistoria y Arqueología, Universidad Nacional de Educación a Distancia. Ciudad Universitaria. Paseo Senda del Rey 7, E-28040 Madrid, Spain; jjorda@geo.uned.es

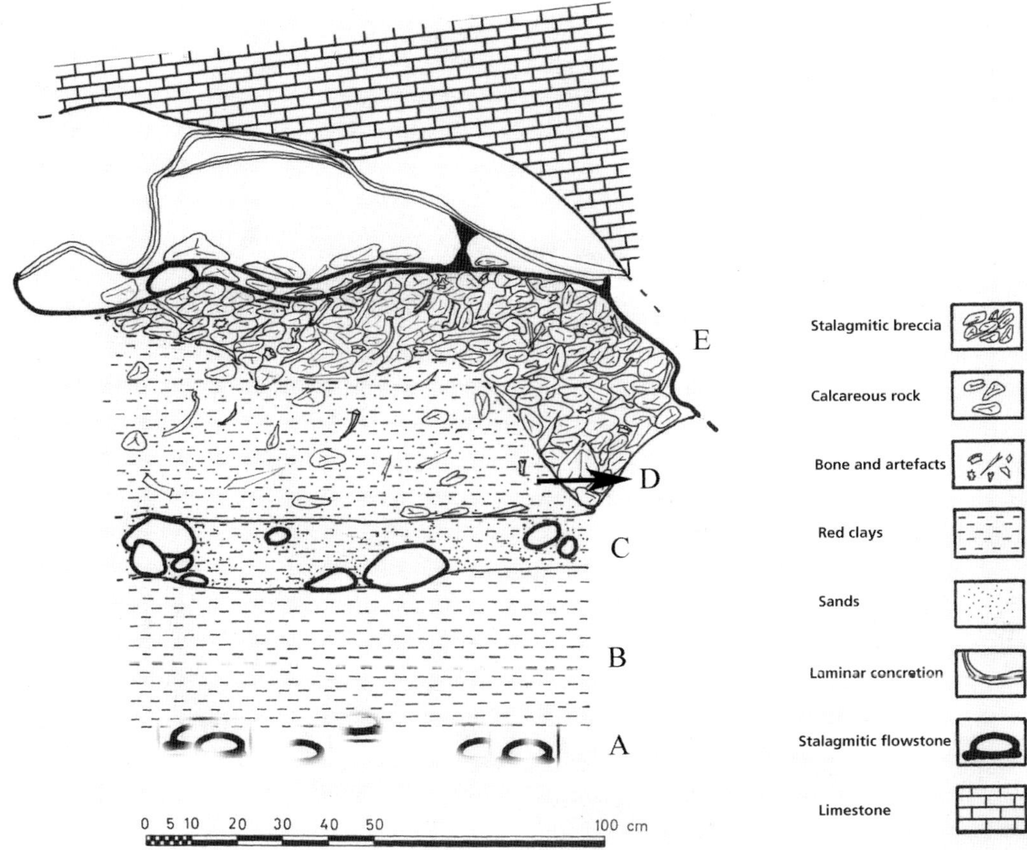

Figure 1. Section of Pleistocene deposits indicating Valdegoba lithostratigraphic units.

Large mammals

Excavations carried out since 1987 have found a large number of faunal remains. The macromammals include: *Homo neanderthalensis*, *Ursus arctos*, *Ursus spelaeus*, *Canis lupus*, *Vulpes vulpes*, *Crocuta crocuta*, *Panthera pardus*, *Felis silvestris*, *Lynx pardina*, *Meles meles*, *Lutra lutra*, *Martes* sp., *Stephanorhinus hemitoechus*, *Equus ferus*, *Equus hydruntinus*, *Sus scrofa*, *Cervus elaphus*, *Capreolus capreolus*, *Rupicapra pyrenaica*, *Capra pyrenaica*, *Bos primigenius* and *Bison priscus*. The micromammals include: *Sorex* sp., *Neomys* sp., *Oryctolagus cuniculus*, *Microtus nivalis*, *Microtus arvalis-agrestis*, *Pliomys lenki*, *Apodemus* cf. *sylvaticus*, *Apodemus* cf. *sylvaticus*, *Arvicola* sp., *Marmota* cf. *marmota*, *Hystrix* cf. *vinogradovii* and *Castor fiber*. The birds are: *Anas* sp., *Aegypius monachus*, *Falco tinnunculus*, *Columba* sp., *Athene noctua*, *Alectoris* sp., *Coturnix coturnix*, *Turdus* sp., *Pyrrhocorax graculus* (Quam *et al.*, 2001).

Herbivores comprise 87% of the fauna. The most abundant species (59%) is chamois, *Rupicapra pyrenaica*. The collection of over 4000 chamois remains from Valdegoba is the second largest on the Iberian Peninsula after the material from the Amalda site, and the best preserved. Age of death and seasonality show intense resource usage. The site was occupied in every season, with young prime-age adults capured predominating over infants. These preferences appear to be related to the social behaviour of the deposited species: after leaving the group in which they were born, wandering individuals with the least experience were the most vulnerable. The mixed environment inferred from the recovered species consisted of rocky zones, mountain forests, deciduous forests and open areas with herbaceous vegetation. This has been corroborated by oxygen isotopes analysed in cattle and goats (Feranec *et al.*, 2010).

Many of the bone remains are the result of action by Neanderthals (cut and percussion marks) and carnivores (bite marks, digested and broken bones). It is difficult to assess the degree of participation by each agent (Díez, 2006).

Human remains (Fig. 2)

A Neanderthal mandible from Level 5 (Unit D), found in 1987. Although found on the surface, its attribution to Level 5 is beyond doubt given that the two incisors discovered in the 2006 match the corresponding gaps in the 1987 jawbone. The individual was about 14 years old. Ten milk teeth from level 6 are from a roughly 8 month old infant. There is also an anterior proximal phalange, two metatarsals –IV and V–, all considered to be *H. neanderthalensis*.

Heavily degraded Mt DNA has been retrieved from one of the molars. Its comparison with another 12 published Neanderthal sequences shows a low genetic diversity in the most recent specimens in Western Europe. The hypothesis that best explains the detected chronological and geographical differences combines a critical decline in Neanderthal populations about 50,000 years ago with a heavy fragmentation of groups and the subsequent recolonization of central and western Europe (Dalen *et al.*, 2012).

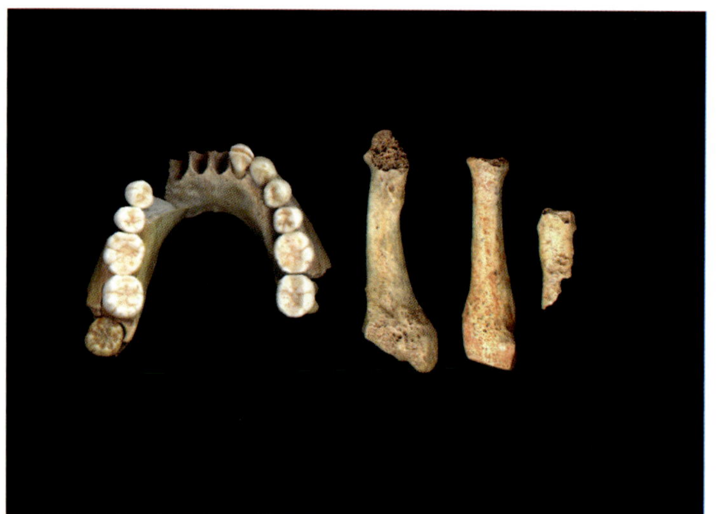

Figure 2. Human remains from Valdegoba (Photo J. Trueba/MSF).

Tools

The lithic industry is abundant, with no major changes between levels. The features of the technocomplex suggest a Middle Paleolithic dating, with little use of the Levallois technique. There is a similar percentage of quartzite and flint, most of the former based on small pebbles brought from the Utrillas facies which outcrops 100 m from the site, hence the high representation of items with cortical zones. There is a similar pattern in the smaller number of quartz items. The flint is exogenous and therefore worked profusely, leaving exhausted cores and a varied repertoire of retouched flakes.

The identified morphotypes are primarily denticulates and sidescrapers, in similar numbers, produced by simple and direct retouch, with many notches amongst the former. There are also several bifaces. Points, endscrapers, undifferentiated abrupts and a few burins complete the typological repertoire. The best finished and most varied items are in flint, with quartzite reserved for simple denticulates and flakes with non-continuous retouch.

Neolithic and early Bronze Age occupations have been documented in the outer area of the cave, with hearths, many pottery shards and sporadic stone items such as millstones and sickle flint flakes, along with domestic fauna and human remains.

In summary, Valdegoba is a rich Mousterian site which is providing extraordinary information for the study of mid-altitude ecosystems during the Upper Pleistocene, Neanderthal lifestyles and their palaeobiological features.

9

PALAEOLITHIC ART IN THE NORTH OF SPAIN

Site	Map numbering
Altamira	1
Cueva de Altxerri	2
Ekain	3
Satimamiñe	4
Cueva de Covalanas	5
La Garma	6
El Pendo	7
El Castillo	8
Las Chimeneas	9
La Pasiega	10
Las Monedas	11
Hornos de la Peña	12
Chufín	13
El Pindal	14
Llonín	15
La Covaciella	16

Site	Map numbering
Tito Bustillo	17
Lluera	18
La Peña de Candamo	19

Marcos García-Diez*,
Pedro Saura Ramos **

Palaeolithic Art in the North of the Iberian Peninsula. World Heritage

About 400 Palaeolithic rock art sites are known in the world and about 160 of them are in the Iberian Peninsula. About a hundred are located in the north of Spain (Fig. 1), in Cantabria and Asturias, with smaller numbers of sites in the Basque Country and Galicia. Most of the sites are located a relatively short distance from the coast, and in altitudes that are generally no higher than 180 m.

The art in the north of the Iberian Peninsula has traditionally been linked with the rock art ensembles in France, within Franco-Cantabrian Palaeolithic art. This name, which implies a certain degree of difference in terms of both numbers and characteristics, is no longer valid. New ensembles are steadily being discovered all over Iberia and long-distance elements of graphic similarity are recognisable that contradict the particularity of Franco-Cantabrian art. This particularity is currently associated with the regions where it is found and with the production technique (both related mainly to the geology and geomorphology), rather than with any graphic uniqueness.

Figure 1. Ceiling in the Hall of the Paintings, Cueva de Altamira (©Pedro Saura).

Palaeolithic art in the north of Spain is primarily found in caves. Not only in the interior zones as used to be thought, but also in exterior or semi-dark zones, where it is harder to identify (and its conservation is more difficult). This change in perspective means that it is possible to propose that there was more art in the open air in the past, as has been documented in the Iberian plateau and in Portugal. Additionally, in several cases the art is associated with the domestic site or dwelling, belying the traditional view of a "dark" art, and instead linking it with daily activities.

The caves with Palaeolithic art can be divided into two groups according to the number of motifs and the graphic diversity. There are ensembles (the largest group) that were produced in a certain moment, although they may have been in use for a long period. In contrast, major sites like Altamira, El Castillo, La Pasiega, Peña de Candamo, Llonín and Tito Bustillo contain figures displaying graphic, technical, stylistic and sometimes even thematic variety representing the re-use of the decorated area for symbolic purposes at different times, even over the course of several millennia. The artists gradually enlarged the ensemble as they incorporated the previous images in the symbolic structure of each

* Dpto. Geografía, Prehistoria y Arqueología, Universidad del País Vasco. c/ Tomás y Valiente s/n, 01006 Vitoria (España). marcos.garcia@ehu.es

** Dpto Dibujo II, Universidad Complutense de Madrid. C/ Greco 2, Ciudad Universitaria 28040 Madrid. pedro-saura@art.ucm.es

period. The images were "atemporal" in the sense that their use/function transcended the time of their creation. In this way, the gradual enlargement reflects the fact that not only the art or the images were important but also, and especially, the place.

From the thematic point of view, the caves in the north of the Iberian Peninsula contain the classic animal figures in Palaeolithic art, above all hinds, bison, horses, stags, aurochs and ibices, while other animals such as bears, mammoths, reindeer, carnivores and even birds are scarce or very scarce. They are mostly animals preferring a eurythermal climate, together with a few examples of cold fauna. In general, all the animals are found in the different periods, although in the older phases hinds are more common whereas in later stages (Magdalenian) the number of bison increases and the themes become increasingly diverse. Despite this, there are ensembles where one species dominates over the others. Human images are very rare, but represented partially by hands and genitals, especially in the Gravettian and Aurignacian. Signs are very abundant and display great diversity; from simple forms like dots, discs, etc. to complex shapes based on geometric forms with internal divisions. In some cases these constitute a regional peculiarity, whereas others are similar to signs found in distant areas.

The figures are distributed inside the caves in varying ways. There are ensembles located near the main routes through the caves, situated in easily-seen places and, in many cases, in large spaces. In general, the large panels in the major ensembles are in this kind of position, ensuring their visibility in a space that can hold several people with a potential common use of the symbolism of the figures. In contrast, other figures are found in small spaces and/or away from the main passages. In these cases, it is necessary to search for them or possess previous knowledge of their existence. These differences suggest public and private uses of Palaeolithic art.

In recent years, the application of absolute dating techniques has allowed, not without some debate, the production of Palaeolithic art to be fixed in time. Uranium-series dates for calcite covering red discs have shown that the interior of El Castillo cave was decorated nearly 41,000 years ago. In general terms, it may be said that the earliest representations were simple signs, and about 32,000 cal BP (based on portable art objects) the first figurative animal depictions were created. At first, these were simple outlined figures, anatomically out of proportion and with no secondary anatomical features. A precise date cannot be given, but by about 17,500 cal BP interior anatomy was represented by internal divisions inside the animals' bodies. The search for realism was consolidated about 15,500 cal BP with great attention to details in the anatomy, proportion and greater naturalism. In late stages of the upper Palaeolithic, the animal depictions tend towards geometric and/or stylised forms, and this trend continued in the Epipalaeolithic.

The Palaeolithic art in the north of the Iberian Peninsula is a reflection of the identity and relationships of human groups. The convergences and divergences enable an understanding of the "cultural geography". Despite Franco-Cantabrian art traditionally being regarded as peculiar to the region, this is no longer considered correct. The graphic construction of the figures exhibits relations over medium and long distances, as do the signs. Despite this, the peculiarities that can be seen are more of a technical nature and not of a formal one, as previously thought. At certain times, such as in the middle Magdalenian, the affinities cover a very large area, from the westernmost part of northern Spain to France. In contrast, the specific cases of peculiarity are occasional and restricted in time, such as the technique of striations used in animal depictions about 16,000 cal BP.

Palaeolithic art in the north of the Iberian Peninsula is one of the greatest cultural manifestations in the history of humankind. It is a masterpiece of human creative genius, of great artistic quality and with a universal value and meaning. It provides a unique visual testimony of a past cultural tradition, directly attesting a way of life and iconographic and religious feelings. The north of the Iberian Peninsula is a fundamental region for the understanding of human creativity, as one of the locations of the birth of Art. It is an outstanding area because of the large number of decorated caves, their excellent state of conservation, their rich iconographic repertoire, diversity of techniques and styles, their survival over millennia and their great age.

In 2008, UNESCO included in the List of World Heritage 17 caves with Palaeolithic art: Peña de Candamo, Tito Bustillo, Covaciella, Llonín, El Pindal, El Castillo, Las Monedas, Las Chimeneas, La Pasiega, La Garma, Covalanas, El Pendo, Hornos de la Peña, Chufín, Santimamiñe, Ekain and Altxerri. The proposal was called *Palaeolithic Cave Art of Northern Spain*, and was an extension of the inscription of Altamira in 1985. The cave of Altamira has been an outstanding example of the universal value of Palaeolithic cave art ever since its discovery, but needs to be understood within a wider cultural phenomenon of the hunter-gatherer-fisher communities that lived in south-west Europe in the Upper Palaeolithic.

Carmen de las Heras*,
José Antonio Lasheras*

Altamira cave (Santillana del Mar, Cantabria)

The Altamira cave is located in Santillana del Mar, Cantabria, in the north of Spain. It is aptly named *Altamira* ("High View") for its panoramic high altitude view overlooking the surrounding sea and hills. It is within easy reach of the coast, the Saja River and its estuary, and the coastal hills. This variety of ecosystems supplied the Palaeolithic communities with sufficient resources for their food and other needs. It was an oft-visited site in the life of Upper Palaeolithic groups for over 9,000 years, as they formed part of a society including the groups who used other nearby caves like La Clotilde, El Linar, Las Aguas, Cualventi, La Meaza, Cudón, El Castillo, La Pasiega, Las Chimeneas, Las Monedas, Hornos de la Peña, Morin, El Pendo, Santián, El Juyo, Camargo, El Ruso, etc., which were occupied during all or some of the same cultural periods.

Altamira cave is located in the upper part of the Santillana del Mar karst, formed in horizontal beds of calcarenites up to a metre thick which were separated by thin layers of clay. Collapse processes have shaped the cave, due to the fall of large orthogonal pieces of bedrock from the roof. A large collapse 13,000 years ago in the first metres of the cave blocked the entrance and sealed the cave off until its discovery in the nineteenth century.

The entrance is located in a gentle slope near the top of the hill and faces north. The cave is 270 metres long, and gently slopes down (Fig. 1). The Hall of the Paintings, (La Sala de Polícromos. Chamber I on the plan) and other side passages are short appendices to a large single passage, dotted with engravings and paintings. Within this single linear cave, in the twentieth century thick walls were built to avoid the roof collapsing in places of greatest structural weakness. The largest of these walls was built to separate the archaeological deposit in the entrance from the chamber with the polychrome (Techo de los Polícromos) paintings, dividing up the original entrance hall. This construction work has given the cave a very different appearance from its original appearance. This Palaeolithic Altamira, however, has been recreated in the replica that can now be visited in Altamira Museum: "the New Cave" (*la Neocueva*).

1. Discovery and archaeology in Altamira: 1875-2003

The entrance hall conserves the remains of what was once a large archaeological deposit

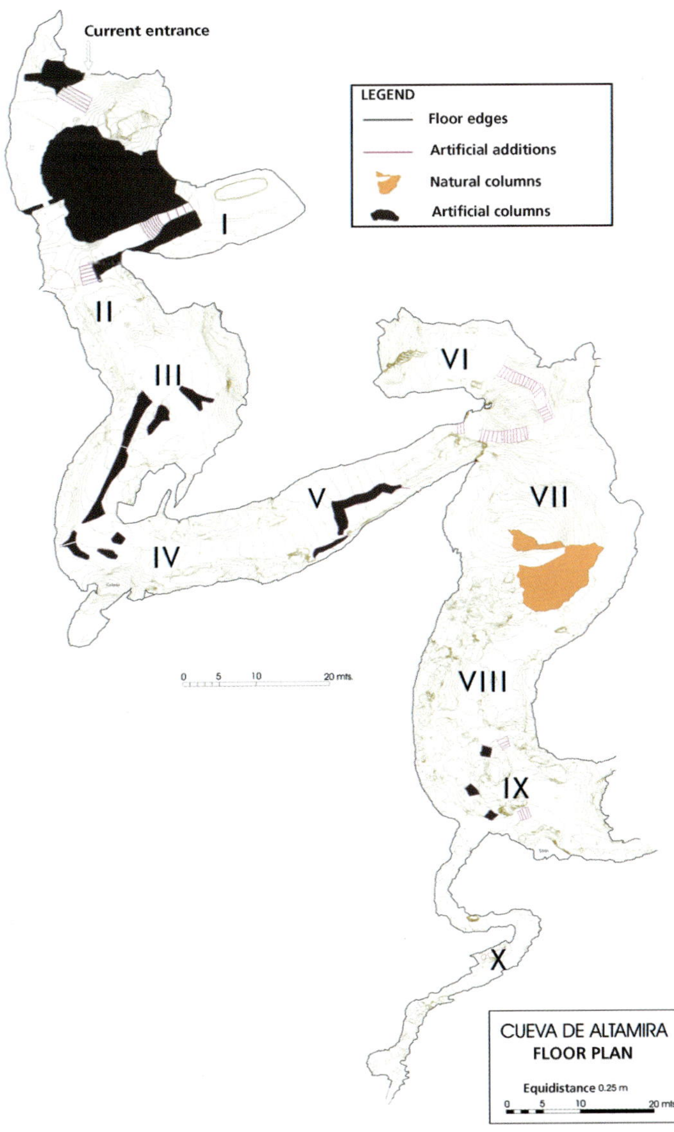

Figure 1. Plan of the Altamira cave © IGN/Altamira Museum.

* National Museum and Research Center of Altamira (39330, Santillana del Mar, Cantabria, Spain). investigacion.maltamira@mecd.es

(Fig. 2). It is now difficult to interpret owing to the natural collapse processes, the initial search for objects and the old excavations. Of these, no log books, inventories, drawings or photographs remain to document the original fieldwork. As such, only the published information remains.

In 1880, Marcelino Sanz de Sautuola published a booklet about the discovery of Altamira. In his descriptions, the floor of the entire entrance hall was covered by a large mass of animal remains, worked bones, stones and shells which extended as far as the Hall of the Paintings. He published an illustration with drawings of a stone pendant, several assegai points and some limpets, but his interest in the objects was limited to using them as a means to establish the age of the spectacular paintings he had just discovered. Sanz de Sautuola's booklet contained some initial revelations for prehistorians of his time. When he examined the figures, he identified bison, which were extinct in the region. He also associated the mineral pigments found on the floor with the colours of the Altamira paintings. He related the figures to those engraved on bones in some French caves. Sautuola even acknowledged the great artistic merit of the ensemble and its artists. For him there was no doubt: everything, artefacts and paintings both, belonged to the Palaeolithic as the first stage of humankind. For Sautuola, this was Art (Sautuola, 1880: 14).

What Sautuola had rightly deduced was unacceptable for most prehistorians of his time. In 1881, Edouard Harlé was sent to Altamira to inform his French colleagues about the paintings. He described the "trenches" dispersed in the cave and took the opportunity to collect a large amount of objects: 140 teeth, 1,200 bones, 600 limpets, 130 periwinkles, and a number of flint implements, including two Solutrean points, which were then sent to various specialists. Harlé dated the occupations at Altamira in the Magdalenian and Solutrean periods according to the typology of the objects. However, he did not assess all of the archaeological information correctly and mistakenly denied the Palaeolithic age of the paintings, despite Sautuola's impeccable analysis.

After 1881, Altamira was ostracized until it was finally recognised scientifically by Cartailhac in 1902. This is when Hermilio Alcalde del Río first visited the cave. He was the director of the Arts and Crafts School in Torrelavega, a town near Santillana del Mar, and he dug in the archaeological deposit between 1903 and 1905. He noted the changes in

Figure 2. Archaeological deposit in the entrance hall of the Altamira cave © Pedro Saura / Altamira Museum.

colour and texture and the greater or lesser presence of limestone rocks, bones, and marine shells. This allowed him to differentiate two levels, one Solutrean and the other Magdalenian (Alcalde del Río, 1906).

In 1924 and 1925, H. Obermaier excavated in the cave again, next to Alcalde del Río's trench. To the levels already known, he added a new one he called *Under the Solutrean*, of which he only published a brief list of fauna which included *Cervus elaphus, Equus caballus* and *Patella vulgata* (Breuil and Obermaier, 1935). In 1929, he mentioned the finding of two Font-Robert points which were never published and are not conserved with the rest of the collection. These artefacts were at that time associated with the Upper Aurignacian (now with the Gravettian) and would have been of great interest for setting the chronology of the occupations and the art in the cave. The existence of a Gravettian level was proven by our archaeological re-examination of the deposit in 2006 (Lasheras *et al.*, 2012).

There were no further excavations in Altamira until the Ministry of Culture created the Altamira National Museum and Research Centre in 1979, to which the cave was affiliated. Over the Christmas period of 1980-1981, J. González Echegaray, the first director of the Museum, and L. G. Freeman conducted fieldwork that only lasted a few days. Their work was interrupted by political tension in Santillana del Mar Town Council, which was concerned about the cave being closed to the public. Consequently, they were only able to excavate the upper part, measuring four square metres, above the stratigraphic section left by Obermaier. The first level with occupation remains is just beneath the pile of fallen rocks that blocked the cave and the calcite that covered them, and it is dated in the Lower Magdalenian. The Solutrean level begins beneath this, but the Echegaray and Freeman did not reach it. However, they differentiated several sub-layers by their colour, texture and composition of the archaeological content, which indicated a more complex archaeological deposit than was known until then (Freeman and González Echegaray, 1996, 2000).

In the Magdalenian level they found numerous pieces of ochre of different colours and sizes, thousands of limpet shells, abundant faunal remains with a large predominance of red deer, and the mandibles and vertebrae of salmon. They confirmed the small proportion of backed bladelets observed by Obermaier. The 106 Magdalenian tools they retrieved allowed the classification and comparison of these deposits and tools with Levels 8 and 9 at El Juyo and Level 4 at El Rascaño, whose diagnostic indices were observed to be very similar (Freeman and González Echegaray, 2000: 126 and following).

During the following years, there was no further archaeological research in the Altamira cave, but research into its conservation was promoted by the Museum and the Ministry of Culture, which signed an agreement with the Spanish National Research Council (CSIC in its Spanish acronym), under the direction of Manuel Hoyos. Under this programme, the calcite covering the collapse that had blocked the entrance was dated. Uranium-series and radiocarbon methodology was used (Labonne *et al.*, 2002), and the results obtained were consistent with the known archaeological data. These findings showed that the calcite began to form 12,900 years ago over rocks covering the Middle Magdalenian level, a time period that coincides with the dates of one of the black bison in the Hall of the Paintings (Table 1). The deposition of the calcite ended approximately 10,700 years ago, according to the dating of the upper part of the layer.

2. Rediscovering Altamira: research from 2003 to 2014[1]

One hundred and twenty years after its discovery, the archaeological understanding of Altamira was insufficient. In order to update the information, further work was required that would not affect the conservation of the cave, which had again been closed to the public in 2002 at the Museo de Altamira request. The research programme "The Times of Altamira", which the Museum carried out after 2003, promoted and coordinated the work of specialists from universities and research centres in Spain and abroad. Some of the findings are presented below.

a. *Dispersed Altamira*[2]

One of the first aspects addressed was the reconstruction of the history of the cave and the documentation of its collections scattered across different museums in Spain, Europe and America. This dispersal of Altamira artefacts was the consequence of the multiple collections after its initial discovery, the acquisition of pieces by various research centres. The reappraisal of the old dispersed collections has proceeded with some success. For example, researchers have identified some tools

1 The authors would like to acknowledge the assistance in this research of all the people and institutions that have supported it over the years. There is currently further ongoing research that is not described in this text.

2 This information coincides partly with the publication Lasheras *et al.*, 2005/2006.

Year	Reference	Material	Lab. Ref.	Provenance	Location	Result ^{14}C BP	Result ^{14}C cal BP (2 sigma)	Date U
1996	Labonne *et al.*, 2002	Calcite		Upper part of calcite	Calcite covering interior deposit	10.7 ky	12.714 – 12.639	11.800 ± 0.8 ky
1996	Labonne *et al.*, 2002	Calcite		Lower part of calcite	Calcite covering interior deposit	12.9 ky	15.571 – 15.256	
1996	Moure *et al.*, 1996	Paint – charcoal	GifA – 96067	Black bison XLIV	Hall of the Paintings	13.130 ± 120	16.100 – 15.329	
1991	Valladas *et al.*, 1992	Paint – charcoal	GifA – 91178	Black bison XLIV	Hall of the Paintings	13.570 ± 190	16.972 – 15.841	
1991	Valladas *et al.*, 1992	Paint – charcoal	GifA – 91179	Large polychrome bison XXXVI	Hall of the Paintings	13.940 ± 170	17.424 – 16.374	
1991	Valladas *et al.*, 1992	Paint – humic fr.	GifA – 91249	Black bison XLIV	Hall of the Paintings	14.410 ± 200	18.037 – 17.008	
2006	Lasheras, *et al.*, 2012	Bone	GrA – 27777	Level 1	Interior deposit	14.070 ± 70	17.398 – 16.837	
1991	Valladas *et al.*, 1992.	Paint – humic fr.	GifA – 91330	Large polychrome bison XXXIII	Hall of the Paintings	14.250 ± 180	17.860 – 16.827	
1991	Valladas *et al.*, 1992	Paint – charcoal	GifA – 91181	Large polychrome bison XXXIII	Hall of the Paintings	14.330 ± 190	17.949 – 16.933	
1990	Valladas *et al.*, 1992	Bone – engraved scapula	GifA – 90057	Lower Magdalenian (A. del Río, 1903-05)	Interior deposit	14.480 ± 250	18.274 – 16.979	
1990	Valladas *et al.*, 1992	Bone	GifA – 90047	Lower Magdalenian (Obermaier, 1924 – 25)	Interior deposit	14.520 ± 260	18.336 – 17.008	
1996	Moure *et al.*, 1996	Paint – charcoal	GifA – 96059	Black line under engraved hind	Gallery III	14.650 ± 140	18.189 – 17.486	
1991	Valladas *et al.*, 1992	Paint – humic fr.	GifA – 91254	Large polychrome bison XXXVI	Hall of the Paintings	14.710 ± 200	18.405 – 17.435	
1996	Moure *et al.*, 1996	Paint – charcoal	GifA – 96060	Large polychrome bison XXXVI	Hall of the Paintings	14.800 ± 150	18.380 – 17.635	
1996	Moure *et al.*, 1996	Paint – charcoal	GifA – 96071	Large polychrome bison XXXIII	Hall of the Paintings	14.820 ± 130	18.360 – 17.700	
2009	Lasheras, *et al.*, 2012	Bone – engraved scapula	GrA – 44928	Under collapse	Exterior deposit	14.830 ± 60	18.237 – 17.857	
2006	Lasheras, *et al.*, 2012	Bone	GrA – 32766	Level 1 - 2	Interior deposit	14.910 ± 60	18.317 – 17.932	
1996	Moure *et al.*, 1996	Paint – charcoal	GifA – 96062	Black hind	Chamber VI	15.050 ± 180	18.692 – 17.895	
2009	Lasheras, *et al.*, 2012	Bone	GrA – 44927	Under collapse (lower)	Exterior deposit	15.370 ± 60	18.785 – 18.500	
2009	Lasheras, *et al.*, 2012	Bone	GrA – 44926	Under collapse (upper)	Exterior deposit	15.400 ± 60	18.805 – 18.533	
2006	Heras, *et al.*, 2012	Bone	GrA – 30329	Level 2	Exterior deposit	15.420 ± 70	18.836 – 18.533	
1991	Valladas *et al.*, 1992	Paint – charcoal	GifA – 91185	Quadrilateral signs	Final gallery	15.440 ± 200	19.168 – 18.258	
1960	Freeman – G. Echegaray, 2001	Bone	M – 829	Lower Magdalenian	Interior deposit	15.500 ± 700	20.634 – 17.208	
2006	Lasheras, *et al.*, 2012	Bone	GrA – 30326	Level 4	Interior deposit	15.580 ± 90	19.021 – 18.638	
2009	Heras, *et al.*, 2012	Bone	Beta – 257006	Under collapse	Exterior deposit	15.610 ± 80	19.037 – 18.686	
1981	Freeman – G. Echegaray, 2001	Bone	I – I2012	Lower Magdalenian level	Interior deposit	15.910 ± 230	19.786 – 18.727	
1996	Moure *et al.*, 1996.	Paint – charcoal	GifA – 96061	Black line	Final gallery	16.480 ± 210	20.449 – 19.394	
2006	Heras, *et al.*, 2012	Bone	GrA – 32760	Level 6	Interior deposit	17.200 ± 70	20.970 – 20.535	
2008	Pike *et al.*, 2012	Calcite	BIG-Uth-O-53	Calcite over red horse	Hall of the Paintings			22.108 ± 0.132
1990	Valladas *et al.*, 1992	Bone	GifA – 90045	Solutrean level (Obermaier, 1924 – 25)	Interior deposit	18.540 ± 540	23.760 – 21.120	
2006	Lasheras, *et al.*, 2012	Bone	GrA – 30324	Level 7 (upper)	Interior deposit	18.750 ± 100	22.887 – 22.404	
2006	Lasheras, *et al.*, 2012	Bone	GrA – 30325	Level 7 (middle)	Interior deposit	19.060 ± 90	23.300 – 22.638	
2006	Lasheras, *et al.*, 2012	Bone	GrA – 32761	Level 7 (lower)	Interior deposit	19.630 ± 80	23.928 – 23.387	
2006	Lasheras, *et al.*, 2012	Bone	GrA – 27739	Level 8	Interior deposit	21.910 ± 90	26.373 – 25.912	
2006	Lasheras, *et al.*, 2012	Bone	GrA – 32765	Level 8	Interior deposit	21.930 ± 100	26.417 – 25.918	
2008	Pike *et al.*, 2012	Calcite	BIG-Uth-O-50	Calcite over red sign	Hall of the Paintings			36.160 ± 0.605

Table 1. Absolute dates obtained at Cueva de Altamira.
The C14 AMS dates were calibrated with the INTCAL13 curve using the OxCal Program, version 4.2 at 95.4% probability (2 sigma).

Figure 3. Palaeolithic airbrushes from the Altamira cave © Pedro Saura / Altamira Museum.

of a very old typology, such as unpublished cleavers, and also some exceptional artefacts, the "airbrushes", which had gone unnoticed because they were initially catalogued as pendants by Hermilio Alcalde del Río. These airbrushes were made from three segments of bones from the leg or wing of a large bird (a raptor or a wading-bird) and display defleshing and cut marks in the form of transverse grooves. Two of the pieces are now understood to fit together because they are part of the same bone, and the three of them measure between 5 and 6mm. They exhibit remains of pigment on both outer and inner surfaces of the tubes, which has led to their identification as tools used to apply red liquid paint. These bone pieces were placed at right angles to each other; by blowing through one section, the other section would absorb the paint and spray it outwards (Fig. 3). Alcalde del Río found these artefacts between some rocks in the passage. The lack of further stratigraphic context prevents any precise dating at this time.

b. *Stratigraphic reappraisal and new dates for the deposit in the cave*[3]

The stratigraphy that has been conserved is 4 metres long and 1 metre thick. At the base it is bounded by a uniform bed of rock and a *roof collapse* (Bajo Colapso), and at its top by the layer of calcite. The sedimentological study confirmed the existence of eight structurally independent levels, which are heterogeneous in their composition and physical-chemical characteristics. The column of AMS radiocarbon dates is also coherent, with no chronological inversions. The absence of any severe alterations to the archaeological deposit meant that the following chrono-cultural sequence could be established:

1. The Lower Magdalenian is represented by Levels 1 to 5, between 14,070 ± 70 BP (GrA-27777) and 15,580 ± 90 BP (GrA-30326).
2. Level 6 exhibits a layer of crushed bones with an erosive contact with Level 5. Its date, 17,200 ± 70 BP (GrA-32760), corresponds to the Upper Solutrean.
3. Level 7 is the thickest layer, and has provided three coherent dates: 18,750 ± 100 BP (GrA-30324), 19,060 ± 90 BP (GrA-30325) and 19,630 ± 80 BP (GrA-32761), which situates it in the Solutrean.
4. Level 8 has been dated twice, to either 21,930 ± 100 BP (GrA-32765) and 21,910 ± 90 BP (GrA-27739) which places it in the late Gravettian.[4]

The contacts between Levels 6, 7 and 8 correspond to erosive processes but a chronology has been definitively established going back to at least 22,000 BP. The discovery of a Gravettian level has supported the correct assignment of the technical and stylistic characteristics of a series of red figures which, until now, had not been precisely dated. This series of figures had originally been attributed as Solutrean as the oldest period known in the deposit. Recently, a Uranium-series date has confirmed their link with the Aurignacian (Pike *et al.*, 2102 and 2013; García Diez *et al.*, 2013), a period that remains yet to be discovered in the deposit (Fig. 4).

c. *Excavations outside the cave*

In 2008-2009, an excavation was conducted in the modern entrance of the cave to determine whether part of the archaeological deposit existed in the area that is now outside the entrance beneath the collapse that blocked it. The end of an archaeological level measuring 20cm thick was located in the outer limit of the collapse, preserved from the erosive processes that had removed the level in the area next to it (Fig. 5). It yielded numerous shells, faunal remains, lithic and bone objects, and a red deer scapula with an engraving of a hind's head, of the same type as those found by Alcalde del Río from 1903 to 1905.

3 This information coincides partly with the publication Lasheras *et al.*, 2012.

4 For further information about the Gravettian level and the oldest art in Altamira, see Heras, Montes and Lasheras, 2013.

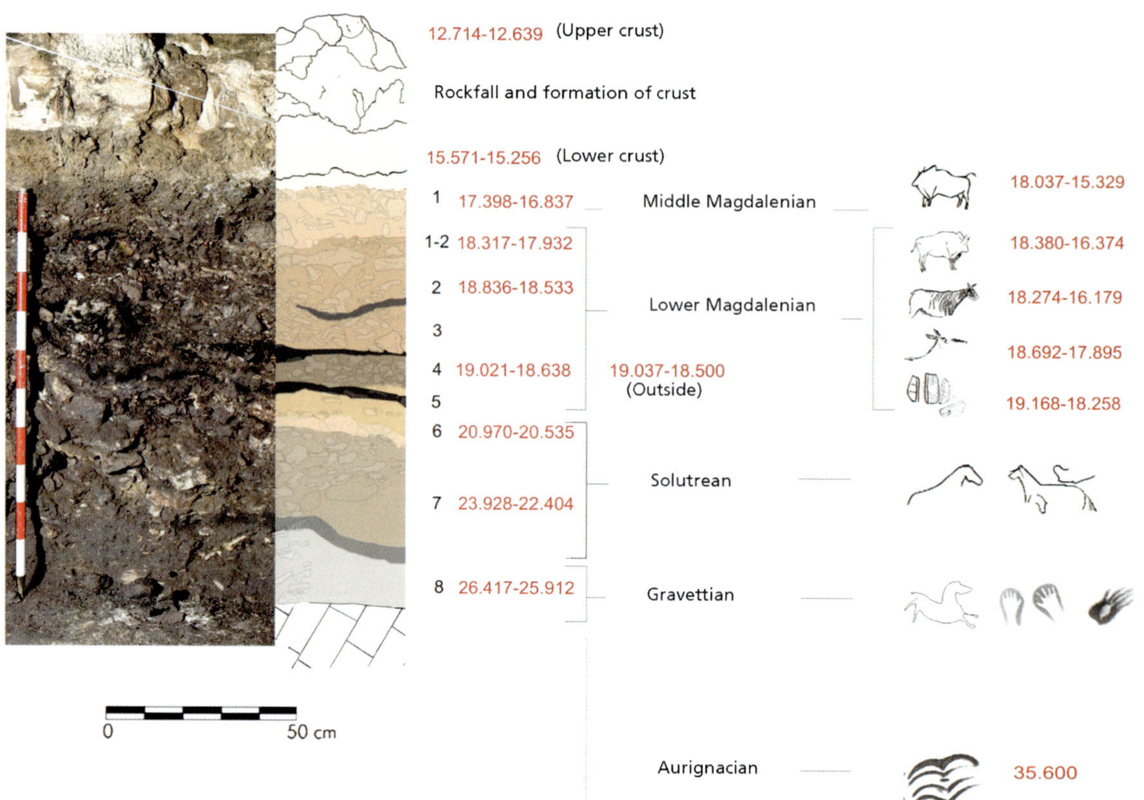

Figure 4. Stratigraphic, chronological and artistic sequence in the Altamira cave © Altamira Museum.

Figure 5. Deposit outside the Altamira cave, buried beneath the collapse of the external part of the entrance at the start of the Upper Magdalenian © Pedro Saura / Altamira Museum.

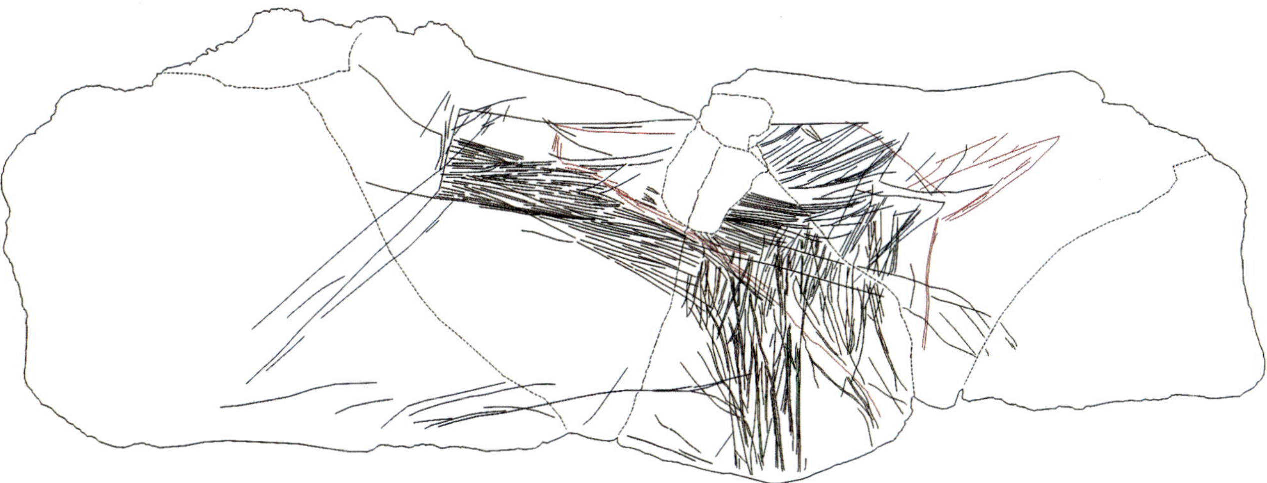

Figure 6. Engraved scapula found in the level *under the collapse* outside the cave. It displays two finely-engraved and superimposed heads of hinds © R. Montes / Museo de Altamira.

The three dates for this level under the collapse place it between 15,370 ± 60 (GrA-44927) and 15,610 ± 80 BP (Beta 257006), coinciding with Levels 2 to 4 in the interior deposit, in the Lower Magdalenian (Table 1).

d. New data for the chronology of engravings with multiple lines in Altamira and Cantabrian Spain[5]

The discovery of the decorated scapula in the level under the collapse has succeeded in reinforcing the chronology attributed to the parietal engravings with multiple lines in Altamira and, therefore, in all Cantabrian Spain (Fig. 6).

Alcalde del Río had found seven scapulae engraved with fine, intermingled lines that represented silhouettes and heads of hinds. In his writings, Alcalde del Río noted that he had found them "in the upper layer [Magdalenian] although in direct contact with typical Solutrean points" (Alcalde del Río in Cartailhac and Breuil, 1906, p. 267). These depictions displayed the same conventionalism as the hinds he had seen engraved in the passages and on the ceiling in the Hall of the Paintings, which caused him to affirm that the parietal and portable ensembles belonged to the same time period. However, doubts remained about the exact stratigraphic position of the scapulae. Later, in the 1924 excavations, Obermaier found engraved scapulae in the Lower Magdalenian level and in the Magdalenian-Solutrean transition layer (Breuil and Obermaier, 1935: 94), but Obermaier decided not to publish them. A note written by Freeman and González Echegaray (2001: 142) now locates them in the Chicago Field Museum. Other objects of this kind have been found in Lower Magdalenian levels (in the caves of El Castillo, Juyo, Cierro and Mirón) and similar engravings on the walls of such caves as El Castillo, Las Aguas, etc.

The three dates obtained directly for these characteristic engravings of Cantabrian Spain

Figure 7. Engraved hind in Passage III/IV with the characteristic multiple lines of these figures © Pedro Saura / Museo de Altamira.

5 This information coincides partly with the publication Heras *et al.*, 2012.

Figure 8. View of the ceiling with the polychrome (Techo de polícromos) paintings © Pedro Saura / Altamira Museum.

(Cantabria and Asturias), both on cave walls and on scapulae, come from Altamira. The first engraved scapula to be dated was one found by Alcalde del Río, and gave a result of 14,480 ± 250 BP (GifA-90057) (Valladas *et al.*, 1992). The second date was for a black line over which one of these characteristic hinds was engraved, on a wall inside Altamira, and the result of 14,650 ± 140 BP (GifA-96059) (Moure *et al.*, 1996) is a *post quem* date for the engraving. These first two dates are very close to those of the decorated scapulae (Fig. 7). The third date, 14,830 ± 60 BP (GrA-44928), corresponds to the scapula found in 2009 in the level under the collapse (Heras *et al.*, 2012). These dates refer to a very precise time, and are of special interest for Altamira as they make the striated engravings of hinds in the cave passages contemporaneous with the polychrome bison on the ceiling in the Hall of the Paintings. It is not possible to determine in which order the two kinds of depictions were produced (Table 1).

3. Altamira and its cave art[6]

The first art of humankind, cave art, was discovered, identified and published with scientific rigour at Altamira by Marcelino Sanz de Sautuola, a member of the gentry who owned a mansion in a nearby town. He possessed a degree in law, but his interest in science led him to the fields of archaeology, history and botany. In 1878, at the Universal Exhibition in Paris, he observed collections of prehistoric objects discovered in France and he decided to search for the same kind of objects in his region. After visiting several caves, he returned to Altamira in 1879 and explored it carefully. It was his seven-year-old daughter, María, the first one to see the paintings. "Papa, oxen!" were her words.

It is in the ceiling of the Hall of the Paintings that Altamira truly becomes spectacular (Fig. 8). It is a large canvas on which Upper Palaeolithic artists expressed their transcendent concerns. For H. Breuil (1935), the art in Altamira was the result of

[6] This information coincides partly with the publication Lasheras J.A., 2010.

a graphic tradition beginning in the Aurignacian/ Perigordian periods and concluding in the Upper Magdalenian, the period to which he attributed the polychrome figures.

Leroi-Gourhan (1965) proposed a shorter chronological framework, as he included all the representations in Styles III and IV, from the Solutrean to the Lower Magdalenian.

In the 1990s, the first absolute AMS radiocarbon dates were obtained for some polychrome bison (Figs. 14 and 15) and other figures painted in black (Figs. 7 and 12, among others) (Table 1). All the results corresponded to the Magdalenian period, between 13,130 ± 120 BP (GifA-96067) and 16,480 ± 210 BP (GifA-96061) (Valladas *et al.*, 1992; Moure *et al.*, 1996). These results coincided with Leroi-Gourhan's proposal, and related the artistic ensembles to the periods of occupation documented in the stratigraphy in the deposit (Bernaldo de Quirós, 1994; Moure, 1994; Lasheras, 2002).

The discovery of the Gravettian level in the recent research meant that the technical and stylistic characteristics of many red and engraved figures, whose direct dating was previously unobtainable, received the coherent support of the longer archaeological sequence. Since then, the application of Uranium-series analysis to figures that could not be dated previously (Fig. 9) lengthened the chronological framework to the Aurignacian period (Table 1).

Figure 9. Red sign dated in the Aurignacian period © Pedro Saura / Altamira Museum.

a. *The First Altamira rock art*

The oldest stage in the decoration of the main ceiling is represented by animals painted in red, engraved signs, hands and several series of dots.

On the right-hand side, juxtaposed curved lines form a large complex red sign. It has been classified as a "claviform sign" but its appearance differs from that of the typical claviform signs in Altamira and other Cantabrian and Pyrenean caves. Indeterminate red stains and the faint partial remains of two large horses of pre-Magdalenian age can be seen around the sign. Breuil (1935, Lamina VI) also included in this area a violet stencilled hand and a foot-shaped sign, equally in violet, which are no longer visible. This complex sign (Fig. 9) was dated by Uranium-series, and the result was older than expected: 36,164 ± 0.605 years (BIG-Uth-O-50) and therefore Aurignacian (Pike *et al.*, 2012 and 2013; García Díez *et al.*, 2013). Currently, only this sign, some large dots and a hand from el Castillo Cave have been dated to such an old time period.

Eleven large red figures, mostly horses (similar to Number 1, 2, 3, 4 and 5 on the plan in Figure 10) were originally dispersed across a large part of the ceiling. They were between 150 and 180cm long. Some of them are partially covered by the later superimposed polychrome figures and they have generally reached the present time with their colours faded by the natural processes that occurred before the discovery of the cave. It should be noted that none of these red figures include any relief or other natural forms of the ceiling.

The largest of these horses projects its fore-legs perpendicular to its chest, its neck is contracted and its head raised. Its back is also contracted, while its belly is stretched and its back legs are open like a pair of compasses; it is a galloping horse, raised on its back legs while its tail hangs from the croup. It is 182cm long, painted in red with a continuous line around its outline in its belly. The head is filled with red colour-wash without any details. The layer of calcite formed over its belly was dated to 22,108 ± 0.132 BP (BIG-Uth-O-53), an *ante quem* date for the drawing of the horse, which means that it must correspond at least to the early Solutrean or, as is thought more likely, to the gravettian (No. 3 on the plan) (Fig. 11).

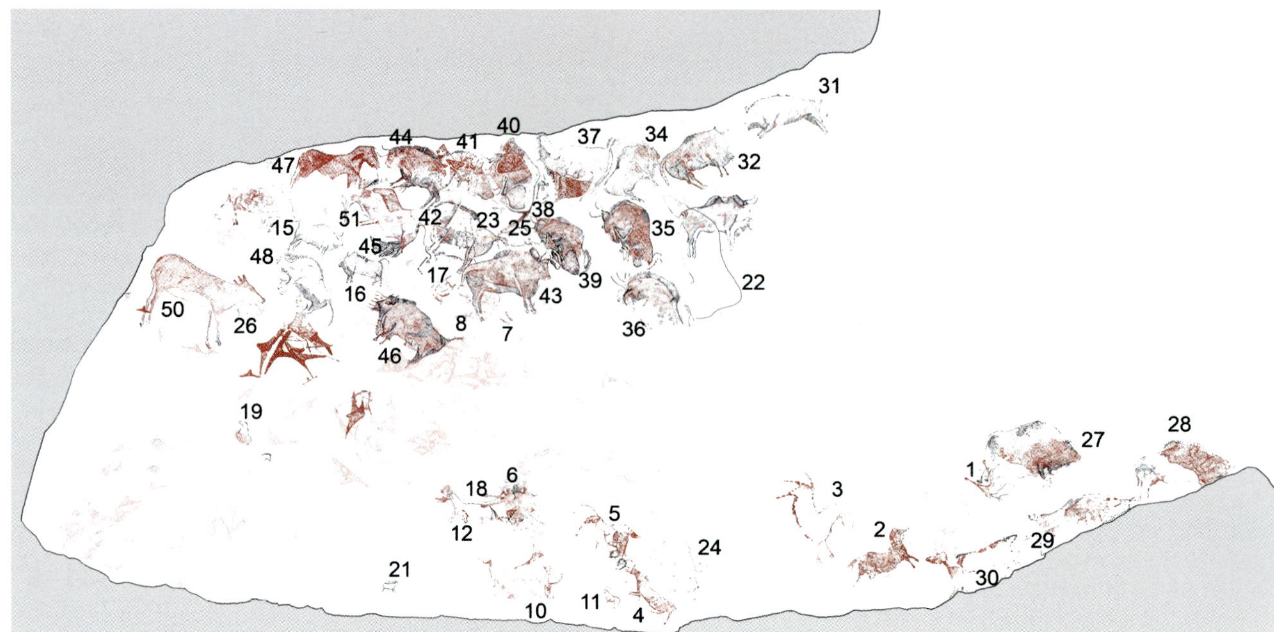

Figure 10. Plan with the location of the painted and engraved representations on the Techo de los Polícromos paintings © Antonio Gómez Laguna / Altamira Museum.

Figure 11. Red horse © Pedro Saura / Altamira Museum.

Another point to bear in mind is the existence of two stencilled hands superimposed on the fore-legs of one of these horses (No. 5 on the plan). As most of the stencilled hands that have been dated in other caves are Gravettian in age, the same date may be extrapolated to these hands and, owing to the superimposition, extended to the other red figures in the ceiling. In this way, they would all be placed in the Gravettian period.

Several series of dots dabbed with a finger tip, in straight and curved lines, as well as a red hand near the two horses facing each other can also be included in this oldest group of representations.

Further inside the cave, 65m from the entrance, a small side-passage measuring little more than one metre wide and five metres long is full of red signs. At the top, a sign consists of four irregular ovals divided up internally. A large red sign measuring three metres long and up to 50 cm wide can be found on the under face of a rock prominence, one metre above the floor. It is formed by long bands of parallel lines crossed by small transversal lines. To see this sign entirely, it is necessary to crouch or even lie on the floor. The narrowness of the space makes it difficult to see this and other signs on one of the walls, and there is not enough room for more than two people at any one time. This should stimulate a reflection on the original function and use of the representations.

On a large flowstone in Gallery II, three large figures were engraved in line, with wide and deep lines. Only the central figure can be identified: it is a stationary horse, over 150 cm long.

b. Magdalenian black and engraved figures

All the black figures in the Altamira Cave were drawn with charcoal, which has allowed to get some of them to be dated by AMS radiocarbon (Table 1). The resulting age, Lower Magdalenian, together with certain stylistic and technical uniformity –charcoal as the pigment and a linear style– means that they are regarded as belonging to the same ensemble. However, their uniformity is relative and they were produced at different times and over a wide span of time.

A group of black horses in the Hall of the Paintings and in Gallery III could not be dated by AMS radiocarbon. Nevertheless, their proportions, the form of their manes and the shape of their muzzle are clearly similar to figures attributed to the Solutrean at other sites in the Iberian Peninsula.

During the Magdalenian, the themes are more varied. Together with the horses, there are aurochs, bison, ibices, red deer stags and hinds, semi-human faces and signs. There are only four aurochs in the whole cave and they all display singular techniques or formal characteristics. On the main ceiling, an enormous bull measuring 270cm long is partially perceptible under a polychrome bison. The head is clearly visible, and its forehead was outlined with a black line that highlights a natural crack. Its dorsal line is a wide band with multiple engravings, almost *sgraffito*. The belly is made to coincide with a natural crack and it is marked by black lines that also indicate the sex. The ceiling in Gallery II was engraved with lines made by the index finger, fore-finger and third finger of a hand in soft clay. Within these lines, the head of a horse nearly a metre long is easily discerned. Near the head, on the face of a bed of rock, fitting between irregularities, a 50-cm-long bull was drawn in black. One last bull, engraved with considerable detail at the start of Gallery V, raises its head, exhibiting its muscular neck.

The bison now begin to populate the cave. On the ceiling there is a huge head drawn with a black line which continues the profile of its hunch, but the rest of the animal is not perceivable (No. 24 on the plan). To outline the horn, a pre-existing strip of calcite was marked in black, while a second parallel black line represents the other horn. The whole figure was conceived around this small natural relief. The other black bison on the ceiling (No. 2, 15, 16, 17 and 25 on the plan) cannot be associated with this series and, because of their technical and stylistic characteristics, they will be studied below in connection with the polychrome figures.

A group of quadrilateral black signs in the final passage were placed by means of AMS-C14 in the Lower Magdalenian (15,440 ± 200 BP GifA-91185) (Fig. 12). Some natural forms of the rock near these signs, in virtually the deepest part of the cave, were made into human-like faces. They are known as "masks", and belong to the same Magdalenian time. Just a few marks were needed to suggest eyes, eyebrows and mouth. The light alone reveals their shape in the natural rock forms, and the black

Figure 12. Quadrilateral signs © Pedro Saura / Altamira Museum.

Figure 13. "Masks". Paint and rock are combined in order to create suggestive, unique images © Pedro Saura / Altamira Museum.

marks suffice to make some uncertain faces appear in places where *nobody* was present before (Fig. 13).

c. *The engraved cave*

Engraved representations are found in all the galleries and sectors of the cave. The red deer is the species most often represented with this technique in Altamira. There is one large group of engravings whose all members seem to belong to the same family. The interior of many of their bodies, heads and necks is either filled with striated lines or shaded. They are comparable with the engravings made on red deer scapulae whose age was discussed above (Fig. 7). On the ceiling, a large stag measuring 70cm long is roaring, opposite a hind's head drawn with the same technique.

Over twenty hinds are engraved on the ceiling (Gran Techo), while others on the wall of the same hall have recently been discovered. There are thirteen of them in Galleries III, IV and V, and nearly the same number in Gallery X, of which six are grouped together in a small panel. This latter grouping is the deepest artistic representation in the cave, and it is located in a place that is so narrow and low that it is necessary to crawl to see them.

d. *The great ceiling (Gran Techo) with the polychrome bison*

The main attraction and interest of Altamira is the large group of figures painted on this ceiling. The paintings, known as *polychromes*, form an outstanding work of art that makes a profound impression on anyone who observes them.

These 25 large figures represent bison, a hind and two horses. They are between 125 and 170 cm long, while the hind (No. 50 on the plan) reaches two metres. The figures were produced by engraving and drawing the outline, the forelegs, hair on the chest and the hunch in black. The engraved lines are wide, with multiple parallel lines defining the outline. By means of deeper lines, further details such as the eyes, the horns and the hair on the neck are engraved. Most of the figures were then filled with red paint, except the bison No. 42 and 48, which were painted with yellow or brown ochre. In some figures, black pigments induce a change of colour in their bellies, and on their legs from the dock to the elbow, representing with naturalistic faithfulness the darker colour of the wet or mud-stained coat of an animal that has been resting on the ground while chewing the cud (No. 33, 34, 43 and 48). Certain lines made by reserving colour separate the legs from the chest, the haunches from the belly or one leg from another.

The natural protuberances on the ceiling, up to 30cm lower than its flat parts, were used to give volume to the figures in their chest (No. 34 on the plan) or in their whole body, as in the case of the bison that seem to be at rest (No. 35, 36 and 39). The belly of the large hind (No. 50) is also over a gentle relief that may have been used to suggest it was pregnant. Cracks were also used to represent the outlines (No. 34). The repeated and constant use of relief and other natural rock forms was not by chance, nor did it only seek the effect of volume. It undoubtedly obeys other symbolic and perhaps transcendental reasons.

The term *polychrome* used to describe these figures is inexact. Indeed, these figures transmit that impression; nevertheless, no more than two pigments were used in any of them. These pigments were charcoal black and ochre red or brown. The polychrome appearance is the result of both the addition of pigment to the rock and the transparency and glazes of the rock through the pigment. However, this transparency was not a technique employed by the Palaeolithic artists, but a consequence of time, of the subtle alteration occurring over millennia due to filtration or condensation of water on the ceiling, which washes away the pigment and re-deposits it or makes it fall to the floor. The interior of these "polychrome" figures was filled with red colour-wash, as can be observed, for example, in the chest and neck of the bison resting on the ground and turning its head round, without the colour of the rock being visible through it (Fig. 14).

The crack dividing up the ceiling longitudinally influenced the work of the Palaeolithic artists. It seems likely that the four bison similar to the other polychrome figures on the right-hand side were the first to be produced. It is also conceivable that the immediately following *discovery* of the natural rock volumes transferred the location of the symbolic creation to the other part of the ceiling. Neither the forms or techniques, or any other details make them different from the rest of the herd (No. 27 to 30 on the plan).

The group of polychrome animals is completed with a huge horse's head (No. 41) and the figure of a foal (no. 46) identified in that way by Freeman and González Echegaray (2001).

e. *The last bison, the last artists*

The date of the monochrome bison Number 16 is the most recent of those obtained so far (13,130 ± 120 BP GifA96067) (Fig. 15). It displays the technique of spreading the charcoal, a direct and firm application in some lines, and a softer touch to achieve grey tones, by using the hand to spread or fade the colour. Thus, particular shades were achieved. This helped to

Figure 14. "Polychrome" bison in Altamira © Pedro Saura / Altamira Museum.

Figure 15. Black bison on the ceiling of the Polychromes © Pedro Saura / Altamira Museum.

create volumes, as if it was a modern charcoal drawing. Certain characteristics relate these figures to the polychrome paintings and thus they become part of its ceiling, whereas others are similar to later types characteristic of the Middle Magdalenian. The collapse that took place at the entrance soon afterwards and the impossibility of re-entering the cave meant that these bison were the epilogue of a masterpiece.

4. Conclusions

Research on the archaeological deposit and new dates for the portable and rock art have provide new information about knowledge of human occupation of the Altamira cave, as can be summarised in the following points:

- The archaeological deposit covers a long period of time, from 13,000 BP to 22,000 BP. Its surface area during Upper Palaeolithic covers the whole original entrance hall, even the area that was covered by the collapse and large area which currently is outside. In total, around 300 m^2.
- The stratigraphic sequence is coherent from the geological, chronological and cultural points of view. However, low intensity post-depositional processes may have caused an occasional movement of the archaeological record, over short distances, from its original place (now beneath the collapse that blocked the cave) to its current position.
- The graphic ensemble, the art, was produced over a long period of 20,000 years, between 35,559 and 15,204 cal BP. This means that the cave was reused, sometimes respecting existing depictions or adding them and using them in new figures. In this way a palimpsest or accumulation of culture and symbolism was formed, suggesting a shrine or, better, a place of discontinuous symbology, given different meanings at different times.
- Paintings and engravings were produced at Altamira from the Aurignacian, in the first stages of Upper Palaeolithic art in Europe.
- Painters, engravers... artists? The answer is undoubtedly *yes*. Somebody created all these figures out of nothing, with artistic elements like paint and lines, and they were achieved with great ability and skill. Not all the figures are masterpieces, but it is difficult to find evidence of clumsiness or incompetence. There are no mistakes and few corrections. The people who painted and engraved in the cave were quite confident in themselves, as a result of their practice and training. The ability of the people who, in these circumstances and with these "canvases", achieved figures that nearly always convey some message cannot be questioned. Current proposals agree on interpreting the symbiosis between art and nature, between the created figures and the natural surface they are on, as described above, in terms of the animism underlying ancient religious systems and, in general, with the animism in all mythical and pre-philosophical thought.

Jesús Altuna*, Koro Mariezkurrena*

Altxerri cave (Aia, Basque Country)

The discovery of Altxerri cave and its cave art ensemble took place in two stages. No caves were known in the area until 1956, when building work was being carried out near Altxerri farm, and limestone was being removed from the hillside behind the farmhouse. One of the dynamite blasts opened a hole 1 m wide and 80 cm wide. A large wide cave was discovered which only seemed to attract local boys who entered it in search of adventure. Fortunately the quarrying ended once enough rock had been obtained.

Six years later, the speleologists Aranzadi, Migliaccio and Vicuña discovered the first figures, 100m from the entrance. They informed Barandiarán of the discovery and the prehistorian confirmed the authenticity of the figures and carried out the first study.

Unfortunately in the time that went by between the discoveries of the cave and the rock art, visitors left graffiti on the walls and even over the Palaeolithic figures.

Twelve years after the first study, Altuna and Apellániz carried out a second investigation, and in 1996 Altuna produced the third study. Since then, Altuna and Mariezkurrena have published the finds of new figures, and more recently González Sainz and Ruiz-Redondo have published a paper on the figures in the upper passage in the cave.

The cave formed in well-jointed stratified limestone. The strata are relatively thin, rarely more than 40cm thick, and have been severely affected by the Tertiary orogeny so that they are folded and fractured. The figures were produced either on the faces and sections of the beds or on the bedding planes. In the former case, the relatively thinness of the beds means that the figures are not too big and are adapted to the size of the rock faces.

Altxerri is an important site for several reasons. Over a hundred animal figures are known in the main passage. A large variety of species are represented; while bison dominate, the inventory of species includes reindeer, red deer, horses, aurochs, ibex, possible saiga antelope, chamois, fox, fish, a bird and a snake. In addition, there are two anthropomorphs, numerous signs that are difficult to interpret and scratched surfaces. The upper passage, to be described in greater detail below, had a different entrance, which is now blocked, and holds a small but very different art ensemble from the one in the main passage.

The first group of figures are located in a small side-passage about 100m from the entrance, on the left-hand side of the main passage. It is preceded by an engraved "barbed" sign and contains over 12 bison, 2 reindeer, 2 ibices, 2 possible saiga antelopes, 2 foxes, 1 horse, 1 hind, 1 probably hare, 1 bird, 4 fish and 2 anthropomorphs, as well as signs and other drawings. All these figures are engraved, except for a few features. One of the largest figures is a reindeer drawn with deeply engraved lines. Its head is very carefully depicted, with the palm-shaped front part of the antler, and the typical mass of hair between the neck and chest. The legs are drawn in detail with the ankles and ending in the fetlocks and hooves (Fig. 1). Inside its neck, a fox is represented. It is almost whole, deeply engraved, and its relatively short ears suggest that, like the reindeer, it is an Arctic species.

Equally of interest in this first group are two flat fish, possibly plaice, and a bird which was represented by using the natural form of the rock which resembles such an animal. Another two fish are opposite it, one of them looks like a bream and the other, which is less clear, is probably a salmonid.

In the case of some figures, especially the bison, the rock was scraped with abundant, structured and much finer lines, which seem to be an expressionist representation of the animals' hair in their fore-quarters, especially their winter coat. The scraping sometimes prepared the wall before the animal figure was engraved.

* Centro de Conservación e Investigación de los Materiales Arqueológicos de Gipuzkoa. Paseo de Zarategi 82-84, 20014 San Sebastián. altuna@arkaios.com

One outstanding bison is almost whole, facing left with its head downwards. Its tail is raised and turned towards the front. Its sex is clearly marked. Two straight lines were drawn above the animal, one over the posterior part of its hunch and the other over the croup. In the point where the first of these touches its body, a thick line of red paint appears to show the blood flowing from the wound caused by the weapon.

Leaving the side-passage, the second group of rock art is in the continuation of the main passage. Here there are more paintings than engravings, unlike in the first group. However, these paintings are in a very damp part of the cave and much of the pigment has been lost, especially in the upper part of a horizontal edge of rock that divides the wall into two parts, one above the other. Several bison and the fore-quarters of an ibex have been identified, while in the lower part another bison consists of its head, the first part of its hunch, and the posterior part of its body and tail; the central part has been covered by a thick stalagmite that has grown over it. Other figures are an engraved head and neck of an ibex and an aurochs painted in black.

On the right-hand wall, opposite these figures and above a scraped area, a painted and engraved bison occupies one of the faces of bedrock. The engraving seems to have been intended to shape the front part of the animal and prepare the wall, before the central and posterior part of the animal was painted. This "wall-preparation" engraving continues over an area behind the figure. A few metres further on, another group of figures, partly painted in black and partly engraved, include some ten bison.

At this point, the main passage divides into two. On one side it slopes down to a shaft, with figures to be described below, while the other side leads to other groups of figures, the furthest from the entrance. To reach these groups it is necessary to climb the wall, crawl under a low arch and descend to a bridge between two shafts.

On one bed of rock there are 7 bison, 1 complete horse, 1 fore-quarters of a horse, 1 chamois, 1 ibex and 1 probable aurochs, as well as scraped surfaces and some signs. The horse occupies a prominent position above the bison (Fig. 2). The scraping accompanies the painting, by preparing the wall and shaping and completing the figures.

On the opposite wall, there is an engraved figure of an almost whole reindeer. Over its neck a serpentiform winds upwards. Other reindeer and bison are also present.

Figure 1. Reindeer and Arctic fox in Altxerri cave.

On the slope to the shaft, there are further figures, including the largest in the passage (engraved fore-quarters of a bison and hind-quarters of a horse) and in the shaft itself, two incomplete bison.

The homogeneity of the figures in the main passage and shaft at Altxerri suggest that they were all produced in a relatively short time, during the late Magdalenian, and they correspond to Leroi-Gourhan's Style IV.

In addition to this passage, there is an upper gallery that is now reached up a metal ladder installed in a vertical chimney. The original entrance, which is now blocked, was higher up. This upper passage contains further figures, above all a large bison 5m long painted in red, which is attributed to a much earlier period than the figures in the main passage. Numerous red dots were discovered

Figure 2. Horse and bison in Altxerri cave.

by Wesbuer and reported to González Sainz. Two of the abundant bone fragments on the floor were dated by Altuna and Mariezkurrena to 29,940 ± 745 BP (Ua-11145) and 34,195 ± 1235 BP (Ua-11144). Recently another burnt bone was dated to 34,370 ± 280 BP (Beta-340768). A short distance away from the large bison, a vertebra of a large bovid is stuck in a crack in the wall.

Jesús Altuna*, Koro Mariezkurrena**

Ekain cave (Deba, Basque Country)

The rock art ensemble of Ekain was discovered by Albizuri and Rezabal in 1969. Inside a small cave that was known to exist, the explorers discovered a long passage, with very difficult access, and in it they found the cave art. They informed Barandiarán and Altuna of the discovery and these certified the authenticity of figures and published the first study. In 1978, a new study was published by Altuna and Apellániz. In 1996, Altuna published a third investigation and in 2008 Altuna and Mariezkurrena brought out a study of new finds produced during the making of the replica of the

* Centro de Conservación e Investigación de los Materiales Arqueológicos de Gipuzkoa. Paseo de Zarategi 82-84, 20014 San Sebastián. altuna@arkaios.com

Figure 1. Main panel with the horses in Ekain cave.

cave. The colouring matter used in the paintings has been analysed by Chalmin, Menu and Altuna.

The archaeological deposit in the cave entrance was excavated by Barandiarán from 1969 to 1972, and by Altuna from 1973 to 1975 and from 2008 to 2011. It includes levels assigned to the lower, middle and upper Magdalenian. In the upper level an engraved plaquette was found with figures of an ibex, a stag and a horse dated to 12,050 ± 190 BP (I-9240). In the most recent excavations, beneath the upper Magdalenian layer was found a *contour decoupé* made from a bovid rib represented a bird with profuse internal shaping. It has been dated to 13,862 ± 29 BP (Ua-39108). Both the date and the characteristics of the object correspond to the middle Magdalenian. This phase, which must correspond to a time when the cave was less frequently visited, was not detected in the old excavation.

The cave consists of a narrow entrance passage which widens after 40 m, where the prehistoric representations start. The first depiction, discovered recently and still unpublished, is a red bison in the centre of the passage.

What was until now believed to be the first figure comes after a black curved line at the end of the passage. It is on the junction with a small side-passage and the continuation of the main passage towards the chamber. It consists of a large head, neck and withers of a horse painted in black colour-wash and situated in the top of a dome in the roof.

At the entrance of the side-passage mentioned above, on the left-hand wall, a hind is followed by a stag. These, and a further two at the far end of the cave, are the only engraved figures. All the others were painted, although engraving occasionally partially complements some of the paintings.

A little further on, using the shape of the rock and a hole for its eye, a salmon is painted in black. Next to it and on the opposite wall, ibices are painted in black; some of them are very schematic

Figure 2. Bears in Ekain cave.

and small and the most complete is no longer than 20 cm. Abundant red stains and dots are seen on both walls.

The main chamber is located 50m from the entrance and divides into two passages. The one on the left is blind, and contains a horse with numerous stains and red and black lines, while the other passage continues along a relatively narrow corridor. At its start, on the right and left, two bison seem to indicate the entry to the main panels of horses. The bison on the right uses the natural silhouette of the rock, which resembles the back of a bison with its tail, and the artist completed the rest of the figure with black paint.

The large panel is on the right in this passage (Fig. 1), with 12 horses, 4 bison, 1 hind at the start of the panel, 1 fish at its end and 1 vulva in the centre. Unlike Altxerri, Santimamiñe and Altamira, where bison are the most numerous animals, complemented by horses, in Ekain, horses predominate and are accompanied by bison. The almost whole hind is in the top part of the panel, on the right and painted in black. The bison are on the right and in the top part; the first one in black follows a rock edge in its croup, raised tail and rump, and another is painted in red and black and partly engraved. Some of the horses are painted in black and others in red and black, accompanied by engravings. Several of them display a band at their withers, an M-shaped line separating the colouring on their sides and stripes on their legs, in which the details of their hooves, fetlocks and hocks are depicted.

In the centre of the panel a large fissure separates the figures into two parts. On the right of the fissure there are three bison and two horses, and on the left more horses and a fish. In its upper part, the fissure widens into an oval shaped hollow, in the shape of a spindle or vulva, filled with red pigment, of the same type as the horse next to it. In the centre, a large bison is engraved and the panel ends with a curved red line.

On the opposite wall, as well as the bison already described, there is another incomplete one, four more or less whole horses and three incomplete ones. They are all in black. The most detailed figures are the central and last ones. The one nearest the end of the cave has been constructed around a series of natural edges and cracks in the rock, marking only a few places with black paint to complete the figure. This completion with paint of natural forms suggested by the rock surface is a characteristic of the art in Ekain.

Further on, in a level part of the main passage, on the left the roof is covered by granulated travertine, on which two bears were painted (Fig. 2). It is necessary to stoop to see the figures on this low roof, otherwise it is possible to walk by them without noticing them. They are both simple silhouettes of thick black lines. Nearly all the horses in the two main panels and all those in the end of the passage face towards the area with the bears.

Some 20m from the bears, the main passage reaches a larger chamber with seven horses in red and black on the right-hand wall. The group begins with a curved black line, followed by the first horse, which is somewhat separated from the others. One of them has an engraved arrow over its heart. The M-shaped line representing the horses' coat, band at the withers and striped legs can also be seen in these figures, just as in the main panel. Continuing to the practicable end of the passage, about 13m further on, some wide and shallow engraved lines may be interpreted, with reserves, as parts of two rhinoceros.

The colouring matter used to paint the horses was charcoal, except in the case of the first large horse's head and the bears, where manganese dioxide was employed. Various kinds of ochre were used to make the red pigments. The realism of the horses, their internal shaping and the careful details, especially in their heads, combined with the correct depiction of the bison, are indicative of Leroi-Gourhan's Style IV. This prehistorian stated that the ensemble at Ekain is one of the major sites in the classical period of cave art.

In the late-final Magdalenian, the most often hunted prey was ibex, followed by red deer. In the other two Magdalenian levels it was red deer followed by ibex. In all the levels, remains of horse are sporadic and bison is very rare. The preferences of the hunters at Ekain when hunting ungulates and depicting them were contradictory.

Marcos García-Diez*

Santimamiñe cave (Guernica, Basque Country)

Figure 1. Main panel in the *Chamber* in Santimamiñe cave (© A. Sánchez, Euskal Museoa – Bilbao – Basque Museum).

Santimamiñe cave, discovered in 1916, is situated in a hill called Ereñusarre. It consists of a straight main passage, with several side passages that are generally small in size. The entrance hall contains a deposit formed by human occupations since the Aurignacian, including a high density of remains belonging to the Magdalenian.

The first examples of rock art are located in the entrance hall. They consist of a hind's head which is now in daylight, combining the use of the natural form of the rock with deep wide engraving, as well as simple red motifs (stains, a series of dots and a dot) a little further inside and closely related to the deposit. The first black paintings are in the main passage: an ibex and another zoomorph possibly representing a bison.

On the left, in a high side sector, a small passage leads to the *Antechamber* and *Chamber (Antecá-*

* Dpto. Geografía, Prehistoria y Arqueología, Universidad del País Vasco. c/ Tomás y Valiente s/n, 01006 Vitoria (España). marcos.garcia@ehu.es

mara and Cámara), where most of the representations are found. The first area contains 6 black bison, a black horse, 2 engraved horses (one of which uses the natural rock surface), 2 black zoomorphs, a series of parallel red lines, non-figurative black, red and engraved lines, and red stains. Continuing into the *Chamber*, the number and thematic diversity of the figures increases, as this is the area with greatest concentration of paintings. The motifs are distributed in several panels, with an outstanding group in the main panel (Fig. 1). A total of 21 bison are known; in black, engraved or combining both technical procedures. They are accompanied by 2 black horses, a black bear, a black stag, 2 black ibices, 6 black zoomorphs (one of them possibly an ibex and another a bovid) as well as black and engraved marks.

The last figures are at the end of the main passage, after a sector 50 m long with no representations. It is a small group consisting of 2 bison, a black horse, a black head associated with a mass of flowstone that generally suggests an animal's body, and black lines.

Santimamiñe cave contains an ensemble that was all produced synchronically, except for the exterior engraving of a hind which may correspond to a different time. Bison are the most common theme, occasionally accompanied by horses, ibices and/or deer. Signs are practically absent, and the few examples are simple as no complex signs have been recorded. The most frequent technical procedure is drawing with charcoal, as well as engraving and occasionally painting in red (only used for non-figurative motifs). In some cases, the engravings and black drawings are combined or complement each other. Some of the animals are treated simply and represented mainly by their outline, and in other cases, especially the bison, they are drawn with more details in their secondary anatomy, especially inside their bodies, which gives the figures a greater sense of volume and anatomy. A few figures make use of the natural form of the rock surface to complete or suggest part of the animals' bodies. Although the ensemble is distributed in different parts of the cave, most depictions are in the *Antechamber* and *Chamber*; small isolated spaces, hidden from the main passage. This is therefore mainly a "reserved" ensemble.

No AMS C14 dates are available for the Palaeolithic. However, the graphic associations with other ensembles that have been dated suggest that the figures in Cueva de Santimamiñe were produced between about 14,800 and 12,000 BP, in the middle-upper Magdalenian.

The ensemble in Santimamiñe is integrated in a graphic tradition with very similar ensembles in other parts of Cantabrian Spain and France. This is evidence for the cultural links, as well as a degree of mobility and social interaction, that existed across south-west Europe in the recent Magdalenian.

Marcos García-Diez*,
Joaquín Eguizabal Torre**

Covalanas cave (Ramales de la Victoria, Cantabria)

This cave is located near the town of Ramales de la Victoria and was discovered in 1903. It is located in an area of rugged relief with high mountains and deep narrow valleys connecting the coast with the interior of the Iberian Peninsula. The cave is formed by two passages with a total length of 195m. Little is known about its archaeological deposit; some non-diagnostic pieces of flint and potsherds were found, and the cave walls also display black marks produced during the Middle Ages.

Of the two passages, in the *Galería de la Musica* only a sinuous red line has been documented,

* Dpto. Geografía, Prehistoria y Arqueología, Universidad del País Vasco. c/ Tomás y Valiente s/n, 01006 Vitoria (España). marcos.garcia@ehu.es

** Cuevas Prehistóricas de Cantabria, Sociedad Regional de Educación, Cultura y Deporte, Gobierno de Cantabria. Cuevas de Monte Castillo, 39670 Puente Viesgo (Cantabria). joaquin.eguizabal@srecd.es

Figure 1. Group of hinds, stag and horse in Covalanas cave (©Pedro Saura).

whereas the *Galería de las Pinturas* contains 18 red deer hinds, 2 equids (1 probable), 1 stag, 1 aurochs, 1 possible hybrid, 4 rectangular shapes, 1 trapeze, 1 triangle, 1 diamond-shape, 4 isolated lines, 16 groups of related small lines, 19 isolated dots, 18 small groups of small dots and 101 concentrations of colouring matter. These are all in red.

Some 60 m from the entrance, the *Galería de las Pinturas* becomes narrower, and this is where most of the Palaeolithic representations are located (Fig. 1). First of all, on the right-hand wall, a hollow contains two hinds. The first and largest figure is complete and uses the natural form of the rock to shape its fore-limbs. The other hind is only partially represented. A few metres further on, new red paintings form another group. The first of these is a hind with its head turned backwards whose body displays internal divisions and red dots. It is closely related to another three hinds. All these are framed by cracks in the wall that define a triangular surface. Very near to it there is another composition of a hind with no fore-limbs and a complete stag. The type of association, orientation and position closely link the figures. About another metre towards the end of the cave, there is an incomplete hind. Beneath it, a horse with no fore-limbs displays many anatomical details in its face (eye, mouth, chin and cheek), mane and hind-limbs (hooves and fetlocks). The impression it transmits with its tail, legs and head suggest that it is galloping. In the area around the horse, there is a small rectangular shape, and four hinds, three of which face the equid; a straight line is associated with one of the hinds. The wall finishes with a rectangle filled with colour-wash, stains of colour and small dots and lines.

On the left hand wall, opposite the hind that is turning its head, an aurochs is represented whole, with part of its outline adapted to the form of the rock. Its body is divided internally and four dots are associated with its belly and one with its mouth. To its left, two complete hinds, one above the other, are closely associated. Beneath these, on a different rock face, a figure displays anatomical traits of a hind, bovid and/or a human. In connection with this latter figure there are seven colour stains and two small dots.

About 70 m from the cave entrance, on the left of the main passage, a side passage has a ledge 110 cm above the floor, in which three hinds were painted with internal divisions. At the end of the side passage, two rectangles are filled with red and there is a series of two small paired marks, as well as stains of colour, a line and an association of four small dots. Opposite the previous hinds, another is painted without back legs, but displays a line marking its shoulder and another line between its head and body. The same wall, but facing into the side passage, contains a probable head of a hind, a vulva-like triangular shape and a trapeze, lines, dots and stains.

Towards the end of the passage, different sectors are decorated with stains of pigment, dots, small lines and, above all, a partial zoomorph (possible equid) in a small oval chamber, while a narrow passage contains a small diamond-shape, small dots, a short line and stains of colour, particularly around a tube-shaped opening that has been interpreted as a kind of vulva.

In Covalanas cave, the least common animals (stag, horse and aurochs) are represented by very complete depictions. In addition, the horse and the aurochs are the largest paintings. The anatomical representation is concentrated on showing the outline and, to a lesser extent, indicating secondary anatomical details, mainly in the head. The greatest care is taken, once more, with the horse and aurochs. Internal divisions are based on lines or bands of colour. The impression of volume or the third dimension was occasionally sought by using the natural form of the rock. The only technique used is painting by dots, in which the pigment was applied with a finger or with some kind of pad, or less often with a dry piece of colouring matter.

It is generally agreed that the figures in Covalanas are in a style characteristic of pre-Magdalenian times, although some authors date them in the lower Magdalenian. The absence of direct absolute dates does not allow great precision, but the scarcity of figurative art in the Aurignacian seems to preclude that period, so that they were probably executed between 32,000 and 19,000 cal BP.

The figures with a red dotted outline in Covalanas cave are linked to a graphic tradition that appears in several caves in the eastern and central sectors of Cantabrian Spain. Figures painted with thick lines, whose stylistic traits are very similar to the dotted outlined figures, are equally known in the same and different caves. Because of this, and the fact that some figures exhibit both approaches to painting the outlines, it is thought that the two techniques were relatively synchronic, which means that close graphic-cultural links must have existed between the human groups who produced these types of paintings.

Pablo Arias*, Roberto Ontañón**

La Garma cave (Omoño, Cantabria)

Introduction

La Garma is the name of a hill that is 186 m high, 5km from the modern coast of Cantabria and 12km to the east-south-east of the city of Santander. It is the location of eleven archaeological sites that have yielded evidence of human activity from the Lower Palaeolithic to the Middle Ages, including most of the intermediary periods (Fig. 1), one of the fullest and most detailed sequences in the Prehistory of Europe. It is particularly important because of one exceptional site, the Lower Gallery, a cave whose original entrance was blocked at the end of the Pleistocene, which has allowed the conservation of Upper Palaeolithic floors and structures in a state that is unique in the world, as well as one of the great ensembles of Palaeolithic rock art. On the basis of its importance, La Garma

* Instituto Internacional de Investigaciones Prehistóricas de Cantabria-Universidad de Cantabria. Av. de los Castros s/n. 39005 Santander. pablo.arias@unican.es

** Instituto Internacional de Investigaciones Prehistóricas de Cantabria-Museo de Prehistoria y Arqueología de Cantabria. Av. de los Castros 65-67. 39005 Santander. ontanon_r@cantabria.es

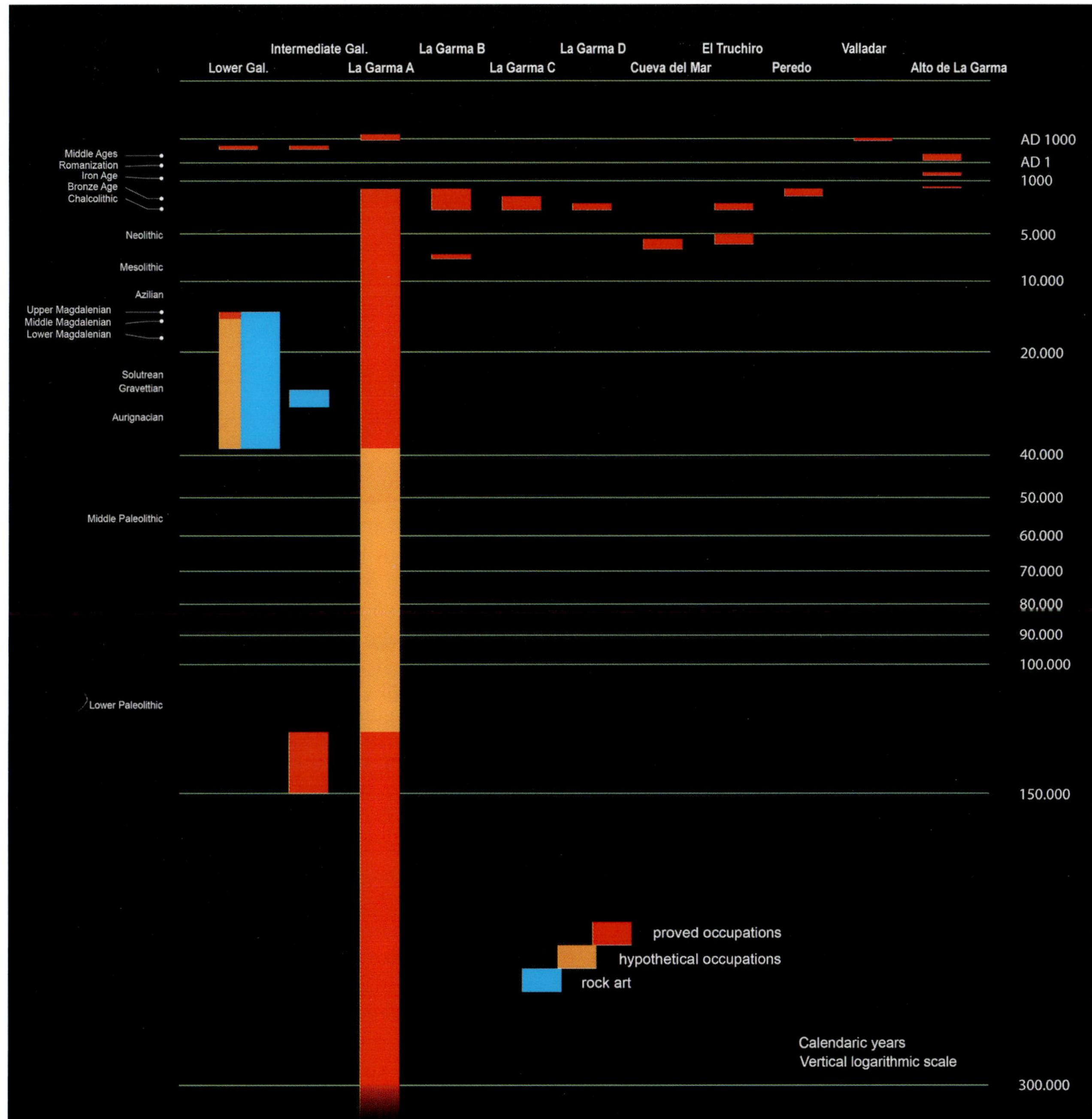

Figure 1. Chronological framework of La Garma Archaeological Zone. Design: Luis C. Teira.

has been included in the World World Heritage List of the UNESCO.

The archaeological sites at La Garma are generally inside caves whose entrances are on the southern side of the hill, mostly belonging to different levels in a karst cave system. Two of them, Cueva del Mar and El Truchiro have been known since the early twentieth century, when they were explored archaeologically by one of the pioneers in Palaeolithic studies in Cantabria, Lorenzo Sierra. However, it was not until the 1990s that the most important sites were discovered: La Garma A, La Garma B and the Intermediate Gallery in 1991, and the Lower Gallery in 1996. Since then, an ambitious inter-disciplinary research project has been carried out, coordinated by the University of Cantabria and funded mostly by the Government of Cantabria, with the participation of some 40 researchers from institutions in Europe and

America. The project is particularly concerned with the conservation of such an outstanding site, and therefore a specific non-invasive methodology has been developed to document the Palaeolithic floors, which are being studied *in situ*, to allow their conservation in a near-original state.

Public outreach has been another priority of the research. Numerous reports have been published by the press, radio, television, and popular magazines, and the work has been presented at conferences in numerous countries in Europe, America and Asia. Two large exhibitions have been held, one devoted monographically to La Garma and the other with a significant presence of the site: "La Garma: a Descent to the Past" (Arias *et al.*, 1999), held in Santander in 1999 and in the Museu d'Arqueologia de Catalunya (Barcelona) in 2001, and "The matter of Prehistoric Language" (Arias and Ontañón 2004), held in Torrelavega in 2004 and in the National Archaeological Museum (Madrid) in 2005. La Garma also occupies a prominent position in the new permanent exhibition of the Museum of Prehistory and Archaeology of Cantabria, and is present in other Spanish and international museums, particularly the National Museum of Nature and Science in Tokyo.

Before *Homo sapiens*: the Lower Palaeolithic at La Garma

The oldest evidence of humans on the hill is located in two sites that apparently were connected during the Pleistocene: the area outside La Garma A and the Intermediate Gallery. The former site is the most significant. There, a thick archaeological deposit, consisting of a succession of silt and flowstone layers containing a typical Acheulian assemblage, with bifaces and cleavers, in association with temperate climate fauna, including the narrow-nosed rhinoceros (*Stephanorhinus hemitoechus*), the straight-tusked elephant (*Palaeoloxodon antiquus*) and Deninger's bear (*Ursus deningeri*), has been found. As the excavation is still in course, its chronology is provisional. However, the study made by a member of our team, Jesús Tapia, shows that it formed completely in the Middle Pleistocene, as suggested by the date of 126,500 BP obtained for the top of the stratigraphic unit. The base has still not been reached, but recent determinations indicate a minimum age of 300,000 years, which means it is one of the oldest deposits indicating human presence in Cantabrian Spain. It should be noted that the deposit, now in the open-air, is really a cave site, as shown by the speleothems found *in situ*. It is the fill of a passage that connected La Garma A (80m a.s.l.) with the Intermediate Gallery (70m a.s.l.) and it would have been protected by a huge rock-shelter which was cut back by erosion on the steep hillside until it reached its current position before 16,000 cal BC.

The Intermediate Gallery is a large part of the 70m level in the cave system, which became separated from its entrance (La Garma B and possibly a second entrance now filled by the archaeological deposit outside La Garma A) during the Pleistocene. Determinations made for palaeontological remains in this passage show that an entrance was still open 30,500 years ago. When the passage was first explored in 1991, the floor of its central part was full of bear hibernation nests which contained numerous bones of *Ursus arctos* associated with Lower Palaeolithic artefacts, including some cleavers. The excavation carried out by R. Montes in 1998 showed that the association of fauna and artefacts was the result of post-depositional processes. The Lower Palaeolithic assemblage comes from a silty layer containing artefacts of that time, probably coetaneous with the deposit outside the cave, which in some places was disturbed by the bears during the Upper Pleistocene.

The Lower Palaeolithic deposits at La Garma are still being studied, and therefore only provisional conclusions can be reached. However, the available information seems to confirm the existence of human activity in the old entrance of La Garma A in the Middle Pleistocene. This is confirmed by the finds of exogenous lithic raw materials (flint, ophite) and evidence of the processing of the faunal remains. The case of the Intermediate Galley is more enigmatic as this is inside the cave beyond the limit of natural light. It is therefore possible that the archaeological materials in this passage correspond to a secondary deposit related to the large rock-shelter mentioned above. But the sedimentological information does not seem compatible with this hypothesis, as these layers were deposited in conditions of very low energy. Consequently, this suggests a direct spatial relationship exists between the artefacts and human activity.

In any case, the archaeological record found in these two sectors shows the presence and activity at La Garma of hominids previous to our species. They were probably Neanderthals, as documented in the nearby cave of El Castillo, or *Homo heidelbergensis*, if the chronology in the central part of the Middle Pleistocene is confirmed.

La Garma's golden age: the Upper Palaeolithic

The period for which La Garma is particularly important is the Upper Palaeolithic. In La Garma A, the Archaeological Zone possesses a very complete stratigraphic sequence with all the classic stages in the period (Fig. 1) and in the Lower Gallery, Magdalenian floors and structures are in a state of conservation that is unique in the world (Figs. 2-4) whilst the walls display a large ensemble of rock art (Fig. 5).

La Garma A provides an excellent perspective of the evolution of Upper Palaeolithic societies. At the start of the period the cave was a rather large rock-shelter about 6m high, and much deeper than the present small vestibule. From about 37,500 to 32,200 cal BC, Aurignacian groups lived there, occupying quite a large surface area (at least some 30 m^2, Stratigraphic Unit C). After that time, the site was abandoned and a thick layer of barren silt accumulated (SU D). The site was occupied again about 30,000 cal BC by Gravettian hunter-gatherers (SU E and F). Two significant and unusual portable art objects were found in these levels: an ibex (*Capra pyrenaica*) metapodial with a wide perforation near the distal epiphysis and a series of engraved marks (Arias and Ontañón 2004), and a large block of limestone with figurative engravings. During the Last Glacial Maximum, in the Solutrean, the cave was occupied intensely, as shown by the thick Stratigraphic Unit G, which has yielded a large collection of points with flat retouching. The occupations continued, apparently without a break, during several Magdalenian phases (lower, middle and upper) until the end of the Pleistocene, when the accumulation of sediments reduced the size of the inhabitable area and even reached the roof in places, so that the large rock-shelter in Aurignacian times had been turned into two small chambers connected by a narrow passage. As we have been able to determine (Arias *et al.*, 2005), in the Middle Magdalenian, they were used for different purposes, with a greater density of activities in the inner chamber, where a semi-circular stone structure was built against the back wall of the cave, which apparently was a rest area.

As mentioned above, the Lower Gallery is a level in the cave system whose entrance became blocked during the late Pleistocene. It contains a large rock art ensemble and an outstanding archaeological document: a number of zones in which the remains of the last occupations in the cave, dated to *ca.* 14,000 cal BC in the Middle Magdalenian, have been conserved *in situ*. When this passage was cut off from the exterior, the processes accumulating sediments, both natural and anthropogenic, were interrupted. In consequence, the cave became a kind of time capsule in which the remains of a Palaeolithic camp (Arias *et al.*, 2011) and several stone structures (Ontañón 2003) have been left on open view. It amounts to some 800 m^2 of a rich Palaeolithic deposit, unique in the world, which can be examined with no need to excavate.

Figure 2. La Garma. Lower Gallery. Magdalenian floor in Zone I. Photo: Pedro Saura.

The Palaeolithic floors in the Lower Gallery cover three sectors of the passage. The largest (Zone I), close to the former entrance, is an area of about 500m^2 where thousands of bones, lithic artefacts, bone and antler tools (including several perforated batons, a spear thrower, numerous assegai points and spatulas), portable art objects, marine mollusc shells and other remains of the daily activity of Magdalenian hunters can be seen (Fig. 2). No less interesting are several structures, made from large pieces of stalagmite and limestone rocks. One subcircular structure is located 40m from the old entrance next to the western wall of the passage and under a ledge of rock. It seems to be the base of a light structure (a kind of tent) made with perishable materials like sticks, branches, bark or skins. An exceptional portable art object was found next to its outer edge: an aurochs phalange with a longitudinal perforation and a superb depiction of a bull, associated with an arrow-shaped sign and a probable anthropomorph (Arias and Ontañón 2004). An antler spear thrower, in the form of a quadruped's leg, was found a short distance away.

Figure 3. La Garma. Lower Gallery. Magdalenian structures in Zone IV

Some 90m from the entrance, in an area that would have been in total darkness, a new concentration of Palaeolithic remains is in an elliptical chamber, 15m long and 8m wide, whose roof slopes down on its western side (Zone III). The floor is carpeted with hundreds of industrial and faunal remains, including several cut fragments of reindeer antler and other signs of bone-working, and a sculpture carved from reindeer antler have been found. Here again there are the remains of Palaeolithic constructions. The clearest structure is sub-circular, next to the western wall of the chamber, under the low roof, and was made with large blocks of limestone and some pieces of flowstone placed upright. The floor inside this structure, of about 5m^2, is lower than the surrounding area, and contains a smaller density of objects than the area outside.

Further inside the cave (130 m from the entrance), Zone IV is the third area with a high density of Palaeolithic objects. These are distributed across a surface of 55 m^2, mostly in an area with a very low roof (from 1.7 to 0.5 m high). Next to the western wall three artificial structures can be seen. Two of them (IV-A and IV-B) were built with large speleothems and slabs of limestone laid on the floor, delimiting two approximately rectangular areas of 3.18 m^2 and 1.5 m^2, respectively (Fig. 3). As can be appreciated in the photograph, there is a certain contrast between the inside of the structures and the surrounding areas, both in the size and shape of the materials and in floor level, which is several centimetres lower inside. In turn, Structure IV-C, located 1.4m to the north-east of the others, is larger (5.35 m^2) and more complex. In this case, the Magdalenian occupants dug out the floor and piled the material, mostly pieces of speleothems, around the sides, in two dry stone walls completed with large upright slabs.

Research carried out in this unusual site has discovered a series of traits that are atypical of the Middle Magdalenian (Arias *et al.*, 2005). Above all, the faunal composition is uncommon, as it is dominated by remains of horse (*Equus caballus*), which make up two thirds of the total, in clear contrast with the usual pattern in Cantabrian deposits of that age, where the predominant species are usually red deer (*Cervus elaphus*) and ibex (*Capra pyrenaica*). Additionally, in Structure IV-B a horse's skull with occipital bone cut out, and remains of the cave lion (*Panthera (Leo) spelaea*) with cut marks were found. It is also noteworthy that in Structure IV-C, two almost complete skeletons of shelduck (*Tadorna tadorna*) marks have been observed. They displayed no processing marks, as if the bodies of two of these attractive anatidae had just been deposited on the cave floor.

We should also highlight that Zone IV has provided a very high amount of objects of adornment (mainly pierced shells and teeth) and portable art objects, which here reach one of the highest densities at Palaeolithic sites in Cantabrian Spain. Some of the outstanding examples are an extraordinary spatula made from a bovine's rib with an ibex represented in relief (Fig. 4), a contour découpé in the form of a male ibex head, a small bone sculpture representing a bear, a rib with two heads of ibices, another with a splendid engraved horse, and a horse incisor with a tiny but highly detailed depiction of a horse. In addition, 17 plaquettes are decorated with engravings representing bison, aurochs, deers and a strange quadruped-human hybrid. Some of these objects appear to have been made in this same area as at least two of them (a pendant made from a bear incisor and the contour découpé) were abandoned without being finished, and the engraved plaquettes seem to be slabs of calcite from the cave itself. The relationship of the structures with graphic expression is not limited to portable art but also includes parietal representations. The low roof over Structure IV-B displays an excellent group of engravings in a clear Magdalenian style, with figures of horse, bison and hind.

It is difficult to interpret Zone IV. However, as expressed elsewhere (Arias 2009), the peculiarities noted above and the comparison with other sites of a similar age in northern Spain and the Pyrenees suggest that it was an area used above all for ritual activities.

The Lower Gallery is also the location of a large Palaeolithic rock art ensemble. Some 500 graphic units have been documented, of which 92 are animal figures, 109 signs and 40 are stencilled hands (and sometimes single fingers) (Fig. 5). The paintings and engravings are found throughout the passage, from the original entrance to its end. However, as C. González Sainz's study has shown, there are chronological differences in their spatial structuring. Thus, while the paintings that can be attributed to the first periods in the development of Palaeolithic art (Aurignacian, Gravettian and Solutrean) are distributed through the whole cave, mostly in the main passage, the Magdalenian representations are concentrated in the part nearest the entrance, and often in small side passages and chambers (González Sainz 2003).

The Lower Gallery also provides extraordinary information about the context in which the rock art was produced. The excellent state of conservation of the Magdalenian floors has allowed data to be gathered about how the pigments were processed. Some stains of paint on the floor, palettes with remains of crushed iron oxide and even some sources of raw materials used to make the paintings in the cave have been studied (Arias *et al.*, 2011). Even more unusual is the evidence to be able to approach the complex problem of visits and activities connected with graphic expression. For example, above the Magdalenian camp in Zone I, in a passage that is difficult to reach but which leads to a group of paintings, a path was worn in the sandy sediment on the floor. This is valuable evidence regarding a matter on which there has been a great deal of speculation but very little solid information: the visits and, generally speaking, activities developed in areas with graphic representations during the Palaeolithic. In turn, the distribution of the Magdalenian floors and paintings questions the traditional theory of spatial separation between the rock art and the living areas, proposed many years ago by such authors as A. Laming-Emperaire and A. Leroi-Gourhan. At La Garma, the large Magdalenian camp in the old entrance hall displays numerous paintings and engravings on the walls, some of them clearly attributable to the same period.

Figure 4. La Garma. Lower Gallery, Zone IV. Spatula with a representation of an ibex. Photo: Pedro Saura.

Figure 5. La Garma. Lower Gallery. Stencilled hands in Zone IX. Photo: Pedro Saura.

The last hunters at La Garma: the Mesolithic

La Garma hill is also a particularly significant site for studying the Mesolithic in the centre of Cantabrian Spain. Research in the Archaeological Zone has revealed Mesolithic occupations from the mid eighth millennium cal BC until the sixth millennium, with the presence of humans attested at La Garma A, La Garma B, Cueva del Mar and El Truchiro, which is one of the main concentrations of sites of this period in Cantabria. In general, the Mesolithic deposits in these caves include large amounts of marine molluscs (shell middens), which is striking bearing in mind the location of the hill, relatively distant from the coast.

However, the importance of La Garma in the context of the Iberian Mesolithic derives from an exceptional archaeological deposit, recently excavated by Ángel Armendariz: the grave in El Truchiro Cave, the only testimony of funerary behaviour in this period in Cantabria. Dated in the first quarter of the sixth millennium cal BC, the burial was of a juvenile individual, laid in a flexed lateral position. Next to the chest there were several beads made from shells (*Cerastoderma* sp. and *Trivia* sp.) and red deer canines, probably the remains of personal adornments accompanying the body, and a set of thirteen flint cores. The burial at El Truchiro also displays another interesting aspect. It suffered a fire, probably indirectly, which affected the conservation of the skeleton negatively but which on the other hand helped to preserve the remains of a structure of oak bark on which the body was lying. This is an exceptional document, unique in the Iberian Peninsula and very rare in Europe as a whole.

La Garma as a necropolis: the Age of Metals

In the second half of the fifth millennium cal BC, a profound change took place in burial rituals in Cantabrian Spain, as in many other parts of Europe: spread of collective inhumations. In the region this practice is manifested in two types of burial places: megalithic monuments and natural caves. La Garma hill constitutes one of the best examples of the latter type. Six caves on the southern hillside were used for burials in the Copper and Bronze Ages, between the early third millennium cal BC and the middle of the second: La Garma A, La Garma B, El Truchiro, La Garma C, La Garma D and Peredo.

The entrance chamber of La Garma A, La Garma B and D, El Truchiro and Peredo are typical examples of the underground spaces used for the successive burials of several bodies without any apparent preparation. The cave itself, with a narrow entrance and passage, sufficed as a burial place. However, the inner chamber of La Garma A and La Garma C provide evidence of more complex funerary practices. In the former, the flowstone layer on the floor was broken through in two places to dig two graves in which five bodies were deposited. The bones were disarticulated, which suggests these were secondary burials. The larger of the two graves also contained several points with flat retouching and a very special object, a flint dagger (Fig. 6) seemingly imported from the south of the Iberian Peninsula. This is one of the clearest examples of the development (or at least of the ostentation) of social inequalities in this part of the Peninsula.

In turn, Ángel Armendariz's excavations in La Garma C also showed that a grave had been dug, in this case in a small chamber which is reached down a narrow ramp. The poorly conserved human remains, were together with typical grave goods for this period, such as pottery, a ground stone axe and a flint arrowhead. The most original aspect in this case is the fact that the entrance to this burial chamber had been covered by a stone wall. The space was therefore sealed off in a way not too different in its conception to megalithic burial chambers.

Alto de la Garma Hillfort

La Garma was also occupied during the Iron Age. On top of the hill, a fortified settlement, visually controlling a large part of the central Cantabrian coastline, has been excavated by the collaborators of the project Esteban Pereda and Juan José Cepeda. The hillfort, one of the key archaeological sites in the study of the formative period of the *Cantabri*, covers a surface area of 18,000m^2, delimited by an oval ring around the top of the hill. In fact, it consists of the remains of two successive structures. The oldest, dated to the seventh century cal BC, is an outer dry stone wall which held back an embankment, which was almost certainly topped by a palisade. This wall was replaced, probably in the early fifth century by another one, 3m wide with a double stone face in most of its length. In some places it was built over the old wall, while

Figure 6. La Garma A. Flint dagger from a Copper Age grave.

in others it was further inside, which slightly reduced the defensive perimeter. It was probably a low wall or embankment completed with a palisade.

Excavations in three areas inside the wall have documented remains of oval-shaped huts, 6-7m in diameter, built against the walls or very near them. They all have stone foundations which would have supported wooden posts and wattle and daub walls, of which numerous fragments have been found in the excavation.

In addition to numerous potsherds and evidence of metallurgy, the excavations have yielded remains of cereals and a large faunal assemblage dominated by cattle. It thus contributes, like other hillforts studied in recent years, to a refutation of the negative image of the subsistence of late Iron Age northern Spanish populations transmitted by Graeco-Latin authors.

A cave epilogue: burials in the early Middle Ages

The archaeological record at La Garma ends in a spectacular medieval finale: a funerary context located in the central part of the Lower Gallery. It consists of five skeletons of young males, dated between the seventh and eighth centuries AD, at the end of the Visigothic realm or the beginning of the Kingdom of Asturias. Three of them are in Zone IV, in small spaces near the shaft connecting with the Intermediate Gallery, and the others are further inside, in Zone V. In all cases, the bodies were simply deposited on the floor, which was not prepared at all, although one of the skeletons is surrounded by pieces of stalagmite which may have held a shroud in place. One of the individuals in Zone IV wore a belt with a damascened lyriform buckle, of a Visigothic type. It should also be mentioned that all of them were subjected to a peculiar post-mortem practice; the skulls were deliberately smashed after the bodies had decomposed, which proves that the cave was visited more than once in this period. A large amount of evidence testifies to these visits, such as hearths and hundreds of pieces of hazel wood charcoal (*Corylus avellana*), probably from the lighting system used by those early explorers, marking the tortuous route by which the bodies were introduced, from the narrow entrance of La Garma A, down a 7m shaft, along the Intermediate Gallery, and down a second 13m shaft.

Such funerary practices are very different from the norm at the time, and therefore they are not easy to interpret. However, our collaborator J.A. Hierro has put forward the interesting hypothesis that this and other coetaneous burials in the Iberian Peninsula might correspond to individuals who died in some of the epidemics of infectious illnesses at that time. The deceased would have been buried, with their belongings, in the most hidden and remote place possible, in order to stop the plague spreading. The destruction of skulls may simply have intended to stop the threat of these accursed and dangerous individuals returning to the world of the living.

Ramón Montes Barquín*

El Pendo cave (Escobedo de Camargo, Cantabria)

El Pendo is one of the best known sites in Cantabrian Spain, largely because of its archaeological deposit, its ensemble of portable art objects and, since 1997, because of its parietal art.

The figures are located in two different sectors and consist of: a) engravings in the final passage of the cave, and b) red paintings, especially at the back of the large entrance chamber.

The engravings found in the narrow final passage, about 180m from the entrance, were discovered by Alcalde del Río in 1907. They were initially identified as two great auks and a vulture, but in a later more detailed study, Barandiarán re-identified them as an anseriform and a possible horse, and this is now widely accepted as the best interpretation.

The series of red paintings was discovered in 1997 and 1998. Most of them are located on a frieze about 80m from the gate in the cave entrance, in the point where the natural daylight fades and the dark zone of the cave begins. Outside this frieze, the only motifs known are a small group of marks on the left wall of the cave and above the area of the 1953-57 excavations, two discs immediately beneath the frieze (on a small section of wall) and some isolated dots on a large block of limestone fallen from the roof.

The main decorated area is thus the face of a horizontal bed of rock, about 25m long (Fig. 1), reaching 3.5m high, although the thickness of the bed averages about 2m. The limestone stratum dips slightly from east to west, as it is thicker on the left and becomes thinner towards the right. It displays a large number of cracks and fractures, some calcite precipitates and other natural alterations. The wall is very dry, while on the right-hand

Figure 1. Left hand side of the Frieze of Paintings in El Pendo cave.

* Unidad Técnica, Itinerario Cultural del Consejo de Europa *Caminos de Arte Rupestre Prehistórico* (RCDR). c/San Martín del Pino 16, 3bajo, 39011 Peñacastillo-Santander. rmontes@prehistour.eu

Figure 2. Large hind and horse in the Frieze of Paintings in El Pendo cave.

side remains of calcite, in the form of small and thin formations of flowstone, partially cover some figures.

When the paintings were discovered, this whole area was covered by dense colonies of micro-organisms that had grown over deposits of dirt accumulated in the cracks and hollows in the wall. The dirt and micro-organisms had masked the figures, causing them to remain unknown until the time of their discovery.

The ensemble of paintings consists of 16 animals figures, 4 graphic units classed as "signs", and another 4 units formed by isolated dots and remains of pigment probably belonging to what were once more complex representations.

The main characteristics of the parietal art are:

- The entire ensemble, apart from some exceptions, is located in a very visible area, the main part in the cave. This does not occur in most of the similar ensembles in Cantabrian Spain. Some of the figures (especially those in the "main panel in the Frieze of Paintings") can be seen with very basic illumination from any point of the large chamber, even from the very entrance of the cave, 80m away.
- The ensemble is dominated by the representations of red deer hinds, with eleven clear figures and one or two probable representations. These make up at least 50% of the total ensemble. In addition, there are figures of other animals that frequently appear in equivalent groups of art: 1 ibex, 1 horse and 2 indeterminate headless quadrupeds (possibly 2 cervids). The four signs (16.6% of the total) are relatively atypical, but not unusual. Indeed, discs, paired marks and depictions in the form of "vulvae" are found relatively frequently at sites in the

region, although they are more common in old ensembles (Tito Bustillo, Pindal, Cudón, Calero II and Sector VI at La Garma) and less typical of sites of this kind (Arco B). Dots, isolated marks and remains of faded pigment, of unrecognisable shape, complete the representations.

- The range of techniques used is limited and simple: colour-wash, single more or less wide lines and, above all dotted lines. Two or even three techniques occasionally appear together in some of the figures. In the most common technique, the dots may be separate or overlap with each other, forming irregular lines. As many as 16 graphic units, including 12 animals, display this technique.
- The pigment used is iron oxide, above all red ochre found locally (there is a seam of ochre on the right hand side of the frieze). The colour sienna, from limonite, appears in the figure of a hind and in some dots located above it.
- The natural form of the rock and cracks in the wall were used to complete or suggest the anatomy of some animal figures or to frame them. This is seen in many of the depictions, which seems to suggest that the wall was studied carefully before it was decorated, and its features were incorporated into the anatomy of the depictions.
- The figures are generally much larger than in most other similar ensembles. Several figures are larger than or equivalent to the maximum standard size of the manual field, about 70 or 80cm in diameter. However, the animals are not ranked according to their size. Figures of hinds are the largest and smallest figures in the ensemble, while the horse is of a quite modest size (Fig. 2) and the size of the ibex is conditioned by the natural form of the rock that suggested the figure.
- No relationship appears to exist between the engravings in the final passage and the group of paintings. Both their location and the differences in technique and style confirm the absence of any stylistic and/or chronological relationship between the two ensembles.
- The conventions used in representing the animal figures are those often recognised in ensembles of the so-called "Ramales School": a generalised use of dotted lines, occasionally together with partial colour-wash (used mainly in the heads and hind-quarters) and continuous lines; very stylised and elongated figures, with small heads and long necks and bodies; the representation of long limbs one place behind the other like open scissors; hinds with V-shaped ears; internal divisions in the area of the chest; a single continuous line representing an ear and the upper part of the head or the cervical line, thus forming an L-shape; and horses with manes painted as a series of parallel vertical dotted lines.

This type of ensemble is normally assigned to the Gravettian period, based on chrono-stylistic comparisons and indirect chronological data, as in the case of the paintings in Arenaza, Covalanas, La Haza, the caves in the Carranza Gorge and certain sectors in La Pasiega. Recent determinations made for calcite covering red dotted paintings (as in the caves of Pondra and Altamira), and the discovery of a portable art object with the figure of a hind in the cave of Antoliñako Koba, are now able to situate the age of this type of ensemble to a middle phase of the Gravettian (*circa* 25 ky BP).

Marcos García-Diez* and Daniel Garrido Pimentel**

El Castillo cave (Puente Viesgo, Cantabria)

The rock art in El Catillo cave was discovered in 1903 by Alcalde del Río, who carried out the first study, Later Breuil and Alcalde del Río undertook a second study in 1911. The Count of la Vega del Sella began a new study in 1934, but the Spanish Civil War curtailed this research. Groenen is currently carrying a revision of the ensemble, as Ripoll did previously.

The cave is about 400 m long and consists of a series of chambers, passages, galleries and ox-bows (Fig. 1). In general the cave is large and of easy access, but some figures are located in more difficult, narrow spaces.

The ensemble is an encyclopaedia of Palaeolithic cave art, with numerous engravings, drawings and paintings, and occasionally sculpture using natural rock forms. It represents at least 35,000 years of artistic and symbolic behaviour.

Sector I

On the rock face in the cave entrance, a small opening has been discovered (*Cueva del Sapo*) containing rock surfaces with a violet colour.

Sector II

The figures in different areas are concentrated mainly in two friezes. The first of these consists of striated figures, mostly representing hinds (several tens of figures), which are in a typical lower Magdalenian style and similar to the figures on the decorated scapulae found in the archaeological deposit in the same cave. Many of the figures are superimposed on each other, representing an "environmental" space. Other figures include a stag using the natural shape of the rock, a probable horse formed by dotted lines, series of dots, rods, and anthropomorphs dated in a post-Palaeolithic time.

To the north, a rock face is in a poor state of conservation. The figures are superimposed, beginning with an infilled rectangle and red lines that might depict an animal. Later, striated figures were produced, especially three closely linked representations. Finally, black figures of a horse and at least one indeterminate animal with a geometric body were painted.

In this sector, the animals are the most important representations, especially the engraved hind

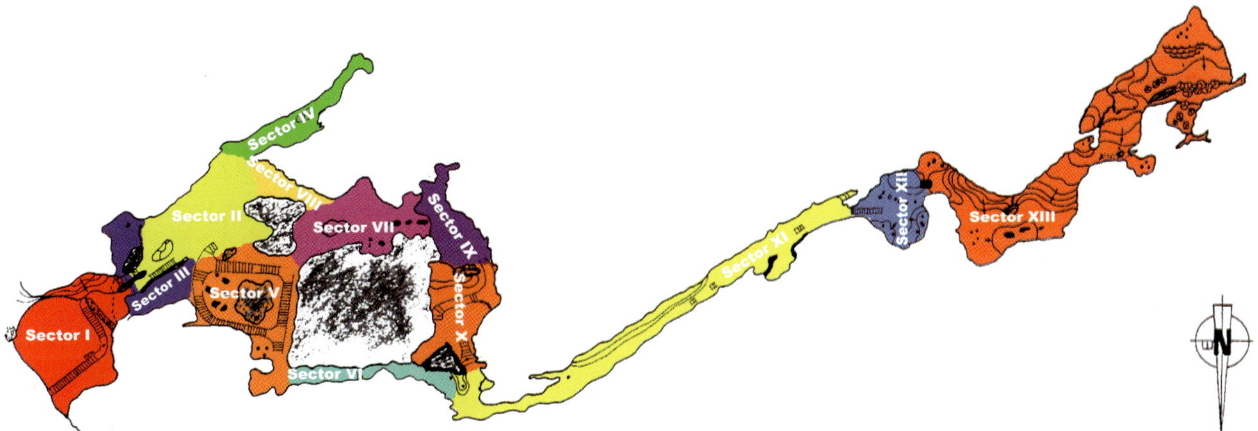

Figure 1. Structure of El Castillo cave.

* Dpto. Geografía, Prehistoria y Arqueología, Universidad del País Vasco. c/ Tomás y Valiente s/n, 01006 Vitoria (España). marcos.garcia@ehu.es

** Cuevas Prehistóricas de Cantabria, Sociedad Regional de Educación, Cultura y Deporte, Gobierno de Cantabria. Cuevas de Monte Castillo, 39670 Puente Viesgo (Cantabria). daniel.garrido@srecd.es

Figure 2. Striated hind's head in El Castillo cave © Pedro Saura

and the painted horse. They are complemented by indeterminate zoomorphs, lines, dots, concentrations of red colour and some "complex" signs. They were produced over a long period of time.

Sector III

Near the start of this sector, an ibex head is on the lower part of a false ledge. Animals were engraved on the roof, such as two incomplete ibices and a horse, as well as a possible aurochs and other lines. Further on, there is a panel with superimposed hinds and stags. All the motifs, consisting of at least 12 zoomorphs, share the techniques of single, wide and deep engraved lines, simply depicting the outline generally with no secondary anatomy.

Sector IV

This begins with an oblique wall, which is completely engraved, above all with caprids, bovids and equids.

Inside the chamber, engravings and paintings are found on both walls. To the south-east, important figures include a large stag in red, a probable aurochs or ibex combining red paint and use of the rock form, a black aurochs, a probable engraved mammoth and a striated hind's head (Fig. 2), as well as engraved lines that might correspond to zoomorphs. Black figures stand out on the opposite wall; horses, caprids and a possible feline, as well as indeterminate animals, corresponding to small animals on the facing wall.

The technical, stylistic and formal variety of the figures on the south-east wall contrasts with the tendency towards homogeneity on the north-west wall. On the first it seems clear that the motifs were produced in several different phases whereas on the opposite wall the ensemble is thought to have been produced in the Magdalenian.

The group of figures is completed by numerous lines (some rods) and dots (some describable as discs).

Sector V

The numerous representations in this sector include the outstanding *Panel de los Polícromos*, about 10 stencilled hands and 20 animals, as well as signs. The hands are the oldest motifs. The red figures are of different ages, with a large violet horse that was repainted in red, leaving five long violet lines in its body, a quadrilateral sign, heads of an aurochs (or horse) and a stag, an incomplete hind and a bison at a nearly natural scale, with anatomical details, that combines red lines with the shape of the rock wall. The central part of the panel exhibits two red hinds and an oval sign. Over these red paintings, four bison were painted in black and also engraved in places. Three of these have been dated to between 17,600 and 14,200 cal BP and the other to between 13,300 and 12,000 cal BP. Finally, the outline and interior of a hollow was coloured in red, suggesting a vulva.

Lower down, the wall displays stencilled hands and red discs as well as dots and small rod-like red lines.

The *Galeria de las Manos* is in the lowest part of the chamber (Fig. 3), with some 40 stencilled hands. These are the oldest figures and the calcite covering them has been dated by uranium series to 37,290 BP. The most numerous motifs are the signs (about 150): quadrilateral, triangular and ellipsoidal shapes, engraved, painted in red or yellow, with colour-wash, filled with vertical lines, segmented by eliminating colour, with an appendix and finished with small straight lines. The animals include the front of a black bison similar to those in Niaux and Covaciella, eight bison in a yellow or reddish tone, six hinds depicted with striations or a simple outline, a headless stag, an engraved ibex, a stag represented by scraping the surface, a red hind and countless engraved lines. On the right at the end, *Tectiforms Corner (Rincón de los Tectiformes)* is a narrow space in which twelve segmented rectangular or sub-rectangular shapes were painted; some of them cross over each other to form a cross. There are also small lines and dots, as well as an engraved chamois and bison.

On the west wall, in a long passage, at least ten animal figures include stags and a bison with its tongue out were engraved, a stag and a large zoomorph were painted in black, an incomplete bison was engraved and a head of a horse or a hind was depicted in red. In addition, the group includes at least four red stencilled hands, small red marks, dots and discs, sometimes associated with an edge or lip of rock.

Sector VI

At the start of this sector, on the right a horse is depicted with long ears reminiscent of an aurochs' horns, in red and yellow and with V-shaped signs over its belly. Above this animal, there is a large red quadrilateral sign, pointed at each end, and an incomplete painted and engraved bison, inside which an aurochs' head appears to be represented. The opposite wall contains red and yellow ellipsoidal signs, while a ledge in the roof is decorated with a yellow horse and a red hind or ibex.

Further on in the same passage, there are red stencilled hands, ovals, dots, lines and discs, some of them violet, as well as animals, such as an engraved ibex head. In this sector some black lines corresponding to an incomplete horse were dated to 19,140 ± 230 BP (GifA98154) and 16,980 ± 180 BP (GifA98153).

Sector VII

This is known as the *Chamber of the Bison Sculpture (Sala del bisonte en escultura)*. A bison in a vertical position was represented in relief on a stalagmite by using the natural convexity of the speleothem, which was retouched by painting and engraving. Inside it there are two red dots. An ibex was drawn too. Around the stalagmite, there are an engraved bison, a horse, an aurochs with its tongue out and some lines that may belong to a quadrilateral sign. Finally, four hinds are striated and superimposed on another speleothem.

Opposite the stalagmite, on the right hand wall, there are 2 black ibices, 2 engraved hinds, 2 violet hinds' heads, a partial animal figure (possibly an aurochs) with prominent genital, a segmented red

Figure 3. *Gallery of the Hands* in El Castillo cave (©Pedro Saura)

quadrilateral, and small red lines, dots and discs, sometimes associated with rock edges and faces.

To the left of the bison sculpture there is a small high-level chamber. In the narrow passage at its entry, in a vertical position there are one black ibex and another one engraved with single lines, both of them next to possible human masks that combine deep engraving and natural rock forms. Inside the chamber, an aurochs and two hinds were engraved with wide deep lines, while at its end, a horse's head, a hind, an aurochs and indeterminate animals were painted in black.

Sector VIII

The *Panel of the Bell-shaped Signs (Panel de los campaniformes)* is in this passage. It consists of five bell-shaped red signs, some of which display a central line, a branching motif and a red horse.

Further up the passage, stags, ibices, hinds and a possible chamois were engraved as simple outlines, together with red dots, lines and discs.

Sector IX

Going up this sector, two or three bison were represented in black in a Pyrenean style, as well as horses and ibices, and even an aurochs. Heading downwards, a bend in the passage and a side-passage are reached. Here, in a hidden space before entering the passage, a small horse is represented

Figure 4. *Gallery of the Discs* in El Castillo cave (©Pedro Saura).

in black colour-wash. Inside the passage, there is a black segmented quadrilateral sign, the fore-quarters of an ibex and the face of an aurochs. The latter depiction displays a sculptural aspect as the eye and nostrils of the animal were painted in black on a rock surface in the shape of its head.

Sector X

After a small chamber, the cave has a space with disperse violet dots, a horse combining black lines to represent its belly and hind-quarters with the shape of the rock, and several red lines, some of which probably represent an animal.

In the lower part of the chamber, the engraving of a horse with deep wide lines and an indeterminate animal have been identified. Finally, five black ibices were drawn on a high wall.

Sector XI

This is known as the *Gallery of the Discs (Galería de los Discos)* (Fig. 4). The decoration begins with an aurochs' head and the hind-quarters of a cervid in red. An oval was represented on a corner, and as the gallery starts, numerous red discs form rows in irregular groups, together with a cross and curved lines. At its end there is a small panel with two diamond-shapes and the last stencilled hand.

From this point on, the motifs are more disperse, although a mammoth (probably a young individual) was painted in red, ibices were engraved and a column is decorated with discs.

Sector XII

This sector displays a large number of discs painted on the stalagmites and columns.

Sector XIII

Although a detailed study is still pending, the engraving of a large deer's head, 2 horses and groups of swirling lines have been documented, represented in a surface of clay.

El Castillo cave contains images representing the origins of symbolic thought about 40,800 years ago, and represents at least 35,000 years in the history of the art of humankind.

The themes depicted include signs (nearly three-quarters of the motifs), animals, and references to humans by stencilled hands. The animal motifs are, in order of their numerical importance, after the indeterminate figures: hinds, bison, horses, stags, ibices, aurochs, chamois, masks and a mammoth, as well as indeterminate cervids and bovids. Among the signs, over 50 of them are complex, consisting of quadrilateral, oval, bell-shaped and branching shapes etc. as well as numerous discs, groups of dots, isolated dots and countless lines, some of which form groups, in addition to concentrations of red pigment.

Various techniques were used. The stencilled hands were produced by spraying red pigment. Charcoal "pencils" were used for the black paintings, and it seems probable that manganese was only used very occasionally. The most common colour used was red, which was applied with a brush, and dotted lines are rare. Different engraving techniques include single deep wide lines, fine lines, multiple outlines and striated interiors.

The natural form of the rock surfaces were often used, sometimes to complete figures and other times to define the general structure of the motif.

Chronologically, most Upper Palaeolithic artistic phases are represented in the cave, and even the production of simple signs and hands in an earlier period cannot be ruled out.

Marcos García-Diez*,
Daniel Garrido Pimentel**

Las Chimeneas cave (Puente Viesgo, Cantabria)

This cave is in the hill of Monte Castillo and was discovered in 1953. It formed on two levels which are connected by a shaft or chimney; the lower level where the cave art is located and the upper level. The original entrance to the lower level (160m long) is blocked, but it connected with the decorated area at the end of the cave along a straight passage. This ends in a circular chamber with a small side-passage re-connecting with the main passage, where most of the representations are located. The absence of archaeological remains and the artefacts found on the surface indicate that the cave was not used as a dwelling.

The first figure, an incomplete engraved caprid, is situated about half-way along the lower passage, near the chimney connecting with the upper passage.

Continuing along the lower passage, numerous marks made with a finger in a clay surface stand out because of their size and their chromatic effect, like a cameo. Above them two possible bovids face each other, and underneath them there is a possible incomplete hind. Opposite this group and a few metres away, a sign, a stag with large antlers in twisted perspective and a grille-shaped sign are equally represented by digital engraving.

In the area immediately before the *Chamber of the Paintings (Sala de las Pinturas)*, some meandering lines were engraved digitally, incised with a pointed object and scraped.

A little further on, under a ledge of calcite, the first painting is an incomplete ibex possibly associated with rounded calcite formations that suggest some kind of fruit or berries that the animal is about to eat.

At the end of the passage, the *Chamber of the Paintings* exhibits two simple quadrilaterals, two simple trapezoidal shapes, two quadrilaterals with a double zigzag on their top side, and two large quadrilaterals divided internally in different ways. To the

* Dpto. Geografía, Prehistoria y Arqueología, Universidad del País Vasco. c/ Tomás y Valiente s/n, 01006 Vitoria (España). marcos.garcia@ehu.es

** Cuevas Prehistóricas de Cantabria, Sociedad Regional de Educación, Cultura y Deporte, Gobierno de Cantabria. Cuevas de Monte Castillo. 39670 Puente Viesgo (Cantabria), daniel.garrido@srecd.es

Figure 1. Stag painted in black in Las Chimeneas cave (©Pedro Saura).

right, two converging lines were drawn which, in combination with the rock surface, might represent the hind leg and rump of a zoomorph, whose cervical-dorsal line is formed by the rock.

Further right, on an overhanging rock and complementing the trapezoidal sign and a quadrilateral partially covered by calcite, more black lines might correspond to an unfinished quadrilateral and a partial figure of a horse in which the maxilla line, chest, fore-limb and anterior part of the belly were drawn and the rest is represented by the natural shape of the rock.

Above all these black figures, in the roof, several lines were engraved, especially a simple quadrilateral and a dashed line. In the roof on the left of the chamber, a large quadrilateral was digitally engraved; it has a smaller quadrilateral inside it, with small parallel lines in its interior.

Behind these representations, there is a small passage which can be reached from two sides. Entering on the left, a horse's head is associated with an edge of the wall and a stag's head. Following this narrow passage, a small chamber is reached with five stags (Fig. 1), together with black lines, a simple quadrilateral and meandering engraved lines. The stags, four complete and one partial, are characterised by their simple outlines and the absence of their muzzles. Their grouping in a small space, the arrangement of two pairs of stags, and the variability in their orientation suggest a composition.

Outside this passage, and again in the *Chamber of the Paintings*, to the right a space is reached with a low sinuous roof which divides up the distribution of the figures as if they were on folds. The surface is soft, and consequently some motifs were drawn with a finger-tip and others with a pointed or blunt implement. Four panels have been differentiated in which, together with numerous lines, several incomplete outlines of zoomorphs with few interior details can be recognised: 8 or 9 aurochs, 4 stags, 2 hinds, 1 or 2 ibices, a chamois, a horse and two indeterminate animals.

Spatial, formal and compositional arguments may be proposed to support, *a priori*, the synchronicity of the ensemble. Similar motifs were engraved and painted, and some of them even combine both techniques. Similar kinds of signs are found in different sectors, such as the meandering lines, although in each sector one or other kind is prioritised.

Taking into account A. Leroi-Gourhan's proposal, the ensemble might be dated in the time between the upper Solutrean and lower Magdalenian. However, the assumption of synchronicity may need to be modified if the C14 AMS dates are to be considered correct, as one of the stags was dated to 15,070 ± 140 BP (GifA95194) and marks on the panel of the quadrilaterals to 13,940 ± 140 BP (GifA-95230).

Rodrigo de Balbín Behrmann*, Cesar González Sainz**, J. Javier Alcolea González*

La Pasiega cave (Puente Viesgo, Cantabria)

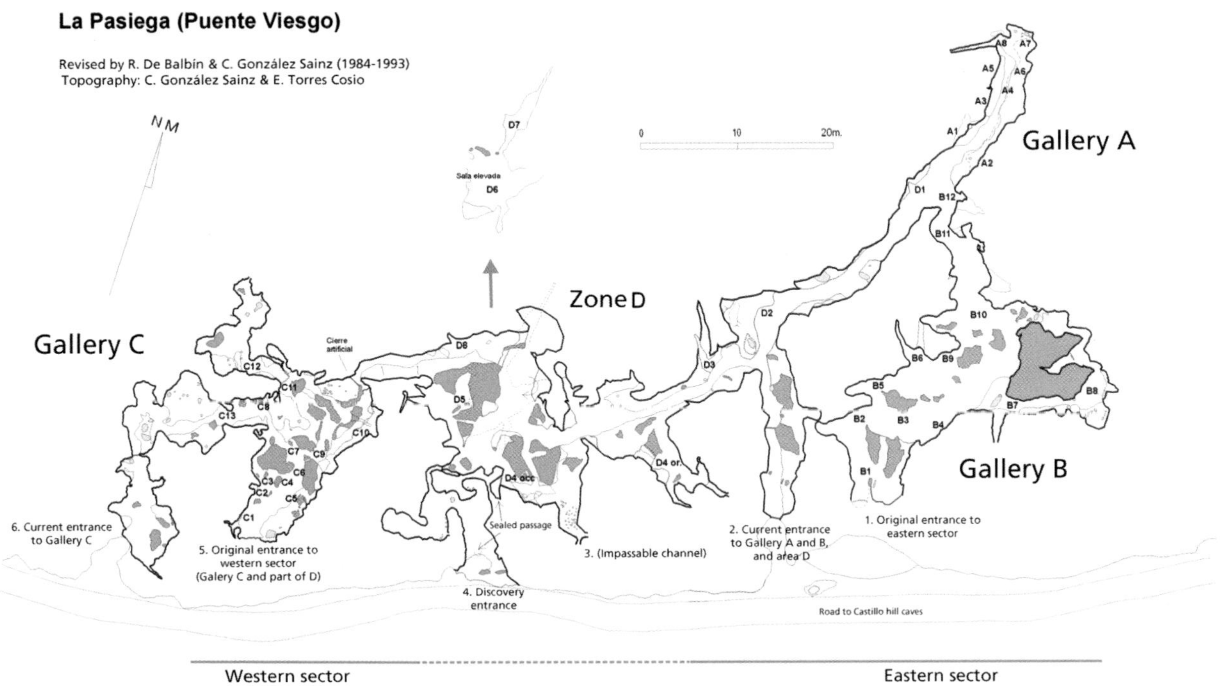

Figure 1. Survey of La Pasiega cave.

The hill of Monte Castillo contains one of the most important groups of caves with Palaeolithic rock art in Europe. La Pasiega (Fig. 1) is located on the steep side of the hill, half way between the caves of Las Chimeneas and Las Monedas and very near to El Castillo Cave. It consists of passages in different directions, sometimes on different levels and connected by shafts.

The cave was discovered in 1911 by the team excavating the deposit in El Castillo cave. A. Leroi-Gourhan's revision was incomplete but fundamental for understanding iconographic structure and chronology of the ensemble. Despite the excellent monograph published in 1913 and the cave's long history, in the 1990s Balbín and González Sainz began a new study which is still ongoing. La Pasiega is one the least well-known great European rock art sites. In addition, work undertaken in the 1950s completely altered the cave by sealing off entrances and blocking passages with artificial walls.

Palaeolithic occupations

Excavations in the 1950s found evidence of human occupation in the Solutrean and lower Magdalenian in the areas around the entrances to Galleries B and C. The names of the passages (Galleries A, B and C) reflected the order in which the rock art ensembles were discovered from Entrance number 4. Leroi-Gourhan's study differentiated four areas, Galleries A, B and C, and Zone D be-

* Dpto. de Historia I, Universidad de Alcalá de Henares. c/ Colegios 2, 28801 Alcalá de Henares, Madrid. rodrigo.balbin@uah.es and javier.alcolea@uah.es

** Dpto. de Ciencias Históricas, Universidad de Cantabria. Avenida Los Castros s/n, 39005 Santander. cesar.González@unican.es

tween the junction of the first two and Gallery C. Bearing in mind the difficulty in moving between the different parts of the cave, the differences between the four main areas, and the position of the original entrances, it is thought that in the Upper Palaeolithic two or three parietal ensembles may have functioned independently of each other: the eastern part, Galleries A, B and the eastern part of Zone D; the western part or Gallery C; and a central ensemble in the western sectors of Zone D.

Eastern series

Gallery B

From its entrance, with Solutrean and probably Magdalenian layers, this passage was the access to deeper parts of the eastern half of the cave (Gallery A and parts of Zone D). The state of conservation of the depictions is poorer nearer the entrance than in the interior area.

It contains over 200 representations: 24 horses, 20 ibices, 16 indeterminate quadrupeds, 11 hinds, 8 stags, 3 aurochs, 2 bison, unidentified bovids, cervids and a carnivore, a giant deer, a bird, a fish and an engraved anthropomorph. The ensemble also includes classic red claviforms, series of dots, several elongated quadrilaterals and a so-called "symbolic inscription". The main panels are on the walls near the entrance with figures of large painted animals and many smaller engravings (Fig. 2).

Gallery A

This refers to the final 20m of the long passage that connects the central and eastern parts of the cave. It displays a "cave-end" ensemble, with one of the region's most outstanding concentrations of animals and signs in red (apart from exceptions in sepia, brown, black and occasional engravings). It is additionally very well conserved.

The density of the representations increases towards the end, with complex compositions on the walls of a narrow passage, domes and side hollows. The first part of the passage is wider and the compositions are simpler, with pairs of animals.

Figure 2. Horse facing a giant deer in the entrance of Gallery B in La Pasiega cave.

Figure 3. Signs at the end of Gallery A in La Pasiega cave.

Gallery A is essentially a pictorial area. It displays 35 hinds, 31 horses and 60 complex signs (elongated quadrilaterals with a pointed protuberance, crescents, ovals, etc.) In addition, there are 14 stags, 5 aurochs, 4 bison, 4 ibices, 2 reindeer, a cervid and 8 indeterminate quadrupeds. The non-figurative motifs also include series of dots, isolated lines, and stains of colour. However the proportion of these motifs is smaller than in the other parts of the cave.

The style of most of the representations is assimilable to pre-Magdalenian art, probably to its later stages. However, they are not synchronic. Some of the black figures, especially in the dome in Sector A6, superimposed on the red figures, evoke the more naturalistic art of the lower Magdalenian.

Eastern part of Zone D

This is a deep part of the cave the prehistoric artists reached from Gallery B. Access must have been easy as far as Sector D2, and more difficulty from there on because of the low roof. At the junction of Galleries A and B, the first group of representations are engraved and painted in red (Sector D1): two hinds, painted signs and several engraved animals. The density of representations decreases towards the centre of Zone D.

Western series

This is the most complex part of Cueva de La Pasiega. In both Gallery C and the western part of Zone D, there are mazes of passages, chambers and high and low level areas. During the Upper Palaeolithic, the usual entrance to this western series was Number 5, which connects with the most decorated part of Gallery C, and where artefacts were found. This entrance was not usable when the cave was discovered, like Number 1 to Gallery B, and today they are both sealed off by a artificial wall.

Gallery C

This contains numerous and diverse representations from the technical, stylistic and chronological points of view. In a small area it condenses the same phases and conventions as in Galleries A and B and Zone D, with the clearest examples of the upper Magdalenian (mainly in Sectors C7 and 8).

The panels in the first 5 m (Sector C1) are complex and diverse in techniques and colours, but also poorly conserved. The complexity increases noticeably from this point. Several animals in an archaic style are painted in red or sienna, together with abundant series of repeated single lines. Then Sectors C2 and 3 display a large group of animal figures, signs in several colours and engravings superimposed on the paintings. In Sector C4 a single panel has been documented, facing the main passage. C5 contains numerous superimposed figures each other and C6 at the end of the first main chamber has a group of small finely-engraved figures. The composition in Sector C7 is clearly Magdalenian and structured, with bovids, horses and some hinds.

Gallery C possesses all the phases that appear in the rest of La Pasiega, as well as others dated in the Magdalenian. Many of the panels in the first part (Sectors C2, 3, 4 and 5) display superimposed figures that usually follow the same sequence (sienna, red or violet, black, and engravings of animals over both the red and violet and the black figures).

Western parts of Zone D

The western Sectors D4 to D8 would have been reached from the end of Gallery C through a narrow passage that connected with the surface, or even from the eastern series. Some remains of representations painted in red and sienna are found in very small passages near the access to western Sector D4. In a small chamber in the middle of a maze (D5), animals are engraved with single lines, with archaic style and conventions, associated with paired finger-marks in red. These are possibly the oldest panels in the whole cave.

Final assessment

In the past, La Pasiega cave had three usable entrances, although the cave must have been difficult to reach from El Castillo cave and even more so from the valley bottom, owing to the steepness of the hillside where it is situated. The remains of industry and fauna belong to the Solutrean and lower Magdalenian, and most of the representations also correspond to that period (21,000-14,500 BP). The Magdalenian style of some animals painted in black and engraved is supported by C14 AMS determinations, which mark the end of artistic production at a little before 12,000 BP.

A total of 41 decorated sectors have been differentiated. The inventory includes over 800 Palaeolithic representations. Among the figures there are 78 horses, 72 hinds, 34 ibices, 28 stags, 18 bison, 15 aurochs, 2 reindeer, 2 anthropomorphs, 2 bovids and 3 indeterminate cervids, as well as a carnivore, chamois, giant deer, bird and fish, and 42 indeterminate quadrupeds. There are also 148 complex signs, above all quadrilaterals, crescents and claviforms, and 32 isolated dots or group of dots. Finally, there are also 284 stains of red or black paint and engraved marks.

The techniques employed were diverse: dotted and simple painted lines, partial or complete colourwash occasionally complemented with engraving, and bichrome paintings. The ways of applying red pigment were more varied than those employed in the black paintings. Yellow, brown and violet were also used. The engravings are equally varied and become more frequent in the Magdalenian.

Marcos García-Diez *,
Daniel Garrido Pimentel **

Las Monedas cave (Puente Viesgo, Cantabria)

This cave, situated in the hill of Monte Castillo, was discovered in 1952. It is 700m long, and contains a number of large chambers as well as evidence of geological processes. Information about its archaeological remains comes from non-systematic research and is scanty. It is known to contain bear bones and pits indicating that these animals hibernated in the cave, humans visited the cave at certain times in the Palaeolithic and also occupied it occasionally in the Bronze Age, and the cave was visited during the sixteenth century AD.

The oldest evidence, for which there is no scientific agreement about its anthropic or natural origin, is located on a column in the entrance chamber. A bison, a mask, a caprid and a hind's head appear to be represented with deep wide engraved lines which, in combination with the rock surface, give the impression of a low relief.

Off the second chamber, a passage contains almost all the black charcoal figures in the cave. They are found in a small space, contrasting with the great size of the chamber, where the figures are located on the walls and a false ceiling. On the right,

* Dpto. Geografía, Prehistoria y Arqueología, Universidad del País Vasco. c/ Tomás y Valiente s/n, 01006 Vitoria (España). marcos.garcia@ehu.es

** Cuevas Prehistóricas de Cantabria, Sociedad Regional de Educación, Cultura y Deporte, Gobierno de Cantabria. Cuevas de Monte Castillo, 39670 Puente Viesgo (Cantabria). daniel.garrido@srecd.es

at the end of the passage there are several lines, some which are reminiscent of a schematic anthropomorph. In this area the rock has several surfaces. On these, two reindeer are outstanding figures because of their naturalism and the use of an interior M-shape to differentiate their coat and give an impression of volume. As the two animals are in an oblique position, they seem to be climbing up the rock where they were drawn. In the centre, a bison and an ibex are represented, and on the right two horses, one of which uses an effect of the rock to represent its eye. A vertical horse is depicted on a higher surface.

Continuing along the left hand wall, a small figure represents a fox or other small carnivore, although it might also be interpreted as a horse. A few centimetres away on a false ceiling, a horse was depicted with an internal division in its shoulder. Above this, in a hidden position, the fore-quarters of a horse is depicted. In sequence along the wall, figures represent 3 ibices (two of them facing each other), a reindeer, another ibex, a horse and a possible mustelid that could be a marten, stoat or weasel. A little further on, the most outstanding composition in the cave consists of a reindeer and a horse (Fig. 1) depicted on two planes of a flake of rock. Both animals, especially the horse, were drawn with full details (coat, internal divisions in their belly and shoulder, facial lines, etc.). The last figure on the wall is a horse.

Figure 1. A horse and reindeer in Las Monedas cave (©Pedro Saura)

Opposite the horse, a panel consists of a mass of curved and straight lines, among which human faces and some animals can be recognised. On this right hand wall of the passage were drawn five horses of different sizes, as well as lines and signs such as a star-shape. The horses display anatomical details and in some cases the figures are completed by the natural form of the rock surface. Two ibices were represented on the same wall, one of which is nearly complete with details in its belly. At the end there are several lines and two animals: one of the few bears in Cantabrian Palaeolithic art and the other an incomplete aurochs. Opposite these animals, some lines were drawn in the form of a grille.

In other sectors of the cave, some isolated black lines may in some cases be interpreted as signs or zoomorphs.

The kind of technique (black drawings) and the formal and stylistic characteristics (naturalistic figures) are indicative of a homogeneous ensemble. As most of the figures are concentrated in certain part of the cave, they may all have been produced in the same period of time. The animals represented are diverse, with reindeer, a bear and a mustelid, which are unusual in Palaeolithic art. However, the most abundant figures are horses. They are not simple outlines, as care is taken with interior anatomy and the correct perspective of the limbs, transmitting photographic realism. Despite this, some figures are out of proportion.

The exact chronology of the ensemble has been defined by the AMS radiocarbon dates obtained. The results of 11,950 ± 120 BP (GifA-95360) for a horse and of 12,170 ± 110 BP (GifA-95203) and 11,630 ± 120 BP (GifA-95284) for an ibex are coherent with the fauna represented.

Marcos García-Diez*,
Daniel Garrido Pimentel**

Hornos de la Peña cave (San Felices de Buelna, Cantabria)

The engravings in Hornos de la Peña were discovered by Alcalde del Río in 1903. In 1909 and 1910, Obermaier and Bouyssonie excavated in the entrance and documented occupations in the Mousterian, Aurignacian, Solutrean, Magdalenian and Neolithic. The parietal art was re-studied from 1971 to 1973 by Ucko.

The cave is about 100 m long. The entrance faces south and the large vestibule continues along a low and narrow corridor, 21m long, leading to the first chamber. From here, another low passage reaches the *Chamber of the Aurochs (Sala del Uro)*, where the cave divides into two passages. The one on the left is on a higher level and it is necessary to climb up flowstone about 15m high. The other on the right leads to *Three Columns Chamber (Sala de las Tres Columnas)*, which communicates with another smaller sector by means of two crawls. These both end in a small chamber, where the first engravings are found. A narrow corridor reaches the final chamber, which is wide and of average height, where most of the engraved figures are located.

In this cave, nearly all the figures are engraved, although a horse in black has been identified. In the vestibule, in full daylight, a horse, a headless bison and several hinds were engraved with deep wide lines.

Inside the cave, the first depiction is an aurochs drawn with a finger in clay, which has given its name to the *Chamber of the Aurochs (Sala del Uro)*, before the cave divides into two. In the left-hand passage, at the top of the flowstone, there is a small chamber with several engravings, particularly an aurochs, two ibices and a horse. A few metres further on, on the right-hand wall, the only drawing in black represents a horse.

Taking the passage on the right in the Chamber of the Aurochs, *Three Columns Chamber (Sala de las Tres Columnas)* is reached. Between the two crawls, a complete detailed stag faces towards the crawl on the left, where an ibex and two horses are engraved.

From this point onwards, the number of engravings increases. On the left, a horse is outstanding for its movement and details. On the right, in the roof, a stag or reindeer is depicted with large antlers. Opposite both figures there are numerous, apparently unconnected lines, some of them sketched with a finger. A group of lines is below them in a hollow. A short distance away, before entering the narrow corridor to the final chamber, there is a possible figure of an elk.

A small hollow in the right-hand wall of the corridor contains another group of engravings, including antlers, the head of an ibex and an aurochs. Above them, a bison is displayed with its horns in twisted perspective and its tongue out as if panting. The upper line of its body is completed with the shape of the rock. A whole bison is represented 1.5m away, at the narrowest point just before reaching the final chamber.

In this chamber, two groups of figures are differentiated by their style, technique and location. On the right, a small ibex was drawn with a finger, while the inside of a hollow was engraved with a toothed implement, forming meandering patterns.

On the left, just before a gently-sloping flowstone leading to a small side-passage, there is a second group of engravings. Two horses were depicted whole. The lower one seems to appear out of the rock, as it is on a second plane with its outline marked by where the wall has flaked away. A hind's head was engraved between the two equids. A serpentiform completes the group. On the right, in a small dome in the roof there is another complete horse. Above this, again in the roof, the relationship between natural hollows and depictions is repeated, as finger marks are located inside a chimney. Further on, a large horse is in the roof, with

* Dpto. Geografía, Prehistoria y Arqueología, Universidad del País Vasco. c/ Tomás y Valiente s/n, 01006 Vitoria (España). marcos.garcia@ehu.es

** Cuevas Prehistóricas de Cantabria, Sociedad Regional de Educación, Cultura y Deporte, Gobierno de Cantabria. Cuevas de Monte Castillo, 39670 Puente Viesgo (Cantabria). daniel.garrido@srecd.es

details in its mane, and with its legs on calcite as if this represented the ground. On the right, another complete horse is depicted in a geometric style. Finally, there is an incomplete bison.

In the roof of the final small passage, there is an indeterminate headless animal, probably a bovid, a grille-shaped sign and a horse's head. This area also displays an anthropomorph (Fig. 1): the raised arm and out-stretched hand suggest a praying posture, while such traits as a tail and the outline of the face give the figure an animal appearance, as if it could represent a shaman. This passage continues for barely 3m in a narrow crawl with a complete, detailed and naturalistic bison.

In Hornos de la Peña, the most abundant figures are bison and horses, occasionally of great realism and anatomical detail. The ensemble also includes one of the few mixed human-animal representations in Iberian Palaeolithic art, a figure located in the innermost and most hidden and restricted part of the cave.

The engravings at the entrance display traits that correspond to an early period, at least 22,000 BP. In contrast, the style and formal characteristics of most of the engravings inside the cave can be attributed to a more recent time, about 15,500-13,000 BP, in the Magdalenian.

Figure 1. Anthropomorph in Hornos de la Peña cave (©Pedro Saura).

Marcos García-Diez *,
Daniel Garrido Pimentel **

Chufín cave (Riclones, Cantabria)

This cave is located 100 m from the confluence of the Rivers Lamasón and Nansa. In the surroundings of its entrance, the landscape of steep slopes would have been an ideal habitat for ibex.

The cave entrance was used as a shelter by shepherds. In 1972, de Cos discovered the exterior engravings and the paintings inside the cave. He then informed Almagro Basch who undertook the first study of the cave art. The name of the cave comes from the legend of Chufín the Moor, who is supposed to have hidden treasure in the cave.

The cave entrance was excavated in 1974 by Cabrera and Bernaldo de Quirós. The main occupation took place in the Upper Solutrean. Laurel-leaf points, notched and concave base points, endscrapers, burins and backed bladelets were found in relation with a circular habitation structure: a two-metre diameter hut associated with remains of ibex,

* Dpto. Geografía, Prehistoria y Arqueología, Universidad del País Vasco. c/ Tomás y Valiente s/n, 01006 Vitoria (España). marcos.garcia@ehu.es

** Cuevas Prehistóricas de Cantabria, Sociedad Regional de Educación, Cultura y Deporte, Gobierno de Cantabria. Cuevas de Monte Castillo, 39670 Puente Viesgo (Cantabria). daniel.garrido@srecd.es

Figure 1. Engraved red deer hinds in the entrance of Chufín cave (©Pedro Saura).

red deer, roe deer, chamois and bovids. Its proximity to the confluence of the rivers explains the finds of fish vertebrae, while the presence of limpets attests contacts with the coast, some 16km away.

The rock art is situated in two sectors; an outer area in daylight and the dark inner area. The first figure is a red deer hind in the arch at the entrance to the cave. Most engravings are closely related to the archaeological deposit. Some of the most interesting figures are a possible fish and line that may represent a horse's back. However, the main panel is in the centre and on a vertical face of rock, near the start of the passage to the inner part of the cave. It contains 16 hinds (Fig. 1), a bison and a triangular shape, as well as other lines. All the figures were engraved by abrasion with deep and wide grooves, so they are easy to see. The hinds, which were at first interpreted as caprids, are superimposed on one another and are characterised by their schematic style. They are represented solely by their outlines with few references to interior anatomical details. Most of them are out of proportion, either because the body is hypertrophied or the neck is elongated, which may represent an expressive attitude.

After crawling through a passage, inside the cave it is possible to stand up in a high and wide chimney. A few metres away, on the right hand wall there is a doubtful Palaeolithic engraving described as a bird with a long beak and lowered wings. A little further on, a zigzag shape was engraved with the finger on the same wall and a series of red figures are also found on this wall, barely 30m from the interior lake. Various themes are represented. First, a horse and an aurochs are partially superimposed. Next to them, a woman is represented using the natural form of the rock to represent her breasts and stomach; claviform signs were painted in the area of the vulva and these may be interpreted as pubic hair. Next, there are two paired marks, a tree-like sign and a figure alternatively interpreted as a horse or a human. Two groups of dots are found at the top of the slope to the lake.

On the left-hand wall, on a raised platform, animals are drawn as simple outlines with fine lines; they consist of at least three depictions of antlers, an incomplete aurochs and three horses. Other engravings were made with a wider line. They represent two headless bison and are located on an inclined frieze. Finally a complex motif has been interpreted, with doubts, as a possible human figure.

Groups of red dots are located on a cornice and are clearly visible from below. They all consist of series of dots arranged in rows and forming clouds of dots. Some of them are associated with the shape, fissures or hollows in the rock, and some of them have been interpreted as vulvas. Before the dots were painted the rock surface was prepared with a light coat of red pigment. The only animal figure painted in red is a partial figure of a stag which, because of its vertical posture, may be considered a humanised representation.

The rock art is currently thought to have been produced in three phases. The first two would have been before 18,000 BP and correspond to the deep wide engravings in the daylight zone and the red paintings inside. The exterior engravings were probably produced in the Gravettian, about 25,000 BP or in the early Solutrean, about 21,000 BP. These hinds are reminiscent of engraved figures in the outer rock-shelters of other caves in northern Spain. Some doubts exist about the age of the red animals, with no interior details and certain lack of proportion. Although it cannot be stated for certain, the red signs formed by dots may also be assigned to the same early phase as the red animal figures, or they are at least relative synchronic. A precise age cannot be given, but they would have been produced during the Aurignacian or Gravettian, between 40,000 and 21,000 years ago. Finally, the finely engraved outlines can be dated in the early Magdalenian, about 16,000 BP.

María González-Pumariega Solís *

El Pindal cave (Pimiango, Asturias)

El Pindal cave is located in the coastal limestone hills, at 23.3 m above sea level. The rock art in the cave was discovered in 1908 and published in 1911.

The cave follows an east-west line over a length of nearly 600m. Nearly all the representations are in the eastern half of the cave, separated into different groups along the passage. The first figures are about 120m from the entrance, on the southern wall, painted in red in the roof. They consist of a horse's head, two lines and two small discs. The other groups are over 200m from the entrance, in four sectors, three on the north wall (the main panel, the panel of the fish, and the panel of the mammoth) and one on the south wall.

The main panel (Fig. 1) comprises 12 bison (1 painted, 3 painted and engraved, and 8 engraved), 5 horses (1 painted and 4 engraved), 1 hind and 1 mammoth, both painted in red, and a probable engraved reindeer antler. In addition, also in red, there are several signs, in the shape of loops and shields, a group of six claviforms, and several groups of dots and lines. Two small claviforms and three lines of dots are in black.

The Panel of the Fish contains 4 horizontal groups of red dots, 2 pairs of black dots and the engraved figures of a fish and a large headless bison. Between the main panel and this one, other representations include a disc and a large bison painted in red, a dotted line and a possible horse's head with some engraved lines accompanying the painting.

The Panel of the Mammoth has the figure of a mammoth and two groups of lines in red. Near this, there is another series of three dots and, a few metres further on, faded stains, a disc and some marks arranged along the wall and on some speleothems, all in red.

* Consejería de Educación, Cultura y Deporte, Principado de Asturias. Apartado de correos 29, 33590 Ribadedeva (Asturias). maria.glez-pumariegasolis@asturias.org

Figure 1. Main panel in El Pindal cave.

Opposite the mammoth, on the southern side of the passage, a block of limestone is decorated with black paintings of a horse's head (related to some engraved lines), a stag, and a probable bison. Near this group, also in black but on the roof, there is a branching sign and a ladder-shaped sign. Some isolated red dots are scattered across the sector and part of a flowstone is stained with the same colour.

The first study and reproduction of the Palaeolithic art in the cave was carried out by Breuil who understood it to be a diachronic ensemble with figures that he attributed to each of his main cycles of prehistoric art, based mainly on stylistic comparisons with other sites in northern Spain and the Pyrenees. In this way, Altamira, Marsoulas and Niaux were points of reference for the most recent Magdalenian representations in El Pindal, while Covalanas and El Castillo were respectively references for figures attributed to the early Magdalenian and those he regarded archaic, such as the mammoth. This diachronic scheme was ratified by Jordá, but not by Leroi-Gourhan, who considered all the representations as a coherent example of his early Style IV, although with some extensions in the start of the recent Style IV. From a thematic point of view, he thought the presence of the mammoth was comparable with certain sites in the Pyrenees (Trois-Frères) and the Périgord (Bernifal, Combarelles and Font de Gaume).

Indeed, one of the least agreed-upon aspects in research about El Pindal is that of its cultural attribution. The different opinions summarised above have been based solely on criteria of relative chronology. The few archaeological data obtained in the cave entrance is limited to a few shells, a truncated Asturian pick and a cobble-stone painted with a red line around its perimeter, all attributed to post-Palaeolithic uses. The result of the only sample taken for a radiocarbon determination (from the stag on the block) gave a post-Palaeolithic date.

In our opinion, the formal, technical and, in some cases, thematic characteristics of all the engravings suggest a middle/upper Magdalenian age, a time with which the claviforms, the groups of dots in the main panel and nearly all the bison can be associated. Owing to the nature of the superimpositions they are involved in and the particular locations, the black representations must have been painted when the red figures and the engravings already existed. The two painted horse's heads, the hind, the only painted bison in the main panel, and the signs and lines in the same panel pose greater doubts. The same can be said of the red dots in the Panel of the Fish and the two mammoth figures, formally identical and with a correlative and significant spatial distribution and orientation (one at the start of the chamber, facing towards the entrance and the other at the finish, facing towards the end of the cave). All these representations make manifest the uncertainties inherent in exclusively comparative arguments and, although based on these a great pre-Magdalenian age has been proposed for the representations, we believe that the graphic activity may have started in the earliest phases of the Magdalenian or in the millennia immediately before.

El Pindal cave contains one of classic Palaeolithic ensembles in Cantabrian Spain. Its great interest lies in the balanced organisation and distribution of the parietal art, as well as in the association of very characteristic elements in this geographical area with others that are more expressive of inter-regional cultural exchange. Above all, over a hundred years after its discovery, part of its art ensemble still defies a chronological definition.

Marco de la Rasilla Vives*, David Santamaría Álvarez**, Vicente Rodríguez Otero***

Llonín cave (Peñamellera Alta, Asturias)

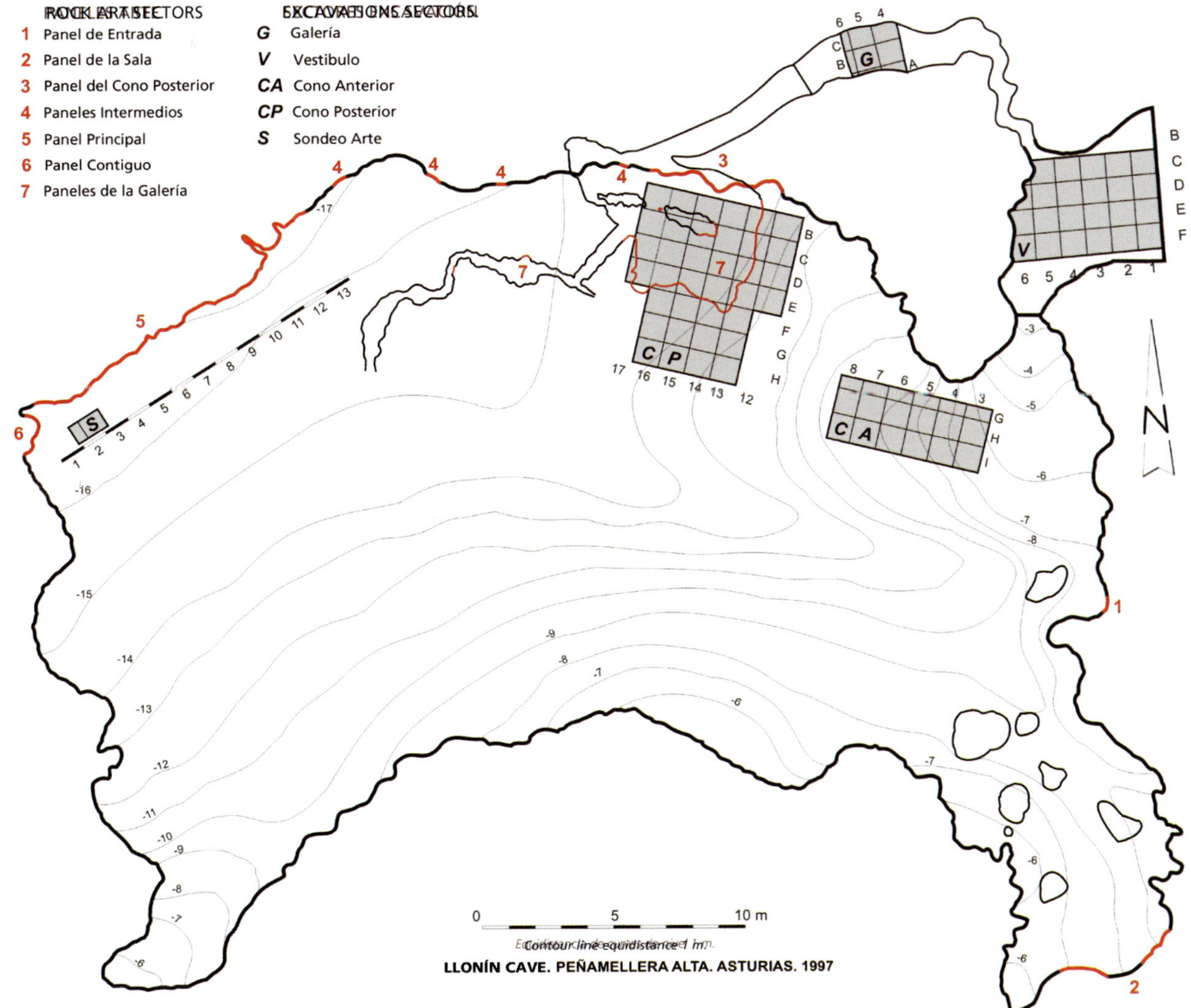

Figure 1. Plan of Llonín cave with the excavation sectors and the cave art panels.

The basins of the Rivers Casaño, Cares and Deva are the location of eleven caves with rock art in addition to Llonín cave. This cave follows an east-north east direction. It is in area of mountains and contains formations with iron, manganese and copper carbonates.

The cave entrance was practically blocked by deposits and calcite formations. However, when searching for a cave where cheese could be fermented, it was discovered in 1957 and prepared for that purpose, causing the destruction of part of the archaeological deposit. The

* Dpto. de Historia, Universidad de Oviedo. c/ Tte. Alfonso Martínez s/n, 33011 Oviedo (España). mrasilla@uniovi.es
** Dpto. de Historia, Universidad de Oviedo. c/ Tte. Alfonso Martínez s/n, 33011 Oviedo (España). santamariadavid@uniovi.es
*** Arqueólogo. Villaviciosa. Asturias. vicente.correo@gmail.com

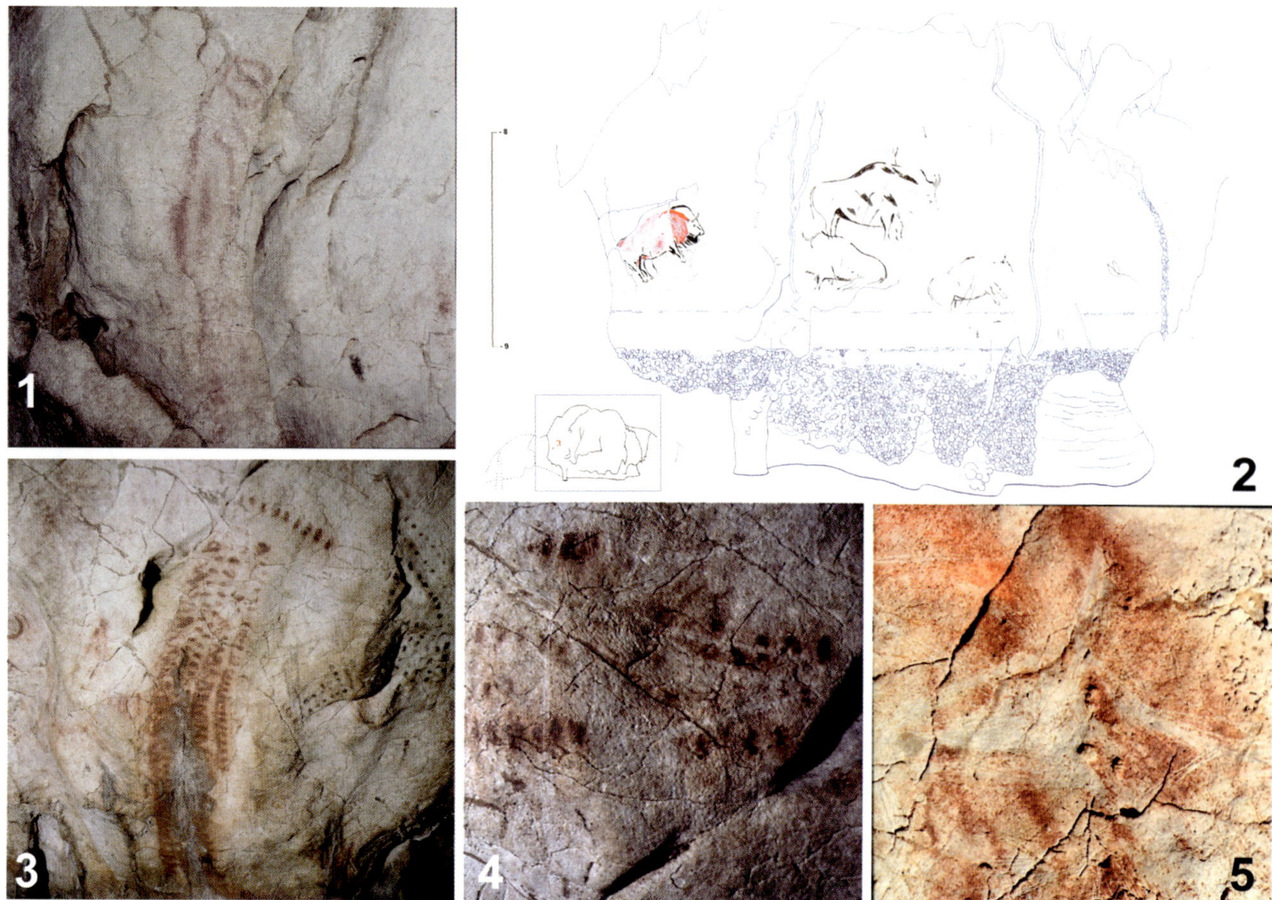

Figure 2. Llonín cave: 1. Female anthropomorph; 2. Copy of the right hand side of the Chamber Panel *(Panel de la Sala)* (by Miranda Duque); 3. Red quadrilateral sign and alignment of black dots; 4. Fore-quarters of a hind; 5. Hind's head. Except for number 2, all the figures are in the Main Panel.

existence of the paintings was announced in 1971.

Research has revealed a rich archaeological and artistic record (Fig. 1). The archaeological sequence includes evidence of the Mousterian, Gravettian, upper Solutrean, Badegoulian, middle Magdalenian, upper Magdalenian, and to a lesser extent, Azilian and Bronze Age. The decoration is divided into different panels: (Gallery Panel, *Panel de la Galería*, Entrance Panel, *Panel de la entrada*, Chamber Panel, *Panel de la Sala*, Back Cone Panel, *Panel del Cono Posterior*, Intermediate Panels, *Paneles intermedios*, Main Panel *Panel principal* and the Panel contiguous *Panel Contiguo* to the interior of the main hall).

The organisation of the depictions, with significant superimpositions, begins a few metres from the entrance with two hinds painted with red dotted lines. The Chamber Panel contains bison above all, some of them wounded and kneeling, represented with black paint and fine engraved lines, as well as one in red that uses the natural form of the rock and was reworked with fine engravings (Fig. 2.2). There is also a black bear inside a small niche in the ceiling where it had to be represented in a crouching position.

The decoration continues in the Back Cone Panel, with linear red paintings of an aurochs and a hind, dots dabbed on the wall with a finger, groups of dots, arrow-shaped red signs and, superimposed on them, the fore-quarters of hinds engraved with multiple lines and striations.

The Intermediate Panels display some smaller figures and signs, and both these and the Back Cone Panel follow the slope of the cone as it was formed by the accumulation of archaeological levels.

Finally the Main and Contiguous Panels are reached, where lithic implements and bones have been found in fissures and hollows in the wall. Figures are painted in two tones of red, including a bison, a female anthropomorph (Fig. 2.1), quadrilateral and meandering signs (Fig. 2.3) vertical lines arranged in a fan shape or in angles and horizontal alignments of single, double or triple rods.

Depicted in black, there are quadrilateral signs created by joining together triangular motifs, as well as bison, reindeer, stags and horses drawn as outlines (although some of them display fine engraving in their outline and other are partially filled with a black colour-wash). There are also outstanding figures engraved with multiple and striated lines, mostly hinds, but also ibices and stags (Fig. 2.4 and 2.5). Other figures, such as horses, are drawn with single lines.

It is suggestive that, of all the caves and rock-shelters in Asturias, Llonín is one with figures produced over a long period. In this respect, the engravings with multiple and striated lines are important as they mark a division between pre-Magdalenian and Magdalenian representations, and furthermore they represent some of the best examples of this technique in Franco-Cantabrian parietal art. The chronological structure is as follows:

Phase 1. Gravettian. The site was very important in symbolic terms as there are depictions in the whole cave, and the ensembles in the Back Cone also belong to this period, but the record is very limited as regards subsistence. A few figures in terracotta red, such as a bison with its horns and front legs in twisted perspective, a poorly-conserved quadrilateral sign and several lines correspond to this time. Also, other figures in vermilion red, such as a female anthropomorph, groups of parallel lines, a meandering sign and another quadrilateral with alignments of triangular motifs can be attributed to the same period.

Phase 2. Solutrean. Corresponding to this period there is a relatively small number of figures, such as black quadrilaterals with internal divisions and zoomorphs drawn with black lines. It is also possible that some of the red paintings were produced in this time. Archaeological evidence is found throughout the cave, with a significant number of pointed lithic implements, but in contrast the cave art is scarcer.

Phase 3. Badegoulian and lower Magdalenian. The technique of engraving with multiple and striated lines has been attributed to the lower Magdalenian by the finds of portable art with the same kind of figures in several archaeological levels. An important and peculiar archaeological record in the cave is attributed to the Badegoulian (Level III in the Gallery), with raclettes, Placard-type assegai points, pseudo-excise technique and the use of local raw materials. This evidence demonstrates a major change that requires an explanation. Is it the result of an autochthonous transition or was there a process of "enculturation"? In this respect, as a hypothesis because they were attributed to the lower Magdalenian, the striated engravings may have been made by a Badegoulian group who deleted the existing art (at least a large red stain and what there might have been under it) whilst at the same time using the red colour for some parts of their figures. This would mark a new form of expression as a prelude to the artistic development in the Magdalenian. This hypothesis would be supported by the fact that no certain evidence of the lower Magdalenian has been found in the deposit, nor in other caves in the river basin. It might be said that the non-existence of levels dated in a period does not mean that the groups at the time did not produce cave art. That is true, but it is at least strange that the cave displays good samples of other periods, yet of one in which the action on the cave walls was very intense, there is no evidence, or the non-artistic activity was so ephemeral that it has not been possible to differentiate the materials belonging to that possible lower Magdalenian.

Phase 4. Middle Magdalenian. This is represented by bison, reindeer, stags and horses painted with black lines and associated with engravings in their outlines or with their interiors filled with black colour-wash; as well as by other figures that were only engraved.

Phase 5. Upper Magdalenian. Belonging to this period are figures engraved with single or multiple lines with naturalistic forms. They are bison (one with its tongue out, and one in the Chamber Panel with arrows and kneeling), horses (especially those with bristling manes), ibices, stags and the bear.

AMS radiocarbon determinations have been obtained in Llonín, and recently samples have been taken to date calcite by Uranium series. As regards the radiocarbon dates, some of them contradict the parietal stratigraphy and relative chronology. Others are compatible with the span of time corresponding to the proposed cultural attribution, but do not add much precision owing to differences between the humic fraction and pure carbon samples. Yet others offer no possibility of analysis as remains had to be added from different parts of the same ensemble. In conclusion, it may be said that, over all, the radiocarbon determinations have not provided high-quality data.

In 2009 a protection area was established around the cave, and a study was carried out that has reached very illustrative results about the presence of several kinds of micro-organisms and also through comparisons and inferences made between the data obtained in this and other regional caves.

Blanca Ochoa*,
Irene Vigiola-Toña**

La Covaciella cave (Carreña de Cabrales, Asturias)

This cave was discovered in 1994 when it was broken into by road works. It tends to slope upwards, on an E-W line, over a total length of about 80m. The cave is divided into three sectors, two chambers and a passage around 35 m long. Remains of bear, and their pits and claw marks have been found, showing that they used the cave for hibernation in the Upper Pleistocene. Since the original entrance became blocked in the Holocene, it is unlikely that humans have entered, but animals may have.

The rock art is located in a passage at the western end of the cave and is reached climbing up a slope of clay. The representations are grouped in four panels, all of them on the left hand wall. Some 13 figurative representations (8 bison, 1 stag, 1 reindeer or caprid, 1 horse and 2 bovids) and 6 non-figurative motifs (3 signs, 1 series of dots and 2 groups of lines) have been documented. In addition, the walls display stains of pigment and isolated lines.

The first figure, an incomplete bovid engraved with fine multiple lines, is located on the clay ramp, inside a hollow that may be intended to complete its fore-quarters.

The second panel is eight metres from the ramp and it is arranged in two areas around a large fissure, on which divides the panel where most of the representations converge (Fig. 1). It begins with a linear

Figure 1. Bison in the main panel in La Covaciella.

* Dpto. Geografía, Prehistoria y Arqueología, Universidad del País Vasco. (UPV/EHU) c/ Tomás y Valiente s/n, 01006 Vitoria (España). blanca.ochoa@ehu.es

** Dépt. de Préhistoire, Muséum national d'Histoire naturelle (MNHN). 1, rue René Panhard, 75013 París (Francia). irvigiola@gmail.com

sign and an incomplete stag, both traced with a finger. On the right, a complete bison was drawn with a finger and with black pigment; a small head of a horse is drawn in black next to the fissure and below the bison. All these figures face right. Above the stag and the bison, there are numerous finger marks and a similar sign to the one at the start of the panel.

On the other side of the fissure, three bison were traced all face left. The upper two are technically the most complete in the cave. They combine an outline drawn in black, engraving to complete some areas, a colour-wash inside their bodies that was later scraped off in places, and finally scraping around their outline. Both animals are complete and were represented with full details. Below them, a third bison is also complete but displays fewer details and is simpler technically. A series of dots and stains were painted in red ochre over its hind limbs and under its belly. On the right, a fourth bison represented by its cervical-dorsal line and part of the head faces right. The group is completed by the engraving of a further bison: only the start of the cervical-dorsal line and its head, but drawn with full details (hair, eye, horns and tongue). On a cornice near this group, using the natural form of the rock to complete the figure, the hind-quarters of a bison were drawn with a finger. The panel is completed by a caprid, or a reindeer if the use of the form of the rock is taken into account, drawn with a finger.

Continuing along the passage, 12m from the previous panel and a few centimetres above the floor, there is a large stain of red ochre. The last panel is at the end of the passage. It consists of two bisons in black, one complete and the other incomplete in a semi-vertical position. They are both in a poor state of conservation due to water and mud running down the wall.

AMS radiocarbon determinations have provided dates for two figures: 17,503-16,620 cal BP (GifA-95281) and 16,400-15,534 cal BP (GifA-95370) for the bison on the right in the central panel, and 17,733-16,973 cal BP (GifA-95364) and 17,123-16,058 cal BP (GifA-95362) for the bison on the left. These results situate the rock art of Cueva de Covaciella in the Middle Magdalenian (17,500/17,200-16,500/16,000 BP). They suggest the figures are contemporaneous and agree with proposals for the chronology of their style.

Covaciella is associated with a European-wide graphic tradition in the middle phases of the Magdalenian. The most similar ensembles are located in other caves in northern Spain (such as Urdiales and Santimamiñe) and the French Pyrenees (Niaux).

Rodrigo de Balbín Behrmann *,
J. Javier Alcolea González **

Tito Bustillo cave (Ribadesella, Asturias)

This cave is located on the left bank of the River Sella, near its mouth, in the Carboniferous limestone of Ardines Hill. It is also known as Pozu'l Ramu and Pozu la Cerezal, the names of entrances before the cave art was discovered. This was found in 1968 by Torreblanca Caving Club and was given the name of Tito Bustillo in memory of one of the club members who died shortly after the discovery.

The Palaeolithic entrance was on the western side of the hill (Fig. 1A) in the village of Ardines and facing south-west. Nowadays, the cave is entered along an artificial tunnel near the estuary, 1km from the coast.

Beginning in the original entrance, a chamber is reached which is blocked at its start by a collapse. The archaeological deposit, of which a small part has been excavated, is located in the south-west of the large chamber that follows, in an intermediate zone between the exterior and interior.

The first archaeological excavation was carried out by García Guinea in 1970 while the system-

* Dpto. de Historia I, Universidad de Alcalá de Henares. c/ Colegios 2, 28801 Alcalá de Henares, Madrid. rodrigo.balbin@uah.es
** Dpto. de Historia I. Universidad de Alcalá de Henares. c/ Colegios 2, 28801 Alcalá de Henares, Madrid. javier.alcolea@uah.es

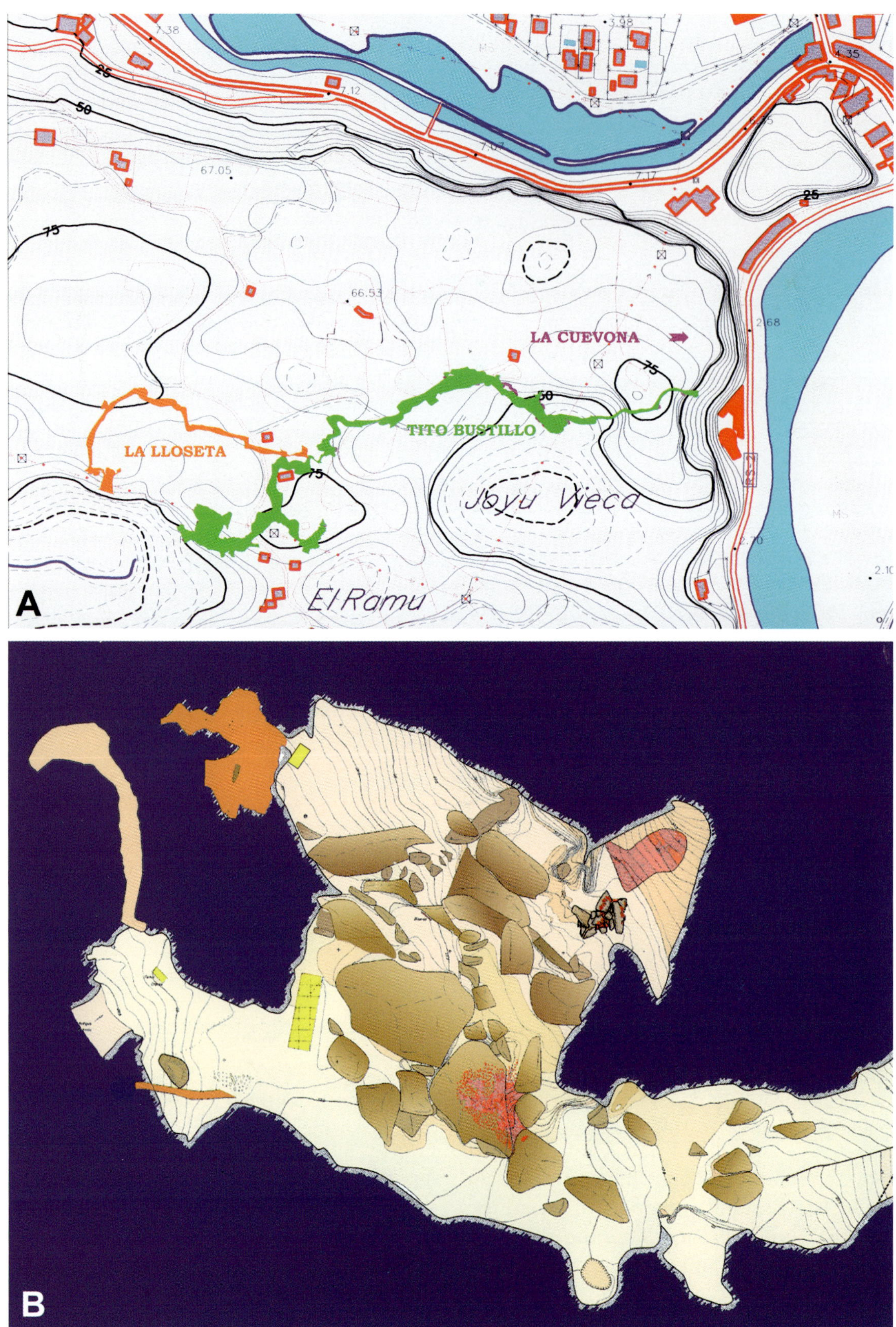

Figure 1. A: Map of Ardines Hill with the surveys of Tito Bustillo and La Lloseta. B: Plan of Zone XI with the entrance hall and the pigment mine.

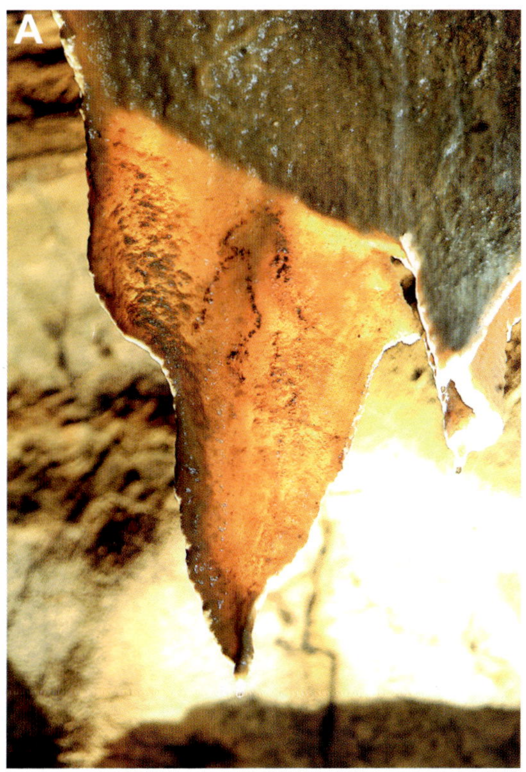

Figure 2. A: Male anthropomorph painted on a limestone crest in the Gallery of the Anthropomorphs and dated by U/Th. B: Female anthropomorph painted on the other side of the same crest.

atic research directed by Moure Romanillo began in 1972. Reports on the first three field seasons were published in 1975 and 1976. The studies on the rock art started in 1974 under the direction of Balbín Behrmann and Moure Romanillo. Work was restarted in 1998 by the authors of this text, in order to verify archaeologically the old excavated areas, investigate new areas and document the art fully. The nearby caves of La Lloseta, La Cuevona and Les Pedroses were also documented.

Since the first publications by Moure and Balbín, the decorated areas have been numbered in order from I to XI, starting in the modern tourist entrance. This distribution is useful for working in the cave, but it is limited as the cave is decorated in its entirety.

Rock art

The graphic composition in the different zones is as follows:

Zone III

This is one of the most important, among other reasons because of its special female sexual significance (Fig. 3A). A single theme is represented in this zone, consisting of different forms of the female genital, sometimes together with the profile of the body.

Zone V

This group is arranged around a part of the main passage, on both its sides. It is therefore defined by its position, beginning with an area of flowstone, after Zone IV, whose columns make a resonant sound and were painted in red. In all this area, several sub-zones exist, discovered in the latest research.

Gallery of the Bison. This is a small side passage, leading off the right of the main passage through an oval opening in the form of the female genital, painted in red. A narrow passage is reached, some 10m long and a maximum of 2m wide, painted and engraved with figures representing bison, horses and signs.

Gallery of the Anthropomorphs. This is a passage following from the previous one and connecting with it. It is about 30m long and on a higher level that the main passage. At its top, a shaft 4m deep is closed off

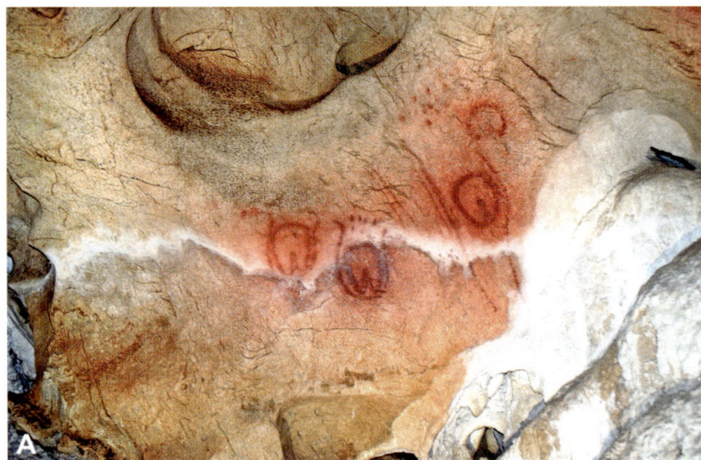

Figure 3. A: Vulvae painted in Zone III, or Chamber of the Vulvae. B: Figures in the Main Panel or Zone X, with three reindeer and three horses.

on its northern side by an artificial wall. It leads to an elongated chamber at the bottom of which a limestone ridge is decorated with red anthropomorphs (Fig. 2 A and B). A large accumulation of bones and burnt limestone, with charcoal and remains of ochre, has been excavated in the shaft.

Contours decoupés

A little further on, on the right-hand ledge, 4m above the floor of the passage, a deliberate deposit of four contours decoupés in the form of hind's heads was found.

Zone VI

This zone starts beyond the area with the contours decoupés. In the whole area and surrounding spaces, there are abundant remains of paintings, including stags, horses and claviform signs, on the walls of the main passage and in shades of red and black.

Zone VII

This zone contains one of the few engravings of a cetacean in Palaeolithic art. It is in a side-passage on the left of the main passage, together with an engraved anthropomorph. The area also exhibits other animal paintings and engravings.

Zone VIII

This displays an ensemble specialised in engravings of horses, bovids and cervids, located in a side-passage on the right-hand side of the main passage. The figures are in a recent style and of outstanding quality.

Zone IX

This is an area between the passage leading to the main panel and the one that goes to the archaeological deposit. A compound quadrilateral sign and a polychrome horse are represented; the latter with the same conventions and colour as those in the main panel in Zone X.

Zone X

This is the main panel, which holds most of the figures in the cave and acts as its centre. It possesses various representations of animals and signs, both painted and engraved, with a predominance of horses and cervids that are sometimes polychrome (Fig. 3B). Among these figures, many of them quite large in size, there are female anthropomorphs like the ones in Zone III, large felines and bison. The figures were superimposed on each other over several thousands of years, and therefore the ones that were produced last are the most easily visible.

Although the representations are now concentrated on the right-hand side of the chamber, they were once distributed all over it, some of the largest were even on the ceiling. The state of conservation is irregular, and deficient in the case of the large figures on the ceiling. However, others painted at the same time are well conserved.

Zone XI

This covers the area between Zone IX and the occupation deposit and further south (Fig. 1B). It contains a passage from the old entrance, separated from the main cave, where an excavation has been carried out since 2005. This leads to Zone XI itself, separated from it by a collapse which partly moved a Mesolithic burial. This indicates, among other things, that the cave was visited at times after the Upper Palaeolithic. The movement that caused this separation also caused blocks to collapse inside the area, interrupting its continuity, although it had all been occupied in the late Pleistocene.

Moure's excavations took place in the centre-south of the space, and we are excavating in the northern part, within an area that is the continuation of the previous excavation. The remains in both areas belong to the same period.

In this chamber, 50 x 50m in size, a pigment mine was found, the source of the colouring matter used in most of the paintings in the cave, with tones going from yellow to violet, and including red.

This is the zone with the largest figures in the cave, mostly on the southern wall and as much as 35m above the floor. The whole area is full of colouring matter, which was piled up and prepared next to the mine and stored on a large flat rock, from where the southern wall was probably painted.

Environment and chronology

Cueva de Tito Bustillo is located in Ardines Hill and communicates directly with La Cuevona and La Lloseta, which also possess cave art. However, the same hill contains a further nine caves and three of them are decorated. Tito Bustillo can only be understood in relation with these neighbouring caves and the whole underground system, which must have been an important centre because of its size and depictions. This hill should be understood as a cultural ensemble, in use from at least the Middle Palaeolithic to the Mesolithic, in unbroken association with its inhabitants and their cultural manifestations, as they quite probably possessed an organisational system above the traditional bands and consisting of several hundred people.

Our first publications proposed a model of a brief use and decoration of the cave, among other reasons because only the most recent levels in its occupation deposit had been excavated. We now know that the entrance was further away from the large area in Zone XI and that the occupation covered a much longer period of time, perhaps in the same dwelling area, beneath the levels that are currently known or more probably under the levels in the entrance passage or hall that that has been excavated in recent years, or even in the outer slope located over La Gorgocera at the entry to the River San Miguel.

The composition of the pigments in the mine and on the walls has been analysed, and the base of all the pigments is the same. In some cases the agglutinants used to dissolve the colours could be identified. These are fats in the stylistically oldest paintings, such as vulvae and circles. In contrast, in the more recent depictions, some of which are polychrome, the pigment was usually dissolved in water, which gives it less consistency and durability.

Tito Bustillo was decorated throughout the whole cave, on the main passages and side-passages, in chambers and passages, on countless occasions, from the start of the Upper Palaeolithic until its end, at least.

Old dates are available for the Gallery of the Anthropomorphs, where the male figure has been dated by U/Th to a period between 36,200 ± 1500 BP and 35,540 ± 390 BP, while the deposit we excavated was dated by radiocarbon to 32,990 ± 450 BP (38,420-36,137 cal BP). These dates are therefore in the first graphic phases in the Upper Palaeolithic, in the Aurignacian culture, when Tito Bustillo was already occupied. For the main panel in Zone X, no such old dates are known for the paintings, but the lowest figures on these walls, that were repainted so often, belong to very old times.

Most of the figures that have been sampled in the main panel are dated in a period between 13,000 and 11,000 BP, with some discordances demonstrating the varying exactness in the C14 AMS methodology. Most of the dates obtained for the occupation levels in the deposit and in the decoration area of the main panel correspond to the same span of time, with some exceptions that do not alter the average age substantially. These are all within the middle-upper Magdalenian, which is coherent with the style of the figures in the ensembles attributed to the late Upper Palaeolithic.

The cave is also known to have been used after the end of the Ice Age, because the burial in Zone XI, called El Coxu, has been dated by C14 to 8,470 ± 50 BP (9,542-9,421 cal BP) in the Azilian.

More needs to be known about the early stages of the occupation, in order to achieve a better understanding of the organisation of the site when its decoration began. However, the human presence and repeated use gives us a much more complete idea of Palaeolithic reality, with fewer divisions and boundaries than was thought. The span of time of its use is also longer than we once proposed.

José Adolfo Rodríguez Asensio *

La Lluera caves (Oviedo, Asturias)

La Lluera I and the small cave of La Lluera II are located near San Juan de Priorio, in Las Caldas on the right bank of the River Nalón.

La Lluera I is a small horseshoe-shaped cave with two passages leading off from the entrance which connect inside the cave to form a small third passage.

In the entrance, on the wall before the start of the passage, en engraving represents a horse in profile with a square head, the cervical-dorsal line forming an S-shape on its side and some anatomical details, like the hock on the hind leg. Inside this figure there are two signs, one of them an angle and the other in the form of a feather. They are clear engravings but not as deep as those inside the cave. In this area, two large panels face each other, one on each wall. Two main zones can be differentiated; in the higher one figures of hinds were engraved insistently. They are depicted with the characteristic stereotypes of the Nalón middle river basin, where hinds are represented by a conventionalism consisting of three lines: two diagonal parallel lines and an oblique one across the top of the other two to represent the head and start of the neck.

Beneath this great frieze, in which there are also some signs, a panel reaching the present floor level is totally engraved, and in which a few figures can be selected as examples. The large figure of a hind continues along its back and in its chest to form the fore leg. Part of the line of this animals' body is used to represent a large bull with its cervical-dorsal line ending in its tail, its head with the detail of its eye and lyre-shaped horns in double perspective. A depiction of a male ibex with its horns spreading from its head is engraved with its body complete. A pachyderm occupies a central place in the panel, inside the hind and the bull. Below these figures a silhouette of a small horse with a triangular head and strong neck appears to leap from an engraved horizontal line that may represent the ground. After this panel, which contains more figures, there is a large hollow in the wall (Fig. 1).

In this natural niche, a herd of aurochs were drawn in perspective, in line from left to right and from bottom to top, so that the figures nearer the floor are larger and they become smaller nearer the right and the top. Each of these aurochs is engraved with a line forming a rather pointed head, which continues along the back to the withers and a raised tail. The hind-quarters were engraved with details in the back leg and marked genital to continue in the belly and front leg.

In the Great Niche, several scenes of animals were represented, which complement each other while, independently each one possesses its own value and strength. Six aurochs face the cave entrance, while 13 hinds on the left hand side complement the aurochs, as the line marking the latter animals' horns is used for the chests of the hinds. Additionally, these are the only figures facing inside the cave, like the other two on the right hand side. In the right hand corner, half-covered by a speleothem, there are two aurochs, one of which has lyre-shaped horns. Finally in the middle and top part on the right, two horses were engraved, one with a rectangular head. As well as these figures, several lines may be interpreted as signs or as the start of unfinished hinds, as documented in the case of an angle in the top central part. The most outstanding figure, because of its position and the skill in its depiction, is a hind with a stylised neck of great beauty which continues in a complete body, although part of the fore-limb has been lost.

Next to the niche but outside it and on the line marking the limit reached by daylight, the last figure is a bison lying down with its legs folded underneath it. That is the last engraving as there are no lines further inside the cave. All the engravings are exterior figures where they are reached by daylight.

On the opposite wall, several figures of hinds are represented, in some cases only by their hind-quar-

* Dpto. de Historia, Universidad de Oviedo. Campus de El Milán, 33011 Oviedo. adolfo@uniovi.es

Figure 1. Engravings in the Niche in La Lluera I (©J. Fortea).

ters and in others by their head. In the entrance area, opposite the panel of the hind and bull, a large hind seems to face the one on the opposite wall. Its head uses two natural cracks for the eye and the ear.

Opposite the Great Niche, in another small hollow, a series of lines are difficult to interpret despite being very suggestive and may represent two proboscideans.

The art in La Lluera I belongs to an early stage, perhaps in the middle Solutrean, in which the hinds in the upper frieze mark the start of a trend of what would be the large exterior shrine. In the following stage, in the upper Solutrean, the opposing walls and the niche were decorated, with the latter a point of reference for this cultural period. Some further figures were possibly added in the Magdalenian. The art in La Lluera I allowed Fortea to define the second artistic phase in the Nalón basin.

Some 50m to the east of the cave of La Lluera I, on a slightly higher level, La Lluera II is a tube draining the hillside that communicates with the river bank formed in the same limestone escarpment. It is a channel that widens a little at its end to form a small chamber with enough room for only two people. On the left hand wall, in a two-metre square panel, a group of engravings develop the same theme, triangles (Fig. 2), in different ways: closed, open, with a vertical central line, with the vertex upwards or downwards, large triangles with small ones inside them, and some that make use of the lines of others. A number of these triangles use protuberances in the rock, and in others cracks are made to coincide with the inside of the triangle. In the centre of this panel full of engraved triangles, a hind was depicted with three lines like those in La Lluera I.

Figure 2. Triangles in the small cave of La Lluera II (©J. Barrera).

Mª Soledad Corchón Rodríguez *,
José Adolfo Rodríguez Asensio**

Cueva de la Peña de Candamo (San Román de Candamo, Asturias)

This cave is located at the top of Peña Blanca Hill, with its entrance facing south, towards the valley of the River Nalón, at the end of its middle course. It therefore looks out over the valley and the medium-high hills around it. It was a privileged position for human habitation in the Palaeolithic. It is not a large cave, but its formations, passages, chambers and halls are of great speleological and archaeological interest. It is the westernmost cave with Palaeolithic art, and the one with the largest number of motifs out of all the sites in the Nalón middle valley: thirteen caves and rock-shelters with exterior engravings and four with interior paintings.

The scientific discovery took place in summer 1914, although it was already well-known in the area and occasionally visited between 1903 and 1911-1914, according to the graffiti on walls in spaces of difficult access (*Galería de las Batiscias*). Its discoverer, Hernández Pacheco, reported the paintings and engravings that same year to the Royal Spanish Society of Natural History and at the Congress of the Spanish Association for Progress in Science (Valladolid, 1915). El Conde de la Vega del Sella independently discovered the paintings on the *Muro de los Grabados* in 1914, and published a brief note in 1929 explaining how he removed the calcite that covered the black dots and yellow aurochs on the left hand side. Hernández Pacheco carried out the study of the cave from 1915 to 1917, with the collaboration of Cabré and Benítez Mellado. The result was the publication of a detailed monograph in 1919. At the same time, he undertook the first excavations in the nearby "Solutrean Small Cave" (1917-1918), with the collaboration of Wernert. This fieldwork recovered Solutrean artefacts and Jordá's excavation in 1957 elaborated on the known sequence by documenting upper Solutrean and lower Magdalenian occupations.

The narrow entrance through which Hernández Pacheco had entered the cave was soon altered and, although the cave was listed as a National Monument in 1923, that did not stop its chambers and passages being modified in the following decade. The building work to facilitate visits, together with the irreversible damage suffered by the most accessible engravings and paintings in the Spanish Civil War, the disproportionate lighting, and inappropriate social use of the cave (1940-1955) caused the loss of figures, especially in the *Muros de los Grabados*, and biological contamination. As a result, the cave was closed between 1979 and 1994. When the problems had been partially solved, the cave was re-opened to the public with restrictions on the restricted visits. In the face of the great demand and the risks caused by large numbers of visitors, the Candamo Cave Interpretation Centre was founded, directed by one of the authors (ARA), in which reproductions of the most important works of art are exhibited.

Since 1919 and until recently, research on the parietal art in the cave has been restricted to certain specific points. The main studies aimed to clarify the chronological sequence of the representation, based on the examination of superimpositions in the *Muros de los Grabados:* Jordá and Moure's decoration phases. In other cases, the interpretation of some figures was changed by Berenguer. More recently, a relative chronology based on the parietal stratigraphy in the Wall of the Engravings has been proposed, with the age of the sequence made more accurate by the direct AMS dating of black figures, carried out by Fortea.

Current research in the cave

The latest research began in 2006, funded by the Ministry of Science and Technology, with the objective of carrying out a study of the possibles engravings of seals, as in the nearby cave of Las Caldas evidence had been found of marine mammals in middle Magdalenian levels (*ca.* 14,000 BP), in the form of pendants made from teeth and portable

* Department of Prehistory, University of Salamanca. c/ Cervantes s/n, 37002 Salamanca (Spain). scorchon@usal.es
** Dpto. de Historia, Universidad de Oviedo. Campus de El Milán, 33011 Oviedo. adolfo@uniovi.es

objects engraved with seals, dolphins and a sperm whale (*Halichoerus grypus, Globicephala melas, Physeter macrocephalus catodon*). The cave was the only site in Europe, besides Tito Bustillo and its disputed engraving, to display parietal representations of this type of marine fauna: two possible engravings of *Halichoerus sp.*, described by Hernández Pacheco and now with a new interpretation. This study led to the discovery of new engravings and paintings, as all the decorated sectors were fully revised. At the same time, an International Conference was held in order to frame the parietal art in La Peña de Candamo within the context of Palaeolithic art in Cantabrian Spain, the Pyrenees and south-west France, and support the candidature of the cave to be included on UNESCO's list of World Heritage, as occurred in 2008, together with a further 17 sites. The conference proceedings, *El Paleolítico superior Cantábrico. Primera Mesa Redonda (San Román de Candamo, Asturias, 26-28 Abril 2007)*, have recently been published.

The continuation of the research, co-financed with European funds, enabled a new plan of the cave to be produced during the full speleological exploration of the cave and the covacho, in order to document the connection between them and find

Figure 1. Old Phase. Chamber under the Red Signs. Triangular ideomorph with curved signs, closed signs and thick red dot. Colour saturation allows the closed structure and internal divisions to be perceived (Photo: Candamo Team).

new entrances. This increased the surveyed length from 60m to 240m. At the same time, new engravings and paintings were found in all the sectors that were re-examined (*Vestíbulo, Galería de Entrada, Sala Baja de los Signos, Entrada al Salón* and *Salón de los Grabados*) (Figs. 1 and 3), some of which were unknown because of their difficult access (*El Hornito, La ventana* and *Galería de las Batiscias*). A new inventory of the representations was carried out, with computerised records, and they were positioned precisely on the new plan of the cave. A petrological, geochemical and biological study programme was started (2009-2013) to detect and monitor alterations (decalcification, biological and chemical pollution) affecting the conservation of the representations. In addition, a three-dimensional map of the geometry and volume of the cave was carried out with a laser (TLE-FARO), with extra infra-red information, which is of great use for analysing degradation and additions, as well as a digital reproduction with a virtual flight and archaeological GIS (TIDOP Groupe). Later, detailed photographs of the most complex panels (*Muro de los Grabados-Talud, Mogote estalagmítico* and *Galería Batiscias*) provided orthographic images that support the interpretation and correction of the motifs.

The complementary research carried out in the following years, in the framework of a new inter-disciplinary project, addressed the study of the mineral components in the pigments used by the Palaeolithic artists. Significant identities were identified in the figures produced in different parts of the cave, enabling the proposal of hypotheses about the decorative process and discriminating phases in the production. In addition, the indirect sampling of red haematite, black charcoal and yellow goethite pigments with RAMAN spectroscopy, ICP Masses (trace elements) and Energy Dispersive X-ray Fluorescence allowed not only the molecular identification of the compounds but also a diagnosis of the degradation of the calcite surfaces. Another interesting aspect is the research aimed at characterising the human occupation in the cave, particularly in the Galería de las Batiscias, an isolated and less altered part of the cave. Numerous evidence of Palaeolithic graphic activity has been located, in the form of remains of pigment, industry and brecciated fauna, as well as new panels of engravings previously unknown. At the same time, the full study of the parietal art in the *Salón de los Grabados* has succeeded in identifying large accumulations of representations, which are true pictorial stratigraphies, with over 250 figures identified in the main wall, or *Muro de los Grabados*, and other emblematic panels, like the *Camarin* (Fig. 2), *El Mogote, El Talud, Los Discos and la Palmera*.

Another important aspect of the art refers to the dating of black paintings and the controversy aroused by the contradictory results obtained by Fortea. Modern techniques allow greater precision and the new programme allows both direct and indirect dating of the parietal graphic activity. Black pigments have been dated with AMS C14, while calcite associated with engravings and paintings have been dated by U/Th, by Valladas and Pons-Branchu. The results suggest that Cueva de La Peña de Candamo was decorated during most of the Upper Palaeolithic and the occupation of the cave reached its deepest parts from the start, in a series of pre-Magdalenian phases (Aurignacian, Gravettian and especially in the Solutrean), until the end of the Magdalenian.

This means that Cueva de La Peña de Candamo can be included within a select group of caves in Cantabrian Spain (Llonín, Tito Bustillo, La Lloseta, Altamira, Castillo, La Pasiega and La Garma) in which the decoration took place over a very long period of time. In all of them, the circumstance of possessing panels with a large concentration of depictions, in intricate chronological superimpositions, as in Candamo, where they form veritable pictorial stratifications, allows motifs and engraving and painting techniques in the different caves to be compared, thus obtaining more information about Palaeolithic artistic activity in northern Spain between *ca*. 30,000 and 11,500 BP.

Acknowledgements

The research in Cueva de la Peña de Candamo has been carried out in the framework of the projects: (PI: Mª Soledad Corchón): *Estudio del Solutrense y Magdaleniense en el centro-oeste de la Cornisa Cantábrica (21.000-10.000 calBC)*. Ministry of Science and Technology (BHA2003-05438); European Project FEDER-MICINN: *Estudio integral del Solutrense Cantábrico: gestión del territorio, movilidad y relaciones culturales en la transición del Pleniglaciar al Tardiglaciar* (HUM2007-66057/HIST). *Aplicación de nuevas Geotecnologías al estudio del Arte Paleolítico y su contexto social en el valle del Nalón (Asturias, España): 20000-13.000 BP*. MICINN (HAR2010-17916). The team acknowledges the valuable collaboration given by the *Laboratoire des Sciences du Climat et de l'Environnement* (LSCE/ IPSL, Gif-sur Ivette, France) in dating the art in the cave.

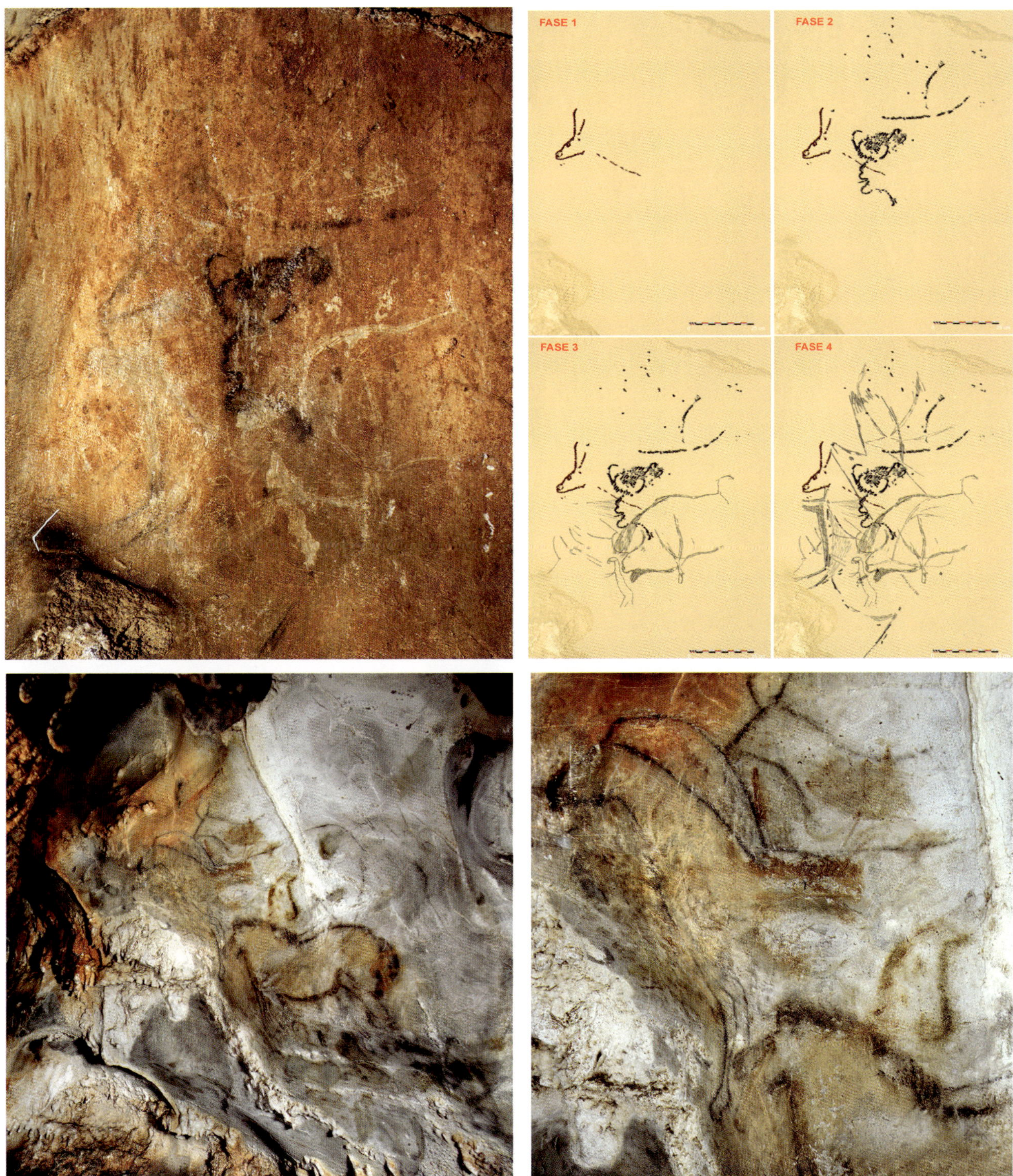

Figure 2. Magdalenian figures. Top, upper part of the *Muro de los Grabados*: computer reconstruction of the artistic process. Bottom, the *Camarin*: modelled horse in sienna and black, over black outlines of a horse and aurochs (Photos: P. Saura and Candamo Team).

Figure 3. Secondary panels in the Main Hall. Top, old phase: details of the columns decorated with discs (palm of the hand prints). Bottom: *Talud*, yellow aurochs in the old phase and later sienna and black figures; *The Palm-Tree*, ibex dated in the upper Magdalenian (Photos: P. Saura and Candamo Team).

10

POST-PLEISTOCENE ART FROM THE IBERIAN LEVANT

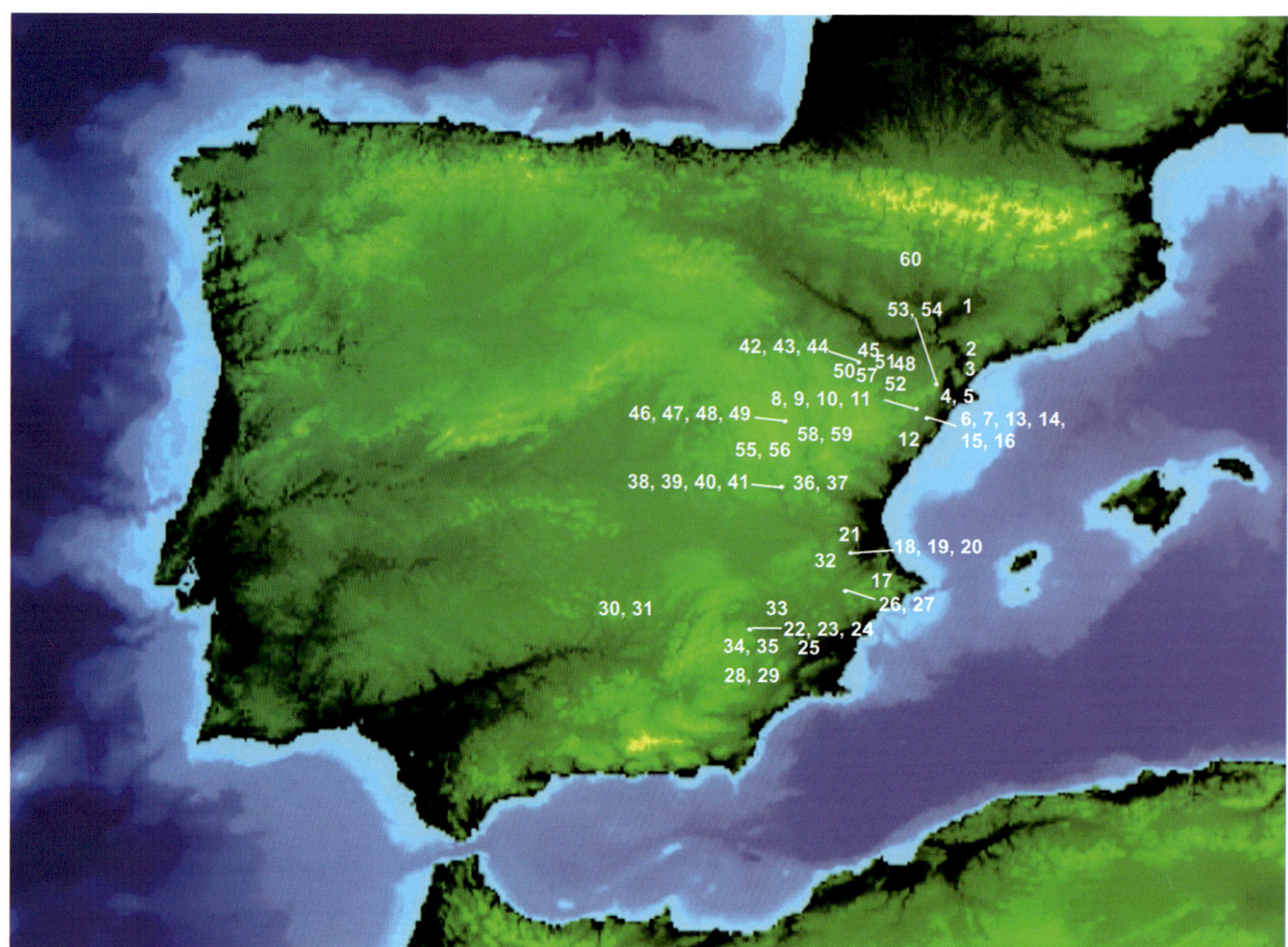

Site	Map numbrering
Roca dels Moros de El Cogull	1
Abrigo de Perellada IV	2
Abrigo de Cabra Feixeta	3
Abrigos d'Ermites en la Serra de la Pietat	4
Conjunto d'Ermites	5
Cova Centelles	6
Cova del Puntal	7
Cingle de la Mola Remigia	8
Cova Remigia	9
Racó Gasparo	10
Racó Molero	11
Abrigos de la Joquera	12
La Saltadora	13
Abrigo d'en Melia	14
Abrigo del Cingle del Barran de l'Espigolar	15
Barranco de la Valltorta	16
La Sarga	17
Abrigo del Lucio	18
Barranco Moreno	19
Cueva de la Araña	20
El Abrigo de la Pareja	21
Cañaica del Calar	22
Fuente del Sabuco	23
La Risca	24
El Milano	25
Cantos de la Visera en Monte Arabí	26
Cueva de los Grajos	27
Estrechos de Santoge	28
Lavaderos de Tello	29
Peñón de la Tabla del Pochico	30
Prado del Azogue	31

Site	Map numbrering
Cueva de la Vieja	32
Minateda	33
Abrigo de los toros de las Bojadillas	34
Solana de las Covachas	35
Abrigo de los Oculados	36
Cueva del Tío Modesto	37
Peña del Escrito	38
Selva Pascuala	39
Abrigo de Selva Pascuala	40
Marmalo	41
Los Trepadores	42
Tia Mona	43
Tio Garroso	44
Los Chaparros	45
Cocinilla del Obispo	46
Doña Clotilde	47
Prado del Navazo	48
Toros de la Losilla	49
Cañada de Marco	50
Val del Cahrco del Agua Amarga	51
Barranco Hondo	52
Roca dels Moros de Calapatá	53
Calapatá	54
Chimiachas	55
Piezarrodilla	56
Cerrao I and II	57
Cabras blancas	58
Prado de las Olivanas	59
Muriecho	60
Fariceu	61

Spanish Levantine Art. The Graphic Legacy of the last Hunter-Gatherers in Western Europe

Ramon Viñas Vallverdú*

1. Introduction

After the authenticity of the Palaeolithic paintings in Altamira cave (Santillana del Mar, Santander) had been recognised scientifically, a chapter of splendour opened up for archaeological research and discoveries of prehistoric art, not only in Spain but in the whole world. Émile Cartailhac's article "*La grotte d'Altamira, Espagne. 'Mea culpa' d'un sceptique*" (Cartailhac, 1902) put an end to two decades of debate between the more sceptical archaeologists and others who supported the authenticity of those prehistoric documents.

There is not the slightest doubt that the suspicion and scepticism towards rock art, expressed by the great personalities of archaeological science in the late nineteenth century, like Gabriel de Mortillet and E. Cartailhac himself, had repercussions on other major discoveries. Some of these, like J. Marconell's discovery (1892) of rock-shelters with rock art, known as "Toros de la Losilla" (Prado del Navazo and Cocinilla del Obispo, in Albarracín, Teruel), went completely unnoticed and aroused no interest in the archaeological world. Those magnificent friezes, with realistic bulls painted in white, were the first evidence of another unknown prehistoric rock art in the pre-littoral area of Mediterranean Spain, which would later be given the name of Spanish Levantine Art.

In 1903, a year after E. Cartailhac's article in *L'Anthropologie*, Juan Cabré published other rock paintings located in a rock-shelter known as Roca dels Moros or "dels Cuartos" in the ravine of Calapatà in Cretas (Teruel). At this site, three stags, represented with great detail and painted in red, were studied and published later by Henri Breuil and Juan Cabré (Breuil and Cabré, 1909). However, it was another find in the area of Las Garrigues in Lleida which caught the attention of international researchers: La Roca dels Moros de El Cogul (Lleida). Although this site had long been known by the local inhabitants in the region, it was the village priest Ramon Huguet who in 1907 sent a note to Carreras Candi informing about some "curiosities", so that they could be included in a geographical dictionary of Catalonia.

Ramon Huguet's information was forwarded to Ceferino Rocafort, who was responsible of the Lleida section of the dictionary, and he went to the site to confirm the existence of the supposed painted figures in a small rock-shelter. C. Rocafort was astonished by the representations and wrote about them in the newspaper "La Veu de Catalunya" (10 April 1908) and in the Bulletin of the *Centre Excursionista de Catalunya* with some drawings of the figures (Rocafort, 1908a and b). The news reached Henri Breuil, who immediately set out for El Cogul to study the frieze. His results were published in the Bulletin of the *Centre Excursionista de Catalunya*. For the French scholar, the frieze at El Cogul dated to the Upper Palaeolithic (Age of the Reindeer) and, more precisely to in the Magdalenian.

According to H. Breuil, the chrono-cultural attribution of this new art in the Mediterranean basin was fully proven by a scene of bison-hunting represented in the panel at Roca dels Moros de El Cogul (Fig. 1A, 1B). However, his Palaeolithic hypothesis, which he always maintained, was argued by researchers in the *Institut d'Estudis Catalans*, like Luis Mariano Vidal, Joaquim Soler and Ceferino Rocafort, who also carried out studies of the frieze at El Cogul. In their paper, published in

* IPHES, Institut Català de Paleoecologia Humana i Evolució Social, C/ Marcel.lí Domingo s/n. Campus Sescelades, (Edifici W3), Tarragona 43007

Figure 1.A. Composition in the frieze at Roca dels Moros de El Cogul (drawing by R. Viñas, A. Alonso, E. Sarriá, 1985). *Servei d'Arqueologia, Generalitat de Catalunya*. This is the best known group, because of its thematic content (supposed phallic dance) and the long controversy over the chrono-cultural attribution of the art.

Figure 1.B. Phallic figure, surrounded by female figures, Roca dels Moros de El Cogul (Photo. R. Viñas).

the Annual of the *Institut*, they rejected the Palaeolithic age of those rock art figures and proposed a more recent date (Vidal. 1908).

In just a few years, this new original style, found in small caves, rock-shelters and walls in the open-air, was discovered at a large number of sites, such as the rock-shelters of Cueva de La Vieja (Alpera, Albacete, 1910); Cantos de la Visea in Monte Arabí, (Yecla, Murcia, 1912); Val del Charco del Agua Amarga (Alcañiz, Teruel, 1913); Cova dels Caballs, Civil, and Saltadora in the Ravine of La Valltorta (Tírig and Coves de Vinromà, Castellón, 1917); Peña del Escrito and Selva Pascuala (Villar del Humo, Cuenca, 1918) (Fig. 2); Cueva de la Araña (Bicorp, Valencia, 1920); and the main ensemble at Minateda (Minateda, Albacete, 1920).

Figure 2. Representation of a bull presiding over the ensemble at Selva Pascuala (Villar del Humo, Cuenca) (Photo J.F. Ruiz).

With those rock art sites, a Levantine area began to be defined, which today contains over a thousand locations. These are archaeological sites that apparently played an important role in the life of post-Palaeolithic hunter-gatherers, as a place for transmitting and communicating historical and cultural concepts and ritual practices.

2. Distribution Area

Up to date, the distribution area of rock-shelters with Levantine Art extends across an area of about 600 x 150km, in the pre-littoral mountains from the Catalan Coastal Chain to the Baetic System, reaching the Iberian System inland, in the mountains of Albarracín and Cuenca and the southern part of La Mancha. It thus covers the mountains and plateaux in the Autonomous Communities of Aragon, Catalonia, Valencia, Murcia, Castilla-La Mancha, and the northern part of Andalusia. Additionally, some rock art sites with figures in a Levantine style are found in other parts of the Iberian Peninsula.

However, no Levantine ensembles have been found in strictly coastal areas, either because the artists never painted in these areas or because the marine climate, which is extremely corrosive, has not allowed the preservation of the rock surfaces until the present time. The sites nearest the sea are the Rock-shelter of La Joquera (Borriol, Castellón), the ensemble of d'Ermites (Ulldecona, Tarragona) and the rock-shelter of Cabra Feixet (Perelló, Tarragona), all less than 10km from the shore line.

The places chosen by the Levantine painters were rock-shelters and walls located at altitudes between 300 and 1000m above sea level, on rugged hillsides and gentler slopes, mostly south-facing and sunny sites. They are places in a strategic position, with sources of water, for hunting wild animals like deer and ibex, or in open gentle areas with a wide panoramic view over the territory (Fig. 3).

The Levantine area displays an intricate ideographic mosaic with formal and thematic differences on regional scales, showing the existence of an ancient common cultural substrate. Despite their intrinsic particularities, it should be noted that it is difficult to draw boundaries between the different areas within this rock-art tradition, as all the regions share conceptual and technical aspects and traits (stylistic and thematic). The art represents the imagination of hunter-gatherers focused on a dual, animal and human, image.

The northern area covers the largest area from the south of Tarragona, Aragon and Valencia to the northern part of Albacete. In this group, an undeniable dynamism of the figures is seen in panels showing hunting activity, expressed in scenes of great movement, and in themes con-

Figure 3. View of the surroundings of Cingle de la Mola Remigia (Ares del Maestre, Castellón), with the location of the rock art ensembles of Cova Remigia and El Cingle in the upper escarpment (Photo. R. Viñas).

nected with honey-collecting or of a ritual and symbolic nature, in which female figures take part. Among these ensembles may be cited the rock-shelters of d'Ermites in Serra de la Pietat (Tarragona); the rock-shelters of La Valltorta, Rossegadors and Polvorin; Remigia, Cingle and Centelles (Castellón); Val del Charco del Agua Amarga, Tio Garroso, Los Trepadores, Tia Mona, Cerrao I and II (Teruel), Muriecho (Huesca); Cueva de la Araña (Valencia); Cueva de La Vieja and Minateda (Albacete).

A second or southern area extends and connects with the northern groups and reaches the regions of Jaen and Almería. In this area, the vital dynamism characterising the figures in the northern group decreases, as well as the percentage of themes connected with hunting. In contrast, there are more social and ritual scenes and compositions. Sites in this area include: La Sarga, some rock-shelters in the Moreno ravine (Valencia); los Grajos, la Fuente del Sabuco, la Cañaíca del Calar, el Milano, la Risca, Cantos de la Visera (Murcia); the main rock-shelter at Minateda and Covachas de la Solana and the Taibilla area (Albacete).

The last area covers the westernmost and inland region. This is to the south of the Iberian System, basically in the mountains of Albarracín and Cuenca. Here are found the large figures of bovids and faunal compositions with some hunting scenes. Some of these sites are the rock-shelters of Prado del Navazo, Cocinilla del Obispo (Albarracín, Teruel), Selva Pascuala, Peña del Escrito and Marmalo (Villar del Humo, Cuenca), Peñón de la Tabla del Pochico and Prado del Azogue (Aldeaquemada, Jaen), Lavaderos de Tello and Estrechos de Santoge (Vélez-Blanco, Almeria). Just as in the other areas, within this group there are ensembles displaying traits of neighbouring areas, like Prado de las Olivanas or Cabras Blancas (Tormón, Teruel) (Fig. 4), Cantos de la Visera I-II (Yecla, Murcia) and Minateda (Minateda, Albacete) (Viñas *et al.*, 1982).

3. Themes and their figures

Levantine art is identified mainly by the innovation of narrative in rock-art scenes contain-

Figure 4. Group of caprids in the rock-shelter of Cabras Blancas (Tormón, Teruel) (Photo R. Viñas).

ing the human figure, which becomes one of the elements articulating much of the content of this artistic tradition. Its study allows us to approach the symbolic thought of the artists and to analyse certain activities of both social and ritual life, as well as material and subsistence aspects.

In the panels we can see, for the first time in European prehistoric art, groups of hunters chasing deer, ibices, bulls and wild boar, gathering natural products, in scenes of violence, ritual sacrifices or executions, and in depictions of a social or ritual kind. Female figures appear in compositions that are apparently symbolic, ceremonial and sometimes of an everyday nature.

This represents a change of paradigm, which without giving up beliefs involving supernatural aspects and sacred animals such as certain figures of bulls or stags, opts to develop, in its sacred or meeting places, themes with a historical facet; fighting between warriors, executions and/or ritual sacrifices, hunting, possible mythical tales with legendary heroes, dances and, naturally, many other aspects of the ceremonial and symbolic realm, which in a certain way may have marked the annual and ritual cycle of these societies.

Several authors have defined the most significant traits of Levantine Art; for instance Herbert Kühn, who stated that: "Man is located in the centre of the Universe and if in the Palaeolithic it was expressed externally, in the Mesolithic the conquest of man was achieved in such a way that in the art it went beyond the purely magical" (Kühn, 1957). Similarly, Hans-Georg Bandi remarked that it is: "... the artistic treasure with the most life of all those we have inherited from the prehistoric people of Europe..." (Bandi, 1962). Antonio Beltrán thought that: "... perhaps the most striking characteristic of Levantine rock art is the joint presence of people and animals in the scenes: people are the subject and main actors in these friezes, lording over them as a hunter or as a warrior, sometimes as a gatherer and more rarely as a domesticator of animals or as a farmer..." (Beltrán, 1968).

With time, the addition and participation of new figures in previous scenes created true palimpsests, such as at Minateda and Cueva de la Vieja, with clear formal changes, especially in the human figures, which express graphic styles with synchronic and diachronic representations that should be studied and analysed in each region to be able to understand the evolutionary process in this tradition.

In short, the thematic content can be divided into: a) scenes with animal figures; b) scenes with human figures; c) scenes with figures of animals and humans; d) particular scenes (related to the supernatural world, anthropo-zoomorphs and ritual specialists or "shamans").

3.1. *Faunal representations*

Fauna is one of the major pillars in the study of Levantine Art. The list of species represented includes ibex, red deer, fallow deer, roe deer, chamois, bulls, wild boar, horses and, in smaller numbers, canids and insects and, sporadically, some birds, rabbits and a possible bear. The distribution of these animals is relatively uniform, although in percentages that vary in each area. However, the pre-eminence of ibices, red deer and bulls should be noted, followed by horses, wild boar and the other species.

In this group of animals, the association of two important species should be highlighted: bovids and cervids play a central role in this rock-art tradition. In numerous panels, these two animals preside over the compositions (Fig. 2 and 5). In some friezes, this relationship even creates a certain metamorphosis of the bovids, which have deer antlers added to their horns (Cueva de la Vieja and the Rock-shelter of the Toros de Las Bojadillas). This link between the two animals is equally seen in the superimposition of a stag on a bull at Cantos de la Visera. The head of the stag is seen over the bull's head, as well as the horns and antlers of them both. In these examples, the body of the bovids predominates, although it is clear that the intention was to express the symbolic alliance of a single entity (Viñas and Saucedo, 2000).

The animals may appear alone or in groups. In the first case, the isolated animal may be larger than the average size and preside over the centre of the panels as if it was a particular being, perhaps a mythical or sacred entity or an intermediary with supernatural forces. Some examples are the majestic stag at Chimiachas, the splendid bulls at Selva Pascuala and Piezarrodilla (in Cuenca and Teruel), the large stag at Minateda, and the fallow deer at Covachas de la Solana (Nerpio, Albacete). In the second case, groups of animals, they are represented in small herds with examples of the same species, in passive attitudes, at resting, trotting quietly and often sharing the

Figure 5. Ensemble in the Rock-shelter of Cañaica del Calar (Moratalla, Murcia) (R. Viñas).

same space with other animals. However, these are sometimes later additions.

At other cases, the animals become hunting prey and appear in frenetic chases harassed by the hunters' arrows. In hunting scenes, the animals take on countless forms and positions depending on the role they play in each composition. For example, the stag with its head turned backwards in an alert posture; the wild boar running, brought down or dead; the wounded ibex escaping from danger leaving a trail of blood; the red deer with an arrow in its side falling over a precipice; the hind that has fallen in a trap; the herd of deer attempting to escape from the hunters; the caprid that turns on the hunters; or the wounded bull chasing the archer; among many other scenes and situations.

3.2. Human representations

Human figures, mainly men and women but sometimes children and adolescents, are subjected to huge variability in stylistic concepts and, like the animals, they are represented in a wide range of positions and attitudes.

They are shown alone or in pairs, small groups and large groups. Most of the human figures are males, many of which appear sexless but are included in this gender because of their general appearance, carrying a bow and several arrows, and sometimes a small bag hanging from their back. In contrast, other figures carry large bags and objects. In general their bodies are naked, while some wear striking attire on their heads, arms, waist and legs consisting of feathers, caps, bent appendices like "aerials", armbands, bracelets, belts, ribbons and suspended elements and possibly shells. The meaning of these ornaments should be attributed to their magic power (Fig. 6A and 6B).

Regarding the scanty clothes of the male figures, it may be noted that the legs of some figures are extremely robust, which suggests that they are wearing breeches or trouser-like protectors.

These hunters are shown in numerous postures and attitudes: standing, walking, running, resting and even climbing. In hunting scenes they are

Figure 6-A. Group of archers at Cova Centelles (Albocassèr, Castellón) (Photo A. Rubio).

Figure 6-B. Couple of archers at Cova dels Rossegadors or "Polvorín" (La Pobla de Benifassa, Castellón) (Photo A. Rubio).

seen following animal tracks, running and attacking their prey. In the southern area, in Castellón and Teruel, some of the bowmen are shown with their legs completely spread wide ("running as if in flight", like a dancer's leap).

They are equally found in scenes of gathering food like honey and perhaps birds' eggs, and climbing walls and trees with ropes. In some rock-shelters they are seen gathering possible fruit or acorns that they shake from the tree with a stick, perhaps to eat them or make traps, bait or decoys to attract prey, a common technique among hunter groups. In the same way, they appear in warrior dances, in skirmishes, wounded with arrows, in executions and even dead (Viñas, 1982; Viñas and Morote, 2011).

The figures regarded as females, although less common than the male figures, generally represent a highly significant role as their participation in the compositions often reveals a less narrative and more symbolic component, possibly connected to rites of passage, fertility, and perhaps presiding over panels in the form of "priestesses" or symbolising goddesses, among other possible roles (Fig. 7). However, they also appear in tasks of food gathering or carrying burdens and objects.

Like the male figures, the females may be shown alone, in pairs or in groups. With some exceptions, they generally appear rather static or passive, as at La Roca dels Moros (Cogul, Lleida); Racó Gasparo (Ares del Maestre Castellón); Cova Centelles (Albocassèr, Castellón); Abrigo del Lucio (Bicorp, Valencia); Val del Charco del Agua Amarga (Alcañiz,

Figure 7. Female figures in the Rock-shelter of La Risca, Moratalla (Photo. M. Loperena).

Teruel); La Risca (Moratalla, Albacete); Solana de las Covachas (Nerpio, Albacete); Cueva de la Vieja (Alpera, Albacete) and Minateda (Minateda, Albacete). Only in Cueva de los Grajos (Yecla, Murcia) do the female figures display certain movement with their arms in a dancing position. However, in this case the ensemble contains traits and figures typical of Schematic Art, belonging to a later time, which means that these female figures correspond to a late or final stage of the Levantine tradition.

Few women appear naked, like the males usually are. Some examples are the seated "venus" at Cova del Puntal in Albocassèr (Castellón), or the apparently pregnant woman at Los Chaparros in Albalate del Arzobispo (Teruel). Most of the figures described as females are shown wearing a long tight or bell-shaped skirt that sometimes ends in triangles that hang down. These skirts reach the knees (e.g. at Cogul, Fig. 1) and occasionally the feet, as can be seen at the Rock-shelter of La Pareja in Dos Aguas (Valencia).

As regards the women's clothes, some figures with tiny breasts appear with a wide upper part of their legs, as if they were wearing a skirt tucked up or breeches in the form of bloomers. These figures are seen carrying burdens or possibly children on their shoulders, in a scene in the Centelles rock-shelter, where the group appear to be moving campsite.

Several researchers have pointed out that the women's torso seems to be uncovered. However, without taking issue with this possibility, it should be said that far too often sexual identification has been made simply on the basis of the figures wearing a skirt or having slightly wider hips. In many of these figures the breasts are not shown, and when they are, they are small or tiny. Large breasts, reaching almost to the waist, have been described at a few sites, such as the rock-shelter of Roca dels Moros (El Cogul, Lleida), but it should be borne in mind that ceremonial attire, such as necklaces and breast adornments, could be confused with breasts. Therefore, on the evidence, it is difficult to demonstrate that the women's upper part of their body was naked. It is true that in the case of small breasts, the images aim to represent adolescents or girls in the initial stage of puberty. However, it would be necessary to examine many other figures not wearing a skirt in order to differentiate the genders.

The adornments worn by the women include a possible diadem holding their hair over their forehead, which produces the typical triangular medium-length hair style. They also wear armbands, short ribbons hanging from their elbows, necklaces and possible breast adornments.

One special trait is represented by certain human figures in the northern area (Castellón, Tarragona and Teruel), which display animal features, sometimes with a mythical or supernatural appearance. These are interpreted as "hunting and forest spirits" (Bandi, 1962); "masked dancers" (Ripoll, 1963), "wizards, sorcerers and masked figures" (Beltrán, 1965) and classed as "anthropozoomorphs" (Viñas and Martínez, 2001). It should be recalled that the terms "wizard" and "sorcerer" have traditionally been applied to all anthropozoomorphs with horns. However, some scholars of Palaeolithic art have noted that they represent a characteristic of Palaeolithic thought and that they involve "something more than a vague magic or an unknown deity" (Leroi-Gourhan, 1984). A very subtle and prudent way of approaching the more symbolic and shamanistic world.

However, among the complex anthropo-zoomorph representations, there are particular and specific traits for each type, which may indicate the role each figure played in ritual acts. Although any interpretation is always risky and hypothetical, some of the sites where these scenes were painted can be described, such as El Cingle, Cova Remigia and Racó Molero (Ares del Maestre, Castellón). At El Cingle, a person-bull is next to an individual with a thick tail, who has deer antlers on his head. The first person, with the bull's head, is carrying a possible bow and has very thin legs, a long tail, a tiny breast and an abdominal bulge. These characteristics, somewhat androgynous, could symbolise a state of pregnancy or the capacity of regeneration. Its physiognomy confers it a role equivalent to the so-called "Spirit of the Forest" or "Lord of the Animals", while the person at its side might personify a ritual specialist or shaman, with his auxiliary spirits that assist him and guide him in his ritual.

The site of Racó Molero is near this rock-shelter and it also contains an ensemble with a solitary man-bull, described as a sorcerer or dancer (Beltrán, 1965). This person, in a static position, has a bull's head with a body with few details, painted with simple lines without highlighting muscles, but indicating a penis, possibly to emphasise his male role. He holds a possible bow and two arrows. His human anatomy, without a tail, suggests he is a possible mediator, a ritual specialist or shaman, perhaps the male counterpart of the supposed "Spirit of the Forest" in El Cingle.

Similarly, at Cova Remigia, a possible rite of passage contains two human figures with thick tails. They seem to be a ritual specialist or teacher and a novice being initiated in contact with the supernatural world through trance.

These interpretative proposals are integrated within a coherent system in the model of hunting as a symbolic exchange. This model expresses how hunting was conceived by these groups as benefiting from the alliance established with the supernatural world by a representative of the group, the ritual specialist or shaman (Viñas and Martínez, 2001).

4. The stylistic concept and technique

The term of Levantine Art has been used for a series of rock-art ensembles with a figurative conception, and a realistic and stylised character. This style is constructed from the images, with are generally small (between 5 and 25cm) but include exceptional miniatures contrasting with colossal figures 50cm or more in size.

Levantine Art basically uses two techniques: painting and engraving. The figures may be painted in one or two colours, while the engravings display a technique of fine, simple lines, sometimes with scraping. There are more painted representations than engravings (Fig. 8).

Both techniques, painting and engraving, may be combined as in the northern area (Teruel and Lleida). The figures show that the process began with the outline of the image being engraved with a fine simple line, and later the painted image filled or was superimposed on this. However, this order was not always followed, as in other cases the engraving seems to have only added details to certain parts of the painted figures. These are nearly always animal figures that were published in old reports (Cabré, 1915; Almagro, 1952).

More recently, several finds of engravings in a Levantine style have been made in Barranco Hondo in Castellote (Teruel) and in the rock-shelter of Perellada IV in Capçanes (Tarragona). The former contains some animals, such as a stag and stylised quadruped, both with striated lines in their head, neck and legs, as well as a schematic human figure and two archers with a stylised body and thick legs. These are the first human figures in a Levantine style to be discovered that were engraved mainly with the technique of scraping (Utrilla and Villaverde, 2004). In the second rock-shelter there are two stags and a headless animal; all three figures are represented by their outlines with striated lines inside their bodies (Viñas and Sarriá, 2009-2010). All these figures are similar technically to other animal depictions that have been dated in late Palaeolithic or Epipalaeolithic times, as at Abric de'n Melia rock-shelter in Castellón (Villaverde, 2005) and the rock-shelter of Cingle del Barranc de l'Espigolar, with engraved deer, signs and quadrupeds, together with some Levantine and Schematic paintings (Guillem and Martínez, 2009).

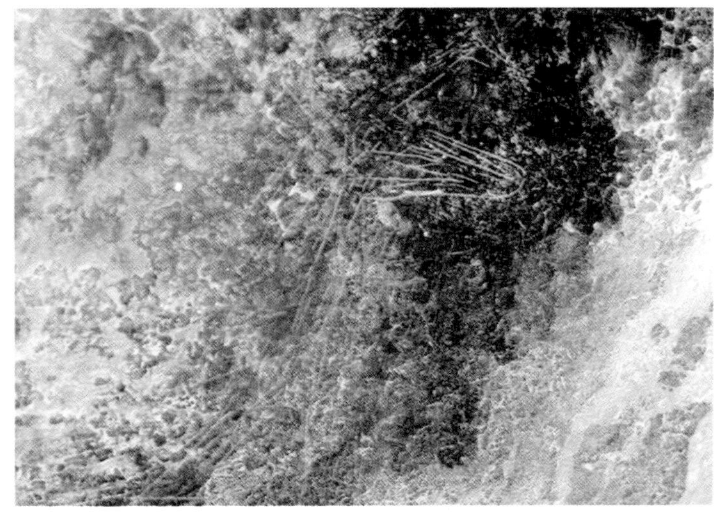

Figure 8. Detail of a stag's head, engraved with fine and multiple lines in the Rock-shelter of Llabería V (Capçanes, Tarragona) (Photo A. Rubio).

The palette of the Levantine painters contained a small range of pigments: red (red-brown, purple and orange), black (blackish and bluish-black) and white (whitish and milky). Most of the figures are painted in a single colour, although in certain regions two different tones were combined or details were added with a second colour; for example, red-brown with details in black (Roca dels Moros de El Cogul), red-brown with details in white (Coves de Centelles, dels Caballs and del Civil in Valltorta-Gasulla), dark brown and blackish with details in white (Coves del Civil). Some of the figures published in the 1930s, with two colours, have lost many of the details added in white (Cabré, 1925, Viñas and Morote, 2013). This suggests that the figures in many other regions may have suffered the same fate.

Numerous figures were restored, repainted and modified, producing a false effect of two colours. However, in some cases, when the figures were repainted part of the body was intentionally respected and the image was thus represented in two tones.

Mineral pigments were used, such as iron and manganese oxides. These were ground up and then mixed with a sticky plant or animal agglutinant. They may also have been diluted in water and applied directly in a liquid state.

If the outline of some human figures and numerous animals are examined in detail, it can be seen that very fine instruments were used to paint them, in order to represent for example the faces of the people or the hooves of the ungulates. Therefore, it is possible that some type of brush was used, made from plant elements, hairs or small feathers. The way the paint was applied can be observed in some animal figures. The outline was painted and then the inside of the body was filled with a colour-wash or with longitudinal, transversal and criss-crossing lines.

In human figures, the same method was used, drawing the outline and filling the body with colour-wash. When two colours were used, in some archers, a milky white pigment was used to add fine details and adornments like diadems, feathered caps, arm-bands, bracelets, belts, ribbons at the knees and body paint in the form of parallel and transversal lines on the torso, paint on the penis, and dots on the thorax and legs. Similarly, white dots are seen on the body and skirts of some female figures (Viñas and Morote, 2013).

The canon of human figures (men, women and some children) concentrates on flat silhouettes with realistic and stylised features, which may even form purely linear and schematic individuals. In general, they consist of an outline with a twisted profile, which is to say the torso is shown from the front or slightly on one side, and the rest of the body in profile and sometimes slightly leaning. In the same way, the animals are shown from the side, with the horns seen from the front or turned, and sometimes the legs are placed in certain perspective. As mentioned above, careful detail is taken in the outline, from the ears to the hooves. In the case of stags, isolated heads have been documented at such sites as Saltadora and Solana de las Covachas.

Human figures display great typological diversity and have been the subject of different classifications based on morphological types and graphic phases. The first scholars to attempt a typological systematisation were P. Wernert and H. Obermaier who in their study of the paintings at La Valltorta established three main types as well as a fourth they called "Alpera". The first type referred to proportioned forms with realistic features and thick robust legs. The second included figures with a stylised body, a thin torso, long legs and clearly marked calves. The third type included both proportioned and stylised figures in a linear style with no indication of muscles. The fourth type (Alpera) designated the most proportioned and realistic figures (Obermaier and Wernert, 1919). However, this classification was overtaken by the large number of morphotypes that have been identified since then.

Some time later, in an old essay, a proposal was made with a typological structure that took the size of the head as the mean unit of the human figures. This corresponds to an eighth of the length of the body, in a proportion taken from the "Golden Ratio and Lamé's theorem". With this method a new classification was established with 11 types (6 for the more proportioned forms and 5 for the disproportioned or stylised figures) (Viñas, 1988).

Other proposals have recently been made for the Valltorta-Gasulla group by I. Domingo, based on graphic phases and enlarging the classification through patterns of superimpositions and additions seen in human figures in the following sequence: 1. Centelles Phase; 2. Civil Phase; 3. Mas d'en Josep Phase; 4. Tolls Phase; 5. Cingle Phase; and 6. Linear Phase (Domingo, 2005).

However, the quantity and changes in the styles of the human figures, with several variations and sub-types across the whole area with Levantine paintings, means that it is necessary to carry out regional research on the evolutionary process (based on superimpositions, compositional studies and chromatic stratigraphies) in order to construct a general typological structure for Levantine Art.

5. Hypotheses on the chrono-cultural attribution

The accumulation, diversity and superimposition of figures at numerous sites like Minateda, Cueva de La Vieja and Cova Remigia among many others, are indicative of a temporal factor in the formation of these palimpsests. However, after a century of research on Levantine Art, the chrono-cultural aspect, about its origin and development, is still a matter of debate and controversy.

However, the main problems faced in this discussion are: a) the absence of portable art (located in dated archaeological deposits) truly comparable with the parietal paintings; and b) the lack of both direct and indirect dating for the rock art.

The history of this debate begins with H. Breuil, a pioneer in the study of Levantine Art, when he claimed that the paintings at Roca dels Moros de El Cogul belonged to the Palaeolithic, because of a hunting scene with a bison that he dated in the Magdalenian period (Breuil, 1908). This researcher attempted to prove the presence of Quaternary fauna at other rock-art sites, as well as their link with an African origin in the Capsian. In 1920, he dated the main rock-shelter at Minateda in the Perigordian (27,000 – 20,000 BC) with a later Magdalenian influence (15,000 – 9000 BC) (Breuil, 1920).

H. Breuil's theories were rapidly accepted by scholars as H. Obermaier, P. Wernert, P. Bosch Gimpera, J. Cabré and L. Pericot, but contested by others, like M. Pallarés, A. Duràn, J. Colominas, E. Hernández Pacheco, M. Santa-Olalla, P. Graziosi, H.G. Bandi, M. Almagro and finally by J. Cabré himself. They held doubts about the Quaternary fauna and their Palaeolithic attribution, and inclined towards a Neolithic date, which coincided with the archaeological deposits known at that time in the surroundings of the rock-art sites. Since that beginning, the chrono-cultural arguments became polarised between those who supported a Palaeolithic origin and those who postulated a Neolithic age. These propositions have been maintained until the present time.

However, some of these authors began to situate the origin of Levantine Art in the post-Palaeolithic periods: the Epipalaeolithic and Mesolithic (M. Almagro, 1952). In the 1960s and 70s, Eduardo Ripoll and Antonio Beltrán added their support to this theory by systematising the development of Levantine Art in four theoretical phases. For Ripoll these were summarised in the following framework:

A. Naturalistic phase: 1. Early period (bulls at Albarracín and large figures). 2. Recent period (deer at Calapatá and other isolated animals).
B. Static stylised phase.
C. Dynamic stylised phase.
D. Transition phase to the schematic facies (Ripoll, 1964 and 2001).

The first phase (A) was produced by Epipalaeolithic populations (6500 – 4000 BC), whereas the next two phases (B and C) would have been in contact with and influenced by the first Neolithic populations on the Mediterranean coast, with simple agriculture and small-scale animal husbandry, which extended towards the hinterland. Finally, the last phase (D) would be contemporary with the first metallurgy.

However, some years later, E. Ripoll stated that: "This working hypothesis, which was valid over a quarter of a century ago, in the light of new discoveries suffers from excessive simplicity, as we have said, but it was accepted in a more or less simplified way by other authors" (Ripoll, 2001: 273-274).

In turn, A. Beltrán noted that: "As a debatable working hypothesis, the following phases could be established".

1. Ancient or naturalistic phase, of an Aurignacian-Perigordian tradition, contemporary with the Epipalaeolithic (6000 – 3500 BC), with its apogee before 5000 BC. It coincides with Ripoll's naturalistic Phase A and his periods 1 (bulls at Albarracín, as well as at La Araña, Minateda and El Cingle, and the deer at Val del Charco) and 2 (deer at Calapatá). It is very likely that this phase, as in Palaeolithic art, would also include geometric signs and figures with a schematic air, as seen in superimpositions at La Sarga, La Araña and Cantos de la Visera, where there is a superimposition of deer-bull-schematic bird.
2. Central phase, with the slow disappearance of bulls and an abundance of deer and i, and the appearance of barely naturalistic human figures, while the animals follow the tradition in Phase I. It can be dated after 4000 BC. It coincides with Ripoll's static-stylised Phase B and one of its clearest examples would be the central panel of large figures in Cueva Remigia. The 0.60m-tall figure of a woman at Val del Charco represents the transition from Phase I to Phase II.
3. Development phase (Ripoll's dynamic-stylised Phase C), between 3500 and 2000 BC, contemporary with the Neolithic on the coastal plains. The running human figures and the correction of animal naturalism through movement would be its most significant characteristics.

4. Final phase, with a return to static figures and a tendency towards schematic forms, as well as the introduction of an early agriculture with straight or angled digging sticks and the domestication of animals (dogs at Alpera and later horses and donkeys). It can be dated after 2000 and at least until 1200, the date of the helmeted horseman at Cingle de la Remigia. This phase would therefore enter in the Eneolithic and Bronze Age I (Beltrán, 1968).

The development of Levantine Art was envisaged with a first phase beginning in the Epipalaeolithic and restricted to large animal figures, bulls and some deer. A phase still without human figures and in which, according to A. Beltrán, some geometric figures and schematic elements, like those at La Sarga and Cantos de la Visera, should be included. This phase was followed in the Neolithic by another with fewer large bulls and the presence of deer, and ibex as well as stylised and static human figures. For Beltrán, the finest stage in Levantine Art would be in the third phase, with greater dynamism in the figures, contemporary with the Neolithic on the coastal plains. The fourth phase, dated in the Eneolithic and early Bronze Age would represent a return to the initial static styles, representing an incipient agriculture with digging sticks and domestic animals. In short, these models proposed a development between the Epipalaeolithic and the Eneolithic (Viñas and Morote, in press).

6. Discussion

Contrasting with these theories, which dated the first Levantine paintings to about 8000 or 6000 BC, M. Santa Olalla and Francisco Jordá situated Levantine Art in the Bronze Age. For F. Jordá, this art had its origin in the Neolithic of the eastern Mediterranean and had been imported in two stages: Syrian-Anatolian and Egyptian-Palestinian. According to this scholar, Levantine Art expressed ranked social structures, with hunting and war chiefs, as well as a religious structure with intermediaries between the deities and humans. In addition, male and female anthropomorphic and phallic deities were associated with hunting and agriculture, and were honoured with dances and games with animals, in short, a society with strong matrilineal roots, typical of agricultural societies (Jordá, 1966, 1975 and 1976).

In the early 1980s, F. J. Fortea compared the portable art discovered in the archaeological deposit in Cueva de la Cocina (Dos Aguas, Valencia) with the rock art at Cantos de la Visera, where square and grille-shaped geometric paintings are found underneath Levantine paintings.

Although the geometric figure at Cantos de la Visera is quite different formally from the incised motifs on the 35 plaquettes at La Cocina, which are decorated with linear lines and radial groups, Fortea deduced the existence of an Epipalaeolithic geometric linear art previous to the Levantine figures, as also seen at La Sarga and Cueva de la Araña. This scholar claimed that the archaeological context of Levantine Art did not go beyond the Epipalaeolithic and that in most cases the materials were dated in the Neolithic and Bronze Age (Fortea, 1974, 1975).

The important discoveries of Macro-schematic art in the area of Alicante, made by members of the *Centre d'Estudis Contestans* in the early 1980s and published by Mauro Hernández (1994-2000), were associated with the praying figures impressed on cardial pottery at Cova de l'Or de Beniarrès (Valencia). This new style unified all the large schematic motifs, like those at Cova de la Sarga, discovered in 1951, with Levantine figures of deer associated with the Macro-schematic types. All these deer were considered later than the Macro-schematic of the cardial Neolithic period. However, other studies have expressed some doubts about the superimpositions at La Sarga and proposed a reversed order in the chromatic stratigraphy, according to which some deer would be later and one of them previous or synchronic with the Macro-schematic figures (Viñas, 2012).

Additionally, among the fragments of epi-cardial pottery in Cova de l'Or there are other impressed designs of an ibex, a bovid and a cervid, which were immediately associated with Levantine Art. However, there are some discrepancies between the zoomorphs on Neolithic pottery and those in Levantine rock art and this need to be studied in detail. For example, the internal decoration of the impressed animals seems to follow a pattern of parallel bands, apparently inherited from ancient Epipalaeolithic forms. The decorations of wild animals on epi-cardial pottery may also be taken from preceding periods and be the result of cultural syncretism. In addition, the Neolithic in Valencia, in the centre of the area of Levantine Art, must have acquired elements deeply rooted in the ancient populations, such as

Figure 9. Frieze at the Cueva de Tío Modesto (Henarejos, Cuenca) with hunting scenes and abstract motifs (Photo. J. F. Ruiz).

deer, bulls and ibex, and simply incorporated them in the pottery (Viñas and Morote, 2011).

In recent years, some research projects have attempted to date Levantine and Schematic paintings indirectly through the calcium oxalate on the superficial layers and calcareous coverings related to the paintings, using the AMS radiocarbon method (Ruiz *et al.*, 2006, 2009, 2012). The presence of calcium oxalate, produced by micro-organisms, had been detected on surfaces with Levantine paintings in the 1970s (Viñas, 1978).

At some rock-art sites in the area of Cuenca, Juan Ruiz has carried out several chronometric studies, and obtained the first dates associated with the paintings. In the frieze in Cueva de Tío Modesto (Henarejos, Cuenca), Levantine and zigzag abstract signs and stripes are mixed together, forming a number of superimpositions. Two samples were dated with the results of 5230 – 5010 cal BC and 4830 – 4610 cal BC for two samples of oxalate layers covering a series of zigzags, thought to be the first phase in the frieze (Ruiz *et al.*, 2006, 2009). However, a later re-examination showed that the zigzags also covered one of the Levantine figures, and in consequence this figure is older than the zigzags and the dates obtained (Viñas, 2012) (Fig. 9).

At other sites, like the Rock-shelter of Marmalo III, a sample that was apparently rejuvenated, taken next to a large Levantine bovid, was dated to 5980 – 5730 cal BC. For now, the sample indicates that the bovid corresponds to an earlier date. Soon afterwards, at the Rock-shelter of Selva Pascuala, Panel 2 (with schematic and semi-figurative motifs) another surface was dated to 2280 – 1440 cal BC (Ruiz *et al.*, 2009) and at the Rock-shelter of Los Oculados, with schematic figures, a period between 910 – 540 cal BC and 3630 -3365 cal BC was determined (Ruiz *et al.*, 2012). It is clear that this line of chronometric research represents a way forwards.

Together with these theories, proposals and research, the matter of the Levantine engravings remains to be studied. There are engravings that precede the paintings or were used as preliminary sketches, and others without any connection with paintings. Most of these are representations of animals, lines, signs and hardly any human figures. This technique, as stated above, mostly involves fine and striated lines, which derives from a technique that was widely used in the late Upper Palaeolithic and therefore this possible link between the last Palaeolithic art and the first Levantine art should be taken into account (Viñas *et al.*, 2012; Viñas, 2012).

Regarding this aspect, other authors like Miguel A. Mateo have commented that figurative art, concentrating mainly on animal figures, did not disappear at the end of the Palaeolithic. On the contrary, it continued during Epipalaeolithic periods until the ninth millennium BP, as indicated by absolute dates provided by some archaeological deposits with portable art, including animals engraved with similar multiple lines, such as at Fariseu in the Vale do Côa (Portugal) with a date of 8930 ± 80 BP (Bueno, Balbín and Alcolea 2007, 2009; Mateo, 2012). For this author, perhaps "... it is not too risky to relate these parietal and portable engravings in the Mediterranean area with the typical figures in Style V [Palaeolithic], with which they share the technique of fine incisions and no few formal conventionalisms..." (Mateo, 2012).

Although there is no doubt that we now possess a vast store of information about the Levantine world, it is equally true that research is still incapable of giving a definitive explanation of the chrono-cultural development of Levantine Art. However, with the evidence and discoveries that are still appearing, our provisional proposal about the origin and evolution of Levantine Art is as follows:

A. Initial stage: 10,000 – 8000 BC

First links between the Palaeolithic and Epipalaeolithic:

1) Final Palaeolithic engravings in such rock-shelters as Melià, Espigolar and Llaberia IV, similar to Palaeolithic parietal and portable art in the Mediterranean basin (Cova del Parpalló, Cova Matutano, Molí del Salt and other sites).

B. Epipalaeolithic: 8000 – 7000 BC

Continuation of Palaeolithic techniques and themes and the first examples of Levantine paintings:

1) Fine engravings of animals in a Levantine style, as at Llabería and Barranco Hondo.
2) Outlines of animals, engraved with fine lines and then painted, as at Albarracín, Calapatà and Cogul.
3) Large isolated animals at Minateda, and some at Albarracín, Piezarrodilla and Covachas de la Solana. It should be borne in mind that the large size of the animals is not an indicator of their age, as they are found throughout the Levantine sequence.
4) Human figures in different formats, depending on the local or regional development: Nerpio, Minateda, Valltorta-Gasulla, Cuenca and Albarracin
5) Some abstract elements should be included in this stage. Grille-shapes at Cantos de la Visera and perhaps some serpentiforms (frequent in the Magdalenian).

C. Epipalaeolithic-Mesolithic: 7500 – 5500 BC

Development of Levantine Art

1) Animal and human figures continue in all types of sizes and styles.
2) Some Levantine figures are added on top of other Levantine figures in all the large assemblages.
3) Finely-engraved and scraped figures continue to be produced, at Llaberia IV and in human figures at Barranco Hondo.
4) The technique of using finely engraved lines to fill animal bodies with longitudinal marks is copied in painting.
5) Human figures are produced in an extraordinary variety of forms and achieve their greatest expressiveness in movement.
6) The themes are varied with animals, archers, some female figures, hunting, fighting and gathering scenes and ceremonies and rituals.
7) Some figures begin to be repainted, as at Piezarrodilla, Olivanas (black bulls), Cogul (red bulls), Cabra Feixet (hind), stags at La Vieja (Alpera), etc.

D. Early Neolithic and Levantine Art: 5500 – 4000 BC

Mesolithic groups continue to come to their sacred sites and meeting places and maintain their tradition of painting, while the neolithisation process begins to develop and a new iconography is introduced with a symbolic content that is the opposite of the Levantine world: Macro-schematic Art.

1) Large Macro-schematic figures are produced and, at La Sarga these partially cover a deer, while some deer are later superimposed on the Macro-schematic figures.
2) It seems that in this stage certain scenes with animals and humans, such as the last female figures at El Cogul, La Vieja, La Risca and later Los Grajos, continue to be repainted and added to.
3) The technique of fine engraving disappears in rock art but is maintained in the painted fill inside the figures.
4) The tradition of the ancient Epipalaeolithic and Mesolithic cults and part of the beliefs expressed in Levantine Art is transferred and survives in the Neolithic, as shown by the cardial pottery in the area of Alicante.
5) The Neolithic groups add some schematic figures and compositions to the old Levantine ensembles.

E. Decline of Levantine Art: 4000 – 3000 BC

During the Chalcolithic-Bronze Age, some Levantine sites were still visited, as can be seen at Cogul. Mainly schematic representations are painted at them, although it seems that in some area the last figures in the Levantine tradition were produced.

1) The last Leventine representations appear to wear some adornments that can be interpreted as Neolithic or Chalcolithic objects.
2) Figures with "semi-schematic" or "semi-figurative" characteristics are produced, reminiscent of the Levantine style, as at Selva Pascuala, Doña Clotilde, Cañada de Marco and some sites in the Province of Cadiz. This concept marks a definitive change and the end of Levantine Art (Viñas, 2012).

We believe that research needs to reappraise and carefully analyse all the data provided by the rock art sites and their archaeological contexts. The origin and development of this phenomenon cannot be explained without comparing the information from each of the areas and, in turn, cross-referencing it with the context of the Iberian Peninsula in which it formed and developed. Only by advancing through new studies and significant discoveries shall we be able to solve the current problems.

11
BIBLIOGRAPHY

Bibliography

Adán, G., Arribas, A., Barbadillo, J., Cervera, J., Estrada, R., García, M.A., Jordá, J.F., Pastor, J., Sánchez, B., Sánchez, A., Sanchiz, B., Sesé, C., 1995. Prospecciones y excavaciones arqueológicas en el Alto Valle del Jarama (Valdesotos, Guadalajara, Castilla - La Mancha). Arqueología en Guadalajara. Patrimonio Histórico - Arqueología Castilla-La Mancha 12, Toledo, pp. 111-124.

Adán, G., Jordá Pardo, J., 1989. Industrias óseas del Paleolítico y postpaleolítico pirenaico en relación con los nuevos hallazgos de Jarama II (Guadalajara), Espacio, Tiempo y Forma, serie I Prehistoria y Arqueología 2, 109-130.

Adserias, M., Bartroli, R., 2007. L'ocupació prehistòrica de la Balma de l'Auferí, Jornades d'Arqueologia, Tortosa 1999, Serv. d'Arqueologia, Barcelona, pp.73-86.

Adserias, M., Bartroli, R., Cebrià, A., Farell, D., Gamarra, A., Miró, J.M., 1996. La Balma de l'Auferí (Margalef de Montsant, Priorat): un nou assentament prehistòric a la Vall del Montsant, Tribuna d'Arqueologia 1994-1995, 39-50.

Aguirre Ruiz de Gopegui, M., 2013. Ocupaciones gravetienses de Antoliñako koba: aproximación preliminar a su estratigrafía, cronología e industrias, in: Pensando el Gravetiense: nuevos datos para la Región Cantábrica en su contexto, Actas del Coloquio Internacional Gravetiense cantábrico: Estado de la Cuestión, Museo de Altamira, 2011, org. Universidades de Oviedo, Cantabria, País Vasco y Ministerio de Cultura, pp.216-228.

Aguirre, E., 1964. Las Gándaras de Budiño. Porriño (Pontevedra). Madrid, Ministerio de Educación Nacional. Dirección General de Bellas Artes. Servicio Nacional de Excavaciones Arquelógicas.

Aguirre, E., Butzer, K. W., 1967. Problematic Pleistocene Artifact Assemblage from Northwestern Spain, Science 157, 430-431.

Aguirre, M., 1996. Resultados de la aplicación de la Estratigrafía Analítica en el sondeo estratigráfico de Antoliñako koba (Gautegiz-Arteaga, Bizkaia), Krei 1, 37-56.

Aguirre, M., 2001. El yacimiento paleolítico de Antoliñako koba (Gautegiz-Arteaga, Bizkaia): secuencia estratigráfica y dinámica industrial. Avance de las campañas de excavación 1995-2000, Illunzar 98/00 4, 39-81.

Aguirre, M., González Sáinz, C., 2011. Canto con grabado figurativo del Gravetiense de Antoliñako koba (Gautegiz-Arteaga, Bizkaia). Implicaciones en la caracterización de las primeras etapas de la actividad gráfica en la región Cantábrica, Kobie (Serie Paleoantropología) 30, 43-62.

Aguirre, M., López Quintana, J.C., Sáenz de Buruaga, A., 2001. Medio ambiente, industrias y poblamiento prehistórico en Urdaibai (Gernika, Bizkaia) del Würm reciente al Holoceno medio. Illunzar 98/00 4, 13-38.

Agustí, B., 1998. Els rituals funeraris en el període calcolí tic-bronze final al nord-est de Catalunya, Tesis doctoral, Universitat de Girona, Girona.

Agustí, J., Blain, H.-A., Cuenca-Bescós, G., Bailón, S., 2009. Climate forcing the first hominid dispersal in Western Europe, Journal of Human Evolution 57, 815-821.

Agustí, J., Blain, H.-A., Furió, M., De Marfá, R., Santos-Cubedo, A., 2010. The early Pleistocene small vertebrate succession from the Orce region (Guadix-Baza Basin, SE Spain) and its bearing on the first human occupation of Europe, Quaternary International 223-224, 162-169.

Agustí, J., Madurell, J., 2003. Los arvicólidos (Muroidea, Rodentia, Mammalia) del Pleistoceno inferior de Barranco León y Fuente Nueva-3 (Orce, Granada). Datos preliminares, in: Toro, I., Agustí, J., Martínez-Navarro, B. (Eds.) El Pleistoceno inferior de Barranco León y Fuente Nueva 3, Orce (Granada). Memoria científica campañas 1999-2002. Arqueología Monografías, Consejería de Cultura, Junta de Andalucía. pp. 137-145.

Alberdi, M.T., 2010. Estudio de los caballos de los yacimientos de Fuente Nueva-3 y Barranco León-5 (Granada), in: Toro, I., Martínez-Navarro, B., Agustí, J. (Eds.), Ocupaciones Humanas en el Pleistoceno inferior y medio de la Cuenca de Guadix-Baza. Junta de Andalucía. Consejería de Cultura. Arqueología Monografías, pp. 291-306.

Alberdi, M.T., Alonso, MA., Azanza, B., Hoyos, M., Morales, J., 2001. Vertebrate taphonomy in circum-lake environments: three cases in the Guadix-Baza Basin (Granada, Spain), Palaeogeogrphy, Palaeoclimatology, Palaeoecology 165, 1-26.

Alberdi, M.T., Bonadonna, FP., 1989. Geología y Paleontología de la Cuenca de Guadix-Baza. Trabajos sobre el Neógeno-Cuaternario, Museo Nacional de Ciencias Naturales, CSIC, Madrid.

Alberdi, M.T., Ruiz-Bustos, A., 1985. Descripción y significado bioestratigráfico del Equus e Hipopótamo en el yacimiento de Venta Micena (Granada), Estudios Geológicos 41, 251-261.

Alcalde del Río, H., 1906. Las pinturas y grabados de las cavernas prehistóricas de la Provincia de Santander. Altamira, Covalanas, Hornos de la Peña y El Castillo, Blanchard y Arce, Santander.

Alcalde del Río, H., Breuil, H., Sierra, L., 1911. Les cavernes de la Région Cantabrique (Espagne), A. Chéne, Mónaco.

Alcalde, G., 1983. Els micromamífers del Cau del Roure (Serinyà, Gironès). Amics de Besalú. IV Assemblea d'Estudis del seu comtat, Besalú, vol. I, pp. 71-72.

Alcalde, G., 1986. Les faunes de Rongeurs du Pléistocène Supérieur et de l'Holocène de Catalogne (Espagne) et leurs significations paléoécologiques et paléoclimatiques. These, Ecole Pratique des Hautes Études, París, p. 114.

Alcaraz-Castaño, M., López-Recio, M., Tapias, F., Rus, I., Baena, J., Morín, J., Pérez-González, A., Santonja, M., e.p., The Late Pleniglacial human occupation of Central Iberia: New technological, chronometric and palaeoenvironmental data from the Solutrean workshop of Las Delicias (Manzanares Valley, Spain), Quaternary International.

Alcolea, J.J., Balbín, R. de., 2003a. Témoins du froid. La faune dans l'art rupestre paléolithique de l'intérieurpéninsulaire, L'Anthropologie 107, 471-500.

Alcolea, J.J., Balbín, R. de., 2003b. El Arte Rupestre Paleolítico del interior peninsular. Elementos para el estudio de su variabilidad regional, in: de Balbín R., Bueno, P. (Eds), Primer Symposium Internacional de Arte Prehistórico de Ribadesella, Ribadesella, 2003, pp. 223-253.

Alcolea, J.J., Balbín, R. de., 2006a. Arte Paleolítico al aire libre. El yacimiento rupestre de Siega Verde, Salamanca. Arqueología de Castilla y León nº 16. Junta de Castilla y León.

Alcolea, J.J., Balbín, R. de., 2006b. Siega Verde y el Arte Paleolítico al aire libre del interior peninsular, in: Delibes de Castro, G., Diez Martin, F. (Eds.), El Paleolítico Superior en la Meseta Española, Studia Archaeologica nº 94, Valladolid, pp. 41-74.

Alday, A., 1996-2007. El yacimiento de Atxoste (Vírgala, Álava), Arkeoikuska (de Arkeoikuska 95 a Arkeoikuska 06). Gobierno Vasco.

Alday, A., 1998. Kanpanoste Goikoa. El depósito prehistórico de Kanpanoste Goikoa (Vírgala, Alava): memoria de las actuaciones arqueológicas 1992-1993. Memorias de Yacimientos Alaveses 5. Diputación Foral de Álava.

Alday, A., 2003. Cerámica neolítica de la región vasco-riojana: base documental y cronológica, Trabajos de Prehistoria 60, 53-80.

Alday, A., 2006. El legado prehistórico de Mendandia: los modos de vida de los últimos cazadores-recolectores en la prehistoria de Treviño, Arqueología de Castilla y León, Memorias 15.

Alday, A., 2006. El mesolítico de muescas y denticulados en la cuenca del Ebro y el litoral mediterráneo peninsular: síntesis de los datos, in: El Mesolítico de muescas y denticulados de la cuenca del Ebro y el litoral mediterráneo peninsular, Memorias de yacimientos alaveses 11, Vitoria, pp. 303-317.

Alday, A., 2007. Mésolithique et Néolithique au Pays Basque d'après l'abri de Mendandia (8500-6400BP): l'évolution de l'industrie lithique, le problème de la céramique et les stratégies d'occupation, L'Anthropologie 111 (1), 39-67.

Alday, A., Castaños, P., Perales, P., 2012. Quand ils ne pas seulement vivaient de la chasse: preuves de la domesticacion ancienne dans les gisements néolithiques d'Atxoste et de Mendandia (País Vasco), L'Anthropologie 116, 127-147.

Alday, A., Cava, A., 2006. La unidad de muescas y denticulados del Mesolítico en el País Vasco: la formalización de un modelo cultural, in: Alday, A. (Ed.), El mesolítico de muescas y denticulados en la cuenca del Ebro y el litoral mediterráneo peninsular, Memoria de Yacimientos alaveses 11, 223-300.

Alday, A., Cava, A., 2009. El Mesolítico geométrico en Vasconia, in: Utrilla, P., Montes, L. (Eds.), El Mesolítico Geométrico en la Península Ibérica, Monografías Arqueológicas 44, 93-130.

Alday, A., Juez, L., Pérez-Romero, A., Adán, G., Santos, E., Galindo-Pellicena, M., Carretero, J. M., Arsuaga, J.L., 2011. La industria ósea del Portalón de Cueva Mayor (Sierra de Atapuerca, Burgos). Biapuntados, puntas de flecha y agujas. Morfología y funcionalidad, MUNIBE (Antropologia-Arkeologia) 62, 227-249

Alday, A., Soto, A., López de Heredia, J., Perales, U., 2013. El abrigo de Martinarri (Obécuri, Treviño): una ocupación del Tardiglaciar en la Cuenca Alta del Ebro, Trabajos de Prehistoria 69 (2), 257-272.

Alférez, F. Roldán, B., 1992. Un molar humano Anteneandertal con patología traumática procedente del yacimiento cuaternario de Pinilla del Valle (Madrid), Munibe 8, 183-188.

Alférez, F., Molero, G., Maldonado, E., Bustos, V., Brea, P., Buitrago, A. M., 1982. Descubrimiento del primer yacimiento cuaternario (Riss-Würm) de vertebrados con restos humanos en la provincia de Madrid (Pinilla del Valle), Coloquios de Paleontología 37, 15-32.

Allué, E., 2002. Dinámica de la vegetación y explotación del combustible leñoso durate el Pleistoceno Superior y el Holoceno del Noreste de la Península Ibérica a partir del análisis antracológico. Tesis doctoral inédita. Universitat Rovira i Virgili, Tarragona.

Allué, E., Angelucci, D.E., Cáceres, I., Fiocchi, C., Fontanals, M., García, M., Huguet, R., Ollé, A., Saladié, P., Vergès, J. M., Zaragoza, J., 2000. La Cativera (El Catllar, Tarragona): datos preliminares sobre el límite Pleistoceno-Holoceno en el sur de Cataluña. Actas do 3º Congresso de Arqueologia Peninsular. Vol. IX. Contributos das ciências e das tecnologias para a arqueologia da Peninsula Ibérica, Porto, pp. 81-98.

Allué, E., Ibáñez, N., Saladié, P., Vaquero, M., 2010. Small preys and plant exploitation by late pleistocene hunter-gatherers. A case study from the Northeast of the Iberian Peninsula, Archaeological and Anthropological Sciences 2 (1), 11-24.

Almagro, M., 1952. El covacho con pinturas rupestres de Cogul (Lérida). Instituto de Estudios Ilerdenses, p. 93.

Almagro, M., 1973. Las pinturas y grabados de la cueva de Chufín (Ciclones, Santander), Trabajos de Prehistoria 30, 9-67.

Almagro, M., 1976. Los omoplatos decorados de la cueva de El Castillo, Puente Viesgo, Santander, Trabajos de Prehistoria 33, 9-112.

Almagro, M., Cabrera, V., Bernaldo de Quirós, F., 1977. Nuevos hallazgos de arte rupestre en Cueva Chufín, Trabajos de Prehistoria 34, 9-30.

Alonso Diago, M.A., Hoyos, M., Alberdi, MT., 2003. Tafonomía del yacimiento de vertebrados pleistocenos de Cúllar de Baza-1 (Granada, España), Revista Española de Paleontología 16, 283-298.

Altuna, J., 1972. Fauna de mamíferos de los yacimientos prehistóricos de Guipúzcoa. Con Catálogo de los Mamíferos Cuaternarios del Cantábrico y del Pirineo Occidental, Munibe 24, 1-464.

Altuna, J., 1989. La subsistance d'origine animale pendant le Moustérien dans la région Cantabrique (Espagne), in: Pathou, M., Freeman, L.G. (Eds.), L'Homme de Neandertal. La Subsistance. Actes du colloque international de Liège, vol. 6, pp. 41-43.

Altuna, J., 1992. El medio ambiente durante el Pleistoceno Superior en la región Cantábrica con referencia especial a sus faunas de mamíferos, Munibe (Antropologia - Arkeologia) 44, 13-29.

Altuna, J., 1996. Ekain und Altxerri bei San Sebastián, Zwei altsteinzeitliche Bilderhöhlen im spanischen Baskenland, Thorbecke Verlag, Sigmaringen.

Altuna, J., 1996. Hallazgo de dos nuevos bisontes en la cueva de Altxerri (Aia, País Vasco), Munibe 48, 3-6.

Altuna, J., 2009. Cueva de Ekain. 2ª fase de excavaciones. I campaña, Arkeoikuska 2008, 358-365.

Altuna, J., 2010. Cueva de Ekain. 2ª fase de excavaciones. II campaña, Arkeoikuska 2009, 345-348.

Altuna, J., Apellániz, J.Mª., 1976. Las figuras rupestres paleolíticas de la cueva de Altxerri (Guipúzcoa), Munibe 28, 1-242.

Altuna, J., Apellániz, J.Mª., 1978. Las figuras rupestres paleolíticas de la cueva de Ekain (Deva, Guipúzcoa), Munibe 30, 7-151.

Altuna, J., Baldeón, A., Mariezkurrena, K. 1985. Cazadores magdalenienses en la cueva de Erralla (Cestona-País Vasco), Munibe (Antropologia-Arkeologia) 37, 7-206.

Altuna, J., Mariezkurrena, K., 1996. Primer hallazgo de restos de antílope saiga (Saiga tatarica L.) en la Península Ibérica, Munibe 48, 3-6.

Altuna, J., Mariezkurrena, K., 2008. Nuevos hallazgos en la cueva de Ekain (Gipuzkoa, País Vasco), Zephyrvs 61, 17-32.

Altuna, J., Mariezkurrena, K., 2010. Altuna, J., Mariezkurrena, K., 2010. Pinturas rupestres en la galería superior de la cueva de Altxerri (Aia, Gipuzkoa), Zephyrus 45, 65-73.

Altuna, J., Mariezkurrena, K., 2012. Macromammalian remains from the Holocene levels in El Mirón Cave, in: Straus, L., González Morales, M. (Eds.), El Mirón Cave. University of New Mexico Press, Albuquerque, pp. 288-318.

Altuna, J., Mariezkurrena, K., 2013. Contour découpé en Ekain, Estudios en homenaje a F. Javier Fortea Pérez, Universidad de Oviedo, pp. 237-245.

Altuna, J., Mariezkurrena, K., Elorza, M., 2001-2002. Arqueozoología de los niveles paleolíticos de la cueva de Abauntz (Arraiz, Navarra), Saldvie 2, 1-26.

Altuna, J., Mariezkurrena, K., Ríos J., 2011. Ocupaciones humanas en Aitzbitarte III (País Vasco 33.600-18.400) (Zona de entrada de la cueva), EKOB 5, 1-536.

Altuna, J., Merino, J. M., 1984. El yacimiento prehistórico de la cueva de Ekain (Deba, Guipúzcoa). Sociedad de Estudios Vascos, Colección Barandiaran 1, 1-351.

Álvarez, E., 2008. The use of Columbella rustica (Class: Gastropoda) in the Iberian Peinsula and Europe during the Mesolithic and the Early Neolithic, in: Hernández, M.S., Soler, M.S., López, J.A. (Eds.), IV Congreso del Neolítico Peninsular, vol II. Alicante, pp. 103-111.

Álvarez-Alonso, D., Arrizabalaga, A., 2012. La secuencia estratigráfica inferior de la cueva de Lezetxiki (Arrasate, País Vasco). Una reflexión necesaria, Zephyrus 69, 5-29.

Álvarez-Fernández, E., Carriol, R.-P., Jordá, J.F., Aura, J.E., Avezuela, B., Badal, E., Carrión, Y., García-Guinea, J., Maestro, A., Morales, J.V., Perez, G., Perez-Ripoll, M., Rodrigo, M.J., Scarffh, J.E., Villalba, M.P., Wood, R., 2013. Occurrence of whale barnacles in Nerja Cave (Málaga, Southern Spain): indirect evidence of whale consumption by humans in the Upper Magdalenian, Quaternary International, doi: 10.1016/j.quaint.2013.01.014

Alvarez-lao, D., Arsuaga, J. L., Baquedano, E., Pérez-González, A., 2013, Last Interglacial (MIS 5) ungulate assemblage from the Central Iberian Peninsula: The Camino Cave (Pinilla del Valle, Madrid, Spain), Palaeogeography, Palaeoclimatology, Palaeoecology 374, 323-337.

Ameijenda, A., 2011. Geomorphology and Relative Chronology of the Human Occupations during the Pleistocene at the Basin of Monforte de Lemos (Lugo, Galicia), in: de Lombera, A., Fábregas, R. (Eds.), To the West of Spanish Cantabria: the Palaeolithic Settlement of Galicia, BAR International Series 2283, Archaeopress, Oxford, pp 81-91.

Anadón, P., Julià, R., de Deckker, P., Rosso, J.C., Soulié-Märsche, I., 1987. Contribución a la Paleolimnologia del Pleistoceno inferior de la cuenca de Baza (sector Orce-Venta Micena), Paleontologia I Evolució, spec. mem. 1, 35-72.

Anderung, A., Bouwman, A., Persson, P., Carretero, J.M., Ortega, A.I., Elburg, R., Smith., C. Arsuaga. J.L., Ellegren, H., Götherström, A., 2005. Prehistoric contacts over the Straits of Gibraltar indicated by genetic analysis of 3 Iberian Bronze Age cattle, Proceedings of the National Academy of Science, 102, 8431-8435.

Angelucci, D., 2003. Geoarcheology and micromorphology of Abric de la Cativera (Catalonia, Spain), Catena, núm. 54, 573-601.

Angelucci, D., 2005. Nuevas aportaciones sobre el límite Pleistoceno-Holoceno en Cataluña: los yacimientos del Abric de la Cativera i de Picamoixons (Tarragona), in: Pérez, Machado, M. J. Santonja, M. (Eds.), Geoarqueología y patrimonio de la Península Ibérica y el entorno mediterráneo, pp. 359-368.

Angelucci, D., Anesin, D., López-Martínez, M., Haber-Uriarte, M., Rodríguez-Estrella, T., Walker, M.J., 2013. Rethinking stratigraphy and site formation of the Pleistocene deposit at Cueva Negra del Estrecho del Río Quípar (Caravaca de la Cruz, Spain), Quaternary Science Reviews 80, 195-199.

Angelucci, D.E., Cáceres, I., Lozano, M., Ollé, A., Rodríguez, X.P., Vergès, J.M., 2004. El jaciment de la Cansaladeta (la Riba, Alt Camp) en el marc del Plistocè mitjà català, Cypsela 14, 151-170.

Angelucci, D.E., Gené, J.M., Ollé, A., Vaquero, M., Vergès, J.M., Allué, E., Fontanals, M., Ibáñez, N., Lozano, M., Rodríguez, X.P., Saladié, P., Zaragoza, J., 2003. Darreres intervencions arqueològiques en jaciments paleolítics de la conca del Francolí: la Cansaladeta (la Riba, Alt Camp) i el Molí del Salt (Vimbodí, Conca de Barberà), Tribuna d'Arqueologia 1999-2000, 23-63.

Angulo, J., García-Díez, M., Gómez, A. 2011. Conoce Chufín. Sociedad Regional de Cultura y Deporte, Consejería de Cultura, Turismo y Deporte, Gobierno de Cantabria. Santander.

Anónimo, 1953. La caverna de las Monedas y sus interesantes pinturas, Publicaciones del Patronato de las Cuevas Prehistóricas de Santander, Santander.

Aparicio Pérez, J., 1992. Los orígenes de Oliva, Xátiva y Benicarló. Serie Histórica, nº 7. Real Academia de Cultura Valenciana, pp.79-82.

Aparicio Pérez, J., 1994. Prehistoria de los Valles del Norte de la provincia de Alicante (Comunidad Valenciana. España). Serie Histórica del Aula de Humanidades, nº 12. Real Academia de Cultura Valenciana.

Aparicio Pérez, J., 2006. La labor de la SEAV de la Diputación Provincial de Valencia hasta 2005. Nº I. Sección de Estudios Arqueológicos V, Diputación Provincial, Valencia, pp. 36-66.

Aparicio Pérez, J., 2010. La labor de la SEAV de la Diputación Provincial de Valencia. 2005-2010. Nº V. Sección de Estudios Arqueológicos V, Diputación Provincial, Valencia, pp.11-60.

Aparicio Pérez, J., 2010. VARIA VII. Serie Arqueológica V. Sección de Estudios Arqueológicos V, Diputación Provincial, Valencia, pp. 10-19.

Aparicio Pérez, J., 2012. La labor de la SEAV de la Diputación Provincial de Valencia. 2011-2012. Nº VI. Sección de Estudios Arqueológicos V, Diputación Provincial, Valencia, pp.13-18.

Aparicio Pérez, J., Gurrea, V., Climent, S., 1983. Carta arqueológica de la Safor. Gandia: Instituto de Estudios Comarcales Duque Real Alonso el Viejo. Ayuntamiento de Gandia, pp. 39-42.

Aparicio Pérez, J., San Valero Aparisi, J., Martinez Perona, J. V., 1983. Actividades arqueológicas (desde 1979 a 1982). Varia II. Departamento de Historia Antigua. Serie Arqueológica, no 9, pp. 201-495.

Apellániz, J.Mª., 1971. La caverna de Santimamiñe, Diputación de Vizcaya, Bilbao.

Aranda, V., 2011. Estudio funcional de los grandes configurados de Pleistoceno Medio del yacimiento de Santa Ana (Cáceres, Extremadura, España). Aproximación metodológica mediante Microscopio Electrónico de Barrido (MEB/MEBA), Tesis de Máster, Departament d'Història i Història de l'Art, Universitat Rovira i Virgili, Tarragona, p. 201.

Aranda, V., Canals, A., Ollé, A., in press. Experimental program for the detection of use wear on quartzite, Use-Wear 2012. Proceedings of the International Conference on Use-Wear analysis, Cambridge Scholars Publishing.

Aranda, V., Ollé, A., Canals, A., 2012. Experimental program for the detection of use wear on quartzite. Actas de International Conference on Use-wear analysis, USE-WEAR 2012, CEOT - Universidade do Algarve, Faro.

Aranzadi, T., Barandiarán, J.M., Eguren, E., 1925. Exploraciones en la caverna de Santimamiñe (Basondo, Cortézubi) I. Figuras rupestres, Bilbao.

Aranzadi, T., Barandiarán, J.M., Eguren, E., 1925. Exploraciones en la caverna de Santimamiñe (Basondo, Cortézubi) I. Figuras rupestres, Bilbao.

Arceredillo, D., 2013. Los ungulados de La Peña de Estebanvela (Ayllón, Segovia), in: Cacho, C. (Coord.), Ocupaciones magdalenienses en el interior de la Península Ibérica. La Peña de Estebanvela (Ayllón, Segovia). Junta de Castilla y León-CSIC, pp. 183-209.

Areso, P., Uriz, A., 2011. Revisión estratigráfica del depósito arqueológico de la cueva de Santimamiñe (Kortezubi, Bizkaia). Sedimentología del relleno, Kobie Serie BAI n.º 1, 343-356.

Arias, P., 2009. Rites in the dark? An evaluation of the current evidence for ritual areas at Magdalenian cave sites, World Archaeology 41 (2) 262-294.

Arias, P., Calderón, T., González-Sáinz, C., Millán: A.,Moure A., Ontañón, R., Ruiz, R., 1998. Dataciones absolutas para el arte rupestre paleolítico de Venta La Perra (Carranza, Bizkaia), Kobie (Paleoantropología) XXV, 85-92.

Arias, P., Corchón, MªS., Menéndez, M., Rodríguez, A. (Eds.), 2012. El Paleolítico Superior Cantábrico. Actas de la Primera Mesa Redonda (San Román de Candamo, Asturias), Monografías 3, 2013, IIIPC -UNICAN, Santander.

Arias, P., González-Sainz, C., Moure, A., Ontañón, R., 1999. La Garma. Un descenso al pasado, Gobierno de Cantabria, Santander.

Arias, P., Laval, E., Menu, M., González-Sainz, C., Ontañón, R., 2011. Les colorants dans l'art pariétal et mobilier paléolithique de La Garma (Cantabrie, Espagne), L'Anthropologie 115 (3-4), 425-445.

Arias, P., Ontañón, R., (Eds.) 2004. La materia del lenguaje prehistórico. El arte mueble paleolítico de Cantabria en su contexto, Gobierno de Cantabria, Santander.

Arias, P., Ontañón, R., Álvarez Fernández, E., Aparicio, M.T., Chauvin, A.M., Clemente, I., Cueto, M., González-Urquijo, J.E., Ibáñez, J.J., Tapia, J., Teira, L.C., 2005. La estructura magdaleniense de La Garma A. Aproximación a la organización espacial de un hábitat paleolítico, in: N.F. Bicho (Ed.), O Paleolítico. Actas do IV Congresso de Arqueologia Peninsular (Faro, 14 a 19 de Setembro de 2004), Universidade do Algarve, Faro, pp. 123-141.

Arias, P., Ontañón, R., Álvarez Fernández, E., Cueto, M., Elorza, M., García-Moncó, C., Güth, A., Iriarte, M.J., Teira, L.C., Zurro, D., 2011. Magdalenian floors in the Lower Gallery of La Garma. A preliminary report, in: Site-internal spatial organization of hunter-gatherer societies: case studies from the European Palaeolithic and Mesolithic, eds. S. Gaudzinski-Windheuser, O. Jöris, M. Sensburg, M. Street, E. Turner, Verlag des Römisch-GermanischenZentralmuseums, Mainz, pp. 31-51.

Arnáiz Alonso, M.A., 1990. Las ocupaciones de San Quirce de Río Pisuerga: Reflexiones sobre la utilización del espacio y sus implicaciones, BSAA LVI, 25-37.

Arnaíz Alonso, M.A., 1996. El Paleolítico inferior en el tramo medio-alto del río Pisuerga: situación actual de la investigación, Actas III Congreso de Historia de Palencia 1, pp.11-33.

Arnold, L.J., Demuro, M., Navazo Ruiz, M., Benito-Calvo, A., Pérez-González, A., 2013. OSL dating of the Middle Palaeolithic Hotel California site, Sierra de Atapuerca, north-central Spain, BOREAS 42, 285-305.

Arriaza Dorado, M.C., 2011. Estudio tafonómico de lagomorfos y quelonios del nivel F del Abrigo de Navalmaíllo (Pinilla del Valle, Madrid). D.EA. UAM (unpublished).

Arribas Herrera, A., Aura Tortosa, J.E., Carrión, J.S., Jordá-Pardo, J.F., Pérez Ripoll, M., 2004. Presencia de hiena manchada en los depósitos basales (Pleistoceno superior final) del yacimiento arqueológico de la Cueva de Nerja (Málaga, España), Revista Española de Paleontología 19 (1), 109-121.

Arrizabalaga, A., 1989a.Orain dela 30.000 urte. Labeko Koba. Hace 30.000 años, Ayuntamiento de Arrasate, Oñate, p. 24.

Arrizabalaga, A., 1989b. Labeko Koba. Auriñaciense en Guipúzcoa, Revista de Arqueología 96, 62-63.

Arrizabalaga, A., 1991. Labeko Kobako aztarnategi arkeologikoaren indusketa (Arrasate, Gipuzkoa), Cuadernos de Sección de Prehistoria y Arqueología 4, 9-39.

Arrizabalaga, A., 1992. Labeko Koba (Arrasate, Guipúzcoa). Nuevos datos sobre el Paleolítico Superior inicial, The Late Quaternary in the Western Pyrenean Region, U.P.V., Bilbao, pp. 285-290.

Arrizabalaga, A., 1993. El yacimiento arqueológico de Labeko Koba (Arrasate-Mondragón, Guipúzcoa). Aportación al Paleolítico superior inicial vasco, El Origen del Hombre Moderno en el SW de Europa, U.N.E.D., Madrid, pp. 195-208.

Arrizabalaga, A., 1995. La industria lítica del Paleolítico superior inicial en el oriente cantábrico. Tesis Doctoral, Universidad del País Vasco, Vitoria, p. 1000.

Arrizabalaga, A., 2005-2006. Las primeras ocupaciones humanas en el Pirineo Occidental y Montes Vascos. Un estado de la cuestión en 2005, Munibe (Antropologia-Arkeologia) 57 (2), 53-70.

Arrizabalaga, A., 2006. Lezetxiki (Arrasate, País Vasco). Nuevas preguntas acerca de un antiguo yacimiento, in: Cabrera, V., Bernaldo de Quiros, F., Maillo, J. M. (Eds.): En el centenario de la Cueva de El Castillo: el ocaso de los Neandertales. Centro Asociado de la UNED-Cantabria, Santander, pp. 291-310.

Arrizabalaga, A., Altuna, J., (dirs.) 2000. Labeko Koba (País Vasco). Hienas y Humanos en los albores del Paleolítico superior, Munibe (Antropologia -Arkeologia) 52, Donostia, p. 398.

Arrizabalaga, A., Altuna, J., Areso, P., Elorza, M., García, M., Iriarte, M.J., Mariezkurrena, K., Mujika, J., Peman, E., Tarriño, A., Uriz, A., Viera, L., 2000. Síntesis cronológica, ambiental y cultural del yacimiento de Labeko Koba (Arrasate, País Vasco), IIIer Congreso de Arqueología Peninsular, Vol. II, Porto, pp. 293-310,

Arrizabalaga, A., Altuna, J., Areso, P., Falgueres, C., Iriarte, M. J., Mariezkurrena, K., Pemán, E., Ruiz-Alonso, M., Tarriño, A., Uriz, A., Vallverdú, J., 2005. Retorno a Lezetxiki (Arrasate, País Vasco): nuevas Perspectivas de la investigación, in: Santonja, M., Pérez-González, A., Machado, A. (Eds.), Geoarqueología y Patrimonio en la Península Ibérica y el entorno mediterráneo, Madrid, pp. 81-98.

Arrizabalaga, A., Alvarez-Fernández, E., Iriarte-Chiapusso, M.J., 2011. Spondylus sp. at Lezetxiki Cave (Basque Country, Spain): First Evidence of its use in Symbolic Behaviour during the Aurignacian in Europe, in: Ifantidis, F., Nikolaidou, M. (Coor.), Spondylus in Prehistory: New Data and Approaches - Contributions to the Archaeology of Shell Technologies, Chapter 2, B.A.R. International Series S2216, Oxford, pp. 11-16.

Arrizabalaga, A., Iriarte, M. J., Villaluenga, A., 2010. Labeko Koba y Lezetxiki (País Vasco). Dos yacimientos, una problemática común, in: Baquedano, E., Rosell, J. (Dirs.), Cubiles de hiena (y otros grandes carnívoros) en los yacimientos arqueológicos de la Península Ibérica, Zona Arqueológica 9, Alcalá de Henares, pp. 262-274.

Arrizabalaga, A., Ríos-Garaizar, J., 2012. First Human occupations in the Basque crossroads, Journal of World Prehistory 25 (3-4), 157-181.

Arsuaga, J.L., Baquedano, E., Pérez-González, A., Sala, N., García, N., Álvarez, D., Laplana, C., Huguet, R., Sevilla, P., Blain, J-A., Quam, R., Ruiz-Zapata, B., Sala, P., Gil-García, M. J., Uzquiano, P., Pantoja, A., 2010. El yacimiento arqueopaleontológico del Pleistoceno Superior de la Cueva del Camino en el Calvero de la Higuera (Pinilla del Valle, Madrid), in: Baquedano, E., Rosell, J. (Eds.), Zona Arqueológica 13 (1ª Reunión de Científicos sobre cubiles de hiena (y otros grandes carnívoros) en los yacimientos arqueológicos de la Península Ibérica), pp. 422-442.

Arsuaga, J.L., Baquedano, E., Pérez-González, A., Sala, N., Quam, R. M., Rodríguez, L., García, R., García, N., Álvarez, D., Laplana, C., Huguet, R., Sevilla, P., Maldonado, E., Blain, J-A., Ruiz-Zapata, B., Sala, P., Gil-García, M. J., Uzquiano, P., Pantoja, A., Márquez, B., 2012. Understanding the ancient hábitats of the last-interglacial (late MIS 5) Neanderthals of central Iberia: paleoenvironmental and taphonomic evidence from the Cueva del Camino (Spain) site, Quaternary International 275, 55-75.

Arsuaga, J.L., Bermúdez de Castro, J.M., 1987. Estudio de los restos humanos del yacimiento de la Cova del Tossal de la Font (Villafamés, Castellón), Cuadernos de Prehistoria y Arqueología Castellonenses 10 (1984), 19-34.

Arsuaga, J.L., Fernández Peris, J., Gracia-Téllez, A., Quam, R., Carretero, J.M., Barciela González, V., Blasco, R., Cuartero, F., Sañudo, P., 2012. Fossil human remains from Bolomor Cave (Valencia, Spain), Journal of Human Evolution 62 (5), 629-639.

Arsuaga, J.L., Gracia, A., Lorenzo, C., Martínez, I., Pérez, P. J., 1999a. Resto craneal humano de Galería/Cueva de los Zarpazos (Sierra de Atapuerca), in: Carbonell, E., Rosas, A. Díez, J.C. (Eds). Atapuerca: Ocupaciones Humanas y Paleoecología del Yacimiento de Galería. Memorias, 7. Junta de Castilla y León. Consejería de Educación y Cultura, Zamora, pp. 233-236

Arsuaga, J.L., Lorenzo, C., Carretero, J.M., Gracia, A., Martínez, I., García, N., Bermúdez de Castro, J.M., Carbonell, E., 1999b. A complete human pelvis from the Middle Pleistocene of Spain, Nature 399, 255-258.

Arsuaga, J.L., Martínez, I., 2004. Atapuerca y la evolución humana. Barcelona: Fundació Caixa de Catalunya.

Arsuaga, J.L., Martínez, I., Gracia, A., Carretero, J.M., Carbonell, E., 1993. Three new human skulls from the Sima de los Huesos Middle Pleistocene site in Sierra de Atapuerca, Spain, Nature 362, 534-537.

Arsuaga, J.L., Martínez, I., Gracia, A., Carretero, J.M., Lorenzo, C., García, N., Ortega, A.I. 1997a. Sima de los Huesos (Sierra de Atapuerca, Spain). The site, Journal of Human Evolution 33, 109-127.

Arsuaga, J.L., Martínez, I., Gracia, A., Lorenzo, C., 1997b. The Sima de los Huesos crania (Sierra de Atapuerca, Spain). A comparative study, Journal of Human Evolution 33, 219-281.

Arsuaga, J.L., Martínez, I., Villaverde Bonilla, V., Lorenzo, C., Quam, R., Carretero, J.M., Gracia, A., 2001. Fósiles humanos del País Valenciano, in: Villaverde Bonilla, V. (Ed.), De Neandertales a Cromañones. El inicio del poblamiento humano en las tierras valencianas, Universitat de València, València, pp. 265-322.

Arsuaga, J.L., Quam, R., Daura, J., Sanz, M., Subirà, M.E., Dalen, L., Götherstrom, A., 2011. Neandertalmt DNA from a Late Pleistocene Human Mandible from the Cova del Gegant (Spain), in: Condemi, S., Weniger, G.C. (Eds.), Continuity and Discontinuity in the Peopling of Europe: One Hundred Fifty Years of Neanderthal Study, Vertebrate Paleobiology and Paleoanthropology, Springer Science, pp. 213-217.

Arsuaga, J.L., Villaverde, V., Quam, R., Gracia, A., Lorenzo, C., Martínez, I., 2002. The Gravettian occipital bone from the site of Malladetes (Barx, Valencia, Spain), Journal of Human Evolution 43, 381-393.

Arsuaga, J.L., Villaverde, V., Quam, R., Martínez, I, Carretero, J. M., Lorenzo, C., Gracia, A., 2007. New Neandertal remains from Cova Negra (Valencia, Spain), Journal of Human Evolution 52, 31-58.

Asquerino, M.D., Araque, F.A., Martos, E., Aguilar, R., Jiménez, M.C., López, N., Muñoz, L., 1991. El Pirulejo. Resultados preliminares de la campaña de 1991, Estudios de Prehistoria Cordobesa 5, 87-130.

Aura, J.E., 1995. El Magdaleniense Mediterráneo: la Cova del Parpalló (Gandía, Valencia), Trabajos Varios del SIP 91, Museu de Prehistòria, Valencia.

Aura, J.E., Carrión, Y., Estrelles, E., Pérez Jordà, G., 2005. Planteconomy ofHunter-gatherergroups at theend of thelast Ice Age: plantmacroremainsfromthe cave of Santa Maira (Spain) ca. 12,000- 9000 BP, Vegetation Hist. Archaeobot 14, 542-550.

Aura, J.E., Carrión, Y., García, O., Jardón, P., Jordá, J.F., Molina, L.,Morales, J.V., Pascual, J.L., Pérez, G., Pérez, M., Rodrigo, M.J., Verdasco, C. C., 2006. Epipaleolítico-Mesolítico en las comarcas centrales valencianas, in: Alday, A. (Ed.), El Mesolítico de muescas y denticulados en la Cuenca del Ebro y el litoral mediterráneo peninsular, Diputación Foral, Vitoria-Gasteiz, pp. 65-120.

Aura, J.E., Jordá Pardo, J. F., Pérez Ripoll, M., Rodrigo García, M. J., Badal García, E., Guillem Calatayud, P., 2002. The Far South: the Pleistocene-Holocene Transition in the Nerja Cave (Andalucía, Spain), Quaternary International 93-94, 19-30.

Aura, J.E., Jordá, J. F., Fortea, F.J., 2006. La Cueva de Nerja (Málaga, España) y los inicios del Solutrense en Andalucía, Zephyrus 59, 67-88.

Aura, J.E., Jordá, J.F., Montes, L., Utrilla, P., 2011. Human responses to Younger Dryas in the Ebro valley and Mediterranean watershed (Eastern Spain), Quaternary International 242, 348-359.

Aura, J.E., Jordá-Pardo, J.F., 2013. Solutrenses del Sur en Transición, Espacio, Tiempo y Forma. Serie I, Prehistoria y Arqueología, Nueva época. doi: 10.5944/etf i.5.10851.

Aura, J.E., Jordá-Pardo, J.F., Pérez Ripoll, M., Badal, E., Morales, J.V., Avezuela, B., Tifagom, M., Jardón, P., 2010. Treinta años de investigación sobre el Paleolítico superior de Andalucía: la Cueva de Nerja (Málaga, España), in: Mangado, X. (Ed.), El Paleolítico superior peninsular. Novedades del siglo XXI. Homenaje al Profesor Javier Fortea. Monografies, 8. Seminari d'Estudis i Recerques Prehistòriques, Universidad de Barcelona, Barcelona, pp. 149-172.

Aura, J.E., Morales, J.V., de Miguel, Mª. P., 2009. Restos humanos con marcas antrópicas de les coves de Santa Maira. (Castell de Castells, la Marina alta, Alicante), in: Pérez, A., Soler, B. (Eds.), Restos de Vida-Restos de Muerte, Museu de Prehistòria de València, València, pp. 169-174.

Aura, J.E., Tiffagom, M., Jordá-Pardo, J.F., Duarte, E., Fernández de la Vega, J., Santamaría, D., de la Rasilla, M., Vadillo, M., Pérez, M., 2012. The Solutrean - Magdalenian Transition: a view from the southwest, Quaternary International 272-273, 75-87.

Averbouh, A., 2000. Technologie de la matière osseuse travaillée et implications palethnologiques. L'exemple des chaines d'explotation du bois de cervide chez les Magdaléniens des Pyrénées. Tesis doctoral inédita. Université Paris I Panthéon-Sorbonne, Paris, p. 247 .

Azanza, B., Baldellou, V., Cuchí, J.A., López, P., Montes, L., Utrilla, P. 1988.Cronoestratigrafía de la cueva musteriense de los Moros (Gabasa, Huesca), Cuaternario y Geomorfología, 2 (1-4), 1-12

Badal, E., 2001. La recolección de piñas durante la Prehistoria en la Cueva de Nerja (Málaga), in: Villaverde, V. (Dir.), De Neandertales a Cromañones. El primer poblamiento en tierras valencianas, Universitat de València, València, pp. 101-104.

Baena Preysler, J., Carrión E., Cuartero F., Fluck H., 2012. A chronicle of crisis: The Late Mousterian in north Iberia (Cueva del Esquilleu, Cantabria, Spain), Quaternary International 247, 199-211.

Baena Preysler, J., Carrión, E., Cuartero, F., Fluck, H., 2012. A chronicle of crisis: The Late Mousterian in north Iberia (CuevadelEsquilleu, Cantabria, Spain), Quaternary International 247(1), 199-21.

Baena Preysler, J., Carrión, E., Ruiz, B., Ellwood, B., Sesé, C., Yravedra, J., Jordá, J., Uzquiano, P., Velázquez, R., Manzano, I., Sánchez, A., Hernández, F., 2005. Paleoecología y comportamiento humano durante el Pleistoceno Superior en la comarca de Liébana: la secuencia de la Cueva del Esqulleu, Occidente de Cantabria, España, in: Lasheras, J.A., Montes, R. (Eds.), Neandertales cantábricos. Estado de la cuestión, vol. 20. Monografías Museo de Altamira, pp. 461-487.

Baena Preysler, J., Polo, J., Bárez, S., Cuartero, F., González, I., Lázaro, A., Nebot, A., Martín Puig, D., Márquez, R., Pérez-González, A., Pérez, T., Rubio, D., Roca, M., Rus, I., 2011. El proyecto arqueológico de El Cañaveral (Coslada-Madrid): gestión e investigación. Actas de las V Jornadas de Patrimonio Arqueológico en la Comunidad de Madrid, Dirección General de Patrimonio Histórico, Madrid, pp. 93-114.

Bagolini, B. 1968. Ricerche sulle dimensione dei manufatti litici prehistorici no ritocati. Anales de l'Universitá di Ferrara.

Balbín, R. de, 1989. L'art de la Grotte de Tito Bustillo (Ribadesella, Espagne). Une vision de synthèse, L'Anthropologie 93 (2), 435-462 .

Balbín, R. de, Alcolea, J.J., 2009. Arte mueble en Tito Bustillo: los últimos trabajos, Veleia 24-25, 131-159.

Balbín, R. de, Alcolea, J.J., González, M.A., 1999. Une vision nouvelle de la grotte de El Pindal, Pimiango, Ribadedeva, Asturias, L'Anthropologie 103(1), 51-92.

Balbín, R. de, Alcolea, J.J., González, M.A., 2003. El Macizo de Ardines, un lugar mayor del arte paleolítico europeo, in: Bueno, P., Balbín, R. de (Ed.), El Arte Prehistórico desde los comienzos del siglo XXI, Amigos de Ribadesella, Ribadesella, pp.91-151.

Balbín, R. de, González, C., 1992. La Pasiega, Monte de El Castillo, Puente Viesgo, Cantabria, in: La Naissance de l'Art, Unión Latine, París, pp. 239-241.

Balbín, R. de, González, C., 1993. Nuevas investigaciones en la cueva de La Pasiega (Puente Viesgo, Cantabria), Boletín S.E.A.A. LIX, 9-34.

Balbín, R. de, González, C., 1994. Un nuevo conjunto de representaciones en el sector D.2 de la cueva de La Pasiega (Puente Viesgo, Cantabria), in: J.A. Lasheras (Ed.), Homenaje a J. González-Echegaray, Altamira 17, Ministerio de Cultura, Madrid, pp. 269-280.

Balbín, R. de, González, C., 1995. L'ensemble rupestre paléolithique de "La Rotonda", dans la Galerie B de la Grotte de La Pasiega (Puente Viesgo, Cantabria), L'Anthropologie 99 (2-3), 296-324.

Balbín, R. de, González, C., 1996. Las pinturas y grabados paleolíticos del corredor B7 de la cueva de La Pasiega (Cantabria), in: Moure, A. (Ed.), El Hombre Fósil 80 años después, Universidad de Cantabria, Santander, pp. 271-294.

Balbín, R. de, Moure, A., 1983. La galería principal de la cueva de Tito Bustillo, Ars Praehistorica I, 47-97.

Balbín, R. de., 1995. L'art paléolithique à l'air libre de la vallée du Douro, Archéologia 313, 34-41.

Balbín, R. de., 2008. (Ed.). Arte Prehistórico al aire libre en el Sur de Europa. Junta de Castilla y León Consejería de Cultura y Turismo. Salamanca

Balbín, R. de., Alcolea, J. J., 1992 a. La grotte de Los Casares et l'Art Paléolithique de la Meseta espagnole. L'Anthropologie 96, (2-3), 397-452.

Balbín, R. de., Alcolea, J. J., 1994. Arte Paleolítico de la Meseta española, Complutum 5, 97-138.

Balbín, R. de., Alcolea, J. J., 1995. L'art paléolithique à l'air libre de la vallée du Douro, Archéologia 313, 34-41.

Balbín, R. de., Alcolea, J. J., 1999. Vie quotidienne et vie religieuse. Les sanctuaires dans l'Art Paléolithique, L'Anthropologie 103, 23-49.

Balbín, R. de., Alcolea, J. J., 2001. L'Art Paléolithique en plein air dans la Péninsule Ibérique: quelques précision sur son contenu, chronologie et signification, in : Les prémiers hommes modernes de la Péninsule Ibérique. Actes du Colloquede la Commision VIII de la U.I.S.P.P. pp. 205-236.

Balbín, R. de., Alcolea, J. J., 2002. L'art rupestre paléolithique de l'intérieur péninsulaire ibérique: une revision chronoculturelle d'ensemble, in: Actes du Colloque L'art Paléolithique à l'air libre: le Paysage modifié par l'image, 07-09/10/1999. Coor. D. Sacchi, pp. 139-157.

Balbín, R. de., Alcolea, J. J., 2005a. Testigos del frío. La fauna en el Arte Rupestre Paleolítico del interior peninsular, in: Santonja, M., Pérez-González, A., Machado, M. J. (Eds.), Geoarqueologia y Patrimonio en la Península Ibérica y el entorno mediterráneo. ADEMA. Soria, pp. 547-566.

Balbín, R. de., Alcolea, J. J., 2005b. Espace d'habitation, espace d'enterrement,espace graphique. Les coïncidences et les divergences dans l'Art Paléolithique de la Corniche Cantabrique, in :Vialou, D., Renault Miskovsky, J., Patou-Mathis, M. (Dirs), Comportements des hommes du Paléolithique moyen et supérieur en Europe. Territoires et milieux. Eraul 111. pp. 193-206.

Balbín, R. de., Alcolea, J. J., Santonja, M., 1994. SiegaVerde y el arte rupestre paleolítico al aire libre. VI Coloquio Hispano-Ruso de Historia. Madrid. pp. 5-19.

Balbín, R. de., Alcolea, J. J., Santonja, M., 1995. El yacimiento rupestre paleolítico al aire libre de Siega Verde (Salamanca, España): una visión de conjunto, Trabalhos de Antropologia e Etnologia 35 (3), 73-102.

Balbín, R. de., Alcolea, J. J., Santonja, M., 1996a. Siega Verde. Un art rupestre à l'air libre dans la vallée du Douro. Dossiers d'Archéologie, n° 209. Diciembre 1995 - enero 1996. Dijon : 98-105.

Balbín, R. de., Alcolea, J. J., Santonja, M., 1996b. Arte Rupestre Paleolítico al aire libre en la cuenca del Duero: Siega Verde y Foz Côa. Fundación Rei Afonso Henriques, Serie monografías y estudios. Zamora.

Balbín, R. de.,Santonja, M., 1992. Siega Verde (Salamanca), in: El Nacimiento del Arte Europa". Catálogo de la Exposición de la Unión Latina, París, pp.250-252.

Baldeón, A., 1990. El Paleolítico Inferior y Medio en el País Vasco. Una aproximación en 1990, Munibe (Antropologia - Arkeologia) 42, 11-22.

Baldeón, A., 1993. El yacimiento de Lezetxiki (Gipuzkoa, País Vasco). Los niveles musterienses, Munibe (Antropologia - Arkeologia) 45, 3-97.

Baldeón, A., 1999. El abrigo de Axlor (Bizkaia, País Vasco). Las industrias líticas de sus niveles musterienses, Munibe 51, 9-121.

Bandi, H.G., 1962. Pinturas rupestres del Levante Español, Arte de los pueblos, Ed. Seix y Barral, Barcelona, pp. 71-98.

Bañuls, S., López-García, J.M., Blain, H.-A., Canals, A., 2012. Climate and landscape during the Last Glacial Maximum in southwestern Iberia: The small-vertebrate association from the Sala de las Chimeneas, Maltravieso, Extremadura, Comptes Rendus Palevol 11 (1), 31-40.

Baquedano, E., Arsuaga, J. L., Pérez-González, A., 2010. Homínidos y carnívoros: competencia en un mismo nicho ecológico pleistoceno: los yacimientos del Calvero de la Higuera en Pinilla del Valle, in: Actas de las Quintas Jornadas de Patrimonio Arqueológico en la Comunidad de Madrid, pp. 61-72.

Baquedano, E., Márquez, B., Pérez-González, A., Mosquera, M., Huguet, R., Espinosa, J. A., Sánchez Romero, L., Panera, J, Arsuaga, J.L., 2011-2012, Neandertales en el Valle del Lozoya: los yacimientos paleolíticos del Calvero de la Higuera (Pinilla del Valle, Madrid), Neandertales en Iberia: Últimos avances en la investigación del Paleolítico Medio Ibérico, Mainake XXXIII, 83-100.

Barandiarán, I., 1967. El Paleomesolítico del Pirineo Occidental. Bases para la sistematización tipológica del instrumental óseo paleolítico, Monografías Arqueológicas, III, Universidad de Zaragoza, Zaragoza, p. 355.

Barandiarán, I., 1972. Arte mueble del Paleolítico Cantábrico. Universidad de Zaragoza, Zaragoza.

Barandiaran, I., 1988. Datation C14 de l'art mobilier magdalénien cantabrique, Préhistoire Ariégoise, XLIII, 63-84.

Barandiarán, I., 1988. Prehistoria: El Paleolítico, Historia General de Euskal Herria, Auñamendi, San Sebastián.

Barandiarán, I., Cava, A., Alday, A., 2006. Ocupaciones de altura e interior durante el Tardiglaciar: la Llanada alavesa y sus estribaciones montañosas, Zona arqueológica 7 (1), 535-550.

Barandiarán, J.M., 1953. El hombre prehistórico en el País Vasco, Ekin, Buenos Aires.

Barandiarán, J.M., 1956. El Hombre Prehistórico en el País Vasco, Buenos Aires.

Barandiarán, J.M., 1960. Exploración de la cueva de Lezetxiki en Mondragón (trabajos de 1957,1959 y 1960), Munibe 12, 273-310.

Barandiarán, J.M., 1963. Exploración de la cueva de Lezetxiki (campaña de 1962), Munibe 15, 87-102.

Barandiarán, J.M., 1964. Exploración de la cueva de Lezetxiki en Mondragón (campaña de 1961), Munibe 16, 56-59.

Barandiarán, J.M., 1964. La cueva de Altxerri y sus figuras rupestres, Munibe 16, 91-141.

Barandiarán, J.M., 1965. Exploración de la cueva de Lezetxiki (Mondragón) (Campaña de 1963), Munibe 17, 52-64.

Barandiarán, J.M., 1976. Obras Completas. Vasconia Antigua –La cueva de Santimamiñe, Tomo IX, Editorial La Gran Enciclopedia Vasca, Bilbao.

Barandiarán, J.M., 1980. Excavaciones en Axlor. 1967-1974, in: Barandiarán, J. M., Obras completas, tomo XVII, pp. 127-384.

Barandiarán, J.M., Altuna, J., 1966. Excavación en la cueva de Lezetxiki (Campaña de 1965), Munibe 18, 5-12.

Barandiarán, J.M., Altuna, J., 1967. Excavación de la cueva de Lezetxiki (Campaña de 1966), Munibe 19, 79-106.

Barandiarán, J.M., Altuna, J., 1967. Excavación de la cueva de Lezetxiki (Campaña de 1967), Munibe 19, 231-246.

Barandiarán, J.M., Altuna, J., 1969. La cueva de Ekain y sus figuras rupestres, Munibe 21, 331-385.

Barandiarán, J.M., Altuna, J., 1970. Excavación de la cueva de Lezetxiki (Campaña de 1968), Munibe 22, 51-59.

Barandiarán, J.M., Boucher, P., Fernández Medrano, D., 1959. 3ª Campaña de excavaciones en el yacimiento prehistórico de Lezetxiki. Campaña en el de Kobatxo. Garagarza-Mondragón, Munibe 11, 17-19.

Barandiarán, J.M., Fernández Medrano, D., 1957. Exploración en la cueva de Lezetxiki en Mondragón (trabajos de 1956), Munibe 7, 69-80.

Barandiarán, J.M., Fernández Medrano, D., 1959. Trabajos de la sección de Prehistoria en las Jornadas Espeleológicas, Boletín de la Institución Sancho El Sabio III, 1-2, 23-29.

Barciela, V., Blasco, R., Cuartero, F., Fernández Peris, J., Hortelano, L., Sañudo, P., 2013. Cova del Bolomor. 25 años en busca de un tiempo perdido. Museu de Prehistòria de Valencia, Valencia, p. 75.

Bárez, S., Rus, I., Pérez-González, A., Vega de Miguel, J., 2011. Los yacimientos achelenses de "Los Ahijones", metodología geoarqueológica y resultados preliminares de la intervención. Actas de las V Jornadas de Patrimonio Arqueológico en la Comunidad de Madrid, Dirección General de Patrimonio Histórico, Madrid, pp. 185-200.

Barnadiaran, J. M., 1961. Excavaciones en Aitzbitarte IV (Trabajos de 1960), Munibe 13, 183-285.

Barris, J., 1983. El jaciment arqueològic del Cau del Roure (Serinyà). Amics de Besalú. IV Assemblea d'Estudis del seu comtat, Besalú, vol. I, pp. 143-154.

Barroso Ruiz, C., (Coord.) 2003. El Pleistoceno Superior de la cueva del Boquete de Zafarraya. Junta de Andalucía. Consejería de Cultura.

Barroso Ruiz, C., de Lumley, Mª. A., Caparrós, M., Verdú Bermejo, L., 2006. Les restes Humains Néandertaliens et Homo sapiens de la grotte du Boquete de Zafarraya, in: Barroso Ruiz, C., de Lumley, H. (Eds.), La Grotte du Boquete de Zafarraya, Consejería de Cultura. Junta de Andalucía, Sevilla.Málaga, Andalousie. T. III, pp.1167-1396.

Barroso Ruiz, C., de Marchi, M.P., Abdessador, S., Bailón, S., Desclaux, E., Gregoire, S., Hernández Carrasquilla, F., Lacombat, F., Lebreton, V., Lecervoisier, B., Moigne, A. Mª., Perrenoud, C., Renault-Miskovsky, J., Riquelme Cantal, J. A., Rodríguez Vidal, J., Saos, T.,Vernet, J.-L., Vilette, Ph., 2006. Contexte Paléoécologique, Paléoclimatique et Paléogéographique des neandertaliens de la grotte du Boquete de Zafarraya, in: Barroso Ruiz, C., de Lumley, H. (Eds.), La grotte du Boquete de Zafarraya, Consejería de Cultura, Junta de Andalucía. Sevilla. Málaga, Andalousie. T. III, pp. 1127-1166.

Barroso Ruiz, C., García Sánchez, M., Ruiz Bustos., A. Medina Lara, P., Sanchidrian Torti, J. L., 1983. Avance al estudio cultural, antropológico y paleontológico de la cueva del Boquete de Zafarraya (Alcaucín, Málaga), Rev. Antropología y Paleoecología Humana 3, 3-7.

Barroso Ruiz, C., Medina Lara, F., 1989. El último neandertal, Investigación y ciencia, Junio 37-39.

Barroso Ruiz, C., Medina Lara, F., Boutié, P., Barsky, D., 2006. Les industries Moustériennes de la grotte du Boquete de Zafarraya. In: Barroso Ruiz, C., de Lumley, H. (Eds.), La grotte du Boquete de Zafarraya, Consejería de Cultura. Junta de Andalucía. Sevilla, Málaga, Andalousie. T. III, pp. 1497-1586.

Barroso Ruiz, C., Medina Lara, F., Caparrós, M., 2006. Cadre Géographique de la grotte du Boquete de Zafarraya:contextes administratif, topographique, climatique, hidrologique et environnemental (flore et faune), in: Barroso Ruiz, C., de Lumley, H. (Eds.), La Grotte du Boquete de Zafarraya, Consejería de Cultura. Junta de Andalucía. Sevilla, Málaga, Andalousie. T. I, pp. 29-51.

Barroso Ruiz, C., Medina Lara, P., Sanchidrian Torti, J. L., Ruiz Bustos, A., García Sánchez, M., 1984. Le gisement mousterienne de la grotte du Boquete de Zafarraya (Alcaucín, Andalousie), L'Anthropologie 88, 133-134.

Barroso Ruiz, C., Riquelme Cantal, J. A. Moigne, A.Mª, Barnes, L., 2006. Les faunes de grands mammifères du pléistocène supérieur de la grotte du Boquete de Zafarraya. Étude paléontologique, paléoécologique et archéozoologique, in: Barroso Ruiz, C., de Lumley, H. (Eds.), La grotte du Boquete de Zafarraya, Consejería de Cultura. Junta de Andalucía. Sevilla, Málaga, Andalousie. T. II, pp. 675-891.

Barroso, C., Bailón, S., 2003. Los anfibios y los reptiles del Pleistoceno superior de la cueva del Boquete de Zafarraya, in: Barroso, C. (Ed.), El Pleistoceno Superior de la cueva del Boquete de Zafarraya. Arqueología Monografías, vol. 15, Consejería de Cultura, Junta de Andalucía, Sevilla, pp. 267-276.

Barroso, C., Botella, D., Caparrós, M., Moigne, A. M., Celiberti, V., Monclova, A., Pineda, L., Monge, G., Testu, A., Barsky, D., Notter, O., Riquelme, J. A., Pozo, M., Carretero, M. A., Khatib, S., Saos, T., Gregoire, S., Bailón, S., García, J. A., Cabral, A., Djerrab, A., Hedley, I. G., Abdessadok, S., Batalla, G., Astier, N., Bertin, L., Boulbes, N., Cauche, D., Filoux, A., Hanquet, C., Milizia, C., Rossini, E., Verdú, L., Pois, V., de Lumley, H., 2012. La cueva del Angel (Lucena, Córdoba): un hábitat Achelense de cazadores en Andalucía, Menga: Revista de Prehistoria de Andalucía 3, 27-56

Barroso, C., Botella, D., Caparrós, M., Moigne, A. M., Celiberti, V., Testu, A,, Barsky, D., Notter, O., Riquelme, J. A., Pozo, M., Carretero, M. A., Monge, G., Khatib, S., Saos, T., Gregoire, S., Bailón, S., García, J. A., Cabral, A. L., Djerrab, A., Hedley, I. G., Abdessadok, S., Batalla, G., Astier, N, Bertin, L., Boulbes, N., Cauche, D., Filoux, A., Hanquet, C., Milizia, C., Moutoussamy, J., Rossoni, E., Verdú , L., de Lumley, H., 2011. The Cueva del Ángel (Lucena, Spain): An Acheulean hunters habitat in the South of the Iberian Peninsula, Quaternary International 243, 105-126.

Barsky, D., Celiberti, V., Cauche, D., Grégoire, S., Lebègue, F., de Lumley, H., Toro-Moyano, I., 2010. Raw material discenment and technological aspects of the Barranco León and Fuente Nueva 3 stone assemblages (Orce southern Spain), Quaternary International 223-224, 201-219.

Barsky, D., Garcia, J., Martínez, K., Sala, R., Zaidner, Y., Carbonell, E., Toro-Moyano, I., 2013. Flake modification in European Early and Early-Middle Pleistocene stone tool assemblages, Quaternary International 316, 140-154.

Barsky, D., Sala, R., Menéndez, L., Toro, I., 2014. Use and re-use: Re-knapped flakes from the Mode 1 site of Fuente Nueva 3 (Orce, Andalucía, Spain), Quaternary International. doi.org/10.1016/j.quaint.2014.01.048

Barsky, D., Vergès, J.M., Sala, R., Toro-Moyano, I., in progress. Limestone percussion tools from the late Early Pleistocene sites of Barranco León and Fuente Nueva 3 (Orce, Spain).

Barton, R. N. E., Jennings, R., 2013. The lithic artefacts assemblages of Gorham's Cave, in: Barton, R. N. E., Stringer, C. B., Finlayson, J. C. (Eds.), Neanderthals in Context: A Report of the 1995-1998 Excavations at Gorham's and Vanguard Caves, Gibraltar. Oxford University Press, Oxford, pp. 151-187.

Barton, R.N.E., 2013. The lithic artefact assemblages of Vanguard Cave, in: Barton, R. N. E., Stringer, C. B., Finlayson, J. C. (Eds.), Neanderthals in Context: A Report of the 1995-1998 Excavations at Gorham's and Vanguard Caves, Gibraltar, Oxford University Press, Oxford, pp. 243-252.

Barton, R.N.E., Stringer, C. B., Finlayson, J. C. (Eds.), 2013. Neanderthals in Context: A Report of the 1995-1998 Excavations at Gorham's and Vanguard Caves, Gibraltar, Oxford University Press, Oxford.

Bartrolí, R., Carbonell, E., Vaquero, M., 2008. Darrers treballs de recerca i adequació a l'Abric Romaní i a la Cinglera del Capelló. El parc prehistòric de Capellades (Anoia), Tribuna d'Arqueologia 2006, 35-57.

Bartrolí, R., Cebrià, A., Muro, I., Riu-Barrera, E., Vaquero, M., 1995. A frec de ciència. L'Atles d'Amador Romaní i Guerra, Ajuntament de Capellades, Capellades.

Basabe, J.M., 1966. El húmero premusteriense de Lezetxiki (Guipúzcoa), Munibe 18 13-31.

Basabe, J.M., 1970. Dientes humanos del paleolítico de Lezetxiki (Mondragón), Munibe 22, 113-124.

Bastir, M., Rosas, A., Tabernero, A.G., Peña-Melián, A., Estalrrich, A., Rasilla, M. de la, Fortea, J., 2010. Comparative morphology and morphometric assessment of the Neandertal occipital remains from the El Sidrón site (Asturias, Spain: years 2000-2008), Journal of Human Evolution 58, 68-78.

Bataller, J.R., 1935. Els darrers treballs geològics a les comarques tarragonines en els darrers anys Revista del Centre de Lectura, 84-96.

Beltrán, A., 1965. Nouveautés dans la peinture rupestre du Levant espagnol: El Racó de Gasparo, el Racó de Molero (Ares del Maestre, Castellón), Bulletin de la Société Préhistorique de l'Ariège XX, 117-125.

Beltrán, A., 1968. Arte Rupestre Levantino, Seminario de Prehistoria y Protohistoria, Facultad de Filosofía y Letras, Monografías Arqueológicas 4, Zaragoza.

Beltrán, A., 1993. Arte prehistórico en Aragón. Zaragoza. Ibercaja. Zaragoza.

Beltrán, A., 2002. Art rupestre dans la grotte du Parpalló (Gandia, Valence, Espagne). International Newsletter on Rock Art, Bulletin de l'I.N.O.R.A. (Foix, Francia) 33, 7-11.

Beltrán, A., Baldellou, V., 1981. Avance al estudio de las cuevas pintadas del Barranco de Villacantal (Huesca), in: Altamira Symposium, Ministerio de Cultura, Madrid, pp. 131-140.

Benito Calvo, A., Martínez-Moreno, J., Mora, R., Roy, M., Roda, X., 2011. Trampling experiments at Cova Gran de Santa: their relevance for archaeological fabrics of the Upper-Middle Paleolithic assemblages, Journal of Archaeological Science 36, 2566-2577.

Benito del Rey, L., 1976. Excavaciones realizadas en el yacimiento musteriense de la cueva de las Grajas (Archidona, Málaga). Noticiario Arqueológico Hispánico 5, Prehistoria, pp.40-52.

Benito del Rey, L., 1979. Nuevas aportaciones al conocimiento del Paleolítico inferior y medio en España. Serie Resúmenes de Tesis doctorales. Facultad de Geografía e Historia, Universidad de Salamanca. pp. 26-27.

Benito del Rey, L., 1981. Fractura intencional de determinados útiles en el Musteriense de la cueva de las Grajas de Archidona (Málaga). Mainake II-III, pp.5-19.

Benito del Rey, L., 1982. Aportación a un estudio tecnomorfológico del bifaz, útil del paleolítico inferior y medio, Studia Zamorensia 3, fig. 5, p. 321.

Benito-Calvo, A., Pérez-González, A., 2014. Geomorphological map of the Sierra de Q5 Atapuerca and the middle Arlanzón valley, Journal of Maps, in press doi:1 0.1080/17445647.2014.909339

Bergadà, M.M., 1998. Estudio geoarqueológico de los asentamientos prehistóricos del Pleistoceno Superior y el Holoceno inicial en Cataluña, BAR International Series 742, 268 p., 201 fig., Oxford.

Bergadà, M.M., 1998. Estudio geoarqueológico de los asentamientos prehistóricos del Pleistoceno Superior y el Holoceno inicial en Cataluña. BAR International Series, 742, Oxford.

Bergadà, M.M., Burjachs, F., Fullola, J.M., 1999. Evolution paléoenvironnnementale du 14.500 à 10.000 BP dans les Pré_Pyrénées catalans: la grotte du Parco (Alòs de Balaguer, Lleida, Espagne), L'Anthropologie 103 (2), 249-264.

Bergadà, M.M., Serrat, D., 2001. Seqüènciasedimentària i paleoambiental de la Cova del Toll (Moià): darreresaportacions. Modilianum, Revista d'Estudis del Moianès 24, 8-22.

Berger, G.W., Pérez-González, A., Carbonell, E., Arsuaga, J.L., Bermúdez de Castro, J.M., Ku, T.L., 2008. Luminescence chronology of cave sediments at the Atapuerca paleoanthropological site, Spain, Journal of Human Evolution 55, 300-311.

Bermejo, L., Canals Salomò, A., González Pérez, J. M., Fernández Amo, F., Campaña, I., Carbonell, E., 2013. Aplicación de técnicas de prospección geofísica al estudio de la Cueva de Santa Ana (Cáceres, España), in: Actas del X Congreso Ibérico de Arqueometría, Museo de Bellas Artes, Castellón.

Bermúdez de Castro, J.M., Arsuaga, J.L., Carbonell, E., Rosas, A., Martínez, I., Mosquera, M., 1997. A hominid from the Lower Pleistocene of Atapuerca, Spain: Possible ancestor to Neandertals and Modern Humans, Science 276, 1392-1333.

Bermúdez de Castro, J.M., Carretero, J.M., García-González, R., Rodríguez-García, L., Martinón-Torres, M., Rosell, J., Blasco, R., Martín-Francés, L., Modesto, M., Carbonell, E., 2012. Early pleistocene human humeri from the gran dolina-TD6 site (Sierra de Atapuerca, Spain), American Journal of Physical Anthropology 147, 604-617.

Bermúdez de Castro, J.M., Martinón-Torres, M., 2013. A new model for the evolution of the human Pleistocene populations of Europe, Quaternary International 295, 102-112.

Bermúdez de Castro, J.M., Martinón-Torres, M., 2013. A new model for the evolution of the human Pleistocene populations of Europe. Quaternary International 295, 102-112.

Bermúdez de Castro, J.M., Martinón-Torres, M., Gómez, A., Prado, L., Carbonell, E., 2010a. New human evidence of the Early Pleistocene settlement of Europe, from Sima del Elefante site (Sierra de Atapuerca, Burgos, Spain), Quaternary International 223-224, 431-433.

Bermúdez de Castro, J.M., Martinón-Torres, M., Gómez-Robles, A., Prado-Simón, L., Martín-Francés, L., Lapresa, M., Olejniczak, A., Carbonell, E., 2011. Early Pleistocene human mandible from Sima del Elefante (TE) cave site in Sierra de Atapuerca (Spain): A comparative morphological study, Journal of Human Evolution 61 (1), 12-25.

Bermúdez de Castro, J.M., Martinón-Torres, M., Gómez-Robles, A., Prado-Simón, L., Martín-Francés, L., Lapresa, M., Olejniczak, A., Carbonell, E., 2011. Early Pleistocene human mandible from Sima del Elefante (TE) cave site in Sierra de Atapuerca (Spain): A comparative morphological study, Journal of Human Evolution 61, 1-11.

Bermúdez de Castro, J.M., Martinón-Torres, M., Prado, L., Gómez-Robles, A., Rosell, J., López-Polín, L., Arsuaga, J.L., Carbonell, E., 2010b. New immature hominin fossil from European Lower Pleistocene shows the earliest evidence of a modern human dental development pattern, Proceedings of the National Academy of Sciences 107, 11739-11744.

Bermúdez de Castro, J.M., Rosas, A. 1992. A human mandibular fragment from the Atapuerca Trench (Burgos, Spain), Journal of Human Evolution 22 (1), 41-46.

Bermúdez de Castro, J.M., Sáenz de Buruaga, A., 1999. Étude préliminaire du site Pléistocène supérieur à hominidé d'Arrillor (Pays Basque, Espagne), L'Anthropologie 103, 4, 633-639.

Bernaldo de Quirós, F, 2006. Symbolism Before the Symbolism: Evidence for the Origins in the Cantabrian Middle Paleolithic, PaleoAnthropology 2006, A38, Paleoanthropology Society, Filadelfia (USA).

Bernaldo de Quirós, F., 1994. Reflexiones en la cueva de Altamira, in: Lasheras (Ed.), Homenaje a Joaquín González-Echegaray. Monografías del Museo Nacional y Centro de Investigación de Altamira, nº 17, Madrid, pp. 261-267.

Bernaldo de Quirós, F., Cabrera Valdés, V., Stuart A.J., 2006, Nuevas dataciones para el Musteriense y el Magdaleniense de la cueva de El Castillo, in: Cabrera V., Bernaldo de Quirós F., Maillo J.M. (Ed.), En el centenario de la cueva de El Castillo: el ocaso de los Neandertales, Centro Asociado de la UNED Cantabria, Santander, pp.- 453-458

Bernaldo de Quirós, F., Castaños, P., Maillo Fernández, J.M., Neira, A., 2012. El Gravetiense de la cueva del Castillo. Nuevos datos, in: de las Heras C., Lasheras, J.A., Arrizabalaga, A., de la Rasilla, M. (Eds.) Pensando el Gravetiense: nuevos datos para la región cantábrica en su contexto peninsular y pirenaico. Monografías del Museo Nacional y Centro de Investigación de Altamira, nº 23, Ministerio de Educación, Cultura y Deporte, Santillana del Mar, Cantabria, pp.- 264-275.

Bernaldo de Quirós, F., Maillo Fernández, J.M., A. Neira, 2008. The place of Unit 18 of El Castillo cave in the Middle to Upper Paleolithic Transition, Eurasian Prehistory 5 (2), 57-71.

Bernaldo de Quirós, F., Maillo Fernández, J.M., Neira, A., 2010. La cueva de El Castillo: perspectivas desde el siglo XXI, El Paleolítico superior peninsular. Novedades desde el siglo XXI, Barcelona, pp. 291- 310.

Biberson, P., 1964. Torralba et Ambrona. Notes sur deux stations acheuléennes de chasseurs d'elephants de la Vieille Castille. Homenaje H. Breuil, v.I. Diputación de Barcelona. Instituto de Prhª y Arqueología, Barcelona, pp. 201-248.

Binder, D., Collina, C., Guilbert, R., Perrin, T., García Puchol, O., 2012. Pressure-Knapping Blade Production in the North-Western Mediterranean Region during the Seventh Millennium cal BC., in: Desrosiers, P.M. (Ed.), The Emergence of Pressure Blade Making: From origin to modern experimentation, Springer, pp. 199-217.

Binford, L. R., 1987. Where There Elephant Hunters at Torralba?, in: Nitecki, M. H., Nitecki, D. V. (Eds.), The Evolution of Human Hunting. Plenum Press, New York, pp. 47-105.

Bird, M.I., Charville-Mort, P.D-J., Ascough, P.L., Wood, R., Higham, T., Apperley, D., 2010. Assessment of oxygen plasma ashing as a pre-treatment for radiocarbon dating, Quaternary Geochronology 5, 435-442.

Bischoff, J., García-Diez, M., González-Morales, M. R., Sharp, W., 2003. Aplicación del método de series de

Uranio al grafismo rupestre de estilo paleolítico de la cavidad de Covalanas (Ramales de la Victoria, Cantabria), Veleia 20, 143-150.

Bischoff, J.L., Julià, R., Mora, R., 1988. Uranium-Series Dating of the Mousterian Occupation at Abric Romani, Spain., Nature 332, 68 - 70.

Bischoff, J.L., Ludwing, K., Garcia, J.F., Carbonell, E., Vaquero, M., Stafford, T.W., 1994. Dating of the basal Aurignacian Sandwich at Abric Romani (Catalunya, Spain) by Radiocarbon and Uranium-Series., Journal of Archaeological Science 21, 541-551.

Bischoff, J.L., Shamp, D.D., Aramburu, A., Arsuaga, J.L., Carbonell, E., Bermúdez de Castro, J.M., 2003. The Sima de los Huesos hominids date to beyond U/Th equilibrium (>350 kyr) and perhaps to 400-500 kyr: New radiometric dates, Journal of Archaeological Science 30, 275-280.

Bischoff, J.L., Soler. N., Maroto-Genover, J., Julià R., 1989. Abrupt Mousterian/Aurignacian Boundary at c. 40 ka bp: Accelerator 14C dates from L'Arbreda Cave (Catalunya, Spain), Journal of Archaeological Science 16, 563-576

Bischoff, J.L., Williams, R.W., Rosenbauer, R.J., Aramburu, A., Arsuaga, J.L., García, N., Cuenca-Bescós, G., 2007. High-resolution U-series dates from the Sima de los Huesos hominids yields 600+8-66 kyrs: implications for the evolution of the early Neanderthal lineage, Journal of Archaeological Science 34, 763-770.

Blain, H.A, Santonja, M., Pérez-González, A., Panera, J., Rubio-Jara, S., 2014, Climate and environments during Marine Isotope Stage 11 in the central Iberian Peninsula: the herpetofaunal assemblage from the Acheulean site of Áridos-1, Madrid, Quaternary Science Reviews 94, 7-21.

Blain, H.A., 2005. Contribution de la paléoherpétofaune (Amphibia and Squamata) à la connaissance de l'évolution du climat et du paysage du Pliocène supérieur au Pléistocène moyen d'Espagne. Tesis Doctoral, Muséum National d'Histoire Naturelle de Paris, Institut de Paléontologie Humaine, París, p. 402.

Blain, H.A., Bailon, S., Cuenca-Bescós, G., Bennàsar, M., Rofes, J., López-García, J.M., Huguet, R., Arsuaga, J.L., Bermúdez de Castro, J.M., Carbonell, E., 2010. Climate and environment of the earliest West European hominins inferred from amphibian and squamate reptile assemblages: Sima del Elefante Lower Red Unit, Atapuerca, Spain, Quaternary Science Reviews 29, 3034-3044.

Blain, H.A., Gleed-Owen, C., López-García, J.M., Carrión, J.S., Jennings, R., Finlayson, G., Finlayson, C., Giles-Pacheco, F., 2013. Climatic conditions for the last Neanderthals: Herpetofaunal record of Gorham's Cave, Gibraltar, J. Hum Evol 64, 289-99.

Blain, H.A., Laplana, C., Sevilla, P., Arsuaga, J. L., Baquedano, E., Pérez-González, A., 2014. MIS5/4 transition in a mountain environment: Herpetofaunal assemblages from Cueva del Camino, central Spain, Boreas 43, 107-120.

Blain, H.-A., López-García, J. M., Cuenca-Bescós, G., Alonso, C., Vaquero, M., Alonso, S., 2009. Première mise en évidence fossile du chioglosse portugais chiglossa lusitánica (Amphibia, Caudata) et son implication pour l'histoire biogéographique de l'espèce. C. R. Paleovol 8, 693-703.

Blain, H.A., Panera, J., Uribelarrea del Val, D., Rubio-Jara, S., Pérez-González, A., 2012. Characterization of a rapid climate shift at the MIS 8/7 transition in central Spain (Valdocarros II, Autonomous Region of Madrid) by means of the herpetological assemblages, Quaternary Science Reviews 47, 73-81.

Blain, H.A., Sesé, C., Rubio-Jara, S., Panera, J., Uribelarrea, D., Pérez-González, A., 2013. Reconstruction paléoenvironnementale et paléoclimatique du Pléistocène supérieur ancien (MIS 5a) dans le Centre de l'Espagne: les petits vertébrés (Amphibia, Reptilia y Mammalia) des gisements de HAT et PRERESA (Sud-est de Madrid), Quaternaire 24, 191-205.

Blasco, F., 1995.Hombres, fieras y presas. Estudio arqueozoológico y tafonómico del yacimiento del Paleolítico Medio de la Cueva de Gabasa 1 (Huesca). Monografías Arqueológicas, 38. Universidad de Zaragoza

Blasco, F., 1997. In the Pursuit of Game: The Mousterian Cave Site of Gabasa I in the Spanish Pyrennees, Journal of Anthropological Research 53 (2), 177-217

Blasco, F., Montes, L., Utrilla, P., 1996. Deux modèles de stratège occupationnelle dans le Moustérien Tardif de la vallée de l'Ebre: les grottes de Peña Miel et Gabasa, in: Carbonell, E., Vaquero, M. (Eds.), The last Neandertals, the first anatomically Modern Humans, pp. 289-313.

Blasco, R., 2011. La amplitud de la dieta cárnica en el Pleistoceno medio peninsular: una aproximación a partir de la Cova del Bolomor (Tavernes de la Valldigna, Valencia) y del subnivel TD10-1 de Gran Dolina (Sierra de Atapuerca, Burgos). Ph. Dissertation, Universitat Rovira i Virgili, Tarragona.

Blasco, R., Blain, H.-A., Rosell, J., Díez, C., Huguet, R., Rodríguez, J., Arsuaga, J.L., Bermúdez de Castro , J.M., Carbonell, E., 2011. Earliest evidence for human consumption of tortoises of European Early Pleistocene from Sima del Elefante, Sierra de Atapuerca, Spain, Journal of Human Evolution 61 (4), 503-509.

Blasco, R., Rosell, J., Arsuaga, J.L., Bermúdez de Castro, J.M., Carbonell, E., 2010. The hunted hunter: the capture of a lion (Panthera leo fossilis) at the Gran Dolina site, Sierra de Atapuerca, Spain, J. Archaeol. Sci. 37, 2051-2060.

Blasco, R., Rosell, J., Domínguez-Rodrigo, M., Lozano, S., Pastó, I., Riba, D., Vaquero, M., Peris, J.F., Arsuaga, J.L., de Castro, J.M.B., Carbonell, E., 2013. Learning by heart: cultural patterns in the faunal processing sequence during the Middle Pleistocene, PlosOne 8, e55863.

Blasco, R., Rosell, J., Fernández Peris, J., Arsuaga, J.L., Bermúdez de Castro, J.M., Carbonell, E., 2013. Environmental availability, behavioural diversity and diet: a zooarchaeological approach from the TD10-1 sublevel of Gran Dolina (Sierra de Atapuerca, Burgos, Spain) and Bolomor Cave (Valencia, Spain), Quaternary Science Reviews 70, 124-144.

Blasco, R., Rosell, J., Made van der, J., Rodríguez, J., Campeny, G., Arsuaga, J.L., Bermúdez de Castro, J.M., Carbonell, E., 2011. Hiding to eat: the role of carnivores in the early Middle Pleistocene from the TD8 level of Gran Dolina (Sierra de Atapuerca, Burgos, Spain), Journal of Archaeological Science 38, 3373-3386.

Boccaccio, G., Utrilla, P., 2013. Du Languedoc à l'Aragon: Analyse technologique comparée du Salpêtrien de la vallée du Rhône et du Solutréen supérieur de la Cueva de Chaves, in: Le Solutréen 40 ans après Smith'66. 47e Supplément à la Revue Archéologique du Centre de la France, Tours.

Bonifay, M.F., 1967. Principales formes caractéristiques du Quaternaire moyen du Sud-Est de la France (grands mammifères), Bulletin du Musée d'Anthropologie Préhistorique de Monaco 14, 49-62.

Bonmatí, A., Gómez-Olivencia, A., Arsuaga, J.L., Carretero, J.M., Gracia, A., Martínez, I., Lorenzo, C., Bérmudez de Castro, J.M., Carbonell, E., 2010. Middle Pleistocene lower back and pelvis from an aged human individual from the Sima de los Huesos site, Spain, Proceedings of the National Academy of Sciences 107: 18386-18391.

Bordes, F., Thibault, Cl., 1977. Thougts on the Initial Adaptation of Hominids to European Glacial Climates, Quaternary Researchs 8, 115-127.

Bordes, F., Viguier, Cl., 1971. Sur la présence de galets taillés de type ancien dans un sol fossile à Puerto de Santa María au Nord-Est de la baie de Cadix (Espagne), C. r. Acad. Sc., 272, 1747-1749.

Botella Ortega, D., Barroso Ruiz, C., Riquelme Cantal, J. A., Abdessadok, S., Caparrós, M., Verdú Bermejo, L., Monge Gómez, G., García Solano, J. A., 2006. La cueva del Ángel (Lucena, Córdoba), un yacimiento del Pleistoceno Medio y Superior del sur de la Península Ibérica, Trabajos de Prehistoria 63 (2), 153-165.

Botella, M., Marqués, I., De Benito, A., Ruiz, A., Delgado MT., 1975. La excavación y sus resultados arqueológicos, Cuadernos de Prehistoria y Arqueología de la Universidad de Granada 1, 25-45.

Botella, M., Martínez, C., 1979. El yacimiento musteriense de Cueva Horá (Darro, Granada): Estudio de las campañas 1977 y 1978 en Cueva Horá, Antropología y Paleoecología Humana 1, 59-74.

Breuil, H., 1908. Les pintures quaternaires de la Roca del Cogul, Butlletí del Centre Excursionista de Lleida, Año I, pp. 10-13.

Breuil, H., 1920. Les peintures rupestres de la Péninsule Ibérique, Les roches peintes á Minateda (Albacete), L'Anthropologie XXX, 1-50.

Breuil, H., 1921. Nouvelles cavernes ornées paléolithiques dans la province de Málaga, L'Anthropologie 31, 239-253.

Breuil, H., Cabré Aguiló, J., 1909. Les peintures rupestres du bassin inferieur de l'Ebre, L'Anthropologie XX, 1-21.

Breuil, H., Obermaier, H., 1935. La Cueva de Altamira en Santillana del Mar. Tipografía de Archivos, Madrid.

Breuil, H., Obermaier, H., Alcalde del Río, H., 1913. La Pasiega à Puente Viesgo (Santander) (Espagne), Institut de Paléontologie Humaine, Chêne, Mónaco.

Briggs, A.W., Good, J. M., Green, R. E., Krause, J., Maricic, T., Stenzel, U., Lalueza-Fox. C., Rudan, P., Brajković, D., Kućan, Ž., Gušić, I., Schmitz, R., Doronichev, V. B., Golovanova, L. V., Rasilla, M. de la, Fortea, J, Rosas, A., Pääbo, S., 2009. Targeted retrieval and analysis of five Neandertal mtDNA genomes, Science 325, 318-321.

Broca, P., 1869. Remarques sur les ossements des cavernes de Gibraltar, Bull. Mem. Soc. Anthropol. 4, 146-158.

Brock, F., Higham, T., Ditchfield, P., Bronk Ramsay,C., 2010. Current Pretreatment Methods for AMS Radiocarbon Dating at the Oxford Radiocarbon Accelerator Unit (ORAU), Radiocarbon 52 (1), 103-112.

Bronk , C.R., 2009. Bayesian analysis of radiocarbon dates, Radiocarbon 51, 337-360 .

Bronk Ramsey, C., 2009. Bayesian analysis of radiocarbon dates, Radiocarbon 51 (1), 337-360.

Brown, A. B., 1867. On the Geology of Gibraltar with special reference to the recently explored caves and bone breccia. Proc. R. A. Institution, 1867.

Brusi, D., Linares, R., Maroto-Genover, J., Pallí, L., Pujadas, R., Ramió, S., Roqué, C., Soler, N., 2005. Las cuevas prehistóricas de Serinyà (Pla de l'Estany, Girona), Boletín Geológico y Minero X, 116, 3, 247-256.

Brusi, D., Maroto-Genover, J., Soler, N., 2002. Zona lacustre de Banyotes, in: Pallí, Ll., Roqué, C., Brusi, D. (Eds.), Geología de Girona: 9 itinerarios de campo. XII Simposio sobre Enseñanza de la Geología, Girona, pp. 168-188.

Bueno Ramirez, P., Balbín Behrmann, R. de., 2009. Marcadores gráficos y territorios tradicionales en la Prehistoria de la Península Ibérica, Cuadernos de Prehistoria y Arqueología de la Universidad de Granada 19, 65-100.

Bueno, P.R., Balbín, R., Alcolea, J.J., 2007. Style V dans le bassin du Duero. Tradition et changement dans les graphies des chasseurs du Paléolithique Supérieur européen, L'Antropologie 11, 549-589.

Bueno, P.R., Balbín, R., Alcolea, J.J., 2009. Estilo V en el ámbito del Duero: cazadores finiglaciares en siega Verde (Salamanca), in: Balbín, R. de (Eds.), Arte Prehistórico al aire libre en el Sur de Europa, Junta de castilla y León, Valladolid, pp. 259-490.

Bukhsianidze, M., 2005. The Fossil Bovidae of Dmanisi. PhD International Doctorate "Environmental, Humans and Compartmental Dynamics" XVI cycle 2001-2004 at the University of Ferrara (Italy), p. 192.

Burbano, H. A., Hodges, E., Green, R.E., Briggs, A. W., Krause, J., Meyer, M., Good, J. M., Maricic, T., Johnson, P.L.F., Xuan, Z., Rooks, M., Bhattacharjee, A., Brizulea, L., Albert, F.W., Rasilla, M. de la, Fortea, J., Rosas, A., Lachmann, M., Hannon, G. J., Pääbo, S., 2010. Targeted investigation of the Neandertal genome by Array-Based sequence capture, Science 328, 723-725.

Burjachs, F., 2002. Paleoecología del Homo antecessor: Palinología de la Unidades TD5, 6 y 7 de la "Gran Dolina" de

Atapuerca (Burgos, Spain)Lengua Española (A.P.L.E), in: Cartagena, U.P.d. (Ed.), XIII Simposio de la Asociación de Palinólogos en Lengua Española (A.P.L.E.), Universidad Politécnica de Cartagena, Cartagena.

Burjachs, F., Julià, R., 1994. Abrupt Climatic Changes during the Last Glaciation Based on Pollen Analysis of the Abric Romani, Catalonia, Spain, Quaternary Research 42, 308 - 315.

Burjachs, F., Renault-Miskovsky, J., 1992, Paléoenvironnement et Paléoclimatologie de la Catalogne durant pres de 30.000 ans (du Würmien ancien au début de l'Holocène d'aprés la palinologie du site de l'Arbreda (Gérone, Catalogne), Quaternaire 3 (2), 1992, 75-85.

Busk, G., 1864. Pithecoid Priscan Man from Gibraltar, The Reader 4, 109-110

Busk, G., 1864. Report on British Association Meeting. Bath Chronicle (special daily edition) 22nd September.

Busk, G., 1865. On a very ancient human cranium from Gibraltar. Report of the 34th meeting of the British Association for the Advancement of Science, Bath 1864, 91-92.

Busk, G., 1868. On the caves of Gibraltar in which human remains and works of art have been found. Trans. Int. Congr. Anthrop. y Prehist. Archaeol., 3rd Session, Norwich.

Butzer, K.W., 1965. Acheulian Occupation Sites at Torralba and Ambrona, Spain. Their Geology, Science 150, 1718-1722.

Butzer, K.W., 1967. Geomorphology and Stratigraphy of the Paleolithic site of Budiño (Province of Pontevedra, Spain), Eiszeitalter und Gegenwart 18 (Ohringen/ Würt, 31-12), 82-103.

Butzer, K.W., 1971. Environment and Archaeology. An ecological approach to prehistory. Aldine, Chicago.

Butzer, K.W., 1980. Investigación preliminar de la geología de la cueva de El Pendo, in: J. González-Echegaray (Ed.), El yacimiento de la cueva de "El Pendo" (excavaciones 1953-57). Biblioteca Praehistorica Hispana, vol. XVII, Madrid, pp. 201-213.

Butzer, K.W., 1981. Cave sediments, Upper Pleistocene stratigraphy and Mousterian facies in Cantabrian Spain, Journal of Archaeological Science 8, 133-183.

C.R.P.E.S., 1985. Sota Palou (Campdevànol). Un centre d'intervenció prehistòrica postglaciar a l'aire lliure, Diputació de Girona, Girona.

Cabanes, D., Mallol, C., Expósito, I., Baena, J., 2010. Phytolith Evidence for Hearths and Beds in the Late Mousterian Occupations of Esquilleu Cave (Cantabria, Spain). Journal of Archaeological Science 37, 2947-2957.

Cabré Aguiló, J., 1915. El arte rupestre en España. (Regiones septentrional y oriental). Comisión de Investigaciones Paleontológicas y Prehistóricas, I.

Cabré Aguiló, J., 1925. Las pinturas rupestres de La Valltorta: Escena bélica de la Cova del Civil, AMSEAEP, pp. 201-233.

Cabrera-Valdés, V., 1984. El yacimiento de la Cueva de "El Castillo. (Puente Viesgo, Santander). C.S.I.C. p. 485

Cabrera-Valdés, V., 1984. El yacimiento de la cueva de El Castillo (Puente Viesgo, Santander), Biblioteca Prehistorica Hispana XXII, Madrid.

Cabrera-Valdés, V., Arrizabalaga, A., Bernaldo de Quirós, F., Maíllo-Fernández, J. M., 2004. La transición al paleolítico Superior y la evolución de los contextos Auriñacienses (50.000-27.000 BP). Kobie Anejos 8, 141-208.

Cabrera-Valdés, V., Bernaldo de Quirós F, 1984. Die Wohnstrukturen von Cueva de Chufín und Cueva del Castillo Kantabrisches Spanien, Structures d'habitat du Paleolithique Superieur en Europe, Urgeschichte Materialhefte, 6, pp.51 57.

Cabrera-Valdés, V., Bernaldo de Quirós, F., 1977. The solutrean site of Cueva Chufín (Santander, Spain), Current Anthropology 18, 780-781.

Cabrera-Valdés, V., Bernaldo de Quirós, Maillo J Fernández, J.M., Valladas, H., Lloret, M., 2006. El Auriñaciense arcaico de El Castillo (Cantabria): descripción tecnológica y objetivos de la producción. En torno a los conceptos de Protoauriñaciense, Auriñaciense Arcaico, inicial y antiguo. Espacio Tiempo y Forma I-15, U.N.E.D., Madrid. 67-86.

Cabrera-Valdés, V., J. Bischoff, J., 1989. Accelerator 14C dates for Early Upper Paleolithic Basal Aurignacian at El Castillo Cave Spain, Journal of Archaeological Science 16, 577 584 .

Cabrera-Valdés, V., Maillo Fernández, J.M., Lloret, M., Bernaldo de Quirós, F., 2001. La transition vers le paléolithique supérieur dans la grotte du Castillo (Cantabrie, Espagne): la couche 18, L'Anthropologie 105, 505-532.

Cabrera-Valdés, V., Múzquiz, M., 2000. El arte rupestre de la cueva de Las Monedas (Puente Viesgo). Resultados preliminares de las campañas 1989-1990, in: Actuaciones Arqueológicas en Cantabria 1984-1999, Gobierno de Cantabria, Santander, pp. 145-146.

Cabrera-Valdés, V., Pike-Tay, A., Bernaldo de Quirós, F., 2004. Trends in Middel Paleolithic settlement in Cantabrian Spain: The Late Mousterian at Castillo Cave. Settlement Dynamics of the Middle Palaeolithic and Midle Stone Age, Vol. II, Kerns Verlag, Tubingen, pp. 437-460.

Cabrera-Valdés, V., Valladas, F., Bernaldo de Quirós, F., Hoyos, M., 1996. La transition Paléolithique moyen-Paléolithique supérieur à El Castillo Cantabrie: nouvelles datations par le carbone-14, Comptes Rendues Academie Sciences de Paris, 322, IIa, 1093-1098.

Cáceres, I., 2002. Tafonomía de yacimientos antrópicos en Karst. Complejo Galería (Sierra de Atapuerca, Burgos), Vanguard Cave (Gibraltar) y Abric Romaní (Capellades, Barcelona). Departament d'Història i Geografiaa. Universitat Rovira i Virgili, Tarragona. p. 659.

Cáceres, I., Huguet, R., Rosell, J., Esteban-Nadal, M., Saladié, P., Díez, J.C., Ollé, A., Vallverdú, J., García-Medrano, P., Carbonell, E., 2010. El yacimiento de Galería (Sierra de Atapuerca, Burgos, España). Un enclave para la obtención de recursos cárnicos en el Pleistoceno Medio, Zona Arqueológica 13, 186-195.

Cáceres, I., Lozano, M., Saladié, P., 2007. Evidence for Bronze Age Cannibalism in El Mirador Cave (Sierra de Atapuerca, Burgos, Spain), American Journal of Physical Anthropology 133 (3), 899-917.

Cacho, C., Fumanal, M.P., López, P., Pérez Ripoll, M., Martínez Valle, R., Uzquiano, P., Arnanz, A.,Sánchez Marco, A., Sevilla, P., Morales, A., Roselló, E., Garralda, M.D., García-Carrillo, M. 1995. El Tossal de la Roca (Vall d'Alcalà, Alicante). Reconstrucción paleoambiental y cultural de la transición del Tardiglaciar al Holoceno inicial, Recerques del Museu d'Alcoi 4, 11-101.

Cacho, I., Grimalt, J.O., Canals, M., Sbaffi, L., Shackleton, N.J., Schönfeld, J., Zahn, R., 2001. Variability of the western Mediterranean Sea surface temperature during the last 25.000 years and its connection with the Northern Hemisphere climate changes, Paleoceanography 16 (1), 40-52.

Cacho, I., Grimalt, J.O., Canals, M., Sbaffi, L., Shackleton, N.J., Schönfeld, J., Zahn, R., 2001. Variability of the western Mediterranean Sea surface temperatures during the last 25,000 years and its connection with the northern hemisphere climatic changes, Paleoceanography 16, 40 - 52.

Cacho, I., Grimalt, J.O., Pelejero, C., Canals, M., Sierro, F.J., Flores, J.A., Shackleton, N., 1999. Dansgaard-Oeschger and Heinrich event imprints in Alboran Sea paleotemperatures, Paleoceanography 14 (6), 698-705.

Cacho-Quesada, C., (coord.) 2013. Ocupaciones magdalenienses en el interior de la Península Ibérica. La Peña de Estebanvela (Ayllón, Segovia). Junta de Castilla y León-CSIC.

Cacho-Quesada, C., de la Torre, I., 2005. Les harpons magdaleniens sur le versant mediterranéen espagnol, in : Dujardin, V. (Coord.), Industries osseuses et parures du Solutréen au Magdalénien en Europe, Mémoire XXXIX de la Societé préhistorique française, pp. 257-266.

Cacho-Quesada, C., Jordá Pardo, J., De la Torre Sáinz,, I., 2001. Tossal de la Roca (Alicante), in: Villaverde, V. (Ed.), De neandertales a cromañones. El inicio del poblamiento humano en tierras valencianas, Universitat de Valencia, Fundació General de la Universitat de Valencia, Valencia, pp. 419- 424.

Cacho-Quesada, C., Jordá Pardo, J., De la Torre, I., Ravedra, J., 2001. El Tossal de la Roca (Alicante. Nuevos datos sobre el Magdaleniense mediterráneo de la Península ibérica, Trabajos de Prehistoria, 58, I, pp. 71-93.Madrid.

Cacho-Quesada, C., Jordá, J., 2009. El Tossal de la Roca. The Pleistocene- Holocene Transition in the Mediterranean Region of Eastern Spain, Journal of Anthropological Research 65, 221-236.

Cacho-Quesada, C., Jordá-Pardo, J.F., De la Torre Sáinz, I. e Yravedra Sáinz de los Terreros, J., 2001. El Tossal de la Roca (Alicante). Nuevos datos sobre el Magdaleniense mediterráneo de la Península Ibérica, Trabajos de Prehistoria 58 (1), 71-93.

Cacho-Quesada, C., Martos, J. A., 2004. Estudio tecnológico de los niveles magdalenienses del Tossal de la Roca (Vall d' Alcalá, Alicante), in: Miscelánea en Homenaje a Emiliano Aguirre, Arqueología, Zona Arqueológica 4, pp. 88- 101.

Cacho-Quesada, C., Martos, J.A., Jordá- Pardo, J., Yravedra, J., Sesé, C., Zapata, L., Avezuela, B., Valdivia, J. Ruiz, M., Marquer, L., Martín- Lerma, I., Tejero, J.M., 2012. Human landscapes of the Late Glacial Period in the interior of the Iberian Peninsula: La Peña de Estebanvela (Segovia, Spain), Quaternary International 272-273, 42- 54.

Cacho-Quesada, C., Pérez Marín, S., 1997. El Magdaleniense de la Meseta y sus relaciones con el Mediterráneo español: el abrigo de Buendía (Cuenca), in: J. M. Fullola, N. Soler (Eds.), El món mediterrani després del Pleniglacial (18.000-12.000 B.P.). Banyoles 18-20 maig 1995. Serie Monogràfica 17. Centre d'investigacions arqueologiques. Girona, pp. 263-275.

Cacho-Quesada, C., Ripoll López, S. 1987. Nuevas piezas de arte mueble en el Mediterráneo español, Trabajos de Prehistoria 44, 35-62.

Cacho-Quesada, C., Ripoll, S., 1987. Nuevas piezas de arte mueble en el Mediterráneo español, Trabajos de Prehistoria 44

Cacho-Quesada, C., Ripoll, S., Muñoz, F.J., (coords.) 2007. La Peña de Estebanvela (Estebanvela-Ayllón, Segovia). Grupos magdalenienses en el sur del Duero. Memorias de Arqueología de Castilla y León 17. Junta de Castilla y León, Valladolid.

Calvo, M., 2004. La memoria del útil. Análisis funcional de la industria lítica de la Cueva del Parco (Alòs de Balaguer, La Noguera Lleida). Monografies del SERP 5, Ed. SERP, Barcelona.

Campillo, D., Eulalia Subirá, M., Chimenos, E., Aparicio, J., Pérez, A., Vila, S., 2002. Estudi de les restes humanes de la campanya 2000 de la Cova Foradà (Oliva, València), Cypsela 14, 143-150.

Canal, J., Carbonell, E., 1978. Nova aportació per l'estudi del Paleolític Inferior i Mig del NE de Catalunya, Revista de Girona 83, 265-288.

Canal, J., Carbonell, E., 1979. Les estaciones prehistòriques del Puig d'en Roca. Girona, Associació Arqueològica de Girona, Girona.

Canal, J., Carbonell, E., 1989. Catalunya paleolítica, Diputació de Girona, Patronat Francesc Eiximenis, Girona.

Canal, J., Soler, N., 1976. El Paleolític a les comarques gironines, Caixa d'Estalvis Provincial de Girona, Girona.

Canals, A., Aranda, V., Barrero, N., Bermejo, L., Donadei, P., García-Vadillo, F.J., Mejías del Cosso, D., Marín, J., Modesto, M., Morcillo, A., Rabazo, A., Rodriguez-Hidalgo, A., Carbonell, E., 2013. La cueva de El Conejar (Cáceres), nuevos datos para la transición del Paleolítico al Neolítico en el interior de la Península. Actas del VI Encuentro de Arqueología del Suroeste Peninsular, Badajoz, Villafranca de los Barros, 2013, pp. 171-192.

Canals, A., Aranda, V., Barrero, N., Bermejo, L., García Vadillo, F.J., Mancha, E., Marín, J., Mejías del Cosso, D.,

Modesto, M., Morcillo, A., Peña, L., Rabazo, A., Rodríguez Hidalgo, A. J., Canals, A., Sauceda, I., Carbonell, E., 2004. The project "The first settlers in Extremadura" and the Paleolithic in the Salor area, BAR International Series. Acts of XIVth U.I.S.P.P. 1239, pp. 157-167.

Canals, A., García, M., Sauceda, I., Carbonell, E., 2005. Actividad arqueológica y conservación del arte rupestre en la Cueva de Maltravieso (Cáceres, España), Boletín del Instituto Andaluz de Patrimonio Histórico 53, pp. 44-57

Canals, A., Rodríguez-Hidalgo, A., Peña, L., Mancha, E., García-Díez, M., Bañuls, S., Euba, I., López-García, J. M., Barrero, N., Bermejo, L., García, F. J., Mejías, D., Modesto, M., Morcillo, A., Aranda, V., Carbonell, E., 2010. Nuevas aportaciones al Paleolítico superior del suroeste peninsular: la cueva de Maltravieso, más allá del santuario extremeño de las manos, in: El paleolítico superior peninsular. novedades del siglo XXI, Barcelona, pp. 199-218.

Canals, A., Sauceda, I., Carbonell, E., 2004. The project "The first settlers in Extremadura" and the Paleolithic in the Salor area, BAR International Series. Acts of XIVth U.I.S.P.P., pp. 157-167.

Canals, A., Sauceda, I., Carbonell, E., Díaz, O., Mejias, D., 2004. Industries of the Middle Paleolithic in open-air sites in Extremadura. Acts of XIVth U.I.S.P.P., BAR International Series 1239.

Canals, A., van der Made, J., Sauceda, I., Carbonell, E., 2003. El conjunto paleontológico de la cueva de Maltravieso (Cáceres): un nuevo yacimiento del Pleistoceno, in: Actas de la IX Reunión Nacional de Cuaternario, Consejería de Cultura, Cajastur, AEQUA, Principado de Asturias, Concejo de Candamo, pp. 313-320,

Cantalejo, P., Espejo, M.-M., Ramos, J., Weniger, G.-C., 2014 (a). Elementos de iluminación, in: Ramos, J., Weniger, G.-C., Cantalejo, P., Espejo, M. M. (Ed.), Cueva de Ardales. Intervenciones Arqueológicas 2011 - 2014. Ediciones Pinsapar, Málaga, pp. 119-146.

Cantalejo, P., Espejo, M.-M., Ramos, J., Weniger, G.-C., Pastoors, A., 2014 (b). Resultados de las Investigaciones sobre el Arte Rupestre Prehistórico, in: Ramos, J., Weniger, G.-C., Cantalejo, P., Espejo, M.-M. (Ed.), Cueva de Ardales - Intervenciones Arqueológicas 2011 - 2014. Ediciones Pinsapar, Málaga, pp. 165-194.

Cantalejo, P., Maura, R., Espejo, M.-M., Ramos, J., Medieranero, J., Aranada, A., 2006. La Cueva de Ardales: Arte prehistórico y ocupación en el Paleolítico Superior. (Ed.) CEDMA, Diputación de Málaga, Málaga.

Cañaveras, J.C., Sánchez-moral, S., Lario, J., Cuezva, S., Fernández Cortés, A., Muñoz, M. C., 2011. El modelo de relleno, o cómo llegaron los restos a la Galería del Osario, in: Rasilla, M. de la, Rosas, A., Cañaveras, J. C., Lalueza-Fox, C. (Eds.), La Cueva de El Sidrón (Borines, Piloña, Asturias). Investigación interdisciplinar de un grupo neandertal, Consejería de Cultura y Turismo y Ediciones Trabe SLU, Oviedo, pp. 43-63.

Caparrós, M., Barroso Ruiz, C., Moigne, A. Mª., Monclova Bohórquez, A., 2012. Did Neanderthals and carnivores compete for animal nutritional resources in the surroundings of the Cave of Zafarraya?, Journal of Taphonomy 10, 395-415.

Carballo, J., 1923. Excavaciones en la cueva del Rey, en Villanueva (Santander). Junta Superior de Excavaciones y Antigüedades, 9, Madrid.

Carballo, J., Larín, B., 1933. Exploración en la gruta de El Pendo (Santander), Junta Superior de Excavaciones y Antigüedades, 123, Madrid.

Carbonell, E., 1985. Méthode d'analyse appliquée aux industries lithiques des gisements du Pleistocene Moyen du Massif de Montgrí (Catalogne, Espagne), Tesis doctoral, Université de Paris VI, Paris, 2 vols., p. 510.

Carbonell, E., 1992. Abric Romaní, nivell H: un model d'estratègia ocupacional al Plistocè superior mediterrani., Estrat 5, 159-308.

Carbonell, E., 2001. La cueva de Santa Ana: las primeras comunidades humanas en El Calerizo, II Jornadas de Arqueología Urbana de Cáceres, Museo de Cáceres, Cáceres.

Carbonell, E., 2002. Abric Romaní nivell I. Models d'ocupació de curta durar de fa 46.000 anys a la Cinglera del Capelló (Capellades, Anoia, Barcelona), Universitat Rovira i Virgili, Tarragona.

Carbonell, E., 2012. High resolution archaeology and Neanderthal behavior: time and space in level J of Abric Romaní (Capellades, Spain), Springer, Dordrecht.

Carbonell, E., Bermúdez de Castro, J.M., Arsuaga, J.L., Díez, J.C., Rosas, A., Cuenca-Bescós, G., Sala, R., Mosquera, M., Rodríguez, X.P. 1995. Lower Pleistocene hominins and artifacts from Atapuerca-TD6 (Spain), Science 269, 826-830.

Carbonell, E., Bermúdez de Castro, J.M., Pares, J.M., Perez-Gonzalez, A., Cuenca-Bescos, G., Olle, A., Mosquera, M., Huguet, R., van der Made, J., Rosas, A., Sala, R., Vallverdu, J., Garcia, N., Granger, D.E., Martinon-Torres, M., Rodriguez, X.P., Stock, G.M., Verges, J.M., Allue, E., Burjachs, F., Cáceres, I., Canals, A., Benito, A., Diez, C., Lozano, M., Mateos, A., Navazo, M., Rodriguez, J., Rosell, J., Arsuaga, J.L., 2008. The first hominin of Europe, Nature 452, 465-467.

Carbonell, E., Cáceres, I., Lozano, M., Saladié, P., Rosell, J., Lorenzo, C., Vallverdú, J., Huguet, R., Canals, A., Bermúdez de Castro, J.M., 2010. Cultural cannibalism as a paleoeconomic system in the european Lower Pleistocene, Current Anthropology 51, 539-549.

Carbonell, E., Canals, A., Sauceda, I., Barrero, N., Carbajo, Á., Díaz, Ó., Díaz, I., Fernández, R., García, F.J., Peña, L., García, M., García, M., Gil, J., Guerra, S., León, L. M., Mancha, S., Mancha, E., Mejías, D., Merino, R. M., Morano, M., Morcillo, A., Muñoz, L., Rodríguez, A., Julià, R., Giralt, S., Falguères, C., 2005. La grotte de Santa Ana (Cáceres, Espagne) et l'évolution technologique au Pléistocène dans la Péninsule ibérique, L'Anthropologie 109 (2), 267-285.

Carbonell, E., Culí, N., Busquets, R., 1976. El Paleolític Mitjà a la conca del Freser, Cypsela 1, 23-27.

Carbonell, E., García-Antón, M.D., Mallol, C., Mosquera, M., Ollé, A., Rodríguez, X.P., Sahnouni, M., Sala, R., Vergès, J.M. 1999. The TD6 level lithic industry from Gran Dolina, Atapuerca (Burgos, Spain): production and use, Journal of Human Evolution 37, 653-693.

Carbonell, E., Guilbaud, M., Mora, R., Muro, I., Sala, R., Miralles, J., 1988. El complex del Plistocè mitjà del Puig d'en Roca, Consejo Superior de Investigaciones Científicas, Girona.

Carbonell, E., Márquez, B., Ollé, A., Rodríguez, X.P., Vallverdú, J., Vergès, J.M., Zaragoza, J., 1992. Els Vinyets. El Catllar (Tarragonès). Els primers pobladors de la Catalunya meridional. Ajuntament del Catllar, El Catllar.

Carbonell, E., Mora, R., 1984. Diacronía y homogeneidad funcional entre dos yacimientos del paleolítico inferior del NE catalán: Pedra Dreta y Puig d'en Roca III, in (Ed.): Arqueología Espacial 2. Coloquio sobre distribución y relaciones entre los asentamientos, Seminario de Arqueología y Etnología Turolense, Colegio Universitario de Teruel, Teruel, pp. 147-158.

Carbonell, E., Mosquera, M., 2006. The emergence of a symbolic behaviour: the sepulchral pit of Sima de los huesos, Sierra de Atapuerca, Burgos, Spain, C.R. Palevol 5, 155-160.

Carbonell, E., Mosquera, M., Ollé, A., Rodríguez, X.P., Sahnouni, M., Sala, R., Vergès, J.M., 2001. Structure morphotechnique de l'industrie lithique du Pléistocène inférieur et moyen d'Atapuerca (Burgos, Espagne), L'Anthropologie 105, 259-280

Carbonell, E., Mosquera, M., Ollé, A., Rodríguez, X.P., Sala, R., Vergès, J.M., Arsuaga, J.L., Bermúdez de Castro, J.M., 2003. Les premiers comportements funéraires auraient-ils pris place à Atapuerca, il y a 350 000 ans?, L'Anthropologie 107, 1-14.

Carbonell, E., Rodríguez, X.P., 2007-2008. El Paleolítico inferior en Cataluña, Veleia 24-25, 331-343.

Carbonell, E., Rodríguez, X.P., Rosell, J., Vallverdú, J., Vaquero, M., 1999. Les VinyesGrans (Perafort, Tarragonès) i els-Vinyets (el Catllar, Tarragonès), Les indústries i el seu context estratigràfic. Jornades d'Arqueologia, Tortosa, p.13.

Carbonell, E., Rodríguez, X.P., Sala, R., Vaquero, M., 1992. New elements of the logical-analitic system, Cahier Noir 6, 3-61.

Carbonell, E., Rosas González, A., Díez Fernández, J. C., 1999. Atapuerca: Ocupaciones humanas y Paleoecología del yacimiento de Galería, Arqueología en Castilla y León 7, Memorias, Junta de Castilla y León. Consejería de Educación y Cultura.

Carbonell, E., Sala, R., Rodríguez, X.P., Mosquera, M., Ollé, A., Vergès, J.M., Martínez- Navarro, B., Bermúdez de Castro, J.M., 2010. Early hominid dispersals: a technological hypothesis for 'out of Africa', Quaternary International 223-224, 36-44.

Cardoso, S., Valverde, L., Palencia, L., Pancorbo, M., López Quintana, J.C., Guenaga Lizasu, A., 2011. Análisis de ADN mitocondrial en los restos humanos de la cueva de Santimamiñe (Kortezubi, Bizkaia), Kobie Serie BAI n.º 1, 383-391.

Carrancho, A., Villalaín, J.J., Pavón-Carrasco, F., Osete, M., Straus, L., Vergès, J., Carretero, J., Angelucci, D., González-Morales, M., Arsuaga, J., Bermúdez de Castro, J., Carbonell, E., 2013. First directional European palaeosecular variation curve for the Neolithic based on archaeomagnetic data, Earth and Planetary Science Letters 380, 124-137.

Carrancho, A., Villalaín, J.J., Pavón-Carrasco, F.J., Oseted, M.L., Straus, L.G. Vergès, J.M. Carretero, J.M., Angelucci, D.E., González-Morales, M.R, Arsuaga, J.L., Bermúdez de Castro, J.M., Carbonell, E., 2013. First direccional European palaeosecular variation curve for the Neolithic based on archaeo magnetic data, Earth and Planetary Science Letters 380, 124-137.

Carretero, J.M., Arsuaga, J.L., Lorenzo, C., 1997. Clavicles, scapulae and humeri from the Sima de los Huesos site (Sierra de Atapuerca, Spain), Journal of Human Evolution 33, 357-408.

Carretero, J.M., Lorenzo, C., Arsuaga, J.L., 1999. Axial and appendicular skeleton of Homo antecessor, Journal of Human Evolution 37, 459-500.

Carretero, J.M., Ortega, A.I., Juez, L., Pérez-González, A., Arsuaga, J.L., Pérez-Martínez, R., Ortega, M.C., 2008. A late Pleistocene-Early Holocene archaeological sequence of Portalón de Cueva Mayor (Sierra de Atapuerca, Burgos, Spain), MUNIBE (Antropologia-Arkeologia) 59, 67-80.

Carrión Marco, Y., 2005. La vegetación mediterránea y atlántica de la Península Ibérica. Nuevas secuencias antracológicas, Trabajos Varios del SIP-Museu de Prehistòria 104.

Carrión Santafé, E., 2002. Variabilidad técnica en el Musteriense de Cantabria. Tesis doctoral microficada. Universidad Autónoma de Madrid. Departamento de Prehistoria y Arqueología.

Carrión Santafé, E., Baena Preysler J., Torres Navas C., 2013. Una tecnología en extinción: procesos técnicos y tecnológicos del final del musteriense en el norte peninsular, Mainake 33, 251-274.

Carrión Santafé, E., Baena Preysler, J., Conde Ruiz, C., Cuartero, F., Roca, M., 2008. Variabilidad tecnológica en el musteriense de Cantabria, Treballs D'Arqueologia 14, 279-318.

Carrión, J.S., Finlayson, C., Fernández, S., Finlayson, G., Allué, E., López-Sáez, J. A., López-García, P., Gil-Romera, G., Bailey, G., González-Sampériz, P., 2008. A coastal reservoir of biodiversity for Upper Pleistocene human populations: palaeoecological investigations in Gorham's Cave (Gibraltar) in the context of the Iberian Peninsula. Quat. Sci. Rev. 27, 2118-2135.

Carrión, J.S., Yll, E.I., Walker, M.J., Legaz, A.J., Chain, C., López, A., 2003. Glacial refugia of temperate, Mediterranean and Ibero-North African flora in south-eastern Spain: new evidence from cave pollen at two Neanderthal man sites, Global Ecology and Biogeography 12, 119-129.

Carrión, J.S., Yll, E.I., Walker, M.J., Legaz, A.J., Chain, C., López, A., 2003. Glacial refugia of temperate, Mediterranean and Ibero-North African flora in south-eastern Spain: new evidence from cave pollen at two Neanderthal man sites, Global Ecology and Biogeography 12, 119-129.

Cartailhac, E., 1902. La grotte d'Altamira, Espagne. *Mea culpa* d'un sceptique, L'Anthropologie 13, 348-354.

Cartailhac, E., 1902. Les cavernes ornées de dessins. La grotte d'Altamira, Espagne. Mea culpa d'un sceptique, L'Anthropologie 13, 348-354.

Cartailhac, E., Breuil, H., 1906. La Caverne d'Altamira à Santillane prés Santander (Espagne). Imprimérie de Mónaco, Mónaco.

Casado, P., 1979. Consideraciones sobre la distribución geográfica de algunos elementos del arte paleolítico, Caesaraugusta 49-50, 89-100.

Casanova, J., Martínez-Moreno, J., Mora R., de la Torre, I., 2009. Stratégies techniques dans le Paléolithique Moyen du sudest des Pyrénées, L'Anthropologie 113, 313-340.

Casanova, J., Martínez-Moreno, J., Mora, R., de la Torre, I., 2009. Stratégies techniques dans le Paléolithique Moyen du sud-est des Pyrénées, L'Anthropologie 113, 313-340.

Casanova, J., Pizarro, J., 2004. La Balma Guilanya (Naves, Solsones). Un yacimiento Paleolítico en el Pre-Pirineo de Cataluña, in: Allué, E., Martin, J., Carbonell, E., Canals, A. (Eds.), Actas del Primer Congreso Peninsular de Estudiantes de Prehistoria, Universitat Rovira i Virgili, Tarragona, pp. 195-203.

Casanova, J., Roda, X., Martínez-Moreno, J., Mora, R., 2014. Débitage, façonnage et diversité des systèmes techniques du Moustérien à Tragó (Pré-Pyrénées de Lleida, Catalogne), in : Brenet *et al.*, (Ed.), Émergence et diversité des techno-complexes au Paléolithique moyen ancien, XXVIIe Congrès Préhistorique de France, Paris, pp. 139-154.

Casas, J., Peña, JA., Vera, JA., 1975. Interpretación geológica y estratigráfica del yacimiento de La Solana del Zamborino, Cuadernos de Prehistoria de la Universidad de Granada 1, 5-15.

Castaños, P., Castaños, J. 2011. Estrategias de caza en la secuencia prehistórica de Santimamiñe, Kobie Serie BAI n.° 1, 197-205.

Castaños Ugarte, P.M., 2005. Revisión actualizada de las faunas de macromamíferos del Würm antiguo en la Región Cantábrica, in: Montes Barquín, R., Lasheras Corruchaga, J.A. (Coord.), Neandertales cantábricos. Estado de la cuestión. Museo de Altamira, Monografías n° 20, Santander, pp. 201-207.

Castaños, P., Murelaga, X., Arrizabalaga, A., Iriarte, M.J., 2011. First evidence of Macaca sylvanus (Primates, Cercopithecidae) from the Late Pleistocene of Lezetxiki II Cave (Basque Country, Spain), Journal of Human Evolution 60, 816-820.

Castellano, S., Parra, G., Sánchez-Quinto, F. A., Racimo, F. Kuhlwilm, M., Kirkher, M., Sawyer, S., Fu, Q., Heinze, A., Nickel, B., Dabney, J., Siebauer, M., White, L., Burbano, H. A., Renaud, G., Stenzel, U., Lalueza-Fox., C., Rasilla, M. de la, Rosas, A., Rudan, P., Brajkovic, D., Kucan, Ž., Gušic, I., Shuncov, M. V., Derevianko, A. P., Viola, B., Meyer, M., Kelso, J., Andrés, A. M., Pääbo, S., 2014. Patterns of coding variation in the complete exomes of three Neandertals, PNAS, Early Edition, doi/10.1073/pnas.1405138111.

Castelló, E.C., 2003. Catálogo Espeleológico del término municipal de Vilafamés, Ayuntamiento de Vilafamés, Vilafamés.

Castellví, M., 1974. La Cueva de les Teixoneres (Moià, Barcelona), in: (Eds.), Miscelánea Arqueológica. XXV Aniversario de los Cursos Internacionales de Prehistoria y Arqueología de Ampurias (1947-1971). Barcelona. I, pp. 229-232.

Castilla, M., Carretero, J.M., Gracia, A., Arsuaga, J.L., 2014. Evidence of rickets and/or scurvy in a complete Chalcolithic Child skeleton from the Site of El Portalón (Sierra de Atapuerca, Spain), Journal of Anthropological Sciences 92, 1-16.

Cava, A., 2004. La ocupación prehistórica de Kanpanoste en el contexto de los cazadores-recolectores del Mesolítico. Memoria de Yacimientos Alaveses 9. Diputación Foral de Álava.

Cazals, N., 2000. Constantes et variations des traits techniques et économiques entre le Magdalénien Inférieur et Moyen. Analyse des productions lithiques du Nord de la Peninsule Ibérique. Unpublished PhD dissertation. Université de Paris I-Pantheon- Sorbonne.

Cendrero, O., 1915. Resumen de los bastones perforados de la Provincia de Santander. Comisión de Inves. Paleontológicas y Prehistóricas. Notas 1 y 2. Madrid.

Cerdeño, E., 1990. Stephanorhinus hemitoechus (Falc.) (Rhinocerotidae, Mammalia) del Pleistoceno Medio y Superior de España, Estudios Geológicos 46, 465-479.

Chaline, A., 1970. Pliomys Lenki, forme relicte dans la Microfaune du Würm ancien de la Grotte de Lezetxiki (Guipúzcoa-Espagne), Munibe 22, 43-49.

Chalmin, E., Menu, M., Altuna, J., 2002. Le matières picturales de la grotte d'Ekain (Pays Basque), Munibe 54, 35-51.

Chimeno, E., Malgosa, A., Subira, M.E., 1992. Paleopatología oral y análisis de elementos traza en el estudio de la dieta de la población epipaleolítica de "El Collado" (Oliva, Valencia), Munibe 55 (8), 177-182

Christensen, M., Tejero, J.-M., in press. La fabrication d'objets en matières dures animales, in: Balasse, M., Reiche, I., Dauphin, Y., Oberlin, C., Geigl, E.-M., Brugal, J.-P. (Eds.), Messages d'os. Archéométrie du Squelette animal et humain, CNRS éditions, Paris.

Clark, G.A., 1976. El Asturiense Cantábrico. Bibliotheca Praehistorica Hispana, 13, Madrid.

Clark, G.A., 1983. The Asturian of Cantabria: Early Holocene Hunter-Gatherers in Northern Spain, Anthropological Papers of the University of Arizona 41, Tucson.

Clemente Conte I, Díez Fernández-Lomana J.C., Terradillos Bernal M., 2012. Productive activities in the Middle Palaeolithic lithic instruments of San Quire site (Alar del Rey, Palencia, Spain), Abstracts book International conference on use-wear analisis. Faro, p. 14.

Cleyet-Merle, J.J., 1996. Duruthy (Sorde-L'Abbaye, Landes), in: Thiault, H., Roy, J.B. (Eds.), L'art préhistorique des Pyrénées. Musée des Antiquités Nationales, Paris.

Collcut, S. N., 2013. Gorham's Cave lithological and lithogenetic patterns. In: Barton, R. N. E., Stringer, C. B., Finlayson, J. C. (Eds.), Neanderthals in Context: A Report of the 1995-1998 Excavations at Gorham's and Vanguard Caves, Gibraltar. Oxford University Press, Oxford, pp. 37-49.

Combier, J., 1977. Dix ans de recherches préhistoriques dans la région Rhône-Alpes (1965-1975), Gallia Préhistoire tome 20, fasc. 2, 576-578.

Consuegra, S., García, C., Serdio, A., González Morales, M., Straus, L., Knox, D., Verspoor, E., 2002. Mitochondrial DNA variation in Pleistocene and modern Atlantic salmon from the Iberian glacial refugium, Molecular Ecology 11, 2037-2048.

Cook, G., 1997. George Busk FRS (1807-1886), nineteenth-century polymath: surgeon, parasitologist, zoologist and palaeontologist. Journal of Medical Biography 5, 88-101.

Coolidge, F.L. and Wynn, T., 2005. Working memory, its executive functions, and the emergence of modern thinking, Cambridge Archaeological Journal 15, 5-26.

Cooper, J.H., 2013a. The late Pleistocene avifauna of Gorham's Cave and its environmental correlates. In: Barton, R. N. E., Stringer, C. B., Finlayson, J. C. (Eds.), Neanderthals in Context: A Report of the 1995-1998 Excavations at Gorham's and Vanguard Caves, Gibraltar. Oxford University Press, Oxford, pp. 112-127.

Cooper, J.H., 2913b. The Late Pleistocene avifauna of Vanguard Cave, in: Barton, R. N. E., Stringer, C. B., Finlayson, J. C. (Eds.), Neanderthals in Context: A Report of the 1995-1998 Excavations at Gorham's and Vanguard Caves, Gibraltar, Oxford University Press, Oxford, pp. 227-235.

Corchón, M.A. (coord.) (in process). La Cueva de las Caldas (Priorio, Oviedo). El Magdaleniense de la Sala II.

Corchón, M.S, González-Aguilera, D., Muñoz, A. L., Gómez, J., Herrero, J.S., 2009a, Documentación, modelado y reconstrucción 3D de la cueva de Las Caldas (Asturias, España). VI. El yacimiento y el Arte parietal. Excavaciones Arqueológicas en Asturias. Oviedo, pp. 355-366.

Corchón, M.S. Tarriño, A. Martínez, J., 2009b. Mobilité, territoires et relations culturelles au début du Magdalénien moyen cantabrique: nouvelles perspectivas, in: Acts of the XVth International Congress UISPP, Lisbon. BAR International Series 1938, pp. 217-230.

Corchón, M.S., 1994. El Magdaleniense con triángulos de Las Caldas (Asturias, España). Nuevos datos para la definición del Magdaleniense inferior cantábrico, Zephyrus XLVI, 77-95

Corchón, M.S., 2007. Investigaciones en la Cueva de Las Caldas. Los niveles del Magdaleniense superior. Excavaciones Arqueológicas en Asturias. Principado de Asturias, Oviedo, pp.45-67

Corchón, M.S., Álvarez, E, Rivero, O., Garrido, D., Ortega, P., 2013b. Reféxions sur le Solutréen Cantabrique. Le cas de la grotte de Las Caldas (Asturies, Espagne). Le Solutréen 40 ans après Smith'66. Actes du Colloque de Preuilly-sur Claise. Revue Archéologique du Centre de la France, pp. 445-462.

Corchón, M.S., Garate, D., 2010. Nuevos hallazgos de arte parietal paleolítico en la cueva de La Peña (San Román, Candamo), Zephyrus 65, 75-102.

Corchón, M.S., Garate, D., González-Aguilera, D., Muñoz, A.L., Gómez-Lahoz, J., Herrero, J. S., 2011. Nouveaux regards sur la grotte de La Peña (San Román de Candamo, Asturies), L'Anthropologie 113 (4), 384-424.

Corchón, M.S., Garate, D., Hernando, C., Ortega, P., Rivero, O., 2012. Vers un modèle décoratif pour la grotte de La Peña de Candamo (Asturies, Nord de l'Espagne) à la lumière des nouvelles découvertes. Préhistoire, Art et Sociétés, Bulletin de la Société Préhistorique Ariège-Pyrénées 65-66, 123-143.

Corchón, M.S., Garate, D., Valladas, H., Pons-Branchu, E., Rivero, O., Hernando, C., Ortega, P., 2014a. La cueva de La Peña (San Román, Candamo). Estudio integral del arte parietal paleolítico (2009-2012), in: Excavaciones Arqueológicas en Asturias 2007-2012, Principado de Asturias, Oviedo, pp. 15-26.

Corchón, M.S., Garate, D., Valladas, H., Rivero, O., Pons-Branchu, E., Ortega, P., Hernando, C., 2014b. Back to the point: new datings for La Peña de Candamo Cave Art (Asturias), Zephyrus LXXIII, 67-82.

Corchón, M.S., Mateos, A., Álvarez, E., Peñalver, E., Delclos, X., Vander Made, J., 2008. Ressources complémentaires et mobilité dans le Magdalénien cantabrique, in: Nouvelles données sur les mammifères marins, les crustacés, les mollusques et les roches organogènes de la Grotte de Las Caldas (Asturies, Espagne), L'Anthropologie 112, 284-327

Corchón, M.S., Ortega, P, Vicente F.J., 2013a. Cadenas operativas y suelos de ocupación. El nivel 9 de la Cueva de Las Caldas (Asturias, España), Munibe 64, 5-20.

Corominas, J.M., 1948. El Mesolítico de la cueva 'd'En Mollet' de Serinyà, Anales del Instituto de Estudios Gerundenses III, 89-98.

Corominas, J.M., 1958. Actividades del Centro de Estudios Comarcales de Bañolas en 1958, Anales del Instituto de Estudios Gerundenses XII, 393-394.

Cortada, T., Maroto-Genover, J., 1990. La dent humana paleolítica de la cova de Mollet I (Serinyà), Quaderns del Centre d'Estudis Comarcals de Banyotes 1988-1989, 135-148.

Cortés Sánchez, M., 2007. El Paleolítico Medio y Superior en el Sector Central de Andalucía (Córdoba y Málaga). Monografías del Museo de Altamira 22, Santander.

Cortés Sánchez, M., Morales Muñiz, A., Simón Vallejo, M.D., Bergadà Zapata, M.M., Delgado Huertas, A., López García, P., López Sáez, J.A., Lozano Francisco, M.C., Riquelme Cantal, J.A., Roselló Izquierdo, E., Sánchez Marco, A., Vera Peláez, J.L., 2008. Palaeoenvironmental and cultural dynamics of the coast of Málaga (Andalucía, Spain) during the Upper Pleistocene and Early Holocene, Quaternary Science Reviews 27 (23-24), 2176-2193.

Cortés, M., Jiménez, F., Simón, M.D., López, J.A., Riquelme, J.A., Fernández, F., Martínez, E., Arroyo, E., Pérez, A., Turbón, D., López, L., Pérez, S., 2008. Cazadores recolectores del Paleolítico Superior en la sierra Subbética. Estudios en homenaje a la profesora María Dolores Asquerino, Antiquitas 20.

Cortés-Sánchez, M., (Ed.) 2007a. Cueva Bajondillo (Torremolinos). Secuencia cronocultural y paleoambiental del Cuaternario reciente en la Bahía de Málaga. CEDMA, Málaga.

Cortés-Sánchez, M., 2007b. El Paleolítico medio y superior en el sector central de Andalucía (Córdoba y Málaga). Monografías Museo de Altamira 22. Ministerio de Cultura, Madrid.

Cortés-Sánchez, M., Morales Muñiz, A., Simón Vallejo, M.D., Lozano-Francisco, M.C., Vera-Peláez, J.L., Finlayson, C., Rodríguez Vidal, J., Delgado Huertas, A., Jiménez-Espejo, F.J., Martínez Ruiz, F., Martínez Aguirre, M.A., Pascual Granged, A., Bergadà Zapata, M.M., Gibaja Bao, J.F., Riquelme Cantal, J.A., López Sáez, J.A., Rodrigo Gámiz, M., Sakai, S., Sugisaki, S., Finlayson, G., Fa, D.A., Bicho, N.F., 2011. Earliest Known Use of Marine Resources by Neanderthals, PLoS ONE 6 (9), DOI: 10.1371/journal.pone.0024026.

Costamagno, S., Théry-Parisot, I., Brugal, J.F., Guibert, R., 2005. Taphonomic consequences of the use of the bones as fuel. Experimental data and archaeological applications, in: O'Connor, T. (Ed.), Biosphere to Lithosphere. New studies in vertebrate taphonomy. Proceeding of the 9th Conference of the International Council of Archaeozoology, Durham, August, 2002, Oxbow books, Oxford, pp. 52-63.

Craighead, A., 1999. Climate change and patterns in the exploitation of economic resources (marine Mollusca and ungulate fauna) in Cantabrian Spain at the end of the Pleistocene, ca. 21-6.5 kyr. BP, in: Driver, J. (Ed.), Zooarchaeology of the Pleistocene/Holocene Boundary. British Archaeological Reports S-800, Oxford, pp. 9-20.

Croitor, R., Bonifay, M.-F., Brugal, J.-P., 2008. Systematic revision of the endemic deer Haploidoceros n. Gen. Mediterraneus (Bonifay, 1967) (Mammalia, Cervidae) from the Middle Pleistocene of Southern France, Paläontologische Zeitschrift 82, 325-346

Crovetto, C., 1994, Le industrie litiche, analisi tecnico-tipologica dei reperti di scavo, in: Peretto, C. (Ed.), Le Industrie Litiche del Giacimento Paleolitico di Isernia La Pineta, la Tipologia, le Tracce di Utilizzazione, la Sperimentazione, Isernia, Cosmo Iannone, "Istituto Regionale per gli Studi Storici del Molise "V. Cuoco", pp. 183-353.

Crovetto, C., Ferrari, M., Peretto, C., Longo, L., Vianello, F., 1994. The carinated denticulates from the Palaeolithic site of Isernia La Pineta (Molise, Central Italy): tools or flaking waste? The results of the 1993 lithic experiments, Human Evolution 9, 175-207.

Cuadra, F., Alcalá, G., 1918. La cueva de Basondo, Comisión de Monumentos de Vizcaya, Bilbao.

Cuartero, F., 2008. Tecnología lítica en la Cova del Bolomor IV: ¿una economía de reciclado?, Saguntum 39, 27-44.

Cuenca-Bescós, G., Canudo, J.I., Laplana, C., 1999. Análisis bioestratigráfico de los roedores del Pleistoceno medio del yacimiento de Galería (Sierra de Atapuerca, Burgos), in: Carbonell, E., Rosas, A., Díez, J.C. (Eds.), Atapuerca: Ocupaciones humanas y paleoecología del yacimiento de Galería, Junta de Castilla y León, Burgos, pp. 189-210.

Cuenca-Bescós, G., García, N., 2007. Biostratigraphic succession on the Early and Middle Pleistocene mammal faunas of the Atapuerca cave sites (Burgos, Spain), Courier Forschunginstitut Senckenberg 259, 99-110.

Cuenca-Bescós, G., Laplana, C., Canudo, I., Arsuaga, J.L. 1997. Small mammals from Sima de los Huesos. Journal of Human Evolution 33, 175-190.

Cuenca-Bescós, G., Rofes, J., López-García, J.M., Blain, H.A., De Marfá, R.J., Galindo-Pellicena, M.A., Bennásar-Serra, M.L., Melero-Rubio, M., Arsuaga, J.L., Bermúdez de Castro, J.M., Carbonell, E., 2010. Biochronology of Spanish Quaternary small vertebrate faunas, Quaternary International 212, 109-119.

Cuenca-Bescós, G., Straus, L., González Morales, M., García, J., 2008. Paleoclima y paisaje del final del Cuaternario en Cantabria: los pequeños mamíferos de la Cueva del Mirón, Revista Española de Paleontología 23, 91-126.

Cuenca-Bescós, G., Straus, L., González Morales, M., García, J., 2009. The reconstruction of past environments through small mammals: from the Mousterian to the Bronze Age in El Mirón Cave, Journal of Archaeological Science 36, 947-955.

Currant, A.P., Fernández-Jalvo, Y., Price, C., 2013b. The large mammal remains from Vanguard Cave, in: Barton, R. N. E., Stringer, C. B., Finlayson, J. C. (Eds.), Neanderthals in Context: A Report of the 1995-1998 Excavations at Gorham's and Vanguard Caves, Gibraltar, Oxford University Press, Oxford, pp. 236-239.

Currant, A.P., Price, C., Sutcliffe, A.J., Stringer, C., 2013a. The large mammal remains from Gorham's Cave. In: Barton, R. N. E., Stringer, C. B., Finlayson, J. C. (Eds.), Neanderthals in Context: A Report of the 1995-1998 Excavations at Gorham's and Vanguard Caves, Gibraltar. Oxford University Press, Oxford, pp. 141-150.

D' Errico, F., Cacho, C. 1994. Notation versus decoration in the Upper Paleolithic. A case study from Tossal de la Roca (Alicante, Spain). Journal of Archaeological Science, 1994 (2):185 - 200.

Dalén, L., Orlando, L., Shapiro, B., Brandström-Durling, M., Quam, R., Gilbert, M.T.P., Díez, J.C., Willerslev, E., Arsuaga, J.L., Götherström, A., 2012. Partial Genetic Turnover in Neandertals: Continuity in the East and Population Replacement in the West, Mol Biol Evol 29 (8), 1893-1897.

Daura, J., 2008.Caracterització arqueològica i paleontològica dels jaciments plistocens del massís del Garraf-

Ordal i cursbaix del riu Llobregat. Tesis Doctoral, Universitat de Barcelona, Barcelona, p. 674.

Daura, J., Sanz, M., 2011-2012. Procedencia estratigráfica de los restos humanos neandertales de la Cova del Gegant (Sitges, Barcelona), Mainake 33, 215-232.

Daura, J., Sanz, M., Font, O., Budó, J., 2006. Restes fòssils de Testudo hermanni al massís del Garraf, Butlletí de la Societat Catalana d'Herpetologia 17, 9-20.

Daura, J., Sanz, M., Pike, A.W.G., Zilhão, J., Subirà, M.E., Fornós, J.J., Fullola, J.Mª., Julià, R., 2010. Stratigraphic context and direct dating of the Neanderthal mandible from Cova del Gegant (Sitges, Barcelona), Journal of Human Evolution 59, 109-122.

Daura, J., Sanz, M., Rosell, J., Julià, R., 2010. Un cubil de carnívoros del Pleistoceno medio y superior con escasa presencia humana: la Cova del Rinoceront (Castelldefels, Barcelona), in: Baquedano, E., Rosell, J. (Eds.), Actas de la 1areunión de científicos sobre cubiles de hiena (y otros grandes carnívoros) en los yacimientos arqueológicos de la Península Ibérica, Zona Arqueológica 13, 494-499.

Daura, J., Sanz, M., Subirà, M.E., Quam, R., Fullola, J.Mª., Arsuaga, J.L., 2005. A Neandertal mandible from the Cova del Gegant (Sitges, Barcelona, Spain), Journal of Human Evolution 49, 56-70.

Daura, J., Sanz, M., Vaquero, M., 2005. El Pleistoceno de la Cova del Rinoceront (Castelldefels, Barcelona), in: Ferreira-Bicho, N. (Ed.), O Paleolítico. Actas do IV Congresso de Arqueologia Peninsular. Promontoria Monográfica 2, pp. 217-227.

Davidson, I., 1989. La Economía del Final del Paleolítico en la España oriental. Serie de Trabajos Varios del SIP 85, Valencia,Valencia.

Davidson, I., 1989. La economía del final del Paleolítico en la España oriental. Trabajos Varios del S.I.P., 85, Valencia.

De la Peña, P., 2013. Estudio estratigráfico y tecnotipòlógico de los niveles basales de la Cueva de les Mallaetes (Barx, Valencia): Nuevas claves para el Paleolítico superior inicial mediterráneo, Zephyrus 61, 61-88.

De la Peña, P., 2013. The beginning of the Upper Paleolithic in the Baetic Mountain area (Spain).Quaternary Internationalhttp://dx.doi.org/10.1016/j.quaint.2013.08.008

De la Peña,P., 2011. Sobre la identificación macroscópica de las piezas astilladas: propuesta experimental, Trabajos de Prehistoria 68 (1), 79-98

De la Rasilla, M. *et al.*, 2013. La cueva de El Sidrón (Piloña). Campañas de excavación e investigación 2007-2012. Excavaciones Arqueologías en Asturias 2007-2012, 69-86.

De La Torre, I., López-Romero, E., Morán, N., Benito, A., Martínez, J., Gowlett, J. S., Vicent, J., 2007. Primeras intervenciones arqueológicas en el yacimiento paleolítico del abrigo de Buendía (Castejón, Cuenca), in: Millán, J.M., Rodríguez, C. (Eds.), I Jornadas de Arqueología de Castilla-La Mancha. Cuenca 13-17 diciembre 2005. Ediciones de la Universidad de Castilla-La Mancha, pp. 531-545.

De la Torre, I., Martínez-Moreno, J., Mora, R., 2012. When bones are not enough: Lithic refits and occupation dynamics in the Middle Palaeolithic level 10 of Roca dels Bous. Seetah, in: Gravina, B. (Ed.), Bones for tools-tools for bones, MacDonald Institute for Archaeological Research, Cambridge, pp. 9-19.

De la Torre, I., Martínez-Moreno, J., Mora, R., 2013. Change and stasis in the Iberian Middle Paleolithic Considerations on the significance of Mousterian technological variability, Current Anthropology 54 (S8), 320-336.

De la Torre, I., Mora, R., 2005. Technological Strategies in the Lower Pleistocene at Olduvai Beds I and II. ERAUL 112, Liège.

De la Torre, I., Mora, R., Domínguez-Rodrigo, M., de Luque, L., Alcalá, L., 2003. The Oldowan industry of Peninj and its bearing on the reconstruction of the technological skills of Lower Pleistocene hominids, Journal of Human Evolution 44, 203-224.

De la Torre, I., Mora, R., Martínez-Moreno, J., 2013. Change and stasis in the Iberian Middle Palaeolithic. Considerations on the significance of Mousterian technological variability, Current Anthropology 54 (8), 320-336.

De Lombera Hermida, A., Fábregas Valcarce, R. (Eds.), 2013. Cova Eirós. Primeras evidencias de arte rupestre Paleolítico en el Noroeste Peninsular, Andavira Editora SL, Santiago de Compostela.

De Lombera Hermida, A., Rodríguez Álvarez, X. P., Fábregas Valcarce, R., Moncel, M. H., 2011. La gestion du quartz au Pléistocène moyen et supérieur. Trois exemples d'Europe Méridionale, L´Anthropologie 115, 294-331.

De Lombera, A., Rodríguez, X. P., Rabuñal, J., Ameijenda, A., Martínez, F., Soares, M., Pérez Alberti, A., Fábregas, R., 2012. El yacimiento de Valverde (Monforte de Lemos, Lugo, Galicia) y las primeras evidencias de poblamiento en el pleniglaciar del NW peninsular, Espacio, Tiempo y Forma (Serie I Prehistoria y Arqueología) 5, 369-388.

De Lombera, A., Rodríguez, X.P. Fábregas, R., Lazuén, T., 2011. The Paleolithic settlement of the Monforte Basin, in: de Lombera, A., Fábregas, R. (Eds.), To the West of Spanish Cantabria: the Palaeolithic Settlement of Galicia, BAR International Series 2283, Archaeopress, Oxford, pp 93-110.

De Lumley, M. A., 1973. Anténéandertaliens et Néandertaliens du bassin méditerranéen occidental européen, Etudes Quaternaires, memoire 2, Marseille.

Dean, M.C., Rosas, A., Estalrrich, A., García-Tabernero, A., Huguet. R., Lalueza-Fox, C., Bastir, M, Rasilla, M. de la, 2013. Longstanding dental pathology in Neandertals from El Sidrón (Asturias, Spain) with a probable familial basis, Journal of Human Evolution 64, 678-686.

Defleur, A., 1993. Les sépultures moustériennes, Éditions du Centre National de la Recherche Scientifique, Paris.

Delgado-Raack, S. 2011. La utilización de cantos rodados y plaquetas en la secuencia estratigráfica de Santimamiñe, Kobie Serie BAI n.° 1, 171-196.

Delibrias, G., Romain, O., Le Hasif, G., 1987. Datation par la méthode du carbone 14 du remplissage de la grotte de l'Arbreda, Quadre cronològic del Plistocè Superior a Catalunya. Paleoambients i cultures prehistòriques, Cypsela 6, 133-135.

Dennell, R.W., 2003. Dispersal and colonisation, long and short chronologies: how continuous is the Early Pleistocene record for hominids outside East Africa?, Journal of Human Evolution 45 (6), 421-440.

Dennell, R.W., 2004. Hominid dispersals and Asian biogeography during the Lower and Early-Middle Pleistocene, c. 2.0-0.5 Mya, Asian Perspectives 43, 205-226.

Dennell, R.W., 2010. The colonization of 'Savannahstan': issues of timing(s) and patterns of dispersal across Asia in the Late Pliocene and Early Pleistocene: in: Norton. C.J., Braun, D.R. (Eds.), Asian Paleoanthropology: From Africa to China and Beyond. Vertebrate Paleobiology and Paleoantrhropology, Springer, Dordrecht, pp. 7-30.

Dennell, R.W., Martinón-Torres, M., Bermúdez de Castro, J.M., 2011. Hominin variability, climatic instability and population demography in Middle Pleistocene Europe, Quaternary Science Reviews 30, 1511-1524.

Dennell, R.W., Roebroeks, W., 2005. An Asian perspective on early human dispersal from Africa, Nature 438, 1099-1104.

Díaz, I., Mejías del Cosso, D., Sanabria, D., Rodríguez-Hidalgo, A. J., 2004. El Paleolítico medio en Extremadura: Yacimiento "Vendimia" (Malpartida De Cáceres), in: Allué, J., Canals, A., Carbonell, E. (Eds.), Primer Congreso Peninsular de Estudiantes de Prehistoria., pp. 82-66

Díaz, O., Barrero, N., Mancha, S., 2004. Yacimientos Paleolíticos en Extremadura: el Yacimiento El Millar (Cáceres). Actas del primer congreso peninsular de estudiantes de prehistoria, Tarragona, 2014, pp. 75-81

Díez, J.C., 1991. La grotte de Valdegoba (Huérmeces, Burgos, Espagne). Un gisement du Paléolithique Moyen avec des restes humaines, L'Anthropologie 95, 329-330.

Díez, J.C., 2006. Huellas de descarnado en el Paleolítico Medio: la cueva de Valdegoba (Burgos), Zona arqueológica 7 (1) (Miscelánea en homenaje a Victoria Cabrera), pp. 305-318.

Díez, J.C., Aguirre, E., Mora, R., 1985. Zooarqueología de Torralba (Soria), Celtiberia 69, 7-34.

Díez, J.C., Alonso, R., Bengoechea, A., Colina, A., Jordá, J. F., Navazo, M., Ortiz, J. E., Pérez, S., Torres, T., 2008. El Paleolítico Medio en el valle del Arlanza (Burgos), Cuaternario y Geomorfología 22 (3-4), 135-157.

Díez, J.C., García, M.A., Gil, E., Jordá, J.F., Ortega, A.I., Sánchez, A., Sánchez, B., 1988-1989. La cueva de Valdegoba (Burgos). Primera campaña de excavaciones, Zephyrus 41-42, 55-74.

Díez, J.C., Jordá, J.F., Sánchez, B., 1988. La cueva de Valdegoba (Huérmeces, Burgos), estratigrafía, industria lítica y fauna, in: II Congreso Geológico de España 1, pp. 379-382.

Díez, J.C., Moreno, V., Rodríguez, J., Rosell, J., Cáceres, I., Huguet, R., 1999. Estudio arqueológico de los restos de macrovertebrados de la unidad GIII de Galería (Sierra de Atapuerca). Atapuerca: Ocupaciones Humanas y Paleoecología del Yacimiento de Galería. E. Carbonell, A. Rosas and J.C. Díez. Junta de Castilla y León. Consejería de Educación y Cultura. Memorias, 7, Zamora, pp. 265-282.

Djindjian, F., 2013, L'apport des données de l'art solutréen dans les problématiques de circulations des chasseurs cueilleurs au Maximum Glaciaire en Europe occidentale, Supplément à la Revue Archéologique du Centre de la France 47, 275-296.

Domènech, E., 2005. La transición del Paleolítico medio al superior en la Cova Beneito (Muro, Alicante). Recientes aportaciones, in: Santonja, M., Pérez González, A., Maldonado, M.J. (Eds.), Geoarqueologia y Patrimonio en la Península Ibérica y el entorno del Mediterráneo, pp. 197-206.

Domènech, E., Bergadà, M. M., Roca de Togores, C., 2012. Nuevas aportaciones al Paleolítico superior medio de la Cova Beneito (Muro, Alacant), Recerques del Museu d'Alcoi 21, 7-18.

Domingo, R., Montes, L., Utrilla, P., 2012. Las puntas de escotadura solutrenses de Chaves y de Fuente del Trucho (Huesca, España), Espacio, Tiempo y Forma 5, 513-522.

Domingo, R., Montes, L., Utrilla, P., 2013. Las puntas de escotadura solutrenses de Chaves y de Fuente del Trucho (Huesca, España), Espacio, Tiempo y Forma. Serie I. De punta a punta. El Solutrense en los albores del siglo XXI, 513-522.

Domínguez Alonso, R.M., Arcos Fernández, S., Ruiz Zapata, B., Gil García, M. J., 2009. Nuevos datos sobre la Terraza Compleja de Butarque en Villaverde Bajo. Actas de las IV Jornadas sobre Patrimonio Arqueológico en la Comunidad de Madrid, Dirección General de Patrimonio Histórico, Madrid, pp. 339-343.

Domínguez-Bella, S., Ramos, J., Bernal, D., Vijande, E., Cantillo, J.J., Cabral, A., Pérez, M., Barrena, A., 2012. Methodological approximation to the archaeological excavation in breccia: the Benzú rock-shelter case (Ceuta, Spain), Antiquity 86, 1167-1178.

Dorta, R., Hernández C.M., Molina F.J., Galván, B., 2010. La alteración térmica en los sílex alcoyanos (Alicante, España). Una aproximación desde la arqueología experimental en contextos del Paleolítico medio: El SALT, Recerques del Museud'Alcoi 19, 33-63.

Duarte, E., Santamaría, D., Rasilla, M. de la, Martínez, L., Fernández de la Vega, J., Suárez, P., Forcelledo, E., Tarriño, A., in press. El sílex como recurso mineral en la Prehistoria de Asturias. Workshop SÍLEX: Trazadores litológicos de larga distancia durante la Prehistoria de la Península Ibérica 2011, Burgos.

Duarte, E., Utrilla, P., Mazo, C., Rasilla, M. de la., 2012. ¿Ecos asturianos en el Magdaleniense de Abauntz?, Trabajos de Arqueología Navarra 24, 5-54.

Duckworth, W.L.H, 1911. Cave Exploration at Gibraltar in September, 1910. J. Roy. Anthrop. Inst. XLI, 350-380.

Dupré, M., 1988. Palinología y paleoambiente. Trabajos Varios del S.I.P., Valencia, p. 84.

Dupré, M., Carrión, J.M., 2001. La Palinología. Paisajes valencianos del Pleistoceno superior, in: Villaverde, V. (Ed.), De Neandertales a Cromañones. El Inicio del Poblamiento Humano en las Tierras Valencianas, Universidad de Valencia, Valencia, pp. 41-44.

Duran, J.-P-, Soler, N., 2006. Variabilité des modalités de débitage et des productions lithiques dans les industries moustériennes de la grotte de l'Arbreda, secteur Alpha (Serinyà, Espagne), Bulletin de la Société Préhistorique Française 103 2, 241-262.

Duval, M., Falguères, C., Bahain, J.-J., 2012. Age of the oldest hominin settlements in Spain: contribution of the combined U-series/ESR dating method applied to fossil teeth, Quaternary Geochronology 10, 412-417.

Duval, M., Falguères, C., Bahain, J.-J., Grün, R., Shao, Q., Aubert, M., Dolo, J.-M., Agustí, J., Martínez-Navarro, B., Palmqvist, P., Toro-Moyano, I., 2012. On the limits of using combined U-series/ESR method to date fossil teeth from two Early Pleistocene archaeological sites of the Orce area (Guadix-Baza basin, Spain), Quaternary Research 77 (3), 482-491.

Duval, M., Falguères, C., Bahain, J.J., Grün, R., Shao, Q., Aubert, M., Hellstrom, J., Dolo, J.M., Austi, J., Martínez-Navarro, B., Palmqvist, P., Toro-Moyano, I., 2011. The challenge of dating Early Pleistocene fossil teeth by the combined uranium serires-electron spin resonance method: the Venta Micena paleontological site (Orce, Spain), Journal of Quaternary Science 26 (6), 603-615.

Duval, M., Moreno, D., Shao, Q., Voinchet, P., Falguères, C., Bahain, J.-J., García, T., Garcia, J., Martínez, K., 2011. Datación por ESR del yacimiento arqueológico del Pleistoceno inferior de Vallparadís (Terrassa, Cataluña, España), Trabajos de Prehistoria 68, 7-24.

Engelken, L., Carnero-Montoro, E., Pybus, M., Andrews, G. K., Lalueza. C., Comas, D., Sekler. I., Rasilla, M. de la, Rosas, A., Stoneking, M., Valverde, M. A., Vicente, R., Bosch, E., 2014. Extreme population differences in the human zinc transporter ZIP4 (SLC39A4) are explained by positive selection in Sub-Saharan African, PLOS Genetics 10(2), 1-14.

Escalon de Fonton, M., Onoratini, G., 1979. Les industries de la filiation magdalenienne dans le Sud-Est de la France et leurs positions geochronologiques, in : La Fin de Temps Glaciaires en Europe, Colloque International du CNRS, 271, pp. 382-415.

Espigares, M.P., 2010. Análisis y modelización del contexto sedimentario y los atributos tafonómicos de los yacimientos pleistocénicos del borde nororiental de la cuenca de Guadix-Baza. Ph.D. Thesis, University of Granada.

Espigares, M.P., Martínez-Navarro, B., Pamqvist, P., Ros-Montoya, S., Toro, I., Agustí, J., Sala. R., 2013. Homo vs. Pachycrocuta: Earliest evidence of competition for an elephant carcass between scavengers at Fuente Nueva-3 (Orce, Spain), Quaternary International 295, 113-125.

Espigares, M.P., Ros Montoya, S., 2011. Estudio paleontológico y tafonómico del material óseo de la cueva de las Grajas, Archidona (Málaga), unpublished, Granada. pp. 68.

Espigares, M.P., Ros-Montoya, S., Martínez-Navarro, B., Palmqvist, P., Toro, I., 2008. Presence of cut marks on large mammal bones from the early Pleistocene sites of Barranco León and Fuente Nueva-3 (Orce, Granada). Abstracts Volume de la Quinta Reunión de Tafonomía y Fosilización, Third Meeting on Taphonomy and Fossilization, pp. 41-42.

Estévez, J., 1979. La fauna del Pleistoceno catalán. Tesis Doctoral, Universitat de Barcelona, Barcelona, p. 1282.

Estrada, A., 2009. La malacofauna marina del jaciments epipaleolítics catalans: Una aproximació als usos simbòlics i culturals. Monografies del SERP 9, Ed. SERP, Barcelona.

Estrada, A., Tejero, J. M., Mangado, X., Petit, M. A., Fullola, J. M., Bartrolí, R., Esteve, X., 2010. From Mediterranean Sea to The Segre River. Perforated shells from magdalenian levels of Parco's (Cave Alòs de Balaguer. Lleida. Spain), in: Alvarez, E., Carvajal, D. (Ed.), Proceedings of 2nd. ICAZ malacological group Meeting. Munibe suplemento 31, Sociedad de Ciencias Aranzadi, San Sebastián, pp. 70-77.

Euba Rementeria, I. 2011. Explotación de los recursos leñosos y reconstrucción de la vegetación desde el Tardiglaciar hasta el Holoceno en la cueva de Santimamiñe (Kortezubi, Bizkaia), Kobie Serie BAI n.° 1, 267-279.

Fabián, J.F., 1997. La difícil definición actual del Paleolítico Superior en la Meseta. El yacimiento de La Dehesa (Salamanca) como exponente de la etapa Magdaleniense final, in: Bueno Ramírez, P., Balbín Behrmann, R. (Eds.), II Congreso de Arqueología Peninsular. Zamora, 24-27 septiembre 1996. 1. Fundación Rei Afonso Henriques, Zamora, pp. 219-238.

Fábregas-Valcarce, R., Alonso Fernández, S., Ameijenda Iglesias, A., Grandal d'Anglade, A., Lazuén Fernández, T., de Lombera Hermida, A., Pérez Alberti, A., Pérez Rama, M., Rodríguez Álvarez, X. P., Serna González, M.R., Vaquero Rodríguez, M., 2010. Completando o mapa. Novas datacións absolutas para o Paleolítico e Mesolítico do interior galego, Gallaecia 29, 5-28.

Fábregas-Valcarce, R., Alonso Fernández, S., Ameijenda, A., Grandal D'Anglade, A., Lazuén, T., de Lombera Hermida, A., Pérez Alberti, A., Pérez Rama, M., Rodríguez Álvarez, X.P., Rodríguez Rellán, C., Serna González, M.R., Terradillos Bernal, M., Vaquero Rodríguez, M., 2009. Novos resultados das intervencións arqueolóxicas no sur lucense. Os xacementos paleolíticos da Depresión de Monforte (Monforte de Lemos), Cova Eirós (Triacastela) e Valdavara (Becerreá), Gallaecia 28, 9-32.

Fábregas-Valcarce, R., de Lombera Hermida, A., Serna González, M. R., Vaquero Rodríguez, M., Pérez Rama, M., Grandal D'Anglade, A., Rodríguez Álvarez, X. P., Alonso Fernández, S., Ameijenda Iglesias, A., 2012. Ocupacións prehistóricas e históricas nas cavidades das

Serras Orientais galegas. As covas de Eirós (Triacastela) e Valdavara (Becerreá), Gallaecia 31, 19-46.

Fábregas-Valcarce, R., Lazuén, T., de Lombera, A., Peña, J. A., Pérez Alberti, A., Rodríguez, X. P., Rodríguez, C., Terradillos, M., 2007. Novos achados paleolíticos no interior de Galicia. A Depresión de Monforte de Lemos e as súas industrias líticas, Gallaecia 26, 7-33.

Falguères, C., Bahain, J.-J., Bischoff, J.L., Pérez-González, A., Ortega, A.I., Ollé, A., Quiles, A., Ghaleb, B., Moreno, D., Dolo, J.-M., Shao, Q., Vallverdú, J., Carbonell, E., Bermúdez de Castro, J.M., Arsuaga, J.L., 2013. Combined ESR/U-series chronology of Acheulian hominid-bearing layers at Trinchera Galería site, Atapuerca, Spain, Journal of Human Evolution 65, 168-184.

Falguères, C., Bahain, J.-J., Pérez-Gonzalez, A., Mercier, N., Santonja, M., Dolo, J.-M., 2006. The Lower Acheulian site of Ambrona, Soria (Spain): ages derived from a combined ESR/U-series model, J. Archaeol. Sc. 33, 149-157.

Falguères, C., Bahain, J.J., Yokoyama, Y., Arsuaga, J.L., Bermúdez, J.M., Carbonell, E., Bischoff, J.L., Dolo, J.M., 1999. Earliest humans in Europe: the age of TD6 Gran Dolina, Atapuerca, Spain, J. Hum. Evol. 37, 343-352.

Falguères, C., Yokoyama, Y., Arrizabalaga, A., 2005-2006. La Geocronología del yacimiento pleistocénico de Lezetxiki (Arrasate, País Vasco). Crítica de las dataciones existentes y algunas nuevas aportaciones, Munibe (Antropologia-Arkeologia) 57 (2), 93-106.

Farrand, W.R., 2012. Sedimentology of El Mirón Cave, in: Straus, L., González-Morales, M. (Eds.), El Mirón Cave. University of New Mexico Press, Albuquerque, pp. 60-94.

Faura i Sans, M., 1920. Recents troballes a Catalunya de mamífers fòssils "Elephas" i "Rhinoceros". Butlletí de la Institució Catalana d'Història Natural III, pp. 38 - 39.

Félix, J., Budó, J., Capalleras, X., Mascort, R., 2006. The fossil register of the genera Testudo, Emys and Mauremys of the Quaternary in Catalonia, Chelonii 4, 47-51.

Feranec, R., García, N., Díez, J.C., Arsuaga, J.L., 2010. Understanding the ecology of mammalian carnivorans and herbivores from Valdegoba cave (Burgos, northern Spain) through stable isotope analysis, Palaeogeogr., Palaeoclimatol., Palaeoecol. 297, 263-272.

Ferguson, J., Henderson, G. M., Fa, D. A., Finlayson, J. C., Charnley, N. R., 2011. Increased seasonality in the Western Mediterranean during the last glacial from limpet shell geochemistry. Earth Planet. Sci. Lett. 308, 325-333.

Fernández de la Vega, J., Rasilla, M., 2012. El Solutrense del Abrigo de La Viña (Asturias, España). Cualidades generales e industria lítica del nivel VI del Sector occidental, Espacio, Tiempo y Forma. Serie I. Prehistoria y Arqueología 5,10.5944/etf i.5.9279

Fernández Peris, J., 2007. La cova del Bolomor (Tavernes de la Valldigna, Valencia). Las industrias líticas del Pleistoceno medio en el ámbito del Mediterráneo peninsular, Serie de Trabajos Varios del SIP (Servicio de Investigación Prehistórica) 108.

Fernández Peris, J., 2007. La Cova del Bolomor (Tavernes de la Valldigna, Valencia). Las industrias líticas del Pleistoceno medio en el ámbito del Mediterráneo peninsular. Serie de Trabajos Varios del SIP (Servicio de Investigación Prehistórica), Valencia.

Fernández Peris, J., 2008. La cova de Bolomor (Tavernes de la Valldigna, Valencia): Las industrias líticas del Pleistoceno medio en el ámbito del mediterráneo peninsular. Serie de Trabajos Varios del Servicio de Investigación Prehistórica 108. Diputación Provincial de Valencia.

Fernández Peris, J., Barciela González, V., Blasco, R., Cuartero, F., Fluck H., Sañudo Die, P., Verdasco, C., 2012. The earliest evidence of hearths in Southern Europe: the case of Bolomor Cave (Valencia, Spain), Quaternary International 247, 267-277.

Fernández Peris, J., Barciela, V., Blasco, R., Cuartero, F., Sañudo, P., 2008. El Paleolítico Medio en el territorio valenciano y la variabilidad tecno-económica de la Cova del Bolomor, Treballs d'Arqueologia 14, 141-169.

Fernández, C., 1993. Los macromamíferos del Pleistoceno y Holoceno inicial en el Noreste peninsular, in: Pérez Alberti, A., Guitián, L., Ramil Rego, P. (Eds), La evolución del paisaje en las Montañas del entorno de los Caminos Jacobeos, Xunta de Galicia, Santiago, pp. 183-191.

Fernández, C., 2000-2001. Industria ósea prehistórica del noroeste de la Península Ibérica. Lancia 4, 71-84

Fernández, E., 2005. Polimorfismos de DNA mitocondrial en poblaciones antiguas de la cuenca mediterránea. Unpublished PhD dissertation, Universidad de Barcelona.

Fernández-Díaz, 2013. Zooarqueologia y tafonomia del subnivel de Pleistoceno inferiro TD6-3 del yacimiento de Gran Dolina, Sierra de Atapuerca (Burgos), Història, Universitat Rovira i Virgili, Tarragona.

Fernández-Jalvo, Y., Díez, J.C., Bermúdez de Castro, J.M., Carbonell, E., Arsuaga, J.L., 1996. Evidence of early cannibalism, Science 271, 277-278.

Fernández-López de Pablo, J., 1999. El yacimiento prehistórico de Casa de Lara. Cultura material y producción lítica. Fundación José María Soler, p. 163.

Fernández-López de Pablo, J., Gómez-Puche, M., Ferrer, C., Yll, R., 2011a. El Arenal de la Virgen (Villena, Alicante). Primer asentamiento perilacustre del Mesolítico de Muescas y Denticulados en la Península Ibérica, Zephyrus LXVIII, 87-114.

Fernández-López de Pablo, J., Gómez-Puche, M., Martínez-Ortí, A., 2011b. Systematic consumption of non-marine gastropods at open-air Mesolithic sites in the Iberian Mediterranean Region, Quaternary International 244, 45-53.

Fernández-López de Pablo, J., Salazar-García, D. C., Subirà, M. E., Roca, C., Gómez, M., Richards, M. P., Esquembre, M. A., 2013. Late Mesolithic burials at Casa Corona (Villena, spain): direct radiocarbon and palaeodietary evidence of the last forager populations in eastern Iberia, Journal of Archaeological Science 40 (1), 671-680.

Fernández-Tresguerres Velasco, J.A., 1976. Enterramiento aziliense en la Cueva de los Azules I, Cangas de Onís,

Oviedo, Bol. del Instituto de Estudios Asturianos, 87, Oviedo, pp. 273-288.

Fernández-Tresguerres Velasco, J.A., 1980. El Aziliense en las provincias de Asturias y Santander, Monografías del Centro de Investigación y Museo de Altamira, nº 2, Santander.

Fernández-Tresguerres Velasco, J.A., 1981. Cantos pintados del Aziliense cantábrico". Altamira Symposium, Madrid, pp. 245-250.

Fernández-Tresguerres Velasco, J.A., 1989. Thoughts on the Transition from the Magdalenian to the Azilian in Cantabria: Evidence from the Cueva de Los Azules, Asturias, in: Bonsall (Ed.), Mesolithic in Europa. Papers presented at the Third International Symposium Edinburgh 1985. Edinburgh: John Donald Publishers LTD, pp. 582-588.

Fernández-Tresguerres Velasco, J.A., 1994. El arte aziliense, Complutum 5, 81-95.

Fernández-Tresguerres Velasco, J.A., 1995. El Aziliense de la región cantábrica, in: Moure, González-Sainz (Eds.), El Final del Paleolítico cantábrico. Transformaciones ambientales y culturales durante el Tardiglaciar y comienzos del Holoceno en la Región Cantábrica. Santander: Servicio de Publicaciones de la Universidad de Cantabria, pp. 199-224.

Fernández-Tresguerres Velasco, J.A., 2003. Arte y territorio durante el periodo aziliense en el occidente Cantábrico, in: Balbín Behrmann, R., Bueno Ramírez, P. (Eds.), El arte prehistórico desde los inicios del siglo XXI. Primer Symposium Internacional de Arte Prehistórico de Ribadesella. Real Instituto de Estudios Asturianos, Ministerio de Educación y Tecnología, Oviedo, pp. 255-261.

Fernández-Tresguerres Velasco, J.A., 2004. El final del paleolítico en los espacios cantábricos: el Aziliense, Kobie Anejos 8, 309-336.

Fernández-Tresguerres Velasco, J.A., 2006. El final del Paleolítico en el Cantábrico: la Cueva de los Azules (Cangas de Onís). Oviedo, Real Instituto de Estudios Asturianos.

Fernández-Tresguerres Velasco, J.A., Junceda Quintana, F., 1992. Informe sobre las campañas de excavación realizadas en la cueva de los Azules entre 1986 y 1990, Excavaciones arqueológicas en Asturias 1987-90. Principado de Asturias, Oviedo, pp. 89-94

Fernández-Tresguerres Velasco, J.A., Junceda Quintana, F., 1994. Los arpones azilienses de la cueva de Los Azules (Cangas de Onís, Asturias), in: Homenaje al Dr. Joaquín González-Echegaray. Monografías nº 17. Museo y Centro de investigación de Altamira, pp. P. 87-95.

Fernández-Tresguerres Velasco, J.A., Rodríguez Fernández, J.J. 1990. La cueva de Los Azules (Cangas de Onís). Excavaciones arqueológicas en Asturias: 1983-86, Principado de Asturias, Oviedo, pp. 129-133

Ferrer, C., 2008. Estudio geomorfológico, in: Estudios sedimentológicos, polínicos, faunísticos, antracológicos, carpológicos y de los restos humanos del yacimiento de La Corona (Villena), dentro de la obra AVE tramo Caudete-Villena P.K. 004+160 al P.K. 004+360 Villena (Alicante). Unpublished report.

Finlayson, C. *et al.*, 2006. Late survival of Neanderthals at the southern most extreme of Europe. Nature 443, 850-853.

Finlayson, C., 2006. Climate, vegetation and biodiversity - a multiscale study of the south of the Iberian Peninsula. PhD Thesis, Anglia Ruskin University, Cambridge.

Finlayson, C., Brown, K., Blasco, R., Rosell, J., Negro, J.J., Bortolotti, G., Finlayson, G., Sánchez-Marco, A., Giles Pacheco, F., Rodríguez-Vidal, J., Carrión, J.S., Fa, D.A., Rodríguez-Llanes, J.M., 2012. Birds of a feather: Neanderthal exploitation of raptors and corvids. Plos One 7, e45927.

Fontanals, M., 2001. Noves aportacions a la intervenció del límit Pliestocè-Holocè al sud de Catalunya: l'estudi de la indústria lítica del jaciment de la Cativera (El Catllar, Tarragonès), Butlletí Arqueològic Època V, 23, Reial Societat Arqueològica de Tarragona, pp. 73-100.

Fontanals, M., Ollé, A., Vergès, J.M., 2009. Les ocupacions del tardiglacial a l'Abric de la Cativera (El Catllar, Tarragonès), in: Els Pirineus i les àrees circumdants durant el tardiglacial. Mutacions i filiacions tecnoculturals, evolució paleoambiental (16000-10000 BP). Homenatge al professor Georges Laplace, XIV Col·loqui Internacional d'Arqueologia de Puigcerdà, Institut d'Estudis Ceretans, Puigcerdà, pp. 537-547.

Fortea, F.J., 1973. Los complejos microlaminares y geométricos del Epipaleolítico mediterráneo español. Memorias del Seminario de Prehistoria y Arqueología de la Universidad de Salamanca, Salamanca.

Fortea, F.J., 1974a. Algunas aportaciones a los problemas del Arte Levantino, Zephyrus XXV, 225-257.

Fortea, F.J., 1974b. En torno a la cronología relativa del inicio del Arte Levantino (avance sobre las plaquetas de la Cocina), in: 50 Aniversario de la Fundación del laboratorio de Arqueología de Valencia, 1924-1974, Papeles núm. 11, Valencia, pp. 185-197.

Fortea, F.J., 1975. En torno a la cronología relativa del inicio del arte levantino (Avance sobre las pinturas rupestres de la Cocina), Sagvntvm 11, 185-197.

Fortea, F.J., 1981. Investigaciones en la cuenca media del Nalón, Asturias (España), Zephyrus XXXII-XXXIII, 5-16.

Fortea, F.J., 1989. Cuevas de la Lluera. Avance al estudio de sus artes parietales, in: González-Morales, M.R. (Ed.), Cien Años después de Sautuola, Gobierno de Cantabria, Santander, pp. 187-202.

Fortea, F.J., 1990. Abrigo de La Viña. Informe de las campañas 1980-1986, Excavaciones Arqueológicas en Asturias 1983-86 1, pp. 55-68.

Fortea, F.J., 1992. Abrigo de La Viña. Informe de las campañas 1987 a 1990, Excavaciones Arqueológicas en Asturias 1987-90 2, pp.19-28.

Fortea, F.J., 1994. Los "santuarios" exteriores en el Paleolítico cantábrico, Complutum 5, 203-220.

Fortea, F.J., 1995. Abrigo de La Viña. Informe y primera valoración de las campañas 1991 a 1994, Excavaciones Arqueológicas en Asturias 1991-94 3, pp.19-31.

Fortea, F.J., 1999. Abrigo de La Viña. Informe y primera valoración de las campañas de 1995 a 1998, Excavaciones Arqueológicas en Asturias 1995-98 4, pp. 31-41.

Fortea, F.J., 2000. El Pindal, vision nouvelle ou fiction?, Préhistoire, art et sociétés, Bulletin de la Société Préhistorique de l'Ariège 55, 35-62.

Fortea, F.J., 2000-2001. Los comienzos del arte paleolítico en Asturias: aportaciones desde una arqueología contextual no postestilística, Zephyrus 53-54, 177-216.

Fortea, F.J., 2001. El Paleolítico superior en Galicia y Asturias (1996-2000), in: Noiret, P. (Ed.), Le Paléolithiquesupérieureuropéen. Bilanquinquennal 1996-2001, ERAUL, Liège, pp. 149-160.

Fortea, F.J., 2001. La Cueva de Llonin. (Peñamellera Alta), in: Enciclopedia Temática de Asturias 13, Silverio Cañada Editor, Gijón, pp. 222-225.

Fortea, F.J., 2002. Trente-neuf dates C14-SMA pour l'art pariétal paléolithique des Asturies, Préhistoire, Art et Sociétés 57, 7-28.

Fortea, F.J., 2007. 39 edades 14C AMS para el arte paleolítico rupestre en Asturias, in: Excavaciones Arqueológicas en Asturias 1999-2002 5, Principado de Asturias, Oviedo, pp. 91-102.

Fortea, F.J., 2007. Cuevas de Covaciella y El Bosque (Cabrales). Campaña de 2000, in: Excavaciones Arqueológicas en Asturias: 1999-2002. Principado de Asturias. Servicio de Publicaciones, Oviedo, pp. 221-226.

Fortea, F.J., de la Rasilla, M., Rodríguez, V., 2004. L'art pariétal et la séquence archéologique paléolithique de la grotte de Llonín (Peñamellera Alta, Asturies, Espagne), Préhistoire, Arts et Societés LIX, 7-29.

Fortea, F.J., *et al.*, 1990. Travaux récents dans les vallées du Nalón et du Sella (Asturies), en Colloque International L'art des objets au Paléolithique, Tome I, L'art mobilier et son contexte. Foix-Le Mas d'Azil 1987, París, pp. 219-244.

Fortea, F.J., Jordá-Pardo, J.F., 1976. La Cueva de Les Mallaetes y los problemas del Paleolítico Superior del Mediterráneo Español, Zephyrvs 26-27, 129-166.

Fortea, F.J., Martí, B., Fumanal, P., Dupré, M., Pérez Ripoll, M., 1987. Epipaleolítico y neolitización en la zonaoriental de la Península Ibérica, in: Guilaine, J., Courtin, J., Roudil, J.-L., Vernet, J.-L. (Dir.), Premières Communautés Paysannes en Méditerranée Occidental. Actes du Colloque International du CNRS (Montpellier, 1983), Éditions du CNRS, Paris, pp. 599-606.

Fortea, F.J., Rasilla Vives, M. de la, Rodríguez Otero, V., 2004. L'art pariétal et la séquence archéologique paléolithique de la Grotte de Llonín (Peñamellera Alta, Asturies, Espagne), Préhistoire, Art et Sociétés LIX, 7-29.

Fortea, F.J., Rasilla, M. de la, D. Santamaría, D., Martínez, L., Duarte, E., Fernández de la Vega, J., Martínez, E., Cañaveras, J. C., Sánchez-Moral, S., Cuezva, S., Lario, J., Rosas, A., Martínez-Maza, C., García-Tabernero, A., Bastir, M., Huguet, R., Estalrrich, A., García-Vargas, S., Sánchez-Meseguer, A., León, S., Lalueza-Fox, C., Torres, T. de, Ortiz, J. E., Julià, R., Grün, R., Valladas, H., Mercier, N., Tisnèrat-Laborde, N., Soler, V., Silva, P.G., Carrasco, P., Ayarza, P., Álvarez, F., Santos, G., Altuna, J., Badal, E., Alonso, J., 2009. La Cueva de El Sidrón (Borines, Piloña, Asturias). Campañas arqueológicas de 2003 a 2006, Excavaciones Arqueológicas en Asturias 2003-2006 6, 367-384.

Fortea, F.J., Rasilla, M. de la, García-Tabernero, A. Gigli, E., Rosas, A., Lalueza-Fox, C., 2008. Excavation protocol of bone remains Neandertal DNA analysis in El Sidrón Cave (Asturias, Spain), Journal of Human Evolution 55(2), 353-357.

Fortea, F.J., Rasilla, M. de la, Martínez, E., Sánchez-Moral, S., Cañaveras, J. C., Cuezva, S., Rosas, A., Soler, V., Julià, R., Torres, T. de, Ortiz, J. E., Castro, J., Badal, E., Altuna, J., Alonso, J., 2007c. La Cueva de El Sidrón (Borines, Piloña, Asturias). Campañas arqueológicas de 2000 a 2002, Excavaciones Arqueológicas en Asturias 1999-2002 5, 191-205.

Fortea, F.J., Rasilla, M. de la, Rodríguez, V., 1992. La cueva de Llonin (Llonín, Peñamellera Alta). Campañas de 1987 a 1990, in: Excavaciones Arqueológicas en Asturias 1987-90 2, Principado de Asturias, Oviedo, pp. 9-18.

Fortea, F.J., Rasilla, M. de la, Rodríguez, V., 1995. La cueva de Llonín (Llonín, Peñamellera Alta). Campañas de 1991 a 1994, in: Excavaciones Arqueológicas en Asturias 1991-94 3, Principado de Asturias, Oviedo, pp. 33-43.

Fortea, F.J., Rasilla, M. de la, Rodríguez, V., 1999. La cueva de Llonín (Llonín, Peñamellera Alta). Campañas de 1995 a 1998, in: Excavaciones Arqueológicas en Asturias 1995-98 4, Principado de Asturias, Oviedo, pp. 60-68.

Fortea, F.J., Rasilla, M. de la, Rodríguez, V., 2007. La cueva de Llonin (Llonin, Peñamellera Alta). Campañas de 1999 a 2002, in: Excavaciones Arqueológicas en Asturias 1995-98 5, Principado de Asturias, Oviedo, pp. 77-86.

Fortea, F.J., Rasilla, M. de la, Santamaría, D., Martínez, L., Duarte, E., Fernández de la Vega, J., 2010. El Paleolítico Superior en Asturias en los albores del siglo XXI, in: Mangado, X. (Coord.), Jornadas Internacionales sobre el Paleolítico Superior Peninsular. Novedades del siglo XXI, Homenaje al Prof. Javier Fortea, Barcelona, 2010, Barcelona, pp. 271-289.

Fortea, F.J., Rasilla, M. de la, Santamaría, D., Rosas, A., 2007a. El Paleolítico Superior Antiguo en Asturias y su contexto, in: Muñoz, J. (Coord.), La Prehistoria en Asturias. Un legado artístico único en el mundo, La Nueva España, Oviedo, pp. 355-388.

Fortea, F.J., Rasilla, M. de la, Santamaría, D., Rosas, A., Lalueza-Fox, C., Martínez, E., Sánchez-Moral, S., Cañaveras, J. C., 2007b. El Sidrón (Borines, Piloña, Asturias). La presencia del Homo Neanderthalensis en Asturias, in: Muñoz, J. (Coord.), La Prehistoria en Asturias. Un legado artístico único en el mundo, La Nueva España, Oviedo, pp. 321-354.

Fortea, F.J., Rodríguez-Otero, V., Hoyos, M., FASE (Federación Asturiana de Espeleología), Valladas, H., Torres, T., 1995. Covaciella, in: Excavaciones Arqueológicas en Asturias 1991-94. Principado de Asturias. Servicio de Publicaciones, Oviedo, pp. 258-270.

Freeman, L.G., 1971a. Estructuras y ocupación Auriñaciense en el sector Este del yacimiento, in: González-Echegaray, J., Freeman, L.G. (Eds), Cueva Morín. Publicaciones del Patronato de las cuevas prehistóricas de la provincia de Santander, VI, Santander, pp. 301-341.

Freeman, L.G., 1971b. Los niveles de ocupación musteriense, in: González-Echegaray, J., Freeman, L.G. (Eds.), Cueva Morín. Publicaciones del Patronato de las cuevas prehistóricas de la provincia de Santander, VI, Santander, pp. 27-161.

Freeman, L.G., 1973. El musteriense, in: González-Echegaray, J., Freeman, L.G. (Eds), Cueva Morín. Publicaciones del Patronato de las cuevas prehistóricas de la provincia de Santander, X, Santander, pp. 13-140.

Freeman, L.G., 1975. Acheulean Sites and Stratigraphy in Iberia and the Maghreb, in: Butzer, K. W., Isaac G. Ll. (Eds.), After the Australopithecines, Mouton Pub., The Hague-Paris, pp. 661-744.

Freeman, L.G., 1975. Acheulian Sites and Stratigraphy in Iberia and the Maghreb, in: Butzer, K.W., Isaac, G. Ll. (Eds.), After the Australopithecines. Mouton Pub., The Hague-Paris, pp. 661-744.

Freeman, L.G., 1991. What mean these stones? Remarks on raw material use in the Spanish Paleolithic, in: Montet-White, A., Holen, A. (Eds.), Raw Materials Economy among Prehistoric Hunter-Gatherers. University of Kansas Press, Lawrence, pp. 73-125.

Freeman, L.G., 1994. Torralba and Ambrona: A Review of Discoveries, in: Corruccini, R. S., Ciochon, R. L. (Eds), Integrative Paths to the Past, Prentice Hall, Englewood Cliffs, New Jersey, pp. 597-637.

Freeman, L.G., Butzer, K. W., 1966. The Acheulean station of Torralba, Spain: A progress report, Quaternaria 8, 9-21.

Freeman, L.G., González-Echegaray, J., 1973. Hallazgo de enterramientos paleolíticos y su localización en la estratigrafía de Cueva Morín, in: González-Echegaray, J., Freeman, L.G. (Eds.), Cueva Morin. Publicaciones del Patronato de las cuevas prehistóricas de la provincia de Santander, X, Santander, pp. 220-254.

Freeman, L.G., González-Echegaray, J., 2000. La grotte d´Altamira. Paris: La Maison des Roches.

Frías, D., 2013. Nuevas aportaciones al estudio del musteriense final cantábrico: el utillaje lítico del nivel D de Axlor (Dima, Vizcaya). Trabajo de Fin de Master, Universidad de Cantabria.

Fullola Pericot, J.M., 1978. L'Hort de la Boquera, un nou jaciment a vall del Montsant, Butlletí de la R.S.A.T. IV 141-144, 3-14.

Fullola Pericot, J.M., 1979. Las industrias líticas del Paleolítico Superior Ibérico. Serie de Trabajos Varios, 60, Servicio de Investigación Prehistórica, Valencia.

Fullola Pericot, J.M., Bartolí, R., Bergadà, M.M., Doce, R., García-Arguelles, P., Nadal, J., Rodon, T., Adserias, M., Cebrià, A., 1993. Nuevas aportaciones al conocimiento del Paleolítico Superior en las comarcas meridionales y occidentales de Cataluña, in: Actas de la VIII Reun. Nac. sobre Cuaternario de AEQUA, Fumanal, M.P., Bernabeu, J. (Eds.), Estudios sobre Cuaternario. Medios sedimentarios. cambios ambientales. Hábitat humano, Valencia, pp. 239-247.

Fullola Pericot, J.M., Bartrolí, R., Bergadà, M.M., Burjachs, F., Meneses, M.D., Nadal, J., 1997. Le Magdalénien ancien en Catalogne: aproche à l'étude des couches inférieures de la grotte du Parco (Alòs de Balaguer, La Noguera, Lleida), in : Fullola, J. M., Soler, N. (Eds.), El món mediterrani després de Pleniglacial (18.000-12.000 BP). Sèrie Monogràfica 17, MAC-Girona, Girona, pp. 303-319.

Fullola Pericot, J.M., García-Arguelles, P., 1980. Primeres notícies de les troballes realitzades a la cova del Filador (Margalef de Montsant) i voltants durant les darrerres campanyes d'excavacions (1979-80). L'Hort d'en Marquet, Butlletí de la R.S.A.T. V (2), 2-22.

Fullola Pericot, J.M., García-Arguelles, P., 1982-83. El Planot: primeres dades pel seu coneixement dins de la Prehistòria del Priorat, Universitas Tarraconensis 5, Fac. de Filosofia i Lletres, Div. de Geogr i Història, Univ. de Barcelona, pp. 63-73.

Fullola Pericot, J.M., García-Argüelles, P., Millán, M., 1988 . Noves aportacions al coneixement de la Cova del Parco (Alòs de Balaguer, La Noguera, Lleida), in: actes del 7è Congrés Internacional d'Arqueologia de Puigcerdà, Homenatge al Dr.J. Maluquer de Motes, juny 1986, Puigcerdà. pp. 29-35.

Fullola Pericot, J.M., Mangado, X., Tejero, J.M., Petit, M.A., Bergadà, M.M., Nadal, J., García-Argüelles, P., Bartrolí, R., Mercadal O., 2012. The Magdalenian in Catalonia (Northeast Iberia), Quaternary International 272-273, 55-74.

Fullola Pericot, J.M., Petit, M.A., Bergadà, M.M., Bartrolí, R., 1998. Occupation épipaléolithique de la grotte du Parco (Alòs de Balaguer, Catalogne, Espagne), in : Proceedings of the XIII International Congress of the UISPP, vol. 2, section 6, Upper Palaeolithic, Forlì, setembre de 1996. ED. ABACO, Forlì, pp. 535-542.

Fullola Pericot, J.M., Petit, M.A., Mangado, X., Bartrolí, R., Albert, R.M., Nadal, J., 2004. Occupation épipaléolithique microlamellaire de la grotte du Parco (Alòs de Balaguer, Catalogne, Espagne). Le Mésolithique, in : Actes du XIV Congrès UISPP, section 7. Lieja 2001. BAR International Series 1302, Oxford, pp. 121-128.

Fullola Pericot, J.M., Viñas, R., 1985. Primer grabado parietal naturalista en cueva de Cataluña: la cueva de la Taverna (Margalef de Montsant, Priorat, Tarragona), Caesaraugusta 61-62, 67-78.

Fumanal, M.P., 1986. Sedimentología y Clima en el País Valenciano. Servicio de Investigación Prehistórica (Serie Trabajos Varios, 83), Valencia, p.207.

Fumanal, M.P., 1988. Sedimentología y clima en el País Valenciano. Trabajos Varios del S.I.P., Valencia, p. 83.

Fumanal, M.P., 1993. El yacimiento premusteriense de la Cova del Bolomor (Tavernes de la Valldigna, País Valenciano), Cuadernos de Geografía 54, 223-248.

Fumanal, M.P., 1994. El yacimiento musteriense de El Salt (Alcoi, País Valenciano). Rasgos geomorfológicos y climatoestratigrafía de sus registros, Saguntum PLAV 27, 39-55.

Fumanal, M.P., 1995. Los depósitos cuaternarios en cuevas y abrigos rocosos. Implicaciones sedimentológicas, El Cuaternario del País Valenciano, pp. 115-124.

Fumanal, M.P., Villaverde, V., 1988. Cova Negra et le milieu du Paleolithique moyen dans le region du Pays Valencien (Espagne), in: Laville, H. (Ed.), L'Homme de Néandertal. Vol. 2. L'environnement. ERAUL, Liege, pp. 73-85.

Fumanal, M.P., Villaverde, V., 1997. Quaternary deposits in caves and shelters in the central mediterranean area of Spain, L'Anthropologie 35, 109-118.

Fusté, M., 1953. Parietal neandertalense de Cova Negra (Játiva), Trabajos Varios del SIP, 17.

Galindo-Pellicena, M.A., Carretero, J.M., Arsuaga, J.L., 2014. Primary or Secondary Products?: The nature of Capra and Ovis exploitation within the Chalcolithic and Bronze Age levels at Portalón site (Atapuerca Hill, Burgos, Spain), in: Haskel, J. Greenfield (Eds.). Animal Secondary Products. Archaeological Perspectives on Domestic Animal Exploitation in the Neolithic and Bronze Age.

Galván, B., Hernández, C.M., Francisco, Mª.I., 2007-08. Elementos líticos apuntados en el musteriense alcoyano. El Abric del Pastor, Alicante, Veleia 24-25, 367-383.

Galván, B., Hernández, C.M., Francisco, Mª.I., Molina, J., Tarriño, A., 2008. La Producción Lítica del Abric del Pastor (Alcoy, Alicante). Un ejemplo de la variabilidad musteriense, Tabona 17, 11-61.

Galván, B., Hernández, C.M., Mallol, C, Mercier, N, Sistiaga. A, Soler, V., in press, New Evidence of Early Neanderthal Disappearance in the Iberian Peninsula, Journal of Human Evolution.

García Aguilar, J.M., 1997. La cuenca de Guadix-Baza (Granada): evolución geodinámica y sedimentarias de los depósitos lacustres entre el turoliense superior y el Pleistoceno. Tesis doctoral. Universidad de Granada, p. 532.

García Catalán, S., 2007. La industria lítica del nivel Asup del Molí del Salt (Vimbodí, Tarragona) y su contextualización en el Paleolítico Superior final de la vertiente mediterránea de la Península Ibérica, Trabajos de Prehistoria 64 (2), 157-168.

García Catalán, S., Gómez de Soler, B., Soto Quesada, M., Vaquero Rodríguez, M., 2013. Los sistemas de producción lítica en el Paleolítico Superior final: el caso del nivel Asup del Molí del Salt (Vimbodí i Poblet, Tarragona), Zephyrus LXXII, 39-58.

García Díez, M., 2013. La exprsión gráfica de La Peña de Estebanvela (Segovia) en el contexto de los últimos grupos cazadores-recolectores europeos, in: Ocupaciones magdalenienses en el interior de la Península Ibérica: La Peña de Estebanvela (Ayllón, Segovia) (C. Cacho, coord.), Junta de Castilla y León – CSIC. Madrid, pp. 471-514.

García Díez, M., Angulo, J. Eguizabal, J., 2011. Conoce Covalanas, Sociedad Regional de Cultura y Deporte, Consejería de Cultura, Turismo y Deporte, Gobierno de Cantabria, Santander.

García González, R., 2011. Elementos para una filogeografía de la Cabra Montés Ibérica (Capra Pyrenaica Schintz, 1838), Pirineos 166 ,87-122.

García González, R., 2011. New Holocene Capra Pyrenaica (Mammalia, Artiodactyla, Bovidae) skulls from the Southern Pyrénées, Comptes Rendus Palevol 11, 241-249.

García Guinea, M.A., González-Echegaray, J., 1966. Nouvelles represèntations d´art rupestre dans la grotte del Castillo, Préhistoire et Spéléologie Ariégeoises XXI, 441-446.

García Morales, M., 1896-1987. Nuevas figuras grabadas en Hornos de la Peña (Cantabria), Bajo Aragón Prehistoria 7-8, 167-178.

García Puchol, O., 2005. El proceso de Neolitización en la fachada mediterránea de la península Ibérica. Tecnología y Tipología de la piedra tallada, British Archaeological Reports, 1430, Oxford.

García, C., 1979. Los roedores de Cueva Horá (Darro, Granada): Nuevos datos sobre la fauna del Pleistoceno superior en Andalucía, Antropología y Paleoecología Humana 1, 79-83.

García, E., Menéndez, M., Quesada, J.M., 2004. Güelga Cave (Narciandi, Cangas de Onís, Asturias, Spain) and the cantabrian lower magdalenian. XIVème Cong. UISPP (Université de Liége. Belgique), BAR International Series, pp. 33-41.

García, E., Richards, M.P., Subira, E., 2006. Palodiets of Humans and Fauna at the Spanish Mesolithic Site of El Collado, Current Anthropology, 47 (3), 549-556

García, J., 2005. Tecnologia lítica i variabilitat de les indústries del Pleistocè mitjà i superior inicial del Nord-est de la Península Ibèrica i Sud-est de França: Nivel G de la Caune de l'Arago, la Selva i conques del Rosselló, Ter i Lacustre de Banyoles. Tesis Doctoral, Dept. Historia i Geografia, Univ. Rovira i Virgili, Tarragona.

Garcia, J., 2008. El Paleolític inferior a Catalunya i al Rosselló, Institut d'Estudis Ceretans, Ripoll.

Garcia, J., 2010. Tecnología lítica del Paleolítico inferior en el noreste de la Península Ibérica y sureste de Francia, BAR Internacional Series S2101, Archaeopress, Oxford.

Garcia, J., 2011. Continuité technologique et traditions techniques au Paléolithique inférieur: un modèle d'occupation territoriale dans le Sud de la France et dans le Nord-Est de la péninsule Ibérique, Bulletin de la Société Préhistorique Française 108 (4), 609-643.

Garcia, J., Landeck, G., Martínez, K., Carbonell, E., 2013b. Hominin dispersals from the Jaramillo subchron in central and south-western Europe: Untermassfeld (Germany) and Vallparadís (Spain), Quaternary International 316, 73-93.

Garcia, J., Martínez, K., Carbonell, E., 2011. Continuity of the first human occupation in the Iberian Peninsula: Closing the archaeological gap, Comptes Rendus Palevol 10, 279-284.

Garcia, J., Martínez, K., Carbonell, E., 2013a. The Early Pleistocene stone tools from Vallparadís (Barcelona, Spain): rethinking the European Mode 1, Quaternary International 316, 94-114.

Garcia, J., Martínez, K., Carbonell, E., Agustí, J., Burjachs, F., 2012. Defending the early human occupation of Vallparadís (Barcelona, Iberian Peninsula): A reply to Madurell-Malapeira *et al.*, (2012), Journal of Human Evolution 63, 568-575.

Garcia, J., Martínez, K., Carbonell, E., Canal, J., 2009. L'escola de Girona de Paleolitistes, Annals de L'Institut d'Estudis Gironins L, 9-26.

García, M., Carbajo, A., Guerra, S., 2004. Metodología aplicada al estudio de las áreas de captación de recursos y distribución de yacimientos al aire libre del Pleistoceno Medio en el término de Malpartida de Cáceres y Cáceres (España), in: Allué E., Martín, J., Canals, A., Carbonell, E. (Eds.), Actas del 1° Congreso Peninsular de Estudiantes de Prehistoria, pp. 368-373.

García, N., 2003. Osos y otros carnívoros de la Sierra de Atapuerca. Oviedo: Fundación Oso de Asturias.

Garcia, N., Arsuaga, J. L., 2001. Ursus dolinensis: a new species of Early Pleistocene ursid from TrincheraDolina, Atapuerca (Spain), Comptes Rendus de l'Académie des Sciences 332, 717-725.

García, N., Arsuaga, J.L., Bermúdez de Castro, J.M., Carbonell, E., Rosas, A., Huguet, R., 2008. The Epivillafranchian carnivore Pannonictis (Mammalia, Mustelidae) from Sima del Elefante (Sierra de Atapuerca, Spain) and a revision of the Eurasian occurrences from a taxonomic perspective, Quaternary International 179, 42-52.

García, N., Arsuaga, J.L., Torres, T., 1997. The carnivore remains from the Sima de los Huesos Middle Pleistocene site (Sierra de Atapuerca, Spain), Journal of Human Evolution 33, 155-174.

García-Antón, M.D., 1998. Reconstrucciones de Paleovegetación en Atapuerca según Análisis Polínico, in: Aguirre, E. (Ed.), Atapuerca y la Evolución Humana, Fundación Ramón Areces, Madrid, pp. 61-72.

García-Antón, M.D., Morant, N., Mallol, C., 2002. L'approvisionnement en matières premières lithiques au Pléistocène inférieur et moyen dans la Sierra de Atapuerca, Burgos (Espagne), L'Anthropologie 106, 41-55.

García-Antón, M.D., Mosquera, M., 2007. Donées préliminaires sur des aires d'approvisionement et de selection des matières premières lithiques dans les occupations du Pléistocene Moyen du niveu TD10-1. En Moncel, M.-H., Moigne, A.-M., Arzarello, M., Peretto, C. in: Aires d'approvisionement en matières premières et aires d'approvisionement en resources alimentaires. Approche intégrée des comportements-UISPP. Actes du XV Congrès Mondial (Lisbonne, 4-9 Septembre 2006). British Archaeological Research International Series 1725, pp.171-185.

García-Arguelles, P., Fullola, J.M., 2002. La Bauma de la Peixera d'Alfés (Alfés, Lleida) y la Cova del Boix (Margalef de Montsant, Tarragona) en el contexto del Paleolítico Superior del nordeste peninsular", Monograf. SERP, n° 3, 97 p., 22 figs.14 gráf, 8 fot. Barcelona.

García-Argüelles, P., Fullola, J.M., Román, D., Nadal, J., Bergadà, M.M., 2013. El modelo epipaleolítico geométrico tipo Filador cuarenta años después: vigència y nuevas propuestas, in: Rasilla, M. (Coord) F. Javier Fortea Pérez. Universitatis Ovetensis Magister. Univ. de Oviedo, pp. 151-166.

García-Arguelles, P., Nadal, J., 1998. The geometrical sequence of the Filador rock shelter (Catalonia, Spain), Proceedings of the XIII Internat. Congr. UISPP, vol. 3, section 7, The Mesolithic, (Forlì 1996), A.B.A.C.O. Edizioni, Forlì, pp. 49-54.

Garcia-Arguelles, P., Nadal, J., Fullola, J. M., 2002. Vint anys d'excavacions a l'abric del Filador (Margalef de Montsant, Priorat, Tarragona), Tribuna d'Arqueologia 1998-1999, 71-96.

García-Arguelles, P., Nadal, J., Fullola, J. M^a^., Bergadà, M^a^.M., Domingo, I., Allué, E., LLoveras, LL., e.p.. Nuevas interpretaciones del Paleolítico Superior inicial de la Cataluña meridional: el yacimiento de l'Hort de la Boquera (Priorat, Tarragona), Trabajos de Prehistoria.

García-Argüelles, P., Nadal, J., Fullola, J.M., 2005. El abrigo del Filador (Margalef de Montsant, Tarragona) y su contextualización cultural y cronològica en el Nordeste peninsular, Trabajos de Prehistoria 62 (1), 65-83.

García-Arguelles, P., Serrat, D., Bergadà, M.M. 1993. Las terrazas fluviales del curso medio del río Montsant (Tarragona) y su relación con los asentamientos prehistóricos, El Cuaternario en España y Portugal, Actes de la 2ª Reun. del Cuaternario Ibérico, vol. 1, Madrid, pp. 493-499.

García-Diez, M., Eguizabal, J., 2003. La cueva de Covalanas. El grafismo rupestre y la definición de territorios gráficos en el paleolítico cantábrico, Consejería de Cultura, Turismo y Deporte, Gobierno de Cantabria, Santander.

García-Díez, M., Garrido, D., 2012. La cronología de las manos parietales en el arte paleolítico, in: de las Heras, C., Lasheras, J. A., Arrizabalaga, A., de la Rasilla, M., (Coords.), Pensando el Gravetiense: nuevos datos para la región cantábrica en su contexto peninsular y pirenaico. M.N.C.I.A., 23 pp. 492-500.

García-Diez, M., González-Morales, M.R., 2003. Reflexiones en torno al llamado "arte esquemático-abstracto": a propósito de unas fechas de Covalanas (Ramales de la Victoria, Cantabria), Veleia 20, 227-241.

García-Diez, M., González-Morales, M., Straus, L., 2012. El grafismo rupestre paleolítico de la Cueva de El Mirón, Trabajos de Prehistoria 69, 21-36.

García-Díez, M., Hoffmann, D.L., Zilhao, J., de las Heras, C., Lasheras, J.A., Montes, R., Pike, A.W.G., 2013. Uranium series dating reveals a long sequence of rock art at Altamira Cave (Santillana del Mar, Cantabria), Journal of Archaeological Science 40, 4098-4106.

García-Diez, M., Ochoa, B., Barandirarán, I, 2013. Neanderthal graphic behaviour: the pecked pebble from

Axlor rockshelter (northem Spain), Journal of Anthropological Research 69 (3), 397-410.

García-Díez, M., Rodríguez-Hidalgo, A., Canals, A., 2012. Arte mueble paleolítico en el interior peninsular: la cueva de Maltravieso (Cáceres, España), Trabajos de Prehistoria 69 (2), 163-171.

García-Diez, M., Vaquero, M., 2006. La variabilite graphique du Moli del Salt (Vimbodi, Catalogne, Espagne) et l'art mobilier de la fin du Paleolithique superieur àl'est de la Peninsule Iberique, L'Anthropologie 110 (4), 453-481.

García-Medrano, P., 2011. Los sistemas técnicos del Pleistoceno Medio en el Oeste de Europa. Cadenas operativas y procesos de configuración en los conjuntos líticos de Galería y Gran Dolina-TD10-1 (Sierra de Atapuerca, Burgos, España) y Boxgrove (Sussex, Inglaterra). Tesis Doctoral. Departamento de Ciencias Históricas y Geografía. Área de Prehistoria. Universidad de Burgos. Burgos. p.495.

García-Medrano, P., Ollé, A., Díez, C., Carbonell, E., 2013. Les matières premières, la technologie lithique et les stratégies d'occupation dans le site du Pléistocène moyen de Covacha de los Zarpazos (gisement de Galería, Sierra de Atapuerca, Espagne), L' Anthropologie 117, 515-540.

García-Medrano, P., Ollé, A., Mosquera, M., Cáceres, I., Díez, C., Carbonell, E., 2014. The earliest Acheulean technology at Atapuerca (Burgos, Spain): Oldest levels of the Galería site (GII Unit), Quaternary International. DOI/10.1016/j.quaint.2014.03.053.

Gardiner. B., 1999. Picture Quiz. Newsletter and Proceedings of the Linnean Society of London 15, 6-13

Garralda, M.D., 1980 El esqueleto aziliense del la Cueva de Los Azules I (Cangas de Onís, Oviedo), in: Esteva, C. (Ed.), I CongresoEspañol de Antropología. Servicio de Publicacionesde la Universidad de Barcelona, Barcelona, pp. 573-580.

Garralda, M.D., 1986. The Azilian man from Los Azules Cave I (Cangas de Onis, Oviedo, Spain), Human Evolution 1 (5), 431-447.

Garralda, M.D., 2005. Los neandertales de la Península Ibérica, Munibe 57, 289-314.

Garralda, M.D., Galván, B., Hernández, C.M., Mallol, C., Gómez, J.A., Maureille, B., in press. Neanderthals from El Salt (Alcoy, Spain) in the Context of the Latest Middle Palaeolithic Populations from the Southeast of the Iberian Peninsula, Journal of Human Evolution.

Garrod, D.A.E., Buxton, L.H.D., Smith, G. Elliot, Bate, D.M.A., 1928. Excavation of a Mousterian Rock-shelter at Devil's Tower, Gibraltar. Journal of the Royal Anthropological Institute 58, 33-113.

Gaudzinski, S., Roebroeks, W., 2000. Adults only. Reindeer hunting at the Middle Palaeolithic site Salzgitter Lebenstedt, Northern Germany, Journal of Human Evolution 38, 497-521.

Gavelas, A. J., 1981. Breves notas sobre el santuario prehistórico del Abrigo de la Manzaneda, Boletín del Instituto de Estudios Asturianos 104, 933-936.

Gibert J., Agustí J., Moyá, S., 1983. Presencia de Homo sp. en el yacimiento Venta Micena, Paleont. Evolució. Publicación Especial, 1-12.

Gibert, A., 1909. Tarragona prehistórica y protohistórica, Tipografia l'Avenç.

Gibert, L., Scott, G., Martin, R., Gibert, J., 2007. The Early to Middle Pleistocene boundary in the Baza Basin (Spain), Quaternary Science Reviews 26, 2067-2089.

Gil Ortiz, C., Calleja de Diós, M., 2009. Seguimiento en el colector margen derecha norte. Actas de las IV Jornadas sobre Patrimonio Arqueológico en la Comunidad de Madrid, Dirección General de Patrimonio Histórico, Madrid, pp. 349-352.

Gil, E., Hoyos, M., 1987. Contexto estratigráfico, in: Aguirre, E., Carbonell, E., Bermúdez de Castro, J.M. (Eds.), El hombre fósil de Ibeas y el Pleistoceno de la Sierra de Atapuerca, Junta de Castilla y León. Consejería de Cultura y Bienestar Social, Valladolid.

Gil, E., Lanchares, E., 1987. Los roedores del yacimiento musteriense de la Cueva de Gabasa (Pirineo Aragonés). Interés paleoecológico, Geogaceta 3, 5-7

Giles Pacheco F., Giles Guzmán, F., Gutiérrez López, J.M., Santiago Pérez, A., Finlayson, C., Rodríguez Vidal, J., Finlayson, G., Fa, D.A., 2012. The tools of the last Neanderthals: Morphotechnical characterization of the lithic industry at level IV of Gorham's Cave, Gibraltar. Quatern. Int. 247, 151-161.

Giles Pacheco, F., Gutiérrez López, J. M., Mata Almonte, E., Santiago Pérez, A., 1996. Laguna de Medina, bassin du fleuve Guadalete (Cádiz, Espagne). Un gisement acheuléen ancien dans le cadre des premières occupations humaines de la Péninsule Ibérique, L´Anthropologie 100 (4), 507-528.

Giles Pacheco, F., Mata Almonte, E., Gutiérrez López, J. M., Santiago Pérez, A., Aguilera Rodríguez, L., 1994. Aportaciones a la ocupación paleolítica de la banda atlántica gaditana, in: J. Ramos *et al.*, (Eds.), Aproximación a la Prehistoria de San Fernando. San Fernando, pp. 69-86.

Giralt, S., Vallverdú, J., Sala, R., Rodríguez, X.P., 1995. Cronoestratigrafia i paleoclimatologia de l'ocupació humana a la vall mitjana del Ter al Pleistocè mitjà i superior inicial, in: Agustí, B., Burch, J., Merino, J. (Eds.), Excavacions d'urgència a Sant Julià de Ramis (Anys 1991-1993), Centro de Investigaciones Arqueológicas de Girona, Serie Monográfica 16, Girona, pp. 23-36.

Gleed-Owen, C.P., Price, C., 2013a. Amphibians and reptiles from Gorham's Cave. In: Barton, R. N. E., Stringer, C. B., Finlayson, J. C. (Eds.), Neanderthals in Context: A Report of the 1995-1998 Excavations at Gorham's and Vanguard Caves, Gibraltar. Oxford University Press, Oxford, pp. 102-111.

Gleed-Owen, C.P., Price, C., 2013b. Herpetofaunal evidence from Vanguard Cave, in: Barton, R. N. E., Stringer, C. B., Finlayson, J. C. (Eds.), Neanderthals in Context: A Report of the 1995-1998 Excavations at Gorham's and Vanguard Caves, Gibraltar, Oxford University Press, Oxford, pp. 224-226.

Goldberg, P., Mallol, C., 2006. Pinilla del Valle- 2006. Micromorphology samples. Informe unpublished.

Gómez-Robles, A., Martinón-Torres, M., Bermúdez de Castro, J. M., Margvelashvili, A., Bastir, M., Arsuaga, J. L., Pérez-Pérez, A., Estebaranz, F., Martínez, L. M., 2007. A geometric morphometric analysis of hominin upper first molar shape, Journal of Human Evolution 53, 272-285.

Gómez-Robles, A., Martinón-Torres, M., Bermúdez de Castro, J.M., Margvelashvili, A., Bastir, M., Arsuaga, J.L., Pérez-Pérez, A., Estebaranz, F., Martínez, L.M., 2007. A geometric morphometric analysis of hominin upper first molar shape, Journal of Human Evolution 53, 272-285.

González R., 2001. Art et espace dans les grottes paléolithiques cantabriques, Jérôme Million, Grenoble.

Gonzalez, J., Freeman, L., 1998. Le Paléolithique inférieur et moyen en Espagne, Serie Prehistoire d'Europe, 6, Jerome Million, Grenoble.

González, M.R., Straus, L.G., 2000.Parietal engravings in Magdalenian stratigraphic context in El Mirón Cave (Ramales de la Victoria, Cantabria, Spain), Bulletin de l'I.N.O.R.A., 27 2-6.

González-Echegaray, J. (Ed.), 1980. El yacimiento de la cueva de "El Pendo" (excavaciones 1953-57). Biblioteca Praehistorica Hispana, vol. XVII, Madrid.

González-Echegaray, J., 1963. Cueva de las Chimeneas, Excavaciones Arqueológicas en España 21, Madrid.

González-Echegaray, J., 1964. Nuevos grabados y pinturas en las cuevas del Monte del Castillo, Zephyrvs XV, 441-446.

González-Echegaray, J., 1969. El paso del Paleolítico Medio al Superior en la costa cantábrica, Anuario de Estudios Atlánticos 15, 273-279.

González-Echegaray, J., 1971a. El Paleolítico Superior, in: González-Echegaray, J., Freeman, L.G. (Eds.), Cueva Morin. Publicaciones del Patronato de las cuevas prehistóricas de la provincia de Santander, VI, Santander, pp. 191-297.

González-Echegaray, J., 1971b. Introducción, in: González-Echegaray, J., Freeman, L.G. (Eds.), Cueva Morin. Publicaciones del Patronato de las cuevas prehistóricas de la provincia de Santander, VI, Santander, pp. 5-24.

González-Echegaray, J., 1972. Notas para el estudio cronológico del arte rupestre en la cueva del Castillo, in: Santander Symposium, Patronato de las Cuevas Prehistóricas de Santander, Santander-Madrid, pp. 409-422.

González-Echegaray, J., 1974. Pinturas y grabados de la cueva de Las Chimeneas (Puente Viesgo, Santander), Monografías de Arte Rupestre 2, Diputación Provincial de Barcelona, Barcelona.

González-Echegaray, J., Freeman, L.G., 1971. Cueva Morín. Publicaciones del Patronato de las cuevas prehistóricas de la provincia de Santander, VI, Santander.

González-Echegaray, J., Freeman, L.G., 1973. Cueva Morín. Publicaciones del Patronato de las cuevas prehistóricas de la provincia de Santander, X, Santander.

González-Echegaray, J., Freeman, L.G., 1978. Vida y muerte en Cueva Morín.Institución Cultural de Cantabria, Santander.

González-Echegaray, J., Freeman, L.G., 1996. Obermaier y Altamira. Las nuevas excavaciones, in: Moure, A. (Ed.), El Hombre Fósil, 80 años después. Santander: Universidad de Cantabria-Fundación M. Botín-Institute for Prehistoric Investigations.

González-Echegaray, J., Freeman, L.G., 1998. Le Paléolithique inférieur et moyen en Espagne. Éditions Jerôme Millon. Grenoble.

González-Echegaray, J., Moure Romanillo, A., 1970. Figuras rupestres inéditas de la cueva del Castillo (Puente Viesgo), Boletín del Seminario de Estudios de Arte y Arqueología XXVI, 441-446.

González-Echegaray, J., Moure, A., 1971. Representaciones rupestres inéditas en la cueva de La Pasiega (Puente Viesgo, Santander), Trabajos de Prehistoria 28, 401-405.

González-Echegaray, J., Ripoll, E., 1953-1954. Hallazgos en la cueva de La Pasiega (Puente Viesgo, Santander), Ampurias XV-XVI, 43-65.

González-Morales, M., Dupré, M., Corchón, M. S., Hoyos, M., Laville, H., Fortea, J., Rodríguez, J. A., Fernández-Tresguerres, J. A., 1989. Neue Untersuchungen in den Flusstälern des Nalón und des Sella (Asturien),Madrider Mitteilungen 30, 1-30.

González-Morales, M., Straus, L.G., 2005. The Magdalenian sequence of El Mirón Cave, in: Dujardin, V. (Ed.), Industrie Osseuse et Parures du Solutréen et Magdalénien en Europe. Mémoire de la Société Préhistorique Française 39, Paris, pp. 209-219.

González-Morales, M., Straus, L.G., 2009. Extraordinary Early Magdalenian finds from El Mirón Cave, Cantabria, Antiquity 83, 267-281.

González-Morales, M., Straus, L.G., 2012. Terminal Magdalenian/Azilian at El Mirón Cave and the Río Asón valley, in: Muñiz, J. (Ed.), Ad Orientem. Ménsula, Oviedo, pp. 189-215.

González-Morales, M., Straus, L.G., 2013a. La ocupació gravetiense de la Cueva de El Mirón y el contexto del arte paleolítico temprano de la cuenca del Asón, in: Heras, C. de la, Lasheras, J.A., Arrizabalaga, A., Rasilla, M. de la (Eds.), Pensando el Gravetiense. Museo Nacional y Centro de Investigación de Altamira, Mongrafías 33, Santander, pp. 305-318.

González-Morales, M., Straus, L.G., 2013b. Colgante decorado con una cabeza de caballo de la Cueva de El Mirón, in: Rasilla, M. de la (Ed.), F. Javier Fortea Pérez. Ménsula, Oviedo, pp. 225-235.

González-Pumariega, M., 2007. La Cueva de Llonín, in: La Prehistoria en Asturias. Un legado artístico único en el mundo, La Nueva España, Oviedo, pp. 321-354.

González-Pumariega, M., 2011. La cueva de El Pindal, 1911-2011. Estudio de su arte rupestre cien años después de Les Cavernes de la Région Cantabrique, Ménsula, Pola de Siero.

González-Pumariega, M., 2013. El arte rupestre paleolítico del Abrigo de La Viña (Oviedo, Asturias). Presentación de su estudio actual dentro del proyecto de investigación del yacimiento,in Medina-Alcaide, M.A., Romero, A.J., (Coord.), Mensajes desde el pasado. Manifestaciones gráficas de las sociedades prehistóricas. Fundación de Servicios Cueva de Nerja, Málaga, pp. 37-38.

González-Pumariega, M., 2013. La figura de pez de la cueva de El Pindal (Asturias): un salmón disfrazado de atún, in: de la Rasilla, M. (coord.), F. Javier Fortea Pérez, Universitatis Ovetensis Magister, Ménsula, Pola de Siero, pp. 363-374.

González-Sainz, C., 2002. Representaciones arcaicas de bisontes en la Región Cantábrica, Spal 9, 257-277.

González-Sáinz, C., 2003. El conjunto parietal paleolítico de la Galería Inferior de La Garma (Cantabria). Avance de su organización interna, in: Balbín, R., Bueno, P. (Coords.), El arte prehistórico desde los inicios del siglo XXI, Ribadesella, pp. 201-222.

González-Sáinz, C., 2005 El punto de vista de los autores estructuralistas: a la búsqueda de un orden en las cuevas decoradas del paleolítico Superior, in: Lasheras, A., González-Echegaray, J., El significado del Arte Paleolítico, Museo de Altamira, Santander, pp. 181-209.

González-Sainz, C. 2011. Industrias en hueso y asta de los niveles magdalenienses de Santimamiñe (excavaciones 2004-2007), Kobie Serie BAI n.º 1, 11-153.

González-Sainz, C. Balbin, R. de, 2000. Revisión de las representaciones paleolíticas de la cueva La Pasiega en el conjunto del Monte Castillo. Topografía y documentación artística, in; Actuaciones arqueológicas en Cantabria 1984-1999, Gobierno de Cantabria, Santander, pp. 69-74.

González-Sáinz, C., Balbín, R., 2002. La Pasiega, in: Las cuevas con arte paleolítico en Cantabria:. A.C.D.P.S. Santander, pp. 165-178.

González-Sainz, C., Cacho, R., Altuna, J., 1999. Una nueva representación de bisonte en la cueva de Ekain (País Vasco), Munibe 51, 153-159.

González-Sainz, C., Ruiz, R., 2010. Una nueva visita a Santimamiñe. Precisiones en el conocimiento del conjunto parietal paleolítico, Kobie anejo 11, Diputación Foral de Bizkaia, Bilbao.

González-Sainz, C., Ruiz-Redondo, A., 2013. Not only Chauvet: dating Aurignacian rock art in Altxerri B Cave (Northern Spain), Journal of Human Evolution 65, 457-464.

González-Sampériz, P., Montes, L., Utrilla, P., 2003. Pollen in Hyena coprolites from Gabasa Cave (Northern Spain), Review of Paleobotany and Palynology 126, 7-15.

González-Sampériz, P., Montes, L., Utrilla, P., 2005. Análisis palinológico alternativo en un yacimiento arqueológico. Los coprolitos de hiena de la Cueva de los Moros de Gabasa (Huesca, España), in: Geoarqueología y Patrimonio en la Pla. Ibérica y el entorno mediterráneo, pp. 587-595.

González-Urquijo, J., Ibáñez, J. J., Rios, J. Bourguignon, L., Castaños, P., Tarriño, A., 2005. Excavaciones recientes en Axlor. Movilidad y planificación de actividades en grupos de neandertales, in: Montes, R., Lasheras, J. A. (Ed.), Actas de la Reunión científica: Neandertales Cantábricos. Estado de la cuestión. Monografías del Museo Nacional y Centro de Investigación de Altamira 20, pp. 527-539.

González-Urquijo, J., Ibáñez, J.J., Ríos, J., Bourguignon, L., 2006 Aportes de las nuevas excavaciones en Axlor sobre el final del Paleolítico Medio, in: Cabrera, V. *et al.*, (Eds.), En el centenario de la cueva de El Castillo: el ocaso de los neandertales, UNED, Madrid, pp. 269-290.

Gorrotxategi, X., 2000. Arte paleolítico parietal de Bizkaia, Kobie anejo 2, Diputación Foral de Bizkaia, Bilbao.

Gracia, F. J., Giles Pacheco, F., Cano Pan, J. A., Santiago Pérez, A. Mata Almonte, E., Gutiérrez López, J. M., 2004. Evolución geomorfológica de la cuenca del río Louro en conexión con el valle del Miño y poblamiento paleolítico (Gándaras de Budiño-Tuy; Pontevedra), in: Homenaje al Profesor Emiliano Aguirre, Museo Arqueológico Regional, Alcalá de Henares, pp. 219-229.

Grandal-D'Anglade, A., 1991. Revisión de los fondos paleontológicos del Museo Provincial de Lugo: nuevos datos sobre fauna cuaternaria de Galicia, Cuadernos do Laboratorio Xeolóxico de Laxe 16, 23-35.

Grandal-D'Anglade, A., Vidal Romaní, J., 1997. A population study of the Cave Bear (Ursus spelaeus Ros.-Hein.) from Cova Eirós (Triacastela, Galicia, Spain), Geobios 30, 723-731.

Green, R.E., Krause, J., Briggs, A. W., Maricic, T., Stenzel, U., Kircher, M., Patterson, N., Li, H., Zhai, W., Fritz, M. H-Y., Hansen, N., Durand, E.Y., Malaspinas, A.S., Jensen, J., Marques-Bonet, T., Alkan, C., Prüfer, K., Meyer, M., Burbano, H. A., Good, J.M., Schultz, R., Aximu-Petri, A., Butthof, A., Höber, B., Höffner, B., Siegemund, M., Weihmann, A., Nusbaum, C., Lander, E.S., Russ, C., Novod, N., Affourtit, J., Egholm, M., Verna, C., Rudan, P., Brajkovi´c, D., Ku´can, Ž., Guši´c, I., Doronichev, V. B., Golovanova, L. V., Lalueza-Fox, C., Rasilla, M. de la, Fortea, J., Rosas, A., Schmitz, R., Johnson, P., Eichler, E. E., Falush, D., Birney, E., Mullikin, J., Slatkin, M., Nielsen, R., Kelso, J., Lachmann, M., Reich, D., Pääbo, S., 2010. A draftsequence of the Neandertal genome, Science 328, 710-722.

GRIP Members 1993. Climate instability during the last interglacial period recorded in the GRIP ice core, Nature 364, 203-207.

Groenen, M., 2006. La grotte d'El Castillo (Puente Viesgo, Cantabrie, Espagne), in: L'archéologie à l'Université Libre de Bruxelles (2001-2005). Matériaux pour une histoire des milieux et des pratiques humaines (coll. Études d'archéologie, 1), CRÉA, Bruxelles, pp. 153-161.

Groenen, M., 2007a. Principios de lectura del arte parietal en las cuevas decoradas del Monte del Castillo, in: Maíllo J.M., Baquedano, E. (Eds.), Miscelánea en Homenaje a Victoria Cabrera vol. 2, Museo Arqueológico Regional, Alcalá de Henares, pp. 42-53.

Groenen, M., 2007b. Voir l'image préhistorique: bilan des travaux dans la grotte ornée d'El Castillo (Cantabrie, Espagne), in: Evin, J. (Ed.), Un siècle de construction du discours scientifique en Préhistoire vol. III, S.P.F, Paris, pp. 307-321.

Grün, R., Aguirre, E., 1987. Datación por ESR y por la serie de U, en los depósitos cársticos de Atapuerca, in: Aguirre, E., Carbonell, E., Bermúdez de Castro, J.M. (Eds.), El Hombre Fósil de Ibeas y el Pleistoceno de la Sierra de Atapuerca. Junta de Castilla y León, Valladolid, pp. 201-204.

Guilaine, J., Martzluff, M., Coularou, J., Rivenq, C., 1995. Les excavacions a la balma de la Margineda (1979-1991), Govern d'Andorra, Andorra.

Guillem, P., 1996. Micromamíferos cuaternarios del País Valenciano: Tafonomía, Bioestratigrafía y reconstrucción paleoambiental. PhD Dissertation, Universitat de València.

Guillem, P.M., 1995. Paleontología continental: microfauna. El Cuaternario del País Valenciano, pp. 227-233.

Guillem, P.M., 1996. Micromamíferos cuaternarios del País Valenciano: Tafonomía, Bioestratigrafía y reconstrucción paleoambiental. Tesis doctoral. Valencia, Dpt. Arqueología y prehistoria. Universidad de Valencia.

Guillem, P.M., Martinez, R., 2009. Arte rupestre en el Cingle del Barranc de l'Espigolar (La Serratella, Castelló), in: El arte rupestre del Arco Mediterráneo de la Península Ibérica, 10 años en la lista del Patrimonio Mundial de la UNESCO, Generalitat Valenciana, pp. 35-48.

Gusi, F., Aguilella, G., 1998. Les ocupacions eneolítiques de la Cova de Dalt del Tossal de la Font (Vilafamés, Castelló), Quaderns de Prehistòria i Arqueologia de Castelló 19, 53-104.

Gusi, F., Carbonell, E., Estévez, J., Mora, R., Mateu, J., Yll, R., 1983. Avance preliminar sobre el yacimiento del Pleistoceno medio, Tossal de la Font (Vilafamés, Castellón), Cuadernos de Prehistoria y Arqueología Castellonenses 7(1980), 7-29.

Gusi, F., Gibert, J., Agustí Ballester, J., Pérez, A., 1987. Nuevos datos del yacimiento Cova del Tossal de la Font (Vilafamés, Castellón), Cuadernos de Prehistoria y Arqueología Castellonenses 10 (1984), 7-18.

Gusi, F., Olària, C., Ollé, A., Saladié, P., Vallverdú, J., Cáceres, I., Made, J.v.d., Expósito, I., Burjachs, F., López-Polín, L., Lorenzo, C., Bennàsar, M., Salazar-García, D.C., Carbonell, E., 2013. La Cova de Dalt del Tossal de la Font (Vilafamés, Castellón): conclusiones preliminares de las intervenciones arqueológicas (1982-1987 / 2004-2012), Quaderns de Prehistòria i Arqueologia de Castelló 31, 17-38.

Gutiérrez-Zugasti, F.I. 2011. Los moluscos alimenticios de la cueva de Santimamiñe (Kortezubi, Bizkaia): campañas de excavación 2004-2006, Kobie Serie BAI nº 1, 247-265.

Gutiérrez-Zugasti, F.I., Cuenca Solana, D., Clemente Conte, I., González Sainz, C., López Quintana, J.C. 2011. Instrumentos de trabajo y elementos de adorno en conchas de molusco de la cueva de Santimamiñe (Kortezubi, Bizkaia), Kobie Serie BAI nº 1, 155-170.

Haber Uriarte, M., 2003. Neandertalenses de la Península Ibérica: estudio arqueológico y paleoantropología. Tesis Doctoral. Universidad de Granada.

Hardy, K., Buckley, S., Collins, M., Estalrrich, A., Brothwell, D., Copeland, L., García-Tabernero, A., García-Vargas, S., Rasilla, M. de la, Lalueza-Fox, C., Huguet, R., Bastir, M., Santamaría, D., Madella, M., Fernández Cortés, A., Rosas, A., 2012. Neanderthal medics? Evidence for food, cooking and medicinal plants entrapped in Neanderthal dental calculus, Naturwissenschaften 99, 617-626.

Harlé, E. 1881. La grotte d'Altamira, Materiaux pour l'Histoire Primitive de l'Homme 17, 275-284

Harlé, E. 1908. Les Grotte d'Aitzbitarte ou Landarbaso à Renteria, près de Saint Sebastien, Bulletin de la Societé Géologique de France 4, (8), 300-302.

Harlé, E., 1920. Restes d'Eléphant et de Rhinocéros trouvés récemement dans le Quaternaire de la Catalogne. Butlletí de la Institució Catalana d'Història Natural. Febrer, pp. 40 - 43.

Haynes, G., 1991. Mammoths, Mastodonts and Elephants. Biology, Behavior, and the Fossil Record. Cambridge University Press, Cambridge.

Hedges, R.E.M., Housley, R.A., Bronk Ramsey, C., Van Klinken, G. J., 1994. Radiocarbon Dates from the Oxford AMS System: Archaeometry Datelist 18, Archaeometry 36, 2, 337-374.

Hennen, J., 1830. Sketches of the Medical Topography of the Mediterranean: comprising an account of Gibraltar, the Ionian Islands and Malta. Thomas y George Underwood, London.

Heras, C., Lasheras, J.A., Rasines, P., Montes, R., Fatás, P., Prada, A., Muñoz, E., 2012. Datation et contexte archéologique de la nouvelle omoplate gravée découverte à Altamira, in: Clottes, J. (Ed.), L'art pléistocène dans le monde / Pleistocene art of the world / Arte pleistoceno en el mundo, Actes du Congrès IFRAO, Tarascon-sur-Ariège, septembre 2010, Symposium «Art mobilier pléistocène». N° spécial de Préhistoire, Art et Sociétés, Bulletin de la Société Préhistorique Ariège - Pyrénées, LXV-LXVI, 2010-2011, livre: pp. 270-271; CD, pp. 1571-1588.

Heras, C., Montes, R., Lasheras, J.A., 2013. Altamira: nivel gravetiense y cronología de su arte rupestre/ Altamira: the gravettian level and the chronology of its cave art, in: de las Heras, C., Lasheras, J. A., Arrizabalaga, Á., de la Rasilla, M., 2013. Pensando el Gravetiense: nuevos datos para la región cantábrica en su contexto peninsular y pirenaico / Rethinking the Gravettian: new approaches for the Cantabrian Region in its peninsular and pyrenean contexts. Monografías del Museo Nacional y Centro de Investigación de Altamira, 23, pp. 501-516

Heras, C., Montes, R., Lasheras, J.A., Rasines, P., Fatás, P., 2008. Nuevas dataciones de la cueva de Altamira y su implicación en la cronología de su arte rupestre paleolítico, Cuadernos de Arte Rupestre de Moratalla 4.

Hernández Pacheco, E., 1919. La caverna de la Peña de Candamo (Asturias), Comisión de Investigaciones Paleontológicas y Prehistóricas, memoria 24, Madrid.

Hernández-Carrasquilla, F., 2001. A new species of vulture (Aves, Aegypiinae) from the Upper Pleistocene of Spain, Ardeola 48 (1), 47-53.

Hernández-Pérez, M. S., 2000. Sobre la religión neolítico. A propósito del Arte Macroesquemático, in: Scriptan in Honorem Enique A. Llobregat Conesa, Vol. I Alicante, pp. 137-155.

Hernández-Pérez, M. S., Ferrer, I., Marset, P., Català Ferrer, E., 1994. L'Art Macroesquemàtic, Edit. Centre d'Estudis Contestans, Cocentaina.

Herrasti, L., Etxeberria, F. 2011. Estudio de los restos humanos de la cueva de Santimamiñe (Kortezubi, Bizkaia). Campañas de 2004 a 2006, Kobie Serie BAI nº 1, 375-382.

Higham, T.F.G., Bronk Ramsey, C., Cheney, H., Brock, F., Douka, K., 2013. The radiocarbon chronology of Gorham's Cave. In: Barton, R. N. E., Stringer, C. B., Finlayson, J. C. (Eds.), Neanderthals in Context: A Report of the 1995-1998 Excavations at Gorham's and Vanguard Caves, Gibraltar. Oxford University Press, Oxford, pp. 62-76.

Hoffmann, D., Utrilla, P., Pike, A., Bea, M., Baldellou, V., García-Díez, M., Zilhão J., e.p. Chronology of Palaeolithic rock art at Fuente del Trucho: style, U-series dates and comparison with Cantabrian sites, in: Actas resumen del Congreso UISPP, Burgos 2014, session A11a, Burgos.

Hoffmeister, D., Zellmann, S., Pastoors, A., Kehl, M., Cantalejo, P., Ramos, J., Weniger, G.-C., Bareth, G., in press. The investigation of the Ardales Cave, Spain - 3D documentation, topographic analyses, and lighting simulations based on terrestrial laser scanning. Remote Sensing.

Hontecillas Tamallo, D., Knoll, F., Arsuaga, J. L., Laplana, C., Pérez-González, A., Baquedano, E., 2012. Reworked remains of mosasauroids (Pythonomorpha, Squamata) in the Pleistocene of Pinilla del Valle (Madrid,Spain), in: Royo-Torres, R., Gascó, F., Alcalá, L., (Coord.), 10th Annual Meeting of the European Association of Vertebrate Palaeontologists, ¡Fundamental!, 20 p. 113.

Howell, F. C., 1965. Yacimiento achelense de Ambrona, Noticiario Arqueológico Hispánico VII, 7-23.

Howell, F. C., 1966. Early Man. Time-Life Int. The Netherlands.

Howell, F. C., Butzer, K. W., Aguirre, E., 1962. Noticia preliminar sobre el emplazamiento achelense de Torralba, Excavaciones Arqueológicas en España, v. 10. Ministerio de Cultura. Madrid.

HowelL, F. C., Butzer, K. W., Freeman, L.G., Klein, R. G., 1995. Observations on the Acheulean occupation site of Ambrona (Soria Province, Spain), with particular reference to recent investigation (1980-1983) and the lower occupation, Jahrbuch des Römisch-Germanischen Zentralmuseum Mainz 38, 33-82.

Howell, F. C., Freeman, L.G., 1982. Ambrona: an early Stone Age site on the Spanish Meseta, The L. S. B. Leakey Foundation News 22, 11-13.

Hoyos, M., 1995. Cronoestratigrafía del Tardiglaciar en la región cantábrica, in: Moure, A. González, C. (Eds.), El final del Paleolítico cantábrico, UCA, Santander, pp.16-76.

Hoyos, M., Laville, H., 1982. Nuevas aportaciones sobre la estratigrafía y sedimentología de los depósitos de la Cueva de El Pendo (Santander): sus implicaciones, Zephyrus 34-35, 249-254.

Hoyos, M., Sáenz De Buruaga, A., Ormazábal, A., 1999. Cronoestratigrafía y paleoclimatologíade los depósitos prehistóricos de la Cueva de Arrillor (Araba, País Vasco), Munibe 51, 137-151.

Hoyos, M., Utrilla, P., Montes, L., Cuchí, J.A., 1992. Estratigrafía, sedimentología y paleoclimatología de los depósitos musterienses de la Cueva de los Moros de Gabasa, Cuaternario y Geomorfología 6 (1-4), 143-156.

Hublin, J. J., Barroso Ruiz, C., Medina Lara, P., Fontugne, M., Reyss, J. L., 1995. The Mousterian site of Zafarraya (Andalucia, Spain): dating and implications on the palaeolithic peopling processes of Western Europe, C.R. Acad. Sci. Paris 321, 931-937.

Huguet, R., 2007. Primeras ocupaciones humanas en la Península Ibérica: Paleoeconomía en la Sierra de Atapuerca (Burgos) y la Cuenca de Guadix-Baza (Granada) durante el Pleistoceno Inferior. Ph.D. thesis, Universitat Rovira i Virgili, Tarragona, Spain.

Huguet, R., Arsuaga, J. L., Pérez-González, A., Arriaza, M. C., Sala-Burgos, M. T. N., Laplana, C., Sevilla, P., García, N., Alvarez-Lao, D., Blain, H-A., Baquedano, E., 2010. Homínidos y hienas en el Calvero de la Higuera (Pinilla del Valle, madrid) durante el Pleistoceno Superior. Resultados preliminares, in: Baquedano, E.M., Rosell, J. (Eds.), Zona Arqueológica 13 (1ª Reunión de Científicos sobre cubiles de hiena (y otros grandes carnívoros) en los yacimientos arqueológicos de la Península Ibérica), pp. 444-458.

Huguet, R., Díez Fernández-Lomana, J.C., Rossell, J., Cáceres, I., Moreno Lara, V., Ibáñez, N. Saladié, P., 2001. Le gisement de Galería (Sierra de Atapuerca, Burgos, Espagne): un modèle archéozoologique de gestion du territoire durant le Pléistocène, L'Anthropologie 105 (2), 237-257.

Huguet, R., Saladié, P., Cáceres, I., Díez, C., Rosell, J., Bennàsar, M., Blasco, R., Esteban-Nadal, M., Gabucio, M.J., Rodríguez-Hidalgo, A., Carbonell, E., 2013. Successful subsistence strategies of the first humans in south-western Europe, Quaternary International 295, 168-182.

Ibáñez, N., 2005. Orígenes de la acumulación de lagomorfos y aves del yacimiento Abric Agut (Cataluña, España), in: Animais na pré-historia e arqueologia da Península Ibérica, Actas do IV Congresso de Arqueologia Peninsular, Faro, IX-2004, Universidade do Algarve, Faro, pp. 169-178.

Ibáñez, N., Saladié, P., 2004. Acquisition anthropique d'Oryctolagus cuniculus dans le site du Molí del Salt (Catalogne, Spagne), in: Brugal, J.-P., Desse, J. (Eds.), Petits animaux et sociétés humaines. Du complément alimentaire aux ressources utilitaires. XXIVe Rencontres Internationales d'Archéologie et d'Histoire d'Antibes, Éditions APDCA, Sophia Antipolis, pp. 255-259.

Iriarte-Chiapusso, M.J. 2011. Polen y vegetación en la secuencia estratigráfica de Santimamiñe (Kortezubi, Bizkaia), Kobie, Serie BAI nº 1, 321-341.

Isaac, G. Ll., 1977. Olorgesailie. Archaeological Studies of a Middle Pleistocene Lake Basin in Kenya. Prehistoric Archeology and Ecology Series, The University of Chicago Press.

Iturbe Polo, G., Cortell Pérez, E., 1992. El Auriñaciense evolucionado en el País Valenciano: Cova Beneito y Ratlla del Bubo, in: Aragón / Litoral mediterráneo. Intercambios culturales durante la Prehistoria. Homenaje a Juan Maluquer de Motes, Zaragoza, pp. 129-138.

Iturbe, G., Fumanal, M.P., Carrión, J.S., Cortell, E., Martínez, R., 1993. Cova Beneito (Muro, Alicante): una perspectiva interdisciplinar, Recerques del Museu d'Alcoi 2, 23-88.

Jardón P., 2000., Los raspadores en el Paleolítico superior. Tipología, tecnología y función en la Cova del Parpalló (Gandía, España) y en la GrotteGazel (Sallèles-Cabardès, Francia). Trabajos Varios del SIP 97, Museu de Prehistòria, Valencia.

Jennings, R., Finlayson, C., Fa, D., Finlayson, G., 2011. Southern Iberia as a refuge for the last Neanderthal populations, Journal of Biogeography 38, 1873-1885.

Jiménez Fuentes, E., Gil, S., Pollos, S., 1995. Quelonios del Pleistoceno Medio de las Grajas (Archidona: Málaga), Stvdia Geologica Salmanticensia, 31, 55-62.

Jiménez, M., 1996. El glaciarismo en la cuenca alta del río Nalón: una propuesta de evolución de los sistemas glaciares cuaternarios en la Cordillera Cantábrica, Sociedad Geológica de España 9 (3-4), 157-168.

Jiménez, M., 1997. Movimientos en masa en la cabecera del río Nalón, Cuaternario y Geomorfología, 11 (3-4), 3-16.

Jiménez-Arenas, J.M., Santonja, M., Botella, M., Palmqvist, P., 2011. The oldest handaxes in Europe: fact or artefact?, Journal of Archaeological Science 38, 3340-3349.

Jiménez-Espejo, F.J., Rodríguez-Vidal, J., Finlayson, C., Martínez-Ruiz, F., Carrión, J.S., García-Alix, A., Paytan, A., Giles Pacheco, F., Fa, D. A., Finlayson, G., Miguel Cortés-Sánchez, M., Rodrigo Gámiz, M., González-Donoso, J.M., Linares, M.D., Cáceres, L.M., Fernández, S., Iijima, K., Martínez Aguirre, A., 2013. Environmental conditions and geomorphologic changes during the Middle-Upper Paleolithic in the southern Iberian Peninsula. Geomorphology 180-181, 205-216.

Jordá, F., 1953. Nuevos hallazgos en Cova Negra (Játiva), Archivo de Prehistoria Levantina, 4, 7-13.

Jordá, F., 1957. Guijarro pintado de tipo aziliense de la cueva del Pindal, Zephyrus 8(2), 269-274.

Jordá, F., 1966. Notas para una revisión de la cronología del Arte Rupestre Levantino, Zephyrus XXVIII, 46-47.

Jordá, F., 1975. La sociedad en el Arte Rupestre Levantino. 50 Aniversario de la Fundación del laboratorio de Arqueología de Valencia, 1924-1974, Papeles núm. 11 Valencia, pp. 159-184.

Jordá, F., 1976. ¿Restos de un culto al toro en el Arte Levantino?, Zephyrus XXVI-XXVII, 198-216.

Jordá, F., Berenguer, M., 1954. La Cueva de El Pindal (Asturias): nuevas aportaciones, Boletín del Real Instituto de Estudios Asturianos 23, 337-364.

Jordá, F., Carral, P., 1988. Geología y Estratigrafía del yacimiento prehistórico de la Cueva de Ambrosio (Vélez-Blanco, Almería), in: Ripoll López, S. (Ed.), La Cueva de Ambrosio (Almería, Spain) y su posición cronoestratigráfica en el Mediterráneo Occidental. Oxford, British Archaeological Reports, International Series, 462, pp. 19-40.

Jordá-Pardo, J. F., Cacho, C., 2013. Radiocarbono y cronoestratigrafía del registro arqueológico pleistoceno de La Peña de Estebanvela (Ayllón, Segovia, España), in: C. Cacho (coord.), Ocupaciones magdalenienses en el interior de la Península Ibérica. La Peña de Estebanvela (Ayllón, Segovia). Junta de Castilla y León-CSIC, pp. 75-92.

Jordá-Pardo, J.F., 2001. Dataciones isotópicas del yacimiento del Pleistoceno superior de Jarama VI (Alto Valle del Jarama, Guadalajara, España) y sus implicaciones cronoestratigráficas. Studien in Memoriam Wilhelm Schüle, Verlag Marie Leidorf GmbH., Rahden/Westf, pp. 225-235.

Jordá-Pardo, J.F., 2007. The wild river and the last Neanderthals: A palaeoflood in the geoarchaelogical record of the Jarama Canyon (Central Range, Guadalajara province, Spain). Geodinamica Acta 20 (4) 209-217.

Jordá-Pardo, J.F., Aura Tortosa, J.E., 2009. El límite Pleistoceno - Holoceno en el yacimiento arqueológico de la Cueva de Nerja (Málaga, España): nuevas aportaciones cronoestratigráficas y paleoclimáticas, Geogaceta 46, 95-98.

Jordá-Pardo, J.F., Avezuela, B., Aura, J.E., Martín-Escorza, C., 2011a. The gastropod fauna of the Epipalaeolithic shell midden in the Vestibulo chamber of Nerja Cave (Málaga, southern Spain), Quaternary International 244 (1), 27-36.

Jordá-Pardo, J.F., Baena, J., Carral, P., García-Guinea, J., Correcher, V., Yravedra, J., 2009. Procesos sedimentarios y diagenéticos en el registro arqueológico del yacimiento pleistoceno de la Cueva del Esquilleu (Picos de Europa, norte de España), Cuaternario y Geomorfología 22 (3-4), 31-46.

Jordá-Pardo, J.F., Cacho Quesada, C., 2008. Cronoestratigrafía y procesos geodinámicos del registro del Pleistoceno superior del Tossal de la Roca (Vall d'Alcalà, Alicante, España), Cuaternario y Geomorfología 22 (3-4), 11-29.

Jordá-Pardo, J.F., Maestro, A., Aura, J. E., Álvarez, E., Avezuela, B., Badal, E., Morales, J. V., Pérez, M., Villalba, M. P., 2011b. Evolución paleogeográfica, paleoclimática y paleoambiental de la costa meridional de la Península Ibérica durante el Pleistoceno superior.El caso de la Cueva de Nerja (Málaga, Andalucía, España), Boletin de la Real Sociedad Española de Historia Natural 105, 137-147.

Jordá-Pardo, J.F., Menéndez, M., Carral, P., Quesada, J.M., Wood, R., 2013. Geoarchaeology and chronostratigraphy of the Middle-Upper Palaeolithic transition at the cave of La Güelga (Cangas de Onís, Asturias, Spain), in: Pastoors, A., Auffermann, B. (Eds.) Pleistocene Foragers on the Iberian Peninsula: Their Culture and Environment, Wiss, Schriften des Neanderthal Museums 7 pp.85-106.

Jöris, O., Street, M., Terberger, T., Weninger, B., 2011. Radiocarbon Dating the Middle to Upper Palaeolithic Transition: The Demise of the Last Neanderthals and the First Appearance of Anatomically Modern Humans in Europe, in: Condemi., S., Weniger, G-. (Ed.), Continuity and Discontinuity in the Peopling of Europe, Springer, pp. 239-298.

Juan Cabanilles, J., García Puchol, O., 2013.Rupture et continuité dans la néolithisation du versant méditerranéen de la péninsule Ibérique: mise à l'épreuve du modèle de dualité culturelle, in : Jaubert, J., Fourmenty, N., Depaepeed, P. (Eds.), XXVIIe Congrès Préhistorique de France. Transitions, Ruptures et Continuité durant la Préhistoire/Transitions, Ruptures and Continuity in Prehistory, 31 mai-5 Juin Bordeaux-Les Eyzies.

Julià, R., 1980. La conca lacustre de Banyoles-Besalú, Centre d'Estudis Comarcals de Banyoles, Banyoles.

Junceda Quintana, F., Fernández-Tresguerres Velasco, J. A., 1995. Cueva de los Azules: 1991-1994. Excavaciones arqueológicas en Asturias 1991-94, Principado de Asturias, Oviedo, pp. 63-64

Kehl, M., Burow, C., Hilgers, A., Navazo, M., Pastoors, A., Weniger, G.-C., Wood, R., Jordá Pardo, J. F., 2013. Late Neanderthals at Jarama VI (central Iberia)?, Quaternary Research 80 (2), 218-234.

Keith, A., 1911. The early history of the Gibraltar cranium. Nature 87, 313-314.

King, W., 1864. The reputed fossil man of the Neanderthal. Quart.J.Sci. 1, 88-97.

Kornprobst, T., Rat, P., 1967. Prémiers résultats d'une étude géologique et paléoclimatique du remplissage paléolithique moyen et supérieur de la grotte de Lezetxiki (Mondragón-Guipúzcoa), Munibe 19, 247-260.

Kostopoulos, D., 1997. The Plio-Pleistocene artiodactyls (Vertebrata, Mammalia) of Macedonia; 1, The fossileferous site "Apollonia-1", Mygdonia Basin of Greece, Geodiversitas 19 (4), 845-875.

Krause, J., Lalueza-Fox, C., Orlando, L., Enard, W., Green, R.E., Burbano, H. A., Hublin, J.-J., Bertranpetit, J., Hänni, C., Rasilla, M. de la, Fortea, J., Rosas, A., Pääbo, S., 2007. The derived FOXP2 variant of modern humans was shared with Neanderthals, Current Biology 17(21), 1908-1912.

Kühn, H., 1957. El arte rupestre en Europa, Ed. Seix y Barral. Barcelona, pp. 71-94.

Küstner, E.C., Vila, S., I de Galdàcano, M., E. S., Pérez, J. A., Fiego, J., Pérez, A. P., Valero, D. C., 2002. Estudio de los restos humanos procedentes de la Cova Foradà (Oliva, Valencia). Antropología y biodiversidad, Ediciones Bellaterrra, pp. 520-528.

Labonne, M., Hillaire-Marcel, C., Ghaleb, B., Goy, J. L., 2002. Multi-Isotopic Age Assessment of Dirty Speleothem Calcite: An Example from Altamira Cave, Spain, Quaternary Science Reviews 21, 1099-1110.

Lacruz, R., Bermúdez de Castro, J.M., Martinón-Torres, M., O'Higgins, P., Paine, M.L., Carbonell, E., Arsuaga, J.L., Bromage, T., 2013. Facial Morphogenesis of the Earliest Europeans, PlosOne 8, 1-7.

Lalueza-Fox, C., 2005. Genes de neandertal, Ed. Síntesis, Madrid.

Lalueza-Fox, C., 2010. El Proyecto Genoma Neandertal; hacia una definición genética del ser humano, Memorias de la Real Sociedad Española de Historia Natural 8, 69-78.

Lalueza-Fox, C., 2011. Desvelando el más íntimo código: los estudios paleogenéticos, in: Rasilla, M. de la, Rosas, A., Cañaveras, J. C., Lalueza-Fox, C. (Eds.), La Cueva de El Sidrón (Borines, Piloña, Asturias). Investigación interdisciplinar de un grupo neandertal, Consejería de Cultura y Turismo y Ediciones Trabe SLU, Oviedo, pp. 117-135.

Lalueza-Fox, C., 2012. Los nuevos genomas de homininos del pasado, in: Mateos, A., Perote, A. (Coords.), Visiones del ser humano. Del pasado al presente. Instituto Tomás Pascual-CENIEH, Madrid, pp. 61-70.

Lalueza-Fox, C., 2013. Palabras en el tiempo. La lucha por el genoma neandertal, Ed. Crítica, Barcelona.

Lalueza-Fox, C., Gigli, E., Rasilla, M. de la, Fortea, J., Rosas, A., Bertranpetit, J., Krause, J., 2008. Neandertal paleogenomics in the ABO blood group gene, BMC Evolutionary Biology 8, 342.

Lalueza-Fox, C., Gigli, E., Sánchez-Quinto, F., Rasilla, M. de la, Fortea, J., Rosas, A., 2012b. Issues from Neandertal genomics: diversity, adaptation and hibridisation revised from El Sidrón case study, Quaternary International 247, 10-14.

Lalueza-Fox, C., Römpler, H., Caramelli, D., Stäubert, C., Catalano, G., Hughes, D., Rohland, N., Pilli, E., Longo, L., Condemi, S., Rasilla, M. de la, Fortea, J., Rosas, A., Stoneking, M., Schöneberg, T., Bertranpetit, J., Hofreiter, M., 2007. A melanocortin 1 receptor allele suggests varying pigmentation among Neanderthals, Science 318, 1453-1455.

Lalueza-Fox, C., Rosas, A., Estalrrich, A., Gigli, E., Campos, P. F., García-Tabernero, A., García-Vargas, S., Sánchez-Quinto, F., Ramírez, O., Civit, S., Bastir, M., Huguet, R., Santamaría, D., Thomas, M., Gilbert, P., Willerslev,

E., Rasilla, M. de la, 2011. Genetic evidence for patrilocal mating behaviour among Neandertal groups, PNAS 108 (1), 250-253.

Lalueza-Fox, C., Rosas, A., Rasilla, M. de la, 2012a. Palaeogenetic research at the El Sidrón Neandertal site, Annals of Anatomy 194, 133-137.

Lalueza-Fox, C., Sampietro, M. L., Caramelli, D., Puder, Y., Lari, M., Calafell, F., Bastir, M., Martínez-Maza, C., Fortea, J., Rasilla, M. de la, Bertranpetit, J., Rosas, A., 2005. Neanderthals evolutionary genetics; mitochondrial DNA data from the Iberian Peninsula, Molecular Biology and Evolution 22 (4), 1077-1081.

Langlais, M., 2004. Réflexions sur la place des différents types de productions lamellaires au sein de la culture magdalénienne du languedoc méditerranéen et des Pyrénées catalanes, Pyrenae 35 (1), 45-73.

Langlais, M., 2010. Les sociétés magdaléniennes de l'Isthme pyrénéen. Collection Documents Préhistoriques, 26. Ed. CTHS, Paris.

Laplace, G., 1971. De l'application des coordonnées cartésiennes à la fouille stratigraphique, Munibe XXIII, 223-236.

Laplana, C., Blain, H.-A., Sevilla, P., Arsuaga, J. L., Baquedano, E. Y., Pérez-González, A., 2013. Un assemblage de petits vertébrés hautement diversifié de la fin du MIS5 dans un environnement montagnard au centre de l'Espagne (Cueva del Camino, Pinilla del Valle, Communauté Autonome de Madrid), Quaternaire 24 (2), 207-216.

Laplana, C., Sesé, C., Sevilla, P., Arsuaga, J.L., Baquedano, E., Cacho Quesada, C., Vega-Toscano, L.G., 2011. Evidence of the presence of the Root vole (Microtus oeconomus) in Central Spain during the Late Pleistocene. Abstracts for Session 42 Ecological Responses to Climatic Change at Decadal to Millennial Timescales: From Genes to Biomes. XVIII INQUA Congress. Berna, Suiza, 22-23 julio de 2011.

Laplana, C., Sevilla, P., Arsuaga, J. L., López-Martínez, N., Blain, H.-A., 2009. Southermost record of Ochotona (Lagomorpha, Mammalia) in Europe, Journal of Vertebrate Paleontology 29, (3), 132A.

Laplana, C., Sevilla, P., Blain, H.-A., Araujo, C., Arsuaga, J. L., Baquedano, E., Pérez-González, A., 2013. Microvertebrados del nuevo yacimiento "Sondeo Galería" del Calvero de la Higuera (Pleistoceno Medio final, Pinilla del Valle, Madrid). XXIX Jornadas de Paleontología, pp. 87-88.

Lasheras, J.A., 2002. El arte paleolítico de Altamira, in: Lasheras, J.A. (Ed.), Redescubrir Altamira Madrid: Turner ediciones, pp. 65 - 91.

Lasheras, J.A., 2010. The cave of Altamira. 22.000 years of history, Revista Adoranten.

Lasheras, J.A., Fernández Valdés, J.M., Montes, R., Rasines, P., Blasco Laffon, E., Soutullo García, B., Heras, C., Fatás, P., 2012. La cueva de Altamira: nuevos datos sobre su yacimiento arqueológico (sedimentología y cronología)/ Altamira cave: new data about the archaeological site (sedimentology and chronology), in: Arias *et al.*, (Coord.), El Paleolítico superior cantábrico, actas de la 1ª Mesa Redonda sobre Paleolítico Superior Cantábrico. San Román de Candamo (Asturias), 26-28 Abril de 2007. Monografías del Instituto Internacional de Investigaciones Prehistóricas de la Universidad de Cantabria., 3, Santander, pp. 67-75.

Lasheras, J.A., Montes, R., Muñoz, E., Rasines. P., Heras, C., Fatás, P., 2005/2006. El proyecto científico 'Los Tiempos de Altamira'. Primeros resultados. En Homenaje a Jesús Altuna: Arte, Antropología y Patrimonio arqueológico, Munibe 57 (3), 143-159.

Laville, H., Hoyos, M., 1994, Algunas precisiones sobre la estratigrafía y sedimentología de cueva Morín (Santander), In: Bernaldo de Quirós, F. (Ed.), El cuadro geocronológico del Paleolítico Superior Inicial. Monografías del Museo y Centro de Investigación de Altamira 13, Madrid, pp. 200-209.

Lazuén Fernández, T., Fábregas Valcarce, R., de Lombera Hermida, A., Rodríguez Álvarez, X.P., 2011. La gestión del utillaje de piedra tallada en el Paleolítico medio de Galicia. El nivel 3 de Cova Eirós, Trabajos de Prehistoria 68, (2), 237-258

Lazuén Fernández, T., González-Urquijo, J., in press a. Análisis de la tecnología, gestión y función de la industria lítica del nivel inferior del yacimiento de Axlor (Dima, Bizkaia), Isturitz.

Lazuén Fernández, T., González-Urquijo, J., in press b. Recycling in the Early Middle Paleolithic: The role of resharpening flakes assessed through techno-functional analysis, Quaternary International.

Leakey, M.D., 1971. Olduvai Gorge, Excavations in Bed I and Bed II, 1960-1963, vol. 3. Cambridge University Press, Cambridge.

Leroi-Gourhan, A., 1965, Préhistoire de l'Art occidental, Mazenod, Paris.

Leroi-Gourhan, A., 1965. La Préhistoire de l'Art Occidental, Mazenod, Paris.

Leroi-Gourhan, A., 1965. La Préhistoire de l'art occidental. Edit. Mazenod, París.

Leroi-Gourhan, A., 1971. Préhistoire de l'art occidental, Mazenod, París.

Leroi-Gourhan, A., 1984. Símbolos, artes y creencias de la Prehistoria, Ed. Istmo, Madrid.

Leroy, S.A.G., Arpe, K., Mikolaiewicz, U., 2011. Vegetation context and climatic limits of the Early Pleistocene hominin dispersal in Europe, Quaternary Science Reviews 30, 1448-1463.

Lewis, C., Waldridge, S., Asmeron, Y., 1998. Neogene artenosphere derived volcanism in noreast Spain: constraints on the geodinamic evolution of the western Mediterranean sea, Unpublished.

Liberda, J., Joroen J., Thompson, W, Jack Rink, W., Bernaldo de Quirós, F., Jayaraman, R., Selvaretinam, K., Chancellor-Madisson, K., Volterra, V., 2010. ESR Dating of Tooth Enamel in Mousterian Layer 20, El Castillo, Spain, Geoarchaeology: An International Journal 25, 4, 467-474.

Lira, J., Linderholm, A., Olaria, C., Durling, M.B., Thomas, M.G., Gilbert, P., Ellegren, H. Willerslev, E., Lidén, K., Arsuaga, J.L., Götherström, A., 2010. Ancient DNA reveals traces of Iberian Neolithic and Bronze Age lineages in modern Iberian horses, Molecular Ecology 19, 64-78.

López Chicano, M., 1985, Estudio hidrogeológico general de la Sierra de Araceli y sectores adyacentes, Lucena (Córdoba). Dep. Hidrogeología, Facultad de Ciencias, Universidad de Granada, 175.

López-García, J. M., Blain, H.-A., Burjachs, F., Ballesteros, A., Allué, E., Cuevas-Ruíz, G. E., Rivals, F., Blasco, R., Morales, J. I., Rodríguez -Hidalgo, A., Carbonell, E., Serrat, D., Rosell, J., 2012. A multidisciplinary approach to reconstructing the chronology and environment of southwestern European Neanderthals: the contribution of Teixoneres cave (Moià, Barcelona, Spain), Quaternary Science Reviews 43, 33-44.

López-García, J. M., Blain, H.-A., Cuenca-Bescós, G., Alonso, C., Alonso, S., Vaquero, M., 2011. Small vertebrates (Amphibia, Squamata, Mammalia) from the late Pleistocene-Holocene of de Valdavara-1 cave (Galicia, northwestern Spain), Geobios 44, 253-269.

López-García, J. M., Cuenca-Bescós, G., Finlayson, C., Brown, K., Giles Pacheco, F., 2011. Palaeoenvironmental and palaeoclimatic proxies of the Gorham's cave small mammal sequence, Gibraltar, southern Iberia. Quat. Int. 243, 137-142.

López-García, J.M., Blain, H.A., Cuenca-Bescós, G., Ruiz-Zapata, M.B., Dorado, M., Gil-García, M.J., Valdeolmillos, A., Ortega, A.I., Carretero, J.M., Arsuaga, J.L., Bermudez de Castro, J.M., Carbonell, E., 2010. Palaeoenvironment and palaeoclimatic reconstruction of the Latest Pleistocene of El Portalón Site, Sierra de Atapuerca, northwestern Spain, Palaeogeography, Palaeoclimatology, Palaeoecology 292, 453-464.

López-García, J.M., Blain, H.-A., de Marfà, R., García, A., Martinell, J., Bennàsar, M.L., Cuenca-Bescós, G., 2011. Small-mammals from the middle pleistocene layers of the sima del elefante (Sierra de Atapuerca, Burgos, Northwestern Spain), Geologica Acta 9, 29-43.

López-García, J.M., Blain, H.-A., Sanz, M., Daura, J., 2011. A coastal reservoir of terrestrial resources for Neanderthal populations in north-eastern Iberia: palaeoenvironmental data inferred from the small-vertebrate assemblage of Cova del Gegant, Sitges, Barcelona, Journal of Quaternary Science 27, 105-107.

López-García, J.M., BlainH.-A., Cuenca-Bescós, G., Arsuaga, J.L., 2008.Chronological, environmental, and climatic precisions on the Neanderthal site of Cova del Gegant (Sitges, Barcelona, Spain). Journal of Human Evolution 55, 1151-1155.

Lopez-Martinez, N., 1980. Los Micromamiferos (Rodentia, Insectivora, Lagomorpha y Chiroptera) del sitio de ocupacion achelense de Aridos-1 (Arganda, Madrid), in: Santonja, M., Lopez, N., Perez-Gonzalez, A. (Eds.), Ocupaciones Achelenses en el valle del Jarama, Arqueologia y Paleontologia 1, Publicaciones de la Diputacion Provincial, Madrid, pp. 161-202.

López-Quintana, J.C. 2011. La ocupación humana de Santimamiñe (Kortezubi): paisaje, recursos y estrategias de explotación del medio desde el Magdaleniense inferior al Calcolítico-Edad del Bronce. Kobie Serie BAI n° 1, 421-446.

López-Quintana, J.C., Guenaga Lizasu, A. 2009. El dolmen de Katillotxu V (Mundaka, Bizkaia): arquitectura y secuencia estratigráfica de un monumento megalítico decorado, Illunzar 7, 87-125.

López-Quintana, J.C., Guenaga Lizasu, A. 2011. Revisión estratigráfica del depósito arqueológico de la cueva de Santimamiñe (Kortezubi, Bizkaia): campañas de 2004 a 2006. Cronoestratigrafía y paleoambiente, Kobie Serie BAI n° 1, 7-70.

López-Quintana, J.C., Guenaga Lizasu, A., Sáenz de Buruaga Blázquez, A. 2011. Dinámica evolutiva de la industria lítica tallada en la secuencia estratigráfica de Santimamiñe. Campañas de 2004 a 2006, Kobie Serie BAI n° 1, 71-110.

López-Recio, M., Silva, P. G., Cunha, P. P., Tapias, F., Roquero, E., Morín, J., Carrobles, J., Murray, A. S., Buylaert, J. P., 2013. Dataciones por luminiscencia de la terraza + 25-30 m del río Tajo en el área de Toledo. El yacimiento achelense de Pinedo, in: Baena, R., Fernández J. J., Guerrero, I. (Eds.), El Cuaternario ibérico: investigación en el s. XXI. Actas de la VIII Reunión de Cuaternario Ibérico, Sevilla, La Rinconada, 2013, AEQUA, Sevilla, pp. 17-21.

Lordkipanidze, D., Jashashvili, T., Vekua, A., Ponce de León, M.S., Zollikofer, C.P.E., Rightmire, G.P., Pontzer, H., Ferring, R., Oms, O., Tappen, M., Bukhsianidze, M., Agusti, J., Kahlke, R., Kiladze, G., Martinez-Navarro, B., Mouskhelishvili, A., Nioradze, M., Rook, L., 2007. Postcranial evidence from early Homo from Dmanisi, Georgia, Nature 449, 305-310.

Lorenzo, C., Navazo, M., Díez, J.C., Sesé, C., Arceredillo, D., Jordá-Pardo, J.F., 2012. New human fossil to the last Neanderthals in central Spain (Jarama VI, Valdesotos, Guadalajara, Spain), Journal of Human Evolution 62 (6), 720-725.

Lorenzo, J.I., 1994. Ensayo de una metodología aplicada al estudio de Paleontología Humana de las poblaciones prehistóricas del Valle Medio del Ebro, Unpublished PhD dissertation. Universidad de Zaragoza.

Lorenzo, J.I., Montes, L., 2001. Restes néandertaliens de la Grotte de los Moros de Gabasa (Huesca, Espagne), in : Zilhao, J. Aubry, Th., Carvalho, A. F. (Eds.), Les premiers hommes modernes de la Péninsule Ibérique. Actes du Colloque de la Commission VIII de l'UISPP, Trabalhos d'Arqueologia1 7, pp. 77-86.

Lozano, M., Subirà, M. E., Aparicio, J., Lorenzo, C., Gómez-Merino, G., 2013. Toothpicking and Periodontal Disease in a Neanderthal Specimen from Cova Foradà Sit (Valencia, Spain), PloS one, 8 (10), e76852

Lozano-Fernández, I., Agustí, J., Cuenca-Bescós, G., Blain, H.-A., López-García, J.M., Vallverdú, J., 2013: Pleistocene evolutionary trends in dental morphology of Mimomys savini (Rodentia, Mammalia) from Iberian peninsula and discussion about the origin of the genus Arvicola. Quaternaire 24 (2), 179-190.

Lumley, H. de, 1971. Le Paléolithique Inférieur et Moyen du Midi Méditerranéen dans son Cadre Géologique. II: Bas-Languedoc-Roussillon-Catalogne, Ve Supplément Gallia Préhistoire, CNRS, Paris.

Luque, C. G., 2001. Geometría y estructura del sistema hidrogeológico kárstico de la sierra del Peñajorao. Descripción física y morfológica de la cueva de El Pendo y proceso de levantamiento topográfico, in: Montes y Sanguino (Dirs.), La Cueva del Pendo, actuaciones arqueológicas 1994-2000, Ayto. de Camargo, Consejería de Cultura y Deporte, Asamblea Regional de Cantabria. Santander, pp. 107-127.

Machado, J., Hernández, C.M., Galván, B., 2011. Contribución teórico-metodológica al análisis histórico de palimpsestos arqueológicos a partir de la producción lítica. Un ejemplo de aplicación para el Paleolítico medio en el yacimiento de El Salt (Alcoy, Alicante), Recerques del Museud'Alcoi 20, 33-45.

Machado, J., Hernández, C.M., Mallol, C., Galván, B., 2013. Lithic production, site formation and Middle Palaeolithic palimpsest analysis: in search of human occupation episodes at Abric del Pastor Stratigraphic Unit IV (Alicante, Spain), Journal of Archaeological Science 40-5, 2254-2273.

Macphail, R.I., Golberg, P., Barton, R.N.E, 2013. Vanguard Cave sediments and soil Micromorphology, in: Barton, R. N. E., Stringer, C. B., Finlayson, J. C. (Eds.), Neanderthals in Context: A Report of the 1995-1998 Excavations at Gorham's and Vanguard Caves, Gibraltar, Oxford University Press, Oxford, pp. 193-210.

Macphail, R.I., Goldberg, P., 2000. Geoarchaeological investigation of sediments from Gorham's and Vanguard Caves, Gibraltar: Microstratigraphical (soil micromorphological and chemical) signatures. In: Stringer, C.B., Barton, R.N.E., Finlayson, J.C. (Eds.), Neanderthals on the Edge. Oxford, Oxbow Books, pp. 183-200.

Made v.d., J., 2013. First description of the large mammals from the locality of Penal, and updated faunal lists for the Atapuerca ungulates-Equus altidens, Bison and human dispersal into Western Europe, Quaternary International 295, 36-47.

Made v.d., J., Aguirre, E., Bastir, M., Fernández-Jalvo, Y., Huguet, R., Laplana, C., Márquez, B., Martínez, C., Martinón, M., Rosas, A., Rodríguez, J., Sanchez, A., S., S., Bermúdez de Castro, J.M., 2003. El registro paleontológico y arqueológico de los yacimientos de la Trinchera del Ferrocarril en la Sierra de Atapuerca.,Coloquios de Paleontología 1, 345-372.

Maíllo-Fernández, J. M., 2001. Aproximación al Fenómeno laminar del Paleolítico Medio: el ejemplo de cueva Morín, Madrid, Espacio, Tiempo y Forma 14, 79-105.

Maíllo-Fernández, J. M., 2003. La Transición Paleolítico Medio-Superior en Cantabria: análisis tecnológico de la industria lítica de Cueva Morín. Tesis Doctoral, UNED, Madrid, p. 547.

Maíllo-Fernández, J. M., 2007a. Le Châtelperronien en Espagne: mythes et réalités. Une approche technologique, in : Evin, J. (Ed.), Congrès du Centenarie. Un siècle de construction du discours scientifique en Préhistoire, Société Préhistorique Française, Paris, pp. 95-103.

Maíllo-Fernández, J. M., 2007b. Aproximacióntecnológica al Musteriense Final de Cueva Morín (Villanueva de Villaescusa, Cantabria), Munibe 57, 21-49.

Maíllo-Fernández, J. M., 2008. El Chatelperroniense en el Noroeste de la Península Ibérica, Férvedes 5, 127-136.

Maíllo-Fernández, J. M., Valladas, H., Cabrera, V., Bernaldo de Quirós, F., 2001. Nuevas dataciones para el Paleolítico Superior de Cueva Morín (Villanueva de Villaescusa, Cantabria), Espacio, Tiempo y Forma 14, 145-150.

Maíllo-Fernández, J.-M., 2012. Missing Lithics: The Role of Flakes in the Early Upper Palaeolithic of the Cantabrian Region (Spain), in: Pastoors, A., Peresani, M (Eds.), Flakes not Blades: The role of flake production at the onset of the Upper Palaeolithic in Europe. WissenschaftlicheSchriftendes Neanderthal Museums, Mettmman, pp. 69-84.

Mallol, C., Cabanes, D., Baena, J., 2010. Microstratigraphy and diagenesis at the Upper Pleistocene site of Esquilleu Cave (Cantabria, Spain), Quaternary International 214, 70-81.

Mallol, C., Hernández, C.M., Cabanes, D., Sistiaga, A., Machado, J., Rodríguez, A., Pérez, L., Galván, B., 2013. The Black Layer of Middle Paleolithic combustion structures.Interpretations and archaeostratigraphic implications, Journal of Archaeological Science 40, 2515-2537.

Mallol, C., Hernández, C.M., Machado, J., 2012. The significance of stratigraphic discontinuities in Iberia Middle-to-Upper Palaeolithic transitional sites, Quaternary International 275, 4-13.

Maluquer de Motes, J., 1951. La Cova de les Llenes de Eriñà (Lérida) in (Eds.), Investigaciones en el Pallars III. . Zaragoza, Monografías del Instituto de Estudios Pirenaicos. Consejo Superior de Investigaciones Científicas, pp. 5-20.

Maluquer de Motes, J., 1983-1984. Un jaciment paleolític a la comarca de la Noguera, Pyreane 19-20, 215-233.

Maluquer de Motes, J., 1985. El primer yacimiento del Magdaleniense Superior en el valle del Segre. Noticia preliminar, in: Symbolae Ludovico Mitxelena Septuagenario oblatae. Pars altera. Vitoria, pp. 1501-1503.

Mancha, E., 2007. La cueva de Maltravieso (Cáceres, España): Geología sedimentaria de los depósitos de entrada de cueva, Tesis de Máster, Departament d'Història i Història de l'Art, Universitat Rovira i Virgili, Tarragona.

Mancha, E., 2011. Geología sedimentaria y lugares de ocupación prehistóricos de la Cueva de Maltravieso (Cáceres, España), Tesis doctoral, Universitat Rovira i Virgili. Tarragona.

Mangado, X., 2005. La caracterización y el aprovisionamiento de los recursos abióticos en la Prehistoria de Cataluña. BAR International Series, 1420, Oxford.

Mangado, X., Petit, M.A., Fullola, J.M., Bartrolí, R., 2006-2007. El paleolític superior final de la Cova del Parco (Alòs de Balaguer, La Noguera), Revista d'Arqueologia de Ponent, 16-17, 45-62.

Mangado, X., Petit, M.A., Fullola, J.M., Bartrolí, R., Bergadà, M.M., Esteve, X., Calvo, M., Tejero, J.M., Estrada, A., 2009. Els caçadors-recol·lectors de la Cova del Parco (Alòs de Balaguer, La Noguera, Lleida), in: Fullola, J.M., Valdeyron, N. (Eds.), Els Pirineus i les àrees circumdants durant el Tardiglacial. Mutacions i Filiacions. XIV CIAP, Homenatge al Prof. G. Laplace, Ed. IEC., Puigcerdà, pp. 565-578.

Mangado, X., Tejero, J.M., Fullola, J.M., Petit, M.A., García-Argüelles, P., García, M., Soler, N., Vaquero, M., 2010. Nuevo territorios, nuevos grafismos: una visión del Paleolítico Superior en Catalunya a inicios del siglo XXI, in: Mangado, X. (Ed.), El Paleolítico Superior peninsular. Novedades del siglo XXI. Monografies del SERP, 8. Ed. SERP, Barcelona, pp. 63-83.

Manzano, I., Baena, J., Lázaro, A., Martín, S., Dapena, L., Albiach, M., Roca, J., Moreno, E., 2005. Análisis de los recursos líticos en la Cueva del Esquilleu: gestión y comportamiento durante el Musteriense (comarca de La Liébana, Occidente de Cantabria, in: Montes, R., Lasheras, J.A. (Ed.), Neandertales cantábricos. Estado de la cuestión. Monografías Museo Nacional de Altamira, 20, pp. 285-300.

Manzano, L., Dapena, L., Expósito, A., Gómez, J., Caro, J., Álvarez, D., Roca, N., Díaz, D., Lillo, J.M., Baena, J., Debenham, N., 2011. Yacimientos paleolíticos en los Berrocales (Proyecto U.Z.P. desarrollo del Este de los Berrocales, Vicálvaro, Madrid). Actas de las V Jornadas de Patrimonio Arqueológico en la Comunidad de Madrid, Dirección General de Patrimonio Histórico, Madrid, pp. 201-212.

Marconell, E., 1892a. Los toros de la Losilla. Miscelánea Turolense, 9. Año II: 160 (Edición facsimilar) 1891-1901, Madrid.

Marconell, E., 1892b. Los toros de la Losilla. Miscelánea Turolense, 10. Año II: 180 (Edición facsimilar) 1891-1901, Madrid.

Mariano Vidal, L., 1908. Las pinturas rupestres de Cogul, Anuari de l'Institut d'Estudis Catalans, pp. 544-550.

Marín, A., 1933. Memoria explicativa de la hoja nº 473 Tarragona. Mapa geológico de España. Instituto Geológico y Minero de España. Tipografia y litografia Coullaut, Madrid, p. 73.

Marín, A.B., 2009. The human use of the montane zone of Cantabrian Spain during the Last Glacial: faunal evidence from El Mirón Cave, Journal of Anthropological Research 65, 69-102.

Marín, A.B., 2010. Arqueozoología en el Cantábrico Oriental durante la Transición Pleistoceno/Holoceno: La Cueva del Mirón. PUbliCan, Santander.

Marks, A.E., Brugal., J-Ph., Chabai, V. P., Monigal, K., Golberg, P., Hockett, B., Pemán, E., Elorza, M., Mallol, C., 2002. Le gisement pléistocène moyen de Galeria Pesada (Estrémadure, Portugal): premiers résultats, Paleo 14, 77-100.

Maroto-Genover, J., 1980. L'estratigrafia de la cova de Mollet III (Serinyà), Amics de Besalú, III Assemblea d'Estudis del seu comtat, Besalú, pp. 227-244.

Maroto-Genover, J., 1994. El pas del paleolític mitjà al paleolític superior a Catalunya i la seva interpretació dins del context geogràfic franco-ibèric, Tesis doctoral, Universitat de Girona, Girona.

Maroto-Genover, J., Julià, R., López-García, J.M., Blain, H.-A., 2012. Chronological and environmental context of the Middle Pleistocene human tooth from Mollet Cave (Serinyà, NE Iberian Peninsula), Journal of Human Evolution 62, 655-663.

Maroto-Genover, J., Soler, N., Fullola, J. M., 1996. Cultural Change between Middle and Upper Palaeolithic in Catalonia, in: E. Carbonell, E., Vaquero, M. (Eds.), The Last Neandertals, the First Anatomically Modern Humans: a Tale about the Human Diversity. Cultural Change and Human Revolution at 40 ka BP, Capellades, pp. 219-250.

Maroto-Genover, J., Soler, N., Mir, A., 1987. La cueva de Mollet I (Serinyà, Gerona), Cypsela VI, 101-110.

Maroto-Genover, J., Terradas, X., 1986. La utilització dels còdols en el Solutrià de la cova de l'Arbreda (Serinyà), Homenatge al Dr. Josep Maria Corominas, Quaderns 1985, vol. 1, Banyoles, pp. 111-123.

Maroto-Genover, J., Vaquero, M., Arrizabalaga, A., Baena, J., Baquedano, E., Jordà, J., Julia, R., Montes, R., Van Der Plicht, H., Rasines, P., Rachel Wood, R., 2012. Current issues in late Middle Palaeolithic chronology: New assessments from Northern Iberia, Quaternary International 247, 15-25.

Maroto-Genover, J., Vaquero, M., Arrizabalaga, Á., Baena, J., Carrión, E., Jordá, J., Martinón, M., Menéndez, M., Montes, R., Rosell, J., 2005. Problemática cronológica del final del Paleolítico medio en el Norte Peninsular. Museo de Altamira. Monografías 20, pp. 101-114.

Maroto-Genover, J., Vaquero, M., Arrizabalaga, A., Baena, J., Carrión, E., Jordá, J.F., Martinón, M., Menéndez, M., Montes, R., Rosell, J., 2006. Problemática cronológica del final del Paleolítico Medio en el norte Peninsular, in: Montes, R., Lasheras, J.A. (Ed.), Neandertales cantábricos. Estado de la cuestión, vol. 20. Monografías del Museo Nacional de Altamira, pp. 101-114.

Márquez, B., Mosquera, M., Baquedano, E., Pérez-González, A., Arsuaga, J. L., Panera, J., Espinosa, J. A., Gómez, J., 2013. Evidence of a Neanderthal-made quartz-based technology at Navalmaíllo rockshelter (Pinilla del Valle, Madrid Region, Spain). Journal of Anthropological Research 69 (3), 373-395.

Márquez, B., Mosquera, M., Panera, J., Bárez, S., Rus, I., Gómez,J., Arsuaga, J. L., Pérez-González, A., Baquedano, E., 2008. El poblamiento humano antiguo en el Valle alto del Lozoya (Madrid), Espacio, Tiempo y Forma. Serie I. Nueva época. Prehistoria y Arqueología 1, 25-32.

Márquez, B., Ollé, A., Sala i Ramos, R., Vergès, J. M., 2001. Perspectives méthodologiques de l'analyse functionnelle des ensembles lithiques du Pléistocène

Inférieur et Moyen d'Atapuerca (Burgos, Espagne), L'Anthropologie 105 (1), 281-299.

Martí, B., Aura, J.E., Juan Cabanilles, J., García Puchol, O., Fernández, J., 2009. El mesolítico geométrico facies Cocina, in: Utrilla, P., Montes, L., (Coord.), El mesolítico geométrico en la cuenca mediterránea. Publicaciones de la Universidad de Zaragoza.

Martín Merino, M.A., Domingo, S., Antón, T., 1981. Estudio de las cavidades BU-IV-A (Sierra de Atapuerca), Kaite. Estudio de Espeleología Burgalesa 2, 41-78.

Martín Penela, A., 1986. Los grandes mamíferos del yacimiento Pleistoceno superior de Cueva Horá (Darro, Granada, España), Antropología y Paleoecología Humana 4, 107-129.

Martín, A., Rodríguez, J., 1979. El yacimiento musteriense de Cueva Horá: Avance del estudio geológico de Cueva Horá (Darro, Granada). Antropología y Paleoecología Humana 1, 75-78.

Martínez Bea, M., 2001-2002. El aprovechamiento de accidentes naturales en el arte rupestre paleolítico. Un nuevo caso en la cueva del Castillo (Puente Viesgo, Santander), Salduie 2, 27-44.

Martínez Navarro, B., Toro Moyano, I., Ros-Montoya, S., Espigares Ortiz, MP., Fajardo Fernández-Palma, B., 2006. Resultados de la prospección superficial del área de Huéscar (Sector Nororiental de la cuenca de Guadix-Baza), Anuario Arqueológico de Andalucía 2003, 54-57.

Martínez Rubio, T., Martorell Briz, X., 2012. La senda heredada: contribución al estudio de la red de caminos óptimos entre yacimientos de hábitat y de arte rupestre neolíticos en el Macizo del Caroit (Valencia), Zephyrus 70, 69-84.

Martínez Valle, R., 1995. Fauna cuaternaria del País Valenciano. Evolución de las comunidades de macromamíferos, El Cuaternario del País Valenciano, pp. 235-244.

Martínez Valle, R., 1996. Fauna del Pleistoceno Superior del País Valenciano; aspectos económicos, huellas de manipulación y valoración paleoambiental. PhD Dissertation, Universitat de València.

Martínez Valle, R., 2001. Los grandes mamíferos pleistocenos. Una aproximación paleoambiental y bioestratigráfca, in: Villaverde, V. (Eds.), De Neandertales a Cromañones. El Inicio del Poblamiento Humano en las Tierras Valencianas. Universidad de Valencia, Valencia, pp. 45-57.

Martínez, J., 1986-1987. Un grabado paleolítico al aire libre en Piedras Blancas (Escullar, Almería), Ars Praehistorica V-VI, 49-58.

Martínez, K., Garcia, J., Burjachs, F., Yll, R., Carbonell, E., 2014. Early human occupation of Iberia: the chronological and palaeoclimatic inferences from Vallparadís (Barcelona, Spain), Quaternary Science Reviews 85, 136-146.

Martínez, K., Garcia, J., Carbonell, E., Agustí, J., Bahain, J.-J., Blain, H.-A., Burjachs, F., Cáceres, I., Duval, M., Falguères, C., Gómez, M., Huguet, R., 2010. A new lower Pleistocene archeological site in Europe (Vallparadís, Barcelona, Spain), Proceedings of the National Academy of Sciences 107, 5762-5767.

Martínez, L., 2010. Estudio tecno-tipológico y tafonómico de las industrias líticas del final del Auriñaciense y comienzo del Gravetiense del abrigo de La Viña (La Manzaneda, Oviedo),Trabajo de máster, Universidad de Zaragoza, Zaragoza, p. 282.

Martínez, L., Rasilla, M. de la., 2013. El Gravetiense en Asturias: revisión y novedades, in: Heras, C. de las., Lasheras, J.A., Arrizabalaga, A., Rasilla, M. de la (Eds.), Pensando el Gravetiense: nuevos datos para la región cantábrica en su contexto peninsular y pirenaico. Museo Nacional y Centro de Investigación de Altamira 23, pp. 276-288.

Martínez, R., 1996. Fauna del Pleistoceno Superior en el País Valenciano. Aspectos económicos, huellas de manipulación y valoración paleoambiental, Tesis Doctoral, Universitat de València, vol. 2

Martínez-Andreu, M., Montes-Bernárdez, R., San Nicolás-del Toro, M., 1989. Avance al estudio del yacimiento musteriense de la Cueva Negra de La Encarnación (Caravaca, Murcia), in: Crónica XIX Congreso Nacional de Arqueología, Castellón de la Plana 1987, Ponencias y Comunicaciones Volumen I, Saragossa, Universidad de Zaragoza, Seminario de Arqueología, Secretariado de los Congresos Arqueológicos Nacionales, "Congresos Arqueológicos Nacionales", pp. 973-983.

Martínez-Moreno, J, de la Torre, I., Mora, R., Casanova, J., 2010. Technical variability and change in the pattern of settlement at Roca dels Bous, in: Conard, N. J., Delagnes, A. (Ed.), Settlement Dynamics on the Middle Paleolithic and Middle Stone Age III, Tubingen, Kerns Verlag, pp. 485-507.

Martínez-Moreno, J., 1990. Informetécnico de los restos óseos de la Cova del Gegant (Sitges, Garraf). Servei d'Arqueologia i Paleontologia de la Generalitat de Catalunya. Centre d'Informació i Documentació del Patrimoni Cultural de la Generalitat de Catalunya. Informe inédito, Barcelona, p. 140.

Martínez-Moreno, J., Miret, J., Mora, R., Muro, I., 1985. Memòria de l'excavaciód'urgència de la Cova del Gegant 1985, Server d'Arqueologia i Paleontologia, Centre d'Informació i Documentació del Patrimoni Cultural de la Generalitat de Catalunya. Informe inédito, Barcelona, p. 98.

Martínez-Moreno, J., Mora, R., Casanova, J., 2004. El marco cronométrico de la cueva de L'Estret de Tragó (Os de Balaguer, La Noguera) y la ocupación de la vertiente sur de los Prepirineos durante el paleolítico medio, Saldvie 4, 1-16.

Martínez-Moreno, J., Mora, R., de la Torre, I., 2010. The Middle-to-Upper Palaeolithic transition in Cova Gran and the extinction of Neanderthals in the Iberian Peninsula, Journal of Human Evolution 58, 211-226.

Martínez-Moreno, J., Mora, R., de la Torre, I., Benito-Calvo, A., 2012. The role of flakes in the early Upper Palaeolithic 497D assemblage of Cova Gran de Santa Linya (Southeastern Pre-Pyrenees, Spain). In:

Pastoors&Peresani (Eds), Flakes not Blades: The role of Flake production at the onset of the Upper Palelolithic in Europe. Wissenschafliche Schriften des Neanderthal Museums 5, Mettmann, pp. 85-104.

Martínez-Moreno, J., Mora, R., Roca, G., y Parcerisas, J., 1990. Memoria d'excavació a la Cova del Gegant 1989, Serveid'Arqueologia i Paleontologia, Centre d'Informació i Documentació del Patrimoni Cultural de la Generalitat de Catalunya, Barcelona. Informe inédito, Barcelona, p. 76.

Martínez-Navarro, B., 1991. Revisión sistemática y estudio cuantitativo de la fauna de macromamíferos del yacimiento de Venta Micena (Orce, Granada). Ph.D. Thesis, Universidad Autónoma of Barcelona.

Martínez-Navarro, B., 2002. The skull of Orce: Parietal bones or frontal bones?, Journal of Human Evolution 42, 265-270.

Martínez-Navarro, B., 2010. Early Pleistocene faunas of Eurasia and Hominin dispersals, in: Fleagle, J.G., Shea, J.J., Grine, F.E., Baden, A.L., Leakey, R. (Eds.), Out of Africa I. The First Hominin Colonization of Eurasia. Contributions from the Second Stony Brook Human Evolution Symposium and Workshop, September 27-30, 2005, (Chapter 13), Springer, pp. 207-224

Martínez-Navarro, B., Espigares, M.P., Ros, S., 2003. Estudio preliminar de las asociaciones de grandes mamíferos de Fuente Nueva-3 y Barranco León-5 (Orce,Granada, España) (Informe de las campañas de 1999e2002), in: Toro, I., Agustí, J., Martínez-Navarro, B. (Eds.), El Pleistoceno inferior de Barranco León y Fuente Nueva 3, Orce (Granada). Memoria Científica Campañas 1999e2002. Junta de Andalucía. Consejería de Cultura. E.P.G. Arqueología Monográfico, pp. 115-136.

Martínez-Navarro, B., Palmqvist, P., 1995. Presence of the African Machairodont Megantereon whitei (Broom, 1937) (Felidae, Carnivora, Mammalia) in the Lower Pleistocene site of Venta Micena (Orce, Granada, Spain), with some considerations on the origin, evolution and dispersal of the genus, Journal of Archaeological Science 22, 569-582.

Martínez-Navarro, B., Palmqvist, P., Madurell, J., Ros-Montoya, S., Espigares, Mª. P., Torregorosa, V., Pérez-Claros, J. A., 2010. La fauna de grandes mamíferos de Fuente Nueva-3 y Barranco León-5: Estado de la cuestión, in: Toro, I. *et al.*, (Eds.), Ocupaciones humanas en el Pleistoceno inferior y medio de la cuenca de Guadix-Baza. Memoria científica, Consejería de Cultura, Junta de Andalucía, pp. 197-236.

Martínez-Navarro, B., Rook, L., 2003. Gradual Evolution in African hunting dog lineage. Systematic implications, C.R. Palevol 2, 695-702.

Martínez-Navarro, B., Ros-Montoya, S., Espigares, M.P., Palmqvist, P., 2011. Presence of the Asian origen Bovini, Hemibos sp. Aff. Hemibos gracilis and Bison sp. At the early Pleistocene site of Venta Micena (Orce, Spain), Quaternary International 243, 54-60.

Martínez-Navarro, B., Sardella, S., Rook, L., Bellucci, L., Ros-Montoya, S., 2012. First occurrence of Soergelia (Ovibovini, Bovidae, Mammalia) in the Early Pleistocene of Italy, Quaternary International 267, 98-102.

Martínez-Navarro, B., Turq, A., Agustí, J., Oms, O., 1997. Fuente Nueva-3 (Orce, Granada, Spain) and the first human occupation of Europe, Journal of Human Evolution 33, 611-620.

Martínez-Pillado, V., Aranburu, A., Arsuaga, J.M., Ruiz-Zapata, M.B., Gil-García, M.J., Stoll, H., Yusta, I., Iriarte, E., Carretero, J.M., R., Lawrence Edwards, R., Cheng, H., 2014. Upper Pleistocene and Holocene palaeoenvironmental records in Cueva Mayor karst (Atapuerca, Spain) from different proxies: speleothem crystal fabrics, palynology, and archaeology, International Journal of Speleology 43 (1) 1-14.

Martínez-Valle, R., 1996. Fauna del Pleistoceno superior del País Valenciano; aspectos económicos, huellas de manipulación y valoración paleoambiental. Tesis doctoral. Universitat de València.

Martín-Lagos. I., 2013. El inicio del Paleolítico medio en Cueva Horá (Darro, Granada): La industria lítica de los niveles LV y LVI. Departamento de Prehistoria y Arqueología, Universidad de Granada. Trabajo Fin de Máster inédito.

Martinón-Torres, M., Bastir, M., Bermúdez de Castro, J.M., Gómez, A., Sarmiento, S., Muela, A., Arsuaga, J.L., 2006. Hominin lower second premolar morphology: evolutionary inferences through geometric morphometric analysis, Journal of Human Evolution 50, 523-533.

Martinón-Torres, M., Bermúdez de Castro, J.M., Gómez-Robles, A., Arsuaga, J.L., Carbonell, E., Lordkipanidze, D., Manzi, G., Margvelashvili, A., 2007. Dental evidence on the hominin dispersals during the Pleistocene, Proceedings of the National Academy of Sciences 104 (33), 13279-13282.

Martinón-Torres, M., Bermúdez de Castro, J.M., Gómez-Robles, A., Arsuaga, J.L., Carbonell, E., Lordkipanidze, D., Manzi, G., Margvelashvili, A., 2007. Dental evidence on the hominin dispersals during the Pleistocene, Proceedings of the National Academy of Sciences of the United States of America 104 (33), 13279 -13282.

Martinón-Torres, M., Bermúdez de Castro, J.M., Gómez-Robles, A., Margvelashvili, A., Prado, L., Lordkipanidze, D., Vekua, A., 2008. Dental remains from Dmanisi (Republic of Georgia): morphological analysis and comparative study, Journal of Human Evolution 55 (2), 249-273.

Martinón-Torres, M., Bermúdez de Castro, J.M., Gómez-Robles, A., Prado-Simón, L., Arsuaga, J.L., 2012. Morphological description and comparison of the dental remains from Atapuerca-Sima de los Huesos site (Spain), Journal of Human Evolution 62, 7-58.

Martinón-Torres, M., Dennell, R., Bermúdez de Castro, J.M., 2011. The Denisova hominin need not be an out of Africa story, Journal of Human Evolution 60, 251-255.

Martos, J. A., Valdivia, J., Cacho, C., 2013. Caracterización tecnotipológica de la industria lítica de La Peña de Estebanvela (Segovia), in: C. Cacho (coord.), Ocupaciones magdalenienses en el interior de la Península Ibérica. La Peña de Estebanvela (Ayllón, Segovia). Junta de Castilla y León-CSIC, pp. 245-394.

Masriera, A., 1975. Observaciones sedimentológicas sobre el depósito cuaternario de la Cova del Gegant (Sitges, Barcelona). Speleon. Monografia I. V Symposium de Espeleología, pp. 35-38.

Mazo, C., 1989. Análisis de huellas de uso en útiles de sílex del Paleolítico. Aplicación del método al estudio del nivel magdaleniense de Abauntz (Arraiz, Navarra). Unpublished PhD dissertation, Universidad de Zaragoza.

Mazo, C., Utrilla, P., Blasco, F.. Mandado, J., Torres, T., Ortiz E., Rink, W.J., 2011-2012. El nivel musteriense de la cueva de Abauntz (Arraitz, Navarra) y su aportación al debate vasconiense. Neanderthales en Iberia: últimos avances en la investigación del Paleolítico Medio Ibérico, Mainake XXXIII, 193-220.

Mazo, C., Utrilla, P., Sopena, M.C., 2008. ¿Cómputos lunares? en el Magdaleniense Medio de la Cueva de Abauntz. Una reflexión sobre marcas en múltiplos de siete, Espacio, Tiempo y Forma, Serie I. Homenaje a E. Ripoll, t. I., 135-154.

Medina, M. A., Cristo, A., Romero, A., Sanchidrián, J.L., 2010. Otro punto de luz. Iluminación estática en los "santuarios" paleolíticos, in: Congrès de l'IFRAO, Symposium L'art pléistocène en Europe (Pré-Actes), Taras con /Foix.

Meese, D., Alley, R., Gow, T., Grootes, P.M., Mayewski, P., Ram, M., Taylor, K., Waddington, E., Zielinski, G., 1994. Preliminary depth-age scale of the GISP2 ice core. CRREL Special Report, 94-1. Hanover, New Hampshire: Cold Regions Research and Engineering Laboratory, p. 66

Meiri, M., Lister, A., Higham, T., Stewart, J., Straus, L., Obermaier, H., González Morales, M., Marín, A.B., Barnes, I., 2013. Late-glacial recolonization and phylogeography of European red deer, Molecular Ecology 22, 4711-4722.

Mejías del Cosso, D., 2009. Tecnocomplejos del pleistoceno en la cuenca media-baja del Tajo. El yacimiento Vendimia en la penillanura del Salor. Zona y afluentes integrados. Tesi doctoral, Departament d'Història i Història de l'Art, Universitat Rovira i Virgili.

Mejías del Cosso, D., Canals, A., Aranda, V., Barrero, N., Bermejo, L., García Vadillo, F.J., Mancha, E., Marín, J., Modesto, M., Morcillo, A., Peña, L., Rabazo, A., Rodríguez Hidalgo, A., Carbonell, E., 2011. La cueva de "El Conejar", las últimas sociedades cazadoras-recolectoras. Actas de las II Jornadas de Arqueología Urbana de Cáceres, Cáceres.

Mejías del Cosso, D., Rodríguez-Hidalgo, A., Canals, A., Mancha, E., Aranda, V., Barrero, N., Bermejo, L., Cánovas, I., Donadeii, P., García, F.J., García, J., Marín, J., Modesto, M., Morcillo, A., Peña, L., Carbonell. E, 2010. Sociedades de transición en el Tajo interior. El registro mesolítico de la cueva de El Conejar, Cáceres (España). Actas Meso 2010: Eighth International Conference on the Mesolithic in Europe, Santander.

Méndez Quintas, E., 2007. El yacimiento achelense de As Gándaras de Budiño. La industria en facies fluviales, Complutum 18, 27-45.

Méndez Quintas, E., 2008. La industria lítica de las facies coluviales del yacimiento achelense de As Gándaras de Budiño: El Locus V en las excavaciones de Vidal Encinas. Zephyrus 62: 41-61.

Menéndez, L., Rosell, J., Canals, A., Mosquera, M., 2009. El nivel G de las Fuentes de San Cristóbal (Huesca, España): nuevas aportaciones al estudio del Paleolítico medio en el Pre-Pirineo aragonés, Cuaternario y Geomorfología 23(1-2), 109-125.

Menéndez, L., Rosell, J., Moncel, M.-H., 2007. Preliminar comparative analysis between Level G of Las Fuentes de San Cristóbal (Pre-Pyrenees of Huesca, Spain) and Level Ga of Payre (Ardèche, France): a similar neanderthal territorial behavior in two different chronological contexts? BAR International Series, pp. 199-206.

Menéndez, M., Jordá, J.F., Kehl, M., Weniger, G-C., Quesada, J. M., 2014. Análisis micromorfológico en la Cueva de La Güelga, in: Excavaciones Arqueológicas en Asturias 2007-2012 (EAA), pp. 377-379

Menéndez, M., Quesada, J.M., Jordá, F.J., Carral, P., Trancho, G.J., García, E., Álvarez-Alonso, D., Rojo, J., Word, R., 2009. Excavaciones arqueológicas en la Cueva de la Güelga (Cangas de Onís), EAA (2003-2006), pp. 209-221.

Meyer, M., Fu, Q., Aximu-Petri, A., Glocke, I., Níkel, I., Arsuaga, J.L., Martínez, I., Gracia, A., Bermúdez de Castro, J.M., Carbonell, E., Pääbo, S., 2013. A mitochondrial genome sequence of a hominin from Sima de los Huesos, Nature doi:10.1038/nature12788

Michel, V., Bard, E., Delanghe, D. El Mansouri, M., Falguères, Ch., Petitt, P., Yokoyama, Y., Barroso Ruiz, C., 2003. Geocronología del relleno de la cueva del Boquete de Zafarraya, in : Barroso Ruiz, C.(Eds), El Pleistoceno superior de la cueva del Boquete de Zafarraya, Arqueología Consejería de Cultura. Junta de Andalucía. Sevilla, Monografías nº 15, pp.113-133.

Michel, V., Delanghe, D., Bard, E., Pettit, P., Yokoyama, Y., Barroso Ruiz, C., 2006. Datation C-14, ESR, des niveaux moustériens de la grotte du Boquete de Zafarraya., in: Barroso Ruiz, C., de Lumley, H. (Eds.), La grotte du Boquete de Zafarraya, Consejería de Cultura, Junta de Andalucía, Sevilla, Málaga, Andalousie. T. I, pp. 487-518.

Michel, V., Delanghe-Sabatier D., Bard, E., Barroso Ruiz, C., 2013. U-series, ESR and 14C studies of the fossil remains from the Mousterian levels of Zafarraya Cave (Spain): a revised chronology of Neandertal presence, Quaternary Geochronology 15, 20-33.

Mir, A., 1975. La industria lítica de la Cova del Gegant. Sitges (Barcelona). Speleon. Monografia I. V Symposium de Espeleología, pp. 39-48.

Mir, A., 1987. Memoria de la quinta campaña de excavaciones en el yacimiento de la Cueva de la Fuente del

Trucho. Asque-Colungo (Huesca), Arqueología Aragonesa 1985, 19-21.

Mir, A., Salas, R., 1976. Tres nuevos carnívoros del yacimiento cuaternario de la Cova d'en Mollet-I Serinyà (prov. de Girona), Publicaciones del Instituto de Investigaciones Geológicas de la Diputación de Barcelona XXXI, 97-124.

Miret Estruch, C., 2007. Estudi de la tecnologia lítica de la Unitat 3 de les Coves de Santa Maira -boca Oest- (Castell de Castells, Marina alta, Països Catalans), Saguntum-PLAV 39, 85-102.

Molina, F.J., Tarriño, A, Galván, B., Hernández, C.M., 2010. Áreas de aprovisionamiento de sílex en el Paleolítico medio en torno al Abric del Pastor (Alcoi, Alicante), a partir del estudio macroscópico de la colección Brotons, Recerques del Museu d'Alcoi 19, 65-79.

Molina, F.J., Tarriño, A., Galván, B., Hernández C.M., 2011. Estudio macroscópico y áreas de aprovisionamiento de la industria silícea del yacimiento mesolítico y neolítico de Benàmer. In Torregrosa, P., Jover, F.J. López, E (Dirs), Benámer (Muro d'Alcoi, Alicante). Mesolíticos y neolíticos en las tierras meridionales valencianas, Serie de Trabajos Varios del SIP 112, 121-131.

Monclova Bohórquez, A., Barroso Ruiz, C., Caparrós, M., Moigne, A. Mª., 2012. Una aproximación a la comprensión de la fauna de macromamíferos de la cueva de Zafarraya (Alcaucín, Málaga), Menga: Revista de Prehistoria de Andalucía 3, 83-105.

Monge, G., 2012. Caracterización mineralógica, geoquímica y textural del relleno Pleistoceno de la Cueva del Ángel en Lucena (Córdoba). Tesis Doctoral (inédita). Universidad de Sevilla, 280.

Monge, G., Carretero, M. I., Pozo, M., Barroso, C., 2014. Mineralogical changes in fossil bone from Cueva del Ángel, Spain: archaeological implications and occurrence of whitlockite, Journal of Archaeological Science 46, 6-15.

Mons, L., 1996. Un atelier de sculpteurs sur pierre. Isturitz, in: Thiault, H., Roy, J.B. (Eds.), L'art préhistorique des Pyrénées. Musée des Antiquités Nationales, Paris.

Montes, L., 1988. El Musteriense en la Cuenca del Ebro. Monografías Arqueológicas, 28. Universidad de Zaragoza.

Montes, L., Utrilla, P., Hedges, R., 2001. Le passage Paléolithique Moyen-Paléolithique Supérieur dans la vallée de l'Ebre (Espagne). Datations radiométriques des grottes de Peña Miel et Gabasa, in: Zilhao, J. Aubry, Th., Carvalho, A. F. (Eds.), Les premiers hommes modernes de la Péninsule Ibérique, Actes du Colloque de la Commission VIII de l'UISPP.Trabalhos d'Arqueologia17, pp. 87-102.

Montes, L., Utrilla, P., Martínez-Bea, M., 2006. Trabajos recientes en yacimientos musterienses de Aragón: Una revisión de la transición Paleolítico Medio/Superior en el Valle del Ebro, Miscelánea en homenaje a Victoria Cabrera-Zona Arqueológica 7, pp. 214-233

Montes, L., Utrilla, P., 2008. Le Paléolithique Supérieur dans la moyenne Vallée de l'Ebre, L'Anthropologie 112, 168-181.

Montes, R., 2010. El Pendo, in: A.C.D.P., Las Cuevas con Arte Paleolítico en Cantabria, Cantabria en imagen, Santander, pp. 221-228.

Montes, R., Sanguino, J. (Dir.), 2001. La Cueva de El Pendo. Actuaciones arqueológicas 1994-2000, Gobierno de Cantabria - Ayuntamiento de Camargo - Parlamento de Cantabria, Santander.

Montes, R., Sanguino, J., Gómez, A. J., Luque, C.G. 1999. New Palaeolithic cave art in El Pendo cave, Cantabrian Region, Spain, Rock Art Research 15(2), pp. 89-97.

Montes, R., Sanguino, J., Martín P., Gómez, A.J., Morcillo, C., 2005. La secuencia estratigráfica de la cueva de El Pendo (Escobedo de Camargo, Cantabria): problemas geoarqueológicos de un referente cronocultural, in: Alfredo Pérez González, Manuel Santonja Gómez, María José Machado, coordinadores, Actas Geoarqueología y patrimonio en la Península Ibérica y el entorno mediterráneo. IV Reunión Nacional de Geoarqueología, Almazán (Soria), 2002, pp. 139-159.

Mora, R., 1988. El paleolítico medio en Catalunya: yacimientos en cueva y al aire libre. Tesis Doctoral, Universitat de Barcelona, Barcelona, p. 888.

Mora, R., Benito, A., Martínez-Moreno, J., González-Marcén, P., de la Torre, I., 2011. Chrono-stratigraphy of the Upper Pleistocene and Holocene archaeological sequence in Cova Gran, Journal of Quaternary Science 26, 635-644

Mora, R., Carbonell, E., 1987. Las industrias del Paleolítico medio en la comarca de La Selva (Gerona), Cyspela VI, 185-190.

Mora, R., Carbonell, E., Cebrià, A., Martínez, J., 1988. Els sòls d'ocupació a l'abric Romaní (Capellades, Anoia). Tribuna d'Arqueologia 1987-1988, 115-123.

Mora, R., Carbonell, E., Martínez, J., 1987. Can Garriga: un tecnocomplejo en contexto estratigráfico (Sant Julià de Ramis, Girona), Cuaternario y Geomorfología 1 (1-4), 195-218.

Mora, R., Martínez-Moreno, J., Casanova, J., 2008. Abordando la noción de variabilidad musteriense en la Roca dels Bous, Trabajos de Prehistoria 65 (2), 13-28.

Morales A., Roselló, E., 1984-1985. Algunas consideraciones de índole zoológica en torno al pez representado en la cueva de El Pindal, Ars Praehistorica 3-4, 247-251.

Morales Pérez, J.V., 2013. La transició del Paleolític Superior Final/Epipaleolític al Mesolític en el territorio Valencià. Aportacions de l'estudizooarqueològic del jaciment de Santa Maira (Castell de Castells, Alacant), in: Sanchos, A., Pascual, J. Ll. (Eds.), Animals i Arqueologia hui. Ieres. Jornades d'Arqueozoologia del Museu de Prehistòria de València, Museu de Prehistòria, València, pp. 181-202

Morales Pérez, J.V., Sanchís Serra, A., 2009. The Quaternary fossil record of the genus Testudo in the Iberian Peninsula. Archaeological implications and diachronic distribution in the western Mediterranean, Journal of Archaeological Science 36, 1152-1162.

Morales, J.I., Burjachs, F.,, Allue, E., Fontanals, M., Soto, M., Exposito, I.,Gassiot, E., Pelachs, A., Perez Obiol, R., Soriano, J.M., Verges, J.M., Yll, E., 2012. Paleogeografia humana durante el Tardiglaciar y Holoceno inicial en el ámbito mediterréneo del NE Ibérico, Cuaternario y Geomorfologia 26, (3-4), 11-28.

Morales, J.I., Verges, J.M., Fontanals, M., Ollé, A., Allue, E., Angelucci, D.E., 2013. Procesos técnicos y culturales durante el Holoceno inicial en el noroeste de la Península Ibérica. Los niveles B y Bb de La Cativera (El Catllar, Tarragona), Trabajos de Prehistoria 70 (1), 54-75.

Morales, J.V., 2008. Estudio zooarqueológico. In: Estudios sedimentológicos, polínicos, faunísticos, antracológicos, carpológicos y de los restos humanos del yacimiento de La Corona (Villena), dentro de la obra AVE tramo Caudete-Villena P.K. 004+160 al P.K. 004+360. Villena (Alicante). Unpublished results.

Morales, J.V., Sanchís, A., 2009. The Quaternary fossil record of the genus Testudo in the Iberian Peninsula. Archaeological implications and diachronic distribution in the western Mediterranean, Journal of Archaeological Science 36, 1152-1162.

Morales-Pérez, J.V., Sanchis-Serra, A., 2009. The Quaternary fossil record of the genus Testudo in the Iberian Peninsula. Archaeological implications and diachronic distribution in the western Mediterranean, Journal of Archaeological Science 31, 1152-1162.

Mosquera, M. 1995. Procesos técnicos y variabilidad en la industria lítica del Pleistoceno Medio en la Meseta: Sierra de Atapuerca, Torralba, Ambrona y Áridos. Tesis Doctoral. Departamento de Prehistoria y Etnología, Universidad Complutense de Madrid, Madrid, p. 370

Mosquera, M., Ollé, A., Pérez-González, A., Rodríguez, X.P., Vaquero, M., Vergès, J.M., Carbonell, E., 2007. Valle de las Orquídeas: un yacimiento al aire libre del Pliestoceno Superior en la Sierra de Atapuerca (Burgos), Trabajos de Prehistoria 64 (2), 143-155.

Moullé, P.E., Echassoux, A., Martínez-Navarro, B., 2004. Ammotragus europaeus: une nouvelle espèce de Caprini (Bovidae, Mammalia) du Pléistocène inférieur à la grotte du Vallonnet (France), Comptes Rendus Palevol 3, 663-673.

Moure, A. 1989. La caverne de Tito Bustillo (Asturies, Espagne). Le gisement paléolithique, L'Anthropologie 93 (2), 73-86.

Moure, A., González Sáinz, C., Bernardo de Quirós, F., Cabrera Valdes, V., 1996. Dataciones absolutas de pigmentos en cuevas cantábricas: Altamira, El Castillo, Chimeneas y Las Monedas, in: Moure, A. (Ed.), El Hombre Fósil, 80 años después, Universidad de Cantabria, Santander, pp. 295-324.

Moure, A., González-Sainz, C., 2000. Cronología del arte paleolítico cantábrico: últimas aportaciones y estado actual de la cuestión, in: Actas del 3er Congreso de Arqueología Peninsular vol. II, ADECAP, Oporto, pp. 461-473.

Moure, A., González-Sainz, C., Bernaldo de Quirós, F., Cabrera, V., 1996. Dataciones absolutas de pigmentos en cuevas cantábricas: Altamira, El Castillo, Chimeneas y Las Monedas, in: Moure, A. (Ed.), El "Hombre Fósil" 80 años después, Universidad de Cantabria, Santander, pp. 295-324.

Moure, A., González-Sainz, C., González-Morales, M.R., 1991. Las cuevas de Ramales de la Victoria (Cantabria). Arte rupestre paleolítico en las cuevas de Covalanas y La Haza, Universidad de Cantabria, Santander.

Moure, A., López, P., 1979. Los niveles preneolíticos del abrigo de Verdelpino (Cuenca), Actas del XV Congreso Arqueológico Nacional, Lugo, pp. 111-124.

Moure, A., Ortega, L., 1994. Grabados de la Galería III de la Cueva de Altamira: Las figuras de la "Gran Colada", in: Lasheras, (Ed.): Homenaje a Joaquín González-Echegaray. Monografías del Museo Nacional y Centro de Investigación de Altamira, 17, pp. 253-259.

Moyà-Solà, S., 1987. Los bóvidos (Artiodactyla, Mammalia) del yacimiento del Pleistoceno inferior de Venta Micena (Orce, Granada, España), Paleontologia i Evolució, Memòria Especial 1, 181-236.

Mozota, M., 2012. El hueso como materia prima: El utillaje óseo del final del Musteriense en el sector central del norte de la Península Ibérica. Tesis Doctoral, Universidad de Cantabria.

Mullens. W. H. (Ed.), 1913. The Introduction to Fauna Calpensis by John White. The Selborne Society, London

Muñoz, E., Montes, R., 2003. El paleolítico en el arco de la Bahía de Santander., in: Fernández, C., Ruiz, J. (Eds.), La Arqueología de la Bahía de Santander, Santander, pp. 177-224.

Muñoz, F.J., 2000. Las puntas ligeras de proyectil del Solutrense Extracantábrico: análisis tecnomorfológico e implicaciones funcionales. Serie Aula Abierta. Universidad Nacional de Educación a Distancia. Madrid.

Muñoz, F.J., Márquez, B., 2006: Las puntas de aletas y pedúnculo del Solutrense peninsular: un programa experimental, in: Sanchidrián, J.L., Márquez, A.Mª., Fullola, J.M. (Eds.), IV Simposio de Prehistoria de la Cueva de Nerja: La cuenca mediterránea durante el Paleolítico Superior. La cuenca mediterránea durante el Paleolítico Superior. Reunión de la VIII Comisión del Paleolítico Superior de la UISPP. Nerja, pp. 234-246.

Muñoz, F.J., Márquez, B., Ripoll, S., 2012. La punta de aletas y pedúnculo del Solutrense Extracantábrico: de los "dimonis" al arco. De punta a punta. El Solutrense en los albores del siglo XXI, Espacio Tiempo y Forma. Serie I, Prehistoria y Arqueología. Nueva época 5, 477-489.

Muñoz, L., Mancha, E., Morcillo, A., 2004. Precedentes Historiográficos del Paleolítico Inferior y Medio de Extremadura, actas del Primer Congreso Peninsular de Estudiantes de Prehistoria, Tarragona, pp. 69-74.

Murchison, C., 1868. Palaeontological memoirs and notes of the late Hugh Falconer, A.M., M. D. Robert Hardwicke, London. Murelaga, X., Bailon, S., Saez de Lafuente, X., Castaños, P., López Quintana, J. C., Guenaga Lizasu, A., Ortega, L. A., Zuluaga M. C., Alonso-

Olazabal, A. 2011. La fauna de microvertebrados de Santimamiñe (Pleistoceno superior- Holoceno) (Kortezubi, Bizkaia), Kobie, Serie BAI nº 1, 291-319.

Múzquiz, M., 1990. El pintor de Altamira pintó en la cueva del Castillo, Revista de Arqueología 114, 14-22.

Nadal, J., 1998. Les faunes del Plistocè final-Holocè a la Catalunya meridional i de ponent. Interpretacions tafonòmiques i paleoculturals. Tesis Doctoral Inèdita. Universitat de Barcelona, Barcelona.

Nakazawa, Y., Straus, L., González Morales, M., Cuenca, D., Caro, J., 2009. On stone-boiling technology in the Upper Paleolithic: behaviorl implications from an Early Magdalenian hearth in El Mirón Cave, Cantabria, Spain, Journal of Archaeological Science 36, 684-693.

Navazo, M., Alonso, R., Benito-Calvo, A., Díez, C., Pérez-González, A., Carbonell, E., 2011. Hundidero: OIS 4 Open Air Neanderthal Occupations in Sierra de Atapuerca. Archaeology, Ethnology and Anthropology of Eurasia 39 (4), 29-41.

Navazo, M., Carbonell, E., 2014. Neanderthal settlement patterns during MIS 4-3 in Sierra de Atapuerca (Burgos, Spain), Quaternary International, .doi.org/10.1016/j.quaint.2014.03.032.

Navazo, M., Colina, A., Domínguez, S., Benito, A., 2008. Raw stone material supply for Upper Pleistocene settlements in Sierra de Atapuerca (Burgos, Spain): flint characterization using petrographic and geochemical techniques, Journal of Archaeological Science 35, 1961-1973

Navazo, M., Díez, C., 2008. Redistribution of Archaeological Assemblages in Plowzones, Geoarchaeology: An International Journal, 23 (3), 323-333.

Obermaier, H., 1916. El Hombre Fósil C.I.P.P. Madrid.

Obermaier, H., 1929a. Altamira, en Investigación y Progreso, 2, pp. 9-11.

Obermaier, H., 1929b. Altamira, in: IV Congreso Internacional de Arqueología con motivo de la Exposición Internacional de Barcelona, Barcelona, pp. 5-23.

Obermaier, H., Wernert, P., 1919. Las pinturas rupestres del barranco de la Valltorta (Castellón) "C.I.P.P", Memoria núm. 23, Madrid.

Olària, C. 1999. Cova Matutano (Vilafamés, Castellón) un modelo ocupacional del magdaleniense superior-final en la vertiente mediterránea peninsular. Monografies de Prehistòria i Arqueología Castellonenques, 5, Castellón, p. 455.

Olària, C., 2008. Grafismo mobiliar magdaleniense en el contexto del Mediterráneo peninsular. Monografies de Prehistòria i Arqueología Castellonenques, 7, Castellón, 206.

Olària, C., Gusi, F., Carbonell, E., Ollé, A., Vallverdú, J., Allué, E., Bennàsar, L., Bischoff, J.L., Burjachs, F., Cáceres, I., Expósito, I., López-Polín, L., Saladié, P., Vergès, J.M., 2007. Noves intervencions al jaciment plistocènic de la Cova de Dalt del Tossal de la Font (Vilafamés, Castelló), Quaderns de Prehistòria i Arqueologia de Castelló 24 (2004-2005), 9-26.

Olivares, M., Castro, K., Garate, D, Corchón, MªS., Sarmiento, A., Etxebarria, N., Murelaga, X., 2013. Non-invasive portable instrumentation to study Palaeolithic rock paintings: the case of La Peña Cave in San Roman de Candamo (Asturias, Spain), Journal of Archaeological Science 40, 1354-1360.

Ollé, A., 2003. Variabilitat i patrons funcionals en les sistemes tècnics de mode 2. Anàlisi de les deformacions d'ús en els conjunts lítics del Riparo Estertno de Grotta Pagglicci (Rignano Garganico, Foggia), Áridos (Arganda, Madrid) i Galería-TN (Sierra de Atapuerca, Burgos). Tesis Doctoral. Departament d'Historia i Geografia. Universitat Rovira i Virgili, Tarragona, p. 589.

Ollé, A., Cáceres, I., Vergès, J.M., 2005. Human occupations at Galería Site (Sierra de Atapuerca, Burgos, Spain) after the technological and taphonimical data, in: Molines, M., Moncel, M.H. Monnier, J.L. (Eds), Les premiers peuplements en Europe. Colloque international: Données récents sur les modalités de peuplement et sur le cadre chronostratigraphique, géologique et paléogéographique des industries du Paléolithique ancient et moyen en Europe. Oxford, British Archaeological Series, International Series, S 1364, pp. 269-280.

Ollé, A., Mosquera, M., Rodríguez, X.P., de Lombera-Hermida, A., García-Antón, M.D., García-Medrano, P., Peña, L., Menéndez, L., Navazo, M., Terradillos, M., Bargalló, A., Márquez, B., Sala, R., Carbonell, E., 2013. The Early and Middle Pleistocene technological record from Sierra de Atapuerca (Burgos, Spain), Quaternary International, 138-167.

Ollé, A., Rodríguez, X.P., Vergès, J.M., 2008. El jaciment de la Cansaladeta: les primeres evidències del poblament a la Catalunya meridional, in: Vergès, J.M., López, J. (Eds.), Prehistòria i història antiga, Institut d'Estudis Vallencs, Valls, pp. 56-67.

Ollé, A., Vergès, J.M., Canals, A., Peña, L., 2007. Outil et fonction. Analyse tracéologique de bifaces de la grotte de Santa Ana (Cáceres, Extremadura, Espagne). Actas de Les cultures à bifaces du Pléistocène Inférieur et Moyen dans le monde. Émergence du sens de l'harmonie, Tautavel, France

Ollé, A., Vergès, J.M., Peña, L., Aranda, V., Pedergnana, A., Canals, A., Carbonell, E., 2012. A microwear analysis of handaxes from Santa Ana cave (Ca_ceres, Extremadura, Spain). Actas de International Conference on Use-wear analysis, USE-WEAR 2012, CEOT - Universidade do Algarve, Faro.

Oms, O., Anadón, P., Agustí, J., 2009. Introduction to the Pleistocene sites of Barranco León, Fuente Nueva 3 and other sites from the Orce area (Guadix-Baza Basin, Spain), SEQS Conference, INQUA-SEQS, Orce and Lucena (Granada, Spain).

Oms, O., Parés, J.M., Martínez-Navarro, B., Agustí, J., Toro, I., Martínez-Fernández, G., Turq, A., 2000. Early human occupation of Western Europe: Paleomagnetic dates for two paleolithic sites in Spain. Proceedings of the National Academy of Sciences, 97 (19), 10666-10670.

Ontañón, R., 2003. Sols et structures d'habitat du Paléolithique supérieur, nouvelles données depuis le Cantabres: la Galerie Inférieure de La Garma (Cantabrie, Espagne), L'Anthropologie 107, 333-363.

Ortega Cobos, D., Soler Masferrer, N., Maroto Genover, J., 2005. La production de lamelles pendant l'Aurignacien archaïque dans la grotte de l'Arbreda: organisation de la production, variabilité des méthodes et des objectifs, in: Le Brun-Ricalens, F., (Coord), Productions lamellaires attribuées à l'Aurignacien: chaînes opératoires et perspectives technoculturelles, Archéologiques, 1, Luxemburg, pp. 359-373.

Ortega, A.I., 2009. Evolución geomorfologica del karst de la Sierra de Atapuerca (Burgos) y su relación con los yacimientos pleistocenos que contiene, Tesis Doctoral, Universidad de Burgos.

Ortega, A.I., Benito-Calvo, A., Pérez-González, A., Carbonell, E., Bermúdez de Castro, J.M., Arsuaga, J. L., 2014. Atapuerca Karst and its Palaeoanthropological Sites, in: Gutiérrez, F., Gutiérrez, M. (Eds.), Landscapes and Landforms of Spain, World Geomorphological Landscapes, © Springer Science+Business Media Dordrecht 2014, pp. 101-110

Ortega, A.I., Benito-Calvo, A., Pérez-González, A., Martín-Merino, M.A., Pérez-Martínez, R., Pares, J.M., Aramburu, A., Arsuaga, J.L., Bermúdez de Castro, J.L., Carbonell, E., 2013. Evolution of multilevel caves in the Sierra de Atapuerca (Burgos, Spain) and its relation to human occupation, Geomorphology 196, 122-137.

Ortega, A.I., Martín, M.A., 2012. Cuevas de Atapuerca. Una visión de la mano del Grupo espeleológico Edelweiss, Publicaciones de la Excma. Diputación Provincial de Burgos y del Grupo Espeleológico Edelweiss, Burgos.

Ortega, P., 2013. Estudio espacial de La Peña de Estebanvela (Ayllón, Segovia), in: C. Cacho (coord.), Ocupaciones magdalenienses en el interior de la Península Ibérica. La Peña de Estebanvela (Ayllón, Segovia), Junta de Castilla y León-CSIC, pp. 515-534.

Palao, G., 1969. Gorham's Cave, Gibraltar. Gibraltar Cave Research Group Report, Unpublished, Gibraltar Museum.

Pallarés, M., Bordas, A., Mora, R., 1997. La Font del Ros en el proceso de neolitización de los Pirineos Orientales, in: de Balbín, R., Bueno, P. (Eds.), II Congreso de Arqueología Peninsular. Tomo I. Paleolítico y Epipaleolítico. Fundación Rei Afonso Henriques, Zamora, pp. 311-325.

Pallarès, M., Wernet, P., 1920. El Solutria de Sant Julia de Ramis: el Cau de les Goges, Anuari de l'Institut d'Estudis Catalans (Secció Històrico-arqueològica) VI, 425-444.

Pallí, Ll. 1982., Mapa geològic de Girona. Girona: Ajuntament de Girona/ Departament de Geologia del Col. legi Universitari de Girona.

Pallí, Ll., 1976. Morfolitología de las terrazas del Ter en Girona, Annals de la Sección de Ciencias del Colegio Universitario de Girona 1, Girona.

Palmqvist, P., Arribas, A., Martínez-Navarro, B., 1999. Ecomorphological study of large canids from the lower Pleistocene of southeastern Spain, Lethaia 32, 75-88.

Palmqvist, P., Martínez-Navarro, B., Toro, I., Espigares, M.P., Ros-Montoya, S., Torregrosa, V., Pérez-Claros, J.A., 2005. A re-evaluation of the evidence of human presence during Early Pleistocene times in southeastern Spain, L'anthropologie 109, 411-450.

Palmqvist, P., Torregrosa, V., Pérez-Claros, J.A., Martínez-Navarro, B., Turner, A., 2007. A re-evaluation of the diversity of Megantereon (Mammalia, Carnivora, Machairodontinae) and the problem of species identification in extinct carnivores, Journal of Vertebrate Paleontology 27, 160-175.

Panera, J., Rubio-Jara, S., Yravedra, J., Blain, H.-A., Sesé, C., Pérez-González, A., 2014. Manzanares Valley (Madrid, Spain): A good country for Proboscideans and Neanderthals, Quaternary International 326-327, 329-343.

Panera, J., Torres, T., Pérez-González, A., Ortíz, J.E., Rubio-Jara, S., Uribelarrea del Val, D., 2011. Geocronología de la Terraza Compleja de Arganda en el valle del río Jarama (Madrid, España), Estudios Geológicos 67, 495-504.

Parcerisas Civit, J., 2006. El aprovisionamiento de materias primas en los yacimientos de Ambrona y Torralba: la base de recursos, in: Martínez Fernández, G., Morgado Rodríguez, A., Marrero, J.A. (Eds.), Sociedades prehistóricas, recursos abióticos y territorio. Actas de la III Reunión de Trabajo sobre aprovisionamiento de recursos abióticos en la Prehistoria, Fundación Ibn-al-Jatib de Estudios de Cooperación Cultural. Granada, pp. 73-86.

Parés, J.M., Duval, M., Arnold, L.J., 2013. New views on an old move: Hominin migration into Eurasia, Quaternary International, 295, 5-12.

Parés, J.M., Pérez-González, A., 1995. Paleomagnetic age for hominid fossils at Atapuerca Archaeological site, Spain, Science 269, 830-832.

Parés, J.M., Pérez-González, A., 1999. Magnetochronology and stratigraphy at Gran Dolina section, Atapuerca (Burgos, Spain), Journal of Human Evolution 37, 325-342.

Parés, J.M., Pérez-González, A., Rosas, A., Benito, A., Bermúdez de Castro, J.M., Carbonell, E., Huguet, R., 2006. Matuyama-age lithic tools from the Sima del Elefante site, Atapuerca (northern Spain), Journal of Human Evolution 50, 163-169.

Patou-Mathis, M., 1996. Techniques d'acquisition et de traitement des grands mammifères par les Néandertaliens européens: exemple de «chaînes opératoires», Quaternaria Nova VI, 187-203.

Pedraza, J. de., 1994. El Sistema Central Español, en Gutiérrez Elorza (Coord.): Geomorfología de España, Rueda, Madrid, pp. 63-100.

Pedraza, J. de., Carrasco, R. M., Martín Duque, J. F., 2003. El macizo de Peñalara. Geomorfología, actividad periglaciar y restauración del paisaje en ambientes fríos de montaña: Guía de la Excursión, VI Reunión IPA-ESPAÑA, pp. 1-17.

Peña, L., 2006. Caracterización y estudio morfotécnico de las industrias líticas del Pleistoceno inferior y medio de los yacimientos en la cueva de Santa Ana y Maltravieso en el Calerizo Cacereño (Cáceres, Extremadura). Comparación de dos conjuntos líticos en cuarzo lechoso: La Sala de los Huesos y el Nivel C de la Cueva de L`Aragó (Tautavel, Francia), Tesis de Màster, Departament d'Història i Història de l'Art, Universitat Rovira i Virgili, Tarragona.

Peña-Chocarro, L., 2012. Neolithic, Chalcolithic, and Bronze Age plant remains from El Mirón Cave, in: Straus, L., González Morales, M. (Eds.), El Mirón Cave. University of New Mexico Press, Albuquerque, pp. 148-173.

Peña, L., Canals, A., Mosquera, M., Lumley, H., 2008. Morpho-technological study of the Lower and Middle Palaeolithic lithic assemblages from Maltravieso and Santa Ana cave (Cáceres, Extremadura). Comparison of two lithic assemblages knapped in milky quartz: Maltravieso cave-Sala de los Huesos-and level C of L'Arago cave (Tautavel, France), Annali dell'Università degli Studi di Ferrara Museologia Scientifica e Naturalistica.

Peña, P. de la, 2011. Sobre la unidad tecnológica del Gravetiense en la Península Ibérica: implicaciones para el Paleolítico superior inicial. Tesis Doctoral. Universidad Complutense de Madrid, Madrid.

Perea, S., Doadrio, I., 2013. Restos ictiofaunísticos del Pleistoceno superior del yacimiento de La Peña de Estebanvela (Ayllón, Segovia), in: C. Cacho (coord.), Ocupaciones magdalenienses en el interior de la Península Ibérica. La Peña de Estebanvela (Ayllón, Segovia). Junta de Castilla y León-CSIC, pp. 133-140.

Peretto, C. (Ed.), 1994, Le Industrie Litiche del Giacimento Paleolitico di Isernia La Pineta, la Tipologia, le Tracce di Utilizzazione, la Sperimentazione, Isernia, Cosmo Iannone, "Istituto Regionale per gli Studi Storici del Molise 'V. Cuoco'".

Peretto, C., Arzarello, M., Gallotti, R., Lembo, G., Minelli, A., Hohenstein, U.T., 2004. Middle Pleistocene behavioural strategies: the contribution of Isernia La Pineta (Molise, Italy), in: Baquedano, E., Rubio Jara, S. (Eds.), Miscelánea en homenaje a Emiliano Aguirre Volumen IV Arqueología, Alcalá de Henares, Museo Arqueológico Regional, "Zona Arqueológica Número 4", pp. 368-381.

Pérez González, A., Karampaglidis, T.,A, J. L.,B, E., Bárez, S., Gómez, J. J., Panera, J., Márquez, B., Laplana, C., Mosquera, M., Huguet, R., Sala, P., Arriaza, M. C., Benito, A., Aracil, E., Maldonado, E., 2010. Aproximación geomorfológica a los yacimientos del Pleistoceno superior del Calvero de la Higuera en el Valle Alto del Río Lozoya (Sistema Central Español, Madrid), Zona Arqueológica 13, 404-419.

Pérez Rama, M., Fernández Mosquera, D., Grandal D´Anglade, A., 2011. Effects of hibernation on the stable isotope signatures of adult and neonate Cave bears, Quaternaire 4, 79-88.

Pérez, M., 1992. Marcas de carnicería, fracturas intencionadas y mordeduras de carnívoros en huesos prehistóricos del mediterráneo español, Instituto de Cultura Juan Gil-Albert, Diputación Provincial de Alicante.

Pérez-González, A., 1994. Depresión del Tajo, in: Gutiérrez Elorza, M. (Ed.), Geomorfología de España, Ed. Rueda, Madrid, pp. 389-436.

Pérez-González, A., Aleixandre, T., Pinilla, A., Gallardo, J., Benayas, J., Martínez, M.J., Ortega, A. I., 1995. Aproximación a la estratigrafía de Galería en la Trinchera de la Sierra de Atapuerca (Burgos), in: Bermúdez, J.M. *et al.*, (Eds.): Actas Evolución humana en Europa y los yacimientos de la Sierra de Atpaureca. Volumen 1, pp. 99-122.

Pérez-González, A., Gallardo-Millán, J.L., Uribelarrea, D., Panera, J., Rubio-Jara, S., 2013. La inversión Matuyama-Brunhes en la secuencia de terrazas del río Jarama entre Velilla de San Antonio y Altos de la Mejorada, al SE de Madrid (España). Estudios Geológicos, 69 (1), 35-46.

Pérez-González, A., Parés, J. M., Carbonell, E., Aleixandre, T., Ortega, A. I., Benito, A., Martín Merino, M.Á., 2001. Géologie de la Sierra de Atapuerca et stratigraphie des remplissages karstiques de Galería et Dolina (Burgos, Espagne), L'Anthropologie 105, 27-43.

Pérez-González, A., Parés, J.M., Gallardo, J., Aleixandre, T., Ortega A.I., Pinilla, A., 1999. Geología y estratigrafía del relleno de Galería de la Sierra de Atapuerca (Burgos). in: Carbonell, E., Rosas, A. Díez, J.C. (Eds), Atapuerca: Ocupaciones Humanas y Paleoecología del Yacimiento de Galería. Memorias, 7, pp. 31-42.

Pérez-González, A., Santonja, M., Gallardo, J., Aleixandre, T., 1991. Los yacimientos pleistocenos de Torralba y Ambrona y sus relaciones con la evolución geomorfológica del poljé de Conquezuela. Resúmenes de las Comunicaciones. VIII Reunión Nacional del Cuaternario (sin paginar). Valencia.

Pérez-González, A., Silva, P., 2009. Plio-Cuaternario y Cuaternario, in Memoria de la Hoja a E. 1:50.000 de Talavera de la Reina (nº 627), Mapa Geológico de España, Instituto Tecnológico GeoMinero de España, Madrid, pp. 18-26.

Pérez-González, A., Uribelarrea, D., 2002. Geología del Cuaternario en los valles fluviales del Jarama y Manzanares en las proximidades de Madrid, in: Panera, J., Rubio-Jara, S. (Eds.), Bifaces y Elefantes. La investigación del Paleolítico inferior en Madrid, Zona Arqueológica 1, 302-317.

Pérez-Ripoll, M., 2004. L'exploitation du lapin pendant le Paléolithique de la región de Valence (Espagne). En Petits animaux et sociétés humaines. XXIV Rencontres Internationales d'Archéologie et d'Histoire d'Antibes, pp. 191-206.

Pérez-Ripoll, M., Raga, J. A., 1998. Los mamíferos marinos en la vida y en el arte de la Prehistoria de la cueva de Nerja, in: Sanchidrián, J. L., Simón, M. D. (Eds.), Las culturas del Pleistoceno superior en Andalucía. Homenaje al profesor F. Jordá Cerdá, Málaga, Patronato de la cueva de Nerja, pp. 251-275.

Pérez-Romero, A., Juez, L., Carretero, J.M., Ortega, A.I., Ortega, M., Arsuaga, J.L., 2010. Una moneda almohade del S. XIII en el yacimiento del Portalón de Cueva Mayor, Sierra de Atapuerca (Burgos), Numisma 254, 85-106.

Pérez-Romero, A., Carretero, J.M., Alday, A., Arsuaga, J.L., 2013. La Cerámica Protohistórica e Histórica en el yacimiento del Portalón de Cueva Mayor, Sierra de Atapuerca. Burgos, Boletín de la Sociedad Española de Cerámica y Vidrio, 52 (4), 183-193. ISSN 0366-3175, eISSN 2173-0431. doi: 10.3989/cyv.242013

Pericot, L., 1942. La cueva del Parpalló (Gandía) Consejo Superior de Investigaciones Científicas, Instituto Diego Velázquez, Madrid.

Pericot, L., 1945. La Cueva de la Cocina (Dos Aguas). Nota preliminar, Archivo de Prehistoria Levantina II, 39-71.

Pericot, L., Pallarès, M., 1931. Els jaciments asturians del Montgrí, Ed. Arts Gràfiques, Barcelona.

Perrin, T., Allard, P., Marchand, G., Binder, D., García Puchol, O., Valdeyron, N., in press. The late Mesolithic of Western Europe: origins and diffusion of blade and trapeze industries, in: Arias, P. (Ed.), Meso 2010. Proceedings of the Eight International Conference on the Mesolithic in Europe, Santander.

Petit, M.A., (Coord.) 1996. El procés de neolitització de la vall del Segre. La cova del Parco (Alòs de Balaguer, La Noguera): estudi de les ocupacions humanes del Vè al IIn mil·leni a.C., Monografies del SERP, 1. Ed. SERP, Barcelona.

Petit, P.B., Baley, R.M., 2000. AMS radiocarbon and luminescence dating of Gorham's and Vanguard caves, Gibraltar, and implications for the middle to upper Palaeolithic transition in Iberia, in: Stringer, C. B., Barton, R. N. E., C. B., Finlayson, J. C. (Eds.), Neanderthals on the edge, Oxbow, Oxford, pp. 155-162.

Pike, Tay A.W.G., Cabrera Valdés, V., Bernaldo de Quirós, F., 1999. Seasonal variations of the Middle-Upper Palaeolithic transition at El Castillo, Cueva Morin and El Pendo (Cantabria, Spain), Journal of Human Evolution 36, 283-317.

Pike, Tay A.W.G., Hoffmann, D. L., García Diez, M., Pettitt, P.B., Alcolea, J., Balbín, R., González-Sainz, C., de las Heras, C., Lasheras, J.A., Montes, R., Zilhao, J., 2012. U-series dating of Palaeolithic Art in 11 Caves in Spain, Science 336 (6087), 1409-1413.

Pike, Tay A.W.G., Hoffmann, D. L., García Diez, M., Pettitt, P.B., Alcolea, J., Balbín, R., González-Sainz, C., de las Heras, C., Lasheras, J.A., Montes, R., Zilhao, J., 2013. On the origins of Paleolithic caves art: U-series dating at Altamira, El Castillo and Tito Bustillo caves, in: de las Heras, C., Lasheras, J. A., Arrizabalaga, Á., de la Rasilla, M., 2013. Pensando el Gravetiense: nuevos datos para la región cantábrica en su contexto peninsular y pirenaico/ Rethinking the Gravettian: new approaches for the Cantabrian Region in its peninsular and pyrenean contexts. Monografías del Museo Nacional y Centro de Investigación de Altamira, n.° 23, pp. 485-500.

Pinilla, L., Pérez-González, A., Sopeña, A., Parés, J. Mª, 1995. Fenómenos de hundimientos sinsedimentarios en los depósitos cuaternarios del río Tajo en la cuenca de Madrid (Almoguera-Fuentidueña de Tajo), in: Aleixandre, T., Pérez-González, A. (Eds.), Reconstrucción de paleoambientes y cambios climáticos durante el Cuaternario, Centro de Ciencias Medioambientales, C.S.I.C., Madrid, pp. 125-139.

Pinto, T., 1975. Complejo cárstico del Sidrón (Borines), Torrecerredo 8, 31-34.

Pinto-Llona A.C., Clark, G., Karkanas P., Blackwell B., Skinner A.R., Andrews P., Reed K., Miller, A., Macías-Rosado, R., Vakiparta, J., 2012. The Sopeña Rockshelter, a New Site in Asturias (Spain) bearing evidence on the Middle and Early Upper Palaeolithic in Northern Iberia, Munibe (Antropologia-Arkeologia), 63, 45-79.

Pinto-Llona, A. C., Clark, G. A., Miller, A., 2005. Sopeña, un nuevo yacimiento de Paleolítico Medio y Superior Inicial en el norte de la Península Ibérica, in: Bicho, N. (Coord.), Centro de Estudos de Patrimonio, Departamento de Historia, Arqueologia e Patrimonio, Universidade do Algarve (Eds.), O Paleolítico, Actas do IV Congresso de Arqueología Peninsula, Faro, 2004, pp. 407-418.

Pinto-Llona, A. C., Clark, G. A., Miller, A., Reed, K., 2009. Neanderthals and Cro-Magnons in northern Spain: ongoing work at the Sopeña rockshelter (Asturias, Spain). Ed. M. Camps and C. Smidtz: The Mediterranean from 50,000-25,000 BP: Turning Points and New Directions. Oxford: Oxbow Books, pp. 312-322.

Pinto-Llona, A.C., Clark, G.A., Miller, A., 2006. Resultados preliminares de los trabajos en curso en el abrigo de Sopeña (Onís, Asturias), in: Cabrera Valdés V., Bernaldo de Quirós, F., Maíllo Fernández, J.M. (Coords.), UNED (Eds.), En el centenario de la cueva de El Castillo: el ocaso de los neandertales, pp. 193-208.

Pitamon, F.J., 1977. Los roedores del Pleistoceno de la cueva las Grajas (Archidona). Tesis de Licenciatura. Universidad de Salamanca 1977. Inédita.

Prat, F., 1977. L'Equidé du gisement Acheuléen de Torralba (Soria,Espagne). Equus caballus torralbae nov. subspec., Bull. Ass. Française pour l'Etude du Quaternaire, Supp. Recherches Françaises sur le Quaternaire (INQUA, 1977), 33-46.

Price, C., 2013. The small mammal fauna of Gorham's Cave. In: Barton, R. N. E., Stringer, C. B., Finlayson, J. C. (Eds.), Neanderthals in Context: A Report of the 1995-1998 Excavations at Gorham's and Vanguard Caves, Gibraltar. Oxford University Press, Oxford, pp. 128-140.

Prieto, J., Abenza, J., Montes, R., Sanguino, J., Muñoz, E., 2001. Hallazgos antropológicos y arqueológicos en el complejo kárstico de El Sidrón (Vallobal, Infiesto, Concejo de Piloña, Asturias), Munibe 53, 19-29.

Prieto, J., Montes, R., Muñoz, E., Sanguino, J., 1998. Hallazgos antropológicos y arqueológicos en el complejo kárstico de El Sidrón (Vallobal, Concejo de Piloña, Asturias), Informe depositado en la Consejería de Educación y Cultura, Principado de Asturias, Oviedo.

Quam, R., Arsuaga, J.-L., Bermúdez de Castro, J.-M., Díez, J.C., Lorenzo, C., Carretero, J.M., García, N., Ortega, A.I., 2001. Human remains from Valdegoba Cave (Huermeces, Burgos, Spain), Journal of Human Evolution 41, 385-435.

Quam, R., Bailey, S., Wood, B., 2009. Evolution of M1 crown size and cusp proportions in the genus Homo, Journal of Anatomy 214 (5), 655-670.

Querol, Mª A., Santonja, M., 1979. El yacimiento achelense de Pinedo, Excavaciones Arqueológicas en España 106, Ministerio de Cultura. Madrid.

Querol, Mª A., Santonja, M., 1983. El yacimiento de cantos trabajados de El Aculadero (Puerto de Santa María, Cádiz), Excavaciones Arqueológicas en España, 130, Madrid.

Quesada, J.M., Menéndez, M., 2009. Revisión cronoestratigráfica de la Cueva de La Güelga (Narciandi, Asturias). Del Musteriense al Paleolítico superior inicial, Espacio Tiempo y Forma, 39-74.

Ramil Rego, P., Llana Rodríguez, C., Fernández Rodríguez, C. 1993. Las Gándaras de Budiño (Pontevedra): una reflexión en su trigésimo aniversario, in: Actas del XXI Congreso Nacional de Arqueología. Teruel-Albarracín, pp. 555-567.

Ramos, J., Bernal, D., Domínguez-Bella, S., Calado, D., Ruiz, B., Gil, M.J., Clemente, I., Durán, J.J., Vijande, E., Chamorro, S., 2008. The Benzu rockshelter: A Middle Palaeolithic site on the North African coas, Quaternary Science Reviews 27, 2210-2218.

Ramos, J., Bernal, D., Vijande, E., Cantillo, J.J. (Eds.), 2013. El Abrigo y la Cueva de Benzú. Memoria de los trabajos arqueológicos de una década en Ceuta (2002-2012), Ciudad Autónoma de Ceuta y Servicio de Publicaciones Universidad de Cádiz, Cádiz.

Ramos, J., Espejo, M.-M., Cantalejo, P., Martín, E., Molina, J.-A., Durán, J.-J., Alcázar, J., Ramírez, F., Vela, A., Grün, R., Ford, D.-C., 1992. Cueva de Ardales. Su recuperación y estudio. Ayuntamiento de Ardales, Málaga.

Ramos, J., Weniger, G.-C., Cantalejo, P., Espejo, M.-M., 2014. Cueva de Ardales. Intervenciones Arqueológicas 2011 - 2014. Ediciones Pinsapar, Málaga.

Ramsey, B.C., 2009. Bayesiananalysis of radiocarbon dates, Radiocarbon 51 (1), 337-360.

Rasilla, M. de la, Rosas, A., Cañaveras, J. C., Lalueza-Fox, C. (Eds.), 2011a. La Cueva de El Sidrón (Borines, Piloña, Asturias). Investigación interdisciplinar de un grupo neandertal, Consejería de Cultura y Turismo, Gobierno del Principado de Asturias y Ediciones Trabe SLU, Oviedo.

Rasilla, M. de la, Rosas, A., Cañaveras, J. C., Lalueza-Fox, C., Martínez, E., Sánchez-Moral, S., Silva, P. G., Santos, G., 2011b. Los interrogantes planteados y su concreción en el proceso de excavación y análisis, in: Rasilla, M. de la, Rosas, A., Cañaveras, J. C., Lalueza-Fox, C. (Eds.), La Cueva de El Sidrón (Borines, Piloña, Asturias). Investigación interdisciplinar de un grupo neandertal, Consejería de Cultura y Turismo y Ediciones Trabe SLU, Oviedo, pp. 35-40.

Rasilla, M. de la, Santamaría, D., 2011-12. El Paleolítico medio en Asturias, Mainake 33, 31-62.

Rasilla, M. de la, Santamaría, D., Martínez, L., Duarte, E., Fernández de la Vega, J., Suárez, P., Díez, A. B., Martínez, E., Cañaveras, J. C., Sánchez-Moral, S., Cuezva, S., Fernández Cortés, A., García Antón, E., Lario, J., Rosas, A., García-Tabernero, A., Estalrrich, A., Huguet, R., Bastir, M., Fernández Cascón, B., Sesé, C., Lalueza-Fox, C., Silva, P. G., Carrasco, P., Santos, G., Huerta, P., Rodríguez, L., Picón, I., Fernández, B., Standing, M., Badal, E., Tarriño, A., Salazar-García, D. C., Fortea J., 2013. La Cueva de El Sidrón (Borines, Piloña, Asturias). Campañas de excavación e investigación 2007-2012, Excavaciones Arqueológicas en Asturias 2007-2012 7, pp. 69-85.

Rasilla, M. de la, Santamaría, D., Martínez, L., Duarte, E., Suárez Ferruelo, P., Suárez Manjón, P, Tormo, C., 2011c. Las intervenciones arqueológicas en el exterior y en otras galerías interiores del complejo cárstico, in: Rasilla, M. de la, Rosas, A., Cañaveras, J. C., Lalueza-Fox, C. (Eds.), La Cueva de El Sidrón (Borines, Piloña, Asturias). Investigación interdisciplinar de un grupo neandertal, Consejería de Cultura y Turismo y Ediciones Trabe SLU, Oviedo, pp. 165-179.

Rasmussen, S.O., Seierstad, I.K., Andersen, K.K., Bigler, M., Dahl-Jensen, D., Johnsen, S.J. 2008. Synchronization of the NGRIP, GRIP, and GISP2 ice cores across MIS 2 and palaeoclimate implications, Quaternary Science reviews 27, 18-28.

Reimer, P.J., Bard, E., Bayliss, A., Beck, J.W., Blackwell, P.G., Bronk Ramsey, C., Buck, C.E., Cheng, H., Edwards, R.L., Friedrich, M., Grootes, P.M., Guilderson, T.P., Haflidason, H., Hajdas, I., Hatté, C., Heaton, T.J., Hoffmann, D.L., Hogg, A.G., Hughen, K.A., Kaiser, K.F., Kromer, B., Manning. S.W., Niu, M., Reimer, R.W., Richards, D.A., Scott, E. M., Southon, J.R., Staff, R.A., Turney, C.S.M., van der Plicht, J., 2013. INTCAL 13 and Marine 13 radiocarbon age calibration curves 0-50.000 years cal BP, Radiocarbon 55 (4), 1869-1887.

Rhodes, E.J., 2013a. OSL dating of sediments from the lower part of Gorham's Cave. In: Barton, R. N. E., Stringer, C. B., Finlayson, J. C. (Eds.), Neanderthals in Context: A Report of the 1995-1998 Excavations at Gorham's and Vanguard Caves, Gibraltar. Oxford University Press, Oxford, pp. 77-88.

Rhodes, E.J., 2013b. OSL age estimates from Vanguard Cave, in: Barton, R. N. E., Stringer, C. B., Finlayson, J. C. (Eds.), Neanderthals in Context: A Report of the 1995-1998 Excavations at Gorham's and Vanguard Caves, Gibraltar, Oxford University Press, Oxford, pp. 211-217.

Rhodes, S.E., Walker, M.J., López-Martínez, M., Haber-Uriarte, M., López.Jiménez, A., Buitrago-López, A.T., Dewar, G., 2013. Analysis of Hystrix specimens recovered from Sima de las Palomas, Murcia, Spain, in: Program with Abstracts, Canadian Association for Physical Anthropology, 41st Annual Meeting, October 17-20 2013 Scarborough, ON (University of Toronto, Scarborough). Scarborough, University of Toronto, and Canadian Association for Physical Anthropology, p. 47.

Rightmire, G.P., Lordkipanidze, D., Vekua, A., 2006. Anatomical descriptions, comparative studies and evolutionary significance of the hominin skulls from Dmanisi,

Republic of Georgia, Journal of Human Evolution 50, 115-141.

Rink, W.J., Schwartz, H.P., Lee H.K., Cabrera Valdés, V., Bernaldo de Quirós F., Hoyos, M., 1995, ESR Dating of Tooth Enamel: Comparison with AMS 14C at El Castillo Cave, Spain, Journal of Archaeological Science 23, 6, 1196, 945-952.

Ríos González, S., García de Castro Valdés, C., Rasilla Vives, M. de la, Fortea, J., 2007. Arte rupestre prehistórico del Oriente de Asturias, Consorcio para el desarrollo rural del Oriente de Asturias, Ediciones Nobel, Oviedo.

Rios-Garaizar J., 2012. Industria lítica y sociedad del paleolítico medio y superior en torno al Golfo de Bizkaia, PUbliCan-Ediciones de la Universidad de Cantabria 564 pp.

Ríos-Garaizar, J., 2007. Industria lítica y sociedad en la transición del paleolítico medio al superior en torno al Golfo de Vizcaya. Tesis doctoral, Universidad de Cantabria.

Ríos-Garaizar, J., 2008. Nivel IX (Chatelperroniense) de Labeko Koba (Arrasate-Gipuzkoa): gestión de la industria lítica y función del sitio, Munibe Antropologia-Arkeologia 59, 25-46.

Ríos-Garaizar, J., Arrizabalaga, A., Villaluenga, A., 2012. Haltes de chasse du Chatelperronien à la Peninsule Ibérique. Labeko Koba et Ekain (Pays Basque), L'Anthropologie 116 (4), 532-549.

Ripoll, S., (Ed.) 1988. La Cueva de Ambrosio (Vélez-Blanco, Almería) y su posición cronoestratigráfica en el Mediterráneo Occidental. British Archaeological Report, Oxford, Inglaterra, 462, 2 vols, pp. 596

Ripoll, S., 1989. Le gisement de La Cueva de Ambrosio: Nouveaux Apports au Solutréen de la Péninsule Ibérique, L'Anthropologie 92 (4), 851-886.

Ripoll, S., 1990. Le Solutréen dans le Sud de la Péninsule Ibérique. Colloque International sur Les industries á pointes foliacées du Paléolithique Supérieur européen, E.R.A.U.L. 42, pp. 449-465.

Ripoll, S., Baldellou, V., Muñoz, F.J., Ayuso, P., 2001. La Fuente del Trucho (Asque-Colungo, Huesca), Bolskan 18, 211-224.

Ripoll, S., Cacho, C., 1990. Art mobilier du Paléolithique mediterranéen espagnol: quelques nouvelles découvertes. Colloque International L'art des objets au Paléolithique, en L'Art des objets au Paléolithique (Ministère de la Culture) Foix, pp. 287-293.

Ripoll, S., *et al.*, 1994. Arte rupestre paleolítico en el yacimiento solutrense de La Cueva de Ambrosio (Vélez Blanco, Almería), Trabajos de Prehistoria 51, 21-39.

Ripoll, S., Muñoz, F.J., Latova, J., 2006. Nuevos datos para el arte rupestre paleolítico de La Cueva de Ambrosio (Vélez Blanco, Almería), in Congreso de arte esquemático en la Península Ibérica., pp. 547- 562.

Ripoll-Perelló, E., 1956, Nota acerca de algunas nuevas figuras rupestres de las cuevas de El Castillo y La Pasiega (Puente Viesgo, Santander), in: Actas del IV Congreso Internacional de Ciencias Prehistóricas y Protohistóricas (Madrid 1954), Zaragoza, pp. 301-310.

Ripoll-Perelló, E., 1963. Pinturas Rupestres de la Gasulla (Castellón), Monografía de Arte Rupestre, Arte Levantino, n.° 2, Barcelona.

Ripoll-Perelló, E., 1971-1972. Una figura de «hombre-bisonte» de la cueva de El Castillo, Ampurias XXXIII-XXXIV, 93-110.

Ripoll-Perelló, E., 1972. La cueva de Las Monedas en Puente Viesgo (Santander), Monografías de Arte Rupestre 1, Diputación Provincial de Barcelona, Barcelona.

Ripoll-Perelló, E., 1972. Un palimpsesto rupestre de la cueva del Castillo (Puente Viesgo, Santander), in: Santander Symposium, Ministerio de Cultura, Santander, pp. 457-465.

Ripoll-Perelló, E., Lumley, H. de, 1965. El Paleolítico Medio de Cataluña, Ampurias XXVIXXVII, 1-70.

Rissetto, J., 2009. Late Pleistocene Hunter-Gatherer Mobility Patterns and Lithic Exploitation in Eastern Cantabria (Spain). Ph.D. dissertation, University of New Mexico.

Riuró, F. 1945., Nuevos hallazgos en dos cuevas de San Julián de Ramis, Ampurias 7-8, 335-339.

Rivera, O., Gárate, D., 2013. Arte parietal paleolítico en la cueva de Hornos de la Peña (Cantabria): nuevos datos sobre su conjunto exterior, Zephyrvs LXXII, 59-72.

Roca, J.R., Juliá, R., 1997. Late Glacial and Holocene climatic changes and desertification expansion based on biota content in the Salines sequence, Southeastern Spain, Geobios 30, 823 - 830.

Rocafort, C., 1908a. Las pinturas rupestres de Cogul, "La veu de Catalunya" 10 de abril de 1908, Barcelona, 3.

Rocafort, C., 1908b. Les peintures rupestres de Cogul, Butlletí del Centre Excursionista de Catalunya XVIII 158, 65-73.

Rodrigo García, M.J., 1991. Remains of Melanogrammus aeglefinus (Linnaeus, 1758) in the Pleistocene-Holocene Passage of the Cave of Nerja (Málaga, Spain), Schriften aus der Archäeologist-Zoologishen Arbeitsgruppe Schleswig 5, 348-351.

Rodríguez de Tembleque, J. M., 2005. El Paleolítico inferior en la cuenca del Tajo (Castilla-La Mancha), in: Santonja, M. (Ed.), Los Primeros Pobladores de Castilla-La Mancha, Fundación Cultura y Deporte de JCCM y Caja de Castilla-La Mancha, Albacete, 74-110.

Rodríguez de Tembleque, J. M., Pérez-González, A., Santonja, M., Ruiz, B., 2010. Yacimiento achelense de Puente Pino: estado de las investigaciones en 2010, Boletín Asociación Española de Amigos de la Arqueología 46, 17-29.

Rodríguez, A., Galván, B., Hernández, C., 2002. Contribución del análisis funcional en la caracterización de El Salt como un centro de intervención referencial de las poblaciones neandertalianas en los valles de Alcoi (Alicante), in: Clemente, Risch Gibaja (Eds): Análisis Funcional: su aplicación al estudio de sociedades prehistóricas. BAR I. S. 1073, 121-132.

Rodríguez, J., Burjachs, F., Cuenca-Bescós, G., García, N., Van der Made, J., Pérez González, A., Blain, H.A., Expósito, I., López-García, J.M., García Antón, M., Allué, E., Cáceres, I., Huguet, R., Mosquera, M., Ollé, A., Rosell, J., Parés, J.M., Rodríguez, X.P., Díez, C., Rofes, J., Sala, R., Saladié, P., Vallverdú, J., Bennasar, M.L., Blasco, R., Bermúdez de Castro, J.M., Carbonell, E., 2011. One million years of cultural evolution in a stable environment at Atapuerca (Burgos, Spain), Quaternary Science Reviews 30, 1396-1412.

Rodríguez, L., García-González, R., Sanz, M., Daura, J., Quam, R., Fullola, J.Mª., Arsuaga, J.L., 2011. A Neanderthal Lower Incisor form Cova del Gegant (Sitges, Barcelona, Spain), Boletín de la Real Sociedad Española de Historia Natural Sección Geológica 105, 25-30.

Rodríguez-Álvarez, X. P., 2004. Technical Systems of Lithic Production in the Lower and Middle Pleistocene of the Iberian Peninsula: Technological variability between north-eastern sites and Sierra de Atapuerca sites. Oxford:John and Erica Hedges Ltd. (British Archaeological Reports, International Series S1323).

Rodríguez-Álvarez, X. P., de Lombera Hermida, A., Fábregas Valcarce, R., Lazuén Fernández, T., 2011. The Upper Pleistocene site of Cova Eirós (Triacastela, Lugo, Spain), in: de Lombera Hermida, A., Fábregas Valcarce, R. (Eds.), To the West of Spanish Cantabria: the Palaeolithic Settlement of Galicia. BAR International series 2283, Archaeopress, Oxford, pp. 123-133.

Rodríguez-Álvarez, X. P., Fábregas, R., Lazuén, T., de Lombera, A., Pérez Alberti, A., Peña, J. A., Rodríguez, C., Terradillos, M., Ameijenda, A., Rodríguez, E., 2008. Nuevos yacimientos paleolíticos en la Depresión de Monforte de Lemos (Lugo, Galicia, España), Revista Cuaternario y Geomorfología 22, 71-92.

Rodríguez-Álvarez, X. P., Lozano, M., 1999. El Pleistoceno medio y superior inicial del Noreste de la Península Ibérica, Pyrenae 30, 39-68.

Rodríguez-Álvarez, X. P., Maroto-Genover, J., Vaquero, M., Ortega, D., Sala, R., García, J., Lozano, M., 2004. El paleolític inferior i mitjà a Catalunya, Fonaments 10-11, 23-66.

Rodríguez-Álvarez, X. P., Rosell, J., 1993. Contribución al conocimiento del Paleolítico inferior del Noroeste de la Península Ibérica: el yacimiento de Nerets (Conca de Tremp, Catalunya), Cuaternario y Geomorfología 7, 15-22.

Rodríguez-Álvarez, X. P., Sala, R., Casellas, S., Vallverdú, J., 1995. Ocupació antròpica de la vall mitjana del Ter en l'inici del Plistocè superior, in: Agustí, B., Burch, J., Merino, J. (Ed.), Excavacions d'urgència a Sant Julià de Ramis (Anys 1991-1993), Centre d'Investigacions arqueològiques de Girona, Girona, pp. 37-65.

Rodríguez-Álvarez, X. P., Vaquero, M., Sala, R., Garcia, J., Maroto-Genover, J., Ortega, D., Lozano, M., 2003/2004. El Paleolític inferior i mitjà a Catalunya. En El Paleolític als Països Catalans, Fonaments 10/11, 23-66.

Rodríguez-Asensio, J. A., 2001. Yacimiento de Cabo Busto. Los orígenes prehistóricos de Asturias. Ed. GEA 2000, S.L. Gijón

Rodríguez-Asensio, J.A., Barrera Logares, J.M., 2013. Las ocupaciones solutrenses de las cuevas de La Lluera, in: Excavaciones Arqueológicas en Asturias, Principado de Asturias, Oviedo, pp. 87-108.

Rodríguez-Baylach, N., unpublished. Aproximació tecnotipològica de la indústria lítica de l'estrat 2 de l'abric de Els Colls (Margalef de Montsant, Priorat, Tarragona), Practicum de master, junio 2011, tutores X. Mangado y L. Klaric, Univ, de Barcelona, p.119.

Rodríguez-Hidalgo, A., 2008. Zooarqueología de los yacimientos kársticos del Complejo Cacereño. La Cueva de Santa Ana y la Cueva de Maltravieso, Tesis de Máster, Departament d'Història i Història de l'Art, Universitat Rovira i Virgili, Tarragona.

Rodríguez-Hidalgo, A., Canals, A., Saladié, P., Garcia, A.B., Garcia-Diez, M., 2010. Upper Palaeolithic ornaments seashells from Sala de las Chimeneas, Maltravieso cave, Cáceres (Spain), Munibe 31, 37-46.

Rodríguez-Hidalgo, A., Muñoz, L., Canals, A., 2008. Una aproximación zooarqueológica al yacimiento de la cueva de Maltravieso, in: Sanabria P.J. (Ed.), El mensaje de Maltravieso 50 años después, Museo Provincial de Cáceres, pp. 153-164.

Rodríguez-Hidalgo, A., Saladié, P., Canals, A., 2013. Following the white rabbit: A case of a small game procurement site in the upper palaeolithic (Sala de las Chimeneas, Maltravieso Cave, Spain), International Journal of Osteoarchaeology 23 (1), 34-54.

Rofes, J., Cuenca-Bescos, G., 2006., First evidence of the Soricidae (Mammalia) Asoriculus gibberodon (Petenyi, 1864) in the Pleistocene of North Iberia, Rivista Italiana Di Paleontologia E Stratigrafia 112, 301-315.

Rofes, J., García-Ibaibarriaga, N., Murelaga, X., Arrizabalaga, A., Iriarte, M.J., Cuenca-Bescos, G., Villaluenga, A., 2012. The southwesternmost record of Sicista (Mammalia; Dipodidae) in Eurasia, with a review of the palaeogeography and palaeoecology of the genus in Europe, Palaeogeography, Palaeoclimatology, Palaeoecology 348-349, 67-73.

Roldán, C., Villaverde, V., Ródenas, I., Novelli, F., Murcia, S., 2013., Preliminary analysis of Palaeolithic black pigments in plaquettes from the Parpalló cave (Gandía, Spain) carried out by means of non-destructive techniques, Journal of Archaeological Science 40, 744-754.

Román, D., Villaverde, V., 2012. The Magdalenian harpoons from the Iberian Mediterranean, base don piecesfromCova de les Cendres (Teulada-Moraira, Valencia región), Quaternary International 272-273, 33-41.

Rook, L., Martínez-Navarro, B., 2010. Villafranchian: the long story of a Plio-Pleistocene european large mammal biochronologic unit, Quaternary International 219, 134-144.

Rosas, A., Aguirre, E., 1999. Restos humanos neandertales de la Cueva de El Sidrón, Piloña, Asturias. Nota preliminar, Estudios Geológicos 55 (3-4), 107-206.

Rosas, A., Estalrrich, A., García-Tabernero, A., Bastir, M., García-Vargas, S., Sánchez-Meseguer, A., Huguet, R., Lalueza-Fox, C., Peña-Melián, A., Kranioti, E. F., Santamaría, D., Rasilla, M. de la, Fortea, J., 2012. Les Néandertaliens d'El Sidrón (Asturies, Espagne). Actualisation d'un nouvel échantillon, L'Anthropologie 116 (1), 57-76.

Rosas, A., Estalrrich, A., García-Vargas, S., García-Tabernero, A., Bastir, M., Huguet, R., Peña-Melián, A., 2011a.

Los fósiles neandertales de la Cueva de El Sidrón, in: Rasilla, M. de la, Rosas, A., Cañaveras, J. C., Lalueza-Fox, C. (Eds.), La Cueva de El Sidrón (Borines, Piloña, Asturias). Investigación interdisciplinar de un grupo neandertal, Consejería de Cultura y Turismo y Ediciones Trabe SLU, Oviedo, pp. 81-116.

Rosas, A., Estalrrich, A., García-Vargas, S., García-Tabernero, A., Huguet, R., Lalueza-Fox, C., Rasilla, M. de la, Fortea, J., 2013. Identification of Neandertal individuals in fragmentary fossil assemblages by means of teeth associations. The case of the El Sidrón (Asturias, Spain), Comptes Rendus Palevol 12(5), 279-291.

Rosas, A., García-Tabernero, A., Estalrrich, A., García-Vargas, S., Bastir, M., Lalueza-Fox, C., Huguet, R., Peña-Melián, A., Santamaría, D., Rasilla, M. de la, Fortea, J., 2011c. La imagen de los neandertales a la luz de los últimos descubrimientos. El caso de El Sidrón (Asturias), in: Fernández Caro, J. J., Baena Escudero, R. (Eds.), Arqueología, Paleontología y Geomorfología del Cuaternario en España, X Aniversario del Seminario Francisco Sousa, Sevilla, La Rinconada, 2013, AEQUA y Ayuntamiento de La Rinconada, Sevilla, pp. 95-122.

Rosas, A., Huguet, R., Estalrrich, A., García-Tabernero, A., García-Vargas, S., Bastir, M., Peña Melián, A., 2011b Fauna de macromamíferos en la Galería del Osario, in: Rasilla, M. de la, Rosas, A., Cañaveras, J. C., Lalueza-Fox, C. (Eds.), La Cueva de El Sidrón (Borines, Piloña, Asturias). Investigación interdisciplinar de un grupo neandertal, Consejería de Cultura y Turismo y Ediciones Trabe SLU, Oviedo, pp. 147-148.

Rosas, A., Huguet, R., Pérez-González, A., Carbonell, E., Bermúdez de Castro, J.M., Vallverdú, J., van der Made, J., Allué, E., García, N., Martínez-Pérez, R., Rodríguez, J., Sala, R., Saladie, P., Benito, A., Martínez-Maza, C., Bastir, M., Sánchez, A., Parés, J.M., 2006. The "Sima del Elefante" cave site at Atapuerca (Spain), Estudios Geológicos 62, 327-348.

Rosas, A., Huguet, R., Pérez-González, A., Carbonell, E., Vallverdú, J., van der Made, J., Allué, E., García, N., Martínez-Pérez, R., Rodríguez, J., Sala, R., Saladie, P., Simón, G., Martínez-Maza, C., Bastir, M., Sánchez, A., Parés, J. M., 2004 . Initial approach to the site formation and Paleoecology of the "Sima del Elefante": a Pleistocene karst locality at Atapuerca Hill, in: Zona Arqueológica. Miscelánea en homenaje a Emiliano Aguirre. Geología. Museo Arqueológico Regional, Alcalá de Henares, pp. 135-155.

Rosas, A., Martínez Maza, C., Bastir, M., García-Tabernero, A., Lalueza-Fox, C., Huguet, R., Ortiz, J. E., Julià, R., Soler, V., Torres, T. de, Martínez, E., Cañaveras, J. C., Sánchez-Moral, S., Cuezva, S., Lario, J., Santamaría, D., Rasilla, M. de la, Fortea, J., 2006. Paleobiology and comparative morphology of a late Neandertal sample from El Sidrón (Asturias, Spain), PNAS 103 (51), 19266-19271.

Rosas, A., Martínez-Maza, C., Bastir, M., García-Tabernero, A., Lalueza-Fox, C., Huguet, R., Estalrrich, A., García-Vargas, S., de la Rasilla, M., Fortea, J., 2007. Paleobiological aspects of El Sidrón (Asturias, Spain) Neandertals, American Journal of Physical Anthropology 132(S44), 202.

Rosas, A., Pérez González, A., Carbonell, E., Made van der, J., Antonio, S., Laplana, C., Cuenca-Bescós, G., Parés, J.M., Huguet, R., 2001. Le gisement pléistocene de la "Sima del Elefante" (Sierra de Atapuerca, Espagne), L'Anthropologie 105, 301-312.

Rose, E.P.F., Rosenbaum, M. S., 1990. Royal Engineer Geologists and the Geology of Gibraltar. Gibraltar Museum, Gibraltar.

Rosell, J., 1998. Les primières occupations humaines à la Sierra de Atapuerca (Burgos, Espagne). Les niveaux TDW-4 et TDW-4b, in: Brugal, J.-P., Meignen, L., Patou-Mathis, M. (Eds.), Économie Préhistorique: les comportements de subsistance au Paléolithique XVIIIe Rencontres Internationales d'Archéologie et d'Histoire d'Antibes. Éditions APDCA, Sophia Antipolis, pp. 153-162.

Rosell, J., Blasco, R., 2009. No cutmarks, no toothmarks. The anatomical connections at the Gran Dolina site, Journal of Taphonomy 7 (1), 53-54.

Rosell, J., Blasco, R., Rivals, F., Chacón, G., Menéndez, L., Morales, J. I., Rodríguez -Hidalgo, A., Cebrià, A., Carbonell, E., Serrat, D., 2010. A stop along the way: the role of neanderthal groups at Level III of Teixoneres Cave (Moià, Barcelona, Spain), Quaternaire 21 (2), 139-154.

Rosell, J., Huguet, R., Aïmene, M., Angelucci, D., Canals, A., Pastó, I., Rodríguez Álvarez, X. P., 2000. El yacimiento de las Fuentes de San Cristóbal (Veracruz, Huesca): un nuevo enclave del Paleolítico medio en el Prepirineo, in: (Eds.), Actas do 3° Congresso de Arqueologia Peninsular. Oporto, II, pp. 235-249.

Rosell, J., Rodríguez, X. P., 1991. Paleolític inferior a la conca de Tremp: la localització arqueològica dels Nerets, Collegats 5, 133-139.

Roselló Izquierdo, E., Morales Muñiz, A. 2011. Evidencias de pesca en las ocupaciones de Santimamiñe, Kobie Serie BAI n° 1, 239-246.

Rossillo, R., Palomo, A., Gómez, B., Vallverdú, J., 2008. Resultats de les excavacions arqueològiques del Turó de la Bateria excavació (TBEX) (Girona). IX Jornades d'Arqueologia de les Comarques de Girona, vol. 1, L'Escala-Empúries, pp. 31-42.

Roy, M., Tarriño, A., Benito Calvo, A., Mora, R., Martínez-Moreno, J., 2013. El aprovisionamiento de sílex en el Prepirineo Oriental: el nivel arqueológico 497C de Cova Gran, Trabajos de Prehistoria 70 (1), 7-27.

Rubio-Jara, S., 2011. El paleolítico en el valle del río Manzanares (Madrid). Caracterización geoarqueológica de depósitos pleistocenos y estudio tecnoeconómico de la industria lítica, Tesis Doctoral inédita, Universidad Nacional de Educación a Distancia, Madrid, p. 607.

Rufí, I., Ventura, H., Rivals, F., Allué, E., Vaquero, M., Maroto-Genover, J., 2014. Les campanyes arqueològiques al cau del Roure durant els anys 2012-2013, XII Jornades d'Arqueologia de les Comarques de Girona, Besalú, pp. 43-48.

Ruiz Bustos, A., 1976. Estudio sistemático y ecológico sobre la fauna del Pleistoceno Medio de las Depresiones Granadinas. El yacimiento de Cúllar de Baza-1. Departamento de Paleontología, Universidad de Granada. Tesis Doctoral inédita.

Ruiz Zapata, B., Gil García, M. J., Uzquiano, P., 2012. Calvero de la Higuera, in: Carrión, J. S. (coord.), Paleoflora y paleovegetación de la Península Ibérica e Islas Baleares: Plioceno-Cuaternario. Ministerio de Economía y Competitividad, pp. 541-545.

Ruiz Zapata, B., Gil García, M.J., 2014. Estudio polínico de la secuencia AD, in: Ramos, J., Weniger, G.-C., Cantalejo, P., Espejo, M.-M. (Ed.), Cueva de Ardales. Intervenciones Arqueológicas 2011 - 2014. Ediciones Pinsapar, Málaga, pp. 85-93.

Ruiz Zapata, B., Gómez-González, C., Gil García, M. J., Pérez-González, A., López-Sáez, J. A., Arsuaga, J. L., Baquedano, E., 2008. Evolución de la vegetación durante el Pleistoceno superior y el Holoceno en el Valle alto del río Lozoya. Yacimiento arqueopaleontológico de la Cueva de la Buena Pinta (Pinilla del Valle, Sistema Central Español), Geogaceta 44, 83-86.

Ruíz Zapata, M.B., Ortega Martínez, A.I., Dorado Valiño, M., Valdeolmillos Rodríguez, A., Gil García, M.J., Arsuaga Ferreras, J.L., Carretero Díaz, J.M., Martínez Mendizábal, I., 2003. Vegetational history during Bronze and Iron Age in Portalón Cave (Sierra de Atapuerca, Burgos, Spain), in: Ruíz Zapata, M.B., Dorado Valiño, M., Valdeolmillos Rodríguez, A., Gil García, M.J., Bardají Azcárate, T., de Bustamante Gutiérrez, I., Martínez Mendizabal, I. (Eds.), Quaternary climatic changes and eviromental crises in the Mediterranean Region, Universidad de Alcalá - Ministerio de Ciencia y Tecnología - INQUA; Alcalá de Henares, pp. 103-106.

Ruiz, J.F., Hernanz, A., Ann, A., Rowe, M. W., Viñas, R., Gavira, J.M., Rubio, A., 2012. Calcium oxalate AMS 14C dating and chronology of pos-Paleolithic rock paintings in the Iberian Peninsula. Two dates from Abrigo de los Oculados (Henarejos, Cuenca, Spain), Journal of Archaeological Science 39 (8), 2655-2667.

Ruiz, J.F., Mas, M., Hernanz, Rowe, M.W., Steelman, K., Gavira, J.M., 2006. First radiocarbon dating of oxalate crusts over Spanish prehistoric rock art, International News of Rock Art 46, 1-5.

Ruiz, J.F., Rowe, M.W., Hernanz, A., Gavira, J.M., Viñas, R., Rubio, A., 2009. Cronología del arte rupestre postpaleolítico y datación absoluta de pátinas de oxalato cálcico. Primeras experiencias en Castilla-La Mancha (2004-2007), in: IV Congreso El Arte Rupestre del Arco Mediterráneo de la Península Ibérica. 10 años en la Lista del Patrimonio Mundial de la UNESCO, Valencia, pp.303- 316.

Ruiz, M.B., Gil, M.J., 2005. Los neandertales cantábricos: su paisaje vegetal, in: Lasheras, J.A., Montes, R. (Ed.), Neandertales cantábricos. Estado de la cuestión. Monografías del Museo de Altamira, pp. 275-284.

Ruiz-Alonso, M., Marquer, L., Peña-Chocarro, L., Sabato, D., Zapata, L., 2013. Paisaje y uso de la vegetación durante el Magdaleniense en La Peña de Estebanvela (Segovia): análisis antracológico y fitolitológico, in: C. Cacho (coord.), Ocupaciones magdalenienses en el interior de la Península Ibérica. La Peña de Estebanvela (Ayllón, Segovia). Junta de Castilla y León-CSIC, pp. 93-126.

Ruiz-Bustos, A., 1999. Biostratigraphy of the continental deposits in the Granada, Guadix and Baza basins (Betic Cordillera), in: Gibert, J., Sánchez, F., Gibert, L., Ribot, F. (Eds.), The hominids and their environment during the Lower and Middle Pleistocene, Museo de Prehistoria y Paleontología, Gibert, J, Granada, pp. 153-174.

Sacchi, D., 1986. Le Paléolithique Supérieur du Languedoc Occidental et du Roussillon, Supplément à Gallia Préhistoire, XXI. CNRS, París.

Sacchi, D., Soler Masferrer, N., Maroto Genover, J., Domènech Faus, E., 1996. La question de l'Aurignacien tardif dans le domaine méditerranéen nord-occidental, in: Montet-White, A., Palma di Cesnola, A., Valoch, K. (Eds.), The Upper Palaeolithic, Colloquia 6, (Colloquium XI: The late Aurignacian. Colloquium XII: The origin of the Gravetian), 23-40.

Sáenz de Buruaga, A., 1989. Cueva de Arrillor (Murua-Zigoitia, Álava). I campaña de excavaciones arqueológicas, Arkeoikuska-1989, 11-16.

Sáenz de Buruaga, A., 1990. Cueva de Arrillor (Murua-Zigoitia, Álava). II campaña de excavaciones arqueológicas, Arkeoikuska-1990, 21-22.

Sáenz de Buruaga, A., 1991. Cueva de Arrillor (Murua-Zigoitia, Álava). III campaña de excavaciones arqueológicas, Arkeoikuska-1991, 21-26.

Sáenz de Buruaga, A., 1992. Cueva de Arrillor (Murua-Zigoitia, Álava). IV campaña de excavaciones arqueológicas, Arkeoikuska-1992, 43-49.

Sáenz de Buruaga, A., 1993. Cueva de Arrillor (Murua-Zigoitia, Álava). V campaña de excavaciones arqueológicas, Arkeoikuska-1993, 43-47.

Sáenz de Buruaga, A., 1994. Cueva de Arrillor (Murua-Zigoitia, Álava). VI campaña de excavaciones arqueológicas, Arkeoikuska-1994, 76-80.

Sáenz de Buruaga, A., 1996. Apuntes provisionales sobre la historia y el concepto de Estratigrafía Analítica, Krei 1, 5-20.

Sáenz de Buruaga, A., 1997. Cueva de Arrillor (Murua-Zigoitia, Álava). VII campaña de excavaciones arqueológicas, Arkeoikuska-1997, 95-102.

Sáenz de Buruaga, A., 2000. El Paleolítico inferior y medio en el País Vasco: síntesis de datos y algunas reflexiones, Spal 9, 49-68.

Sáenz de Buruaga, A., Aguirre, M., Grima, C., López Quintana, J.C., Ormazabal, A., Pastor, B., 1998. Método y práctica de la Estratigrafía Analítica, Krei 3, 7-41.

Sahly, A., 1975. La grotte préhistorique de Gargas, Rieumes, Imp. J. Cucuron.

Sala-Burgos, M.T.N., 2012. Tafonomía de yacimientos kársticos de carnívoros en el Pleistoceno. Tesis Doctoral, Universidad Complutense de Madrid

Saladié, P., 2009. Mossegades d'omnívors. Aproximació experimental i aplicació zooarqueològica als jaciments de la Sierra de Atapuerca, Geografia i Història, Universitat Rovira i Virgili, Tarragona.

Saladié, P., Cáceres, I., Ollé, A., Vallverdú, J., Made, J.v.d., Vergès, J.M., Bennàsar, M.L., López-Polín, L., Lorenzo,

C., Expósito, I., Burjachs, F., Olària, C., Gusi, F., Carbonell, E., 2010. Primeros resultados tafonómicos de las asociaciones fósiles de la Cova de Dalt del Tossal de la Font (Vilafamés, Castellón), Zona arqueológica 13, 526-537.

Saladié, P., Huguet, R., Díez, C., Rodríguez-Hidalgo, A., Cáceres, I., Vallverdú, J., Rosell, J., Bermúdez de Castro, J.M., Carbonell, E., 2011. Carcass transport decisions in Homo antecessor subsistence strategies, Journal of Human Evolution 61, 425-446.

Saladié, P., Huguet, R., Rodríguez-Hidalgo, A., Cáceres, I., Esteban-Nadal, M., Arsuaga, J.L., Bermúdez de Castro, J.M., Carbonell, E., 2012. Intergroup cannibalism in the European Early Pleistocene: The range expansion and imbalance of power hypotheses, Journal of Human Evolution 63, 682-695.

Saladié, P., Rodríguez-Hidalgo, A., Huguet, R., Cáceres, I., Díez, C., Vallverdú, J., Canals, A., Soto, M., Santander, B., Bermúdez de Castro, J.M., Arsuaga, J.L., Carbonell, E., 2014. The role of carnivores and their relationship to hominin settlements in the TD6-2 level from Gran Dolina (Sierra de Atapuerca, Spain), Quaternary Science Reviews 93, 47-66.

Saladié, P., Vallverdú, J., Bennàsar, L., Cabanes, D., Mancha, E., Menéndez, L., Blain, H., Ollé, A., Vilalta, J.F., Mosquera, M., Cáceres, I., Expósito, I., Esteban, M., Huguet, R., Rosas, A., Solé, A., López-Polín, L., Martinell, J., García, A., Martínez, B., Agustí, J., Ros, S., Carbonell, E., Capedevila, E., 2009. Resultats preliminars del nivell 2 del sondeig en el Centre de Convencions del Barranc de la Boella, Cota Zero 23, 13-19.

Salazar-García, D. C., Aura, J. E., Olària, C. R., Talamo, S., Morales, J. V., Richards, M.P., 2014. Isotopeevidenceforthe use of marine resources in the Eastern Iberian Mesolithic, Journal of Archaeological Science 42, 231- 240.

Salazar-García, D.C., Power, R.C., Sanchis Serra, A., Villaverde, V., Walker, M.J., Henry, A.G., 2013. Neanderthal diets in central and southeastern Mediterranean Iberia, Quaternary International 318, 3-18.

Samper-Carro, S.C., Martínez-Moreno,J., 2014. Who let the hyenas out? Taphonomic analysis of the faunal assemblage from GL-1 of Cova del Gegant (Sitges, Spain), Quaternary International 330, 19-35.

Sánchez Fernández, G., Bernaldo de Quirós F., 2008. El final del Musteriense cantábrico: el nivel 20e de la cueva de El Castillo (Cantabria), Férvedes 5, in: Ramil Rego, E. (Ed.), I Congreso Internacional de Arqueoloxia de Vilalba, Museo de Prehistoria e Arqueoloxia de Vilalba, pp.- 117-126.

Sánchez Fernández, G., Maillo Fernández, J.M., 2006. Soportes laminares en el musteriense final cantábrico: el nivel 20e de la cueva de El Castillo (Cantabria), in: Maíllo-Fernández, J.M., Baquedano, E. (Ed.), Miscelánea en Homenaje a Victoria Cabrera, Zona Arqueológica 7 (vol 1), Alcalá de Henares, pp. 264-273.

Sánchez Goñi, M.F., Harrison, S.P., 2010. Millennial-scale climate variability and vegetation changes during the Last Glacial: Concepts and terminology, Quaternary Science Review 29, 2823-2827.

Sánchez Marco, A., 1999. Aves del yacimiento mesopleistoceno de Galería (Sierra de Atapuerca). Patrones ecológicos en el Pleistoceno Medio. Atapuerca, in: Carbonell, E., Rosas, A. Díez, J.C. (Eds), Atapuerca: Ocupaciones Humanas y Paleoecología del Yacimiento de Galería. Memorias 7, pp. 211-224.

Sánchez Marco, A., 2004. Avian zoogeographical patterns during the Quaternary in the Mediterranean region and paleoclimatic interpretation, Ardeola 51, 91-132.

Sánchez Marco, A., 2005. Avifaunas cuaternarias de la Península Ibérica: Sistemática, Paleocología, Paleozoografía. Tesis Doctoral, Universidad Autónoma de Madrid, Madrid, p. 505.

Sánchez Marco, A., 2013. Avifauna finipleistocena de La Peña de Estebanvela (Segovia), in: C. Cacho (coord.), Ocupaciones magdalenienses en el interior de la Península Ibérica. La Peña de Estebanvela (Ayllón, Segovia). Junta de Castilla y León-CSIC, pp. 149-155.

Sánchez Marco, A., Cacho Quesada, C., 2010. Avian wings as ornaments in a Magdalenian population, Archaeofauna 19, 133-139.

Sánchez-Cervera, B., Santonja, M., Pérez-González, A., Domínguez-Rodrigo, M., Sánchez-Romero, L., e.p. La industria lítica del yacimiento achelense de Torralba (Soria, España). Colecciones Cerralbo y Howell. Trabajos de Prehistoria.

Sánchez-Goñi, M. F., 1991. Analyses palynologiques des remplissages de grotte de Lezexiki, Labeko et Urtiaga (Pays Basque espagnol). Leur place dans le cadre des séquences polliniques de la region cantabrique et des Pyrénées Occidentales, Tesis Doctoral Ciencias I.P.H., Paris, p. 275.

Sánchez-Moral, S., Cañaveras, J. C., Lario, J., Cuezva, S., Silva, P. G., Rasilla, M. de la, Fortea, J., 2007. Caracterización del relleno sedimentario de la Galería del Osario (Cueva de El Sidrón, Asturias, España), in: Lario, J., Silva, P. G. (Eds.), XII Reunión Nacional de Cuaternario, AEQUA, Ávila, 2007, AEQUA, pp. 123-124.

Sanchidrián, J.L., 1994, Arte rupestre de la Cueva de Nerja, Málaga.

Sanchidrián, J.L., Márquez, A.Mª., Valladas, H., Tisnerat, N., 2001. Dates directes pour l'artrupestred'Andalousie (Espagne), Bulletin de l' I.N.O.R.A. 29, 15-19.

Sanchis Serra, A., 2010. Los lagomorfos del Paleolítico medio de la región central y sudoriental del Mediterráneo Ibérico. Caracterización tafonómica y taxonómica. Tesis Doctoral, Universitat de València, Valencia, p. 586.

Sanchis Serra, A., Fernández Peris, J., 2011. Nuevos datos sobre la presencia de Lepus en el Pleistoceno Medio y Superior del Mediterráneo Ibérico: Cova del Bolomor (Valencia), Saguntum 43, 9-20.

Sanchiz, B., Martín, C., 2011. La herpetofauna del yacimiento de El Sidrón, in: Rasilla, M. de la, Rosas, A., Cañaveras, J. C., Lalueza-Fox, C. (Eds.), La Cueva de El Sidrón (Borines, Piloña, Asturias). Investigación interdisciplinar de un grupo neandertal, Consejería de Cultura y Turismo y Ediciones Trabe SLU, Oviedo, pp. 155-157.

Sanguino, J., Montes, R., 2005. Nuevos datos para el conocimiento del Paleolítico medio en el centro de la Región cantábrica: la Cueva de Covalejos (Piélagos,Cantabria), in: Montes, R., Lasheras, J.A. (Ed.), Neandertales cantábricos. Estado de la cuestión, vol. 20. Monografías del Museo Nacional de Altamira, pp. 489-504.

Sanguino, J., Montes, R., Martín, P., 2005. El marco cronoestratigráfico y paleoclimático del Pleistoceno superior inicial de la región cantábrica, ¿Un gigante con pies de barro?, in: Santonja, M., Pérez-González, A., Machado, P. (Eds.), Geoarqueología y Patrimonio en la Península Ibérica y el entorno mediterráneo. Adema, Soria, pp. 127-138.

San-Pedro, Z., Cáceres, I. 2011. Tafonomía del registro fósil de macromamíferos del Magdaleniense inferior tardío de la cueva de Santimamiñe (Kortezubi, Bizkaia), Kobie Serie BAI nº 1, 207-238.

Santafé, J. V., Casanovas, M. L., 1993. Dicerorhinus hemitoechus (Falconer, 1868) (Mammalia, Perissodactyla) del yacimiento pleistocénico de la Cueva del Gegant (Garraf, Barcelona), Empuréis 48-50, 310-322.

Santamaría, D., 2006. Clasificación y estudio de los materiales musterienses de la Cueva de El Sidrón, Trabajo de Investigación, Universidad de Oviedo, Oviedo, p. 378.

Santamaría, D., 2012. La Transición del Paleolítico medio al superior en Asturias. El abrigo de La Viña (La Manzaneda, Oviedo) y la cueva de El Sidrón (Borines, Piloña). Servicio de Publicaciones de la Universidad de Oviedo, Oviedo.

Santamaría, D., de la Rasilla, M., 2013. Datando el final del Paleolítico medio en la Península Ibérica. Problemas metodológicos y límites de la interpretación, Trabajos de prehistoria 70 (2), 241-263.

Santamaría, D., Fortea, J., Rasilla, M. de la, Martínez, L., Martínez, E., Cañaveras, J. C., Sánchez-Moral, S., Rosas, A., Estalrrich, A., García-Tabernero, A., Lalueza-Fox, C., 2010. The technological and typological behaviour of a Neanderthal group from El Sidrón Cave (Asturias, Spain), Oxford Journal of Archaeology 29(2), 119-148.

Santamaría, D., Montes, L., Utrilla, P., 2008. Variabilidad técnica del Paleolítico Medio en el valle del Ebro: la cueva de los Moros 1 de Gabasa (Peralta de Calasanz, Huesca), in: Mora, R., Martínez, J., de la Torre, I., Casanova, J. (Eds), Variabilidad técnica del Paleolítico Medio en el Sudoeste de Europa, Treballs d'arqueologia 14, 319-329.

Santamaría, D., Rasilla, M. de la, Martínez, L., Tarriño, A., 2011. Las herramientas y su interpretación cultural y económica, in: Rasilla, M. de la, Rosas, A., Cañaveras, J. C., Lalueza-Fox, C. (Eds.), La Cueva de El Sidrón (Borines, Piloña, Asturias). Investigación interdisciplinar de un grupo neandertal, Consejería de Cultura y Turismo y Ediciones Trabe SLU, Oviedo, pp. 135-144.

Santonja, M., 1989. Torralba y Ambrona, nuevos argumentos, BSAA LV, 5-13.

Santonja, M., López, N., Pérez-González, A. (Eds.), 1980. Ocupaciones achelenses en el valle del Jarama, Arqueología y Paleontología 1. Diputación Provincial de Madrid, Madrid.

Santonja, M., Pérez-González, A., 2001. Cuesta de la Bajada (Teruel) and human occupation of the eastern zone of the Iberian Peninsula in the middle Pleistocene, in: D. Büchner (Ed.), Von den Meseta-Kulturen zur Paläo-Ökologia. Festschrift für Wilhelm Schüle, anlälich seines siebzigsten Geburtstags, gewidmet von seinen Freunden, Schülern und Kollegen. Wissenschaft y Öffentlichkeit, Freiburg, pp. 418-426

Santonja, M., Pérez-González, A., 2005 (Eds.). Los yacimientos Paleolíticos de Ambrona y Torralba (Soria). Zona Arqueológica 5, Museo Arqueológico Regional de Madrid. Alcalá de Henares.

Santonja, M., Pérez-González, A., 2006. La industria lítica del miembro estratigráfico medio de Ambrona (Soria, España) en el contexto del Paleolítico antiguo de la Península ibérica. Zephyrus LIX, 95-108.

Santonja, M., Pérez-González, A., 2010. Precisiones en torno a la edad y la industria lítica de El Aculadero (Puerto de Santa María, Cádiz), in: Mata Almonte, E. (Ed.), Cuaternario y Arqueología: Homenaje a Francisco Giles Pacheco, Servicio de Publicaciones de la Diputación Provincial de Cádiz. Cadiz, pp. 19-26.

Santonja, M., Pérez-González, A., 2010a. Mid-Pleistocene Acheulian industrial complex in the Iberian Peninsula. Quat Int 223-224, 154-161.

Santonja, M., Pérez-González, A., Domínguez-Rodrigo, M., Sesé, C., Soto, E., Panera, J., Rubio-Jara, S., Arnold, L. J., Duval, M., Demuro, M., Ortiz, J. E., de Torres, T., Mercier, N., Barba, R., Yravedra, J., i. p. Among the oldest evidence of Ancient Middle Paleolithic occupation in Europe: Cuesta de la Bajada site (Teruel, Spain). Journal of Archaeological Science. Submitted.

Santonja, M., Pérez-González, A., Vega, G., Rus, I., 2001. Elephants and stone artifacts in the Middle Pleistocene terraces of the Manzanares River (Madrid, Spain), in: Cavarretta, P. *et al.*, (Eds.), Proceedings of the 1st International Congress, The World of Elephants, Roma, pp. 597-601.

Santonja, M., Pérez-González, A., Villa, P., Sesé, C., Soto, E., Mora, R., Eisenmann, V., Dupre, M., 2000. El yacimiento paleolítico de Cuesta de la Bajada (Teruel) y la ocupación humana de la zona oriental de la Península ibérica en el Pleistoceno Medio, in: Homenaje a E. Llobregat, Instituto Alicantino de Cultura Juan Gil Albert, Alicante, pp. 79-101.

Santonja, M., Vega, G., 2002. La investigación del valle del Manzanares (1862-1975) en el contexto del Paleolítico español, in: Panera, J., Rubio-Jara, S. (Eds.), Bifaces y Elefantes. La investigación del Paleolítico inferior en Madrid, Zona Arqueológica 1, 242-275.

Santonja, M., Vega, G., 2002. La investigación del valle del Manzanares (1862-1975) en el contexto del Paleolítico español, in: Panera, J., Rubio-Jara, S. (Eds.), Bifaces y Elefantes. La investigación del Paleolítico inferior en Madrid. Zona Arqueológica 1, Museo Arqueológico Regional de Madrid, Alcalá de Henares, pp. 242-275.

Santos, G., Martínez, J., Silva, P. G., Sánchez-Moral, S., Cañaveras, J. C., Rasilla, M. de la, 2012b. Contribución al conocimiento de la Cueva de El Sidrón (Piloña, Asturias) con técnicas de láser escáner 3D. Avances de la Geomorfología en España 2010-2012. XII Reunión Nacional de Geomorfología, Santander, 2012, PUbliCan Ediciones de la Universidad de Cantabria, Santander, pp. 255-258.

Santos, G., Silva, P. G., Standing, M., Huerta, P., Fernández, B., Cañaveras, J. C., Sánchez-Moral, S., Rasilla, M. de la, 2012a. Análisis topográfico y geomorfológico del complejo kárstico de El Sidrón (Piloña, Asturias), in: VIII Congreso Nacional de Geología, Oviedo, 2012, Geotemas, 13, p. 224.

Sanz de Sautuola, M., 1880. Breves Apuntes sobre algunos objetos prehistóricos de la Provincia de Santander. Santander: Imp. y Lit. de Telesforo Martínez

Sanz, M. 2013. Patrons d'acumulació de restes de fauna del Plistocè superior al nord-est peninsular (àrea del Massís del Garraf-Ordal). Tesis Doctoral, Universitat de Barcelona, Barcelona, p. 505.

Sanz, M., 2006. Patron sd'acumulació de restes de fauna en el Plistocè mig i superior. Diploma d'Estudis Avançats, Universitat de Barcelona, Barcelona, p 111.

Sanz, M., 2013. Patrons d'acumulació de fauna del Plistocè superior al nord-est peninsular (àrea del Massís del Garraf-Ordal). Tesis Doctoral, Universitat de Barcelona, Barcelona, p. 505.

Sanz, M., Daura, J., Brugal, J.-P., 2014. First occurrence of the extinct deer Haploidoceros in the Iberian Peninsula in the Upper Pleistocene of the Cova del Rinoceront (Castelldefels, Barcelona). Comptes Rendus Paleovol13, 27-40.

Sanz, M., Daura, J., Terrado, E., Méndez, M., Fullola, J.M^a., 2011. La geotecnia vertical aplicada a la rehabilitación de yacimientos Pleistocenos. Treballs del Museu de Geologia de Barcelona 18, 25-35.

Sarrión, I., Fernández Peris, J., 2006. Presencia de Ursus thibetanus mediterraneus (Forsyth Major, 1873) en la Cova del Bolomor (Tavernes de la Valldigna, Valencia), Arch. Prehistoria Levantina 26, 25-38.

Schabereiter-Gurtner, C., Saiz-Jimenez, C., Piñar, G., Lubitz, W., Rolleke, S., 2004. Phylogenetic diversity of bacteria associated with Palaeolithic paintings and surrounding rock walls in two Spanish caves (Llonín and La Garma), FEMS Microbiology Ecology 47, 235-247.

Scott, G.R., Gibert, L., 2009. The oldest hand-axes in Europe, Nature 461, 82-85.

Serna, L. M., Valle, A., Obregón, F., Toca, M. A., González, C., 2001. Las cuevas del valle de Villaescusa. Asociación para la defensa del patrimonio de Villaescusa. Santander.

Serra, J. d. C., Villalta, J. F., Thomas, J., Fusté, M., 1957. Livret Guide des excursions B2-B3. Alentours de Barcelona et Moià, in : (Eds.), V Congrés International del INQUA. Madrid-Barcelona.

Serra, S., Gutiérrez, R., Carbonell, E., Canal, J., 1981. Puig d'en Roca III. Un nuevo lugar de ocupación del Paleolítico Inferior en el Valle Medio del Ter (Girona), Butlletí de l'Associació Arqueològica de Girona 4, 4-15.

Sesé, C., 2005. Aportación de los micromamíferos al conocimiento paleoambiental del Pleistoceno Superior de la Región Cantábrica: Nuevos datos y síntesis, in: R. Montes Barquín, J.A., Lasheras Corruchaga (Eds.), Neandertales Cantábricos, estado de la cuestión. Monografías del Museo Nacional y Centro de Investigación de Altamira 20, pp. 167-200.

Sesé, C., 2011. Los pequeños mamíferos del yacimiento de El Sidrón, in: Rasilla, M. de la, Rosas, A., Cañaveras, J. C., Lalueza-Fox, C. (Eds.), La Cueva de El Sidrón (Borines, Piloña, Asturias). Investigación interdisciplinar de un grupo neandertal, Consejería de Cultura y Turismo y Ediciones Trabe SLU, Oviedo, pp. 148-155.

Sesé, C., 2013. Micromamíferos (Rodentia, Insectivora, Lagomorpha y Chiroptera) de La Peña de Estebanvela (Segovia), in: C. Cacho (coord.) 2013, Ocupaciones magdalenienses en el interior de la Península Ibérica. La Peña de Estebanvela (Ayllón, Segovia), Junta de Castilla y León-CSIC, pp.157-182.

Sesé, C., Panera, J., Rubio-Jara, S., Pérez-González, A., 2011. Micromamíferos del Pleistoceno Medio y Pleistoceno Superior en el valle del Jarama: yacimientos de Valdocarros y HAT (Madrid, España), Estudios Geológicos 67, 131-151.

Sesé, C., Sevilla, P., 1996. Los micromamíferos del Cuaternario peninsular español: cronoestratigrafia e implicaciones bioestratigráficas, Revista Española de Paleontología, n° extraordinario, 278-287.

Sesé, C., Soto, E., 2002. Vertebrados del Pleistoceno del Jarama y Manzanares, in Panera, J., Rubio-Jara, S. (Eds.), Bifaces y elefantes. La investigación del Paleolítico Inferior en Madrid, Zona Arqueológica, vol. 1, 318-337.

Sesé, C., Soto, E., Pérez-González, A., 2000. Mamíferos de las terrazas del valle del Tajo: primeras notas de micromamíferos del Pleistoceno en Toledo (España central), Geogaceta 28, 137-140.

Sevilla, P., 1983. Los quirópteros de la cueva de Las Grajas (Archidona, Málaga).Tesis de Licenciatura. Universidad Autónoma de Madrid.1983. Inédita.

Sevilla, P., 1988. Estudio paleontológico de los Quirópteros del Cuaternario Español. Paleontologia i Evolució, n° 22, Sabadell 1988. pp.113-133.

Sevilla, P., 2012. Evidence of the presence of the Root vole (Microtus oeconomus) in Central Spain during the Late Pleistocene Quaternary International 279-280, 442-443.

Sevilla, P., Laplana, C., Araujo, C., López, N., 2012. Reconstucting early Mousterian environments in Spain. The contribution of the late middle Plesitocene small mammal assemblages of Las Grajas Cave (Málaga, Spain), in: Liao, J.C.,Vintaned, J.A.,Valenzuela-Ríos, J.I., García-Foerner, A. (Eds.), XXVIII Jornadas de la Sociedad Española de Paleontología. Valencia-Sóller 1-6 de octubre de 2012. Universitat de València. Sociedad Española de Paleontología, Madrid. pp. 253-256.

Shipton C., Clarkson, C., Bernal, M.A., Boivin, N., Finlayson, C., Finlayson, G., Fa, D., Giles Pacheco, F., Petraglia, M., 2013. Variation in lithic technological strategies among the Neanderthals of Gibraltar. PLoS One 8(6): e65185.

Silva, P. G., López-Recio, M., Tapias, F., Roquero, E., Morín, J., Rus, I., Carrasco-García, P., Giner-Robles, J.L., Rodríguez-Pascua, M.A., Pérez-López, R., 2013. Stratigraphy of the Arriaga Palaeolithic sites. Implications for the geomorphological evolution recorded by thickened fluvial sequences within the Manzanares River valley (Madrid Neogene Basin, Central Spain), Geomorphology 196, 138-161.

Silva, P. G., Santos, G., Carrasco, P., Huerta, P., Ayarza, P., Álvarez, F., Fernández, B., Standing, M., 2011. La geomorfología, topografía y prospección geofísica del complejo de El Sidrón. La búsqueda del lugar de procedencia de los restos fósiles, in: Rasilla, M. de la, Rosas, A., Cañaveras, J. C., Lalueza-Fox, C. (Eds.), La Cueva de El Sidrón (Borines, Piloña, Asturias). Investigación interdisciplinar de un grupo neandertal, Consejería de Cultura y Turismo y Ediciones Trabe SLU, Oviedo, pp. 65-79.

Smith, J., 1846. On the Geology of Gibraltar. Quart. J. Geol. Soc. Lond. 2, 41-51

Soler, J., Soler, N., Agustí, B., Bolus, M., 2013. The Gravettian calvaria from Mollet III cave (Serinyà, Northeastern Iberian Peninsula), Journal of Human Evolution 65, 322-329.

Soler, J., Soler, N., Solés Coll, A., Niell Ciurana, X., Coromina Bujons, N., Medina Boronat, B., 2012. Les excavacions a la cova de l'Arbreda (Serinyà) durant les campanyes de 2010 i 2011, in: Onzenes Jornades d'Arqueologia de les comarques de Girona, Generalitat de Catalunya, Girona, vol I, pp. 47-58.

Soler-Masferrer, N., 1982. Cau del Duc, Torroella de Montgrí. Les Excavacions Arqueològiques a Catalunya en els darrers anys, Generalitat de Catalunya, Departament de Cultura, Barcelona.

Soler-Masferrer, N., 1986. Les indústries del Paleolític Superior en el Nord de Catalunya, Tesis doctoral, Universitat de Barcelona, Barcelona.

Soler-Masferrer, N., 1986. Les industries del Paleolitic Superior en el Nord de Catalunya. Tésis Doctoral. Universidad Central de Barcelona. Inédita.

Soler-Masferrer, N., 1999. Le Paléolithique des grottes de Serinyà (Gérone, Catalogne, Espagne), in: Sachi, D. (Dir.), Les faciès leptolithiques du nord-ouest méditerranéen: milieux naturels et culturels. XXIVe Congrès Préhistorique de France, Société Préhistorique, Carcassonne, pp. 195-228.

Soler-Masferrer, N., Maroto Genover, J., 1987. L'estratigrafia de la cova de l'Arbreda (Serinyà, Girona), Cypsela 6, 53-66.

Soler-Masferrer, N., Maroto Genover, J., 1993. Les nouvelles datations de l'Aurignacien dans la Péninsule Ibérique, in: Pavúk J. (Ed.), Actes du XIIe Congrès International des Sciences Préhistoriques et Protohistoriques, Institut Archéologique de l'Académie Slovaque des Sciences, Bratislava, pp. 162-173.

Soler-Masferrer, N., Maroto-Genover, J., Ramió, S., 2001. Les coves prehistòriques de Serinyà, Guies del Museu d'Arqueologia de Catalunya, Consell Comarcal del Pla de l'Estany, Banyoles.

Soler-Masferrer, N., Maroto-Genover, J., Ramió, S., 2009. The Prehistoric caves of Serinyà. Archaeology Museum of Catalonia guidebooks, Barcelona.

Soler-Masferrer, N., Soler Masferrer, N., Maroto-Genover, J., 2009. L'Arbreda's archaic Aurignacian dates clarified, Eurasian Prehistory 5 (2), 45-55.

Soler-Masferrer, N., Soler Subils, J., 2013. Cabezas de fémur perforadas en la cueva del Reclau Viver (Serinyà, Girona) y el Gravetiense final en el norte de Cataluña, in: de la Rasilla, M. (Ed.), F. Fortea Pérez. Universitatis Ovetensis Magister. Estudios en homenaje, Ménsula ed., Pola de Siero, 317-334.

Sollas, W., 1907. On the cranial and facial characters of the Neanderthal race. Phil.trans.R.Soc. London B, 199, 281-339.

Soria, F.J., López-Garrido, A.C., Vera, J.A., 1987. Análisis estratigráfico y sedimentológico de los depósitos neógeno-cuaternarios en el sector de Orce (derpesión de Guadix-Baza), Paleont i evol., Mem. Esp. 1, 11-34.

Soto, A., Alday, A., Montes, L., Utrilla, P., Perales, U., Domingo, R., i. p. Epipalaeolithic assemblages in the Ebro basin (Spain). The difficult identification of cultural identities, Quaternary International.

Soto, M., Gómez de Soler, B., Vallverdú, J., Vaquero, M., 2011. El territori d'aprovisionament del sílex dels caçadors i recol·lectors del Molí del Salt (Vimbodí i Poblet - Conca de Barberà), Aplec de Treballs 29, 31-52.

Soto, M., Gómez de Soler, B., Vallverdú, J., Vaquero, M., 2013. Aplicación experimental de sistemas de información geográficos a la prospección y análisis de áreas de captación de rocas silíceas en la prehistoria. El caso práctico del Abric romaní y el Molí del Salt, in: Palomo, A., Piqué, R., Terradas, X. (Eds.), Experimentación en Arqueología. Estudio y difusión del pasado, Sèrie Monogràfica del MAC, Barcelona, pp. 501-508.

Sowers, T., Bender, M., Labeyrie, L., Martinson, D., Jouzel, J., Raynaud, Pichon, J.J., Korotkevich, A., 1993. A 135.000 year Vostok-Specmap common temporal Framework, Paleoceanography 8, 737-766.

Staff, S.S., 2010, Keys to Soil Taxonomy, Washington D.C., p. 338.

Stein, J., (Ed.), 1981. Random House Dictionary of the English Language The Unabridged Edition, New York, Random House, p. 537.

Stewart, J.R., Stringer, C.B., 2012. Human evolution out of Africa: the role of refugia and climate change. Science 335, 1317-1321.

Straus, L.G., Clark, G.A., 1986. La Riera Cave: Stone Age Hunter-Gatherer Adaptations in Northern Spain. Anthropological Research Papers 36, Arizona State University, Tempe.

Straus, L.G., González-Morales, M.R., 2001. The year 2000 excavation campaign in El Mirón Cave (Ramales de la Victoria, Cantabria, Spain), World Arcaheology Newsletter 23, 1-8.

Straus, L.G., González-Morales, M.R., 2003. El Mirón Cave and the 14C chronology of Cantabrian Spain, Radiocarbon 45, 41-58.

Straus, L.G., González-Morales, M.R., 2007. Further radiocarbon dates for the Upper Paleolithic of El Mirón Cave, Radiocarbon 49, 1205-1214.

Straus, L.G., González-Morales, M.R., 2009. A preliminary description of Solutrean occupations in El Mirón Cave, Munibe 60, 117-137.

Straus, L.G., González-Morales, M.R., 2010. The radiocarbon chronology of El Mirón Cave (Cantabria, Spain): new dates for the Initial Magdalenian occupations, Radiocarbon 52, 33-39.

Straus, L.G., González-Morales, M.R., 2012. El Mirón Cave, Cantabrian Spain. University of New Mexico Press,

Straus, L.G., González-Morales, M.R., Carretero, J.M., 2011b. Lower Magdalenian secondary human burial in El Mirón Cave, Cantabria, Spain, Antiquity 85, 1151-1164.

Straus, L.G., González Morales, M.R., Fontes, L.n.d. Initial Magdalenian artifact assemblages in El Mirón Cave (Ramales de la Victoria, Cantabria, Spain): a preliminary report. Unpublished manuscript

Straus, L.G., González-Morales, M.R., Gutiérrez, I., Marín, A.B., 2011a. Further Solutrean evidence in El Mirón Cave, Munibe 62, 117-133.

Straus, L.G., González-Morales, M.R., Higham, T., Richards, M., Talamo, S., n.d.a. Radiocarbon dating the Late Upper Paleolithic of Cantabrian Spain: El Mirón Cave date list IV. Unpublished manuscript.

Straus, L.G., González Morales, M.R., Marín, A.B., Iriarte, M.J., 2013. The human occupations of El Mirón Cave (Ramales de la Victoria, Cantabria, España) during the Last Glacial Maximum/Solutrean period, Espacio, Tiempo y Forma. Serie I, Nueva Epoca, Prehistoria y Arqueología 5, 19-432.

Straus, L.G., González-Morales, M.R., Stewart, E., 2008. Early Magdalenian variability: new evidence from El Mirón Cave, Cantabria, Spain, Journal of Field Archaeology 33, 197-218, 367-369.

Stringer C., Finlayson C., Barton R.N.E., Fernández-Jalvo Y., Cáceres I., Sabin R.C., Rhodes E.J., Currant A.P., Rodríguez-Vidal J., Giles-Pacheco F., Riquelme-Cantal J.A., 2008. Neanderthal exploitation of marine mammals in Gibraltar. Proc. Natl. Acad. Sci. USA 105(38), 14319-14324.

Stuckenrath, R., 1978. Dataciones de Carbono 14, in: González-Echegaray, J., Freeman, L.G. (Eds.), Vida y muerte en Cueva Morín, Institución Cultural de Cantabria, Santander, pp. 215.

Stuiver, M., Grootes, P.M., 2000. GISP2 oxygen isotope ratios. Quaternary Research 53, 277 - 284.

Stuiver, M., Polach, H.A., 1977. Reporting of 14C Data, Radiocarbon, 19(3), 355-363.

Stuiver, M., Reimer, P. J., Reimer, R. W., 2000. CALIB 4.3. [WWW program and documentation] URL:<http://www.calib.org>, using the data set given by Stuiver, M., Reimer, P. J., Bard, E., Beck, W. E., Burr, G. S., Hughen, K. A., Kromer, B., McCormac, F. G., Plicht, J. v.d., Spurk, M., 1998. INTCAL98 radiocarbon age calibration 0-24,000 BP, Radiocarbon 40, 1041-1083.

Suárez Ferruelo, P., 2013. Definición tecno-tipológica y funcional de las laminillas Dufour: el caso de los niveles IX y VIII del Sector Central del abrigo de La Viña, CKQ, Estudios de Cuaternario 3, 101-121.

Subirà, M.E., Campillo, D., Chimenos, E., Aparicio, J., Fiego, J., Pérez-Pérez, A., Vila, S., 2003. Estudio de los restos humanos procedentes de la Cova Foradà (Oliva, Valencia), Antropología y biodiversidad, Bellaterra, pp. 520-528

Sverrisdóttir, Oddný Ósk, Timpson, A., Toombs, J., Lecoeur, C. Froguel, Ph. Carretero, J.M. Arsuaga, J.L., Götherström, A., Thomas, M.G., 2014. Direct Estimates of Natural Selection in Iberia Indicate Calcium Absorption Was Not the Only Driver of Lactase Persistence in Europe. Molecular Biology and Evolution, doi:10.1093/molbev/msu049.

Tarriño, A., 2006. El sílex en la cuenca vasco-cantábrica y pirineo navarro: caracterización y su aprovechamiento en la Prehistoria, Monografías del Museo Nacional y Centro de Investigación de Altamira, 21, Ministerio de Cultura.

Tarriño Vinagre, A. 2011. Procedencia de los sílex de la industria lítica del yacimiento en cueva de Santimamiñe (Kortezubi, Bizkaia), Kobie Serie BAI nº 1, 281-289.

Tarriño, A., Duarte, E., Santamaría, D., Martínez, L., Fernández de la Vega, J., Suárez, P., Rodríguez, V., Forcelledo, E., Rasilla, M. de la, 2013. El Sílex de Piloña. Caracterización de una nueva fuente de materia prima en la Prehistoria de Asturias, in: Rasilla, M. de la (Coord.), F. Javier Fortea Pérez. UniversitatisOvetensis Magister. Estudios en Homenaje, Ediciones de la Universidad de Oviedo y Ménsula Ediciones, S.L., Oviedo, pp. 115-132.

Tarriño, A., *et al.*, 2013. El Sílex de Piloña. Caracterización de una nueva fuente de materia prima lítica en la Prehistoria de Asturias. F. Javier Fortea: Universitatis Ovetensis Magister, Oviedo, pp. 115-132.

Tarriño, A., Yusta, I., Aguirre, M., 1998. Indicios de circulación a larga distancia de sílex en el Pleistoceno superior. Datos petrográficos y geoquímicos de materiales arqueológicos de Antoliñako koba, Boletín de la Sociedad Española de Mineralogía 21-A, 200-201.

Tarrús, J., 1978. Els nivells ceràmics de les coves de Serinyà, Tesis de licenciatura, Universitat de Barcelona, Barcelona.

Tarrús, J., 1986. El paratge del Reclau Viver (Serinyà) del Neolític Antic al Bronze Final, Quaderns del Centre d'Estudis Comarcals de Banyoles 1985, I, 232-239.

Teira Brión, A., Martín Seijo, M., de Lombera Hermida, A., Fábregas Valcarce, R., Rodríguez Álvarez, X.P., 2012, Forest resources management during Roman and Medieval cave occupations in the Northwest of the Iberian Peninsula: Cova do Xato and Cova Eirós (Galicia, Spain). Wood and charcoal. Evidence for human and natural history, Sagvntvm extra-13, 159-166.

Tejero, J.M., 2005. El treball de l'os a la Prehistòria. Anàlisi tecnomorfològica de la industria en matèries dures animals de la Cova del Parco (Alòs de Balaguer), 2ª Edició Premi Memorial Josep Barberà. Ed. SCA, Barcelona.

Tejero, J.M., Bernaldo de Quirós F., 2008. Evidencias de trabajo en materias duras animales en el Auriñaciense de transición (Unidad 18) de la cueva de "El Castillo" (Puente Viesgo, Cantabria), VELEIA 24-25, 415-424.

Tejero, J.M., Estrada, A., Nadal, J., Fullola, J. M., Mangado, X., Petit, M. A., Bartrolí, R., Calvo, M., 2010. Chasseurs et artisans au Tardiglaciaire. L'exploitation des ressources animales dans le Magdalénien de la grotte du Parco (Alós de Balaguer, Lleida), in : Fontana, L., *et al.*, (Eds.), Exploitation du monde animal par les sociétés de chasseurs-cueilleurs préhistoriques. Environnements, subsistance et comportements techniques. BAR International Series 2040, Oxford, pp. 91-99.

Tejero, J.M., Fullola, J. M., 2006. Las agujas en hueso de la cueva del Parco (Alòs de Balaguer, Lleida). Un ejemplo de gestión no alimentaria de los recursos animales en el Magdaleniense, Zona Arqueológica 7 (I), 496-503.

Tejero, J.M., Fullola, J.M., 2008. L'exploitation non alimentaire des ressources animales pendant le Magdalénien au NE de la péninsule Ibérique. L'exemple de la grotte du Parco (Alòs de Balaguer, Lleida, Espagne), L'Anthropologie 112 (2), 328-345.

Tejero, J.M., Morán, N., Cabrera Valdés, V., Bernaldo de Quirós F., 2005. Industria Ósea y arte mueble de los niveles auriñacienses de la Cueva del Castillo (Puente Viesgo, Santander), Pyrenae 36-1, 35-56.

Terradillos-Bernal, M., 2010. El Paleolítico inferior en la Meseta Norte: Sierra de Atapuerca, La Maya, El Basalito, San Quirce y Ambrona. Estudio tecnológico y experimental. Tesis Doctoral. Dpto. Ciencias Históricas y Geografía. Universidad de Burgos. Burgos.

Terradillos-Bernal, M., Díez Fernández-Lomana, J.C., 2012. La transition entre les Modes 2 et 3 en Europe. Le rapport sur les gisements du Plateau Nord (Péninsule Ibérique), L´Anthropologie 116, 348-363.

Terradillos-Bernal, M., Rodríguez, X.-P., 2012. The Lower Palaeolithic on the northern plateau of the Iberian Peninsula (Sierra de Atapuerca, Ambrona and La Maya I): a technological analysis of the cutting edge and weight of artefacts. Developing an hypothetical model, Journal of Archaeological Science 39 (5), 1467-1479.

Terrado, E., Sanz, M., Daura, J., Méndez, M., 2013. Estabilización del contorno rocoso de un yacimiento arqueológico (Cova del Rinoceront) ubicado en un antiguo frente de excavación de una cantera de roca caliza en Castelldefels (Barcelona), in: Alonso, E., Corominas, J., Hürlimann, M. (Eds.), VII Simposio Nacional sobre Taludes y Laderas Inestables (Palma de Mallorca, Junio 2013), Centre Internacional de Mètodes Numèrics en Enginyeria (CIMNE), Barcelona, vol. II pp. 649-660.

Théry-Parisot, Costamagno, S., Brugal, J. P., Fosse, P., Guilbert, R., 2005. The use of bone as fuel during the palaeolithic, experimental study of bone combustible properties. 9th ICAZ Conference, Durham, 2002, in: Mulville, J., Outram, A. (Eds.), The Zooarchaeology of Milk and Fats, Oxbow books, Oxford, pp. 50-59.

Tiffagom M., 2006. De la Pierre à l'Homme. Essai sur une Paéoanthropologie solutréenne. ERAUL, 113.

Tissoux, H., 1999. Géochronologie de sites paléolithiques de Catalogne. Résultats préliminaires obtenues par les méthodes U-Th et ESR sur les sites de l'Arbreda, de Cau del Duc d'Ullà et de Cau del Duc de Torroella de Montgrí. Diplôme d'Études Approfondies, Muséum National d'Histoire Naturelle, Paris.

Tissoux, H., Falgueres, C., Bahain, J.-J., Rosell, J., Cebrià, A., Carbonell, E., Serrat, D., 2006. Datation par les séries de l'Uranium des occupations moustériennes de la Grotte des Teixoneres (Moià, Province de Barcelone, Espagne), Quaternaire 17, 27-33.

Toledo, A., 1990. La utilització de les coves des del Calcolitic fins al Bronze Final al N.E. de Catalunya (2.200-650 a.C.), Tesis doctoral, Universitat Autònoma de Barcelona, Bellaterra.

Tormo, C., 2010. Los roedores e insectívoros de los niveles gravetienses de la Cova de les Cendres (Teulada-Moraira, Alicante). Implicaciones paleoclimáticas, Archivo de Prehistoria Levantina XXVIII, 47-71.

Toro-Moyano, I., Barsky, D., Cauche, D., Celiberti, V., Grégoire, S., Lebegue, F., Moncel, M.H., Lumley, H. de, 2011. The archaic stone tool industry from Barranco Léon and Fuente Nueva 3, (Orce, Spain): Evidence of the earliest hominin presence in southern Europe, Quaternary International 243, 80-91.

Toro-Moyano, I., de Lumley, H., Fajardo, B., Barsky, D., Cauche, D., Celiberti, V., Grégoire, S., Martínez-Navarro, B., Espigares, M.P., Ros-Montoya, S., 2009. L'industrie lithique des gisements du Pléistocène inférieur de Barranco León et Fuente Nueva 3 à Orce, Grenade, Espagne, L'Anthropologie 113, 111-124.

Toro-Moyano, I., Lumley, H. de, Barrier, P., Barsky, D., Cauche, D., Celiberti, V., Grégoire, S., Lebègue, F., Mestour, B., Moncel, M.H., 2010a. Les industries lithiques archaïques du Barranco León et de Fuente Nueva 3, Orce, bassin du Guadix- Baza, Andalousie. Monography. CNRS Editions.

Toro-Moyano, I., Lumley, H. de, Barsky, D., Cauche, D., Celiberti, V., Moncel, M.H., 2003. Las industrias líticas de Barranco León y Fuente Nueva 3. Estudio técnico y tipológico. Las cadenas operativas. Análisis traccológico. Resultados preliminares, in: Toro-Moyano, I., Agustí, J., Martínez Navarro, B. (Eds.), El Pleistoceno inferior de Barranco León y Fuente Nueva 3, Orce (Granada). Junta de Andalucía. Consejería de Cultura. E.P.G.P.C. Arqueología Monografías, Memoria Científica campañas 1999-2002, Sevilla, pp. 173-183.

Toro-Moyano, I., Lumley, H. de, Fajardo, B., Barsky, D., Cauche, D., Celiberti, V., Grégoire, S., Martínez-Navarro, B., Espigares, M.P., Ros-Montoya, S., 2009. L'industrie lithique des gisements du pléistocène inférieur de Barranco León et Fuente Nueva 3 à Orce, Grénade, Espagne, L'Anthropologie 113 (1), 111-124.

Toro-Moyano, I., Martínez-Navarro, Agustí, J. (Eds.), 2010 b. Ocupaciones Humanas en el Pleistoceno inferior y medio de la cuenca de Guadix-Baza. Memoria Cientifica. Junta de Andalucía, Consejería de Cultura, EPG, Arqueología Monográfico.

Toro-Moyano, I., Martínez-Navarro, B., Agustí, J., Souday, C., Bérmudez de Castro, J.M., Martinón-Torres, M., Fajardo, B., Duval, M., Falguères, C., Oms, O., Parés, J.M., Anadón , P., Julià, R., García-Aguilar, J.M., Moigne, A-M., Espigares, M.P., Ros-Montoya, S., Palmqvist, P., 2013. The oldest human fossil in Europe dated to ca. 1.4 Ma at Orce (Spain), Journal of Human Evolution 65 (1), 1-9.

Torrente Casado, R., 2010. El yacimiento de Cúllar-Baza 1 (Cúllar, Granada). Síntesis historiográfica y nuevos aportes al estudio de las primeras ocupaciones humanas en el sur de la Península Ibérica. Departamento de Prehistoria y Arqueología, Universidad de Granada. Trabajo Fin de Máster inédito.

Torres, T., de Ortiz, J. E., Fernández, E., Arroyo-Pardo, E., Grün, R., Pérez-González, A., 2014. Aspartic acid racemization as a dating tool for dentine: A reality, Quaternary Geochronology 22, 43-56.

Torres, T., de, Ortiz, J. E., Grün, R., Eggins, S., Valladas, H., Mercier, N., Tisnérat-Laborde, N., Julià, R., Soler, V., Santamaría, D., Rasilla, M. de la, 2011. La datación de los fósiles de El Sidrón: una compleja aproximación multidisciplinar, in: Rasilla, M. de la, Rosas, A., Cañaveras, J. C., Lalueza-Fox, C. (Eds.), La Cueva de El Sidrón (Borines, Piloña, Asturias). Investigación interdisciplinar de un grupo neandertal, Consejería de Cultura y Turismo y Ediciones Trabe SLU, Oviedo, pp. 159-165.

Turq, A., Martínez-Navarro, B, Palmqvist, P., Arribas, A., Agustí, J., Rodríguez-Vidal, J., 1996. Le Plio-Pléistocène de la région d' Orce, province de Grenade, Espagne: bilan et perspectives de recherche, Paléo 8 (1), 161-204.

Ucko, P., 1987. Débuts illusoires dans l´étude de la tradition artistique, Bulletin de la Société Préhistorique Ariège-Pyrénées 42, 15-81.

Ucko, P., 1989. La subjetividad y el estudio del arte parietal paleolítico, in: González-Morales, M.R. (Ed.), Cien Años después de Sautuola, Gobierno de Cantabria, Santander, pp. 283-358.

Utrilla, P., 1982. El yacimiento de la cueva de Abauntz (Arraiz, Navarra), Trabajos de Arqueología Navarra 3, 203-346.

Utrilla, P., 2000. Acerca del Hombre más antiguo de Aragón: una cuestión de publicidad, Naturaleza Aragonesa 6, 80-86.

Utrilla, P., 2004. Evolución histórica de las sociedades cantábricas durante el Tardiglacial: el Magdaleniense inicial, inferior y medio (16.500-13.000 BP), Kobie (serie anejos) 8, 245-276.

Utrilla, P., 2005 El Arte Rupestre en Aragón. 100 Años después de Calapatá, in: Hernández, M.S., Soler, J. (Eds.), Arte Rupestre en la España Mediterránea, MARQ, Alicante, pp. 341-377.

Utrilla, P., Baldellou , V., Bea M., Viñas R., 2012. La cueva de la Fuente del Trucho (Asque- Colungo, Huesca). Una cueva mayor del arte gravetiense, in: de las Heras, C. Laceras, J. A. Arrizabalaga, A., de la Rasilla, M. (Coords.), Pensando el Gravetiense: nuevos datos para la región cantábrica en su contexto peninsular y pirenaico. M.N.C.I.A., 23, pp. 526-537.

Utrilla, P., Blasco, F., 2000. Dos asentamientos magdalenienses en Deza, Soria, Boletín del Seminario de Arte y Arqueología LXVI, 9-63.

Utrilla, P., Blasco, F., Rodanés, J.M., 2006. Entre el Ebro y la meseta: el magdaleniense de la cuenca del Jalón y la placa de Villalba, in: G. Delibes, F. Díez (Eds.), El Paleolítico superior en la Meseta Norte española. Studia Archaeologica 94. Universidad de Valladolid, Secretariado de Publicaciones e Intercambio Científico. Valladolid. pp. 173-213.

Utrilla, P., Martínez Bea, M., 2008. Sanctuaires rupestres comme marqueurs d'identité territoriale : Sites d'agrégation et animaux « sacrés », in: Sauvet, G., Fritz, C. (Eds.), Art rupestre et communication: espaces symboliques et territoires culturels, Préhistoire, Arts et Sociétés LXIII, 109-133.

Utrilla, P., Mazo, C., 1992. L'occupation de l'espace dans la grotte d'Abauntz (Navarra, Espagne). Le peuplement magdalénien, Paléogéographie physique et humaine (Chancelade, 1988). CTHS, Paris, pp. 365-376.

Utrilla, P., Mazo, C., 1996a. Le versant Sud des Pyrénées, in: L'art préhistorique des Pyrénées. Musée des Antiquités Nationales, pp. 60-69.

Utrilla, P., Mazo, C., 1996b. Arte mueble sobre soporte lítico de la cueva de Abauntz. Su aportación a los estilos del Magdaleniense Tardío, Complutum 6, 41-62.

Utrilla, P., Mazo, C., 1996c. Le Paléolithique Supérieur dans le versant Sud des Pyrénées. Communications et influences avec le monde Pyrénéen français, in: Pyrénées Préhistoriques. Arts et Societés. CTHS, Paris, pp. 243-262.

Utrilla, P., Mazo, C., 1996d. Non flint raw materials in La Rioja. A tentative interpretation, in: Moloney, N., Raposo, L. and Santonja, M. (Eds.), Non-Flint Stone Tools and the Palaeolithic Occupation of the Iberian Peninsula. British Archaeological Reports 649, pp. 63-80.

Utrilla, P., Mazo, C., 2011. Los cantos pintados de la cueva de Abauntz y algunas nuevas lecturas del bloque 1. VII Congreso de Historia de Navarra. SEHN. Príncipe de Viana 253, pp. 23-42.

Utrilla, P., Mazo, C., 2014. La Peña de las Forcas (Graus, Huesca). Un asentamiento estratégico en la confluencia del Ésera y el Isábena. Monografías Arqueológicas. Prehistoria, 46. Universidad de Zaragoza, pp. 435.

Utrilla, P., Mazo, C., Domingo, R., 2003. Les structures d'habitat de l'occupation magdalénienne de la grotte d'Abauntz (Navarre, Espagne). L'organisation de l'espace, in: Vasil'ev, S.A., Soffer, O., Kozlowski, J. (Eds.), Perceived Landscapes and Built Environments. The Cultural Geography of Late Paleolithic Eurasia. British Archaeological Reports 1122, pp. 25-37.

Utrilla, P., Mazo, C., Domingo, R., i.p. Fifty Thousand Years of Prehistory at the Cave of Abauntz (Arraitz, Navarre): a Nexus Point Between the Ebro Valley, Aquitaine and the Cantabrian Corridor, Quaternary International

Utrilla, P., Mazo, C., Lorenzo, J.I., 2007. Enterramientos humanos en el Calcolítico de Abauntz. In: La tierra te sea leve. Arqueología de la Muerte en Navarra, Museo de Navarra, pp. 66-72.

Utrilla, P., Mazo, C., Lorenzo, J.I., i. p. Rituales funerarios en el calcolítico de Abauntz. Un ejemplo de lesión con supervivencia, Saldvie 11.

Utrilla, P., Mazo, C., Rivero, O., Lombo A., 2013. Mirando de nuevo a Isturitz. El tema del alisador del bisonte en el Magdaleniense medio de Abauntz, in: de la Rasilla, M. (Ed.) F. Javier Fortea Pérez. Universitatis Ovetensis Magister. Estudios en Homenaje. Universidad de Oviedo, pp. 247-261.

Utrilla, P., Mazo, C., Sopena, M.C., Domingo, R., Martínez-Bea, M., 2007-2008. Ríos, montañas y charcas: una representación de paisaje en el bloque 1 de la cueva de Abauntz, Veleia 24-25, 229-260.

Utrilla, P., Mazo, C., Sopena, M.C., Domingo, R., Nagore, O., 2004. L'art mobilier sur pierre du versant Sud des Pyrénées: les blocs gravés de la grotte d'Abauntz, in: Lejeune, M., Welté, A.-C. (dir.). Art mobilier paléolithique supérieur en Europe occidentale, ERAUL 107, Liège, pp. 199-218.

Utrilla, P., Mazo, C., Sopena, M.C., Martínez-Bea, M., Domingo, R., 2009. A palaeolithic map from 13,660 calBP: engraved stone blocks from the Late Magdalenian in Abauntz Cave (Navarra, Spain), Journal of Human Evolution 57 (2), 99-111.

Utrilla, P., Montes, L., 1987. Las cuevas de los Moros de Gabasa (Huesca). I. El yacimiento musteriense, Bolskan 3, 3-16.

Utrilla, P., Montes, L., 1989. La grotte moustérienne de Gabasa (Huesca, Espagne). L'Homme de Neandertal. 6. La subsistence, Lieja, pp. 145-153.

Utrilla, P., Montes, L., 1993. El final del musteriense en el Valle del Ebro. Datos y reflexiones, in: Cabrera, V. (Ed.), El origen del Hombre Moderno en el suroeste de Europa, Madrid, pp. 219-246.

Utrilla, P., Montes, L., Blasco, M.F., Torres y Ortiz, J.E. (2010): La cueva de Gabasa revisada 15 años despuúes: un cubil para las hienas y un cazadero pra los Neandertales. Zona Arqueológica, 13: 376-390.

Utrilla, P., Montes, L., Gonzalez-Sampériz, P., 2004. Est-ce que c'était l'Èbre une frontière à 40-30 ka? BAR International Series (Actes du XIVéme Congrès UISPP. Section 6. Le Paléolithique supérieur: Sessions générales et posters) 1240, pp. 275-284.

Utrilla, P., Montes, L., Gonzalez-Sampériz, P., 2006. Est-ce que c'était l'Èbre une frontière à 40-30 ka?, in: Cabrera, V., Bernaldo de Quirós, F., Maillo, J. (Eds.), En el Centenario de la Cueva del Castillo: el Ocaso de los Neandertales, Centro Asociado a la UNED en Cantabria, pp. 165-191.

Utrilla, P., Montes, L., Hoffmann, D., Baldellou, V., Bea, M., Domingo, R., Pike, A., 2014. La Fuente del Trucho. Ocupación, estilo y cronología: in Congreso Internacional Cien Años de Arte Rupestre Paleolítico. Centenario del descubrimiento de la Cueva de la Peña de Candamo. 3-5 julio de 2014, Oviedo.

Utrilla, P., Montes, L., Mazo, C., Alday, A., Rodanés, J.M., Blasco, M.F., Domingo R., Bea, M., 2010. El Paleolítico Superior en la Cuenca del Ebro a principios del s. XXI. Revisión y novedades, in: Mangado, X. (Ed.) El Paleolítico superior Peninsular. Novedades del siglo XXI. Homenaje a Javier Fortea. Barcelona, pp. 23-62.

Utrilla, P., Redondo, G., 1979. Monedas de bronce de época constantiniana halladas en la cueva de Abauntz (Navarra), Príncipe de Viana 40, 31-39.

Utrilla, P., Villaverde, V., 2004. Los grabados levantinos del Barranco Hondo, Castellote (Teruel). Gobierno de Aragón, Departamento de Educación, Cultura y Deporte, 159.

Uzquiano, P., Yravedra, J., Ruiz Zapata, B., Gil García, M. J., Sesé, C., Jordá, J., Baena, J., 2010. Bones experiences at El Esquilleu Cave (Western Cantabria, Northern Spain): Domestic hearths management, human behaviour and adaptations to environmental trends between 53-30 Kyrs BP. ICAZ Congress, Paris, 23-28 August 2010. S S O Session S4-3: Hominin subsistence in the Old World during Pleistocene and Early Holocene.

Uzquiano, P., Yravedra, J., Ruiz Zapata, B., Gil, Mª. J., Sese C., Baena, J., 2012. Human behaviour and adaptations to MIS 3 environmental trends (>53-30 ka BP) at Esquilleu cave (Cantabria, northern Spain), Quaternary International, 252: 82-89

Valladas, H., Cachier, H., Maurica, P., Bernaldo de Quirós, F., Clottes, J., Cabrera, V., Uzquiano, P., Arnold, M., 1992. Direct radiocarbon dates for prehistoric paintings at the Altamira, El Castillo and Niaux caves, Nature 357, 68-70.

Vallverdú, J., Carrancho, A., 2004. Estratigrafia del Molí del Salt, in: Vaquero, M. (Ed.), Els darrers caçadors-recol·lectors de la Conca de Barberà: el jaciment del Molí del Salt (Vimbodí). Museu-Arxiu de Montblanc i Comarca, Montblanc, pp. 61-68.

Vallverdú, J., Saladié, P., Bennàsar, L., Cabanes, D., Mancha, E., Menéndez, L., Blain, H., Ollé, A., Vilalta, J.F., Mosquera, M., Cáceres, I., Expósito, I., Esteban, M., Huguet, R., Rosas, A., Solé, A., López-Polín, L., Martinell, J., García, A., Martínez, B., Agustí, J., Ros, S., Carbonell, E., Capedevila, R., 2009. El barranc de la Boella de la Canonja (Tarragonès) revisitat en la intervenció arqueològica preventiva de l'any 2007, Tribuna d'Arqueologia (2008-2009), 7-28.

Van Klinken, G.J., 1999. Bone collagen quality indicators for palaeodietary and radiocarbon measurements, Journal of Archaeological Science 26 (6), 687-695.

Vaquero, M. (Ed.), 2004. Els darrers caçadors-recol·lectors de la Conca de Barberà: el jaciment del Molí del Salt (Vimbodí), Museu-Arxiu de Montblanc i Comarca, Montblanc.

Vaquero, M., 2004. La Bauma dels Pinyons (Capellades, Anoia), in: Actes de les Jornades d'Arqueologia i Paleontologia 2001. Comarques de Barcelona 1996-2001. La Garriga, 29 i 30 de novembre, 1 de desembre de 2001, Generalitat de Catalunya, Barcelona, pp. 60-66.

Vaquero, M., 2006. El Mesolítico de facies macrolítica en el centro y sur de Cataluña, in: Alday, A. (Ed.), El Mesolítico de muescas y denticulados en la cuenca del Ebro y el litoral mediterráneo peninsular, Diputación Foral de Álava, Álava, pp.137-160.

Vaquero, M., 2013. Expedient reduction strategies in the late Pleistocene and early Holocene of the Iberian Peninsula, in: Pastoors, A., Auffermann, B. (Ed.), Pleistocene foragers on the Iberian Peninsula: Their culture and environment. Festschrift in honour of Gerd-Christian Weniger for his sixtieth birthday. Neanderthal Museum. Mettmann. Wissenschaftliche Schriften des Neanderthal Museums 7, pp. 163-182.

Vaquero, M., Allué, E., Alonso, S., Bischoff, J. L., Burjachs, F., Vallverdú, J., 2006. El Abric Agut (Capellades, Barcelona) y el Mesolítico de muescas y denticulados en el noreste de la Península, in: Bicho, N. F., Veríssimo, H. (Eds.), Do Epipaleolítico ao Calcolítico na Península Ibérica. Actas do IV Congresso de Arqueologia Peninsular (Faro, 14 a 19 de Setembro de 2004), Universidade do Algarve, Faro, pp. 113-126.

Vaquero, M., Allué, E., Alonso, S., Campeny, G., Estrada, A., García, M., Gené, J. M., Merino, G. G., Ibáñez, N., Martínez, K., Saladié, P., Sarró, M. I., Vallverdú, J., Vilalta, J., 2005. Una nueva secuencia del Paleolítico Superior final en el Sur de Cataluña: el Molí del Salt (Vimbodí, Tarragona), in: Bicho, N. F. (Ed.), O Paleolítico. Actas do IV Congresso de Arqueologia Peninsular (Faro, 14 a 19 de Setembro de 2004), Universidade do Algarve, Faro, pp. 493-508.

Vaquero, M., Allué, E., Bischoff, J.L., Burjachs, F., Vallverdú, J., 2013. Environmental, depositional and cultural changes in the Upper Pleistocene and Early Holocene: the Cinglera del Capelló sequence (Capellades, Spain), Quaternaire 24 (1), 49-64.

Vaquero, M., Alonso, S., Alonso, C., Ameijenda, A., Blain, H., Fábregas, R., Gómez, G., Lombera, A., López-García, J. M., Lorenzo, C., Lozano, M., Rodríguez, C., Rosell, J., Serna, M., 2009. Nuevas dataciones radiométricas para el Paleolítico Superior en Galicia: La cueva de Valdavara (Becerreá, Lugo), Trabajos de Prehistoria 66 (1), 99-113.

Vaquero, M., Alonso, S., Alonso, C., Ameijenda, A., Gómez, G., Lombera, A., Lorenzo, C., Rodríguez, C., 2008. Nuevos datos sobre el Paleolítico Superior en Galicia: la cueva de Valdavara (Becerreá, Lugo), in: Ramil Rego, E. (Ed.), 1 Congreso Internacional de Arqueoloxía de Vilalba, Férvedes 5, 137-141.

Vaquero, M., Alonso, S., Ameijenda, A., 2011. Archaeological Excavations in the Becerreá Sites (Eastern Lugo): Valdavara Cave and Valdavara 3, in: de Lombera, A., Fábregas, R. (Eds.), To the West of Spanish Cantabria. The Palaeolithic Settlement of Galicia, BAR International Series 2283, Archaeopress, Oxford, pp. 133-143.

Vaquero, M., Alonso, S., García-Catalán, S., García-Hernández, A., Gómez de Soler, B., Rettig, D., Soto, M., 2012. Temporal nature and recycling of Upper Paleolithic artifacts: the burned tools from the Molí del Salt site (Vimbodí i Poblet, northeastern Spain), Journal of Archaeological Science 39 (8), 2785-2796.

Vaquero, M., Esteban, M., Allué, E., Vallverdú, J., Carbonell, E., Bischoff, J.L., 2002. Middle Palaeolithic Refugium, or Archaeological Misconception? A New U-series and Radiocarbon Chronology of Abric Agut (Capellades, Spain), Journal of Archaeological Science 29, 953-958.

Vaquero, M., García Díez, M., Allué, E., Gené, J.M., Ibáñez, N., Saladié, P., Vallverdú, J., 2004. Conclusions, in: Vaquero, M. (Ed.), Els darrers caçadors-recol·lectors de la Conca de Barberà: el jaciment del Molí del Salt (Vimbodí). Excavacions 1999-2003, Museu-Arxiu de Montblanc i Comarca, Montblanc, pp. 285-326

Vaquero, M., Maroto-Genover, J., Arrizabalaga, A., Baena, J., Baquedano, E., Carrión, E., Jordá, J. F., Martinón, M., Menéndez, M., Montes, R., Rosell, J., 2006. The neanderthal-modern human meeting in Iberia: a critical view of the cultural, geographical and chronological data, in: N. J. Conard (Eds.), When Neandertals and Modern Humans Meeting. Tübingen, Kerns Verlag, pp. 419-439.

Vaquero, M., Pastó, I., 2001. The definition of spatial unit in middle palaeolithicsites : The Hearth-related assemblage, Journal of Archaeological Science 28, 1209-1220.

Vega del Sella, Conde de la, 1921. El Paleolítico de Cueva Morín (Santander) y Notas para la climatología Cuaternaria. Comisión de Investigaciones Paleontológicas y Prehistóricas, Memoria 29, Madrid.

Vega del Sella, Conde de la., 1930. Las Cuevas dé La Riera y Balmori. Comisión de Investigaciones Paleontológicas y Prehistóricas, Memoria 38, Madrid.

Vega Toscano, LG., 1988. El Paleolítico Medio del Sureste español y Andalucía Oriental. Madrid: Universidad Complutense, Serie Tesis Doctorales.

Vega Toscano, LG., 1990. Le fin du Paléolothiqueau sud de l'Espagne: sesimplications dans ler contextre de la PéninsuleInérique, in: C. Farzy (Eds.), Paléolithique moyen récent et Paléolithique supérieur ancien en Europe. Mémoires Musée de Préhistoire de l'Ile de France 3, pp.169-176.

Vega, C., 2012. The ceramics of El Mirón Cave, in: Straus, L., González Morales, M. (Eds.), El Mirón Cave. University of New Mexico Press, Albuquerque, pp. 372-425.

Vega, L.G., Sevilla, P., Colino, F., Gutiérrez, F., Peña, P., Rodríguez, R., Bárez, S., 2008. Nuevas investigaciones sobre los yacimientos paleolíticos en la Sierra Norte de la Comunidad de Madrid, in: Resúmenes V Jornadas de Patrimonio arqueológico en la Comunidad de Madrid. Los primeros pobladores: arqueología del Pleistoceno. Museo Arqueológico Regional. Alcalá de Henares, pp.21-22.

Vekua, A., 1995. Die Wirbeltierfauna des Villafranchian von Dmanisi und ihre biostratigraphische Bedeutung, Jarhb. Ger.- Röm. Zentralmuseum Mainz 42, 77-180.

Vera, J. A., 2004. Geología de España. Instituto Geológico y Minero de España/Sociedad Geológica de España, Madrid.

Vera, J.A., Fernández, J., López-Garrido, A.C., Rodríguez. Fernández, 1985. Geología y estratigrafía de los materiales plio-pleistocenos del sector de Orce-Venta Micena (Prov. Granada), Paleontologia i evolució, 18 (1984), 3-11

Verdasco Cebrián, C., 2002. Man: agent of accumulation and alteration of natural deposits, Quaternary International 93-94, 215-220.

Vergès, J.M., Allué, E., Angelucci, D., Burjachs, F., Carrancho, A., Cebrià, A., Expósito, I., Fontanals, M., Moral, S., Rodríguez, A., Vaquero, M., 2008. Los niveles neolíticos de la Cueva de El Mirador (Sierra de Atapuerca, Burgos): nuevos datos sobre la implantación y el desarrollo de la economía agropecuaria en la submeseta norte, in: Actas del IV Congreso del Neolítico Peninsular, Alicante, pp. 418-427.

Vergès, J.M., Allué, E., Angelucci, D., Cebrià, A., Díez, C., Fontanals, M., Manyanós, A., Montero, S., Moral, S., Vaquero, M., Zaragoza, J., 2002. La Sierra de Atapuerca durante el Holoceno: datos preliminaries sobre las ocupaciones de la Edad del Bronce en la Cueva de El Mirador (Ibeas de Juarros, Burgos), Trabajos de Prehistoria 59 (1),107-126.

Verner, W., 1919. Article in Gibraltar Chronicle of 14th May, 1919.

Vidal Encinas, J. M., 1982. Las Gándaras de Budiño: Balance preliminar de dos campañas de excavaciones (1980-1981). El Museo de Pontevedra XXXVI, pp. 91-114.

Vidal, L.M., 1911-1912. Abric Romaní, Estació Agut, Cova de l'Or o dels Encantats. Estacions prehistòriques de les époques mosteriana, magdaleniana i neolítica a Capellades i Sta. Creu d'Olorde (Barcelona), Anuari de l'Institut d'Estudis Catalans IV, 267-302.

Vilaseca, S. 1949. Avance al estudio de la cueva del Filador, de Margalef (provincia de Tarragona), A.E.A., nº 33, Madrid, pp. 347-361.

Vilaseca, S. 1953. Las industrias del sílex tarraconenses, Consejo Superior de Investigaciones Científicas, Madrid.

Vilaseca, S., 1936. La indústria del sílex a Catalunya. Les estacions tallers del Priorat i extensions, ed. Llibreria Nacional i Estrangera, Reus, p. 128.

Vilaseca, S., 1952. Mústero-levalloisiense en Reus, Archivos de Prehistoria Levantina 3, 31-36

Vilaseca, S., 1953. Las industrias del sílex tarraconenses, ed. C.S.I.C., Inst. Rodrigo Caro, Madrid, p. 526

Vilaseca, S., 1954. Nuevos yacimientos tarraconenses de cerámica acanalada. Instituto de Estudios Tarraconenses Ramón Berenguer IV, Reus, p. 87

Vilaseca, S., 1968. Cuatro días en la cova del Filador, (Margalef), in: La Préhistoire, problèmes et tendances, ed. CNRS, París pp. 476-490.

Vilaseca, S., 1973. Reus y su entorno en la Prehistoria, Rosa de Reus 48-49 (1-2), Reus, pp. 282-174.

Vilaseca, S., 1973. Reus y su entorno en la Prehistoria. Asociación de Estudios Reusenses, Reus, p. 283.

Vilaseca, S., Capdevila, R., 1968. Las estaciones prehistóricas del Pla del Maset (Cap de Salou) y les Gavarres (Constantí). Instituto de Estudios Tarraconenses "Ramón Berenguer IV", Reus, p. 52.

Villalta, J. F. de, 1964. Datos para un catálogo de las aves fósiles del cuaternario español, Speleon 15, 79-102.

Villaluenga, A., Arrizabalaga, A., Ríos-Garaizar, J., 2013. Multidisciplinar Approach to two Chatelperronian Series: Lower IX Layer of Labeko Koba and X Level of Ekain (Basque Country, Spain), Journal of Taphonomy 10 (3-4), 499-520.

Villaverde, M., 2005. Las primeras manifestaciones artísticas: el Arte Paleolítico, in: Martínez Valle, R. (Eds.), Arte rupestre en la Comunidad Valenciana, Generalitat Valenciana, pp. 91-115.

Villaverde, M., Martínez Valle, R., Badal, E., Guillem, P., García, R., Menargues, J. 1999. El Paleolítico Superior de la Cova de les Cendres (Teulada-Moraira, Alicante). Datos proporcionados por el sondeo efectuado en los cuadros A/B-17, Archivo de Prehistoria Levantina, XXIII, Valencia, pp. 9-65.

Villaverde, V., 1984. La Cova Negra de Xàtiva y el Musteriense de la región central del Mediterráneo español, Trabajos Varios del SIP, 79.

Villaverde, V., 1994. Arte paleolítico de la Cova del Parpalló. Estudio de la colección de las plaquetas y cantos grabados y pintados, Museu de Prehistòria, Valencia.

Villaverde, V., 1995. El Paleolítico en el País Valenciano: Novedades y breve síntesis. In: Actas de las Jornadas de Arqueología del Alfaç del Pi (Alicante). Consellería de Cultura, pp. 13-36.

Villaverde, V., Aura, J.E., Barton, C.M., 1998. The Upper Paleolitihc in Mediterranean Spain: A Review of Current Evidence, Journal of Word Prehistory 12 (2), 121-198.

Villaverde, V., Fumanal, M., 1990. Relations entre le Paléolithique Moyen et le Paléolithique Supérieur dans le versant Méditerranéen espagnol. In: Paléolithique Moyen Récent et Paléolithique Supérieur Ancien en Europe, Mémoires du Musée de Préhistoire de l'Ille de France, vol. 3, pp. 177-183.

Villaverde, V., Martínez Valle, R., 1992. Economía y aprovechamiento del medio en el Paleolítico de la región central del Mediterráneo español, in: Moure, A. (Ed.), Elefantes, ciervos y ovicaprinos. Economía y aprovechamiento del medio de la Prehistoria de España y Portugal. Universidad de Cantabria: 77-96.

Villaverde, V., Martínez Valle, R., Guillem, P., Fumanal, M., 1996. Mobility and the role of small game in the Middle Paleolithic of the central region of the Spanish Mediterranean: a comparison of Cova Negra with other Paleolithic deposits, in: Carbonell, E., Vaquero, M. (Eds.), The Last Neandertals, the First Anatomically Modern

Humans: A Tale about the Human Diversity. Universitat Rovira i Virgili, Tarragona, pp. 267-288.

Villaverde, V., Martínez, R., Badal. E., Guillem, P.M., García, R., Menargues, J., 1999. El Paleolítico superior de la Cova de les Cendres (Teulada-Moraira, Alicante). Datos proporcionados por el sondeo efectuado en los cuadros A/B-17, Archivo de Prehistoria Levantina XXIII, 9-65.

Villaverde, V., Martínez-Valle, R., 1995. Características culturales y económicas del final del Paleolítico superior en el Mediterráneo español. En Los últimos cazadores. Transformaciones culturales y económicas durante el Tardiglaciar y el inicio del Holoceno en el ámbito mediterráneo, Colección Patrimonio, 22. Alicante, pp. 79-117.

Villaverde, V., Martínez-Valle, R., Badal, E., Guillem, P.M., García, R., Menargues, J., 1999. El Paleolítico superior de la Cova de les Cendres (Teulada-Moraira, Alicante). Datos proporcionados por el sondeo efectuado en los cuadros A/B-17, Archivo de Prehistoria Levantina XXIII, 9-65.

Villaverde, V., Román, D., 2004. Avance al estudio de los niveles gravetienses de la Cova de les Cendres. Resultados de la excavación del sondeo (cuadros A/B/C-17) y su valoración en el contexto del Gravetiense mediterráneo ibérico, Archivo de Prehistoria Levantina XXV, 19-59.

Villaverde, V., Roman, D., 2013. El Gravetiense de la vertiente mediterránea ibérica: estado de la cuestión y perspectivas, in: de las Heras, C., Lasheras, J.A., Arrizabalaga, A., de la Rasilla, M. (Eds.), Pensando el Gravetiense: nuevos datos para la región cantábrica en su contexto peninsular y pirenáico, pp. 34-54.

Villaverde, V., Román, D., Martínez, R., Badal, E., M.M. Bergadà, P.M. Guillem, Pérez-Ripoll, M., Tormo, C., 2010. El Paleolítico superior en el País Valenciano. Novedades y perspectivas. En El Paleolítico superior peninsular, Novedades del siglo XXI, 85-113.

Villaverde, V., Román, D., Pérez Ripoll, M., Martínez, R., Badal, E., Bergadà, M.M., Guillem, P.M., Pérez, M., Tormo, C., 2010. El Paleolítico superior en el País Valenciano. Novedades y perspectivas, in: Mangado, X. (Ed.): El Paleolítico superior peninsular. Novedades del siglo XXI. Homenaje al Prof. Javier Fortea. Monografíes 8, SERP, Barcelona, pp. 85-113.

Villaverde, V., Román, D., Pérez-Ripoll, M-, Bergada, M.M., Real, C., 2012. The end of the Upper Palaeolithic in the Mediterranean Basin of the Iberia Peninsula, Quaternary International 272-273, 17-32.

Viñas R. Ullastre, J., Quereda, J., Camarasa, J.M., Español, F., Filella, S., Miquel, D., Gusi, F., 1982. La Valltorta, Arte Rupestre del Levante Español, Ed. Castell, Bacelona.

Viñas R., Morote, J.G., 2011. Arte Rupestre Valltorta-Gasulla, Museo y Parque Cultural, Asociación de Amigos del Parque Cultural de La Valltorta y su Museo, Bancaja, Cuenca, 264.

Viñas R., Morote, J.G., 2013. La aplicación de pintura blanca en los conjuntos levantinos de la Valltorta-Gasulla, Sección de Estudios Arqueológicos V. Serie Arqueológica, Varia XI, Diputación Provincial de Valencia, pp. 219-255.

Viñas R., Morote, J.G., in press. Asociaciones escénicas y tipológicas en el Arte Levantino de Valltorta-Gasulla. Sección de Estudios Arqueológicos V. Serie Arqueológica, Varia XII, Diputación Provincial de Valencia.

Viñas R., Rubio, A., Ruiz, J.F., 2012. La técnica paleolítica del trazo fino y estriado entre los orígenes del estilo levantino de la Península Ibérica. Evidencias para una reflexión, in: L'art pléistocène dans le monde / Pleistocene art of the world / Arte pleistoceno en el mundo, Congrès IFRAO, Tarascon-sur-Ariège, septembre 2010, Symposium «Art pléistocène en Europe». N° spécial de Préhistoire, Art et Sociétés, Bulletin de la Société Préhistorique Ariège-Pyrénées, pp. 165-178.

Viñas R., Sarria, E., 2009-2010. Documentació dels nous conjunts d'art rupestre del Priorat (Tarragona), Arte Rupestre del Levante Español, Ed. Castell, Barcelona, pp. 53-84.

Viñas R., Saucedo, E.R., 2000. Los cérvidos en el arte rupestre postpaleolítico Quaderns de Prehistòria i Arqueologia de Castelló, Servei d'Investigacions Arqueològiques i Prehistòriques, Diputació de Castelló, pp. 53-68.

Viñas, R., 1972. Observaciones sobre los depósitos cuaternarios de la Cova del Gegant. Sitges (Barcelona), Speleon 19, 115-126.

Viñas, R., 1978. Informe sobre un microorganismo detectado en las pinturas rupestres del Barranco de la Valltorta, Cuadernos de Prehistoria y Arqueología Castellonense 5, 361-367.

Viñas, R., 1988. Programa y codificación de una base de datos para la documentación e investigación del arte postpaleolítico, Caesaraugusta 65, 111-146.

Viñas, R., 2012. Superimpositión in Spanish Levantine Rock Art: previous proposals and new evidence for a reassessment; Las superposiciones en el arte rupestre levantino: antiguas propuestas y nuevas evidencias para un periodo de reflexión. The Levantine Question, El problema "Levantino", Archaeolingua, Budapest-Cáceres, pp. 55-80.

Viñas, R., Martínez, R., 2001. Imágenes antropo-zoomorfas del postpaleolítico castellonense. Quaderns de Prehistòria i Arqueologia de Castelló, Servei d'Investigacions Arqueològiques i Prehistòriques, Diputació de Castelló, pp. 365-392.

Viñas, R., Villalta, J.F. de, 1975. El depósito cuaternario de la Cova del Gegant. Speleon. Monografia I, V Symposium de Espeleología, p. 19-33.

Viñes, G., 1942. Cova-Negra de Bellús. Notas sobre las excavaciones practicadas, Trabajos Varios del SIP, 6.

Viseras, C., Soria, J. M., Durán, J. J., Pla, S., Garrido, G., García-García, F. and Arribas, A., 2006. A large-mammal site in a meandering fluvial context (Fonelas P-1, Late Pliocene, Guadix Basin, Spain): Sedimentological keys for its paleoenvironmental reconstruction, Palaeogeography, Palaeoclimatology, Palaeoecology 242 (3-4), 139-168.

Vives, E., 1986. Les restes òssies humanes del Bronze de Mollet III (Serinyà), Quaderns del Centre d'Estudis Comarcals de Banyoles 1985, II, 157-161.

VV.AA., 2008. La Necrópolis Mesolítica de El Collado (Oliva, Valencia), in: Serie arqueológica Varia VIII, Sección de estudios Arqueológicos V, José Aparicio Pérez (Ed.), Diputación Provincial de Valencia.

Waechter, J. D'A., 1951. Excavations at Gorham's Cave, Gibraltar. Proceedings of the Prehistoric Society 17, 83-92.

Waechter, J. D'A., 1964. The excavations at Gorham's Cave, Gibraltar, 1951-1954. Bulletin of the Institute of Archaeology of London 4, 189-221.

Walker, M.J, López-Martínez, M.V., Carrión-García, J.S., Rodríguez-Estrella, T., San-Nicolás-del-Toro, M., Schwenninger, J-L., López-Jiménez, A., Ortega-Rodrigáñez, J., Haber-Uriarte, M., Polo-Camacho, J-L., García-Torres, J., Campillo-Boj, M., Avilés-Fernández, A., Zack, W., 2013. Cueva Negra del Estrecho del Río Quípar (Murcia, Spain): A late Early Pleistocene hominin site with an "Acheulo-Levalloiso-Mousteroid" Palaeolithic assemblage, Quaternary International 294, 135-159.

Walker, M.J., Angelucci, D., Anesin, D., Berna, F., Fernández-Jalvo, Y., Haber-Uriarte, M., López-Martínez, M., Rhodes, S.E., Rodríguez-Estrella, T., Schwenninger, J-L., and Skinner, A.R., Evidence of Early Palaeolthic fire at the late Early Pleistocene site of Cueva Negra del Estrecho del Río Quípar (Caravaca de la Cruz, Murcia, Spain). In preparation for XVII UISPP Session Congress B53 The Archaeology of Early Fire Use, XVII UISPP Congress, Burgos. September 1-7 2014.

Walker, M.J., Gibert, J., López Martínez, M., Lombardi, A.V., Pérez-Pérez, A., Zapata, J., Ortega, J., Higham, T., Pike, A., Schwenninger, J-L., Zilhão, J., Trinkaus, E., 2008. Late Neandertals in Southeastern Spain: Sima de las Palomas del Cabezo Gordo, Murcia, Spain, Proceedings of the National Academy of Sciences USA 105, 20631-20636.

Walker, M.J., Gibert, J., Sánchez, F., Lombardi, A.V., Serrano, I., Eastham, A., Ribot, F., Arribas, A., Sánchez-Cabeza, J-A., García-Orellana, J., Gibert, L., Albaladejo, S., Andreu, J.A., 1998. Two SE Spanish middle palaeolithic sites with Neanderthal remains: Sima de las Palomas del Cabezo Gordo and Cueva Negra del Estrecho del Río Quípar (Murcia province). Internet Archaeology 5 (autumn/winter 1998) http://intarch.ac.uk/journal/issue5/walker_index.html

Walker, M.J., Lombardi, A.V., Zapata, J., Trinkaus, E., 2010a. Neandertal mandibles from the Sima de las Palomas del Cabezo Gordo, Murcia, southeastern Spain, American Journal of Physical Anthropology 142, 261-272.

Walker, M.J., López Martínez, M., Ortega-Rodrigáñez, J., Haber-Uriarte, M., López-Jiménez, A., Avilés-Fernández, A., Polo-Camacho, J.L., Campillo-Boj, M., García-Torres, J., Carrión-García, J.S., San Nicolas-del Toro, M., Rodríguez-Estrella, T., 2012a. The excavation of the buried articulated Neanderthal skeletons at Sima de las Palomas (Murcia, SE Spain), Quaternary International 259, 7-21.

Walker, M.J., Ortega Rodrigáñez, J., Agut Giménez, A., Soler Laguía, M., Zollikofer, C.P.E., Ponce de León, M.S., 2012b. The Sima de las Palomas Neanderthal skeletons: First steps towards "virtual" reconstruction, in: Proceedings of the European Society for the Study of Human Evolution 1, 191 special issue, J-J.Hublin, W.Roebroeks, M.Soressi, T.Terberger, F.Spoor, Eds., Proceedings of the 2nd Annual Meeting of the European Society for the Study of Human Evolution ESHE 21-22 September 2012 Bordeaux/France). Max-Planck Institute for Evolutionary Anthropology, Society for the Study of Human Evolution, Leipzig.

Walker, M.J., Ortega Rodrigáñez, J., López Martínez, M., Parmová, K., Trinkaus, E., 2011b. Neandertal postcranial remains from the Sima de las Palomas del Cabezo Gordo, Murcia, southeastern Spain, American Journal of Physical Anthropology 144, 505-515.

Walker, M.J., Ortega, J., Parmová, K., López, M., Trinkaus, E., 2011a. Morphology, body proportions, and postcranial hypertrophy of a female Neandertal from the Sima de las Palomas, southeastern Spain, Proceedings of the National Academy of Sciences USA 108, 10087-10091.

Walker, M.J., Rodríguez-Estrella, T., Carrión García, J.S., Mancheño-Jiménez, M-A., Schwenninger, J-L., López-Martínez, M., López-Jiménez, A., San Nicolás-del Toro, M., Hills, M.D., Walkling, T., 2006. Cueva Negra del Estrecho del Río Quípar (Murcia, Southeast Spain): An Acheulian and Levalloiso-Mousteroid assemblage of Palaeolithic artifacts excavated in a Middle Pleistocene faunal context with hominin skeletal remains, Eurasian Prehistory 4, 3-43.

Walker, M.J., Zapata, J., Lombardi, A.V., Trinkaus, E., 2010b. New evidence of dental pathology in 40,000 year old Neandertals, Journal of Dental Research 90, 428-432.

Warburton, J., Alvarez, C. 1989. A thrust tectonic interpretation of the Guadarrama Mountains, Spanish Central System, en AGGEP (Eds.) Libro Homenaje a R. Soler, Madrid, pp. 147-155.

Ward, S., Gale, R., Carruthers, W., 2013. Late Pleistocene vegetation reconstruction at Vanguard Cave, in: Barton, R. N. E., Stringer, C. B., Finlayson, J. C. (Eds.), Neanderthals in Context: A Report of the 1995-1998 Excavations at Gorham's and Vanguard Caves, Gibraltar, Oxford University Press, Oxford, pp. 218-223.

Weninger, B., Jöris, O., 2004. Glacial Radiocarbon Calibration. The CalPal Program, in: Higham, T., Ramsey, Ch. B. Owen C. (Eds.), Radiocarbon and Archaeology, Fourth International Symposium, Oxford.

Wood, R.E., Arrizabalaga, A., Camps, M., Iriarte-Chiapusso, M.-J., Jones, R., Maroto-Genover, J., de la Rasilla, M., Santamaría, D., Soler, J., Soler, N., Villaluenga, A., Higham, T.F.G., 2014. The chronology of the earliest Upper Palaeolithic in Northern Iberia: New insights from L'Arbreda, Labeko Koba and La Viña, Journal of Human Evolution 69 (4), 91-109.

Wood, R.E., Arrizabalaga. A., Camps, M., Fallon, S., Iriarte-Chiapusso, M-J, Jones, R., Maroto-Genover, J., de la Rasilla, M. Santamaría, D., Soler, J., Soler, N., Villaluenga, A., Higham, T.F.G., 2014. The chronology of the earliest Upper Palaeolithic in northern Iberia: New insights from L'Arbreda, Labeko Koba and La Viña, Journal of Human Evolution 91-109.

Wood, R.E., Barroso-Ruiz, C., Caparrós, M., Jordá-Pardo, J.F., Galván Santos, B., Higham, T.F.G., 2013. Radiocarbon dating casts doubt on the late chronology of the Middle to Upper Palaeolithic transititon on southern Iberia, PNAS 110 (8), 2781-2786.

Wood, R.E., Higham, T., Torres, T. de, Tisnérat- Laborde, N., Valladas, H., Ortiz, J. E., Lalueza- Fox, C., Sánchez-Moral, S., Cañaveras, J. C., Rosas, A., Santamaría, D., Rasilla, M. de la., 2013, A new date of the Neanderthals from El Sidrón Cave (Asturias, Northern Spain), Archaeometry 55 (1), 148-158.

Yanes, Y., Gómez-Puche, M. Esquembre-Bebia, M.A., Fernández López de Pablo, J., 2013. Younger Dryas-early Holocene transition in the south-eastern Iberian Peninsula: insights from land snail shell middens, Journal of Quaternary Science.

Yll, E.I., Carrión, J.S., Pantaleón-Cano, J., Dupré, M., La Roca, N., Roure, J.M., Pérez-Obiol, R., 2003. Palinología del Cuaternario reciente de la Laguna de Villena (Alicante), Anales de Biología 25, 65 - 72.

Yll, E.I., Watson, J., Paz, M.A., 1994. Les darreres excavacions al Roc del Migdia (Vilanova de Sau, Osona): estat de la qüestió i noves perspectivas, Tribuna d'Arqueologia 1992-1993, 15-24.

Yravedra, J., 2006. Acumulaciones biológicas en yacimientos arqueológicos: Amalda VII y Esquilleu III-IV, Trabajos de Prehistoria 63 (2) 55-78.

Yravedra, J., Andrés, M., 2013. Estrategias de subsistencia entre los grupos magdalenienses de La Peña de Estebanvela (Ayllón, Segovia), in: C. Cacho (coord.), Ocupaciones magdalenienses en el interior de la Península Ibérica. La Peña de Estebanvela (Ayllón, Segovia). Junta de Castilla y León-CSIC, pp. 211-243.

Yravedra, J., Baena, J., Arrizabalaga, A., Iriarte, M. J., 2005. El empleo de material óseo como combustible durante el Paleolítico medio y superior en el Cantábrico. Observaciones experimentales, in: Actas de la Reunión Científica Neandertales cantábricos. Estado de la cuestión. El Paleolítico medio cantábrico: hacia una revisión actualizada de su problemática, Monografías del Museo y Centro de Investigación de Altamira, 20, Madrid, pp. 369-383.

Yravedra, J., Domínguez-Rodrigo, M., 2009. The shaft-based methodological approach to the quantification of long limb bones and its relevance to understanding hominid subsistence in the Pleistocene: application to four Palaeolithic sites, Journal of Quaternary Science 24, 85-96.

Yravedra, J., Domínguez-Rodrigo, M., Santonja, M., Pérez-González, A., Panera, J., Rubio-Jara, S., Baquedano, E., 2010. Cut marks on the Middle Pleistocene elephant carcass of Áridos 2 (Madrid, Spain), Journal of Archaeological Science 37, 2469-2476.

Yravedra, J., Gómez Castanedo A., 2013. Taphonomic implications for the Late Mousterian of South-West Europe at Esquilleu Cave (Spain). Quaternary International, DOI:10.1016/j.quaint.2013.09.030.

Yravedra, J., Rubio-Jara, S., Panera, J., Uribelarrea, D., Pérez-González, A., 2012. Elephants and subsistence. Evidence of the human exploitation of extremely large mammal bones from the Middle Palaeolithic site of PRERESA (Madrid, Spain), Journal of Archaeological Science 39, 1063-1071.

Yravedra, J., Uzquiano P., 2013. Burnt bone assemblages from El Esquilleu cave (Cantabria, Northern Spain): deliberate use for fuel or systematic disposal of organic waste?, Quaternary Science Reviews 68, 175-190.

Yusta, I., Velasco, F., Aguirre, M., Orue, I., 2005. Aparición de niveles ricos en fosfatos en el registro paleolítico de la Cueva de Antoliña (Gautegiz-Arteaga, Vizcaya). Macla 3, Actas de la XXV Reunión de la Sociedad Española de Mineralogía 2005, pp. 221-223.

Zack, W., Andronikov, A., Rodríguez-Estrella, T., López-Martínez, M., Haber-Uriarte, M., Holliday, V., Lauretta, D., Walker, M.J., 2013. Stone procurement and transport at the late Early Pleistocene site of Cueva Negra del Estrecho del Río Quípar (Murcia, SE Spain). Quartär, Internationales Jahrbuch zur Eiszeitalter- und Steinzeitforschung, International Yearbook for Ice Age and Stone Age Research 60, 7-28.

Zaidner, Y., 2013. Adaptive flexibility of Oldowan hominins: secondary use of flakes at Bizat Ruhama, Israel, Plos One 8 (6), 66851.

Zapata, L. 2009. Agricultura prehistórica en el País Vasco litoral, Munibe (Antropologia-Arkeologia) 57, 553-561.

Zazo, C. 1989. Los depósitos marinos cuaternarios en el golfo de Cádiz, in: Díaz del Olmo, F., Rodríguez Vidal, J. (Eds.), El Cuaternario en Andalucía Occidental, AEQUA Monografías 1, Sevilla, pp. 113-122.

Zazo, C., Goy, J. L., Dabrio, C. J., 1983. Medios marinos y marino salobres en la bahía de Cádiz durante el Pleistoceno, Mediterránea 2, 29-52.

Zilhão, J., 2006. Chronostratigraphy of the Middle-to-Upper Paleolithic transition in the Iberian Peninsula, Pyrenae 37 (1), 7-84.

Zilhao, J., D'Errico, F. 1999. The chronology and taphonomy of the earliest Aurignacian and its implications for the understanding of Neandertal extinction, Journal of World Prehistory 13, 1-68.

Zubeldia, H., Murelaga, X., Bailón, S., Aguirre, M., Sáez de la Fuente, X., 2003/07. Microinvertebrados de la secuencia superior de Antoliñako koba (Pleistoceno superior) (Gautegiz-Arteaga, Bizkaia), Kobie (Serie paleoantropología) 27, 5-49.